W9-AEC-343

THE ROUTLEDGE HISTORY
OF SEX AND THE BODY

The Routledge History of Sex and the Body provides an overview of the main themes surrounding the history of sexuality from 1500 to the present day. The history of sex and the body is an expanding field in which vibrant debate on, for instance, the history of perversions is developing. This book examines the current scholarship and looks towards future directions for the field.

The volume is divided into 14 thematic parts, which are split into two chronological chapters: 1500–1750 and 1750 to the present day. Focusing on the history of sexuality and the body in the West but also interactions with a broader globe, these thematic parts survey the major areas of debate and discussion. Covering themes such as science, identity, the gaze, courtship, reproduction, sexual violence and the importance of age and race, the volume offers a comprehensive view of the history of sex and the body. The book concludes with an afterword in which the reader is invited to consider some of the 'tensions, problems and areas deserving further scrutiny'.

Including contributors renowned in their field of expertise, this ground-breaking collection is essential reading for all those interested in the history of sexuality and the body.

Sarah Toulalan is a senior lecturer in early modern history at the University of Exeter, UK. Her previous publications include *Bodies, Sex and Desire from the Renaissance to the Present* co-edited with Kate Fisher (2011) and *Imagining Sex: Pornography and Bodies in Seventeenth-Century England* (2007).

Kate Fisher is Professor of Modern History at the University of Exeter, UK. Her previous publications include *Bodies, Sex and Desire from the Renaissance to the Present* co-edited with Sarah Toulalan (2011), *Sex before the Sexual Revolution: Intimate Life in England 1918–1963* with Simon Szreter (2010) and *Birth Control, Sex and Marriage in Britain 1918–60* (2006).

THE ROUTLEDGE HISTORIES

The Routledge Histories is a series of landmark books surveying some of the most important topics and themes in history today. Edited and written by an international team of world-renowned experts, they are the works against which all future books on their subjects will be judged.

THE ROUTLEDGE HISTORY OF SEX AND THE BODY

1500 to the Present

Edited by
Sarah Toulalan and Kate Fisher

Routledge
Taylor & Francis Group

LONDON AND NEW YORK

First published 2013
by Routledge
2 Park Square, Milton Park, Abingdon, Oxon OX14 4RN

Simultaneously published in the USA and Canada
by Routledge
711 Third Avenue, New York, NY 10017

Routledge is an imprint of the Taylor & Francis Group, an informa business

British Library Cataloguing in Publication Data
A catalogue record for this book is available from the British Library

Library of Congress Cataloging in Publication Data
The Routledge history of sex and the body, 1500 to the present / edited by
Sarah Toulalan and Kate Fisher.
p. cm. — (The routledge histories)
Includes bibliographical references and index.
1. Sex–Western countries–History. 2. Sexology–Western countries–History. 3. Human
body–Western countries–History. 4. Western countries I. Toulalan, Sarah. II. Fisher, Kate.
HQ12.R69 2013
306.709182'1–dc23
2012037890

ISBN: 978-0-415-47237-1 (hbk)
ISBN: 978-0-203-43686-8 (ebk)

Typeset in Baskerville
by Taylor & Francis Books

Printed and bound in the United States of America by Publishers Graphics,
LLC on sustainably sourced paper.

CONTENTS

CONTENTS

CONTENTS

LIST OF ILLUSTRATIONS

CONTRIBUTORS

Helen Blackman is a freelance writer and historian based in Exeter. She has published on the reproductive sciences in Victorian and Edwardian Britain and teaches medical humanities at the Peninsula Medical School. She is currently writing a book about the Rolle family of Devon, commissioned by Clinton Devon Estates. Her blog is at http:// helenblackman.wordpress.com.

Antoinette Burton teaches in the History Department at the University of Illinois, where she is Bastian Professor of Global and Transnational History. Her most recent books are *Empire in Question: Reading, Writing and Teaching British Imperialism* (Duke University Press, 2011) and *A Primer for Teaching World History: Ten Design Principles* (Duke University Press, 2012).

Jonathan Burton is the author of *Traffic and Turning: Islam and English Drama, 1579–1624* (2005) and co-editor with Ania Loomba of *Race in Early Modern England: A Documentary Companion* (2007). He has published articles on Shakespeare, travel writing, and religious difference, and he is currently working on a book entitled *High School Shakespeare*. He teaches in the English Department at Whittier College.

Richard Cleminson is Reader in the History of Sexuality in the Department of Spanish, Portuguese and Latin American Studies, University of Leeds. He is also currently Deputy Director of the Centre for Interdisciplinary Gender Studies at the same University. He has published primarily on the history of sexuality in Spain and his books include *Hermaphroditism, Medical Science and Sexual Identity in Spain, 1850–1960* (Cardiff: University of Wales Press, 2009), *'Los Invisibles': A History of Male Homosexuality in Spain, 1850–1939* (Cardiff: University of Wales Press, 2007) (both with F. Vázquez García) and *Anarquismo y sexualidad (España, 1900–939)* (Cadiz: Universidad de Cádiz, 2008). He is also editor with Jamie Heckert of *Anarchism and Sexuality: Ethics, Relationships and Power* (Abingdon and New York: Routledge, 2011). He is currently working on a history of eugenics in Portugal.

Harry G. Cocks is Lecturer in British History at Nottingham University and the author of *Nameless Offences: Homosexual Desire in Nineteenth Century England* (2003), *The Modern History of Sexuality* (2005, with Matt Houlbrook), and *Classified: The Secret History of the Personal Column* (2009).

Katherine Crawford is Professor of History at Vanderbilt University. She is interested in the ways that gender informs sexual practice, ideology, and identity, both in normative and non-normative formations. Among her on-going research are projects exploring the presumptions about corporeal color as a product of gender and recuperating the history of pleasure. Her most recent book is *The Sexual Culture of the French Renaissance* (Cambridge University Press, 2010).

Ivan Crozier is Senior Lecturer in the Science Studies Unit at the University of Edinburgh, UK and holds a Future Fellowship at the History Department of the University of Sydney, Australia (2012–16). His research interests include the history of psychiatry, especially the construction of sexual categories, and the cultural history of the body and sexuality. These interests occasionally align, as in his current project on the history of koro, a culture-bound syndrome that is used to understand how psychiatrists think about culture and the body. Most of his work is concerned with the history of sexology, particularly Havelock Ellis's work – and to this end he edited the original *Sexual Inversion* for Palgrave (2008). He also edited vol. 6 of Berg's *Cultural History of the Human Body* (2010).

Shani D'Cruze is currently Honorary Reader in the Research Institute for Law, Politics and Justice at Keele University. She has published on the history of gender and violent crime and on the history of the family since the eighteenth century. After more than 15 years as an academic historian in UK universities, Shani D'Cruze moved to Crete in 2005 where she combines olive farming with research, writing and editing. Recent academic publications include: *Murder: Social and Historical Approaches to Understanding Murder and Murderers* (with Sandra Walklate and Samantha Pegg, Cullompton: Willan, 2006), *Women, Crime and Justice since 1660* (with Louise Jackson, Basingstoke: Palgrave, 2009) and 'Sexual Violence in History; A Contemporary Heritage?' in S. Walklate and J. Brown, *Handbook of Sexual Violence* (Abingdon: Routledge, 2011).

Paul R. Deslandes is an Associate Professor of History at the University of Vermont. He is the author of *Oxbridge Men: British Masculinity and the Undergraduate Experience, 1850–1920* (Bloomington: Indiana University Press, 2005) and a number of articles and essays on the history of British education, masculinity, and male sexuality that have appeared in the *Journal of British Studies, History of Education Quarterly, Gender and History, History Compass,* and the *Journal of Women's History*. Deslandes is currently writing a new book on the cultural history of male beauty in Britain from the 1840s to the present. He also serves as Associate Executive Secretary for the North American Conference on British Studies.

Lisa Downing is Professor of French Discourses of Sexuality at the University of Birmingham, UK. Her research specialisms include the history of sexology, psychiatry and psychoanalysis; the diagnostic history of 'perversion' and 'paraphilia'; modern critical theory, especially queer theory, feminist philosophy, and the work of Michel Foucault; and the history of murder. She is the author of five books and over 30 academic journal articles and chapters, and the editor of nine books and special journal issues. Her most recent monograph is *The Subject of Murder: Gender, Exceptionality, and the Modern Killer* (Chicago University Press, 2013). She is currently working on a co-authored book (with Iain Morland and Nikki Sullivan) on US sexologist John Money's diagnostic concepts.

Tanya Evans is a Lecturer in the Department of Modern History at Macquarie University. Prior to this she was a Research Fellow at the Institute of Historical Research in London. Her publications include *'Unfortunate Objects': Lone Mothers in Eighteenth-Century London* (Palgrave Macmillan, 2005) and (with Pat Thane) *Sinners, Scroungers, Saints: Unmarried Motherhood in Twentieth-Century England* (Oxford, 2012). She co-edited a Special Issue of *Australian Historical Studies* on Biography and Life-Writing published in March 2012. She is curating an exhibition on 'Family Life in Nineteenth-Century New South Wales' for the Museum of Sydney and writing *Family Life in Nineteenth-Century Australia* to be published by Allen & Unwin in 2014.

Kate Fisher is Professor of Modern History at the University of Exeter. Her research focuses on the history of sexuality, and particularly on intimacy within marriage during the twentieth century. She has published widely on changing birth control practices and has also co-edited with Sarah Toulalan *Bodies, Sex and Desire from the Renaissance to the Present* (Palgrave, 2011). She co-directs, with Rebecca Langlands (Department of Classics and Ancient History), an interdisciplinary study entitled *Sexual Knowledge, Sexual History* which explores how both popular and academic ideas about sex and sexuality have been articulated from the eighteenth century to the present day with reference to erotic material from ancient civilizations, and is working with Jana Funke on a study of the uses of the past in sexological debates.

Laura Gowing is Reader in Early Modern British History at King's College, London, and author of *Domestic Dangers: Women, Words, and Sex in Early Modern London* (OUP, 1996) and *Common Bodies: Women, Touch and Power in Seventeenth-century England* (Yale, 2003). Her most recent book is *Gender Relations in Early Modern England* (Pearson, 2012) and she is currently working on female apprentices.

Lesley A. Hall is Senior Archivist at the Wellcome Library and Honorary Lecturer in History of Medicine, University College London. She has published extensively on questions of sexuality and gender in nineteenth- and twentieth-century Britain: her works include *Sex, Gender and Social Change in Britain since 1880* (2000: second edition 2012), *Outspoken Women: Women Writing about Sex, 1870–1969* (2005), *The Life and Times of Stella Browne, Feminist and Free Spirit* (2010); and the edited volumes *Sexual Cultures in Europe: National Histories* and *Themes in Sexuality* (with F. Eder and G Hekma, 1999), and (with Roger Davidson) *Sex, Sin and Suffering: Venereal Disease and European Society Since 1870* (2001). Her website is http://www.lesleyahall.net and her blog is at http://www.lesleyahall.blogspot.com.

Martin Ingram is Emeritus Fellow in History at Brasenose College, Oxford. His publications include *Church Courts, Sex and Marriage in England, 1570–1640* (Cambridge, 1987), and numerous articles on crime and the law, sex and marriage, religion and popular customs. He is currently completing a book on sexual regulation in England before, during and after the Reformation. He has also published on the history of climate.

Lauren Kassell is Senior Lecturer in the Department of History and Philosophy of Science and Fellow of Pembroke College, University of Cambridge. Her first book focuses on Simon Forman, the Elizabethan astrologer-physician (Oxford, 2005) and she is now working on a book on magical practitioners in early modern England. She directs the Casebooks Project, a digital edition of the 85,000 medical records kept by Forman and his protégé, Richard Napier (http://www.magicandmedicine.hps.cam.ac.uk). Since 2004, she has contributed to the Wellcome-funded project on Generation to Reproduction (http://www.reproduction.group.cam.ac.uk), a major collaborative initiative to systematically reassess the history of reproduction.

Maria Luddy is Professor of Modern Irish History at the University of Warwick, where she is also Chair of the History Department. She has written extensively on the social history of Ireland in the nineteenth and twentieth centuries. She is currently completing a book on the history of marriage in Ireland.

Lianne McTavish is Professor in the Department of Art and Design at the University of Alberta in Canada, where she offers courses on early modern visual culture, the history of the body, and critical museum theory. She has published two monographs, *Childbirth and the Display of Authority in Early Modern France* (Ashgate, 2005), and *Defining the Modern Museum: A Case Study in the Challenges of Exchange* (University of Toronto Press, 2012).

Ian Frederick Moulton, Head of Interdisciplinary Humanities in the School of Letters and Sciences at Arizona State University, is a cultural historian and literary scholar whose research focuses on the representation of gender and sexuality in early modern literature. He is the author of *Before Pornography: Erotic Writing in Early Modern England* (Oxford University Press, 2000), and the editor and translator of Antonio Vignali's *La Cazzaria*, an erotic and political dialogue from Renaissance Italy (Routledge, 2003). He is currently writing a book on the cultural dissemination of conflicting ideas about romantic love and sexuality in sixteenth-century Europe.

Malcolm Nicolson is Professor of the History of Medicine at the University of Glasgow. His research interests are in the history of medicine, technology and diagnosis, Scottish medicine in the nineteenth and twentieth centuries, and the history of obstetrics. He has published extensively, including most recently on James Young Simpson (1811–70) and the development of physical diagnosis.

Kathryn Norberg is Associate Professor of History and Gender Studies at the University of California, Los Angeles. She is currently working on two projects: the first deals with prostitution in seventeenth-century France; the second is based on the journal of a Parisian madame who describes life in her brothel from 1751 to 1758. Recent publications include 'In Her Own Words: An Eighteenth-Century Madame Tells her Story', in *Prostitution and Eighteenth-Century Culture: Sex, Commerce and Morality*, edited by Anne Lewis and Markman Ellis (London: Pickering & Chatto, 2012).

Kevin Siena is Associate Professor of History at Trent University. He is the author of *Venereal Disease, Hospitals and the Urban Poor: London's 'Foul Wards' 1600–1800* (2004) and editor of *Sins of the Flesh: Responding to Sexual Disease in Early Modern Europe* (2005). His articles and chapters explore the histories of eighteenth-century medicine, welfare and sexuality, analyzing issues like hospital visitation, same-sex spread of syphilis, workhouse medicine, illness and suicide, and female death inspectors. He is currently co-editing a collection on the medical history of skin and writing a monograph on class and contagion in eighteenth-century London.

Lisa Z. Sigel is Associate Professor in the Department of History at DePaul University. She works on the history of pornography, obscenity and sexuality. She has published three books, *Governing Pleasures: Pornography and Social Change in England, 1815–1914*, *International Exposure: Perspectives on Modern European Pornography, 1800–2000*, and *Making Modern Love: Sexual Narratives and Identities in Interwar Britain*.

Michael Stolberg is Chair of the History of Medicine at the University of Würzburg, Germany. His research focuses on the history of early modern medicine, the history of body and gender and, more recently, the history of medical ethics. He is the author, amongst others, of *Experiencing Illness and the Sick Body in Early Modern Europe* (Basingstoke, 2011; original German edition 2003) and is currently conducting two major research projects on early modern physicians' correspondences and on the history of early modern medical practice.

Julie-Marie Strange is Senior Lecturer at the University of Manchester. Her publications include *Death, Grief and Poverty in Britain, 1870–1914* (Cambridge University Press, 2007) and *Fatherhood and Attachment in the British Working Class, 1870–1914* (Cambridge University Press, 2013).

Sarah Toulalan is Senior Lecturer in the Centre for Medical History at the University of Exeter. Her previous publications include *Imagining Sex: Pornography and Bodies in Seventeenth Century England* (Oxford: Oxford University Press, 2007) and (ed. with Kate Fisher) *Bodies, Sex and Desire from the Renaissance to the Present* (Palgrave, 2011). She is currently working on a second monograph entitled *Children and Sex in Early Modern England: Knowledge, Consent, Abuse c. 1550–1750* funded by a Leverhulme Major Research Fellowship.

Randolph Trumbach is Professor of History at Baruch College and the Graduate Center, City University of New York. He has published *The Rise of the Egalitarian Family: Aristocratic Kinship and Domestic Relations in Eighteenth-Century England* (1978) and *Sex and the Gender Revolution, Volume 1: Heterosexuality and the Third Gender in Enlightenment London* (1998). He has published many articles on the history of homosexuality, most recently 'Male Prostitution and the Emergence of the Modern Sexual System: Eighteenth-Century London', in *Prostitution and Eighteenth Century Culture*, eds Ann Lewis and Markman Ellis (2012). These articles are to be the basis for *Volume 2: The Origins of Modern Homosexuality*.

Susan Vincent is Research Associate at the Centre for Renaissance and Early Modern Studies (CREMS) at the University of York. While working primarily on the cultural history of dress in early modern England, she has expanded her research interests to include dress practices up to the present day. Author of *Dressing the Elite: Clothes in Early Modern England* and *The Anatomy of Fashion: Dressing the Body from the Renaissance to Today*, she is currently writing a book about hair.

Garthine Walker is Senior Lecturer in History at Cardiff University, where she teaches early modern cultural and social history and historical theory. Her research focuses primarily on crime and gender in the early modern period. Her publications include *Crime, Gender and Social Order in Early Modern England* (CUP, 2003), (ed.) *Writing Early Modern History* (Arnold/Bloomsbury, 2005), (co-edited with Alex Shepard) *Gender and Change: Agency, Chronology and Periodisation* (Blackwell, 2009), and (co-edited with Angela McShane) *The Extraordinary and the Everyday in Early Modern England* (Palgrave Macmillan, 2010).

ACKNOWLEDGEMENTS

The production of this book has been a team effort: it could not have come together without the hard work and goodwill of a great number of people. The idea for this book originated with Eve Setch at Routledge, and we are very grateful to Eve both for her original inspiration and her confidence in us as editors to bring it to completion, despite delays and setbacks along the way. We are also grateful to Laura Mothersole at Routledge for her support, and especially for all her hard work in arranging image permissions and dealing with copyright issues. The volume would not, of course, have come together without the commitment, energy, knowledge and expertise of the contributors. It has been a very great pleasure to work with them, and to get to know them better, over the several years that the book was in the making – thank you all for your patience, perseverance, and generosity of time and effort. Lisa Downing deserves special thanks for reading the entire book and generously offering comments and corrections in addition to her thoughtful critique in the book's Afterword. Many thanks also to Victoria Bates for her editorial assistance and to Claire Keyte in the Centre for Medical History at the University of Exeter for administrative and other support. Sarah would also like to thank Tim Rees particularly for his unflagging support and encouragement throughout.

The Publisher would like to thank the Wellcome Trust Library, Staatliche Museen, the British Museum, Tate Gallery and the National Portrait Gallery for their kind permission to reproduce the images in this book.

INTRODUCTION

Sarah Toulalan and Kate Fisher

The history of love is the history of mankind, of civilization.[1]
(Iwan Bloch)

For sexologists seeking to understand human sexuality and its variations (frequently from a medical perspective) at the beginning of the twentieth century, history was important. As German sex reformer Iwan Bloch argued (see quotation above) the history of civilization, and the progress of man towards higher forms of existence were fundamentally affected by changing sexual practices. Sexologists sought to demonstrate the importance of studying the history of sexuality, both because it was essential to contextualizing contemporary problems of human sexuality, but also because it was key to understanding the nature of European history (framed in terms of civilization and progress) itself. Among historians, however, the serious and scholarly investigation of sex and the body is relatively new, and its integration into mainstream historical practice even more recent.[2] A specialist journal devoted to the 'history of sexuality' has only been in existence for a little over 20 years. In establishing this journal, published by the University of Texas Press, the editorial board sought to shift the tradition for work on the history of sexuality to be undertaken by sexologists whose focus was predominantly medical. In 1990 this new journal, recognizing that a new approach to the study of sexuality was evolving, invited scholars from the humanities (rather than from the sciences) to come together. The journal made an explicit call in its opening edition for 'social historians, sociologists, anthropologists, philosophers, psychologists, literary scholars, classicists, art and film historians (and others)' to put historically variable, social and cultural frameworks at the forefront of the analysis of sexuality.[3] The response was impressive, and since then the history of sexuality has developed rapidly and is now a vibrant field of scholarly activity, raising few eyebrows or concerns about its scholarly legitimacy.[4] This book surveys (indeed, it celebrates) the emergence of the histories of sex, sexuality and the body. Within the book the particular subjects are contextualized in the key areas of debate that have structured the field. Employing a range of theoretical and empirical approaches and perspectives, paired chapters dealing with different time periods (the first part pre-1750, the second post-1750) both assess current understanding of each topic and point to areas of neglect or questions for future research.

It is the interdisciplinary, theoretically rigorous and conceptually challenging nature of much of this work in the history of bodies and sex that makes it such a vibrant and exciting field to work in, but it also highlights the importance of accessible collections such as this one. The field is broad and covers a large variety of themes and areas. As Jeffrey Weeks has pointed out, over the past 30 years, we have seen the focus of scholarly attention spread, to a point at which it is increasingly difficult to contain its remit within identifiable key themes.[5] Similarly, Kim Phillips and Barry Reay have observed, 'the history of sexuality is at once a history of a "category of thought", and a history of "changing erotic practices, subjective meanings, social definitions, and patterns of regulation whose only unity lies in their common descriptor"'.[6] Harry Cocks and Matt Houlbrook concur: the history of sex 'is about far more than sex itself'; indeed, they argue that 'rather than being content to occupy a narrow and marginal sub-discipline, historians of sexuality have had greater aspirations – aspirations to write a total history of modern Western culture'.[7]

All this can make the landscape rather difficult for students and readers to navigate. The conceptual debate about the very nature of human sexuality and the assumptions scholars bring to its investigation provides further complications that can confuse the reader. Many students are startled to read at the beginning of their studies, for example, that sexuality has not always existed, but was instead a medical construction of human behaviour that emerged towards the end of the nineteenth century. Grappling with such unsettling ideas at the same time as confronting claims that sex and sexuality are implicated in all areas of history can at first seem daunting. This book seeks to provide a helpful route through some of the intellectual frameworks that have been used to study sex in historical contexts from 1500 to the present and to outline the key arguments that have dominated – and continue to dominate – historical debate. It will explore the conceptual frameworks contested by historians and highlight the various different contexts, situations and behaviours that have been associated with sex in times past, and the different understandings of human bodies that underpinned them.

The legacy of Foucault is threaded throughout this collection and few of the topics considered in its chapters ignore his work (though not all authors may reference him explicitly). From the outset historians' reactions to Foucault's various writings relevant to the history of sexuality have been ambivalent. Foucault's lack of attention to historical specifics irked empirically focused historians and the suggestion, as Harry Cocks and Matt Houlbrook have pointed out, that the history of sexuality is invariably only a story of power was difficult to accept.[8] However, as these essays show, it is almost impossible to exaggerate the influence of Foucault in establishing the framework for debate in almost all areas of the historical investigation of sex and sexuality, and his work remains an important and challenging point of engagement with sex in the past. Particularly stimulating has been Foucault's identification of a fundamental shift in thinking about sex and the body which presents the very idea of sexuality as a product of scientific thinking, increasingly dominant from the end of the nineteenth century, that had little or no purchase in earlier periods. This idea has provided a basic (although not universally accepted) framework for understanding the different meanings and significance of sexual behaviours and experiences of the body in many of the following chapters, and explored in detail by Harry Cocks in chapter 2. Foucault's enduring legacy, as illustrated by this book, lies not so much in particular historical narratives, which are accepted or rejected, but in the establishment of a conceptual framework for thinking about the ways in which people have considered sex or understood their bodies differently in the past. Ivan Crozier, for example, provides a nuanced development of Foucault's focus on the medical categories used to define and construct sexual types and identities, charting the ways in which such categorizations have been resisted and reworked by individuals in the pursuit of pleasure. Garthine Walker and Shani D'Cruze employ insights drawn from Foucault in the discussion of the history of rape. As D'Cruze explains, if we follow Foucault in seeing a shift from understanding sexual behaviours as acts to understanding them as governed by identities, then conceptions of rape change as well – rape becomes psychologized, perpetrators are identified and labelled by their acts and the harm to the 'victim' becomes less about damage to chastity or honour but now a fundamental attack on the person and her – or his – psychological well-being.

Many treatments of the history of sexuality begin by acknowledging the difficulties historians face in finding suitable sources to chart changing sexual attitudes and behaviours. Acceptable but private, or illicit and needing to be hidden, much sexual behaviour does not leave a large paper trail documenting its contours or details. Comparatively few individuals record details of their sexual behaviour and feelings, even in the modern world. However, as this volume shows, the centrality of sex to the workings of European society ensures that a variety of relevant documents that provide insights into various sexual cultures, customs, thoughts, rules and regulations, experiences and emotions can be mined by scholars. In charting the work of earlier scholars, the essays in this volume are testament to the rich and inventive use of sources by historians and the extraordinary insights they can provide despite their limitations and lacunae.

For the reader looking for an entry point to this field a number of existing introductory volumes, textbooks and survey works already exist. For the most part these focus on particular regions, nations, and time periods.[9] Some works have been more ambitious in their scope, such as Robert Nye's collection of primary sources, and key works in the recent historiography entitled simply *Sexuality*, Angus McLaren's *Twentieth-Century Sexuality* or the double-volume collection *Sexual Cultures in Europe* edited by Franz X. Eder, Lesley Hall and Gert Hekma. Particularly impressive studies of modern European sexuality are Harry Cocks and Matt Houlbrook's short collection of essays which consider the key themes, approaches and areas of debate in the history of sexuality in western European countries and north America since 1750. This is an extremely valuable set of well-written essays that is particularly strong on collapsing an artificial distinction between experience and ideologies and ideas, and highlighting the intimate relationship between categorizations of sex and the various ways it is experienced.[10] Unique in paying due attention to the whole of Europe (including the East) is Dagmar Herzog's lively and exceptionally well-informed overview of sexuality in the twentieth century, which is remarkable in its accessible yet nuanced presentation of the complexities of European sexual history and the refusal to let the dominant framing of changes in sexual attitudes and behaviours in terms of liberation or repression structure her analysis.[11] For the early modern and medieval periods, Kim M. Phillips and Barry Reay's *Sex Before Sexuality: A Premodern History* provides a sophisticated analysis of the complicated understandings of sexual behaviour in a premodern world which shared very few of the frameworks for thinking about sex with those of our modern western world, while their earlier *Sexualities in History: A Reader* (2002) brought together many key articles on the history of sexuality published in the previous decade.[12] Katherine Crawford's *European Sexualities* encompasses all regions of western Europe without over-generalizing. Anna Clark's *Desire* is a concise but engaging overview of the history of sexuality in Europe from ancient to modern times, and Stephen Garton provides a sophisticated summary of the history of the history of sexuality, across all time periods, since the first sexual histories written by sexologists.[13] Peter Stearns' *Sexuality in World History* is the only serious attempt to provide a truly global and transnational perspective on sex in the past, but such a short volume inevitably focuses on rather broad shifts, what Stearns calls the 'great transformations in sexuality', even while it attempts to resist over-generalization.[14]

This book examines a long time period, from 1500 to the present with occasional glimpses back to the late medieval and early Renaissance worlds. The nature of much academic work is such that the areas of expertise that scholars develop often reflect the conventions of historical periodization. We wished to put such periodization under the microscope, and examine continuities across time as well as the complex trajectories of historical change. Without asking scholars to write about periods whose literature they are unfamiliar with, we split the book into linked chapters covering the same theme. In structuring the book around paired chapters considering the same topic in earlier and later periods this book aims to ensure that major continuities or significant transitions are apparent, without glossing over the specifics of period, place and the complexities of change over time. In so doing, however, we are aware that we have imposed a rough (and artificial) mid-eighteenth-century division onto our map of European sexual cultures. In part this reflects the dominant historiographical idea that there is something profoundly different about the early modern and modern worlds, and which structures the framework through which scholars tend to situate themselves/be situated. Phillips and Reay also identify the mid-eighteenth century as a pivotal point in the dominant narratives of the history of sexuality, the point at which many scholars date a shift towards recognizable 'modern' sexuality, including a reconfiguration of women's bodies, a new interpretation of anatomical differences between male and female, and the emergence of a phallocentric model of sex and desire.[15] In doing this, however, we are not seeking to accept this division – indeed many of the chapters point out the ways in which historians remain sceptical of this neat division between early modern and modern – but rather to interrogate it. By placing together chapters which look at the same theme from either side of a crude 1750 divide, the book forces us to think about the strengths and weaknesses of the periodizations which have structured the field and its development. The notions of modernity and tradition and the teleological assumptions which underpin the questions frequently asked of the past are juxtaposed, highlighting tensions and contradictions caused by the tendency of historians to work from within narrower timeframes.

In some cases, the relevance of a mid-eighteenth-century shift in attitudes towards sex and the body is deemed appropriate. Kathryn Norberg, for example, regards the mid-eighteenth century as a pivotal point in attitudes towards prostitution, a time when a variety of forces coalesce into the construction of the prostitute as a different creature – separated and isolated from 'ordinary women' as both a social and biological evil. In other cases an easy separation of European narratives of change into premodern and modern disintegrates, and the fragility of key trajectories of change are highlighted, as by Kate Fisher in her analysis of the historiography of marriage in chapter 18. The juxtapositions of these chapters enable a particularly productive approach to constructing histories over a long timeframe, indicating both continuities as well as both large and smaller changes over time. Each chapter is embedded in a detailed understanding of the period, written by an author who is an expert in that particular literature. Yet, each chapter directly speaks to and about longer term changes and the broad patterns of change and continuity.

Other traditions of scholarship that this book reflects (and reproduces) are more problematic. The rich historiography of the history of sexuality has its limitations. This volume is not a guide to what the history of sexuality should look like, but rather is indicative of the shape the field has taken during the past 40 years or so – it reveals its strengths and its weaknesses. The dominance of Anglo-American literature on the framework of the debates is clear, with literature on European cultures comparatively less well developed or well known. For example, there is less scholarship available in English on eastern Europe and Russia, and what exists has not yet been fully integrated into the grand narratives of European change, although two recent works which try to trouble this historically ingrained western-centricism in sexuality studies are Lisa Downing and Robert Gillett's *Queer in Europe: Contemporary Case Studies* and Robert Kulpa and Joanna Mizielińska's *De-Centring Western Sexualities: Central and Eastern European Perspectives*.[16] Dagmar Herzog argues that the study of post-Communist sexuality is well under way, some of which looks back to the Communist period,[17] but we await a body of scholarship on sex and the body within the European Communist experience.[18] In the history of sexuality as in much of European historiography, the integration of studies of western Europe, with those of central eastern European nations is a further important undertaking. As Stefan Berger argues: 'It remains one of the most important tasks of the post-Cold War Europe to reintegrate the histories of Western and Eastern Europe.'[19] A rich literature also exists on Scandinavia which remains insufficiently incorporated into European narratives of sexuality.[20]

The geographical focus on the West (North America, Britain and continental Europe, with occasional references to Australia and New Zealand), and the rest of the world considered only from a imperial perspective – and that predominantly in the separate set of chapters on race by Jonathan Burton and Antoinette Burton – is indicative of the arbitrary and indeed unsatisfactory dominance of this framework in the development of the history of sexuality, which has allowed the ideologically based division of the world into the West and the Rest to structure the writing of history. This framework is 'imaginary', as it glosses over many of the transnational and global exchanges informing sexual cultures, attitudes and behaviours (as both Jonathan Burton and Antoinette Burton point out). But it is also at the same time self-fulfilling in constructing boundaries between cultures, attitudes and behaviours as part of the construction of sexuality itself. As Jonathan Burton succinctly puts it: 'Sexual cultures … were never unique to particular geographies or cultures but instead were produced along criss-crossing pathways, and woven in and out of various spaces and times.'[21] Some other chapters, in addition to the close examinations in chapters 27 and 28, illustrate the insights that can be gained through exploring such transnational threads. Susan Vincent, in her chapter on clothing and the body in the early modern period, notes that the discovery of the new world also made itself felt in the world of costume and fashion, as exotic dress found its way into the costume books that started to be printed in the sixteenth century. The discovery of peoples of different skin colour, cultures and mores, and the development of colonialism brought new differentiations in the history of rape law where the rape of white women by black men was treated more seriously and with more severity than was the rape of indigenous women by white men.[22] Racialized ideas about sexual appetite and lack of chastity infused attitudes towards rape and prostitution and the spread of sexual disease. Kevin Siena notes that one of the effects of the virulent strains of venereal disease that travelled to Europe following the discovery of the new world was the demonizing of indigenous peoples, who were seen as requiring domination, through the emergence of the trope of the hypersexual native.

It is to be hoped that the future of the history of sexuality will grapple with these themes more satisfactorily – as it is already increasingly doing – challenging and reworking these geographical distinctions and exploring the intersections between sexual cultures across the world. Yet in seeking to explore the state of our research into the history of sexuality and the body, the structure and framing of this book inevitably reproduces such traditions. The reader will encounter many recurring themes and issues throughout the book, too many for us to enumerate and discuss in this introduction. What we want to do here instead is to draw attention to just a few of the issues that emerge from the discussions set out in the chapters to follow. One of these issues is to do with the way that authors engage with recurring questions of change over time, challenging and modifying existing narrative trajectories or giving greater emphasis to continuities. In doing so, these narratives are also further enmeshed within the existing histories of bodies and sex. This can be seen, for example, in the way that historians discuss changing understandings about bodies and sex/ gender: whether they disagree with Thomas Laqueur's thesis of a shift from a one-sex model of the body differentiated hierarchically and by heat to two incommensurate sexes, or challenge only the timing of such a shift in thinking about the body, nevertheless the concept is thoroughly embedded within the discussion. We also want to draw readers' attention to some new directions in research and analysis. These new directions are not only to do with new subjects that are only now beginning to be explored in greater depth by historians (such as body size and sex, for example, touched on only very briefly in passing by Sarah Toulalan in chapter 15 and, regrettably, a notable omission from this collection), but are rather concerned with shifts in focus to take greater account of a particular category of analysis such as age, for example, or heterosexuality.

Throughout this collection, it is clear that, along with Foucault, one of the most influential scholars to have informed histories of the body and sex/gender has been Thomas Laqueur. The argument of a transition from a premodern one-sex model of the body to a modern two-sex one made in his *Making Sex: Body and Gender from the Greeks to Freud*, published in 1990, has profoundly influenced subsequent discussions of bodies, sex and gender.[23] Although historians have subsequently debated and modified his thesis it nevertheless remains a cornerstone of body history, informing discussions of a very wide range of subject matters. As Lauren Kassell notes, 'Laqueur's legacy has been most enduring amongst modern historians of sex and the body for whom the transition from the one-to two-sex model serves as a sort of creation myth for binary ideas about sex difference.'[24] Michael Stolberg is most explicit in rejecting Laqueur's thesis, asserting that 'The major anatomists and the overwhelming majority of late medieval and early modern physicians clearly did not advocate a one-sex model. On the contrary, they stressed anatomical difference and its fatal effects on female health.'[25] Restricted to discussions of anatomy, ideas of physical difference according to disease have rarely featured in this debate, but as Stolberg reminds us, 'Due to the peculiar nature of their genitals and breasts, women … suffered from many diseases which were unknown in men.' Laura Gowing argues that one-sex and two-sex models co-existed with ideas about sexual difference that were embodied from head to toe and determined by the balance of humours in the body. She further notes that Laqueur's argument that an emerging differentiation through language between male and female sexual parts from the eighteenth century indicates this increasing differentiation of bodies ignores the huge variety of vernacular and slang terms for male and female body parts that existed prior to this.[26] While Katherine Crawford agrees that 'The critics are not wrong', she nevertheless concedes that 'aspects of Laqueur's thesis remain persuasive,' for 'The difficulty of re-imagining the female body as anatomically specific, for instance, was stubbornly persistent, with gendered assumptions about bodies and roles seemingly limiting new approaches to understanding human anatomy.'

Ideas about the nature of seed, who produces it and what is its nature, infuse discussions of sex and the body, especially in the construction of one-sex or two sexes where homology necessitates female seed, but where difference in body heat affects its nature and efficacy. Ideas about female subordination, in which women are the same but inferior, meant that they therefore produced inferior seed in both quality and substance. Furthermore, as Kevin Siena argues, the shift from a one-sex to a two-sex model of reproduction, where women's production of seed disappears, facilitated the construction of models of transmission of sexual disease in which women's promiscuity could be blamed. However, Sarah Toulalan points out that understandings about the nature of seed were not only gendered, but also infused ideas about age and fitness for sexual activity and successful reproduction. Katherine Crawford's point that gendered ideas about male superiority and female inferiority were inscribed on the body and rationalized as innate characteristics can be applied equally to distinctions made by age. While gender has long been central to analysis of ideas about constructions of bodies and sex, consideration of age as a category of analysis has been slower to emerge, but needs more attention – and in conjunction with race and class as well as gender.

Histories of clothing and dress have so far only appeared on the margins of the one-sex to two-sex debate, where sex differentiation was insufficiently achieved through the body alone and its organization of sexual characteristics. But clothing too had a part to play in making visible to the outside world a person's sex and gender role. Early modern historians have noted that infancy and the early years of childhood occupied a kind of neutered space where bodies were warm and moist, not yet having solidified into the constitutional difference of cold/moist, hot/dry that differentiated women from men. Clothing thus took on an important role in differentiating between the two – which also intersected with age in the practice of breeching boys between the ages of 5 and 8, changing their clothing from the skirts of early childhood worn by both girls and boys to the breeches worn by men that served to differentiate the place in the world occupied by male and female children, and the worlds that they would go on to inhabit in future as they grew. Susan Vincent further notes, 'if garments contributed so much to the normative performance of masculinity and femininity – as glimpsed, for example, in the ritual of breeching – then the wrong clothes perverted that performance and ushered in the effeminate man and the manly woman.' Such concerns for differentiation of gender through clothing were particularly acute in relation to the hermaphrodite and the potential threat it posed to the sex/gender order. However, Vincent also points out that it was not so much an anxiety that bodies might *really* change from one sex to another with the increase or decrease of bodily heat that made bodies either masculine or feminine, but rather 'that appearances no longer clearly mirrored the truth beneath. It is the disruption of the sign that is at stake, not a fear that the sign may, upon examination, prove to be empty.'[27] Clothing was intimately connected to later questions of sexual rather than gender identity, as Paul Deslandes points out, where women's mannish clothing was conflated with lesbian desire.

In writing a history of bodies and sex over a long period of time one of the primary approaches that the reader might anticipate would be for chapters to set out how (and what) knowledge has expanded, or been gained, altered and 'improved'. Here we might expect a story of progression, of improvement of the human condition, as technological development – particularly – has enabled greater penetration of the interior of the body, even down to the level of cells and DNA, allowing subsequent development of new and 'better' ways of understanding and, consequently, of treating and thinking about bodies and sex. Although information of this nature is to be found within the following chapters, broader questions that authors address are to do with what constitutes knowledge and expertise in such matters, who has what kinds of knowledge, and how this shapes under-standing. Although there is a part of this book (part VII, by Laura Gowing and Tanya Evans) that deals specifically with the questions of knowledge and experience, in practice all the chapters in the book address these questions to a greater or lesser extent. At one level everyone has some knowledge of bodies – their own and the bodies of those they come into close contact with – but what constitutes 'expert' knowledge, and who is able to acquire and disseminate knowledge, and to whom, has varied over time. Those authors writing about the pre-1750 period often note how in early modern Europe 'expert' knowledge was not limited simply to those (men) educated in formal institutions of learning and through literacy, especially Latin, the language in which learned anatomies were circulated. 'Expert' knowledge was the province of both this educated elite of medical practitioners but also of ordinary women to whom learned medicine was mostly closed. Through their practice of midwifery and of kitchen physick or medical care in the household – the production and administration of remedies for a very wide variety of illnesses and bodily disorders – women of lesser education and much lower down the social scale than those university-educated men who practised medicine and surgery professionally, also gained knowledge about the body, and particularly of the sexual body. Women were not only thought to be repositories of sexual knowledge and expertise, but they also had more informal networks in which such knowledge might be disseminated. Midwives were subject to ecclesiastical control in England, and to a mix of municipal, state, ecclesiastical and physician supervision in different parts of Europe in the seventeenth century and into the eighteenth, reflecting the huge importance of the Church at this time in matters of the body; the body was not simply about biology but was also thoroughly enmeshed in legal, religious, and other social and cultural beliefs and practices – as it remains today, albeit in differing proportions and ways.[28]

Who had better knowledge of the female body and who was therefore better qualified to manage labour became a site of contestation between female midwives and male medical practitioners who sought to increase their authority in this area and to take over as primary birth attendants, as Lianne McTavish and Helen Blackman discuss in part X. The increasing professionalization and specialization of medical practice in the nineteenth and twentieth centuries saw the ascendancy of male practitioners and the development of obstetrics as well as other medical specialisms. However, as Lauren Kassell notes, making 'public' knowledge of the body, of its private parts and reproduction through the medium of print was problematic. Early modern physicians and surgeons met opposition to the publication of anatomies that included the reproductive parts of the body, as did Ambroise Paré in late sixteenth-century France and Helkiah Crooke in early seventeenth-century London. It was apparently one thing for learned physicians and surgeons to describe and discuss the organs of generation in the 'professional' sphere of the anatomy theatre among other learned men, but quite another to bring this knowledge into a wider 'public' sphere, and in the vernacular, so that potentially anybody who had access to print, whatever their station in life, level of education and occupational identity, could therefore also access and discuss it. Concern seemed to focus upon the potential 'misuse' of knowledge, particularly of the sexual body – that it might be used for erotic purposes, to titillate, rather than to educate and to honour God's creation. Such concerns persisted into the twentieth century over the contents of books about sex both scholarly and intentionally erotic, and over information about contraceptives, and still erupt today in concerns about the nature and extent of sexual education in schools.

Similar concerns, not surprisingly, also fed into anxieties about the availability and circulation of far more self-evidently erotic or pornographic material. Here the secrets of sex and generation were more obviously displayed for pleasure rather than for learning, however much an author might have denied this as his primary purpose. Before the mid-seventeenth century when cheap print became more widely available, images of the sexual body had a much more restricted circulation. Paintings or frescos painted on walls, and erotic engravings were only seen by those who were wealthy enough to be able to afford and display them (although perhaps also to servants in these wealthy households), although bawdy verse and graffiti would have circulated at the lower levels of society on the streets and in taverns. Explicitly erotic texts originated in high-class culture, in court cultures of poetry and Latin medical texts, that were limited to a minority of elite men (and some women) who were able to read texts that circulated in other languages, as Ian Moulton points out. The circulation of manuscript texts also necessarily restricted such material to elite culture. Lower down the social scale, sexual knowledge or information might be expressed socially rather than textually, so leaving fewer traces and less material for the historian to draw upon in attempting to write a history of sexual and bodily knowledge that encompasses all classes (and ages) of society. Such knowledge would have been revealed in public oral and physical exchange, in games, gestures, bawdy songs or rhymes rather than in the manuscripts and printed books to be found in private libraries and collections. Such differentiation of genres and audiences increasingly collapsed with technological advances in the twentieth century, and especially the later development and spread of the internet, making pornographic material ubiquitous and easily accessed, as Lisa Sigel discusses in chapter 12. A number of authors refer to changes in technology bringing changes in ways of knowing, understanding, thinking about and representing bodies and sex. The introduction of the printing press at the beginning of the period, and later improvements that brought about greater dissemination of (cheaper) printed matter, shifted access to imagery and other representations of bodies and sex from the purview of the educated and wealthy elites who circulated manuscript and paintings, to a more 'mass market'. Technology has also changed the nature of the representations themselves, allowing new and different images and narratives (and identifications) to emerge. The rise of print culture that first allowed the diffusion of ancient ideas about bodies and sex subsequently enabled the circulation of new ideas and the development of a secular discourse, particularly in popular literature, alongside medical treatises, as Katherine Crawford sets out in chapter 1. Such concerns about access to this kind of material and for whom it is thought to be inappropriate and potentially damaging has changed over time, becoming more narrowly focused by age today rather than by class and gender as in the past.

Who looked at whose body was also a matter not just of expertise but also of decorum. Knowledge of women's bodies and of generation had been the province of women – birth attendants and midwives – partly because it was not judged seemly for male practitioners to look at or to touch these parts of the body. Monica Green has demonstrated that gynaecology was always the province of male expertise (and Lauren Kassell shows how male medical knowledge of the menstrual cycle was considered central to making a correct diagnosis of female disorders and to provide appropriate remedies), but nevertheless, looking and touching were problematic.[29] As Michael Stolberg and Malcolm Nicolson both demonstrate, knowledge about bodies and the technologies devised to enable knowledge about bodies to be gained was thoroughly grounded in social and cultural 'norms' about learning on the one hand, and about looking at and touching bodies on the other. Central to these considerations were issues of propriety, as well as of class and gender. It may have been easier for male medical practitioners to look at and to touch a male body, though men, too, may have been reluctant to have their private parts handled by another man, in however professional a capacity. Particularly problematic were male investigations of female private parts, as Malcolm Nicolson points out: 'The stethoscope was devised because of anxieties surrounding the proper deportment of men toward women. It has its origins in gender relations.'[30] Such barriers may only have been overcome when bodily conditions had become so intolerable that shame and decorum were overcome by necessity. Further developments were made in the light of anxieties about class and contagion: the stethoscope could be extended to further remove the diagnosing physician from too close a physical proximity to the patient; for the sake of higher social status clients to preserve modesty and distance from lower rank surgeons and physicians, but also, in the case of lower class patients where the physician himself was reluctant to get too close, and had anxieties about contagion through contact. Nicolson also demonstrates how particular diagnostic techniques were developed as a result of particular social and cultural considerations and not because they offered any specific diagnostic advantage. For example, the positioning of a woman on her left side for examination of her private parts was advocated because it allowed the woman to remain covered by clothing and bedclothes so that she was never fully exposed to the physician's gaze. Physicians thus learned to diagnose disorders of the female reproductive parts through touch rather than by sight.

Such a distinction between sight and touch to gain knowledge of the body can be found in earlier periods, hinting at the perceived relative intrusiveness of different kinds of examination. Similarly, use of the speculum was restricted and the investigating physician attempted to use it in such a way that his view was confined to the internal organs rather than also encompassing the external privities. Thus social and gender considerations thoroughly moulded both examination of the body leading to knowledge of its workings and the development of techniques and instrumentation to allow such examination. Michael Stolberg also points to shifts in the status of medical men towards an increasing professionalization that may have contributed to a greater willingness on the part of patients to allow visual and manual examination of the body: an expectation of professional 'objectivity' and standards of behaviour mitigated feelings of shame and embarrassment, and allowed the patient to feel safe from any improper attention. Furthermore, the growth of hospitals throughout the eighteenth and into the nineteenth century gave physicians greater access to bodies through which diagnostic practice and skills could be honed without having to give consideration to patients' feelings of shame or embarrassment; such feelings could not be ignored when patients were private and paying a physician for care – and might take their custom elsewhere if they felt that due care and attention was not being paid to their comfort. The development of a professional, 'objective', medical gaze to overcome embarrassment and consequent reluctance to allow examination and treatment of the most private parts of the body has been particularly important in emerging specialisms such as gynaecology and obstetrics, venereology, and colo-rectal medicine. The medical profession's desire to overcome feelings of shame and embarrassment in their patients and the consequent reluctance to expose oneself for examination and diagnosis seems to have gained pace in very recent years with the production of TV programmes such as *Embarrassing Bodies*, which has encouraged people with conditions affecting the genitals and processes of excretion especially (though not exclusively) to reveal them not only in the privacy of the doctor's surgery but to an audience of millions on national TV.

Looking at the naked body was not solely a consideration of the medical professions as we have seen, but was also enmeshed in religion and politics. What is meant by 'naked' has varied over time: in early modern Europe it did not necessarily mean the body entirely unclothed but referred to the body in varying states of undress, as Susan Vincent points out. Paul Deslandes develops this discussion further, articulating debates in art historical scholarship about the meanings of 'naked' and 'nude' in relation to painting and the 'idealized' nude form. One of the major difficulties with representations of the body unclothed in art – as elsewhere – is the inability to decouple the naked body from eroticism and hence from imputations of moral depravity. Such a concern was central to those involved in promoting 'nudism' and who aligned ideas about health and purity, and optimizing human reproduction – including racial purity – with the body unclothed as Richard Cleminson also discusses in part II on the sexual sciences. Thus at the same time as nudist movements emphasized health and purity, distancing themselves from associations with sexual titillation and moral laxity, they were nevertheless concerned with sexual and reproductive matters. Ideas about non-European people encountered through exploration were also shaped by responses to their shamelessly unclothed bodies (to European Christian eyes) which were understood as indicative of sexual depravity.

Numerous chapters point to one of the clearest shifts in understandings about bodies and how they worked (including sex and reproduction) that began to take place from the late seventeenth century and which picked up pace during the eighteenth century. Early modern knowledge and understanding based upon the classical humoural model of the body was gradually displaced by more modern conceptualizations, although new discoveries and theorizations were initially often incorporated into the humoural framework. This shift in understanding was not completed by the end of the eighteenth century, neither was it so rapid as historians have often suggested, as humoural ideas continued to inform newer understandings into the nineteenth century, and also remained in language and descriptions of temperament into the twentieth century. As new discoveries and theories about bodies shifted understandings, older ideas about heat and cold nevertheless lingered, albeit in a far less dominant fashion than previously. The humoural model of the body was still informing understandings of sex and conception into the later eighteenth century, where infertility from cold was still a key idea. Julie-Marie Strange notes that in the eighteenth century this model of the body was beginning to be replaced by 'mechanistic paradigms of bodies that ran on vital energy, transmitted via a complex nervous system'. However, there were nevertheless continuities. Strange also notes that 'the dominant medical paradigm of sexed bodies in this period was preoccupied with fertility', as Toulalan argues it had been in early modern Europe, and hence 'to demonstrate modern medicine's tendency to imagine sexed bodies in relation to reproductive destinies'. There is further continuity also in the tendency, as Strange remarks, 'to pathologize the female body against an assumed masculine norm'.[31] Just as in early modern times the female body was measured against and found inferior to a normative male body, this continued, albeit in different forms, into the nineteenth and twentieth centuries.[32]

With regard to sex, the normative body is also a sexually mature body, but one that is also potentially reproductively capable; one that is post-pubescent but not yet 'too old'. However, whereas in early modern Europe pre-pubescent bodies were understood to be characterized by a lack of sexuality – of unreadiness for sex and therefore unsuitability to engage in sexual activity – by the nineteenth century little girls were not always regarded in this way. Strange notes that despite a new tendency to idealize the child and childhood and to separate pre-from post-pubescent children, some pre-pubescent girls might not be thought exempt from sexualization, particularly poor, working-class girls who were perceived as liable to be lacking in morality, at risk of incestuous relationships or to be enticed or coerced into prostitution. Such anxieties manifested themselves in concerns about prostitution and a 'white slave trade' of girls for sex and the raising of the age of consent, initially to 13 and then to 16. However, as Kathryn Norberg points out, no evidence has been found that girls younger than 16 were involved in prostitution, and the average age was usually around 25.

Ideas about bodies and how they work changed again in the early twentieth century with the discovery of hormones and the development of endocrinology. Helen Blackman and Julie-Marie Strange both note that understandings of menstruation now changed from being understood as precipitated by nerves to hormones. With this understanding came other developments such as the ability to control conception through the use of hormones and the contraceptive pill that had broader social implications for female liberty from childbearing and their greater participation in economic life, as Tanya Evans discusses in chapter 14. However, there were nevertheless continuities in perceptions of bodies at times of sexual development. Puberty and adolescence continued to be understood as a transitional period of danger and difficulty that was fraught with pitfalls, although now couched in different terms and concerns, such as, for example, cultures of consumption.[33]

Understandings of, and attitudes towards, old age and sex also changed over time. Whereas Toulalan identified cultures of mockery towards the old, particularly to do with sexuality, Strange noted a change 'from ridicule to investing maturity with dignity'. Another shift identified as occurring from the late eighteenth century was in the management of menopause as a time of life. While early modern medicine identified it as bringing bodily changes and often causing illness, from the late eighteenth century medical men began to think about it as a time of life that needed to be managed, though there was some continuity in the perception that it heralded increasing decrepitude and the withering of not only the reproductive function but also the reproductive organs. But from the nineteenth and into the twentieth century these were regarded as not just physical changes, but also changes to temperament and behaviour. It was thought that such psychological and behavioural changes could amount to as much as insanity, making this a particularly difficult and dangerous time for women. Whereas older women's sexual desires were ridiculed and cause for stereotyping in the figure of the early modern 'lusty widow', now such desires were indicative of pathology. As in the earlier period, though, such desires were problematic because they decoupled sex from maternity, suggesting persistence in perceptions of women's bodies as bound up with their fertility and reproductive role.

As will be apparent from the previous discussion, a significant issue raised by a number of authors is that more attention needs to be paid to age as a category of analysis in the histories of the body and sexuality, alongside considerations of gender, class and race. This argument underpins part VIII on life cycles but also features elsewhere. It is most directly addressed by Randolph Trumbach who argues that in early modern Europe sexual relations were organized around age: 'In 1500 in western societies sexual desire was as likely to be organized by differences in age as by differences in gender.'[34] Although Ivan Crozier does not specifically do so, arguing for a realignment of thinking about sex around acts rather than identities ('focusing on bodies and the sexual pleasures for which they are used is a way out of the categorical imperative that still haunts us with the use of labels first constructed by nineteenth-century sexologists'[35]), he nevertheless raises the issue in his discussion of masochism and conceptions of sexual flagellation. A behaviour that was understood in the early modern period in somatic terms as producing pleasure, and so enabling intercourse and orgasm in older men who had difficulties in achieving physical congress, was transformed by the late nineteenth century into one that was understood through psychological mechanisms for transforming pain into pleasure. Understandings about sexual behaviours might therefore be re-aligned around age categories (older men) as much as by the type of sexual activity itself. Age also intersects with race, as we see in part XIV by Jonathan Burton and Antoinette Burton, where the bodies of those living in hotter climes were understood to mature sexually earlier than colder European bodies, and where the practice of child marriage contributed to perceptions of Asian men as 'failed men'.[36]

The chapters by Toulalan and Strange that examine ideas about sexual development and decline also argue for an organization of sexuality around fertility and reproduction, where age necessarily becomes foregrounded as it governs readiness and capacity for sexual and reproductive life. The centrality of fertility and reproduction to these ideas about sexual development and decline thus necessarily restricts their discussions to sex between male and female, precluding consideration of same-sex sexual behaviours as non-reproductive. Trumbach's discussion, however, focuses upon same-sex sexual encounters and argues specifically for an early modern organization of same-sex sexual behaviour around age for both men and women, where older men sought relations with boys, women with girls: 'sexual behavior between males and between females was in both cases organized predominantly by differences in age, men with boys and women with girls.' Scholars are alert to the necessity of considering questions about class, gender and race in their analyses of bodies and sex, but have not yet integrated age as a category of analysis in quite the same way. Yet age has fundamentally conditioned thinking about bodies and sex. As Stephen Robertson has pointed out, 'Against the tendency to restrict the concern with age to the history of childhood, we have to be alert to its broader resonance. Ideas about age were not only located in the legal system … they flowed to that site from medicine, psychology, education, and popular culture, fields that had been permeated by a consciousness of age.'[37]

Trumbach argues that 'The sexual passivity of the adolescent boy was acceptable because he had not yet become a man.'[38] Becoming a man was, as Toulalan shows, bound up with the physical development of the male body where achieving manhood was to achieve fully functioning reproductive capacity in the ability to not only ejaculate seed, but seed that was 'prolifick', hot and vigorous, and able to spark new life. Trumbach notes that the sodomy practised by men in early modern Florence was strictly organized by age with the active, penetrating role being almost always taken by a man older than his passive, penetrated partner, very rarely the reverse, as 'it was taken as a normal part of human development that when a beard had grown on an individual male, he was able to change from passive boy to active man'. He also points out this age differential in contemporary plays which frequently included references to sodomy, where nearly all such references or scenes were 'structured by differences in age between an adult man and an adolescent boy'. Furthermore, most, though not all, transvestite prostitutes were likely to have been adolescent boys who could pass as 'maids', often drawn from the ranks of young enlisted soldiers and drummer boys, aged 14 to 16, from the London regiments. Similarly, paintings also eroticized the body of the boy: 'The body of the naked adolescent male, and men's desire for that body, was central to that art.'[39] Due to the paucity of sources we can be less certain that women's same-sex sexual relationships were organized in similar ways, but in pornography and erotica, as both Ian Moulton and Kathryn Norberg point out, female same-sex sexual activities were frequently represented as an older woman initiating a younger girl into the pleasures of sex. Trumbach argues that it is not unlikely that the same organization by age may have applied in Europe as other studies for other parts of the world have shown that such sexual cultures were not unknown.

Various essays in this collection show that age was also a key category in cultures of knowledge, intersecting with gender, at least as they were represented in pornography and erotica, where, as we have seen above, sexual knowledge was passed – or at least represented as passed – from older, experienced woman to young, inexperienced girl. Older women were regarded as repositories of sexual and reproductive knowledge, serving on juries of matrons to establish virginity, impotence or pregnancy. Norberg, as we have seen, has noted that the average age of the early modern prostitute was around 25, and despite contemporary rhetoric, girls below the age of 16 have not been identified. It would therefore seem that pre-pubescent girls did not engage in selling sex – or were not sold for sex by others – suggesting that sexual readiness was a precondition for prostitution, as it appears to have been for marriage; Martin Ingram similarly notes that 'very young marriages were uncommon' in north-west Europe, with couples usually waiting until they had sufficient resources to set up a new household except among wealthier, higher class families where earlier alliances might be forged for political or economic advantage.[40] Similarly, age (as well as marital status) influenced attitudes towards and reactions to rape (noted by both Walker and D'Cruze), where the rape of minors under the age of consent – and usually therefore pre-pubescent until it was raised in stages from 12 to 16 in the late nineteenth century – was generally prosecuted more keenly and more likely to achieve conviction. However, as previously noted, in the nineteenth century some children, especially girls, were understood to 'display premature and precocious sexuality' so that they might be seducers and blackmailers of respectable men.[41] This kind of negative construction of the girl-child was, however, inflected by class where only working-class girls were likely to display such behaviour. Concerns about children and sex have emerged again in the late twentieth century with child sexual abuse and paedophilia seeming to receive disproportionate media coverage: 'By 2000 the psychopathic rapist-murderer of children was the quintessential monster.' Cases of abduction and abuse that are sensationalized have raised public concerns, and the growth of the internet has allowed greater production and dissemination of pornographic materials involving children to an unprecedented level. Studies have indicated that the consumption of child pornography is not confined to stereotypical pathologized 'monsters', but can be found at all levels of society.[42] Age has thus emerged as a key category of analysis to which historians of bodies and sex need to pay attention as much as they do to gender, class and race.

Barry Reay and Kim Philips have recently argued convincingly that historians have underplayed the extent to which heterosexuality also has a history and has been variously constructed over time and place. Ian Moulton in this volume further points out that the privileging of heterosexuality in representations of bodies and sex has continued until at least the late twentieth century. In erotic and pornographic representation heterosexual sexual encounters were the norm, with homosexual sex generally treated as an aberration and harshly condemned. Lisa Sigel notes that the proliferation of differing kinds of erotic representation, not only homosexual, is a relatively recent development. The primary frame of reference for sex and sexual pleasure was marriage and the production of children, and this did not really change until the late twentieth century. Sexual pleasure within marriage was understood as an important part of binding a couple together and ensuring the stability and endurance of marriage, and hence of wider society, particularly through children and inheritance: 'Marriage law, sodomy law, the distinction between licit and illicit sexual activities, even the distinction between what was sex and what was not, all depended on the relation of a given practice to the possibility of procreation.'[43] This can also be seen in attitudes towards sexual activity throughout the life cycle, where sex at either the beginning or the end was problematic as it was non-procreative sex – pre-menarche for girls, or not yet sufficiently procreative male seed (and female in the two-seed model before the eighteenth century) and post-menopause or in many older men whose seed became less potent as they aged. Such concerns with sex and the possibility of procreation meant that successful conjugal sexual relations was promoted as other expressions of sexual desire were increasingly attacked or constructed as deleterious to both sexual health and health more generally, and, from the nineteenth century, pathologized. Thus Harry Cocks concludes that 'sexual infractions tended to follow the modern pattern of moving from being treated first as sins, then as crimes and finally as diseases or psychological disorders'.[44] The separation of marriage from reproduction and property transmission is a modern – late twentieth-century – shift that has come with reliable contraception to separate sex from reproduction, with easier divorce so that marriage is a dissoluble contract, and with changes in inheritance practices so that wealth and property are no longer necessarily retained within the family but can legitimately be willed elsewhere, to extra-familial persons, organizations and even non-human legatees. Such an examination of the varieties of ways that heterosexuality has been constructed owes much, Harry Cocks points out, to queer theory which suggests that 'we reject the apparent self-evidence of modern sexual categories and identities, and that we pay attention to the specific ways in which each society creates rules about sex and the body'.[45]

Modern historians of the body, working within a predominantly secular tradition – especially one where biology underpins understanding of how bodies work and reproduce (reproduction is now taught in schools in biology lessons) – has often obscured the extent to which religion was enmeshed with understandings about bodies and shaped and constrained experience of sex. Several authors remind us how religious ideas have shaped sexual morality and discipline throughout western European history, and continue to do so despite the rise of secular thought about the body and sexuality. Martin Ingram identifies a shift from religious to secular sexual discipline towards the end of the seventeenth century as the 'coercive power' of the church courts waned, but religious bodies as well as individuals motivated by Christian morality continued to be involved in moral campaigns for sexual regulation, as is apparent through the attempts to deal with venereal disease and prostitution in the nineteenth century that Maria Luddy and Lesley Hall discuss in chapters 22 and 26. Increasing globalization and emigration in more recent decades has thrown conflict between religious and secular approaches to the body and sex into greater relief, reminding historians of the continuing importance of religion in shaping perceptions and attitudes.

In early modern Europe, not only was the body understood first and foremost as exemplary of God's handiwork – the microcosm in which the workings of the universe were displayed – and sex intended to reproduce the species as 'He' had intended, but when 'natural' explanations for bodily disorders reached their limits, spiritual or diabolical ones came to the fore. This can be seen especially, Lauren Kassell argues, in the disorder of hysteria, or 'suffocation of the mother' where the womb was thought to wander and bring out various symptoms including breathing difficulties as it pressed on the breathing passages. When natural remedies were unable to relieve symptoms and sufferings then diabolical causes could be suspected, with cure having spiritual remedies – prayer and fasting. In representations of the body, religion too had an impact upon its interpretations: anti-Catholic erotica, for example, was interpreted differently in Catholic countries than in Protestant ones – a legitimate criticism of an unacceptable faith in England but an unacceptable attack on the status quo in France. However, Kathryn Norberg argues that Catholic and Protestant attitudes towards prostitutes were similar, but after the Protestant Reformation and Catholic Counter-Reformation, Catholic attitudes became more strict. While arguing that prostitutes might be saved through repentance, Catholic theologians nevertheless also argued for the abolition of brothels and the condemnation of prostitution, anxious that they might be regarded as less 'righteous' than their intolerant Protestant brothers. Both Catholic and Protestant authorities found it impossible completely to remove prostitution and so resorted to limiting it to certain areas as far as was possible. Maria Luddy's discussion of the 'wrens of the Curragh', however, demonstrates the harsh treatment and lack of tolerance shown towards these women, and the shelters in which they lived, by the Catholic clergy. The idea of regulation and toleration of prostitution gained new ground in the nineteenth century but was now based upon medical rather than moral reasons, regarding it as a growing health issue. It was believed that prostitutes spread venereal disease and therefore that regulation and treatment of prostitutes would reduce the number of cases, particularly among the military whose strength was depleted through illness, as Lesley Hall also shows in more detail in her discussion of the Contagious Diseases Acts.

Religion too was implicated in understanding the advent of the new sexual disease to Europe: it had been sent by God to punish sinners and it has been argued that it contributed to more stringent moral policing in the era of reformations, and to the declining toleration of brothels and regulated prostitution that had been characteristic of the medieval period: 'Whereas medieval prostitutes had been seen to offer a kind of necessary service, providing an outlet for unmarried men, saving respectable wives and daughters from sexual predation, they were increasingly portrayed as a threat.'[46] The division between Protestant and Catholic Europe was also apparent in differing attitudes towards treatment of the disease and of those suffering from it. Catholic teaching allowed for redemption through good works while that of Protestants emphasized salvation through faith alone. Catholic institutions for the care of those suffering from venereal diseases thus placed emphasis on moral and spiritual redemption as well as physical care and cure, while Protestants focused only upon physical healing. Kevin Siena argues that this may have also led to a more forgiving attitude towards those with the disease, where sinners might be welcomed 'back into the fold' and 'even diseased prostitutes might be forgiven, albeit within a very constrained institution'.[47] However, as Lesley Hall points out, attempts to regulate prostitution in the nineteenth century to prevent the spread of sexual disease were also perceived as an affront to Christian morality in 'rendering vice safe'.

Authors in this volume invite us to think about bodies not just as they may have been differently 'constructed' at different times but also – and more importantly – about the significances of different bodies, the ideas and cultural valences that they embody, at different times. As Richard Cleminson points out, 'The body of an aristocratic Englishman in the late 1700s was understood to be subject to, literally to embody, different mechanisms and finalities, particularly in respect of the mind, than the body of a black slave in a European colony.' He goes on, 'The truths thus apparently derived from the body participate in narratives that construct overlapping boundaries between health and ill health, the pathological and the normal, the sexually deviant and the sexually normative and the hierarchy of races and sexes.'[48] We may only 'know' bodies therefore through situating them in the specificities of time and place, and the particularities of societies and cultures. Thus the use of terms and categories is highlighted throughout this volume as problematic. Not only can they be anachronistic but they also serve to obscure different understandings in different times and places. Ian Moulton notes succinctly that 'if sexuality has a history at all, it consists precisely in the different and changing ways that various sexual acts are culturally represented, categorized, and understood'.[49] This is particularly applicable to discussions of sexual representations, as both Ian Moulton and Lisa Sigel remark. Historians have spent a lot of time debating the meaning of particular terms – pornography, erotica, obscenity – but the early modern period had no single term to categorize texts or images that were sexual in nature, but rather a variety of different terms with varying meanings. Similarly, the meanings of words for sexual categories also change over time and place. The word 'gay' is an obvious case in point – used in the nineteenth and early twentieth centuries to denote a woman who was a prostitute, or 'upon the town', it is now used to denote homosexuality, a significant shift in meaning over time.

The eighteenth and nineteenth centuries are still seen as pivotal times of change in how the body and sex were understood. Kathryn Norberg pinpoints the mid-eighteenth century as a pivotal point in attitudes towards prostitution changing as they were seen as the primary means of transmission of venereal disease that was understood to be undermining public health; not only the health of the men who frequented prostitutes but also that of 'honest' married women who were infected by a husband: 'The French worried that syphilis was undermining the French population because it killed babies and rendered adults infertile. The future of France, not just a rake's health, was now at risk.'[50] Norberg also argues that it was then that prostitutes came to be seen as fundamentally different to other women, whereas earlier the early modern sexually voracious woman was likely to commit adultery, fornication or fall into prostitution to satisfy her lust. As women came to be understood rather as maternal and domestic, the prostitute became a different creature, separated and isolated from 'ordinary' women as both a social and a biological evil.

Explaining the timing of change and what it meant is also found to be problematic. In particular, as Garthine Walker remarks in the conclusion to her discussion of rape and sexual violence in early modern Europe, the same explanation – 'the emergence of modern sensibilities' – has been found for two different changes taking place at the same time: a reduction of prosecutions for child rape in England and a new recognition of its occurrence and a need to deal with it in France.[51] Similarly in terms of punishment, removing the death penalty is seen in terms of modernization, but in some places it was imposed in the eighteenth century for rape, thus contradicting such arguments. Moreover, as Shani D'Cruze continues, if taking rape seriously as a crime against the person is an indicator of modernization where violence, including sexual violence, is taken more seriously, then sexual violence cannot always be seen to follow this trend as it continued to be ignored or its seriousness downplayed. However, again following Foucault, the key point of change is the late nineteenth century and sexological developments: the categorization of sexual 'types' and the development of ideas about 'perversion'. With reference to rape, 'Sexology privileged and naturalized a model of sexual practice based on sharp gender dichotomies, where masculinity was the active, aggressive principle.' This meant that some sexual violence became hidden within 'normal' heterosexual practice, and was only distinguished as pathological when violence became extreme or when it was directed towards 'inappropriate' victims such as children. Although clearly not a new phenomenon, a much more recent concern has arisen about the use of sexual violence in war as part of 'the spectrum of torture, killing and mutilation visited on defeated and often civilian populations'.[52] Here rape becomes a bonding mechanism for combatants and is deliberately used as a means of social, cultural and ethnic destruction, fracturing social bonds and patrilineal descent to further defeat weakened states. Rape, then, does not fit so neatly into arguments about progress and modernization.

The following chapters thus encourage the reader to think about both how the field has been shaped so far – the ideas that have informed understandings about bodies and sex in the past – and those that are now emerging to shape future research and the questions we ask about the past. The book concludes with a short afterword by Lisa Downing that invites the reader to consider some of the 'tensions, problems and areas deserving further scrutiny' that emerged in her reading of the book. It also looks at the historical analyses in the chapters that follow in the light of some contemporary thinking and debates about sex, gender and the body, reminding us that history is never just about the past.

Notes

1 Iwan Bloch, *The Sexual Life of Our Time: In Its Relations To Modern Civilization*, London: Rebman, 1909; translated from the German *Das Sexualleben unserer Zeit in seinen Beziehungen zur modernen Kultur*, Berlin: Marcus Verlagsbuchhandlung, 1906.
2 Peter Stearns argues in *Sexuality in World History* that 'serious work on the history of sex is only a few decades old'. Peter Stearns, *Sexuality in World History*, New York and London: Routledge, 2009, p. 1.
3 *Journal of the History of Sexuality* 1:1, 1990.
4 Many early works were self-consciously pioneering and positioned themselves on the margins of legitimate or respectable historical activity. Many of these works comment on the place of the history of sex and sexuality as at the margins of respectable academic work.
5 Jeffrey Weeks, 'Sexuality and History Revisited' in Kim M. Phillips and Barry Reay, *Sexualities in History: A Reader*, New York and London: Routledge, 2001, pp. 27–41.
6 Phillips and Reay, 'Introduction' in *Sexualities in History*, p. 4.
7 Harry Cocks and Matt Houlbrook, 'Introduction' in *The Modern History of Sexuality*, Basingstoke: Palgrave, 2005, pp. 1–18 (16, 3). This point is explored by Sigel in chapter 6.
8 Cocks and Houlbrook, 'Introduction', p. 9.
9 There are far too many to list here. For those looking at British history, in the modern period, Jeffrey Weeks' remarkably enduring *Sex Politics and Society*, first published in 1981 and revised and reissued in 1989, remains an essential starting point. It has been joined by others including Lesley Hall, *Sex Gender and Social Change in Britain since 1880*, Basingstoke: Macmillan, 2000. For earlier periods see (for example) Ruth Mazo Karras, *Sexuality in Medieval Europe: Doing unto Others*, London: Routledge, 2005; Katherine Crawford, *Sexual Cultures of the French Renaissance*, Cambridge: Cambridge University Press, 2010; Tim Hitchcock, *English Sexualities, 1700–1800*, Basingstoke: Macmillan, 1997.
10 Cocks and Houlbrook, *The Modern History of Sexuality*.
11 Dagmar Herzog, *Sexuality in Europe: A Twentieth Century History*, Cambridge: Cambridge University Press, 2011.
12 Kim M. Phillips and Barry Reay, *Sex Before Sexuality: A Premodern History*, Cambridge: Polity, 2011.
13 Anna Clark, *Desire: A History of European Sexuality*, London: Routledge, 2008. See also her *The History of Sexuality in Europe: a Sourcebook and Reader*, New York: Routledge, 2010.

14 Stearns, *Sexuality in World History*.

15 See especially Tim Hitchcock, 'Re-defining Sex in Eighteenth Century England', *History Workshop Journal* 41, 1996, pp. 73–92.

16 Their focus is, however, more contemporary than historical. Lisa Downing and Robert Gillett (eds), *Queer in Europe: Contemporary Case Studies*, Farnham: Ashgate, 2011, and Robert Kulpa and Joanna Mizielińska, *De-Centring Western Sexualities: Central and Eastern European Perspectives*, Farnham: Ashgate, 2011. We are grateful to Lisa Downing for pointing us towards these two works.

17 Studies of the post-communist period in Russia and eastern/central Europe include Aleksandar Štulhofer and Theo Sandfort (eds), *Sexuality and Gender in Postcommunist Eastern Europe and Russia*, New York: The Haworth Press, 2005; Janet Elise Johnson and Jean C. Robinson, *Living Gender after Communism*, Bloomington, IN: Indiana University Press, 2007; Igor S. Kon, *The Sexual Revolution in Russia: From the Age of the Czars to Today*, New York: The Free Press, 1995; Judit Takács, '(Homo)Sexual Politics: Theory and Practice' in Miklós Hadas and Miklós Vörös (eds), *Ambiguous Identities in the New Europe*, Budapest: Republika Circle, 1997, pp. 93–103.

18 Although see Kulpa and Mizielińska, *De-Centring Western Sexualities*. Dan Healey's *Homosexual Desire in Revolutionary Russia* (Chicago: The University of Chicago Press, 2001) is a notable exception, in his words, 'the first full-length study of same-sex love in any period of Russian or Soviet history'.

19 Stefan Berger, *Writing the Nation: A Global Perspective*, Basingstoke: Palgrave, 2007, p. xxvi.

20 A very small indication of the wealth of writing on Scandinavia includes the following on early modern Sweden: Jonas Liliequist, 'Masculinity and Virility – Representations of Male Sexuality in Eighteenth-Century Sweden' in Anu Korhonen and Kate Lowe (eds), *The Problem with Ribs: Women, Men and Gender in Early Modern Europe*, Helsinki: Helsinki Collegium for Advanced Studies, 2007, pp. 57–81, and Liliequist, 'Peasants Against Nature: Crossing the Boundaries Between Man and Animal in Seventeenth- and Eighteenth-Century Sweden', *Journal of the History of Sexuality* 1:3, 1991, pp. 393–423. For modern Sweden see, for example: Jens Rydström, '"Sodomitical Sins are Threefold": Typologies of Bestiality, Masturbation, and Homosexuality in Sweden, 1880–1950', *Journal of the History of Sexuality* 9, 2000, pp. 240–76, and his *Sinners and Citizens: Bestiality and Homosexuality in Sweden, 1880–1950*, Chicago: Chicago University Press, 2003. On prostitution and sexuality see, for example: Yvonne Svanström, 'Criminalising the John: A Swedish Gender Model?' in Joyce Outshoorn (ed.), *The Politics of Prostitution: Women's Movements, Democratic States and the Globalisation of Sex Commerce*, Cambridge: Cambridge University Press, 2004, pp. 225–44, and Svanström, *Policing Public Women: The Regulation of Prostitution in Stockholm, 1812–1820*, Stockholm: Atlas Akkademi, 2000; Anna Lundberg, 'Passing the "Black Judgement": Swedish social policy on venereal disease in the early twentieth century' in Roger Davidson and Lesley A. Hall (eds), *Sex, Sin, and Suffering: Venereal Disease and European Society Since 1870*, London: Routledge, 2001, pp. 21–43. Davidson and Hall's edited volume is exemplary in its coverage of Europe, including essays on Sweden and Russia as well as Italy, Spain and Germany.

21 Jonathan Burton, chapter 27.

22 Karen Vieira Powers, *Women in the Crucible of Conquest: The Gendered Genesis of Spanish American Society, 1500–1600*, Albuquerque, NM: University of New Mexico Press, 2005, p. 95; John F. Chuchiak, 'The sins of the fathers: Franciscan friars, parish priests, and the sexual conquest of the Yucatec Maya, 1545–1808', *Ethnohistory* 54, 2007, pp. 69–127; Matthew Restall, *The Maya World: Yucatec Culture and Society, 1550–1850*, Stanford, CA: Stanford University Press, 1997.

23 As also has Judith Butler, referenced by a number of contributors but not discussed here. See her *Gender Trouble: Feminism and the Subversion of Identity*, London: Routledge, 1990; *Bodies that Matter: On the Discursive Limits of 'Sex'*, New York: Routledge, 1993.

24 Kassell, chapter 3.

25 Stolberg, chapter 5. Thomas Laqueur, *Making Sex: Body and Gender from the Greeks to Freud*, Cambridge, MA: Harvard University Press, 1990; Michael Stolberg, 'A Woman Down to her Bones: The Anatomy of Sexual Difference in the Sixteenth and Early Seventeenth Centuries', *Isis* 94, 2003, pp. 274–99; Katherine Park, *Secrets of Women: Gender, Generation, and the Origins of Human Dissection*, New York: Zone Books, 2006.

26 Gowing, chapter 13.

27 Vincent, chapter 9.

28 Doreen Evenden, *The Midwives of Seventeenth-Century London*, Cambridge: Cambridge University Press, 2000, pp. 24–25.

29 Monica H. Green, *Making Women's Medicine Masculine: The Rise of Male Authority in Pre-Modern Gynaecology*, Oxford: Oxford University Press, 2008.

30 Nicolson, chapter 6.

31 Strange, chapter 16.

32 See Ornella Moscucci, *The Science of Woman: Gynaecology and Gender in England, 1800–1929*, Cambridge: Cambridge University Press, 1990; Geoffrey Chamberlain, *From Witchcraft to Wisdom: A History of Obstetrics and Gynaecology*, London: RCOG Press, 2007; Thomas Laqueur, *Making Sex: Body and Gender from the Greeks to Freud*, Cambridge, MA; London: Harvard University Press, 1990.

33 See Strange, chapter 16.

34 Trumbach, chapter 7.

35 Crozier, chapter 8.

36 Antoinette Burton, chapter 28.

37 Stephen Robertson, *Crimes against Children: Sexual Violence and Legal Culture in New York City, 1880–1960*, Chapel Hill and London: University of North Carolina Press, 2005, p. 133.

38 Trumbach, chapter 7.

39 Trumbach, chapter 7.

40 Ingram, chapter 17.

41 Strange, chapter 16.

42 D'Cruze, chapter 24.

43 Moulton, chapter 11.

44 Cocks, chapter 2.

45 Cocks, chapter 2.

46 Siena, chapter 25.

47 Siena, chapter 25.

48 Cleminson, chapter 4.

49 Moulton, chapter 11.

50 Norberg, chapter 21.

51 Walker, chapter 23.

52 Dagmar Herzog (ed.), *Brutality and Desire: War and Sexuality in Europe's Twentieth Century*, Basingstoke: Palgrave, 2009, p. 4.

Part I

STUDYING THE BODY
AND SEXUALITY

1

THE GOOD, THE BAD, AND THE TEXTUAL

Approaches to the study of the body and sexuality, 1500–1750

Katherine Crawford

The sex advice manual, *Aristotle's Masterpiece*, advised readers: 'When the Husband commeth into his Wives Chamber, he must entertain her with all kind of dalliance, wanton behaviour, and allurements to Venery, but if he perceive her to be slow and more cold, he must cherish, embrace, and tickle her … intermixing more wanton Kisses with wanton Words and Speeches, handling her Secret Parts and Dugs, that she may take fire and be inflamed to Venery.'[1] *Aristotle's Masterpiece* was not by Aristotle, but it was something of a masterpiece. It was, with adaptations for the changing times, a best seller until well into the nineteenth century.[2] Aimed at a popular audience, *Aristotle's Masterpiece* exemplifies several of the salient developments in the shifting understandings of the study of the body and sexuality that began in the Renaissance, and also provides a good focus for understanding the ways in which the study of the history of sex and the body have developed in the past 30 years of scholarship. *Aristotle's Masterpiece* exemplifies the complicated and contested developments in thinking about sex and sexuality, challenging the assumption that sex before the 'Enlightenment' period of the seventeenth/eighteenth century was 'playful', 'unihibited', or unmedicalized. First, *Aristotle's Masterpiece* shows the effects of the rise of secular thought about the body and sexuality that took place during the period referred to as the Renaissance (including developments such as the spread of print culture and the recovery of Antiquity) in undermining earlier presumptions about corporeal knowledge. Second, it highlights the contradictory impulses such shifts created in which the expanding language about sexuality encountered attempts to define, control, and regulate 'proper' sexuality. Finally, in its reliance on sensory experience and a fundamental trust in the reliability of the body to behave as nature intended, *Aristotle's Masterpiece* echoes the new corporeal and sexual regime of the European Enlightenment.

Despite all that it can reveal about the culture of its day, a text like *Aristotle's Masterpiece* has only recently come to the attention of scholars, as a result of methodological and conceptual changes in approaches to history. The study of sex and the body has emerged and transformed since the 1970s. The field has been dominated in particular by Michel Foucault's work, despite his relatively low interest in early modernity. However, as we shall see, Foucault established a set of conceptual and methodological frameworks that have proved extremely stimulating, while painting a particular image of the medieval and early modern worlds which historians have spent considerable energy revising, modifying and challenging. Since the 1970s, following the work of Foucault and others, a whole new range of sources for thinking about the medieval and early modern periods have come to dominate studies along with new ways of interrogating more familiar sources. In the 1970s, the shift away from high politics and toward the history of everyday life and ordinary people prompted inquiries into the history of the family, the history of women, and to a degree, the history of sexuality. After all, families continue because of sex, and women, historians found, were largely defined in terms of their sexual status as virgins, wives, widows, nuns, or prostitutes, just to name the more common iterations.[3] Second, historians of women, coming out of the social tradition, filled in empirical data about women's lives and formulated narratives about sexually inflected practices.

This chapter explores the compelling intellectual framework for studying sex and the body provided by Foucault's *History of Sexuality* (1978). It examines the body of critical historical works, which, while indebted to Foucault's conceptual challenges, reworked his idea that the Renaissance was a period when sexuality, as an attribute of the person, was absent and the mechanisms for controlling behaviour were based on acts and not on identities, in a way which meant that behaviour itself could be viewed as less inhibited and more playful. In recent work, the Renaissance is revealed as a period of intense debate about sexual matters that drew upon, for example, ancient texts and medical models of male and female nature. In particular, the idea that such understandings of sex enabled a form of 'sexual freedom' has been revised and the important ways in which sexuality was policed have been stressed. A focus on *Aristotle's Masterpiece* provides an exceptionally clear route through these themes, highlighting the ways in which the shifting understandings of sex and the body in the period 1500–1750 did not follow Foucault's model. Rather, the text illustrates the ways in which the 'Renaissance' ushered in a period of new contestations around sex and the body, new forms of control, and new anxieties: configurations of sex which were both a form of science and an art at the same time.

Foucault argued that discourse, made up of both language and silences around language, constituted a technology of power. In the case of sexuality, discourse was largely organized by and around such institutional structures as the church, the state, the family, and 'science'.[4] In addition to the understanding of power as a matter of discourse, Foucault argued two central premises that continue to motivate historical scholarship and are of particular importance for this chapter. As Harry Cocks explores in greater detail in the companion chapter to this one, Foucault maintained that sexual identity was a product of modernity and prompted by the rise of interest in sexuality as a matter of population politics and 'morality'. In early modernity, individuals committed sexual 'acts' but did not regard their sexual behaviour as constituting their identity. In contrast, a modern person defined himself (for Foucault, the subject in question was almost always male) by reference to his sexual behaviour. Terms like 'homosexual' came to have meaning as identity categories as never before. Second, Foucault argued that the distinction between the science and art of sex (*scientia sexualis* and *ars erotica*) was crucial for understanding how people obfuscated around sex. The development of scientific language around the biology of reproduction and the medicine of sex led to the articulation of sexual knowledge as 'fact'. The modern west, he maintained, sought to understand sex as a matter of truth generated through confession. Other cultures (Rome in the past and the 'East' broadly construed) understood sexual knowledge in terms of sensual pleasure. Where western subjects understood sex as constraint, those in the East accepted pleasure without separating 'good' sexual acts from 'bad' ones.

Provocative as these claims were, Foucault asserted them more than proved them. Lacking empirical precision, Foucault's work was both the target of historians and an inspiration to them.[5] Historical study of sexuality prompted by Foucault has attempted to fill the empirical gaps, challenged aspects of Foucault's chronology, and inspired inquiry into patterns of meaning with respect to sexuality and sexual behaviour. For example, scholars have highlighted important Renaissance texts which challenged Judaeo-Christian assumptions about sex long before the period Foucault highlighted as significant. The Renaissance is conventionally understood as an intellectual movement that recuperated ancient texts and spread knowledge of Antiquity through the teaching and learning of Latin, Greek, and Hebrew texts. Less conventionally, scholars have found that many of these texts considered sexual matters.[6] In 1417, Poggio Bracciolini unearthed a manuscript of the *De rerum natura* by Lucretius. For the first time since the sixth century, significant remains devoted to supporting the philosophy of Epicurus became available in the west. Lucretius' poem was published in 1473, and the surviving letters of Epicurus appeared in print in 1533. Epicurus inspired supporters initially. Bartholomaeus De Sacchi Platina's *De honesta voluptate* focused on pleasures of the body with special attention to corralling desire so that it did not cause discomfort by allowing pleasures to control the body.[7] Lorenzo Valla wrote *De voluptate* in defence of Epicurean ideas, and his notion that pleasure rather than virtue was the highest good caused him to be regarded askance by the hierarchy of the Catholic Church.[8] For Thomas Creech, Epicurean pleasure was a travesty. Of Epicurus, Creech warns: 'Sometimes his Books declare him a most loose and dissolute Voluptuary', while Lucretius was devoted to, 'his share in sensual Pleasures'.[9] The Epicurean rejection of notions of the divine and immortality of the soul that could be cast as compatible with Christian ethics meant that the emphasis on corporeal pleasure caused tremendous discomfort.

These sorts of discourses did not figure in Foucault's account. He had little to say about the Renaissance. He thought the crucial development toward modern sexuality occurred in the seventeenth century with the rise of auricular confession. In his narrative, the practice of describing the self in confession, of understanding sexual acts as expressed in language, produced the internalization of sexual norms. A more relaxed, playful attitude toward sex, he argued, gave way to the modern practice of disciplining the self. Indeed, there are plenty of examples that suggest this process of identification through confession did occur. A transcript of proceedings by the Inquisition in Mexico reveals how confession could work in dramatic terms. Marina de San Miguel came to the attention of the Inquisition in 1598. When asked why she had been arrested, Marina initially offered minor transgressions of church law. The officials remained unimpressed until Marina seemed to fall into a trance and then explained she had a vision of assisting Christ releasing souls from Purgatory. Still, Marina's story did not satisfy, and she was enjoined to examine her conscience. Left to do so for six weeks, Marina requested an interview. And the dam broke. She had engaged in sexual relations with several men and another *beata*. She had masturbated and looked at her genitals with a mirror. As for her spiritual trance, that was a fake, she said. She just wanted to maintain her reputation for piety, and both the trance before witnesses and denying her sexual depravity (as she now saw it) were part of her effort to do so. Marina defended herself by arguing that she did not intend to sin, and that her actions were accordingly not sinful. The Inquisition did not agree, and Marina was convicted.[10] While the process of turning Marina's experiences into 'sin' and 'crime' through confession illustrates aspects of Foucault's point about the power of discourse to create identity, it undermines his assertion that sex was more playful and uninhibited. Marina knew to hide her sexual experiences, recognized that revealing them would be dangerous, and discovered that the Inquisition understood her desire to hide as evidence of her knowledge that she was in fact guilty, regardless of her intentions.

Marina's self-protection is not surprising. Contrary to what Foucault implies, discourse about sex and the body had been prominent in the west since Antiquity. Aristotelian logic and ancient physiology organized ideas about sexuality and the body derived from presumptions about men and women. Aristotle's philosophy with respect to sex was articulated most fully in *De generatione animalium* (On the Generation of Animals). Among Aristotle's assertions was the idea that only men produce seed necessary to reproduce human life. Aristotle reasoned that men were superior, and since nature created everything for a purpose – a *telos* – men must provide the important parts in procreation. Seed for Aristotle meant the soul and principal characteristics. Women provided the locus for generation (the womb) and the basic matter to enable the foetus to develop. These were inferior aspects in Aristotle's view, in which all things have four causes: material, formal, efficient, and final. Material causes are the most basic; formal causes (and the male contribution was the formal cause) were more advanced and therefore more important. The key difference was humoural, Aristotle believed. Every person had a 'complexion', which was the balance of their humours. Each humour (blood, phlegm, black bile, and yellow bile) had a quality (dry, wet, hot, or cold). Based on the four basic elements (earth, water, fire, and air), the humours had qualities that reflected the balance of elements of which they were composed. The balance could be altered by environment, diet, and physical activity, but in general, women were colder and wetter, while men were hotter and dryer. While there were functional differences between male and female bodies, in humoural terms, all bodies were on a spectrum from hot to cold and dry to wet.

Aristotelian ideas continued to dominate through the Middle Ages. Despite the concerns of Christian ascetics, sexuality remained a lively issue and debates about sex and the body peppered the intellectual exchanges of scholastics. As Joan Cadden notes, problems raised by ancient physicians and natural philosophers motivated much scholastic discussion.[11] With Constantine the African's (c. 1020–87) translations of Islamic medical texts that brought the Graeco-Arabic medical corpus into the Latin west, basic truisms about sexuality came into the learned tradition.[12] Constantine reiterated the notion elaborated in the Greek medical tradition of the Hippocratic corpus and by the highly influential Roman physician Galen (131–201) that physical pleasure provided humans with a motive for intercourse so that the species would not die out.[13] Discussions of the gendering of corporeal pleasure regularly appeared in scholastic texts. Constantine maintained that women derived greater pleasure from intercourse because they were both expelling their own sperm and receiving the male's.[14] William of Conches in the *Dragmaticon* followed Constantine's lead. William wondered why women have greater sexual heat even though they are cooler in complexion. He answered that women derive pleasure from both emission and reception of seed.[15] Petrus de Abano Pativinus opined that men have more intense pleasure, while women enjoy a more extensive version. Petrus noted that encounters with the penis (*virge*) give women 'great delectation'.[16] Hildegard of Bingen insisted that men have more focused pleasure, while women have more diffuse experience of it.[17] The examples could be multiplied, with interlocutors turning questions of physiology, pleasure,

26

and desire over and over within a fundamentally Aristotelian and humoural frame.[18] The discourse of sexuality and the body, in short, was abundantly present long before modernity.

The discoveries and recoveries of the Renaissance, of which the revival of Epicurus was just one, threatened entrenched beliefs about the body and sexuality built up by scholastic debate. As Julia Haig Gaisser has indicated, the rediscovery of Catullus caused all kinds of trouble with his sexually explicit, often raunchy poems.[19] The explicit erotics of the poems attributed to Anacreon prompted one editor to suppress poems he found offensive and to rearrange the collection to downplay others.[20] Plato, James Hankins has noted, was bowdlerized to render his ideas about marriage and homosexuality in suitable form.[21] Ovid, never lost in the west but often grossly distorted to make him palatable for Christians, appeared in Renaissance commentaries with the sexually titillating bits no longer allegorized into oblivion.[22] As more accurate versions of ancient texts emerged, both the volume of voices at odds with Christian beliefs and the development of more sophisticated methods for understanding the ancient context gradually undermined earlier certainties about sexuality and the body.

Ideas that conflicted with Christian sexual mores did not immediately destroy the Aristotelian synthesis or the humoural system. Old debates continued to appear in popular medical literature. The relative roles of male and female in reproduction, for instance, still exercised commentators. Thomas Vicary emphasized mutual contribution: '[A]s the Renet and Milke make the Cheese, so both the Sparme of man and woman make the generation of Embreon.'[23] Nicholas Culpeper describes not mutuality but competition: 'The reason why sometimes a *Male* is conceived, sometimes a *Female*, is, The strength of the Seed; for if the Mans Seed be strongest, A Male is conceived; if the Womans, a Female: The greater light obscures the lesser by the same rule; and that is the reason weakling men get most Girls, if they get any.'[24] Manuals devoted to facilitating procreation through teaching basic physiology, instruction in foreplay, and maintaining sexual health routinely addressed questions of pleasure as well as function.

The mix of distinctions between men and women and the propensity to see all human beings on a humoural spectrum has prompted debate among historians about early modern understandings of the sexed body. Emphasizing the continued dominance of Galenic medicine with its foundation in the humours, Thomas Laqueur has argued that Europeans largely understood male and female bodies as emanations of one sex along a spectrum. The differences between men and women were of degree (hotter vs. colder; dryer vs. moister) rather than of kind. This way of thinking, Laqueur argues, led to the presumption among anatomists that the female body was an inverted version of the male body (Aristotelian teleology again prevails in making the male the standard, which the female fails to attain). Anatomists following Galen described the uterus as an inverted penis, and the ovaries as female testicles that remained inside the body because the female lacked sufficient heat to push them out. The homologies worked intellectually for the most part, Laqueur notes, and problems such as the clitoris (in the homology argument, it was redundant) were simply overlooked.[25] While there is much that is compelling about Laqueur's argument, historians have pointed to several areas in which the presumptive dominance of the one-sex model must be questioned. Laura Gowing argues from extensive archival work that men and women recognized difference experientially.[26] Karen Harvey has found that Laqueur's central period of representational change, the eighteenth century, is actually marked by extensive continuity in the representation of bodies, and the female body in particular.[27] Katharine Park and Robert Nye dissent on the grounds that multiple, often competing notions of human physiology coexisted.[28] The critics are not wrong, but aspects of Laqueur's thesis remain persuasive. The difficulty of re-imagining the female body as anatomically specific, for instance, was stubbornly persistent, with gendered assumptions about bodies and roles seemingly limiting new approaches to understanding human anatomy.

But the infusion of 'new' texts and the development of textual practices that yielded more reliable information about Antiquity did facilitate questioning of paradigms about the body and sexuality. Take, for instance, the 'rediscovery' of the clitoris. Several anatomists 'found' the clitoris: Charles Estienne identified it in 1545; Gabriele Falloppia claimed he had spotted it first in a treatise written in 1550 and published in 1561; Realdo Colombo argued for priority, publishing his 'discovery' in 1559. Katharine Park recounts these assertions as part of her argument that the clitoris, understood as functionally duplicative of the penis, prompted discussion of women as necessarily hermaphroditic. This both undermined the presumptive gender hierarchy of traditional anatomy and encouraged fantasies about female sexuality.[29] Detailed anatomical study in general moved beyond the wisdom of the ancients, with attention to sexual anatomy eventually countering ancient axioms, including the belief that the womb could move about inside a woman and strangle her if her humours were unbalanced.[30] More texts, better texts, and an understanding of Antiquity as rooted in its specific time and place encouraged Renaissance inquiries to move beyond the truisms about the body and sexuality that had long prevailed.

The infusion of new ideas and new understandings of old ideas about sexuality and the body played into two related developments: the rise of print culture and the elaboration of secular discourse about corporeal matters. As Mary Fissell has found, popular medical tracts, pamphlets, and books provided information in both words and pictures for the less literate.[31] Images of male and female reproductive parts, examples of foetal mishaps, and descriptions of healthy vs. diseased bodies became available even for those for whom reading was not an option. For the growing number of the literate, Latinate culture gradually gave way to vernacular literatures, of which *Aristotle's Masterpiece* was but one example. Books of all sorts advised people on sexual matters. Jacques Guillemeau told readers that a man might recognize if his wife had conceived, 'If he [the husband] finde an extraordinarie contentment in the companie of his Wife; and if he feele at the same time a kind of sucking or drawing at the end of his yard.'[32] Advice on how to assure that the woman will carry to term, ways to control unusual appetites during pregnancy, and warnings about when it is acceptable to have intercourse before the child is born. In his advice, Giovanni Marinello explained about optimal positions for achieving pregnancy, the importance of moderation in coitus, and how to select a partner based on physiological compatibility.[33] Eucharius Roesslin advised copiously on sexual dysfunction, with explanations made more vivid by the addition of images derived from the anatomical studies of Vesalius.[34] Michele Savonarola emphasized that venereal relations are 'escrementi utili' [exceedingly useful], and not just to keep the human race afloat. Coitus can help with conditions such as melancholy, retention of urine for men, and retention of menses for women. Sex must be moderate, but its therapeutic value was not to be denied.[35] Savonarola, and indeed all the popular medical texts, made a point of asserting that procreative sex was congruent with Christian teaching, but the texts make scant reference to God amidst elaborate discussions of sexual techniques and the physiology of male and female sex organs.

The Renaissance altered perceptions of the body, expanded knowledge of ancient sexuality, and undermined the dominant understandings of physiology and sexuality. These changes did not go unnoticed or unanswered, and Foucault was not quite correct in positing early modern freedom around sexuality. Historians have found that rulers and ruling bodies installed new and newly intense disciplinary structures around sexuality supported by moralists bent on conveying the notion that social order rested on sexual propriety. One of the areas of heightened interest was the policing of sodomy. Officials treated sodomy as a sin, occasionally executing men (female sodomy was another matter), usually for what we would recognize as male homosexual intercourse.[36] Several jurisdictions in which fines or jail sentences had sufficed as punishment for those convicted of sodomy opted to make it a capital crime. Venice made such a change in 1464. In 1532, the Holy Roman Empire declared same-sex sodomy by either men or women a capital crime. Municipalities in the Empire followed the lead from the centre, and confessional preference does not seem to have made a difference. England made 'buggery' a capital crime in 1533, but declined to include women in its provisions when the law was revised in 1548. Examples could be multiplied, and the rhetoric accompanying sodomy took on apocalyptic proportions. Venetian authorities hinted that the survival of the city depended on catching perpetrators:

> To eliminate the vice of sodomy from this our city is worth every concern and as there are many women who consent to this vice and are broken in the rear parts and also many boys are so broken and all these are treated, yet still none of the accused and their deeds go unpunished; therefore, because it is wise to honor God, just as blows with weapons are denounced to the Signori di Notte [by medical practitioners], so too those who are broken in those parts be they boys or women are to be denounced.[37]

The promulgation of harsh laws and efforts to publicize them indicated that sexual expression had its limits.

The results of such efforts were mixed. States gained or appropriated a great deal of power over sexuality, and while they did not choose to exercise it in many instances, the coercive threat remained. Portuguese officials investigated over 4,000 cases of sodomy between 1587 and 1794, but only executed 30 individuals out of 400 cases brought to trial. Geneva was more likely to execute if matters got to trial: 12 sodomy trials (several with multiple defendants) led to nine executions, three banishments, and 12 sentences for corporal punishment.[38] As Maria R. Boes has argued, the draconian quality of the law meant that denunciations were less, rather than more, common. Cases in Frankfurt, she found, only reached a crisis point when the accused sodomite additionally outraged the general social order.[39] The state may have refrained for the most part, but as Gayle Rubin pointed out, the dangers of regulating sexuality always fall most heavily on the most vulnerable.[40] Moreover, official condemnation gave sanction to stigmatizing 'deviant' sexuality of all kinds. By way of early modern example, the Society for the Reformation of Manners in England led campaigns against 'sodomites' and prostitutes, with occasional jabs at adulteresses, unmarried pregnant girls, and libertines. Denouncing London's 'molly-houses' (establishments where men looking to enjoy sexual encounters with other men met), Ned Ward revealed the gendered background of his hatred for sodomites:

There was a particular Gang of *Sodomitical* Wretches in this town, who call themselves the *Mollies*, and are so far degenerated from all masculine deportment, or
manly exercise, that they rather fancy themselves women, imitating all the little
vanities that custom has reconciled to the female sex, affecting to speak, walk,
tattle, curtsy, cry, scold, and mimic all manner of effeminacy, that ever has fallen
within their several observations.[41]

Ward's vitriol, and the efforts of the Society and its various continental cousins to eradicate
sexual deviance, indicate that sexual norms were considered to be under threat.

At the same time, the very visibility of 'deviant' sexuality and contestation over definitions of proper bodily comportment suggest that the 'moralists' had something of a point.
The spread of print culture had multiple effects on the public discussion of sexuality, of
which three will serve as examples. First, among traditional literary domains, some poets
wrote exceedingly sexual poetry. The most famous exemplar was Pietro Aretino (1492–
1556), who penned sonnets to accompany engravings that imitated classical models.
Despite the patina of respectability in their design, the engravings were sexually explicit
images with visible erections and unmistakable signs of physical pleasure. Aretino's raunchy
poems deepened the scandalous potential of the engravings by praising anal sex, repeatedly
using profanity in his rhyme schemes, and celebrating non-procreative, areligious sexual
intentionality.[42] Aretino was notorious, famous, and wealthy for his literary activities, and a
veritable flood of obscene poetry soon appeared. The range of sexual material was vast.
A poem like 'A un soupçonné de sodomie' [To One Suspected of Sodomy] worked by
suggestion:

> Antoine, je ne sçai pourquoi
> Tu escris souvent au femelles,
> Mais je sçai que pas une d'elles
> N'a point affaire aveques toy.[43]
> [Antoine, I do not know why/you write often to women/But I know why none of
> them/Have had relations with you].

Other poems were far more explicit, as one which included the lines: 'Je sçai que vous
dirés que le Grand Juppiter/Ne fait rien dans le Ciel que Culs et Cons fouter' [I know that
you say that Great Jupiter/Does nothing in Heaven but fuck asses and cunts].[44] Love
poetry with references to consummation, satires of aspiring lovers on the make, jokes about
flagging penises and sagging breasts, attacks on monks and priests and nuns for lascivious
behaviour, ribald accounts of lecherous virgins, mock praise for successful copulation,
mock praise for failed copulation, mock praise for self-pleasuring, and wicked denunciations of sexual pretence abound. John Wilmot, Earl of Rochester, died young (at 33), but
left a reasonable collection of obscene poetry, including 'Signior Dildo', 'The Disabled
Debauchee', 'To His Mistress', and 'A Song of a Young Lady to Her Ancient Lover', to
suggest a few of his themes. Rochester excoriated marriage routinely, and satirized sexual
and social mores.[45] As with all print culture, the learned few were the primary consumers,
but similar themes and material in popular ballads and poetry suggest that sexually explicit
poetry had points of contact at several levels of society.

Prose erotica also provided lessons about sexuality and the body.[46] Among the many
forms of prose erotica that appeared were texts that purported to reveal older women

teaching younger ones about sex. *The School of Venus* (1680) features Katherine teaching the innocent Frances by means of extended conversations about genitals, coitus, and sexual games.[47] The educational dynamic is apparent between Tullia and Octavia in *A Dialogue Between A Married Lady and A Maid* (1740) as well.[48] Both pieces invoke Antiquity throughout, with references to Priapus, Juvenal, and debauched Roman emperors drawing on the Renaissance recovery of knowledge about the ancient past. In a different vein, the experienced Sister Angelica tutors Sister Agnes in all things sexual in *Venus in the Cloister* (1725).[49] The implicit anti-clericalism of featuring over-sexed nuns was in part an excuse for voyeuristic accounts of extensive sexual activity behind convent walls. Lesbianism features in all these texts, providing titillation and possibly education for interested readers. Another genre, the 'whore biography', often included a lesbian episode as part of the 'life' story of a woman who becomes a prostitute and 'describes' her sexual adventures. John Cleland's *Fanny Hill* (1750) is perhaps the most famous example of this mode of providing sexual information in a titillating format.[50] Even the public discussion of venereal disease could provide erotic information. Precisely as Foucault suggested, condemnations of venereal disease in medical texts were part of a proliferation of sexual debate and discussion. Works like John Marten's 1704 *Treatise of all the Degrees and Symptoms of the Venereal Disease in Both Sexes* invited voyeuristic examination of the self and one's sexual partners in order to prevent encounters that might lead to infection.[51]

Nor was sex only in print. Libertines on stage provided models of lives organized around the pursuit of sexual pleasure. As with the literature on venereal disease, the official intention was to condemn libertine sexual practices. But the theatre also put them on display. Maximillian Novak has argued that Théophile de Viau (1590–1626) formulated the basic premises of libertinism, which were the rejection of social conventions and a preference for bodily experience rather than reliance on traditional learning and knowledge.[52] The intellectual framework of libertinism was Epicurean. After rejecting Aristotle, Pierre Gassendi (1592–1655) turned to Epicurus to explain the organization of matter in terms of atoms as the basic building blocks of all things. Epicurus, as we have seen, was morally dubious in Christian Europe because of his insistence that the highest good is pleasure. Gassendi downplayed the moral implications, but he could not alter the fact that Epicurus understood pleasure in entirely self-regarding terms.[53] The value of pleasure is that it informs reason and prudence: that which provides pleasure to the self is good.[54] Although a Catholic priest, Gassendi associated with a group of free thinkers and libertines in Paris, including Pierre Charron and François Luillier.[55] The ideas propounded by Gassendi and his fellows appeared on stage in several guises. In France, Molière's *Dom Juan ou le Festin de Pierre* premiered in 1665 at the Palais-Royal. Dom Juan was the French version of the Spanish Don Juan, and Molière's play was one of several that highlighted social hypocrisy. Despite the properly moralizing ending with the nefarious Dom Juan consigned to hell for his flouting of religious belief, the play was initially withdrawn after 15 performances because of objections to the free-thinking main character who regularly seduces and marries women to their ruin. As Molière's experience indicated, contemporaries were not blind to the potential dangers of portraying libertines on stage even if the depictions were highly negative. Thomas Shadwell's *The Libertine* (1675) features the character of Don John advocating that life should be devoted to pleasure: 'My business is my pleasure: that end I will always compass without scrupling the means. There is no right or wrong but what conduces or hinders pleasure.'[56] For Don John and his friends, sexual pleasure is high on the list. Don Antonio impregnated both of his sisters, and Don

Lopez is excited by the thought of sexual conquest. For his part, Don John kills Octavio to gain access to Maria. Don Antonio expresses the horrific logic of libertine pleasure: 'She'll endure a rape gallantly. I love resistance: it endears the pleasure.'[57] Don John seduces and drops women wherever he goes, and kills any who challenge him to live up to his promises.[58] The Epicurean emphasis on pleasure is evident, although the frenzied sequence of dangerous encounters was hardly in keeping with Epicurus' notions of pleasure. Don John is meant to be sufficiently monstrous to be off-putting: Shadwell's preface to the printed version included the disclaimer, 'I hope that the severest reader will not be offended at the representation of those vices on which they will see a dreadful punishment inflicted', but Don John's attitude of entitlement remained plainly on display.[59]

Epicurean libertinism, no matter how altered on stage, figured centrally in the development of new paradigms relative to sexuality and the body in the Enlightenment. Rejecting the reverence for the past and the reliance on tradition (whether religious or emerging out of pagan Antiquity), Enlightenment philosophers turned to the natural world as the basis for their truth.[60] Epicurus' materialism – all things are made of atoms that obey basic physical laws – fit with aspects of Enlightenment philosophy that emphasized understanding the world through sensory experience and rational judgement. Materialism appealed to those who rejected organized religion as superstition because the idea that matter obeyed the dictates of nature obviated the need for an active, anthropomorphic god.[61] The effects of such thinking on understandings of sexuality and the body were several. The willingness to think of bodies as matter facilitated reconsideration of the humoural system. Biology moved forward on many fronts, but among them, William Harvey's finding that all animals produced eggs and Antonie van Leeuwenhoek's turning his microscope on male seed to discover sperm moved human anatomy toward understanding two separate biological sexes. Laqueur has argued that the development of language for and representations of female sexual organs as distinct from male ones indicates the intellectual separation into two sexes.[62] Laqueur is right in that modern perceptions of the body usually see it as two distinct, incommensurate sexes, both of whom are required for procreation. He grants less space to the persistence of humoural ideas about bodies, not the least of which is the recurrence of the term 'human' rather than 'male' and 'female' in a variety of contexts.

From a different perspective, the instantiation of sexual incommensurability that Laqueur highlights was very much in place by the middle of the eighteenth century. In much Enlightenment thought, 'nature' made men and women different, and thus, social differences were 'natural' as well. A panoply of corollaries about bodies and sexuality followed in the form of social logic of sexual differentiation. Thinkers like Jean-Jacques Rousseau and Immanuel Kant maintained that men, being rational and stronger, belonged in public capacities while weaker, 'naturally' irrational women were properly domestic.[63] Instead of believing that women's weakness made them sexually voracious and lascivious, the idea became that women were sexually vulnerable. The image of prostitutes as victims of unscrupulous men became a staple of moral discourse and informed efforts to address prostitution. Institutions such as the Magdalen Hospital in London, founded in 1758, tried to rehabilitate 'fallen' women and girls on the assumption that they were seduced and abandoned.[64] If women became victims because of sex, same-sex sexuality became more than a crime against nature – it became unnatural. The lieutenant-general of police in Paris deliberately set about entrapping men seeking sex with other men under Louis XV.[65] In Holland, officials stepped up prosecutions of women engaged in sexual activities with other women.[66] In 1828, England passed a law making prosecution of male homosexual sodomy much easier to pursue. Domestic heterosexuality, resting on presumptions about male and female bodies as constitutionally different, was both the 'natural' norm and apparently in constant need of protection against 'unnatural' alternatives.

To a degree, the above characterization of eighteenth-century sexuality seems to end up back in Foucault's chronology in which modernity is more restrictive about sex than the seventeenth century. But one argument of this chapter is that interrogating Foucault's framework reveals a rather different picture of how the study of sexuality and the body developed in early modern Europe. Instead of a period of comparative sexual freedom preceding modern sexual identity, the Renaissance dislocated the presumptive sexual order. The study of sexual practices in ancient texts, the development of knowledge that exceeded the limits of Antiquity, and the broadening of access to information about sex and bodies disrupted aspects of accepted belief. This set the stage for contestation over the meanings of sex and the sexed body. Disciplinary practices emerging in law were met with evasion since it seems implausible that framers of laws against sodomy, for instance, expected sodomites to remain unmolested unless they made other kinds of trouble. At the same time, the spectre of punishment for sexual misconduct prompted self-protective group creation in urban molly-houses, while the lack of enforcement prompted moralists and the activists they inspired to attack 'deviants'. The self-conscious sexual profligacy of libertine drama points to another reaction, in which (mostly) men of privilege denied the disciplinary mechanisms around sex entirely. This is not a world of sexual freedom even for libertines. Contestation over sexuality and the body took new and newly complex forms beginning in the Renaissance.

Moreover, the Enlightenment shift away from reflecting on the textual tradition that marked the Renaissance and toward 'nature' as the baseline reference point for 'truth' was not such a clear or decisive break with the past. Enlightenment thinkers inherited much from the Renaissance, including conflicting ideas about how sexuality and the body could be understood and addressed in cultural practice. Enlightenment libertines reworked the idea of sexual pleasure by reference to nature, but Renaissance developments enabled the formulation of that position. Epicurean ideas recovered in the Renaissance were among those that informed Enlightenment ideas about the 'natural' pleasures of sex. The Enlightenment revisions of understanding of the body in scientific terms also owed much to the prolonged discussions of sexuality and the body in the literature spawned by the expansion of print culture. To return for a moment to a text that encompasses several of the impulses around the study of sex, *Aristotle's Masterpiece* can be understood as an exemplar of *scientia sexualis*: it tells readers how to procreate and implicitly – by telling them what to do – it indicates what should not be done. But *Aristotle's Masterpiece* is also *ars erotica* in a way. Like many texts of the past it might not 'work' for us as a prompt book, if you will, but who is to say that it did not work like that for someone else? To put it another way, 'bad' sexual acts can be mighty 'good', and knowledge of the body and its sexual possibilities are often both at once.

Notes

1 Anon., *Aristotle's Masterpiece, or, The Secrets of Generation Displayed in All the Parts Thereof*, London: J. How, 1684, p. 189. Nicolas Venette's *Tableau de l'amour conjugal* (first published in France in 1686) was only slightly less popular.

2 Roy Porter and Lesley Hall, *The Facts of Life: The Creation of Sexual Knowledge in Britain, 1650–1950*, New Haven, CT: Yale University Press, 1995, pp. 33–64, discusses the textual history of *Aristotle's Masterpiece*.

3 On social history and the family, see, for instance, Tamara K. Hareven, 'The History of the Family and the Complexity of Social Change', *American Historical Review* 96:1, 1991, pp. 95–124. This essay is especially helpful for tracing the various influences and developments in the history of the family through the 1980s. Hareven lays out the debates and points of controversy within family history studies evenly and lucidly. For a longer view, see Peter N. Stearns, 'Social History Present and Future', *Journal of Social History* 37:1, 2003, pp. 9–19.

4 Michel Foucault, *History of Sexuality, Vol. 1: An Introduction*, trans. Robert Hurley, New York: Pantheon Books, 1978 [1976]. Initially, Foucault planned six volumes, but completed only two more before his death, and these represented a shift from the original plan he had articulated. The completed volumes addressed sexuality in ancient Greece and Rome.

5 Examples abound throughout this chapter, but for direct engagement with Foucault on questions pertaining to the body, see, for instance, Colin Jones and Roy Porter (eds), *Reassessing Foucault: Power, Medicine and the Body*, London and New York: Routledge, 1994.

6 The term 'Renaissance' is controversial. See William Caferro, *Contesting the Renaissance*, Oxford: Blackwell Publishing, 2011, for a multifaceted discussion. Nonetheless, I retain it as having some useful meaning, even as I acknowledge that much of what the Renaissance was about was rote language learning and the development of a secularly trained administrative class. See Anthony Grafton and Lisa Jardine, *From Humanism to Humanities: The Institutionalizing of the Liberal Arts in Fifteenth- and Sixteenth-Century Europe*, Cambridge, MA: Harvard University Press, 1986.

7 The text circulated in the late fifteenth century, but it is accessible in a modern reprint as B. Platinae Cremonensis, *De Honesta Voluptate, De Ratione Victus*, Cologne: Eucharii, 1529.

8 Lorenzo Valla, *On Pleasure. De voluptate*, trans. A. Kent Hieatt and Maristella Lorch, intro. Maristella de Panizza Lorch, New York: Abaris Books, 1977. Originally published in 1431 and reworked under different titles and with variations thereafter.

9 Lucretius, *Titus Lucretius Carus His Six Books of Epicurean Philosophy, Done into English Verse, with Notes*, trans. Thomas Creech, 3rd edn, London: Thomas Sawbridge, 1683, sigs. a1v, a2v. The first edition appeared in 1682. Creech reiterates his concerns. See, for instance, 'the Wantonness of the *Epicureans* is as Notorious' (p. 1) and 'Epicurean Principles are Pernicious to Societies' (p. 50) in the midst of a section on meanings of pleasure.

10 Jacqueline Holler, 'The Spiritual and Physical Ecstasies of a Sixteenth-Century *Beata*: Marina de San Miguel Confesses Before the Mexican Inquisition Mexico, 1598' in *Colonial Lives: Documents on Latin American History, 1550–1850*, ed. Geoffrey Spurling and Richard Boyer, Oxford: Oxford University Press, 1999, pp. 77–100.

11 Joan Cadden, *Meanings of Sex Difference in the Middle Ages: Medicine, Science, and Culture*, Cambridge: Cambridge University Press, 1993. See also Danielle Jacquart and Claude Thomasset, *Sexuality and Medicine in the Middle Ages*, trans. Matthew Adamson, Princeton: Princeton University Press, 1988; Mary Frances Wack, *Lovesickness in the Middle Ages: The Viaticum and Its Commentaries*, Philadelphia: University of Pennsylvania Press, 1990; and Brian Lawn, *The Salernitan Questions: An Introduction to the History of Medieval and Renaissance Problem Literature*, Oxford: Clarendon Press, 1963.

12 See *Constantine the African and Ali ibn al'Abbas al-Magus: The Pantegni and Related Texts*, ed. Charles Burnett and Danielle Jacquart, Leiden and New York: Brill, 1994.

13 Paul Delany, 'Constantinus Africanus' *De coitu*: A Translation', *Chaucer Review* 4, 1969, pp. 55–65.

14 Constantine the African, *Pantegni*, fol. 28rb. The question of whether female sperm was actually seed created much consternation among medieval scholastics and medical writers. Aristotle said that women did not produce seed; the Hippocratic corpus indicated that they sort of did. See Cadden, *Meanings of Sex Difference*, pp. 25, 34, 62, 79, 97, and 200–201. Cadden treats both ancient and medieval iterations of the issue.

15 William of Conches, *A Dialogue on Natural Philosophy, Dragmaticon Philosophiae*, trans. and intro. Italo Ronca and Matthew Curr, Notre Dame, IN: University of Notre Dame Press, 1997, p. 135.

16 Petrus de Abano Pativinus, *Conciliator differentiarum philosophorum et precipue medicorum*, Venice: Luce Antony Junta Fiorentini, 1526, fol. 49v–50v. Differentia 34. The first printed edition was in 1476.

17 Hildegard of Bingen, *Causae et curae*, ed. Paul Kaiser, Liepzig: Teubner, 1903, pp. 76–77.
18 The epitome of such discussions is Albert the Great, *Questions Concerning Aristotle's On Animals*, trans. Irven M. Resnick and Kenneth F. Kitchell, Jr., Washington, DC: Catholic University of America Press, 2008. See especially pp. 185–202, Book V, which addressed human reproduction, but also Book I, Q. 13, 'Why all animals except the human are very noisy during intercourse', and Q. 39, which maintains that big feet in a man are good because they indicate a large penis, but a woman with big feet has a big womb, which is apparently very bad.
19 Julia Haig Gaisser, *Catullus and his Renaissance Readers*, Oxford: Clarendon Press, 1993.
20 *Anacreonis Teii Odae. Ab Henrico Stephano luce et Latinitate nunc primum donatae*, Paris: Henri Estienne, 1554.
21 James Hankins, *Plato in the Renaissance*, 2 vols, Leiden and New York: Brill, 1990, vol. 1, pp. 70, 80, 137–38.
22 Katherine Crawford, *The Sexual Culture of the French Renaissance*, Cambridge: Cambridge University Press, 2010, ch. 1.
23 Thomas Vicary, *The English-mans Treasure: with the true Anatomie of Mans bodie*, London: George Robinson for Iohn Perin, 1587, p. 50.
24 Nicholas Culpeper, *A Directory for Midwives: Or, A Guide for Women, In their Conception, Bearing and Suckling their Children*, London: Peter Cole, 1651, p. 57.
25 Thomas W. Laqueur, *Making Sex: Body and Gender from the Greeks to Freud*, Cambridge, MA: Harvard University Press, 1990.
26 Laura Gowing, *Common Bodies: Women, Touch and Power in Seventeenth-Century England*, New Haven and London: Yale University Press, 2003.
27 Karen Harvey, 'The Substance of Sexual Difference: Change and Persistence in Representations of the Body in Eighteenth-Century England', *Gender and History* 14:2, 2002, pp. 202–23.
28 Katharine Park and Robert Nye, 'Destiny is Anatomy', *New Republic* 18:2, 1991, pp. 53–57.
29 Katharine Park, 'The Rediscovery of the Clitoris' in David Hillman and Carla Mazzio (eds), *The Body in Parts: Fantasies of Corporeality in Early Modern Europe*, New York and London: Routledge, 1997, pp. 170–93.
30 Strangulation by the womb appears in the Hippocratic corpus along with suggested remedies to restore the womb to its proper position. Plato also expresses support for the idea.
31 Mary Fissell, 'Readers, Texts, and Contexts: Vernacular Works in Early Modern England' in Roy Porter (ed.), *The Popularization of Medicine, 1650–1850*, London and New York: Routledge, 1992, pp. 72–96.
32 Jacques Guillemeau, *The Happy Deliverie of Women*, London: Hatfield, 1612, p. 3.
33 Giovanni Marinello, *Le Medicine Partenenti alle infermità delle donne*, Venice: Gio. Bonfadino & Compagni, 1610.
34 Eucharius Roesslin, *The birth of mankinde, otherwise named the Womans Booke. Set forth in English by Thomas Raynalde Phisition, and by him corrected, and augmented*, London: Thomas Adams, 1604. The original English version appeared in 1512. Raynalde supplied the Vesalius images.
35 Michele Savonarola, *Libro della natura et virtu delle cose, che nutriscono, & delle cose non naturali, Con alcune osservationi per conservar la sanità, & alcuni quesiti bellissimi da notare*, Venice: Domenico & Gio. Battista Guerra, 1576, p. 261. See also pp. 265–66, 270–71.
36 Sodomy meant any non-procreative sex, including masturbation, anal penetration, oral sex, same-sex encounters, and bestiality.
37 Quoted Guido Ruggiero, *The Boundaries of Eros: Sex, Crime and Sexuality in Renaissance Venice*, New York and Oxford: Oxford University Press, 1985, pp. 117–18.
38 For a more detailed discussion, see Katherine Crawford, *European Sexualities, 1400–1800*, Cambridge: Cambridge University Press, 2007, pp. 155–62.
39 Maria R. Boes, 'On Trial for Sodomy in Early Modern Germany' in Tom Betteridge (ed.), *Sodomy in Early Modern Europe*, Manchester and New York: Manchester University Press, 2002, pp. 27–45.
40 Gayle Rubin, 'Thinking Sex: Notes for a Radical Theory of the Politics of Sexuality' in Carole S. Vance (ed.), *Pleasure and Danger: Exploring Female Sexuality*, London: Pandora, 1992, pp. 267–93.
41 Ned Ward, *History of the London Clubs*, London: n.p., 1709, p. 284.
42 For the sonnets in Italian and with an English translation, see Bette Talvacchia, *Taking Positions: On the Erotic in Renaissance Culture*, Princeton: Princeton University Press, 1999. Talvacchia lays

out the circumstances around the production of the sonnets and provides cogent analysis of their content.

43 *Le Cabinet secret du Parnasse. Recueil de poésies libres, rares ou peu connues, pour servir de Supplément aux Oeuvres dites complètes des poètes français*, ed. Louis Perceau, 3 vols, Paris: Au Cabinet du Livre, 1928, vol. 1, p. 235. This modern collection represents a small but reasonably representative sample of the sexual poetry that appeared in print in France. I have counted 16 separate collections, most of which went into multiple editions. Many poems appear repeatedly, sometimes with attribution.

44 Bibliothèque nationale de France MS n.a.f. 6888, 128.

45 John Wilmot, Earl of Rochester, *The Complete Poems*, ed. David M. Vieth, New Haven: Yale University Press, 2002.

46 There has been much debate over whether such texts are erotica or pornography. For a summary, see Crawford, *Sexual Culture*, pp. 174–76. For English early modern pornography, see especially Sarah Toulalan, *Imagining Sex: Pornography and Bodies in Seventeenth-Century England*, Oxford: Oxford University Press, 2007. For Italian counterpoints, see David O. Frantz, *Festum Voluptatis: A Study of Renaissance Erotica*, Columbus: Ohio State University Press, 1989. For an insightful corrective to the ahistorical tendency in feminist criticism regarding pornography, see Manuela Mourào, 'The Representation of Female Desire in Early Modern Pornographic Texts, 1660–1745', *Signs* 24, 1999, pp. 573–602, which contends that early modern pornography is not necessarily oppressive to women and thus can be used to challenge the view of women as powerless victims posited by anti-pornography feminists. See also chapter 11 by Ian Moulton in this volume.

47 Anon., *The School of Venus, or the Ladies Delight, Reduced into Rules of Practice*, London[?]: n.p., 1680. The title page acknowledges the French original, *L'Ecole des Filles*.

48 Nicolas Chorier, *A Dialogue Between A Married Lady and A Maid*, London: n.p., 1740. The English edition is an abridgement of Chorier's *Satyra sotadica*, 1660.

49 Anon., *Venus in the Cloister: or, The Nun in her Smock*, London: n.p., 1725. The French original was *Venus dans le cloître, ou la religieuse en chemise* by Jean Barrin, 1683. The English publisher was probably Edmund Curll, who specialized in publishing erotica and pornography.

50 John Cleland, *Fanny Hill: or, Memoirs of a Woman of Pleasure*, ed. Peter Wagner, London: Penguin, 1986. For a sense of the range and extent of this literature, see Julie Peakman (ed.), *Whore Biographies, 1700–1825*, 8 vols, London: Pickering & Chatto, 2006–7. Part I includes biographies of English prostitutes, both famous and obscure. Part II features courtesans' autobiographies, which reveal much about what the women thought about gender issues around sale of sex. Attitudes toward chastity, promiscuity, men, and the double standard recur. These volumes are well presented, and much of the material has been unavailable in unexpurgated form.

51 Roy Porter, '"Laying Aside Any Private Advantage": John Marten and Venereal Disease' in Linda E. Merians (ed.), *The Secret Malady: Venereal Disease in Eighteenth-Century Britain and France*, Lexington, KY: University of Kentucky Press, 1996, pp. 51–67.

52 Maximillian E. Novak, 'Libertinism and Sexuality' in Susan J. Owen (ed.), *A Companion to Restoration Drama*, Oxford: Blackwell, 2001, pp. 53–68; see p. 55. Viau paid dearly for his beliefs, falling foul of Louis XIII and dying young after spending two years in the Conciergerie prison.

53 Pierre Gassendi, *De vita et moribus Epicuri libri octo*, Lyons: Guillaume Barbier, 1647; *Syntagma philosophiae Epicuri cum refutationibus dogmatum quae contra fidem christianam ab eo asserta sunt*, Lyon: Guillaume Barbier, 1649; and *Animaadversiones in decimum librum Diogenis Laertii*, Lyon: Guillaume Barbier, 1649.

54 Epicurus, 'Letter to Menoeceus' in *The Essential Epicurus: Letters, Principal Doctrines, Vatican Sayings, and Fragments*, trans. and intro. Eugene O'Connor, Amherst, NY: Prometheus Books, 1993, p. 65.

55 René Pintard, *Le Libertinage érudit dans la première moitié du XVIIe siècle*, Paris: Slatkine, 2000, pp. 127–29; Lisa Tunick Sarasohn, 'Epicureanism and the Creation of a Privatist Ethic in Early Seventeenth-Century France' in Margaret J. Osler (ed.), *Atoms, Pneuma, and Tranquility*, Cambridge: Cambridge University Press, 1991, pp. 175–96.

56 Thomas Shadwell, *The Libertine* in Deborah Payne Fisk (ed.), *Four Restoration Libertine Plays*, Oxford: Oxford University Press, 2005, 1.1, ll., pp. 123–25.

57 To be fair, Don Lopez is not only about sex: he killed his older brother to appropriate his inheritance. See Shadwell, *The Libertine*, 1.1, ll., pp. 65–74. For the rape comment, see 2.1, ll., pp. 328–29.

58 See, for instance, Shadwell, *The Libertine*, 1.1, ll., pp. 108–13; 2.1, ll., pp. 165–380; 4.1, ll., pp. 1–231.

59 Shadwell, *The Libertine*, preface, ll., pp. 14–16. While I make no claims to be able to trace influence from stage to street, the cultural context does seem telling. Randolph Trumbach has argued that a popular form of libertinism is visible in the historical records of crime in seventeenth-century London. See *Sex and the Gender Revolution, Vol. 1*, Chicago and London: University of Chicago Press, 1998, pp. 90–111. See also Lawrence Stone, 'Libertine Sexuality in Post-Restoration England: Group Sex and Flagellation among the Middling Sort in Norwich in 1706–7', *Journal of the History of Sexuality* 2, 1992, pp. 511–26.

60 This is a tremendous condensation of a complicated intellectual movement. For a sense of the range of questions and answers raised by Enlightenment thinkers, see Jonathan I. Israel, *Enlightenment Contested: Philosophy, Modernity, and the Emancipation of Man, 1670–1752*, New York: Oxford University Press, 2009.

61 Some Enlightenment thinkers were more adamant about materialist atheism than others. Julien Offray de La Mettrie (1709–51), for instance, was outspoken in his materialist-based atheism, as is apparent in his *L'Homme Machine* (1748). In contrast, François-Marie Arouet Voltaire (1694–1778) was representative of a more common line of thought, which maintained that belief in the divine was not at odds with understanding the natural world. Organized religion, however, was worthy of nothing but scorn. See, for instance, the entries in his *Philosophical Dictionary* under 'Atheism', 'Devout', 'Ecclesiastical Ministry', 'Faith', 'God', 'Mohammedans', 'Religion', 'Sect', and 'Theist'.

62 Laqueur, *Making Sex*, ch. 5.

63 See Jean-Jacques Rousseau, *Emile, or On Education* (1762), Book 5; Immanuel Kant refers to women as 'the fair sex' in 'What is Enlightenment?' (1784) and elaborates on the differences between men as noble and women as beautiful.

64 See also Timothy J. Gilfoyle, 'Prostitutes in History: From Parables of Pornography to Metaphors of Modernity', *The American Historical Review* 104:1, 1999, pp. 117–41, which argues that the regulation of prostitution goes hand-in-hand with the expansion of state power.

65 Michel Rey, 'Police and Sodomy in Eighteenth-Century Paris: From Sin to Disorder' in Kent Gerard and Gert Hekma (eds), *The Pursuit of Sodomy: Male Homosexuality in Renaissance and Enlightenment Europe*, New York: Haworth Press, 1989, pp. 129–46.

66 Theo van der Meer, 'Tribades on Trial: Female Same-Sex Offenders in Late Eighteenth-Century Amsterdam', *Journal of the History of Sexuality* 1:3, 1991, pp. 424–45.

2

APPROACHES TO THE HISTORY
OF SEXUALITY SINCE 1750

Harry G. Cocks

The history of modern sexuality is about sexual behaviour but not only that. It also deals with the changing way that sexuality is constituted as a field of knowledge and a set of power relations. It therefore sets itself the complex task of trying to examine the way in which dominant conceptions of sexuality interact with personal identity and the self. It asks two key questions: first, is there something distinctive about the way bodies and desires are thought about and experienced in the modern period, and second, does the way that sexuality is represented, thought about and described affect the way it is experienced, and if so, how? There are several answers to this question, the broad outlines of which I will set out below. Perhaps the dominant response of historians is to assume that there is a direct link between moral and social rules and the actual experience of the body. However, there are many others who dispute this, and suggest that there is something constant about sexual behaviour and identity across cultures and time periods. There are also a number of viewpoints in between and refinements of these broad positions. In general, though, the idea that there is something distinctive about modern sexuality has survived decades of critical scrutiny.

What is sexuality?

The modern history of sexuality can only really be understood if we appreciate that the word 'sexuality' has a specific modern meaning. When we in the contemporary West talk about sexuality, we are using it as an umbrella term to refer to behaviour, orientation, identity, desire, anatomy and other matters that relate to individuality. However, within that, we usually assume that its primary significance relates to personal identity. It is possible to say that you have 'a sexuality', by which we mean a form of sexual orientation or a type of personal identity and we often also imply that it has some kind of (often mysterious) relationship to anatomy and psychology. Sexuality also refers to a field of knowledge that inquires into this relationship between sexual behaviour and individual identity and encompasses most of the 'psy' sciences – psychology and psychiatry, as well as related fields like psychoanalysis, criminology or social policy. Part of the point of the psy sciences is to investigate the relationship between sexual behaviour and psychological health, to inquire into what makes us well or badly adjusted to social norms.

Sexual behaviour or identity has not always been understood in this way. It was only in the 1890s, when sexual and psychological science were emerging, that the word 'sexuality' took on its key modern meaning. In the eighteenth century, the term 'sexuality' was used in a scientific sense to refer to the reproductive capacity of an organism, especially of plants, and until well into the twentieth century 'sex' was used not to discuss behaviour, but to refer to anatomical characteristics (the differences between the sexes).[1] The term 'sexuality' was not the term employed to refer to the body and its desires. Sexual behaviour and feeling was essentially disaggregated into categories like the 'natural passions', morals, marriage, or the collection of medieval sins known as 'luxuria', which refer mainly to forms of fornication such as non-missionary-position sex or sodomy. Our use of the word 'sexuality' assumes that it is a coherent field of knowledge all to itself, and can in fact be removed from the context in which it appears and studied as a thing in itself.

By contrast, in the medieval and early modern periods, sexual behaviour and attitudes towards it could not be disentangled from their immediate context. They mattered because of their relationships to social questions like reproduction, marriage, property, morals, patronage, religion or kinship. Similarly, if you wanted to inquire into the nature of sexual behaviour or psychology, you would have to see it in relation to these questions and deal just as much with them as with matters of behaviour or inclination. If one looks at any history of morals or behaviour, the development of the modern way of thinking can be followed. In pre-industrial peasant societies or less complex tribal groupings, for instance, the history of marriage has been inseparable from the transmission of property, reproduction, or issues of status and alliance. In the modern period, however, and especially in western Europe and America since 1900, marriage (or any long-term partnership) has increasingly come to be seen as a form of dissoluble contract between equals, the significance of which lies primarily in their mutual emotional satisfaction. The other meanings of marriage still matter of course, especially outside the global north, but we recognize that they are in many ways subordinate to psychological health and adjustment. Love, as the historian Stephanie Coontz puts it, has conquered marriage across the world.[2]

Central to the history of modern sexuality, then, in my view is the attempt to show how this specific idea of sexuality emerged and how it affected the way people behaved and thought of themselves. In short, how did it become possible for sexuality to be notionally separated from the wider context of kinship, reproduction, alliance or inheritance, to be constituted as a separate domain of knowledge? To ask this question is not to say that sexual behaviour in the modern world has no relevance for these wider questions – in many ways we know that it does. But the set of assumptions that goes with 'sexuality' understood in this way is of course a kind of willing fiction. We know that sex and the body have a political and social significance that exceeds questions of personal identity, but we often assume that this is not the case. Part of the point of a history of sexuality is to resist that fiction, to show again that sexuality does have a broader relevance, and to restore the earlier idea that desire does have an ethical and political significance.

Explaining modern sexuality

One of the key questions posed by historians is how this meaning of 'sexuality' – what we might call the modern way of treating, experiencing and understanding the body and its desires – developed. It is often said that the historians who aim to answer this question can be called a broadly 'social constructionist' school, in that they assume that the body and its desires do alter in profound ways according to the social and moral rules which seek to govern them. However, we should bear in mind that there are other historians who disagree with the idea that sexuality is either thought of or experienced differently by different societies. They argue that sexual behaviour, attitudes and categories are fixed in some way, probably by our biological make-up, and that as a result they are transhistorical or always roughly the same throughout history. In this 'essentialist' view, the nature of personal experience and psychology is also broadly the same through the ages, while the categories that we use to describe individuals – gay, straight, bisexual – can be plausibly applied to any period. We can call this position an 'essentialist' one, in that it suggests that there is something essential about sexual desire and behaviour that is always the same and does not alter fundamentally – only the meanings attributed to it change. This view has been taken up recently by those associated with evolutionary explanations of human behaviour and I will explain all these in greater detail below.

This characterization of the history of sexuality as a war between essentialism and social constructionism is, however, somewhat crude – in particular it ignores the fact that there are many different gradations of each position and that neither is as straightforward as it sounds. For instance, there are broadly two distinct ways of understanding what modern sexuality is. They are both often seen as social constructionist in approach; they are however quite different from each other. Both assume that there is something distinctive about modern sexuality, but they draw very different conclusions about personal identity and experience from that premise. Put simply, one suggests that modern ideas of sexuality resulted from the rise and expansion of personal freedom, and that the sphere of sexual freedom has expanded correspondingly. In that reading, sexuality has been progressively 'liberated'. The second position, associated with the French theorist and historian Michel Foucault and his followers, argues (in broad terms) that sexuality represents an arena for the play of power relations in which states and their agencies seek to administer and direct sexual behaviour.

The first position argues that since the eighteenth century there has been a vast increase in the sphere of personal freedom and people have simply had more time to devote to themselves. As communal social forms have declined, the individual has gained a new primacy. In this view, the long-term decline in working hours, the corresponding expansion of leisure time, the development of publicly funded education, health and welfare systems and of mechanical contraception, the rise of print and other media devoted to discussing social and political questions, the expansion of democracy and related developments all helped to create a space in which personal identity and individual wants mattered more than ever before, and could also be examined at length. In this view, sexuality which was once repressed and controlled, punished, or regarded as sinful could increasingly be expressed. As the modern world saw an expansion in the sphere of liberty, so there was a corresponding decline in the communal and collective ties that bound pre-industrial society. Symptoms of these changes can be seen in the rise of individualism as an ideology, as well as in changes to the intimate sphere, for example, in the idea of marriage primarily as an emotional tie between equal partners, in the smaller modern family, in gay rights, women's rights and a broad rhetoric of sexual freedom.[3]

This interpretation tends to assume two things that, as we will see, are often criticized, and which also in fact link this approach to the conceptual framework found in the 'essentialist' school. First, that sexual freedoms have expanded in a more or less linear fashion – there are more of them, and we are less repressed as every century passes – and second, that the only thing that changes about sex is the nature of its expression – the experience itself is always roughly the same. The latter reading has often been dubbed the 'hydraulic' view as it assumes that sex – like water – can only ever be channelled or diverted; its essence cannot be significantly altered. It can be either repressed or dammed up, or released and set free. As the great social historian Lawrence Stone put it, the modern period was characterized by 'remarkable release of the libido'.[4] If you assume that sex in the past was repressed in this way, then the corresponding assumption is that there is a 'normal' level to which sexual behaviour will naturally gravitate. Some historians argue that this is what has happened since the eighteenth century, suggesting that previously outlawed sexual behaviour has been allowed and encouraged. So in that sense, this version of modern history assumes that modern sexuality is different, but only in the respect that there is more of it, and that it has therefore become more important in people's lives.[5]

Even though in this view sexuality changes, and is 'socially constructed' in a simple sense in that it follows moral rules, it does not usually assume that the actual experience of desire changes that much. So what exactly does it mean to say something is 'socially constructed'? First of all, it is important to realize that the idea that sexuality, gender and the body are altered in their essence by cultural rules is not a recent, or late twentieth-century view. The 'common-sense' view of the body and its desires as essentially the same across cultures was popular, but never entirely dominant, even in early histories of sexual behaviour and attitudes. In fact it was frequently asserted to the contrary, even by eighteenth-century writers, that behaviour and gender was in some way 'socially constructed'. The eighteenth-century collector Richard Payne Knight (1751–1824), for instance, who wrote a treatise on ancient fertility rituals (and has some claim to be one of the first historians of sexuality), argued both ways. Although he suggested that sensibility (feeling or emotion) was essentially transhistorical ('Men, considered collectively, are at all times the same animals, employing the same organs, and endowed with the same faculties'), he also conceded that their 'passions, prejudices and conceptions' would be 'directed to various ends, and modified in various ways, by the variety of external circumstances operating upon them'.[6] Similarly, early feminist writings such as *The Vindication of the Rights of Woman* (1792) by Mary Wollstonecraft argued that women's apparently weak and passive nature owed more to social rules than their physical make-up.

Payne Knight's assumption that 'external circumstances' affect the passions in a variety of ways can be taken as a succinct summary of the case for the idea of the body as a social construction. He suggests that rules and customs do have an effect on experience and sensibility, but is unable to specify exactly what it is. Similarly, modern social constructionists suggest that the way in which something is understood or described will have an effect on how it is experienced – but then often struggle to describe the minute processes that could show exactly how that might work. This uncertainty means that within the idea of 'social constructionism' there may be a 'weak' version of the argument and a 'strong' one. The 'weak' version states that social-cultural rules and mores have some kind of effect which mainly relates to either the release or repression of desires. The 'strong' position, on the other hand, points out that desire is not merely released or repressed, but constantly shaped, and the entire process has a profound effect on personal identity. Therefore, simply saying something is socially or culturally constructed is clearly only the beginning of the argument. One needs to determine in a detailed way how exactly this process of 'construction' happens, if at all.[7] How are bodily desires enmeshed within the manifold complexity that we call culture and society? Can we draw out individual examples of how this 'construction' might happen?

Michel Foucault's *History of Sexuality*

One of the major approaches to the history of sexuality, that associated with Michel Foucault, has tried to address this problem by taking this 'strong' position. Although, as we have seen, the idea of the body as a social construction was not new, Foucault's writings broadened out the question of how bodies and societies interact into a much wider analysis of changing power relations in modern western societies, and as such offered a revelatory account of the history of sexuality. As we have already said, conventional histories of modern western societies have tended to outline the growth of liberty and personal freedom. As Foucault points out in *Discipline and Punish* (1975), state power in early modern Europe was exemplified by spectacular, violent and public forms of terror such as execution or torture that acted in an exemplary way to demonstrate the overwhelming power of the sovereign, and hence the state. Most historians would suggest that over the course of the next two centuries, the terrifying power of the state gave way to more pluralistic societies (in which power might be held by a variety of people and institutions), alongside the rise of modern forms of democracy, individualism and a growing sphere of personal autonomy, in which individuals were seen as the bearers of universal rights. The rise of these freedoms seems to show modern societies progressing from forms of government which relied on primitive terror to ones that rest on the active consent of those governed. While Foucault does not explicitly disagree with this account, he suggests that while one form of power declined, another – what he calls 'biopower' – emerged; one that was more suitable to governing a notionally free population. The threat of endless terror from either the state (torture, execution, physical punishment) or God (the fires of Hell) was replaced by continual measurement and monitoring.

At the beginning of the nineteenth century, states like Britain began to take a systematic interest in the size and quality of their population for the first time. This led in turn, Foucault suggests, to an interest in the health of that population, and to various measures to encourage public health. Put simply, biopower describes this attempt on the part of the state and its agencies to measure, map, administer or direct the natural forces of life and death. An interest in sexual behaviour is part and parcel of these inquiries, and therefore is a central aspect of the rise of biopower. For instance, one of the key ways of measuring population was via the birth rate, which itself was dependent on sexual behaviour in (and outside of) marriage. States that sought to measure their population and its health therefore automatically took a broad interest in sexual behaviour and morality.

It is important to note, however, that biopower in Foucault's account does not involve repression or coercion and is more like a set of administrative processes. Such processes required extensive statistical and medical knowledge of society: only armed with information could the business of life be directly managed. This kind of number-crunching was first done by groups outside the remit of the state but was gradually taken over by it; states began to develop mechanisms for measuring birth rates and maternal health (and their 'normal' distribution), the capacities of individuals as workers, parents or children, or rates of disease and mortality. The development of such knowledge can be seen in the emergence across nineteenth-century Europe of attempts to count populations and to map their natural characteristics – a sign of which was the establishment by the British state of the General Register Office in 1836 in order to collate all such statistics. As a consequence of this interest in population and public health, the question of whether someone behaved 'normally' in sexual terms became a matter of pressing social concern. The result during the course of the nineteenth century was a series of investigations into sexual behaviour, culminating in the application of scientific methods to its study – the rise of what Foucault calls *scientia sexualis* (sexual science).

This, Foucault says, is where the modern preoccupation with sexuality comes from – the rise of biopower as an administrative process. Foucault also identifies one of the specific ways in which *scientia sexualis* was devised – that is, through the emergence of a broad field of inquiry that we can call sexology. At the end of the nineteenth century, Foucault suggests, a number of medical, scientific, legal, psychiatric and other writers began to inquire into the nature of sexual behaviour. Some of this began with the state or those allied to it. One of the first people to write systematically about sexual normality and abnormality was the Austrian doctor Richard von Krafft-Ebing, who in his work with the Viennese police came across a wide variety of sex offenders. He compiled his inquiries into the most comprehensive account of sexual behaviour then written, entitled *Psychopathia Sexualis* (1886). Others, such as the German writer Karl Ulrichs, who wanted to remove the social stigma from homosexuality and argued for its legalization in the German states, came up with further new ways to categorize sexual behaviour. More followed these examples, applying this method of categorization and drawing upon individual case studies. This work was popularized in Britain in the 1890s by progressive thinkers like the doctor and writer Havelock Ellis, who began to publish his own encyclopedia of sexual behaviour in 1895, his collaborator John Addington Symonds, and most successfully, by the socialist Edward Carpenter.

Sexology like that pioneered by Krafft-Ebing generally applied a specific method. This was the categorization of different classes of sexual behaviour and psychology, along with the investigation of individual case histories – what Foucault calls the 'specification' of different types of sexual desire. Inquiries like this looked back into an individual's past to find the roots of his or her behaviour in childhood, or examined their subject's anatomy for equally telling signs of 'inversion' – the physical symptoms of effeminacy in a man or manliness in a woman. These investigations, Foucault says, symbolize a new way of seeing the body and its desires – they show an entirely new concept of 'sexuality' coming into being, one that defines it as the mysterious mainspring of the personality, the core of the self.

For Foucault, 'sexuality' has a particular meaning. It is not the same as the entirety of all biological drives and urges, and neither is it merely equivalent to the capacities and pleasures of the body. In addition to those things, 'sexuality' refers to a way of knowing ('the will to knowledge') which assumes that individual psychology can be read from sexual behaviour or anatomy, and that these things will always be in some way homologous – an assumption found in most sexological texts. Foucault resists the attempt to set out causes for these developments in the usual way of historians, and for this reason students often find him puzzling. Instead, his interest is in the coalescence of a particular way of thinking, acting and being, an apparatus of thought and action with its own set of powerful assumptions, its own internal unity, rules and patterns – what Foucault calls a discourse.

Thus the discourse of sexuality emerged from biopower and sexology and its development is symbolized by four key areas of thought that developed in part from the increasing professionalization of medicine and science in the nineteenth century. More doctors and scientists simply meant more inquiries into the physical body, and Foucault sees this process producing four vital elements of *scientia sexualis*. First, the medical notion that women were especially prone to hysteria as the result of their reproductive organs (the 'hysterization of women's bodies'); second, the supervision of children's sexuality ('the pedagogization of children's sex'), such as the control and scrutiny of masturbatory tendencies or precocious sexual behaviour; third, the centrality of reproductive fertility to a social body ('the socialization of procreative behaviour'); and finally the 'psychiatrization of perverse pleasure', that is, the specification, supervision and treatment of different kinds of sexual 'abnormality'.[8] Sexuality is not, then, a 'natural given', and neither is it a biological or psychological secret at the heart of the self which is gradually uncovered. It is instead 'a great surface network' covering the body, its place in the world, and the ways of knowing about it.[9] Medical, legal and other networks of surveillance and supervision created a desire to both 'extort' the truth of the body from their subjects and patients, and a corresponding need to continually 'confess' the truth of one's self.

The rise of 'sexuality' in this sense is marked by a series of apparent 'inventions'. In the course of the eighteenth and early nineteenth centuries, modern medicine produced the notion of the hysterical woman and the adolescent masturbator as particular characters with specific psychological and anatomical characteristics, while the state's interest in public health compelled it to examine 'normal' rates of marriage, birth and death, and inquiries into criminality produced the idea that the sexual pervert was not merely the perpetrator of particular (illicit) sex acts, but a type of person with a telling anatomy and psychology – no longer merely criminal, but 'the pervert', 'the paedophile' or 'the homosexual'. As the historian Chris Waters has pointed out, the entire modern vocabulary of perversion and sexual abnormality began to be created at this time – one that coined terms like sexual perversion (1885), masochism, sadism and paedophilia (all 1890). By the end of the century each of these, Robert Nye suggests, 'had crystallized into distinct types, each with its own symptomatology, archive of clinical cases, and small army of medical and legal specialists devoted to studying, curing or punishing them'.[10]

One reason that this transition, from acts to types, is significant is that it represents what Foucault calls the 'government of individualization'. What we often assume to be natural, private processes involving the simple exercise of autonomy and free choice, Foucault says, are in fact the objects of rule in many different ways. For instance, many forms of legislation, custom and tradition try to prevent people from committing certain sexual acts, and to regulate, maintain and encourage others regarded as useful and good, such as the prudent marriages imagined by early Victorian thinkers in Britain, or the large families beloved of pro-natalist or fascist regimes. Specific programmes designed to bring these ends about are what Foucault calls 'biopolitics'. Inherent to these programmes are statistical and scientific notions of what constitutes normal behaviour – a process Foucault calls 'normalization' as it encourages individuals to measure themselves against the same standards. These forms of biopower and 'normalization' are employed not to merely control and suppress, but to try and bring into being certain types of person. Instead of seeing sexuality as being repressed by these forces, Foucault describes a decentred network of power that attempts to shape it, and that is creative and inventive, not automatically authoritarian or destructive. For instance, many democracies that adopted pro-natalist biopolitics tried in the twentieth century to encourage motherhood partly by establishing a positive maternal identity and linking it to racial health and progress. This was not only fostered by the state, but also by pressure groups and campaigns unaffiliated to the state. This is an example, Foucault concludes, of how power works in the modern world – it tries to create useful and productive individuals through a series of incentives, boundaries, norms and rewards, and the rise of 'sexuality' in the modern sense is a key example of how this process works. We might imagine that desires are natural and autonomous processes, but individual decisions take place within a historically specific set of practices and forms of knowledge that have emerged relatively recently, and which set limits to what can be thought, said and done. Therefore, Foucault suggests, when we assume that we are 'liberating' ourselves by saying yes to sex, we are merely ever more enmeshed in networks of power and surveillance, more than ever the inheritors of those who invented *scientia sexualis*, more than ever caught up in the modern idea that 'sexuality' is a secret that must be continually confessed.

The latter, Foucault suggests, is a key technique in the modern regime of sexuality. The assumption frequently made in the present is that sex in the past has always been repressed in some way, and therefore to express it is to 'liberate' it, along the lines of the hydraulic model of desire. However, as he points out, sex was constantly discussed even during the supposedly repressed nineteenth century, and the continual demand that we 'confess' the truth of our being is actually a form of intense self-government that is a characteristic of modern societies. While we are no longer terrorized by harsh laws, Foucault says, we instead scrutinize and govern ourselves in line with the norms established through bio-power. To take one example, sexology gave rise to an idea of the homosexual as a type of person which then for much of the twentieth century became a key way of measuring and understanding one's own desires. The classic example of this is Xavier Mayne's early sexological treatise on *The Intersexes* (1909), which was influenced by Ellis as well as Ulrichs and Edward Carpenter, and which includes a survey in which one could examine the question 'Am I at all Uranian?'[11] The questionnaire asked the male reader to examine his anatomy and psychology for anatomical signs of femininity – thought at the time to be a key manifestation of homosexuality or 'sexual inversion'. Did your parents exhibit 'simisexual traits', was your teething 'normal and timely', were you a 'distinctly beautiful child', were the lines of your bosom 'flat or curved, compared with the average model of your sex'?[12] This kind of examination and self-scrutiny began at the margins with the perverts, hysterics and homosexuals, Foucault says, and gradually extended its reach across western society as a whole. Its power is seen in the way we interrogate ourselves, continually demand the truth of ourselves, scrutinize our identities for moments of incoherence, perversity or homosexual tendency, or more recently, for the absence of desire or a failure to demonstrate its proper quantity. These are signs, Foucault concludes, that we are bound by historically established norms and regimes of surveillance almost as securely as any coercive laws.

Foucault's critics and queer theory

It is often pointed out that Foucault did not invent the idea that sexuality is a field of power relations, or that the body is an object of rule, and nor did he pioneer the notion that sex is socially constructed. While this is true, and the latter idea in particular dates back to the Enlightenment, Foucault was pioneering in attempting to provide an explanation for our modern idea of what 'sexuality' is. He also attempted to show how it developed not simply by vague reference to the rise of individualism, but as a consequence of specific developments like biopower and sexual science. Finally, he tried to show that this regime of knowledge has had specific effects on personal identity. There have been other, more telling criticisms of his work though. The basic assumption underlying Foucault's

History is that the way that something is thought about or described directly and pro-foundly affects the way it is experienced, an idea that by no means commands universal assent. Foucault's essentialist critics are particularly unsympathetic to his suggestion that the writings of elite theorists affected the ways in which ordinary people lived their lives. People, they argue, are not the passive dupes of theorists, and sexuality is not made in the laboratory or the library, but from lived experience.

Also, Foucault's account of sexual identity and its creation has been undermined in other ways. His *History* makes two key assumptions: first, that the 'regime of sexuality' or *scientia sexualis* is defined by the delineation of types. This is epitomized by the distinction between the early modern sodomite – someone who commits certain proscribed acts – and the modern homosexual, who is defined as a type of person, a species, and a specific anatomy. Therefore, the implication is that there is a distinction between medieval and early modern history which organized sexual behaviour around good and bad acts, and modern history in which good and bad identities mattered. Second, Foucault implies that these 'regimes' or systems of sexual categorization succeeded each other in time – the one giving way to the other. Many of his critics take a broadly essentialist position and argue that some people thought of sexuality and sexual orientation as a sort of primary identity long before the nineteenth century. This, it is sometimes argued, can be seen in the ancient Roman figure of the male *cinaedus*, who had a supposed inherent preference for passive sex with men, or in those accounts of medieval sodomy that presume the effeminacy of the sodomite.[13]

Similarly, the idea that ancient or medieval societies mainly organized sexuality around good and bad acts while modern ones assume that the coherence of sexual identity has also been scrutinized. For example, it is often argued that in early modern societies it was possible for a man to have sex with another man and retain his masculine identity as long as he remained the active partner. If he did so, he would not necessarily see himself as belonging to a separate category of person – a sodomite or homosexual.[14] Sexual beha-viour and identity, it is suggested, was much more fluid, and as there was no 'homosexual role', neither could there have been an equally well-defined heterosexual one. This way of understanding sex, it has often been argued by Foucauldian historians, has tended to die out in the modern West, to be replaced by the view that any same-sex desire probably made one homosexual, while not being attracted in this way made one solidly hetero-sexual. Clear hetero/homo divisions, therefore, were said to be quintessentially modern. However, it has been shown that in homosexual subcultures at least, the distinction between active intercourse (good) and passive (bad) that goes back to ancient Greece was still alive for much of the twentieth century, and still is in many countries. The work of George Chauncey on New York subcultures in the 1920s and 1930s, and Matt Houlbrook on the same period in London, shows that many working-class men had sex with other men, but by retaining the active role in sex preserved their self-image of masculine 'normality'. In these cases it was gender and not sexual preference that determined how you behaved and thought of yourself – you were a man first and not a homosexual, and if you remained a man in almost every respect other than choice of sexual partner, you could not be a 'queer'.[15]

This evidence has undermined the idea that coherent sexual identities, 'systems' or models of sexual behaviour and identity succeed each other in chronological sequence. The 'sodomite' defined by his acts alone did not necessarily give way to the 'modern homosexual' defined by his effeminacy. Foucault's essentialist critics have said that such evidence shows that homosexuality (and sexuality as a whole) is historically constant, and remains broadly the same in any culture. For a long time, histories of sexuality were caught up in this eternal battle between social constructionist and essentialist interpretations and not much headway was made.

The impasse was bypassed, however, by the emergence of queer theory. One of the founding texts of queer theorizing, Eve Kosofsky Sedgwick's *Epistemology of the Closet* (1991), argued that it was simply wrong to take dogmatic positions on either side of the constructionist/essentialist divide. It was also overly dogmatic to assume either that homosexuality is one thing that can be identified in all societies or that one model of sexuality or identity simply dies out when another is invented. In the modern West, she says, there are at least two contradictory ideas about homosexuality – on the one hand it is assumed to be the preserve a specific group of people (a 'minoritizing' or essentialist discourse), and on the other it is thought to be within the capability of anyone given the right conditions (a 'universalizing' and constructionist discourse). This incoherence should, Sedgwick suggests, make us question the self-evidence of the distinction between homo and hetero, minority and majority. These categories may not apply at all in the past, and may therefore also be questioned in the present. As Sedgwick argues, if homosexuality as a category suffers from this vagueness, then so does heterosexuality, and so does western culture in general. In fact, Sedgwick says, modern western history makes no sense without this realization, and the effects of such indeterminacy can be found everywhere you look.

Queer theory offers some way out of the old essentialist/constructionist debate by undermining both the essentialist idea that sexuality is one thing at all times, and the Foucauldian notion that there is something specific about modern sexuality that is not found in previous periods. Instead, queer theory suggests two things: that we reject the apparent self-evidence of modern sexual categories and identities, and that we pay attention to the specific ways in which each society creates rules about sex and the body. Further, it says that these moral rules should not be assumed to correspond in any way with modern categories or identities. Queer theory suggests that such identities are never all-encompassing, and are always exceeded and disrupted in some way. Many past experiences and attitudes lie far outside such familiar categories and are therefore strange to us, or 'queer' in a real sense.

More recently, the classicist David Halperin has added to this view by suggesting that we see sexual history as a collection of different coexisting categories and types. He sees it as a kind of palimpsest – a type of text which has been written over earlier type and on which the traces of those previous marks are still readable. In that view, the history of sexuality is a sort of accumulation of all its previous incarnations. Halperin uses the example of homosexuality's history to make his point. For him, 'homosexuality' is an umbrella term that includes many different past ideas.[16] He proposes that male homosexuality has been structured historically by five different models of desire and selfhood. These are age-differentiated, for example, the institutionalized pederasty of ancient Greece; role-specific, in which the 'effeminate' sexual partner is the one penetrated and in which the active partner retains his masculinity; effusive same-sex friendship traditions; gender crossing – effeminacy, cross-dressing and all forms of gender deviance; and homosexual, or the modern assumption that sexual acts and inner psychology always align. Homosexuality, Halperin says, has a superficially coherent appearance (as does heterosexuality), but really has only a 'specious unity' and in fact contains within it all the earlier ideas relating to same-sex desire.[17] Each of these ideas has come to the fore at various times in western history but without fully displacing the others. Halperin points out that the history of sexuality, and especially of homosexuality, no longer has a stable subject (*the* homosexual, *the* heterosexual). But in many ways that is liberating, as it frees us from having to constantly return to the essentialist/constructionist dilemma and allows historians to examine the specifics of past sexual mores, identities and behaviours without assuming (as Foucault tended to do) that they will evolve into some version of what exists now.

Foucault's concentration on western Europe and America has also been revised by historians of European empires. This work brings race into the creation of modern sexuality in a way that Foucault's *History* did not. As many historians have pointed out, European ideas of the normal and healthy body were made in dialogue with other races and through the process of colonization. For instance, encounters with the New World from the sixteenth century onwards exposed Europeans to radically different moral systems and sexual practices. When British and French sailors made contact with the inhabitants of Tahiti at the end of the eighteenth century, for instance, they found a society in which nudity and sexual display was common as part of a formal greeting, and in which sex did not seem to be private or restricted.[18] As a result, explorers like Joseph Banks or Philippe de Bougainville produced a vision of a sexually free tropical paradise that still lives on. When these societies were compared with the restrictions of European morals, it began to seem that the existence of such stricter moral systems was a sign of civilization or higher evolutionary development. In the nineteenth century sexual promiscuity therefore became a sign of primitivism.[19]

Foucault's account and that of many historians also leaves religion largely out of the picture. Although Foucault states that the practice of religious confession was an important precursor to modern regimes of knowledge and surveillance, he and others have tended to assume that secular discourses are far more influential than any other. In the longer term that is true, and sexual infractions tended to follow the modern pattern of moving from being treated first as sins, then as crimes and finally as diseases or psychological disorders. However, we cannot merely assume the inexorable secularization of the modern world, or the corresponding irrelevance of religion or spirituality, as these were key factors in the making of sexual attitudes and behaviour until well into the twentieth century, and, with the rise of religious fundamentalism across the world, they still have a place in contemporary societies.[20]

The decline of the old Foucaldian certainties – or at least the widening of Foucault's picture through the addition of specific studies – has opened up a huge territory of historical inquiry. Much of this work focuses on identities and relationships that do not fit squarely into the hetero/homo binary. In particular, the history of homosexuality has been rethought in the way Halperin envisaged, with an increased stress on same-sex relations as a kind of continuum. This means that instead of searching for identifiable 'homosexuals' (or heterosexuals for that matter) in a past that did not use such terms, historians have instead focused on other kinds of same-sex passion, such as the friendship tradition or the construction of queer families and marriages, and have stopped insisting on discovering detailed evidence of sexual acts or preferences as a conclusive reason to study these men and women. They can simply be read as outside ordinary categories, as 'queer'.[21]

However, although interesting work has come out of queer theory it has also been a victim of its own success in defining a contemporary sensibility. When it first emerged it was deeply influenced by Foucault's suggestion that embracing sexual identity was not necessarily a good thing and in fact implicated you in the perpetuation of biopower. Among Foucault's many pithy slogans was his injunction to reject identity, to become aware that our bodies and desires had been the object of government, and therefore to 'refuse ourselves' instead of becoming ourselves. We should, he said, think of the self as a historical and political battlefield and therefore 'think differently' in order to escape this violent history. This rejection of identity did seem radical, opening the way for an attack on the historically produced categories of homo and hetero. Queer theory promised a world of radical and uncategorizable otherness beyond these suffocating assumptions. However, more recently the success of queer as an idea has led to its appropriation by other, less radical voices. Transcending one's identity, picking up and putting down different kinds of mentality as required, has become one of the clichés of neo-liberal consumerism, and therefore no longer seems as radical as it once appeared. 'Think differently', for instance, some time ago became a slogan used by Apple Computers. Queer theory, in acquiring these strange bedfellows, has therefore lost some impetus as a critique of gender and sexuality, and as a result is in something of a quandary.

Materiality, biology and evolution

Although Foucault may be regarded by some as no longer central to the history of sexuality, much recent work is a development of his thought, rather than a direct contradiction of it. The broader story of biopower, and its implementation via specific techniques or programmes of 'biopolitics', is widely accepted and documented, although its implications for personal identity are disputed. For all their differences with Foucault, most of his critics from queer theory agree that the natural body is best viewed through the prism of culture. As John Boswell noted, the social constructionist position doesn't assume the natural body or natural world has no existence, rather that it is always expressed through culture, and that its biological facts are therefore essentially ignorable.[22] However, one powerful objection to this is that thinking of the 'social' in this way reifies the natural. In the reading of social constructionism, the body or the natural world can never be anything other than a passive surface on which human plans and intentions are played out. Dissatisfaction with such an approach has led some historians to try and understand the social world as a set of multiple interactions with natural and material objects, in which the capacities and inherent tendencies of natural phenomena have direct and indirect effects on the social world, producing new possibilities and situations. In Bruno Latour's terms, the apparent modern divide between nature and culture is actually a permeable boundary – neither nature nor culture are ever entirely separate from each other, and we cannot wall off or reify nature in the way that classic social constructionist ideas have done. Instead, nature should be reclassified into a series of 'non-natural objects' whose existence and life is dependent on interactions with social structures and forms. To try and understand how this nature–culture interaction takes place, Latour says, we need very specific and detailed studies of how these allegedly 'natural' facts are made. We also need to realize that society is literally made up of these processes of construction.[23]

A similar effort to explore the world of things has been made by those influenced by human geography. This work tries to demonstrate that sexuality and identity are inseparable from the material networks and spaces – especially urban ones – that they inhabit. In this sense, sexuality has to be located in a particular place and a way of using or regulating particular spaces – streets, bars, clubs, etc. – (what geographers call 'spatial practices') in order to exist. This 'spatial turn' was itself constructed out of an earlier recognition that sexual identity was based on the autonomy which resulted from the growth of capitalism, cities and free labour.[24] Modern forms of sexual identity, which assume that entire lives can be lived according to sexual preferences or individual wishes, rather than the demands of procreation or family, rely on the existence of (mainly urban) networks of sociality, friendship, employment and leisure. These urban spaces are then held to be constitutive of sexual identities – it is implied that there would, for instance, be no gay identity without the bars, clubs, houses, salons, etc. of the modern city. To take one example used by Matt Houlbrook, a man named Cyril came to London in the 1930s and there discovered a 'queer' world where sexuality was fluid, and men could have sex with other men and not think of themselves as homosexual as long as they remained the active partner in sex and maintained an image of tough masculinity. All these assumptions were located in particular places, communities and social practices. For Cyril, who until that point had been a family man, this was a revelation. As he put it in 1934, 'I have only been queer since I came to London about two years ago, before then I knew nothing about it.'[25]

This turn to the material world has been influenced by a disenchantment with questions of meaning and representation, but also responds to the increasing dominance of science as the master narrative of modernity. By the late 1990s, the sway of cultural-constructionist approaches had been challenged by the rise of evolutionary biology and psychology, and the application of these ideas to the history of sexuality. These ideas rest on Darwin's idea of natural selection, which states that the organism best adapted to its environment will survive and pass on its evolutionary advantages to the next generation, thereby refining these adaptations over a great length of time. It does so through sexual reproduction which, compared to asexual reproduction (in which the organism reproduces 'by itself' from its own genes), confers the evolutionary advantages of disease resistance and genetic diversity. Darwin always suspected that these advantages descended down the generations from the mixture of some inherent physical quality that resided in the parents, but it wasn't until the twentieth century that this genetic component was recognized, and not until 2001 that the human genome was fully mapped. This seemed at first to promise that human conduct could be explained fully by reference to the genome – that there would be a 'gene for' all kinds of behaviour, including homosexuality.[26] While these have not materialized, it has given further force to the argument that all human traits, behavioural or otherwise, are subject to natural selection.

This view rests on the fact that genes make bodies, not the other way round. Put simply, genes are what survive through generations of the evolutionary process, and are therefore the basic building blocks of natural selection. That which enables an advantageous gene to survive will be selected for over time. As Richard Dawkins puts it, 'genes are immortal, while bodies and all other higher units are temporary'. Individuals, then, are mere 'survival machines' for genes.[27] Genetic properties define the physical characteristics of individual animals, and these in turn ensure the success or otherwise of the organism. Therefore over the long term, those genetic properties that assist survival will be selected, and unsuccessful ones selected out, the consequence being that all traits and behaviours can be seen as subject to the process of natural selection, including sexual and courtship behaviours of all kinds. This was first suggested by Darwin in the *Descent of Man* (1871), when he observed that among animals, courtship was driven by competition for females among the strongest males, and by the preference of females. This also applies to humans, neo-Darwinists argue, so that all forms of sexual and courtship behaviour should be seen as part of the process of natural selection. If it exists now, the argument goes, and we can see examples of it through human history, then, as humans have barely evolved since they began to walk upright, it must confer some kind of evolutionary advantage. In this view, the most powerful men in any society will try and ensure their genes survive either by monopolizing women (via harems, polygamy or concubinage) or by demonstrating their power and wealth in such a way as to attract the most fecund women. The attractiveness of such women is, it is argued, estimated according to an unconscious preference for those who appear to be most fertile. Women, on the other hand, will seek out these powerful and wealthy men in order to ensure that their offspring will have access to sufficient resources. Gender characteristics, such as the allegedly natural nurturing capacities of women, and the equally 'natural' aggression and competitiveness of men, derive from these evolutionary pressures, and are only ever directed and not determined by cultural processes. This explains, according to some evolutionary biologists, why men like women with big breasts and narrow waists (this is said to offer the suggestion of fertility, which all men who seek to propagate their genes will be after), why men compete and display wealth, and why indeed they 'want BMWs, power and money in order to pair-bond with women who are blonde, youthful and narrow-waisted'.[28] Even rape is said to be traceable to a male evolutionary impulse to spread genes as widely as possible.[29] Although neo-Darwinist writers like the psychologist Steven Pinker are careful to say that evolution is only one part of human nature and that he and his fellow evolutionary theorists are not genetic determinists, they nevertheless argue that 'there are major spheres of human experience' including sexuality, 'in which evolutionary psychology provides the only coherent theory'.[30]

The problem with these models is not only one of causation – for instance, how do we know that such specific behaviour as driving a BMW can be traced to an organic rather than a cultural cause, even if we admit that this might be part of the explanation? And can such causes ever be separated? In addition to those objections, the basis of 'gene-for' arguments has actually been undermined by the sequencing of the human genome. This showed that it contained many fewer genes than was thought: 30,000–40,000 rather than the 100,000–300,000 that had been predicted. As Nikolas Rose has pointed out, this figure was only around double the number possessed by a fruit fly, and therefore exploded the idea of genes as determinants of specific human behaviours.[31] The biggest problem for evolutionary approaches, however, is that although we may have been 'programmed' by our evolutionary history, it is our development and environment that determines which programmes run. It is now generally accepted that the way genes and brains work and develop, even at a cellular level, is affected by environmental conditions.[32] Similarly, not all features of human life are evolutionary adaptations. It has been argued, famously, by Stephen Jay Gould and Richard Lewontin, that some features of life and culture may simply be by-products of other evolutionary processes. For instance, we developed large brains in order to deal with the complex processes at work on the African savannah during the Pleistocene, and not to dance the rumba or play snooker.[33]

So the jury is still out on evolutionary approaches to human behaviour and sexuality. Even if one accepts this view, it can only explain historical change in the broadest sense, and is very difficult to apply to specific events, thoughts or actions. Similarly, it returns us to a view of sexual behaviour – the 'hydraulic' interpretation that it can only be repressed or channelled – that was repeatedly found unsatisfying by historians. It remains the case, then, that the history of sexuality continues to be about something different. In Foucaldian terms it is about biopower and the development of the modern 'regime of sexuality' as a strategy of rule. Since Foucault historians have offered a more complex picture that takes in empire, race, geography, and more complex accounts of identity and history. They have also, through queer theory, mounted a concerted attack on conventional ideas of sexual identity that has been immensely productive in questioning the self-evidence of the homo/hetero binary, but has also had some unpredictable consequences. More recently there has been a turn towards the material in the form of human geography, spatial theories and evolutionary psychology. The latter, for all its extravagant claims, has yet to find that many adherents among historians. All these methods are attempts to draw out the relationship between culture, power, material things, and the individual self. This can only be an ongoing inquiry, and in many ways historians of sexuality are in search of a new method, a new theoretical framework. In such circumstances diverse and exciting work is likely to be produced.

Notes

1 Arnold Davidson, 'Sex and the Emergence of Sexuality' in Edward Stein (ed.), *Forms of Desire: Sexual Orientation and the Social Constructionist Controversy*, New York: Routledge, 1992, pp. 89–132 (99).
2 Stephanie Coontz, *Marriage, A History: How Love Conquered Marriage*, New York: Penguin, 2006.
3 The most sophisticated accounts and explanations of expanding modern sexual freedom are: Lawrence Stone, *The Family, Sex and Marriage*, London: Weidenfeld and Nicolson, 1977, repr. 1979; Philippe Ariès, Georges Duby *et al.* (eds), *A History of Private Life*, 5 vols, Cambridge, MA and London: Belknap Press of Harvard University Press, 1987; Randolph Trumbach, *The Rise of the Egalitarian Family: Aristocratic Kinship and Domestic Relations in Eighteenth Century England*, New York: Academic Press, 1978; Alan Bray, *Homosexuality in Renaissance England*, London: Gay Men's Press, 1982; Faramerz Dabhoiwala, 'Lust and Liberty', *Past and Present* 207, 2010, pp. 89–179; Michael Mason, *The Making of Victorian Sexual Attitudes*, Oxford: Oxford University Press, 1994. Earlier versions include Gordon Rattray Taylor, *Sex in History*, London: Thames & Hudson, 1953.
4 Stone, *The Family, Sex and Marriage*, p. 543.
5 For a version of this view see Hera Cook, *The Long Sexual Revolution: English Women, Sex and Contraception, 1800–1975*, Oxford: Oxford University Press, 2004.
6 Richard Payne Knight, *An Account of the Remains of the Worship of Priapus.*, London: T. Spilsbury, 1786, pp. 21–22. A similar point on the variability of mores was made by Michel de Montaigne in his essay 'Of Custom' for which see Dabhoiwala, 'Lust and Liberty', p. 124. On Payne Knight see G.S. Rousseau, 'The Sorrows of Priapus: Anticlericalism, Homosocial Desire, and Richard Payne Knight' in G.S. Rousseau and Roy Porter (eds), *Sexual Underworlds of the Enlightenment*, Manchester: Manchester University Press, 1987, pp. 101–55.
7 On the question of social constructions see Nikolas Rose, *Powers of Freedom: Reframing Political Thought*, Cambridge: Cambridge University Press, 1999, introduction, and Ian Hacking, *The Social Construction of What?*, Cambridge: Cambridge University Press, 1999.
8 Michel Foucault, *The History of Sexuality, Vol. 1. An Introduction*, trans. Robert Hurley, Harmondsworth: Penguin, 1990 [1976], pp. 104–5. On Foucault and the tradition of sociology that reached similar conclusions see Mary McIntosh, 'The Homosexual Role' in Ken Plummer (ed.), *The Making of the Modern Homosexual*, London: Hutchinson, 1981; Jeffrey Weeks, *Coming Out: Homosexual Politics in Britain from the 1890s to the Present*, London: Quartet Books, 1977; Jeffrey Weeks, *Sex, Politics and Society: The Regulation of Sexuality in Britain Since 1800*, London: Longman, 1989; 2nd edn, with additional chapter and new bibliography.
9 Foucault, *History*, p. 105.
10 Robert Nye (ed.), *Sexuality*, Oxford: Oxford University Press, 1999, p. 143. See also Harry Oosterhuis, *Stepchildren of Nature: Krafft-Ebing, Psychiatry, and the Making of Sexual Identity*, Chicago: University of Chicago Press, 2000.

11 Xavier Mayne [Edward Prime Stevenson], *The Intersexes: A History of Simisexualism as a Problem in Social Life*, privately printed, 1908, quoted in Chris White (ed.), *Nineteenth Century Writings on Homosexuality, A Sourcebook*, London: Routledge, 1999, p. 110.

12 Mayne, *Intersexes*, quoted in White, *Nineteenth Century Writings*, pp. 111–12.

13 On this see Amy Richlin, 'Not Before Homosexuality: The Materiality of the *Cinaedus* and the Roman Law Against Love Between Men', *Journal of the History of Sexuality* 3:4, 1993, pp. 523–73. Key statements of the 'essentialist' case include John Boswell, 'Revolutions, Universals and Sexual Categories' in Martin Duberman, Martha Vicinus and George Chauncey (eds), *Hidden From History: Reclaiming the Gay and Lesbian Past*, London: Penguin, 1991, pp. 17–36; John Boswell, *Christianity, Social Tolerance and Homosexuality: Gay People in Europe From the Beginning of the Christian Era to the Fourteenth Century*, Chicago: University of Chicago Press, 1980; John Boswell, *The Marriage of Likeness: Same-sex Unions in Pre-modern Europe*, London: Harper Collins, 1995; Rictor Norton, *Mother Clap's Molly House: The Gay Subculture in England, 1700–1830*, London: Gay Men's Press, 1992; Graham Robb, *Strangers: Homosexual Love in the 19th Century*, London: Picador Press, 2003; Louis Crompton, *Homosexuality and Civilization*, Cambridge, MA: Harvard University Press, 2003. See also Stein, *Forms of Desire*.

14 On this see Michael Rocke, *Forbidden Friendships: Homosexuality and Male Culture in Renaissance Florence*, New York and Oxford: Oxford University Press, 1996; Randolph Trumbach, 'Modern Sodomy, 1700–1800: The Origins of Homosexuality' in Matt Cook (ed.), *A Gay History of Britain*, Oxford: Greenwood World Publishing, 2007; Randolph Trumbach, *Sex and the Gender Revolution Vol. 1, Heterosexuality and the Third Gender in Enlightenment London*, Chicago and London: University of Chicago Press, 1998.

15 George Chauncey, *Gay New York: Gender, Urban Culture and the Making of the Gay Male World, 1890–1940*, New York: Basic Books, 1995; Matt Houlbrook, *Queer London: Perils and Pleasures in the Gay Metropolis, 1918–1957*, Chicago: University of Chicago Press, 2005; H.G. Cocks, 'Safeguarding Civility: Sodomy, Class, and the Limits of Moral Reform in Early 19th Century England', *Past and Present* 190, 2006, pp. 121–46.

16 David M. Halperin, *How to do the History of Homosexuality*, Chicago: University of Chicago Press, 2002, p. 106.

17 Halperin, *How to do the History of Homosexuality*, p. 107.

18 The most recent account is Anne Salmond, *Aphrodite's Island: The European Discovery of Tahiti*, Berkeley: University of California Press, 2010.

19 See, for example, Ann Laura Stoler, *Race and the Education of Desire: Foucault's History of Sexuality and the Colonial Order of Things*, Durham, NC: Duke University Press, 1995; Antoinette Burton and Tony Ballantyne (eds), *Bodies in Contact: Rethinking Colonial Encounters in World History*, Durham, NC: Duke University Press, 2005; Ross Forman, 'Race and Empire' in Matt Houlbrook and H.G. Cocks (eds), *The Modern History of Sexuality*, Basingstoke: Palgrave Macmillan, 2005, pp. 109–32; Robert Aldrich, *Colonialism and Homosexuality*, London, New York: Routledge, 2003, pp. 187–89; Ronald Hyam, *Empire and Sexuality: The British Experience*, Manchester: Manchester University Press, 1990; Mrinalini Sinha, *Colonial Masculinity: The 'Manly' Englishman and the 'Effeminate' Bengali in the late Nineteenth Century*, Manchester: Manchester University Press, 1995; George W. Stocking, *Victorian Anthropology*, New York: Free Press, 1987.

20 See on this H.G. Cocks, 'Religion and Spirituality' in Houlbrook and Cocks, *The Modern History of Sexuality*, pp. 157–79; Dabhoiwala, 'Lust and Liberty' in *The Origins of Sex*, pp. 95–120; John Maynard, *Victorian Discourses on Religion and Sexuality*, Cambridge: Cambridge University Press, 1995.

21 For some of these histories of friendship and family see Martha Vicinus, *Intimate Friends: Women Who Loved Women, 1778–1928*, Chicago: University of Chicago Press, 2004; Alan Bray, *The Friend*, Chicago: University of Chicago Press, 2003; Katherine O'Donnell and Michael O'Rourke (eds), *Love, Sex, Intimacy and Friendship Between Men, 1550–1800*, Basingstoke: Palgrave Macmillan, 2003; Laura Gowing, Michael Cyril William Hunter and Miri Rubin (eds), *Love, Friendship and Faith in Europe, 1300–1800*, Basingstoke: Palgrave Macmillan, 2005.

22 John Boswell, 'Concepts, Experience and Sexuality' in Stein, *Forms of Desire*, pp. 133–74.

23 See Bruno Latour, *We Have Never Been Modern*, trans. Catherine Porter, Cambridge, MA: Harvard University Press, 1993; Bruno Latour, *Reassembling the Social: An Introduction to Actor-Network Theory*, Oxford and New York: Oxford University Press, 2005; Timothy Mitchell, *Rule of Experts: Egypt, Techno-Politics, Modernity*, Berkeley: University of California Press, 2002.

24 John D'Emilio, *Sexual Politics, Sexual Communities: The Making of a Homosexual Minority in the United States, 1940–1970*, Chicago: University of Chicago Press, 1983; John D'Emilio and Estelle B. Freedman, *Intimate Matters: A History of Sexuality in America*, New York: Harper & Row, 1988.

25 Houlbrook, *Queer London*, pp. 2–3; see also Rebecca Jennings, *Tomboys and Bachelor Girls: A Lesbian History of Post-war Britain 1945–71*, Manchester: Manchester University Press, 2007.

26 On the alleged existence of a 'gay gene', see Dean Hamer and Paul Copeland, *The Science of Desire: The Search for the Gay Gene and the Biology of Behaviour*, New York: Simon & Schuster, 1994; Garland E. Allen, 'The Double-edged Sword of Genetic Determinism: Social and Political Agendas in Genetic Studies of Homosexuality, 1940–94' in Vernon A. Rosario (ed.), *Science and Homosexualities*, New York, London: Routledge, 1997, pp. 242–70; Glen Wilson and Qazi Rahman, *Born Gay: The Psychobiology of Sex Orientation*, London: Peter Owen, 2005. For a sceptical overview see Nikolas Rose, *The Politics of Life Itself: Biomedicine, Power and Subjectivity in the 21st Century*, Princeton: Princeton University Press, 2007.

27 Richard Dawkins, *The Selfish Gene*, 30th anniversary edn, Oxford: Oxford University Press, 2006 [New York: OUP, 1976], pp. 40, 44.

28 Bobbi Low, R.D. Alexander and K.M. Noonan, 'Human Hips, Breasts and Buttocks: Is Fat Deceptive?', *Ethology and Sociobiology* 8, 1987, pp. 249–57, quoted in Matt Ridley, *The Red Queen: Sex and the Evolution of Human Nature*, London: Viking, 1993; repr. London: Penguin, 1994, pp. 154–56. The BMW quote is from the *Independent* review of *The Red Queen*, and is proudly displayed on the cover.

29 Randy Thornhill and Craig Palmer, *A Natural History of Rape: Biological Bases of Sexual Coercion*, Cambridge, MA and London: MIT Press, 2000.

30 Stephen Pinker, *The Blank Slate: The Modern Denial of Human Nature*, London: Penguin, 2002, p. 135.

31 Rose, *The Politics of Life Itself*, p. 46.

32 For a summary of the science see Rose, *Politics of Life Itself*, p. 47; Steven Rose, *Lifelines: Biology beyond Determinism*, Oxford and New York: Oxford University Press, 1997; repr. as *Lifelines: Life beyond the Gene*, Oxford and New York: Oxford University Press, 2003, ch. 5. He concludes that, 'Far from being isolated in the cell nucleus, magisterially issuing orders by which the rest of the cell is commanded, genes, of which the phenotypic expression lies in lengths of DNA distributed among chromosomes, are in constant dynamic exchange with their cellular environment' (*Lifelines*, p. 125). For a serious discussion of what historians can do with evolutionary psychology see Daniel Lord Smail, *On Deep History and the Brain*, Berkeley: University of California Press, 2007.

33 Stephen Jay Gould and Richard Lewontin, 'The Spandrels of San Marcos and the Panglossian Paradigm: A Critique of the Adaptationist Programme', *Proceedings of the Royal Society of London B* 205, 1979, pp. 581–98; For a critique of Dawkins *et al.* see Stephen Jay Gould, 'More Things in Heaven and Earth' in Steven and Hilary Rose (eds), *Alas, Poor Darwin: Arguments Against Evolutionary Psychology*, Westminster, MD: Harmony Books, 2000, pp. 101–25 (116–17).

Part II

SEXUAL SCIENCE AND THE MEDICAL UNDERSTANDINGS OF THE BODY

3

MEDICAL UNDERSTANDINGS OF THE BODY, *C*.1500–1750[1]

Lauren Kassell

What are the differences between the parts of generation in men and women? Helkiah Crooke, a London physician, asks this question in the midst of his 1615 book on anatomy, *Microcosmographia. A Description of the Body of Man.* This is a huge book, running to more than a thousand folio pages and filled with illustrations. It was in many ways a typical anatomical book. Following Andreas Vesalius' groundbreaking work of 1543, *On the Fabric of the Human Body*, anatomies were often printed in a large format and amply illustrated. Anatomy had become the ultimate investigation of nature, laying bare the secrets of God's most wondrous creation. To understand the body of man was complex. The body of woman, and its hidden capacity to generate new life, was an even greater challenge. This is an era when 'generation' – a term that I will use throughout this chapter – encompassed the processes of development and growth as well as the act of reproduction. Sex, gender and sexuality were not defined simply in terms of 'biology'. What it meant for a body to be 'natural' was itself at stake. Emerging discourses of objectivity were tied to constructions of subjectivity.[2] The differences between men and women and between masculinity and femininity were inscribed and enacted within understandings of the natural world as God's creation. Social relations were regulated by the Church and mediated through notions of patrilineage and patriarchy which informed governance from the state to the family. Questions about sex, generation and sexuality were debated within universities, in legal courts, and by laypeople. By publishing books that exposed knowledge about generation, physicians demonstrated their mastery of the natural world and displayed their prowess as men of learning.[3]

This chapter considers the major questions that physicians and natural philosophers asked about sex and generation in early modern Europe. Were men and women different in nature or in kind? Were they physically and psychologically distinct? What bearing did their generative functions have on their health? Where did semen, the seeds of generation, come from and did both sexes produce it? Why was sex pleasurable and was it equally so for men and women? What determined whether a foetus was male or female, and why did some children resemble their parents?[4] These questions were framed in terms of learned debates in Latin books as well as the local politics of sex, generation and medicine. Medical understanding of the body was informed by and enacted through medical practice. The best histories of early modern medicine treat ideas and practices as two sides of the same coin.

Crooke's book provides an ideal case for introducing the history of early modern generation. It was a compendium of leading anatomical knowledge, engaged with the recovery of ancient texts and the rise of experimental philosophy. It has featured as a source for Anglophone historians of medicine, sex and the body. And it was published amidst disputes about the status of vernacular medical knowledge and the politics of women's health in early modern London. These disputes were common throughout Europe, and a convergence of events brought them into the historical record in England. Crooke's *Microcosmographia* did not advance knowledge or change practice, but through it we can survey competing ideas about sex and the body and chart the shifting medical, theological and natural philosophical discourses which produced this knowledge. We can also glimpse moments when the health of men and women was tied to their generative and sexual functions, and when a woman's womb defined her being and became the locus of attention of her medical practitioners.

Anatomical books, the parts of generation and the politics of medicine

Microcosmographia looked much like the other grand anatomical works of the preceding century, with one important difference. It was the first comprehensive anatomy published in English. It described the anatomy of the human body in full, including the generative parts in men and women, with illustrations. This caused a scandal. Who was this bold physician? Crooke had studied in Cambridge, then in Leiden under Peter Paw, a distinguished anatomist, before taking an MD at Cambridge in 1604 and then settling in London. Around this time he began working on *Microcosmographia*.[5] In 1613 he became a candidate for a fellowship with the College of Physicians, a role that authorized him to practise medicine in the city and entrusted him with maintaining the medical hierarchy. Delayed in part because of his irreverent and litigious behaviour, he would not become a full fellow until 1620.[6]

Medical practice in London was regulated according to a hierarchy based on privilege, knowledge and expertise. This model was established first in the Italian cities, where physicians set up colleges, claiming a professional status like lawyers and asserting their authority over the medical trades. Physicians studied at universities and advised their clients on the management of health and the treatment of diseases. The College of Physicians of London licensed the practice of physic within seven miles of the city. Surgeons and barber-surgeons were trained through apprenticeships and regulated through the guild structure. They treated wounds and fractures and attended the outside of the body. Their status had fluctuated over the preceding centuries, as their place within universities and at royal courts shifted. Throughout the fifteenth century, anatomy had been associated with the manual, lowly work of surgeons. As humanist physicians, prompted by the recovery of ancient medical texts, became more interested in anatomy and began to publish vernacular surgical works, the status of practical knowledge of the body increased. Vesalius' work was part of a trend to promote knowledge gleaned from the senses, particularly sight. Like surgeons, apothecaries were trained and regulated through the guild structure. They ran shops selling drugs and related wares and made up remedies prescribed by physicians, who also oversaw the quality of their drugs. Midwives were regulated by the Church. Numerous practitioners worked outside of, and in some cases in opposition to, the medical hierarchy.[7] They ranged from illiterate bonesetters to highly educated foreigners, often practising medicine alongside other trades. In Jacobean London, relations between the physicians and surgeons were in flux, in part over the regulation of midwives. For instance, in 1616 Peter Chamberlaine the Elder and Peter Chamberlaine the Younger, brothers who worked as surgeons and specialized in midwifery, supported an unsuccessful petition from the London midwives to form a college.[8] Crooke championed greater education for surgeons, and he dedicated *Microcosmographia* to them.

Anatomical instruction had been specified in the surgeons charter of 1540, and the physicians began giving anatomical lectures in 1565. As Crooke notes, a physician was to deliver an anatomical lecture twice a week, partly in Latin, partly in English for the benefit of the surgeons.[9] The surgeons also organized anatomies for themselves, employing a physician or surgeon.[10] In 1617 the physicians instituted an annual anatomy lecture for midwives, delivered 'in private on the organs of parturition'.[11] Knowledge could also be acquired through private study or from the handful of English books on the subject. It seems that dead bodies were opened in Elizabethan and Jacobean London more frequently than is generally considered to be the case.[12] Access to anatomical knowledge was central to the wrangling over status between physicians and surgeons.

In the autumn of 1614 John King, the Bishop of London, sent the College proof-sheets of Crooke's anatomy. In his capacity as licensor to the press, he wanted their advice on whether it was fit for publication. Book IV, 'Of the Naturall Parts belonging to generation, as well in Men as in Women', was a concern. The College discussed Crooke's use of the vernacular, his inclusion of illustrations of the generative organs, and his reliance on other authors. They concluded that the volume should be condemned and recommended that all copies be burned. Failing which, they suggested that two physicians could correct the offending pages. The work on generation by Ambrose Paré, the famous French surgeon, had encountered the same opposition in Paris in the 1570s which Crooke met in London in the 1610s.[13] The London physicians' objections went unheeded and in the summer of 1615 the whole book was published.[14] It was reprinted the following year and reissued in 1618, 1631 and 1651. In 1616 and 1634 William Jaggard, Crooke's (and Shakespeare's) printer, issued the illustrations in a separate volume, *Somatographia anthropine. Or, A description of the body of man*. As Alexander Read, a surgeon, noted in a preface to this book, the images uninterrupted by text better served the memory and the smaller format could be easily carried to a dissection and used to follow the anatomy.

Crooke answered the physicians' objections in the front matter to *Microcosmographia*. The title page specifies that the work is based on translated material from the recently published anatomies of his Gaspard Bauhin and André du Laurens. Bauhin was professor of anatomy and botany in Basel and du Laurens was professor of medicine at Montpellier and physician to Henry IV. Crooke says that he did not write an anatomy afresh because it was not possible to access the number of bodies necessary to do so in England.[15] In the preface to the surgeons, Crooke defends his decision to publish this work in the vernacular. For him, physic and surgery are sister arts, and anatomical knowledge is crucial to them both. In other countries, he notes, it is common for physicians to write vernacular books to instruct surgeons who cannot read Latin, as well as to instruct them through lectures and dissections.[16] Abroad and in England, Crooke says in a Latin dedication to the king, he has seen physicians display the anatomy of the generative organs and heard them discuss them in the vernacular.[17] In the preface to Book IV he insists that parts of generation are crucial to anatomy. Just as the human body is the epitome of the universe, so human seed is the epitome of the body. Generation is central to the conceit of the book. The life of the individual is limited, but generation renders it perpetual. Diseases of these parts, especially amongst women, provoke anxiety and are difficult to cure. Without lifting the veils of nature and modesty that conceal these parts, medical ignorance will persist. While acknowledging the commonplace that naughty-minded boys read medical books as sex manuals, Crooke insists that he includes this material not to titillate the prurient reader, but to instruct surgeons in their art, to inform laypeople about their own bodies and to honour God's creation. Even divines, says Crooke, have endorsed his whole anatomy. For those readers who wish to do so, moreover, the book is set out so that Book IV can be separated from the rest and studied in private.[18]

Testicles, heat, seeds and hermaphrodites

What do these 'obscene' 60 pages contain? They are divided into two parts: the 'History', which describes the generative parts of men, then women, linking the two with a comparative chapter, and the 'Controversies', which sets out questions about the generative parts. The first part glosses Bauhin and borrows his illustrations. We see images of the testicles and penis removed from a man's body (Table I), situated as part of an open torso (Table II) and details of the testicles and seminal vessels (Table III) and the muscles of the penis and fundament (Table IV). We see a woman's torso, opened to reveal the generative organs and the vascular structure of the breasts (Tables V, VI, VIII), details of her generative organs (Tables VII, IX), a pregnant woman with her womb exposed (Table X, this is the same as on the title page), details of the pregnant womb (Tables XI–XIII), and the wombs of a dog and cow (Table XIV). The first image of the woman's torso, Table V, illustrates Chapter IX, which compares the anatomy of men and women (see Figure 3.1).

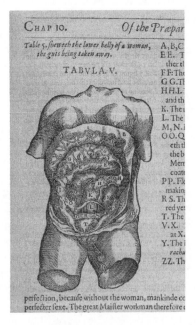

Figure 3.1 Helkiah Crooke, *Microcosmographia, a description of the body of man*, 1615, p. 217. Wellcome Library, London.

Crooke, following Bauhin, who follows Galen, describes a homology between the generative organs of men and women. Galen, the second-century Roman physician who had systematized the writings attributed to Hippocrates and rationalized the doctrines of medicine, was the standard point of reference for early modern physicians. Together with Aristotle's works on animal generation and Hippocratic texts on gynaecology, these provided the major works against which new ideas about sex and generation were defined. The homology between the sexes explains the mirror structure of Book IV: there are two chapters on the testicles, one for each sex. Both men and women have testicles, placed differently in the body. The penis corresponds to the vagina and the scrotum corresponds to the womb.[19] The differences are determined by heat, as it affects the conception and development of an infant and as it defines the physiology of the different sexes. Without enough heat to bring the female body to perfection, her generative organs remain lodged within. As Crooke explains:

> The Testicles in men are larger and of a hotter nature then in women; not so much by reason of their scituation, as because of the temperament of the whole body, which in women is colder, in men hotter. Wherefore heat abounding in men thrusts them foorth of the body, whereas in women they remain within, because their dull and sluggish heate is not sufficient to thrust them out.[20]

In this situation, her womb provides the blood from which an infant is formed and the vessel in which to grow it.[21] Women are imperfect men who, with enough heat, have the potential to transform into men. 'The trueth of this appeareth by manifold stories of such women, whose more active and operative heate hath thrust out their Testicles, and of women made them men.'[22]

The second part of Book IV, the 'Controversies', is largely drawn from du Laurens.[23] This sets out questions about the function of the testicles, the workings of the womb, and other differences between the sexes. Question VIII addresses 'How the parts of generation in men and women do differ', the question with which I began this chapter. Here there is a shift in mode from the discursive arguments of the anatomists to the collection of curiosities of the natural historians. Parts idealized or pathological are replaced by extraordinary cases. To answer how the generative parts of men and women differ, Crooke, following du Laurens, recounts a series of cases in which a woman turned into a man. In ancient Rome, a maid turned into a man and, like other monsters, was banished to the island of the soothsayers. In Argos, a married woman turned into a man, grew a beard, married a woman and produced offspring. Pliny, the great Roman natural historian, described a woman in Africa who changed sex overnight. In fifteenth-century Rome, a cardinal reports a case of a woman who grew a virile member on her wedding day. In Vasconia lived a grey-haired, strong and hairy 60-year-old man, who was previously a woman. At the age of 15, she fell, the ligaments between her legs broke, 'her privities came outward, and she changed her sex'. In fifteenth-century Naples, a pair of 15-year-old daughters changed into sons.[24] These cases, as the anatomists note, are typically taken to demonstrate that the generative organs in men and women are the same, only differently situated, as we saw explained, following Galen, in Chapter IX above.

This part of *Microcosmographia*, however, provides a different explanation. Following du Laurens, Crooke sets out a contrary position. Anatomically, men have a prostate and women do not. Plus the neck of the womb (vagina) is structurally different from the penis.

Inverting one will never make the other. Nor is the clitoris a reduced version of the penis. The womb is not the scrotum. The ovaries are not the testes. How is it, Crooke asks, that so many anatomists recount cases of the women turned into men? One answer is that some of the stories are fabulous. Another is that these are hermaphrodites, people who have the organs of both sexes, often with one set latent until some sort of accident or crisis. A third answer is that a woman has an enlarged clitoris, making it seem like a penis.[25] Whatever the explanation, du Laurens' account of the differences between the sexes departs from Galen and his followers' focus on form and heat and shifts the evidence to observed structures and reason. For him, the explanation of the differences between the sexes is less a question about anatomy and more about metaphysics. Is woman, as she is described in the Aristotelian tradition, imperfect?[26]

The explanatory frameworks which allow for the vagina to be described as an inverted penis and for a woman who over-exerts herself to suddenly turn into a man have come to be known as the one-sex model. This term was coined by Thomas Laqueur in his controversial book, *Making Sex: Body and Gender from the Greeks to Freud* (Harvard, 1990). Building on work which historicized the body, Laqueur argues that at some point during the eighteenth century there was a major shift in how sex and gender were understood.[27] Prior to this the one-sex model dominated, in which males and females were seen as part of a continuum of heat and perfection. This was replaced by a two-sex model, in which the sexes were biologically distinct and women were defined by their maternal function and lesser rational faculties, differences instantiated in wider pelvises and weaker nerves. Through the eighteenth century, parallel arguments were extended to differentiate people according to race and social status. Laqueur's argument is compellingly schematic. The one-sex model has informed a range of readings from the stylistic effeminacy of humanist scholars, to the feminized body of Christ, to boys playing women on the Shakespearean stage.[28] Laqueur's legacy has been most enduring amongst modern historians of sex and the body for whom the transition from the one- to two-sex model serves as a sort of creation myth for binary ideas about sex difference.[29]

Laqueur's critics countered that he was working with a reductive chronology and conflated Aristotelian ideas about function with Galenic ideas about form, producing a unified tradition of homology where there had not been one.[30] Aristotle's woman was a receptacle, cool, passive, and filled with blood which, when animated by the hot, male seed was formed into a foetus. She is inferior to man, an imperfect being. Galen's woman was also cooler and weaker but her differences centred on her womb, which, following the Hippocratic writings, made her erratic and lascivious. The Galenic homology was typically depicted in anatomical images of the woman's generative organs, such as in Table VII, which has been taken as the iconic representation of this homology (see Figure 3.2).[31]

Scholars generally concur that major cultural changes in how sex and generation were understood had occurred by the end of the eighteenth century and that these shifts were associated with trends amongst physicians and natural philosophers to see the body as defined by essential, natural attributes. The ways in which different traditions – ancient or modern, medical or legal or cultural – contributed to these shifts, how they are periodized, and whether the body entailed or reflected gender roles continues to be disputed.[32] Anatomical practices are increasingly understood as embedded within the local politics of religion, medicine and patriarchy.[33] Historians of early modern medicine have reframed questions about sex and gender to draw attention to the fluidity of the male body,

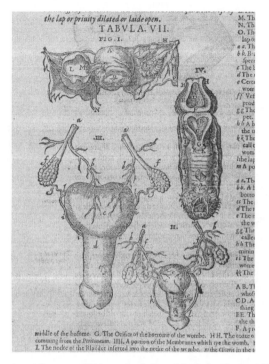

Figure 3.2 Helkiah Crooke, *Microcosmographia, a description of the body of man,* 1615, p. 220. Wellcome
Library, London.

demonstrate the creation by men of a textual tradition about women's bodies, and situate
medical practices within broader cultures and economies of body work.[34] More research is
needed on health as it relates to sex, sexuality and the life cycle.[35]

Crooke makes perennial appearances in historical studies of anatomy, sex and the body.
Sometimes he is cited as a voice in support of the one-sex model; sometimes he is cited as a
voice against such a model, lauding the perfection of women and dwelling on the inconsistencies in Galenic accounts of the homologies between the generative organs of men and
women.[36] As we have seen, both are present in his work because of its composite structure;
nor, in the passages which can be identified as Crooke's, is he consistent.[37] More particularly, attentive scholars have noted that Crooke's work reflects the controversy about sex
difference conducted in anatomical works precisely because, as Crooke notes, he draws
directly from Bauhin and du Laurens.[38] In relation to the generative parts, Bauhin
speaks of similarities between the sexes, du Laurens about differences. Bauhin follows
Galen, a position which Crooke endorses in part in complaining that Vesalius was too
critical of the ancient doctor.[39] Du Laurens presents the first unequivocal challenge to the
Renaissance notions of correspondence.[40] Regardless, Crooke's book has served as a
mine of information about anatomy, particularly the generative organs, the brain and
bodily identity.[41] Most recently, his work has been read as presenting subjectivity as
sex-specific. The male body is the epitome of the universe; the female body is defined
by the single organ, the womb.[42] Crooke's work embodies debates about the anatomy
of men and women. It speaks, in words and images, whatever modern authors have sought
there.

Anatomists' descriptions of the differences between men and women were rooted in their observations of dissected cadavers, guided by their study of medical and natural philosophical texts and, for those who practised medicine, informed by their encounters with their patients. The uterus and the testicles embodied the differences between the sexes, differences defined in terms of generative function and in relation to the rest of the body. The penis and the vagina had secondary functions as conduits of seed. However, the ways in which the uterus and the testicles contributed to generation eluded observation. Similarly, determining pregnancy was the purview of women and midwives, and was done through signs such as missed periods, sore breasts, swollen belly and the motion of the foetus, known as 'quickening'. Distinguishing a true from a false, or 'molar', pregnancy was important. These were caused by a weakness or impurity of the seed, male or female, and other factors which highlighted the links between an orderly marriage and the healthy production of an heir.[43] Seed was produced from blood, but explanations varied for how it was produced. Within the Aristotelian tradition, the heart was the seat of physiological processes and semen was a refined form of blood. Galen defined the brain, heart and liver as the principal parts, corresponding to the animal, vital and natural faculties. The liver produced blood, which was refined into seed in the testicles; sometimes, as Crooke notes, Galen included the testicles as a principal part, because they were essential, not to the vitality of an individual, but to the perpetuation of the kind.[44]

Before anatomists derived techniques to see the seeds of generation in the late seventeenth century, they postulated analogies between these hidden workings and visible realms.[45] They also drew on the writings of physicians, natural philosophers and theologians about the maternal imagination, embryology and monstrosity. Crooke includes Book V, 'The historie of the infant', because he is following du Laurens. Book V focuses on questions particular to the process of generation. The similarities and differences between the sexes are defined by as well as expressed through generation, and accordingly many of the same topics occur here as in Book IV. Children were expected to resemble their parents, and when they did not the theory of maternal imagination was typically invoked.[46] Through her imagination, a woman imprinted what she saw or felt on her child. Famously, if a woman looked on a painting of a Moor at the moment of conception, she might give birth to a black child; if she was frightened by a rabbit, her child might have a harelip. Monstrous births were extreme examples, often read as signs of providence and discussed in sensational pamphlets and serious works of demonology and natural philosophy.[47] The case of Mary Toft who, in 1726, reputedly gave birth to 17 rabbits was the subject of medical, natural philosophical and popular speculation about the workings of providence, the natural processes of generation, and the intellectual weaknesses of women.[48]

For Crooke, the differences between male and female bodies are defined in terms of heat, and their differing quantities of heat determine their differing contributions to generation.[49] That their bodies are different in kind relates to their function, according to which each is perfectly formed. The idea that men and women are equally perfect, following du Laurens, breaks with Aristotle. The purpose of sex is procreative; to this end, men and women are differently suited. Sexual desire is designed to entice people into intercourse. Without it, men would shun such brutish actions, and women would not risk the pain of childbirth. Sexual pleasure is necessary for the preservation of mankind.[50] Sexual arousal brings heat to the genitals, increased through the friction of the act, resulting in orgasm and the release of seed. Whether women produced seed had been debated since antiquity. Anatomists, Crooke notes, dispute whether women's seed is fruitful, but he is certain that both sexes produce it. Aristotle described a one-seed model in which the male provided the seed that acted upon the matter, or blood, provided by the female, as rennet coagulates milk into cheese. Galen, following Hippocratic writings, set out a two-seed model, in which both sexes produced seed, albeit of different qualities. Because the testicles of men and women differ in size and situation, male semen is thicker, globular, hot and active, and female semen is cooler, thinner and wetter.[51] In some traditions, seed from the man's right testicle, which lies closest to the liver, the seat of digestion, produces a male child, seed from the left a female child. In other traditions, a female child lies on the left side of the womb and only moves after 90 days.[52] For the woman's seed to be released, she, like a man, needed to experience pleasure.[53] Throughout the early modern period, theories of generation informed legal cases. Some legal courts dismissed accusations of rape when the alleged act resulted in a pregnancy. For women, such as nuns or virgins, who did not have routine sexual pleasure, physicians could argue that illnesses resulting from retained seed could be treated by manual release.[54] Through the sixteenth century, most traditions concurred that seeds, whatever their source, needed to be nurtured by a woman's blood to grow. Women are colder and moister than men because they have more blood precisely so that they can nurture an infant.

The generations following Crooke would become especially interested in seed, using new experimental practices and innovative technologies (fixing specimens in wax, the microscope) to bear on pressing philosophical questions. In 1651 William Harvey finally published his research on generation, arguing that all organisms come from an egg, '*ex ovo omnia*'. By 'egg' he meant the whole conceptus, constituted by the foetus, membranes and placenta.[55] His experiments on chickens and deer failed to demonstrate the presence of male or female seed in the uterus after coition in fertile animals. He followed earlier anatomists in studying the development of chicks, and concluded that they form and shape their own matter, rather than developing out of pre-existing parts. He termed this process 'epigenesis', meaning parts budding out of one another. What came to be known as 'preformationism' presented a competing model, in which seed or sperm contained an entire being which simply grew bigger during the generative process. Other questions were debated. Was generation better understood as a form of propagation, leading through the generations to the original man and woman? How was the ability of some female insects to breed without males, known as parthenogenesis, to be explained? Did pangenesis, the idea that any part of an organism could become a new one, make sense? The spontaneous generation of insects occupied Jan Swammerdam, Francesco Redi and others through the 1660s. In 1667, comparing oviparous and viviparous generation, Niels Steno noted that the testicles of viviparous animals contained eggs. The testicles of women, he concluded, are like ovaries. His work was the subject of a priority dispute in the Royal Society in 1672–73 and the existence of human eggs was not visually proven until 1827. From the 1670s, with the consensus that women contributed eggs rather than menstrual blood or semen to generation, what remained of the disputes between the Aristotelian and Galenic models dissipated. Male seed was also investigated and in 1677 Anthonie van Leeuwenhoek wrote to the Royal Society reporting that he had seen what he called spermatozoa through a microscope. By the end of the seventeenth century, it had been established that animals come from animals of the same sort and that males and females contribute not seeds, but spermatozoa and eggs to this process. The nature of the eggs and sperm and their contributing role in generation continued to be debated. 'Spermists' credited the sperm as the primary agent in generation, with the egg providing nutrition. 'Ovists' treated the sperm as an animating force, nudging the egg awake. From 1749, following the writings of Georges-Louis Leclerc, Comte de Buffon, the term reproduction began to replace generation. Scientific research began to focus less on the processes of growth and development and more on fertilization and inheritance.[56] Generation had become a subject of experimental inquiry and political economy, but it remained tied to the politics of sex, sexuality and reproduction.

Hysteria, menstruation and the diseases of women

Crooke fashions *Microcosmographia* as an anatomy book to sit beside the major works in the field from Mondino de Luzzi to Vesalius to du Laurens. He also situates it alongside vernacular works, in French and in English. It is time, he suggests, for worthy anatomists to turn their attention westwards to England. His book is the taper at which they might light their torches.[57] The story which conventional histories of learned medicine tell begins in Italy and moves northwards, climaxing with William Harvey's publication on the motion of the blood in 1628. Medical discoveries followed the path of the Renaissance, beginning with the recovery of the teaching and ideals of classical antiquity, their reconciliation with Christian humanism, and culminating with the rise of modern commerce, political systems, scientific inquiry and cultural expression. These are traditions formed through and documented by big Latin books and the epistolary networks that linked men of learning throughout early modern Europe. Increasingly historians have become attentive to the production of this knowledge, in material terms, amidst questions of politics and patronage, and as expressed across different cultural registers. Crooke prompts us to consider the place of generation in vernacular works and in the economy of medical knowledge and expertise more generally.

From the late fifteenth century, the promotion of vernacular works and the rise of printing were part of the humanist programme. In England, from the 1540s vernacular medical works discussed sex and generation within the conventions of midwifery texts, natural histories and books of wonders. These texts dovetailed with devotional writings and conduct books about Eve, Mary and the roles of women as wives and mothers. The production of books about women's bodies peaked in the 1650s.[58] Crooke's work was the first comprehensive English anatomy, but, as he signalled in the preface to the surgeons, he was building on John Banister's 1578 *The Historie of Man, sucked from the sappe of the most approved anathomistes*. ... Banister had been an eminent London surgeon, also licensed by the College of Physicians.[59] His anatomy explicitly avoids the generative organs of women. Book VI is about the instruments of propagation, and reveals 'as much as of the Male may commodiously be spoken' and omits women 'because I am from the begynnyng perswaded, that, by liftyng up the vayle of Nature's secrets, in womens shapes, I shall commit more indecencie agaynst the office of *Decorum*, then yeld needefull instruction to the profite of the common sort'.[60] Crooke, as we have seen, insists that it is appropriate and necessary to the study of anatomy and to the health of women to include this information. His work would be lame if it lacked this limb.[61] Comparing Crooke and Banister's works provides a simple explanation for why the Fellows of the College of Physicians proposed to censor, ban and burn *Microcosmographia*. It broke with decorum, a decorum that Banister had upheld. Yet in the first decade of the seventeenth century, while Crooke was writing his book, medical, legal and religious men in London were debating the extent to which women's diseases were caused by their wombs. We cannot be certain whether these debates informed Crooke's work or the College's opposition to it, but it is clear that Crooke was writing in a climate in which learned men talked about women's bodies.

With the recovery of Hippocratic gynaecological texts in the 1520s, women's health became increasingly tied to the uterus and defined in terms of sex, menstruation and childbirth.[62] Women produced excess blood to nourish the child, initially in the womb and then it was concocted into breast milk. Healthy women menstruated, and regular menstruation was a sign of fertility.[63] A woman who was not pregnant periodically excreted excess blood, and with it the foul humours that had accumulated in her body. If this process was impeded, she sickened. Menstruation was a mainstay of Galenic medical theory, according to which a healthy body had the appropriate balance of the four humours: blood, black bile, yellow bile and phlegm. Cases of men who suffered periodic bleeding from the nose, haemerrhoids, or other sources, have been studied as evidence for the natural and pathological definitions of flow in the early modern period. Such cases of 'male menstruation' signal the ways in which gender was understood and enacted in terms of bodies bounded and unbounded.[64] Practitioners often inquired about the menstrual status of a woman, sometimes too about her sexual activity. And women consulted practitioners about menstrual irregularity, though practitioners sometimes suspected that this was a means of controlling fertility. Just as stopped menses was a sign of pregnancy, so there was suspicion that efforts to provoke menstruation might be intended to prevent pregnancy. Pregnancy, however, was typically defined as beginning when the child quickened, as movement signalled the ensoulment of the foetus.[65] Unless a woman was pregnant, menstruation was central to her health. Girls on the cusp of menarche were especially prone to diseases such as greensickness, and hysteria typically afflicted older women.[66]

In 1603 Edward Jorden published *Briefe Discourse of a Disease called the Suffocation of the Mother*. 'Mother' was another term for womb, and 'suffocation of the mother' was hysteria, a disease caused by the womb restricting the function of the brain either by wandering from its natural place within the body or by producing noxious humours from retained seed or menses.[67] A woman with this affliction lost her senses, typically appearing dead, having fits or howling. These were the same symptoms as demonic possession, and practitioners who could not cure the disease through natural remedies often concluded that the patient was bewitched and could only be healed through prayer and fasting, actions which expelled demons from the body. Remedies for the hysterical woman variously attempted to return her womb to the correct location through coercion (tying down the woman), attraction (placing sweet-smelling herbs between her legs) or the expulsion of the retained blood and seed (bloodletting, orgasm). As the *Problems of Aristotle*, a popular collection of medical and natural questions and answers apocryphally bearing the philosopher's name, explained, carnal copulation is healthy because 'it doth ease and lighten the body, cheere the minde, comfort the head and the sence, take away many griefes of melancholy, because it doth expell the fume of the seede from the braine, and it doth expel the matter of impostume [e.g. blockages]'.[68]

Jorden, a physician writing at the behest of the Bishop of London, Richard Bancroft, sets out the evidence that the 'suffocation of the mother' has natural causes. His emphasis on psychological explanations of illness has won him a place in the history of psychiatry. As Michael MacDonald has shown, however, this work also needs to be read as an intervention in the local politics of possession, witchcraft and medicine. Jorden's work was prompted by the case of Mary Glover, though he does not name her. In 1602 Glover, aged 14, began to suffer from hysteria. When she failed to respond to the treatment of physicians, possession was suspected. Glover became a spectacle, prompting Londoners to debate whether the case was natural, demonic or fraudulent. Ultimately, Elizabeth Jackson was accused and convicted of bewitching Glover, although the judgment was contentious and she was soon released. Numerous physicians testified at Jackson's trial, on both sides. Jorden was amongst them, and he argued that Glover suffered from hysteria, a natural disease. The Bishop of London solicited Jorden's work to settle tensions in the capital about the politics of possession.[69]

Jorden's pamphlet was aimed at a lay audience. It begins by baldly stating that women are subject to more diseases than men. This is because the womb is subject to diseases, and it in turn corrupts the rest of the body. Drawing on the major learned authorities on the subject and on recent accounts by other physicians, Jorden sees the womb primarily as an organ of excretion. It is like a sink or drain through which bodily waste passes. If it becomes blocked, health is compromised. Second, the womb has a reproductive function.[70] While much of the obstetrical and gynaecological literature produced during the Protestant Reformation portrayed the womb in positive terms, works like Jorden's cast a darker vision about women's bodies and their maternal roles.[71] Jorden's primary concern is not with the function of the womb, but with the 'consent', or sympathy, between the womb and other parts of the body. There are, Jorden explains, two sorts of consent between parts of the body. First, a malignancy creeps from one part to another, and alters the quality of the part. Second, two parts share nothing, but one partakes of the grief of the other, like mutual compassion, as all nervous parts have with the brain. It is the second sort of consent which the womb conveys to other parts, especially the brain, heart and liver. These, as noted above, are the principal parts. Jorden is asking his readers to see the woman's body as subject to her womb. A woman with a diseased womb risks losing her animal, vital and natural faculties; the majority of Jorden's work sets out the dangers of this affliction. The comforts provided by a woman's friends and family, Jorden stresses, are essential to her cure.[72]

Any physician living in London in the first decade of the seventeenth century would have been aware of the Glover case, and Crooke is no exception. He notes 'A strange case like a possession in Mary Glover of Thames Street' next to a passage explaining that the womb is fixed in the body and causes convulsions by pressing on adjacent organs.[73] In the 'Controversies' Crooke does not mention the Glover case, but he echoes Jorden's arguments on 'the wonderfull consent betweene the wombe and almost all the parts of womens bodis'. Crooke begins, following the Hippocratic tradition, with the premise that 'the wombs of women are the causes of all diseases'.[74] He departs from du Laurens' text, cites English cases and promises to tell his readers more about how to treat a prolapsed uterus in a forthcoming book on surgery which seems not to have been published.[75] His work on morbid anatomy is informed by and perhaps in dialogue with current concerns about the health of women. For Crooke, like Jorden, a woman's health depended on her womb, which depended on her role as a wife and mother. Mary Glover's convulsing body became the locus of disputes in which physicians exercised their authority to judge whether a disease was natural or demonic. Physicians and divines seem to have concurred that this young woman's body was subject either to the evils of the devil or to the ills of her womb. A further account illustrates the extent to which Glover's body was subject to medical scrutiny.

Stephen Bradwell, another member of the College of Physicians who had been called by the court to examine Glover (and who, incidentally, was Banister's son-in-law), wrote a reply to Jorden. This work was never printed.[76] Bradwell argued that Glover's affliction was demonic. His argument hinges on details of his careful consideration of Glover's menstrual cycle and her physical symptoms. When the fits began, he notes, Glover had not yet reached menarche. Three months later she began to have regular periods, a sign, according to the Hippocratic writings, that the convulsions would cease. They did not. Jorden, Bradwell suggests, did not know this: 'he is here to understand, that which (perhaps) he never enquired, that *M. Gl.* bodie enjoyed this dew of womanhoode about the end of Julie next after the day of her heavie visitation [i.e. convulsions]: and from thenceforth continued by orderly periodes, well encreasing measures for a yeare after, that I was privie unto'.[77] Bradwell also reports on his physical examination of Glover. As she lay on her back, a movement 'began in the middest of her bellie: it moved as if it had beene some living creature, or ones hand within a bed, first obscurelie lifting up the cloathes, and then more manifestly; so did it make the middest of her bellie to lifte upwards, from her back; not arise upwarde, towards her stomach'.[78] Such motions were typical signs of demonic possession. Bradwell is suggesting that had Jorden attended to Glover's menstrual cycle or observed the motion of her womb, he would not have judged her disease natural. Here we glimpse a physician enquiring about a woman's menstrual cycle, examining her body, and complaining that his colleague's failure to do so led to an incorrect diagnosis.[79] For male medical practitioners to examine women's bodies risked breaching decorum, while failing to do so risked malpractice. Female medical practitioners, typically midwives, often examined a woman's body and provided legal testimony in cases where a woman accused of a crime pleaded the belly or was accused of infanticide or witchcraft, searching her body for signs of pregnancy or the suckling of demonic familiars.[80] Glover was not the accused and there is no evidence that the expertise of women was sought in this case. Glover's body, like the anatomized body, was the object of medical inquiry. This inquiry centred on her womb.

Conclusion

Perhaps the most emblematic image of early modern medical knowledge about generation is the title-page to Vesalius' monumental work of 1543. The anatomist is dissecting a woman, her uterus open to the audience. Through his skill, he can see into the hidden parts of a woman and the wonders of creation. He knows that the woman before him is not pregnant, knowledge which confirms the judgement of the midwives who rejected the woman's claim that she was with child, a circumstance which would have stayed her execution.[81] Crooke's title-page, in contrast, includes paired figures of a man and a woman, the woman is pregnant, neither figure is subject to the hand of the anatomist, and the woman's womb remains closed. In 1631 Crooke prepared a new edition of *Microcosmographia*, reissuing the sheets from the earlier editions, with some expanded front matter and a new title-page. This elaborate engraving includes the images of male and female bodies from the original edition, and adds scenes of an apothecary and a surgeon at work at the top and an anatomical scene at the bottom. The seated man in a hat is reputed to be Crooke. Before him is a head, the brain exposed and explained by the anatomist. The brain had long been the princely organ, but by greeting his readers with it, Crooke signals the increasing sense that the brain, as the locus of the soul, was the new frontier of natural knowledge.[82] The bodies which Crooke encountered as a student of anatomy and practitioner of medicine were defined as male and female, masculine and feminine, healthy and unhealthy according to their generative function and within a Christian cosmology. Forward lay an era when women, from the perspective of physicians and natural philosophers, were physically delicate and intellectually feeble beings, in contrast to men who were strong and rational. The differences between the sexes had become fixed, objective and natural and medical men needed to find new means to rule women's bodies.

Notes

1 This work was supported by the Wellcome Trust [grant 088708] and enriched by the many students who have read *Microcosmographia* with me. Thanks to Karin Ekholm, Mary Fissell and the editors for comments on a draft of this chapter.
2 This is the legacy of the works of Michel Foucault, discussed throughout this volume. For the history of early modern medicine, the landmark work on the body is Barbara Duden, *The Woman Beneath the Skin: A Doctor's Patients in Eighteenth-Century Germany*, trans. Thomas Dunlap, Cambridge, MA: Harvard University Press, 1991 [1987].
3 Katharine Park, *Secrets of Women: Gender, Generation, and the Origins of Human Dissection*, New York: Zone Books, 2006.
4 The best introductions to these questions are Joan Cadden, *Meanings of Sex Difference in the Middle Age: Medicine, Science, and Culture*, Cambridge: Cambridge University Press, 1993; Ian Maclean, *The Renaissance Notion of Woman: A Study in the Fortunes of Scholasticism and Medical Science in European Intellectual Life*, Cambridge: Cambridge University Press, 1980, ch. 3.
5 Crooke, *Microcosmographia*, 'Preface to the Chyrurgeons', unpaginated.
6 William Birken, 'Crooke, Helkiah 1576–1648', *Oxford Dictionary of National Biography*, Oxford: Oxford University Press, 2004, [http://www.oxforddnb.com/view/article/6775] (accessed 12 April 2012); Margaret Pelling, *Medical Conflicts in Early Modern London: Patronage, Physicians, and Irregular Practitioners 1550–1640*, Oxford: Oxford University Press, 2003, pp. 126–27n.
7 For varying accounts of medical hierarchies in early modern Europe, see Laurence Brockliss and Colin Jones, *The Medical World of Early Modern France*, Oxford: Oxford University Press, 1997; David Gentilcore, *Healers and Healing in Early Modern Italy*, Manchester: Manchester University Press, 1998; Pelling, *Medical Conflicts*.
8 The Chamberlaines were the family later thought to have originated the secret of the forceps. Helen King, 'Chamberlen family per. c.1600–c.1730', *Oxford Dictionary of National Biography*, Oxford: Oxford University Press, 2004 [http://www.oxforddnb.com/view/article/58754] (accessed 12 April 2012).
9 Crooke, *Microcosmographia*, 'Preface to the Chyrurgeons', unpaginated. See also Pelling, *Medical Conflicts*, pp. 69, 102.
10 Lynda Payne, '"A Spedie Reformation": Barber-Surgeons, Anatomization, and the Reformation of Medicine in Tudor London' in Gerhild Scholz Williams and Charles D. Gunnoe, Jr. (eds), *Paracelsian Moments: Science, Medicine and Astrology in Early Modern Europe*, Kirksville, MO: Truman State University Press, 2002, pp. 71–92.
11 Pelling, *Medical Conflicts*, p. 221.
12 Andrew Cunningham, 'The Kinds of Anatomy', *Medical History* 19, 1975, pp. 1–19; David Harley, 'Political Post Mortems and Morbid Anatomy in Seventeenth Century England', *Social History of Medicine* 7:1, 1994, pp. 1–28; Carol Loar, 'Medical Knowledge and the Early Modern English Coroner's Inquest', *Social History of Medicine* 23, 2010, pp. 475–91; Lynda Payne, *With Words and Knives: Learning Medical Dispassion in Early Modern England*, Aldershot: Ashgate, 2007.
13 Susan Broomhall, *Women's Medical Work in Early Modern France*, Manchester: Manchester University Press, 2004, p. 233.
14 Royal College of Physicians, *Annals*, Bk. 3, 1608–29, trans. J. Emberry and S. Heathcote, 1953–55, 11 November 1614, p. 65; 22 December 1614, p. 65; 3 April 1615, p. 71.
15 Crooke, *Microcosmographia*, 'Preface to the Chyrurgeons', unpaginated. For his debt to Bauhin and du Laurens, see also pp. 25–26, 257, [1113].

16 Crooke, *Microcosmographia*, 'Preface to the Chyrurgeons', unpaginated; see also pp. 25, 197.

17 Crooke, *Microcosmographia*, 'Serenissimo potentissimo … ', unpaginated. The Physicians later held this against Crooke: *Annals*, 21 April 1618, p. 111.

18 Crooke, *Microcosmographia*, p. 197.

19 Crooke, *Microcosmographia*, pp. 216–17.

20 Crooke, *Microcosmographia*, p. 204.

21 Crooke, *Microcosmographia*, pp. 198–99.

22 Crooke, *Microcosmographia*, p. 204.

23 See n. 15 above; Winfried Schleiner, 'Early Modern Controversies about the One-Sex Model', *Renaissance Quarterly* 53, 2000, pp. 180–91 (181).

24 Crooke, *Microcosmographia*, pp. 249–50.

25 Cathy McClive, 'Masculinity on Trial: Penises, Hermaphrodites and the Uncertain Male Body in Early Modern France', *History Workshop Journal* 68, 2009, pp. 45–68 (esp. 58). Crooke omits the often cited case of Germain Garnier, called German Marie, because he was christened Marie: Ambrose Paré, *On Monsters and Marvels*, trans. Janis L. Pallister, Chicago: Chicago University Press, 1982 [1573], pp. 31–32.

26 Rebecca M. Wilkin, *Women, Imagination and the Search for Truth in Early Modern France*, Aldershot: Ashgate, 2008, ch. 3.

27 Laqueur's work should be read in parallel with Londa Schiebinger's: 'Skeletons in the Closet: The First Illustrations of the Female Skeleton in Eighteenth-Century Anatomy', *Representations* 14, 1986, pp. 42–82; Londa Schiebinger, *The Mind Has No Sex? Women in the Origins of Modern Science*, Cambridge, MA: Harvard University Press, 1989; Londa Schiebinger, *Nature's Body: Gender in the Making of Modern Science*, Brunswick, NJ: Rutger's University Press, 1993.

28 Patricia Parker, 'Gender Ideology, Gender Change: The Case of Marie Germain', *Critical Inquiry* 19, 1993, pp. 337–64; Jonathan Sawday, *The Body Emblazoned: Dissection and the Human Body in Renaissance Culture*, London: Routledge, 1995, pp. 213ff; Janet Adelman, 'Making Defect Perfection: Shakespeare and the One-Sex Model' in Viviana Comensoli and Anne Russell (eds), *Enacting Gender on the English Renaissance Stage*, Urbana, IL: University of Illinois Press, 1999, pp. 23–52.

29 See, for instance, Myra J. Hird, *Sex, Gender and Science*, Basingstoke: Palgrave, 2004.

30 See especially Katharine Park and Robert Nye, 'Destiny is Anatomy', *The New Republic*, 18 February 1991, pp. 53–57. The debate was rekindled a decade later: Michael Stolberg, 'A Woman Down to Her Bones: The Anatomy of Sexual Difference in the Sixteenth and Seventeenth Centuries', *Isis* 94, 2003, pp. 274–99, published with responses from Laqueur, 'Sex in the Flesh', pp. 300–306 and Schiebinger, 'Skelettestreit', pp. 307–13. For recent advances on this debate, see Helen King, *Midwifery, Obstetrics and the Rise of Gynaecology: The Uses of a Sixteenth Century Compendium*, Aldershot: Ashgate, 2007.

31 Laqueur, 'Sex in the Flesh', p. 301.

32 On the overemphasis on medical traditions, see Faramerz Dabhoiwala, *The Origins of Sex: A History of the First Sexual Revolution*, London: Allen Lane, 2012.

33 Giovanna Ferrari, 'Public Anatomy Lessons and the Carnival: The Anatomy Theatre of Bologna', *Past & Present* 117, 1987, pp. 50–106; Park, *Secrets of Women*.

34 For instance, Caroline Bicks, 'Stones like Women's Paps: Revising Gender in Jane Sharp's Midwives Book', *Journal for Early Modern Cultural Studies* 7, 2007, pp. 1–27; Sandra Cavallo, *Artisans of the Body in Early Modern Italy: Identities, Families and Masculinities*, Manchester: Manchester University Press, 2007; Harold J. Cook, 'Markets and Cultures: Medical Specifics and the Reconfiguration of the Body in Early Modern Europe', *Transactions of the Royal Historical Society* 21, 2011, pp. 123–45; McClive, 'Masculinity on Trial'; Monica H. Green, *Making Women's Medicine Masculine: The Rise of Male Authority in Pre-Modern Gynaecology*, Oxford: Oxford University Press, 2008; Lisa Wynne Smith, 'The Body Embarrassed? Rethinking the Leaky Male Body in Eighteenth-Century England and France', *Gender and History* 23, 2010, pp. 26–46.

35 See chapter 15, 'Bodies, sex and the life cycle', this volume.

36 Laqueur, *Making Sex*, pp. 90, 105; Schiebinger, *The Mind has No Sex?*, pp. 170, 178, 187–88; Adelman, 'Making Defect Perfection', pp. 36–39; Stolberg, 'A Woman Down to Her Bones', pp. 279, 282, 286–87.

37 E.g. Crooke, *Microcosmographia*, pp. 198–99. I have been judicious in attributing passages to Crooke and have noted his debt to other authors unless there is clear evidence to the contrary.

38 Schleiner, 'Early Modern Controversies', p. 181.
39 Crooke, *Microcosmographia*, p. 25.
40 Schleiner, 'Early Modern Controversies', pp. 183–84.
41 See, for instance, Patricia Crawford, 'Sexual Knowledge in England, 1500–1750' in Roy
    Porter and Mikulas Teich (eds), *Sexual Knowledge, Sexual Science: The History of Attitudes to Sexuality*,
    Cambridge: Cambridge University Press, 1994, pp. 82–106; David Hillman and Carla Mazzio
    (eds), *The Body in Parts: Fantasies of Corporality in Early Modern Europe*, New York and London:
    Routledge, 1997; Sawday, *The Body Emblazoned*.
42 Eve Keller, *Generating Bodies and Gendered Selves: The Rhetoric of Reproduction in Early Modern England*,
    Seattle: University of Washington Press, 2007, esp. ch. 2.
43 Cathy McClive and Helen King, 'When is a Foetus not a Foetus? Diagnosing False Concep-
    tions in Early Modern France' in Véronique Dasen (ed.), *L'Embryon humain à travers l'histoire:
    Images, saviors et rites*, Paris: CNRS, 2007, pp. 223–38.
44 Crooke, *Microcosmographia*, p. 44.
45 Thanks to Karin Ekholm for sharing this argument with me.
46 Silvia De Renzi, 'Resemblance, Paternity, and Imagination in Early Modern Courts' in Staffan
    Müller-Wille and Hans-Jörg Rheinberger (eds), *Heredity Produced At the Crossroads of Biology,
    Politics, and Culture, 1500–1870*, Cambridge, MA: MIT Press, 2007, pp. 61–83; Katharine
    Park, 'Impressed Images: Reproducing Wonders' in Caroline A. Jones and Peter Galison
    (eds), *Picturing Science, Producing Art*, London: Routledge, 1998, pp. 254–71; cf. Gianna Pomata,
    'Blood Ties and Semen Ties: Consanguinity and Agnation in Roman Law' in M. J. Maynes
    et al. (eds), *Gender, Kinship, Power: A Comparative and Interdisciplinary History*, London: Routledge,
    1996, pp. 43–64; Justin E. H. Smith, *The Problem of Animal Generation in Early Modern Philosophy*,
    Cambridge: Cambridge University Press, 2006.
47 There is an extensive literature on monsters. See especially Lorraine Daston and Katharine
    Park, *Wonders and the Order of Nature 1150–1750*, New York: Zone Books, 1998, ch. 5.
48 Lisa Forman Cody, *Birthing the Nation: Sex, Science, and the Conception of Eighteenth-Century Britons*,
    Oxford: Oxford University Press, 2005, ch. 5.
49 Crooke, *Microcosmographia*, p. 274.
50 Crooke, *Microcosmographia*, pp. 285–86; Cadden, *Meanings of Sex Difference*, ch. 3, esp. pp. 161–62.
51 Crooke, *Microcosmographia*, pp. 218–19, 241–46.
52 Cadden, *Meanings of Sex Difference*, p. 41, citing Pliny.
53 Laqueur, *Making Sex*, pp. 43–52; Thomas Laqueur, 'Orgasm, Generation, and the Politics of
    Reproductive Biology', *Representations* 14, 1986, pp. 1–41.
54 Winfried Schleiner, *Medical Ethics in the Renaissance*, Washington, DC: Georgetown University
    Press, 1995, ch. 5.
55 William Harvey, *Exercitationes de generatione animalium*, London: n.p., 1651.
56 These debates and discoveries are set out in a lively fashion in Matthew Cobb, *The Egg and
    Sperm Race: The Seventeenth-Century Scientists Who Unravelled the Secrets of Sex, Life and Growth*, London:
    The Free Press, 2006; see also Clara Pinto-Correia, *The Ovary of Eve: Egg and Sperm and Preformation*,
    Chicago: Chicago University Press, 1997. On medieval theological embryology, see Maaike
    van der Lugt, *Le ver, le démon et la vierge: les théories médiévales de la génération extraordinaire: une étude sur
    les rapports entre théologie, philosophie naturelle et médecine*, Paris: Les Belles Lettres, 2004. On the
    discourse and politics of the study of eggs and sperm in the seventeenth century, see Cody,
    Birthing the Nation, ch. 4; Keller, *Generating Bodies*, chs 4 and 5. The standard work on eighteenth-
    century debates is Jacques Roger, *The Life Sciences in Eighteenth Century French Thought*, trans. Keith
    R. Benson, Stanford: Stanford University Press, 1997.
57 Crooke, *Microcosmographia*, pp. 25–26.
58 See especially Mary Fissell, *Vernacular Bodies: The Politics of Reproduction in Early Modern England*,
    Oxford: Oxford University Press, 2004; Fissell, 'Hairy Women and Naked Truths: Gender and
    the Politics of Knowledge in Aristotle's Masterpiece', *William and Mary Quarterly* 60, 2003,
    pp. 43–74. On gynaecology, see Green, *Making Women's Medicine Masculine*; King, *Midwifery,
    Obstetrics and the Rise of Gynaecology*; cf. Special Issue, 'Women, Health, and Healing in Early
    Modern Europe', *Bulletin of the History of Medicine* 82, 2008. On advice literature, see Randolph
    M. Bell, *How to Do It: Guides to Good Living for Renaissance Italians*, Chicago: Chicago University
    Press, 1999. On gender, generation and female sexuality, see also Katherine Crawford,

European Sexualities, 1400–1800, Cambridge: Cambridge University Press, 2007; Kathleen M. Crowther, *Adam and Eve in the Protestant Reformation*, Cambridge: Cambridge University Press, 2010, ch. 4; Danielle Jacquart and Claude Thomasset, *Sexuality and Medicine in the Middle Ages*, trans. Matthew Adamson, Cambridge: Polity, 1988 [1985]; Robert Martensen, 'The Transformation of Eve: Women's Bodies, Medicine and Culture in Early Modern England' in Porter and Teich, *Sexual Knowledge, Sexual Science*, pp. 107–33; Katharine Park, 'The Rediscovery of the Clitoris: French Medicine and the Tribade, 1570–1620' in Hillman and Mazzio, *The Body in Parts*, pp. 171–93.

59 Andrew Griffin, 'Banister, John 1532/3–1599?', *Oxford Dictionary of National Biography*, Oxford: Oxford University Press, 2004; online edn, October 2008 [http://www.oxforddnb.com/view/article/1280] (accessed 13 April 2012).

60 Banister, *The Historie of Man*, fols. 85, 88v.

61 Crooke, *Microcosmographia*, p. 197.

62 King, *Midwifery, Obstetrics and the Rise of Gynaecology*.

63 Lisa Wynne Smith, 'Imagining Women's Fertility before Technology', *Journal of Medical Humanities* 31, 2010, pp. 69–79. On menstruation, see Patricia Crawford, 'Attitudes to Menstruation in Seventeenth-Century England', *Past & Present* 91 1981, pp. 47–73; Bethan Hindson, 'Attitudes towards Menstruation and Menstrual Blood in Early Modern England', *Journal of Social History* 43, 2009, pp. 90–114; Cathy McClive, 'Menstrual Knowledge and Medical Practice in France, c. 1555–1761' in Andrew Shail and Gillian Howie (eds), *Menstruation: A Cultural History*, Basingstoke: Palgrave, 2005, pp. 76–89.

64 See especially McClive, 'Menstrual Knowledge and Medical Practice'; Gianna Pomata, 'Menstruating Men: Similarlity and Difference of the Sexes in Early Modern Medicine' in Valeria Finucci and Kevin Brownlee (eds), *Generation and Degeneration: Tropes of Reproduction in Literature and History from Antiquity to the Enlightenment*, Durham, NC: Duke University Press, 2001, pp. 109–52; Smith, 'The Body Embarrassed?', pp. 26–46; Michael Stolberg, 'Menstruation and Sexual Difference in Early Modern Medicine' in Shail and Howie, *Menstruation: A Cultural History*, pp. 90–101.

65 Jennifer Evans, '"Gentle Purges corrected with hot Spices, whether they work or not, do vehemently provoke Venery": Menstrual Provocation and Procreation in Early Modern England', *Social History of Medicine* 25, 2012, pp. 2–19; Laura Gowing, *Common Bodies: Women, Touch and Power in Seventeenth-Century England*, New Haven: Yale University Press, 2003, ch. 4.

66 Helen King, *Hippocrates' Woman: Reading the Female Body in Ancient Greece* London: Routledge, 1998; King, *The Disease of Virgins: Green-Sickness, Chlorosis and the Problems of Puberty*, London: Routledge, 2003.

67 King, *Hippocrates' Woman*, ch. 11, esp. pp. 244–46.

68 *The Problemes of Aristotle*, 1595, sig. [E7v].

69 Michael MacDonald, *Witchcraft and Hysteria in Elizabethan London: Edward Jorden and the Mary Glover Case*, London: Routledge, 1991.

70 Jorden, *Briefe Discourse*, fol. 7.

71 Fissell, *Vernacular Bodies*, ch. 2.

72 Jorden, *Briefe Discourse*, fols. 7ff, 23v–25v.

73 Crooke, *Microcosmographia*, p. 225; see p. 251. For similar readings of Jorden and Crooke, see Keller, *Generating Bodies*, pp. 94–97.

74 Crooke, *Microcosmographia*, p. 252.

75 Crooke, *Microcosmographia*, pp. 225, [1113].

76 For an edition of Bradwell's text, see 'Mary Glover's Late Woeful Case, Together with her Joyful Deliverance', British Library, Sloane MS 831, ed. MacDonald, *Witchcraft and Hysteria*.

77 Bradwell, 'Mary Glover's Case', ed. MacDonald, *Witchcraft and Hysteria*, p. 102.

78 Bradwell, 'Mary Glover's Case', ed. MacDonald, *Witchcraft and Hysteria*, p. 86.

79 Roy Porter, 'The Rise of the Physical Examination' in W. F. Bynum and Roy Porter (eds), *Medicine and the Five Senses*, Cambridge: Cambridge University Press, 1993, pp. 179–97.

80 Cathy McClive, 'Blood and Expertise: The Trials of the Female Medical Expert in the Ancien Regime Courtroom', *Bulletin for the History of Medicine* 82, 2008, pp. 86–108; Gowing, *Common Bodies*.

81 Park, *Secrets of Women*, ch. 5.

82 On the solidity of the brain and women's 'nervous bodies', see Martensen, 'The Transformation of Eve'. For representations of the anatomized brain, see also the title-page of Alexander Read, *The manuall of the anatomy or dissection of the body of man*, 1638; Rembrandt, 'The Anatomy Lesson of Dr Joan Deyman', 1656. On Rembrandt, Descartes and this painting, see Sawday, *Body Emblazoned*, pp. 154–57.

4

MEDICAL UNDERSTANDINGS
OF THE BODY

1750 to the present

Richard Cleminson

> Although we struggle for rights over our own bodies, the very bodies for which we struggle are not quite ever only our own.[1]

Is it possible to write a history of the body for a particular period of time? What constitutes the subject of our analysis? What, after all, is signified by the body? Such questions invite us to think less about the different types of body that may have existed over time and more about the meanings that bodies have been accorded in different cultures and places historically. Thinking about the body in this way means that rather than analysing a single body, we focus on numerous kinds of body that inhabit particular periods of time. These periods are in turn subject to changing understandings of factors such as race, gender, sex and sexuality, qualities that are often presented as essential but differentiated characteristics of particular bodies. Instead of the body remaining an 'elusive presence' in history, recent sociological and historical research has placed the body in a central location and has shown that such differences arise not necessarily because of any fundamental physical or anatomical distinctions between bodies, say between Asian bodies and white European bodies or between heterosexual or homosexual bodies, but because the significances that are invested in these bodies and in the persons that inhabit them vary over time in accordance with social and cultural dynamics.[2] The body of an aristocratic Englishman in the late 1700s was understood to be subject to, literally to embody different mechanisms and finalities, particularly in respect of the mind, than the body of a black slave in a European colony.[3]

The body, then, becomes not an unchanging physical self-contained entity but a realm in which certain understandings elevated to the category of 'truths' are performed and exacted in an ever-changing process. The truths thus apparently derived from the body participate in narratives that construct overlapping boundaries between health and ill health, the pathological and the normal, the sexually deviant and the sexually normative and the hierarchy of races and sexes.[4] Thus, one sex should be ascribed to one body, eliminating the possibility of hermaphroditism; one form of sexuality should be championed, heterosexuality, and deviations from the norm pathologized or punished; and the social attributes of the sexes – encapsulated by what we may now term 'gender' – carefully allocated or prescribed to each sex. But these arrangements are not mere 'representations'; they do not somehow exist outside of day-to-day life and experience. As Roger Chartier has stated: 'The representations of the social world themselves are the *constituents of social reality*'.[5] Within these narratives scientific discourses on the body have been hugely influential and have made up bodies and the understandings around them; indeed, as one recent account has argued, the 'life sciences and medicine *construct* those bodies and give rise to social beliefs'.[6] Bodies, therefore, are never simple, 'natural', or pre-existing in any way, but are only knowable through the workings of culture and history.[7] However, we should not think of this relation as a one-way street with powerful discourses of science on the one hand and a passive audience on the other. People deploy their bodies, not as autonomous elements but as deeply embedded material and discursive entities, as a means of ordering their own experiences and as a way of understanding their world and their part in it: the body has shifted from being a mere *signifier* of something else to become understood as a 'site of experience, memory, or subjectivity'.[8] In such reasoning, individual and collective agency as an experiential process can be analysed, rejecting notions of the body as a 'passive recipient of cultural practices, denied even the agency of experience' and emphasizing the *lived body* in a dynamic analysis.[9]

Such understandings grow out of much earlier attempts to argue that the body, sex and gender exist in a mutually constitutive relationship.[10] Although some of these early feminist accounts viewed the sex of the body as something intrinsic and biologically grounded, with gender being understood as a set of cultural practices emerging from the sexed nature of the body, more recent analyses have revised their interrelationship.[11] It is now argued that sex and gender differences, rather than being grounded in nature or culture respectively, 'arise from specific histories and from specific divisions of labour and power between the sexes'.[12] If, as Joan Scott argues, sex, gender and sexual difference are effects which are discursively and historically produced, it is not possible to take these categories as our starting points of analysis. Rather, we need to ask how 'laws, rules and institutional arrangements refer to and implement differences between the sexes ... '; how medical or legal discourses have 'produced knowledges said to reflect the truth about the nature of women and men'.[13] It is then possible to determine 'the fragile and fleeting significances' that notions of gender, sexuality, masculinity and femininity take on.[14]

Such thoughts invite us to eschew any simple explanation of the relation between sex and gender, nature and nurture and the cultural and material dimension in the sexed and gendered body, allowing us to interrogate specific historical instances of the emergence of the body as a subject of the sexual sciences.[15] The remit of the sexual sciences, their field of intelligibility and sphere of influence exceeded any single branch of science to range over physiology, anatomy and psychoanalysis. Their rise has been understood by different authors as a male-led curtailment and assault on women's autonomy and freedom, part of a change from the *ars erotica* of Ancient Greece to the care of the self of the medieval period to encapsulate new expressions of *scientia sexualis* in the eighteenth century, and as part of a 'biopolitical' project, characteristic of western European societies, which managed the health of bodies as a resource integral to their good health as part of the articulation of the political apparatus of modern states.[16] Historians generally agree that the nature of the representation of the body and sexuality changed form and organizational principle significantly during the eighteenth century. A dual process entailed whereby a particular form of science intervened in the body and people made sense of their world through the articulation of the new field of 'sexuality'. The distinct field of the 'sexual sciences' was born, accompanied by the notion that each individual and population possessed a form of sexuality. This new area of knowledge-in-construction inserted the body in modes of regulation, containment and incitement, as Michel Foucault has argued, but it also engendered resistance whereby the body and human beings were anything but passive subjects; they can be read as 'archives' of sexual knowledge.[17]

In the changing logics of scientific thought, the importance of human nature as the driver of the thought process of the mind, the customs and the body moved to centre stage in a naturalistic, empirical and analytical interpretation, providing a map of natural knowledge of the mind that was far removed from the theological study of the immortal soul.[18] As professor of moral philosophy, Francis Hutcheson, stated in 1747: 'we must search accurately into the constitution of our nature to see what sort of creatures we are'.[19] This deep focus on interiority allowed for an analysis whereby instead of human progress and failure being overseen or determined by God, human pasts and futures were explained by chains of being, developmental stages and evolutionary doctrines.[20] Complexity and the multiple roles of body parts – the anatomist Bichat identified 21 types of different tissue according to appearance and function in his *Anatomie générale* (1801) – suggested a different set of relations between the part and the whole and between the individual and society.[21] The workings of sexuality came to be an integral part of these relations.

The roots of these changes in scientific thought can be understood in three principal innovations entailed in Enlightenment investigations of sexuality. First, natural philosophers and medical writers addressed themselves to phenomena in the natural world such as reproduction, behaviour and diseases. Second, science and medicine held privileged epistemological positions in society as powerful explanatory discourses. Third, as activities, science and medicine were understood through sexual metaphors, for example, by designating nature as female needing to be undressed and examined.[22] On the back of four great organizational principles guiding science in the nineteenth century (biogenetic law, understandings of sexual selection, theories of energy conservation and force, and the gendered and racialized division of labour), the sexual sciences of this century differentiated themselves from scientific thought of previous periods.[23] This appreciation has allowed historians to argue that the new turn in the sexual sciences resulted in a different kind of knowledge. As Cynthia Russett states:

> the sexual science that arose in the nineteenth century was something more than simply another chapter in that history. It was distinctive in a number of ways. In the first place, it attempted to be far more precise and empirical than anything that had gone before. In addition, it was able to draw on new developments in the life sciences as well as on the new social sciences of anthropology, psychology, and sociology. And, finally, it spoke with the imperious tone of a discipline newly claiming, and in large measure being granted, decisive authority in matters social as well as strictly scientific.[24]

As the eighteenth century progressed, gender polarities were presented as increasingly firm and naturally ordained. Whole fields, not just human anatomy, became infused with notions of sexual difference as a device for the understanding not only of anatomy but of human social arrangements in general.[25] In this way, the differently sexed body and its role in reproduction was 'read' to behold certain truths about fundamental differences between men and women.[26] By the early nineteenth century, the new science of gynaecology, for example, had legitimized different male and female fields in reproduction and society and the presentation of these differences as the fruit of unbiased, scientific observation served to conceal the social conditions that had underscored those differences in the first place.[27] Previous ideas on the inferiority of women and the superiority of men were challenged, sometimes overturned, and complementarity together with incommensurability between men and women was harnessed to ground separate spheres and separate functions for the two sexes, particularly within the context of evolutionary theories.[28]

As a synchronic process, nineteenth-century sexual psychopathology, psychiatry and sexology steadily identified an ever-more complex and intricate taxonomy of disorders related to the body and sexuality. Emblematic of this phenomenon is the work by Richard von Krafft-Ebing, *Psychopathia Sexualis* (1886), whose extensive taxonomy, often presented in Latin, details sadism, zooerasty, bestiality, fetishism and tens of other practices or conditions.[29] The combination of ideas on evolution, sex and sexuality also posited a racial hierarchy, whereby the white male European was represented as an exemplar of the highest form of civilization with the black African, 'intermediate' sexual forms and expressions such as hermaphroditism and homosexuality being depicted as hangovers from primitive, primeval times. It is no mere coincidence that the immutable characteristics of homosexuals were formulated at the same time as the debate over the supposedly immutable characteristics of separate races.[30] Homosexuality, as Rudi Bleys has illustrated, acted both as a degeneration away from an original heterosexual drive and a regression into a polymorphous sexuality characteristic of a distant and rather more bleak human past.[31]

In order to examine how these new sets of knowledge were mobilized and how the debates were literally fleshed out, three main examples occupy the remainder of this chapter. First, changes from the eighteenth century onwards on the conceptualization of sexual difference are examined. The second example will illustrate by means of some concrete contextualized examples how sexual differences were made to matter in individuals deemed to be hermaphrodites or between the sexes. Finally, the processes whereby some interpretations of the sexual sciences became popularized in the context of diverse European 'body culture' movements such as nudism are discussed. In providing these examples, one aim is to show that the constitution of sexual knowledge, as Porter and Hall have pointed out, is not an accretive process or 'a flight of steps towards truth or as some sudden epiphany'.[32] Sexual knowledge is different from knowledge gained in some sciences like astronomical inquiry, for 'heavenly bodies are just objects; human bodies', the authors write, 'are subjects and objects simultaneously'.[33] In other words, as suggested above, bodies have been the object of the sexual sciences but people have also created a discourse and practice about their own bodies in relation to, or in resistance to, the sexual sciences. Another aim of the remainder of the chapter is to show that the sexual sciences did not constitute a monolithic entity. There were dissidences and differences of opinion in their articulation. In these disputes we can see how the slippery concepts of sex and gender are evoked and brought into being, sometimes reaffirmed, at other times disavowed. Finally, these examples aim to show that the sexual sciences do not enjoy an autonomous existence outside of social and political demands and social usages. They do not constitute themselves from a pure base that emerges axiomatically from 'science'.

The sexed body

The relationship between biology and culture has given rise to many different interpretations in which biology has often been viewed as an unchanging entity and culture as inherently plastic and malleable. But if biology is understood, at least to some degree, as contingent upon cultural interpretations, not only is the biological basis of gender distinctions revised but the very distinctions between nature and culture and between men and women are questioned. As Epstein and Straub have argued: 'distinctions between male and female bodies are mapped by cultural politics onto an *only apparently clear biological foundation*. As a consequence, sex/gender systems are always unstable sociocultural constructions.'[34] Such constructions, apart from their fragility in the present, can also be shown to have been less than solid in the past: 'Historical research into the discursive functions of gender ambiguity reveals the periodic failure (as well as the laboriously maintained force) of rigidly oppositional categories such as male/female or hetero/homosexual.'[35]

Any construction of sexual or gendered difference does not, however, merely exist in textbooks and in discourses in the academy. They have very real implications for people who live within such systems and particularly for those that do not conform to them. As Cheryl Chase points out: 'The insistence on two clearly distinguished sexes has calamitous personal consequences for the many individuals who arrive in the world with sexual anatomy that fails to be easily distinguished as male or female.'[36] The seeming exclusivity of the two sexes, however, not only needs to be denaturalized in the present but needs to be examined historically in order to show how the notion is contingent upon the social and scientific circumstances of a given society, as Herdt has pointed out with respect to the existence of a 'third gender' in various societies.[37] Today, in the scientific West there are biologists such as Anne Fausto-Sterling who have argued that we should be thinking in terms of at least five human sexes rather than two.[38] New studies on transgender and intersexuality, for example, have pointed out how forcible compliance to two genders, sexes and sexualities can have deleterious effects not only on the individual but on broader society.[39]

That the existence of two sexes, with fundamental, incommensurable anatomical and mental differences between them, is a recent notion would appear at first sight to be counter-intuitive. So accustomed are we in western societies to talking about men and women that it is difficult to appreciate that before the 1700s, as a number of historians have recently argued, human beings were represented by one sex, the male sex, from which the female sex would be derived as an imperfect form. However, the suggestion that males and females were so similar anatomically that it was merely a question of their genitalia being turned outwards rather than inwards appears to be a logical formulation that 'makes sense'.[40] Thomas Laqueur has argued that a 'one-sex' model prevailed in European societies up to the beginning of the eighteenth century, whereby the virile male represented perfection and all others, including women, children and, in some branches of medical thought, hermaphrodites, were deemed less perfect.[41] This older model allowed for the differentiation of humanity into two groups and while society could speak of men and women as displaying no major differences in terms of anatomy, males and females were considered to embody fundamental differences in terms of bodily organization. By the start of the eighteenth century, the 'discovery' of foundational mental and anatomical differences, such as between the skeletons, brains and craniums of men and women, would no longer allow for this 'one-sex' model and the detailing of incommensurable differences signified the steady rise of a 'two-sex' dichotomous model. In the ensuing lively debate on these questions, it has been argued, however, that the shift between the two models not only obscures the historical diversity of ideas of 'sex' and its relation to 'gender' but also that it entails an over-idealized periodization depicting these changes.[42]

Laqueur states in his *Making Sex* that sex, or the body, must be understood as an epi-phenomenon, while gender would be the primary or 'real' category to distinguish the sexes within the one-sex model.[43] Two genders, in this reading, would correspond to one sex before 1700.[44] But in foregrounding the social roles arising from the two genders, Laqueur seems to underestimate the materiality of the body and how differences such as activity/passivity, warmth/coolness and dryness and moistness were seen as distinct modes of organization which resulted in particular social roles for men and women within a natural order ordained by God. In his formulation 'So-called biological sex does not provide a solid foundation for the cultural category of gender, but constantly threatens to subvert it', the gendered category stands in for a foundational marker.[45] One critic, Michael Stolberg, while disagreeing about the periodization of the shift between the two models – despite arguing that notions of sex need to be historicized and 'cannot be understood as an ahis-torical natural given' – opposes the notion of sex to gender, which is 'understood as a social and cultural category'.[46] However, for the period referred to here by these authors, it makes no sense to talk about 'gender' as a foundational or a constructed category, being as it was a set of signifiers that only emerged in contradistinction to 'sex' from the eight-eenth or even nineteenth century onwards. If, however, gender is viewed not as either merely culturally constructed or as foundational but as properly constitutive of sex, whereby sex becomes a regulatory ideal in the sense that Judith Butler has outlined, a different understanding is arrived at whereby sex and gender cannot be considered, respectively, as categories that emerge from 'nature' and 'culture'.[47] Rather, our under-standings of both arise from our interpretation of nature; indeed, notions of gender, that is, the performance of gendered acts, actually make up what sex we are.

With respect to the historical period we refer to here, Londa Schiebinger, in her dis-cussion of different representations of male and female skeletons, argues that the eighteenth century saw the rise of a new kind of biological determinism wherein 'gender and notions of gender roles were seen as grounded in the sex of the physical body – and it is here that representations of female skeletons found their significance'.[48] At a time when profound social changes were in operation with respect to the role of women and men in post-Enlightenment liberal articulations of the state, such sexual differences took on a new significance. Schiebinger once more:

> My point in discussing the revolution in views of sexual difference in the eight-eenth century was not that sexual dimorphism had not previously been recog-nized but that male and female bodies in this later period were resexualized along profoundly different lines from those of the Galenic world.[49]

The constructivism of the social sciences gives us indispensable tools in order to re-politicize the polar and dualistic model (there are only two sexes and two genders), to show their contingency, and their status as historical inventions.[50] But social constructionism must get over the antagonism between biology and culture, of the representation of the body as a thing or piece of property, and must avoid the pitfall of dissolving the material world as if it 'did not matter'. Recently, authors such as Myra Hird have begun to do this: bodies are material but not in ways that justify continuous emphasis on 'sexual difference'. The very diversity, openness and variation of the material world and its interpretation, Hird argues by drawing on 'a loosely configured group of analyses called "new materialism"', allow us to construct narratives that go beyond positing a 'changeable culture against a stable and inert nature'.[51]

Constructing sex

The purpose of the previous section has been to suggest, first, that by the nineteenth century the two sexes were deemed to inhabit different bodies, and second, that the sexual sciences posited that there was a particular natural and discernible correlation between body, sex, gender and sexuality that would be constructed on the artifice of masculinity, femininity and heterosexuality.[52] Those sexual practices and bodies that fell outside of these constraints were pathologized along a continuum of the sexual perversions and deviations, including sexual inversion, atypical gender behaviour and hermaphroditism or intersexuality. Some branches of the sexual sciences lend themselves very clearly to an analysis that illustrates how the perceived sex and gender of the subject were made up, not as a simple ahistorical set of cultural attributes but as discourses and materialities that literally made up the kind of body that one was deemed to be. This mutually dependent framework of intelligibility can be seen in studies of hermaphrodites or intersex people in the twentieth century. The next section of this chapter shows by means of a number of examples how the anatomy of gender difference was made real for sexual scientists but also how fragile these constructs were.

Alice Dreger has shown how hermaphroditism and intersexuality became an issue for medical scientists in the late nineteenth and early twentieth centuries. Despite national and cultural differences, doctors in France, Germany and England sought to match up sexed and gendered traits in those individuals deemed of doubtful or indeterminate sex in order to produce sound masculinities and femininities and to guarantee functioning heterosexuality. This was a complex process, drawing on a number of possibly conflicting and competing frameworks and protocols stemming from early nineteenth-century 'Teratology', which revised medieval and early modern considerations of those 'in between' the sexes. The determination of the 'real sex' of the individual was the task of the medical doctor and his medico-legal assistant: 'The years from around 1860 to 1870 were precisely one of those periods when investigations of sexual identity were carried out with the most intensity, in an attempt not only to establish the true sex of hermaphrodites but also to identify, classify, and characterize the different types of perversions.'[53] This process, however, became increasingly complex as established frameworks were constantly revised in the light of new case studies and insights. By looking at the development of such a science it is possible to confirm the impression of a set of knowledge very much under construction, with medical specialists feeling their way, quite literally, towards a consensus and a firmer knowledge base. Sex and gender differences were not self-evident; they had to be discursively and materially inscribed on the body.[54] This was particularly evident when the possibility of 'homosexual hermaphrodites' was entertained. How could it be that even if the real sex of the individual could be identified, he or she could be erotically oriented to members of the same sex? Such an alignment may seem perfectly possible to us now, but in the early twentieth century, the existing models found themselves unable to process such an eventuality.[55]

This 'ontologising via embodiment of sex and racial difference' can also be seen in the articulation of endocrinological and hormonal theories from the 1900s to the 1940s.[56] As noted above, nineteenth-century sexual scientists were informed by a dual conception of essential differences between men and women and by the idea that sexual dimorphism was a mark of advanced development. Those individual human beings and races that had not managed such differentiation were deemed throw-backs to an ancestral primitiveness. But scientists also believed that the 'germs' of one sex resided, although latent or dormant, in the other sex and that through the action of these 'residua' it was possible to collapse back into an atavistic state.[57] But these conceptualizations did not necessarily coincide at the same time across all countries. The renowned Spanish endocrinologist and historian of science Gregorio Marañón, for example, believed that while there were certain differences between the sexes, these resulted from the most complete differentiation along a horizontal and vertical plane between masculinity and femininity and between the male and the female. Perfection, as in the classical Greek model, would be obtained by the most virile male. The possibility of slipping back into a less differentiated state was always present in the battle that both sexes waged inside any one body; women could improve by approximating towards the male sex as they got older, but not too much because of the danger of lesbianism; men could negotiate the 'crisis' of adolescence and a possible fall into femininity, only to decay into effeminacy as they grew older.[58]

Alongside the evident physical characteristics highlighted to prove the sex of hermaphrodites (the genitalia, internal organs, body hair and general demeanour, amongst other criteria), the presence of certain hormones deemed 'male' and 'female' was understood as a failsafe criterion for determining sex in the early twentieth century. Hence, oestrogen was identified in the female as a sex marker and androgen in the male. Homosexuals could have a mix or incorrect proportion of these hormones. However, in the early 1930s it was discovered that 'normal' men and women did not possess exclusively the hormones assigned to their real sex; men, for example, secreted ample quantities of oestrogen. Yet another set of criteria was torn asunder and conceptualizations of sex difference once again shifted.[59] In the 1950s, other developments took place to categorize a lack of normative alignment between body, gender and sex with more complex categories for the determination and meaning of sex.[60] Notions of the 'transsexual' and 'gender dysphoria' moved to centre stage. What had changed, however, by the 1970s and 1980s was that 'patients' themselves had begun to rationalize their own situation in the very terms that medical doctors and sexologists drew up. Transgenderism and transsexuality would not be confined to the high echelons of medical expertise; like homosexuality in the earlier part of the century, theories would be born as a result of dialogue between patient and practitioner.[61] Rather than ideas of two sexes or one sex inhabiting the body as in the eighteenth and nineteenth centuries, some practitioners and 'patients' now refer to the 'best sex' where gender, sexuality and the body are much more flexible categories.[62]

'Body work' or nudism in contemporary European societies

The old model, whereby pure science was generated in an elite centre and subsequently 'diffused' into wider circles, whether society at large or 'non-professional' scientific circles, has given way to more nuanced accounts of science in action whereby scientific knowledge needs to be understood as part of 'a communicative process, involving appropriation, resistance and cultural contestation'.[63] The sexual sciences, often conceived as enjoying unprecedented power, are usefully analysed from this perspective. Not only does the reception of the sexual sciences vary from country to country over historical time, their very constitution and *modus operandi* emerge as a result of a complex interplay of factors. Therefore, we should go beyond any supposed schism between 'sexual science proper' and any 'popularized' form in order to recognize that the sexual sciences were configured by an inextricable process of construction between 'expert' and more 'popular' domains in which any mutual exclusivity between the two is lost. Indeed, the very notion of elite and popular fields can entail 'an unfortunate dualism, with "knowledge" and those who produce it on one side, and a diluted form of that knowledge and its consumers on the other'.[64] Discourse on homosexuality and transvestism, for example, has been shown to have been constructed not from a set of knowledge established a priori by specialists but rather in interaction with the subjects which these expert domains sought to describe and regulate.[65]

This employment or 're-signification' of the premises and logics of the sexual sciences can be seen in bodily and sexual practices such as the twentieth-century sex-reform, eugenics and nudist movements in various countries across Europe. The last of these, nudism, can be understood as a kind of praxis of the body, or a set of techniques of the body, developed in order to attain some higher aim (the purification of the nation, the incarnation of the indomitable spirit of the proletariat or the realization of racial purity), which is seen to be encapsulated, literally 'corporealized' by the body.[66] In this attempt to unite material culture (the body, the sun, the elements) with the development of lived subjectivities as part of a drive towards political and biological betterment, the body was cast as a raw material to be fashioned in conjunction with a set of knowledges drawn from strong, health-oriented, eugenic and scientific discourses on sexuality. Such common ground signified that '[p]rogressive, conservative, racist and even religious perspectives' could coexist within the nudist culture of any given country.[67]

While nudism was in part a response to the tensions encapsulated by modernity, it was also understood to be a route to the 'truth' of the race and to be in harmony with 'nature'.[68] Furthermore, since nudism was to be practised both individually and collectively it took on a dimension far beyond that of the care of the individualized body and the diseases the body suffered and its sexual disorders were writ large on the collective 'social body'.[69] The scientific organization of sexuality in the midst of these considerations moved to centre stage as did the reform of sexual, social and cultural mores: 'The perception of the body and sexuality within nudist writing did not simply reflect a discursive message; rather, the physical techniques of nudism became a means of cultural criticism.'[70] Nudism, therefore, can be understood as a kind of 'body work', whereby 'corporeal itineraries' are realized within the spaces etched out between political ideologies, agency and sexual knowledge.[71]

In England, while 'mainstream' nudists were limited to 'educating young people about the biological differences between the sexes', others, such as the anarchist-socialist Edward Carpenter, advocated a form of 'socialism of sandals and sun' and revolution in all quarters of human life in which nudism would play a driving role.[72] Carpenter's utopian message would involve 'sexual equality and freedom, closeness to Nature, direct relations between human beings, "by plain living, friendship with the Animals, open-air habits, fruitarian food and such degree of Nudity as we can reasonably attain to"'.[73] In other countries, the nudity of the body, as well as demystifying its taboos, was also perceived as a strategy in a broader attempt to foster the optimum conditions for the reproduction of human beings. As such, many nudist movements emerged in conjunction with the sexual sciences of the age and, in particular, with one of the two 'great innovations in the technology of sex' of the nineteenth century: eugenics.[74] Eugenics, a diffuse sexual science that drew on biological thought, evolutionary theories, moral concerns and conceptions of disease, colonized the popular imagination and became in some European countries, such as Germany and Spain, an influential field with a profound reception in society as well as in specific movements for change such as nudism. In England, however, such linkages between nudism and eugenics were not explicitly forged.[75]

Chad Ross argues that nudism in Germany became increasingly infused with racial hygienic discourse, especially from the mid-1930s onwards as the Nazis came to power.[76] One nudist explained that the improvement of the race was inseparable from 'National renewal, Nordification and improving the character and nature of Germans either psychotechnically, morally or through racial hygiene and eugenics is not in the least possible without *körperkultur* [sic]'.[77] Nudism would allow people to get to know their future spouse and determine their reproductive compatibility through a process of mate selection, whereby the 'healthy and racially acceptable' partner would also be the most beautiful.[78] In Spain, too, such linkages between eugenics and nudism were made explicit. Here, the nudist 'movement' was broad, often leftist in political inspiration, and it provided a critique of contemporary society and civilization by advocating vegetarianism and nudism and voicing opposition to the use of tobacco. The Barcelona-based 'Friends of the Sun', in addition to organizing gymnastics in the main city square and leading excursions into the countryside, advocated a form of nudism that aspired to encapsulate 'eugenic sentiments of brotherhood' in order to improve human health.[79] Other organizations, such as the Pentalfa School, advocated a form of eugenics coupled with a strict sexual morality: syphilis, pederasty, lasciviousness and the corruption that supposedly brought down the Roman Empire were all put down to youth's ignorance in not following 'a true natural lifestyle'.[80]

More explicitly connected to a political project, the anarchist naturist *Iniciales* (Barcelona, 1929–37) presented itself as a monthly review combining 'anarchism, sexual education, naturism, nudism and free love'. As such, the 'undressing of body and spirit', whereby humanity would be freed from clothes as well as of its 'moral and personal prejudices and miseries', would entail a revolution in sexual morality and sexual relations.[81] The French anarchist E. Armand, writing in *Iniciales*, explicitly linked nudism and sexuality, hoping that such an 'exaltation' would be 'pure, natural, instinctive', nothing to do with the 'fictitious excitation' provided by those half dressed or dressed up to titillate.[82] While the political and social content of different nudist movements varied, they all coincided in their attempt to move towards a utopian horizon for the ordering of human reproduction. As in other scenarios, such as the feminist use of phrenology to buttress claims for equality with men in the mid-nineteenth century, or the feminist use of sexology, nudism drew on a popularized form of sexual scientific knowledge that was put to use for a particular political project of 'racial' or sexual purification.[83]

Conclusion

The sexual sciences of the 1750s were different in nature and expression to those of the late twentieth century. Not only did the notion of female inferiority decline, but sex traits were no longer seen as necessarily and exclusively connected to one sex or the other. While the role of the sexual sciences is still strongly connected to the production of sexual normativity – whether by assigning the 'best' sex to one body, finding the specificities of the biological basis of homosexuality, or managing sexual satisfaction for troubled couples – the strict correlation between body, gender and sexuality has been eroded. As the mission of the sexual sciences in the West has moved away from charting the perversions, they have concentrated instead on providing balance and harmony to sexual relations and not prejudice, legal sanction or persecution. The subtlety and all-pervasiveness of the sexological logic, however, by no means signify its lack of potency. Sex is still posited by the sexual sciences as the secret or the truth that informs personality, the basis for personal and social well-being and the route to individual and collective happiness and fulfilment.

Notes

1 Judith Butler, *Precarious Life*, London and New York: Verso, 2004, p. 26.
2 Kathleen Canning, 'The Body as Method? Reflections on the Place of the Body in Gender History', *Gender & History* 11:3, 1999, pp. 499–513 (499).
3 Bryan Turner, *The Body and Society: Explorations in Social Theory*, Oxford: Blackwell, 1984; R. W. Connell, 'Bodies, Intellectuals and World Society' in Nick Watson and Sarah Cunningham-Burley (eds), *Reframing the Body*, Basingstoke: Palgrave, 2001, pp. 13–28.
4 Ann Laura Stoler, *Race and the Education of Desire: Foucault's History of Sexuality and the Colonial Order of Things*, Durham, NC: Duke University Press, 1995.
5 Roger Chartier, 'Intellectual History or Sociocultural History? The French Trajectories' in Dominick LaCapra and Steven L. Kaplan (eds), *Modern European Intellectual History*, Ithaca and London: Cornell University Press, 1982, pp. 13–46 (41), emphasis added. With respect to gender, Joan Scott has argued that 'Knowledge is a way of ordering the world; as such it is not prior to social organization, it is inseparable from social organization'; Joan Scott, *Gender and the Politics of History*, New York: Columbia University Press, 1999, p. 2.
6 Jennifer Terry and Jacqueline Urla, 'Introduction: Mapping Embodied Deviance' in Jennifer Terry and Jacqueline Urla (eds), *Deviant Bodies: Critical Perspectives on Difference in Science and Popular Culture*, Bloomington, IN: Indiana University Press, 1995, pp. 1–18 (3).
7 Terry and Urla, 'Introduction', p. 3.
8 Canning, 'The Body as Method?', p. 501.
9 Lynda Birke, *Feminism and the Biological Body*, Edinburgh: Edinburgh University Press, 1999, p. 34; Elizabeth Grosz, *Volatile Bodies: Toward a Corporeal Feminism*, Bloomington, IN: Indiana University Press, 1994; Iris Marion Young, *On Female Body Experience: 'Throwing Like a Girl' and Other Essays*, Oxford: Oxford University Press, 2005.
10 Anne Oakley, *Sex, Gender and Society*, London: Maurice Temple Smith, 1972; Gayle Rubin, 'The Traffic in Women: Notes on the "Political Economy" of Sex' in Rayna R. Reiter (ed.), *Toward an Anthropology of Women*, New York and London: Monthly Review Press, 1975, pp. 157–210.
11 Birke, *Feminism and the Biological Body*, pp. 1–2; Bernice Hausman, *Changing Sex: Transsexualism, Technology, and the Idea of Gender*, Durham, NC and London: Duke University Press, 1995, pp. 8–9; Sally Hines and Tam Sanger (eds), *Transgender Identities: Towards a Social Analysis of Gender Diversity*, London: Routledge, 2010. Oudshoorn argues that the effect of assigning sex to the biomedical sciences and gender to the social sciences has been the maintenance of sex 'as an ahistorical attribute of the human body and the body ... excluded from feminist analysis'; Nelly Oudshoorn, *Beyond the Natural Body: An Archeology of Sex Hormones*, London: Routledge, 1994, p. 2.
12 Londa Schiebinger, *Feminism and the Body*, Oxford: Oxford University Press, 2000, p. 1.
13 Scott, *Gender and the Politics of History*, pp. 201–2.
14 Ludmilla Jordanova, *Sexual Visions: Images of Gender in Science and Medicine between the Eighteenth and Twentieth Centuries*, New York and London: Harvester Wheatsheaf, 1989, p. 4.
15 Cf. Julia Epstein, 'Either/Or – Neither/Both: Sexual Ambiguity and the Ideology of Gender', *Genders* 7, 1990, pp. 99–142.
16 Janice G. Raymond, *The Transsexual Empire*, London: The Women's Press, 1980, p. xvi; Michel Foucault, *The History of Sexuality, Vol. 1. An Introduction*, trans. Robert Hurley,

Harmondsworth: Penguin, 1990 [1976], pp. 51–73, 139–40; Mitchell Dean, *Governmentality: Power and Rule in Modern Society*, London: Sage, 1999.

17 Michel Foucault, *Discipline and Punish: The Birth of the Prison*, trans. Alan Sheridan, New York: Pantheon, 1977; Alan Sekula, 'The Body and the Archive', *October* 39, 1986, pp. 3–64 (7).

18 Roy Porter, *Enlightenment: Britain and the Creation of the Modern World*, London: Penguin, 2001, pp. 183, 170.

19 Porter, *Enlightenment*, pp. 162–63.

20 Roy Porter, *The Greatest Benefit to Mankind: A Medical History of Humanity from Antiquity to the Present*, London: HarperCollins, 1997, p. 253.

21 Porter, *The Greatest Benefit to Mankind*, p. 265.

22 Jordanova, *Sexual Visions*, p. 24.

23 Cynthia E. Russett, *Sexual Science: The Victorian Construction of Womanhood*, Cambridge, MA; London: Harvard University Press, 1989, p. 49.

24 Russett, *Sexual Science*, pp. 3–4.

25 Londa Schiebinger, *The Mind has no Sex? Women in the Origins of Modern Science*, Cambridge, MA; London: Harvard University Press, 1989.

26 Jordanova, *Sexual Visions*, pp. 24, 51.

27 Ornella Moscucci, *The Science of Woman: Gynaecology and Gender in England, 1800–1929*, Cambridge: Cambridge University Press, 1990, p. 2.

28 It is important to point out that this was no hegemonic position. 'Sexual characters' were not necessarily seen as fixed properties. See the debate between commentators such as Patrick Geddes and J. Arthur Thomson, authors of *The Evolution of Sex* (1889), who posited fundamentally different make-ups for men and women, described respectively as katabolic and anabolic, and Harry Campbell, *Differences in the Nervous Organisation of Man and Woman* (1891), who argued for more flexible traits; Russett, *Sexual Science*, pp. 77, 89–92.

29 Jeffrey Weeks, *Sex, Politics and Society: The Regulation of Sexuality since 1800*, London and New York: Longman, 1989, pp. 141–59; Porter, *The Greatest Benefit to Mankind*, pp. 702–3.

30 Russett, *Sexual Science*, p. 7; Siobhan B. Somerville, 'Scientific Racism and the Invention of the Homosexual Body' in Lucy Bland and Laura Doan (eds), *Sexology in Culture: Labelling Bodies and Desires*, Cambridge: Polity, 1998, pp. 60–76 (73).

31 Rudi C. Bleys, *The Geography of Perversion: Male-to-Male Sexual Behaviour outside the West and the Ethnographic Imagination, 1750–1918*, London: Cassell, 1996, p. 189 cited in Merl Storr, 'Transformations: Subjects, Categories and Cures in Krafft-Ebing's Sexology' in Bland and Doan (eds), *Sexology in Culture*, pp. 11–26 (14).

32 Roy Porter and Lesley Hall, *The Facts of Life: The Creation of Sexual Knowledge in Britain, 1650–1950*, New Haven; London: Yale University Press, 1995, p. 8.

33 Porter and Hall, *The Facts of Life*, p. 8. Of course, it could be argued that the conception of the 'heavenly bodies' is indeed another cultural or scientific construction.

34 Julia Epstein and Kristina Straub, 'Introduction: The Guarded Body' in Julia Epstein and Kristina Straub (eds), *Body Guards: The Cultural Politics of Gender Ambiguity*, New York; London: Routledge, 1991, pp. 1–28 (2), emphasis added.

35 Epstein and Straub, 'Introduction: The Guarded Body', p. 19.

36 Cheryl Chase, 'Hermaphrodites with Attitude: Mapping the Emergence of Intersex Political Activism', *GLQ: A Gay and Lesbian Quarterly* 4:2, 1998, pp. 189–211 (189).

37 Gilbert Herdt (ed.), *Third Sex, Third Gender: Beyond Sexual Dimorphism in Culture and History*, New York: Zone Books, 1996.

38 Anne Fausto-Sterling, 'The Five Sexes: Why Male and Female Are Not Enough', *The Sciences* 33:2, 1993, pp. 20–25.

39 Katrina Karkazis, *Fixing Sex: Intersex, Medical Authority, and Lived Experience*, Durham, NC; London: Duke University Press, 2008; Catherine Harper, *Intersex*, Oxford; New York: Berg, 2007.

40 Barbara Brook, *Feminist Perspectives on the Body*, London; New York: Longman, 1999, p. x.

41 Thomas Laqueur, *Making Sex: Body and Gender from the Greeks to Freud*, Cambridge, MA; London: Harvard University Press, 1990.

42 Schiebinger, *The Mind has no Sex?*, pp. 189–213; Thomas Laqueur, 'Sex in the Flesh', *Isis* 94:2, 2003, pp. 300–306; Michael Stolberg, 'A Woman Down to her Bones: The Anatomy of Sexual

Difference in the Sixteenth and Early Seventeenth Centuries', *Isis* 94:2, 2003, pp. 274–99; Londa Schiebinger, 'Skelettestreit', *Isis* 94:2, 2003, pp. 307–13; Richard Cleminson and Francisco Vázquez García, *Hermaphroditism, Medical Science and Sexual Identity in Spain, 1850–1960*, Cardiff: University of Wales Press, 2009; Richard Cleminson and Francisco Vázquez García, 'Subjectivities in Transition: Gender and Sexual Identities in Cases of "Sex Change" and "Hermaphroditism" in Spain, *c.* 1500–1800', *History of Science* 48, 2010, pp. 1–38.

43 Laqueur, *Making Sex*, p. 8.

44 Laqueur, *Making Sex*, p. 25.

45 Laqueur, *Making Sex*, p. 124.

46 Stolberg, 'A Woman Down to her Bones', p. 276.

47 Butler writes: 'The category of "sex" is, from the start, normative; it is what Foucault has called a "regulatory ideal". In this sense, then, "sex" not only functions as a norm, but is part of a regulatory practice that produces the bodies it governs […] Thus, "sex" is a regulatory ideal whose materialization is compelled, and this materialization takes place (or fails to take place) through certain highly regulated practices. In other words, "sex" is an ideal construct which is forcibly materialized through time'; Judith Butler, *Bodies that Matter: On the Discursive Limits of 'Sex'*, New York; London: Routledge, 1993, p. 1.

48 Schiebinger, 'Skelettestreit', p. 309.

49 Schiebinger, 'Skelettestreit', pp. 310–11.

50 Francisco Vázquez García, 'Del sexo dicotómico al sexo cromático. La subjetividad transgenérica y los límites del constructivismo', *Revista Latinoamericana de Sexualidad, Salud y Sociedad* 1, 2009, pp. 63–88 (69); Jay Prosser, *Second Skins: The Body Narratives of Transsexuality*, New York: Columbia University Press, 1998.

51 Myra J. Hird, *Sex, Gender and Science*, Basingstoke; New York: Palgrave Macmillan, 2004, pp. 145–46.

52 As Foucault has written: 'Biological theories of sexuality, juridical conceptions of the individual, forms of administrative control in modern nations, led little by little to rejecting the idea of a mixture of the two sexes in a single body'; Michel Foucault, *Herculine Barbin, Being the Recently Discovered Memoirs of a Nineteenth-Century French Hermaphrodite*, trans. Richard McDougall, New York: Pantheon Books, 1980, p. viii.

53 Foucault, *Herculine Barbin*, pp. xi–xii.

54 Alice D. Dreger, *Hermaphrodites and the Medical Invention of Sex*, Cambridge, MA; London: Harvard University Press, 1988; Geertje Mak, '"So We Must Go behind Even What the Microscope Can Reveal": The Hermaphrodite's "Self" in Medical Discourse at the Start of the Twentieth Century', *GLQ: A Journal of Lesbian and Gay Studies* 11:1, 2005, pp. 65–94.

55 Alice D. Dreger, 'Hermaphrodites in Love: The Truth of the Gonads' in Vernon A. Rosario (ed.), *The Erotic Imagination: French Histories of Perversity*, New York and Oxford: Oxford University Press, 1997, pp. 46–66.

56 Nancy L. Stepan, 'Race, Gender, Science and Citizenship', *Gender and History* 10, 1998, pp. 26–52 (29) cited in Karen Harvey, 'The Substance of Sexual Difference: Change and Persistence in Representations of the Body in Eighteenth-Century England', *Gender and History* 14, 2002, pp. 202–23 (203).

57 Storr, 'Transformations', pp. 13–14.

58 Richard Cleminson and Francisco Vázquez García, 'Breasts, Hair and Hormones: The Anatomy of Gender Difference in Spain, 1880–1940', *Bulletin of Spanish Studies* 86:5, 2009, pp. 627–52.

59 Nelly Oudshoorn, 'Endocrinologists and the Conceptualization of Sex, 1920–40', *Journal of the History of Biology* 23:2, 1990, pp. 163–86 (170–71).

60 Money provides definitions of 'sex' as chromosomal, anatomical, morphological, genital, gonadal, legal, endocrinological, hormonal and psychological; John Money, 'Sex Reassignment as Related to Hermaphroditism and Transsexualism' in Richard Green and John Money (eds), *Transsexualism and Sex Reassignment*, Baltimore, MD: Johns Hopkins University Press, 1969, pp. 91–93, cited in Raymond, *The Transsexual Empire*, pp. 6–8.

61 Harper, *Intersex*; Karkazis, *Fixing Sex*.

62 Hird, *Sex, Gender and Science*, pp. 127–28.

63 Jonathan R. Topham, 'Rethinking the History of Science Popularization/Popular Science' in Faidra Papanelopoulou, Agustí Nieto-Galan and Enrique Perdiguero (eds), *Popularizing Science*

and Technology in the European Periphery, 1800–2000, Farnham; Burlington, VT: Ashgate, 2009, pp. 1–20 (20).

64 Ludmilla Jordanova, 'The Popularisation of Medicine: Tissot on Onanism' in Ludmilla Jordanova (ed.), *Nature Displayed: Gender, Science and Medicine, 1760–1820*, London; New York: Longman, 1999, pp. 103–17 (103).

65 Harry Oosterhuis, *Stepchildren of Nature: Krafft-Ebing, Psychiatry, and the Making of Sexual Identity*, Chicago; London: University of Chicago Press, 2000; Alison Oram, *Her Husband was a Woman! Women's Gender Crossing in Modern British Popular Culture*, London: Routledge, 2007.

66 Richard Cleminson, 'Making Sense of the Body: Anarchism, Nudism and Subjective Experience', *Bulletin of Spanish Studies* 81:6, 2004, pp. 697–716; Marcel Mauss, 'Techniques of the Body' in Jonathan Crary and Sanford Kwinter (eds), *Incorporations*, New York: Zone, 'Techniques of the Body' [1934], pp. 455–77.

67 Evert Peeters, 'Authenticity and Asceticism: Discourse and Performance in Nude Culture and Health Reform in Belgium, 1920–40', *Journal of the History of Sexuality* 15:3, 2006, pp. 432–61 (434).

68 Cf. Marshall Berman, *All That Is Solid Melts Into Air: The Experience of Modernity*, London: Verso, 1983; S. N. Eisenstadt, 'Multiple Modernities', *Daedalus* 129:1, 2000, pp. 1–29; George Mosse, *Nationalism and Sexuality: Middle-Class Morality and Sexual Norms in Modern Europe*, Madison, WI; London: University of Wisconsin Press, 1985, pp. 48–65; Karl Toepfer, *Empire of Ecstasy: Nudity and Movement in German Body Culture*, London; Berkeley, CA: University of California Press, 1997, pp. 6, 10; John Alexander Williams, *Turning to Nature in Germany: Hiking, Nudism, and Conservation, 1900–1940*, Stanford, CA: Stanford University Press, 2007.

69 Chad Ross, *Naked Germany: Health, Race and the Nation*, Oxford; New York: Berg, 2005, p. 153; David G. Horn, *Social Bodies: Science, Reproduction, and Italian Modernity*, Princeton, NJ: Princeton University Press, 1994.

70 Peeters, 'Authenticity and Asceticism', p. 435; cf. Glenn Smith and Michael King, 'Naturism and Sexuality: Broadening our Approach to Sexual Wellbeing', *Health & Place* 15, 2009, pp. 439–46; David Bell and Ruth Holliday, 'Naked as Nature Intended', *Body and Society* 6:3–4, 2000, pp. 127–40.

71 Loïc Wacquant, 'Pugs at Work: Bodily Capital and Bodily Labour among Professional Boxers', *Body & Society* 1:1, 1995, pp. 65–93 cited in Mari Luz Esteban, *Antropología del cuerpo. Género, itinerarios corporales, identidad y cambio*, Barcelona: Edicions Bellaterra, 2004, p. 12; Esteban argues that 'corporeal itineraries' enable people to be viewed 'as agents of their own life and not exclusively as victims of a particular system of gender and of a hegemonic bodily culture in the West' (my translation); Esteban, *Antropología del cuerpo*, p. 10.

72 Smith and King, 'Naturism and Sexuality', p. 439; Sheila Rowbotham, *Edward Carpenter: A Life of Liberty and Love*, London: Verso, 2008, p. 145.

73 Rowbotham, *Edward Carpenter*, p. 6; Rowbotham cites Carpenter's *My Days and Dreams* (1916).

74 Foucault, *The History of Sexuality*, p. 118.

75 J. C. Hardwick, 'Nudism in England', *Eugenics Review* 25:2, 1933, p. 122. This short piece reviews two books: Rev. Norwood's *Nudism in England* (1933) and Jan Gay's *On Going Naked* (1933). The first of these is deemed not to advocate too close an identification with eugenics, although Hardwick cites Norwood to state that nudism 'undoubtedly has a contribution to make towards the improved health of the race, and it will in time make for a more beautiful mankind'.

76 Ross, *Naked Germany*, p. 10.

77 Ross, *Naked Germany*, p. 146.

78 Ross, *Naked Germany*, pp. 146, 153, 155.

79 '¿Qui són els "amics del sol?"', *Amics del Sol* 1, 1922–23, unpaginated.

80 N. Capo, 'Eugenesia y desnudismo', *Pentalfa* 170, 1933, pp. 5–6.

81 Xavier Díez, *Utopia sexual a la premsa anarquista de Catalunya: la revista 'Etica-Iniciales' (1927–1937)*, Lleida: Pagès Editors, 2001, p. 41.

82 E. Armand, 'El Nudismo', *Iniciales* 6, 1932, pp. 5–6.

83 Russett, *Sexual Science*, p. 21; Lucy Bland, *Banishing the Beast: English Feminism and Sexual Morality, 1885–1914*, London: Penguin, 1995, pp. 278–80.

Part III

EXAMINING THE BODY

Science, technology and the exploration
of the body

5

EXAMINING THE BODY,
C. 1500–1750

Michael Stolberg

In modern medical practice, the physical examination of the patient's body plays an important part. Though the range of available diagnostic technologies has widened substantially over the last years, inspection, palpation and auscultation have remained at the centre of the typical medical consultation. Medical historians have commonly considered the rise of physical examination as a fairly recent phenomenon, closely linked to the 'birth of the clinic' in the early nineteenth century. In early modern medicine, by contrast, authors like Roy and Dorothy Porter, Eve Keller and Edward Shorter have found, physicians were 'reluctant to get closely to grips with the body.'[1] There was a 'nearly complete absence of physical contact' and 'medical diagnosis made almost no use of physical examination of the patient'.[2] Indeed, in 'the routine clinical encounters of the seventeenth or eighteenth century, anything more than the most perfunctory and formal physical contact – as for example that involved in pulse-taking – was extremely unusual between doctor and patient.'[3] 'A physician who routinely laid hands upon his patients would have appeared "eccentric, and possibly offensive".'[4] 'When a physical examination actually occurred,' there was 'no palpation of the abdomen, no careful inspection of the veins in the neck ... no rectal or vaginal exams.'[5] In eighteenth-century France, Brockliss and Jones have found, physicians 'still touched their patients as little as possible'.[6] Malcolm Nicolson has shown that palpation figures with remarkable frequency in the case histories of Giovanni Battista Morgagni's '*De sedibus et causis morborum*' (1761) but even he has come to the conclusion that only 'relatively rarely would the physician examine the patient's body manually'.[7] In the early nineteenth century, according to Stanley J. Reiser, 'failure of doctors to examine the body in the presence of internal disease, and the reluctance of patients to allow it', were still common.[8]

Historians have identified a number of reasons for the limited role of physical examination in traditional bedside medicine. First, they have pointed out that the prevailing disease theories – and in particular those of humoural pathology – made a physical examination seem largely irrelevant. Early modern doctors, as Charles Newman has put it bluntly, quite simply 'paid no attention to physical examination because it would have been of no interest to them.'[9] Second, the role of shame, the influence of 'deeply felt notions of decency' around baring the body, especially among female patients, has been highlighted.[10] 'The maintenance of human dignity and physical privacy', as Reiser has put it, 'placed limits on human interaction through touch'.[11] In her study of the women who consulted the eighteenth-century German physician Johann Storch, Barbara Duden has remarked a striking contrast between the frankness with which patients spoke even about genital or menstrual complaints on the one hand and a virtual taboo when it came to touching the female body on the other.[12] Third, and for some historians most importantly, manual examination has been described as being at odds with the learned physicians' self-fashioning as scholars, as thinkers who left manual activities to the barber-surgeons. Physicians prided themselves on their ability to arrive at a precise diagnosis just based on their careful interpretation of the patient's narrative. They did not need to perform a physical examination.[13]

My following analysis of the place and rationale of examining the body in early modern medicine will not fundamentally challenge this established account but it will modify it in important respects. I will not question that physical examination – and manual palpation in particular – played a smaller role in early modern medicine than in the late nineteenth and early twentieth centuries. As I will show, however, a closer look at sources which, in contrast to general textbooks, reflect early modern physicians' actual practice, reveal that touching the patient's body was more widespread and important than historians have so far assumed. Not only did the barber-surgeons and midwives by nature of their profession constantly touch their patients' bodies to treat wounds or injuries, to let blood or apply a clyster, or to feel for the cervix and the baby's head. Academic physicians' casebooks as well as their published consilia and medical observations – a very popular genre at the time – show that they, too, already in the sixteenth and seventeenth centuries frequently resorted to physical examination and palpation to establish, confirm or reject a diagnosis. And they may well have been even more commonly applied than these sources suggest, because the results were presumably mentioned above all when they yielded important diagnostic results. In other words, the question is not whether early modern physicians performed a physical examination at all but to what extent and for what reasons they resorted to it and why its recognition among physicians grew. In what follows, I will first take a general look at the role of physical examination in early modern medical practice, and I will then try and assess the impact and relative importance of the three major obstacles to physical examination outlined above and identify developments which promoted an even more widespread reliance on physical examination in the course of the early modern period.

Diagnosing diseases

Traditional bedside medicine has quite rightly been described as relying heavily on the patient narrative. Physicians frequently based their diagnosis and treatment almost exclusively on the sufferer's account of his or her subjective sensations. Since the physicians prided themselves on their skill in tailoring medicines and regimen specifically to their patients' constitution or temperament, they also enquired extensively into eating habits and personal life style, earlier disease episodes, the reactions to previous therapeutic efforts, idiosyncratic preference for or aversiveness to certain foods or drugs, etc. Many physicians took their time. As early modern physicians' practice journals make clear, it was quite common that they only visited two or three patients per day.[14] In most cases, the patient narrative was not the only source of diagnostic information, however. To start with, looking at the patient's external appearance, the colour and appearance of the skin, the facial expression, the state of the tongue or for signs of general weakness or strength provided valuable additional clues. Physicians frequently went into fair detail in this respect.

The 40 year-old Count Friedrich of the Rhenopalatinate, for example, was described in the following words:

> His whole body is meagre. His neck is somewhat long and slender and bent forward. His shoulder-blades are bare of flesh. His chest is narrow and hairy. He has a low and soft voice … He is pale in his face and yellowish all over his body. He [once] was strong and agile in all parts of his body, though he always had small muscles, which now have been much consumed by his previous illness.[15]

Often a wealth of information was also gained from the careful inspection of blood and excrements. Vomit might be full of mucus or other corrupt matter which had accumulated in the stomach. Stools might be liquid or hard, or bloody, or mixed with mucus, or yellowish suggesting an abundance of bile. The blood which issued forth from the vein in blood-letting might be 'blackish', 'thick' or 'slimy'. And, most importantly, uroscopy, inspecting the patient's urine, provided a welcome access to the nature of the disease and the strength of the innate heat. Even if the patient did not undress, the physician could furthermore elicit diagnostic signs with his hands. In order to determine a patient's temperament or complexion he could touch the patient's tongue or skin – though the results were known to be somewhat unreliable due to the influence of the physician's own temperament.[16] Especially in fevers, he might feel the pulse to assess whether it was particularly fast, or weak, or irregular,[17] or, in the eighteenth century, count the pulse rate.[18]

When historians describe a virtual absence of physical examination in early modern medicine they are referring above all, of course, to an examination of the (largely) naked body and its manual exploration in a modern sense. But also in this respect the widely asserted 'almost complete lack of interest in physical exam'[19] stands in marked contrast to early modern medical casuistic writing. In the literally thousands of medical 'observations', 'casus' and 'consilia' of the sixteenth and seventeenth centuries as well as in early modern physicians' personal casebooks or notebooks – unfortunately a much rarer source – we encounter a very considerable number of cases of men and women whose chests, breasts and bellies were palpated or who had even their private parts examined. Manual exploration seems to have been so widespread in fact that it shaped the public perception of the medical profession. When the physician visited a patient, Agrippa von Nettesheim (1486–1535) noted in his critical account of contemporary medicine, he inspected the urine, felt the pulse, had a look at the tongue – and touched the patient's sides.[20]

'In omnibus morbis exploranda tactu hypocundria [sic]', i.e. 'in all diseases the upper belly is to be explored by touching', Georg Handsch, a Bohemian apprentice physician in Prague, noted in 1556.[21] Andreas Gallus and Pietro Andrea Mattioli, the physicians he was following in their practice in Prague at the time, quite frequently resorted to a manual examination; for example, to exclude an obstruction in the hypochondria of a count with malignant fever, or to decide who was right about the Archduchess' sickness, which Gallus attributed to the liver and Mattioli to the uterus, or to make sure there was still some sensation left in the foot of Gallus' daughter Magdalena who risked losing her toes to gangrene, or to identify the cause of the swollen belly and feet of a cachectic merchant, or to exclude an abdominal scirrhus in a moribund bishop, or to diagnose a tumour at the base of the stomach in another dying patient.[22]

Gallus and Mattioli were not exceptional in this respect. They only put into practice what students already, in Padua and elsewhere, were taught to do by their professors.[23] Especially the belly as the site of liver, stomach and spleen was frequently palpated. Thus, to cite one of many examples from printed observations, Michael Ettmüller, in the case of a woman who consulted him with shortness of breath and hiccups, found the upper belly tense and full and identified a soft swelling which gave way to the touch.[24] Zacharias Geitzcofler von Geilenbach recounted how his physician probed a bladder stone with his own hands and thus successfully resolved the controversy between two barber-surgeons who could not agree whether the stone was firmly attached to the wall of the bladder (and therefore inoperable) or not.[25] Sometimes the examining physician would also use palpation to elicit local pain as a further diagnostic sign. Johann Frank in the German town of Ulm, for example, found a fist-sized swelling in a young patient which was painful when he touched it.[26] Similarly, the attending physician of a priest about whom E. F. Geoffroy was asked for advice in the early eighteenth century found that the liver could 'hardly be felt' but that there was slight pain when the area was pressed.[27] Even the patients and their relatives sometimes reported that they had felt a tumour or hardening. Guido von Boetzelaar, in 1591, for example, resolutely rejected his physicians' claim that he suffered from a disease of the spleen. He could feel a hardening around his belly button which was also where his pain was located. The spleen, he argued, could never extend so far. He was sure his suffering originated from his stomach.[28] There was no swelling or hardening in his wife's breast, Mordecai Cary could assure James Jurin, after he had 'felt it very freely this morning'.[29]

As an important piece of evidence for the presumed neglect of manual palpation in early modern medicine, historians have pointed to the common practice of consulting by letter, where physicians were frequently prepared to express their judgement and prescribe medicines just on the basis of a written report, without ever seeing the patient.[30] At closer analysis this is not quite so convincing an argument for the physicians' general disregard for manual exploration, however. After all, the patient could be examined by the local physician or surgeon and the results could then be communicated in writing. Thus Dr Alliot, in 1689, asked for more detailed information about the case of a patient with a tumour of the breast. Before he expressed his judgement, he wanted to know whether the tumour was hard and indeed hard as stone, how big it was and how deeply rooted. 'It will be necessary' he concluded, 'that this lady takes the trouble of asking her physician or her surgeon to examine the state of her entrails, whether there is no tension or hardening in the area of the liver, the spleen, the uterus [or] towards the area of the pancreas.'[31] Asked for advice about a severely ill female patient who suffered, among others, from a reduced urinary excretion, E. F. Geoffroy, in 1728, similarly recommended that her belly be palpated and that especially the area of the bladder be examined for swelling or pain. This would make it easier to decide whether the kidneys were producing insufficient amounts of urine or whether the urine was held back in the bladder, in which case it could be catheterized.[32]

Diagnostic relevance

The widely shared assumption that early modern physicians touched their patients as little as possible clearly has to be taken with more than a grain of salt. As we have seen, one major reason for the (alleged) reluctance of learned physicians to perform a physical examination was its perceived lack of relevance within the context of contemporary medical theory. There is some truth to this argument but it is based, in part, on a misconception. Early modern humoural medicine, we are told over and over again, attributed diseases to an imbalance of the four humours (yellow and black bile, blood and phlegm) and/or their respective qualities (warm, cold, moist and dry).[33] This would indeed have accorded very limited relevance to physical examination and virtually none to manual palpation. This is an extremely simplified and misleading account of the complexity of early modern disease theories, however. The notion of a balance of humours and qualities or temperament was and remained important for the understanding of individual bodily constitution. When it came to explaining diseases and their underlying causes, however, this notion was largely irrelevant. In sources from actual practice, it is difficult to find even a single case in which an early modern physician diagnosed a patient's disease simply in terms of such a humoural imbalance of his or her body. More frequently, individual organs like the liver or the stomach were described as too hot or too cold, but even then this imbalance was usually only one of several explanatory elements. Ultimately the overwhelming majority of diseases was attributed to a more or less specific morbid matter, to impure, corrupt, putrid, adust or acrid humours which moved through the body and settled down in its various parts. Even when one of the four natural humours was assigned a major part, such as in melancholy or biliary fevers, the disease was not explained as resulting from a lack or excess of the respective humour but to its pathological accumulation in individual parts of the body or, much more commonly, to its alteration or degeneration, as in the case of excessively 'heated' or 'burnt' yellow or black bile frequently cited as the cause of melancholy.[34]

Of course, morbid, putrid humours flowing through the body or the hot, smoky vapours which were thought to sometimes arise from them were hardly more accessible to the physician's touching hand than a humoural imbalance. In 'fevers', whatever the specific nature of the morbid matter, the physician might only feel the warmth of the skin. Similarly, in cases of consumption, probably the most widespread chronic disease, the coughing and the copious yellowish, greenish and sometimes bloody expectoration and the increasing emaciation and weakness provided much better diagnostic evidence than the changed form of the finger nails sometimes observed in advanced consumption[35] or the 'sharp heat' which could be felt when the patient's skin was touched.[36]

Based on the prevailing concept of morbid matter, humoural medicine offered much more room than is commonly assumed also for the notion of local pathology, however, because in many cases the morbid humours were found to settle down in one or several parts of the body. As the cases in Gallus' and Mattioli's practice already suggested, a very common diagnosis which could be confirmed or excluded by palpation were 'obstructions' and 'apostemes'. In the case of Johann von Mengkwitz's sick wife, for example, Matthias Ratzenberger, in 1544, diagnosed a coarse melancholical humour as the underlying cause, which had resulted in an obstruction and 'hardening' of the spleen.[37] When morbid matter settled and accumulated in a particular area of the body or organ for some time it could harden into a 'scirrhus' or even worse develop into a cancer. In such cases, manual exploration of the belly and, if necessary, of the genitals was often deemed decisive to confirm or exclude the diagnosis. In 1603, for example, physicians from Montpellier were consulted about the case of a young woman who suffered from lacerating, abdominal pain. When a 'hard and resistant tumour in the very same area of the uterus' could be palpated it was concluded that she suffered not from cancer but from 'uterine dropsy'.[38] The Italian physician Peregrini Capponi was able to exclude, in turn, the possibility that a patient's complaints might be due to her liver, because 'in the seat of the liver no tumour is perceived from the outside.'[39]

Manual exploration also played a crucial role in the diagnosis of dropsy, another common and widely feared disease. In cases of suspected dropsy, medical textbooks almost routinely recommended that the physician press a finger onto the skin of a swollen extremity. If the patient suffered from dropsy the resulting pit would remain visible for quite a while.[40] Casuistic sources show that this advice was followed in ordinary practice.[41] Dropsy of the belly, i.e. ascites, and of the chest could also be revealed by 'succussion', i.e. by moving or shaking the patient, a technique recommended already in Hippocratic writing.[42] Zacutus Lusitanus, for example, reported how he provoked a sound like that of water in a hose in a woman with severe ascites.[43] Sometimes the water inside could already be heard moving when the patient was asked to turn from one side to the other.[44] For diagnostic and prognostic reasons it was also important to distinguish ascites due to accumulated fluid in the abdominal cavity from 'tympanites' and, at times, from pregnancy. In ascites, the reader was told, the belly felt thicker, more solid. In tympanites, by contrast, which was also considered as a type of dropsy but one which was caused by air or winds, there was no fluctuation inside and percussion – already recommended by Aretaeus of Cappadocia in the first century AD.[45] – gave forth a sound 'like a drum'.[46] According to Daniel Sennert this drum-like sound also helped distinguish tympanites from pregnancy.[47] In addition, one could put a light close to one side of the belly of a patient: in tympanites the light would shine through to the other side.[48] Sixteenth- and early seventeenth-century humoural theory thus accorded considerable importance to manual examination above all in certain types of diseases, namely in those which were attributed to a local accumulation of morbid matter. In the course of the early modern period, however, changes in contemporary medical theory made the diagnostic relevance of the physician's touching hand grow further when the focus of medical attention shifted from the humours and vapours to the solid parts, to the individual organs and the pathological processes which affected them.

A major impetus for this shift came from the growing importance of dissection.[49] In retrospect, the discoveries of the 'anatomical revolution' were of rather limited use for the understanding, let alone for the treatment of internal diseases. For good reasons, even Vesal's famous 'De humani corporis fabrica libri septem' were rarely mentioned in contemporary observations or casebooks. While physicians successfully staged their claims to superior knowledge of the innermost secrets of the human body in public anatomies of executed criminals, many more dissections were performed in private on the bodies of deceased patients, however. Dissecting the bodies of patients who had succumbed to their disease rather than the bodies of healthy criminals sharpened attention for the lasting, visible effects of diseases on the various parts or organs of the body. Nicolaus Tulpius, the Amsterdam physician immortalized in Rembrandt's famous painting, introduced his 'Observationes medicae' in 1641 with the programmatic call: 'Climb down to the interior parts and inquire not only into the nature of the viscera, but above all into the places and causes of the hidden diseases.'[50] In 1509, already several decades before Vesal, Antonio Benivieni published his 'De abditis nonnullis ac mirandis morborum et sanationum causis', containing 111 case histories. Some of them included the results of post-mortems which had unearthed evidence of local pathological change, such as a massive corrosion of the 'pelvic bone', an abscess, a perforation of the intestine, bladder- and gall-stones, or in the case of

Antonio Bruno, a relative of his, who vomited everything he ate, a hardened, callous tumour in the lower part of the stomach which blocked the passage into the duodenum.[51] Others followed suit. By 1679, Théophile Bonet was already able to draw on about 3,000 published post-mortems in his 'Sepulchretum'[52] and presumably many more were performed whose results were never made public.

Long before the rise of the much-acclaimed 'anatomical-clinical' method in the Paris hospitals around 1800,[53] physicians thus came to pay more and more attention to the lasting, solid morbid changes inside the body underlying the distinct clinical features of many diseases. This was bound to strengthen, in turn, the role of the physical examination as a means to identify the pathological changes in the living patient which autopsy brought to light in the corpse. Based on an increasingly sophisticated pathoanatomical knowledge, diagnosis by manual palpation became, at times, remarkably subtle. For example, when E. F. Geoffroy, in 1725, was consulted about a lady who complained of abdominal pain, fever, weakness and emaciation and whose right hypochondria seemed tense, resistant and slightly painful, he concluded that probably the patient's right ovary was affected and most likely scirrhous and disposed to inflammation, with a risk of suppuration.[54]

The rise of anatomy and the growing interest in local, organic, pathological change had a particularly profound effect on the physicians' perception of the female body and its diseases. Medieval anatomists had already pointed out anatomical differences between the sexes. Based on numerous dissections and, from the seventeenth century onwards also on microscopic analysis, early modern physicians elaborated on this theme. Even the skeleton of women was shown to differ from that of the men, but above all their genitals were unique. As many readers may know, Thomas Laqueur has argued, quite to the contrary, that pre-Enlightenment learned medicine adhered to a one-sex model: ovaries and testicles, penis and vagina, uterus and scrotum were perceived to be essentially the same except that man's stronger vital heat pushed his genitals outside while, in women, they remained inside the belly. Laqueur's account beautifully suits modern notions of a cultural construction of sex and gender and has proved extremely attractive especially to literary historians but it has collapsed under the weight of historical evidence. It is based on a virtually complete ignorance of the extensive writings on the topic in Latin, the principal language of medico-scientific publication of the time, and, on top of that, on a rather selective reading of vernacular sources. The major anatomists and the overwhelming majority of late medieval and early modern physicians clearly did not advocate a one-sex model. On the contrary, they stressed anatomical difference and its fatal effects on female health.[55] Due to the peculiar nature of their genitals and breasts, women, they argued with Hippocrates, suffered from many diseases which were unknown in men. 'Diseases of women' developed into a respected subfield for which a growing number of physicians claimed particular expertise.[56] The crucial role of the female genitals and breasts as principal sites of local and general female pathology gave manual or digital exploration paramount diagnostic importance, and this is precisely what early modern 'gynaecologists' recommended and practised.[57]

Shame and embarrassment

This brings us to the second major barrier to a more widespread reliance on physical examination. Early modern physicians frequently complained especially about their female patients' reluctance to allow them a physical examination. Palpation of the belly and even more a vaginal examination performed by a male physician challenged established norms of female modesty and honour.[58] Even when they suspected a serious, potentially life-threatening disease of the female private parts, sixteenth- and seventeenth-century physicians sometimes had to be content with what a midwife could tell them. Rainer Solander, for example, trusted the midwife who found that his lady's uterus was lying across in her belly and that she could only feel the sides and not the mouth of the uterus.[59] Raymund Fortis also arrived at his diagnosis of a uterine cancer based only on the midwife's account of what she could feel with her fingers and concluded that he had to limit himself to a palliative treatment, a '*palliativam curationem*' in this case.[60] While contemporary French women were described as somewhat more 'accessible',[61] Italian women, Giovanni Battista Morgagni still complained in the eighteenth century, only rarely allowed him to perform a vaginal examination.[62] Similarly Johann Storch in Germany reported of women who only reluctantly bared their breasts or their bellies to let him examine a tumour or hernia.[63]

As Storch's account indirectly makes clear, however, some women were, under certain circumstances, nevertheless prepared to expose their naked breasts, bellies or private parts to the gaze or touch of a male physician – provided they suspected a serious or indeed potentially deadly disease which they thought could be diagnosed that way. The barriers were high but they could be overcome. Some women eventually placed their wish to regain health above their shame and allowed or even asked the male physician to explore their 'private parts', to even introduce his finger to palpate the vagina and the cervix. The seventeenth-century physician Christopher Guarinonius, for example, recounted, as if it were the most natural thing in the world, how he examined the breasts of the daughter of the Duke of Bavaria's chancellor. Her personal physician had come to the conclusion – presumably based on a physical examination as well – that the patient suffered from true cancer. Guarinonius 'examined and touched' the breast closely, however, and also found some inflammatory and oedematous areas around the tumour, which in his view spoke against a purely cancerous nature.[64] And when the Duchess of Massa suffered from abdominal pain and no stones could be found, Giovanni Maria Lancisi and his colleagues decided to examine her uterus, 'as far as the delicacy of these parts' allowed. The surgeon Marco Antonio Collegiano introduced his finger into her vagina, touched the mouth of the uterus and found it harder than in its natural state. This touching produced an uncomfortable sensation and some bleeding; in the right part of the vagina also a thickening or shrinking of the fibres could be seen. A year later the Duchess died 'with clearer signs of a carcinoma'.[65] In the unusual case of a female satyriasis, Dr Chauvel in Avignon, according to his colleague Cabrol of Montpellier, was even allowed to see the effects of excessive sexual intercourse on the woman's lacerated genitals; a married woman with extraordinary sexual desire she had demanded that her husband 'watered her garden' four times in one night.[66]

Some women even accepted rather embarrassing postures when they felt this was necessary. Johann Frank described in the seventeenth century how he positioned a patient suspected of suffering from a tumour of the uterus. 'In order to inspect the affected part more precisely, I made her lie on her back, with her buttocks raised higher than her head.' This allowed him to see the whole 'neck of the uterus' which 'appeared reddish, with little veins swollen with blood everywhere'.[67] As early modern physicians remarked, women generally found being exposed to the gaze of a male physician even more embarrassing than manual exploration.[68] Thus Felix Platter reported the case of a lady from Basel who developed a growth in the area of the clitoris, similar to a goose-neck. She would not let Platter see her secret parts but she did allow him to touch the growth with the adjacent areas well covered.[69] The particular embarrassment caused by visual exposure to the male physician – in this case aggravated by the similarity to sexual penetration – may also account for the marginal role of the vaginal speculum in early modern medicine. The instrument had been known since antiquity and its use was still recommended in sixteenth- and seventeenth-century medical textbooks, for example, to diagnose tumours and ulcers of the cervix. But it seems to have been used only rarely – if at all – in actual practice.[70]

The degree to which the feelings of shame and embarrassment caused by physical examination changed over the early modern period remains controversial. Norbert Elias' account of the 'process of civilization' would suggest that the taboos surrounding nudity and bodily functions became increasingly powerful, at least until their partial breakdown in postmodern consumer society. Against Elias the cultural anthropologist Hans Peter Duerr has argued, however, that in all societies, from the most 'primitive' to the most 'civilized', the way in which individuals deal with emotions, bodily functions and nudity is to a large degree shaped and sanctioned by norms and taboos. He has cited a range of medical sources which attest to women's consistent resistance to a physical examination of their naked bodies throughout western history.[71]

Even if we accept the idea of a long-term shift from external sanctions towards internal self-control which, according to Elias, is at the heart of the process of civilization, quite different conclusions can be drawn. The increasing internalization of social norms of decency could have promoted a growing sense of shame but, combining with codes of professional ethics, it could also have created the necessary conditions under which women would more readily permit a physician to examine and touch their denuded bodies in the absence of any witnesses, without the fear that the physician might abuse the situation.[72] Furthermore, Elias suggests that nudity in front of socially superior persons was generally experienced as more embarrassing than in front of people from the lower ranks. While noble, aristocratic patients should thus have been less reluctant to undress or be touched by a learned physician, shame would have become a stronger barrier, the more also lower- and middle-class patients came to prefer the learned physicians' advice, and would have made a compulsory physical examination as in cases of suspected rape particularly traumatic.[73] More research on the role of class in this context is needed but some of the casuistic evidence points into this direction. In Samuel Auguste Tissot's copious patient correspondence, for example, we find quite a number of (mostly French) female upper-class patients who accepted a vaginal examination by a male physician or surgeon or even, like a 40-year-old who suffered from colics, had themselves examined 'by all the most able' physicians.[74] In 1794, in southern Germany, on the other hand, an itinerant healer who targeted primarily the lower-class, rural population hoped to attract female patients by offering that his wife would see and examine them.[75]

The growing role of the hospital in obstetrics and general medical care finally gave the physicians increased access also to the bodies of large numbers of lower-class women. Hospital physicians could afford to ignore, at least to a large degree, their patients' narratives and their feelings of shame. The poor, unmarried women in lying-in hospitals knew that this was indeed the price they would have to pay; in contrast to his 'private' practice, these patients' esteem for the individual physician had hardly any impact on his income and career. This brings us to the third and final potential obstacle to physical examination: professional considerations.

Professional considerations

The third factor to which, as we have seen, the 'rudimentary state of intimate physical examination' in early modern medicine has been attributed were physicians' concerns for their professional dignity. The learned physician, as Roy and Dorothy Porter have put it, wanted to distinguish himself from the less-learned surgeon 'whose skill lay in his fingertips, not in his mind'. The physician, by contrast, arrived at a more precise diagnosis thanks to his skill in interpreting the patient narrative. He was 'a thinker, not a toucher'.[76] Undoubtedly early modern physicians fashioned themselves as the proponents of a 'rational' medicine based on 'method'. They contrasted their medicine as a superior intellectual activity against the more manual – and thus supposedly more menial – work of barber-surgeons and other less-learned competitors on the medical market, who routinely opened veins, applied clysters, prepared bandages and plasters, probed wounds, repositioned fractures and the like and thus constantly touched the patients' bodies, including the most shameful, embarrassing areas. Though learned physicians commonly did leave the manual aspects of therapy to the barber-surgeons, there is very little evidence in the sources to suggest, however, that physicians also felt that touching a patient's belly or calves for diagnostic purposes was below their dignity. On the contrary, as we have seen, leading medical authorities of the time explicitly recommended doing so and instructed their students in this art and high-ranking court physicians like Gallus and Mattioli showed no reservations whatsoever in this respect.

With regard to professional dignity, there were, in fact, powerful incentives for the learned physicians to resort even more consistently to physical examination. After all, other well-established and widely expected diagnostic procedures, such as inspecting the urine and stirring the patients' stools with a stick, were in many ways much less dignified. And the paramount role of uroscopy in early modern medical culture, apart from associating the learned physician with fetid excrements, also jeopardized physicians' professional authority on a very fundamental level. When people suspected a sickness or pregnancy they almost routinely had, first of all, their urine examined, frequently without even seeing the physician. As the physicians complained, they put such great trust in uroscopy, in fact, that they sometimes refused to reveal any further information on the patient's sex, age, complaints or way of life. The truly skilful uroscopist, they claimed, saw everything in their 'waters'. Most learned physicians grew increasingly sceptical of uroscopy and, in particular, of diagnosing diseases just from a patient's urine. In numerous publications they expressed their worries about the dangers of blatant misdiagnosis or, even worse, of becoming the laughing-stock of the whole area when someone deliberately tricked them with cow urine or Malvasian wine. But they often had no choice but to comply. Otherwise they risked losing their patients, because many among their less-learned competitors continued to rely above all on uroscopy and were even prepared to predict the sex of a future child just from looking at the mother's urine.[77] In this situation, physical examination, feeling for the hidden pathological processes inside the body, was an attractive alternative. It not only promised to reduce the risk of an embarrassing misdiagnosis, it also enabled the learned physicians to stage their medical and anatomical learning and their privileged access to the secrets of the human body and its diseases much more impressively than uroscopy.

In the long run, their increasing recognition of manual skills and anatomical knowledge also helped learned physicians to conquer new territories and thus attract new patients and open new sources of revenue. Surgery, though still practised mostly as a manual craft by apprenticed barber-surgeons in the sixteenth and seventeenth centuries, gradually gained growing recognition among learned physicians.[78] First in the Italian universities, where students could even get a doctorate in 'surgery', and later also north of the Alps medical students could obtain a training in surgery.[79] In Leiden, for example, they were instructed amongst others how to insert a urinary catheter.[80] Authorities like Barthélemy Cabrol, Wilhelm Fabricius of Hilden and Pieter van Foreest published extensive collections of surgical observations to serve as a guide to others.[81] In the eighteenth century, the advice of famous physician-surgeons like Johann Heister was sought by elite patients all over Europe.

More controversial, also within the medical profession, was the rise of midwifery. Reservations and, at times, outright rejection of man-midwifery were due above all to gender ambiguities – male physicians took on a professional role which was traditionally reserved for women – and to fears of sexual transgression.[82] Once more upper-class women initiated a trend towards a growing reliance on learned physicians; however, even in uncomplicated deliveries.[83] Man-midwifery – like surgery before – became 'newly aligned with the masculine attributes of reason and decorous action',[84] and learned physicians and surgeons became increasingly familiar figures in middle- and upper-class lying-in chambers.

Conclusion

As this chapter has outlined, physical examination, including manual palpation and vaginal examination, played a much more prominent role in pre-nineteenth-century medical practice than historians have widely assumed. Due to notions like 'obstruction', 'aposteme', 'scirrhus' and 'cancer', inspecting and touching the body was appreciated as an important diagnostic tool already within humoural pathology. It became in many cases almost indispensable after the rise of anatomy and the post-mortem had prompted a shift of focus from morbid humours to organic change, a shift which affected in particular the diagnosis of women's diseases which were attributed above all to the uterus and the breast, i.e. to those parts in which the anatomy of the female body differed fundamentally from the male. Shame was and remained a major obstacle, especially, it seems, in the encounter between lower-class and rural female patients and male middle-class physicians, but it could and was in many cases overcome, sometimes by force, but much more frequently due to the patients' hope for a more precise diagnosis and an effective therapy. Historians' assumption, finally, that learned physicians abstained from physical examination and palpation out of fear for their dignity and professional authority seems largely mistaken. Conventional means of diagnosis like uroscopy and coproscopy posed a comparatively greater threat to the physician's dignity and authority and physical examination and exploration of the body, quite to the contrary, offered a welcome alternative in this situation. Based on detailed anatomical knowledge and on a growing body of insights gained from post-mortems, early modern physicians could successfully self-fashion themselves as having privileged access to the pathological events inside the bodies and they could extend their professional domain to surgery and obstetrics, in a process which, in the long run, led to the virtual monopoly which nineteenth- and twentieth-century academic physicians came to enjoy in the whole of medicine.

Notes

1 Dorothy Porter and Roy Porter, *Patient's Progress: Doctors and Doctoring in Eighteenth-Century England*, Cambridge and Oxford: Polity Press, 1989, p. 74.

2 Eve Keller, 'The Subject of Touch: Medical Authority in Early Modern Midwifery' in Elizabeth D. Harvey (ed.), *Sensible Flesh: On Touch in Early Modern Culture*, Philadelphia: University of Pennsylvania Press, 2003, pp. 62–80 (69).

3 Roy Porter, 'A Touch of Danger: The Man-Midwife as Sexual Predator' in G. S. Rousseau and Roy Porter (eds), *Sexual Underworlds of the Enlightenment*, Chapel Hill: University of North Carolina Press, 1988, pp. 206–32 (212).

4 Roy Porter, 'The Rise of Physical Examination' in W. F. Bynum and Roy Porter (eds), *Medicine and the Five Senses*, Cambridge: Cambridge University Press, 2004, pp. 179–97 (179).

5 Edward Shorter, *Bedside Manners: The Troubled History of Doctors and Patients*, New York: Simon & Schuster, 1985, pp. 41f; similarly Saul Jarcho, 'Morgagni and Auenbrugger in the Retrospect of Two Hundred Years', *Bulletin of the History of Medicine* 35, 1961, pp. 489–96 (491).

6 Laurence W. B. Brockliss and Colin Jones, *The Medical World of Early Modern France*, Oxford: Oxford University Press, 1997, p. 566.

7 Malcolm Nicolson, 'Giovanni Battista Morgagni and Eighteenth-Century Physical Examination' in Christopher Lawrence (ed.), *Medical Theory, Surgical Practice: Studies in the History of Surgery*, London and New York: Routledge, 1992, pp. 101–34; Malcolm Nicolson, 'The Art of Diagnosis: Medicine and the Five Senses' in W. F. Bynum and Roy Porter (eds), *Companion Encyclopedia of the History of Medicine*, London and New York: Routledge, 1993, pp. 801–25 (808).

8 Stanley Joel Reiser, *Medicine and the Reign of Technology*, Cambridge: Cambridge University Press, 1978, p. 6.

9 Charles Newman, 'Diagnostic Investigation Before Laennec', *Medical History* 4, 1960, pp. 322–28 (328); similarly Porter, 'A Touch of Danger', pp. 212–13.

10 Porter and Porter, *Patient's Progress*, pp. 74–75.

11 Reiser, *Medicine and the Reign of Technology*, p. 4.

12 Barbara Duden, *Geschichte unter der Haut. Ein Eisenacher Arzt und seine Patientinnen um 1730*, Stuttgart: Klett,1987, p. 102.

13 Porter and Porter, *Patient's Progress*, pp. 74–75; Nicolson, 'The Art of Diagnosis'; see also N. D. Jewson, 'Medical Knowledge and the Patronage System in 18th-Century England', *Sociology* 8, 1974, pp. 369–85; Mary E. Fissell, 'The Disappearance of the Patient's Narrative and the Invention of Hospital Medicine' in Roger French and Andrew Wear (eds), *British Medicine in an Age of Reform*, London and New York: Routledge, 1991, pp. 92–109.

14 Early modern practice journals are currently at the centre of major research initiatives, such as the German-Austrian-Swiss research network 'Medical Practices (17th to 19th Centuries)' (www.medizingeschichte.uni-wuerzburg.de/aerztliche_praxis/index.html) and the 'Casebooks Project' on Richard Napier and Simon Forman in Cambridge (www.hps.cam.ac.uk/casebooks/).

15 Bayerische Staatsbibliothek, Munich, Ms. Clm 456.

16 Brian K. Nance, 'Determining the Patient's Temperament: An Excursion into Seventeenth-Century Medical Semiology', *Bulletin of the History of Medicine* 67, 1993, pp. 417–38 (426–29).

17 For a list of the different pulse qualities see, for example, Gaspar Bravo de Sobremonte Ramirez, *Resolutionum et consultationum medicarum tertia editio*, Lyons: Borde and Arnaud, 1662, p. 624.

18 John Floyer, *The Physician's Pulse Watch, or an Essay to Explain the Old Art of Feeling the Pulse, and to Improve It by the Help of a Pulse-Watch*, London: Smith and Walford, 1707.

19 Shorter, *Bedside Manners*, p. 41.

20 Agrippa von Nettesheim, *Die Eitelkeit und Unsicherheit der Wissenschaft und die Verteidigungsschrift*, ed. Fritz Mauthner, 2 vols, Munich: Müller, 1913, vol. 2, p. 74.

21 Österreichische Nationalbibliothek, Vienna, Cod. 11207, fol. 236.

22 Österreichische Nationalbibliothek, Vienna, Cod. 11207, fols 17r, 22r, 79v, 97r, 97v, 107v and an unnumbered, inserted leaf.

23 Jerome J. Bylebyl, 'The Manifest and the Hidden in the Renaissance Clinic' in Bynum and Porter, *Medicine and the Five Senses*, pp. 40–60 (47); for seventeenth-century teaching of manual examination in Leiden see Franciscus Sylvius, 'Casus medicinales sive historiae aegrotorum', in Sylvius, *Opera omnia*, Geneva: de Tournes, 1698 (separate page numbers).

24 Michael Ettmüller, *Opera omnia Theoretica et Practica*, 2 vols, Lyons: n.p., 1685, part 3, p. 143; Carolus Musitanus, *Opera omnia, Seu Trutina Medica, Chirurgica, Pharmaceutico-Chymica*, 2 vols, Geneva: Cramer & Perachon, 1716, p. 288.

25 Wilhelm Fabricius, *Längst begehrt vollkommene Leib-und Wund-Artzney*, trans. F. Greiff, Frankfurt, 1652, pp. 1258–60, letter from Z. Geitzcofler von Geilenbach, 18 March 1609.

26 Stadtarchiv Ulm, Ms. Franc 8b, fol. 232r; Paul de Sorbait, *Praxis medica plurimis observationibus rebusque scitu dignissimis aucta et correcta*, Vienna: Voigt, 1680, p. 388.

27 Bibliothèque Interuniversitaire de Médecine, Paris (BIM), Ms. 5241, fols 38r–42r, Angers, 16 November 1718.

28 Universiteitsbibliotheek Leiden, Ms. Marchand 3, letter from G. van Boetzelaar, 13 October 1591.

29 Letter from Mordecai Cary, 12 June 1733 in James Jurin, *The Correspondence of James Jurin (1684–1750). Physician and Secretary to the Royal Society*, ed. Andrea Rusnock, Amsterdam and Atlanta: Rodopi, 1996, p. 399.

30 Duden, *Geschichte*, p. 106; Porter, 'The Rise of Physical Examination', p. 183.

31 Bibliothèque Municipale d'Avignon, Ms. 3192, fols 184r-v (late seventeenth century).

32 BIM, Ms. 5241, fol. 274v.

33 See, however, Andrew Wear, *Knowledge and Practice in English Medicine, 1550–1680*, Cambridge: Cambridge University Press, 2000 and Michael Stolberg, *Experiencing Illness and the Sick Body in Early Modern Europe*, Basingstoke: Palgrave, 2011.

34 For an overview see Stolberg, *Experiencing Illness*.

35 Musitanus, *Opera omnia*, p. 186.

36 Musitanus, *Opera omnia*, p. 185.

37 Universitätsbibliothek Erlangen Ms. 997, fols 58v–59v.

38 Sächsische Landes- und Universitätsbibliothek Dresden, Ms. C337, fols 274v–275v.

39 Biblioteca Universitaria di Bologna, Ms. 391, vol. I, fol. 75r.

40 Sorbait, *Praxis medica*, p. 381; Ettmüller, *Opera omnia*, vol. 2, p. 32; Michael Bernhard Valentini, *Praxis medicinae infallibilis*, 2nd edn, Frankfurt: von Sand, 1721 [1704], p. 98.

41 Österreichische Nationalbibliothek, Vienna, Cod. 11207, fol. 108r; Sylvius, 'Casus medicinales sive historiae aegrotorum', p. 52 (case 140).

42 Renate Wittern, 'Zur Krankheitserkennung in der knidischen Schrift "De internis affectionibus"' in C. Habrich, F. Marguth and J. H. Wolf (eds), *Medizinische Diagnostik in Geschichte und Gegenwart*, Munich: Fritsch, 1978, pp. 101–19.

43 Amatus Lusitanus, *Curationum medicinalium centuria prima, multiplici variaque rerum cognitione referta*, Florence: Torrentinus, 1551, p. 182.

44 Ettmüller, *Opera omnia*, vol. 2, p. 32.

45 Kenneth D. Keele, *The Evolution of Clinical Methods in Medicine*, London: Pitman, 1963, p. 19.

46 Musitanus, *Opera omnia*, vol. 1, p. 288; cf. Raymundi Io. Fortis, *Consultationum et responsionum medicinalium centuriae quatuor*, Padua: Bolzetta de Cadorinis, 1669, p. 500f, on the case of an 18-year-old girl whose swollen belly 'percussus instar tympani resonat'.

47 Danniel Sennert, *Opera omnia*, 2 vols, Lyons: Huguetan and Ravaud, 1656, vol. 2, p. 643.

48 Fortis, *Consultationum*, p. 498.

49 Andrew Cunningham, *The Anatomical Renaissance: The Resurrection of the Anatomical Projects of the Ancients*, Aldershot: Scholar Press, 1997; Roger French, *Dissection and Vivisection in the European Renaissance*, Aldershot: Ashgate, 1999.

50 Nicolaus Tulpius, *Observationum medicarum libri tres*, Amsterdam: Elzevier, 1641.

51 Antonio Benivieni, *De abditis nonnullis ac mirandis morborum et sanationum causis*, trans. Charles Singer, Springfield, IL: Thomas, 1954 [1507]; several dozen other observations were later found among his papers; see the edition by Giorgio Weber, Florence: Olschki, 1994.

52 Theophile Bonet, *Sepulchretum anatomicum seu anatomia practica ex cadaveribus morbo denatis proponens historias et observationes, quae pathologiae genuinae tum nosologiae orthodoxae fundatrix dici meritur*, Geneva: Chouët, 1679.

53 Michel Foucault, *La naissance de la clinique*, 7th edn, Paris: Quadrige, 2003 [1973].

54 BIM Ms. 5245, fols 27r–28v.

55 Thomas Laqueur, *Making Sex: Body and Gender from the Greeks to Freud*, Cambridge, MA: Harvard University Press, 1990; Michael Stolberg, 'A Woman Down to her Bones: The Anatomy of

Sexual Difference in the Sixteenth and Early Seventeenth Centuries', *Isis* 94, 2003, pp. 274–99; Katharine Park, *Secrets of Women: Gender, Generation, and the Origins of Human Dissection*, New York: Zone Books, 2006.

56 Cf. Helen King, *Midwifery, Obstetrics and the Rise of Gynaecology. The Uses of a Sixteenth-Century Compendium*, Aldershot: Ashgate, 2007.

57 See, for example, Jacques Guillemeau, *De la grossesse et accouchement des femmes; du gouvernement de celles-ci et moyen de survenir aux accidents qui leur arrivent, ensemble de la nourriture des enfans*, Paris: Pacard, 1621, p. 670; François Mauriceau, *Traité des maladies des femmes grosses et de celles qui sont nouvellement accouchées*, Paris: n.p., 1682, pp. 130, 143, 355 and 358; Johann Jacob Manner, *De exploratione per tactum utilissima et summe necessaria artis obstetricae enchiresi*, praes. G.F. Sigwart, Tübingen: Schramm, 1761.

58 For example, Michiel Boudewijns, *Ventilabrum medico-theologicum*, Antwerp: Woons, 1666, pp. 360–64; see Hans Peter Duerr, *Intimität: Der Mythos vom Zivilisationsprozeß*, Frankfurt: Suhrkamp, 1994, pp. 53–94 and 387–404 for further medieval and early modern references.

59 Staatsbibliothek Berlin, Ms. germ. quart. 58, fols 284r–285v.

60 Fortis, *Consultationum*, p. 663.

61 Duerr, *Intimität*, p. 29.

62 Giovanni Battista Morgagni, *De sedibus et causis morborum per anatomen indagatis*, Venice: Typographia Remondiana, 1761, book 3, letter 48.

63 Duden, *Geschichte*, pp. 94 and 102–3.

64 Christophorus Guarinonius, *Consilia medicinalia in quibus universa praxis medica exacte pertractatur*, Venice: Baglioni, 1610, pp. 600–602.

65 Biblioteca Lancisiana, Rome, Ms. 259, vol. 3, fols 630–33, report, 29 July 1703 and fol. 708, note about the Duchess' death.

66 Barthélemy Cabrol, *Alphabeton anatomikon*, Geneva: Chouët, 1604, p. 100.

67 Stadtarchiv Ulm Ms. Franc 8b, fol. 235v.

68 Cf. Duerr, *Intimität*, pp. 80–94.

69 Felix Platter, *Observationum in hominis affectibus plerisque, corpori et animo, functionum laesione, dolore, aliave molestia et vitio incommodantibus, libri tres*, Basel: König, 1614, p. 626; Felix Platter, 'Felicis Plateri observationes et curationes aliquot affectuum partibus hisce accidentium' in I. Spachius (ed.), *Gynaeciorum sive de mulierum tum communibus, tum gravidarum, parientium, et puerperarum affectibus et morbis libri*, Strasbourg: Zetzner, 1597 (pages not numbered).

70 Guillemeau, *De la Grossesse et accouchement des femmes*, p. 703; Mauriceau, *Traité des maladies des femmes grosses*, p. 358; Musitanus, *Opera omnia*, p. 480; see also Victor Deneffe, *Le speculum de la matrice à travers les âges*, Antwerp: Caals, 1902; Duerr, *Intimität*, pp. 35–43.

71 Duerr, *Intimität*; on the debate between Elias and Duerr see also Michael Schröter, 'Scham im Zivilisationsprozeß. Zur Diskussion mit Hans Peter Duerr' in H. Korte (ed.), *Gesellschaftliche Prozesse und individuelle Praxis: Bochumer Vorlesungen zu Norbert Elias' Zivilisationstheorie*, Frankfurt: Suhrkamp, 1990, pp. 42–85.

72 Norbert Elias, *Über den Prozess der Zivilization: soziogenetische und psychogenetische Untersuchungen*, Berne: Franke Verlag, 1969; Duerr, *Intimität*.

73 Cf. Duerr, *Intimität*, pp. 62–63.

74 Bibliothèque Cantonale et Universitaire de Lausanne-Dorigny, Fonds Tissot, letter from Mme de Dureville [?], 8 January 1774.

75 Flysheet distributed by J. K. Hoffmann, reprinted in *Journal von und für Franken* 4, 1792, pp. 729–34.

76 Porter and Porter, *Patient's Progress*, pp. 74–75.

77 Cf. Camille Vieillard, *L'urologie et les médecins urologues dans la médecine ancienne*, Paris: Rudeval, 1903; Michael Stolberg, *A Cultural History of Uroscopy, 1500–1800*, Farnham: Ashgate, 2013 [in press].

78 Reiser, *Medicine and the Reign of Technology*, p. 19; cf. Christopher Lawrence, 'Democratic, Divine and Heroic: the History and Historiography of Surgery' in Lawrence, *Medical Theory*, pp. 1–47.

79 Nancy G. Siraisi, 'The Faculty of Medicine' in H. de Ridder-Symoens (ed.), *A History of the University in Europe. Vol. I: Universities in the Middle Ages*, Cambridge: Cambridge University Press, 1992, pp. 360–87 (381).

80 Olaus Borrichius, *Olai Borrichii itinerarium 1660–1665*, ed. H. D. Schepelern, vol. 1, Copenhagen: Danish Society of Language and Literature, 1983, p. 119.

81 Cabrol, *Alphabeton*; Fabricius, *Längst begehrt vollkommene Leib-und Wund-Artzney*; Pieter van Foreest, *Observationum et curationum chirurgicarum libri quinque*, Frankfurt: Palthenius, 1610; Pieter van Foreest, *Observationum et curationum chirurgicarum libri quatuor posteriores. I. De plagis, seu vulneribus cruentibus […] II De ulceribus, III. De fracturis, IV. De luxationibus*, Frankfurt: Palthenius, 1610.
82 Porter, 'A Touch of Danger'.
83 Adrian Wilson, *The Making of Man-Midwifery: Childbirth in England 1660–1770*, London: UCL Press, 1995.
84 Keller, 'The Subject of Touch', p. 70.

6

EXAMINING THE BODY
SINCE 1750

Malcolm Nicolson

In 1776, the Scottish philosopher David Hume, having been ill for some time, visited Bath to take the waters. He had consulted several physicians, who had made various conjectures as to the nature of his condition but had not been able to agree upon a diagnosis. The issue was not resolved until Hume's abdomen was directly examined. This procedure was, however, not undertaken by any of his attendant physicians but by a famous surgeon: 'John Hunter ... coming accidentally to Town Dr Gusthart proposed that I should be inspected by him: He felt very sensibly [i.e. palpably] as he said a Tumour or swelling in my Liver.'[1] True to his own doctrine of the priority of direct experience, Hume immediately accepted Hunter's diagnosis: 'This Fact, not drawn by reasoning, but obvious to the Senses, and perceived by the greatest Anatomist in Europe must be admitted as unquestionable and will alone account for my situation.'[2] Hume's physician, Dr Gusthart, did not dispute the validity of Hunter's findings. Evidently he did not oppose physical examination in principle; nor did he doubt its relevance to medical therapy. Palpation was, however, not a procedure that he was prepared to undertake himself. Such methods were in his view, it must be supposed, the business of surgeons. Gusthart remained optimistic regarding his patient's condition but Hume reconciled himself to Hunter's diagnosis and duly prepared for his death, which occurred two months later.

Such reluctance to undertake a thorough scrutiny of the bodies of patients was not confined to fashionable English physicians. John Rutherford (1695–1779), Professor of the Practice of Physic at the University of Edinburgh, impressed upon his students the value of noting the patient's facial appearance. For instance, in the course of a clinical lecture upon the case of a young woman newly admitted to the Edinburgh Royal Infirmary, he remarked: 'If it had been daylight, I would have examined her gums and the internal canthus of her eyes ... for by looking into the internal canthus and the gums and finding them in a florid state then the blood is in a good state.'[3] Rutherford's careful inspection of the woman's face was not, however, extended to other parts of her body. He concluded, 'The disease seems to be owing to the mismanagement she underwent in childbed. She says she was lacerated and probably it was her vagina.' But he made no attempt to confirm his supposition with an examination of her genitalia nor, it seems, did any other member of the hospital's staff.

It is instances such as these (they could be multiplied many times over) that have led historians to argue that diagnostic practice in the eighteenth century was generally based upon methods other than physical examination. Charles Newman argued that the physician relied upon four basic techniques.[4] First, he noted the patient's general behaviour and demeanour, and visually inspected those parts of the body not normally hidden under clothes or bedclothes. Second, he took the pulse at the wrist, a procedure that also allowed him to ascertain whether the skin was hot, dry or clammy, and so on. Third, he inspected faeces and urine, and also, when available, blood, vomit, pus and sputum. Fourth and most importantly, he listened carefully to the patient's account of her ailment. As Bynum put it, 'the patient's own description of his illness was the pivotal point in the diagnostic process'.[5] Reiser has likewise concluded that, while the eighteenth-century physician might occasionally palpate, he would accord considerably less significance to the direct evidence of his senses than to his client's verbal testimony.[6] Jewson has influentially argued that the most important feature of the eighteenth-century physician's professional context was the economic power of individual patients.[7] Thus, within each consultative encounter, the physician's behaviour at the bedside was generally constrained by the authority of his client. The patient could insist that, unless she decreed otherwise, the physician should abide by the normal social conventions governing physical contact between non-intimates. Even surgeons might have their activities at the bedside restricted by a patient's unwillingness to allow visual inspection or manual examination of the affected parts.[8]

However, evidence can readily be pointed to which seems to run counter to this received account of eighteenth-century diagnostic practice. For instance, the Dutch physician, Gerhard van Swieten, provided the following account of the swelling of the lymphatic glands in the groin subsequent upon the contraction of syphilis:

> I have often and carefully observed buboes at their rise. The patients begin to complain of a certain tension in the groin ... I could feel the glands deep down, as yet but a little increased, distinct, and ranged lengthwise along the groin: they are soon increased in bulk, and unite almost into one mass, which afterwards rises into a tumour, often very great.[9]

Van Swieten made this type of observation in patients of both sexes: 'I have often been an eye-witness of the external skin of the penis, and the exterior part of the pudenda in women, having been attacked by venereal shankers.'[10] Furthermore, a reading of what is certainly one of the major medical texts of the latter half of the eighteenth century, *De Sedibus et Causis Morborum per Anatomen Indagatis* (The Seats and Causes of Diseases as revealed by Anatomy), by the Italian physician, Giovanni Morgagni, furnishes many examples of its author laying his hands upon the living bodies of his patients.[11] Morgagni's palpation seems to have been, at least on occasion, an active form of examination:

> If you handled it, you perceived it to be an unequally tuberous tumour in its whole surface ... just as it has been made up of granular bodies; which seem'd also to be confirmed by the resistance it gave when you press'd it. When it was press'd upon ... a sense of pain ... arose in the tumour ... by laying hold of the tumour with both hands, I easily drew it to one side or other.[12]

Furthermore, Morgagni palpated confidently and vigorously in bodily areas not normally accessible to non-intimates, 'And although it is very difficult in very fat and full-breasted women ... to distinguish this disorder; unless perhaps by pressing your fingers very strongly against the chest, at the sides of the breasts.'[13]

As Stolberg argues, touching the patient's body was evidently 'more widespread and important than historians have so far assumed'.[14] Nevertheless it should be noted that, even in Morgagni's case, diagnostic practice was modulated and controlled by patients' agency. Certain parts of the body were more accessible than others. Vaginal examination was often prohibited. Morgagni regarded hardening of the os uteri, detected by the physician's finger, as the least equivocal sign of pregnancy in the early months: 'Wherefore I have made use of this sign when it was in my power; but I have it in my power very seldom; the women of our country being for the most part repugnant to an examination of that kind.'[15] Van Swieten's diagnostic practice was circumscribed in a similar fashion. Some patients cooperating unproblematically, and might even take the initiative: 'A man ... flew to me ... to show me a swelling ... in his right testicle.'[16] But others did not. Like Morgagni, van Swieten found that gaining permission for vaginal examination was particularly difficult.

What the Morgagni and van Swieten examples show is that we have to modify the assumption that diagnostic practice took the same form wherever and whenever physic was practised in the eighteenth century. While certainly accepting that Newman's description is valid for many contexts, we ought to recognize that the exact configuration of the interplay between patients' agency and physicians' behaviour at the bedside was a cultural variable. It is likely that there existed considerable diversity of diagnostic procedures, dependent upon the different professional and social circumstances within which eighteenth-century physic was practised. Moreover, real as the effect of the patient's authority undoubtedly was in modulating the behaviour of the practitioner, the importance of these social conventions can be exaggerated. Patients must have consented, at least on occasion and perhaps reluctantly, to being examined intimately by surgeons; otherwise operations for anal fistula, bladder stone or hernia would not have been possible. Although infrequently performed, these procedures were part of the surgical repertoire of the eighteenth century, as was bladder catherization.

I have argued elsewhere that among the circumstances most relevant to whether or not physical examination was routinely undertaken was the relative social status of surgery, together with the epistemological significance accorded to pathological anatomy, in particular historical and geographical contexts.[17] Both van Swieten and Morgagni practised in professional environments in which physic and surgery were closely associated. Morgagni was an active research anatomist and van Swieten, while only occasionally performing autopsies, shared the Italian's commitment to the central significance of post-mortem dissection.[18] Both men attempted to correlate internal pathological abnormalities, tumours, abscesses, and so forth, revealed after death, with the symptoms observed during the patient's final illness. In other words, their interest in physical examination was encouraged and complemented by a structural understanding of disease processes.

Both the importance of an anatomical approach in stimulating interest in physical examination, and the problematic nature of physicians' responses to such diagnostic innovations, can be illuminated by considering the trajectory of the novel technique of thoracic percussion. In 1761, Leopold Auenbrugger, an Austrian physician who had been a student of van Swieten, published an account of his 'inventum novum'.[19] By tapping his fingers against his patients' chests and listening to the sounds produced, he could determine whether the part of the chest that had been struck was hollow (i.e. filled with air) and therefore healthy, or otherwise. Auenbrugger confirmed the significance of the various percussive sounds by post-mortem observation. However, his colleagues in Vienna, even van Swieten, responded with indifference to his innovation and it was generally ignored for the remainder of the century.[20] Thoracic percussion does not seem to have fitted easily into the culture of much of late eighteenth-century medicine. William Cullen's *First Lines on the Practice of Physic*, a major textbook which provides a comprehensive introduction to the medical practice of the period, contains only two instances in which physical examination is discussed. In one, Cullen advises that, when seeking to differentiate between tympanites and anasarca, a physician should note that, in the former, the swelling 'being struck, it gives a sound like a drum'.[21] Cullen is, in other words, describing the technique of abdominal percussion. However, despite his awareness of the value of this form of investigation, Cullen did not seek to add further manual techniques to his diagnostic repertoire, as is evidenced by his reaction to the suggestion of thoracic percussion. In the 1778 edition of *First Lines*, he wrote: 'How far the method proposed by Auenbrugger will apply to ascertain the presence of water and the quantity of it in the chest, I have not had occasion or opportunity to observe.'[22] In the 'corrected and enlarged' edition of 1784, exactly the same statement may be found.[23] Throughout the period between these two editions, Cullen, as a professor in the Edinburgh Medical School, had the resources of the Royal Infirmary at his disposal. Making a trial of thoracic percussion was evidently not high on his list of priorities.

However, in the last decades of the eighteenth century, with the continuing development of pathological anatomy, as evidenced, for example, by the work of Matthew Baillie, interest in correlating post-mortem observations with clinical signs and symptoms grew.[24] But, as Duffin has pointed out, this process was not unproblematic – many physicians struggled with the challenge of how to integrate the older disease concepts with the information gained from dissection.[25] Nevertheless, in the aftermath of the French Revolution, with the abolition of the traditional divisions between surgery and internal medicine in the Paris School, the so-called 'anatomico-clinical' method became institutionalized to an extent that was to prove irrevocable. One of the most successful practitioners of the new structural approach was Jean-Nicholas Corvisart.[26] Beginning in the 1790s, Corvisart studied the *Inventum Novum* assiduously and began to experiment with Auenbrugger's technique on his patients at the Charité hospital. Soon he was able, in many cases, to predict, before the patient died, what would eventually be found within the thorax, feats of diagnostic acumen that greatly enhanced his reputation among his colleagues and students. Corvisart took a special interest in heart disease and was able, by percussion, to ascertain the presence and extent of cardiac hypertrophy. He also taught himself to identify some disorders of the heart by placing his hand against a patient's ribcage and detecting unusual vibrations. This was a particularly impressive achievement, since previously heart disease had seldom been reliably diagnosed in life.

Pulmonary tuberculosis was a major cause of morbidity and mortality in the early nineteenth century. It provided the pioneers of physical examination with much material upon which to hone their skills. Gaspard-Laurent Bayle, for instance, is said to have undertaken approximately 900 autopsies on victims of tuberculosis.[27] His extensive knowledge of the pathological anatomy of the disease led him to emphasize the importance of the percussion sounds in making a definitive diagnosis. Bayle's younger colleague, René Laennec, was also inspired by Corvisart to take up the twin studies of pathological anatomy and physical examination. Laennec adopted the practice, known to the Ancient Greek physicians, of applying his ear directly to the patient's chest (immediate auscultation) to listen to the sounds of the heart and the lungs. However, he regarded this technique as not always applicable. The dirty condition of many poorer patients made such an examination unattractive and 'it was scarcely to be suggested for most women patients, in some of whom the size of the breasts also posed a physical obstacle'.[28] In 1816, Laennec was consulted by a young woman who seemed to be suffering from heart disease. She was plump and Laennec was unable to get her chest to resonate upon percussion. Nor was palpation effective. He felt inhibited from pressing his ear firmly against the bosom of his young patient. Laennec was in his mid-thirties but he was single, having led a life of almost monastic devotion to medicine. So, remembering how sound was transmitted through solid materials, he picked up some sheets of paper, rolling them into a cylinder, and applied that to the woman's chest. He was amazed to hear the sounds of her heart clearly and distinctly. The stethoscope had been invented.[29]

Laennec experimented with various materials and shapes for his new instrument, eventually finalizing upon a simple hollow wooden cylinder, about 25 centimetres long. With this tool, Laennec undertook a comprehensive investigation of the sounds to be heard emanating from the heart, comparing his findings, wherever possible, with pathological alterations observed upon autopsy. From late 1817 onwards, he moved to concentrate upon the pathology of the lung, identifying sounds diagnostic of bronchitis, pneumonia, pleurisy and tubercular cavity. As Grmek has pointed out, a key discovery was 'pectoriloquy', the enhanced transmission of the patient's voice through the stethoscope from within the chest.[30] Wherever Laennec heard that sound, he asserted that he would later find, upon autopsy, a tubercular cavity in the lung. The results of these extensive clinical and pathological investigations were published in 1819 in Laennec's major work, *De l'auscultation médiate,* which formed the basis of our modern understanding of the pathology of the lung and, to an extent, of the heart.[31] Laennec claimed that he had placed 'the internal organic lesions on the same plane as the surgical diseases with respect to diagnosis', in other words rendered them directly accessible to the senses.[32]

While there was a certain amount of opposition to the employment of the stethoscope, by conservative doctors who felt the use of an instrumental aid would compromise their professional dignity or who were unable to educate their ears sufficiently to apply the technique, Laennec's innovation came into general use quite quickly.[33] The expansion of clinical teaching in the hospitals that occurred in the nineteenth century provided students with the necessary supply of patients upon whom to gain experience with the instrument. By the second half of the century, the stethoscope had become an indispensable badge of office of the medical practitioner, as it remains. It should, however, be noted that, despite Laennec's claims to the contrary, his stethoscope possessed few acoustic advantages over the older technique of applying one's ear directly to the patient's chest. In most clinical applications, the instrument did not enable one to hear the thoracic sounds any louder or clearer than one could with the naked ear. One important exception is the detection of cavitation in the apex of the lung, an early sign of pulmonary tuberculosis, for which the doctor would have to insert an ear into the patient's armpit to investigate by direct auscultation, a procedure both physically difficult and aesthetically unappealing. Nevertheless, what was attractive about Laennec's invention was that it enabled the physician to examine the thorax conveniently and hygienically, while preserving his personal and professional dignity and respecting the modesty of his patients, particularly female ones. In other words, the real improvement that the stethoscope brought to medical practice was a social one. It sanitized physical examination, making it less embarrassing for doctor and patient alike. The circumstances of its invention are telling about the social relations of the technology. The stethoscope was devised because of anxieties surrounding the proper deportment of men toward women. It has its origins in gender relations.

Considerations of social and professional convenience were to shape further developments of stethoscope design. In 1829, N. P. Comins, physician to the Edinburgh Royal Infirmary, was concerned at 'the great difficulty of attaining the accurate knowledge of which it [the stethoscope] is the medium of communication, notwithstanding the numerous cases of thoracic disease that have been treated in the Infirmary'.[34] The root of this difficulty lay in the fact that application of the short cylinder was often uncomfortable to the patient, who had to adopt awkward positions, for considerable periods of time, to accommodate the novice stethoscopist. Comins designed a longer instrument with a hinge between its two tubes, to enable the exploration of 'any part of the chest, in any position, and in any stage of disease, without pressure or inconvenience to the patient or to himself'.[35] As well as its utility to the student, Comins presented his new design as also having significant advantages to the experienced physician: 'As it does not require the head of the stethoscopist over the chest of the sick person, and as another tube may be screwed to the instrument, it can be used in the highest ranks of society without offending fastidious delicacy.'[36] Thus, the second tube could be replaced with a longer one if the patient was particularly shy or modest, or indeed if the patient was particularly dirty. Comins continued:

> Timidity or disgust is unpardonable on the part of the physician when engaged in the discharge of his duty. But, as it is often necessary in contagious diseases to explore the chest of the poorest of individuals, may not reasonable precaution and the feelings of a gentleman be so far complied with as to use the cylinder with the additional tube, in cases manifestly contagious or miserably wretched.[37]

Numerous other modifications were suggested to improve the ease of use or the acoustics of the instrument.[38] C. J. B. Williams (1805–89) constructed a binaural stethoscope in the 1840s, but it was not until the introduction of flexible rubber tubes in the 1880s that employing both ears in auscultation became wholly practical.[39] Another innovation was the provision of a bell-shaped end, often incorporating a diaphragm.

The introduction of percussion and stethoscopy began a process by which the basis of the understanding of disease was taken away from the patient and invested in signs and symptoms that were accessible and intelligible only to the doctor. As Duffin notes, the stethoscope was the 'first instrument of medical technology to distance and diminish the role of the patient in her own illness experience'.[40] Disease was no longer understood principally in terms of symptoms experienced by the patient but in terms of structural changes detected by an examining physician. Laennec could, for instance, identify signs of serious illness even in persons who felt well, a historic transformation of the doctor's cognitive authority. From 1840 onwards, a new scrutinizing impulse came to characterize elite medicine. Auscultation and percussion were developed to new levels of sophistication, notably by Carl von Rokitansky and Joseph Skoda in Vienna.[41] Skoda demonstrated, on the basis of much pathological and acoustic evidence, that particular sounds were not necessarily associated with specific diseases but rather with specific alterations to the physical structure of the lung. His description of what became known as Skodiac resonance, whereby unaffected portions of the lung become more tympanic upon percussion owing to reduction in their volume from compression by fluid elsewhere in the thorax, was indicative of the more thorough processes of physical examination to which the body was now being subjected.

While the widespread adoption of the stethoscope accustomed laypeople to being examined by the doctor and stimulated the development of other methods of physical diagnosis, the introduction of physical examination into private, as against hospital, practice could be problematic. Some misgivings arose as to the motives of doctors – why did they wish to transgress the bounds of social conventions regarding bodily contact between non-intimates, and expose the bodies of their patients to visual scrutiny or manual examination? The stethoscope did not obviate all these problems but the imposition of a physical barrier between doctor and patient certainly helped. Moreover the stethoscope could be applied quite effectively through a nightdress or thin shirt. On occasion, other technologies might be utilized to mediate, as this example from mid-century Paris exemplifies:

> A gentleman who had married a young and handsome lady, of whom he was extremely jealous, was obliged to apply to a surgical celebrity of Paris on account of a boil which caused the lady great agony, and was situated about the cardiac region. To allow of an inspection was out of the question, nothing could induce the husband to sanction it. The surgeon declined prescribing blindfold; but the difficulty was overcome by the gentleman's skill in photography and tinting. He presented to the doctor the exact facsimile of the affected part, was told what course to pursue, and to report progress in a few days. This was done very punctually, and a second photograph presented. After three or four visits of this kind the wife was well, and the husband much pleased with the success of his contrivance.[42]

As this passage exemplifies, the extent to which, in the nineteenth century, the body, particularly the female body, was exposed to the medical gaze can be exaggerated. Of interest in this respect is the diagnostic practice of James Young Simpson, who became Professor of Midwifery [i.e. obstetrics] at the University of Edinburgh in 1839. As a gynaecologist, Simpson's professional attention was directed to a region of the body where exposure and contact are fraught with social and interpersonal tensions. How Simpson gained and utilized diagnostic access to the female pelvis is, thus, revealing of the character and social context of physical examination in the Victorian era.[43]

Some historians of gynaecology and obstetrics have enjoyed describing how the eighteenth-century man-midwife conducted his examinations by fumbling blindly under bedclothes or within petticoats. It is asserted that the removal of such prudish hindrances was a necessary condition of the arrival of a newly rational, modernized gynaecology in the nineteenth century. Myrtle Simpson, for instance, assumes that Simpson, as a disinterested scientific clinician, would have expected as a matter of course to have unrestricted access to the bodies of his patients and, moreover, would have instilled such confidence in his patients that such access would have been willingly granted.[44] But this was not necessarily the case. In some respects, Simpson's practice was constrained in ways quite similar to that of Giovanni Morgagni.

Simpson considered that it was in diagnostics that medicine had made its greatest advances in the first half of the nineteenth century. This improvement was exemplified, he contended, by the enhancement in the understanding of diseases of the heart and lungs that had been achieved by means of percussion and auscultation. This transformation stood as proof of the superiority of physical means of diagnosis over other methods:

> Surgical diagnosis is, as a whole, more accurate than medical diagnosis. But why is the surgeon more accurate in the discrimination of the affections which he treats than the physician? Merely because he can, and does, found his diagnostic deductions far more upon physical symptoms.[45]

Simpson made extensive use of the stethoscope in his obstetric practice. He sought to detect the foetal heartbeat to confirm pregnancy and recognized slowing or irregularity of the beat, during labour, as an indication of foetal distress. He listened for the 'placental souffle', the distinctive sound that obstetricians attributed to the highly vascularized nature of the placenta, and believed that thereby he could, at least on occasion, localize that organ. However, to Simpson, it was the enhanced understanding of the pathology of the non-gravid uterus that had been the major diagnostic achievement of gynaecology in his time. He argued that the uterine sound, a metal probe that could be inserted through the cervix into the cavity of the womb, revealed the organ to the medical examiner in a manner analogous to that by which the stethoscope had revealed the heart and lungs to the chest physician.

Simpson's uterine sound was a thin, flexible rod, made of silver, about nine inches long, with an ivory handle. Near its end, the rod was bent to a curve, the angle of which could be altered according to the configuration of individual patients. Its tip was rounded to minimize the risk of damage to the walls of the womb. Simpson preferred to perform his gynaecological examinations with the woman lying on her left side with her upper body positioned across the bed and her knees drawn up. Standing behind the woman's buttocks, Simpson could locate the os uteri by introducing the forefinger of his left hand into the vagina and searching for the central indentation of the cervix. He held the uterine sound in his right hand and guided it into position along the left forefinger. Once the probe was in position, the natural mobility of the womb could be exploited to bend it either ventrally, to be palpated by a hand placed upon the abdominal wall, or dorsally, to make it accessible to a finger inserted into the rectum. If the uterus could not be easily moved, that was also of diagnostic interest. If there were a tumour in the pelvis, Simpson would attempt to move the uterus relative to it, seeking thereby to ascertain whether the mass was inside the womb, attached to its outer wall, or located elsewhere in the pelvic cavity. This procedure could help, for instance, in the distinguishing of uterine fibroids from 'ovarian dropsy', i.e. ovarian cysts.

It is important to note that Simpson conducted these investigations by touch rather than by sight. In his undergraduate lectures, he gave precise instructions as to how best to examine a woman in the early stages of labour:

> The examination *per vaginam* must be done with much care ... The more delicacy you exhibit the higher will you be esteemed by the patient ... do it with all care and caution. You anoint the finger for this purpose. Place the patient on the left side ... Examine always in bed and covered. You need never expose the patient. You do it at your peril both as a practitioner and gentleman. Do it with one finger the index.[46]

On another occasion, writing of the advantages of inserting a probe into the uterus rather than the bladder, Simpson explained that the os uteri is easier to locate than the opening of the urethra. This would only have been the case if he were finding his way by touch rather than by sight. It is evident from Simpson's accounts that, in the mid-nineteenth century, the practitioner's ability to scrutinize the female body and expose it to the medical gaze still remained somewhat limited by social conventions and the patient's agency. Indeed, one of the reasons that Simpson preferred a woman to lie on her side, rather than on her back, to be examined was that this position made it easier for him to work within the bedclothes.

Simpson was also an accomplished exponent of the technique of bimanual examination. In this procedure, one hand is pressed against the abdominal wall while a finger of the other hand is introduced into the vagina or, on other occasions, into the rectum. Obtaining consent to touch could not, however, be taken for granted. Simpson gave the following cautionary advice about the diagnosis of pregnancy:

> No medical man would venture to form a definite … judgement upon the matter until he was allowed to make some physical diagnosis of the condition of the uterus, – that is, until he had ascertained by sight or touch, or both, that the abdomen was really enlarged; until, probably, by a careful external examination of the abdomen by the hand and the stethoscope, he had ascertained that the existing tumour really was uterine, and really contained a foetus; or, in the earlier months, until, perhaps, he was permitted to make a vaginal examination, in order to make out the state of development, size … [47]

Simpson is arguing for the utility and necessity of physical diagnosis and simultaneously acknowledging that gaining permission for abdominal examination might be somewhat problematic and gaining permission to perform a vaginal examination might be even more so.

When he deemed it clinically indicated, Simpson sought to visualize the internal surfaces of the reproductive tract by means of the speculum. The vaginal speculum provides a good example of how changes in diagnostic practice may be affected by changes in social attitudes rather than solely by technical or clinical innovation. It is an old piece of technology, having been developed to a high standard by the surgeons of the Roman Empire. The speculum had however fallen somewhat into disuse by the early modern period and the instrument was only occasionally employed by surgeons in the seventeenth and eighteenth centuries. Its utility as a practical surgical tool was re-established by Marion Sims in the course of his work on the repair of vesico-vaginal fistula and the speculum gradually came back into common use in diagnosis from the middle of the nineteenth century onwards. The renewed interest in the application of the speculum was not, however, without controversy, as Simpson was well aware.

> In this country, great difficulties have been placed against the more general introduction of the speculum into practice, in consequence of the very disagreeable and revolting exposure of the person of the patient, which is usually considered necessary in its employment. We have latterly in our own practice endeavoured to avoid this very natural objection, by teaching ourselves to introduce … the instrument when the patient was placed on her left side … with

the nates [buttocks] near the edge of the bed ... [W]ith attention to the management of the bed-clothes, we have found that the instrument can be perfectly
employed with little, or indeed without any, exposure of the body of the patient.
The speculum is introduced easily without the assistance of sight, and the mouth
of it only requires to be afterwards uncovered, in order to enable us to examine
the *cervix uteri* and the top of the vagina.[48]

To a twenty-first-century observer, it may seem odd that a gynaecologist could visualize
the cervix with less difficulty than he could the external genitalia. But that apparent paradox vividly demonstrates that, by the 1850s, the medical gaze had gained only partial and
conditional access to the female body.

It was not only the sensitivities of individual patients that Simpson and his colleagues
had to take cognizance of, when proposing clinical interventions. As the above quotation
illustrates, the activities of some gynaecologists had aroused misgivings within the wider
medical profession. The nature of these concerns is indicative of anxieties regarding the
ethical behaviour of medical men toward the women in their care, as well as contemporary
social attitudes toward female sexuality. Simpson's most formidable opponent was the
eminent surgeon, Marshall Hall. Hall strongly opposed the use of the speculum on moral
grounds. He was not impressed by the argument that the instrument could be discreetly
deployed under the bedclothes:

But, if there be no exposure of the person ... is there, at first, no wounding of the
feelings, and is there, afterwards, no deterioration and blunting of those feelings,
by the daily or weekly use of the speculum vaginae in the virgin, and in the very
young even among the married? I loudly proclaim that ... the female who has
been subjected to such treatment is not the same person in delicacy and purity
that she was before.[49]

Hall concluded with a call to professional probity:

Let us ... throw aside this injurious practice with indignant scorn, remembering
that it is not mere exposure of the person, but the dulling of the edge of the virgin
modesty, and the degradation of the pure minds of the daughters of England,
which are to be avoided.[50]

Concerns as to possible impropriety in the use of the speculum were not confined to
medical professionals. An alternative practitioner, the 'hygeist' James Morison, conducted
a long campaign against orthodox medicine, accusing doctors of exploiting their patients
by deceiving them into submitting to unnecessary medical and surgical interventions. He
was particularly exercised to warn the public against the gynaecologist as sexual predator.
It certainly behoved all doctors who treated women to guard themselves against the suspicion
of an ulterior motive in seeking greater access to the female body.[51] Often it was better to
touch discreetly than intrude with the eye. A fine line had to be walked. Simpson noted,
with evident puzzlement, that his predecessor as Professor of Midwifery, James Hamilton,
was prepared to undertake vaginal examinations but thought it improper to apply the
stethoscope to the female abdomen. But Hamilton's prudence is merely evidence that, like
Simpson, he was trying to proceed carefully in complex professional and moral terrain.

Simpson's greatest professional achievements date from the 1840s and 1850s. Simpson thus represents an early phase of the evolution of modern diagnostic practice, in which the trained ear, applied to the stethoscope, and the '*tactus eruditus*', the practised hand, employed in palpation and percussion, were the primary tools of examination. As we have seen, important innovator as Simpson undoubtedly was, his modes of investigation display as many continuities with the practice of the previous century as they do with that of the gynaecologist of 50 or 100 years later. In his time, physical examination still had to be proselytized for.

·Another important nineteenth-century diagnostic innovation was thermometry.[52] In the eighteenth century, thermometers that could potentially have been clinically useful were available but they were expensive, slow to give an accurate reading, and fragile. However, the principal reason that the clinical thermometer did not come into common use in the eighteenth century was the central reliance that was placed upon the patient's testimony. More often than not, the patient said she felt cold while the thermometer registered her as being hot.[53] Under these circumstances it was the patient who was believed and not the diagnostic instrument. A major step in establishing the thermometer as a clinical tool was the publication, in 1868, of *The Characteristics of Body Heat in Disease* by Carl Wunderlich.[54] Having observed thousands of fever patients, Wunderlich established that diseases had characteristic temperature curves, and that graphically recording these changes could have diagnostic and prognostic value. Recurrent fever could be distinguished from malaria, for instance; the latter displaying a smoother temperature curve than the former. Similar distinctions were found between typhoid and typhus. Pneumonia was shown to have a very characteristic curve, with a distinctive crisis on the eighth day or so. If the patient survived this period and his temperature began to fall, then the relatives could be reassured that recovery could be confidently expected. Wunderlich's curves are the origin of the temperature chart that used to hang on the frame of every bed in every hospital in the western world and woe betide the nurse who failed to keep the temperature record up to date. The position of the chart, at the end of the bed facing away from the patient, is symbolic of the way in which, as the century progressed, the basis of the understanding of disease was taken away from the patient and invested in signs and symptoms that were accessible and intelligible only to the doctor.

In the latter half of the nineteenth century, several more tools were devised to augment further the physician's senses. The ophthalmoscope was invented in 1850, again exposing disorders of the living that could previously have been seen only on post-mortem dissection. An effective laryngoscope was introduced in 1857. The invention of electric light in the 1880s made endoscopes much easier to use and, in the following decades, the urinary bladder, the rectum, the sigmoid and descending colon, and the stomach were all exposed to the medical gaze. Artificial illumination made the vaginal speculum a much more effective clinical tool. Some authors, both in the nineteenth century and more recently, have argued that the deployment of the clinical thermometer set in motion a trend in physical diagnosis that was radically distinct in character from the legacy of the stethoscope and the visualizing devices.[55] The difference was that effective deployment of the stethoscope was dependent on the physician's senses, and was thus to an extent subjective, whereas the graphical recording of temperature data could be regarded as objective and scientific. In 1863, Etienne-Jules Marey devised an instrument, the sphygmograph, which recorded the arterial pulse waves on to smoked paper. By the 1890s, accurate numerical readings of blood pressure could be obtained with the newly improved sphygmomanometer. The electrocardiograph was introduced in the first decade of the twentieth century.

It is undoubtedly true that the emergence of the 'graphical method', together with the greater range and availability of chemical and, later, bacteriological laboratory tests, diminished, to an extent, the role of clinical acumen in certain aspects of the diagnostic process. However it should be remembered that, simultaneously to these innovations, an ever closer visual and manual scrutiny of the body was enhancing rather than diminishing the role of physical examination in the clinical encounter. I refer to the development, especially in the latter half of the nineteenth century, of an extensive inventory of clinical semiology. For instance, in 1869, the Scottish physician, Argyll Robertson, described the ophthalmological sign that bears his name.[56] An Argyll Robertson pupil, unlike a normal one, does not contract in response to light but will, nevertheless, contract to focus on a near object. The sign became regarded as pathognomonic for various forms of neurosyphilis, which association led to an alternative name, 'the prostitute's pupil'. Many of the most impressive achievements in the understanding of clinical signs occurred in the rising specialty of neurology. The work of Joseph Babinski (1857–1932) might be taken as an example.[57] Babinski prided himself on his ability to arrive at a diagnosis while asking the patient very few questions – the contrast with eighteenth-century practice was deliberate. Instead he conducted a meticulous neurological examination. Babinski described several new clinical signs, the most famous of which is named after him. Eliciting 'Babinski's reflex' entails pricking the sole of the foot. In a healthy adult, this produces bending of the big toe. Straightening of the toe is an indication of damage to the central nervous system. This test continues to be an important part of the present-day neurological 'exam'. Another of Babinski's chief concerns was to distinguish, by means of similar forms of physical examination, organic disease from hysterical, i.e. psychiatric, disorders. The development of clinical signs continued into the twentieth century, with hundreds being added to the clinical repertoire. Orthopedics, for instance, gained the Lachman test for detecting a rupture of the anterior cruciate ligament.[58]

Access to patients' bodies was not however necessarily straightforward, at least in certain circumstances. Queen Victoria died in 1901 and it was only upon post-mortem that her physician learned that she had a prolapse of the uterus.[59] She had never consented to a gynaecological examination. The great slaughter of young men in the First World War created a surplus of women in the 1920s, many of whom never married or had much to do with men. The female members of that generation were still creating access problems for their (still predominantly male) doctors into the second half of the twentieth century. But gradually, throughout the nineteenth and twentieth centuries, being examined by the doctor became regarded as different from other forms of bodily contact between non-intimates. The doctor became a licensed examiner of his (and later, her) patients' bodies. The character and extent of clinical examination came to be controlled, not by social norms, still less by jealous husbands or elderly virgins, but by professional standards of training and ethics, ultimately sanctioned by the disciplinary committees of the General Medical Council.

On the other hand, it is sometimes argued that the advent of sophisticated forms of diagnostic imaging, in the twentieth century, has relegated physical examination to a more secondary position in clinical practice.[60] It is certainly true that, for instance, the development of soft-tissue x-radiology and echocardiology provided information about the state of the heart and lungs far beyond what could be obtained by the stethoscope. Likewise, magnetic resonance imaging (MRI) has rendered some of the rarefied aspects of neurological semiology virtually obsolete. However, the stethoscope, the otoscope (for examining the ear) and the ophthalmoscope retain their value for the general physician and, as tools of first approximation, for the specialist. In general practice and in certain specialties, the ability to perform manual diagnostic procedures accurately and tactfully remains an essential skill. Trainee paediatricians, for instance, have impressed upon them the value of digital rectal examinations, a form of investigation they are often reluctant to perform. Hence the admonitory rubric, 'If you don't put your finger in it, you'll put your foot in it.'

It should be noted, also, that the relation between physical examination and technologically mediated imaging is often closer than might be supposed. Obstetric ultrasound imaging, for instance, is essentially an interactive cognitive process, almost a form of technologically assisted palpation.[61] The Polaroid images given to expectant women to take away, and put in the family album, are not, in most cases, the actual basis of diagnosis. The real diagnostic image is three-dimensional and largely mental, built up in the operator's understanding not only from the two-dimensional images on the screen but also by spatial and proprioceptive feedback, as she moves her probe over the patient's abdomen, coupled with previous clinical experience and knowledge of the underlying anatomy. Obstetric ultrasound is thus similar in practice to older forms of physical examination in which the hidden, internal structures of the body are revealed to the imagination of the examining physician by means of her educated hand and eye. Ultrasound scanning thus links modern medicine to the anatomico-clinical innovations of Auenbrugger and Laennec and displays the continued importance of physical examination in the competent and humane practice of medicine.

Notes

1 Quoted in Roy Porter, 'The rise of physical examination' in W. F. Bynum and Roy Porter (eds), *Medicine and the Five Senses*, Cambridge: Cambridge University Press, 1993, pp. 179–97 (181).

2 Porter, 'The rise of physical examination'.

3 J. Rutherford, 'Clinical lectures', MS notes (undated), Edinburgh University Library, Dc.10.28, p. 20.

4 Charles Newman, 'Physical Signs in the London Hospitals: A Chapter in the History of the Introduction of Physical Examination', *Medical History* 2, 1958, pp. 195–201; Charles Newman, 'Diagnostic investigation before Laennec', *Medical History* 4:4, 1960, pp. 322–29.

5 W. F. Bynum, 'Health, disease and medical care' in G. S. Rousseau and R. Porter (eds), *The Ferment of Knowledge: Studies in the Historiography of Eighteenth-Century Science*, Cambridge: Cambridge University Press, 1980, pp. 211–54 (232).

6 Stanley Joel Reiser, *Medicine and the Reign of Technology*, Cambridge: Cambridge University Press, 1978, pp. 11–22.

7 N. D. Jewson, 'Medical Knowledge and the Patronage System in 18th Century England', *Sociology* 8, 1974, pp. 369–85.

8 Malcolm Nicolson, 'The art of diagnosis: Medicine and the five senses' in W. F. Bynum and Roy Porter (eds), *Companion Encyclopedia of the History of Medicine*, London: Routledge 1993, pp. 801–25.

9 Gerard van Swieten, *Commentaries on Boerhaave's aphorisms*, 18 vols, Edinburgh: Elliot, 1776, vol. 17, p. 113.

10 Van Swieten, *Commentaries*, p. 65.

11 Malcolm Nicolson, 'Giovanni Battista Morgagni and eighteenth-century physical examination' in Christopher Lawrence (ed.), *Medical Theory, Surgical Practice: Studies in the History of Surgery*, London: Routledge, 1992, pp. 101–34.

12 G. B. Morgagni, *The seats and causes of diseases investigated by anatomy*, trans. B. Alexander, London: Miller, 1769, vol. 2, p. 382.

13 Morgagni, *The seats and causes of diseases*, vol. 2, pp. 638–39.

14 Stolberg, this volume.

15 Morgagni, *The seats and causes of diseases*, vol. 2, p. 696.

16 Van Swieten, *Commentaries*, vol. 17, p. 127.

17 Nicolson, 'Giovanni Battista Morgagni'; Nicolson, 'Gerhard van Swieten and the innovation of physical examination' in Ilana Löwy *et al.* (eds), *Medicine and Change: Historical and Sociological Studies of Medical Innovation*, Paris: Inserm, 1993, pp. 49–68; Nicolson, 'The art of diagnosis'.

18 Van Swieten, *Commentaries*, vol. 1, p. 20.

19 Henry E. Sigerist, 'On Percussion of the Chest: A Translation of Auenbrugger's Original Treatise by John Forbes', *Bulletin of the History of Medicine* 4, 1936, pp. 373–403.

20 James B. Herrick, 'A note concerning the long neglect of Auenbrugger's *Inventum Novum*', *Archives of Internal Medicine* 71:6, 1943, pp. 741–48.

21 William Cullen, *First lines of the practice of physic*, 4 vols, Edinburgh: Elliot, 1786, vol. 4, p. 228.

22 See Saul Jarcho, 'The introduction of percussion in the United States', *Journal of the History of Medicine* 13, 1985, pp. 259–60.

23 Jarcho, 'The introduction of percussion'; also Saul Jarcho, 'Auenbrugger, Laennec and John Keats: some notes on the early history of percussion and auscultation', *Medical History* 5, 1961, pp. 167–72.

24 Alvin E. Rodin, *The influence of Matthew Baillie's morbid anatomy: Biography, evaluation and reprint*, Springfield: Thomas, 1973; Malcolm Nicolson, 'Matthew Baillie' in William F. Bynum and Helen Bynum (eds), *Dictionary of Medical Biography*, Westport: Greenwood Press 2007, vol. 1, pp. 146–48.

25 Jacalyn Duffin, *To See with a Better Eye: a life of R. T. H. Laennec*, Princeton: Princeton University Press, 1998, p. 29.

26 Duffin, *To See with a Better Eye*, pp. 32–33; Erwin H. Ackerknecht, *Medicine at the Paris Hospital, 1794–1848*, Baltimore: Johns Hopkins Press, 1967, pp. 83–88.

27 Duffin, *To See with a Better Eye*, pp. 96–101; Ackerknecht, *Medicine at the Paris Hospital*, pp. 85–89.

28 Duffin, *To See with a Better Eye*, p. 122.

29 Malcolm Nicolson, 'The stethoscope' in Robert Bud, Stephen Johnston and Deborah Warner (eds), *Instruments of Science: A Historical Encyclopedia*, London: Science Museum 1998, pp. 584–86.

30 Mirko D. Grmek, 'L'invention de l'auscultation mediate, retouches à un cliché historique', *Revue palais de la découverte* 22, 1981, pp. 107–16.

31 R. T. H. Laennec, *A treatise on the diseases of the chest*, trans. J. Forbes, London: Underwood, 1821.

32 Duffin, *To See with a Better Eye*, p. 207.

33 Malcolm Nicolson, 'The introduction of percussion and stethoscopy to early nineteenth-century Edinburgh' in Bynum and Porter, *Medicine and the Five Senses*, pp. 134–53.

34 N. P. Comins, 'New stethoscope', *London Medical Gazette* 4, 1829, pp. 427–30 (427).

35 Comins, 'New stethoscope', p. 429.

36 Comins, 'New stethoscope', p. 429.

37 Comins, 'New stethoscope', p. 429.

38 Nicolson, 'The stethoscope'; Stanley Joel Reiser, 'The science of diagnosis: diagnostic technology' in Bynum and Porter, *Companion Encyclopedia of the History of Medicine*, pp. 826–51.

39 C. J. B. Williams, 'On the acoustic principles and construction of stethoscopes', *Lancet* 2, 1873, pp. 664–66 (655); Nicolson, 'The stethoscope'.

40 Jacalyn Duffin, 'Laennec, René Théophile Hyacinthe' in Bynum and Bynum, *Dictionary of Medical Biography*, pp. 757–61 (760).

41 A. Sakula, 'Joseph Skoda', *Thorax* 36, 1981, pp. 404–11.

42 Anon, 'Photographic surgery', *Lancet* 2, 1867, p. 146.

43 See Malcolm Nicolson, 'James Young Simpson and the development of physical diagnosis' in Alison Nuttall and Rosemary Mander (eds), *James Young Simpson: A lad o'pairts*, Edinburgh: Scottish History Press, 2011, pp. 57–75.

44 Myrtle Simpson, *Simpson, the obstetrician: A biography*, London: Gollancz, 1972, p. 57.

45 J. Y. Simpson, *Clinical lectures on the diseases of women*, Edinburgh: Black, 1872, p. 6.

46 J. Y. Simpson, 'Notes of lectures on midwifery by Dr J.Y. Simpson, taken by William MacNeil', 1863, Royal College of Surgeons of Edinburgh Archive, unpaginated.

47 Simpson, *Clinical lectures*, p. 27.

48 J. Y. Simpson, 'Case of amputation of the neck of the womb', *Edinburgh Medical and Surgical Journal* 55, 1841, pp. 104–12 (105).

49 M. Hall, 'On a new and lamentable form of hysteria', *Lancet* 1, 1850, pp. 660–61 (660).

50 Hall, 'On a new and lamentable form of hysteria', p. 661.

51 Nicolson, 'James Young Simpson and the development of physical diagnosis'.

52 Reiser, *Medicine and the Reign of Technology*, pp. 116–21.

53 Reiser, *Medicine and the Reign of Technology*, p. 113.

54 C. A.Wunderlich, *On the temperature in diseases: a manual of medical thermometry*, trans. W. Bathurst Woodman, London: New Sydenham, 1871.

55 Merriley Borell, 'Training the senses, training the mind' in Bynum and Porter, *Medicine and the Five Senses*, pp. 244–61; Reiser, *Medicine and the Reign of Technology*, pp. 91–121.

56 J. M. S. Pearce, 'The Argyll Robertson Pupil', *Journal of Neurology, Neurosurgery and Psychiatry* 75, 2004, p. 1345.

57 P. Koehler, 'Babinski, Joseph-Félix-François' in Bynum and Bynum, *Dictionary of Medical Biography*, vol. 1, pp. 142–43.

58 Anon., 'History of the Lachman test', *Clinical orthopedics and related research* 216, 1987, pp. 302–3 (302).

59 Michaela Reid, 'Sir James Reid, Bt: royal apothecary', *Journal of the Royal Society of Medicine* 94:4, 2001, pp. 194–95.

60 Reiser, *Medicine and the Reign of Technology*, pp. 228–31.

61 Malcolm Nicolson and J. E. E. Fleming, *Imaging and Imagining the Fetus: The Development of Obstetric Ultrasound*, Baltimore: Johns Hopkins Press, forthcoming.

Part IV

BODY AND MIND

Sexuality and identity

7

FROM AGE TO GENDER, *C.* 1500–1750

From the adolescent male to the adult effeminate body

Randolph Trumbach

In 1500 in western societies sexual desire was as likely to be organized by differences in age as by differences in gender, and the bodies of men, women, and hermaphrodites were likely to be seen as profoundly similar. This sexual system was of long standing. In western societies it was directly linked with the world that had existed in the ancient Mediterranean. This western system was also in many ways similar to the sexual systems that could be found elsewhere in the world, for instance, in East and South Asia. The way in which the western system operated was influenced by the Christian religion, but it is likely that Christianity had for the most part accepted a system that had long existed independently of it. In western societies a masculinist system that made honourable for adult men sexual acts in which they sexually penetrated others but were not themselves penetrated, coexisted with a Christian moral and legal system that made sinful and illegal all sexual acts that occurred outside of marriage between a man and a woman. Sources suggest that many adult men might desire and penetrate both women and adolescent males. It is likely that women also desired both males and females. This desire for both genders is harder to demonstrate among women because sexual behaviour between women appeared less often in the legal sources than did behaviour between males. But sexual behaviour between males and between females was in both cases organized predominantly by differences in age, men with boys and women with girls. The study of this same-sex behaviour is the easiest way to see the difference between the traditional sexual system and the modern sexual system that came into existence in the first generation after 1700.

By 1750 there was no longer a unitary sexual system in western societies. Between 1700 and 1750 a new sexual system came into existence in north-western Europe, in England, France, and the Dutch Republic.[1] The traditional sexual system that had prevailed in 1500 continued to exist throughout the eighteenth century in central, southern, and eastern Europe. By 1800 it is likely that the modern system had come to prevail in Germanic Europe and North America.[2] But it is not until about 1900 that it can be documented in southern and eastern Europe and in Latin America.[3] Over the course of the twentieth century something like the system of European sexual modernity that first appeared in the generation after 1700 in north-western Europe has come to prevail in many societies that are not western. In East Asia it appeared in Japan in the first half of the twentieth century but in China probably not until after World War II.[4] It still does not prevail in South Asia[5] or in most of the Muslim world,[6] and the situation in sub-Saharan African societies is extremely difficult to describe.[7]

The presence or absence of the modern sexual system can most easily be established by asking whether there has come into existence in a society a minority of adult men who desire only other males and who do not desire women. These men usually wished sexually both to penetrate and be penetrated. They often expressed their sexual desire by adopting some of the characteristics of women in their speech, gait, and dress. This effeminacy was viewed by the rest of society as their defining mark, but some men were not effeminate, and some men could display or conceal their effeminacy at will. These men desired both adult and adolescent males, and their sexual objects might be either men like themselves or men from the majority. The latter were often available to them because a difficult to establish percentage (perhaps as many as a third) of men from the majority who were supposed to desire only women, occasionally had sexual relations with the new male sexual minority. The men from the minority usually organized themselves into urban subcultures, and a great deal of the evidence for their having come into existence as a group is drawn from the legal sources which document the hostile actions by public authorities against the public subculture. But men in the countryside or in small towns were unlikely to have the support of a subculture, and the men who preferred adolescents to adult men were also likely to meet their partners outside of a public subculture. The effeminacy of these adult men needs to be distinguished from the sexual effeminacy of adult men which occasionally appeared in the traditional system that had prevailed around 1500. In the traditional system boys were passive (and often effeminate) and men active, and boys were supposed to move from one role to the other at the end of their adolescence in their early twenties. But some boys failed to make this transition and became adult passive men who either hid their desire in a marriage to a woman or became openly transvestite prostitutes. But the desire of a man for a boy did not lead him to adopt women's ways, whereas in the modern system, it was presumed that only a minority of effeminate men desired sex with another male and that the males they desired might be either adults or adolescents.

The presence or absence of the modern sexual system can be established more easily by studying the nature of same-sex behaviour than by studying relations between men and women. Female prostitution in 1500 and 1750 can look superficially the same, and this is even more true of sexual relations in marriage. The nature of male prostitution, on the other hand, can be shown to have changed profoundly between 1500 and 1750. Men who in 1500 went to female prostitutes or married wives were also likely to have sexual relations with adolescent boys. But by 1750 the men who went to female prostitutes and who married women were unlikely to have sexual relations with any kind of male, whether adult or adolescent, and these men were very likely to use their sexual behaviour with women to establish in their own eyes and in the eyes of others that they never experienced sexual desire for other males.

The traditional system in 1500

In traditional sexual systems in which same-sex relations were structured by differences in age, four roles can be distinguished for both males and females. Among males, there was first the adult man who penetrated three kinds of passive males. The sexual passivity of the adolescent boy was acceptable because he had not yet become a man. The two kinds of passive adult males were used but viewed with contempt. The man who sought to hide his passivity by marrying a woman (the ancient Roman *cinaedus*) was the more despised of the two since he undermined the role of the paterfamilias. The transvestite who left the world of the family and became a prostitute (the Roman *gallus*), sometimes joining a band to replace his family, received greater acceptance.[8] Some historians have doubted that women ever organized same-sex relations by differences in age, but Gill Shepherd's study of women in twentieth-century Mombasa plainly shows that they have. The transvestite female husband who penetrated her partner with an artificial phallus is the best documented of the four roles among women: she, like the passive married man, undermined the family and she was therefore treated with great contempt. The transvestite virgin, on the other hand, by her virginity secured the right to act as a man in society (neatly reversing the role of transvestite male prostitute): she can be documented in ancient Egypt and in the Balkans and Iraq in the twentieth century.[9] This system of four roles can be found widely distributed in many societies and survives to the present in South Asia and in the Muslim world.

There was a second less widely distributed system of same-sex relations organized by gender in which adult and adolescent males penetrated a small group of transvestite passive men who have been classically described by anthropologists as present among the native North American peoples with the passive men usually being labeled as 'berdaches', as Jonathan Burton discusses in his investigation of bodies, sex and race later in this volume.[10] This second system was not present in Europe before 1700. It might look superficially like the modern European system that came into being after 1700 since the men who desired men in this system were occasionally transvestite and usually presumed to be effeminate in other ways. But these effeminate Europeans were despised in their societies whereas the berdache was accepted and often highly valued. Furthermore, the sexual partners of the men in the new European minority were most usually other men from the minority, whereas one berdache never had sex with another but only with men from the majority. The traditional North American system does demonstrate, however, that it was not unprecedented to have a system of same-sex relations organized around a minority gender role.

The evidence from Italy, and above all from Florence, most clearly documents the traditional European system around 1700. Michael Rocke has brilliantly demonstrated what can be done when the arrests and denunciations for late fifteenth-century Florence are played against the demographic information in the catasto. At least 15,000 Florentine males were accused of sodomy and over 2,400 were convicted by the principal magistracy responsible for overseeing sodomy. From this Rocke has estimated that at least two-thirds of all Florentine males were implicated by the time they reached the age of 40, and these figures do not cover all the magistracies. This strongly suggests that almost all males in this society had sexual relations with other males at some point in their lives and did so repeatedly. Sodomy was nonetheless illegal in Florence. Preachers such as Bernardino of Siena regularly denounced it. But Bernardino also accepted that it was widespread. He even said that mothers were proud that their attractive adolescent sons caught men's eyes and deliberately sent them into the streets dressed in their most alluring clothes. The Florentines apparently lived out their sexual lives under two different moralities, one that was Christian and disapproved of sodomy, and another that was masculinist and patriarchal and promoted it.[11]

The distinction between a homosexual minority and a heterosexual majority cannot have existed in Florence. If this distinction can be shown not to have existed in a single

European society, it is very unlikely to have existed in any of them. It is apparent when one compares Florence with either the ancient pagan or the later Muslim Mediterranean that the sodomy of Florence was nothing new; but it appears to have been more open than elsewhere and therefore better documented. The question thus needs to be asked whether it had grown more open in the course of the fifteenth century. There had certainly been relatively few cases in the fourteenth century when the penalties had been far more severe. But as the penalties were moderated into a series of graduated fines (which were often not paid), the number of denunciations increased. Many Florentines therefore thought that sodomy was wrong, but they did not think it was so wrong as to merit a severe punishment. This was the compromise between the two moralities by which many Florentines lived. But in their adolescence and young manhood, most Florentine males lived entirely according to the masculinist morality and not the Christian one.

The sodomy which most Florentine males practised was strictly organized by differences in age. From the time boys entered puberty around the age of 15 until their beards began to grow at around 19 or 20, they were anally penetrated by older men. These older men were usually unmarried and in their later twenties. Between 19 and 23 there seems to have been a transitional phase when a young man could be both active and passive, but he was always active with someone younger and passive with someone older. Adolescent boys occasionally took turns at being active and passive with each other. But young adult men never allowed themselves to be passive with their adolescents. Older men sometimes fellated their adolescent partners instead of penetrating them. Most men seem to have stopped pursuing boys once they married in their thirties. A few adult men (estimated at about 12 per cent) never married, and some of these had relations with boys throughout their lives. Some men in their twenties had sex with both female prostitutes and boys. Very few adult men (around 3 per cent) allowed themselves to be penetrated; they had presumably failed to make the transition from passive boy to active man. No adult transvestite men appear in the fifteenth-century Florentine records, but such men do very occasionally appear in Venetian and English sources. Rolandino Ronachaia, after his marriage to a woman had failed, moved to Venice and worked and lived as a prostitute called Rolandina, having relations with an 'infinite number of men'. In London, John Rykener in 1395 called himself Eleanor, dressed as a woman, and prostituted himself to a number of men. A century and a half later, Robert Chestwyn did much the same thing in London. Here one can see the evidence for all four of the male roles in age-structured systems: active man, passive boy, passive married man, transvestite prostitute.[12]

The English evidence cannot produce anything like the statistical certainty one finds in Florence, but Henry VIII's visitation of the English monasteries suggests a compelling story for the north of England. In ten houses monks or canons were accused of having sex with males. The Augustinians, the Cistercians, and the Benedictines each had three such houses; the Premonstratensians had one. In six houses there was only one canon or monk who pursued boys. Two houses had two such canons or monks, one house had three, and one house had four. Six of the 16 canons or monks are listed as having been with one boy. Three of them had each had two boys, one had had four, one five, one six, and one of them had had ten boys. One canon was said to have had 'diverse' boys and another 'many' boys, and a monk was charged with simply having 'boys'. Eight of the 16 monks or canons who went with boys were also charged with masturbation, and of these, Richard Stubbs, a Benedictine at Holy Trinity at York, had also had sex with six women as well as with his six boys. In all these ten houses the total number of canons or monks who had been sexually active through voluntary pollution, sodomy with males, or incontinency with women, varied. The Augustinian canons at Thurgarton in Nottinghamshire were by far the most sexually active house. In 1536 there was a total of 16 canons and a prior in the house. Fourteen of these (82.3 per cent) were charged with sexual activity. Eight had committed voluntary pollution. Two of these and five more, for a total of seven, had been with women. Five of these women at least were married. The subprior had been with several women, as had three other canons. One canon had had four boys and another had had many boys. It is difficult to say what the dynamic was in an individual house that produced men who had sex with boys. It is unlikely to have been the ethos of any particular order, and was more probably the result of the situation in an individual house. But for a canon who wished to pursue boys, it must certainly have been easier to do so in an Augustinian house like Thurgarton where 14 of 16 canons were engaged in some sort of sexual activity.[13]

Individual religious houses apparently had quite different sexual cultures even when they might belong to the same order and be in the same city. Richard Stubbs at Holy Trinity, York, with his six boys and six women, also masturbated in what seems to have been the typical Benedictine fashion, along with six of his brother monks, making two-thirds (or seven of eleven) of this house sexually active. But in the much larger Benedictine house of St Mary's in the same city of York, only 14 per cent of the 51 monks were sexually active and masturbated. It was probably only in one of the smaller houses that one found almost all the religious in a house engaged in sexual activity. This was most likely to happen among the Augustinians since they had the largest number of smaller houses in the northern province. In the 1530s there were 24 houses with 326 canons. Among the Augustinian houses, it is therefore not surprising to find that in one-third of them, a half or more of the canons were sexually active, and that these houses had from 17 to five members. In the larger Augustinian houses of 23 to 28 canons, less than one third of the canons appear to have been sexually active. The sexually active canon or monk was probably therefore likely to be thought of as being an Augustinian. It was perhaps for this reason that Geoffrey Chaucer made his pardoner, who was a sexually passive adult sodomite, into an Augustinian canon. There were certainly more sexually active Augustinians spread out among a greater number of houses in a greater number of communities than there were of any other kind of enclosed religious. But they do not seem to have produced more men who had sex with boys than did the Benedictines or the Cistercians. Given that sex with boys was relatively infrequent compared to masturbation or sex with women, it is striking that in two out of three houses among both Cistercians and the Augustinians in which monks had sex with boys, there should have been more than one monk who did so. Was it the case that when one monk started such an involvement, it encouraged others in a house to do so? Did men attracted to boys tend to choose a house known to have others like themselves? Or was it simply that some houses were more likely than others to notice and report the behaviour? The monks who had relations with boys were usually older, experienced monks. It is likely that it took a degree of self-confidence to move on from masturbation to either boys or women, or to both, but that more monks moved on to women than to boys. From this one may argue that this was possibly a common practice among sixteenth- and seventeenth-century Englishmen. For, as Robert Burton put it in *The Anatomy of Melancholy*, 'if it was like this among votaries, monks, and such-like saintly little men', that there were so many 'whoremongers, cinaedi, debauchees, buggers, lovers of boys, pederasts, sodomites, … and Ganimedes', what 'may one suspect to have happened in market places and in palaces? What among noblemen, what in brothels, how much nastiness, how much filth?'[14]

The English literary evidence is much better than the legal. The most sympathetic discussion of sexual relations between males in the seventeenth century appeared in the plays of the London stage, and a good deal of the opposition to the theatres by the Puritans was inspired by this tolerance for what they viewed as a crying sin. On the London stage women's roles were played by transvestite boys and it was often claimed that this excited men's desire for boys. The plays also had sodomitical exchanges between men and boys who were playing the role of a boy. In a number of plays a young girl (played by a transvestite boy) dressed as a boy or a page. With these girls dressed as boys, men in the play often flirted, thinking them actual boys. The potential sodomy of these scenes was redeemed when the boy was revealed to be a girl; the man (and the playwright) could then say that they had been reacting to a girl's good looks and not a boy's. But, of course, the good looks of the young actor were in fact those of a boy: the potential sodomy could never be entirely displaced. These plays with girls dressed as boys have been counted. Between 1590 and 1642 there were 74 such plays. In 14 years (26 per cent) there were none, but in the remaining 39 years there were from one to four each year. If to this list one adds the other plays with sodomitical references, it is likely that in about 120 plays of the surviving 300 plays there was some reference to sodomy.[15]

In the plays there were several kinds of sodomy presented, but almost all of it was structured by differences in age between an adult man and an adolescent boy. The adult male characters in the plays are for the most part gentlemen and therefore the evidence cannot be used to document relations between poorer males. Many of the boys in relationships with men are represented as poor boys, but some pages have the same social standings as their masters. When the man and boy are of the same social class, it is expected that the master will see to the page's education. As the boy grows up the master will promote his marriage. Boy and master are sometimes represented as deeply in love, with one boy longing to marry his master. A page will be expected to sleep in the same bed as his master, to dress and undress him, to accompany him in public, to entertain him by playing on the lute, by singing, and by reading him to sleep. Pages who are poor boys are most likely to be represented as crafty and their sexual relations with their masters are less likely to be idealized. Boy actors are represented as the sexual companions of the adult actors who are their masters. It is often said that they are prostituted for the men who have come to see them act. Some of them seem to have worn women's clothes in the street. There is evidence of transvestite boy prostitutes in the street but they were not necessarily young actors. The page's body size and his clothes were so sexually appealing to men that some female prostitutes dressed as pages in the street. It was suggested that transvestism in boys could affect their gender identity as men. Women seem to have found these adolescent pages as appealing as men did, and they sought to seduce them and even to keep them. The pages could therefore be sexually responsive to women. The men who pursued pages are also usually represented as being attracted to women as well. Very occasionally there are representations of adult men who are sexually passive with another adult man, but this attraction is usually explained as the result of drunkenness or bewitchment. In all these presentations sodomy is shown in a relatively matter-of-fact way as a fairly typical male behaviour. It can never be directly praised, though, for that would be contrary to the law and true religion. This is the unofficial masculinist position on sodomy, the alternative that men believed, felt and often practised, when they were not being officially Christian.

The Puritans were therefore correct to say that on sodomy the theatre presented an alternative morality to which many, if not most, men at some moment in their lives probably subscribed.

Since the differences between male prostitution before and after 1700 can be used to document the replacement of the traditional sexual system by the modern one, it is useful to look at its description in the seventeenth-century London plays and satires. In Ben Jonson's plays the transvestite boys of the playhouses are the most usual boy prostitutes or 'ingles'. 'Ingle' in Jonson is sometimes a word simply for friend: Juniper in *The Case is Altered* (1599) calls both Antonio and Valentine 'sweet ingle' and 'my ingle', and they are both adult men and not one of the pages in the play. The three boys who introduce *Cynthia's Revels* (1600), on the other hand, call themselves 'such fine ingles as we' in a context full of sexual innuendo that boys are desired by men. The third of them says to the others, 'what will you ravish me'; he continues 'I'lde crie, a rape, but that you are children'; and takes for granted that the audience has come to ogle the boys: 'I wonder that any man is so mad, to come see these rascally Tits play here … not the fift part of a good face amongst them all.' Ovid in *Poetaster* (1601) similarly ties ingle to the sexual desirability of boy actors: 'What? Shall I have my sonne a stager now? And enghle for players? a gull? a rooke? A shot-clogge? To make suppers and be laughed at?' Later in the play, Tucca offers at first to sell or rent his two boy actors, but after Histrio asks to 'let one of them do a little of a ladie', and then inquires what Tucca will charge for a week of the boys' services, Tucca withdraws his offer, saying, 'No, you mangonizing slave, I will not part from 'hem: you'll sell 'hem for engles you.' In *The Devil is an Ass* (1616) Merecraft proposes to hire a boy actor to play the Spanish lady and suggests Dicke Robinson. Robinson was an actor who by 1616 was no longer a boy, and who in real life seems to have been a rake, since in September of the year the play was performed, he was 'charged with incontinency' at the Middlesex sessions. Merecraft in the play describes Robinson as 'a very pretty fellow' who went often to the chamber of a gentleman who was a friend of Merecraft's. With this gentleman the boy goes to a supper party dressed as a lawyer's wife. Does this show that boy actors visited gentlemen and went about the street dressed as women? Merecraft describes it as all high spirits. But it does suggest that a boy's stage transvestism might move into the real world and become part of his attraction for his adult male admirers.[16]

Boy prostitutes are referred to by others in their satires. John Marston in one of his satires writes 'But ho, what Ganimede is that doth grace the gallants heeles. One, for two daies space is closely hyred.' Thomas Dekker has a mock dedication to Sir Nicholas Nemo 'the now-onely-onely-Supper-maker-to Enghles & Plaiers-Boys', and Everard Guilpin mocks Licus 'who is at every play and every night sups with his Ingles'. Taking a 'play-boy' to supper was evidently a part of prostituting him and something the man about town might be inclined to do. But some texts suggest there were boy prostitutes who were not young actors. Thomas Heywood adds an anti-Semitic detail by writing that the English Jews 'make money of their own children; the male stewes can witness that'. In 'Ingling Pyander' (1599) Thomas Middleton bitterly tells of a man who has fallen in love with a boy he then encounters 'ingling' or whoring in the street dressed in 'a nymphs attire', or in women's clothes. Once the man had 'lov'd Pyander well', so he 'loathes my soul to seek Pyander's shame', but in retrospect he feels what a 'fool that I was in my affection'. With a woman it would not have been so bad: 'for had he been a she injurious boy, I had not been so subject to annoy'. He warns other men, 'trust not a painted puppet, as I've done'

(Sir Simonds D'Ewes in 1622 told a friend 'that boyes were growen to the height of wickedness to paint'). The streets, Middleton said, 'are full of iggling parasites' dressed as women. If you must hire a boy, 'be curious in your choice, the best will tire'. The best boy prostitutes are bad, 'therefore hire none at all'. Thomas Randolph similarly writes a poem in which 'a woman (as I thought)' passes him by in Somerset Garden, runs her hand in the fountain, and looks at the roses. Daringly the woman raises her gown and looks at her crimson stockings, blushing at 'her open impudence'. The poet asks the gardener who she is and is told that she is 'a maide of honour' at the court. He concludes, however, that the answer to the riddle is that here is neither 'mayde, nor honour, sure noe honesty'. She is instead a male prostitute and probably (as a modern commentator suggests) a transvestite boy actor. The poem was daring enough that Randolph's brother did not print it in 1638 when he edited a volume of Randolph's verse after his early death possibly because it might have been seen as criticizing the stage transvestism of the Queen who lived in Somerset House.[17]

William Prynne pointed out that every playhouse was surrounded by a group of bawdy-houses to which men took their 'strumpets and adulteresses': 'witnesses the Cock-pit, and Drury-Lane: Black-friers Playhouse, and Duke-humfries: the Red-bull, and Turnbull-street: the Globe, and Bank-side Brothel-houses'. Prynne did not mention any brothels specifically for boys, but Clement Walker in 1649 knew of 'new-erected sodoms and spintries at the Mulberry Garden', a spintry (a word from Tacitus) being a brothel for boys. In 1649 the playhouses had been closed for seven years, but in 1654 the Mulberry Gardens was the one place left 'for the ladys & Gallants' when John Evelyn went there to seek 'refreshment' since 'Cromwell & his partisans' had shut up Spring Garden. It is likely enough that in Prynne's day, as in the 1640s and 1650s, the female strumpets and the boys had also mixed together in bawdy-houses adjacent to playhouses.[18] In a system of sexual relations structured by differences in age, most male prostitutes would have been adolescent boys, although it is apparent (from the three earlier cases) that there would also have been the occasional adult male transvestite prostitute.

The best visual evidence for the traditional system comes, of course, from the world of Italian Renaissance painting which established the canons of western visual art. The body of the naked adolescent male, and men's desire for that body, was central to that art. It makes a neat parallel with the centrality of the adolescent male body for the plays and theatre of early seventeenth-century England. Together the two bodies of evidence confirm what the legal evidence from both Italy and England has also shown, that many men desired both boys and women, and that they acted on both desires. It might even be possible to argue that in the public world of painting and the theatre it was easier to represent the bodies of boys than the bodies of women. This was probably a consequence of the requirement that women should be virgins until marriage. The sexuality of boys was more malleable than the sexuality of women. A woman's virginity once lost could never be restored. But it was taken as a normal part of human development that when a beard had grown on an individual male, he was able to change from passive boy to active man. It was rather like the stories of those individuals who, by leaping over an object, had caused the sexual organs hidden in their bodies to descend into open sight, transforming them from women into men. In this world there was often (though not always) thought to be only male genitals with women's inside the body and men's outside as Thomas Laqueur has maintained.[19] In such a world the bodies of boys, small and hairless like women's but with their male genitals in plain view, might easily substitute for women, especially when their arses allowed men to penetrate them with their penises. Boys' genitals were always the same but their minds were hermaphroditical, allowing them to change from being penetrated to being the penetrator.

The drawings of naked male adolescent studio assistants (using the published collections) made by Italian artists ranging from Filippino Lippi at the end of the fifteenth century to Guercino in the early seventeenth century establish some of this argument. Between Lippi and Guercino, there are the drawings of Leonardo, Raphael, Andrea del Sarto, Pontormo, Parmigianino, Bronzino, Barocci, Annibale Carracci, and Domenichino. These drawings were made either in preparation for a painting in which the nude boy might eventually be transformed into a sorrowing Virgin Mary standing at the foot of the Cross, as Barocci did (see Figure 7.1);[20] or they might be made by students and their teachers in academies to train their eyes and hands.[21]

The latter kinds of drawings were often more finished than those made in preparation for a painting, where only the boy's body and not his head was fully realized. This world of looking at naked youths sometimes plainly became the basis of erotic encounters. Leonardo seems to have made a drawing of his assistant Sulai, in which the boy is presented with an erect penis (an image circulated on the Internet) and this model was then transformed into the finished John the Baptist in the Louvre. This must have been known and may explain why the painting was denounced in the early seventeenth century.[22] Parmigianino made a drawing (now in the Louvre) of two naked headless youths in which one boy with a flaccid penis masturbates with his left hand the very large erection of another. In another drawing a censor has made several strokes with a pen through the erect penis of another youth who

Figure 7.1 Federico Barocci, Study for the Virgin Mary in the Bonarelli *Crucifixion*. Courtesy of Berlin, Staatliche Museen, inv. 2–1974 [4176].

is part of a group of youths which includes a naked woman with her legs open to reveal her vagina.[23] Pontormo drew one youth seated and pointing at the viewer: the boy's legs are open and his trunk pushed backwards, so that the entrance to his anus can be seen beneath his penis.[24] It is similar to the finished painting of Cupid that Caravaggio later made of his young lover and assistant, which was found so erotic that a curtain was hung in front of it.[25] In two other drawings, a boy lies on his stomach with his arse offered in one by the position of his legs, and in the other with the boy raising himself on his elbows to look at the viewer.[26]

In finished sacred painting the relationship between Christ and his male followers, both adolescent and adult, could be eroticized by those who had eyes to see. Throughout Europe men justified their love of boys by pointing to the love of Jesus and St John, especially as it was described at the Last Supper in John's gospel (13: 23–25), where the Vulgate describes John as lying *in sinu Jesu*, in Jesus's lap.[27] Painters always presumed that John was an adolescent, sometimes just entering puberty at 14 or 15, sometimes when his voice would have been breaking at 17 or 18. Tintoretto painted the scene nine times between 1546 and 1592. His John is sometimes the younger adolescent sometimes the older, asleep on the table next to Jesus. But in the version for San Rocco, it is hard at first to find John, until one sees that he is the younger adolescent lying in Jesus's lap with the Lord resting his left hand on the boy's shoulder as with his right hand he gives a Communion wafer to St Peter.

The relationship between Christ and later adult male saints was often presented as a mystical marriage. Anthony of Padua was often painted in this way: Guercino did four versions, Murillo did ten. These scenes were relatively unproblematic since Jesus was always represented as an infant, as he was in his marriages to Catherine of Alexandria.[28] The scenes between St Francis and the crucified Jesus were more difficult. Murillo did one of these, but Guercino did not, even though he painted Francis ten times. In Murillo's picture Jesus in his loincloth has his left arm still nailed to the cross: his free right arm is bent over to embrace Francis's shoulder as Francis embraces Jesus with both arms. Earlier in the century Francisco Ribalta had painted a more revealing version of Francis's embrace in which Jesus with his right arm places his crown of thorns on Francis as an angel flies to place a crown of roses on Jesus: marriage wreaths have been exchanged and the cross has become a marriage bed. Ribalta also painted a marriage between Christ and St Bernard, in which with both arms Christ embraces Bernard who returns the gesture with his eyes closed in ecstasy. Bernard was the hero whose sermons on the Song of Songs were read throughout Europe by Catholic monks and English Puritan men seeking to understand the marriage of their souls to Christ as his bride.[29] These men were prepared to express their submission by undertaking the despised role of the passive adult man: their submission carried its force because they knew the treatment such men received in the sexual economy of Europe.

The transformation of sexuality and gender after 1700

In the first generation of the eighteenth century between 1700 and 1730 a new sexual role appeared in the cities of north-western Europe, in London, Paris and Amsterdam. In London the men who fulfilled this role were called mollies. They were adult effeminate men who were sexually interested only in men. They were first brought to public attention in London in a play by Thomas Baker, *Tunbridge-Walks*, which was performed in 1703. In the years that followed, especially in 1707 and 1709, and again between 1726 and 1732, there was a series of cases inspired by the Societies for the Reformation of Manners, in which men of this new effeminate kind were brought to public attention, especially in the newspapers and in the public punishments in which these effeminate men stood in the pillory and were stoned and mocked in the theatre of the streets. Some of these men seem to have been attracted to boys and some to other adult men. Those who sought out other adult men met them in the streets, the parks, the boghouses or the public toilets, at church and in alehouses that especially catered to these men and were called molly-houses. From the very first appearance of these men, the masculine men of the male majority who were supposed to desire only women stood in an adversarial position to the new sexual minority. The majority of men were now obliged to play a new role, the role that we might anachronistically call the exclusively heterosexual man. Occasionally men from this majority did sometimes have sex with these adult effeminate men. As a result two kinds of male heterosexual/homosexual interaction appear in the English legal sources. Some heterosexual men blackmailed homosexual men, but they also blackmailed heterosexual men who were too timid to resist. It may have been that it was not always easy for an observer to distinguish a heterosexual male from a homosexual one. This made the patrolling of sexual boundaries difficult. Some sodomites knew that some heterosexual men would agree to have sex with them, but it is apparent that a sodomite could not always tell which men would. Those who rejected these advances from sodomites often seized them and had them charged with making a sodomitical assault.[30]

In the London newspapers between 1720 and 1799 there were nearly 500 cases reported of men in London who had been caught either having sex with another man or trying to pick up an unwilling man. Since the search engine for the Burney newspapers is imperfect, 500 is a minimum figure: there may well have been twice as many. Each case would also have appeared several times since newspapers reprinted reports from other papers. The terms in which the acts were reported changed significantly in the 1760s. The acts ceased to be called sodomy or sodomitical and instead were labelled 'unnatural crimes', which remained the standard term in the newspapers throughout the nineteenth century. About 170 cases were reported from outside of London. Against these more than 600 cases of men who attempted sodomy, there have to be placed 150 instances in which a man attempted to blackmail another man in London for attempting sodomy with himself or someone else. In many of these cases the blackmailers were drawn from the body of soldiers stationed in London. These soldiers (as will become apparent) were often found highly desirable by men from the new male sexual minority. The soldier's body, clothed and unclothed, and presumed to belong to the new heterosexual majority, became an object of fascination to English society and was thereby made in a real sense into a prostituted body.

In Thomas Baker's 1703 play *Tunbridge-Walks*, Maiden is described as a 'nice fellow that values himself upon his effeminacies'. He was distinguished from Squib, who was a 'fluttery' or frivolous military fop. Maiden has many ladylike accomplishments, can sing, dance, play the guitar, do fancy work, and dress a woman since he was once apprenticed to a milliner. But a 'gentleman took a fancy' to him and left him an estate. Maiden likes women's company but does not 'desire any private love-favours from 'em'. He admits that he has never had sex with a woman. When he was a boy he 'loved mightily to play with girls and dress babies'. He and his friends, who are called beaus, meet together in his chambers in the Temple, where they 'play with fans and mimic the women', scream 'hold up your tails', make curtsies, and call one another 'Madame'. He also says that he has gone to the theatre dressed as a woman. Male milliners like Maiden who made women's clothes became the stereotypical sodomite in the public mind. Baker himself in *The Female Tatler* (1709) described them as 'the sweetest, fairest, nicest, dished out creatures; and by their elegant address and soft speeches, you would guess them to be Italians'. Two generations later Fanny Burney found the mercers more 'entertaining' than the clothes; they 'recommended caps and ribbons with an air of so much importance, that I wished to ask them how long they had left off wearing them'.[31]

The word 'effeminate' acquired a new meaning. In the newspapers between 1680 and 1720 the word effeminate was used as synonymous with weak and referred to collectives, so that one could write of an 'effeminate nation' or an 'effeminate nobility', and attribute effeminacy to the Persians or the Venetians. But, between 1720 and 1750, in 20 per cent of the cases a new usage appeared in which it characterized some aspect of an individual Englishman. It turned up especially in advertisements that attempted to find a robber, or a soldier who had run away from his regiment. Individuals were described as having an effeminate face, countenance or looks, and most often as having effeminate voices or speech. In 1737 effeminate was for the first time clearly associated with sodomites, and used to describe the women's names taken by a band of sodomitical robbers who had come down to Bristol from London. An effeminate voice in a man became a burden, and by 1749 Samuel Angier, an expert in speech impediments, advertised that he could relieve 'men speaking in an effeminate, and women in a masculine tone' of voice. The traditional communal use of effeminacy continued to come strongly to the fore during moments of national crisis like the American or French Revolutions. But the new meaning of effeminacy as a characteristic of male sodomites was clearly demonstrated in the 1750s by *The Public Advertiser*'s notice (4 March 1756) that 'on Tuesday night last information being brought to John Fielding and Saunders Welch Esqrs, that an assembly of men of the effeminate kind, were to have a dance at a public house, a warrant was immediately granted … and [the constable's officers] apprehended about fourteen persons of the above stamp'. The old and new meanings of effeminacy coexisted throughout the next century and a half, but at some point in the twentieth century, effeminacy as a personal characteristic of men associated with homosexual desire entirely won out.

Thomas Baker's play had 24 performances between 1703 and 1711. For the next decade it did not play but, after the trials of the late 1720s brought mollies again to public attention, it played 33 times between 1729 and 1749. It was then replaced by David Garrick's *Miss in Her Teens* (1747) which became the stage's favourite representation of the effeminate sodomite, playing 324 times over the rest of the century with Garrick playing the role of Fribble 59 times. In *Miss in Her Teens* Fribble describes to the 16-year-old Miss Biddy, whom he is courting, a scene in the street when he was offered a coach by two 'hackney-coach fellows', 'I'll carry you and your doll too', says he, 'Miss Margery for the same price'. Fribble, like Maiden, plays with dolls. Fribble turns on the coachman and threatens him; the coachman 'makes a cut at me with his whip, and striking me over the nail of my little finger it gave me such exquisite torter that I fainted away'. In his faint his pocket is picked of his purse, his scissors, his Mocoa smelling bottle, and his 'huswife', which was a pocket case for needles, pins and threads. When Biddy expresses her surprise that Fribble uses a huswife, Fribble tells her 'there is a club of us, all young bachelors, the sweetest society in the world, and we meet three times a week at each other's lodgings, where we drink tea, hear the chat of the day, invent fashions for the ladies, make models of 'em and cut out patterns in paper'. At one of these meetings at Billy Dimple's 'three drunken naughty women of the town burst into our clubroom, cursed us all, threw down the china, broke six looking-glasses, scalded us with the slop-basin, and scrat poor Phill Whiffle's check in such a manner that he has kept his bed these three weeks'. This club is directly modelled on Maiden's club in Thomas Baker's play. Biddy tells him that these happy bachelors offer little to the ladies to 'wish and sigh' for. Fribble responds that his interest in her is genuine and that his friends see him leaving them: 'I am prodigiously rallied about my passion for you, I can tell you that, and am looked upon as lost to our society already.' But Biddy does not take him seriously. There are no descriptions of the mannerisms with which Garrick played the role. The text of the play seems to indicate that Fribble spoke in a simpering tone. There is a print representing a diminutive Fribble preparing to duel a gigantic Captain Flash, his loud polar opposite. The two editions of Garrick's *Fribbleriad* in which he denounced his enemies as sodomites do carry frontispieces of a Fribble, and in these Fribble stands poised with his backside suggestively stuck out for its public reception. This must have seemed to mimic a woman's stance with a bosom thrust forward and a backside stuck out. Fribble in a print from 1747 (*Christmass Gambolls*) has been drawn in this way and Charles Towsend caricatured the effeminate second Earl of Bristol (Lord Hervey's son) in the same pose (National Portrait Gallery). By 1793 Fribble and the man-milliner could be brought together and mocked in a print in which a female customer denounces the man-milliner as Mr Fribble, objects that he has cheated her by cutting her ribbon too short, and, playing on the meaning that a man's 'yard' was his penis, tells him that 'his yard is too short by an inch' (see Figure 7.2).

From among the boys of 14 to 16 who were the drummers for the London regiments, and from among the young enlisted soldiers of 18 and over, were drawn many of eighteenth-century London's male prostitutes. It seems to have been the case that these military boys and young men were not themselves sodomites. There were also young sodomitical male prostitutes who met men in the molly-houses; and there were adult transvestite male prostitutes who went with men who were not sodomites. Soldiers seemed most available as they stood immobile and on guard in the various London parks. This is what Richard St George Mansergh St George wished to indicate in his satirical print. A small elegant man observes through a glass a large ferocious grenadier. Lest the point was missed the print was accompanied by satirical verses against sodomy. These were credited to Tobias Smollett's novel *Roderick Random* in which Lord Strutwell tried to seduce Random with a reference to Petronius. Soldiers used their knowledge of sodomites gained in the Park to blackmail them. The two themes came neatly together when three soldiers tried to blackmail Henry Sharpe. Thomas Williams, a private in the Coldstream regiment, said that Sharpe had come up to him between 10 and 12 at night as he stood sentry in the Green Park and asked whether he 'had been done lately'. Williams claimed he told Sharpe he did not know what the phrase meant; Sharpe explained he 'wanted to know whether any man had anything to do with me lately'. Williams replied that he was a married man and detested such things. To this Sharpe's lawyer protested that since Williams had been a soldier for three years, it was not believable that he had not known from his own experience, or from his fellow soldiers, what the phrase 'if

Figure 7.2 'The Man-Milliner' as Fribble, 1793. Courtesy of the British Museum (1861, 0518.978).

you had been done lately' meant.[32] But did it mean anal intercourse, fellatio, or masturbation?

When the Royal Academy began to conduct life classes, it was soldiers and older female prostitutes who agreed to be paid to remove their clothes and to sit naked and immobile so that their bodies could be sketched by young male students. Johann Zoffany painted such a life class as the setting for his group portrait of the older members of the Academy (see Figure 7.3).

A naked man, probably about 30, with one hand raised over his head and the other behind his back, sits with his genitals exposed (in another life class scene Zoffany had placed a drape over the model's sexual organs), but a leg is raised so that the viewer of the picture cannot see the model's genitalia. A second, younger, model waits his turn and is taking off his clothes, with his shirt off, and one stocking gone as he removes the other. In the preparatory watercolour now in the British Museum, the older model looks no older than a newly enlisted guardsman. The younger boy is most likely a drummer. The clothes of both models lie discarded on the floor: the man and the boy have undressed before their male audience. In the world of female prostitution, women removed their clothes to 'show postures', but they were not always immobile as they also enacted various positions in sexual intercourse. Still, the Academicians must have known that both their male and female models had acted as prostitutes. The life class was an acceptable form in which the men from the sexual majority crossed over into the new minority world of same-sex desire between adult men.[33]

Figure 7.3 The Academicians of the Royal Academy, 1771–72 (oil on canvas), Zoffany, Johann (1733–1810). The Royal Collection 2011 Her Majesty Queen Elizabeth II/The Bridgeman Art Library.

Women and same-sex desire

It is likely that sexual relations between women, like those between men, passed from being organized by difference in age before 1700 to being organized by differences in gender after 1700; but it is difficult to be certain since the evidence, compared with that for men, is exiguous. Comparing women's experience with men's is further complicated because among women the two less prevalent roles of the masculine penetrating woman and the masculine virgin are better documented than the likely more widespread roles of actions between women (without penetration) and passive adolescent girls. With men, on the other hand, the active man and the passive boy appear far more frequently than the adult penetrated man and the transvestite prostitute. Inquisition records do occasionally document groups of women who were not penetrators before 1700. In 1560 in Aragon a group of women were charged with sexual relations, but since these had occurred 'without any instrument', the charges were dropped because such acts could not be seen as sodomy. The Brazilian inquisition between 1591 and 1595 did charge 29 women with relations with women; their actions seemed to have been organized by differences in age. The literary and visual sources centred on Jupiter's seduction of Callisto, when he took on the appearance of Diana, that Valerie Traub has collected complements the inquisition records. Jupiter appears as a brunette woman and Callisto as a blonde adolescent girl in the paintings, and Jupiter was played by a woman and Callisto by a girl in John Crowne's masque. The women who married women and used an artificial penis appear in the sources well into the eighteenth century, and were always condemned. But the woman soldier who maintained her virginity was highly idealized. At some point in the eighteenth century, and most clearly by the 1770s, a new sapphist role appeared in which one woman took on some masculine characteristics in speech, gait, and dress and had as a partner a more conventionally feminine woman. These partially masculinized women thrived on their gender ambiguity and in this differed from the female husbands of the traditional system who had tried to pass entirely as men, and had even sometimes managed to hide their female genitals from their wives.[34]

Neither the traditional nor the modern system of same-sex relations seem to have had for women the importance that such relations had for men. This was almost certainly because women's sexual relations with men as virgins, wives, or prostitutes were viewed by men as having greater significance than any sexual relations women might have with each other. Before 1700 it does seem likely that women may have desired both girls and men, but unlike with men and boys, no evidence has yet been gathered that suggests that women acted on their desire for girls. An age of marriage in the late twenties in northern Europe would have given a social space for such action; an age of marriage at 15 in the south would have made it more difficult. There is no sign that sexually active but passive girls were given anything like the roles that sexually passive boys acted out in the theatre or in painting. If sexual activity between girls and women usually occurred without penetration, physical virginity could have been maintained.

Conclusion

In the sexual system before 1700, males could be both passive and active sexually, and might, as part of the normal course of life, switch from one role to the other. After 1700 most men were sexually active only with women. A minority of men were both passive and active with boys or men. Some of these men also married women. Some of the men from the majority, like the soldiers in London, might occasionally have sexual relations with the new passive sexual minority of men. The sexual majority (as I have tried to show in *Sex and the Gender Revolution*) sought to prove their exclusive desire for women by going to female prostitutes and seducing unmarried women. It is also likely that the new demographic regime in England, in which marriage became universal and the age of marriage fell from the later to the earlier twenties, began in the 1720s just at the moment that the new sexual minority became firmly established in the public mind.

It is probably an impossible task to seek causes for this transition, and it is easy to confuse the consequences of the transition with its supposed causes. Since the transition seems to have occurred only in north-western Europe but among all social classes in that area, any causation would have to take those two factors into consideration. If this transition is conceptualized as a movement from a system organized by age to one organized by gender, it is appropriate to remember that before 1700 a system like that of native North America in which relations between males were organized by gender existed in relatively egalitarian hunter-gatherer societies, whereas the age-structured systems of Europe and Asia existed in societies divided between elites and subjugated groups. The transition in Europe after 1700 might therefore have occurred because European social structures had begun to move to a more nearly egalitarian system of social relations. And, as an example of this, the English elite (as I suggested 30 years ago in *The Rise of the Egalitarian Family*) had begun by 1750 to organize relations between spouses and between parents and children in a more egalitarian direction.

Notes

I would like to thank T. Scott Johnson for help in preparing the text of this essay.

1 Randolph Trumbach, 'The heterosexual male in eighteenth-century London and his queer interactions' in Katherine O'Donnell and Michael O'Rourke (eds), *Love, Sex, Intimacy and Friendship between Men, 1550–1800*, London: Palgrave Macmillan, 2003, pp. 99–127 (122–25) lists and discusses the historiography.

2 For Germany, see Trumbach, 'Afterword' and the essays in Katherine M. Faull (ed.), *Masculinity, Senses, Spirit*, Lewisburg: Bucknell University Press, 2011; for North America see Thomas A. Foster (ed.), *Long Before Stonewall: Histories of Same-Sex Sexuality in Early America*, New York: New York University Press, 2007.

3 Dan Healey, *Homosexual Desire in Revolutionary Russia: The Regulation of Sexual and Gender Dissent*, Chicago: University of Chicago Press, 2001; Cristian Berco, *Sexual Hierarchies, Public Status: Men, Sodomy and Society in Spain's Golden Age*, Toronto: University of Toronto Press, 2007; Richard Cleminson and Francisco Vázquez García, *'Los Invisibles': A History of Male Homosexuality in Spain, 1850–1940*, Cardiff: University of Wales Press, 2007; James N. Green, *Beyond Carnival: Male Homosexuality in Twentieth-Century Brazil*, Chicago: University of Chicago Press, 1999; Robert Irwin McKee, Edward J. McCaughan and Michelle Rocio Nasser (eds), *The Famous 41: Sexuality and Social Control in Mexico,1901*, London: Palgrave Macmillan, 2003.

4 Gary Leupp, *Male Colors: The Construction of Homosexuality in Tokugawa Japan*, Berkeley: University of California Press, 1995; Gregory M. Pflugfelder, *Cartographies of Desire: Male-Male Sexuality in Japanese Discourse*, Berkeley: University of California Press, 1999; Matthew H. Sommer, *Sex, Law and Society in Late Imperial China*, Stanford: Stanford University Press, 2000; Wenqing Kang, 'Male same-sex relations in China 1900–1950', Ph.D. thesis, University of California, Santa Cruz, 2006.

5 For South Asia, see the work of Serena Nanda, Lawrence Cohen, and especially Shivananda Khan, cited in Randolph Trumbach, 'Renaissance Sodomy, 1500–1700' in Matt Cook, Robert Mills, Randolph Trumbach and H. G. Cocks (eds), *A Gay History of Britain: Love, and Sex between Men since the Middle Ages*, Oxford: Greenwood, 2007, pp. 45–75, 227–30 (227).

6 Walter G. Andrews and Mehmet Kalpakli, *The Age of Beloveds: Love and the Beloved in Early-Modern Ottoman and European Culture and Society*, Durham, NC: Duke University Press, 2005; Khaled El-Rouayheb, *Before Homosexuality in the Arab-Islamic World, 1500–1800*, Chicago: University of Chicago Press, 2005; Arno Schmitt and Jahoeda Sofer (eds), *Sexuality and Eroticism among Males in Moslem Societies*, New York: Harrington Park Press, 1992.

7 Stephen O. Murray and William Roscoe (eds), *Boy Wives and Female Husbands: Studies in African Homosexualities*, New York: St Martin's Press, 1998; Marc Epprecht, *Hungochani: The History of Dissident Sexuality in Southern Africa*, Montreal: McGill Queens University Press, 2004.

8 Craig A. Williams, *Roman Homosexuality: Ideologies of Masculinity in Classical Antiquity*, New York: Oxford University Press, 1999.

9 Bernadette Brooten, *Love Between Women: Early Christian Responses to Female Homoeroticism*, Chicago: University of Chicago Press, 1996; Valerie Traub, *The Renaissance of Lesbianism in Early Modern England*, Cambridge University Press, 2002; Gill Shepherd, 'Rank, gender, and homosexuality: Mombasa as a key to understanding sexual options' in Pat Caplan (ed.), *The Cultural Construction of Sexuality*, London: Routledge, 1987, pp. 240–70; Susanna Elm, *'Virgins of God': The Making of Asceticism in Late Antiquity*, Oxford: Clarendon, 1994; Antonia Young, *Women Who Become Men: Albanian Sworn Virgins*, New York: Berg, 2000; René Gremaux, 'Woman becomes man in the Balkans' in Gilbert Herdt (ed.), *Third Sex, Third Gender: Beyond Sexual Dimorphism in Culture and History*, New York: Zone Books, 1994, pp. 214–81; Sigrid Westphal-Hellbusch, 'Transvestiten bei arabischen stamen', *Sociologus* 6, 1956, pp. 126–37.

10 Walter L. Williams, *The Spirit and the Flesh: Sexual Diversity in American Indian Culture*, Boston: Beacon, 1986; Will Roscoe, *The Zuni Man-Woman*, Albuquerque: University of New Mexico Press, 1991; Sabine Lang, *Men as Women, Women as Men: Changing Gender in Native American Cultures*, Austin: University of Texas Press, 1998.

11 Michael Rocke, *Forbidden Friendships: Homosexuality and Male Culture in Renaissance Florence*, New York: Oxford University Press, 1996.

12   Guido Ruggiero, *The Boundaries of Eros: Sex Crime and Sexuality in Renaissance Venice*, New York: Oxford University Press, 1985, p. 136; Ruth Mazo Karras and David Lorenzo Boyd, '"*Ut cum muliere*": a male transvestite prostitute in fourteenth-century London' in Louise Fradenburg and Carla Freccero (eds), *Premodern Sexualities*, London: Routledge, 1996; Michael Shapiro, *Gender Play on the Shakespearean Stage: Boy Heroines and Female Pages*, Ann Arbor: University of Michigan Press, 1994, p. 226.

13   The National Archives, London, SP 1/102/84–104; David Knowles and R. Neville Hadcock, *Medieval Religious Houses, England and Wales*, New York: St Martin's, 1971; Anthony Shaw, 'The Compendium Compertorum and the Making of the Suppression Act of 1536', Ph.D. Thesis, University of Warwick, 2003; G. W. Bernard, *The King's Reformation: Henry VIII and the Remaking of the English Church*, New Haven: Yale, 2005.

14   Robert Burton, *The Anatomy of Melancholy*, ed. T. C. Faulkner, N. K. Klessling and R. L. B. Blair, 6 vols, introduction and commentary by J. M. Bamborough and M. Dodsworth, Oxford: Clarendon, 1989–2000 [1621], vol. III, p. 50; vol. VI, pp. 33–34.

15   Trumbach, 'Renaissance Sodomy', pp. 55–66.

16   C. H. Herford and Percy and Evelyn Simpson (eds), *Ben Jonson*, Oxford: Clarendon Press, 1925–51, 11 vols: 'The Case is Altered', vol. III, pp. 106, 137, 156, 174–77; 'Cynthia's Revels', vol. IV, pp. 38–40, induction ll. pp. 165–66, 99–103, 120–23; 'Poetaster', vol. IV, pp. 209, 252–54; 'The Devil is an Ass', vol. VI, pp. 221, 208.

17   Arnold Davenport (ed.), *The Poems of John Marston*, Liverpool: Liverpool University Press, 1961, p. 78; F. P. Wilson (ed.), *The Plague Pamphlets of Thomas Dekker*, Oxford: Clarendon Press, 1925, p. 65; Everard Guilpin, *Skialetheia*, ed. D. A. Carroll, Chapel Hill: University of North Carolina Press, 1974, p. 49; Thomas Heywood, *Dramatic Works*, ed. R. H. Shepherd, New York: Russell and Russell, 1964, 6 vols, 'A Challenge for Beauty', 1636, vol. V, p. 26; Thomas Middleton, *Works*, ed. A. H. Bullen, New York: AMS Press, 1964, 8 vols, 'Ingling Pyander', Satire V in *Micro-Cynicon*, 1599, vol. VIII, pp. 130–34; Elizabeth Bourcier (ed.), *The Diary of Sir Simonds D'Ewes 1622–1624*, Paris: Didier, 1974, pp. 92–93; W. C. Hazlitt (ed.), *Poetical and Dramatic Works of Thomas Randolph*, London: Reeves and Turner, 1875, 2 vols, vol. II, pp. 661–62; Lisa Jardine, *Still Harping on Daughters: Women and Drama in the Age of Shakespeare*, New York: Columbia University Press, 1989, 2nd edn, pp. 10–13.

18   William Prynne, *Histrio-Mastrix*, New York: Johnson Reprint, 1972 [1633], pp. 390–91; Clement Walker, *Relations and Observations, Historical and Politick*, London: R. Royston, 1661, 2 vols, vol. II, p. 257; E. S. De Beer (ed.), *The Diary of John Evelyn*, Oxford: Clarendon Press, 2000 reprint, 6 vols. vol. III, pp. 96–97.

19   Thomas Laqueur, *Making Sex: Body and Gender from the Greeks to Freud*, Cambridge, MA: Harvard, 1990; Londa Schiebinger, *The Mind Has No Sex? Women in the Origins of Modern Science*, Cambridge, MA: Harvard, 1989.

20   Andrea Emiliani, *Federico Barocci (Urbino 1535–1612)*, Ancona: Ars, 2008, I, pp. 160–73, #19.

21   Nikolaus Pevsner, *Academies of Art Past and Present*, New York: Da Capo, 1973.

22   Alessandro Vezzosi, *Leonardo e lo Sport*, Florence: Giunti, 2004, reproduces the drawing; Frank Zöllner, *Leonardo da Vinci 1452–1519*, London: Taschen, 2011, II, pp. 199–209.

23   David Ekserdjian, *Parmigianino*, New Haven: Yale, 2006, pp. 111–17.

24   Janet Cox-Rearick, *The Drawings of Pontormo*, Cambridge, MA: Harvard, 1964, 2 vols, #136.

25   Catherine Puglisi, *Caravaggio*, London: Phaidon, 1998. This is one among many discussions.

26   Cox-Rearick, *Pontormo*, #179, #289.

27   Randolph Trumbach, 'The transformation of sodomy from the Renaissance to the modern world and its general sexual consequences', *Signs* 37:4, 2012, pp. 832–48.

28   David M. Stone, *Guercino*, Florence: Cantini, 1991; Diego Angulo Iñiguez, *Murillo*, Madrid: Espasa-Calpe, 1981, 3 vols.

29   Fernando Benito Domenech, *The Paintings of Ribalta 1565/1628*, New York: Spanish Institute, 1988; Trumbach, 'Transformation'.

30   Randolph Trumbach, *Sex and the Gender Revolution. Volume 1: Heterosexuality and the Third Gender in Enlightenment London*, Chicago: University of Chicago Press, 1998; Randolph Trumbach, 'Modern sodomy: the origins of homosexuality 1700–1800' in Cook *et al.* (eds), *Gay History of Britain*, pp. 77–105, 230–33; Trumbach, 'Transformation'. Three recent works take different views. Katherine Crawford, *The Sexual Culture of the French Renaissance*, Cambridge: Cambridge

University Press, 2010, finds male heterosexuality in the sixteenth and seventeenth centuries, but this ignores the evidence that men continued to like both boys and women, for which, see Jeffrey Merrick and Bryant T. Ragan Jr., *Homosexuality in Early Modern France*, New York: Oxford, 2001. Phillips and Reay stress the continuity between medieval and early modern same-sex attraction but they do not offer an account of the emergence of the heterosexual/homosexual world; see Kim M. Phillips and Barry Reay, *Sex before Sexuality: A Premodern History*, Cambridge: Polity, 2011. Dabhoiwala sets up a straw man of a repressive Christian sexuality which he knocks down with a liberating Enlightenment. He does not see the conflict between masculinist and Christian views before 1700, and that the Christian restriction of sex to pro-creative marriage still operated within the presumption that men liked both boys and women. The Enlightenment is an unlikely cause of change since it was an elite movement to be found throughout Europe, whereas the early eighteenth-century transformation occurred among all classes and was limited to north-western Europe. Dabhoiwala notably does not make same-sex relations central to his study. See Faramerz Dabhoiwala, *The Origins of Sex: A History of the First Sexual Revolution*, London: Allen Lane, 2012.

31 Trumbach, 'Modern sodomy', p. 89.

32 Randolph Trumbach, 'Male prostitution and the emergence of the modern sexual system: eighteenth-century London' in Ann Lewis and Markman Ellis (eds), *Prostitution and Eighteenth-Century Culture: Sex, Commerce and Morality*, London: Pickering & Chatto, 2012; Trumbach, 'Blackmail for sodomy in eighteenth-century London', *Historical Reflections* 33, 2007, pp. 23–39; for Thomas Williams see *Old Bailey Proceedings Online*: www.oldbaileyonline. org (accessed 17 May 2012), December 1790, trial of George Platt, Philip Roberts (t17901208-35).

33 For life class models see James Fenton, *School of Genius: A History of the Royal Academy of Arts*, London: Royal Academy of Arts, 2006, pp. 131–48; Ilaria Bignamini and Martin Postle, *The Artist's Model: Its Role in British Art from Lely to Etty*, Nottingham: Nottingham University Art Gallery, 1991, p. 82; for Zoffany see Penelope Treadwell, *Johan Zoffany: Artist and Adventurer*, London, Paul Halberton, 2009; Mary Webster, *Johan Zoffany 1733–1810*, New Haven: Yale University Press, 2011; Martin Postle (ed.), *Johan Zoffany RA, Society Observed*, New Haven: Yale University Press, 2011.

34 William Monter, *Frontiers of Heresy: The Spanish Inquisition from the Basque Lands to Sicily*, Cambridge: Cambridge University Press, 1990, pp. 281–82; Ligia Bellini, *A Coisa Obscura: mulher, sodomia e inquisição no Brasil colonial*, São Paulo: Brasilense, 1987; Traub, *Renaissance of Lesbianism*; Randolph Trumbach, 'London's Sapphists: from three sexes to four genders in the making of modern culture' in Julia Epstein and Kristina Straub (eds), *Body Guards: The Cultural Politics of Gender Ambiguity*, New York: Routledge, 1991; Emma Donoghue, *Passions between Women: British Lesbian Culture 1668–1801*, London: Scarlet Press, 1993. Since 1993 a large literature has appeared; see Phillips and Reay, *Sex Before Sexuality*.

8

(DE-)CONSTRUCTING SEXUAL KINDS SINCE 1750

Ivan Crozier

Historians of sexuality have addressed a number of hotspots since the 1970s: pornography, birth control, prostitution, and venereal diseases. All of these foci have more or less explicitly shown us the ways in which power (exercised through morality, social sanctioning, the law, etc.) have constrained the expressions of sexual pleasures and desires. A key part of this focus in sexual historiography has been directed towards the medicalization of 'sexual perversions' during the nineteenth century, especially homosexuality, but also other 'aberrant' forms of pleasure including sadism and masochism (hereafter S/M unless being discussed separately), cross-dressing, necrophilia, bestiality, as well as general medical understandings of the sexual impulse. Nevertheless, there remains much to explore with other 'perverse' manifestations of the sexual impulse, such as urolagnia, fetishism, sexual 'self-harm', and other sexual desires that have come under a medical gaze. Historians, like other social commentators, have largely remained in the comfort zone of describing more common (and therefore more acceptable) sexual acts, and so it is unlikely that there will be the same historical interest in these rarely depicted subjects (and subjectivities), despite the availability of (pornographic, medical, literary) material portraying water sports, latex fetishes, or giving and receiving enemas, and regardless of the possibilities for using these sexual practices to explore past manifestations of the sexual impulse. It seems, scanning the historiography of sexuality, that the same kinds of sexual categories developed by nineteenth-century sexologists such as Richard von Krafft-Ebing, Havelock Ellis, Albert Moll, Jean-Martin Charcot, and Alfred Binet have been reified, regardless of the common slippage between these apparently naturally occurring separate categories and the actual practices of individuals classified into them, leaving us with a situation that continues to artificially construct (historical) experience in essentialist terms, as if all homosexual men are incapable of enjoying sexual situations involving women, or as if all masochists cannot occasionally switch and deliver a hard caning. Despite the fact that nineteenth-century sexologists adhered to these categories, seeking out the primary perversion in an individual case,[1] the historian is in something of a privileged position to read through these categories, and to (re-)construct narratives of past sexual pleasures without the necessary recourse to ideas of fixed sexual identities promulgated in sexological discourses. The methodological issues surrounding this tendency to equate a sexual act with a fixed sexual identity will be discussed below, but suffice it to say here that focusing on bodies and the sexual pleasures for which they are used is a way out of the categorical imperative that still haunts us with the use of labels first constructed by nineteenth-century sexologists.

These sexual categories, as almost every serious commentator since Michel Foucault has shown, are not simply objective descriptions of the reality of particular sexual variations; they are manifestations of power, and as such are limited to a specific time and place (nineteenth-century European sexological discourses, despite the efforts in these discourses to adopt a universal position, and to assume similar sexual acts in other cultures and times to be manifestations of an identical perverse sexual impulse).[2] The psychopathological construction of sexual 'perversions' in the late nineteenth and early twentieth centuries was based squarely on conceptions of a variation from the 'normal' impulse (which was taken to mean heterosexual, reproductive, uxorious, non-excessive). As Georges Canguilhem has shown, conceptions of the pathological presuppose ideas of the normal: the two are co-constructed, even if (as in the case of so-called normal sexuality) a proper understanding of the 'normal' could only be developed after the full extent of 'abnormal' manifestations had been understood.[3] Such was the explicit aim of Havelock Ellis's seven-volume *Studies in the Psychology of Sex* (1897–1928). But the efforts of sexologists to describe 'kinds of people' were based on the fundamental link between what people do for sexual pleasure – their sexual acts – and a notion of fixed sexual identities.[4] As Foucault has famously said of the emergence of the homosexual, 'The sodomite had been a temporary aberration; the homosexual was now a species.'[5] What is lacking from these early sexological discourses, and from the work of many of the historians who have unproblematically assumed the existence of these categories in their subjects, is that sexual lives vary; that people can do different things sexually, and that they do not always stay comfortably in these categories throughout the course of their lives, or even from one sexual encounter to the next. These categories also largely fail to adapt to the historical specificity of the concept: i.e. a masochist now is not the same as a masochist in the nineteenth century; the nominalism, to quote Ian Hacking, is 'dynamic'.[6] This standpoint does not mean that there is something aberrant in the sexual behaviour because it is either incomplete or excessive (they are not completely gay, or they also play with S/M or other fetishes), as much as there is a problem with the category being employed. There are (and always have been) many varieties of sexual play involving pain – it is a multiple practice that does not reduce to a fixed identity. The sexual pleasures of these 'perverts' (which have so fascinated sexologists and historians) are what really happen, even if these practices are very messy and resist neat categorization. Psychopathological discourses about them are *post hoc* theorizations written for the benefit of other psychiatrists, and as such should be approached with care by historians, even when they appear to contain first-person narratives of sexual practices under the rubric of some sexual category.[7] The problem that historians of sexuality face is that these medical discourses are the primary sources in which traces of past sexual desire may be found. These sources are not pure: they are heavily filtered by the selection processes employed by doctors to construct their objects for the readership of other sexologists. Their descriptions of sexual encounters, of body types, of dreams, of desires, while building up notions of sexual typologies, are not naïvely objective, but are the product of active (scientific) choices, and are constrained by the commitments, theories, and accepted methodologies of the field for which they are written.

It is, however, important to note that in many of the histories that have utilized medical interventions in sexual practices for their source material, sexuality has been located in the body. In addition to the largely psychological modelling of sexual aberration, the doctors who produced the medical discourses that are the foundation of sexual typologies often (but not always) sought corporeal evidence for their assertions (e.g. the lesbian with the large clitoris, the prostitute who could not blush, the sexual invert who could not whistle).[8] These kinds of signifiers were of course the hallmarks of the positivistic school of criminal anthropology, although they were often adopted into other strands of sexological research.[9] Thus we have conceptions in these sexological writings of the homosexual body that displayed a stereotypical, gender-inverted form; or the masochistic body, with its particular ability to receive physical pain (which is always assumed to be negative); or the fetishization of certain body parts or physical attributes (hair colour, piercings, penis or breast size, the shape of someone's bottom, etc.). These attentions to the sexual body originally derived from the earlier forensic medical writings that were used to identify and corroborate other evidence of sexual crimes, such as sodomy or rape.[10] Focusing on the body was of limited use in discovering the basis for sexual experience, however, as many people were not submitted to the medico-legal examinations that emphasized corporeal signs, and from the 1870s and 1880s, sex psychologists began to explore the mental typologies associated with particular sexual behaviours that had been grounded in special body types. These discourses fell under the rubric of a newly emerging field: sexology. Sexologists did much to standardize the discursive objects that we live with today: the homosexual, the masochist, the sadist, the fetishist, etc. This history of the emergence of sexological theory has been well traced.[11]

For historians to use bodies as a focus makes some sense for two reasons: not only is there a significant historiography of the body on which to draw[12] but also it is through their corporeal practices that people themselves resist constructions of their desires as psychopathological: how they have sex and what they think of it is determined by their corporeal limits, and not by the abstractions of sexologists. The medical material on which the history of sexuality has so long feasted is only of use in constructing a very specific understanding of past sexuality: the psychopathological understanding of sexual acts. In the same way that historians of pornography are necessarily limited by the imaginations of their authors, scientific discourses about sexuality are written for particular purposes, and therefore are subject to a very specific 'grammar'.[13] We need to understand that although these two sources both describe sexual practices, their aims are not the limits of sexual experiences. They are both idealized representations. As historians focus on more recent periods, new sources open up (diaries, letters, blogs, which position the author in relation to these psychopathological discourses, sometimes, or in relation to the practices and emotions that they experience, on other occasions). The medicalization of sexual variations set up particular typologies, but the various practices of individuals can be very much underdetermined by these discourses. Although these acts are what sexologists categorize when they label people, and submit their desires to psychological dissection, explaining their 'perversions' in terms of a variety of scientific theories (degeneration, heredity, upbringing, psychological complexes, hormones, brain structure, and so on), these discursive constructions are never the totality of the individual, or even necessarily the extent of their sexual practices.

The 'perverts' found in psychiatric discourses are trapped between the freedom of succumbing to their pleasures, the sanctioning gaze of the medical discourses (and other social apparatuses of power) that affect their own identities, and the (social) meanings of their acts. As such, control is exerted over the uses to which they put their bodies (through legal limitations on acts that can be performed, people on whom they can be performed, the circulation of images of these acts, and the control of substances that may be used to enhance these experiences). All these 'perverts' can do is go forward into the illicit mazes they have built up around their desires, seeking pleasures to which they can return again and again, extending the limits of their pleasures as they bury themselves deeper in the experiences they seek. This 'total embodiment' is the only way that they can resist psychopathological power. Their bodies are suspended between pathologizing discourses and the orgasms they desperately chase. But the participants in these 'aberrant' sexual acts are not free: they have to negotiate their relationships with heteronormative discourses that describe their most cherished sexual outlets as perverse, and sometimes effect the ban of these acts entirely. The pleasures the 'perverts' seek come at a price: social sanctioning, from legal control, medical pathologization, social ostracism from beneficial social structures (marriage, the nuclear family, being 'normal', being 'sane'). By becoming a 'pervert' – by being a kind of person who seeks specific, 'deviant', sexual acts rather than those acceptable to the majority – spaces of relative freedom need to be found in the evening's empire where these pleasures can be pursued. It is in the anonymous darkness of the club, with cries obscured by the pounding rhythms of other bodies in motion, that these pleasures and the people who enjoy them thrive. It is here, as will be seen in the penultimate section of this chapter, that freedom from psychopathological discourses may be encountered, fragmented by the flicker of strobe lighting, but clear to those who are present deep in their bodies, writhing in incalculable pleasures. It is these bodies, broken down so as to be rebuilt outside of the slavery of being 'normal', that best illustrate how resistance operates, and the possibilities that may be had by following one of the long, shaded paths to corporeal pleasure. Official categories are of little help in understanding these practices.

Thinking about (sexual) bodies

Since Judith Butler's work on gender performativity, and its general acceptance for understanding sexual identities as fluid, non-essentialist, and perpetually evolving through practices of reiteration, sexual categories are best thought of as artificial kinds.[14] Likewise, these performative analytic standpoints underline that it is impossible to think about sexuality outside of the above-mentioned power structures – especially the psychopathological discourses used to construct ideas of sexual aberration, by impacting on the 'perverts' themselves. This position is sound, although it assumes a lot when it comes to explaining *how* these institutions of power affect sexual performativity. It is here that Ian Hacking's work on 'kinds of people' and 'looping effects' can help.

Ian Hacking suggests that the human sciences at certain times make up people that did not exist before. The human sciences effectively produce kinds of people. Hacking elaborates:

> We think of these kinds of people as definite classes defined by definite properties. As we get to know more about these properties, we will be able to control, help, change, or emulate them better. But ... they are moving targets because our investigations interact with them, and change them. And since they are changed, they are not quite the same kind of people as before.[15]

The existence of these categories, as they became more widely known by practitioners of these sexual possibilities, were increasingly incorporated into sexual identities. People became homosexual or masochist, to use two examples that I will amplify below. They used these labels, they explained themselves in these scientific terms and according to the various (psychological, heritable, gendered, genetic, etc.) models that were posited by psychopathologists. The process, as Hacking has shown, is not unidirectional. It loops back into the scientific claims. But what the scientists are studying is not natural, it is an artificial, or human, kind. People have an awareness of their own subjectivities, which is how they react to discourses about them (by accepting them, by understanding themselves in these scientific terms, by resisting them, by actively ignoring them).

Power is linked to resistance, as Foucault often noted.[16] While power acts directly on the body of the subaltern, the body can also be a site of resistance. This performing the sexual body, reiterating past sexual acts and pleasures, is therefore doubly articulated by psychopathological power, and resistance to that power. To put it bluntly: how people fuck determines their relationship to power. If they utterly abandon themselves to their bodies, they are – for those brief hours and minutes – outside of psychiatric power and submerged in pleasure. Pleasure is an escape. The bodies and pleasures that sexologists examined to establish norms are precisely the place to fight battles, to resist psychopathological categories through sexual activity which signifies something utterly different to the pleasure-seeker than to the psychopathologist.[17]

Making sexuality: two examples

In order to illustrate the ways in which sexological discourses of the nineteenth and twentieth centuries constructed sexual typologies that both had a corporeal aspect, and increasingly emphasized psychological characteristics, I will focus upon two problems: homosexuality and masochism. The first of these is extremely well known in the historiography of sexuality, and indeed homosexuality may well be considered the initial sexual 'aberration' around which the field of sexology first emerged in the 1870s and 1880s. Masochism, on the other hand, entered the sexological field in the 1890s as a much less studied object until it was taken up as a fundamental part of psychoanalytic theory. These two objects will be studied in turn, first to show how such categories were developed, and later to show how these categories fail to adequately capture the complexities of either homosexual or masochistic sexual pleasures.

Homosexuality

Much argument has been had over whether homosexuality is a universal characteristic of human nature, or a momentary form of sexual being.[18] My position is that homosexuality is a collective achievement between sexological discourses and the people who have sex with people of the same sex, and identify themselves as homosexual (or gay, or lesbian, etc.). This category is not fixed. Nor do I suggest that some people of one sex have not always enjoyed physical pleasures with others of the same sex. The power of sexological discourses lies in the ways that 'facts' of homosexuality (the hereditary discourses, the psychological cases, etc.) are incorporated into people's understandings of themselves. As the theories change, as different values are put on the explanatory power of some fact or other in these scientific discourses, so the objects – the people – change. Men enjoying sodomy in the Port of Amsterdam, as Theo van der Meer has shown us, are not the same as Freud's lesbian case, or gays and lesbians taking part in an ACT UP action to raise HIV treatment awareness, or two men arranging on the Internet to meet up in a hotel to suck each other off anonymously.[19] As discussed above with reference to Hacking's work, looping effects change both the kinds of people and the medical discourses that discuss them. With this in mind, the following sketch of the historical development of theories of homosexuality illustrates how each time a new concept is developed, new people are described by doctors who do not quite fit the category; each time a new theory is developed which challenges these older theories, new case material is enrolled to support this theory. In all of these theories, there are different homosexuals: the object is not stable, and indeed, until the psychiatric consensus of the twentieth century, it had had different names. Additionally, many people who engaged in same-sex pleasures reacted to these psychopathological discourses. Homosexuals reacted to their medicalization in a number of ways: by criticizing it directly (as in the case of John Addington Symonds or Edward Carpenter); by submitting themselves to these psychosomatic technologies that identified and 'treated' their homosexuality; by accepting these scientific justifications of homosexuality as 'natural' (which was the basis of the criticisms of legal prohibitions); or they simply carried on their pursuit of same-sex pleasure, regardless of the known consequences (in legal or in medical terms, the two sometimes working closely in conjunction). In all of these instances, the homosexuality produced is in a power relation with these pathologizing discourses. It is an artificial kind.

In the last decades of the eighteenth century, as psychiatry was emerging in Europe from the mangled collection of mad doctors who ran asylums into a medical specialism with some pretension to scientific standards, a number of medical discussions about sexuality emerged. These discourses first focused on medical sexual problems – masturbation, prostitution, venereal diseases. Samuel Tissot had already addressed the problem of masturbation, and its associations with debilitating diseases in 1760, and by the nineteenth century, spermatorrhoea, the uncontrolled leaking of seminal fluids from the penis that was believed to eventually kill, was treated through a variety of techniques, such as cauterizing the penis, or introducing several regimes to prevent boys masturbating, from health advice and scare mongering to chastity devices and electric alarms.[20] Psychiatrists soon began looking at sexuality too, reconstructing sexuality from a medical-corporeal problem into a psychological one, although it was not until the 1880s that Alfred Binet would link masturbation to sexual perversions via his model of the fetish, which linked an individual to the history of their own sexual pleasure.[21]

Writing about homosexuality medically increased from the late eighteenth century. Joseph Häussler, Claude François Michea, and Heinrich Kann all struggled with the idea that the sexual impulse could turn towards people of the same sex.[22] A number of psychiatrists, such as Forbes Winslow, following Jean Etienne Dominique Esquirol's notion of a form of sexual monomania called erotomania, described the ways in which the sexual impulses could be deflected away from heterosexual intercourse towards other pleasures.[23] Many of these psychiatrists were simply describing masturbation, but increasingly an awareness of homosexual sex was articulated in these discourses. Forensic doctors, such as Ambroise Tardieu and Johann Casper, developed forensic proofs that could be used to identify the homosexual, especially on the basis of the assumed appearance of their gaping anuses and (in Tardieu's writing) the pointy, dog-shaped penis of the active sodomite.[24] Such caricatures of the body of the homosexual lasted a long time in forensic medical circles.

These forensic discourses rarely framed sexual deviance in terms of a specific psychological type, although Casper was an exception to this trend, and from his work a whole tradition emerged. Sodomy, homosexual and heterosexual, was often illegal, and was described in forensic medical texts under the heading of rape. There was no need for an aetiology of why people would want to engage in practices that were regarded with basic horror – for these were the days before anal sex became mainstream in heterosexual relationships and in garden-variety pornography, as it is today. To engage in such an act was considered perverse and, in most jurisdictions, illegal. It was often described within the discourses of degeneration that were taking hold in Europe from the mid-nineteenth century. One of the psychiatric doyens of this position, Wilhelm Griesinger, encouraged the search for brain lesions in the sexual pervert that had been passed on through the generations.[25] Griesinger's descriptions of homosexuality were taken further by his student and successor at the Charité Hospital in Berlin, Carl Friedrich Otto Westphal, who described the first psychiatric case of *conträre Sexualempfindung* (contrary sexual feeling): Fräulein N.[26]

Fräulein N. exhibited many of the traits that are found in nineteenth-century sexological discourses. She had a persistent sexual desire for other women that was manifest both in physical and psychological terms. She had a history of masturbation fuelled by fantasies of kissing and holding other girls; she embodied many of the corporeal traits that were found, and subsequently sought, in sexological descriptions of lesbians: clitoral hypertrophy, a tight vagina, a masculine mien. She also had never entertained any sexual feelings for men. These physical and psychological attributes became the standard features of pre-psychoanalytic constructions of homosexuality. The basic attribute in these discourses was sexual (and gender) inversion: with all manner of corporeal, social and psychological features uncovered in homosexuals, described in sexological discourses, and used to develop notions of a 'normal' (heterosexual, reproductive, 'properly' gendered) sexual impulse. The works of Lombroso, Ellis, Krafft-Ebing and other sexologists, as many historians have shown, consistently produced models of the homosexual that effectively set the scene for understanding same-sex practices not as acts of pleasure, but as indicative of a type of person who could be fastidiously examined in order to better understand the modes of their sexual transgressions.[27]

These sexological discourses – based on case histories that described in minute detail the first appearances of these sexual aberrations, the content of homosexual dreams, the manifestations of their desires in dark encounters, the bodies (especially the genitalia), the physical appearance, tastes, and artistic preferences – produced a new species of sexual aberration: the homosexual. Less attention was generally paid to the endless searches for the acceptance of homosexual loves, and to the social risks of blackmail, opprobrium, and hatred that affected sexual inverts, although more liberal-minded sexologists such as Havelock Ellis used their works to alter such social opinion. These discourses instead had the effect of tying people who enjoyed same-sex encounters to a specific identity that became the totality of their worth in society – perverted creatures against whom notions of normality were raised to establish pathology, further bolstering centuries of legal, religious and moral persecution of such practices. Constructing 'pathological' sexual categories, such as homosexuality, produces difference that underlies social inequality.[28]

Sexological understandings of sexual perversions did not exclusively maintain their (generally) more biologically grounded sexual categories. A number of hypnotherapists such as Albert von Schrenk-Notzing and Lloyd Tuckey argued that homosexuality was simply a matter of improper sexual object choice, and had attempted to cure their patients' desires through techniques of suggestions (before sending the gay men they had hypnotized off to a prostitute to test the effectiveness of the cure).[29] But by the beginning of the twentieth century, Freudian models of homosexuality, with their particular technologies of understanding (and constructing) the subject in psychoanalytical terms, soon dominated sexological ideas about sexual perversions – despite the fact that Freud's own models of sexual aberration owed much to the work of sexologists.[30] These psychoanalytic models emphasized individual histories, paying close attention to familial relationships, sexual fantasy, mild psychosexual dysfunction such as hysteria, psychological complexes such as the Oedipus complex, narcissism, and so on, and especially notions of sexual immaturity that underlay a new conception of homosexuality which was seen as a partially developed sexual impulse that had been channelled in the wrong direction. These models, while offering a different set of reasons for the development of sexual perversion, remained committed to rigid ideas of sexual normality from which homosexuality deviated.[31] These psychoanalytic models overshadowed other biological and sociological psychosexual discourses for many years, with psychotherapy being the main choice of therapy in order to come to terms with same-sex desire. Psychoanalytic categories were the basis of the classification of mental disorders in the first edition (1952) of the *Diagnostic and Statistic Manual* of the American Psychiatric Association (hereafter DSM), and so homosexuality remained a mental disorder until it was removed from the DSM in 1973. This was not before various 'treatments' for homosexuality under a basically psychoanalytical framework had been introduced, for example, aversion therapies, where homosexual men were shown gay pornographic images that were expected to excite them while also being given drugs that made them feel physically sick, so that the association between their sexual desires and overpowering nausea would encourage them to seek other forms of sexual satisfaction.[32]

The dominance of psychoanalysis in the conceptual formation of homosexuality was not complete, however. From the late nineteenth century, physiologists had been studying newly discovered biological agents: hormones. The hormonal body was a new under-standing of physiology that could explain sexual desires in gendered terms. Indeed, some of the first work on hormones was aimed at understanding gendered differences, and crude hormonal extracts (in the form of puréed animal testicles) were noted for their effects on the increase in sexual desire by Parisian endocrinologist Charles Édouard Brown-Séquard in 1889.[33] In terms of treating homosexuality, the old tropes of effeminacy in gay men were very much alive. The assumption that homosexuals were not 'real men' was blamed on their lack of the 'male' sex hormone, testosterone (which is present in both men and women, although in higher volume in men, and which affects the levels of things such as hirsuteness, sexual desire, and depth of voice). A solution to the existence of homosexual desire was sought in giving hormonal injections to gay men. The result was not, however, that effeminate gay men became macho and indulged in 'proper' heterosexual sex; rather, they shaved several times a day, had higher sex drives, and indulged in more gay sex than they had been hitherto able. The psychologist who first drew attention to the problems in this regime of treatment, Evelyn Hooker, emphasized a social model of homosexuality.[34] Expanding the work of Alfred Kinsey and his team, Hooker saw the ubiquity of homosexuality as a complex social role (Kinsey, however, also attended to the non-homosexual exclusivity of same-sex sexual practices, and as such found a much higher incidence of homosexuality in America than has been comfortably accepted in some quarters).[35] Hooker's position was echoed by British sociologist Mary MacKintosh, who also studied the social aspects of homosexuality. It was no longer simply a case of a biolo-gical urge, or a series of psychological complexes, that made someone homosexual. Rather, the community of homosexuals that gelled around shared sexual pleasure also provided social support for members of the community.[36] These social studies had the effect of de-pathologizing homosexuality, suggesting that many of the lifestyles that could flourish in the gay community were the same as those found in heterosexual couples, thus further suggesting that homosexuality was not a minor part of society, indulged in by a select group of degenerated individuals, but was a significant social factor – a point that Havelock Ellis made in 1897.

The recent general acceptance of homosexuality – resulting in the decriminalization of some homosexual practices in many jurisdictions, the extension of some heterosexual social privileges to same-sex couples, and the de-pathologization of homosexuality by psychiatrists[37] – has not prevented a number of scientific studies from being conducted that seek a biological basis for understanding homosexual desire, falling into the same kinds of thinking that was first noted in the nineteenth century. Examples of this are the various genomic studies of genes that predisposed people to the enjoyment of homosexual sex; finger length studies, by which lesbians and homosexuals are believed to have different finger ratios to 'normal' people; different brain structures of homosexuals, and so on.[38] These studies still start from the assumption that fixed sexual identities exist, that all people who enjoy certain types of sexual pleasure are a kind of subspecies with shared biological, genetic, and neurological differences.

The reconstruction of homosexuality since the change in medico-legal attitudes has been led by public health regimes in response to HIV/AIDS. This response to the virus, which was first linked to homosexual groups before it was expanded to include other risks groups including intravenous drug users, sex-workers and haemophiliacs, and eventually the main transmitters of the virus, heterosexual men and women, involved rethinking ideas about sexual behaviours. Psychiatric categories were of little use to prevent the spread of the virus amongst heterosexuals, and instead public health officials instituted education campaigns about HIV/AIDS that promoted safer sex practices, especially the use of condoms outside of monogamous relationships. Other 'at-risk' groups, including men who have sex with men but who do not identify as gay or bisexual, were targeted as requiring particular education in order to stop the spread of HIV/AIDS. Extremely active in these campaigns were groups such as ACT UP and the Terence Higgins Trust, which worked with medical authorities (not always uncritically) to develop the best methods for treating and spreading knowledge about HIV/AIDS.[39] These encounters demonstrate the ways in which active participation by both medical and lay groups, combined with active resistance of the psychopathologization of homosexuals in the ways they themselves determined the kinds of things that they would do with their own bodies, involves a reconstruction of conceptions of homosexuality. The wider acceptance of homosexuality as a normal part of (western) societies, although not yet complete, required a resistance of psychopathological constructions of effeminate, or aberrant, individuals based on their physical appearance and psychological profile. These older characterizations are not the totality of people found in the complex and evolving varieties of same-sex practices that exist today (for an overview of contemporary homosexual issues, see one of the many prevalent gay magazines, such as *Têtu*).

Masochism

Donatien-Alphonse-François, Marquis de Sade, used sexual violence both to subvert the natural order and to construct a philosophical resistance to rationality where the body becomes the site of extreme experience, and where the dynamics of pleasure were played out beyond their acceptable limits. This underbelly of the Enlightenment created a space where tortured bodies shattered accepted morality and conventional heteronormative notions of sexual experience.[40] Sade's position extended the bodily conceptions of Réné Descartes's mechanical philosophy expressed in *Discours de la méthode* (1637) and Julien Offray de la Mettrie's *L'homme machine* (1748), where corporeality was separated from pure thought. It produced new possibilities for the subject through their (voluntary or forced) participation in violent sexual encounters.[41] Sade's portrayal of the body at the limit of rationality and experience produced new forms of sexual pleasure in these scenes of sexual violence.[42] His writings made such new identities possible.

Sade's visions of sexual excess were much messier than those of the eponymous Baron Leopold von Sacher-Masoch, whose protagonist of *Venus im Pelz* (1870), Severin, indulged his submissive propensities not only through the threat of whippings by his Mistress, Wanda, but through an elaborate series of contracts drawn up to extend the attentions typical of 'normal' enamoured relations. His construction of subservience (and utter devotion) through humiliation and pain expanded the complex psychological interplay between the two parties in a relationship. It is not insignificant (although it was missed by the sexologists who wrote about masochism) that it is the masochist who makes the rules of engagement, and thus also is an active participant in the relationship.[43] This is not the same as other forms of sexual degradation, such as Sade's, which use pain primarily as an expansion of corporeal sensation, combining sexual exploration with the limits of bodily experience. Nor does it echo the widely adopted expressions of pain play encounters that can exist in contemporary S/M sexualities, which do not revolve around power exchange (although complex Dom(me)/sub, Mistress (or Master)/Slave, relationships flourish in these milieux as well).

Medical understandings of sexual pain in the mid-nineteenth century were much less elaborate. William Acton, the Victorian venereologist now famed for his disparaging remarks about female sexual enjoyment, addressed the dissolution of the sexual impulse over the course of the life cycle, and raised the spectre of old men needing to be beaten with canes to reawaken their flagging sexual powers.[44] Such *roués de coups* are commonly found haunting the pages of Victorian pornography as devotees of the specific sexual services involving pain that were available in Victorian brothels.[45] It was not until the end of the century that sexologists began to reformulate sexual aspects of pain in psychological terms.

In 1881, Shobal Vail Clevenger posited a radically different model of the sexual impulse to those being offered in European discussions of homosexuality seen above. This model claimed that the origin of the sexual impulse was hunger. Desire could be traced back to amoebae, some of which exhibited 'cannibalistic' habits that were reminiscent of copulation when they enveloped smaller bacteria, assimilating their genetic material as well as their proteins.[46] Studying a number of higher animals, from praying mantises to crabs (which 'confuse the two desires by eating portions of each other while copulating'), Clevenger exposed the atavism of S/M practices: 'The bitings and even the embrace of the higher animals appears to have reference to this derivation.'[47] Clevenger's model made explicit the association between femininity and submission. It was used to explain a variety of sexual experiences: sodomy was a degeneration towards the cloacal apposition in reptiles; sexual violence was the atavistic degeneration towards animals that employed violent means in copulation; inversion was a throwback to hermaphroditic animals; fetishes were extreme forms of the existing modes of love.[48]

Clevenger's biological model of the sexual impulse (and others, such as that of American psychiatrist James Kiernan) were expanded in the 1890 edition of Richard von Krafft-Ebing's *Psychopathia Sexualis*, in which sadism and masochism were named after Sade and Sacher-Masoch respectively.[49] For Krafft-Ebing, masochism was:

> A peculiar perversion of the psychical *vita sexualis* in which the individual affected, in sexual feeling and thought, is controlled by the idea of being completely and unconditionally subject to the will of a person of the opposite sex, of being treated by this person as by a master, humiliated and abused. This idea is colored by sexual feeling; the masochist lives in fancies in which he creates situations of this kind, and he often attempts to realize them.[50]

It is important to note that S/M for Krafft-Ebing was predominantly a heterosexual phenomenon. His conception was widely adopted. For example, for Charles Féré, the Parisian psychologist, masochism was 'an affection of emotivity consisting in the research for painful manœuvres practised upon them by members of the other sex in order to provoke satisfaction of their venereal appetites. The physiological act is not even attempted, ... these individuals find no pleasure except in painful or shameful acts.'[51] Féré also held that the relationship between love and pain was the result of diminished excitation. It was 'the seeking of real and imaginary sufferings, whether for the purpose of exciting and facilitating sexual pleasure, or for obtaining an actual equivalent of sexual excitations that provoke[d] orgasm.'[52]

These sexological models emphasized a gendered coupling between sadism and masochism, with sadism the masculine, active, pain-giving, dominating form of desire, and masochism its alter-ego, finding pleasure in being dominated, humiliated, and beaten in ways that were considered archetypically feminine because they adopted a submissive role. In these early sexological discourses, sadism and masochism combined neatly.[53] They are fixed, gendered identities, a part of a continuum with masculine desire at one end, and feminine at the other. In this way, women were naturalized as being receptive to dominance and pain (and much was made of their ability to cope with the pain of childbirth, in terms of submitting to and receiving this pain, rather than conquering it), while men were 'naturally' considered to be active, dominant, and violent (and in their ability to deal with pain, this was seen to be bravely conquering rather than passively submitting to it). The true perversion, in sexological conceptions of these sexual archetypes, is a gendered perversion, where women adopt dominant roles and start hurting their lovers, and where men become subservient, receptive to the beatings being administered.[54] Just as homosexuality inverted gendered norms through reversal of 'natural' sexual tastes, so do S/M desires in these discourses, where S/M reversed 'natural' sexual roles.

Masochism was more complex than just involving enjoyment of receiving pain. It was also quickly seen to be symbolic, especially in Havelock Ellis's conception.[55] A love of humiliation and an assumption of submission, rather than actual violence, was considered to be emblematic of the masochistic mindset. These symbolic and self-harming features were quickly elaborated by psychoanalytic models of masochism, which continued to emphasize this form of sexual desire as feminine, and to naturalize female masochistic tendencies. We find this trope in a long line of psychoanalytic theorists from Sigmund Freud, to Sandor Rado, Karen Horney, and Helene Deutsch, which for a long time sufficed as the main conceptualization of masochistic personalities, and which were used to explain sexual encounters involving pain in psychiatric circles.[56] More nuanced studies of masochistic behaviour were advanced recently by Robert Stoller, a Californian psychoanalyst, whose work on masochism explored the extent of sexual pain play, and the construction of subjectivities around such pleasures.[57]

Reconstructing masochism in the DSM III and DSM IV

The DSM is now main repository of psychiatric standards used by medicine and health insurance companies in the US and elsewhere. The original DSM (1952) was adapted from the US Army Medical Board classifications, and like the DSM II was heavily psychoanalytical in approach. The DSM II (1968) simply placed masochism under 'sexual deviations', with the expectation that other psychiatric sources would be read to amplify the subject. The reconstruction of the DSM III (1980) under the direction of Robert Spitzer gave masochism its own entry:

> Sexual masochism could be diagnosed if one of the following is true:

1. A preferred or exclusive mode of producing sexual excitement is to be humiliated, bound, beaten, or otherwise made to suffer.
2. The individual has intentionally participated in an activity in which he or she was physically harmed or his or her life was threatened, in order to produce sexual excitement.[58]

By the DSM IV (1994, text revised 2000), the definition of masochism depended on 'the act (real, not simulated) of being humiliated, beaten, bound, or otherwise made to suffer'.[59] These definitions do not take account of the sexual pleasure involved, or of issues of consent. They are predicated on the pathology of the masochistic subject. And they do not recognize that masochistic experience may only be a part of an individual sexual repertoire. Further, they rely on a sexual ethic that pathologizes some forms of sexual pleasure rather than others (i.e. non-masochistic heterosexual).[60] However, these discourses also describe as pathological some situations in which some people (usually women) can find themselves, particularly forms of sexual abuse relying on humiliation and punishment. These sexually abusive relationships differ from masochistic ones in ways that have prompted feminist groups to criticize psychiatry, as the DSM does not take into account the differences in social circumstance by which people will find themselves in submissive sexual relationships.

Masochism as a sexual practice that involves pain, rather than those forms of submissive behaviour that are associated with masochistic character-types or which involve humiliation (although these two elements can of course coexist or be incorporated into pain play), centres around the body: the pain it can undergo, the limits that can be pushed, the psychological effects of intimacy and trust that are produced when one's body is handed over to the sexual will of the other partner to be hurt and played with as they desire, using sundry instruments (whips, scalpels, ropes, needles, hooks) in order to push their masochist deep into their body in highly sexualized ways. The body in pleasure and pain is central to the encounter. The coital imperative of heteronormative sex that is focused on the orgasm, especially of the male partner, is far from the aim of the encounter. Pleasure, coming to terms with the sensations of pain, control, self-affirmation, intimacy: these are sought by the masochist. But there is much more to the (sexual) lives of these masochists than is implied in the psychopathological discourses; pain play is not (usually) the only form of sexual practice engaged in by those categorized as masochists. Indeed, for the DSM, one transgression is enough for a diagnosis.

Masochistic resistance

These psychopathological constructions of S/M sexualities have not been taken lying down. Two active campaigns have been launched at the DSM: by S/M practitioners, who insist that their forms of sexual enjoyment are normal and ethically sound. These groups have adopted the maxim 'safe, sane, consensual' to explain their practices (and to act as a code of conduct), where sexual play is to involve prior negotiation, and not to involve dangerous situations (mentally or physically), such as drug use, or a real risk of permanent injury.[61] Additionally, there is significant feminist resistance to constructing masochism as passive and normally feminine. These ideals of feminine sexual desire, it is argued, have a double effect of limiting female sexual expression on the one hand (making it pathological to be a domme), while also being used to normalize female sexual submission to the point that it can be seen to institutionalize domestic violence. Both views have been widely challenged.[62]

The picture of the masochist as a sorry being in pain, or pathetically seeking situations in which pain will be administered like Sacher-Masoch's Severin, is far from complete. Within the S/M community there are a great number of artistic corporeal forms that celebrate the masochist, such as artistic bondage and erotic photography. These genres owe much to two different traditions: Japanese bondage art, *shibari*, but with specific modern twists, such as using brightly coloured ropes rather than the traditional jute; and fetish photography, deriving from the ubiquitous images of S/M model Betty Page, with her adaptations of burlesque, replete with whips when playing a *domme*, or with images of her hog-tied, waiting to be dominated, when in a submissive feminine role. Not only are these images adapted by professional erotic photographers, who often maintain the interest in feminine underwear typical of the 1950s (corsets, stockings), and by performers at fetish clubs, who adopt similar fashion, although often with modern twists in terms of materials (latex, bright colours and prints); they are also re-enacted (and often uploaded onto the Internet) by 'regular' participants in S/M sex. Celebrating S/M artistically, showing images of beauty that rely on uses and constraints of the masochist's body, or showing the effects of these practices – whip marks, rope burns on the skin, scars, brands, erotic images of masochists with dilated pupils typical of the subject deep in 'sub-space' (a condition of being high on endorphins deriving from the pain experienced) – are all very different from psychiatric descriptions of 'abnormal' sexual personalities. Many of the participants in these activities, although often self-identifying in terms of categories such as sadism and masochism (and with many subtle gradations and variations in between), resist the psychopathological construction of their sexual experiences in psychiatric discourses. What these people do, and how they understand their practices, is often positive and affirms a sense of control over their bodies and desires through journeys of self-exploration. These standpoints are often – but not always – informed by feminist and queer theory, and as such often consciously resist the power structures that represent these practices as aberrant. Resistance in these cases involves using both theory in daily life, and the body and its representation to celebrate S/M pleasures.

Gay S/M: new forms of pleasure?

As suggested throughout this chapter, there has been a tendency to treat the sexual categories that emerged in the nineteenth century as natural entities: historically fixed kinds of people. Even the above histories of the concepts of homosexuality and masochism fell into this historiographical trap by adopting psychiatry as a starting point for understanding experience, as if these are more real than the experiences of individuals. In order to briefly illustrate how to read beyond these psychiatric discourses, I will describe a variety of gay masochistic pleasure to show the multiplicity of practices that resist the categories forged by psychiatrists over a century ago. This standpoint derives much from Foucault's oft-quoted comment on S/M sex:

> I think that S/M is ... the actual creation of new possibilities of pleasure that one might never have imagined before ... The idea that physical pleasure is always a matter of sexual pleasure and the idea that sexual pleasure is the base of all possible pleasures is something that I think is truly something false. What S/M practices show us is that we can produce pleasure beginning with very strange objects and using certain bizarre parts of our bodies in very unusual situations.[63]

Around this description of new forms of pleasure, which are not transhistorical realities, but which emerged through very specific social practices, we can begin to undermine the singularity of both 'masochism' and 'homosexuality' (not all masochists are men into hard S/M play with other men, and not all homosexuals are either). Identity is not tied to a single category, and neither category adequately fits all practitioners. In the S/M scene, older ideas of sexual pleasure and gender that were central to nineteenth-century typographies of homosexual men (effeminacy, etc.) are rendered irrelevant, especially regarding performances of masculinity, as either dominant, and pain- and pleasure-giving (playing as a top) or as submissive or pain- and pleasure-receiving (playing as a bottom). In such scenes, emphasis is placed upon giving into and extending the body and pleasure – not on the 'identity' of the individual in the encounter. And it is important to note that nor are these roles enacted in S/M games necessarily fixed beyond the particular encounter – tops and bottoms in one scene can switch in different sexual encounters, seeking different pleasures.[64]

To illustrate these points, I will focus on a new form of pleasure, which is prevalent in, but not exclusive to, the gay scene: anal fisting. This practice had a recent emergence in the 1970s (although fisting had been described in Sade's *Philosphie dans le boudoir*, 1795). My observations stem from a conversation I had with two friends at a club just off Nollendorfplatz in Berlin in 2002. We discussed the now-common prevalence of fisting within these spaces, with anonymous men bent over pool tables covered in black latex sheets having hands inserted deep into their arses, and especially we discussed the increasingly younger ages of men who could 'take a fist'. Historically, this anecdote is interesting in precisely the ways that Foucault has described S/M: new forms of pleasure become new standards for 'being' a particular kind of gay man into S/M practices.

> What all these people are doing is not aggressive; they are inventing new possibilities of pleasure with strange parts of their body – through the eroticization of the body. I think it's ... a creative enterprise, which has as one of its main features what I call the desexualization of pleasure.[65]

Younger guys, my friends observed, were pushing themselves further. These practices are a good example of looping effects, with ideals being put into practice by an increasing number of people, except that the sanctions (and rewards) within the subcultures in which these practices are accepted activities are not determined according to psychopathology. Rather, it is the group of practitioners that determines what is acceptable, and increasingly provides spaces for these activities (leather bars, S/M saunas, *La Fistinière*, a hotel in France devoted to a gay male clientele into fisting). We do not find descriptions of this practice in the sexological texts, either under S/M or homosexuality. The fister and the person who can take a fist are new kinds of people; their achievements are of a particular social value within the community in which they engage in these practices (which are often, but not exclusively, performed in social spaces, such as clubs, hotels, and in pornographic films). They differ from both the gay man or lesbian who marries their lover and adopts a lifestyle that in many ways echoes traditional heterosexual (and heteronormative) relationships, as much as they differ from the heterosexual S/M couples using the dungeon equipment (slings, padded tables, revolving wheels for restraint; whips, crops, floggers for inflicting pain) for bondage and discipline scenes at fetish nights in clubs. When these people are indulging such pleasures, they are outside of psychiatric power.[66]

These bodily practices are an optimum site of resistance, in Foucault's sense. These people pay no heed to the categories that supposedly explain the self (to the subject, or to society), such as gender, or the classic descriptions of homosexuality or S/M. By playing in such ways, these categories are subverted. The man being fisted is no less masculine than the person pushing their hand into the soft folds of his rectum. If anything, the bottom is adopting many of the classical tropes of masculinity: an ability to come to terms with pain (when conquering it, rather than submitting to it), and the ability to use his body to actively seek pleasure. Yet at the same time, classical feminine tropes are also enacted: being penetrated, giving into the pleasures being forced upon him, etc. I am not here suggesting that the bottom in this scene is a kind of intersexual being, but rather that sexological categories are uselessly narrow for understanding this practice. Likewise the fister is also inadequately described in accepted sexological terms as active or dominant: while they are indeed pushing their hand(s) deep into their partner, and thus in a sense dominating them by forcing them to come to terms with extraordinary sensations, they are doing so in an extremely attentive, caring way, following the reactions of their partner in minute detail, allowing them to expand the boundaries of their bodies and pleasures. Neither of these people is focusing on a coital imperative to ejaculation; neither of them is adopting a typically gendered position. Yet it cannot be said that they are not engaging in the pursuit of pleasure. Their intimate, sexual bodies are sites of resistance. The categories they supposedly embody fail to adequately describe the scene.

Conclusions

This chapter has used two examples – homosexuality and masochism – to show the power embodied in sexological understandings of sexuality. It has also addressed practices of resistance. After describing the emergences of two sexological categories, homosexuality and masochism, and after suggesting points where these powerful psychopathological discourses are resisted, it was argued by focusing on recently emerged practices within the gay S/M community that sexological categories failed, because of the totalizing effects that they sought. The efforts of psychopathologists to set up categories such as homosexuality or masochism as fundamental to identity were selective constructs based on a commitment to unifying ideas of the individual based on a narrow view of sexual activity as fixed. Rather than accept these psychopathological categories, it was argued that gay S/M sex practices, such as fisting, problematized these categories. I am not trying to dismantle sexological reasoning just for the sake of it – but rather to show how resistance operates.

The problem is understanding this situation in relation to identity. Sexual identity – a political construct of both 'perverts' and their scientists – emerges from the adoption of these psychopathological categories, and from their resistance, as seen in the looping effects that can be traced through history. On the one hand, we see the positive effects of power – with psychiatric and other medical interventions (as well as legal and social sanctioning) used with people deemed to be perverse at different points in time. But on the other hand, these same people have ultimate control over how they use their bodies: for sex, to modify, to extend their pleasures. These new bodies – tattooed, pierced, ripped, adorned, and photographed for circulation on the Internet – are emerging from these historically entrenched interactions between discourses and pleasures, shattering psychiatric categories as they writhe in ecstasy, but it is unwise to imagine that these people are eternal, or that their practices, desires, acts, are stable or have a fixed meaning. They, too, will be washed away.

Notes

I would like to thank Chiara Beccalossi, Casey Gifford, Jennifer Burns Levin, Marissa Ochsner, Amanda Sordes, Eva Wong and students from Dr Levin's class on Obscene Literature at the Robert D. Clark Honors College at the University of Oregon (May 2011) for reading and discussing this paper with me. Your comments and criticisms helped a lot. Any faults are, of course, my own.

1 Havelock Ellis, 'Eonism' in *Studies in the Psychology of Sex*, vol. 7, Philadelphia: FA Davis & Co., 1928; Ivan Crozier 'Havelock Ellis, Eonism and the Patients' Discourse', *History of Psychiatry* 11, 2000, pp. 125–54.

2 David Halperin, *How to Do the History of Homosexuality*, Chicago: University of Chicago Press, 2002; Arnold Davidson, *The Emergence of Sexuality*, Cambridge, MA: Harvard University Press, 2002.

3 Georges Canguilhem, *The Normal and Pathological*, New York: Zone Books, 1989; for a study of this basic idea in sexual terms, see Jonathan Katz, *The Invention of Heterosexuality*, Chicago: University of Chicago Press, 2007; Elizabeth Stephens and Chad Parkhill, 'Heterosexuality: An Unfettered Capacity for Degeneracy' in Chiara Beccalossi and Ivan Crozier (eds), *A Cultural History of Sexuality in the Age of Empire*, Vol.5, Oxford: Berg, 2010, pp. 27–42.

4 Ian Hacking, 'Kinds of People: Moving Targets', *Proceedings of the British Academy* 151, 2007, pp. 285–318.

5 Michel Foucault, *History of Sexuality, Vol I: An Introduction* (*La volonté de savoir*), trans. Robert Hurley, New York: Pantheon, 1984 [1976], p. 43.

6 Ian Hacking, 'Making Up People' in *Historical Ontology*, Cambridge, MA: Harvard University Press, 2002.

7 Ivan Crozier, 'Pillow Talk: Credibility, Trust and the Sexological Case History', *History of Science* 46, 2008, pp. 375–404.

8 Carl Friedrich Otto Westphal, 'Die Conträre Sexualempfindung', *Archiv für Psychiatrie und Nervenkrankenheiten* 2, 1869–70, pp. 73–108; Cesare Lombroso and Guglielmo Ferrero, *Criminal Woman, the Prostitute, and the Normal Woman* [*La donna delinquente*], trans. and ed. Nicole Hahn Rafter and Mary Gibson, Durham, NC: Duke University Press, 2004; Havelock Ellis and John Addington Symonds, *Sexual Inversion*, introduced by Ivan Crozier, Basingstoke: Palgrave, 2008 [1897].

9 See David Horn, *The Criminal Body: Lombroso And The Anatomy Of Deviance*, New York: Routledge, 2003 for one of many studies on the embodiment of aberration.

10 Ivan Crozier, '"All the Appearances Were Perfectly Natural": The Anus of the Sodomite in Nineteenth-Century Medical Discourse' in Christopher E. Forth and Ivan Crozier (eds), *Body Parts: Critical Explorations in Corporeality*, Lanham, MD: Lexington Books, 2005.

11 For an overview of the emergence of sexology, see Davidson, *The Emergence of Sexuality*; Gert Hekma, '"A Female Soul in a Male Body": Sexual Inversion as Gender Inversion in Nineteenth-Century Sexology' in Gilbert Herdt (ed.), *Third Sex, Third Gender: Beyond Sexual Dimorphism in Culture and History*, New York: Zone Books, 1994, pp. 213–40; Crozier, 'Introduction' to Ellis and Symonds, *Sexual inversion*; Harry Oosterhuis, *Stepchildren of Nature*, Chicago: Chicago University Press, 1999.

12 Thomas Laqueur, *Making Sex: The Body and Gender from the Greeks to Freud*, Cambridge, MA: Harvard University Press, 1990; Ivan Crozier, 'Performing the Western Sexual Body after 1920' in Crozier (ed.), *Cultural History of the Human Body, 1920–Present*, vol. 6, Oxford: Berg, 2010, pp. 43–70.

13 Michel Foucault, *Archaeology of Knowledge*, trans. Alan Sheridan, New York: Pantheon Books, 1972.

14 In Martin Kusch's sense of an artificial kind. See his *Psychological Knowledge*, London: Routledge, 1995. For use of this theory in understanding the sexual body in the twentieth century, see Crozier, 'Performing the Sexual Body'. For Judith Butler, see *Gender Trouble*, London: Routledge, 1990 and *Bodies that Matter*, London: Routledge, 1992.

15 Ian Hacking, 'Making up People', *London Review of Books*, 17 August 2006.

16 Michel Foucault, 'Nietzsche, Genealogy, History' in the *Michel Foucault Reader*, ed. Paul Rabinow, London: Vintage, 1984.

17 See Arnold Davidson, 'Foucault, Psychoanalysis and Pleasure' in *Emergence of Sexuality*, pp. 209–15.

18 See Halperin, *How to Do the History of Homosexuality*.

19 Theo van der Meer, 'The Persecutions of Sodomites in Eighteenth-Century Amsterdam: Changing Perceptions of Sodomy' in Kent Gerard and Gert Hekma (eds), *The Pursuit of Sodomy: Male Homosexuality in Renaissance and Enlightenment Europe*, New York: Harrington Park Press, 1989, pp. 263–305; Sigmund Freud, 'Über die Psychogenese eines Falles von weiblicher Homosexualität' [The Psychogenesis of a Case of Homosexuality in a Woman], *International Zeitschrift für Psychoanalyse* 6:1, 1920, pp. 1–24; Steven Epstein, *Impure Science*, Berkeley: California University Press, 1997; Mark Davis, *Sex, Technology and Public Health*, Basingstoke: Palgrave, 2009.

20 Thomas Laqueur, *Solitary Sex*, New York: Zone Books, 2004; Ivan Crozier, '"Rough winds do shake the darling buds of May": a note on William Acton's conception of childhood sexuality', *Journal of Family History* 26, 2001, pp. 411–20.

21 Alfred Binet, *Le Fétichisme dans l'amour*, Paris: Octave Doin Editeur, 1888.

22 Hekma, 'A Female Soul in a Male Body'.

23 J. E. D. Esquirol, 'Érotomanie', *Dictionnaire des sciences médicales*, t. XIII, Paris: CLF Panckoucke, 1815, pp. 186–92; Forbes B. Winslow, *On obscure diseases of the brain and disorders of the mind*, London: John W. Davies, 1861.

24 Ambroise Tardieu, *Etude médico-légale sur les attentats aux mœurs*, Paris: Baillière, 1857; Johann Casper, 'Ueber Nothzucht und Paderastie und deren Ermittelung Seitens des Gerichtesarztes', *Vierteljahrschrift für gerichtliche und öffentliche Medizin* 1, 1852, pp. 21–78; Crozier, 'All the Appearances'; Vernon Rosario, 'inversion's Histories/history's Inversions' in Vernon Rosario (ed.), *Science and Homosexualities*, London: Routledge, 1997, pp. 89–107.

25 Wilhelm Griesinger, 'Vortrag zur Eröffnung der Psychiatrischen Klinik', *Archive für Psychiatrie und Nervenkrankheiten* 1, 1868, pp. 143–58.

26 Westphal, 'Die conträre Sexualempfindung'.

27 E.g. Oosterhuis, *Stepchildren of Nature*; Chiara Beccalossi, 'Female Same-sex Desires: Conceptualizing a Disease in Competing Medical Fields in Nineteenth-century Europe', *Journal of the History of Medicine and Allied Sciences* 67:1, 2012, pp. 7–35; Jennifer Terry, *An American Obsession*, Chicago: Chicago University Press, 2000.

28 At the same time, these discourses also provided resources by which homosexuals and other 'sexually aberrant' individuals could construct ideas about their own identities and desires, as Harry Oosterhuis has argued in *Stepchildren of Nature*.

29 Albert von Schrenck-Notzing, *Therapeautic Suggestion in Psychopathia Sexualis With Special Reference to Contrary Sexual Instinct*, trans. C. G. Chaddock, Philadelphia: F. A. Davis & Co, 1898; Lloyd Tuckey, *Psychotherapeutics: Or, Treatment by Hypnotism and Suggestion*, London: Ballière, Tindall and Cox, 1890.

30 See Frank Sulloway, *Freud: Biologist of the Mind*, Cambridge MA: Belknap Press, 1979; Ivan Crozier, 'Taking Prisoners: Havelock Ellis, Sigmund Freud, and the politics of constructing the homosexual, 1897–1951', *Social History of Medicine* 13, 2000, pp. 447–66.

31 See Sigmund Freud, *Three Essays on a Theory of Sexuality* in Sigmund Freud, *On Sexuality*, London: Penguin, 1977.

32 H. L. Minton, *Departing From Deviance*, Chicago: Chicago University Press, 2001; Michael King, 'Treatments of homosexuality in Britain since the 1950s – an oral history: the experience of professionals', *British Medical Journal* 328, 2004, p. 429.

33 For more on the hormonal body, see Chandak Sengoopta, *The Most Secret Quintessence of Life: Sex, Glands, and Hormones, 1850–1950*, Chicago: University of Chicago Press, 2006.

34 Minton, *Departing from Deviance*.

35 See Alfred Kinsey *et al.*, *Sexual Behaviour in the Human Male*, Philadelphia: W. B. Saunders, 1948; James Jones, *Alfred Kinsey: A life*, New York: Norton & Co, 1997.

36 Mary McIntosh, 'The Homosexual Role', *Social Problems* 16, 1968, pp. 182–92.

37 See Minton, *Departing From Deviance* for a recent history of homosexuality.

38 Timothy F. Murphy, *Gay Science: the ethics of sexual orientation research*, New York: Columbia University Press, 1997; Simon LeVay, *Gay, Straight, and the Reason Why*, Oxford: Oxford University Press, 2010; Garland Allen, 'The Double-Edged Sword of Genetic Determinism: Social and Political Agendas in Genetic Studies of Homosexuality, 1940–94' in Vernon A. Rosario (ed.), *Science and Homosexualities*, New York, London: Routledge, 1997, pp. 242–70.

39 Epstein, *Impure Science*.

40 These ideas are put most forcefully in Donatien Alphonse François de Sade, *Philosophie dans le boudoir*, 1795.

41 See Sade, *Justine*, 1787.

42 See Dorinda Outram, *The Body in the French Enlightenment*, New Haven: Yale University Press, 1989.

43 See Gilles Deleuze, *Coldness and Cruelty*, New York: Zone Books, 1991.

44 William Acton, *Functions and Disorders of the Reproductive Organs*, 3rd edn, London: John Murray, 1865. Since Johann Meibom, *A Treatise on the Use of Flogging in Medicine and Venery* (1639), a number of commentators have also discussed the use of flagellation as a sexual stimulant, but this is in terms of increasing blood flow to the genital area, rather than a psychopathological discussion of masochism, and so is outside the scope of the present study. For an analysis of early modern understandings of sexual flagellation see Sarah Toulalan, *Imagining Sex: Pornography and Bodies in Seventeenth-Century England*, Oxford: Oxford University Press, 2007, ch. 3.

45 Iwan Bloch, *Sexual Life in England*, Alfred Aldor: London, 1938.

46 S. V. Clevenger, 'Hunger: the Primitive Desire', *Science* 2, 15 January 1881, p. 14.

47 Clevenger, 'Hunger', p. 14. For similar ideas see Patrick Geddes and J. A. Thomson in their *Evolution of Sex*, London: Walter Scott, 1889, pp. 279–81.

48 S. V. Clevenger, *The Evolution of Man and his Mind*, Chicago: Evolution Publishing Co, 1903, pp. 333–47.

49 See Oosterhuis, *Stepchildren of Nature*; James Kiernan, 'Responsibility in Active Algophily', *Medicine*, April 1903.

50 Richard von Krafft-Ebing, *Psychopathia Sexualis*, trans. C. G. Chaddock, Philadelphia: FA Davis & Co, 1893, p. 115.

51 Charles Féré, *The Pathology of Emotions: Physiological and Clinical Studies*, trans. Robert Park, London: The University Press, 1899, p. 400.

52 Charles Féré, *Evolution and Dissolution of the Sexual Instinct*, 2nd edn, Paris: Charles Carrington, 1901, pp. 163–64.

53 The logic of this model has been effectively challenged by Deleuze, *Coldness and Cruelty*.

54 For an overview of sexological models of S/M, see Ivan Crozier, 'Philosophy in the English Boudoir: contextualising Havelock Ellis' discourses about sexuality, with particular reference to his writing on algolagnia', *Journal of the History of Sexuality* 13, 2004, pp. 275–305.

55 Havelock Ellis, *Love and Pain* in *Studies in the Psychology of Sex*, vol. III, Philadelphia: FA Davis & Co., 1903.

56 See John K. Noyes, *The Mastery of Submission*, Ithaca: Cornell University Press, 1997; Crozier, 'Philosophy in the English Boudoir'.

57 Robert Stoller, *Perversion: The Erotic Form of Hatred*, New York: Pantheon, 1975.

58 Cited in Noyes, *Mastery*, p. 16.

59 Cited in Noyes, *Mastery*, p. 23. The latest draft of this category for the DSM V (due to be published in 2013) is at: 'Sexual Masochism Disorder | Proposed Revision | APA DSM-5': http://www.dsm5.org/ProposedRevisions/Pages/proposedrevision.aspx?rid=187 (accessed 18 January 2011). This category is further discussed by Richard B. Krueger, 'The DSM Diagnostic Criteria for Sexual Masochism', *Archives of Sexual Behavior* 39, 2010, pp. 346–56. A powerful argument against the inclusion of the paraphilias in the DSM V is presented by Charles Moser and Peggy J. Kleinplatz, ' DSM-IV-TR and the Paraphilias: An argument for removal', *Journal of Psychology and Human Sexuality* 17, 2005, pp. 91–109.

60 Lisa Downing, 'The Measure of Sexual Dysfunction: A Plea for Theoretical Limitlessness', *Transformations: Region, Culture, Society*, Special Issue on 'Regions of Sexuality', ed. Iain Morland and Wendy O'Brien, 8 July 2004 at: [http://transformations.cqu.edu.au/journal/issue_08/article_02.shtml] (accessed on 5 March 2011).

61 See [http://en.wikipedia.org/wiki/Risk-aware_consensual_kink] (accessed on 5 March 2011).

62 See Gayle Rubin, 'Studying Sexual Subcultures: the Ethnography of Gay Communities in Urban North America' in Ellen Lewin and William Leap (eds), *Out in Theory: The Emergence of Lesbian and Gay Anthropology*, Urbana: University of Illinois Press, 2002, pp. 17–68; Noyes, *Mastery*.

63 Michel Foucault, *Dits et ecrits*, II, pp. 1556–57.

64 Gayle Rubin, 'Elegy for the Valley of the Kings: AIDS and the Leather Community in San Francisco, 1981–96' in Martin P. Levine, Peter M. Nardi and John H. Gagnon (eds), *In Changing Times: Gay Men and Lesbians Encounter HIV/AIDS*, Chicago: University of Chicago Press, 1997, pp. 101–44; James Miller, *The Passion of Michel Foucault*, New York: Basic Books, 1993; Keith Robinson, 'The Passion and the Pleasure: Foucault's Art of Not Being Oneself', *Theory, Culture & Society* 20, 2003, pp. 119–44.

65 Originally in an interview with Michel Foucault, 'Sex, Power and the Politics of Identity' conducted by B. Gallagher and A. Wilson in Toronto in June 1982. It appeared in *The Advocate*, 7 August 1984, pp. 26–30 and 58.

66 As Friedrich Nietzsche put it: 'one does not get over a passion: rather it is over *when* one is able to represent it.' Nietzsche, *Will to Power*, New York: Vintage Books, 1968, p. 431.

Part V

CLOTHING AND NAKEDNESS

9

FROM THE CRADLE TO THE GRAVE

Clothing the early modern body

Susan Vincent

Until relatively recently the study of dress in the past confined itself to explorations of changing styles and material composition, and histories of production and consumption. Examination of clothing's social and cultural meanings in historical context, and in particular their significance in the formation of embodied identities, emerged in the wake of sociological studies from the 1980s on, but are still relatively under-explored compared to other histories of the body and sexual identities. This chapter briefly examines the approaches to the subject taken by other scholars to date, and then turns to map some of the relationships between clothing and the body in early modernity: the importance of garments to good health, the intimate involvement of cloth and clothing in the experience of maturation and bodily transition, and the role of dress in the understanding and performance of gender. While the examples used here are primarily English, the map may equally be employed to navigate the conceptual terrain of other early modern societies in Europe, for while the specifics of fashion varied across borders, underlying dress practices and ways of conceptualizing the clothed – and unclothed – body reached over regional, political and religious divides.

The relatively recent appearance of dress within History belies an intellectual tradition that in Europe stretches back to the latter part of the sixteenth century and the appearance of illustrated costume books.[1] The discovery of the New World, a growing impulse towards the encyclopedic categorization of knowledge, and a fascination with the ancient, the unusual and the exotic, all combined to fuel the popularity of this new genre: costume books 'took their place in the gallery of marvels of nature and prodigies of human creation'.[2] Beginning with Cesare Vecellio's *Habiti Antichi, et Moderni di Tutto il Mondo* of 1598, some of these texts also included examples of historical dress.[3] Right from the start then, an antiquarian impulse established itself in relation to costume studies, and would prove to be of major importance.[4] From the seventeenth century onwards the researches of individual antiquaries not only constituted the field of knowledge, but the methodological approaches of future generations. Thanks to antiquaries who worked as engravers and painters, in time a link was also forged between costume studies and art. In the nineteenth century history painters in particular turned to published surveys of dress, evidencing a new desire for authenticity in historical recreation that was apparent also on the stage and which created an enduring association between costume studies, the theatre, and, more latterly, film and television. Interest in dress carried through into the twentieth century with unabated vigour,[5] and in the new millennium the republication of Cesare Vecellio's sixteenth-century costume book that over 400 years ago started the whole ball rolling, illustrates the field's astonishing longevity and continuing appeal.

Costume study thus forms an unbroken tradition, remarkable for its consistency of content and form. It was not a tradition, however, that found any favour within the newly developing profession of History, and in Anglophone scholarship particularly it was many years before the study of clothing found its way into History departments in any capacity at all. Under the influence of the Annales school, French historians were open earlier to the idea of dress forming an area of valid research, Fernand Braudel being one of the first to urge its significance, and Daniel Roche following with his masterful treatment of the clothing practices of the *Ancien Régime*.[6] Meanwhile in England, understandably given its long-held links with drawing and painting, the study of fashion within the academy instead developed with traditional art history.

There were two strands to this intellectual programme: the first dealing with representations of dress and concerned, often, with the dating of paintings; and the second, based on the study of artefacts in a museum context, dedicated to an understanding of the technological aspects of surviving garments.[7] In both strands of endeavour, dress has been presented as a decorative art and with little overt interpretation. The contribution of these object-based studies, in either the form of graphic representation or as material remains, is typified by the articles in the periodical *Costume*, the journal of the Costume Society. Most usually these are short, descriptive discussions of specific artefacts or presentations of archival documents (transcriptions of inventories, accounts and so on), which have put valuable source material into the public domain. Although the journal deals with a wide chronology, there is much that is relevant to the early modern period, and although primarily English, does include material of a wider European reach. Mention must be made at this point of the exemplary work by Janet Arnold, to whose knowledge of costume artefacts and their textual remains scholars are deeply indebted.[8] This approach to dress in history has therefore tended to produce scholarship of a detailed and descriptive nature.[9] As the discipline has moved away from connoisseurship and aesthetics, however, more analytical studies relating to dress have also emerged.[10] In line with this, *Costume*'s recent change of editor seems also to be shifting the tenor of this periodical towards more analysis and a greater consideration of dress artefacts within their cultural context.

While anthropology, sociology and psychology had meanwhile all turned their attention to costume and fashion, dress first made its appearance in history departments in economic analyses of textile production, and then later discussions of consumption.[11] *Textile History*, the journal of the Pasold Foundation, is a valuable site for studies of this nature. One aspect of clothing consumption of particular relevance to the period concerns the legal restraints on display and expenditure, known collectively as sumptuary laws, on which there is a substantial literature.[12] Studies of the cultural meanings attached to clothing, its role in the formation of identities and relationships, and its value as a window on society in general have, however, been much slower to come forth. Only in the last decade or so has a sudden flowering of scholarship in this area occurred, and even so the sixteenth and seventeenth centuries – with some notable exceptions[13] – remain a period of relative neglect when compared to the main focus on modernity. This concentration on the post-1700 period is reinforced by the curricula of institutions that teach fashion/dress studies, which seldom stray into an earlier chronology. The most significant journal in the area, *Fashion Theory: The Journal of Dress, Body and Culture*, has a very wide ethnic and geographical reach, but only infrequently ventures into early modernity. This is not a reflection of editorial policy, but of the nature of the majority of articles submitted. Even as recently as 2010 this oversight in cultural history has led to the dress and appearances of early modernity being described as a 'hitherto neglected subject'.[14] The future however looks more promising thanks to the recent upswing in the scholarship of material culture – a nexus of interest for historians, art historians, archaeologists and museum conservators alike. Although concerned with a wider field of study, clothes and the varying practices surrounding their making, (re)use and disposal occupy a significant position.[15] However, to date the biggest contribution to the discussion of the cultural significance of dress in the Renaissance, especially the relationship of clothes to embodied identity, has come from literary history. From the 1990s onwards, the politics and performance of gender and sexuality as expressed through the medium of clothing has proved a fertile ground for literary studies, with challenging and transgressive practices providing a particular lure for scholarly interest. Concentrating on textual representations of dress, primarily as expressed through dramatic writing and the theatre, this scholarship has approached the topic with a relish that matches the energy of much contemporary discussion.[16]

Although, then, there is an extremely long tradition of interest in the 'when' and 'what' of historical dress, in contrast to other disciplines the study of clothing is a relative late-comer to History, and a rare guest indeed in that branch of it concerned with the sixteenth and seventeenth centuries. However, the significance of this aspect of material culture – its relevance to issues of corporeality and sexuality under consideration in this volume – would be difficult to overestimate. While we are used to conceptualizing dress as a category that can be separate from wearers (as instanced, for example, by concepts like 'the clothing industry' and 'the fashion designer'), for early modernity dress was nearly always imagined in conjunction with the body.[17] Garments were not retailed in mass-produced and identical abundance, but were usually created or altered singly for individual wearers. Ownership was also relatively modest: most people had a small number of garments that were a familiar part of their social persona.[18] Dress was about corporeality in general, and specific garments could conjure specific bodies. The selection of these garments was also made with regard to prevailing norms of gender, health, decency, attractiveness and physical comfort. These norms, to return to the image with which we started, form a conceptual landscape to which we will now turn.

This exploration starts from the detail of a single point: a lone figure that stands in the midst of this conceptual landscape naked. When we picture this figure's nakedness, however, what exactly do we see? Probably, utilizing a binary opposition between being naked and being clothed, we imagine a figure that is entirely undressed. The choice is between either being clothed with garments or being naked without: you can have one or other, but not both. Scrutiny of the early modern language of nakedness, however, shows the concept to have been a much more variable construct. Instead of hinging on revelation or concealment, being clothed centred about a notion of *sufficiency*. Being insufficiently covered or equipped was to be naked, a state that thus changed in different contexts and might describe a bodily appearance that we would consider to be dressed.[19] As Sarah Toulalan has noted, even in pornographic images, what we term as nudity was depicted only infrequently, adding that in real life the complete removal of clothes was rare.[20]

From this understanding of nakedness we can step back for a wider view, to begin to appreciate the fundamental position of clothing in relation to the early modern body. For if being inadequately clad left one vulnerable – or 'naked' – the converse also applied.

Appropriate and sufficient clothing not only covered its wearers, it also sustained and protected them. Seen in this way, clothing was an ingredient in the recipe for well-being, a necessary pre-condition for welfare. Garments were not put on and cast off, but lived through, mediating an individual's experience of the surrounding world. A healthy, safe and attractive body was a body which was clothed. In the most fundamental terms, apparel guarded its wearer from environmental influences, helping to prevent him or her from becoming too hot, too cold, or too wet. It is easy for us to shrug aside the significance of this. Partly this is because the site of temperature regulation has now to a large extent been displaced from the immediate locus of the body to the wider surroundings of place and technology. With a push of a button buildings are either heated or cooled, the laundering and drying of garments is simple and quick, abundant hot water is to be had for the mere turning on of a tap, and even the European climate is without its former extremes of cold.[21] In Britain at least, this conspires to minimize the attention we pay, meteorologically, to what is going on around us. As the occasional extreme weather shows, we are surprised when the climate intrudes on the comfort and easy running of our lives. In addition to such changed material and meterological circumstances, the modern medical vision has further displaced apparel's significance for physical well-being. The humoural tradition that dominated early modern healthcare, however, was well alive to the protective properties of dress. In the struggle to balance the four internal humours the environment was a powerful influence, and with such external phenomena as temperature and weather profoundly affecting an individual's humoural balance and therefore health, the manipulation of clothing to warm and cool the body was a matter of common sense.[22] Garments were in fact the first line of defence against ill health.

What this meant in the practical day-to-day unfolding of people's lives is best glimpsed through documents like diaries and letters. In the autumn of 1622, for example, John Winthrop (1588–1649) wrote to his 16-year-old son studying at Trinity College, Dublin: 'You may line your gowne with some warm bayes […] and if you be not allreadye in a freese Jerkin, I wishe you to gett one speedylye, and how soeuer you clothe your self when you stirre, yet be sure to keepe warme when you studye or sleepe.'[23] This was not an overprotective parent unhelpfully micro-managing what should have been left well alone, but simply sound medical advice, and the consequences of ignoring it might, without exaggeration, prove fatal. 'When he was about fourteen daies old,' wrote gentry housewife Alice Thornton (1627–1707), 'my pretty babe broake into red spots, like the smale pox, and through cold, gotten by thinner clothing then either my owne experience or practice did accustom to all my children.'[24] This thin clothing, Alice decided, combined with the bitter weather of an extremely cold December, caused the child to fall seriously ill. Five days later little Christopher Thornton was dead.

I have suggested elsewhere that this conceptualization of clothing led it to become a means of self-medication, a way of manipulating the humours to prevent or even cure indisposition.[25] Available to all, it was an empowering strategy, being neither dependent on specialist knowledge nor beyond the reach of those of even quite modest means. If we turn to Sir William Vaughan's (c.1575–1641) self-help manual on health, therefore, we should not be surprised to find discussion of apparel. The text adopts a handy question-and-answer format, a kind of FAQ for seventeenth-century readers. One of the questions runs: 'Declare vnto me a daily Diet [i.e. course of life], whereby I may liue in health, and not trouble my selfe in Physicke.' 'I Will', writes Vaughan with a rhetorical flourish, before enumerating 16 points for healthy living. Two of Vaughan's first four recommendations involve cloth and clothing: rubbing the body with a linen cloth on first rising, and dressing in handsome garments appropriate to the season and comprising particular fabrics that will resist vermin and contagious airs.[26] Gervase Markham, author of the domestic manual *The English Housewife*, neatly summed up this relationship of garments to bodily well-being. In delineating the housewife's duties, he wrote that she ought to clothe her family 'outwardly and inwardly'. Outward garments were 'for defence from the cold and comeliness to the person': for protection therefore, and for an attractive appearance. Inwardly, and it is to this characteristic of clothing we will now turn, apparel was 'for cleanliness and neatness of the skin'.[27]

The basic inward, or under, garments were the shift for women (sometimes known as a smock, and later as a chemise), and for men the shirt and drawers. Shirts and shifts were voluminous garments, long-sleeved and extending in length anywhere from mid-thigh to mid-calf, and were nearly always made of linen. Functionally, as well as being softer on the skin than the, predominantly, woollen outer garments, underclothes served to absorb the body's sweat and other secretions. While the skin itself was washed rarely, personal linen was changed, or shifted, as often as circumstances allowed. For the poorer sort this might mean they had only one change available – a shirt or smock to wear, and one to launder. The very wealthy would have fresh linen every day. This 'dry wash' and the quality and cleanliness of personal linen was fundamental to hygiene and also, by extension, to manners and civility.[28] In addition, linen formed part of the routines of dental hygiene – 'take a linen cloath and rub your teeth well within and without, to take away the fumosity of the meat and yellownesse of the teeth'[29] – and was recommended as a rub for the body to warm it before exercise or as a daily practice on rising.[30] Finally, and it is understandable with garments so closely associated with the body and worn intimately next to the skin, linens carried an erotic promise, a significance that Daniel Roche has called linen's 'carnal value'.[31] Following exactly the same fashionable logic as hundreds of years later drives the display of bra straps or the waistbands of underpants, from the late fifteenth century shirts and shifts began to be glimpsed at the margins of the dressed body. At the neck and wrists, or perhaps seen teasingly through the slashes of outer garments, tantalizing scraps of white played with the idea of disclosure. In a society in which the body's surface was almost always covered, and being entirely without garments was rare, such partial revelation was rich in allusive possibilities, inviting the imagination to consider the reality of the body while keeping it still carefully hidden from view. These points of sensual significance, the halfway position between cloth and skin, sartorially speaking grew in importance, collars and cuffs of expensive garments becoming heavily and elaborately embroidered, with the small ruches of linen growing, eventually, into those decorative and detachable items known as ruffs and bands.

The gendered nature of the production of these garments is also worth noting. Unlike heavy outerwear tailored by men, the making of linen garments was almost always the province of the seamstress, either a professional or a needlewoman in her own home.[32] Irrespective of social status, in many households wives and sisters therefore made not only their own shifts, but also the shirts of their husbands and brothers (a practice that continued into the nineteenth century). Like the actual sewing, decorative embroidery could also be worked by the amateur or the professional.[33] Even elite women might, therefore, decorate their own and their family's undergarments with fancy work. The nature of this production could only deepen the significance of underclothing. The busy needle piercing the cloth, the garment resting on the lap: this was fabric touched by familiar hands and imbued with relationships.

As is becoming apparent, the relationship between clothing and the body in early modernity was dense with possibility. Whereas in western culture today bodies have their own visibility and logic, in the sixteenth and seventeenth centuries clothing acted much more as the body's proxy, mediating particularly between the realms of corporeal and social experience. We can see this in the way that cloth and clothing participated in the process of maturation, helping to frame the understanding and performance of bodily transitions. This started right at the beginning of the life cycle with the collection of childbed linens. In midwifery manuals the arrangement and ample supply of linen and cloths, so they could be changed as soon as they were soiled, forms the vital first stage in the preparations for a successful delivery.[34] For the expectant mothers themselves, this gathering of materials for the birthing process and the newborn was enormously significant. Female family members and friends were called on for contributions, so that the gathering of these practical items had also an emotional function, announcing the imminence of the birth, and readying both the mother and concerned others for the coming experience – a practical and a psychological preparation in one.[35] So fundamental was this that the absence or presence of cloth and clothing for the newborn could be used as evidence in cases where women were accused of infanticide: linens constituted material proof that a mother intended to care for the delivered child, rather than of disposing of it. When Sarah Nicholson was prosecuted 'for the Murder of her Male Bastard Child' in December 1719, she was acquitted following evidence from several witnesses that she had made preparations for the birth, including one witness who said 'that she saw the Child's Linnen', and another that she 'saw Linnen the next Day'.[36]

After the delivery, the new infant was cleaned, examined and swaddled, bound gently with soft cloths to ensure strong and straight growth (see Figure 9.1). Without the corrective of these cloth bindings, it was felt the vulnerable and pliant newborn was at risk of developing poorly, like a young plant which as it grows is trained against a stake and without which will either sag or snap. Midwifery practice might similarly swaddle

Figure 9.1 The Cholmondeley Ladies, British School seventeenth century, c. 1600–1610. © World History Archive/Alamy.

the post-partum mother, laying napkins over her belly, raising her pelvis with folded cloths and swathing her from the thighs to the abdomen.[37] The textual evidence is supported here by pictorial sources, for as Louis Haas has observed of Renaissance paintings that depict natal scenes, they all show 'an abundance of cloth present at the birth for washing, swaddling, and cleaning'.[38] Letters and recorded recollections suggest that clothing continued to play a fundamental part in understanding a child's development as he or she grew. These are private experiences, important only to the family, and although of no consequence in the greater scheme, they are moments of pride and hope for the individuals concerned. One such was when the swaddling bands of the newborn were unwrapped for good and the infant, now considered sturdy enough for its limbs to cope unaided, was dressed instead in petticoats. It was this event that clergyman Ralph Josselin (1617–83) was referring to when he wrote in his diary on 14 January 1663/4, 'this day Rebekah was coated, lord clothe us with the garments of thy righteousnes in Christ Jesus'.[39] Certainly a moment worthy of celebration that a new child had successfully negotiated those often perilous first weeks of life, which – as was sadly the case with Alice Thornton's baby – might easily also be their last. The actual moment of readiness for this transition was decided by a combination of personal judgement and community practice, rather than according to precise calendar reckoning. As the letters of Charlotte de la Tremoille in 1628 show, readiness could therefore be interpreted differently. The French wife of the Earl of Derby wrote: 'As for our little one he is very well [...] in this country children are short-clothed at a month or six weeks old. I am considered out of my senses that he is not yet short-coated.'[40] This therefore was a developmental milestone understood, or performed, sartorially.

There is one other such milestone that I want to touch on, which concerns the assumption of a gendered identity: the breeching of young boys. Occurring anywhere between 5 to 8 years old – again the milestone was not based on a simple calculation of age, but the judgement of the family – this was an especially important transition. In a society in which all youngsters were swaddled and then dressed in petticoats, childhood represented a kind of neuter category. There *were* distinguishing features between the garments of boys and girls[41] – though in portraits this is not always self-evident for modern viewers – but the obvious correspondence of their full skirts signifies a conceptual framework that categorized primarily according to age rather than sex. By being breeched, boys were able to stride, literally and metaphorically, away from this neuter category and into the realm of men. This supports the findings of historians who in looking at early modern understandings of life stages have identified the undifferentiated periods, gender-wise, of infancy and childhood, and also the ages relating to the attribution of gender-specific terms like 'boy', 'girl', 'lad', and 'maid'. It is significant that for males the use of these gendered descriptors correlates precisely with the typical age of breeching.[42] Family letters reveal that for many parents this was a moment of considerable pride. As Sir Henry Slingsby wrote of his wife's impatience to see their son Thomas in his new doublet and breeches, she 'had a desire to see him in ym [them] how proper a man he would be'.[43] To borrow Judith Butler's notion of gender as performative, something created and re-created daily through behaviour and appearance, in the early modern period breeches were an essential part of that performance, a manifestation of masculinity.[44]

While there are other significant moments of transition marked in some way by dress – the giving of gloves at a marriage, for instance, or the wearing of veils when women were churched after childbirth – I want to look briefly at the last event in the life cycle: death.[45]

Sartorially, this could almost be said to represent a return to life's anonymous beginnings. Certainly, all traces of individuality were removed as the body was washed and then wrapped, not in the linen bands of the newborn, but in the linen shroud of the newly dead.[46] Sometimes the shroud was made by using a sheet from the household store, but most often it was a separate commodity. By the last quarter of the seventeenth century it was even possible to purchase them as off-the-peg, ready-made items.[47] In Ian Mortimer's transcription of Berkshire probate accounts covering nearly 130 years straddling the seventeenth century, he found that in almost all of them the cost of the shroud or winding sheet was included among the funeral expenses, thus showing the item to have been purchased in some form, and not to have been made from existing household linen.[48] Using linen for dressing the body in death drew on the qualities with which this fabric was imbued: linen was decent, clean, intimate and comely.

In the interactions between body and dress mapped so far, clothing has been conceptualized as entirely beneficial, essential to physical well-being and present from the moment of birth to the moment of burial. Sometimes, however, apparel was dangerous; sometimes within the folds of fabric lurked terrible suffering. One such moment was during bouts of contagious sickness, especially the plague. In a Jekyll and Hyde inversion, at such times the intimate relationship between body and garments turned out to have its malevolent side, as absorbing disease from its wearers clothing invisibly spread the sickness further afield. An account of the plague outbreak of 1603 described the viciousness of some who, doomed to die, were determined to take others with them, and cast off garments like scraps of mortality, little pieces of wearable death:

> Here do they Gloues, and there they Garters fall
> Ruffs, Cuffs, & handkerchers, and such things
> They strow about, so to endanger all.[49]

Some fabrics were more prone to infection than others: porous, open weaves and soft, absorbent textiles like wool, fur and linen were more dangerous than the shiny, repellent surfaces of, for example, satins and leather.[50] This explains William Vaughan's advice above, that summer garments be made of such fabrics as will resist contagion and vermin. He advises silk for this purpose, or buff leather.[51] The role of apparel in the breeding and spread of disease was met head-on by Elizabeth's Privy Council in 1578, when it issued orders directing the national response to plague.[52] These measures set the pattern, and over the next 100 years or so were repeated in subsequent government orders, medical treatises and private advice. The orders, recognizing that the contagion was spread 'by the vse and handling of such clothes, bedding and other stuffe as hath bene worne and occupyed by the infected of this disease, during the time of their disease', required Justices of the Peace to seize this material and preferably incinerate it or, failing that, air the goods in an approved fashion. Guidance from physicians, appended to the orders, included instructions as to how this should be undertaken. In addition, this medical advice recommended as a preventative measure the perfuming of garments to keep them from being infected, and also advised after contact with anyone suspected of the plague, the changing of such apparel as had been worn.

A second danger in apparel manifested itself through the phenomenon of monstrous births.[53] This was a fairly common topos in early modern society, sometimes presented as a natural marvel, but at other times following an eschatological principle in which the sins of the fathers and mothers were visited upon the next generation. In an incarnation of thought, 'monstrous' beliefs – often false doctrine and irreligious lives – were made flesh as horribly misshapen offspring, doomed to die if not yet dead already. In one particular variation on this theme, lust for fashion is somatized in the particularity of the newborn's physical deformity: fleshy ruff-like growths about the neck, skulls squeezed to look like headdresses, waists malformed with grotesque farthingales of skin.[54] Although too great an interest in dress – usually labelled pride of apparel – was a moral rather than physical danger and monstrous birth accounts were sometimes clearly satirical warnings rather than serious reportage, it is interesting that discursively at least, they literalized the connection between spiritual and corporeal sickness and, quite literally, embodied the sartorial temptation.[55]

The tensions between 'good' apparel (comely, protective and cleansing) and 'bad' apparel (a conduit for physical and spiritual sickness) arise from a wider ambivalence about dress, an ambivalence that rests on the shaky foundations of clothing's origins. For apparel was the direct result of sin: in Eden, Adam and Eve existed in happy and unclothed innocence; it was only at the first bite of that fateful apple that they knew their nakedness and in shame sought to cover it. The first clothes therefore were the garments of guilt, and although in the post-Edenic wilderness clothing kept its wearers warm and decent, its very existence was only owing to humanity's big act of disobedience, their initial turning from God. This fundamental problem with the teleology of dress is glimpsed in other conflicting responses that it generated. Dressing the body in a comely and attractive fashion, for example, was both self-respecting and respectful of God, for the body was a divine creation, a gift to be cherished and, like all God's gifts, husbanded well. However, dressing the body was also merely decking a stinking sepulchre with the gaudy rags of shame, for all corporeal things were doomed to die and rot, and the body was but a charnel-house prison for the soul. Clearly there are very different attitudes to the body at work here and, by extension, two very different attitudes as to how it ought to be clothed.[56] Picking a cautious way between these positions led most commentators to pronounce that it was with *excessive* clothing that the fault lay. Dress that was excessively expensive, that exceeded an individual's rank, garments that were excessively fashionable or showy or immodest were the sorts of clothing to be abhorred, and the pursuit of which threatened society's civil and moral order. This, of course, opens up immense areas for discussion, and the evidence can be sought and followed in sumptuary legislation, sermons, church and state edits, and moral comment. Two points with regard to the body should be noted, however.

The first is that excessive clothing was an incitement to lust. Foregrounding the corporeal in what was already imbued with physicality, one could say that fashionable clothes, to subvert the saying, made a vice out of necessity. Dress of this sort was a sensual business: its forms and colour caught the eye, the sounds of rustling teased the ear, and its textures played with the touch. And beneath it lay the invisible promise of the body. Sometimes, with women's costume this promise became declaration, as in the low neck-lines of the early seventeenth century, or the exposed forearms of Caroline dress. These revelatory styles were the focus of repeated moral criticism, and attacks levelled from the pulpit charged them with immodesty and want of shame. The second point – and in the vocabulary of sixteenth- and seventeenth-century dress forms this made particular sense – is that excessive clothing refashioned the human body made in God's own image, and distorted it into something grotesque. Ruffs, farthingales and trunk hose – stylized

SUSAN VINCENT

Figure 9.2 Portrait of Mary Kytson, Lady Darcy of Chiche, later Lady Rivers, British School sixteenth century 1500–1599. Tate London.

garments that were padded, stiffened and extended with minimal reference to the body beneath – made a mockery of God's creation (see Figures 9.2 and 9.3). This was a satanic and monstrous remaking.

Again, this aspect of dress excited energetic and appalled complaint, and was voiced through texts as different as sermons and sumptuary laws. One particular perversion of form involved the confusion of gender. For if garments contributed so much to the normative performance of masculinity and femininity – as glimpsed, for example, in the ritual of breeching – then the wrong clothes perverted that performance and ushered in the effeminate man and the manly woman (see Figure 9.4). In the most extreme act of sartorial conjuring, these combined, in text at least, to form the monstrous hermaphrodite.[57] As the future Archbishop of York John Williams (1582–1650) complained in his 1619 sermon on apparel, God had divided male and female but the devil had joined them, creating '*mulier monstrosa supernè*, halfe man halfe woman'.[58] Some scholars, in looking at Renaissance society, have suggested that the ubiquity of the hermaphroditic figure (intersexed or transvestite) indicated a widespread unease about gender and sexuality, especially the fear that these categories were unstable and under threat.[59] In the context of complaints about dress, however, I feel they reveal rather the anxieties of an essentialist position assailed by the ability of clothing to shock and mislead.

172

Figure 9.3 Robert Dudley, 1st Earl of Leicester, unknown artist, oil on panel, c. 1575, NPG 447. © National Portrait Gallery, London.

The garments that provoked moral condemnation were those that were conspicuously unnecessary, or that borrowed motifs or accessories usually associated with the opposite sex: ruffs set with coloured starch; women's bodices that in look resembled male doublets; hair that on women was too short and on men too long; men with fans or ribbon knots, and women with feathered hats or perhaps carrying small knives (see Figure 9.4). These were fashionable forms that pushed at the boundaries of acceptability and forced a confrontation with more traditionally gendered appearances.

The worry was not that sexed bodies were in reality mutable, but that appearances no longer clearly mirrored the truth beneath. It is the disruption of the sign that is at stake, not a fear that the sign may, upon examination, prove to be empty.[60] If in doubt, one has only to look at authority's response to rare cases of real cross-dressing, instances where men, but more usually women, have attired themselves in the specific and usually humble garments of a member of the opposite sex.[61] Such cases were generally punished as a challenge to morals and good order, though in certain life-threatening situations the cross-dressing stratagem was a perfectly acceptable way of avoiding detection, particularly if the cross-dresser was of elite status – and here we might think of the young Duke of York, the future James II, escaping England in the Civil War dressed as a gentlewoman in mohair skirts with an under petticoat of scarlet.[62] Either way, however, such real-life instances provoked neither moral panic nor the language of monstrosity and hermaphroditism. Censure of this sort was reserved for flagrant, disrespectful, 'in-your-face' dress that played with traditionally gendered motifs and accessories as a matter of fashion.

Figure 9.4 Frontispiece to *Haec-Vir; Or, The Womanish-Man.* Courtesy of the British Library.

This essentialist desire of early modernity to inscribe the inner truth on the outer form is evident in other areas of culture: its juridical branding and maiming punishments, for example, and also in the provisions of sumptuary laws that, above all other things, sought to regulate appearance according to social rank. But this distrust of disguise was also, paradoxically, what made disguise possible – for the masking of identity presupposed that a stable and knowable identity existed in the first place. As a motif, disguise typifies Renaissance drama, but it also figures remarkably frequently in real-life accounts of secret ventures and escapes. In memoirs and letters borrowed clothes and false beards happen along more often than one might imagine, as king transforms to commoner, and men and women exchange positions.

As well as being fundamental to the contemporary experience of the body, it will be clear by now that dress overlapped with many other aspects of culture. Like a thread in a garment, discursively apparel ran through many assumptions and debates: about social relationships, personal and group identities, religious belief, theology, economic enterprise, and moral and civic order. Given its overt, declared significance – arguably more than in any other period – the relative paucity of secondary literature is striking. There are many areas where scholars have only just begun to venture, and, in terms of the relation-ship of apparel to embodied experience, there are very few pathways indeed. The areas sketched in this chapter, for instance – the interactions between dress and health, the use of garments to articulate physical and maturational transitions, the dangers of dress – have hardly been acknowledged, let alone adequately charted. Other dimensions are equally, if not more, mysterious: the somatic experience of historical dress, for one – the impact and implications of its weight, feel, sound and sight.[63] If the past is a foreign and fascinating country, then so are the ways in which it was clothed.

Notes

1 Ulrike Ilg, 'The Cultural Significance of Costume Books in Sixteenth-Century Europe' in Catherine Richardson (ed.), *Clothing Culture, 1350–1650*, Aldershot: Ashgate, 2004, pp. 29–47.
2 Daniel Roche, *The Culture of Clothing: Dress and Fashion in the 'ancien régime'*, trans. Jean Birrell, Cambridge: Cambridge University Press, 1994, p. 12.
3 Tawny Sherrill, 'Who was Cesare Vecellio? Placing *Habiti Antichi* in Context' in Robin Netherton and Gale R. Owen-Crocker, *Medieval Clothing and Textiles* 5, Woodbridge: The Boydell Press, pp. 161–88. For the most recent edition of Vecellio's text, see Margaret F. Rosenthal and Ann Rosalind Jones, *The Clothing of the Renaissance World: Europe, Asia, Africa, The Americas; Cesare Vecellio's Habiti Antichi et Moderni*, London: Thames and Hudson, 2008.
4 Aileen Ribeiro, 'Antiquarian Attitudes – Some Early Studies in the History of Dress', *Costume* 28, 1994, pp. 60–70. Also on the early development of costume studies, Valerie Cumming, *Understanding Fashion History*, London: Batsford, 2004.
5 Notable are C. Willett and Phillis Cunnington's Handbooks of English Costume for the sixteenth and seventeenth centuries, published by Faber in various reprints.
6 Fernand Braudel, *Civilisation and Capitalism 15th–18th Century*, trans. Siân Reynolds, vol. 1 *The Structures of Everyday Life: The Limits of the Possible*, London: Collins, 1981; Roche, *Culture of Clothing*; also Philippe Perrot, *Fashioning the Bourgeoisie: A History of Clothing in the Nineteenth Century*, trans. Richard Bienvenu, Princeton: Princeton University Press, 1994.
7 See Jennifer Harris, 'Costume History and Fashion Theory: Never the Twain Shall Meet?', *Bulletin of the John Rylands University Library of Manchester* 77, 1995, pp. 73–79 (73).
8 Janet Arnold, *Queen Elizabeth's Wardrobe Unlock'd*, Leeds: Maney, 1988; and her *Patterns of Fashion* volumes. More recently Maria Hayward's *Dress at the Court of King Henry VIII*, Leeds: Maney, 2007 and *Rich Apparel: Clothing and the Law in Henry VIII's England*, Farnham: Ashgate, 2009.
9 Including Jane Ashelford, *Dress in the Age of Elizabeth I*, London: Batsford, 1988 and *The Art of Dress: Clothes and Society 1500–1914*, London: The National Trust, 1996; Avril Hart and Susan North, *Historical Fashion in Detail: The 17th and 18th Centuries*, London: V&A Publications, 1998.
10 Including Aileen Ribeiro, *Fashion and Fiction: Dress in Art and Literature in Stuart England*, New Haven and London: Yale University Press, 2005. Art historian Evelyn Welch's contributions include her leadership of two research networks: The Early Modern Dress and Textiles Research Network, <http://www.earlymoderndressandtextiles.ac.uk>; and Fashioning the Early Modern: Creativity and Innovation in Europe, 1500–1800, a collaborative project involving the V&A and the Universities of Stockholm, Copenhagen and Helsinki <http://www.fashioningtheearlymodern.ac.uk/>.
11 There is a large literature concerning textile production in the early modern period. As a starting point see the summaries and bibliography in David Jenkins (ed.), *Cambridge History of Western Textiles*, 2 vols, Cambridge: Cambridge University Press, 2003. Key texts looking more to the production and consumption of garments include Margaret Spufford, *The Great Reclothing of Rural England: Petty Chapmen and their Wares in the Seventeenth Century*, London: Hambledon Press, 1984; Joan Thirsk, *Economic Policy and Projects: The Development of a Consumer Society in Early Modern England*, Oxford: Clarendon Press, 1978. For the long eighteenth century, see Beverly Lemire, *Fashion's Favourite: The Cotton Trade and the Consumer in Britain, 1660–1800*, Oxford: Pasold Research Fund and Oxford University Press, 1991, and *Dress, Culture and Commerce: The English Clothing Trade before the Factory, 1660–1800*, Basingstoke: Macmillan, 1997; Giorgio Riello, *A Foot in the Past: Consumers, Producers and Footwear in the Long Eighteenth Century*, Oxford: Pasold Research Fund and Oxford University Press, 2006; John Styles, *The Dress of the People: Everyday Fashion in Eighteenth-Century England*, New Haven and London: Yale University Press, 2007.
12 Including Wilfrid Hooper, 'The Tudor Sumptuary Laws', *English Historical Review* 30, 1915, pp. 433–49; Frances Elizabeth Baldwin, *Sumptuary Legislation and Personal Regulation in England*, Baltimore: Johns Hopkins University Press, 1926; N. B. Harte, 'State Control of Dress and Social Change in Pre-industrial England' in D. C. Coleman and A. H. John (eds), *Trade, Government and Economy in Pre-Industrial England*, London: Weidenfeld and Nicolson, 1976, pp. 132–65; Alan Hunt, *Governance of the Consuming Passions: A History of Sumptuary Law*, London: Macmillan, 1996; Hayward, *Rich Apparel*.

13 Including Christopher Breward, *The Culture of Fashion: A New History of Fashionable Dress*, Manchester: Manchester University Press, 1995; Ann Rosalind Jones and Peter Stallybrass, *Renaissance Clothing and the Materials of Memory*, Cambridge: Cambridge University Press, 2000; Susan Vincent, *Dressing the Elite: Clothes in Early Modern England*, Oxford: Berg, 2003; Richardson, *Clothing Culture*, see esp. summary of historiography, pp. 1–19; Ulinka Rublack, *Dressing Up: Cultural Identity in Renaissance Europe*, Oxford: Oxford University Press, 2010. The *Medieval Clothing and Textiles* series, ed. Robin Netherton and Gale R. Owen-Crocker, The Boydell Press, overlaps with the sixteenth century (volumes published annually since 2005). Note the stated intention for a subsidia series on medieval and early modern dress and textiles, Preface to Volume 5, 2009, p. xi.

14 Rublack, *Dressing Up*, p. xx.

15 E.g. Tara Hamling and Catherine Richardson (eds), *Everyday Objects: Medieval and Early Modern Material Culture and its Meaning*, Farnham: Ashgate, 2010.

16 Including Jones and Stallybrass, *Renaissance Clothing*; Peter Stallybrass, 'Worn Worlds: Clothes and Identity on the Renaissance Stage' in Margreta de Grazia, Maureen Quilligan and Peter Stallybrass (eds), *Subject and Object in Renaissance Culture*, Cambridge: Cambridge University Press, 1996, pp. 289–320; Stephen Orgel, *Impersonations: The Performance of Gender in Shakespeare's England*, Cambridge: Cambridge University Press, 1996; Laura Levine, *Men in Women's Clothing: Anti-Theatricality and Effeminization 1579–1642*, Cambridge: Cambridge University Press, 1994; Jean E. Howard, 'Cross-dressing, the Theatre, and Gender Struggle in Early Modern England' in Lesley Ferris (ed.), *Crossing the Stage: Controversies on Cross-Dressing*, London: Routledge, 1993; Lisa Jardine, *Still Harping on Daughters: Women and Drama in the Age of Shakespeare*, 2nd edn, New York and London: Harvester Wheatsheaf, 1989; Will Fisher, *Materializing Gender in Early Modern English Literature and Culture*, Cambridge: Cambridge University Press, 2006; Amanda Bailey, *Flaunting: Style and the Subversive Male Body in Renaissance England*, Toronto: University of Toronto Press, 2007.

17 A point Rublack also makes, *Dressing Up*, p. 31.

18 The middling sort probably had two or three sets of clothes: Maria Hayward, 'A Shadow of a Former Self: Analysis of an Early Seventeenth-Century Boy's Doublet from Abingdon' in Hamling and Richardson, *Everyday Objects*, pp. 107–18 (108).

19 See also Lucy Gent, '"The Rash Gazer": Economies of Vision in Britain, 1550–1660' in Lucy Gent (ed.), *Albion's Classicism: The Visual Arts in Britain, 1550–1660*, New Haven and London: Paul Mellon and the Yale Centre for British Art, 1995, p. 381.

20 Sarah Toulalan, *Imagining Sex: Pornography and Bodies in Seventeenth-Century England*, Oxford: Oxford University Press, 2007, esp. pp. 233, 262–65.

21 Brian M. Fagan, *The Little Ice Age: How Climate Made History 1300–1850*, New York: Basic Books, 2000.

22 Mary Lindemann, *Medicine and Society in Early Modern Europe*, Cambridge: Cambridge University Press, 1999; Andrew Wear, *Knowledge and Practice in English Medicine, 1550–1680*, Cambridge: Cambridge University Press, 2000; Roy Porter, *Disease, Medicine and Society in England, 1550–1860*, 2nd edn, Cambridge: Cambridge University Press, 1993.

23 John Winthrop, *Winthrop Papers Vol. 1 1498–1628*, Massachusetts: Massachusetts Historical Society, 1929, p. 276, 16 October 1622. Bays and frieze were both warm woollen fabrics.

24 Alice Thornton, *The Autobiography of Mrs. Alice Thornton*, Durham: Surtees Society, vol. 62, 1875, p. 166. This occurred in 1667.

25 Susan J. Vincent, *The Anatomy of Fashion: Dressing the Body from the Renaissance to Today*, Oxford: Berg, 2009, pp. 153–54.

26 Sir William Vaughan, *Approved directions for health, both naturall and artificiall*, London: T. S[nodham] for Roger Iackson, 1612, p. 143.

27 Gervase Markham, *The English Housewife* (1615), ed. M. R. Best, Montreal: McGill–Queen's University Press, 1986, p. 146.

28 Georges Vigarello, *Concepts of Cleanliness: Changing Attitudes in France since the Middle Ages*, trans. Jean Birrell, Cambridge: Cambridge University Press, 1988. On linen generally, see Roche, *Culture of Clothing*, pp. 151–83; Kathleen Brown, *Foul Bodies: Cleanliness in Early America*, New Haven: Yale University Press, 2009, esp. pp. 26–32, 98–117.

29 Girolamo Ruscelli, *The secretes of the reuerende Maister Alexis of Piemount*, London: Iohn Kingstone for Nicolas Inglande, 1558, fol. 83v; Vaughan, *Approved directions for health*, p. 144.

30 See Thomas Elyot, *The castel of helth*, London: Thomae Bertheleti, 1539, sig. G1r–v, fol. 49r–v; or Vaughan, *Approved directions for health*, p. 143.

31 Roche, *Culture of Clothing*, p. 154.

32 On the professional seamstress, Naomi Tarrant, see *The Development of Costume*, Edinburgh: National Museum of Scotland, 1994, pp. 116–24.

33 For the classic feminist account of embroidery, see Rozsika Parker, *The Subversive Stitch: Embroidery and the Making of the Feminine*, rev. edn, London: The Woman's Press, 1996.

34 *Aristotle's compleat and experienc'd midwife*, London: n.p., 1700, p. 59; Jane Sharp, *The Midwives Book*, London: Simon Miller, 1671, p. 187. On delivery and lying-in, including the use of linen, see Doreen Evenden, *The Midwives of Seventeenth-Century London*, Cambridge: Cambridge University Press, 2000, pp. 79–86; Adrian Wilson, 'The Ceremony of Childbirth and its Interpretation' in Valerie Fildes (ed.), *Women as Mothers in Pre-Industrial England*, London: Routledge, 1990, pp. 68–107, esp. 70–83; David Cressy, *Birth, Marriage and Death: Ritual, Religion and the Life-Cycle in Tudor and Stuart England*, Oxford: Oxford University Press, 1997, pp. 80–84.

35 Cressy, *Birth, Marriage and Death*, pp. 50–51.

36 *The Proceedings on the King's Commission of the Peace, and Oyer and Terminer, and Goal-Delivery of Newgate, held for the City of London, and County of Middlesex, at Justice-Hall in the Old Bayly*, 10 December 1719, p. 12. My thanks to Sarah Toulalan for this information.

37 Sharp, *Midwives Book*, p. 210. On swaddling's corrective power, Georges Vigarello, 'The Upward Training of the Body' in Michel Feher, Ramona Naddaff and Nadia Tazi (eds), *Fragments for a History of the Human Body*, 3 vols, New York: Zone, 1989, vol. II, pp. 148–99 (171).

38 Louis Haas, *Renaissance Man and his Children: Childbirth and Early Childhood in Florence 1300–1600*, Basingstoke and London: Macmillan, 1998, p. 100. Also Jacqueline Marie Musacchio, *The Art and Ritual of Childbirth in Renaissance Italy*, New Haven: Yale University Press, 1999, esp. pp. 8, 47.

39 *The Diary of Ralph Josselin 1616–1683*, ed. Alan Macfarlane, Records of Social and Economic History, new series 3, London: Oxford University Press, 1976, p. 504.

40 Quoted in Phillis Cunnington and Anne Buck, *Children's Costume in England 1300–1900*, London: A. & C. Black, 1965, p. 69. Short coats referred to the petticoats of young children, which reached to their feet, p. 68.

41 On the detail of this, see Cunnington and Buck, *Children's Costume*.

42 Paul Griffiths, *Youth and Authority: Formative Experiences in England 1560–1640*, Oxford: Clarendon Press, 1996, pp. 24–25.

43 Quoted in Cunnington and Buck, *Children's Costume*, p. 71.

44 Judith Butler, *Gender Trouble: Feminism and the Subversion of Identity*, New York: Routledge, 1990.

45 While only here considering the dressing of the deceased, mourners had a large and complicated sartorial vocabulary of their own to help them manage the process of mortality and grieving. Claire Gittings, *Death, Burial and the Individual in Early Modern England*, London: Croom Helm, 1984; Julian Litten, *The English Way of Death: The Common Funeral Since 1450*, London: Robert Hale, 1991; Nigel Llewellyn, *The Art of Death: Visual Culture in English Death Ritual c.1500–c.1800*, London: Reaktion, 1991; Ralph Houlbrooke, *Death, Religion, and the Family in England, 1480–1750*, Oxford: Clarendon Press, 1998.

46 Cressy has also noted the parallels between swaddling a child and winding a corpse: *Birth, Marriage and Death*, pp. 428–29.

47 Litten, *English Way of Death*, pp. 72, 74.

48 Ian Mortimer, *Berkshire Probate Accounts, 1583–1712*, Reading: Berkshire Record Society, 1999, pp. 83, 106, 121.

49 John Davies, 'The triumph of death: or, the picture of the plague; according to the life, as it was in Anno Domini. 1603' in *Humours Heau'n on Earth*, London: A[dam] I[slip], 1609, p. 4.

50 Wear, *Knowledge and Practice*, p. 329.

51 Vaughan, *Approved directions for health*, p. 143.

52 *Orders, thought meete by her Maiestie, and her priuie Councell, to be executed throughout the counties of this realme, in such townes, villages, and other places, as are, or may be hereafter infected with the plague*, London: Christopher Barker, 1578. See Paul Slack, *The Impact of Plague in Tudor and Stuart England*, London: Routledge and Kegan Paul, 1985.

53 David Cressy, *Travesties and Transgressions in Tudor and Stuart England: Tales of Discord and Dissension*, Oxford: Oxford University Press, 2000, pp. 29–50.

54 H.B., *A true discripcion of a childe with ruffes borne in the parish of Micheham*, London: Iohn Allde and Richarde Iohnes, 1566; Anon., *A true relation of the birth of three monsters … in Flanders*, London: n.p., 1609; Anon., *A wonder vvorth the reading*, London: William Iones, 1617.

55 Anon., *Prides fall: or, A warning for all English women*, London: F. Coles, T. Vere and W. Gilbertson, n.d.; repr. between 1658–64; repr. F. Coles, T. Vere and I. Wright, 1663–74, and 1700.

56 On these different strands in contemporary Christian thought see J. W. Blench, *Preaching in England in the Late Fifteenth and Sixteenth Centuries*, Oxford: Basil Blackwell, 1964; and Frank Bottomley, *Attitudes to the Body in Western Christendom*, London: Lepus Books, 1979.

57 See Lorraine Daston and Katherine Park, 'The Hermaphrodite and the Orders of Nature: Sexual Ambiguity in Early Modern France' in Louise Fradenburg and Carla Freccero (eds), *Premodern Sexualities*, New York: Routledge, 1996, pp. 117–36; Ruth Gilbert, *Early Modern Hermaphrodites*, Basingstoke: Palgrave, 2002; Kathleen P. Long, *Hermaphrodites in Renaissance Europe*, Aldershot: Ashgate, 2006.

58 John Williams, *A sermon of apparel*, London: Iohn Bill, 1620, p. 7.

59 Levine, *Men in Women's Clothing*; Howard, 'Cross-Dressing'; Daston and Park, 'The Hermaphrodite'.

60 For more on this and cross-dressing see Vincent, *Dressing the Elite*, pp. 153–88.

61 Cross-dressing is further explored in Rudolf Dekker and Lotte van der Pol, *The Tradition of Female Transvestism in Early Modern Europe*, Basingstoke and London: Macmillan, 1989. A transcription of 13 cases from the Repertories of the Aldermen's Court of London and the Minute Books of Bridewell Hospital are included as an appendix to Michael Shapiro, *Gender in Play on the Shakespearean Stage: Boy Heroines and Female Pages*, Ann Arbor: University of Michigan Press, 1994. F. G. Emmison's work with church courts has thrown up a few cases: *Elizabethan Life II: Morals and Church Courts*, Chelmsford: Essex County Council, 1973. Other documented cases are discussed in David Cressy, 'Gender Trouble and Cross-Dressing in Early Modern England', *Journal of British Studies* 35, 1996, pp. 438–65; Patricia Crawford and Sara Mendelson, 'Sexual Identities in Early Modern England', *Gender and History* 7, 1995, pp. 363–77; and Stephen Greenblatt, 'Fiction and Friction' in Thomas Heller, Morton Sosna and David E. Wellbery, *Reconstructing Individualism: Autonomy, Individuality, and the Self in Western Thought*, Stanford: Stanford University Press, 1986, pp. 30–52.

62 *The Memoirs of Anne, Lady Halkett and Ann, Lady Fanshawe*, ed. John Loftis, Oxford: Clarendon Press, 1979, pp. 24–25.

63 Donald Clay Johnson and Helen Bradley Foster (eds), *Dress Sense: Emotional and Sensory Experiences of the Body and Clothes*, Oxford: Berg, 2007, represents a beginning, although the historical reach of this anthropological text is mostly confined to a period accessible through living memory.

10

EXPOSING, ADORNING, AND DRESSING THE BODY IN THE MODERN ERA

Paul R. Deslandes

In a 1978 article that appeared in the British socialist magazine, *Gay Left*, Gregg Blachford, while giving voice to emerging feminist critiques of pornography, also recognized the pleasures and political functions of looking and scrutinizing the unclothed, sexualized body. With reference to his first experience of viewing a gay pornographic magazine, he notes:

> I remember the very exciting feeling I got when I first saw one of these magazines before I came out. There I saw men kissing and holding and loving each other; something that I never thought possible as the mainstream culture manifests itself in overwhelmingly heterosexual and macho terms. It was proof of a homosexual community and it was through porn that I learned of its existence.[1]

Contained in this brief statement are a number of useful assertions that remind us that the acts of viewing, consuming, clothing, and undressing the body in the modern visual age have been vitally important to the articulation of desire, understandings of the gendered self, and the formation of modern sexual identities.

The complexities of looking at the body have, in fact, generated intense interest over the past several decades among historians, art historians, literary critics, and film studies scholars, to mention but a few of the academic disciplines affected by this turn toward the human body. In her, now famous, essay from 1975, the cinema scholar Laura Mulvey utilizes the psychoanalytic theories of both Sigmund Freud and Jacques Lacan and the lens of feminism to describe the experience of viewing films. In its simplest formulation, her work establishes that the acts of looking and of being looked at (what Freud defined as scopophilia) are pleasurable.[2] Cinema, like the many other forms of visual culture that will be discussed below, focuses the attention of the viewer on the 'human face, the human body, [and] the relationship between the human form and its surroundings', an emphasis on looking that is both erotic and constitutive of conceptions of the self.[3] Mulvey's most significant, and most controversial, insight in this work articulates the distinctions between the active male gaze and the passive female subject: 'The determining male gaze projects its phantasy on to the female figure which is styled accordingly.'[4] Women as erotic objects (for both characters in films and spectators) function for Mulvey then as a central narrative trope and key marker of gender difference in movies.

Mulvey's work, like most influential scholarly concepts, has sparked considerable debate. In a 1989 article by Edward Snow, the monolithic nature of Mulvey's conceptualization of the male gaze, and that of other feminist scholars, was scrutinized closely. While Snow recognizes the merits of Mulvey's position, he questions the use of the term 'male' as 'almost entirely negative' and argues that '[a]t times it seems ... that the female can function for the male only as an object of sadistic spectatorial possession.'[5] In rethinking feminist ideas about the male gaze, Snow turns to a reading of Diego Velazquez's (1599–1660) painting, *The Toilet of Venus*, or *Rokeby Venus* (1647–51), arguing that in this rendering of the reclining female nude the subject's back is to the sitter and her face is obscured, appearing only as a reflection in a mirror into which she gazes to examine her own body and, in Snow's analysis, the viewer. This perspective forces a reconceptualization of the differences between viewer and viewed and the distinctions between male and female audience and subject. Similar attempts have been made to revise Mulvey's theory by individuals working within her own field – film studies. In his 1995 study of British and American popular culture, *Male Myths and Icons: Masculinity in Popular Culture*, Roger Horrocks argues that men frequently function as spectacles in popular films and that the 'male body is considerably fetishized in cinema.'[6] Recent work, informed by insights from queer studies, has also reminded us that the gaze could operate between members of the same sex when, for example, queer men celebrated the aesthetics of guardsmen in mid-twentieth-century Britain or women fetishized and eroticized fashion plates and dolls in the Victorian age.[7]

Building on some of these interventions, this chapter focuses on the acts of looking at and displaying the body in modern western culture. With an emphasis on the nude in art and the relationship between dress and personal identities or subjectivities, it seeks to both highlight some crucial developments in this field of study and provide some of the insights that I have been able to draw from my own research on the history of male beauty and masculine self-fashioning in Britain from the 1840s to the present. In so doing, this chapter seeks to establish several overarching arguments. First, it asserts that the richness of this particular area of study is rooted, to a very large degree, in both its interdisciplinarity and its simultaneous reliance on textual evidence, material artifacts, and visual culture for source material; a situation that highlights the multidimensionality of the European past and the diversity of approaches taken in exploring the twinned histories of self-presentation and the manipulation of the body. Its second, and most important, argument asserts the primacy of the relationship between bodily presentation and adornment of the body as essential performative gestures in the articulation of modern gender and sexual subjectivities.[8] Narratives about nakedness and the fashioned body, as we shall see below, are intimately connected to ideas about the gendered and sexed body. In fact, historians who ignore issues of appearance and the materiality (in terms of fashion accessories, clothing, and other types of artifacts) of gender and sexuality run the risk of constructing incomplete analyses that ignore the complexity of these immensely important areas of human subjectivity.[9] In addition to arguing for the centrality of these topics to all considerations of gender and sexuality in the modern period, this chapter also illustrates how the scholarly attention associated with looking at the body helps to transform our understanding of the Enlightenment, the rise of industrial capitalism, imperialism, war, and the articulation of modern sexual subjectivities, to mention but a few of the areas that are illuminated through the scrutiny of the naked and adorned human form.

Attitudes towards and representations of the naked body in art

The scrutiny of bodies has figured prominently in the history of Europe since 1750. While one might turn to close inspections of the body in medicine or to new technologies for examining the human form externally and internally, as others do in this book, the focus in this section is on attitudes about and representations of the unclothed body in art, focusing particularly on scholarly approaches to nakedness and nudity in the western artistic tradition. In pursuing this topic, many have picked up the mantle of art historian Kenneth Clark, who famously asserted in his 1956 study of the nude in western artistic traditions that while nakedness was traditionally associated, for many, with exposure, embarrassment, and a feeling of defenselessness, nudity (particularly in its idealized artistic forms) tended to imply beauty of form, confidence, and artistic propriety. In addition to establishing this distinction, Clark traces the shift away from the classical male nude to the female nude in artistic representations, a development that he dates to the production of Raphael's (1483–1520) print, *Judgment of Paris* (c. 1510–20).[10] The sixteenth, seventeenth, and eighteenth centuries witnessed the emergence of new artistic influences that all had an impact on depictions of the female nude. While sensuous portrayals of gods and goddesses and depictions of unclothed nymphs and cherubs in Baroque and Rococo paintings and sculptures influenced how the human form was represented, the artistic movement that had the greatest impact on attitudes towards the nude was, undoubtedly, neoclassicism.

Among the major proponents of this movement was Johann Joachim Winckelmann (1717–68), a German archaeologist who immigrated to Italy in 1755 to pursue his study of the ancient world.[11] Within his *History of Ancient Art* (1764), Winckelmann not only articulated his conception of beauty (which he called 'the loftiest mark and the central point of art'[12]) but also provided an avowedly male-focused and homoerotic description of the ideal human form, effectively linking, according to Whitney Davis, sexuality and aesthetics.[13] In building towards his discussion of the attributes of the idealized nude, Winckelmann makes clear his admiration for the homosocial worlds of ancient Greek gymnasia and military institutions, 'where the young exercised naked in athletic and other games' and where those who 'desired to see beautiful youth … in nude and in perfection' could find it in great abundance.[14] While Winckelmann's focus was clearly on the male form and face, he did not avoid discussions of the female body in his dissection of beauty, even as he proclaimed that he found 'less to notice in the beauty of the female sex' and that ancient statues depicting women required less explication because they were frequently draped.[15]

Winkelmann's veneration of the ancient nude was accompanied by other intellectual developments in the eighteenth century, including a growing emphasis on individuality and increasingly complex scientific mappings of the human body. Indeed, the intellectual traditions and changes of the Enlightenment, of which Winckelmann was but one small part, produced a growing obsession with both corporeality and sensuality. Science, as Thomas Laqueur has noted in his important work *Making Sex: Body and Gender from the Greeks to Freud*, redefined male and female anatomies in this period by replacing the one-body model of gender and sexuality with a two-body one that privileged physiological and sensory differences, not similarities, between men and women.[16] Furthermore, depictions of the body were not confined to scientific texts or works of art criticism and history. The eighteenth century witnessed the spread of pornography across Europe, a trend that has been linked to both the challenges to convention embodied in the radical perspectives of the philosophes and the political transformations of the period. Indeed, the obsession with nude bodies reflected in the work of Winckelmann should remind us that looking at the body should be anything but a marginal concern to historians of eighteenth-century Europe.[17]

Scholars who have examined the place of the exposed body in more recent artistic traditions and developments, and even contemporary artists themselves (who are, as Leslie Bostrom and Marlene Marlik note in a 1999 *Art Journal* article,[18] still frequently trained using nude models) have certainly not allowed Winckelmann or Clark to have the final say on the place of the nude in western art. Beginning in the 1970s, art historians and critics inspired by emergent feminist discourses began to question not only Clark's distinction between the nude and the naked but also what Marcia Pointon has identified as his 'evident distaste for the human (and particularly the female) biological body which is described variously without specific reference as "huddled together and defenceless," "shapeless" and "pitiful."'[19] In 1972, John Berger, Sven Blomberg, Chris Fox, Michael Dibb, and Richard Hollis published *Ways of Seeing*, a collection of essays based on Berger's BBC television series, which aired in that same year. In this work, the authors challenge Clark's distinctions between the naked and the nude by characterizing nakedness as an act of revelation and nudity as a type of display that hinted at both passivity and vulnerability. In examining (particularly female) naked bodies, the authors do consider gender and sexuality (albeit from a decidedly masculinist perspective). In their formulation, men, as the preeminent consumers of art, always view the female nude, which is a passive figure intended to both entertain and flatter them.[20]

Despite some points of agreement in approach, Pointon's 1990 book *Naked Authority: The Body in Western Painting, 1830–1908* questions the certainty of some of the assertions in *Ways of Seeing*. In offering a more nuanced perspective on the unclothed body in art, she notes, for example, that the 'nude functions not as a category with clear parameters but as a form of rhetoric' in which the 'body functions in a grammar of representation'.[21] For Pointon, the presumed passivity of the female subject discussed in *Ways of Seeing* is especially problematic. Taking Palma Vecchio's (*c.* 1480–1528) *Venus* (*c.* 1520) as a starting point, Pointon attempts to demolish assumptions that the painting is 'an unambiguous image of woman as passive object of possession'.[22] Instead, she interprets the reclining figure – set in a landscape with luminous hair, exposed breasts, and partially draped legs and genitals – not simply as a stand-in for the natural world, but rather as a kind of intermediary between nature and culture. Instead of being overwhelmed or consumed by flora and fauna, the figure is assumed to dominate the landscape or, to use Pointon's own words, to be a subject 'endowed with power in the circuit of sexual desire'.[23]

Other art historians have weighed in on this consideration of the (particularly female) nude in post-Renaissance art, including, most famously, Lynda Nead and, more recently, Alison Smith. Nead's influential essays on the nude engage directly with feminist art criticism as well as the ideas of three influential theorists: the art historian Kenneth Clark, the anthropologist Mary Douglas, and the literary critic Jacques Derrida. Central to her consideration of the female nude are the concepts of outlines, margins, and frames which she sees operating in a variety of artistic traditions and, more generally, in mass culture. Nead is principally interested in showing how artistic representations of women's physical forms often serve to contain them. In her view, art 'performs a kind of magical regulation of the female body'.[24] She is careful, however, to illustrate how feminist artists in the 1960s,

1970s, and 1980s began to challenge some of these conventions with work that provoked, inspired, and ultimately subverted traditional ideas about artistic authority. Of greatest interest, perhaps, is Nead's insistence that we consider the interconnectedness of high art, mass culture, and, even, pornography, which she positions as the illicit and marginal display of the female body (as opposed to sanctioned and public artistic displays of the nude).[25]

Nead's influence is clearly evident in the scholarship of Alison Smith, whose own work on the nude has been more chronologically and geographically bounded, focusing as it does on Britain in the nineteenth century; a period during which, as Kenneth Clark notes, the dominance of the female nude was 'absolute'.[26] Smith's research uncovered the ubiquity of images and physical objects depicting the unclothed human body in British culture during the latter years of Victoria's reign. In dissecting this particular component of artistic life, Smith's work reveals that the nude could function simultaneously as 'one of the most prestigious categories within Victorian art' and as a marker of moral danger and depravity, an assertion that follows closely some of Nead's observations about the blurring of artistic categories and the interrelationship of connoisseurship and desire.[27] Smith's interest in the subject did not end with the publication of her 1996 book *The Victorian Nude: Sexuality, Morality, and Art* but, rather, culminated in an exhibition on the subject that opened at Tate Britain in November 2001, and then travelled to Germany, the United States, and Japan in 2002 and 2003.

It was the erotic possibilities associated with the nude, noted in the work of art critics like Théophile Gautier (1811–72) who frequently mused on the sensuous pleasures of Jean-Auguste-Dominique Ingrès's (1780–1867) work, that made it a controversial subject for many in the nineteenth century.[28] Much recent scholarship on the topic has, in fact, highlighted the fraught status of the nude in artistic circles and popular culture. In chronicling the steps that led to this moment of intense debate, Smith dates the nude's appearance in modern British art to the 1820s and 1830s, when Royal Academician William Etty (1787–1849) produced a number of paintings relying on naked or semi-clothed models, including his 1830 work, *Candaules, King of Lydia, Shews his Wife by Stealth to Gyges, One of his Ministers, As She Goes to Bed*. Given the occasionally controversial nature of artistic depictions of nude women and men, it is not surprising that Etty's productions were unable to escape contemporary criticism.[29] In a consideration of the Royal Academy Exhibition where some of his nudes were displayed, *The Times* opined (also in 1830):

> Representations of the human form become disgusting, unless spiritualized by the purest taste and judgment … and that … the end of art should be to make us better and wiser, and which may be made to fortify our morals, and not excite feelings that had better be repressed.[30]

Unclothed models and paintings and sculptures of nude subjects prompted numerous discussions that highlighted a variety of social and cultural tensions around questions of morality and national identity at the *fin de siècle*.[31] The public discourse on the nude continued throughout the century in Great Britain, particularly in the 1860s and 1870s as artists in that country came under the influence of French paintings and the French system of atelier education, and the use of life models became increasingly important.[32] In the 1880s, for example, purity campaigners targeted sculptural and painterly depictions of the nude by linking them to degeneracy and pernicious social problems, such as child prostitution.[33] Despite these concerns, artists persisted in depicting naked bodies in their work throughout the 1880s and 1890s. In 1886, for example, a less classically inspired type of nude, identified as the 'modern life' nude (who was depicted in informal and frequently natural settings, such as the seaside), was exhibited in a show organized by the French-inspired and unconventional New English Art Club at the Marlborough Gallery in Pall Mall, London.[34]

The nude was a fraught figure elsewhere. In her study of French fine art, print culture, and censorship during the Third Republic, Heather Dawkins sets out to dissect the distinctive components of spectatorship in the late nineteenth century which she defines as 'the complex entanglement of social relations and subjectivity in the experience of looking at images'.[35] Working within both feminist and the social history of art traditions, Dawkins seeks to link the history of the nude in France to discourses of republicanism and democracy but also attempts to show how women themselves engaged with representations of the unclothed or partially clothed female body. In discussing the status of the nude in France, Dawkins chronicles an important change that took place over the course of the 1870s and 1880s. While a select jury reviewed the work of artists intending to show at the Paris Salon (the most prominent of the annual exhibitions in Europe), the printing and distribution of potentially scandalous images of women were reviewed and approved throughout the 1870s by a government body – the censorship administration. Beginning in 1881, 'images suspected of affronting public decency were evaluated by the court after the images had circulated in public'; a judicial process that Dawkins characterizes as both more complicated and more easily challenged.[36]

While Dawkins illuminates the processes of judicial censorship that affected painters and printers alike, she also reminds readers, instructively, that images of female nudes were not produced exclusively for men by men. Suzanne Valadon (1865–1938) who modeled in the 1880s for, among others, Henri de Toulouse-Lautrec (1864–1901) and Pierre-Auguste Renoir (1841–1919) turned her hand to drawing female nudes in the 1890s; an act that allowed her to transfer 'the model's unself-conscious confidence about the female body and the freedom to scrutinise it into images'.[37] While women of the upper and middle classes were largely excluded from the life study or the major institution of art education in France, the École des Beaux-Arts (until 1897), there were some who, nonetheless, transgressed boundaries of bourgeois propriety by pursuing an artistic education at Paris's Académie Julian, where they could paint nude models, or by collecting nudes, as the wealthy American Louisine Elder Havemeyer (1855–1929) did during lengthy excursions to Paris throughout the late nineteenth and early twentieth centuries.[38] The nude, like the fashion plate, the doll, and even pornographic images, then, could also possess homoerotic appeal for women who, in the nineteenth century, occupied a sexual and gender landscape in which, as Sharon Marcus has recently noted, 'female marriage, gender mobility, and women's erotic fantasies about women were at the heart of normative institutions and discourses'.[39]

Opportunities for viewing the nude were expanded dramatically with the rise of photography as both a method of representation and a new art form.[40] The emergence of photographic depictions of the nude from the 1840s produced a number of interesting discussions and debates about the nature of this new technology and whether it should be viewed as an art form or an unmediated and wholly accurate representation of the human body. Many within the scientific community viewed photography as a helpful tool, almost from its inception. The Victorian asylum physician and photography pioneer, Hugh Welch

Diamond (1809–86), saw photography, as he noted in an 1856 paper, as a way to delineate and record 'the characteristic features of different mental diseases in their commencement, continuance, and cure'.[41] Eadwaerd Muybridge (1830–1904), the British-born but American-based photographer, was also seen as contributing to scientific knowledge in North America and Europe through his nude photographic studies, most notably those published in his 1887 portfolio, *Animal Locomotion, An Electro-Photographic Investigation of Consecutive Phases of Animal Movement*. Muybridge's work on the movements of animals, and more centrally for the purposes of this chapter, human beings, relied on nude studies of the body in motion and was shielded from moral censure, as Janine Mileaf has noted, as a result of Muybridge's association with the veterinary department at the University of Pennsylvania.[42] Still, as many have observed with reference to the cultural meaning of scientific photographs, there was always more artifice (in the form of posing, cropping, and artistic subjectivity) in this particular form of documentation than contemporaries were often willing to admit.[43]

Photographs of the nude female and male form also served a variety of other purposes in the nineteenth century. Artists, for example, routinely used photographic studies of nudes in addition to, and sometimes in place of, live models. Occasionally, these nude studies were subject to regulation and censorship by the state. Under the Obscene Publications Act of 1857, British photographers and retailers were subject to censorship and, occasionally, prison terms, for purveying images of nude men and women, even when it was claimed, as was the case in 1882, that these studies 'were for the benefit of art students who could not afford living models'.[44] As Lisa Sigel has observed, these images of artists' models could, in fact, be used for purely erotic purposes on occasion.[45] Titillation also occurred through the circulation of photographic studies of colonial subjects. Possessing and looking at these photographs was not, however, simply a pleasurable diversion. As Philippa Levine has reminded us in her recent work, the act of acquiring and consuming these images functioned as a cultural expression of imperial power and served to underscore the association between nakedness, primitiveness, and inferiority in the discourses of colonialism. Sentiments of this sort are reflected in a simple statement made by the colonial administrator and anthropologist Harry Johnston (1858–1927) who, in 1910, noted: 'the lowly Australoids still lead a savage, naked existence'.[46] From these few brief examples, it is thus possible to see how the artifacts surrounding the nineteenth-century culture of the nude or partially clothed body acquired multiple purposes and meanings.

While, as I have indicated, the female (and to some extent the colonial) nude achieved unparalleled supremacy in the European artistic world of the nineteenth century, the male nude did not, of course, disappear entirely. High art and illicit images of naked men in fact appeared throughout the period under examination in this chapter. Kenneth Clark pays considerable attention to the male body in his examination of the nude in 1956, focusing primarily on the figure of Apollo in the western artistic tradition. In his exploration, he describes how the god of light and sun came, by the fourth century BCE, to be represented in sculptures that combined perfect balance and symmetry with humanity, grace, and defined musculature; an ideal that possesses continued relevance today.[47] While depictions of this form of masculine beauty fell out of favour, according to Clark, from the third century CE until the fifteenth century, it never disappeared entirely. During the Renaissance, the male body came to be viewed, in artistic works depicting the masculine archetypes of energetic and kinetic athletes and martial heroes as well as Apollo (once again), Adam, and David (the biblical King of Israel), as 'something divine', to borrow, as

Clark does, from Giorgio Vasari's (1511–74) sixteenth-century biography of Michelangelo.[48]

Work on the male nude has, of course, developed substantially since the 1950s. In recent years, scholars have tackled not only the male nude in painting and sculpture but also the tradition of photographing the naked male body in the nineteenth and twentieth centuries. The scope of writing on the subject has been varied indeed, ranging from Germaine Greer's broad survey of the beautiful, adolescent boy in western art from the ancient world to the present day[49] to Edward Lucie-Smith's examination of the male figure, in which he articulates the broad contours of the history of nude masculine representations:

> Given a central role by the Greeks, then banished for a long period by Christian asceticism and hatred of the body, it was revived by the Renaissance, only to fall victim, but only very gradually, to the social and economic forces which created modern society. Now [1998] that very society is beginning to feel a need for this range of imagery again, while remaining somewhat afraid of some of the darker forces to which it seems to appeal.[50]

Of greatest significance in this work on the male nude, perhaps, is the open discussion of both same-sex and opposite-sex desire in, particularly, photographic representations of the male body. The emphasis on the eroticism and sexuality of the male nude has, in large part, been spurred on by the emergence of both feminist historiography and, more importantly, by the rise of lesbian and gay history. Looking at and decoding nude and/or semi-clothed images can, for some, serve a valuable political function. According to Allen Ellensweig, whose own work has examined nineteenth- and twentieth-century male photographic representations, dissecting the homoerotic image enables an explication of the forms of oppression that same-sex desiring men have experienced over 150 years and 'the visual strategies photographers have used to deal with subject matter that has left them vulnerable to censure and to professional handicap'.[51] Looking at images of beautiful men did not just serve a political function for gay or queer-identified men. It could also advance, according to Germaine Greer, 'women's reclamation of their capacity for and right to visual pleasure'.[52] Far from being a disconnected or esoteric task, we should understand the act of looking (with the intent, in the instances cited above, of deep analysis and interpretation) to be anything but ephemeral indulgences or merely pleasant diversions.[53]

In some ways, understanding the modern male nude helps us to comprehend the changes in the representation of the unclothed body that have occurred since the late nineteenth century. Like the female nude, the male nude was able to elicit strong and censorious responses from many, who worried about the corruptive possibilities inherent in the display of the male nude body and the anxieties about same-sex desire between men that permeated most discussions of, especially, genital displays.[54] The history of western art is replete with concerns about the dangers of the male nude ranging from Edward Burne-Jones's (1833–98) display and forced removal of his painting *Phyllis and Demophoon* from an exhibition at the Old Water-Colour Society in 1870 to the intense reactions generated by the work and display of Robert Mapplethorpe's photographs in the late 1980s and early 1990s.[55]

Even with the concerns that some expressed about the morality of male nudes, there was, nonetheless, an awareness that this was a meritorious tradition with a long history

Figure 10.1 Henry Scott Tuke, *August Blue* (1894). SOTK2011/Alamy.

indeed. Many contemporaries found within Henry Scott Tuke's (1858–1929) open-air, naturalist, and nude paintings of young fishermen and seaside youths on the Cornish coast of England (see figures 10.1 and 10.2) considerable relief from 'the tedious monotony of the female nude studies'. In one instance, an unidentified reviewer of Tuke's famed 1894 work *August Blue* (Figure 10.1) commented on the aesthetic value of painting the 'neglected male body' in recent artistic productions: 'The firm masculine lines are quite as beautiful in their way as the soft curves of feminine beauty, and have been far too long relegated to an inconspicuous place in art.' Before completing his review, the author indicated that the Greeks would have been dumbfounded by the late Victorian reluctance to paint the nude male body and praised both Tuke and the French artist, Gustave Claude Étienne Courtois (1853–1923), for having 'deliberately chosen the nude male figure as their subject'.[56]

Despite this final claim, Tuke and Courtois were not, of course, alone in working on the nude male. Sculptors at the same time produced statues that derived inspiration from and celebrated the male form, even as they moved away from the formal ideals of neoclassicism by focusing on naturalism and the pleasures of the skin, a development associated with the so-called New Sculpture Movement of Great Britain and epitomized in Frederic Leighton's (1830–96) *An Athlete Wrestling with a Python* (1877). This tendency is also clearly evident in the work of Hamo Thornycroft (1850–1925), whose own sculptures like *The Mower* (c. 1882–94) served to celebrate the physique of the agricultural labourer while reinforcing conceptions of masculinity that in the late nineteenth century privileged activity and musculature.[57] New Sculpture, which art historian David Getsy sees as the beginning of modern art in Britain, did not function in a vacuum and was clearly influenced by continental work, including that of Jules Dalou (1838–1902), a French sculptor who taught at several British institutions in the 1870s and 1880s.[58] The French sculptor Auguste Rodin

Figure 10.2 Henry Scott Tuke, *Boys Bathing* (1912). Falmouth Art Gallery, Cornwall, UK/The Bridgeman Art Library.

(1840–1917) also depicted the male nude in sculptures like *The Bronze Age (The Vanquished)* and *The Thinker*, which were first modelled (with multiple bronze casts completed later) in 1876 and 1880, respectively.[59]

The twentieth century ushered in a number of crucial changes with regard to representations of the nude in different artistic traditions. While the abstractions associated with the emergence of modernism tended to minimize the importance of the classical nude and realistic representation, artists continued to look to the unclothed body for inspiration or to highlight the trauma of modern warfare. The Spanish modernist Pablo Picasso (1881–1973) turned to the nude model in several notable works from the early twentieth century. His *Les Demoiselles d'Avignon* (1907) depicts the naked female form as a series of angles and curves and draws inspiration for its facial compositions from African tribal masks while his 1905 *Two Youths* utilizes slightly more representational techniques in depicting the adolescent male body.[60]

Art, in the form of drawings, paintings, photographs, and sculptures, produced during and in the immediate aftermath of World War I served to depict the male body at war as simultaneously vulnerable, permeable, and injured but also as heroic, muscular, and resilient. The precarious and damaged body provided subject matter for numerous war artists, including the British painter C. R. W. Nevinson (1889–1946) whose 1916 painting *The Doctor* conveys both the pain of war injuries and the dangers the exposed male body could face, and the watercolours of Henry Tonks (1862–1937), who captured, in telling detail, the ravages of facial injuries.[61] The heroic body could also be an antidote for the devastation of war or, as Ana Carden-Coyne recently put it: 'Beautiful bodies displace death with hope.' This was especially evident in Francis Derwent Wood's (1871–1926) classically inspired sculpture of David prominently displayed on the Machine Gun Corps Memorial (1925) in London's Hyde Park. In this instance, commemorating the dead required a toned example of physical perfection to remind viewers of the bravery and superiority of British manhood.[62]

The nude male and female body also appeared in other works of art and media in the twentieth century. While photography continued to grow in popularity after 1900, filmic portrayals of the nude became another mode of representation in displaying the body. The French film company Pathé Frères (founded in 1896) distributed films that featured nude figures, including a 1903 picture called *Five Ladies*, which contained a vignette of a painter and his nude model. Film thus served to further the status of the nude as an appropriate subject for artists working with a variety of purposes and audiences in mind.[63] Twentieth-century artists like David Hockney (1937–) and Lucien Freud (1922–2011) continued to depict nudes in their work. In Hockney's case, the focus, especially in the 1960s, on youthful male bodies in swimming pools and showers was intended to articulate, more openly, homosexual desire in an era of social change. Lucien Freud's depictions of female, and more particularly, male nudes were influenced, according to Edward Lucie-Smith, by the work of the Austrian Expressionist Egon Schiele (1890–1918), and rely, in part, on the technique of 'genital confrontation' for their power.[64]

Bodily and genital confrontation was also evident in a number of cultural products of the 1950s, 1960s, and 1970s. In Great Britain, physique pictorial magazines with titles like *Male Model Monthly* and *Man Alive* provided consumers with idealized versions of the muscular body that harkened back to the classical period. The 1960s provided female audiences with celebrity magazines like *Boyfriend* that allowed them to indulge in fantasies about male pop culture idols and movie stars while articulating new post-war visions of heterosexuality and heterosociability. Similarly, gay pornographic magazines in the 1970s allowed same-sex desiring men to state aesthetic preferences while celebrating the political act of consuming, openly, nude (and highly sexualized) images of men.[65] The scholarly and artistic works and popular cultural forms surveyed in this section should, thus, remind us to think about, as Richard Leppert has noted, the 'representation of the naked body as a sight – and sometimes as a spectacle – that is, as an object of display and intense interest upon which the viewer obsessively gazes'.[66]

Clothing and adorning the body

It was, of course, not just the naked body that interested viewers and functioned as an important spectacle and sight. Just as frequently, it was the clothed and adorned body that generated intense scrutiny and interest. Ruminations on the value of personal beauty, stylish dress, and the necessity of impeccable grooming proliferated in European societies by the latter part of the nineteenth century. Prompted, in part, by fears of degeneration brought about by modern urban life and anxieties regarding the quality of Europe's racial stock, this obsession with observing and improving the body led many contemporaries to reflect on the primacy of the naked and clothed human form as both a sign of national health and an appropriate topic for public discussion. Bourgeois French women were reminded in a dazzling array of manuals published in the 1880s and 1890s that it was their 'mission ... to please, charm, love and be loved'.[67] The British were not immune to these preoccupations either, as a fellow of the Royal College of Surgeons noted when he commented on the commercial value of looking good:

There is hardly any walk of life in which personal appearance will not be found rated by business people at a considerable money value. The shopkeeper choosing a young woman to wait behind the counter, the doctor engaging an assistant, the solicitor picking out a barrister, seldom forget the power of good looks.[68]

Contained within these reflections on the nature of beauty and the value of physical appearance is an obsession with viewing and assessing the body that bears at least some resemblance to the preoccupations that guided the work of painters, sculptors, and photographers. While there was nothing new in reflecting on the form, shape, and comeliness of a man or woman's adorned body or personal style (one need only think about the admiration for George Villiers, Duke of Buckingham's (1592–1628) impressive legs), the connections that were assumed to exist between attractiveness, fashionability, and a definition of the self that extended beyond the mere demarcation of one's social status, in the years after 1750, was indeed novel.[69] The emergence of this association and the evolution of the body as a marker of and vehicle for the expression of complex social identities were spurred on by a number of key developments. The first of these related to new conceptions of the individual, promoted, in part, by Enlightenment philosophes and other thinkers, in the eighteenth century. According to this view, early eighteenth-century conceptions of dress as something that might distance the wearer's true self from a discerning viewing public gave way, by the turn of the century, to ideals that eschewed artifice in favour of authenticity and, ultimately, a 'sense that dress and appearance should be related to one's identity emerged'.[70] Intellectual shifts aside, the eighteenth century was also marked by increasingly varied urban landscapes in cities like London, Paris, and Vienna, where expansive new forms of consumption were privileged by the wealthy (and those who sought to emulate them) and elaborate public dress became an essential marker of sociability.[71]

The nineteenth and twentieth centuries ushered in transformative changes that altered styles of dress and conceptions of the relationship between clothing and modern social identities. The rise of the middle classes in the nineteenth century led to a growing understanding that they, not the aristocrats who dominated the fashionable world in the eighteenth century, were the new arbiters of style and taste. Riding the economic wave generated by industrial capitalism, bourgeois citizens in Europe set new standards at the same time as factory production led to the proliferation of fashionable items that were purchased by an ever-expanding consumer base that 'placed a new emphasis upon the self and stimulated the rise of privatized individualism'.[72] The emergence of new forms of photographic representation and the production of lavishly illustrated magazines and newspapers, beginning in the 1840s, furthered this focus on the relationship between consumption, clothing, and the markers of selfhood. Furthermore, the rise of the film industry and the emergence of modern celebrity cultures in the twentieth century and, more recently, the proliferation of fashion and lifestyle advice websites has fuelled a preoccupation with physical appearance and the social and cultural significance of dress and bodily adornment. Indeed, by the twentieth century it was firmly established, to borrow from the work of Christopher Breward and Caroline Evans, that fashion was a key mechanism for 'interrogating the subjective experience of modern life'.[73]

Approaches to the history of clothing and fashion have been transformed, in recent decades, by the intervention of new methodological perspectives that seek to relate the study of clothing to broader historical processes and employ a range of theoretical insights ranging from feminism to poststructuralist literary criticism. Styles of dress have, indeed, altered dramatically since 1750, with a tendency for men to wear suits and trousers (as opposed to breeches and more elaborate overcoats) and for women to expose a greater amount of their body or, as Anne Hollander has noted, try 'to approach the male ideal [of the suit] more closely, using an assortment of its motifs'.[74] While a complete history of men's and women's fashions, processes of adornment, and grooming practices since 1750 is beyond the purview of this chapter, a few developments are worth mentioning to indicate the relationships that have existed, over a fairly expansive period of time, between dress and gender and sexual subjectivities. In discussing these developments, my intention is to explore key moments when the adornment and dress of the human form was meant to elicit specific reactions from those who were gazing upon the body.

Of the more significant developments that historians of fashion have attempted to document are changes in men's sartorial choices, particularly with reference to what the psychologist J. C. Flügel called, in the 1930s, the 'Great Masculine Renunciation'; a process whereby men rejected the frivolity of fashion in favour of a sober suit of clothes usually consisting of a coat, trousers, occasionally a vest/waistcoat, and a sombre shirt and neck cloth or, by the late nineteenth century, neck tie. In France, as Flügel noted, the rejection of lace, brightly coloured silks, delicate stockings, and embroidered slippers was associated with the political radicalism of the French Revolution with its 'doctrine of the brotherhood of men' and its attempts to minimize distinctions of rank.[75] The idea that one's dress could reveal not only political allegiances but also one's level of manliness was also evident in Great Britain, where excess in dress throughout the eighteenth and nineteenth centuries was critiqued by those who were seeking to grab a greater share of political and economic power.[76]

While it is often assumed that these discussions of men's sartorial choices were primarily held in the eighteenth and early nineteenth centuries, David Kuchta's work on the rise of the three-piece suit in England locates their origins in the seventeenth century (1666, to be precise), when the restored Stuart monarch Charles II inaugurated a dress reform movement which rejected the French-inspired 'doublet, stiff collar, and cloak' in favour of a 'comely vest'.[77] This precursor to the three-piece suit became, according to Kuchta, a marker of elite masculinity that relied on conceptions of manly thrift and 'modesty and plainness in dress'.[78] The eschewal of supposedly feminine modes of display was adopted first by members of the aristocracy who were seeking to claim masculine authority and legitimize their hold on power by proving their seriousness of purpose in leading the nation. In the years after 1750, as they rose to greater prominence in Great Britain, the emergent middle classes began to embrace this sartorial style and renunciation of conspicuous consumption in an effort to support their own claims to power. In Kuchta's work, the experience of looking is considered both a historically significant act and central to his examination of the three-piece suit. As he notes in his introduction, 'this is a history of the power of appearances, of the way in which attitudes toward men in the public eye were shaped by and in turn helped shape, political, economic and cultural change.'[79]

Despite the compelling nature of a number of Kuchta's claims, it is important to note, as some historians of the nineteenth century have, that, rather than being an era of complete renunciation, this was a period in which the masculine embrace of fashion continued for many. The influence of figures like George Bryan ('Beau') Brummell (1778–1840), with his corseted and stiff torso and high, stiff, and immaculately white neck cloth, or the French poet and essayist Charles Baudelaire's (1821–67) perpetually black wardrobe (punctuated with splashes of colour in cravats or gloves).[80] While the dandy Brummell and his followers could be ridiculed in cartoons and the popular press for their excesses, their influence was undeniable, as noted in the writings of one German aristocrat who visited Great Britain in the early part of the nineteenth century. With reference to Brummell's contributions to fashion (as well as his departure from England), he observed, somewhat wryly: 'he left to his native land, as a parting gift, the imperishable secret of the starched neckband ... Brummell's starch remains visible at the neck of every fashionable, and proclaims his lofty genius.'[81]

The desire for adornment by men was also evident in the taste for military embellishments that accompanied the Napoleonic Wars (1803–15), when the influence of armies and navies was felt throughout Europe and evident in the pantaloons, epaulets, and tailored jackets that became commonplace in men's wardrobes at the time. As Susan Vincent describes it: 'military and dandy chic – with their shared aesthetic of tightly fitting garments revealing a broad chest and narrow waist – were extremely significant, and found their way into the average male wardrobe and onto the average male body.'[82] Fashionable clothing was also affected by other developments in the nineteenth century. The Arts and Crafts movement that influenced architecture and design, painting, and sculpture in the latter decades of the nineteenth century also had a substantial impact on dress, especially in northern Europe and North America.

A related movement, Aestheticism, which privileged the 'claim of art's autonomy', influenced styles of dress even more profoundly.[83] Aesthetes like Gautier and Baudelaire in France and Walter Pater and Oscar Wilde in Britain aspired to create beauty everywhere in society. For Wilde, personal style enabled the expression of Aesthetic principles. This was clearly evident during his tour of America in 1882, when he chose to wear for his lectures knee breeches and richly textured velvet jackets. His Yankee audience was never entirely comfortable with this. In one instance, described in Richard Ellmann's biography of Wilde, a group of Harvard students attending a lecture delivered by the poet, essayist, and playwright in Boston, mocked him by dressing in 'the high aesthetic line with breeches, dinner jackets, Whistler locks of white hair, hats like Bunthorne's, each bearing, in a stained-glass attitude, a sunflower'.[84] With this example, we should be reminded that dress could, on occasion, be fraught with tensions that display, in broad relief, the contested battles that occasionally surrounded the display and performance of gender subjectivities.

Men's preoccupation with fashion in the late nineteenth century was also revealed in their participation in the urban consumer cultures of the period. This engagement with the flourishing trade in clothing and beauty products was evident in print advertisements that used visually stimulating images to sell items like shaving soap to men.[85] It was even more apparent in men's visits to the large, elaborate, and spectacular department stores of London, Paris, Berlin, and Vienna. While frequently described as female spaces, owing in part to Emile Zola's depiction of a large Paris department store in his 1883 book *Au Bonheur des Dames* (*The Ladies' Paradise*),[86] these institutions, as scholars like Christopher Breward, Erika Rappaport, and Brent Shannon note, were also utilized by men. When the American-born entrepreneur Harry Gordon Selfridge (1858–1947) opened his department store in London in 1909, he sought to cultivate men's participation in this new consumer spectacle by promoting his store not just as a place of pleasure for women but also as 'The Man's Best Buying Centre'.[87] In Breward's work on male consumption in London between 1860 and 1914, the author established the relationship between the articulation of class identities, the visual markers of dress, and the masculine pleasures of shopping in an attempt to correct the historical record which, he notes, has tended until quite recently to assume that nineteenth-century men spent 'minimal time and attention ... on sartorial matters'.[88]

Men's dress and modes of self-presentation in the twentieth century have also received considerable attention in recent work. Two areas have generated particular interest among historians over the past few years: the issue of dress reform and nudism and the relationship between dress, self-presentation, and gay sexual identities. Anxieties about the effects of modern life and the degeneration of German society brought about by industrialization and urbanization at the end of the nineteenth and beginning of the twentieth centuries led, according to Michael Hau, to a life reform movement (promoted by both establishment medical practitioners and alternative medicine advocates) that focused on improving the health and physical beauty of the nation through exercise, dieting, outdoor activities, and, for some, a rejection of traditional forms of dress and an embrace of nudism. Advocates of nudism (or '*freikorperkultur*', translated as 'free physical culture') during the experimental years of the Weimar Republic (1919–33) saw within this movement the opportunity to erase class and status boundaries, effectively creating a people's community whereby equality, not distinctions based on wealth and dress, predominated.[89] Hans Surén (1885–1972), a prominent advocate of physical culture and nudism during the Weimar and Nazi periods in Germany, promoted gymnastics as a path to national recovery during the 1920s. Furthermore, he argued that nudism could promote body discipline and allow those who had not achieved financial or professional success to nonetheless earn a place of pride in society through physical development.[90]

Other calls for reform emerged in the 1920s and 1930s, an era when, as we shall see below, the conventions of female fashion were also shifting. In Great Britain, according to Ina Zweiniger-Bargielowska, '[d]ress reformers strove to liberate men from the constraints of tradition' by founding, in 1929, the Men's Dress Reform Party. Intended as a reaction to the conventions of male dress that privileged tight collars and ties, heavy suits, and trousers, dress reformers advocated that men wear open collared shirts, shorts, and lighter fabrics. In so doing, Zweiniger-Bargielowska notes, they challenged 'conventional gender hierarchies' by embracing a style (shorts) associated with boys and fabric choices normally considered to be exclusively feminine.[91] While attempts to reform men's dress in Britain were made in earlier periods, the 1920s witnessed the rise of growing concerns about the unhealthy and unhygienic nature of heavy suits for men. Viewed as cranks by some and as challengers to the economic livelihood of tailors and producers of traditional menswear by others, dress reformers nonetheless were instrumental in ushering in changes in leisurewear. Even with the existence of these noteworthy criticisms, many contemporaries remained steadfast defenders of the suit. Modernist designers like the architect Le Corbusier (1887–1965), for example, 'idealised the modernity of the masculine suit with its white shirt as the epitome of modern dress: a uniform ideally adapted to the streamlined speed and minimalist interiors of the twentieth century, and moreover, an unchanging, utopian one.'[92]

Recent interventions into the new queer history, which has privileged the study and dissection of lesbian and gay cultures across geographical and chronological spans, have accorded pride of place to the role of personal appearance and dress in the articulation of sexual identities. As Shaun Cole notes in his study of gay men's fashion in Great Britain and the United States: 'Apparel and adornment had provided an indication of homosexuality or of a tendency toward same-sex sexual activity since the seventeenth century.'[93]

In the eighteenth century, same-sex desiring men frequently relied on cross-dressing and gender play to signal their desires, usually in prescribed settings such as the molly-houses of London and the taverns of Paris.[94] Cross-dressing continued at public balls and dance halls (such as the Eldorado in Berlin and the Magic-City in Paris) in the late nineteenth and early twentieth centuries.[95] It was also during this period, as Cole notes, that dress came to be invested with greater symbolic meaning for queer men, noting as one simple example the propensity of Oscar Wilde and his followers to wear green carnations as signifiers of both aesthetic predilections and desires.[96]

The twentieth century witnessed a number of important changes to queer fashions that have been ably documented in the work of several historians, particularly in Britain where the field of queer history has been most developed (outside the United States). Matt Houlbrook's work on queer London between the end of World War I and the issuance of the Wolfenden Committee's report on homosexual offences and prostitution in 1957 shows how queer men used certain sartorial symbols (including light-coloured suits, fur coats, turtle-neck jerseys, jewellery, or judiciously applied makeup) to make themselves visible to others.[97] Especially effeminate or excessively flamboyant fashion choices could, however, also render men susceptible to police scrutiny and prosecution in an era when male homosexuality was still criminalized.[98] In work published since his 2005 book *Queer London: Perils and Pleasures in the Sexual Metropolis, 1918–1957* appeared, Houlbrook has also examined queer men's engagement with the emerging beauty culture of the 1920s, noting not only how they utilized makeup but also how police chose to read this component of urban queer life as a marker of gender deviance and dangerous sexuality.[99]

The work of Cole and Clare Lomas brings this story closer to the present by examining how sartorial symbols operated in the 1950s, 1960s, 1970s, and 1980s. Based on a series of carefully recorded oral histories, Cole's discussion of the markers of male homosexuality references his subjects wearing suede shoes and camel hair coats in mid-century Britain.[100] Among the other developments reported by his informants were the embrace, in the 1950s, of Italian styling, which emphasized tight-fitting trousers that accentuated men's crotches and posteriors and short jackets, identified as 'bum-freezers'.[101] As gay liberation took hold in the 1960s and 1970s, two other developments with regard to the outer markers of sexual identity occurred. While some more radical queers engaged in what they referred to as 'gender-fuck' (combining both masculine and feminine styles – think dresses and facial hair), the majority of gay men in Britain and elsewhere sought to assert their masculinity by adopting the American-style 'clone look' inspired by masculine archetypes including cowboys and bikers or wearing the 'preppy' outfit of chinos and a Lacoste shirt.[102] Lomas, who also relies on oral histories, explores the 1950s through the 1970s, noting the role that newly established men's boutiques in London's Soho (like Vince Man's Shop and the establishments of John Stephen) played in the lives of queer men seeking to negotiate, simultaneously, their sexual, class, occupational, and generational identities.[103]

While the emphasis on the clothed male body has grown exponentially in recent decades, the focus on women's engagement with fashion and dress has a much longer history. Developments in this field (too vast to cover comprehensively here) have been transformed in recent years by historians employing a range of methodological perspectives drawn from the fields of cultural and gender and sexuality studies. Much of the recent work on the history of women's fashion has, in fact, firmly established the central role that dress has played in the cultural processes associated with sexing the body. As Joanne Entwistle notes in *The Fashioned Body: Fashion, Dress, and Modern Social Theory*, '[p]ractices of dress evoke the sexed body, drawing attention to bodily differences between men and women that might otherwise be obscured'. Western Europeans and North Americans are so reliant on using dress to read gender and the human body, Entwistle continues, that individual articles of clothing (such as skirts for women and trousers for men) 'can come to stand for sexual difference in the *absence* of a body'.[104]

Two articles of female clothing have generated intense scrutiny among historians of dress and come to be associated, explicitly, with the construction and fashioning of femininity in modern Europe: the full skirt and the corset. Both have been the subject of considerable scholarly interest, dialogue, and debate. With regard to the skirt, historian Susan Vincent has observed that the enlargement of women's hips and posterior was commonplace for over 400 years between 1500 and 1900: 'Enlargement was not the sartorial exception, it was the anatomical rule.'[105] While the form that this enlargement took varied over time, complicated technologies of support and expansion were required to make this particular fashion happen. Initially dome-shaped, by the 1740s women's hooped petticoats were flattened and oblong, jutting out from a woman's sides in, sometimes extreme, ways. The nineteenth century witnessed the emergence of a new technology: crinolines constructed of stiff horsehair and woollen fabric that were used to expand the diameter of skirts. Cage petticoats (also referred to as artificial crinolines) replaced the horsehair version in the 1850s. These were made first of flexible whalebone and then of metal and took on a variety of forms, depending on prevailing styles. Contemporaries noted the changes in skirt fashions that occurred over the course of the nineteenth century. When they were at their largest in the 1850s and 1860s, the effects produced by cage petticoats were lampooned in Great Britain in the satirical magazine *Punch* and even disparaged in a popular ballad titled: 'Crinoline: or What a Ridiculous Fashion'.[106]

In her discussion of skirts, Vincent is careful to note that while the sometimes ridiculous fashions of the nineteenth century may have appeared wholly oppressive, especially when one considers women's mobility, this may not have been the entire story. In the eighteenth century, according to Erin Mackie, satirical depictions of hoop petticoats were the result of concerns about these garments as emblems of feminine assertiveness and, perhaps even, sexual autonomy, not restrictiveness.[107] Vincent picks up on this line of analysis in her survey of fashion from the Renaissance to the present when she notes that large skirts actually kept men at a distance and protected women, giving them the opportunity to travel more safely and comfortably on trains and omnibuses, to mention but two facets of life affected by the wearing of these garments.[108] Of course, as Vincent correctly notes, the enormity of skirts could open men to charges of indecent assault as they attempted to negotiate their way around women who could block entrances to public buildings and inhibit access to various modes of transportation as a result of their fashionable excesses. Like all garments, Vincent asserts, petticoats and crinolines were 'capable of sustaining multiple overlapping and conflicting meanings'.[109]

Another female garment in possession of multiple and conflicting meanings was, of course, the corset. In the nineteenth century, controversies abounded about the advisability of corset-wearing, with defenders arguing that corsetry was a way to maintain propriety, femininity, and a proper carriage and detractors arguing that the garment adversely affected the health of women, particularly their reproductive capacities, as the French author Charles Roux noted in his 1855 tract, *Contre le Corset*.[110] In the 1980s, David Kunzle's and Valerie Steele's studies of corsetry also identified a third group in discussing this particular fashion: the tight-lacers who were either extreme followers of fashion or, according to Kunzle, assertive women who embraced a marginalized aesthetic and form of sexual pleasure that could be seen as an act of defiance and self-expression.[111] Despite this range of controversies, many women in the nineteenth century believed that corsets 'served some useful function'.[112] In an era before the brassiere, corsets helped to shape and augment breasts, slim waists, and conceal what many women perceived as physical imperfections.

The corset did not just generate controversy in the nineteenth century. In fact, long after it was abandoned in favour of girdles and slimming diets, it became the subject of intense scholarly interest. As the writing of history came under the influence of second-wave feminism in the 1960s and 1970s, women's historians turned their attention to the study of everyday life and aspects of the female experience like dress and beauty culture. For some writing in this vein, the corset was torture, pure and simple. In a 1977 article by Helene Roberts in the feminist journal *Signs: Journal of Women in Culture and Society*, women's clothing of the Victorian age, in general, and the corset, more specifically, 'projected the willingness to conform to the submissive-masochistic pattern, but dress also helped to mould female behavior to the role of the "exquisite slave"' (as an indication of her interpretive perspective, it is important to note that Roberts also argues that the cage crinoline of the 1850s and 1860s turned women 'into caged birds surrounded by hoops of steel').[113]

Responses to Roberts's work were extensive, both in *Signs* and elsewhere. David Kunzle, as indicated above, attempted to assign a degree of positive agency to women who embraced the tightly laced corset while, in a recently revised edition of his 1982 book *Fashion and Fetishism: Corsets, Tight-Lacing and Other Forms of Body-Sculpture*, giving fuller credence to arguments about the oppressive nature of corsetry.[114] Valerie Steele's highly innovative and beautifully nuanced study, published in 2001, functions as a response to what she sees as the excesses of both perspectives. She articulates her interpretive stance pointedly on the first page of *The Corset: A Cultural History*:

> Corsetry was not one monolithic, unchanging experience that all unfortunate women experienced before being liberated by feminism. It was a situated practice that meant different things to different people at different times. Some women did experience the corset as an assault on the body. But the corset also had many positive connotations – of social status, self-discipline, artistry, respectability, beauty, youth, and erotic allure.[115]

Steele also attempts, in her work, to refute the idea that most women achieved impossibly small waists, noting that such images are largely the subject of fantasy not historical reality. In establishing this point, she observes that the average corset size in the nineteenth century was between 20 and 26 inches (when the average women's waist was thought, by medical professionals, to measure between 27 and 29 inches).[116]

Steele rightly notes the challenges to corseted fashions embodied in the form of organizations like the Rational Dress Society (founded in London in 1881) and advocates of Artistic and Aesthetic dress. For women, the latter movements advocated loose-fitting dresses with voluminous sleeves, muted natural colours, and simple ornamentation (usually handcrafted and nature-inspired embroidery). Embraced and advocated by artists like the British designer William Morris (1834–96), the Belgian architect Henry van de Velde

(1863–1957), and the Austrian artist Gustav Klimt (1862–1918) as an expression of a new philosophy of beauty, this form of dress for women provided an alternative to the more tightly corseted fashions of the day.[117] Other developments of the late nineteenth century would present challenges to the corseted. Calls for greater athleticism among women and a desire to take advantage of the cycling craze of the 1890s led some to abandon corseted fashions in favour of more loose-fitting clothing.[118] Steele reminds us, however, that we should not assume that this transition automatically represented a rejection of restriction in favour of liberation.

Indeed, some who have looked at changes to styles of dress in the twentieth century have been careful to highlight what they see as the underside of the rejection of nineteenth-century conventions and fashions. In examining female dress and hairstyles in post-World War I France, for example, Mary Louise Roberts explores the debates and familial arguments that occurred as women embraced bobbed hair; wore shorter skirts, more revealing dresses, and pyjama-like trousers; and abandoned corsets. Roberts is careful to highlight how these concerns about changes in style acquired weight in French society as a sign of the gender turmoil generated by four years of devastating war. Much as Steele does in her discussion of the corset, however, Roberts rejects uncritical readings of the new boyish silhouette that French women strove for in the years after 1918 as an unproblematic sign of liberation or emancipation. Roberts notes that new beauty regimens and beliefs in the individual's ability to change her body meant that women spent increasing amounts of time grooming themselves. New styles of dress also necessitated that women be rail thin, an expectation that led to excessive dieting, the use of elasticized girdles, and the adoption of the bust bodice.[119]

The changes with regard to women's dress in the years immediately preceding and following World War I also had direct bearing on how questions of sexual identity were discussed in the era of Radclyffe Hall's (1880–1943) infamous novel *The Well of Loneliness* (1928), a book in which the central female character, Stephen Gordon, embraces a decidedly masculine aesthetic. In a recent article on this very issue, though, Laura Doan cautions historians about making the links too explicit between gender deviance and sexual deviance in World War I and post-war Britain. In her exploration of female ambulance drivers, Doan argues that female mannishness was not always a challenge to the sexual order, nor did it possess one simple meaning. In establishing this point, Doan argues that historians must resist the temptation to equate the embrace of masculine poses and styles of clothing (frequently a necessity for female ambulance drivers at the front) with sexual inversion, as many sexologists and Hall herself did at the time. In the end, Doan asserts that the tendency of historians to immediately label these women as part of an identity-based form of lesbian history (and thus assert that their gender inversion always implied sexual inversion) is problematic, given that such links were elusive at the time. Rather, she notes, attention paid to dress and gendered poses, as opposed to the acquisition of a self-reflexive sexual identity might yield a new kind of lesbian historiography altogether:

> [the] scrutiny of cultural topsy-turvydom in the early twentieth century – the utter confusion over gender – points with some clarity to the possibilities of a lesbian historiography that takes more fully into account how gender and sexuality might be interrelated in order to understand sexual identity itself as a historical and historicized process.[120]

Doan and other practitioners of the new queer history like Rebecca Jennings, who has examined butch/femme dynamics at London's Gateways Club in the 1950s, 1960s, and 1970s, remind us that much stands to be gained from considering gender performances in the past and their relationship to the outwardly and self-consciously fashioned body.[121]

The relationship between sexual identities, social mores, and dress is also reflected in the changes to women's fashion that occurred in the 1960s, an era when London superseded, albeit briefly, Paris's status as the 'world's fashion capital'.[122] The short dresses and mini-skirts associated with Mary Quant and her King's Road boutique Bazaar came to epito-mize swinging London. Partly a response to the calls of British and international teens and twenty-somethings for a style that was more youthful, less traditional, and celebratory of the more liberal sexual attitudes of the era, Quant's clothes were also a self-conscious creation of the designer herself. As she noted, with reference to the modern aesthetic she espoused: "'I want free-flowing, feminine lines that compliment a woman's shape, with no attempt at distortion. I want relaxed clothes, suiting to the actions of normal life.'"[123] Clearly, there was much potential in Quant's designs for young women who desired to participate in the freer lifestyles of the era. These styles have also been seen, by historians like Marcus Collins, as contributing to a 'sexualization of society' that occurred in the 25 years or so after the conclusion of World War II. For Collins, fashion's role in this process was indisputable. As he notes, with reference to new types of pornographic repre-sentations in glossy and upmarket magazines: 'From fashion, the new pornography gained glimpses of masculine and feminine emancipation and in turn won plaudits from fashion designers like Mary Quant who saw similarities between pornographic images of women and their own.'[124] Like so much else discussed in this chapter, the act of looking at the body on display in fashion magazines and pornographic magazines performed vital cultural work in an era of intense social and cultural change.

Conclusion

This chapter has addressed the possibilities associated with examining attitudes towards nakedness and nudity, developments in fashion, and the consumption of the body as a visual spectacle in European societies since 1750. Focusing, in particular, on efforts to prepare the body for being viewed and the act of viewing itself, it has introduced readers to major developments and highlighted some of the points of debate and disagreement that this rich area of study has produced in the historical profession. In so doing, it serves to bolster a central assertion of this entire book: that the study of the body has generated great vibrancy within a broad range of interrelated disciplines and that continued research in this field will likely yield surprising new results that will continue to transform our understandings of the European past. While we know much now about how dress served as a marker of social status (and are learning more still about the relationship between both the naked and the clothed body and the articulation of gender and sexual identities) recent considerations of clothing and fashion, as both hybrid subjects and 'situated bodily practice[s]' should remind us of the rich possibilities associated with looking at undressed and dressed men and women.[125] Closer inspection of the body in its various states as text, artifact, and subject of scholarly interest[126] should help us to understand the historical complexities of the human form and the relationship between what Mary Douglas labelled 40 years ago as the social body and the physical body.[127] Examining, historicizing, and contextualizing the body then should help us to understand that it is neither an exclusively physical entity nor merely a cultural construction. The words of the feminist philosopher Elizabeth Grosz serve as an instructive final reminder about the importance of this particular analytical perspective: 'animate bodies are objects necessarily different from other objects; they are materialities that are uncontainable in physicalist terms alone. If bodies are objects or things, they are like no others, for they are centers of perspective, insight, reflection, desire, agency.'[128]

Notes

1 Gregg Blachford, 'Looking at Pornography: Erotica and the Socialist Morality', *Gay Left: A Gay Socialist Journal* 6, 1978, pp. 16–20 (19).

2 Laura Mulvey, 'Visual Pleasure and Narrative Cinema', *Screen* 16:3, 1975, pp. 6–18 (8).

3 Mulvey, 'Visual Pleasure', p. 9.

3 Mulvey, 'Visual Pleasure', p. 11.

4 Edward Snow, 'Theorizing the Male Gaze: Some Problems', *Representations* 25, 1989, pp. 30–41 (30).

6 Roger Horrocks, *Male Myths and Icons: Masculinity in Popular Culture*, New York: St Martin's Press, 1995, p. 44.

7 On guardsmen, see Matt Houlbrook, 'Soldier Heroes and Rent Boys: Homosex, Masculinities, and Britishness in the Brigade of Guards, Circa 1900–960', *Journal of British Studies* 42:3, 2003, pp. 351–88. See also Randolph Trumbach, this volume. On women and fashion plates, see Sharon Marcus, *Between Women: Friendship, Desire, and Marriage in Victorian England*, Princeton, NJ: Princeton University Press, 2007, pp. 109–66.

8 I am relying here on ideas developed by Judith Butler. See Judith P. Butler, *Gender Trouble: Feminism and the Subversion of Identity*, New York: Routledge, 1990, pp. 128–41.

9 On the relationship between materiality and gender, see Ariel Beaujot, *Victorian Fashion Accessories*, London: Berg, 2012, p. 9.

10 Kenneth Clark, *The Nude: a Study in Ideal Form*, New York: Pantheon Books, 1956, p. 356.

11 On Winckelmann's contributions, see Elizabeth Prettejohn, *Beauty and Art 1750–2000*, Oxford: Oxford University Press, 2005, pp. 15–39.

12 Johann Joachim Winckelmann, *The History of Ancient Art Among the Greeks*, trans. G. Henry Lodge, London: Chapman, 1850, p. 31.

13 Whitney Davis, *Queer Beauty: Sexuality and Aesthetics from Winckelmann to Freud and Beyond*, New York: Columbia University Press, 2010, pp. 1–50.

14 Winckelmann, *The History of Ancient Art*, p. 47.

15 Winckelmann, *The History of Ancient Art*, pp. 121–22.

16 Thomas W. Laqueur, *Making Sex: Body and Gender from the Greeks to Freud*, Cambridge, MA: Harvard University Press, 1990.

17 Lisa Z. Sigel, 'Introduction: Issues and Problems in the History of Pornography' in Lisa Z. Sigel (ed.), *International Exposure: Perspectives on Modern European Pornography, 1800–2000*, New Brunswick, NJ: Rutgers University Press, 2005, pp. 1–26 (9). See also Ian Moulton and Sigel, this volume.

18 Leslie Bostrom and Marlene Malik, 'Re-Viewing the Nude', *Art Journal* 58:1, 1999, pp. 43–48.

19 Marcia R. Pointon, *Naked Authority: The Body in Western Painting, 1830–1908*, Cambridge: Cambridge University Press, 1990, p. 13.

20 John Berger, Sven Blomberg, Chris Fox, Michael Dibb, and Richard Hollis, *Ways of Seeing*, London: British Broadcasting Corporation and Penguin Books, 1972, pp. 55–64. My reading of Berger, here, is clearly influenced by the work of Marcia Pointon. See Pointon, *Naked Authority*, pp. 15–17.

21 Pointon, *Naked Authority*, p. 14.

22 Pointon, *Naked Authority*, p. 18.

23 Pointon, *Naked Authority*, p. 20.

24 Lynda Nead, *The Female Nude: Art, Obscenity, and Sexuality*, London: Routledge, 1992, p. 7.

25 Nead, *The Female Nude*, p. 99.

26 Clark, *The Nude*, p. 356.

27 Alison Smith, *The Victorian Nude: Sexuality, Morality, and Art*, Manchester: Manchester University Press, 1997, p. 2.

28 Prettejohn, *Beauty and Art*, pp. 94, 98. Prettejohn's general discussion of these issues appears on pp. 89–101.

29 Smith, *The Victorian Nude*, pp. 86–92.

30 'Royal Academy Exhibition', *Times*, 12 July 1830, p. 5.

31 Smith, *The Victorian Nude*, p. 2.

32 Martin Postle and William Vaughan, *The Artist's Model from Etty to Spencer*, London: Merrell Holberton, 1999, pp. 9–11, 14.

33 Alison Smith, 'The Nude in Nineteenth-Century Britain: "The English Nude"' in Alison Smith (ed.), *Exposed: The Victorian Nude*, New York: Watson-Guptill Publications, 2001, pp. 11–20 (12).

34 Smith, *The Victorian Nude*, p. 3. For the influence of this club on one late Victorian artist, Henry Scott Tuke, see Catherine Wallace, *Catching the Light: The Art and Life of Henry Scott Tuke, 1858–1929*, Edinburgh: Atelier Books, 2008, pp. 49–50.

35 Heather Dawkins, *The Nude in French Art and Culture, 1870–1910*, New York: Cambridge University Press, 2002, p. 1.

36 Dawkins, *The Nude in French Art and Culture*, p. 2.

37 Dawkins, *The Nude in French Art and Culture*, p. 90.

38 Dawkins, *The Nude in French Art and Culture*, p. 124.

39 Marcus, *Between Women*, p. 13.

40 The literature on the history of nude photography is extensive. For examples of different approaches, see Pierre Borhan and Gilles Mora, *Men for Men: Homoeroticism and Male Homosexuality in the History of Photography, 1840–2006*, London: Jonathan Cape, 2007; Emmanuel Cooper, *Fully Exposed: The Male Nude in Photography*, 2nd edn, London: Routledge, 1995; Michael Kohler (ed.), *The Body Exposed: Views of the Body: 150 Years of the Nude in Photography*, trans. John S. Southard and Glen Burns, Zurich: Edition Stemmle, 1995; Jorge Lewinski, *The Naked and the Nude: a History of the Nude in Photographs, 1839 to the Present*, New York: Harmony Books, 1987.

41 Sharrona Pearl, *About Faces: Physiognomy in Nineteenth-Century Britain*, Cambridge, MA: Harvard University Press, 2010, p. 149. Pearl is quoting from Hugh W. Diamond, 'On the Application of Photography to the Physiognomic and Mental Phenomena of Insanity' in Sander Gilman (ed.), *The Face of Madness: Hugh W. Diamond and the Origin of Psychiatric Photography*, New York: Brunner/Mazel, 1976, pp. 19–24 (22–23).

42 Janine A. Mileaf, 'Poses for the Camera: Eadweard Muybridge's Studies of the Human Figure', *American Art* 16:3, 2002, pp. 31–53 (34).

43 Edward Lucie-Smith, *Adam: The Male Figure in Art*, New York: Rizzoli, 1998, p. 119.

44 Martin Myrone, 'Prudery, Pornography, and the Victorian Nude (Or, what do we think the butler saw?)' in Smith (ed.), *Exposed*, pp. 23–36 (32). On nude photographs and the consumption of obscenity in nineteenth-century London, see Lynda Nead, *Victorian Babylon: People, Streets, and Images in Nineteenth-Century London*, New Haven, CT: Yale University Press, 2000, pp. 160–61.

45 Lisa Z. Sigel, *Governing Pleasures: Pornography and Social Change in England, 1815–1914*, New Brunswick, NJ: Rutgers University Press, 2002, pp. 4, 90.

46 Philippa Levine, 'States of Undress: Nakedness and the Colonial Imagination', *Victorian Studies* 50:2, 2008, pp. 189–219 (195). See also Ian Moulton, Lisa Sigel, Jonathan Burton and Antoinette Burton, this volume.

47 Clark, *The Nude*, p. 30.

48 Clark, *The Nude*, p. 59. For Clark's full discussion of the nude male, see pp. 173–224.

49 Germaine Greer, *The Beautiful Boy*, New York: Rizzoli, 2003.

50 Lucie-Smith, *Adam*, p. 187.

51 Allen Ellenzweig, *The Homoerotic Photograph: Male Images from Durieu/Delacroix to Mapplethorpe*, New York: Columbia University Press, 1992, p. 3.

52 Greer, *The Beautiful* Boy, p. 11.

53 Lucie-Smith, *Adam*, p. 141.

54 Lucie-Smith, *Adam*, p. 39.

55 On Burne-Jones, see Prettejohn, *Beauty and Art*, p. 136. On Mapplethorpe, see Arthur Coleman Danto, *Playing with the Edge: The Photographic Achievement of Robert Mapplethorpe*, Berkeley: University of California Press, 1996 and Richard Meyer, 'Mapplethorpe's Living Room: Photography and the Furnishing of Desire', *Art History* 24:2, 2001, pp. 292–311.

56 'In the Picture-Galleries. The Royal Academy (Second Notice)', Unidentified Clipping (1894), *Register of Paintings, etc. by Henry Scott Tuke*, Tate Gallery Archives 9019/1/2/1.

57 Michael Hatt, 'Thoughts and Things: Sculpture and the Victorian Nude' in Smith (ed.), *Exposed*, pp. 37–49 (46–48) and Michael Hatt, 'Near and Far: Homoeroticism, Labour and Hamo Thornycroft's Mower', *Art History* 26:1, pp. 26–55.

58 David J. Getsy, *Body Doubles: Sculpture in Britain, 1877–1905*, New Haven, CT: Yale University Press, 2004.

59 Lucie-Smith, *Adam*, p. 147.

60 Lucie-Smith, *Adam*, p. 151.

61 Ana Carden-Coyne, *Reconstructing the Body: Classicism, Modernism, and the First World War*, Oxford: Oxford University Press, 2009, pp. 89–100.

62 Carden-Coyne, *Reconstructing the Body*, pp. 137–38.

63 Tim Batchelor, 'Pathé Frères: *Five Ladies—Peintre et Modèle* (France 1903)' in Smith (ed.), *Exposed*, p. 180.

64 Lucie-Smith, *Adam*, p. 152. The idea about 'genital confrontation' is borrowed from Richard D. Leppert, *The Nude: The Cultural Rhetoric of the Body in the Art of Western Modernity*, Boulder, CO: Westview Press, 2007, pp. 188–94.

65 Paul R. Deslandes, 'Physique Models, Cinema Idols, and Porn Stars: Selling the Beautiful Man in Britain, 1954–80', unpublished paper, 2012. On pornography in the 1970s, see Paul R. Deslandes, 'The Cultural Politics of Gay Pornography in 1970s Britain' in Brian Lewis (ed.), *British Queer History: New Approaches and Perspectives*, Manchester: Manchester University Press, forthcoming 2013.

66 Leppert, *The Nude*, p. 3.

67 Mary Lynn Stewart, *For Health and Beauty: Physical Culture for Frenchwomen, 1880s–1930s*, Baltimore, MD: Johns Hopkins University Press, 2001, p. 67. Stewart is quoting from Jean d'Auteuil, *A Travers la beauté: Hygiène et Beauté. Secrets inédits*, Paris: n.p., n.d., pp. 8, 13.

68 Fellow of the Royal College of Surgeons, *Kallos: A Treatise on the Scientific Culture of Personal Beauty and the Cure of Ugliness*, London: Simpkin, Marshall, and Co., 1883, p. 4.

69 Susan J. Vincent, *The Anatomy of Fashion: Dressing the Body from the Renaissance to Today*, Oxford: Berg, 2009, pp. 98–100.

70 Joanne Entwistle, *The Fashioned Body: Fashion, Dress and Modern Social Theory*, Cambridge: Polity Press, 2000, p. 73.

71 Entwistle, *The Fashioned Body*, pp. 96–105.

72 Entwistle, *The Fashioned Body*, p. 108.

73 Christopher Breward and Caroline Evans, 'Introduction' in Christopher Breward and Caroline Evans (eds), *Fashion and Modernity*, Oxford: Berg, 2005, pp. 1–7 (2).

74 Anne Hollander, *Sex and Suits*, New York: Knopf, 1994, p. 8.

75 John Carl Flügel, *The Psychology of Clothes*, London: Hogarth Press, 1930, p. 112. Flügel's discussion of renunciation appears on pp. 110–21. Flügel's influence is also discussed in Brent Alan Shannon, *The Cut of His Coat: Men, Dress, and Consumer Culture in Britain, 1860–1914*, Athens, OH: Ohio University Press, 2006, p. 23.

76 For discussions of this process see Leonore Davidoff and Catherine Hall, *Family Fortunes: Men and Women of the English Middle Class, 1780–1850*, Chicago: University of Chicago Press, 1987, pp. 22, 410–15; Susan Kingsley Kent, *Gender and Power in Britain, 1640–1990*, London: Routledge, 1999, pp. 60–63; and Valerie Steele, *Fashion and Eroticism: The Ideals of Feminine Beauty from the Victorian Era to the Jazz Age*, New York: Oxford University Press, 1985, pp. 52–53.

77 David Kuchta, *The Three-Piece Suit and Modern Masculinity: England, 1550–1850*, Berkeley: University of California Press, 2002, p. 1.

78 Kuchta, *The Three-Piece Suit*, pp. 1–2.

79 Kuchta, *The Three-Piece Suit*, p. 6.

80 Valerie Steele, *Paris Fashion: a Cultural History*, 2nd edn, Oxford: Berg, 1998, pp. 79–83.

81 Vincent, *The Anatomy of Fashion*, p. 22. Vincent is quoting from *Pückler's Progress: The Adventures of Prince Pückler-Muskau in England, Wales, and Ireland as Told in Letters to His Former Wife*, trans. Flora Brennan, London: Collins, 1987, pp. 238–40.

82 Vincent, *The Anatomy of Fashion*, p. 54.

83 Allison Pease, 'Aestheticism and Aesthetic Theory' in Frederick Roden (ed.), *Oscar Wilde Studies*, Basingstoke: Palgrave Macmillan, 2004, pp. 96–118 (98).

84 Richard Ellmann, *Oscar Wilde*, New York: Knopf, 1988, p. 182.

85 See, for example, a Pears Soap advert c. 1890s, Soap 6 (6a), John Johnson Collection, Bodleian Library, Oxford.

86 Emile Zola, *The Ladies' Paradise*, Berkeley: University of California Press, 1992.

87 Erika Diane Rappaport, *Shopping for Pleasure: Women in the Making of London's West End*, Princeton, NJ: Princeton University Press, 2000, p. 171–72.

88 Christopher Breward, *The Hidden Consumer: Masculinities, Fashion and City Life 1860–1914*, Manchester: Manchester University Press, 1999, pp. 10–11.

89 Michael Hau, *The Cult of Health and Beauty in Germany: A Social History, 1890–1930*, Chicago: University of Chicago Press, 2003, p. 176. See also Richard Cleminson, this volume.

90 Hau, *The Cult of Health and Beauty*, p. 191. For another perspective on this development, see Erik N. Jensen, *Body by Weimar: Athletes, Gender, and German Modernity*, Oxford: Oxford University Press, 2010.

91 Ina Zweiniger-Bargielowska, *Managing the Body: Beauty, Health, and Fitness in Britain, 1880–1939*, Oxford: Oxford University Press, 2010, p. 223.

92 Breward and Evans, 'Introduction', *Fashion and Modernity*, p. 12.

93 Shaun Cole, *'Don We Now Our Gay Apparel': Gay Men's Dress in the Twentieth Century*, Oxford: Berg, 2000, p. 2.

94 On molly-houses, see Randolph Trumbach, 'Modern Sodomy: The Origins of Homosexuality, 1700–1800' in Matt Cook (ed.), *A Gay History of Britain: Love and Sex Between Men Since the Middle Ages*, Oxford: Greenwood World Publishing, 2007, pp. 78–94. On French taverns, see 'Documents from the Archives of the Bastille, 1706–52' in Jeffrey Merrick and Bryant T. Ragan, Jr. (eds), *Homosexuality in Early Modern France: A Documentary Collection*, New York: Oxford University Press, 2001, pp. 52–60.

95 Florence Tamagne, 'The Homosexual Age, 1870–1940' in Robert Aldrich (ed.), *Gay Life and Culture: A World History*, New York: Universe, 2006, pp. 167–95 (181–82).

96 Cole, *'Don We Now Our Gay Apparel'*, p. 4.

97 Matt Houlbrook, *Queer London: Perils and Pleasures in the Sexual Metropolis, 1918–1957*, Chicago: University of Chicago Press, 2005, pp. 144–49.

98 Houlbrook, *Queer London*, p. 77.

99 Matt Houlbrook, '"The Man with the Powder Puff" in Interwar London', *Historical Journal* 50:1, 2007, pp. 145–71.

100 Cole, *'Don We Now Our Gay Apparel'*, p. 62.

101 Cole, *'Don We Now Our Gay Apparel'*, p. 71.

102 Cole, *'Don We Now Our Gay Apparel'*, pp. 93–106.

103 Clare Lomas, '"Men Don't Wear Velvet You Know!": Fashionable Gay Masculinity and the Shopping Experience, London, 1950–Early 1970s' in Peter McNeil and Vicki Karaminas (eds), *The Men's Fashion Reader*, Oxford: Berg, 2009, pp. 168–78.

104 Entwistle, *The Fashioned Body*, p. 141.

105 Vincent, *The Anatomy of Fashion*, p. 65.

106 Vincent, *The Anatomy of Fashion*, pp. 77–78.

107 Erin Skye Mackie, *Market à La Mode: Fashion, Commodity, and Gender in The Tatler and The Spectator*, Baltimore, MD: Johns Hopkins University Press, 1997, pp. 104–43.

108 Vincent, *The Anatomy of Fashion*, p. 81.

109 Vincent, *The Anatomy of Fashion*, p. 96.

110 Steele, *Fashion and Eroticism*, p 164.

111 David Kunzle, *Fashion and Fetishism: A Social History of the Corset, Tight-Lacing, and Other Forms of Body-Sculpture in the West*, Totowa, NJ: Rowman and Littlefield, 1982; Steele, *Fashion and Eroticism*, pp. 161–91.

112 Valerie Steele, *The Corset: a Cultural History*, New Haven, CT: Yale University Press, 2001, p. 54.

113 Helene E. Roberts, 'The Exquisite Slave: The Role of Clothes in the Making of the Victorian Woman', *Signs: Journal of Women in Culture and Society* 2:3, 1977, pp. 554–69 (557).

114 David Kunzle, *Fashion and Fetishism: Corsets, Tight-Lacing, and Other Forms of Body-Sculpture*, new edn, Stroud, Gloucestershire: Sutton, 2004, p. xii.

115 Steele, *The Corset*, p. 1.

116 Steele, *The Corset*, p. 103.

117 Steele, *The Corset*, pp. 61–62.

118 On aspects of the cycling craze, from a gendered perspective, see Sheila Hanlon, 'The Lady Cyclist: A Gender Analysis of Women's Cycling Culture in 1890s London', Ph.D. Thesis, York University, 2009.

119 Mary Louise Roberts, *Civilization Without Sexes: Reconstructing Gender in Postwar France, 1917–1927*, Chicago: University of Chicago Press, 1994, pp. 63–87.

120 Laura L. Doan, 'Topsy-Turvydom: Gender Inversion, Sapphism, and the Great War', *GLQ: A Journal of Lesbian and Gay Studies* 12:4, 2006, pp. 517–42 (537).

121 Rebecca Jennings, 'The Gateways Club and the Emergence of a post-Second World War Lesbian Subculture', *Social History* 31:2, 2006, pp. 206–25.

122 Steele, *Paris Fashion*, p. 277.

123 Jenny Lister, 'Kaleidoscope: Fashion in Sixties London' in Christopher Breward, David Gilbert, and Jenny Lister (eds), *Swinging Sixties: Fashion in London and Beyond, 1955–1970*, London: Victoria and Albert Publications, 2006, pp. 22–41 (40). The Quant quote is unattributed in this work.

124 Marcus Collins, *Modern Love: Personal Relationships in Twentieth-century Britain*, Newark: University of Delaware Press, 2006, p. 142.

125 Joanne Entwistle, 'The Dressed Body' in Joanne Entwistle and Elizabeth Wilson (eds), *Body Dressing*, Oxford: Berg, 2001, pp. 33–58 (35).

126 Butler, *Gender Trouble*, pp. 128–31.

127 Entwistle, *The Fashioned Body*, p. 14. Entwistle is quoting from Mary Douglas, *Natural Symbols*, Harmondsworth: Pelican Books, 1973, p. 93

128 Elizabeth Grosz, *Volatile Bodies: Toward a Corporeal Feminism*, Bloomington: Indiana University Press, 1994, p. xi.

Part VI

PORNOGRAPHY AND EROTICA

11

EROTIC REPRESENTATION, 1500–1750

Ian Frederick Moulton

The two and a half centuries from 1500 to 1750 saw a huge range of social changes all across western Europe. The Reformation and Counter-Reformation shattered religious unity, creating an intellectual climate of debate, doubt, and contention, as well as a heightened level of censorship and regulation of thought and feeling. Wars of religion ravaged the continent: the Sack of Rome, the French civil wars of the sixteenth century, the Thirty Years War in Germany, the English Civil War and Puritan interregnum – all tore apart families and communities, and disrupted established social and political structures. The period also saw major economic shifts – massive price inflation in the six-teenth century, probably caused by the influx of American silver into Spain, and a historic reorientation of commerce as international trade networks shifted from the Mediterranean to the Atlantic. As an integral part of the larger culture, erotic representation could not help but be influenced by these transformative events. Throughout this period, erotic writing was implicated in the debates and struggles over religion and morality engendered by the Reformation and Counter-Reformation. Some of the most explicit erotic writing from the period is found in polemical texts attacking the supposed hypocrisy and corrup-tion of either a particular sect or organized religion in general. The close connection between erotic discourse and religious controversy can be seen in the evolution of the word 'libertine'. Originally used to describe religious non-conformity, over time it came to refer primarily to a particular form of rebellious sexuality that privileged the passions of the elite male individual over established social and ethical norms.[1]

As wealth and power migrated from Italy and the Mediterranean to the North Atlantic countries – England, France, and the Netherlands – so too did erotic writing. In the early sixteenth century, the most influential erotic texts are Italian. After the Tridentine reforms and the establishment of the Papal Index of Prohibited Books in the 1560s, Italian influ-ence declined, but early Italian texts served as models for later French ones, which in turn were translated and adapted in England and elsewhere. This process follows larger trends both in the development of the book market and the general transmission of cultural models. Indeed, one could argue that erotic writing in this period begins with copies of Aretino's *Sonetti lussuriosi* circulating at the Papal Court in 1527 and ends with Cleland's *Fanny Hill* sitting on the bookstalls of London in 1748. Moving from the *Sonetti* to *Fanny Hill*, one moves from the Mediterranean to the Atlantic, from the sonnet to the novel, from the court to the marketplace, and from the coterie to the public sphere. This movement is pregnant with meaning, and its general trajectory towards modernity is clear enough.[2] But nonetheless it is only one strand in the history of erotic representation in the period. For one thing, focusing on the cultural progression from Italy to England via France slights the substantial production of erotic texts in the Netherlands, especially in the later seventeenth century.[3] Furthermore, a narrow focus on a few influential literary texts neglects widespread popular traditions of bawdy ballads and jests, and ignores obscene verse and popular invective, not to mention medical and legal texts with definite and documented erotic appeal.[4] The variety of erotic writing in the early modern period is vast, and to understand the place and function of erotic representation one must look at a wide range of texts, some innovative and daring, others normative, some sophisticated, others sophomoric.

As far as writing in general is concerned, of course, the greatest upheaval of the period 1500–1750 was technological and economic: the introduction of the printing press and the subsequent development of a market for printed vernacular books. The book market not only allowed wider dissemination of existing texts, it also provoked translation of texts from Latin to the vernacular, and from foreign to domestic languages. It facilitated the broad social dissemination of texts that would otherwise have had limited or specialist audiences, such as sexually detailed medical texts,[5] or printed collections of bawdy coterie verse.[6] Indeed, the book market allowed all forms of writing to proliferate much more widely than was previously possible. In doing so, it transformed both the scope and availability of erotic writing – although in ways difficult to quantify, since many erotic texts were printed clandestinely and many no longer survive.[7] Samuel Pepys's famous destruction of his copy of *L'Ecole des filles* highlights the fact that erotic books tend by their nature to be disposable.[8] And besides, it was the common fate of all sorts of cheap books to end up as wrapping paper for fish or pies, or even to be used as toilet paper.[9] Given the protean nature of the early modern book market, perhaps the best way to understand erotic writing in the period is not as a genealogical series of influential texts but as an array of competing voices and traditions, some elite and relatively narrow in appeal, others popular and broadly accessible, some funny, others serious, some witty and pleasant, others violent and cruel.[10] This diversity of material gives rise to one of the greatest problems in historically evaluating erotic representation in the early modern period: what is one to call such material? Is it pornography?

Certainly the early modern period did produce texts that can seem pornographic to a twenty-first-century reader. Aretino's *Ragionamenti* contain passages of graphicly explicit sexual description; poems like John Marston's 'Metamorphoses of Pygmalion's Image'[11] and even Shakespeare's 'Rape of Lucrece'[12] objectify their female characters and feature a leering, voyeuristic sexuality that seems familiar to those acquainted with later forms of pornography. But whatever they may seem to us, these texts did not seem 'pornographic' to their original readers, because such a concept did not exist at the time. Coined in the nineteenth century and brought into widespread use in the twentieth, 'pornography' was not a word used in the early modern period.[13] Of course, things can exist and be understood even if a culture doesn't name them. The investigation of the origins of pornography is an important historical project in its own right, and it would be naive to assume that pornography first appeared at the same moment the term was coined. But the absence of the term leads to a crucial historical question: lacking the concept of pornography, in what ways did early modern culture structure its understanding of sexuality and its representation?

An analogous problem of terminology exists in the case of homoeroticism: relations that we call homosexual clearly existed in periods before the term was coined in the nineteenth century. Some will argue that 'homosexuality' therefore existed in those earlier periods. Others argue that while the acts we call 'homosexual' existed, the identity we call 'homosexual' did not; while the acts may have been the same as they are today, they were culturally understood using different vocabularies, different systems of categorization, different frames of reference.[14] In terms of our historical understanding of different periods and cultures, the stakes in these debates around terminology are fairly high. One's own cultural biases on fundamental and emotional things like sexuality tend to be quite strong. They also have a tendency to seem natural and obvious. If we simply project our own cultural categories onto earlier periods in unreflective ways, we will lose sight of the differences between our own understanding of things and those of other, earlier cultures. We will fundamentally misread the culture we are trying to understand (all history is to some extent a misreading, but that does not necessarily mean the tendency ought to be encouraged). And if sexuality has a history at all, it consists precisely in the different and changing ways that various sexual acts are culturally represented, categorized, and understood.

Leaving aside the issue of anachronism, 'pornography' is arguably not a particularly useful category with which to describe the erotic writing of the early modern period.[15] To begin with, it is an imprecise term, and one that has proved notoriously hard to define. The difficulty arises in part because the term is fundamentally contradictory: it describes both writing and visual images; it refers both to a genre and a type of content; it denotes a subject matter, but connotes a precise range of attitudes towards that subject matter; it is descriptive, but also pejorative.[16] Although the word 'pornography' is often used to refer to a work's erotic content, most formal definitions focus instead on the intention of those who produced it. The *Oxford English Dictionary*, for example, defines pornography as 'the explicit description or exhibition of sexual subjects or activity in literature, painting, films, etc., in a manner intended to stimulate erotic rather than aesthetic feelings'.[17] This may seem straightforward, but although the 'intent' of an online porn site may seem clear enough, determining the authorial intention behind a 300-year-old literary text may be considerably more difficult. The *OED* definition also relies on an implied opposition between erotic and aesthetic value – if something is sexually arousing, it cannot be beautiful, and vice versa. Again, this principle may seem simple enough, and certainly would apply to many photographs on Internet porn sites, but surely some sexually arousing representations are also beautiful – photographs by Robert Mapplethorpe, paintings by Titian, Courbet, or Boucher, statues by Michelangelo, and drawings by Klimt, for example.[18]

In current usage, 'pornography' refers primarily to photographic or cinematic images rather than writing. Given the flood of pornographic pictures and videos available on the Internet, almost no one now uses the term to describe narrative text – let alone bawdy verse. This strong contemporary connection to digital visual technologies makes pornography particularly problematic as a term of historical analysis. Assuming that contemporary pornographic websites and videos serve the same social function or are governed by the same formal principles as seventeenth-century erotic writing is dubious, to say the least. Using the same term to refer to both forecloses important questions of cultural difference between the present and the past and obscures the place of the erotic in early modern culture. So, if the term pornography is problematic, what is the alternative? Discussions about sexually explicit writing and images in the twentieth century often relied on a distinction between 'pornography' (aggressive, masculine, and exploitative), and 'erotica' (sensual, feminine, and celebratory). This distinction has been much critiqued, but whatever its merits, 'erotica' has the same limitations as 'pornography' if one is attempting a historical analysis of the early modern period.[19] It is another anachronistic term that implies a clear value judgement about the moral and cultural worth of the material under analysis.

The early modern period itself provides no single term to refer to the explicit representation of sexual acts or the texts containing such representations. In English such texts were referred to as 'bawdy' and 'lewd',[20] or were abused as 'filthy', 'nasty', or 'vile'.[21] Perhaps the most specific term used to describe such writing in English was 'Aretine' – referring to the Italian writer Pietro Aretino, and especially to the illustrations of various sexual positions he was widely (though falsely) believed to have drawn.[22] But this term referred to behaviour as well as images and texts. In eighteenth-century France, the words used to describe sexually explicit texts included 'érotique' [erotic], 'licencieux' [licentious], 'obscène' [obscene], 'lascif' [lascivious], and 'lubrique' [lubricious].[23] These terms connected sex to dirt and filth, but also to pleasure, and – perhaps most interestingly – to rebelliousness, individuality,[24] and self-indulgence.

Faced with this intractable problem of terminology, I have resorted to the somewhat anodyne phrase 'erotic writing' to describe writing representing sexuality in the early modern period. The term is meant to be descriptive rather than judgemental. Erotic writing is writing, of whatever kind, genre, or quality, that deals with or describes sexual activity. It is writing about Eros – sexual passion. By using the term 'erotic writing' I am not trying to connote some softer, gentler, more polite form of sexuality. In much early modern writing, in fact, Eros appears as a terrifying and powerful destructive and creative force, in the face of which human beings are generally helpless. Shakespeare's Sonnet 129 gives a classic description: sexual passion, the speaker attests, is

> Mad in pursuit, and in possession so,
> Had, having, and in quest to have, extreme;
> A bliss in proof and proved, a very woe;
> Before, a joy proposed; behind a dream.
>
> (lines 9–12)

And, as the poem famously concludes, knowing that Eros is dangerous does not help us avoid it:

> All this the world well knows, yet none knows well
> To shun the heaven that leads men to this hell.
>
> (lines 13–14)

'Erotic writing' was not a phrase used in early modern England, but the term 'erotic' or 'erotical' does come into English in the early modern period. It appears in Burton's *Anatomy of Melancholy* (III.ii.I.ii) in the 1620s, and in the title, *Erotomania*, coined for the 1640 English translation of Jacques Ferrand's medical treatise *On Lovesickness*. It remained a somewhat technical term, however, until the late nineteenth century – a period when much of our current descriptive vocabulary for sexuality came into common use.

Just as there was no single early modern term that defined erotic writing as a specific genre or subject for discourse, there was no separate legal category to describe erotic works. In early modern Europe texts and images were subject to censorship if they were considered subversive, but little distinction was made between political, religious, or moral subversion.[25] The charges brought against the French painter Jean Hubert in 1721 were typical: he was arrested 'for having drawn plates that were contrary to religion, the State and public morals'.[26] Although all three categories – religion, state, and morality – tended to be seen as intrinsically connected, before the late seventeenth century, censorship in western Europe was almost entirely concerned with religious and political expression. Sexually explicit content in itself was not singled out for prosecution. It is true that authors of sexually explicit works were sometimes harshly punished: Aretino's adversary and emu-lator Niccolò Franco was executed by the Papal authorities in 1570, as was Ferrante Pallavicino, author of *La Retorica delle puttane* (*The Rhetoric of Whores*) in 1644, but both were punished for their outspoken attacks on the Papacy rather than for the specifically sexual content of some of their texts. Similarly, in Restoration England prosecutions of authors for their political views were far more common than prosecutions for obscenity.[27] Throughout the early modern period, the enforcement of censorship in England was relatively weak; individual booksellers or publishers might be prosecuted, but there was no systematic effort to police the book market or printing industry as a whole.[28] In France, the authorities were far more concerned to control the unorthodox religious publications of Jansenists and others than to police erotic expression.[29] And especially in France, erotic and political subversion often went together: the same clandestine printers produced both erotic and Jansenist texts.[30] To a greater degree than in other countries, French erotic texts carried an anti-clerical or politically subversive charge, a tendency particularly marked in the years leading up to the French Revolution.[31]

Indeed, the political valence of early modern erotic texts is often dependent on national and cultural context: in France, explicitly erotic texts arose in conjunction with anti-clerical and anti-establishment satire, often combining the two forms. Such a systematic attack on the national church was much less common in England and the Netherlands. French erotic writing is radical and even revolutionary in its attack on Catholicism and its assertion of the rights of individual upper-class males, but in England, where anti-Catholicism and elite individuality were encouraged rather than condemned, these quali-ties make the very same texts seem relatively conservative – in terms of social values if not of polite discourse.[32] The figure of the lascivious nun, for example, was a generally acceptable stereotype in Protestant countries and a scandalous attack on religion in Catholic ones.

In recent times, especially since the development of the Internet and digital photo-graphy, erotically arousing material is likely to consist primarily of images. In the early modern period, on the other hand, erotic texts were more common than images. Erotic paintings were an elite art form with very little circulation in larger culture. The frescos by Raphael and Giulio Romano at the Villa Farnesina, for example, were seen only by those in the social circle of the house's owner, wealthy banker Agostino Chigi.[33] Paintings of voluptuous female nudes by Titian, Velasquez and others had a similarly limited and elite circulation.[34] Erotic engravings were, of course, printed and circulated more widely than paintings, but they were nonetheless an expensive luxury product.[35] On a less elevated level, it seems likely that erotic graffiti was relatively common in the streets and in broth-els.[36] There are also accounts of erotic playing cards.[37] But little evidence of such ephem-eral material has survived. In England, before 1650, even erotic texts without illustrations were too expensive to be purchased frequently by a large percentage of the literate popu-lation.[38] But from that point on, the price of books in general declined, and there was a corresponding increase in supply and sales of all sorts of printed material, including erotic texts. These economic factors may account in part for the outpouring of published erotic texts in the turbulent middle decades of the seventeenth century. As the book market developed, illustration became cheaper and more common, but it remained comparatively expensive well into the eighteenth century.[39] Some inexpensive texts were accompanied by lewd woodcuts, as was the case with a series of English pamphlets from the Civil War period satirizing non-conformist sects, but this was relatively rare.[40] In any case, frontispieces to erotic texts tend to be relatively chaste by modern standards: figures are often embracing, but clothed.[41] Of course, in a society where bodies in public tended to be entirely covered by clothes, such illustrations could seem more provocative than we find them now. More explicit images were produced, but generally speaking they were a luxury item intended for an elite market.

In fact, most surviving explicitly erotic representation from the early modern period has its origin in high rather than low culture. This may seem surprising: sex often tends to be thought of as 'low', involving as it does the lower body and base desires,[42] and this notion can lead to the assumption that cultural discourses about sexuality are therefore socially 'low' – that is, lower class or vulgar. Certainly, in contemporary culture, pornography is generally seen as antithetical to high culture, either parodying the excesses of new money (*Penthouse*) or defiantly lower class (*Hustler*). In the early modern period, on the other hand, the explicitly erotic texts that have survived mostly originated in elite rather than popular culture. The engravings and poems of *I modi* had their origins at the Papal Court. Antonio Vignali's homoerotic dialogue *La Cazzaria* was the product of an elite academy in Siena. Much surviving early modern English erotic poetry, including some of the crudest in content and language, came not from the streets or fields but from Oxbridge colleges and the Inns of Court.[43] Early seventeenth-century French erotic verse originated in similar circles.[44] Seventeenth- and eighteenth-century libertinism was a largely aristocratic phenomenon, from the Earl of Rochester to the Marquis de Sade and Lord Byron. Indeed, libertinism saw sexuality primarily in terms of the unrestricted power and pleasure of individual elite men. As a practical matter, at least in England, many of the most influential libertine texts were initially available only in foreign languages (French, Italian, and Latin), and their circulation was thus limited to an educated elite. Eroticism in popular culture, although widely prevalent, tended to be more humorous, and less graphic in its language.[45] It was also expressed socially rather than textually – in public courting at fairs, games of leapfrog, and bawdy songs, rather than in clever poems or outrageous dialogues – and so it has left fewer written traces. Although they circulated relatively broadly over time, in a partially literate society, erotic texts necessarily originated as a minority and elite pleasure.[46]

The social diversity of erotic expression and representation is crucial to keep in mind, precisely because it has left such ephemeral traces. What has survived from the period tend to be elite texts that reflect a libertine perspective. So, for better or worse, these libertine texts have come to define the field for many readers and scholars. In his groundbreaking 1965 bibliographic study *Libertine Literature in England, 1660–1745* David Foxon identified a series of key texts crucial to the development of erotic literature in western Europe in the early modern period. Although the notion that these texts form some sort of canon of early modern writing is problematic, the texts themselves have been at the core of debates over early modern erotic representation, and thus it is worth briefly describing them here, especially since they circulated under so many names and in such different forms that it can be difficult to keep them straight.

I modi [The Positions][47] (*c.* 1525), later infamous all over Europe and known in England as 'Aretine's Pictures' or 'Postures'.[48] These were a series of 16 engravings of heterosexual couples having intercourse in various positions. The engravings were by Marcantonio Raimondi after drawings by Giulio Romano and were later published accompanied by erotic sonnets by Pietro Aretino known as the *Sonetti lussuriosi*.[49] The volume seems to have been effectively suppressed, and the 'postures' were much better known by their legendary reputation than by actual acquaintance. Over time, the visual artists were forgotten, and the entire enterprise was popularly ascribed to Aretino, whose name became shorthand for any erotic text or image.[50]

Aretino's *Ragionamenti* [Dialogues] (1534), were also known as the *Sei giornati* [Six Days].[51] These are dialogues by Pietro Aretino in which an experienced whore named Nanna relates her sexual life to a younger whore named Antonia. The first and more famous volume consists of three days during which Nanna and Antonia compare the three ways of life available to women – as nuns, wives, and whores – in an attempt to determine which would be the best for Nanna's teenage daughter Pippa. The volume contains a certain amount of explicit sexual description, mostly employed in an attack on clerical and monastic corruption (Aretino was not a Protestant, but had a personal and political quarrel with the Papal Court). The volume explicitly describes heterosexual intercourse, male and female homosexual relations, group sex, and masturbation. Despite its provocative licentiousness, the volume is a serious social and political examination of power and gender, as well as of the influence of market forces on traditional morality.[52]

La Puttana errante [The Wandering Whore], also known as *Dialogo di Giulia e di Maddelena* [The Dialogue of Giulia and Maddelena] (before 1660), was often, though probably falsely, ascribed to Aretino.[53] In this brief text, a whore named Giulia describes her sexual life and experiences to her companion Maddalena. In doing so, she provides a catalogue and list of possible positions for heterosexual intercourse, as well as brief descriptions of lesbian encounters and sex between men. The dialogue's date is uncertain. The earliest printed edition is from 1660, though a manuscript exists that may date from the late sixteenth century.[54] The title, *Puttana errante*, which has little relation to the content of the text, is taken from a narrative poem on a completely different subject written in the 1530s by Lorenzo Venier, a Venetian nobleman and disciple of Aretino.[55] Unlike the *Ragionamenti*, the dialogue between Giulia and Maddelena has few social or political concerns and is focused primarily on the detailed description of sexual activity.

L'École des filles [The School for Girls] (1655),[56] whose author is unknown, was published in Paris by Michel Millot and Jean L'Ange, who were subsequently prosecuted for their efforts.[57] The text consists of a pair of dialogues between two young women, the virginal Fanchon and her older, more experienced kinswoman Suzanne. In the first dialogue, Suzanne explains sex to Fanchon and encourages her to make love with her suitor Robinet. In the second dialogue, held one week later, Fanchon tells Suzanne about her sexual experiences with Robinet and questions her about their significance. The focus of the volume is almost entirely on heterosexual relations, and the speakers are middle-class young women, not prostitutes. Translated into English as *The School of Venus* in 1688, this text is also primarily sexual in content.[58]

Satyra Sotadica de Arcanis Amoris et Veneris [A Sotadic[59] Satire on the Secrets of Love and Venus] (*c.* 1659), was written in Latin by the Frenchman Nicholas Chorier, and falsely ascribed to Luisa Sigea, a sixteenth-century Spanish nun, poet, and linguist.[60] The volume is a collection of seven dialogues, primarily between two women, Octavia and her older, more

experienced cousin Tullia. The interlocutors are respectable aristocratic women, not prostitutes. The *Satyra Sotadica* is a complex, lengthy, libertine text that begins by describing the
genitals, and then expands to deal with lesbian, marital, and extra-marital sex, ending with
philosophical and explicit descriptions of rape, sodomy, incest, domination and much more
besides. The full Latin text was not translated in the early modern period, but various
sections and adaptations circulated quite widely. The first French version, *L'Académie des
dames* [The School for Ladies] was published in 1680. English translations appeared under
several names: *A Dialogue between a Married Lady and a Maid* (1688), *The School of Love* (1707),
and *Aretinus Redivivus* (1745).[61]

Venus dans le cloître [Venus in the Cloister] (1683), ascribed to Father Jean Barrin,[62] consists of three dialogues between two young nuns: Sister Angélique (aged 19) and Sister
Agnès (aged 16). This volume has less erotic description than the preceding texts, stressing
instead anti-clerical and anti-monastic philosophical and social views. An English
translation, *Venus in the Cloister or the Nun in her Smock*, appeared almost immediately (1683).
A 1725 English edition published by Edmund Curll was successfully prosecuted for
obscene libel.[63]

Memoirs of a Woman of Pleasure, or Fanny Hill (1749) is a novel by John Cleland, recounting
the sexual exploits of the title character.[64] Although sexually explicit texts of various kinds
had been written and published in England for hundreds of years, *Fanny Hill* is often seen
as the first widely influential pornographic work written in English. In its celebration of
sexual pleasure, the novel can be seen as part of the libertine tradition, but it also owes
much to the bourgeois values of the novel as a genre. Fanny may begin as a prostitute, but
she ends up married to her true love Charles, who, not coincidentally, is the man with
whom she originally lost her virginity.

Taken together these texts have frequently been used to construct the compelling but in
some ways dubious teleology I alluded to at the outset of this chapter: a movement
towards modernity, the market, and the public sphere. They also arguably demonstrate
an increasing focus on sexual activity as an end in itself, at times creating what Stephen
Marcus has memorably called a 'pornotopia' in which sex has no relation to procreation,
family, society, or politics, but exists only as a utopian source of physical delight: a fantasy
world primarily structured to stimulate the masturbatory fantasies of heterosexual male
readers.[65] Leaving aside *I modi*, which in any case was more influential as a legend in the
popular imagination than as an actual text that could be read and imitated, all these texts
share certain features. All were written by men, yet all are written from the imagined
perspective of women. All are structured on the notion of an initiation or erotic education,[66] in which a younger and less experienced woman learns from an older and more
experienced one. These texts tend to be anti-clerical, criticizing the supposed hypocrisy of
the church in matters of sexuality. They also tend to privilege heterosexual over homosexual activity, often seeing homosexual encounters (and masturbation) as a preliminary
step on the path to normative heterosexual relations. Lesbian encounters, in particular,
are seen as initiatory rites, part of the learning process for the female protagonists, but
ultimately unsatisfying because no penis is involved. Indeed, the key feature of these texts
may be their obsessive focus on the penis as the ultimate source of pleasure for both men
and women.[67] Despite their celebration of masculinity, in these texts sex between men is
usually seen as an aberration, often a curiosity observed by the female protagonist.[68] The
one episode of male homoeroticism in *Fanny Hill* was suppressed by the author himself
after the first edition, and although the incident is described in some detail, it is framed in

very harsh terms. After watching the men, the narrator Fanny describes their encounter as a 'criminal scene' that leaves her 'burning with rage and indignation'.[69]

As Foxon's title indicates, all these texts are in some sense 'libertine'. That is, they set themselves in opposition to organized religion; they celebrate passion and physical pleasure; they challenge or reject traditional notions of family and duty. And although the speakers are almost all women, the values endorsed are those of elite, rebellious, and self-indulgent young men. Libertine texts tend to be materialist: they focus on the body and physical desires as the fundamental ground of human experience. They are often Machiavellian in their politics: the physical realities of power are more important than idealism, and the naked workings of power are concealed behind a smooth, hypocritical façade. Whether or not libertinism constitutes a coherent philosophy is an open question, but James Grantham Turner is surely right to see libertinism as a performance, a series of cultural gestures adopted primarily by elite young men to increase their social power and define their cultural identity.[70] The libertine disassociation of sexuality from procreation, in particular, marks a huge shift from traditional thinking on the subject. From a modern 'post-pill' perspective, when birth control is readily available for both men and women, seeing sex primarily in terms of pleasure seems natural and obvious. In earlier periods and cultures, although sex was presumably just as pleasurable as it is now, the primary frame of reference for sexual behaviour remained the production of children. Marriage law, sodomy law, the distinction between licit and illicit sexual activities, even the distinction between what was sex and what was not, all depended on the relation of a given practice to the possibility of procreation. Procreation structured traditional cultural understandings of sexuality, while libertinism minimized or ignored it.

Although all the texts Foxon discusses are important and influential, there are serious objections that may be made to the notion that they constitute some sort of canon of early modern erotic writing. As with all attempts at tracing such genealogies, the relations between the texts are at times arbitrary. The connection of the sonnets and engravings of *I modi* with the later narrative texts is unclear, for example, as is the relation of the sixteenth-century Italian texts to the later French ones. If one assumes a late date for the dialogue known as *La Puttana errante*, there is a gap of at least 50 years between the publication of Aretino's *Ragionamenti* and the subsequent texts. Rather than seeing all these texts as a progression or tradition, one could argue that the erotic works of Aretino were to a certain extent *sui generis*, and focus instead on the remarkable outpouring of explicitly erotic texts in the middle years of the seventeenth century – a period marked by the political and social instability of the Fronde rebellions in France and the Civil War and Interregnum in England.[71]

Foxon himself was somewhat reluctant to include *Fanny Hill* in his list, since, unlike most of the other texts he deals with, it is a novel, not a dialogue. There is also a marked difference in tone, for while the Italian and French texts all use a coarse sexual vocabulary ('*cazzo*', '*potta*', '*vit*', '*con*', etc.) *Fanny Hill* avoids the use of vulgar terms, instead employing elaborate metaphors to describe genital organs and their functions: the penis is an 'enormous machine', and a 'furious battering ram'; the vagina, a 'pleasure-thirsty channel' and 'nethermouth', and so on.[72] Moreover, in the Italian texts, the speakers are all prostitutes, whereas in the French and English texts the women are more respectable, middle-class girls, aristocratic wives, and nuns. Even the whore Fanny Hill ends up properly married to her beloved Charles. So, as a canon, Foxon's list is a useful starting point, but it is neither entirely coherent in its categories nor comprehensive in its scope. Even if, for a moment, we limit eroticism to libertinism, there were many influential libertine texts circulating in the period beyond those that Foxon lists. One might cite, for example, Gervaise de Latouche's *L'Histoire du Dom Bougre, portier des Chartreux* (1741–42), available in English almost immediately as *The History of Don B.* (1743), a strongly anticlerical text, written in the form of a confession. And of course, there were libertine writings in other genres than narrative fiction: the poems and drama of Rochester, for example, and satiric parodies such as the 1684 *Parliament of Women*.[73]

Because of their literary qualities and perceived modernity, libertine texts have attracted ample attention from literary scholars. But libertine narrative constitutes only a part of early modern erotic writing as a whole. Not only were erotic texts written in a wide range of genres – verse satire, lyric poetry, epigrams, and drama, as well as dialogues and novels – their content went well beyond the limits of libertinism, if by libertism we mean the celebration of rebellious elite masculine sexuality. Libertinism was only part of a large and public discourse about sex, a discourse that in many ways blended imperceptibly into the larger culture. Although *Fanny Hill* provides a particularly extreme example, eighteenth-century novels often focused on eroticism. In France, the mid-eighteenth century saw a plethora of erotic narratives located in the orient, beginning with Crébillon's *Tanzaï et Néadarné* (1734; English translation 1735). The most famous of these may well be Diderot's *Bijoux indiscrets* [The Indiscreet Jewels] (1748; English translation 1749), about a sultan who has a magic ring that makes women's genitals speak and compels them to reveal their secrets. There were also texts, like Antonio Vignali's *La Cazzaria* (*c.* 1525) and Antonio Rocco's *L'Alcibiade fanciullo a scuola* [Alcibiades the Schoolboy], written before 1630 and published in 1652, that thoroughly reject heterosexual eroticism and celebrate sexual relations between men. Libertine texts in general are fiercely misogynistic, frequently taking the view that women exist primarily to pleasure men. But these texts go further, rejecting women as sexual partners altogether. As such, they run counter to the general early modern trend to connect sexuality very closely with procreation and fertility.[74] Although texts advocating male homosexuality did not circulate as widely and were not imitated as broadly as other forms of erotic texts, they nonetheless constitute important evidence of male sexuality in the period.

Though much in the early modern erotic poetry of France and England supports a male fantasy of limitless potency and easy sexual conquests, the tone is often humorous.[75] There is a knowing hubris in many of the boasts, and many poems mock the sexual shortcomings of both men and women. In England, authors as diverse as Thomas Nashe, the Earl of Rochester, and Aphra Behn explored issues of sexual failing, incompatibility, and dissatisfaction.[76] French poets of the early seventeenth century such as Mathurin Régnier and Théophile de Viau did the same.[77] If the penis is all-powerful, it is also unreliable and fickle, beyond the control of its male masters and female admirers. Such poems drew on classical models by Catullus, Ovid, and Martial, but also on native traditions of bawdy humour and invective.[78] They are popular as well as literary, crude as well as refined, comic as well as sexual. The humorous self-mockery of much of this material sets it apart from the serious intensity of both libertine literature and subsequent pornography.

Divisions between erotic writing and other forms of discourse are particularly hard to define when it comes to poetry. When does a love poem become erotic writing? In writing the sexually explicit *Sonetti lussuriosi*, Aretino was engaging in a sly subversion of the most elegantly Petrarchan of poetic forms. And over time the boundaries between decorous love poetry and salacious eroticism were increasingly blurred. Is Donne's Elegy 19, 'To his

Mistress Going to Bed', an erotic poem? What about Shakespeare's Sonnet 20, to his 'master-mistress'? Strict boundaries between literary and erotic texts do not seem to have been observed by English readers; the manuscript collections in which such 'literary' texts initially circulated are full of erotic texts of varying length, sophistication, and explicitness.[79] In Elizabethan and Jacobean England, erotic poetry circulated primarily in manuscript; most surviving manuscript miscellanies belonged to young men at the Universities and the Inns of Court. In France, this sort of material began to appear in print in the early seventeenth century, published in collections like *Les Muses Gaillardes* (1609), *Le Cabinet Satyrique* (1618), *Le Cabinet Secret du Parnasse* (1618), and *Le Parnasse Satyrique* (1622). These volumes included seduction poems, *carpe diem* poems, humorous *double entendres*, poems about impotence, and poems about dildos. They celebrate physical pleasure and heterosexual desire, and like many texts of the period, focus on both the ubiquitous nature of sexual desire and on the perceived necessity of a penis for both men's and women's sexual satisfaction. In language they are crude and explicit, in tone often comic and satiric.

And early modern erotic writing was not exclusively literary. There were non-literary texts with demonstrated erotic appeal, including many published catalogues of whores. Perhaps the earliest is the 1535 *Tariffa delle puttane di Venegia* [Rates of the whores of Venice] attributed to Antonio Cavallino.[80] Another Venetian list, *Il Catologo di tutte le principale e piu honorate cortigiane di Venezia* [A Catalogue of all the Principal and Most Honoured Courtesans in Venice] appeared in 1565.[81] John Wolfe's 1584 London edition of Aretino's *Ragionamenti* includes the anonymous *Ragionamenti di Zoppino*, a catalogue of Roman prostitutes.[82] Catalogues of London whores were included as appendices in several volumes of the *Wandering Whore* pamphlets that appeared from 1660–63, and other, more detailed catalogues appeared before the end of the century.[83] And *t'Amsterdamsch Hoerdom* [Amsterdam's Whoredom], a descriptive catalogue of prostitutes in Amsterdam, was originally published in Dutch in 1681 and soon translated into several languages.[84] Such books provided some practical information, but also a certain amount of titillation. Like Elizabethan cony-catching pamphlets and other forms of rogue literature, they gave respectable readers a voyeuristic glimpse of an illicit subculture.

From the mid-seventeenth century onward there was an outpouring of books dealing more or less discretely with sexual advice and information: books on courtship,[85] midwifery,[86] lovesickness, and fertility. Whether or not individual readers found these texts arousing, they nonetheless structured and shaped cultural knowledge of sexuality for large numbers of people. Jacques Ferrand's *Treatise on Lovesickness* (Toulouse, 1610; Paris, 1623) provides the most sustained and detailed treatment of the traditional notion that excessive sexual desire was a physical disease requiring medical treatment. His text, published in two different French versions, was translated into English in 1640 under the splendid title of *Erotomania*. Ferrand describes female masturbation,[87] sex with evil spirits, and the notion that in some cases lovesickness can only be cured with intercourse. Although it was an intellectually serious medical text written by a physician, the first edition of Ferrand's treatise was condemned as sacrilegious by the Ecclesiastical Tribune of Toulouse in 1620 because of its discussion of astrology, its recipes for love-potions, and its description of ointments to increase genital pleasure in both men and women.[88] To make matters worse, all this was made available not in scholarly Latin, but in the vernacular. The second edition was less provocative, and the subsequent English translation prudently put some of the most scandalous passages in Latin. Ferrand himself admitted that 'those works that discuss sperm, human reproduction, and … male impotency and female infertility' can sometimes arouse their readers.[89]

Although Ferrand's text provides important insights into early modern medical thinking about sexuality, it was not nearly as popular as later volumes of what might be called medical folklore such as *Aristotle's Masterpiece* (1684), an anonymous book on sex and pregnancy that gave detailed instructions on ways to ensure fertility, including which postures were thought more likely to conceive male children.[90] The text circulated in various versions into the nineteenth century. It had, of course, no actual connection to the works of Aristotle. The most widely circulated early modern medical text dealing with sexuality was Nicolas Venette's *Tableau de l'amour conjugal* [The Picture of Conjugal Love] (1686), translated into all major European languages, and published in modified form into the twentieth century.[91] Venette's book gives detailed descriptions of the genital organs and the mechanics of sexual intercourse. Although he is generally conservative in medical matters and his understanding of the body is Galenic and humoural, Venette promotes the relatively novel idea that love and marriage and sex can all exist harmoniously in one relationship.[92] He sees sex primarily as a natural urge that, because it is natural, cannot be denied or rejected. The notion that sex is a healthy part of a normative and loving companionate marriage marks a total departure from the earlier idea, elaborated by Ferrand, that sex is at its root a disease, as well as the notion, so well expressed in Shakespeare's Sonnet 129, that sexual desire is necessarily a hellish torment.

Venette's praise of conjugal sexuality can also be seen as part of a larger process whereby procreative sex between husband and wife is privileged and other forms of sexuality are increasingly attacked and disparaged. Beginning in the early eighteenth century popular texts begin to appear attacking masturbation, an activity previously ignored in almost all written records, medical, devotional, or fictional.[93] This period also sees an increase in flagellant fiction, in part because, as Sarah Toulalan has shown, beating was believed to heighten sexual heat, and thus increase fertility.[94]

By any measure, the range of erotic representation available in 1750 was vastly expanded from that in 1500. In France, England, the Netherlands, and elsewhere the book market was facilitating the dissemination of a broad range of vernacular texts dealing in relatively explicit terms with erotic activity and sexual desire. Such texts, many and various as they were, still made up a small portion of the overall number of texts printed. And they were, by modern standards, relatively restricted in their view of sexuality: they were, for a start, almost all written by men and focused primarily on male desire, and male heterosexual desire at that. Yet there is no question that, facilitated by the book market, sexual discourse was becoming more public and accessible.

While this proliferation of erotic material is amply documented, it is much more difficult to determine how erotic books were read. There is little evidence of reader reactions to erotic texts, and this paucity of data is part of the reason the example of Pepys and *L'École des filles* is cited in almost every study of erotic representation in the early modern period (including this one). We know that texts were sometimes read against the grain, and that some readers took erotic pleasure from reading texts that we would consider primarily informational. But fragmentary evidence cannot verify a general trend. How many readers responded to *L'École des filles* the way Pepys did, masturbating and then destroying the shameful text? How many were not ashamed at all? How many were simply repulsed by such texts? How many were indifferent? How many laughed at them? The great challenge for scholars of early modern sexuality is to understand the particular ways sexual behaviour was understood in the period given the miniscule surviving evidence of readers' experiences.

Notes

1 James Grantham Turner, *Libertines and Radicals in Early Modern London: Sexuality, Politics, and Literary Culture, 1630–1685*, New York: Cambridge University Press, 2002, pp. x–xii.

2 The notion that erotic writing is fundamentally modern is evident in the subtitle of Lynn Hunt's influential edited collection of essays, *The Invention of Pornography: Obscenity and the Origins of Modernity, 1500–1800*, New York: Zone Books, 1993.

3 Wijnand W. Mijnhardt, 'Politics and Pornography in the Seventeenth and Eighteenth Century Dutch Republic' in Hunt, *The Invention of Pornography*, pp. 283–300.

4 On the eroticism of medical texts, see Roy Porter and Lesley Hall, *The Facts of Life: The Creation of Sexual Knowledge in Britain, 1650–1950*, New Haven, CT: Yale University Press, 1995, pp. 33–90; and Peter Wagner, *Eros Revived: The Erotica of the Enlightenment in England and America*, London: Secker & Warburg, 1988, pp. 8–15. On legal texts, see Peter Wagner, 'Trial Reports as a Genre of Eighteenth-Century Erotica', *The British Journal of Eighteenth Century Studies* V:1, 1982, pp. 117–23.

5 For example, Nicolas Venette, *Tableau de l'amour conjugal*, Paris: n.p.,1686. Dutch translation 1687; German translation 1698; English translation 1703. See also Porter and Hall, *The Facts of Life*, pp. 65–90.

6 For example, Francis Kirkman, *The Wits, or Sport upon Sport*, London: Henry Marsh, 1662.

7 David Foxon, *Libertine Literature in England, 1660–1745*, Hyde Park, NY: University Books, 1965, pp. vi–ix.

8 Samuel Pepys, *The Diary of Samuel Pepys*, ed. Robert Latham and William Matthews, Berkeley: University of California Press, 1970–83, entry dated 9 February 1668.

9 Margaret Spufford, *Small Books and Pleasant Histories: Popular Fiction and its Readership in Seventeenth-Century England*, Athens, GA: The University of Georgia Press, 1981, pp. 48–50.

10 On the diversity of erotic discourses in eighteenth-century England, see Tim Hitchcock, *English Sexualities, 1700–1800*, New York: St Martin's Press, 1997, pp. 21–23.

11 John Marston, *The Metamorphosis of Pigmalions Image. And Certaine Satyres*. London: James Roberts, 1598.

12 All references to the works of Shakespeare are to *The Norton Shakespeare*, ed. Stephen Greenblatt *et al.*, New York: Norton, 1997.

13 The term was used in French earlier than in English. One of the earliest uses appears in Etienne Gabriel Peignot's *Dictionnaire critique, littéraire et bibliographique des principaux livres condamnés au feu, supprimés ou censurés*, Paris: Renouard, 1806. See Lynn Hunt, 'Introduction', *The Invention of Pornography*, pp. 14–15.

14 This debate about the nature of homoeroticism before the nineteenth century goes back to Michel Foucault, *The History of Sexuality, Vol. 1, An Introduction*, trans. Robert Hurley, New York: Vintage, 1980, and Alan Bray, *Homosexuality in Renaissance England*, London: Gay Men's Press, 1982.

15 Sarah Toulalan, *Imagining Sex: Pornography and Bodies in Seventeenth Century England*, New York and Oxford: Oxford University Press, 2007, pp. 1–17, gives a contrary view, arguing that the concept of pornography, if historicized, is a useful category of analysis for the early modern period. Turner, *Libertines and Radicals*, p. xii, coins the term 'pornographia' to refer specifically to early modern writing about prostitution.

16 Roger Thompson's *Unfit for Modest Ears: A Study of Pornographic, Obscene and Bawdy Works Written and Published in England in the Second Half of the Seventeenth Century*, Totowa, NJ: Rowman and Littlefield, 1979, separates pornography, writing 'intended to arouse lust', from 'bawdy', writing 'intended to provoke amusement about sex' (p. ix). Thompson considers bawdy 'healthy' (p. 6), and pornography disgusting (p. 77).

17 Italics added. Webster's definition, 'writings, photographs, movies, etc., intended to arouse sexual excitement, esp. such materials considered as having little or no artistic merit' is

fundamentally similar to the *OED*'s. Thompson's *Unfit for Modest Ears* also bases its definition of pornography 'on the intention of the author': pornography for Thompson is 'writing or representation intended to arouse lust ... The pornographer aims for erection at least in the pornophile' (p. ix). But what of works intended to arouse women?

18 Of course, beauty, like pornography, is arguably in the eye of the beholder. This list is neither definitive nor absolute.

19 For a particularly fierce rejection of the distinction between male pornography and female erotica see Pat Califia, *Public Sex: The Culture of Radical Sex*, San Francisco: Cleis Press, 1994.

20 Samuel Pepys referred to *L'Ecole des filles* as 'the most bawdy, lewd book that I ever saw'. Pepys, *Diary*, entry dated 13 January 1668.

21 Gabriel Harvey attacked Thomas Nashe for writing 'filthy rhymes in the nastiest kind'. Gabriel Harvey, *Pierce's Supererogation*, London: John Wolfe, 1593, sig. F4r. In 1750, Thomas Sherlock, the Bishop of London, referred to Cleland's *Fanny Hill* as 'this vile book'. John Cleland, *Fanny Hill or Memoirs of a Woman of Pleasure*, ed. Peter Wagner, New York: Penguin, 1985, p. 14.

22 On the use of the term 'Aretine' see Ian Frederick Moulton, *Before Pornography: Erotic Writing in Early Modern England*, New York: Oxford, 2000, pp. 158–68.

23 Jean Marie Goulemot, *Forbidden Texts: Erotic Literature and its Readers in Eighteenth-Century France*, trans. James Simpson, Cambridge, UK: Polity Press, 1994, pp. 2–4.

24 In early modern England, Aretino was often described as 'singular', a pejorative term meaning idiosyncratic or antisocial. Moulton, *Before Pornography*, pp. 161–62.

25 Robert Darnton, *Édition et sédition: L'Univers de la littérature clandestine au XVIIIe siécle*, Paris: Gallimard, 1991, pp. 13–16.

26 Goulemot, *Forbidden Texts*, p. 18.

27 Foxon, *Libertine Literature*, p. 9.

28 Toulalan, *Imagining Sex*, pp. 43–45.

29 Goulemot, *Forbidden Texts*, pp. 14, 18–19.

30 Goulemot, *Forbidden Texts*, p. 20.

31 Lynn Hunt, 'Pornography and the French Revolution' in Hunt, *Invention of Pornography*, pp. 301–39.

32 Hitchcock, *English Sexualities*, p. 19.

33 Ingrid D. Rowland, *The Roman Garden of Agostino Chigi*, Gerson Lecture 13, Groningen, 2005. On the elite visual culture of sexuality in early modern Italy, see Linda Wolk-Simon, '"Rapture to the Greedy Eyes": Profane Love in the Renaissance' in Andrea Bayer (ed.), *Art and Love in Renaissance Italy*, New York: Metropolitan Museum of Art, 2008, pp. 42–58.

34 Many early modern female nudes were probably marriage paintings, celebrating fertility in wedlock rather than promiscuity or prostitution. See Rona Goffen, 'The Problematic Patronage of Titian's Venus of Urbino', *Journal of Medieval and Renaissance Studies* 24, 1994, pp. 301–21.

35 For example, an expensive *c.* 1690 Latin copy of Chorier's *Satyra Sotadica* in the British Library contains 32 erotic engravings, BL PC.30.i.10; Toulalan, *Imagining Sex*, pp. 235–41.

36 The existence of erotic drawings on walls is attested by literary sources: in Ben Jonson's 1610 play *The Alchemist*, for example, a nobleman returns to his house to find that squatters have defaced it, leaving 'Madam with a dildo writ o' the walls', 5.5.42. A seventeenth-century poem in Harvard Mss Eng. 636 F*, f. 275 refers to 'a Damn'd Debauch Picture upon Alehouse wall'. See Thompson, *Unfit for Modest Ears*, pp. 176–89.

37 Thompson, *Unfit for Modest Ears*, p. 179.

38 Keith Wrightson, *Earthly Necessities: Economic Lives in Early Modern Britain*, New Haven, CT: Yale University Press, 2000, p. 195; Toulalan, *Imagining Sex*, pp. 51–52.

39 Philip Stewart, *Engraven Desire: Eros, Image, and Text in the French Eighteenth Century*, Durham, NC: Duke University Press, 1992, pp. ix–xi.

40 Toulalan, *Imagining Sex*, pp. 243–70.

41 Toulalan, *Imagining Sex*, pp. 241–43.

42 Mikhail Bakhtin, *Rabelais and His World*, trans. Hélène Iswolsky, Bloomington, IN: Indiana University Press, 1984, pp. 318–23; Peter Stallybrass and Allon White, *The Politics and Poetics of Transgression*, Ithaca, NY: Cornell University Press, 1986, pp. 21–23.

43 Moulton, *Before Pornography*, pp. 44–54.

44 See, for example, many of the texts excerpted in Michel Loude, *Littérature érotique et libertine au XVIIIe siècle*, Lyon: Aléas, 1994.

45 Hitchcock, *English Sexualities*, pp. 8–12.

46 Porter and Hall, *Facts of Life*, p. 92.

47 Translations in square brackets give a literal rendering of the foreign title, rather than referring to a particular English edition of the work. *L'Ecole des filles* [The School for Girls] was first published in English under the title *The School of Venus*, for example.

48 Text and English translation in Bette Talvacchia's *Taking Positions: On the Erotic in Renaissance Culture*, Princeton: Princeton University Press, 1999, pp. 198–227.

49 Talvacchia, *Taking Positions*, pp. 3–19, 71–100.

50 Moulton, *Before Pornography*, pp. 144–60.

51 Pietro Aretino, *Ragionamento Dialogo*, ed. Giorgio Barberi Squarotti and Carlo Forno, Milan: Rizzoli, 1988. English translation: *Aretino's Dialogues* 1971, trans. Raymond Rosenthal, New York: Marsilio, 1994.

52 Margaret Rosenthal, 'Epilogue' to *Aretino's Dialogues*, trans. Raymond Rosenthal, New York: Marsilio, 1994; Ian Frederick Moulton, 'Whores as Shopkeepers: Money and Sexuality in Aretino's *Ragionamenti*' in Diane Wolfthal and Juliann Vitullo (eds), *Money, Morality, and Culture in Late Medieval and Early Modern Europe*, New York: Ashgate, 2010, pp. 71–86.

53 Galderisi, Claudio (ed.), *Il piacevol ragionamento de l'Aretino: Dialogo di Giulia e di Maddelena*, Rome: Salerno, 1987. Galderisi ascribes the text to Aretino and speculates that the text was written before the *Ragionamenti*, but the surviving texts of the dialogue do not support that claim. This text has never been translated into English.

54 Musée Condé, Chantilly, MS 677. The manuscript is not attested as being in the Condé collection until 1673, though it may date from the sixteenth century, possibly from the years before 1572. See Galderisi (ed.), *Il piacevol ragionamento*, pp. 9–12.

55 Foxon, *Libertine Literature*, pp. 27–30. Moulton, *Before Pornography*, pp. 148–52.

56 Pascal Pia (ed.), *L'Ecole des filles ou la philosophie des dames*, Paris: L'Or du Temps: 1969; English translation: *The School of Venus*, trans. Donald Thomas, New York: Panther, 1971.

57 Pia, *L'Ecole des filles*, pp. 177–203, reproduces documents from the trial. Foxon, *Libertine Literature*, pp. 27–30. James Grantham Turner, *Schooling Sex: Libertine Literature and Erotic Education in Italy, France, and England, 1534–1685*, New York: Oxford University Press, 2003, pp. 106–64.

58 Turner, *Schooling Sex*, pp. 106–64, nonetheless provides an intellectual analysis of the volume's philosophy.

59 'Sotadic' refers to Sotades, a Greek sodomite and poet referred to in the epigrams of Martial.

60 Nicholas Chorier, *Aloisiae Sigeae Tolentanae Satyra Sotadica de Arcanis Amoris et Veneris*, ed. Bruno Lavignini, Catania: Romeo Prampolini, 1935. No modern or complete English translation exists. Modern French translation: *Satire sotadique de Luisa Sigea de Tolède*, trans. André Barry, Paris, 1969. On early modern English adaptations see Turner, *Schooling Sex*, pp. 335–43.

61 Foxon, *Libertine Literature*, pp. 38–43; Turner, *Schooling Sex*, pp. 165–220.

62 B. V. (ed.), *Vénus dans le cloître*, Réimpression de l'édition de Cologne, 1719, Paris: Coffret du Bibliophile, 1934. No modern English translation.

63 Foxon, *Libertine Literature*, pp. 13–14.

64 John Cleland, *Fanny Hill, or the Memoirs of a Woman of Pleasure*, New York: Penguin, 1985.

65 Stephen Marcus, *The Other Victorians: A Study of Sexuality and Pornography in Mid-Nineteenth Century England*, New York: Basic Books, 1964, pp. 266–86.

66 This educational theme is the focus of Turner's *Schooling Sex*.

67 Tim Hitchcock, 'Redefining Sex in Eighteenth Century England', *History Workshop Journal* 41, 1996, pp. 72–90, sees this phallocentrism as becoming more pronounced as the eighteenth century progresses. See Toulalan, *Imagining Sex*, pp. 62–91, on the notion that ejaculation of semen was a key component in female sexual pleasure, in part because in the period sexual pleasure and fertility were seen to be closely connected.

68 Aretino, *Aretino's Dialogues*, p. 36. Galderisi (ed.), *Il piacevol ragionamento*, pp. 63–64.

69 Cleland, *Fanny Hill*, p. 195.

70 Turner, *Libertines and Radicals*, pp. x–xi.

71 Foxon, *Libertine Literature*, p. ix.

72 Cleland, *Fanny Hill*, pp. 118–19.

73   Turner, *Libertines and Radicals*, pp. 265–74.

74   Toulalan, *Imagining Sex*, pp. 62–91.

75   Toulalan, *Imagining Sex*, pp. 194–232.

76   Thomas Nashe, 'The Choice of Valentines'; Rochester, 'The Imperfect Enjoyment'; Aphra Behn, 'The Disappointment'.

77   Loude, *Littérature érotique*, pp. 175–78.

78   For example, Ovid, *Amores* 3.7; Catullus, *Carmen* 3; Martial, 1.46.

79   Moulton, *Before Pornography*, pp. 35–69.

80   Antonio Cavallino, *Tariffa delle puttane di Venegia, accompagné d'un catalogue des principales courtisanes de Venise*, 1535, ed. Guillaume Appolinaire, Paris: Bibliothèque des curieux, 1911.

81   This text is reproduced in Rita Casagrande de Villaviera, *Le cortegiane veneziane del Cinquecento*, Milan: Longanesi, 1968. On the *Catalogo* and the *Tariffa*, see Margaret F. Rosenthal, *The Honest Courtesan: Veronica Franco, Citizen and Writer in Sixteenth-Century Venice*, Chicago: University of Chicago Press, 1992, pp. 39–42.

82   Pietro Aretino, *La prima seconda parte de Ragionamenti*, London: John Wolfe, 1584.

83   For example, *A Catalogue of Jilts, Cracks, Prostitutes, Night walkers, Whores, She-friends, King Women and others of the Linnen-lifting Tribe*, London: n.p., 1691; *An Auction of Whores*, London: n.p., 1691.

84   Simon Schama, *The Embarrassment of Riches: An Interpretation of Dutch Culture in the Golden Age*, New York: Random House, 1987, pp. 469–75.

85   English examples include, John Gough, *The Academy of Complements*, London: T.P. for Humphrey Mosley, 1639 (and frequently reprinted); W.S., *Cupid's Schoole*, London: n.p., 1642; Edward Phillips, *The Mysteries of Love and Eloquence, or the Arts of Wooing and Complementing*, London: N. Brooks, 1658.

86   Jane Sharp, *The Midwives Book*, London: Simon Miller, 1671.

87   Jacques Ferrand, *A Treatise on Lovesickness*, ed. and trans. Donald A. Beecher and Massimo Ciavolella, Syracuse, NY: Syracuse University Press, 1990, pp. 263–65, 308–10, 334.

88   Ferrand, *Treatise on Lovesickness*, pp. 26–38.

89   Ferrand, *Treatise on Lovesickness*, p. 243.

90   Porter and Hall, *Facts of Life*, pp. 33–64.

91   Jean Flouret, *Nicholas Venette, Médecin Rochelais*, 1633–98, La Rochelle: Editions Rupella, 1992.

92   Porter and Hall, *The Facts of Life*, pp. 65–90.

93   Most prominently the anonymous *Onania, or the Heinous Sin of Self-Pollution*, 1710. See Porter and Hall, *The Facts of Life*, pp. 91–105.

94   Toulalan, *Imagining Sex*, pp. 92–131.

12

LOOKING AT SEX

Pornography and erotica since 1750

Lisa Z. Sigel

One might think that 'Looking at Sex' would be an easy essay to write given the prevalence of pornography and the long history of campaigns against it. Such essays generally review historical periodization, define terms, mention sources, and then discuss generations of scholars as they work through methods, arguments, and questions. Usually these essays conclude with the need for future work so that scholars new to the field have a clear idea of how to proceed. This essay will follow that organization but it will show the ways that the topic refuses to follow parameters – even simple essay-writing parameters – much as it refuses to conform to other expectations. Thus, the messy essay you get will stand both as descriptor and as evidence of a broader chaos of the topic. This messiness demonstrates what has been a central problem in understanding pornography – too many scholars have tried to find universals about the genre and too few historians have written about its particularities. Thus, even while showing the problems in writing a classic historiographical essay, this essay will focus on the gaps in historiography to show what historians have yet to do. In doing so, it will chart out the areas into which historians – with their penchant for focusing on specifics and particularities – can usefully intervene.

The messiness begins with the issue of periodization and the question of how historians mark out the emergence of pornography as a form. In *The Invention of Pornography* Lynn Hunt suggests that pornography emerged as a genre over the course of the eighteenth century. According to Hunt, before that period pornography 'was almost always an adjunct to something else'.[1] A change began to occur as writing primarily interested in sexual arousal emerged from the intellectual currents provided by humanism, the scientific revolution, and the Enlightenment. As the sexual realm became the main focus of certain writings, it created a new type of literature – pornography. Hunt's work thus dates the emergence of the genre to around 1750, creating a certain felicity to the chronological break between Ian Moulton's essay and my own. However, Walter Kendrick in *The Secret Museum* suggests that pornography names an argument, not a thing in and of itself, and that this argument was first made in the nineteenth century. According to Kendrick, pornography emerged from the older term 'pornographos' meaning 'to write about whores'. In banning such writings, authorities labelled them as pornographic. According to Kendrick, the term denoted a form of cultural censure even as it emerged from its older linguistic roots.[2] Thus, the two most prominent scholars on the topic date the emergence of pornography to different centuries and to two distinct phenomena. What began as a review of periodization becomes muddled before the discussion even gets under way.

The search for clarity collapsing into a confused wrangle continues when one turns to definitions. Basic definitions of 'erotica', 'pornography', and 'obscenity' remain deeply theorized and contested. The need for clear and universal definitions has preoccupied multiple generations of scholars but has not generated a lasting consensus. Early scholars of pornography charted censorship and legalization as a free speech issue. Scholars such as David Foxon, Peter Fryer, and Edward de Grazia, for example, did valuable work looking at the court records to understand the great obscenity battles. Their approach characterized history as a continuous battle between control of morals and freedom of expression – one that the state won during the nineteenth century, but that the radical pressmen continued to wage (at great costs to the themselves) over the course of the twentieth. According to this model, through a series of legal battles, the radical press beat back the state and established freedom of expression as a fundamental human right during the twentieth century. As part of this campaign, scholars and legal activists worked to legitimate art and literature on the basis of its redeeming value. They also suggested that pornography lacked any such value; as Charles Rembar, the attorney who successfully defended *Lady Chatterley's Lover*, *Tropic of Cancer*, and *Memoirs of a Woman of Pleasure* against charges of obscenity in the American courts, argued: 'obscenity is worthless trash' and that pornography is in 'the groin of the beholder'.[3] While the argument that high art has redeeming value and should not be censored has allowed for the importation and publication of literary classics, scholars have not been able to find the marker that separates the obscene from the erotic despite years of trying. This model of linking pornography with free speech campaigns galvanized legal historians to historicize obscenity campaigns and court battles, but it also limited historical scholarship by placing the location of inquiry in the courts and elevating legal records as a primary source for understanding the past. For that generation of scholars, obscenity mattered but sex did not.

In the 1980s and 1990s, feminist scholars began to reconsider the harm caused by such representations. During the 1980s, anti-pornography feminists in the US and, to a lesser degree, the UK, tried to redefine pornography as works that subjugate and degrade women. Anti-pornography efforts, spearheaded by Catherine MacKinnon and Andrea Dworkin, insisted that pornography taught men how to treat women like objects. In the phrase that best captured the ethos, Robin Morgan stated that 'Pornography is the theory, rape is the practice'.[4] A spate of scholarship testifies to the avalanche of work done on definitions and the political volatility of the issue. Despite the fierceness of these accounts and the time spent on definitions and counter-definitions, no lasting accord was reached.[5] The issue of definitions continued to influence scholarly discussions in the 1990s and 2000s as new perspectives from queer studies, cultural studies, and post-colonial studies were brought to the topic. For example, Marcus Wood, in *Slavery, Empathy, and Pornography*, suggests that renderings of slavery functioned as a form of pornography even when located within the abolitionist movement. According to his work, pornography becomes a particularly powerful watchword for sexually loaded cultural ideas.

Recently scholars have moved from defining terms to recognizing the contingent nature of such definitions. According to Thomas Waugh, for example, it might be easy to argue that 'consent is distinguished from non-consent, the real from the simulated, the degrading from the ennobling, mutuality from control, the naked from the nude, the commercial from the personal – in short, the erotic from the pornographic'. These distinctions would be flawed, however, as his further discussion makes clear: 'As recent advances within the feminist and post-feminist debates about pornography have confirmed, most such distinctions are based in class or gender bias, or else in the historical myopia of homo-phobia, cultural snobbery, political instrumentality, or personality (my erotica is your por-nography).'[6] This quagmire has been noted by others. Clarissa Smith suggested that 'In most studies of pornography it is usual to offer some definitions: what is "pornography"?; how does it differ from "erotica" and what is its relationship to the "obscene"? The parti-cular answers given by individual authors to these questions are intimately linked to the further development and substance of their thesis.'[7] Scholars have thus demonstrated that the process of defining one's terms is politically loaded at the outset. The straightforward step of defining one's terms becomes part of preparing an argument about the nature of sexual materials.

Thus, for the last 50 years, scholars have struggled to define pornography, obscenity, and erotica on sound grounds that will provide universal standards. These discussions have been useful in court battles and in illuminating hidden elements in texts, but they have not created foolproof definitions. Instead, as scholars have come to recognize, the whole prac-tice becomes a political exercise. While these battles over terminology have dominated the scholarship, few of the scholars quoted above are historians, even if they do historically oriented works. If historians have done little to make sense of this quagmire, then at least they have also done little to add to it. Instead, historians tend to define their terms provi-sionally. For example, Iain McCalman in *Radical Underworld* buries his definition of obscence materials, erotica, and pornography in a footnote to chapter ten. He offers a clear defence of provisional definitions: 'what matters most to historians is pornography in particular societies'.[8] This use of localized definitions allows McCalman to examine the overlapping political goals of radicals and pornographers in late eighteenth- and early nineteenth-century Britain. By using localized definitions, McCalman can include sexual satires that the state outlawed as obscene and seditious libel but that later generations might not think of as either sexually or politically radical. His provisional definitions provide a path for the rest of us to follow. Historical specificity thus allows an alternative to universal definitions. By focusing on particular definitions, historians can escape the quagmire of defining one's terms that has trapped other sorts of scholars who look for universals.

Even at the level of sources, historians should remain a bit wary, but for very different reasons. Sources on pornography carry a particular set of risks. Publishers lied about the author, the place of publication, and the date in order to escape arrest and prosecution. Moral authorities lied as well to make the problem of immorality appear larger and therefore more threatening. Further, current publishers are well aware of the appeal of historically minded materials and are willing to create such fantasies of past sexual esca-pades. Besides lying there is also the problem of illegality. There are few areas of scholar-ship in which sources can remain legally problematic. Though theft in the past might have been illegal, the documents detailing theft are perfectly legal today. Not so with porno-graphy. Sources can remain illegal. For example, research on child pornography remains legally and culturally suspect and sources that detail child pornography remain illegal, at least in theory. Thus, historians need to be aware of the problems with their sources before they begin their work.

Having said this, historians use a few basic types of sources like bibliographies, extant collections, and legal records to create chronologies, understand materials in context, and explore the geographical spread of materials. Bibliographies are particularly important in this field of study because of the rarity of the works and the problems with publication information: those nations with a strong bibliographic tradition that establishes the existence of materials in time and place and that distinguishes true publication information from the false are not coincidently the same countries with the most clearly documented history. Henry Spenser Ashbee published a three-volume bibliography *Index Librorum Prohibitorum*, *Centuria Librorum Absconditorum*, and *Catena Librorum Tacendorum*, in 1877, 1879, and 1885, respectively. Hugo Hayn published *Bibliotheca Germanorum Erotica* in 1875; it was later expanded and then further supplemented between 1912 and 1929. Jules Gay's six-volume work entitled *Bibliographie des ouvrages relatifs à l'amour* was published in 1871–73 and was supplemented by J. Lemonnyer between 1894 and 1900. These works on English, German, and French pornography, respectively, have formed the backbone for historical examinations in those countries.

A standing collection is the second important source in the field. Oftentimes, the existence of a bibliography overlaps with the existence of the collection established or used by the bibliographer. For example, Henry Spencer Ashbee donated his volumes to the Private Case Collection housed in the British Library. Though some of his materials were burned rather than accessioned, most were saved. The Bibliothèque Nationale in France also has an important collection called 'l'enfer'. The importance of the British Library and the Bibliothèque Nationale as cultural institutions and the prominence of individual collectors have saved such collections from attack by social authorities.[9] The accumulation of works over time allows scholars to recreate patterns of publication, republication, and circulation. Scholars can also compare changes to works between editions; an important tactic for works that are frequently pirated and often reprinted both in complete versions and in edited form. Standing collections at institutions can sometimes provide documentary evidence about the provenance of materials. Such documentation can allow scholars to see how materials circulate through time and space, the costs and places of purchase, and the relationships between sources.

The third source is the legal record. This type of source includes materials that go into the making of laws and policies and those that document the breaking of laws and policies. Thus, everything from police records, customs forms, policy reports, lawyers' briefs, drafts of bills, etc., can form part of the legal record. Case files amassed by government officials can discuss circulation patterns, document the impact of obscene materials (as officials understood them), and collect evidence from various agencies about the ways that a certain law or statute functioned. Parliamentary records can debate policy and the shifts in support for given policies. Police and trial records documenting illegal activities can reveal the extent of trade, the types of productions, the number of workers involved in an enterprise, shop records, capital attached to an enterprise, the age, gender, and nationality of both users and producers. Though every claim made by authorities should be critically examined, the legal record provides some of the best materials about the production and dispersal of sexualized representations.

These three sets of materials – bibliographies, standing collections, and legal records – allow historians to triangulate the trade in time and space. Though every one of them is problematic in some way, each nonetheless offers a foothold into the past. A larger failure arises from the absence of these sources. Those regions and those time periods that are missing one or more of these sources have had few scholars working on the topic and often lack basic histories. In nineteenth-century America, for example, Anthony Comstock burned materials by the ton but did not document what he immolated. Historians can tell that there is a history, but documenting that history without a bibliographic record, a standing collection, or a detailed legal record becomes quite hard. The loss of the historical record has retarded the scholarship. Such gaps in the sources have created serious challenges to working on the topic.

The next stage in this chapter should involve describing generations of historians as they respond to each other, as they address central questions, and as they find new approaches to the topic. However, historians have only begun to do the painstaking work necessary to explain the history of the erotic image or text. We know pornography exists so that it must have a history; how it emerged, though, has yet to be documented. Rather than following historiographical patterns, the lack of scholarship suggests that it might be more efficacious to discuss how the topic changed over time. In this process, this section will emphasize what historians still need to examine. According to Lynn Hunt, the spread of sexualized representations followed the spread of Enlightenment beliefs. Not every nation developed its own pornographic works – indeed, most countries lacked one at least until the nineteenth century – but most had smuggled works that circulated among the wealthy. Despite this gap in the production of new materials, pornography made its way across Europe. Pornography followed patterns of elite learning as works of pornography seeped across porous borders creating an international libertine community. David Stevenson, using the records of the Beggar's Bennison, engages the economics of this early trade. Starting in the port town of Anstruther, Scotland in 1732, the convivial society lasted until 1836 and advocated a hedonism based on shared bawdy erudition. Its all-male membership read aloud bawdy works and engaged in sexual rites dedicated to the priapus. Its members engaged in both free trade (that is, smuggling) and free expression, such as when the membership drank, cavorted, and read aloud pornographic verses. According to Stevenson, club members formed links across Europe that spread from the backwaters of the Scottish countryside all the way to Russia through erotic expression, free trade, and informal ambassadors.[10] This linking of sex and freedom remained emblematic of eighteenth- and early nineteenth-century pornographic circulation.

Using the archives of the Société typographique de Neuchâtel, Robert Darnton has examined the history of publishing to understand how ideas spread across France. As part of a larger history of book trades and publishing, Darnton explores the overlap between Enlightenment philosophers and erotic pamphleteers to examine how publishing contributed to political and sexual expression.[11] According to his analysis, the French government solidified the relationships between philosophies and works of pornography and between the writers and publishing houses that engaged in their production and trade when the state outlawed the two genres in tandem. However, the overlap between the two genres went deeper than their joint restriction. Like philosophers, pornographers chiseled away at the corrupt foundations of society. They accused the Church of perversions and insisted that it had little right to restrict lay sexual practices since members of the clergy corrupted their own innate passions with extravagant vices. As well as attacking sexually corrupt elements in society, pornographers fantasized about positive sexuality and free pleasures. Enlightenment ideals like rationality and natural rights could be applied to sexuality; free-thinking political ideals could overlap with free-thinking sexuality according to G. S. Rousseau.[12] The dramatic cultural changes that occurred during the French Revolution – from new attitudes to divorce, to the repudiation of the monarchy, to the curtailment of Church control – can be tied in part to the critiques found within the French pornography that preceded and accompanied it. This type of political pornography reached its apex (or nadir) in the 1790s in France and ebbed after the trial of Marie Antoinette according to Lynn Hunt.[13] The trial itself can be seen as a platform for pornography's efficacy as Marie Antoinette stood accused of sexual crimes like incest – accusations that had been made in obscene pamphlets.

As these examples demonstrate, historians have used pornography to make claims about the spread of ideas and the meanings of sexuality in context. However, none of the scholars discussed above were historians of pornography or sexuality; instead, their subject areas led them to the topic. Areas that more centrally focus on sexuality, however, have been less well examined by historians. For example, the infamous Marquis de Sade (1740–1814), who seems to embody the pornographic excesses of the age, has become the province of the literary critics and philosophers rather than historians.[14] Sade's imprisonment at the behest of the *ancien régime*, the republic, and Napoleon makes him appear as if he fought and lost a one-man war against state control. His novels – *The 120 Days of Sodom*, *Justine*, *Philosophy of the Boudoir*, and *Juliette* – explore the extremes of liberty and cruelty, self and other. Sade wrote *The 120 Days of Sodom* while imprisoned in the Bastille. Just days before *sans culottes* stormed the prison, Sade was moved from the prison and the incomplete manuscript fell into private hands and was not published until the twentieth century. In his best-known works, *Justine* and *Juliette*, he uses women's bodies to consider the relations between self and society. His work undermines the idea of God's plan on earth by rewarding vice and punishing virtue. Although some of Sade's work was published and dispersed during his lifetime, it experienced a lull in appreciation during the early nineteenth century. His works rebounded in popularity as his name became synonymous with emerging sexual identities (such as sado-masochism) in the late nineteenth century and then gained even more cogency as surrealists and other modernists engaged the convolutions of desire in the wake of the Great War. Though the history of Sade and Sadean philosophy seems like a natural place for historical intervention, historians have yet to embrace the project. In a review essay in the first volume of *The Journal of the History of Sexuality*, Gert Hekma, a sociologist, encouraged historians to take up the work of engaging the Sadean legacy: 'it has become the task of historians of politics and sexuality to delineate the meaning of Sade'.[15] However, historians have not responded, leaving the examination to others in the related genres of literary studies, modern languages, and philosophy.

As well as not having explored single writers of great import like Sade, historians have not done justice to the histories of single volumes of great importance. One could explore a single work, such as John Cleland's *Memoirs of a Woman of Pleasure* (1748 or 1749) and the impact that such a volume had on the erotic tradition, but alas, historians have not.[16] *Memoirs of a Woman of Pleasure*, better known as *Fanny Hill*, illustrates broader literary developments in the transformation of the epistolary into the novel based upon plotting, character development, and description. In two long letters, the title character recounts her journey from innocent country girl, to prostitute, and finally to respectable matron. *Fanny Hill* illustrates the overlap of two forms of pornography – to write about whores and to write salacious art and literature. Bradford Mudge, Professor of British Literature, suggests that a shared dishonesty tied whores and pornography together in the eighteenth century: 'whore and novel alike are in it for the money: Both sell pleasures that are sullied by the selling; both are at once active agents and passive commodities; both are feminized, things at once desired and despised'.[17] The inability to separate truth from falsity emerges from the novel's very premise as Julia Epstein, another English professor, demonstrates in her article 'Fanny's Fanny'.[18] The immediacy of the work and the way the prose purports to show not only what Fanny thinks but also feels, both emotionally and physically, suggests a truth-telling at multiple levels. However, the ability to get at the truth of identities and desires unravels on further reflection. For Cleland, a man, to adopt the persona of a woman suggests a certain transexualism. When Cleland writes of Fanny's longing for Charles (her lover) the authorship of those desires raises the question of queer longings: is it about a woman who desires a man, a man who wants to be a woman, or about a man masquerading as a woman who desires a man? These convolutions of desire dissolve any certainty of analysis and illustrate the complexity of the subject position.

Historians could gain a great deal by engaging with these questions and with these seminal texts. *Fanny Hill* continued to gain prestige in the nineteenth century and editions in English, French, Italian, and German poured off the presses.[19] Its successes contributed to the belief that memoirs allowed readers to peer into boudoirs. Other volumes contributed to the genre of fictitious memoir, including the *Exhibition of Female Flagellants* (1777) supposedly reprinted by Mary Wilson in 1827, *Birchen Bouquet* (1770), and *Venus School Mistress* (1788) attributed to Theresa Berkeley. The fiction of female investment in the texts and the layers of false publication information highlight the focus on female sexuality as a central mystery.[20] Historians have only touched on these issues and have largely left the relationships of memoirs and subjectivities to scholars in literary studies and the history of publishing and readership to bibliographers.

The consideration of subjectivities and fictitious memoirs can be very productive as Sarah Leonard's work has demonstrated. In the German states, the fictionalized memoir became emblematic of obscene wares and demonstrated the political mutability of the form. As Sarah Leonard shows, popular medical works and memoirs, in particular, became the focus of investigations by the state. The 'moral police', who regulated sumptuary displays and monitored public spaces, began to focus on them by the mid-nineteenth century.[21] Works such as *Memoirs of Lola Montez* recounted the personal history of the dancer and consort to King Ludwig of Bavaria. Montez's fictitious memoirs denounced radicalism and extolled the value of loyalty in the fragmenting political world; however, the conservatism of Montez did not preclude the works' reception as 'immoral'.[22] The fictionalized memoir maintained its status as corrupting even as the basis of political and sexual corruption began to change. Leonard's work maps out what historians can do with fictitious memoirs by showing how lived experience can be transformed through fictionalized memoirs into new political realities.

Other scholars extend the chronology of politics and sexuality forward from Leonard's case study. Both Gary Stark, writing about Germany, and Annie Stora-Lamarre, writing about France, show the ways that the consolidation of state control hinged on sexuality.[23] By the 1860s, most governments began national campaigns to control their populations through the censorship of sexual ideas. The state intervened with the justification that they needed to help the weak who remained susceptible to immorality. In France, the outpouring from the pornographic press and the importation of works that detailed ever more perverse practices created a crisis in democratic ideals. According to critics, the masses' familiarity with pornography could only corrupt reason and thereby corrupt the body politic. Pornography became caught in the ebb tide of political alignments; once outlawed because it served the revolution, by the late nineteenth century it was outlawed because it endangered people's abilities to rule themselves.

The process of social control occurred at multiple levels as my own work on nineteenth-century British pornography shows. In the late nineteenth century, for example, the elite had a capacity to both legislate about morality and to imagine others' sexuality; two activities that overlapped in hidden ways. Members of the so-called 'Cannibal Club', an offshoot of the Anthropological Society of London, presented scholarly papers about varied sexual practices, wrote obscene letters, pornographic tracts and essays, and then colonized, governed, legislated, and condemned. The members' status in society provided them with leeway to explore sexual fantasies as part of a shared cultural enterprise.[24] The authority of these men meant that they stood above state surveillance. The police would not inquire into the legality of their possessions despite the open secret of one member's well-stocked library and another's publication of the *Kama Sutra*. Yet these men could legislate on the very intimate details of others' lives. Their fascination with sexuality and their central place in the production and consumption of pornography shows an important relationship between science, arts and letters, government, and pornography that has frequently been overlooked.

Though historians have done little with visual evidence that began to proliferate during the second half of the nineteenth century, new technologies of reproduction, such as early calotypes, made erotic images widely available. The flood of materials began slowly with the development of daguerreotypes, but then picked up speed as calotypes allowed multiple prints from a single negative and mail order allowed the sale of dozens of images per order. As well as affecting the number of images available, these types of reproductions transformed the nature of seeing erotic images as such images purported to mirror nature. At the same time, the rapidly expanding European empires provided new opportunities for a popular, symbolic imperialism as Malek Alloula, an anthropologist, has suggested.[25] Photographs and illustrations from Asia, Central America, and Africa flooded back to Europe allowing all levels of European society to see concrete images of imperial expansion. Images of naked or disrobing women, and occasionally men, permeated the metropolises of Europe, corroborating fictional accounts of non-white sexuality. Even stamps produced by the imperial governments showed images of naked natives well into the twentieth century. Here, too, patterns have to be pieced together from anthropological accounts and from the occasional art historian who specializes in photography because historians have avoided these sorts of ephemeral sources.[26]

The rise of film provides yet another area with which historians might engage. By the turn of the century, cinematic depictions of sexuality began to augment literary productions and still images. According to Joseph Slade, a professor of communications turned porn historian, by the turn of the century, peep shows displayed films of nude women.[27] Shortly thereafter hardcore films began to circulate, though it remains impossible to date the first one. The first might be *Le Voyeur* (1907) or *A l'Ecu d'Or ou la Bonne Auberge* (1908), though no living scholar admits to having seen either film.[28] In Slade's estimation, the first surviving stag film is an Austrian film entitled *Am Abend* (c. 1910).[29] Such silent films erected few linguistic barriers and became staple fare at brothels and other sites of male convivial pleasures, according to Slade's account. Such histories of film have not been done by historians. Slade, Linda Williams, and Laura Mulvey, three scholars most widely associated with the field, are not historians. Historians' concerns with charting change and continuity over time, provenance of documents, and the ways that state structures affect social organization and cultural production could all contribute to robust analysis, but historians have not yet done the work.

Historians have also avoided working with high art despite the thematic importance of sexuality in modernist representations. Modernism's embrace of sexual theory and modernists' confrontational stance towards bourgeois ideas of respectability contributed to the sexual saturation of interwar culture. Maria Tatar demonstrates that Otto Dix, in the

series 'Sex Murder', envisioned the violent repudiation of sexual symbols through the dis-
memberment of a prostitute.[30] So, too, did George Grosz's photographic self-portrait in
which he and his future wife recreated attacks by Jack the Ripper. For such painters, sex
and violence worked to tap into the supposedly primordial energies of the psyche.
Surrealists also embraced the libidinal in the interwar period according to art historians
like Alyce Mahon. When translations of Freud appeared in the 1920s, French surrealists
adapted his ideas to their art in the embrace of Eros and Thanatos.[31] Modernism's willingness to focus on the knife-edge between pleasure and pain further accounts for a good
bit of the resurgent popularity of Sade.[32]

Though historians have been slow to engage art, when images of sexuality overlap with
politics, historians have taken note.[33] Images of the nude body gained more currency as a
reaction to repression, the war, and the problems of modern, urban society according to
Karl Toepfer. This nude body withstood political divisions of the times as artists, intellectuals, and ideologues looked to the body to speak to the human condition. The symbol of
the body was strengthened by the rise of nudism, the back to nature movement, and the
increase in youth groups that sought to combat the degeneration of industrial capitalism
and urbanization.[34] According to these movements, individuals needed to re-attune their
bodies to the outdoors and reject the poison of industrial society. These claims were made
against commercial culture, but magazines, photographs, pulp fiction, films and books followed suit and touted the beauties of the nude physique, as Peter Jelavich demonstrates in
his discussion of Berlin culture.[35]

As the political landscape became more fraught in the 1920s and 1930s, battles over
obscenity began to take on an additional importance as both liberal and authoritarian
regimes articulated a need for a national morality to back up a flagging social cohesion.
Carolyn Dean, in *The Frail Social Body*, linked the failures of the French state with the rising
attacks on homosexuality and pornography in the interwar world. This approach was followed by fascist and authoritarian governments across Europe as they took power, though
the repudiations of modernism and sexual liberalization were often more illusory than real
as Dagmar Herzog has shown.[36] When the National Socialists seized power in Germany in
1933, one of their first acts was to burn the Institute of Sexual Science's books and papers.
Nevertheless, they developed their own 'cult of the body' during the interwar years. Nazi
ideals incorporated elements of pornography into public art. Thus, fascist regimes took
pornography, and the liberal reaction to it, as emblematic of the excesses of liberalism but
could not avoid its persuasive power.

The persuasive power of the eroticized body links together the pre- and post-war world
as historians who chart the spread of consumer goods have shown. Elizabeth Heineman
has demonstrated a continuity of goods from Weimar to post-war Germany through the
mail order business.[37] In post-war Germany, mail order firms including Beate Uhse and
Gisela distributed a wide range of sexual products including contraception, creams and
ointments, informational literature, medical literature, rubber goods, lingerie, and erotica
(both fiction and photographs). The mail order business allowed customers to buy a wide
range of sexual products without distinguishing between the scientific, the medical, and the
erotic realms. The consumption of sexual articles in Germany after World War II emerged
as part of the post-war legacy. Mail order goods allowed the sexualized family to stand as a
bulwark against the totalitarian state and as a restorative to a traumatic past.

The post-war world also saw an emergence of a literary pornography for women,
though the exploration of this area has been left to other disciplines. A pornographic

literature by women for the female market is no small development since inventing female desires to fit with men's fantasies has formed a mainstay of the pornographic tradition. Rewriting sexual tropes has allowed women to create their own sense of sexual subjectivity, but these attempts must be placed in historical context. Works such as Pauline Réage's *The Story of O* (1954) might very well explore the female masochist impulse, but Réage wrote the book for her lover, Jean Paulhan – a man well familiar with the works of the Marquis de Sade. While disentangling true desire from the pressures placed on women to recreate their desires to fit within a male world remains impossible, ignoring the ways that the male world has conditioned female desires – as well as male desires – seems just as wrongheaded. Literary critics like John Phillips and psychologists like Jessica Benjamin have examined these ideas; historians could do more to disentangle the histories of gender, sex theory, philosophy, and publishing.[38]

Another area that deserves exploration would be American cultural influence. When the American culture industry began to dominate European markets during the post-war years, so too did an American influence begin to affect pornography, as magazines such as *Playboy* reached Britain and the continent. Begun in 1953, *Playboy* offered a swinging alternative, or supplement, to marital conformity. *Playboy*'s first printing of 70,000 sold out and the magazine passed the million-copy mark within a few years, according to Barbara Ehrenreich.[39] Recent work by Elizabeth Fraterrigo has demonstrated that *Playboy* articulated a lifestyle for affluent single men that began to articulate distinctly American ideals of consumer aspirations.[40] When joined by *Penthouse* in the 1960s and *Hustler* in the 1970s, such magazines offered semi-legitimate displays of sexuality for all classes of men in America. Laura Kipnis sees these magazines as developing carefully articulated rejections to feminine and feminist culture, though Kipnis sees the working-class *Hustler* as the more Rabelaisian of the lot.[41] These magazines were relatively inexpensive, ubiquitous, and legal, and they allowed individuals to consume a plethora of images and ideas as part of daily life. Though scholars have begun to consider the national impact of the spread of magazines, such materials began to have a global impact that has been less well charted.

The global impact becomes apparent in the spread of film, though here, too, historians have not entered into the conversation. According to Joseph Slade and Katalin Milter, when the Scandinavian countries decriminalized pornography in the late 1960s, Americans entered the market, driving out local producers. In response to American cultural dominance, France erected trade barriers by taxing imports, which encouraged a resurgence of the French pornographic film.[42] Most nations, however, did not develop a platform for the defence of indigenous pornography and allowed their products to be swamped by American imports. With the advent of video, American dominance over the market only grew. Roughly 150 companies clustered together in an area affectionately or derisively called 'Silicone Valley' in California.[43] These companies vertically consolidated production and distribution allowing them to control the global market. The study of the economics and history of the moving image has been left to scholars who specialize in film studies.[44]

One area in which historians seem to be gaining ground, though, is queer studies. With the study of gender, historians began to chart a history of masculinity through its artefacts, like pornography. Furthermore, the rise of the gay liberation movement moved gay pornography from the back alley to the front stacks of the newsagents. This process has alerted historians to the existence of queer desires and encouraged them to find evidence of these longings in older forms of pornography, as current works by Thomas Waugh and Paul Deslandes illustrate.[45] Queer studies has also given new tools for examining the ways that bodies make meaning together. Despite this gain, historians are not keeping up. As the number of historians working on the topic grows arithmetically, the number of artefacts seems to grow geometrically. How much pornography there is and what the global market looks like remains conjectural. Given new web-based methods of delivery that remain anonymous and untracked, scholars can only estimate the extent of the market and the directions it takes. Nonetheless, according to Jonathan Coopersmith, chat rooms and bulletin boards that allowed for open sexual conversation formed one of the bases for early Internet companies' successes.[46] The Internet allowed easy access to pornography from home and falling prices helped dismantle the economic limitations to computer access in Europe and America. The search for images accelerated economic consolidation by large firms because such firms could better provide archives of sexual images, video on demand, interactive games, and video conferencing that consumers demanded. How historians will approach this explosion of materials remains an open problem. Twenty-first-century pornography features an extraordinarily wide array of sexual acts including gay sex, straight sex, transsexual sex, S/M, gonzo features, and multiple partners of all varieties. It includes still images and moving pictures, made-to-order fantasies, interactive media, literature, and glossy high-end photos, and it travels on the web, through the mails, on TV, at newsstands, and in retro red-light districts.

As a result, pornographic forms have grown while studies of those forms have not. Historians have not managed to write the histories of ephemeral publications, of postcards, of glossies, of films, of videos, or of web-based pornography. We have not produced good histories of Silicon Valley, of early films, or of the places that showed the films. We have not considered nudism and its relationship to erotica in most national, local, or transnational contexts. We have not done the histories of the book, histories of readers, or histories of most publishers. We have not studied the economics of the trade or the economics of individual businesses in any depth. We have not considered what subjectivities means to our field. We have not managed to engage with most eastern European producers, distributors, or consumers. We have not considered the circulation between empire and imperial centre. We have not constructed histories of those regions that lack a strong erotic bibliographic tradition, and we have not been successful at recreating libraries that might have existed in the past. We have not even written the history of Sade but have left that project to philosophers and literary scholars. We have few methods for dealing with unnamed visual images; and we have even fewer methods for dealing with electronic circulation. What historians have done is look at the history of the state and how it regulated sexuality. Beyond that sort of project, historians have here and there added pieces of knowledge, as this chapter has illustrated. The occasional history of the book, a history of a single publishing firm, a study of a group of memoirs, for example, have been projects that historians have undertaken and those projects have been well received. The problem is not the reception of such histories but the willingness of historians to start long-term projects that engage with particularities.

Thus, this project that began with a muddle ends with a list of possibilities for future work, as such essays usually do. As part of an advisement for future work, I would suggest that historians should carefully step over the problems of definitions, periods, and other contentious issues. Perhaps the search for clarity has stood in the way of research and has been a central, if paradoxical, part of the problem in understanding pornography. If historians seize the field by going to the archives, we might say not what pornography, obscenity, and erotica are, but what they have been and how they arrived there. Instead of showing how pornography works, we might show how it worked at a particular time and in a particular place. And instead of showing what pornography means, we can show what it meant to a particular group at a certain moment in time. If the search for universalities has impeded historical examinations, perhaps well-documented historical research can impede a proliferating search for universals. Such close examinations certainly won't hurt and they just might help the academy make sense of this much-contested topic.

Notes

1 Lynn Hunt (ed.), *The Invention of Pornography*, New York: Zone Books, 1993, p. 10.
2 Walter Kendrick, *The Secret Museum: Pornography in Modern Culture*, New York: Viking, 1987, p. 31.
3 Quoted in Elisabeth Ladenson, *Dirt for Art's Sake: Books on Trial from Madame Bovary to Lolita*, Ithaca: Cornell University Press, 2007, p. 225.
4 Robin Morgan, 'Theory and Practice: Pornography and Rape' in Laura Lederer (ed.), *Take Back the Night: Women on Pornography*, New York: William Morrow, 1980, pp. 134–40; Andrea Dworkin, *Pornography: Men Possessing Women*, New York: Putnam, 1982; Catherine MacKinnon, *Only Words*, Cambridge, MA: Harvard University Press, 1996.
5 For discussions of the porn wars see: Carole S. Vance (ed.), *Pleasure and Danger: Exploring Female Sexuality*, Boston and London: Routledge and Kegan Paul, 1984; Susan Guber and Joan Hoff (eds), *For Adult Users Only*, Bloomington: Indiana University Press, 1989; Lisa Duggan and Nan Hunter, *Sex Wars: Sexual Dissent and Political Culture*, London and New York: Routledge, 1995.
6 Thomas Waugh, *Hard to Imagine*, New York: Columbia University Press, 1996, p. 8.
7 Clarissa Smith, *One for the Girls! The Pleasures and Practices of Reading Women's Porn*, Bristol: Intellect Books, 2007, p. 15.
8 Iain McCalman, *Radical Underworld: Prophets, Revolutionaries, and Pornographers, 1795–1840*, Oxford: Clarendon, 1993, p. 286, n. 2.
9 Though the Milford Haven collection, with its distinctive book plate, was broken up, the postcard collection resides at the Victoria and Albert Museum. Sarah Liberty Leonard, 'The Cultural Politics of "Immoral Writings": Readers, Peddlers and Police in Germany, 1820–90', Ph.D. dissertation, Brown University, 2001, p. 27.
10 David Stevenson, *The Beggar's Benison: Sex Clubs of Enlightenment Scotland and Their Rituals*, East Lothian: Tuckwell Press, 2001, pp. 33–35, 41–45, 183–85.
11 Robert Darnton, *The Literary Underground of the Old Regime*, Cambridge, MA: Harvard University Press, 1982, pp. 207–8; Robert Darnton, *The Forbidden Best-Sellers of Pre-Revolutionary France*, New York: W. W. Norton & Company, 1995, p. 21.
12 For discussions of sexuality, the Enlightenment and libertinism see: G. S. Rousseau (ed.), *Sexual Underworlds of the Enlightenment*, Chapel Hill: University of North Carolina Press, 1988; James G. Turner, 'The Properties of Libertinism', *Eighteenth-Century Life* 9:3, 1985, pp. 75–87; Catherine Cusset (ed.), *Libertinage and Modernity*, New Haven and London: Yale University Press, 1998, *Yale French Studies* 94.
13 Hunt, 'Pornography and the French Revolution' in Hunt, *The Invention of Pornography*, pp. 312–14.
14 For discussions of Sade see John Phillips, *Sade: The Libertine Novels*, London: Pluto Press, 2001. He also wrote a very nice essay about Sade in Gaetan Brulotte and John Phillips (eds), *Encyclopedia of Erotic Literature*, London and New York: Routledge, 2006, pp. 1152–61.
15 Gert Hekma, 'Rewriting the History of Sade', *Journal of the History of Sexuality* 1, 1990, pp. 131–36 (131).
16 For publication information about *Fanny Hill* see David Foxon, *Libertine Literature in England, 1660–1745*, New York: University Books, 1965; William H. Epstein, *John Cleland: Images of a Life*, New York: Columbia University Press, 1974; Patrick J. Kearney, *A History of Erotic Literature*, Hong Kong: Dorset Press, 1993.
17 Bradford K. Mudge, *The Whore's Story: Women, Pornography, and the British Novel, 1684–1830*, Oxford and New York: Oxford University Press, 2000, p. 226.

18 Julia Epstein, 'Fanny's Fanny: Epistolarity, Eroticism, and the Transsexual Text' in Elizabeth Goldsmith (ed.), *Writing the Female Voice*, Boston: Northeastern, 1989, pp. 135–53.
19 Henry Spenser Ashbee, *Cantena Librorum Tacendorum*, 1885; reprint, New York: Documentary Books, Inc., 1962, pp. 60–91.
20 Julie Peakman, *Mighty Lewd Books: The Development of Pornography in Eighteenth-Century England*, Basingstoke: Palgrave Macmillan, 2003, pp. 172–76.
21 Leonard, 'The Cultural Politics of "Immoral Writings"', pp. 97–98.
22 Sarah Leonard, 'Wanderers, Entertainers, and Seducers: Making Sense of Obscenity Laws in the German States, 1830–51' in Lisa Z. Sigel (ed.), *International Exposure: Perspectives on Modern European Pornography, 1800–2000*, New Brunswick: Rutgers University Press, 2005, pp. 27–47.
23 Gary D. Stark, 'Pornography, Society, and the Law in Imperial Germany', *Central European History* 14:3, 1981, pp. 200–229 (206); Annie Stora-Lamarre, *L'Enfer de la Troisième République: Censeurs et Pornographes, 1880–1914*, Paris: Imago, 1990.
24 Lisa Z. Sigel, *Governing Pleasures: Pornography and Social Change in England, 1815–1914*, New Brunswick: Rutgers University Press, 2002.
25 Malek Alloula, *The Colonial Harem*, Minneapolis: University of Minnesota Press, 1986.
26 See, for example, Heather Waldrup, 'Photographs from an American Album: The *Albatross Nudes, 1899–1900*', *Photography and Culture* 3:1, 2010, pp. 19–40, and Heather Waldrup, 'The Golden Age of Gay Porn: Nostalgia and the Photography of Wilhelm von Gloeden', *GLQ: A Journal of Gay and Lesbian Studies* 12:2, 2006, pp. 237–58.
27 Joseph Slade, 'Eroticism and Technological Regression: The Stag Film', *History and Technology* 22:1, March 2006, pp. 27–52 (32).
28 Al di Lauro and Gerald Rabkin, *Dirty Movies: An Illustrated History of the Stag Film, 1915–1970*, New York: Chelsea House, 1976, pp. 43–46, 52–54.
29 Joseph Slade, 'Eroticism and Technological Regression', p. 34.
30 Maria Tatar, *Lustmord: Sexual Murder in Weimar Germany*, Princeton: Princeton University Press, 1995.
31 Alyce Mahon, *Surrealism and the Politics of Eros, 1938–1968*, New York: Thames and Hudson, 2005, p. 16.
32 See, for example, Hans-Jürgen Döpp, *Paris Eros: The Imaginary Museum of Eroticism*, New York: Parkstone Press Ltd, 2004, ch. 6.
33 See, for example, Karl Toepfer, *Empire of Ecstasy: Nudity and Movement in German Body Culture, 1910–1935*, Berkeley: University of California Press, 1998; Terri J. Gordon, 'Fascism and the Female Form', *Journal of the History of Sexuality* 11:1/2, 2002, pp. 164–200; Michael Hau, *The Cult of Health and Beauty in Germany: A Social History, 1890–1930*, Chicago: University of Chicago Press, 2003.
34 Editors' note: see chapter 4, this volume, by Richard Cleminson.
35 Peter Jelavich, *Berlin Cabaret*, Cambridge, MA: Harvard University Press, 1993, pp. 176–83, 154–65.
36 See, for example, Dagmar Herzog (ed.), *Sexuality and German Fascism*, Oxford and New York: Berghahn, 2004, particularly her introduction, 'Hubris and Hypocrisy, Incitement and Disavowal'; Victoria de Grazia, *How Fascism Ruled Women: Italy, 1922–1945*, Berkeley: University of California Press, 1993; Claudia Koonz, *Mothers in the Fatherland: Women, the Family and Nazi Politics*, New York: St Martin's Press, 1987.
37 Elizabeth Heineman, 'The Economic Miracle in the Bedroom: Big Business and Sexual Consumer Culture in Reconstruction West Germany', *Journal of Modern History* 78:4, 2006, pp. 846–77.
38 See, for example, John Phillips, *Forbidden Fictions: Pornography and Censorship in Twentieth Century French Literature*, London: Pluto Press, 1999; Jessica Benjamin, *The Bonds of Love: Psychoanalysis, Feminism, and the Problem of Domination*, New York: Pantheon, 1988.
39 Barbara Ehrenreich, *The Hearts of Men: American Dreams and the Flight From Commitment*, Garden City, NJ: Anchor Press/Doubleday, 1983.
40 Elizabeth Fraterrigo, *Playboy and the Making of the Good Life in Modern America*, Oxford: Oxford University Press, 2009.
41 Laura Kipnis, *Bound and Gagged: Pornography and the Politics of Fantasy in America*, New York: Grove Press, 1996.

42 Joseph W. Slade, 'Pornography in the Late Nineties', *Wide Angle* 19:3, July 1997, pp. 1–12.
43 Katalin Szövérfy Milter and Joseph W. Slade, 'Global Traffic in Pornography: The Hungarian Example' in Sigel, *International Exposure*, pp. 173–204.
44 Linda Williams (ed.), *Porn Studies*, Durham, NC: Duke University Press, 2004.
45 Thomas Waugh, 'Homosociality in the Classical American Stag Film: Off-Screen, On-Screen' in Williams, *Porn Studies*, 127–41; Paul Deslandes, 'The Cultural Politics of Gay Pornography', British Queer History Conference, McGill University, 16 October 2010.
46 Jonathan Coopersmith, 'Does Your Mother Know What You *Really* Do? The Changing Nature and Image of Computer-Based Pornography', *History and Technology* 22:1, March 2006, pp. 1–25 (5).

Part VII

KNOWLEDGE AND EXPERIENCE

13

KNOWLEDGE AND EXPERIENCE, *C.* 1500–1750

Laura Gowing

Sexual knowledge is always hard to recapture; in a time of low literacy the challenges can seem almost insuperable. In an era before reliable contraception, sexual knowledge often also meant reproductive knowledge. The earliest historians of this topic worked with the printed books that were available to only a minority.[1] More recently a history of popular medicine has turned to cheap print, attempting to reconstruct how ordinary people encountered and read chapbooks, almanacs and recipes.[2] A close textual analysis of the vocabulary and concepts used by doctors and patients has revealed a model of the body now almost entirely lost, where fluxes, fluids and obstacles explain the disruptions of reproduction.[3] Others have tried to reimagine the social world in which knowledge was passed by word, with a particular attention to the knowledge and experience of women, who were so often understood to be particularly closely identified with bodily mysteries.[4] Another useful move has been in the concept of knowledge itself. The modern understanding of reproduction is so recent – the timing of ovulation was only discovered in the early twentieth century, for example – that a history of sexual and reproductive knowledge must recapture a world of different knowledges. Rather than a simple model of transmission from elite to vernacular, historians have begun to consider how information and ideas were appropriated and reworked in a variety of forms: printed words, images, songs, jokes, recipes and folklore.[5] Finally, 'knowledge' and 'facts' are themselves concepts with a history. The late seventeenth century saw a changing understanding of what was meant by 'fact' and 'truth'.[6] Ideas about the body stood at the juncture of biblical, natural and experimental knowing; certainty was hard to attain, and sexual knowledge was inescapably part of the dynamics of power. This chapter traces some of those dynamics. It argues that, for many people, sexual knowledge was determined less by scientific discovery than by the power of secrecy, mystery and magic. Rather than a progress towards 'enlightenment', we will see a series of overlapping sets of ideas about sex and models of the body, with ancient systems maintaining their hold on popular thought at the same time as new discoveries had an impact in some circles, and a continuous interaction between print and oral culture. Sexual knowledge was a social process, involving power and subordination; but more than facts were at stake.

Questions

Why are twins but half men, and not strong as other men?
Why is the seed of a man white, and the seed of a woman red?

Why do women of very hot complexions seldom conceive with child?
Why do women have longer hair than men?
Why do the terms run the first 3 months in women with child?
Why is carnal copulation not good after a bath?[7]

These peculiar questions were part of the common currency of sexual culture from around the fifteenth century to the nineteenth. *The Problems of Aristotle*, published across Europe in vernacular languages and in Latin from the late fifteenth through the eighteenth centuries, offered its readers hundreds of questions and answers, about bodies, sex and the natural world, ranging from digestive processes to hairiness, skin colour to death, eyes and teeth.[8] Not only was it not by Aristotle, of course, but it did not present itself as such: the possessive in its title denotes, rather, 'associated with'.[9] It is a long book – 150 pages – but also a populist one, and it seems reasonable to suppose its question-and-answer format would have given it if not a didactic function, then a way of circulating outside the printed object. The *problemata* were an important genre of natural philosophy in the early modern period, meant to open the doors of knowledge to the popular reader, and sometimes criticized for undermining learned truth. In the context of sexual knowledge, the *Problems* are part of a culture of questions, where the dynamics of authority and ignorance are part of the structures of social and sexual power. For early modern people, the 'facts of life' were a matter for debate, question and secrecy. And in a time of great change in the meaning and uses of knowledge, someone born in the eighteenth century could turn to a text in circulation for 300 years, and find the same questions and answers that had puzzled or reassured her ancestors.

At the heart of the *Problems of Aristotle* was the touchstone of early modern bodies: the humours. In the ancient medical tradition that provided the basis of natural philosophy, the body was composed of fluid humours: blood, phlegm, black bile (or melancholy) and yellow bile (or choler). Each was defined by a combination of hot or cold, wet or dry qualities, and the balance of humours determined the physical constitution of the human body and its sex. Men combined the qualities of hot and dry, women, those of cold and wet. Disease of all kinds was the result of an unbalanced constitution, manifested in an excess of one kind of humour. This basic system was articulated in all the medical texts of the time, and formed the basis of medical practice. Yet we have little evidence of its meaning in the everyday world. Because early modern people talked to physicians, astrologers, cunning folks and surgeons, visited apothecaries and bought cheap medical books or took remedies, we know that the model was constantly in use. We can only speculate about how it shaped the experience of sexual embodiment, and the management of the sexual body.

The ancient texts of Galen and Aristotle, in their different ways, provided a context for sexual difference in which men and women were portrayed as differing not in kind, but in degree. Extra heat in the womb made a foetus male; extra heat in the body gave men more bodily hair, greater height, and a propensity to swift action and anger. Thomas Laqueur's influential *Making Sex* demonstrated the power of the 'one-sex' model before 1750: in anatomical illustrations and descriptions that were reproduced in medical texts across Europe, male and female appear as commensurable opposites, with the masculine external genitals mapped onto the female internal ones.[10] This was a powerful rhetorical model for sexual difference, and it enabled people to visualize the body in compellingly heterosexual terms. But there were other languages for speaking about sexual difference.

The Aristotelian model of conception, for example, in which women contributed no seed to the foetus, but functioned rather as an incubator, was at least as powerful as the idea that conception required the seed of both sexes. The 'two-sex model' that forms the basis of modern sexual frameworks coexisted, in a number of contexts, with the ancient 'one-sex' one.[11]

The *Problems of Aristotle* suggests a picture of sexual difference that reaches further than the genital-based 'one-sex' model. It pursues the nature of difference from head to toe, starting with the hair, and relating it to the whole natural world. Every answer depends on the balance of humours. Women do not have beards, because their 'humidity and superfluity' is expelled through the monthly terms; men go bald, because, like trees in winter, they are short of moisture. Sexual difference is just part of a bigger picture of differences of race, age and complexion: Ethiopians, too, are more likely to have the curly hair that is caused by heated constitutions; red-haired men go grey sooner; bald men are deceitful.[12] Combining the obvious with the (to us) absurd, the *Problems* at once asked questions and invented knowledge. Its persistence throughout the early modern period and across Europe, like its parallel, more sexual text, *Aristotle's Masterpiece*, testifies to the variety of traditions that remained open to early modern people throughout the period.[13] Sexual knowledge was a series of questions – many destined to remain unsolved.

Secrets

The 'facts of life' were hardly secret to early modern people. Most people grew up in rural areas, surrounded by breeding animals; even urban dwellers were unlikely to be insulated from the animal world. Most households lived with a minimum of privacy. Bedrooms were also passages to other rooms; beds were shared; not just sex, but menstruation and child-birth were part of domestic life. There is little to suggest that childhood or adolescence was punctuated by a moment of sexual enlightenment. Certainly accurate sexual knowledge does not seem to have been taken as a danger sign for children. The evidence of rape trials records children (under 14) being more explicit than adult victims. Sometimes ignorance was hard to maintain and modesty had to be learned.

An early sixteenth-century Latin phrasebook for schoolchildren, written by the head-master of Eton in 1519, features one section on vices, and one on marriage, both of which are startlingly specific about sexual and reproductive matters.[14] Sentences set for translation included 'He kept his syster openly as she had been his true wedded wyfe'; 'Common women, with oft misusing of their body, be made barren'; 'He was cutte out of his mothers bely (*Caeso est*)'; 'She had a child before her tyme'; and the useful advice, 'When a woman begynneth to travell: agenst deliverance: it shal ease her/to kepe her breth styffe'. None of this, it seems, was considered 'adult' enough to be kept out of the reach of young scholars. The mechanics of reproduction, and most importantly their moral import, are portrayed explicitly. This seems to be characteristic of late medieval approaches to both teaching, and sexual knowledge. And indeed, at least some of those young men would need the vocabulary for sexual misconduct in later life: as magistrates dealing with sexual crimes and illegitimacy, if not as readers of erotic manuscripts or books. By the later sixteenth century, the method of set sentences was disappearing, so there is no evidence that such exercises persisted. But the continued use of Latin for sexual matters in men's correspondence (and some women's, too) suggests that the boundaries of classical learning played an important part in learning and talking about sex.

The revolution of print put sexual knowledge into a new realm.[15] Books, broadsides, and ballads about sex and reproduction were printed in Latin and in every vernacular language. The first sixteenth-century midwives' book, such as Eucharius Roesslin's *Der Rosengarten* (Strasburg, 1513; translated into English by Thomas Raynalde as *The Birth of Mankind* in 1540), were reprinted, reused and combined into many more editions, some aimed at the literate lay population, both male and female.[16] The medical treatises that have formed the principal source of historians' enquiries into sexual knowledge in this period were a minority text for professional attention. But they were beginning to be part of vernacular culture too. The Council of Trent instructed local clergy to instruct their parishioners more clearly on how to conduct their personal lives: priests may have lent out the popular advice books which focused, for example, on the payment of the conjugal debt and the timing of sex.[17] By the later seventeenth century, titles like *Every Woman Her Own Midwife* were directly encouraging lay women and men to interest themselves in the science of sex and reproduction. Throughout the eighteenth century, *Aristotle's Masterpiece* circulated a combination of classical medicine, myth and popular folklore, keeping sexual knowledge pluralistic. Printed books were not separate from oral culture: they both reflected and fed into the currents of popular knowledge. Vernacular medical treatises were clearly structured for occasional reference use, and their questions, advice and myths about monsters were ideal matter for absorption into popular culture. Material culture – from drinking cups to alehouse graffiti – added another dimension, of which barely anything remains. There is no need to draw a dichotomy between popular and elite knowledge: everyone had a body to experiment with.

But there were also barriers to knowledge, and the power play of knowledge and authority lit frequently on sexual matters. The earliest printed midwifery texts were by men who complained that female midwives were incapable of explaining their own knowledge: from the start a distinction between the customary practice of experienced women and the understanding of men was set up and challenged.[18] Throughout early modern Europe, the workings of the reproductive body were characterized with one word: 'secrets'. In some sense, of course, all bodies were mysterious. There was no way of seeing what went on inside them, except through post-mortem anatomical examinations, which were closely controlled and unusual. But it was the secrets of women that aroused popular and scholarly interest. The noun 'secrets' began to be used about women's sexual parts in the thirteenth century, symbolizing a shift towards a presumed male readership. At once, the term 'secrets' reminded readers of the shame expected to surround a woman's sexual organs, and urged them to explore those secrets themselves.[19] It also drew on the meaning of secrets in natural philosophy: arcane, ultimately unknowable mysteries of nature.

By the beginning of our period, the 'secrets of women' had one definitive meaning: matters of reproduction. This was an age of demographic concern, as well as of anatomical discovery and media revolution. The reproductive body was an absorbing mystery: reading and looking offered a means to manage and control it. To put a body in a book was simultaneously to open it to public scrutiny, and to remind readers of its secrecy. The illustrations of female anatomy in pocket-size midwives' manuals often come folded up, the act of unfolding itself a drama of exploration (see Figure 13.2).

The language of analogy in which descriptions of anatomy were couched must, for some, have mystified as much as clarified. At the same time as early modern people grasped the opportunity of investigating bodily secrets, they were powerfully reminded of the shame and secrecy surrounding the female 'pudenda'. Thomas Raynalde's translation

Figure 13.1 Ivory anatomical model of a pregnant female with removable parts; possibly German, seventeenth century. Wellcome Library, London.

of *Der Rosengarten* into English devoted three pages of his prologue to navigating the dilemma of privacy. He criticized those who suggested that reading of 'privie secrets' might make men find women loathsome, but also concluded that no woman wanted to hear of such things from any man but her 'honest husband' or a physician. Raynalde's prologue also told a persuasive story of the ways such a book could be used:

> many honourable Ladies, and other worshipful Gentylwomen, whiche have not disdayned the oftener by the occasion of this booke, to frequent and haunt women in theyr labours, carrying with them this booke in theyr handes, and causyng suche part of it as doth cheefely concerne the same purpose, to be read before the Mydwyfe, and the reste of the women then beyng present.[20]

This is an ideal narrative, which neatly inserts a new book into an old scenario, so print can replace faulty traditional knowledge: we have no evidence that books were actually used like this. Cheaper print relayed a rather different set of ideas. There is nothing in cheap print to echo the images of foetuses in wombs and anatomical diagrams that punctuate the midwives' manuals. Ballads and broadsides laid out much rougher outlines of knowledge. They told warning tales which reminded the audience of the dangers of sexual ignorance counterposed with promiscuity: young maids seduced and abandoned, new husbands cuckolded by cunning wives or midwives. The widespread and popular tales of monstrous birth, which were also repeated in midwives' books and *Aristotle's Masterpiece*, depicted a female body in which any maternal sin or accident could be inflicted on the body of a child. The mysterious womb was, in this context, actively dangerous.

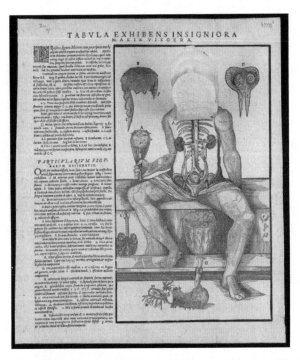

Figure 13.2 Anatomical fugitive sheet of a skeleton, male figure, with moveable flaps which can be raised to show cut-outs of the viscera attached beneath. Image shown with flaps up. Wittenberg, 1573. Wellcome Library, London.

The recipients of knowledge about reproduction were also guarded. If young children were not protected from sexual knowledge, by adolescence, that knowledge was seen as potentially dangerous. Youths, and particularly 'lewd boys', were frequently identified as unsuitable recipients of sexual knowledge, both in conversation and in books. In practice, the limits on such knowledge were less about sex than about reproduction and, particularly, contraception. In London in 1624, an apprentice named Nathan Webb came to ask Ann Barton, a widow who worked in the kitchen of one of the inns of court, 'what was the reason ... whie maides were lett bloode in the foote'. She 'reproved him for ytt and told him it was not fitting for boyes to know it'.[21] Letting blood in the foot was established as a remedy for irregular menstruation, and therefore as an abortifacient. Nathan Webb's question was part of a series of rumours started by Anne Pomeroy – his master's wife – about Elizabeth Maskell, a maidservant at the inn, alleging that she was not a virgin. In another claim to sexual knowledge, Anne Pomeroy told the kitchen that she could look at Elizabeth Maskell's hand and tell she was not a maid. Ann Barton was 60 and described herself as a 'poor widow ... little or nothing worth ... she doth belong to Seargeants Inn ... [and] is employed by the cook of the house in the terme tyme to turne the spitt and washe the dishes and suche like drudgery'. Nathan Webb, by contrast, was the apprentice of Hugh Pomeroy, and in the domestic economy as well as in the urban one, stood some way higher than a kitchen drudge. The claims of popular sexual knowledge were apt to encourage scrutiny of young women for evidence of their moral status; they also gave even poor and old women a card to play.

Modest girls were expected to be innocent, too. If sex was not a mystery, reproduction might be. Infanticide cases across Europe feature pregnant single women and their friends who insisted they had noticed nothing amiss, or had confused the symptoms of pregnancy with wind or gout.[22] Whether or not they were telling the truth, their stories were sufficiently convincing to be heard in court: it was not implausible to reach the end of a pregnancy without knowing what was happening, or to live innocently at close quarters with a pregnant woman. Pregnancy was hard to define objectively for all women: its early stages were always uncertain, the symptoms confusing until quickening, or later.[23] What was kept most secret, then, was not sex, or anatomy, but reproduction. The ability to control procreation was potentially dangerous: as every midwife's book noted, the information it provided could be misused to prevent conception or cause miscarriage. The Renaissance sources are surprisingly reticent about contraception, compared to their ancient and medieval predecessors: not only were the church's proscriptions becoming influential, but the chain of knowledge may have been breaking, as university-educated physicians distanced themselves from women's problems.[24] More broadly, generation was a matter of political and religious controversy across Europe in this period. The mystery of reproduction, at the beginning of the sixteenth century, was a sacred affair. The question of whether women, or men, had more influence in conception bore on the role of Mary: debates about the physical nature of the sacrament were paralleled in debates about the nature of Mary's conception of the son of God. Theologians, heretics and physicians were directly and controversially concerned with the question of how to describe the part Mary played in Christ's incarnation: was it like a pipe carrying water that imbued it with lead, or a bag of saffron that merely retained the spice's colour?[25] Theology and sexual knowledge bore directly and troublingly on each other.

Throughout this period, the sense of women as the guardians of reproductive knowledge was under debate. The genre of almanacs – the earliest printed calendars, cheap and much used – provides an interesting case study here. In late seventeenth-century England the student of astrology, Sarah Jinner, offered advice on sexual and reproductive problems in her almanacs alongside an outline calendar. Remedies were offered for problems of miscarriage, postpartum haemorrhage and uterine prolapses. The 1659 almanac gave four separate recipes for the increase of 'fruitfulness': not being fertile enough was perceived as much more of a problem than an ill-timed pregnancy. Venereal disease was another concern, with several remedies for the whites or 'running of the reines'. Problems with milk and breasts took up three pages in her 1664 almanac, followed by remedies for those bewitched into impotence.[26] She also gave recipes for 'pills to expel a dead child' – ingredients included the herb pennyroyal, which would have been an effective abortifacient as well.[27] Pennyroyal was also suggested for making menstruation regular, following the ancient and useful elision of irregular periods and inconvenient pregnancy (the fact that some medical authorities, of whom the midwife Jane Sharp was one, talked of periods continuing for the first three months of pregnancy confused the issue still further). This is information that comes directly from more substantive, expensive medical treatises: Jinner's work passed it directly into a much more readily available form. Her almanacs were paralleled by a much more sexually explicit, and parodic, version, which actually called itself *The womans almanack*.[28] It has a quite different tone, with much more sex and speculative suggestions, and much less astrology: the very idea of a 'women's almanac' seems to be a joke akin to the satirical 'parliaments of ladies' of the same period, although it also offers its own version of sexual knowledge.

The identification of Jinner's almanacs as female-oriented did not exclude men's physical problems: the 1659 edition had three remedies for a 'fomentation for the cods', using several of the same ingredients central to women's remedies (agnus castus and pennyroyal), and three versions of a 'confection to cause fruitfulness in man or woman'. But the effect, if we take the idea of women's almanacs seriously, is both to safeguard a female authority over generation, and to pass it into the hands of experts. Jinner's qualification as both a woman and a 'student in astrology' also marks her as a repository of sexual authority. Astrology was, of course, already a discipline identified with sexual knowledge: the power of the planets was well known to be authoritative over generation, not just menstruation. Jinner wrote self-consciously of the significance of her publications for sexual knowledge: a book was the solution to those too modest to ask a physician. Her second almanac advised the reader: 'It is not fit the world should be deprived of such helps to Nature; for want of which, many, by their Modesty, suffer much.' Both men and women were 'very shie of acquainting Physitians' of their sexual problems, able to do no more than take their water to a physician 'and tell him they have a pain in the bottom of their bellies'.[29] She recommends, for further directions, Levinus Lemnius's *Secret Miracles of Nature*: 'that our Sex may be furnished with knowledge: if they knew better, they would do better'.

Jinner was echoing a familiar story, where the political conflagrations of the 1640s and 1650s reflected a troublesome politics of reproduction: the state of the nation could be read in the state of its wombs. But her concerns are also echoed in many midwifery manuals, where the alleged ignorance of midwives, mothers, wetnurses, or all three are the target. Jane Sharp deplores the inability of women to keep track of their menstrual cycle, and the high mortality rates of cities: she preaches moderation and labour to urban parents, to ensure their children are born healthy and survive.[30] Nicholas Culpeper lists the whimsical habits of midwives, such as counting the knots in the navel-string to predict how many children a woman would have.[31] Such claims were the bread and butter of print advice: we should read them as one of the causes of declining faith in women's customary expertise, rather than as evidence of popular knowledge or ignorance. The circulation of reproductive knowledge was also an issue of the politics of the public sphere. Midwives were the guardians of inheritance in royal families as well as amongst the poor. The role of midwives in testifying to the truth of the birth of James II's heir in 1688 made clear their public authority, and their awkward position as women in a world of male authority. By the late seventeenth century, the authority of women had been devalued: by the enclosures of the Counter-Reformation, the idea of the bourgeois and male public sphere, and in England by the reaction to the vociferous participation of women in the civil war sects.[32]

Language

However powerful the rhetoric of secrecy was, early modern culture was replete with knowing sexual language.[33] Throughout early modern Europe, a world of oral culture enabled men and women to share what they knew about sex and reproduction. Southern and northern Europe may have differed in the potential for mixed-sex or mixed-age conversations. The spinning bees in barns common to central Europe provided a mixed-sex forum notorious for courtship and sexual licence, a place where sexual norms and sexual knowledge could be transmitted, particularly amongst the young.[34] The *passeggiata* of southern Europe may have performed a similar function, although honest women seem to have been expected not to participate. Gossip was integral to communities, particularly when social mobility was high: it was always worth hearing what people knew about new-comers. In both Protestant and Catholic countries, intensive prosecution of sexual sins made everyone responsible for their neighbours' morals. On the streets and in the fields, arguments could swiftly generate sexual accusations: cuckoldry, bastardy and whoredom were part of the vernacular language of abuse. Graffiti and libellous rhymes elaborated allegations. Sexual jokes, told by both men and women, made fun of those who were ignorant of double meanings.[35]

The most useful and valued, or controversial, scraps of sexual knowledge may have been exchanged in more private locations. The birthing chamber was one. The long lying-in period characteristic of most European cultures allowed plenty of time for neighbours, usually only matrons, to visit and discuss the length of pregnancy, the similarities or dis-similarities between child and father, and perhaps also miscarriage, contraception and abortion. Younger and single people remained on the outside of these conversations, but working life was likely to bring them into contact with knowing jokes and taunts. The institution of service meant that many adolescents reached sexual maturity at a point when they were not living with their parents. Instead servants and apprentices must have learned useful information in conversation from their peers, or while they shared beds with them: one young woman in seventeenth-century England said that her bedfellow, suspecting herself to be pregnant, had felt her stomach at night to see if it matched her own.[36]

The print culture of sex of early modern Europe shares recognizable features through the Latin and vernacular versions of classical ideas and common myths. Oral culture may well have been less homogenous. Not only were there distinctive local languages for sex and body parts, but different social contexts offered different opportunities for sharing knowledge. Two dynamics made a difference: the contact between men and women, and that between married and unmarried. The daily life of northern European communities, particularly in towns, kept men and women in close contact. Workplaces were only loosely differentiated by gender. The young and unmarried also spent their time close to the married. Mediterranean culture was more protective of female honour; more practical emphasis was placed on confining virtuous women within the walls of the household, and keeping them from lewd conversation. Court records from the Italian Renaissance record secret conversations and assignations. But the greater levels of women-only and men-only social contexts in the Mediterranean world might have meant more opportunities to share 'women's secrets' – if fewer to make lewd jokes with men.

The words that shaped and reflected early modern sexual knowledge are no longer entirely visible: the gestures that must have accompanied them, enhancing words with suggestive signs, are even more hidden. Early modern language, both verbal and physical, was rich in metaphor and double meanings.[37] Homologies and binary oppositions were central to early modern culture. Metaphor and comparison pervade every medical text and much of popular literature. Their themes give some indication of the reference points that helped people conceptualize sex and reproduction. Agricultural imagery – the ploughing of fields, the fertile land, the growing of plants – reflected a sense of fertility permeating human, animal and vegetable life; it extended from gynaecological literature to pornography. It reinforced the bond between sex and reproduction. The imagery of war presented sex as a battle, often one in which the female body was conquered by the male warrior, but also one in which men's lances or swords could be 'broken'. The terminology of labour – hammers on anvils, or needles in buttonholes – made sex part of a productive economy, but also like a craft, with its own rules. In these metaphors, the female body was usually the passive part or a dangerous trap. If metaphor was a help to understanding, it also had the effect of instituting sexual relations, and the gender roles that accompanied them, as a model for the world at large.

Language also gave bodies an intriguing flexibility, which reflected the idea of commensurate sexual organs. Words like the English 'tail', 'gear' and 'privates' could be used about both men and women. 'Nature' could refer to the fluids emitted by either sex; Jane Sharp's *Midwives Book* spoke of women's 'nightly Pollutions'.[38] The breadth of reference, the comparisons between male and female organs, and the frequency with which sexual bodies featured in popular culture, meant women's genitals were very far from unnameable. Laurent Joubert's catalogue of 'popular errors' about reproduction includes a long section on virginity, which claims to reproduce three depositions by the sworn matrons who examined assault and rape victims. Here are four Parisian matrons, deposing in 1532, about their examination of Henriette Peliciere, aged 15, who accused Simon le Bragard of forcing and deflowering her:

> And all having been seen and examined with the fingers and with the eyes, we find that she has the *barres* broken, the *halerons* displaced, the *dame* du *milieu* withdrawn, the *pouuant* rent, the *toutons* out of place, the *enchenart* turned up, the *babolle* beaten down, the *entrepet* wrinkled, the *arrierefosse* opened, the *guilboquet* split, the *lippion* flattened, the *guilheuart* dilated, the *balunaus* hanging down.[39]

These terms, many impossible to translate simply, use images of bars and ditches, hair and beards, mouths and trifling small things ('*babolle*'). The attack on the virginal body was also phrased, as so often, as a military assault, with the body in retreat, cleaved, and sundered.[40] The clattering vernacular words convey a much more detailed sense of the assaults that these young women were complaining of: not simply a broken hymen, but a whole catalogue of assaults on the body. English rape depositions create a rather similar effect, by talking about damage to clothes and goods more than the physical attack.[41] These might be metaphors that gave women a better way of understanding the trauma of assault.

For Joubert, as for other authorities, these are superfluous details: it was the hymen (the '*dame* du *milieu*' or dame of the middle) that mattered. The point of words like this was as evidence of the absurd claims of female popular knowledge, akin to the increasingly familiar trope of the ignorant midwife. For the historian, they may be amongst the few remnants of a vanished vernacular: Alison Klairmont Lingo suggests that this period saw the superseding of common or local knowledge by official anatomy, the lively, meaningful metaphors of popular vernacular replaced by single Latin-derived terms.[42] A modern list of parts of the body in Germanic dialects, for example, records 22 classes of meaning for the female genitalia.[43] Contemporaries doubted Joubert's veracity, as have later historians: nothing similar survives.[44] Others complained of the immodesty of publishing such words, and in response, later editions enclosed this section within asterisks, to enable modest maids to skip it – assuming a level of self-control that few would have granted to young women in regard of sex, never mind reading. But from their publication in Joubert's text, these words, wherever they came from, passed into other midwives' books, broadsides, erotic texts and dictionaries: they depicted a world in which there was much more to know about the female genitalia than could be imagined, or spoken, in later centuries.

The role of language in understanding the body is complicated. Did the breadth and sophistication of the vernacular help ensure women's ownership of, or investment in, their own sexuality? Little else in popular culture suggests so. More naming, more metaphors, might also – in identifying women's natures very intricately with their genitalia – be a means of alienation, suppression or difficulty. The erosion of female expertise, the medicalization and professionalization of bodily knowledge, and the refinement of bawdy language all shifted the ground on which sex and gender were constructed.

The early modern period was a time of sexual discovery, but new knowledge helped rekindle old controversies, and the impact of scientific discoveries on popular knowledge was minimal. The new understanding of reproduction inspired by Leeuwenhoek's discovery of spermatozoa under the microscope in 1677, and de Graaf's discovery of eggs in ovarian follicles in 1672, coexisted with preformationism, where the egg contained the elements of life and the sperm provided the spirit. The debate over whose essence, the man's or the woman's, contributed the most vital part to conception, left the meaning of paternity contestable, and reverberated through the popular politics of patriarchy.[45] The popular understanding of the mystery of conception was, however, best expressed in the vernacular term 'nature', which in seventeenth-century English was used for semen, women's sexual fluid, excrement, and menstruation.

This was also a period in which the clitoris began to be spoken of again. Ignored in medieval medical texts, it reappeared in scientific texts from 1559, giving women's bodies another homologue to the penis: by the early seventeenth century, one English writer was describing it as the 'woman's yard'. It became, also, the foundation for fears about sex between women. One seventeenth-century text claimed that French prostitutes called the clitoris the 'godemiché', or dildo.[46] While most historians agree that the concept of sexual identity is a modern one, knowledge about sex between two people of the same sex was spread both orally and in print. In a notorious sodomy trial in London in the late seventeenth century, Edward Rigby was alleged to have told the man he was pursuing that sodomy was 'no more than was done in our Fore-fathers time', and that 'the French King did it, and the Czar of Muscovy made Alexander, a Carpenter, a Prince for that purpose'.[47] Stories of sex between women were passed on in travel literature, pornography and midwives' books and, by the late seventeenth century, were being used as libel.[48]

Sexual ambiguity was a fact of Renaissance sexual culture. Celebrated cases of hermaphroditism were discussed in court documents and popularized in medical books. The idea of imperfect men, imperfect women, people of a double sex or uncertain gender was well accepted by contemporary opinion.[49] The public discourses around hermaphroditism stressed not just the necessary organs, but their performance: to be truly male, a penis had to be capable of ejaculating fertile seed. In comparison to the uncertain secrets of the female sexual organs, the penis seems straightforward; but it, too, was a topic of discussion and investigation.[50] The role of ejaculation and orgasm was one of the most prominent inconsistencies in the corpus of sexual knowledge that circulated between print and oral culture. Every early modern popular medical text reiterated the point that conception required the contribution of both male and female seed, both produced by orgasm. Legal responses to rape recognized the problem this posed for pregnancies resulting from rape: it may well be for this reason that, while pregnancy would otherwise be a primary reason for trying to prosecute rape, pregnant women felt themselves unlikely to receive a positive hearing in court. If they were pregnant, they must have consented and experienced pleasure. Legal theory confirmed this problem with equivocal reflections on the possible separation of bodily and mental consent: women's bodies could let them conceive, even if their minds were refusing. The concept of rape itself is far from clear-cut, and the seventeenth century was a time of transition in the formulation of an idea of female consent. Looking for rape leads the historian to ravishment, passivity, or senselessness – all models that were part of the construction of female subjectivity, but some way from a modern understanding of rape.[51]

A peculiar ballad of the late seventeenth century makes some of the fluidities of sexual knowledge clearer. *A new ballad, Intituled a warning to youth* tells the admonitory tale of a young merchant's son who, after spending his money on cross-dressed London wantons, takes himself to Antwerp and seduces a widow's virgin daughter. He forces her to drink till she is drunk, 'as maiden's head is weak'; he ravishes her when 'she could no resistance make'. Senseless, she conceives, and the reader is warned:

> Therefore good virgins take good heed
> lest you be thus beguiled
> When wine is settled in your brain
> you may be got with child.

The reader learns, too, of her way out: wine is to be both the cause of conception, and the end of it. She vows to 'wash away with wine/my scarlet spots of shame', drinking hot wine to scald the unborn babe to death, and kills herself in the process. A further seven stanzas tell of her mother's revenge (a widow's curse) by cursing the man with agonizing torments. Drunkenness is essential here: it makes the maiden a senseless victim. But it also warns the reader that willing consent is not, by any means, essential to conception, and that a woman's 'sense' – a word that recurs frequently in the text – is easily lost. The female voice bemoaning her fate describes herself as 'a Strumpet in disgrace/though one against my will'.[52] A woman's will is weak indeed here. Warnings to 'youth' come frequently in ballads and broadsides: it was one way of introducing horror stories. At the same time, the oral context in which ballads were presented, and their circulation as disposable cheap print, might easily lead to discussion of matters like the avoidance of pregnancy and the risks of conception.

Less explicitly discussed in popular literature was menstruation. To some degree this may have been because of its lack of definition as a discrete sex characteristic: blood was part of the ebbs and flows typical of all human life. It was compared to fermentation, and as a release of impurities it was a sign of health – quite the opposite of diseases like 'the running of the reines' and 'the whites'.[53] It was the rhythmic nature of menstruation that made it unique to women, and this rhythm was often a subject for concern.[54] The importance of a healthy periodic discharge also made it possible for women to express anxiety about missing periods, without going so far as to consider pregnancy; and for them to seek remedies for it that did not come under the category of abortifacients. Outside the realm of medical texts, which discussed remedies for menstrual disorders, little textual record is left of the meaning of menstruation. In most households it could hardly be kept a secret: 'menstrual cloths' were part of domestic life. For Princess Anne, later Queen Anne, in contrast, the frequency and interruption of menstruation, and hence the chances of her bearing a child, had political significance and required secrecy, and she discussed it in letters to her close friend, using a code. August, 1692, saw her worrying:

I am at this time in very splenetic way for lady Charlotte is not yet come to me and I doubt if I should prove with child, tis too soon after my illness to hope to go on with it, and if I am not, tis a very ugly thing to be so irregular.[55]

She went on to consult her doctors. From the evidence of diaries, the oft-repeated taboos of Leviticus on sex during menstruation seem to have been absorbed by men, wives and prostitutes.[56] Women, and sometimes men, seem to have kept track of menses, at least when they were considering the possibility of pregnancy: almanacs would be one obvious place to do so. But references in almanacs also suggest that women were thought to menstruate all at the same time, in relation to the moon's cycle. This may simply mean that what almanacs said about the body was to be taken with a pinch of salt.

Managing the body

How did this mass of information and discussion translate into bodily experience? One of the concomitants of the humoural system, and the obverse of the obstacles to sexual knowledge, was an impulse to manage the body, its balance and its health. It's a truism to say that early modern women's lives were defined, in part, by their lack of control over reproduction. But this might not reflect their own experience. The amount of expertise, both formal and informal, to which they had access must have given many married women, at least, a sense that they *did* have the ability to control conception and pregnancy. Herbal remedies for and against conception were widespread and readily available; recipes were exchanged both orally and on paper. Single women found information harder to access. In court, some confessed to miscarriages caused by mistresses or lovers. Joan Michell came to London as a servant from Somerset in 1606, already pregnant. When she was six months pregnant her mistress, a gentlewoman named Anne Ellis, gave her 'a drink to purge her head which she took three mornings'; she then had a 'scape' (miscarriage) and that evening both her mistress and another maid where she lived asked her how she did and 'if the drincke did worke with her'. Another woman implicated the matron of Bridewell prison: Elizabeth Brian, imprisoned for illegitimate pregnancy by her master, said that a few days after her arrest 'the Matron gave hir a drinck in a pewter pott which was warme and she thinkes that destroyd the child within hir'.[57] Another Bridewell prisoner, Sara Anderson, said that the silkweaver who fathered her child also advised her 'to make away her Childe in her and prescribed her a drinck for that purpose', although she either did not use it or it did not work.[58] Other men told women they would be able to prevent them from getting pregnant. Knowledge, and access to herbs, was very clearly a tool of power in sexual relationships.

Amongst the more diverse claims to knowledge exchanged between people in early modern Europe, those about the management of potency and fertility were prominent. It was here that the most unpredictable ideas could surface. Fertility remained an absorbing mystery, to which any lay person could contribute. In Somerset in 1620, a woman was overheard 'jesting' that she would try to conceive a girl by 'making trial' with men from two neighbouring villages who, she knew, 'can begett maidens'.[59] In Hereford in 1688, a woman told her neighbours she 'was a twin and should never be with child'.[60] Diet loomed large in the popular imagination, echoing the significance of dietary management in contemporary literature. A London woman told a man not to eat too much cheese 'for fear his ware will be to short';[61] a Somerset man bragged that his potency came from eating stewed prunes and preserves in mead when he was a schoolboy.[62]

This was also a world in which magic remained one of the obvious resorts for mysterious problems. Witches were alleged to cause miscarriages as well as infanticide, by a look or a touch. In Renaissance Rome, a courtesan known as 'Lucrezia the Greek' kept carefully the scraps of cloth she sponged her body with after sex, to cast spells to make her lover, a servant of the Pope, fall in love with her. She sent her servant to find pieces of church bell rope for the same purpose, and swept the dust from successful whores' doors to bring her luck. On one occasion, according to her servant, she had tied pieces of cloth to her genitals after sex with another lover, to protect herself from the syphilis she said his sperm carried.[63] Witch trials in seventeenth-century Friuli exposed a heritage of superstitions and spells, passed between women, that used the magic of the female body to protect crops and health. Women reported lifting their skirts to frighten away storms or caterpillars, using menstruating girls to heal a child's illness, and riding naked on a yoke. Only a faint trace of the power of the phallus appeared, with memories of women who had used a man's member to make the sign of the cross over swollen breasts to release the milk.[64]

Popular sexual knowledge in early modern Europe made the body manageable, but also guarded and honoured its mystery. New facts rarely managed to undermine old models; the model of humours and flows was capacious enough to encompass plenty of apparent contradictions. Those contradictions also left room for individual assertion. Some knew that cheese was an aphrodisiac, others swore by preserves: expertise and authority was everywhere. The veneration of ancient authorities made knowledge a collective, often contradictory affair: there was never just one voice. Print did something to homogenize those voices. One of the features of the *Womens Almanac* was a formula for deducing the sex of a child by adding the numbers of the letters of the father's and mother's names to the month of conception and dividing by seven (if the remainder was even, it was a girl, if odd, a boy); the same formula appeared in a French 'secrets of nature' book, and doubtless in many other places too.[65] What made it work, and last, was the mystery that numerical and symbolic calculations (ones which would be quite complex if you did not know the order of letters of the alphabet, for example) conferred: it transformed straightforward guesswork (with a 50 per cent chance of success) into a 'secret of nature'.

Conclusion

Over our period, the actual state of sexual knowledge remained virtually unchanged. It was as difficult to plan conception, prevent it, or diagnose pregnancy at the end of the period as at the beginning. It is hard to see crucial scientific discoveries like that of sperm having any visible impact on sexual knowledge: the existing model was too flexible and powerful. The very idea that science and experiment could uncover the 'truth' of the body was a dubious one, impinging on divine authority. The meaning of knowledge, though, was shifting. Modesty was an increasingly valued aspect of politeness. Reproduction was a matter of political and religious controversy; the authority of midwives and mothers was being eroded. The expansion of print had a dual effect: sexual facts in print were everywhere, yet the rhetoric of secrecy in midwives' books and other texts made women's bodies more private and more shameful, and women's authority more dubious. The power of vernacular words, popular expertise, traditional ideas and magic remained, and many of the ideas expressed by early modern people were still convincing into the last century. For those reading a fourteenth-century text in the eighteenth century, accuracy was probably not their first concern. The body remained intractable to a search for fixed knowledge, and immensely fertile for questions, stories and meaningful myths.

Notes

1 Early examples include Hilda L. Smith, 'Gynecology and Ideology in Seventeenth-Century England' in Berenice A. Carroll (ed.), *Liberating Women's History: Theoretical and Critical Essays*, Urbana: University of Illinois Press, 1976, pp. 97–114; Audrey Eccles, *Obstetrics and Gynaecology in Tudor and Stuart England*, London: Croom Helm, 1982; Angus McLaren, *Reproductive Rituals: The Perception of Fertility in England from the Sixteenth Century to the Nineteenth Century*, London: Methuen, 1984.

2 Mary Fissell, 'Readers, Texts, and Contexts: Vernacular Medical Works in Early Modern England' in Roy Porter (ed.), *The Popularization of Medicine, 1650–1850*, London: Routledge, 1992, pp. 72–91.

3 Barbara Duden, *The Woman beneath the Skin: A Doctor's Patients in Eighteenth-Century Germany*, Cambridge, MA: Harvard University Press, 1991 [1987]; Ulinka Rublack, 'Pregnancy, Childbirth and the Female Body in Early Modern Germany', *Past & Present* 150:1, 1996, pp. 84–110.

4 Patricia Crawford, 'Sexual Knowledge in England, 1500–1750' in Roy Porter and Mikulas Teich (eds), *Sexual Knowledge, Sexual Science: The History of Attitudes to Sexuality*, Cambridge: Cambridge University Press, 1994, pp. 82–106.

5 Roger Chartier, 'Culture as Appropriation: Popular Cultural Uses in Early Modern France' in Steven L. Kaplan (ed.), *Understanding Popular Culture: Europe from the Middle Ages to the Nineteenth Century*, Berlin: Mouton, 1984, pp. 229–53.

6 Contrasting arguments are presented by Steven Shapin, *A Social History of Truth: Civility and Science in Seventeenth-Century England*, Chicago: Chicago University Press, 1995, and Barbara J. Shapiro, *A Culture of Fact: England, 1550–1720*, Ithaca: Cornell University Press, 2003.

7 *The Problems of Aristotle*, London: n.p., 1647.

8 The first Latin edition was in 1490; in German, from 1492; in English, from 1595; but previous editions existed in manuscript; see Ann Blair, 'Authorship in the Popular "Problemata Aristotelis"', *Early Science and Medicine* 4:3, 1999, pp. 189–227 (195).

9 Blair, 'Authorship', p. 190.

10 Thomas Laqueur, *Making Sex: Body and Gender from the Greeks to Freud*, Cambridge, MA: Harvard University Press, 1990; Joan Cadden, *Meanings of Sex Difference in the Middle Ages: Medicine, Science, and Culture*, Cambridge: Cambridge University Press, 1993.

11 Karen Harvey, 'The Substance of Sexual Difference: Change and Persistence in Representations of the Body in Eighteenth-Century England', *Gender and History* 14:2, 2002, pp. 202–23.

12 *Problems of Aristotle*, ch. 1.

13 On *Aristotle's Masterpiece*, see Mary E. Fissell, 'Hairy Women and Naked Truths: Gender and the Politics of Knowledge in Aristotle's Masterpiece', *William and Mary Quarterly* 60:1, 2003, pp. 43–74; Roy Porter and Lesley Hall, *The Facts of Life: The Creation of Sexual Knowledge in Britain, 1650–1950*, New Haven: Yale, 1995, pp. 33–64.

14 William Horman, *Vulgaria*, London: n.p., 1519, chapters headed 'De viitis et improbia moris' and 'De coniugialibus'.

15 Patricia Crawford, 'Sexual Knowledge in England'; Katherine Crawford, *European Sexualities, 1400–1800*, Cambridge: Cambridge University Press, 2007; Tim Hitchcock, *English Sexualities 1700–1800*, London: Macmillan, 1997; Merry E. Wiesner, 'Disembodied Theory? Discourses of Sex in Early Modern Germany' in Ulinka Rublack (ed.), *Gender in Early Modern German History*, Cambridge: Cambridge University Press, 2002, pp. 152–76; Rudolph M. Bell, *How to Do It: Guides to Good Living for Renaissance Italians*, Chicago: Chicago University Press, 1999.

16 The *Rosengarten* was in no sense a new work, nor originally authored by Roesslin: on its manuscript sources, see Monica H. Green, 'The Sources of Eucharius Rösslin's "Rosegarden for Pregnant Women and Midwives" (1513)', *Medical History* 53:2, 2009, pp. 167–92.

17 Bell, *How to Do It*, p. 34.

18 As in the rhymed prologue to Roesslin's *Rosengarten*.

19 Monica H. Green, 'From "Diseases of Women" to "Secrets of Women": The Transformation of Gynecological Literature in the Later Middle Ages', *Journal of Medieval and Early Modern Studies* 30:1, 2000, pp. 5–39.

20 Thomas Raynalde, *The Birth of Mankynde*, London: n.p., 1565, sig. C1.

21 London Metropolitan Archives, Maskall c Pomeroy, 6 February 1624, MS 9189/1, f. 130v.

22 Laura Gowing, 'Secret Births and Infanticide in Seventeenth-Century England', *Past and Present* 156, 1997, pp. 87–115.

23 Ulinka Rublack, *The Crimes of Women in Early Modern Germany*, Oxford: Oxford University Press, 1999, ch. 5.

24 John M. Riddle, *Contraception and Abortion from the Ancient World to the Renaissance*, Cambridge, MA: Harvard University Press, 1992, pp. 154–57.

25 Mary Fissell, *Vernacular Bodies: The Politics of Reproduction in Early Modern England*, Oxford: Oxford University Press, 2004, pp. 25, 40.

26 Sarah Jinner, *An Almanack for the Year of our Lord 1664*, London: n.p., 1664.

27 Sarah Jinner, *An Almanack and Prognostication for the Year of our Lord 1659*, London: n.p., 1659.

28 Sarah Ginnor, *The Womans Almanack or, Prognostication for ever ... With Several Predictions Very Useful for the Female Sex*, London: n.p., 1659.

29 Jinner, *Almanack 1659*.

30 Jane Sharp, *The Midwives Book: or the Whole Art of Midwifry Discovered*, ed. Elaine Hobby, Oxford: Oxford University Press, 1999 [1671], pp. 76, 81.

31 Nicholas Culpeper, *Culpeper's Directory for Midwives: or, a Guide for Women*, London: Peter Cole, 1656, p. 19.

32 Patricia Crawford, 'Public Duty, Conscience and Women in Early Modern England' in John Morrill, Paul Slack and Daniel Woolf (eds), *Public Duty and Private Conscience in Seventeenth-Century England*, Oxford: Oxford University Press, 1993, pp. 57–76.

33 On the sexual culture of Stuart England, for example, see James Grantham Turner, *Libertines and Radicals in Early Modern London: Sexuality, Politics and Literary Culture, 1630–1685*, Cambridge: Cambridge University Press, 2002.

34 Hans Medick, 'Village Spinning Bees: Sexual Culture and Free Time among Rural Youth in Early Modern Germany' in Hans Medick and David Warren Sabean (eds), *Interest and Emotion: Essays on the Study of Family and Kinship*, Cambridge: Cambridge University Press, 1984, pp. 317–39.

35 Nicholas L'Estrange, *'Merry Passages and Jeasts': A Manuscript Jestbook of Sir Nicholas L'Estrange*, ed. H. F. Lippincott, Salzburg: University of Salzburg, 1974 [1603–55].

36 Lichfield Record Office, Office c. George Fox, B/C/5/ 1685.

37 See, for example, Gordon Williams, *A Dictionary of Sexual Language and Imagery in Shakespearean and Stuart Literature*, 3 vols, London: Athlone Press, 1994.

38 Sharp, *Midwives Book*, p. 225.

39 Laurent Joubert, *Popular Errors*, trans. Gregory David de Rocher, Tuscaloosa: University of Alabama Press, 1989, p. 212.

40 Alison Klairmont Lingo, 'The Fate of Popular Terms for Female Anatomy in the Age of Print', *French Historical Studies* 22:3, 1999, pp. 335–49 (341).

41 Miranda Chaytor, 'Husband[ry]: Narratives of Rape in the Seventeenth Century', *Gender and History* 7:3, 1995, pp. 378–407.

42 Lingo, 'Fate', p. 349.

43 Barbara Duden, *Woman beneath the Skin*, p. 203 n. 85.

44 Lingo, 'Fate', pp. 342–43; see also Cathy McClive, 'Blood and Expertise: The Trials of the Female Medical Expert in the Ancien-Régime Courtroom', *Bulletin of the History of Medicine* 82:1, 2009, pp. 86–108 (99).

45 On the political implications of these discoveries, see Susan C. Greenfield and Carol Barash, *Inventing Maternity: Politics, Science and Literature, 1650–1865*, Lexington: University Press of Kentucky, 1999.

46 Katharine Park, 'The Rediscovery of the Clitoris' in David Hillman and Carla Mazzio (eds), *The Body in Parts: Fantasies of Corporeality in Early Modern Europe*, London and New York: Routledge, 1997, pp. 171–93 (186).

47 *An Account of the Proceedings Against Capt Edward Rigby*, London (1698) in Rictor Norton (ed.), *Homosexuality in Eighteenth-Century England: A Sourcebook* [http://www.rictornorton.co.uk/eighteen/rigby.htm, accessed 22 April 2012].

48 Valerie Traub, *The Renaissance of Lesbianism in Early Modern England*, Cambridge: Cambridge University Press, 2002; Sarah Toulalan, 'Extraordinary Satisfactions: Lesbian Visibility in Seventeenth-Century Pornography in England', *Gender and History* 15:1, 2003, pp. 50–68; Emma Donoghue, *Passions between Women: British Lesbian Culture, 1668–1801*, London: Scarlet Press, 1993.

49 See, for example, Patricia Crawford and Sara Mendelson, 'Sexual Identities in Early Modern England: The Marriage of Two Women', *Gender and History* 7:3, 1995, pp. 362–77; and more widely, Kathleen P. Long, *Hermaphrodites in Renaissance Europe*, Aldershot: Ashgate, 2006.

50 Cathy McClive, 'Masculinity on Trial: Penises, Hermaphrodites and the Uncertain Male Body in Early Modern France', *History Workshop Journal* 68, 2009, pp. 45–68.

51 See Barbara J. Baines, *Representing Rape in the English Early Modern Period*, Lewiston: Edwin Mellen Press, 2003; Garthine Walker, 'Rereading Rape and Sexual Violence in Early Modern England', *Gender and History* 10:1, 1998, pp. 1–25, and Chapter 23, this volume.

52 Bodleian Library, Oxford, *A new ballad, intituled, a warning to youth*, London: n.p., 16 –, Wood 401 (103).

53 Patricia Crawford, 'Attitudes to Menstruation in Seventeenth-Century England', *Past and Present* 91, 1981, pp. 47–73; Sharp, *Midwives Book*, p. 225.

54 Duden, *Woman beneath the Skin*, p. 113.

55 Patricia Crawford and Laura Gowing, *Women's Worlds in Seventeenth-Century England: A Sourcebook*, London: Routledge, 1999, p. 18.

56 Crawford, 'Attitudes to Menstruation', p. 64.

57 London Metropolitan Archives, Bridewell Court Book 5, 25 September 1606 (Michell), f. 134v; Bridewell Court Book 6, 16 May 1605 (Brian), f.30.

58 Bridewell Court Book 5, 23 May 1607 (Anderson), f. 186.

59 Somerset Record Office, 5 May 1620 (Henry Skane), DD/cd 54.

60 Hereford Record Office, 3 September 1688 (Office c. Peach alias Blackpath), HD 4/30.

61 Bridewell Court Book 4, 20 May 1598 (Underhill), f. 21r, 23r.

62 Somerset Record Office, May 1633 (Lewes c. Andrewes), D/D/cd 75.

63 Elizabeth Cohen and Thomas Cohen, *Words and Deeds in Renaissance Rome: Trials before the Papal Magistrates*, Toronto: Toronto University Press, 1993, p. 192.

64 Luisa Accati, 'The Spirit of Fornication: Virtue of the Soul and Virtue of the Body in Friuli, 1600–1800' in Guido Ruggiero and Edward Muir (eds), *Sex and Gender in Historical Perspective*, Baltimore: Johns Hopkins University Press, 1990, pp. 110–40.

65 *Le Secret des Secrets de Nature* (Rouen: n.p., 1700), p. 118.

14

KNOWLEDGE AND EXPERIENCE

From 1750 to the 1960s

Tanya Evans

Dissemination and acquisition of sexual knowledge

Historians of the body and sex have long been indebted to Foucault and his assertion that sexuality is an historical construct rather than a timeless constant.[1] He argued that in the nineteenth century sexual identity became crucial to modern individuals and a new 'technology of power' and 'science of sexuality' emerged that labelled certain categories of sexual activity as illicit and dangerous. A wealth of writing on sexuality surfaced during the nineteenth century as the printed revolution took hold, literacy rates increased and individuals increasingly consumed written sources of knowledge about sex. Foucault and his followers, many of whom focused on the production and impact of elite discourses of sexuality, established that an assumed prevailing discourse of Victorian prudishness and sexual repression was far from monolithic and suggested instead that a proliferation of knowledge at certain authorized sites about sexuality characterized the nineteenth century.[2] It was Foucault's work which revolutionized the history of sexuality and led to an explosion of studies of licit and illicit sexual behaviour. Foucault's scholarship emerged at the same time that the sexual revolution of the late twentieth century, despite having roots much earlier, brought sex into public discussion. The passage of anti-censorship legislation allowed sex to be more openly explored in the print and broadcast media, literature and the theatre.[3]

Technological change occurred at the same time with the introduction of the pill into Europe and Australia towards the end of 1961, now available to single women in the late 1960s and free in many countries from the 1970s.[4] The women's and gay liberation movements also had an important impact on what we know about sexual knowledge and experience in the past. From the 1960s, sexuality became central to human identity and experience.[5] Feminists were quick to question essentialist understandings of the body and sex and argued that specific historical, cultural and social factors played an enormous role both in changing discourse and ideologies of sex and the body and in individual women's and men's experiences of their bodies and sexual practices.[6] In their demands for sexual equality these movements used history, especially the techniques of social history, to explain the oppression of women and homosexuals and in so doing detailed a variety of historical sexual practices and experiences, encouraged greater sexual confidence amongst men and women which meant that more experiences came to light and greater knowledge was demanded.[7] The Women's Health movement, which emerged in Europe, America and

Australia in the 1970s but grew in strength in the 1980s, was instrumental to transforming understandings and knowledge of women's bodies and sex by producing literature, advice, well-woman centres and health groups targeted at women's needs and requirements.[8]

In the last ten years a body of scholars, using a variety of sources, have moved away from an exclusive focus on discourse to one, broadly speaking, focused on sexual experiences and the relationship between discourse and behaviour. Using a blend of demographic, social and cultural historical approaches, they have claimed that instead of an explosion of sexual knowledge in the nineteenth century, throughout this period there was much continuity in the widespread lack of sexual knowledge. They suggest that most people remained remarkably ignorant about sexual matters until the 1960s. Cook emphasizes the continued ignorance of men and women until the late twentieth century and points out the regularity with which people described themselves as having felt ignorant when approaching sexual matters. Cook, Fisher and Szreter all argue that it was not until the 1960s, when women knew more about sex and how to prevent pregnancy, that abstinence and withdrawal declined in prevalence. Up until this point, they argue, knowledge and technology played little part in the sex lives of most people in the past.[9] These historians also explore tensions in the extent of ignorance professed by many men and women and the twentieth-century increase in accessible information about sex; a tension which has led some historians to doubt the veracity of individuals' claims to profound ignorance.[10]

Historians of sexuality have tended to focus on either texts (mostly medical and religious discourse) or experience, and few have successfully integrated an analysis of the complex relationship between texts and behaviour. Scholars influenced by Foucault and Judith Butler, and their critiques, suggest that the history of sexuality requires a twin focus on ideas as well as experience and an awareness of multiple sites of power and resistance as well as the contradictions inherent in the practice of sex and the formation of sexual identities. Knowledge about sexuality throughout this period is framed by the tensions between elite and experiential knowledge. All historians of sexual practice in the past suffer from a dearth of sources. It is hard for historians to discover when, where or what people spoke about sex or how they practised it. Historians have used publications on sex and the dissemination of medical knowledge but it is difficult to discover the impact of these texts.[11] Literacy was a skill learned slowly by most people until, at least, the nineteenth century.[12] Formal education remained limited for most boys and girls until the education acts of the late nineteenth century increased access for primary school ages. Schooling did not become universal for older children and teenagers until the mid-twentieth century. Elite men, and some women, up until the twentieth century were educated extensively in the classics which provided them with an education and some sexual knowledge, including about homoeroticism, as well as other subjects that may have had some influence on practice and identity, but many individuals were excluded from this knowledge. Ulrichs used his knowledge of the classics to publish pamphlets on homosexuality in late nineteenth-century Germany for which he was prosecuted and Wilde referred to him frequently in his widely read work.[13]

There was a public and private language of sex before the 1960s but both were mediated by context. Evidence shows us that stories about sex could be consumed in street literature and the news, both orally and in print.[14] Lawrence Stone and Gail Savage have described how women used remarkably sexually explicit language in late nineteenth-century courts when hoping to obtain divorces from sexually violent husbands and these were widely reported in the press.[15] But what people wrote, said or say, about sex was, and

257

is, often not related to what they did or do. Diaries and letters rarely discuss sexual practice until the late twentieth century, but a handful provide evidence of powerful sexualities, including among women, in the nineteenth century; although, of course, these texts are rarely representative.[16] Only from the 1970s are we able to use a plethora of sources, including biographies, memoirs and oral histories that describe people's own sexual identities and practices in detail, as well as the print and broadcast media. Overall though, it is much easier to discover how sexuality was represented rather than experienced, controlled rather than enjoyed. We will always know more about what was forbidden than what was not, and the move to greater respectability in the mid-nineteenth century meant that more sexual practices came to be labelled as transgressive. Public discussion of sex as a source of pleasure, amongst people of all social classes, was not dominant until the late twentieth century.

The poorest groups within society were mostly dependent upon the oral transmission of knowledge from family and friends, informed mostly by experience. It is difficult, as a result, for historians to access it.[17] We continue to know little also, for the most part, of the experiences of people who lived outside of cities and the far-flung regions of both Europe and Australia, although some of the best recent studies have paid careful attention to regional specificity.[18] Throughout much of the period, sources of knowledge and its consumption varied according to class, race, age, gender and region. We know that middle- and working-class sexual cultures differed, with more working-class men and women likely to have experimented sexually before marriage but historians also know more about what was perceived as 'transgressive' sex (defined differently in different periods) than about 'normal' sexual activity other than what we can glean from fertility statistics. For much of the Victorian period working-class sexuality was increasingly problematized and regulated.[19] Black, Aboriginal in the Australian context, and working-class women were believed to have – and were represented as having – more savage, animal sexualities, to be more promiscuous than white women and women of the middling and upper classes who were represented as naturally more restrained. Indeed, black women were consistently conceptualized as sexual bodies, never as maternal bodies, during the nineteenth century.[20]

Work by women's, feminist and gender historians has shown us how women and men inhabited different sexual cultures throughout this period and that women remained the weakest actors in the drama of sex. For the early modern period, as Laura Gowing's essay shows, men and women understood women's bodies differently than did elite men, informed by their own understandings, readings or discussions. Knowledge was usually dependent upon age, sex, education and level of literacy. The Church remained an important source of information both oral and written, more so in the early modern than the modern period, about menstruation and correct and moral sexual behaviour, which was defined as only possible within marriage and always exclusively heterosexual. For centuries men and women were taught that sex was only appropriate in marriage and that its result should be reproductive.[21]

The good woman was a wife and mother and the good man a husband and father. This behaviour continued to be preached in pulpits throughout the nation and abroad for a long time after the Church's role in regulating sexual behaviour through Church courts waned, but an emergent professional class of medical men became increasingly authoritative towards the end of the eighteenth century and the Church, in any period, was never without its challengers when it came to the message of the sinfulness of sex.[22] Few women contributed to public sexual discourse until the early twentieth century. Women were expected to 'perform' ignorance about sexual matters, though many also remained actually ignorant of such subjects. It is for this reason that recent historians have argued that men dominated cultures of sexual knowledge as well as contraception despite a huge literature previously suggesting that women controlled cultures of contraceptive knowledge and practice.[23] Other historians acknowledge the disadvantages of sexual ignorance for women but they also assert that women were not entirely powerless. Gail Savage's recent discussion of marital rape in Victorian England shows how women could negotiate some power over men who abused their authority in the courts by appealing to Victorian codes of appropriate sexual conduct.[24] It was not until the late nineteenth century that women were seen in public articulating their rights to sexual equality and knowledge.[25]

The significant scholarship of historians of medicine and the body, influenced enormously by Thomas Laqueur's *Making Sex: Body and Gender from the Greeks to Freud* (1990), have allowed us to understand the impact of the medical transformation in ideas about bodies and sexuality in elite scientific and medical texts upon people's lives. Medical discourse influenced some men's and women's understandings of their bodies throughout this period, not least because it informed the law on illicit sexual behaviour. Medical texts continued to be published in Latin until the nineteenth century and remained expensive to buy, but increasingly they became cheaper and were being published in vernacular languages.[26] By the mid-nineteenth century, the influence of the ancient medical writers Aristotle, Hippocrates and Galen became less important as the West moved from a one-sex to a two-sex model of sexual difference. By the nineteenth century medical writers no longer believed in this model (indeed not all of them did prior to this period either), nor that men and women needed to produce seed in order to conceive a child.[27] A woman's supposed passionlessness was crucial to this system, which was rooted in the rise of evangelical religion, and many medical texts claimed that women were no longer required to orgasm in order to conceive.[28] However, competing models of sexuality sat side-by-side. Popular texts on sex and the body (particularly the enduring classic *Aristotle's Compleat Masterpiece* that was read, it is widely claimed, by people of all social classes, which was first published in London in 1684 and underwent numerous repeated publications until the early twentieth century), continued to utilize the one-sex model to describe sexual difference and to celebrate women's capacity for sexual passion.[29] It remained the best-selling guide to pregnancy and childbirth in the eighteenth century and there is no doubt that women's passion remained central to ways in which many men and women thought about sex and texts such as these helped to affirm this.[30] Both Angus McLaren and Roy Porter have suggested that although *Aristotle's Masterpiece* was written to encourage pro-natalism it is clear that many of its readers read it in order to learn how to limit the size of their families and to learn something about sex.[31]

Although there remained a distinction between learned and popular culture throughout this period, they were more interlinked than one might have expected in terms of authorship, language and market from the 1750s. Both medical and popular literature overlapped in significant ways. Medical literature was mostly consumed by the elite until the twentieth century and was shared amongst doctors rather than filtered down to a wide readership. Moreover, most of Europe's and Australia's population avoided visits to the doctor because of their expense until the mid-twentieth century, so we remain uncertain of the impact of medical discourses.[32] Nonetheless, some medics were keen to proselytize their expertise and wrote for a general audience. Jane Sharp's midwifery manual (first published in 1671) and French doctor Nicholas Venette's *Conjugal Love* (published in English translation in 1703 from the original French of 1686) became important sources of knowledge for people from the late seventeenth century.[33] The print revolution and the expansion of the publishing industry resulted in more widespread consumption of texts about sex. Short pamphlets often summarized learned publications and became cheaper in the nineteenth century. Courtship and love had also long been a preoccupation of popular literature.[34] In eighteenth-century chapbooks and ballads premarital sex was represented as commonplace and female sexual desire as a given.[35] This genre burgeoned from the eighteenth century. Reading could be a private or a communal activity and texts could be shared at work and leisure. Nineteenth-century domestic servants accessed elite as well as popular culture by enjoying texts, both books and serials, in the homes of their middle-class employers.[36] Texts could always be used for multiple purposes. Cheap medical tracts that purported to teach couples how best to conceive could also teach them how best not to – as well as to titillate in the process. But could the information be trusted? During the nineteenth century there was little medical consensus in beliefs about female sexuality and the body.[37] The medical profession remained widely ignorant of the reproductive process. Only from 1845 were the reproductive practices of people separated from that of animals. Throughout the nineteenth century many doctors continued to believe that women were at their most fertile just following their periods despite evidence discussed by some that suggested otherwise.[38] By the mid-twentieth century it was accepted that the menstrual cycle could be used to control conception.[39] In Australia, publications such as Patterson's *Physical Health of Woman* (1890), W. Balls-Headley's *The Evolution of the Diseases of Women* (1894) and Warren's *The Wife's Guide and Friend* informed many readers of potential contraceptive and abortion techniques as well as about sex. Dr James Beaney's, *The Generative System and its Function in Health and Disease* (originally published in 1872 and which went through four editions during the 1880s) disseminated a new scientific and secular approach to the body and sexuality and coupled male and female sexual pleasure with reproduction, but its critics were appalled by its supposed pornographic nature. It took until the twentieth century for female sexuality to be uncoupled from maternity in most medical texts, but texts such as these were being written and read more widely across the world from the late nineteenth century.[40] An explosion of pornographic and erotic literature in eighteenth-century Europe, particularly in Britain and France, became an important source of some knowledge about sex for those who consumed it. Though this was mostly for those who could afford it, presumably the elite's servants might have accessed this literature and it was also readily available in brothels (for those who visited them). These texts often portrayed women with voracious sexual appetites and instructed both men and women about how they might pursue their desires.[41]

Women spoke publicly about sex in the campaign against the Contagious Diseases Acts from the 1870s.[42] As a result of this and other social purity campaigns, it was argued that men's sexual desires required an outlet, that their lustfulness and aggressive sexuality needed to be controlled within marriage. From the 1870s the social purity movement in Britain, which contributed to as well as reflected medical discourse, highlighted the widespread sexual discrimination and exploitation, in the form of prostitution and sexual abuse, experienced by women. It was increasingly suggested that male sexuality required containment and control.[43] This 'energy-control' model of sexuality dominated many people's understanding of sexuality well into the twentieth century. Sexology and medicine, rather than religion, began to reform most elite as well as popular understandings of sex and the body from the late nineteenth century.[44] In Britain the writings of sexologists were passed between intellectuals rather than working people because publishers were prosecuted for the publication of their works, though in Germany their work was more widely available.[45] It has been argued that sexological literature was responsible for the creation of a homosexual identity, indeed of sexual identities. It was sexologists who first stated categorically that sex could be divorced from reproduction, though of course until the emergence of the pill this was not achievable for many heterosexual women. Homosexual sexual practices were no longer understood merely as one sexual practice among many others but as a specific social and cultural identity. Some gay male historians have celebrated the ways in which sexology, particularly the work of Havelock Ellis in his *Sexual Inversion* (1897) and Edward Carpenter in his *The Intermediate Sex* (1908), created the basis for the construction of gay male identity which was taken up by campaigners working towards acceptance of homosexuality. It is clear, in grateful letters sent to Edward Carpenter by a number of lesbians, that many individuals experienced relief in recognizing and reading about their sexuality.[46] Some lesbian scholars have suggested that it was from this moment that lesbian sexuality began to be labelled and lesbians became targets of discrimination that fed the furore that surrounded the publication of Radclyffe Hall's *The Well of Loneliness* in 1928 and discrimination towards spinster teachers in the interwar period.[47] Informed by sexological literature, lesbians, writers and consumers of their work were increasingly masculinized by a variety of thinkers but also often took on masculine identities themselves until well into the 1930s and beyond.[48]

The writings and activities of first wave feminists, informed by secular rather than religious ideals, particularly the work of sexologists, and as the twentieth century progressed that of psychoanalysts such as Freud, were crucial to an increasing focus on the importance of female sexual pleasure in a world which increasingly demanded that sexual relationships between men and women be mutually rewarding.[49] Knowledge most certainly spread through the efforts of these early feminists, eugenists and birth control campaigners.[50] This was part of an articulated need to rethink relations between the sexes as well as the marital relationship, men's use of prostitutes, sexual abuse as well as the effects of constant child-bearing on women. In Europe and Australia debates about marriage and sexuality took place in a wealth of journals and newspapers, often articulated and consumed by white, middle-class women.[51] Pioneer women doctors and nurses were often, but not always, feminists. They also played an important role in the reassessment of sexuality and reproduction within the medical profession as well as of social and state welfare provision.[52] Feminism was not responsible for wholesale demographic change from the late nineteenth century, but it was clear that the women's movements in Australia, Europe and the US articulated a widespread and overwhelming desire for a transformation in sexual relations between men and women.

Modern cinema and early twentieth-century popular culture facilitated the commercialization of sex and many young women seemed desperate to reject the sex lives of their mothers. Historians have attempted to dissect the oral cultures of the early twentieth century to learn more about what people spoke about and did. It would seem that old and new sources of knowledge and language about sex co-existed side-by-side. Many early twentieth-century letter and memoir writers drew on an ancient language, mostly from the Bible, but other words came from a variety of sources, many of which had been used for centuries to describe bodily processes, including menses, courses and connections.[53] Although some individuals found sex a source of amusement, entertainment and pleasure, the evidence shows that many experienced immense misery as a result of their ignorance. Few young women seemed to learn about the facts of life from their mothers or other members of their family, but oral cultures amongst friends and colleagues became more significant sources of knowledge in the early twentieth century.[54] The oral historian Elizabeth Roberts interviewed 160 women about sex in the 1970s and 1980s and discovered that most talked about their sex lives in conservative terms and many were overwhelmingly prudish about sex.[55] Nonetheless, many of her interviewees spoke of the prevalence of sexual relations before marriage and its acceptance within their communities.[56] Most learned what they knew from peers, sometimes older siblings but most often from their school and work friends.[57] Celia Wilmot learned all she knew from her older sister; she said:

> I didn't have any knowledge of babies. I assumed listening that a baby popped out like a shell out of me belly, and I had no knowledge of periods and things like that. But my mother never told me anything. My sister ... where she gleaned it from I don't know. But there was this sort of protection.[58]

As young girls increasingly worked with other women in factories, offices and shops and less as isolated domestic servants in other people's houses, they increasingly talked and shared their knowledge of bodies and sex.[59] However, those women who did not work outside the home and who lived in rural areas found themselves excluded from these sources of knowledge.[60] In the early twentieth century learning from friends, family and colleagues continued but these sources were augmented by other outlets such as the cinema, novels, popular sex manuals and plays that revealed more sexual information.[61] Others looked for information elsewhere. In Germany, many Berliners visited sex-reformer Magnus Hirschfield's Institute for Sex Research to learn more about the sexual practices of others.[62] Despite the increase in the dissemination of knowledge, certain historians argue that ignorance remained widespread amongst all social classes and that sex was mostly perceived negatively, especially by women. This changed in the 1950s when the sexual culture remained conservative but people, particularly married men and women, heterosexual and homosexual were becoming increasingly experimental about their sexuality. In the 1960s more variety of sexual cultures crept in amongst different classes, races and regions.[63]

Until the 1960s sex manuals, many written by progressive campaigners, often influenced by feminism, may have situated sexual practice within marriage but they increasingly depicted female sexuality as separate from male sexuality as well as from reproduction.[64] Though expensive, these manuals sold in large numbers throughout the 1940s and 1950s, culminating in the best-selling Alex Comfort's *The Joy of Sex* in 1972. However, most of these earlier texts were consumed in libraries and clinics which restricted their access.[65] The mediums of knowledge about sex transformed during this period and, though most texts were read and shared between middle-class men and women, the popularization of these messages in newspapers and women's magazines spread their messages more widely. These manuals overwhelmingly depicted sex more positively than had been the case in the past.[66]

Recent research on the history of the third sector has revealed how voluntary organizations became crucial conduits of information for couples hoping to pursue a successful and trouble-free sex life, and reformers such as Mary Scharlieb and Marie Stopes were formidable campaigners in the early twentieth century.[67] In Britain in 1927 the Board of Education, under pressure from voluntary organizations, sanctioned sex education in schools. It was not compulsory and by the 1940s only a third of secondary schools across the country provided it. Many schools had to wait until the 1970s to receive any at all. In Australia from the 1930s the Racial Hygiene Association which later morphed into the Family Planning Association of Australia spearheaded the transmission of sex education in schools as well as elsewhere.[68] Voluntary organizations continued – and still continue – to campaign to increase access to sex education but many powerful groups within society, mostly religious, remain opposed to its provision.[69]

The popular press, especially women's magazines and their advice columns, and the broadcast media, radio and then television, became much more important conduits of information about sex in the twentieth century as the messages of passionate reformers reached much wider audiences through these new mediums. The immense efforts of Norman Haire, Evelyn Home and Marie Stopes were significant because their use of these media meant that the knowledge they imparted was either cheap or free, which 'constituted both new audiences and new interpretive possibilities'.[70] From the 1940s magazines became crucial arenas for the dissemination of knowledge about sex, bodies, and reproductive choices when writers responded to thousands of letters from anxious readers. Columnists, many of them influenced by a liberalization of ideas and publications about sex within the US, imparted their knowledge of sex to a mass readership. They also frequently sat on the management committees of voluntary organizations that supported and propagated their views.[71] Dr Norman Haire, Australian-born and educated but also German-speaking, caused controversy with his articles on sex and birth control in *Woman* magazine in the UK and returned to Australia in 1939 to continue his work. Here he lectured publicly to large audiences, personally responded to the many letter writers who wrote asking him for advice, and insisted that women had as much right to sexual pleasure as men. He was one of the few sexologists who bridged the worlds of continental-European as well as Anglo-Australian sexology.[72] This meant that in the twentieth century, experiential forms of knowledge were increasingly mixed with medical information and all fed into people's everyday language of sex and the body.[73]

Contraception and family limitation

From 1750 until the 1960s in both Britain and Australia, people's knowledge and experience of sex and the body was rarely separated from reproduction because sex was mostly conceptualized as marital. The most prevalent sources of knowledge remained religion, medicine and experience. Many couples spent centuries trying to discover how to avoid children and to experience 'Freedom from Fear'.[74] It is difficult for current generations to understand, as well as for historians to convey accurately, the impact of the fear of pregnancy on the sexual pleasures of men and women, particularly of women, married as well as single, in the past. Nonetheless, as we have seen, both sexes challenged to some extent prescriptive literature produced by the medical profession, religious and legal writers on reproduction and illicit sex by using contraception and abortion and by practising illicit sex when religious authorities, the state and numerous other groups and individuals exhorted them not to.[75] Contraceptive cultures also disseminated knowledge about sex. The widespread publicity which accompanied the publications and consequent scandal of Charles Bradlaugh and Annie Besant's *Fruits of Philosophy* (1877), as well as other reformers who advertised the utility of barrier methods of contraception, brought the language of birth control into the public arena.[76] It was at this time that birth control became increasingly separated from sexuality. Some historians have argued that the fall in fertility rates in the nineteenth century suggests that couples were having sex less than they were in the eighteenth century, and that abstinence was widely practised by families desperate not to have more children because they could not afford to rear them and they were concerned to display their sexual morality.[77] Birth rates that were on the decline from the late nineteenth century reached an historic low across Europe and Australia during the 1930s.[78] Widespread frustration about sexual ignorance was articulated by some in the early twentieth century. Women interviewed for the New South Wales Bicentennial Oral History project described their frustration at knowing so little about their bodies and sexuality more broadly.[79] A number of people stepped forward to address the thirst for knowledge about contraception including in Australia, Brettena Smyth and Jessie Street.[80] Marie Stopes (like other campaigning eugenists) in Britain and across the empire was enormously influential in the dissemination of knowledge through the popular press to thousands of men and women who wrote to her or read about her efforts to provide birth control and sex education.[81] This knowledge was exchanged between campaigners across the world in a wide range of media including magazines and films.[82] In Australia, Marion Piddington corresponded often with Marie Stopes and wrote widely read parental advice manuals such as *Tell Them!* (1925) which aimed to enable parents to inform their children about sex.[83] Many men and women found that their doctors often suggested merely that sex should be avoided if they did not want babies.[84] Individuals committed to popular education played an important part in disseminating knowledge about sex and the body, though it has been argued by some that most people continued to remain ignorant of their teachings. While middle-class men and women may have had access to these sources of knowledge, the working classes mostly did not.[85] Some men and women utilized the knowledge they gained training as medical professionals.[86] Within this discourse of increasing knowledge about sex women were increasingly exhorted to demand sexual pleasure.[87]

The campaign to prevent the spread of venereal diseases during World War I and II, as discussed in Chapter 26 by Lesley Hall, led to the first formal sex education classes across the world. For some women, war work during World War II opened their hearts and minds to 'a whole new world in which bodies and sex were explicitly acknowledged, in language, in jokes and in everyday conversation'.[88] And it was also during the war that sexual practice became more conspicuous as the illegitimacy rate increased because fewer women could marry their sexual partners. The widespread dissemination of psychological theories during and following the war also allowed for an increasing division to be established between sex and reproduction.[89] By the 1970s, sex education within schools (limited though it may have been), the dissemination of printed materials, and the popularization of sexual information within the media had, to some extent, freed men and women from their ignorance of their bodies.

Sexuality and sexual behaviour

Recent research has revealed more about the sexuality and sexual behaviour of the poor than about the middle and upper classes because it was they who were most often identified as practising illicit sex. There has been a wealth of studies on illegitimacy, prostitution and sodomy because all these practices were increasingly regulated by the state from the nineteenth century and many of these practices have therefore left a trail of fascinating documentation. Throughout Europe from 1750, and in Australia following settlement, there was an enormous increase in the birth rate, both in and out of wedlock, though rates varied enormously depending upon different regions, but declined at the end of the nineteenth century. Despite the stigma of unwed motherhood that was experienced by some women throughout this period, it is important to acknowledge that many women actively participated in courtship relations and many working-class girls approached the altar pregnant. Women and men from higher social groups were perhaps less likely to practise pre-marital sex until the later twentieth century but it remained relatively widespread amongst the poor, despite increasing concerns with respectability in the nineteenth century,[90] and anxieties about moral status and the risk of pregnancy that Cook, Fisher and Chinn suggest continued into the twentieth century.[91] Nonetheless, others believe that at all times women actively sought acquaintances, friends, lovers and future husbands and many fell pregnant before marriage as a result.[92]

Despite the need to acknowledge the articulation of female desire and passion in a variety of historical sources there is no doubt, as historians have been at pains to prove, that cultural ideas of woman as mother overwhelmed ideas about women as sexual beings by the end of the eighteenth century, and that this was in marked contrast to earlier periods.[93] This cult of maternity was thought to have directly affected the behaviour of middle-class women. But working-class women were also regulated in this way.[94] Despite evidence of Victorian prudishness, many social and cultural historians have shown us that there is plenty of evidence, in the writings of doctors as well as in Victorian novels and erotic and pornographic literature, not to mention the records of births both of legitimate and illegitimate children detailed in parish settlement examinations and petitions submitted to London's Foundling Hospital, of women's and men's continued sexual passion, desire and activity throughout this period.[95]

While scholarship on women's bodies and sexuality has proliferated in recent years, largely as a result of the developments outlined above, there remains little on discourses and the experiences of men, especially heterosexual men, although pioneering studies of male homosexuality have led the way with regard to the history of sexuality more generally.[96] Nonetheless, much of what we know is based on assumptions about heterosexual sex which paralleled the naturalization of heterosexuality over the course of the nineteenth century. Homosexuality was usually represented as a sin and for men, but not women, a crime.[97] Until the late nineteenth century sodomy was defined as an act, punishable by death (until 1860 in England, and from the mid-1860s to the late 1880s in Australia's colonies).[98] Though the death penalty ceased, homosexuality became more intensively policed. The law was one of the major sources of knowledge, albeit one that was constantly shifting its definitions and not applied monolithically, about what sexual practices were acceptable, and which were not, and fundamentally helped to shape people's sense of their sexuality.[99] The law both shaped sexual practice and reflected the practices themselves. The 1885 Criminal Law Amendment Act raised the age of female consent but introduced the Labouchere Amendment which criminalized certain homosexual sexual practices in private as well as public. Germany passed the restrictive paragraph 175 in 1871 which outlawed 'fornication between men'. Homosexual encounters were increasingly and heavily policed up until the mid-twentieth century as a result of this amendment, but people's experiences of the law continued to vary enormously.[100] Australian law was modelled on British law though it was shaped to local needs.

Lesbian sexuality was far less represented in this range of material than male homosexuality, though reference was made to lesbian sexual practices in nineteenth-century medical literature. Women managed to remain under the legal radar and some lesbian women, especially if they were financially independent, were able to practise energetic and passionate sex lives usually labelled, if at all, as 'passionate friendships' with other women. Anne Lister learned about her sexuality, how to name and think about her desire, through her readings and interpretations of the classics and romantic writers.[101] Others used different cultural referents. In the mid-twentieth century, as we have seen, lesbians could utilize the literature produced by the medical profession and psychiatrists to identify their desire for other women. The explosion of writings on sexuality in the late nineteenth century produced by psychiatrists, sexologists and others created a new language for people, mostly middle and upper class, to explore their inner worlds. It is clear, that while homosexual activity was not widely discussed or condoned in the eighteenth and nineteenth centuries, men and women found spaces – men more than women, and perhaps more easily if they were wealthy – to practise their desires. Gay male subcultures were a familiar feature of urban, particularly metropolitan, life throughout these three centuries, although they were perhaps less obvious in Australia than in Europe.[102]

It is much harder for us to discover information about sexual practices that were unlikely to leave their mark on the historical record. In this regard it is important that we highlight how important non-penetrative sexual practices, both solitary and in the course of courtship, were for boys and girls, men and women in the past as well as now. Masturbation intensely bothered both religious and medical authorities from 1750 until World War I. Historians have shown that masturbation was perceived as a sin throughout the eighteenth, nineteenth and early twentieth centuries because of the resultant waste of seed and warnings against the practice were directed at mostly young, single men and women.[103] This waste of seed preoccupied many writers on sexuality and reproduction during this period and was represented in a number of popular pamphlets including *Onania and Onanisme*.[104] Nonetheless, these texts could also be read in multiple ways.[105] Few individuals, however, heeded the warnings of 'experts', especially as literacy increased and the sources of their knowledge and pleasure broadened. Control and liberation coexisted for many. Despite Australia's masculinist and racist culture, sexual independence had long been sought and gained by certain women. The historical evidence of interracial relationships enables us to question the regulatory power of normative definitions of acceptable sexuality. Ann McGrath's research has pointed to the existence and significance of sexual relationships between Aboriginal women and white men from the earliest days of the colony, while Kat Ellinghaus, Vicky Haskins and John Maynard have unpicked the meanings of the much more controversial relations between white women and Aboriginal men in Australian history.[106] Interracial, homosexual, and cross-class sexual relationships enable us to question many of our assumptions about the experience of sex and power in the past.

The passage of legislation, social surveys and the widespread publicity that surrounded them also revealed sexual activities and desires which were widely practised but supposedly illegal which helped, in turn, to shape sexual identities. Kinsey's 1948 American research, *Sexual Behaviour in the Human Male*, the British 'little Kinsey report' which originated within the Mass Observation organization, the Church of England's 1954 report *The Problem of*

Homosexuality: An Interim Report, and the publicity that surrounded the trial of Lord Montagu of Beaulieu and Peter Wildeblood as well as the workings of the Wolfenden Committee brought to light the widespread enjoyment of homosexual sex and a wide variety of sexual practices and their regulation.[107] The gay liberation movement across the western world strengthened the boundaries between homosexual and heterosexual practices and identities and allowed more people to identify themselves as homosexual.[108] Homosexuality was widely discussed in the mainstream press as well as medical, legal and religious literature.[109] Increasing opposition to the discrimination against homosexuals led to the passage of the Sexual Offences Act 1967 (UK) and the decriminalization of homosexual activity in South Australia in 1975, the Australia Capital Territory in 1976, Victoria in 1980, New South Wales in 1984, Western Australia in 1989/90, Queensland in 1990 and Tasmania in 1997. The legitimation of children born out of wedlock in 1959 and divorce law reform in 1969 in the UK as well as elsewhere helped to legitimize other previously illicit sexual activities. The emergence, activism and work of the Gay and Women's Liberation Movement increased understanding of gay as well as heterosexual sexuality, although they were not without their challengers especially under the banner of morality politics in the 1980s. The response to the AIDS crisis, throughout the world, also resulted in the widespread discussion of sexual practices by the state, cultural commentators, a variety of voluntary and educational organizations as well as the media.

White heterosexuality remained central to the message of sex reformers. Geoffrey Gorer's 1955 survey *Exploring English Character* established that most men and women believed sexual pleasure to be an important component of married life. Dr Eustace Chesser's *Love and Marriage* (1946) and *Women* (1958) also established that many people valued good sex within marriage and the importance of communication, verbal as well as physical, within the marital unit. As the meanings of marriage transformed in the mid-twentieth century, so too did the meanings of sex. The world wars had revealed that women were increasingly pursuing sexually satisfying relationships, sometimes outside of marriage.[110] The popularity of the Marriage Guidance Council's (MGC) pamphlet *Sex in Marriage* (1947) which had sold over half a million copies by the late 1960s in Britain and the increasing resort of unhappily married couples to the counsellors of the MGC attested to the increasingly expressed significance of good sex within marriage.[111] Only in the late 1960s and 1970s was gender equality to some extent achieved with increasing economic independence through work and political change. With sexual autonomy gained through the use of reliable contraception women could finally make active choices regarding marriage, conception, education and work. Many women, nonetheless, remained ignorant of how to think and talk about their relationships with men. As Sheila Rowbotham stated, even in 1967, 'I knew that I could simply want sex physically and not emotionally, but this was more or less impossible to assert publicly.'[112] However, more women and men from the 1960s were able to have, to think and to talk about sex without thinking about marriage.[113] Nonetheless, ignorance remained widespread as proven in the findings of Gorer's survey *Sex and Marriage in England Today* and The Royal Commission on Human Relationships, colloquially called the 'fucking commission' which sat in 1970s Australia.[114] Real change did occur in the 1960s but scholars have urged us to question the impact of the so-called 'sexual revolution' and point to the significance of the experience and knowledge of a variety of sexual and marital practices before this period.[115]

By the end of the twentieth century a discourse prioritizing sexual pleasure and experience was widely accepted and embraced by many. Religion was no longer the prominent language that people used to speak about sex, which was now informed by a wealth of sources experiential as well as discursive, transmitted through a variety of sources, via welfare campaigns, the press, government commissions, literature, plays, cinema, radio, television, and sexological literature, with often diverse and conflicting results. Knowledge and experience of sex was embedded within distinct economic, political, social and cultural contexts but by the end of the twentieth century experiential knowledge was widely mixed with medical and sexological cultures for everyone. We know a good deal more about the history of sexual knowledge than we did 20 years ago, but there is still much that we need to discover. The gendered dynamics of sexual cultures have engaged a number of recent scholars and it will be interesting to see how those debates develop as more research on masculinity comes to light, especially in the light of research suggesting the negative impact of new cultures of pornography on men's expectations and experiences of sex. The cross-class nature of knowledge transfer, particularly between employers and servants, is also a significant characteristic worthy of further exploration to question the stark division between the knowledge cultures of different classes that have been created by most historians working in the field. How is sexual pleasure conceptualized by individuals today, and why is it deemed to be central to modern subjectivities? To what extent has the proliferation of sexual knowledge and the increasing emphasis on an individual's rights/demands for pleasure impacted upon sexual knowledge and experience? More significantly, has the tyranny of the search for sexual pleasure replaced that of the consequences of sexual ignorance?

Notes

1 Michel Foucault, *The History of Sexuality, Vol 1. An Introduction*, trans. Robert Hurley, Harmondsworth: Penguin, 1990 [1976].

2 Roy Porter and Lesley Hall, *The Facts of Life: The Creation of Sexual Knowledge in Britain, 1650–1950*, New Haven: Yale University Press, 1995, p. 9, part 2.

3 Rebecca Jennings, 'Sexuality in Postwar Britain' in Julie-Marie Strange and Francesca Carneval (eds), *Twentieth-Century Britain: Economic, Cultural and Social Change*, Harlow: Pearson, 2007, pp. 293–307; Porter and Hall, *The Facts of Life*, ch. 11. Discussion of contraception was subject to censorship until the 1960s in Australia as well as in Europe. Nicole Moore, 'Treasonous Sex: Birth Control Obscenity Censorship and White Australia', *Australian Feminist Studies* 20:48, 2005, pp. 319–42.

4 Hera Cook, 'The English Sexual Revolution: Technology and Social Change', *History Workshop Journal* 59:1, 2005, pp. 109–28 (115–18).

5 Germaine Greer, *The Female Eunuch*, London: Paladin, 1970.

6 Denise Riley, *Am I that Name? Feminism and the Category of Women in History*, Basingstoke: Macmillan, 1988; Barbara Duden, *The Woman Beneath the Skin: A Doctor's Patients in Eighteenth-Century Germany*, Cambridge, MA: Harvard University Press, 1991 [1987]; Ludmilla Jordanova, *Sexual Visions, Images of Gender in Science and Medicine between the Eighteenth and Twentieth Centuries*, Madison: University of Wisconsin, 1989; Londa Schiebinger, *The Mind Has No Sex? Women in the Origins of Modern Science*, Cambridge, MA: Harvard University Press, 1989; Londa Schiebinger, *Nature's Body: Gender in the Making of Modern Science*, Boston: Beacon Press, 1993.

7 Stephen Garton, *Histories of Sexuality, Antiquity to Sexual Revolution*, London: Equinox, 2004, ch. 1; Robert Reynolds, 'Queer Histories' in Wayne Hudson and Geoffrey Bolton (eds), *Creating Australia: Changing Australian History*, Sydney: Allen and Unwin, 1997, pp. 52–60; Elizabeth D. Heineman, 'Sexuality and Nazism: The Doubly Unspeakable?', *Journal of the History of Sexuality* 11:1–2, 2002, pp. 22–66 (23, 34).

8 Joni Lovenduski and Vicky Randall, *Contemporary Feminist Politics: Women and Power in Britain*, Oxford: Oxford University Press, 1993, pp. 233–44. In Australia see Lisa Featherstone, 'Birth in Sydney', *Sydney Journal* 1:1, 2008, pp. 20–26 (23).

9 Simon Szreter, *Fertility, Class and Gender in Britain 1860–1940*, Cambridge: Cambridge University Press, 1996; Kate Fisher, *Birth Control, Sex and Marriage in Britain 1918–60*, Oxford: Oxford University Press, 2006; Hera Cook, *The Long Sexual Revolution: English Women, Sex and Contraception 1800–1975*, Oxford: Oxford University Press, 2004; Simon Szreter and Kate Fisher, *Sex Before the Sexual Revolution: Intimate Life in England, 1918–1963*, Cambridge: Cambridge University Press, 2010.

10 Cook, *The Long Sexual Revolution*, pp. 90, 167. For more sceptical accounts see Thomas Laqueur, 'Simply Doing it', *London Review of Books*, 22 February 1996; Kate Fisher, '"She was Quite Satisfied with the Arrangements I Made": Gender and Birth Control in Britain 1920–50', *Past and Present* 169:1, 2000, pp. 161–93 (168–69).

11 Chris Waters, 'Sexology' in Matt Houlbrook and Harry Cocks (eds), *The Modern History of Sexuality*, Basingstoke: Palgrave, 2006.

12 David Vincent, *Literacy and Popular Culture: England 1750–1914*, Cambridge: Cambridge University Press, 1989.

13 Anna Clark, *Desire: A History of European Sexuality*, London: Routledge, 2008, pp. 152–53; Alastair J. L. Blanshard, *Sex, Vice and Love from Antiquity to Modernity*, Chichester: Wiley-Blackwell, 2010, pp. 113, 147; Sebastian Matzner, 'From Uranians to Homosexuals: Philhellenism, Greek Homoeroticism and Gay Emancipation in Germany, 1835–1915', *Classical Receptions Journal* 2:1, 2010, pp. 60–91; Daniel Orrells, *Sex: Antiquity and Its Legacy*, Oxford: I. B. Tauris/Oxford University Press, 2010 and his forthcoming *Classical Culture and Modern Masculinity*, Oxford: Oxford University Press.

14 Tim Hitchcock, *English Sexualities: 1700–1800*, Basingstoke: Macmillan, 1997, p. 16.

15 Gail Savage, '" … The Instrument of an Animal Function": Marital Rape and Sexual Cruelty in the Divorce Court, 1858–1908' in Lucy Delap, Ben Griffin and Abigail Wills (eds), *The Politics of Domestic Authority in Britain since 1800*, Basingstoke: Palgrave Macmillan, 2009, pp. 43–60; Lawrence Stone, *Road to Divorce: England 1530 to 1987*, Oxford: Oxford University Press, 1990; Peter Wagner, 'Trial Reports as a Genre of Eighteenth-Century Erotica', *British Journal for Eighteenth-Century Studies* 5:1, 1982, pp. 117–23.

16 For men's accounts see James Boswell, *Boswell's London Journal, 1762–3*, ed. Frederick A. Pottle, London: William Heinemann, 1950; Francis Place, *The Autobiography of Francis Place (1771–1864)*, ed. Mary Thale, Cambridge: Cambridge University Press, 1972; Cook, *The Long Sexual Revolution*, p. 97.

17 Melanie Tebutt, *Women's Talk? A Social History of Gossip in Working-Class Neighbourhoods, 1880–1960*, Aldershot: Scholar Press, 1995.

18 There are several very useful local/regional studies of sexual cultures across the western world referenced throughout this chapter. See also Franz X. Eder, Lesley Hall and Gert Hekma, *Sexual Cultures in Europe: Themes in Sexuality*, Manchester: Manchester University Press, 1999, p. 199. The pioneering demographic studies on family life and sexuality remain important: see the work of the Cambridge Group for Study of Population and Social Structure. Peter Laslett, *The World We Have Lost: English Life before the Industrial Age*, New York: Charles Scribner's Sons, 1965; Peter Laslett, *Family Life and Illicit Love in Earlier Generations*, Cambridge: Cambridge University Press, 1977; Andrew Blaikie, *Illegitimacy, Sex and Society in North-East Scotland, 1750–1900*, Oxford, Oxford University Press, 1994; Szreter, *Fertility, Class and Gender*. But we have much more to learn about the difference between rural and urban areas.

19 Françoise Barret-Ducrocq, *Love in the Time of Victoria: Sexuality, Class and Gender in Nineteenth-Century London*, London: Verso, 1991.

20 Carol Groneman, 'Nymphomania: The Historical Construction of Female Sexuality', *Signs* 19:2, pp. 337–67 (342); Frank Mort, *Dangerous Sexualities: Medico-Moral Politics in England since 1830*, London: Routledge, 1987, p. 47. On Aboriginal female sexuality see Lisa Featherstone, 'Imagining the Black Body: Race, Gender and Gynaecology in Late Colonial Australia', *Lilith* 15, 2006, pp. 86–96; Ann McGrath, 'The White Man's Looking Glass: Aboriginal-Colonial Gender Relations at Port Jackson', *Australian Historical Studies* 24:95, 1990, pp. 189–206.

21 See Gowing, this volume, Clark, *Desire*, pp. 4, 102 and Hitchcock, *English Sexualities*.

22 Patricia Crawford, 'Sexual Knowledge in England, 1500–1750' in Roy Porter and Mikulas Teich (eds), *Sexual Knowledge, Sexual Science: The History of Attitudes to Sexuality*, Cambridge: Cambridge University Press, 1994, pp. 82–106.

23 Fisher, *Birth Control*; Cornelie Usborne, *Cultures of Abortion in Weimar Germany*, Munich: Berghahn Books, 2007, ch. 7; Hera Cook, 'Demography' in Houlbrook and Cocks (eds), *Modern History of Sexuality*, 19–40. For discussion of women's role in contraceptive cultures see Gowing, this volume and the later section in this chapter on contraception.

24 Savage, '" … The Instrument of an Animal Function"'.

25 Cook, *The Long Sexual Revolution*, p. 90.

26 Clark, *Desire*, p. 104.

27 Mary Fissell, 'Gender and Generation: Representing Reproduction in Early Modern England', *Gender and History* 7, 1995, pp. 433–56.

28 Nancy F. Cott, 'Passionlessness: An Interpretation of Victorian Sexual Ideology, 1790–1850', *Signs* 4:2, 1978, pp. 219–36.

29 Porter and Hall, *The Facts of Life*, ch. 2.

30 Mary E. Fissell, "Hairy Women and Naked Truths: Gender and the Politics of Knowledge in 'Aristotle's Masterpiece'", *William and Mary Quarterly* 60:1, 2003, pp. 43–74.

31 For discussion of this point see Hitchcock, *English Sexualities*, p. 51.

32 Lesley Hall, *Sex, Gender and Social Change in Britain Since 1880*, Basingstoke: Macmillan, 2000, p. 3.

33 Clark, *Desire*, p. 104.

34 Mary Spufford, *Small Books and Pleasant Histories: Popular Fiction and its Readership in Seventeenth-Century England*, Cambridge: Cambridge University Press, 1981, pp. xix, 157, 158.

35 New York Public Library (hereafter NYPL), *The Unco Bit Want*, *KVD p.v.5 and in British Library (hereafter BL), London, TB 11621.i.12; NYPL, *When I Was Young*, * KVD p.v.20; Houghton Library, Harvard (hereafter HL), *The Maiden's Complaint*, 25252.6 Penny Garlands; HL, *Delightful Thomas: or Weeping Kate's Lamentation*, Alph. Broadsides Box C-D; NYPL, *The Cottage Lays Distant a Mile*, * KVB Ballads, Box 2. On a widow's desire for a young man see NYPL, *Charming Widow*, *KVD p.v.20; all undated. See also Spufford, *Small Books*, p. 63; Joy Wiltenburg, *Disorderly Women and Female Power in the Street Literature of Early Modern England and Germany*, Charlottesville: University of Virginia Press, 1992, p. 68; Clark, *Desire*, p. 103. On the nineteenth century see Anna Clark, *The Struggle for the Breeches: Gender and the Making of the British Working Classes*, London: Routledge, 1995, p. 47; *Onagh's Lock*, n.d., BL Cup.402.i.31, vol. II. For further discussion see Tanya Evans, '"Blooming Virgins all Beware": Love, Courtship, and Illegitimacy in Eighteenth-Century English Popular Literature' in Alysa Levene, Thomas Nutt and Samantha Williams (eds), *Illegitimacy in Britain, 1700–1920*, Basingstoke: Palgrave Macmillan, 2005, pp. 18–33.

36 Margaret Beetham, 'Domestic Servants as Poachers of Print: Reading, Authority and Resistance in Late Victorian Britain' in Lucy Delap, Ben Griffin and Abigail Wills (eds), *The Politics of Domestic Authority in Britain Since 1800*, Basingstoke: Palgrave Macmillan, 2009, pp. 185–204.

37 Carl N. Degler, 'What Ought to Be and What Was: Women's Sexuality in the Nineteenth Century', *American Historical Review* 79, 1974, pp. 1467–90.

38 Crawford, 'Sexual Knowledge', p. 95, and Suellen Murray, '"Being Unwell": Menstruation in Early Twentieth-Century Australia' in Jane Long, Jan Gothard and Helen Brash (eds), *Forging Identities: Bodies, Gender and Feminist History*, Nedland, WA: University of Western Australia Press, 1997, pp. 136–55.

39 Stefania Siedlecky and Diana Wyndham, *Populate and Perish: Australian Women's Fight for Birth Control*, Sydney: Allen and Unwin, 1990, p. 58.

40 As discussed in more detail below. Hall, *Sex, Gender and Social Change*, and for Australia see Kerreen Reigger, *The Disenchantment of the Home: Modernizing the Australian Family 1880–1940*, Melbourne: Oxford University Press, 1985, pp. 114, 179–83, and Frank Bongiorno, *The Sex Lives of Australians: A History*, Collingwood: Black Inc, 2012, ch. 3.

41 Julie Peakman, *Mighty Lewd Books: The Development of Pornography in Eighteenth-Century England*, London: Palgrave, 2003; Lisa Z. Sigel, *Governing Pleasures: Pornography and Social Change in England, 1815–1914*, New Brunswick: Rutgers University Press, 2002; Karen Harvey, *Reading Sex in the Eighteenth Century: Bodies and Gender in English Erotic Culture*, Cambridge: Cambridge University Press, 2004; Steven Marcus, *The Other Victorians: A Study of Sexuality and Pornography in Mid-Nineteenth-Century England*, London: Weidenfeld and Nicolson, 1966; Lynn Hunt (ed.), *the Invention of Pornography: Obscenity and the Origins of Modernity, 1500–1800*, New York: Zone Books, 1993.

42 Judith Walkowitz, *Prostitution and Victorian Society*, Cambridge: Cambridge University Press, 1980; Judith Walkowitz, 'Male Vice and Feminist Virtue: Feminism and the Politics of in Nineteenth Century Britain', *History Workshop Journal* 13, 1982, pp. 79–93; Marilyn Lake, 'Frontier Feminism and the Marauding White Man', *Journal of Australian Studies* 49, 1996, pp. 12–20.

43 Judith Walkowitz, *City of Dreadful Delight: Narratives of Sexual Danger in Late-Victorian London*, London: Virago, 1994.

44 Sheila Jeffreys, 'Women and Sexuality' in June Purvis, *Women's History: Britain, 1850–1945*, London: Routledge, 2000, 163–83, and Matt Houlbrook, *Queer London: Perils and Pleasures in the Sexual Metropolis, 1918–1957*, Chicago: University of Chicago Press, 2005, pp. 246–53.

45 Clark, *Desire*, p. 154, and Rita Felski, 'Introduction' in Lucy Bland and Laura Doan (eds), *Sexology in Culture: Labelling Bodies and Desires*, Cambridge: Polity, 1998, pp. 1–8 (3).

46 Rebecca Jennings, *A Lesbian History of Britain: Love and Sex between Women since 1500*, Oxford; Westport, CT: Greenwood World Publishing, 2007, p. 87. Havelock Ellis spent three and a half of his teen years in Australia; see Bongiorno, *The Sex Lives*, ch. 3. For gay men see Houlbrook, *Queer London*, pp. 197–98.

47 Jeffrey Weeks, *Coming Out: Homosexual Politics in Britain from the Nineteenth Century to the Present*, London: Quartet, 1977; Alison Oram, '"Embittered, Sexless or Homosexual": Attacks on Spinster Teachers 1921–39' in Lesbian History Group (ed.), *Not a Passing Phase: Reclaiming Lesbians in History 1840–1985*, London: The Women's Press, 1989, pp. 99–118, and Jeffreys, 'Women and Sexuality'.

48 Jennings, *A Lesbian History*, p. 78; Ruth Ford, 'Lesbians and Loose Women: Female Sexuality and the Women's Services During World War II' in Joy Damousi and Marilyn Lake (eds), *Gender and War*, Cambridge: Cambridge University Press, 1995, pp. 81–104 (82).

49 This trend was shared throughout Europe: see Rachel Mesch, 'Housewife or Harlot? Sex and the Married Woman in Nineteenth-Century France', *Journal of the History of Sexuality* 18:1, 2009, pp. 65–83.

50 Sally Alexander, 'The Mysteries and Secrets of Women's Bodies' in Mica Nava and Alan O'Shea (eds), *Modern Times: Reflections on a Century of English Modernity*, London: Routledge, 1995, pp. 161–75.

51 Susan Magarey, *Passions of the First-Wave Feminists*, Sydney: UNSW Press, 2001, p. 97; for Britain Lucy Bland, 'Marriage Laid Bare: Middle Class Women and Marital Sex 1880s-1914' in Jane Lewis (ed.), *Labour and Love, Women's Experience of Home and Family, 1850–1940*, Oxford: Basil Blackwell, 1986, pp. 123–46; Lucy Bland, *Banishing the Beast: English Feminism and Sexual Morality, 1885–1914*, London: Penguin, 1995. On newspapers see Adrian Bingham, *Family Newspapers? Sex, Private Life, and the British Popular Press 1918–1978*, Oxford: Oxford University Press, 2009.

52 On Australia see Louella McCarthy, 'All This Fuss about a Trivial Incident? Women, Hospitals and Medical Work in New South Wales, 1900–920', *Women's History Review* 14:2, 2005, pp. 265–83; Louella McCarthy, 'Filtered Images: Visions of "Pioneering" Women Doctors in Twentieth-Century Australia', *Health and History* 8:2, 2006, pp. 91–110; Reiger, *The Disenchantment of the Home*, p. 9. On Britain see Brian Harrison, 'Women's Health and the Women's Movement in Britain, 1840–1940' in Charles Webster (ed.), *Biology, Medicine and Society, 1840–1940*, Cambridge: Cambridge University Press, 1981, pp. 15–71.

53 Alexander, 'The Mysteries and Secrets', pp. 162–63, 170.

54 Diana Gittins, *Fair Sex, Family Size and Structure, 1900–1939*, London: Hutchinson, 1982; Robert Roberts, *The Classic Slum: Salford Life in the First Quarter of the Century*, Manchester: Penguin, 1971.

55 Elizabeth Roberts, *A Woman's Place, An Oral History of Working Class Women, 1890–1940*, Oxford: Basil Blackwell, 1984, ch. 3.

56 Elizabeth Roberts, *Women and Families*, Oxford: Blackwell, 1995, pp. 67–69. Centre for North West Regional Studies, Elizabeth Roberts' Early Collection based on interviews with men and women born before the start of the twentieth century, Mrs M3P, ER. Later collection based on interviews that took place in 1988–90 with 98 men and women born predominantly in the 1920s and 1930s and living in Preston, Lancaster and Barrow, Mr P5P, Mrs S6L, Mrs B11P, Mrs C8P, Mrs E2P, Mr B4B.

57 Alexander, 'The Mysteries and Secrets', pp. 164–65; on Australia see Bongiorno, *The Sex Lives*, ch. 7.

58 Celia was born in 1914 and grew up in Drury Lane, Central London. Interviewed by Sally Alexander and cited in 'The Mysteries and Secrets', p. 165. On widespread ignorance amongst Australian women in the early twentieth century see Lisa Featherstone, *Let's Talk About Sex: Histories of Sexuality in Australia, 1901–1961*, Newcastle: Cambridge Scholars Press, 2012.

59 Steve Humphries, *A Secret World of Sex: Forbidden Fruit: The British Experience 1900–1950*, London: Sidgwick and Jackson, 1988, pp. 60–62.

60 Diana Gittins, 'Married Life and Birth Control between the Wars', *Oral History* 3, 1975, pp. 53–64, pp. 54–58, Fisher, *Birth Control*.

61 Clark, *Desire*, p. 169.

62 Clark, *Desire*, p. 170.

63 Cook, *The Long Sexual Revolution*, pp. 182, 185.

64 Cook, *The Long Sexual Revolution*, p. 192.

65 Alison Bashford and Carolyn Strange, 'Public Pedagogy: Sex Education and Mass Communication in the Mid-Twentieth Century', *Journal of the History of Sexuality* 13:1, 2004, pp. 71–99 (72).

66 Cook, *The Long Sexual Revolution*, pp. 207, 227.

67 See Tanya Evans and Pat Thane, *Sinners, Scroungers, Saints: Unmarried Motherhood in Twentieth-Century England*, Oxford: Oxford University Press, 2012. Scharlieb worked for the Racial Hygiene Association and the National Council for the Unmarried Mother and her Child and wrote a number of important books on sex education, including *What Parents Should Tell their Children*, Sydney: Racial Hygiene Association of NSW, 1934. See also Cook, *The Long Sexual Revolution*, p. 227.

68 Stefania Siedlecky, 'Sex Education in New South Wales: The *Growing Up* Film Series', *Health and History* 8:2, 2006, pp. 111–23.

69 Cate Haste, *Rules of Desire: Sex in Britain World War I to the Present*, London: Pimlico, 1994 [1992], pp. 72–73.

70 Bashford and Strange, 'Public Pedagogy', p. 73.

71 For examples of letters related to sexual matters in the 1950s and 1960s see *Woman*, 13 May 1950; 15 March 1958; 19 March 1960; 17 June 1961; 16 September 1961; 9 March 1963; 2 December 1967; 27 September 1969 and *Woman's Own*, 22 September 1949; 10 December 1953; 27 October 1955; 15 February 1964 and 5 April 1969. Evelyn Home, the pseudonym of the agony aunt, Peggy Makin for *Woman*, worked as a conduit passing on information from the National Council for the Unmarried Mother and her Child to unmarried mothers who wrote to her and shared details of the organization and how it might help women who needed it. On Makin's American influences see Cook, *The Long Sexual Revolution*, p. 225. Late in the twentieth century Marje Proops who was *The Mirror's* agony aunt informed many readers about sex and also advised the government on sex education policy and lone motherhood. See Evans and Thane, *Sinners, Scroungers, Saints*. On the impact of an Irish agony aunt via *The Sunday Press* see Paul Ryan, 'Asking Angela: Discourses about Sexuality in an Irish Problem Page, 1963–80', *Journal of the History of Sexuality* 19:2, 2010, pp. 317–39.

72 Siedlecky and Wyndham, *Populate and Perish*, p. 39; Bongiorno, *The Sex Lives*, chs 7 and 8; Bashford and Strange, 'Public Pedagogy', pp. 71–99.

73 Porter and Hall, *The Facts of Life*, ch. 9.

74 Madge, interviewed by Dr Wallace on 21 October 1943, WP, cited in Lisa Featherstone, 'Sexy Mamas? Women, Sexuality and Reproduction in Australia in the 1940s', *Australian Historical Studies* 126, 2005, pp. 234–52 (243). *Love Without Fear* was the title of Eustace Chesser's book targeted at those who were married or about to be married. It was prosecuted in 1942 for obscenity. See Porter and Hall, *The Facts of Life*, p. 261. On the long-term search for contraception see Angus McLaren, *A History of Contraception from Antiquity to the Present Day*, Oxford: Basil Blackwell, 1991.

75 See John M. Riddle, 'Contraception and Abortion in the Middle Ages' in Vern L. Bullough and James A. Brundage (eds), *Handbook of Medieval Sexuality*, London: Garland Publications, 1996, pp. 261–79; Angus McLaren, *Reproductive Rituals: The Perception of Fertility in England from the Sixteenth Century to the Nineteenth Century*, London: Methuen, 1984, pp. 58–85. There is some evidence of women's desire to learn how to control their reproduction; see Patricia Crawford, 'The Construction and Experience of Maternity in Seventeenth-Century England' in Valerie Fildes (ed.), *Women as Mothers in Pre-Industrial England*, London: Routledge, 1990, pp. 3–38

(16, 20); Patricia Crawford, 'Attitudes to Menstruation in Seventeenth-Century England', *Past and Present* 91, 1981, pp. 47–73 (70); Patricia Crawford and Laura Gowing, *Women's Worlds in Seventeenth-Century England*, London: Routledge, 2000, pp. 14–15. On the use of abortion see Lawrence Stone, *The Family, Sex and Marriage,1500–1800*, London: Penguin, 1990 [1977], pp. 54, 262–63, 266, 307–8, 315; Hitchcock, *English Sexualities*, pp. 52–53; Tanya Evans, *Unfortunate Objects: Lone Mothers in Eighteenth-Century London*, Basingstoke: Palgrave, 2005, p. 111.

76 Carol Smart, 'Disruptive Bodies and Unruly Sex: The Regulation of Reproduction and Sexuality in the Nineteenth Century' in Carol Smart (ed.), *Regulating Womanhood: Historical Essays on Marriage, Motherhood and Sexuality*, London: Routledge, 1992, pp. 7–32; Bongiorno, *The Sex Lives*, ch. 4.

77 Cook, *The Long Sexual Revolution*, pp. 63, 92.

78 R. Sauer, 'Infanticide and Abortion in Nineteenth-Century Britain', *Population Studies* 32, 1978, pp. 81–93; Mass Observation, *Britain and Her Birth Rate*, London: John Murray, 1945. For Britain see Anna Davin, 'Imperialism and Motherhood', *History Workshop Journal* 5, 1978, pp. 9–65. For Australia see Neville Hicks, *'This Sin and Scandal': Australia's Population Debate 1891–1911*, Canberra: Australian National University Press, 1978; The Women's Library, London Metropolitan University (hereafter TWL), Archives of One Parent Families, 'General Committee Minutes', 7 November 1933, 5/OPF/2/1/3/1e; Reiger, *The Disenchantment*, p. 113; Magarey, *Passions*, pp. 112–13; Kate Murphy, '"Very Decidedly Decadent": Elite Responses to Modernity in the Royal Commission on the Decline of the Birth Rate in New South Wales, 1903–4', *Australian Historical Studies* 126, 2005, pp. 217–33.

79 State Library New South Wales, NSW Bicentennial Oral History Project. For Western Australia see Sue Murray, 'Breaking the Rules: Abortion in Western Australia, 1920–50' in Penelope Heatherington and Philippa Maddern (eds), *Sexuality and Gender in History*, Nedlands, WA: University of Western Australia Press, 1993, pp. 223–41.

80 Magarey, *Passions*, p. 103. Ann McGrath, 'Sexuality and Australian Identities' in Wayne Hudson and Geoffrey Bolton (eds), *Creating Australia: Changing Australian History*, Sydney: Allen and Unwin, 1997, pp. 39–51.

81 Marie C. Stopes, *Mother England: A Contemporary History, Self-written by Those Who Have No History*, London: J. Bale, Sons & Danielsson Ltd, 1929, pp. 179, 181, cited by Sally Alexander, 'War of Nerves: Women and the New Age', Inaugural Lecture, Goldsmith's College, 23 May 2000, p. 11; Ruth Hall (ed.), *Dear Dr Stopes, Sex in the 1920s*, Harmondsworth: Penguin, 1979 [1920s], pp. 13–14; Lesley A. Hall (ed.), *Outspoken Women: An Anthology of Women's Writing on Sex, 1870–1969*, London: Routledge, 2005.

82 Clark, *Desire*, p. 177.

83 McGrath, 'Sexuality and Australian Identities', p. 48. Ann Curthoys, 'Eugenics, Feminism and Birth Control: The Case of Marion Piddington', *Hecate* 15:1, 1989, pp. 73–89. See also Vera Irwin Smith, *The Story of Ovum and Sperm: And How They Grew into the Baby Kangaroo Stories of Birth and Sex for Children*, Sydney: Australasian League of Honour, 1920.

84 Alexander, 'The Mysteries and Secrets', p. 170.

85 Szreter and Fisher, *Sex Before the Sexual Revolution*. See Cook's use of the Mass Observation Survey on Sexuality in 1949 in her *The Long Sexual Revolution*, p. 168.

86 Jill Ker Conway, *The Road From Coorain*, Port Melbourne: William Heinemann Australia, 1993 [1989], pp. 23, 27.

87 Susan Kingsley Kent, *Sex and Suffrage in Britain 1860–1914*, London: Routledge, 1987; Lesley Hall, 'Introduction' in Hall, *Outspoken Women*, pp. 1–10 (3).

88 Penny Summerfield and Nicole Crockett, '"You Weren't Taught that with the Welding": Lessons in Sexuality in the Second World War', *Women's History Review* 1:3, 1992, pp. 435–54 (440).

89 Reigger, *The Disenchantment of the Home*, p. 122.

90 Evans, *Unfortunate Objects*; Rachel Fuchs, *Poor and Pregnant in Nineteenth Century Paris*, Berkeley: New Brunswick, 1992; John Knodel, 'Law, Marriage and Illegitimacy in Nineteenth-Century Germany', *Population Studies* 20, 1967, pp. 279–94; Dagmar Herzog, 'Hubris and Hypocrisy, Incitement and Disavowal: Sexuality and German Fascism', *Journal of the History of Sexuality* 11:1–2, 2002, pp. 3–21; Heinemann, 'Sexuality and Nazism', pp. 29–33; Bongiorno, *The Sex Lives*, ch. 3; Timothy Augustine Coghlan, *The Decline in the Birth-Rate of NSW and Other*

Phenomenon of Child-Birth: An Essay in Statistics, Sydney: William Applegate, 1903, pp. 7–12. On prostitution see Julia Laite, *Common Prostitutes and Ordinary Citizens: Commercial Sex in London, 1885–1960*, Basingstoke: Palgrave, 2012; Paula Bartley, *Prostitution, Prevention and Reform in England, 1860–1914*, London: Routledge, 2000.

91 Cook, *The Long Sexual Revolution*, p. 106; Fisher, '"She was Quite Satisfied with the Arrangements"'; Carl Chinn, *They Worked All Their Lives: Women of the Urban Poor in England, 1880–1939*, Manchester: Manchester University Press, 1988, pp. 142–43.

92 Tanya Evans, '"Unfortunate Objects": London's Unmarried Mothers in the Eighteenth Century', *Gender and History* 17:1, 2005, pp. 127–53; Lyndal Roper, 'Will and Honour: Sex, Words and Power in Augsburg Criminal Trials' in Lyndal Roper (ed.), *Oedipus and the Devil: Witchcraft, Sexuality and Religion in Early Modern Europe*, London: Routledge, 1994, pp. 54–79; Gowing, *Domestic Dangers*, p. 257. For other work on female sexual agency see Birthe Kundrus, 'Forbidden Company: Romantic Relationships between Germans and Foreigners, 1939 to 1945', *Journal of the History of Sexuality* 11:1–2, 2002, pp. 201–22.

93 Ruth Perry, 'Colonising the Breast: Sexuality and Maternity in Eighteenth-Century England', *Journal of the History of Sexuality* 2, 1991, pp. 1–27; Felicity Nussbaum, *Torrid Zones: Maternity, Sexuality, and Empire in Eighteenth-Century English Narratives*, Baltimore: Johns Hopkins University Press, 1995; Toni Bowers, *The Politics of Motherhood: British Writing and Culture, 1680–1760*, Cambridge: Cambridge University Press, 1996.

94 Hitchcock, *English Sexualities*, ch. 3; Anna Clark, *The Struggle for the Breeches*, Berkeley: University of California Press, 1995, p. 51.

95 Harvey, 'Sexuality and the Body', pp. 86–88; Roy Porter, 'The Literature of Sexual Advice before 1800' in Porter and Teich (eds), *Sexual Knowledge, Sexual Science*, pp. 134–57. On nineteenth-century petitions for the admission of children into the Foundling Hospital see John R. Gillis, 'Servants, Sexual Relations, and the Risks of Illegitimacy in London, 1801–1900', *Feminist Studies* 5, 1979, pp. 142–73. On working-class women's sexuality in eighteenth-century London see Evans, *Unfortunate Objects*.

96 Claire Scrine, 'Body and Sexuality' in Mary Spongberg, Barbara Caine and Ann Curthoys (eds), *Companion to Women's Historical Writing*, Basingstoke: Palgrave, 2005, pp. 62–74 (72). For example, see Weeks, *Coming Out*; H. G. Cocks, *Nameless Offences: Homosexual Desire in the Nineteenth Century*, London: I.B.Tauris, 2003; Houlbrook, *Queer London*. On Australia see Robert Reynolds, *From Camp to Queer*, Carlton: Melbourne University Press, 2002; Graham Willett, *Living Out Loud: A History Of Gay and Lesbian Activism in Australia*, St Leonards, NSW: Allen and Unwin, 2000.

97 Emma Donoghue, *Passions Between Women: British Lesbian Culture, 1668–1801*, London: Scarlet Press, 1993.

98 On Australia see Bongiorno, *The Sex Lives*, ch. 5.

99 Matt Cook, 'Law' in Houlbrook and Cocks (eds), *The Modern History of Sexuality*, pp. 64–87.

100 Porter and Hall, *The Facts of Life*, ch. 10.

101 Anne Clark, 'Anne Lister's Construction of Lesbian Identity', *Journal of the History of Sexuality* 7:1, 1996, pp. 23–50.

102 On men see Randolph Trumbach, *Sex and the Gender Revolution: Heterosexuality and the Third Gender in Enlightenment London*, vol. 1, Chicago: University of Chicago Press, 1998; Matt Cook, *London and the Culture of Homosexuality*, Cambridge: Cambridge University Press, 2003; Houlbrook, *Queer London*; Jeffrey Merrick and Bryant T. Ragan (eds), *Homosexuality in Modern France*, New York: Oxford: Oxford University Press, 2001; Yvonne Ivory, 'The Urning and His Own: Individualism and the Fin-De-Siècle Invert', *German Studies Review* 26, 2003, pp. 333–52; Dan Healey, 'Masculine Purity and "Gentlemen's Mischief": Sexual Exchange and Prostitution between Russian Men, 1861–1941', *Slavic Review* 60, 2001, pp. 233–65; Bongiorno, *The Sex Lives*, ch. 3. On women see Jennings, *Tomboys and Bachelor Girls*; Helena Whitbread (ed.), *I Know my Own Heart: The Diaries of Anne Lister, 1791–1840*, London: Virago, 1988. On Australia, see David Phillips and Graham Willett (eds), *Australia's Homosexual Histories: Gay and Lesbian Perspectives V*, Melbourne: Australian Centre for Lesbian and Gay Research and the Australian Lesbian and Gay Archives, 2000; Ruth Ford, 'Contested Desires: Narratives of Passionate Friends, Married Masquerades and Lesbian Love in Australia, 1918–45', Unpublished Doctoral Thesis, La Trobe University, 2000; Jennings, *A Lesbian History of Britain*, p. 131; Jennings, 'Lesbians in

Sydney', *Sydney Journal* 2:1, 2009, pp. 29–38; Jennings, 'It was a Hot Climate and it was a Hot Time', *Australian Feminist Studies* 25: 63, 2010, pp. 31–45.

103 Porter and Hall, *The Facts of Life*, p. 151.

104 For Australia see James George Beaney, *The Generative System and its Function in Health and Disease*, 4th edn, Melbourne: George Robertson, 1883, p. 108, cited in Lisa Featherstone, 'Sex and *The Australian Legend*: Masculinity and the White Man's Body', *Journal of Australian Colonial History* 10, 2009, pp. 73–90.

105 Porter, 'Sexual Advice Before 1800', pp. 140–48.

106 McGrath, 'The White Man's Looking Glass', pp. 189–206; Ann McGrath, *Born in the Cattle*, Sydney: Allen and Unwin, 1987; Victoria Haskins and John Maynard, 'Sex, Race and Power: Aboriginal Men and White Women in Australian History', *Australian Historical Studies* 126, 2005, pp. 191–216; Katherine Ellinghaus, 'Absorbing the Aboriginal Problem: Controlling Marriage in Australia in the Late Nineteenth and Early Twentieth Century', *Aboriginal History* 27, 2003, pp. 185–209; Katherine Ellinghaus, *Taking Assimilation to Heart: Marriages of White Women and Indigenous Men in Australia and the United States, 1887–1937*, Lincoln: University of Nebraska Press, 2006.

107 Jennings, 'Sexuality', p. 296. Alfred C. Kinsey, Wardell B. Pomeroy and Clyde E. Martin, *Sexual Behaviour in the Human Male*, London: W. B. Saunders and Co., 1948; '1949 Sex Report', *Sunday Pictorial*, July 1949; University of Sussex, Mass Observation Topic Collection.

108 Weeks, *Sex, Politics and Society*, pp. 285–88.

109 Graham Willett, 'The Origins of Homosexual Politics in Australia' in Phillips and Willett (eds), *Australia's Homosexual Histories*, pp. 67–78; Robert Reynolds, 'CAMP Inc and the Creation of the "Open" Homosexual' in Phillips and Willett (eds), *Australia's Homosexual Histories*, Sydney: Australian Centre for Lesbian and Gay Research, pp. 133–48.

110 Clark, *Desire*, p.168; Dagmar Herzog, *Sex After Fascism: Memory and Morality in Twentieth Century Germany*, Princeton: Princeton University Press, 2005; Cornelie Usborne, *The Politics of the Body in Weimar Germany: Women's Reproductive Rights and Duties*, Ann Arbor: University of Michigan Press, 1992.

111 Geoffrey Gorer, *Exploring English Character*, London: The Cresset Press, 1955; Geoffrey Gorer, *Sex and Marriage in England Today: A Study of the Views and Experience of the Under-45s*, London: Nelson, 1971; Weeks, *Sex, Politics and Society*, p. 237.

112 Sheila Rowbotham, *Promise of a Dream: Remembering the Sixties*, London: Allen Lane, 2000, p. 160.

113 Hera Cook, 'No Turning Back: Family Forms and Sexual Mores in Modern Britain', *History and Policy*, November 2003. [http://www.historyandpolicy.org/papers/policy-paper-17.html] (accessed 24 April 2012); John Ermisch, 'An Economic History of Bastardy in England and Wales', *Institute for Social and Economic Research* Working Paper, Colchester: University of Essex, 15 April 2006, http://www.iser.essex.ac.uk/files/iser_working_papers/ 2006–15.pdf (accessed 24 April 2012).

114 Bongiorno, *The Sex Lives*, ch. 9. Gorer's study was published in 1971.

115 Martin P. M. Richards and B. Jane Elliott, 'Sex and Marriage in the 1960s and 1970s' in David Clark (ed.), *Marriage, Domestic Life and Social Change: Writings for Jacqueline Burgoyne (1944–88)*, London: Routledge, 1991, pp. 33–54; Economic and Social Research Council (ESRC) Seminar Series on the 1950s, 2009. Much of this work is forthcoming in publications reassessing in particular the 1950s. Jennings, 'Sexuality', pp. 300, 302.

Part VIII

LIFE CYCLES

15

'AGE TO GREAT, OR TO LITTLE, DOETH LET CONCEPTION'[1]

Bodies, sex and the life cycle, 1500–1750

Sarah Toulalan

> But when we speak of Ages most fit for to undertake a marry'd state, we must shut out, as uncapable, Eunuchs, and others of both sexes, render'd unfit by accident, or that are born defective; neither is every Age, tho' never so well equipt, fit to tast the pleasures of a Matrimonial State. Young People are too feeble, and the Old too languishing; Infancy and Puerility are too ignorant as to the productive part, and old Age, tho' well acquainted with the manner, yet are destitute of the Matter which Nature requires for Procreation.[2]

When writing about the suitability of bodies for sexual activity and procreation, authors in early modern Europe, such as the English surgeon John Marten (*d.* 1737) quoted above, invariably paired the old and the young, designating both as unsuitable for this purpose. Such comparisons were common to writing about reproduction – or generation as it was termed at this time – where we find also bodies categorized as too fat and too thin similarly linked. Young bodies and old bodies (like fat and thin bodies) were both significantly different from each other – one just at the very beginning of life and yet to grow towards maturity, the other having passed the pinnacle of physical development and now declining towards death – but yet also shared one very significant physical characteristic as identified by Marten above: neither was regarded as fit for the act of sex and for its outcome, the generation of offspring, the young being 'too feeble', the old 'too languishing'. The reasons advanced for this similarity of non-reproductive suitability were likewise characterized at the same time by sameness and difference – the sexual and reproductive bodies of both young and old people suffered from very similar deficiencies, but these had different causes due to the stage of life each body occupied. The stage of development of the body at each end of the life cycle rendered its reproductive parts unfit for sex and infertile: in both girls and old women the breasts were small and did not produce milk, the womb and ovaries were too small and shrunken, the neck of the womb or vagina was too straight and dry, and there was no generative matter in the form of menstrual blood or seed for conception; in boys and old men the genitals were not fully functional and the seed was either wanting or deficient. However, a major difference in the relationship of these bodies to reproductive life was that the barrenness and unfitness for sexual activity of the young body was something that was temporary ('too ignorant as to the productive part') and likely to be remedied by its sexual development that was understood to occur over a period of time usually between the ages of 12 and 20, while that of the old body ('destitute of the Matter') was, for post-menopausal old women a permanent state, and for old men a highly likely, if not entirely certain, development. This difference in the status of infertility at each end of the life cycle was also something that was acknowledged by those who wrote on these subjects: the French physician and professor of medicine, Lazare Rivière (1589–1655) noted, 'And in the first place, Tenderness of Age hinders conception only for a time, which cannot be expected till the Woman is more grown. But Elderly years cause a Total dispaire of Conception.'[3] This chapter will focus upon these two stages of the life cycle only, omitting any discussion of its central portion – adulthood and maturity – which is thoroughly dissected throughout the rest of this book, and will focus specifically upon their shared characteristics in relation to the body and sex as they were understood in this period: their impaired fertility and the unsuitability of young and old bodies for sexual intercourse.

Although a great deal has now been written about both the histories of childhood and of old age, the issue of sex in relation to both children and the old still remains relatively underexplored. The histories of young and old bodies, both more generally and specifically in relation to sexual life, have almost entirely separate historiographies and are very rarely discussed by historians in direct relation to each other.[4] Where they do appear together as part of a larger work on 'life cycles', they are discussed separately in sections on childhood and old age, and little attention is paid to the body or to sexuality at either end of the life cycle, apart from very brief discussions of physical changes at puberty and menopause.[5] Demographic historians have considered the two together in their examinations of changes to the ages of menarche and menopause over time, and especially as these are relevant to questions of population growth, stagnation or decline,[6] as also have anthropologists where menarche and menopause are considered as 'rites of passage' or 'taboo'.[7] Where social histories of old age and childhood have converged is through the discussion of parents and children, usually focusing upon to what extent children may have taken care of their aged parents, and how they reacted to the illness and death of a parent, neatly reflecting the focus of much early debate about children and childhood over whether or not parents in this period loved their children.[8] By bringing the examination of young and old bodies together in a thematic discussion of how they were both understood at this time in relation to sex and reproduction, this chapter further demonstrates the centrality of fertility to early modern thinking about bodies and sex.[9] It also argues for the importance of age as a category of analysis in the histories of the body and sexuality. Given the importance of fertility in early modern thinking about these issues, it can be argued that age and its relationship to fertility had a primary significance that has hitherto received insufficient attention.

The most recent work on children and sex for the early modern period is my own discussion of pre-pubescent children's bodies, puberty and sexual development, preceded by William Naphy's investigation of children and sexual activity in Reformation Geneva and George Rousseau's examination of an incident of sodomitical assault at Wadham College in Georgian Oxford.[10] Neither Naphy nor Rousseau, however, included any consideration of contemporary knowledge and understandings about children's bodies and their fitness for sexual activity. Other writing on the subject of children and sex in this period has considered it as child sexual abuse, its nature and incidence, or in the context of the sexual activity most usually associated with the young, masturbation.[11] In relation to children's bodies, most recent work has examined the diseases of children and, in particular, whether physicians understood children's bodies to be significantly different from those of adults, and consequently arguing for a concept of 'children's physic' as their particular constitutions required specific kinds of treatment tailored to their more delicate or tender bodies.[12] Some historians have examined contemporary knowledge and understanding about menstruation, including its onset at puberty and what this may have meant for girls' health and development,[13] while others, such as Cathy McClive, have examined the role and significance of menstruation in the lives of young women, noting that it was not the onset of menstruation alone that conferred 'womanhood' on a young girl, but rather the establishment of its regularity, and the experience of sex and childbearing.[14]

Similarly, much writing about old women's bodies has focused upon the issue of menopause and the physical changes it brought, arguing that post-menopausal women were now likely to be regarded as old.[15] Whether or not menopause actually marked the entry into old age for early modern women, the cessation of menstruation and the end to a woman's fertility that it brought were nevertheless characteristic of this stage of life. It has been noted that the ending of a woman's fertility particularly negatively affected women's social status at this stage of life giving rise to perceptions of old women as disruptive to households shared with younger kin, no longer serving any useful function, and associated with witchcraft.[16] Michael Stolberg has outlined changing understandings of menstruation and menopause from the sixteenth through to the eighteenth centuries and how menopause was thought to bring a host of maladies, some, such as menorrhagia, potentially fatal. Stolberg also briefly noted that menopause, as a major critical stage in a woman's life, was similar to menarche, but did not explore the comparison in any greater depth.[17] Like more recent explorations of medicine and children's bodies, old age has also been examined in the context of medical constructions of ageing as a disease, and as a time of life that is subject to a variety of particular physical maladies, and of the ways in which life might be prolonged.[18] Explorations of female sexuality in later life have paid attention to the stereotype of the 'merry widow', accustomed to sexual activity through marriage and unable to exercise self-restraint in curbing her now 'highly sexed' nature, and to the challenges this posed to 'the social and moral order' of early modern patriarchal society.[19] It has been similarly remarked that the loss of old men's sexual virility generated the stereotype of the foolish old man who lusted after a younger wife, but who, unable to satisfy her desires, was inevitably cuckolded.[20] This chapter aims to examine the bodies of the young and the old in the context of contemporary ideas about their sexual and reproductive suitability, demonstrating that at the forefront of such anxieties and concerns was their relationship to fertility – the fact that both were understood to be infertile or sub-fertile, and therefore inappropriate for sexual activity. At a time when the primary aim of marriage and sexual intercourse was procreation, with the production of offspring essential for the preservation of family and state, lands, inheritance and economic stability, the regulation of sexual behaviour was an important aspect of all western European societies.

As this chapter focuses specifically upon early modern ideas about the sexual body, reproduction and fertility, it inevitably draws primarily upon medical writings, both those aimed at other physicians, surgeons and midwives, and those which appear to have been written with a broader audience in mind. Although the texts cited here are from English language editions, they are not confined to those that originated in English for an English readership but include many that originated on the continent in a shared western European medical tradition. Writings on generation in English, available to both lay and professional readers, consisted not only of original works but also of a wide array of translations of European-authored works, both from vernacular languages and from Latin, the international language of knowledge and culture. Authors read and borrowed from each other, circulating not only ideas but also words, phrases, sentences and sometimes whole paragraphs or sections in a shared culture of medical knowledge, learning and innovation. Although primarily appearing in medical, anatomical and midwifery texts, information and advice about sex, reproduction and childbearing also appeared in many other sources more widely accessible to a non-medical audience, such as ballads, chap-books, almanacs and other less specialized texts (as we have seen in previous chapters), so that knowledge and information about these matters circulated at all levels of society. Records of book ownership have also indicated that some medical and midwifery books were possessed by men and women without professional medical training, suggesting that such works were not confined to a specialized readership of those with a medical educa-tion.[21] The ideas uncovered here were therefore not restricted only to those who practised medicine, surgery and midwifery, but had a wider circulation, however generalized and simplified for the non-specialist.

Although new ideas, such as those to do with chemical medicine, and theories about generation, were developed, discussed, debated, accepted and rejected during these two and a half centuries, overall there was little change in how young and old bodies were thought of in relation to sex and reproduction. We can see that later eighteenth-century writers repeated the words and ideas – sometimes almost word for word – of much earlier sixteenth-century authors (who were themselves repeating earlier classical ideas) such as the German physician and author of one of the earliest books of midwifery printed in a ver-nacular language, Eucharius Roesslin (c.1470–1526), Dutch physician and author Levinus Lemnius (1505–58), and the French surgeon Ambroise Paré (c.1510–91), indicating that their influence stretched well beyond their lifetimes, even as earlier knowledge was usurped by new discoveries and theories. Ideas about chemical medicine were frequently incorpo-rated into the dominant humoural framework, while from the later seventeenth century and into the eighteenth century references to eggs and ovaries gradually replaced those to female seed.[22] Understanding of the body and how it worked was based upon the classical humoural model wherein it was composed of the four humours blood, yellow and black bile, and phlegm. These four humours corresponded to the four qualities of hot, dry, cold, and wet, to the four seasons (spring, summer, autumn, winter) and by analogy to four stages of life (infancy, youth, maturity and old age). The constitution of a body was thus understood as relating to the particular balance of these humours in the body, with the two sexes on a continuum between more naturally hot and dry men and more cold and moist women. The balance of humours also altered throughout the life cycle, shifting from the warm, moist bodies of infancy and childhood, to the cold and dry bodies of old age, as 'heat without any the least intermission or pause, worketh upon our moisture, and by little and little consumeth it, it selfe also in time decaying'.[23] Each stage of life thus had its own physical characteristics and brought particular kinds of disorders according to its humoural constitution:

> *infancy* ful of moisture, as the fluid soft substance of our flesh manifestly declareth: our *youth* bringeth a farther degree of solidity: our *riper age* euer te[m]perate: thence still declineth our body vnto colde and drinesse, till at length death ceaseth vpon our bodies, being the last end and period of our life.[24]

The ages and stages of life at this time were flexibly organized into three, or four, or seven, as some stages were further subdivided at particular ages.[25] Different authors might specify slightly different age boundaries for each stage, but generally agreed that sexual development took place around the ages of 14 or 15 (but could be earlier or later), and the decline into old age began around the age of 50 'by reason of our heats and moistures decay'.[26] Death came when both heat and moisture were expended: 'when moysture is all wasted a man falleth into a cold and drye distemperaunce, and finally thereby brought to his death.'[27] The gradual loss of the body's vital heat heralded the end of life because 'death is nothing els, but the extinction of nature, that is to saye, of the naturall Heate, a[nd] naturall Humour'.[28] Each stage of life was thus constitutionally different, producing different effects in the body, but both young and old bodies shared the characteristic of not having sufficient heat for successful generation: the young body because it had not yet grown to full maturity, the old body because it had grown past matureness of years and was now decaying towards death.

In the humoural model of the body a satisfactory balance of the humours was essential for conception to take place. Authors from the sixteenth to the eighteenth century advised that too much hot, cold, dryness or moistness in the generative parts, particularly in the humoural balance of the womb for women or the nature of the seed in men, could prevent successful generation. In the early sixteenth-century midwifery treatise *The Byrth of Mankynde*, translated into English from a Latin translation of the original German text, Eucharius Roesslin wrote that

> yf the matrice be distempered by the excesse of any of these foure qualities then must ye reduce it agayne to temperancie by suche remedyes as I shall shewe you hereafter. Lykewyse maye there be defecte and lacke in the man as yf the seade be ouer hote the which the woman shall feale as it were burning hote or to cold the which he shall feale as it were in maner colde.[29]

In the mid-eighteenth century the French physician and professor of medicine Jean Astruc (1684–1766) continued to write in humoural terms about impediments to conception, where 'very cold, languid and insensible Women' had difficulties conceiving and should be treated with remedies that were heating to rectify this deficiency.[30] Heat was a crucial ingredient in both sexual pleasure and successful conception. Raising the body's heat was essential to engender desire and make the genitals ready for sexual intercourse, and also to make the seed vigorous and procreative. Heating foods, herbs and wines might arouse lust in both men and women, as might the use of oils and ointments with heating properties rubbed onto the genitals.[31] The friction of intercourse also further raised heat in both sexes leading to orgasm, and, for a woman, the special properties of semen itself, ejaculated into the vagina at orgasm, having vital heat in three elements, again increased heat, encouraging a conception.[32] Infertility due to the coldness of the seed was a variety of barrenness that was identified by authors from the sixteenth century into the eighteenth, and was remarked upon as common to both young and old.[33] The young had not yet developed sufficient vital heat to engender procreative seed, thus, a boy, 'if he want a Beard', that is, had not yet reached puberty, would not be fertile,[34] while the seed of old bodies was likely to diminish in procreative power with the decrease of vital heat as they aged. According to the English surgeon, Philip Barrough (d.1600), 'It is of the mans part, when his seede is either hote, & as it were burned, or else cold, thinne, waterie and feeble, as is the seede of old and feeble men'.[35] As the English physician Helkiah Crooke (1576–1648) had noted in his compendium of anatomy, *Microcosmographia*, in 1615, 'children and decrepit old men do not yeeld seed'.[36] However, if they did, it was very likely to be deficient being insufficiently hot, although those who were of a hotter constitution might be fertile earlier and retain sexual and procreative vigour into their old age. For girls and old women, in addition to these issues to do with heat and seed (in the two-seed model of conception, where women, too, emitted seed), infertility at these two ends of the life cycle was caused by the lack of menstrual blood which also supplied generative matter for conception and to nourish the growing foetus in the womb (in the Aristotelian, one-seed model of conception, menstrual blood alone was contributed by the woman to the conception). But menstrual blood also had the further function of moistening and dilating the reproductive parts of the body, so that before menarche girls were 'unripe' and unready for the sexual act, while post-menopause, women's sexual parts were understood to become increasingly dry and withered making sexual activity more difficult. Thus fertility and readiness for, or capability to engage in, the sexual act were interlinked at this time, and both were issues pertinent to young and old bodies.

Fertility: the development and decay of generative matter

When writing about the signs and causes of barrenness, authors invariably noted that both the first and the last stages of life were characterized by this state, although the causes were differently determined by the particular stage of life and the body's constitution at that stage. In a definition that echoed sources from the early sixteenth century and which was repeated into the eighteenth century, Thomas Chamberlayne wrote in 1659 that,

> Barrennesse is an impotence to conceive, coming from defect either of the Geni-tals, or of the blood, or of the menstruous blood. First, through the defect of the Genitals, either by the closing up of the Orifice of the womb ... or through the narrownesse of the parts, for so they will not admit the yard; ... Or by reason of some fault in the seed, either the woman being too young, or too old.[37]

The next section of this chapter will discuss defects of the genitals in both sexes and at both ends of the life cycle and how they rendered young and old bodies unsuitable for sex. This section will explore defects of the generative materials – seed and menstrual blood – that caused barrenness in both young and old bodies.

Seed

Seed was understood to be made from blood through a process of 'concoction' that required heat. Seed, as explained by the Dutch physician and professor of medicine and anatomy Isbrand van Diemerbroeck (1609–74), was concocted in a complicated process from the blood into '*a frothy Liquor*' whose composition was mainly salty, from which derived 'its fruitfulness and balsamic Power' and the term 'salacity' for lust.[38] Both young and old bodies were understood to lack sufficient heat to perfect this process and so create seed that was 'prolifick' and capable of producing a successful conception. In young, pre-pubescent bodies, though constitutionally warm and moist, neither girls nor boys were yet hot enough to breed seed for conception; the increasing heat at puberty precipitated the ripening of the seed, though this was understood to be a gradual process that took place over a period of time. Though seed might be emitted, it was not necessarily yet hot and vigorous enough for successful generation. Levinus Lemnius noted that, 'there be some yonge men, who maryinge to soone, and ere they be fully rype, are unfruictfull and not able to get any children, for that they lacke manly strength, a[nd] theyre seede to cold and thinne.'[39] As seed was made from blood, there needed to be sufficient blood available for this purpose, but in both young and old bodies, this was lacking. Helkiah Crooke in the early seventeenth century explained that 'children and decrepit old men do not yeeld seed, for that in these there is no ouerplus [of blood] left'.[40] In boys there was no surplus to 'breed' seed because it went instead into nourishing the growth of the body: 'For in Boyes there is no remainder of lawdable blood of which seede should bee made, because one part of the blood is consumed in their nourishment and the rest in their growth.'[41] Later that century Diemerbroeck explained that seed was not engendered in the young because,

> The same cause that promotes and cherishes the growth of the Body, hinders the Generation of Seed in Children. Hence it is that the Blood is more moist and oily; and the Animal Spirits themselves less sharp, and fewer in quantity, flow to the Stones, so that there is only enough for the growth of the Parts, but not for the Generation of Seed.[42]

As the child grew, the increase in bodily heat had a drying effect that perfected the separation of the 'the salter Particles more fit for the Generation of Seed' from the blood. These were then condensed and mixed 'into a thin Liquor' by the testicles and so 'concocted into Seed'.

Similarly, '*by reason of their abated heat*', in old age '*very little, or watery, or no Seed at all is made in the Stones*'.[43] These earlier understandings continued to be repeated into the eighteenth century: Joannes Groeneveld, a Dutch physician practising in London, published in 1715 an English adapted edition of van den Zype's seventeenth-century text, *Fundamenta Medicinæ*, in which he noted,

> before that Age the Blood was more employed in the Increase of the Bulk of the Body, when the Heat and Pulse were too weak to drive on, and force the Blood through such winding Passages, that were then not by much so enlarged … in old and decrepid Persons, by the Defect of the Natural Heat, and by the Driness of the Spermatick Vessels, by the previous Heat shrunk up and destiture of a rich Blood, the Seed is altogether deficient.[44]

Not only did the 'force and heat of Procreating matter' diminish so that 'the Seed by little and little becoming unfruitful' was no longer fit for generation, but its watery consistency also meant that it could not be retained within the womb to join with the female generative matter. The French surgeon Ambroise Paré remarked how the seed of both boys and old men had a 'more liquid and flexible consistence thereof, so that it cannot stay in the womb, but will presently flow out again: for such is the seed of old men and striplings'.[45] The seed of both young and old was thus defective in both quantity and quality. However, those who were of a hotter constitution therefore might be fertile at an earlier age than other boys, while some old men may have remained 'vigorous in their old Age' so that they were able to father children into their seventies and eighties – as authors frequently remarked – whereas others were either impotent, or if capable of the act, yet unable to beget children.[46]

Authors were frequently unspecific about whether they were discussing male or female seed or both, and when they did specify a sex, it was usually to refer to the seed of men and boys, as we have seen above. This did not, however, exclude girls and old women from these ideas about defects in the seed, who in the two-seed model of generation were also understood to emit seed for conception, as can be seen in the excerpt from Thomas Chamberlayne's midwifery treatise quoted at the beginning of this section where he refers to defects of the female seed ('Or by reason of some fault in the seed, either the woman being too young, or too old').[47] Some authors, like Chamberlayne, did specifically relate their discussion of seed to women. For example, reflecting developments in theorizing about generation that attributed eggs to women rather than seed, Diemerbroeck added that,

> The same Consideration may extend it self to womens Eggs, which so long as they are unripe, will not admit the generative Principle of the male Seed, which is the reason that many young Women of cold Constitutions, do not conceive in several Months after they are married, because their Eggs are unripe and unfit to receive the generative part of mans Seed, which afterwards they do when they come to full Maturity.[48]

For both boys and girls, then, the process of 'ripening' to produce fully fertile and pro-creative seed – or eggs – took place over a period of time as the body developed and matured during the teen-aged years. Similarly, the loss of fertility as the quality and quantity of seed also declined with increasing age was a process that took place over time so that some men retained procreative 'force' longer than others according to constitution and health. For girls and old women, though, fertility was not governed only by the 'ripening' of the seed, but by the onset and cessation of menstruation at menarche and menopause.

Menstrual blood

For both young and old women, there were two material defects that rendered them infertile according to the Galenic-Hippocratic two-seed model of generation: 'seed and menstrual bloud, which two are the originals and principals of generation'.[49] In both Aristotelian and Galenic-Hippocratic models of generation the menstrual blood played a role in conception and gestation, providing matter to the foetus and then subsequently nourishing it within the womb during pregnancy. Whichever model of generation early modern authors may have promoted – and many, like Helkiah Crooke, explained both to their readers – the lack of menstrual blood was understood to be an indication of a woman's inability to conceive. The stages of life that came before menarche and after menopause were thus noted by all authors as characterized by barrenness. For example, like Paré, Riverius listed,

> The Fourth and last Cause of Barrenness, viz. When the woman doth not yield convenient matter to form the Conception, and to augment the same, depends upon a want of Seed and Menstrual blood; so over yong women and over old, do not conceive, through want of both those Materials.[50]

Authors' discussions of the age at which girls would begin to menstruate, signalling the ability to conceive, were thus invariably coupled with the age at which it ceased and the loss of women's generative ability.[51] Lemnius in *The Secret Miracles of Nature*, translated and published in English in 1658 but originally published on the continent in Latin in 1559, and from which other authors borrowed throughout this period, described how

> Mayds in the 14th. year of their age, or somewhat later, shew some signes of maturity, their courses then running, so that they are fit to conceive, which force continues with them till 44, yeares of their age; and some that are lusty and lively will be fruitfull till 55.[52]

Continuing menstruation beyond the usual age of menopause, however, did not mean a continuation of fertility. Rather it was yet another indicator of its ending, as it was a symptom of 'some affect that is contrary to Nature, which also hinders all conception'.[53] The onset of menstruation thus signalled the readiness of a young girl for her reproductive life: it provided matter for conception and, subsequently, for the nourishment of a foetus in the womb as well as preparing her body for the act of sexual intercourse by moistening and dilating the sexual parts. Menstruation was usually thought to occur around the age of 14, as Lemnius above had asserted, but might be earlier at 12 years: in a formulation that was repeated in many texts throughout the sixteenth, seventeenth and eighteenth centuries, Barrough told his readers that 'in manie the floures beginne to flowe the fourtenth yeare, and in verie fewe before the thirtenth or twelfth yeare. And to most women they burst out after the fourtenth yeare.'[54] The establishment of a regular and moderate flow was there-fore regarded as crucial to successful reproduction, and women (and physicians) were concerned to regulate this aspect of their reproductive function in order to optimize their fertility once they had reached menarche. Susan Broomhall identified this as a key issue in deciding whether or not a girl was ready to commence a regular sexual relationship with the anticipation that this would lead to a pregnancy.[55] The lack of menstruation was thus understood as preventing conception and so girls before the age of menarche were clearly understood as unable to conceive, as were post-menopausal women in whom menstruation had ceased.

As noted earlier, in the humoural model of the body and of generation, barrenness was understood to be caused by too much or too little of the four qualities of heat, cold, wet and dry. The cessation of menstruation at menopause not only removed one of the essen-tial generative substances but also meant that the womb now became more dry as well as more cold, as the woman's constitution shifted into that characteristic of old age. The increasing constitutional desiccation of old age together with the cessation of menstruation whose blood no longer moistened the womb, meant that the womb became smaller and shrivelled. William Salmon in his discussion of barrenness from a 'dry Distemper of the Womb' noted that, 'IN this Distemper, the Womb, which of it self is soft and fleshy, and moisten'd by Blood for Conception, is made hard and scirrhous: This Distemper proceeds sometimes from the Birth, and sometimes from old Age, when Child-bearing is over.'[56] Barrenness caused by a dry womb that had become so through age was thus not something that could be remedied as it might in a younger woman by the prescription of moistening treatments, for 'It is incurable in old Persons'.[57] Both the beginning and the end of the life cycle, then, were characterized as non-reproductive years, the young because their bodies had not yet grown to full ripeness, the old because they had passed the full flower of their years in which they had been fruitful and were now withered, dried up, and daily losing the vital heat that had made them sexually vigorous. Daniel Sennert succinctly summed up the ages at which defects in seed and lack of menstrual blood meant that children could not be conceived as, 'In men at eighteen, in women at fourteen, and men seldom get children after sixty, and women seldom bear them after sixty.'[58] Sennert here noted the very upper end of women's fertile age range, which most authors noted as ending much earlier, usually between the ages of 45 and 50.

Sex and the organs of generation

> For as in green raw Youth it is unfit and unseasonable to Marry, so to marry in old Age is altogether as preposterous; for as they that enter upon it too soon are presently exhausted, grow Consumptive, &c. so those that defer it till they are old, are alike liable to the same inconveniencies, besides forfeiting their gravity and conduct, losing that honour due to their years.[59]

Here again we find John Marten in the early eighteenth century advising that sexual activity was neither healthy nor appropriate for both the young and the old, and for similar reasons. The old, however, suffered the further indignity of losing all dignity should they continue to pursue sexual relations, making themselves ridiculous as numerous stories and jokes about cuckolds and old women marrying much younger men attested.[60] Neither young nor old bodies were understood to be fully capable of the sexual act: the young because not yet sexually developed or 'ripe', the old because now past their 'ripenesse' of years and beginning to decay, thus losing the necessary vigour and 'fruitfulnesse' that was characteristic of the middle stage of life. Sexual desire was also problematic for young and old bodies. In young bodies it was thought that sexual desire – and pleasure – was absent until after the changes and developments of puberty. In both boys and girls the physical changes to the sexual and reproductive parts of the body stirred desire for sexual activity and made it now capable of experiencing sexual pleasure: Peter Chamberlain noted, 'About that time young men begin to grow hairy, to change their voyce, and to have lustfull imaginations, maidens paps begin to swell, and they to think upon – &c.'[61] In girls this was brought about by the onset of menstruation, signalled by the growth of the pubic hair and breasts, and in the two-seed model of the body, the emission of seed. In boys it was the emission of seed that brought sexual pleasure due to the properties of semen; and the growth of facial and bodily hair indicated that male bodies were now developing this capability. For the old, although desire might diminish due to the loss of vital heat, it did not necessarily disappear altogether. The desire for sexual activity could continue into old age but was likely to be tempered by the decline in physical vigour and the drying up of the sexual parts making it more difficult to achieve. Old bodies, in their increasing decrepitude, were also perceived as unattractive and sexually undesirable and were frequently represented as such in literature and other writings.[62] They were thus likely to make themselves ridiculous by seeking that for which their bodies were no longer fit, as John Marten noted.

In both young pre-pubescent and old post-menopausal female bodies the genitals were understood to be unsuitable for the act of sexual intercourse for the same reason: in both bodies the vagina, or 'neck of the womb', was understood to be too narrow or 'streight' and dry to allow penetration. Helkiah Crooke described, in words that were repeated in other medical and midwifery texts throughout the seventeenth century and into the eighteenth, how in the vagina 'These folds are in yong women smoother and narrower, and the passage straighter, that it will scarse admit a finger'.[63] Girls' bodies before the developments of puberty were thus unfit for sexual intercourse because they were physically unready for penetration. The growth of the pubic hair was the sign that the body was becoming ready, that it would now become more open to allow the passage of the menstrual blood and seed for conception. Crooke thus further noted that,

> *Pubes* doeth more properly signifie the Downe or Cotton when it ariseth about those parts in men, neare vppon the fourteenth yeare; in women about the twelfth; and it is a signe of maturity or ripenesse. For ... as soone as the passages are open for the seede & monthly courses; the hayre or downe in a boy or girle starteth vp, the skinne being rarefied or made thin.[64]

The passage of the menstrual blood through the vaginal passage served to lubricate and dilate it making it ready for the act of sexual intercourse. Jane Sharp in her *Midwives Book* (1671) noted that 'the younger the maids are the greater the pain, because of the dryness of the part, ... the elder they are, by reason of their courses that have often flowed, the moisture is more and the pain less, by reason of the wetness and looseness of the Hymen'.[65] English physician James Drake (1666–1707) in the early eighteenth century also repeated this earlier understanding of one of the functions of menstruation, when he stated that, 'Just behind the *Nymphae* is the Orifice of the *Vagina*, which in Virgins, especially such as have not yet had the *Catamenia*, or but very rarely, is very streight, but in those that have had them often it grows larger'.[66] This was thus a temporary physical impediment to sexual intercourse that was removed by the child's growth to maturity: 'And in the first place, the straitness of the Genital Parts in regard of youngness of Age, needs no cure; for as Age encreases, they attain to a convenient wideness.'[67]

Before menarche, then, girls' bodies were not sexually ready, and penetration could not be achieved without force and violence causing injury and 'very great pain, which makes her worse for Genital Embracements'.[68] This understanding was not only theorized in medical and midwifery texts, but demonstrated in practice in trials for the rape or sexual assault of pre-pubescent girls where successful prosecutions depended upon evidence of physical injuries to the genitals for proof of forcible penetration or of attempted penetration.[69] Some of those who gave medical evidence at such trials testified that, although there had clearly been a sexual assault upon a child, it had not constituted rape because it was not possible to penetrate a young child who had not yet reached sexual maturity. In 1751, a surgeon, Henry Tompson, testified at the trial of Christopher Larkin for the rape of 11-year-old Jane Gallicote, that she had not been raped because 'no man could penetrate her body, she is of too tender an age for that; it was the opinion of all the surgeons there had been no penetration.'[70] If penetration was forced in such a young body that had not yet matured to allow it, there would be lasting signs of injury including 'unnatural' dilation of the vagina before the regular flow of menstrual blood 'naturally' brought about its loosening so allowing penetrative sex. A surgeon, Mr Dove, who gave evidence at the trial of John Hunter for the rape of the 10-year-old Grace Pitts at the Old Bailey in 1747, testified that he believed she had been penetrated because he found 'her Parts very much distended much enlarged and foul'.[71]

When describing the nature of the vagina in the pre-pubescent girl authors invariably remarked upon its development throughout a woman's life cycle, noting its readiness for sex and childbirth in the middle period of maturity and then its decreasing suitability into old age as it became drier and contracted with the body's increasing loss of heat and moisture. Ambroise Paré in his book on anatomy described how,

> [i]n process of age it grows harder, both by use of venery, and also by reason of age, by which the whole body in all parts thereof becomes dry and hard. But in growing and in young Women it is more tractable and flexible for the necessity of Nature.[72]

Other authors, both English and continental, using the same or very similar words, clearly borrowing from previous publications throughout the period, noted that 'old women, have it hard, callous, and as it were gristly, by reason of the often attrition, and frequent flowing of their Courses'.[73] The later eighteenth-century author of *The Ladies Dispensatory* in 1739 explicitly reflected on how young, 'unripe' female bodies and old women were thus similarly unfit for reproduction:

> The Reception of the Seed is hindered by many Causes; as, immature Age, when by reason of the Narrowness of the genital Passages, the Woman cannot admit the virile Member, or at least not without great Pain, which makes her dislike Copulation: And Old Age hath sometimes the same Effect; for, in elderly Virgins, the Parts are so st[r]aitened for Want of Use, that they cannot, without Difficulty, contribute to the Means of Generation.[74]

This author was repeating an almost identical passage from Riverius in the mid-seventeenth century which was more explicit in asserting that in 'elderly Virgins ... the Genital Parts, ... do become withered, flap, and flaggy, and so strait, that they cannot afterwards easily admit a mans Yard'.[75] Similarly, Thomas Gibson in his *Anatomy of Humane Bodies* (1682) had remarked that it was more difficult to penetrate an old woman if she was still a virgin because, 'Sometimes in elderly Maids the Hymen grows so strong that a Man is glad to make many essays before he can penetrate it'.[76] Thus, like pre-pubescent female bodies, post-menopausal old women were understood as having sexual parts that were not physically suitable for sexual and procreative activity; they were too hard, dry and narrow, lacking the essential moisture and flexibility that were required for the easy admittance of the male member for the act of intercourse.

Authors also wrote that boys before sexual maturity and old men similarly shared the characteristic of being physically unsuitable for sexual intercourse. Boys were understood to begin to mature sexually around the age of 14 but did not come to full 'ripenesse' until their later teens or early twenties when their seed achieved its full procreative force. Paré was very precise about when a boy's seed was ready for conception, using the seven-year division of the stages of life: 'For in them, although the seed be genitable for the most part in the second seventh year, yet it is unfruitful until the third seventh year.'[77] Like girls, the growth of bodily hair signalled this developing sexual maturity, but boys also grew facial hair and saw changes to their voices which deepened and took on the lower timbre of a man. Chamberlain also timed these developments at the age of 14, when 'About that time young men begin to grow hairy, to change their voyce, and to have lustfull imaginations',[78] though other authors, like Lemnius, cited Hippocrates in putting it slightly later at the age of 16 onwards, when 'they have much vitall strength, and their secrets begin to be hairy, and their chins begin to shoot forth, with fine decent down, which force and heat of procreating Children increaseth daily'.[79] Full sexual maturity for boys, though, was not achieved until they were capable of the emission of semen which brought with it the experience of sexual pleasure connected to the qualities of the seed itself, which brought an 'uncommon titillation' that 'was pleasing to a great Degree'.[80] Thus, although heterosexual sexual activity for a boy could not be injurious to the body in the same way as it was for pre-pubescent girls (although sodomy clearly could, also leaving signs of tearing and bruising when forcible), it was nevertheless understood to be inappropriate because boys' bodies were not fully ready as they were not yet capable of emitting seed for procreation.[81] The absence of the seed also meant, as for girls, that neither were they able to experience sexual desire or pleasure. It was the 'prolifick' nature of the seed in bodies that were sexually 'ripe' that engendered sexual desire and pleasure.

Despite authors' assertions that men were able to continue to reproduce well into old age, this physical unsuitability for sexual intercourse was not restricted only to boys, girls and old women. Men's diminishing vital heat as they grew old meant that they were increasingly likely to suffer from impotence. This association of old men with impotence was a staple of jokes and anxieties about cuckolds, particularly where there was a disparity of age when an older man married a younger woman; she would inevitably commit adultery because he would be unable to satisfy her sexually. Authors from the sixteenth to the eighteenth century identified impotence as a particular issue for old men where, 'In some the want of Erections are from a fault in the Spirits, as when they are universally weak and languid, as in old Age and Sickness'.[82] This author, John Marten, went on to further identify the decline in the quality of the man's semen, as it grew more cold with age, as a cause of such impotency: 'In others, want of Erections is from a faulty unprepa-redness in the *Genital Juice*, falling short of its spirituous stimulating Quality, either from Superannuation or old Age'.[83] Authors nevertheless were keen to reassure their readers that old age did not necessarily mean impotence for all men, and included comments to the contrary, often in the same sentence, such as Diemerbroeck who added, 'I except some sort of old men, vigorous in their old Age, who at fourscore and fourscore and ten have begot Children'.[84] Remedies for male impotence thus aimed to increase heat and hence to stimulate lust, but they could be dangerous if taken by the elderly, especially if very strong, such as the commonly discussed aphrodisiac cantharides, or Spanish Fly.[85]

Conclusion

Those at both ends of the age spectrum thus were categorized as unfit for generation, and sexual activity involving both young and old people engendered comment, discussion, prosecution, mockery and disapproval. It disrupted contemporary social and cultural understandings that the primary purpose of sex was for procreation and that it was there-fore an activity that was only suitable for those who were at the ages and stages in the life cycle when the body was ready, fit and able to reproduce. Contemporary understandings of bodies and sex and how they worked excluded both young and old from the category of people who were reproductively capable, so that discovery of sexual activity involving those at both the beginning and the end of the life cycle invariably prompted anxiety and concern as it fell outside social and cultural norms for such behaviour. Representations of sex and the young characterized it as difficult, painful, injurious and lacking in pleasure, while those of sex and the old ranged from suggesting admiration for the vigorous old man who continued to father children despite expectations of dwindling virility and fertility with increasing age, to mocking and reviling male impotence and old women's lust.

Notes

I am very grateful to the British Academy for a Small Research Grant that allowed me to begin the research on which this chapter is based, and to The Leverhulme Trust for a Major Research Fellowship to complete my research on children.

1 Philip Barrough, *The Methode of Phisicke*, London: Thomas Vaurroullier, 1583, p. 157.

2 John Marten, *Gonosologium Novum: Or, A New System Of all the Secret Infirmities and Diseases, Natural, Accidental, and Venereal in Men and Women* … , London: n.p., 1709, p. 90.

3 Often styled in Latin form as Lazarus Riverius, *The Practice of Physick, In Seventeen Several Books*, London: Peter Cole, 1655, p. 506.

4 A notable exception, albeit for a different time and place, is Carroll Smith-Rosenberg, 'Puberty to Menopause: The Cycle of Femininity in Nineteenth-Century America', *Feminist Studies* 1:3/4, 1973, pp. 58–72; republished in her *Disorderly Conduct: Visions of Gender in Victorian America*, Oxford: Oxford University Press, 1986, pp. 182–96.

5 See, for example, Mary Abbott, *Life Cycles in England 1560–1720: Cradle to grave*, London and New York: Routledge, 1996; Deborah Youngs, *The Life Cycle in Western Europe, c.1300-c.1500*, Manchester: Manchester University Press, 2006.

6 J. B. Post, 'Ages at Menarche and Menopause: Some Mediaeval Authorities', *Population Studies* 25:1, 1971, pp. 83–87; E. A. Wrigley, 'Family Limitation in Pre-Industrial England', *Economic History Review*, 2nd series, 19:1, 1966, pp. 82–109.

7 Mary Douglas, *Purity and Danger: An analysis of concepts of pollution and taboo*, London: Routledge & Kegan Paul, 1978; first published 1966.

8 For example, Steven R. Smith, 'Growing Old in an Age of Transition' in Peter N. Stearns (ed.), *Old Age in Preindustrial Society*, New York and London: Holmes & Meier Publishers, 1982, pp. 191–207 (202–5). Most histories of children and childhood discuss the debate over parental love for their children; for a recent collection see Anja Müller (ed.), *Fashioning Childhood in the Eighteenth Century: Age and Identity*, Aldershot: Ashgate, 2006.

9 Sarah Toulalan, '"The Act of Copulation Being Ordain'd by Nature as the Ground of all Generation": Fertility and the Representation of Sexual Pleasure in Seventeenth-Century Pornography in England', *Women's History Review* 15:4, 2006, pp. 521–32; Sarah Toulalan, *Imagining Sex: Pornography and Bodies in Seventeenth Century England*, New York: Oxford University Press, 2007, ch. 2.

10 Sarah Toulalan, '"Unripe" bodies: children and sex in early modern England' in Kate Fisher and Sarah Toulalan (eds), *Bodies, Sex and Desire from the Renaissance to the Present*, Basingstoke: Palgrave, 2011, pp. 131–50; William G. Naphy, '"Under-Age" Sexual Activity in Reformation Geneva' in George Rousseau (ed.), *Children and Sexuality From the Greeks to the Great War*, Basingstoke: Palgrave Macmillan, 2007, pp. 108–27; George Rousseau, 'Privilege, Power and Sexual Abuse in Georgian Oxford' in Rousseau (ed.), *Children and Sexuality*, pp. 142–65.

11 Martin Ingram, 'Child sexual abuse in early modern England' in Michael J. Braddick and John Walter (eds), *Negotiating Power in Early Modern Society: Order, Hierarchy and Subordination in Britain and Ireland*, Cambridge: Cambridge University Press, 2001, pp. 63–84; William Naphy, *Sex Crimes: From Renaissance to Enlightenment*, Stroud: Tempus, 2002, ch. 4; Sterling Fishman, 'The History of Childhood Sexuality', *Journal of Contemporary History* 17, 1982, pp. 269–83.

12 Hannah Newton, 'Children's Physic: Medical Perceptions and Treatment of Sick Children in Early Modern England, *c.* 1580–1720', *Social History of Medicine* 23:3, 2010, pp. 456–74. See also Hannah Newton, *The Sick Child in Early Modern England, 1580–1720*, Oxford: Oxford University Press, 2012.

13 Helen King, *The Disease of Virgins: Green sickness, chlorosis and the problems of puberty*, London and New York: Routledge, 2004; Alexandra Lord, ' "The Great *Arcana* of the Deity": Menstruation

and Menstrual Disorders in Eighteenth-Century British Medical Thought', *Bulletin of the History of Medicine* 73:1, 1999, pp. 36–63.

14 Cathy McClive, 'L'âge des fleurs: le passage de l'enfance à l'adolescence dans l'imaginaire médical du XVIIe siècle', *Biblio* 17, 2007, pp. 171–85. See also Susan Broomhall, '"Women's Little Secrets": Defining the Boundaries of Reproductive Knowledge in Sixteenth-century France', *Social History of Medicine* 15:1, 2002, pp. 1–15 (3).

15 Lynn Botelho, 'Old age and menopause in rural women of early modern Suffolk' in Lynn Botelho and Pat Thane (eds), *Women and Ageing in British Society Since 1500*, Harlow: Longman, 2001, pp. 43–65 (esp. 51–59).

16 L. A. Botelho, 'Images of Old Age in Early Modern Cheap Print: Women, Witches, and the Poisonous Female' in Susannah R. Ottaway, L. A. Botelho and Katharine Kittredge (eds), *Power and Poverty: Old Age in the Pre-Industrial Past*, Westport, CT, and London: Greenwood Press, 2002, pp. 225–46. On old women, menopause and witchcraft see Lyndal Roper, 'Witchcraft and Fantasy in Early Modern Germany' in Lyndal Roper, *Oedipus and the Devil: Witchcraft, Sexuality and Religion in Early Modern Europe*, London and New York: Routledge, 1994, pp. 199–225 (208–11); Alison Rowlands, 'Witchcraft and Old Women in Early Modern Germany', *Past & Present* 173:1, 2001, pp. 50–81 (57–60).

17 Michael Stolberg, 'A Woman's Hell? Medical Perceptions of Menopause in Preindustrial Europe', *Bulletin of the History of Medicine* 73:3, 1999, pp. 404–28 (416).

18 Daniel Schäfer, *Old Age and Disease in Early Modern Medicine*, trans. Patrick Baker, London: Pickering & Chatto, 2011.

19 Charles Carlton, 'The Widow's Tale: Male Myths and Female Reality in 16th and 17th Century England', *Albion* 10:2, 1978, pp. 118–29; Dagmar Freist, 'Religious difference and the experience of widowhood in seventeenth- and eighteenth-century Germany' in Sandra Cavallo and Lyndan Warner (eds), *Widowhood in Medieval and Early Modern Europe*, Harlow: Longman, 1999, pp. 164–78 (165); Katherine Kittredge, '"The Ag'd Dame to Venery Inclin'd": Images of Sexual Older women in Eighteenth-Century Britain' in Ottaway, Botelho and Kittredge, *Power and Poverty*, pp. 247–63.

20 Elizabeth Foyster, *Manhood in Early Modern England, Honour, Sex and Marriage*, London and New York: Longman, 1999; Toulalan, *Imagining Sex*, pp. 213–17; David Turner, *Fashioning Adultery: Gender, Sex and Civility in England, 1660–1740*, Cambridge: Cambridge University Press, 2002.

21 Michael Hunter and Annabel Gregory (eds), *An Astrological Diary of the Seventeenth Century: Samuel Jeake of Rye 1652–1699*, Oxford: Clarendon Press, 1988. Samuel Jeake, a merchant from Rye, Sussex, possessed several medical books.

22 For an extended discussion of both old and new theories see Thomas Gibson, *The Anatomy of Humane Bodies Epitomized*, London: M. Flesher for T. Flesher, 1682, pp. 134–45. On emerging theories and discoveries about reproduction see Matthew Cobb, *The Egg & Sperm Race: The Seventeenth-Century Scientists Who Unravelled the Secrets of Sex, Life and Growth*, London: Pocket Books, 2007; orig. published by The Free Press, 2006; and Maryanne Cline Horowitz, 'The "Science" of Embryology Before the Discovery of the Ovum' in Marilyn J. Boxer and Jean H. Quataert (eds), *Connecting Spheres: European Women in a Globalizing World 1500 to the Present*, New York and Oxford: Oxford University Press, 2000, pp. 104–12. The roles of eggs and sperm in reproduction were not completely understood and accepted until the nineteenth century.

23 Henry Cuffe, *The Differences of the Ages of Mans Life*, London: Arnold Hatfield for Martin Clearke, 1607, p. 117.

24 Cuffe, *Differences*, p. 114.

25 Cuffe sets out each of these, pp. 114–20. Medieval theorists divided childhood into three parts: *infantia* from birth to 7; *pueritia*, 7 to 14; *adoloscentia* from 14 to the age of majority. Old age also could be divided again into three stages to represent the varying stages of decay of the old body. There are numerous discussions of how the stages of life were divided, and especially in the historiography of old age, the different stages of old age, from 'green' to 'decrepit'. See, for example, Phyllis Gaffney, 'The Ages of Man in Old French Verse Epic and Romance', *The Modern Language Review* 85:3, 1990, pp. 570–82; Smith, 'Growing Old in an Age of Transition', pp. 195–97. For an explanation of the different divisions and their origins see Shulamith Shahar, 'Who Were Old in the Middle Ages?', *Social History of Medicine* 6:3, 1993, pp. 313–41 (316–20).

26 Cuffe, *Differences*, p. 120. Much debate has centred around what age was regarded as the start of old age. Shulamith Shahar has argued that it was 60 ('Who Were Old') while others have argued for a cultural rather than chronological construction, particularly differentiating experience according to gender. See Botelho, 'Old age and menopause'. Margaret Pelling has similarly discussed the age of 50 as a milestone age that indicated the beginnings of old age. Pelling, 'Old Age, Poverty and Disability in Early Modern Norwich: Work, Remarriage and Other Expedients' in Margaret Pelling (ed.), *The Common Lot: Sickness, Medical Occupations and the Urban Poor in Early Modern England*, Harlow: Longman, 1998, pp. 134–54 (137–38).

27 Levinus Lemnius, *The Touchstone of Complexions*, trans. Thomas Newton, London: Thomas Marsh, 1576; first published in Latin, Antwerp, 1561, p. 80.

28 Lemnius, *Touchstone*, p. 28.

29 Eucharius Roesslin, *The Byrth of Mankynde newly translated out of Laten into Englysshe*, trans. Richard Jonas, London: I.R., 1540; from *De Partu Hominis* (1532) from the German *Der Swangern frawen und Hebammen Roszgarten* (1513), pp. xiir–xiiv. Roesslin's text was not itself entirely original and drew on other sources; see Monica H. Green, 'The Sources of Eucharius Rösslin's "Rosegarden for Pregnant Women and Midwives" (1513)', *Medical History* 53:2, 2009, pp. 167–92.

30 John Astruc, *A Treatise on all the Diseases Incident to Women*, trans. J. R – n., London: T. Cooper, 1743, pp. 337, 344–45.

31 Jennifer Evans, '"Gentle Purges corrected with hot Spices, whether they work or not, do vehemently provoke Venery": Menstrual Provocation and Procreation in Early Modern England', *Social History of Medicine* 25:1, 2012, pp. 2–19 (7–9); Toulalan, '"Unripe" bodies', pp. 143–44. See also Moulton, Chapter 11, this volume, note 88.

32 Thomas Laqueur, 'Orgasm, Generation, and the Politics of Reproductive Biology', *Representations* 14, 1986, pp. 1–41 (7); Toulalan, *Imagining Sex*, pp. 74–77.

33 In witchcraft it also explained why sex with the devil was barren as it was cold. See Toulalan, *Imagining Sex*, p. 76.

34 Riverius, *Practice of Physick*, p. 506.

35 Barrough, *Methode of Phisicke*, p. 157. By 1652 *The Methode of Phisicke* had reached its seventh edition, attesting to its popularity.

36 Helkiah Crooke, *Microcosmographia: A Description of the Body of Man*, London: William Iaggard, 1615, p. 278.

37 Thomas Chamberlayne, *The Compleat Midwife's Practice Enlarged*, London: Nath. Brook, 1659; 2nd edn, p. 242.

38 Also spelt Ysbrand or Ijsbrand. Isbrand de Diemerbroeck, *The Anatomy of Human Bodies, Comprehending the most Modern Discoveries and Curiosities in that Art*, trans. William Salmon, London: Edward Brewster, 1689, pp. 190–91.

39 Lemnius, *Touchstone*, p. 43.

40 Crooke, *Microcosmographia*, p. 278.

41 Crooke, *Microcosmographia*, p. 286.

42 Diemerbroeck, *Anatomy*, p. 206.

43 Diemerbroeck, *Anatomy*, p. 206.

44 Joannes Groeneveld, *The Grounds of Physick*, London: J. Dover, 1715, p. 40. Translated from Groeneveld's adapted edition of François van den Zype's (Zypaeus) *Fundamenta Medicinæ* (1683; further editions in 1687, 1692 and 1693). Harold Cook describes this book as 'his plagiarized Latin textbook and its English translation' in Harold J. Cook, *Trials of an Ordinary Doctor: Joannes de Groenevelt in Seventeenth-Century London*, Baltimore and London: The Johns Hopkins University Press, 1994, p. 203.

45 Ambroise Paré, *Of the Generation of Man* in *The Works of Ambrose Parey*, trans. Thomas Johnson, London: Jos. Hindmarsh, 1691, p. 566.

46 Diemerbroeck, *Anatomy*, pp. 206–7.

47 Chamberlayne, *Compleat Midwife's Practice*, p. 242.

48 Diemerbroeck, *Anatomy*, p. 204.

49 Paré, *Works*, p. 567.

50 Riverius, *Practice of Physick*, p. 504.

51 See Patricia Crawford, 'Menstruation in Seventeenth-Century England', *Past and Present* 91, 1981, pp. 47–73.

52 Levinus Lemnius, *The Secret Miracles of Nature: In Four Books*, London: Jo Streeter, 1658, p. 308. *Aristotle's Masterpiece* (1684), for example, drew on Lemnius.
53 Lemnius, *Secret Miracles*, p. 309.
54 Barrough, *Methode of Phisicke*, p. 145.
55 McClive, 'L'âge des fleurs', esp. pp. 177–82; Broomhall, '"Women's Little Secrets"', p. 3.
56 William Salmon, *Aristotle's Compleat and Experience'd Midwife*, London: n.p., 1700, p. 145.
57 Salmon, *Aristotle's … Midwife*, p. 146.
58 Daniel Sennert, *The Fourth Book of Practical Physick. Of Womens Diseases*, trans. Nicholas Culpeper and Abdiah Cole from the fourth book of *Practica Medicinae*, London: Peter Cole, n.d. (but dated 1684 in British Library Catalogue), p. 133.
59 Marten, *Gonosologium Novum*, p. 90.
60 See Foyster, *Manhood*, pp. 107–15, 197–98; Kittredge, '"The Ag'd Dame"', pp. 256–61.
61 Peter Chamberlain, *Dr. Chamberlain's Midwifes Practice: Or, A Guide for Women In that high Concern of Conception, Breeding, and Nursing Children*, London: Thomas Rooks, 1665, p. 69.
62 Kittredge, '"The Ag'd Dame"'; Lynn A. Botelho, 'The 17th Century' in Pat Thane (ed.), *A History of Old Age*, Los Angeles: The J. Paul Getty Museum, 2005, pp. 113–73 (135–40).
63 Crooke, *Microsomographia*, pp. 234–35. For example, in Jane Sharp's *The Midwives Book*, London: Simon Miller, 1671, p. 54 and in Nicolas Venette, *Conjugal Love Reveal'd*, 7th edn, London: n.p., 1720; first published in 1686 as *La Génération de l'homme, ou tableau de l'amour conjugal considéré dans l'état du mariage*, p. 20.
64 Crooke, *Microcosmographia*, p. 65.
65 Sharp, *Midwives Book*, p. 50.
66 James Drake, *Anthropologia Nova: Or, A New System of Anatomy*, 2nd edn, 2 vols, London: W. Innys, 1717, p. 150.
67 Riverius, *Practice of Physick*, p. 506.
68 Riverius, *Practice of Physick*, p. 503.
69 See Toulalan, 'Unripe bodies', pp. 140–44.
70 *The Proceedings of the Old Bailey*, Old Bailey Online, Ref. t17510703–21, Trial of Christopher Larkin for rape, 3 July 1751.
71 *OBSP*, Ref. t17470429–28, John Hunter, 29 April 1747.
72 Ambroise Paré, *Of the Anatomy of Mans Body*, in *Works*, p. 86.
73 Chamberlain, *Dr. Chamberlain's Midwifes Practice*, p. 43. See also for almost identical words: Thomas Bartholin, *Bartholinus Anatomy*, London: Peter Cole, 1663, p. 72; and Sharp, *Midwives Book*, p. 53.
74 Anon., *The Ladies Dispensatory: Or Every Woman Her Own Physician*, London: James Hodges, 1739, pp. 186–87.
75 Riverius, *Practice of Physick*, p. 503.
76 Gibson, *Anatomy*, p. 155.
77 Paré, *Of the Generation of Man*, in *Works*, p. 568.
78 Chamberlain, *Dr. Chamberlain's Midwifes Practice*, p. 69.
79 Lemnius, *Secret Miracles*, p. 309.
80 Anon., *A Supplement to the Onania, Or the Heinous Sin of Self-Pollution, And all its frightful Consequences, in the two Sexes, consider'd, &c.*, London: n.p., 1724 (date in B.L. catalogue; but probably later as it includes letters dated 1725), p. 90.
81 Although William Naphy records a case from 1565 in Geneva of a woman who confessed to having rubbed a boy so hard that he was 'injured in his penis, his little member'; Naphy, *Sex Crimes: From Renaissance to Enlightenment*, Stroud: Tempus, 2002, p. 111. See also my discussion in 'Unripe bodies' of a case mentioned by John Marten, pp. 141–42.
82 Marten, *Gonosologium Novum*, p. 42.
83 Marten, *Gonosologium Novum*, p. 43. For the same idea in the mid-seventeenth century see Diemerbroeck, *Anatomy*, p. 206.
84 Diemerbroeck, *Anatomy*, p. 206.
85 On aphrodisiacs see Evans, 'Gentle Purges'.

16

FAIRY TALES OF FERTILITY

Bodies, sex and the life cycle, *c.* 1750–2000

Julie-Marie Strange

In her analysis of Little Red Riding Hood the anthropologist Mary Douglas contrasted ribald sixteenth-century French versions of the tale with the saccharine adaptations of the modern period. In the rural-peasant rendering, Hood is tricked into eating and drinking her grandmother's flesh, enticed into bed with the wolf and subjected to his rakish attempts to seduce her. Using her initiative, the girl escapes with the assistance of washerwomen on the riverbank. Linguistic clues indicate that Hood is not so little, but at the age of puberty. The wolf seeks to initiate the girl into the world of sex but a network of older women assist Hood in retaining her virginity. The transition from girl to woman is fraught with sexual danger, embodied in the form of the wolf with his lusty masculine desire, which must be navigated by a combination of youthful guile and older women's wisdom. Douglas notes that Mother Goose stories operated to transmit generational beliefs about physiology, sex and culture. Allegorical tales regarding pubescent boys depicted crude and brutal associations between male sexuality and culture (epitomized, Douglas tells us, in vulgar anecdotes about pigs' testicles at the annual slaughter season). On what she terms a dignity register, in genre and goriness, Douglas suggests that stories ranging from the gross to the refined can indicate the level of dis/respect and dis/honour shown for different parts or stages of different bodies. The dignity index is pivotal to interpreting the meanings of stories. Thus, early versions of the Little Red Riding Hood story indicate respect for the alignment of female physiology with Nature and identify a coherent feminine world pitched against the vulgar world of corporeal masculinity.[1]

Subsequent versions of the story wrested Little Red Riding Hood from Nature and substituted female cooperation for Hood's timely rescue by a woodcutter. The pubescent girl remained distant from association with boyish vulgarity but Hood and the older women became incapable of cunning defence and relied, instead, on the man with equipment and expertise. What remained constant was the sacrifice of the grandmother. As Douglas notes, in older versions of the story, the wolf not only kills the grandmother but serves her sexual organs to the girl. In nineteenth-century versions, the grandmother is consumed by the wolf but climbs out of his stomach, alive and well, when the woodcutter comes to the rescue. In both tales, the grandmother holds little, if any, sexual allure for the wolf. In this, the consumption of an aged woman's sex organs by a pubescent girl is richly suggestive of the seasonality of the individual life cycle, responsibilities for generation, and the literal 'unsexing' of the older woman. Similarly, modern versions of the story sanitized the crudity of earlier versions but masculinity continued to be depicted as active and independent in comparison to the new passivity assigned to womanhood.

The transformation of Red Riding Hood from a story of women's agency and affiliation with Nature, contingent with lusty masculine corporeality, into an anodyne tale on the dangers lying in wait for unwitting young girls offers a useful analogy to cultural shifts in understanding bodies, sex and the life cycle in the period after 1750. Appeals to Nature as a superior force for the good of humanity did not disappear after the mid-eighteenth century but were increasingly couched in a language of complexity that necessitated the skills of an expert to interpret and help implement the 'laws' of Nature for a confused public. As the model of the humoural body receded in the early eighteenth century, it was replaced by mechanistic paradigms of bodies that ran on vital energy, transmitted via a complex nervous system. Of particular importance in this period was puberty which 'ripened' the unformed sexual body and facilitated the transition of children into predetermined sex roles. In contrast, the aged as sexual agents received relatively little medical attention, not least because the dominant medical paradigm of sexed bodies in this period was preoccupied with fertility.[2] This chapter charts sexual life cycles in the modern period to demonstrate modern medicine's tendency to imagine sexed bodies in relation to reproductive destinies and, second, to pathologize the female body against an assumed masculine norm. While medical advice for men circulated after 1750, it paled in comparison to the burgeoning specialism of the 'diseases of women' whereby female sexuality was understood overwhelmingly in relation to ensuring woman's fulfilment of her assumed vocation as Mother.[3]

Before puberty

The modern child, as we recognize it, emerged from the late eighteenth century, identifiable in the work of Jean-Jacques Rousseau on education and the Romantics who remodelled childhood away from Calvinist notions of inherited sin toward an idealized state of innocence. As Louise Jackson points out, the pure child of romantic imagination had an 'ugly twin', born around the same period: the juvenile delinquent.[4] This did not necessarily diminish notions of children's innate innocence but highlighted the degrading influence of environment on childhood, a concept that proved pivotal to legislative campaigns to reform child labour. The children of industrial England, growing up in poverty, filth and hard labour, were not children at all. In addition, the Evangelical revival at the end of the eighteenth century ensured that notions of childhood never entirely dispensed with belief in children's inborn capacity for moral deviance. Children's literature in this period was often didactic, urging children to strive for goodness and repent of their sins. Similarly, the alignment of children with Nature did not mean that child development could be left to Nature's auspices. An expanding consumer market from the late eighteenth century not only identified childhood as a special age category with particular clothing, leisure and educational needs, but also a period that demanded careful guidance. Childcare management books emphasized the government, preservation and education of infants and children to bind political, moral and economic concerns with medical paradigms to establish the medical practitioners' authority in guiding treatment, not just of the sick, but all children.[5]

The age span of childhood in this period was dependent on biological, social and economic factors. Within a bourgeois and artisan world of education or apprenticeship, childhood was prolonged by financial dependency upon parents. In contrast, working-class and poorer children often began contributing to the family economy at a young age, thereby curtailing notions of childhood grounded in dependency. Even after the Education Act of 1870 and the subsequent introduction of free schooling, most working-class children began part-time work by the time they were 13. For girls, childhood could also be dependent on marital status. For much of the eighteenth and nineteenth centuries, middle-class females in particular were expected to exchange the care and protection of fathers for that of husbands. In the latter half of the nineteenth century, the average age of marriage for women was estimated to be 26 meaning that, for some, girlhood extended well beyond puberty while the lack of economic independence for married and single women arguably kept women in the position of children for much of their lives.[6] Childhood was also defined physiologically: sentimental portrayals of children typically emphasized 'littleness' to promote an association with defencelessness, fragility and innocence. As James Kincaid notes, however, one of the most ubiquitous definitions of childhood in the modern period rested on notions of puberty: childhood was the period before puberty.[7]

For all the romantic idealization of the child and the separation of childhood from the (post)pubescent, the pre-pubescent child was not always sexless. In particular, girls in poverty were vulnerable to sexualization, not least in the imaginations and anxieties of middle-class commentators who perceived working-class environments as synonymous with moral instability: overcrowded homes fostered incest, girls were liable to be sold into prostitution and feckless parents failed to provide moral guidance. Paradoxically, children's welfare campaigns were active in sexualizing children. Dr Barnardo notoriously photographed children in various states of undress, with tousled hair, to intimate their poverty but, also, their moral vulnerability.[8] Anxieties about a 'slave trade', where children were used as sexual objects, recurred throughout the nineteenth century but gained particular publicity in the later decades. The age of consent was raised from 12 to 13 in 1875 and to 16 in the Criminal Law Amendment Act of 1885. As Jackson notes, the age of criminal responsibility, 14, functioned for much of the nineteenth century as the implicit age of consent for boys although the Assault of Young Persons Act, 1880, fixed the age of consent to indecent assault at 13 for boys and girls. This was raised for boys in 1922 when the age of consent for indecent assault for boys was raised to 16. Anxieties about boy morality focused on criminal behaviour whereas social unease about girls rested almost exclusively on sexual immorality. This does not mean that boys were not sexualized but that contemporary anxieties about the sexualization of children grew from a mid-Victorian reform movement preoccupied with double standards and fallen women.[9]

The extent to which middle-class commentators intended to actively sexualize children is subject to debate, especially with regard to the bourgeois child or 'sugarplum'. Approximately 500,000 people bought the *Graphic* Christmas Annual in 1880 for the John Everett Millais centrefold, 'Cherry Ripe', an image of pre-industrial, mob-capped girlhood. As Carol Mavor notes, this was a rural idyll of innocence yet the image contained hints of latent sexuality. The girls' cherries suggested ripe, soft fruits, much like the soft roundness of the budding feminine form; the black lacy gloves on the child's hands were at odds with the pure whiteness of her frock, and it was unclear whether the title referred to the little girl or the fruit.[10] A less ambiguous version of 'Cherry Ripe' appeared in *The Children's Treasury of Pictures and Stories* (1899), a religious collection for small children, featuring an infant girl secretly eating cherry pie. Here, the emphasis was on the naughtiness of small children, reiterated by the incorporation of a children's rhyme into the accompanying text: 'I've lots of purple cherries/Baked within a pie/Like four and twenty Blackbirds/We'll share them you and I.' The feature was probably intended as a moral lesson on gluttony but the (modern) adult viewer can see a moral on purity too: the little girl in a white dress gorging on cherry pie is likely to acquire red stains on her spotless frock, intimating latent sexuality before first menstruation (menarche).[11]

Cherry ripe: sexing puberty

Puberty was manifest in secondary sexual characteristics (for example, the growth of breasts, pubic or facial hair) that indicated development of primary sexual organs (such as ovaries). The extent to which medical and lay writers perceived degrees of similarity between boys and girls in pre-pubescent childhood was inextricable from models of puberty. For some, puberty revolutionized the sexless 'ramping girl' (who, but for dress, was indistinguishable from her brother) into a 'shy and retiring' woman with 'nobler impulses'; the 'angular, gawky girl' became 'a creature of graceful and symmetrical curves'.[12] Little wonder the wolf took a fancy to Hood. For others, puberty was the final fruition of Nature's grand design: a girl's innate submission to, and admiration of, her brother evolved into distinct sex-role difference at puberty.[13] For boys, puberty represented a life cycle stage at which they learned self-control but wherein their sexuality was active and normative. For girls, puberty marked the beginning of their transformation into a mother. As medical philosophers noted, girls' puberty had national significance. Marc Colombat (1838) likened puberty to the 'springtime' of woman's life when she was delivered into the service of humanity to perpetuate the race (seemingly alone).[14] Such representations were tenacious. Writing in the 1880s, Willoughby Wade, a Senior Physician, located developing ovaries as 'the central point of the human race, that round which all revolves, from which all radiates'.[15] Almost 50 years later, Professor R. W. Johnstone addressed the British Medical Association (1927) on the national and social significance of puberty: menarche represented the ripening of Nature's 'star performers' (the ovaries) in the destiny of the race.[16]

Puberty enabled boys to become active sexual agents whereas it transformed asexual girls into objects of desire. Gendered expectations were embedded in understandings of physiological change. William Carpenter (1842) drew attention to the lush pubescent girl: puberty gave girls the 'roundness and fullness which are so attractive to the opposite sex at the period commencing womanhood'. His account of puberty in boys focused on emerging sexual passions that boys were to master, the 'much increased' development of their organs and the amplified power of the voice.[17] As Helen King has observed, male authors were 'barely able to resist [the] charms' of the developing girl, emphasizing her rosy complexion and plump body as erotic indicators of the fertility blossoming within.[18] Addressing a transatlantic audience, D. H. Jacques (1859) exclaimed, 'the bosom expands into luxuriant fullness, the features acquire new and expressive lines, the cheeks become more fresh and rosy, and the lips glow in tempting ripeness'.[19] George Napheys (1871) eulogized: 'Wonderful metamorphosis! The magic wand of the fairy has touched her and she comes forth a new being, a vision of beauty to bewitch the world.' The girl's eyes brightened to 'acquire unwonted significance' as 'windows of the soul', betraying new emotions arising within; her voice became 'rich, melodious, soft' to make 'the sweetest music man ever hears'.[20] Ironically, Napheys's later publications castigated the medical profession for focusing on the diseases of women at the expense of those associated with men.[21]

As medical practitioners had increasingly discredited humoural theories of medicine, they turned to mechanistic or economic models that conceived of body and spirit as a system of checks and balances. The body contained a fixed amount of vital energy that was regulated through nerves; expenditure of energy in one department had to be compensated by credits. The growth of sexual characteristics in puberty severely taxed the nervous system. For boys, over-studying could impede sexual development, while sexual purity could strengthen the body because the loss of semen, through nocturnal emissions or masturbation, depleted the body's vital force. Others argued that the release of semen could provide an outlet for sexual energies that threatened to subsume the mind. For girls, the same physiological model was utilized to restrict access to education, particularly after the age of 12: the establishment of menarche necessitated concentrated amounts of energy and once the menses were established, girls experienced monthly depletions of energy. The development of reproductive organs, inextricable from woman's very purpose, could not be jeopardized by allowing a dual tax on the nerves.

For boys and girls, puberty was also inextricable from moral anxieties. Puberty in boys was a process of steady civilization to socialize them into becoming good men, that is, men who would provide for and protect their families.[22] The active responsibility conferred on boys at puberty is reflected in medical depictions of semen. As Elizabeth Grosz observes, semen is overwhelmingly represented in social and medical texts as a function rather than a fluid. As such, it has purposeful properties: to fertilize, to father and produce an object. Puberty for boys is a self-elected period of sexual maturity. In contrast, female genitalia are imagined as the receptacle for male fluids and the nesting place of their products. At puberty, the female body becomes an uncontrollable form that bleeds and, in twentieth-century parlance, is at the behest of hormones: puberty is not a moment of self-selected sexual maturity but a symbol of imminent reproductive capacity.[23] Advice on how to manage puberty was embedded in general health books and didactic literature for children. Maria Edgeworth's story 'The Purple Jar' (1796) warned young girls against caprice as the protagonist Rosamund ignores her father's instructions to buy new shoes to purchase a purple glass jar instead. On delivery, Rosamund realizes that the jar is not purple but clear glass filled with sticky coloured fluid. Rosamund suffers the disappointment of her purchase while being confined indoors because her shoes are too small. Ostensibly a story that chastises Rosamund for disobedience, the story can also be read as an allegory for menstruation. Rosamund's desire for the frivolous thing of beauty denotes the fickle nature of the girl-woman, the importance of patriarchal authority and the necessity of maternal foresight in warning girls about sticky coloured fluids. This story adopted new currency in Henry Tonks's painting 'Rosamund and the Purple Jar' (1900). Tonks's visualization of the story mirrors the paradox of puberty: the glass jar is at once beguiling but fraught with potential disappointment; the girl's desires outgrow the confines of childhood while she is still trapped within children's clothing and space; and, as a vessel, the womb is only truly valuable when stopped and full.[24]

For Edward Tilt, the father of British gynaecology, puberty meant loss of innocence: capriciousness, flirtatious and potentially wanton behaviour jostled with the pure characteristics of the virginal girl. The senses were 'mysterious portals' influencing the nervous system and predisposing the girl to disease and instability. For Tilt, the danger could be managed by keeping the pubescent girl a 'child' for as long as possible: burgeoning bodies were best contained within childish clothes, and girls should have the diet and routine of the nursery. Sexual maturity was inextricable from sensibility: girls should be prohibited from reading romances, dances, theatre trips, opera, feather beds, rich food, social pleasures and frequent associations with men. Above all, the process of sexual maturation manifest in first menstruation must not be hurried. Asserting that the relative value of a being was estimated from the time it took to 'attain perfection', Tilt observed that such criteria lent 'man' a high value because it took 'so many tedious years to achieve the fullness of his permitted power'. The longer menarche was delayed in women, the stronger their constitution, the more 'harmonious' menstruation and the closer to 'full perfection' they would be.[25] In contrast, the medical and lay assumption that boys had greater capacity for self-regulation facilitated a degree of youthful independence although, of course, the consequences of boyish sexual indiscretion were hardly comparable to those for girls. The archives of Thomas Coram's Foundling Hospital teem with case notes of young, single mothers with ruined characters and appalling job prospects who presented illegitimate babies for adoption, fathered by blithely indifferent and unaffected men.[26]

As more women qualified as medical practitioners in Britain and America at the end of the nineteenth century, new research agendas sought to identify the normative health of girls' bodies in puberty. The Medical Women's Federation, established in 1917, was especially active in promoting research that modelled menarche and menstruation as a hygienic and healthy experience. This was enhanced by campaigns to provide sanitary facilities (towels and bins) in girls' washrooms in schools to divest early menstrual experiences of embarrassment and unhygienic practices. Concurrently, coherent programmes of sex education in schools and through General Practitioners from the 1920s sought to demystify puberty and sexual development for girls and boys. By the latter decades of the twentieth century, the dissemination of information about reproductive life cycles was held as a universal principle in state education.[27] Likewise, in light of expanding occupational opportunities for women, puberty no longer represented the gateway to motherhood as destiny. Sexual development could be viewed outside limited models of feminine roles and, especially in light of second-wave feminist calls for women to reclaim their bodies from medicine, as a period of self-development.

Paradigms of puberty had long noted the emotional turmoil of this period. Rousseau observed that maturing youth was often accompanied by heightened sensibilities and intense creativity. This emotive element of puberty was identified as 'adolescence' in 1904 by Stanley Hall who characterized it as a period of 'storm and stress' for boys and girls. It was this that made young people volatile and socially awkward. With the emergence of endocrinology, the study of hormones, in the early twentieth century, medical paradigms of puberty and adolescence shifted again. Throughout the twentieth century, adolescence became the principal arena for discussing the moral anxieties of puberty, not least because, although related to physiological change, adolescence was an elastic category that could accommodate a range of behaviours over a long period of time. Indeed, the adolescent became the identity for young people around the age of puberty, especially once American market researchers identified the 'teenager' as a distinct consumer group in the 1940s. While the Victorian conception of puberty as dangerous may have receded, adolescence remains understood as a fraught transitional phase for young people with gendered expectations about emerging sexual identities manifest in cultures of consumption.

Bearing up: optimizing fertility

As Henry Allbutt noted in his *Wife's Handbook* (1886), good health was vital to both sexes but the tasks of marriage and maternity invested women's health with extra significance.[28] In a culture where maternity was the apogee of a woman's career, menstruation was the chief signifier of reproductive health. Practitioners' estimates of the age of menarche, roughly between 13 and 16 for most of the nineteenth century, responded to, but also cemented, anxieties about sexual precocity and potential infertility. Thomas J. Graham (1834) noted the numerous 'vulgar prejudices' and relentless nagging of 'incorrigible' mothers concerning the age of menarche.[29] Edward Tilt bemoaned maternal talk of 'bringing girls forward' to 'bring down the courses'; the successful management of menarche was 'best calculated' to 'second Nature in her cautious attempts to inaugurate this new and important epoch'.[30] If practitioners urged parents to relax about menarche, they were less sanguine about irregular periods: the absence of menstruation implied a reproductive system gone awry. According to Helen King, the absence or irregularity of menstruation in girls was alarming because of its ambiguity: the loss of monthly periods might indicate that a girl had evaded parental control and become pregnant.[31]

Some practitioners advised affianced women with poor menstrual performance (scanty or painful periods) to marry quickly as sexual congress would dilate the cervix to permit the easier flow of blood; alternatively, ripping the hymen could release trapped blood clots.[32] According to Allbutt, the first 'conjugal embraces' would cure painful or distressing periods and he encouraged early marriage for girls with menstrual irregularities.[33] Menstrual health as a measure of fertility epitomized the extent to which nineteenth-century medical practitioners equated female sexuality with maternity. As issues of eugenics and Empire became increasingly prominent towards the end of the century, practitioners advised women diagnosed as sterile to avoid marriage: there was little chance of 'happy union' and the question of fertile marriage was a 'matter of some social importance'.[34] One practitioner argued that in India, women who failed to conceive risked replacement by another wife. If the colonial subject took such care in securing progeny, it was the duty of the Englishman to protect reproduction of his own race.[35]

Within a physical economy, menstruation was normal but also erratic and dangerous. Medical treatises described menstruation as a repeated sapping of strength that women must bear up against. Yet menstruation must also be 'performed' to ensure optimum fertility; it was both beyond and within the realm of personal influence, a paradox that justified the need for expert advice while placing responsibility for poor menstruation on women. Pye Henry Chavasse cautioned that failure to 'duly and properly perform' menstruation was causing epidemic proportions of sterility in England: young women preferred frivolity to nurturing their health with sleep, moderate exercise and a good diet.[36] Some practitioners pointed to working-class women who could not rest at menstruation to draw correlations between luxury and poor menstrual performance, identifying cosseted affluent women as the social group most in need of medical treatment for menstrual problems.[37] Practitioners' notions of pursuing an optimum menstrual performance necessarily problematized normative menstruation, especially when the perfect cycle proved so elusive, a paradox that remained in the twentieth century with sex and health education normalizing a 28-day cycle that did not match most women's experience.[38]

Paradigms of menstruation in the nineteenth and early twentieth centuries assumed that painful menstruation (dysmenorrhoea) was normative, although there was wide disagreement on the degrees of pain constituting 'normal' menstruation. The American physician Silas Weir Mitchell (1888) contended that male pain was accidental and depended on the chances of life; for women it was 'incidental' to their sex.[39] The majority of practitioners urged that surgical procedures such as artificial dilation were reserved for married women or extreme cases only. Most practitioners recommended pregnancy as an effective cure. This had a pragmatic effect in that childbirth dilated the cervix and uterus. Yet it also supported notions that women's place was at the domestic hearth. In the early twentieth century research into metabolic rates and periodicity, alongside studies of women's industrial fatigue during the menstrual cycle, challenged generic conceptions of menstruation as an illness to emphasize the health of women at this time and the minimal changes in performance. By the mid-twentieth century, advertisements for sanitary products traded on the assumption that the only barrier to women's full participation in socio-occupational life at menstruation was lack of suitable tampons or towels.

For most of the period prior to the twentieth century, the precise relationship between menstruation and ovulation was unclear with many practitioners equating menstruation with 'heat' in warm-blooded mammals, thereby cementing the relationship between fertility and female sexuality. When medical research by Herman Knaus and Kyusaku Ogino independently confirmed that ovulation and menstruation were separate events in 1929, it had profound implications for women's sex lives, not least for contraceptive technologies and notions of the 'safe' time of the month (the Ogino-Knaus method). The development of endocrinology facilitated identification and understanding of the importance of hormones in fertility and sexual desire, revolutionizing models of male and female periodicity. Endocrinology also facilitated the development of synthetic hormones to promote the management of bodies for health purposes and, notably, in the manufacture of the contraceptive pill which became available in Britain in 1961. The twentieth century was, increasingly, a time when new technologies and medical research enabled women to forge a self-consciously 'modern' approach to sexual life cycles whereby sexuality was not dependent on fertility but on personal choice.

When ripe fruit falls: menopause

Throughout the modern period, older men and women benefited from shifts in medical understandings that demystified ageing and increasingly, from the late eighteenth century, separated older populations into categories: the mature, sick, poor and unwanted. Social historians have correlated these emerging categories with shifts in popular attitudes to the aged: from ridicule to investing maturity with dignity.[40] The notion that ageing was a social process that affected men and women is encapsulated in the gender-neutral term, 'the climacteric'. Medical paradigms of men's sexual life after puberty were relatively stable: older men may experience some impotency or declining sexual ardour but there was little sense of a physiological or psychological 'revolution' in the middle-aged man's life cycle. Even after the emergence of endocrinology in the early twentieth century which enabled researchers to track hormonal changes in ageing men, it remained unclear whether men experienced 'male menopause'. While some medical writers identified a male 'change of life', notably Marie Stopes's *The Change of Life in Men and Women* (1936), the subject of a physiological male menopause remained contested throughout the century.

Women's sexual life cycle, however, had two clear physiological termini: puberty and menopause.

One of the first 'modern' publications on menopause, John Fothergill's 'Of the management proper at the cessation of the menses' (1774), noted the difficulties some women experienced in menopause and sought to give guidance to practitioners consulted on such matters. Although Fothergill noted many potential complaints of menopause, the keynote of his text was reassurance that the process was natural and temporary.[41] The first book dedicated exclusively to menopause (1839) explained the process as a response to the death of the womb. The terminology of menopause from the late eighteenth century suggested turbulence and decline: 'widows' disease', 'old maid's insanity', 'climacteric', 'critical time', 'turn of life', 'sexual involution', 'change' or 'last revolution'.[42] Menopause was synonymous with decay: it was an 'epoch of sexual decrepitude', a time of 'genital insufficiency' and a 'critical age'.[43] Descriptions of symptoms emphasized menopause as loss. Writing in the 1830s, Michael Ryan identified menopausal women as having 'collapsed' breasts, shrinking fullness of habit, and shrivelled skin that lost colour and softness.[44] The 'Change of Life' entry for *A Dictionary of Medicine* (1885) standardized the conflation between loss of femininity and fertility: menopause made women grow fat and coarse, sprout facial hair, breasts became 'large and pendulous' and the abdomen expanded; ovaries 'shrivelled up' and lost their 'smooth outline', fallopian tubes diminished, and uterus walls atrophied.[45] Much of this language was reproduced in advice manuals for lay readers: feminine characteristics 'diminished', tempers became 'austere'; all that was dynamic dissipated; women lost their 'spring and vigour'; vivacious women became 'dejected and downcast'; others became irritable, peevish, and restless; some became a great annoyance to their friends.[46]

Within the model of vital energy, menopause exacted a startling toll upon women's entire nervous system. Tilt estimated that four-fifths of women suffered some illness at menopause, sometimes leading to prolonged, intense debility. Symptoms ranged wildly so that almost any illness in middle age could be attributed to menopause. Although most symptoms were simply 'annoying', the menopausal 'revolution' frequently entailed 'very serious ill health'.[47] Menopause was not all bad, however: some women, previously of bad temper, improved their disposition and the post-menopausal woman's body became more like that of a man, rendering her physiologically stable for the first time since before puberty.[48]

The idea that menopause predisposed women to depression and melancholia was common and menopause was incorporated into medical understandings of precipitating causes of insanity.[49] Obstetrician Robert Barnes lamented that menopause was 'rarely effected' without some nervous disturbance which sometimes amounted to 'absolute' insanity.[50] Some women displayed 'menopausal hypochondria' and 'most' women suffered some neurosis at menopause; anything that nurtured isolation and self-analysis led to 'hysterical rages'.[51] Occasionally, menopause was manifest in suicidal thoughts, alcoholism and sensitivity to smells, sounds, light or taste. The *Students' Handbook of Gynaecology* (1908) suggested that the cumulative 'strain' of the reproductive organs rendered women 'especially liable to insanity': depression, hypochondria and headaches were more common at menopause than at any other time in women's lives.[52] Such were the 'special dangers' of menopause that the British Gynaecological Society suggested that questions of responsibility ought to be admitted when women at the climacteric were charged with criminal offences.[53]

According to the alienist George Savage, writing at the turn of the twentieth century, both sexes underwent a change of life. For men, the change was social and equated with retirement from business. For women, the 'change' was a 'crisis' because biological retirement from women's work, bearing children, was inextricable from cultural conceptions of femininity. Male retirement was self-selected but menopause enforced change. This explained women's increased disposition to mental instability at menopause. Women at menopause offered 'insane interpretations' of normative symptoms, for example, a headache was a cancerous tumour, or they were jealous and violent towards innocent husbands suspected of committing misdemeanours. One of the 'really dreadful' symptoms of menopause was the development of amorous passions for the physician or parson. Worse, some menopausal women imagined sexual offences had been committed against them. Savage advised practitioners to take such accusations lightly as they rarely amounted to more than 'romantic lying'. Lust and masturbation were common 'disorders' of the menopause and women who conceived during their menopause were often ashamed of themselves.[54]

From the late eighteenth century, depictions of older people increasingly noted their valued status as family members, particularly emphasizing their relationships with grandchildren. The exception to these positive shifts was the depiction of post-menopausal women who manifested sexual desire. If Little Red Riding Hood's grandmother held little sexual allure for the wolf, other older female figures in Mother Goose stories, such as the stepmothers in Snow White and Cinderella, wielded sinister levels of sexual power. Liberated from the fear of pregnancy, the older woman could be re-imagined as a sexual predator in that, biologically, she became more like a man. This was apparently distasteful to many medical and lay commentators, not least when contrasted with the smooth and peachy ripeness of youthful femininity. But, more disturbingly, the dislocation of female sexuality from fertility suggested that women had sexual desires independent of maternity. Advice writers urged women to take up hobbies, develop new interests, and spend time with grandchildren and, if anything, post-menopausal bodies did not herald sexual freedom but reverted to a pre-pubescent mould whereby an absence of fertility was matched by nonexistent or illicit sexual desire.

Shifting paradigms of the reproductive life cycle have complicated this model of ageing, health and sexual desire. Since the early twentieth century, research on menopause, and women's reproductive health more generally, was increasingly dominated in Europe and America by the study of internal gland secretions (hormones) and how these influenced the 'periodicity' of women's physical and mental health.[55] By the 1930s, medical paradigms of the reproductive life cycle for men and women were firmly located in the framework of endocrinology. This had the potential to release women's health from the pathological models favoured by earlier practitioners, but early twentieth-century research increasingly identified woman as the 'plaything' of her glands as endocrinologists remodelled menopause as a hormone deficiency disease.[56] Most of the cutting-edge research on menopause in the interwar years debated the use of synthetic hormones and radiation in the treatment of menopausal symptoms, and the possible carcinogenic risks of such therapies. To a much lesser extent researchers also contemplated the potential use of hormone therapies for ageing men, but there was little consensus over the usefulness or necessity of this.[57] The emergence of endocrinology did not harmonize medical understandings of menopause or how best to treat it.[58] Rather, advances in endocrinology in the 1930s demonstrated just how little the change of life was understood.[59]

In 1926, the Medical Women's Federation called for an investigation into women's experiences of menopause. The results, published in 1933, made powerful claims for rethinking menopause in terms of normative signs of change rather than pathological symptoms.[60] The Federation noted that literature on menopause gave the 'general impression' of turbulence. It was surprising, then, that 90 per cent of 1,000 randomly sampled women stated that they had 'carried on their daily routine without a single interruption' due to menopause. While the research sought to challenge negative stereotypes of menopause, it also placed emphasis on outlook and education as factors in managing menopause, potentially reinforcing practitioners' tendencies to devolve responsibility for menopausal experience onto women.[61] This also endorsed the vast market for commercial tonics and 'pick-me-ups' that fused 'modern' hygiene with older models of menopause. The significance of the survey is evident, however, in the feminist critiques from the late 1960s that identified it as a milestone in women's attempts to reconfigure menopause as a process rather than a pathology.[62]

Advances in pharmaceutical technologies alongside sophisticated paradigms of the physiological function led to the development of a range of medications to treat the side effects of ageing. The development of drugs in the 1990s to treat erectile dysfunction made a significant impact on men's capacity to fulfil their sexual desires in middle and older age. These drugs were marketed largely on the assumption that men wanted sex lives after middle age and that the only barrier to sexual activity was physiological error: advertising and research did not question whether older men were intrinsically sexually appealing. In contrast, the significant development in treatment for menopause traded on social and medical assumptions that ageing rendered women sexually unattractive or uninterested. Models of menopause rooted in health and hygiene acknowledged that menopause enabled women to be sexual agents without fear of pregnancy. This legitimated female sexual desire outside of fertility but, inadvertently, confirmed anxieties that post-menopausal women were not sexually attractive. From the mid-twentieth century, advice publications by the Medical Women's Federation and in more populist media, such as *Woman's Own* magazine and the *Daily Mirror*, increasingly ran features emphasizing the normality and health of menopause while reassuring women that they could remain useful and attractive to their husbands, implicitly confirming the notion that women of menopausal age and after were prone to what earlier practitioners unhesitatingly called 'decrepitude' and decay.

Endocrinology compounded the issue with the development and aggressive marketing of hormone replacement therapy in the 1960s and 1970s. The publication in America of *Feminine Forever* (1966) by a medical practitioner, Robert Wilson, vigorously advocated the use of hormones to 'treat' the 'living decay' of menopause. The book, widely reviewed and quoted in women's and medical magazines on both sides of the Atlantic, generated heated debate. Wilson was accused of developing a 'disease' model of menopause that rested on inaccurate physiological paradigms of menopause and negative assumptions about older women's inherent lack of sexual appeal/desire. Others, including self-identified feminists, heralded Wilson as a knight in shining armour to boost female sexual confidence, attractiveness and well-being.[63] That Wilson continued to generate controversy at the turn of the twentieth-first century suggests that the 'problem' of women ageing has not been resolved. The idea that Little Red Riding Hood's Granny could prevent her sex organs from being made into stew if only she took HRT suggests the persistence of a disjuncture in the sexing of life cycles: a man is his body while a woman remains tied to notions of 'coping' with hers.

Conclusion

It is tempting to see the period after 1750 as one of progress whereby changes in medical paradigms and socio-economic patterns brought freedom from superstition, fear and ignorance. Certainly, there were some significant changes, not least, the heteronormative model of reproductive life cycles that characterized much of this period was increasingly destabilized by the rise of gay parenting and individuals opting to remain child-free. There are, however, notable continuities, recurring themes and new problems that emerge throughout this period. Since the 1980s, some scholars have warned that childhood is under threat as children become increasingly sexualized in mass media and marketing. Advances in technology ended the heartbreak of infertility for many people but, simultaneously, created high expectations that, not infrequently, clash with the cost and success rates of such technologies for different people, at different stages of life. Finally, it is doubtful how far women have been liberated from perceptions of puberty, menstruation and menopause as problematic. The anthropologist Emily Martin noted that in the late twentieth century medical and popular books continued to identify female reproductive systems as wasteful, inefficient and intrinsically chaotic in contrast to the vitality and purpose of male organs. Reproduction continued to be imagined as a fairy story with the egg cast as damsel in distress awaiting rescue by the gallant sperm.[64] In a context where a man is his body but a woman remains tied to 'coping' with hers, it is hardly surprising that Little Red Riding Hood still depends on the woodcutter for rescue.

Notes

1 Mary Douglas, 'Red Riding Hood: An Interpretation from Anthropology', *Folklore* 106, 1995, pp. 1–7.
2 This is reflected in historical literature: see Susannah R. Ottoway, *The Decline of Life: Old Age in Eighteenth-Century England*, Cambridge: Cambridge University Press, 2004; Karen Chase, *The Victorians and Old Age*, Oxford: Oxford University Press, 2009; Pat Thane, *Old Age in English History: Past Experiences, Present Issues*, Oxford: Oxford University Press, 2000; and Kay Heath, *Ageing by the Book: The Emergence of Midlife in Victorian Britain*, Albany: State University of New York Press, 2009.
3 See Ornella Moscucci, *The Science of Woman: Gynaecology and Gender in England, 1800–1929*, Cambridge: Cambridge University Press, 1990; Marjorie Levine-Clark, *Beyond the Reproductive Body: The Politics of Women's Health and Work in Early Victorian England*, Ohio: Ohio University Press, 2004; Ruth Robbins (ed.), *Medical Advice for Women, 1830–1915*, London: Routledge, 2009; Geoffrey Chamberlain, *From Witchcraft to Wisdom: A History of Obstetrics and Gynaecology*, London: RCOG Press, 2007; Diane Price Herndl, *Invalid Women: Figuring Feminine Illness in American Fiction and Culture, 1840–1940*, Chapel Hill: University of North Carolina Press, 1993; Thomas Laqueur, *Making Sex: Body and Gender from the Greeks to Freud*, Cambridge, MA; London: Harvard University Press, 1990; Barbara Ehrenreich and Deidre English, *For Her Own Good: 150 Years of the Experts' Advice to Women*, London: Pluto Press, 1979.
4 Louise Jackson, *Child Sexual Abuse in Victorian England*, London: Routledge, 2000.
5 Adriana Benzaquén, 'The Doctor and Medical Preservation and Management of Children in the Eighteenth Century' in Anja Müller (ed.), *Fashioning Childhood in the Eighteenth Century: Age and Identity*, Aldershot: Ashgate, 2006, pp. 13–24 (14).
6 Michèle Mendelssohn, '"I'm Not a Bit Expensive": Henry James and the Sexualisation of the Victorian Girl' in Dennis Denisoff (ed.), *The Nineteenth-Century Child and Consumer Culture*, Aldershot: Ashgate, 2008, pp. 81–94 (86).
7 James Kincaid, *Child-Loving: The Erotic Child and Victorian Culture*, London: Routledge, 1992, p. 69.
8 Lydia Murdoch, *Imagined Orphans: Poor Families, Child Welfare, and Contested Citizenship in London*, London: Rutgers University Press, 2006.

9   Jackson, *Child Sexual Abuse*, pp. 4–5, 14.
10 Carol Mavor, *Pleasures Taken: Performances of Sexuality and Loss in Victorian Photographs*, London: I. B. Tauris, 1996, p. 14.
11 *The Children's Treasury of Pictures and Stories*, London: Nelson, 1899.
12 J. C. Webster, *Puberty and the Change of Life: A Book for Women*, Edinburgh: E. & J. Livingstone, 1892, p. 7.
13 Willoughby F. Wade, 'Ingleby Lectures on Some Functional Disorders of Females', *Lancet*, 5 June 1886, pp. 1054–58.
14 Marc Colombat, *A Treatise on the Diseases and Special Hygiene of Females*, trans. Charles Meigs, Philadelphia: Lea and Blanchard, 1845 [1838].
15 Wade, 'Some Functional Disorders of Females'.
16 R. W. Johnstone, 'Hygiene and Menstruation in Adolescents', *Lancet*, 20 August 1927, pp. 382–84.
17 William B. Carpenter, *Principles on Human Physiology with their Chief Applications to Psychology*, London: J. & A. Churchill, 1855 [1842], pp. 793–96.
18 Helen King, *The Disease of Virgins: Green Sickness, Chlorosis and the Problems of Puberty*, London: Routledge, 2004, p. 90.
19 D. H. Jacques, *Hints Toward Physical Perfection, or, The Philosophy of Human Beauty*, New York: Fowler and Wells, 1859, p. 202.
20 George H. Napheys, *Physical Life of Woman: Advice to the Maiden, Wife and Mother*, London: The Homeopathic Publishing Company, 1895 [1871], pp. 13–15.
21 Gail Pat Parsons, 'Equal Treatment for All: American Medical Remedies for Male Sexual Problems, 1850–1900', *Journal of the History of Medicine* 32:1, 1977, pp. 55–71.
22 Stephanie Olsen, 'The Authority of Motherhood in Question: Fatherhood and the Moral Education of Children in England, *c.* 1870–1900', *Women's History Review* 18:5, 2009, pp. 765–80.
23 Elizabeth Grosz, *Volatile Bodies: Towards a Corporeal Feminism*, Bloomington, IN: Indiana University Press, 1994, pp. 198–204.
24 Hollis Robbins, 'A Menstrual Lesson for Girls: Maria Edgeworth's *The Purple Jar*' in Andrew Shail and Gillian Howie (eds), *Menstruation: A Cultural History*, Basingstoke: Palgrave Macmillan, 2005, pp. 213–24.
25 Edward John Tilt, *On the Preservation of the Health of Women at the Critical Periods of Life*, London: John Churchill, 1851, pp. 25–31. See also Jacques, *Hints Toward Physical Perfection*, p. 203; Webster, *Puberty and the Change of Life*, p. 34; and Pye H. Chavasse, *Advice to a Wife on the Management of her Own Health and on the Treatment of her Own Health and the Treatment of Some of the Complaints Incidental to Pregnancy, Labour and Suckling*, London: J. & A. Churchill, 1889.
26 Françoise Barret-Ducrocq, *Love in the Time of Victoria: Sexuality, Class and Gender in Nineteenth-Century London*, London: Verso, 1991.
27 Julie-Marie Strange, 'The Assault on Ignorance: Teaching Menstrual Etiquette in England, *c.*1920s to 1960s', *Social History of Medicine* 14:2, 2001, pp. 247–65.
28 H. Arthur Allbutt, *The Wife's Handbook: How a Woman Should Order Herself during Pregnancy in the Lying-In Room and after Delivery*, London: W. J. Ramsay, 1886, p. i.
29 Thomas J. Graham, *On the Diseases Peculiar to Females: A Treatise Illustrating Their Symptoms, Causes, Varieties and Treatment*, London: Simpkin & Marshall, 1834, pp. 47–52.
30 Tilt, *On the Preservation*, pp. 17–20, 30, 48–49.
31 King, *The Disease of Virgins*, p. 9.
32 'Reviews and Notices of Books: T. A. Emmet, "Vesico-Vaginal Fistula from Parturition and Other Causes with Cases of Recto-Vaginal Fistula"', *Lancet*, 20 February 1869, pp. 260–62 (260).
33 Allbutt, *The Wife's Handbook*, p. 52.
34 J. Bland-Sutton, 'Discussion on the Menopause', *Lancet*, 19 August 1899, pp. 524–25.
35 J. L. van Geyzel, 'Amenorrhoea Depending on the Absence of the Uterus', *Lancet*, 29 September 1883, pp. 538–39.
36 Chavasse, *Advice to a Wife*, p. 89.
37 W. Tyler Smith, *Parturition and the Principles and Practice of Obstetrics*, London: John Churchill, 1849, pp. 88–89; T. J. Sturt, *Female Physiology: A Treatise on the Diseases of Women*, London: James Gilbert, 1854, p. 177.
38 Karen Houppert, *The Curse: Confronting the Last Unmentionable Taboo*, London: Profile, 2000.

39 S. Weir Mitchell, *Doctor and Patient*, London: J. B. Lippincott Company, 1888, p. 137.
40 See for instance, David Troyansky, 'Long Live the Republic Where Old Men Preside: The Eighteenth Century' in Pat Thane (ed.), *The Long History of Old Age*, London: Thames and Hudson, 2005, pp. 175–210.
41 See Louise Foxcroft, *Hot Flushes, Cold Science: The History of the Modern Menopause*, London: Granta, 2009, p. 2.
42 Tilt, *On the Preservation*, p. 82.
43 Robert Barnes, 'An Address on General Physiology and Pathology, Illustrated by Study of Gestation and Menstruation', *Lancet*, 1 December 1894, pp. 1261–66 (1265); 'Reviews and Notices of Books', *Lancet*, 7 September 1929, pp. 502–3; 'Hunterian Society', *Lancet*, 3 April 1897, pp. 959–60 (959).
44 Michael Ryan, *A Manual of Midwifery or Compendium of Gynaecology and Paidonsology*, London: Runshaw & Rush, 1831, p. 45.
45 Clement Godson, 'Change of Life' in Richard Quain (ed.), *A Dictionary of Medicine including General Pathology, General Therapeutics, Hygiene and the Diseases Peculiar to Women and Children*, London: Longmans, Green and Co., 1885, pp. 228–29.
46 See Sturt, *Female Physiology*, p. 76; Napheys, *Physical Life of Women*, p. 10; Webster, *Puberty and the Change of Life*, pp. 36–56.
47 Edward John Tilt, 'On the Change of Life in Health and Disease: A Practical Treatise on the Nervous and Other Affection Incidental to Women at the Decline of Life', *Lancet*, 22 November 1855, pp. 564–66; Tilt, *On the Preservation of the Health of Women*, pp. 89–102.
48 Webster, *Puberty and the Change of Life*, pp. 36–38; Godson, 'Change of Life', p. 228.
49 See Elaine Showalter, *The Female Malady: Women, Madness and English Culture, 1830–1980*, London: Virago, 1987.
50 Barnes, 'An Address on General Physiology and Pathology', p. 1265.
51 See 'Medical Society of London: Some Mental Disorders Associated with the Menopause', *Lancet*, 4 November 1893, p. 1128; 'British Gynecological Society: Exhibition of Specimens – The Latent Gout of the Menopause', *Lancet*, 28 November 1896, p. 1529; 'Hunterian Society: Cerebellar Tumour – Mental Disorders of the Climacteric Period', *Lancet*, 3 April 1897, pp. 959–60.
52 George Ernest Herman, *The Students' Handbook of Gynaecology*, London: Cassell & Co Ltd, 1908, p. 369.
53 British Gynaecological Society, 'Correlations between Sexual Functions, Insanity and Crime', *Lancet*, 20 January 1900, p. 169.
54 George H. Savage, 'Some Mental Disorders Associated with Menopause', *Lancet*, 4 November 1893, p. 1128; George H. Savage, 'A Lecture in the Mental Diseases of the Climacteric', *Lancet*, 31 October 1903, pp. 1209–13.
55 Wendy Mitchinson, 'No Longer the Same Woman: Medical Perceptions of the Menopause, 1900–950', *Canadian Bulletin of Medical History* 23:1, 2006, pp. 7–47.
56 Barbara Brookes, 'The Glands of Destiny: Hygiene, Hormones and English Women Doctors in the First Half of the Twentieth Century', *Canadian Bulletin of Medical History* 23:1, 2006, pp. 49–67.
57 Foxcroft, *Hot Flushes*, pp. 182–203.
58 Mitchinson, 'No Longer the Same'.
59 H. R. Donald, 'The Female Climacteric and the Menopause', *British Medical Journal*, 2 April 1938, pp. 727–29.
60 'An investigation of the menopause in one thousand women', *Lancet*, 14 January 1933, pp. 106–8.
61 For example, W. Langdon-Brown, 'Royal Society of Medicine Lecture: Medical Aspects of the Menopause', *Lancet*, 28 March 1936, pp. 719–20.
62 J.-M. Strange, 'In Full Possession of Her Powers: Researching and Rethinking Menopause in early Twentieth-Century England and Scotland', *Social History of Medicine* online, 2012.
63 Judith A. Houck, '"What Do These Women Want?" Feminist Responses to Feminine Forever, 1963–80', *Bulletin of the History of Medicine* 77:1, 2003, pp. 103–32; Judith A. Houck, *Hot and Bothered: Women, Medicine and Menopause in Modern America*, Cambridge, MA: Harvard University Press, 2006.
64 Emily Martin, 'The Egg and the Sperm: How Science has Constructed a Romance Based on Stereotypical Male-Female Roles' in Evelyn Fox Keller and Helen Longino (eds), *Feminism and Science*, London, New York: Oxford University Press, 1996, pp. 103–20.

Part IX

COURTSHIP AND MARRIAGE

17

COURTSHIP AND MARRIAGE, C. 1500–1750

Martin Ingram

In marriage the bodies of two individuals became one flesh and the couple, usually ripe for reproduction, took its place within the wider social body. It was an enticing yet daunting prospect for men and women in early modern Europe. Proverbially the choice of partner was the 'weightiest action', both for individuals and their families; indeed it was 'resembled to war, in which it is said, you cannot err twice'.[1] This powerful image takes us straight to some of the key features of the institution of marriage and its pivotal role in the social and political structure of sixteenth- and seventeenth-century Europe. The pattern is at the same time both simple and complex. While a few fundamental principles are recognizable everywhere, there were infinite variations in diverse parts of the continent, at different points in time, at varying social levels, and depending on the vagaries of inclination and behaviour from family to family, couple to couple, and individual to individual. Since a short survey cannot do justice to all these niceties, the following discussion establishes the broad framework, offering examples from Germany, Italy and elsewhere, but for detailed discussion of key issues gives rather more attention to two particularly well-researched areas, England and France.[2]

Essentially marriage was 'till death us do part'. Indeed in 1500 in the whole of western Europe, divorce in the modern sense – the dissolution of a valid union with the right to remarry – was anathema. The Church was prepared to grant annulments on narrowly defined grounds, such as the existence of a prior union, marriage within the forbidden degrees of kinship or affinity, forced union, or permanent inability to consummate the union. Contrary to what has often been assumed, such 'divorces' were hard to obtain and few in number, not least because there existed procedures to enable people to obtain beforehand a dispensation from the most common 'impediment' (kinship or affinity), if there were good grounds and the relationship was not too close. The adultery of either party – but usually it was men who sued – and severe cruelty – mainly the prerogative of female litigants – were grounds for 'separation from bed and board': that is, the couple were allowed to live apart but not to remarry. Unquestionably many couples cut through these rules simply by making their own arrangements for separation, and some went further and married again. But to do so was a risk, which could lead to serious social and legal consequences.

These rules became controversial during the Reformation. Protestants rejected the idea that marriage was a sacrament and subjected existing matrimonial law to penetrating scrutiny. Hence Protestant leaders in Germany and Switzerland asserted the right of the innocent party to remarry in cases of divorce for adultery. Some even extended the principle to other causes of marital breakdown. In Catholic Europe, on the other hand, the Council of Trent strongly reasserted the indissolubility of marriage. Protestant England, too, retained a basically conservative position. In the mid-sixteenth century the issue of remarriage after divorce for adultery was hotly debated by English lawyers and divines, while powerful individuals tried to pre-empt discussion by simply doing what they wanted. This assault on established conventions provoked a backlash and the ecclesiastical canons of 1604 strongly reaffirmed the traditional position. But it proved hard to say no to the very rich. From the late seventeenth century it became possible to obtain an Act of Parliament to dissolve a valid marriage, though only a few were in a position to avail themselves of this procedure. The significance of all these variations in Europe as a whole should not be overstated. Even the more extreme Protestants regarded divorce as an aberration, to be granted only in highly exceptional circumstances. For the great majority of people across the whole of the continent, splitting up and getting married again in due legal form was simply not an option.[3]

An irony of the situation around 1500 was that, whereas the escape routes from marriage (short of death) were few and narrow, it was perilously easy to get into. In the twelfth century canon lawyers had decided that the defining act of marriage was the free consent of the couple expressed in words of the present tense. To use the formula current in marriage ceremonies in the Lisieux area of France in the fifteenth century, 'I Jean give thee Jeanne my body as a faithful husband'; 'I Jeannne give thee Jean my body as a faithful wife'. In practice it was expected that a couple intending marriage would act with the advice and consent of their parents or other kin; the doctrine was not as individualistic as it sounds. Moreover marriages were supposed to be blessed by a priest, in a church or at the church door, and preceded by the publication of 'banns' on three successive Sundays or holy days. This was to ensure that the couple's intentions were known, so that if there existed impediments to lawful marriage the facts could be brought to light. However, in principle a bare declaration by the man and the woman could constitute a binding union, so long as they had reached the canonical age for marriage – 14 for a male and 12 for a female.

By the early sixteenth century such 'clandestine' unions were a matter of great controversy. Debate peaked at the Reformation, with diverse outcomes in different parts of Europe. In England, the legal position in theory remained more or less unchanged throughout the sixteenth and seventeenth centuries. It was not until 1753 that Lord Hardwicke's Marriage Act prescribed that unions could only be celebrated in church within specified times, and following due procedures, by a properly constituted clergyman of the Church of England after publication of the banns on three Sundays in church or the issue of an authorized licence. Before then, a mere declaration between the parties remained sufficient to create a binding union. Yet the principle was of limited social and even legal significance. By the late sixteenth century, and probably long before, it was in practice usual for people to solemnize their unions. When people spoke of getting married, therefore, they meant marriage in church. Hardwicke's Act was passed, not because people in any significant numbers were not getting married in church, but to eliminate the fraud and deceit associated with 'clandestine' marriage ceremonies, celebrated by a priest but at times and places that evaded the usual safeguards of publicity. Such marriages were relatively few at the start of the period, but after 1600 they became more common, till by the late seventeenth century very large numbers of people were procuring clandestine celebrations in 'lawless' churches or chapels, such as the Fleet Prison in London – where banns or licence were usually unnecessary and often no questions were asked. Some of these marriages were elopements and an unknown number were fraudulent.[4]

On the continent sixteenth-century Protestant reformers mostly legislated swiftly to ensure that unpublicized unions, especially those without parental consent, could be declared invalid. Though practice was not quite so clear cut, in contrast to England this did represent a decisive shift. In Catholic Europe the decree *Tametsi* of the Council of Trent (1563), where the matter had been hotly debated, did not go that far but did decree that only marriages celebrated before the parish priest and two or three witnesses after public announcement were valid. This represented a far-reaching change in some areas. For example, in many parts of fifteenth-century Italy it had been common, especially among richer families, for marriages to be performed by a notary in the house of the bride's family; sometimes there had been an ecclesiastical blessing in addition, but it does not seem to have been regarded as essential and the main emphasis of marriage rituals was secular – family based and closely related to the transmission of property. On the other hand, the French crown resisted the introduction of the Tridentine decrees, not because of opposition to ecclesiastical solemnization – which was already widely practised and simply became universal in the climate of the Counter-Reformation – but precisely because the new regulations did not adequately safeguard family interests. Already in 1556 an edict of Henry II had declared that marriage made without parental consent, when the wife was below 25 and the husband below 30, made the couple liable to disinheritance. The ordinance of Blois in 1579 made the matter a criminal offence, while subsequent edicts further strengthened parents' control. But despite these changes and variations, there remained at the heart of European ideas about marriage the principle that the free consent of the couple was integral.[5]

These features of marriage formation need to be seen in broader context. Much of the continent conformed to the so-called north-west European marriage pattern, the main features of which were a high age at first marriage for both men and women (on average the mid- to late twenties) and a relatively high proportion of people (up to 20 per cent in some areas) who never married. Much emphasis has been placed on the demographic consequences of this pattern, which by removing a decade or so from the reproductive span of the average woman inevitably restricted fertility. But the cultural and social structural implications are equally remarkable. The pattern was usually found in association with the institution of service, whereby young people between puberty and the customary age of marriage could reside in the houses of masters and mistresses as domestic or farm servants, or as apprentices. There they could both accumulate resources (wages could be hoarded as board and lodging were part of the contract) and acquire skills which, if they were lucky, would eventually serve them as married householders.[6]

But the homogeneity of this pattern should not be overstated, not least because its relationship to economic and social development was ambiguous. It has been suggested that the north-west European marriage pattern resulted from the demand for wage labour in the period after the Black Death, allowing young people, especially women, to break free of the trammels of family control.[7] This 'girl power' thesis sits uneasily with the observation that in much of seventeenth-century Europe delayed marriage, involuntary celibacy and widespread service were the result of *limited* employment opportunities and powerful patriarchal pressures that bore hard on young people of either sex. Within north-west Europe there were considerable variations in the pattern from area to area and among different social groups. In a classic article, Vivien Brodsky Elliott revealed that in the early seventeenth century London-born women, characteristically living with their parents, married at much younger ages than female migrants to the city; in either case the bridegrooms were mostly in their late twenties.[8] In Europe as a whole, women from richer families tended to marry at an earlier age than their poorer counterparts, but even so very young marriages were uncommon. Even among the aristocracy there was a tendency as the period wore on for marriage ages to drift upwards, in part because it took time to inculcate the educational skills and social graces that the prevailing culture increasingly demanded, even of women. In any case, as the term implies, the north-west marriage pattern was never universal. Eastern Europe was different, in this as in many other respects. Moreover, in parts of southern Europe, notably Sicily, Apulia, and some other parts of south Italy, women were expected to marry at a much younger age, and living-in service and apprenticeship were far less common features of the social structure.[9]

Cross-cutting these patterns were a variety of different forms of family household, some of which inevitably affected courtship and marriage practices. In parts of Austria, Germany and south-west France the so-called stem family was found, a form well adapted to peasant economies in which rural mobility was limited and family (as opposed to wage) labour predominated. The key feature was that at certain stages of the developmental cycle, two (but only two) married couples of succeeding generations dwelt together in the same household. It was understood that the farm or holding would pass to a designated heir, usually the eldest son. He was allowed to marry and lived with his wife in the ancestral house, even while the parents of the older generation remained alive and in charge of the family enterprise. Siblings, on the other hand, could reside only while they remained unmarried.

Less common was the so-called joint family household, consisting of two or more married couples of the same generation. Even more than the stem family, the arrangement was likely to breed tension and stunt individual freedom. Where this family structure existed, it seems often to have been the result of necessity: brothers banding together for mutual defence or to reopen lands ravaged by war in fifteenth-century France, for example, or where families had to join forces to work the large share-cropping tenancies imposed on them by rapacious landlords in parts of Italy and central France. Rarer still were various forms of communal organization resulting in very large family groupings. Their existence is well attested in certain parts of France. But, although some examples survived till the nineteenth century, they were on the whole in decline after 1500. Indeed this was true of all multi-couple family forms. The increasing availability of wage labour undermined their economic *raison d'être*; more peaceful conditions made them less necessary as a defensive measure; while legal changes – insisting that they should be based on formal written contracts – made them less easy to establish and more vulnerable to disputes among disgruntled participants.[10]

Very common all over western Europe was what modern historians have dubbed the 'nuclear' or 'conjugal' family household, which, when complete, consisted of a husband and wife and their co-resident children. This was associated with a powerful customary expectation that when they were old enough to marry, members of the younger generation would set up a new household rather than living with parents or in-laws. This in itself tended to delay marriage, since this was dependent on the availability of a dwelling and the ability of the couple (with or without family assistance) to equip it with household goods and utensils. But many so-called 'nuclear' households were radically different from modern understandings of this term, since they included the living-in servants or apprentices that, as has been seen, were usually the concomitant of the north-west European marriage pattern. Characteristically these were in their teens or early twenties, contributing to the household economy by doing domestic tasks, farm labour, working at their master or mistress's trade, or helping to keep shop. They received wages as well as board and lodging, but part of the bargain was some degree of training – indeed to become, in the case of apprentices, the master of a trade. Sometimes servants were relatives of the householder, mostly they were not. Nonetheless the master and mistress were usually held to be *in loco parentis*, responsible for the behaviour of their servants and apprentices, who were in turn subject to their discipline, which could well take the form of corporal punishment. They were part of the 'family'.

Households with servants and apprentices were mostly found in the middling and upper ranks of urban and rural society. The simple 'nuclear' families were mostly those of the poor. At the other extreme were the large and highly complex households of urban patricians, nobles and (above all) the great aristocracy. Their 'families' might include large numbers of servants, household officers with specialized functions, tutors, retainers, and various relatives, including married couples. Such great households were particularly prominent features of society around 1500, but were only a little less so at the close of the period. According to a writer at the end of the seventeenth century, the household of a great *seigneur* in Paris should contain at least 35 officers and servants; if he had a wife, the number would increase by 16; while the needs of children would bring the total to well over 50. One way in which large households did change, however, was in the use of space. At the start of the period living areas tended to be large, fulfilling numerous overlapping functions, and the lives of servants were closely intermeshed with those of their masters and mistresses. As time went on, houses were increasingly divided into a series of more specialized and more intimate spaces; servants were still prominent, but backstairs and servants' quarters kept them in their place. On a smaller scale, a similar evolution occurred in middling households.[11]

While the household was important it was not autonomous. Sexual conduct and even husband–wife relations were subject to regulation by churches, guilds, city councils, royal or princely lawcourts, and a variety of more or less informal mechanisms of 'neighbourhood watch'. Numerous transgressions that are today regarded as matters of private morality, subject only to personal conscience or to religious exhortation, were in this period treated as crimes, or at least as public scandals, subject to formal censure. Bearing or begetting a child out of wedlock was regarded as a serious antisocial offence. Even more serious was adultery, a form of behaviour akin to the theft of the husband's property, an assault on his honour, and likely to lead to violence or murder. Hence adultery was often subject to severe penalty at the hands of state authorities, the Church, or both. At least that was the theory. Practice was sometimes more lax – in seventeenth-century France, for example, actual prosecutions were quite rare – or else vengeance was tacitly assumed to lie in the hands of the wronged husband.[12]

But it was not merely for their social consequences that such sins were condemned. Open sin was seen as an affront to God, who might visit his wrath not only on errant individuals, but also on nations, cities and communities. The doctrine of divine Providence, shared across the confessional divide, was developed particularly strongly among Protestants. But in Catholic countries too, it was seen as the responsibility of the public authorities in Church and state to bridle sin. If they were negligent, they were themselves liable to divine punishment. The power of these ideas was such that this system of public jurisdiction over sexual morality only slowly decayed from the late seventeenth century onwards, and did so at an unequal rate in different parts of Europe. Meanwhile there developed in some areas a very elaborate system of social discipline exercised by a complex of overlapping jurisdictions. In England the church courts were the main forum for sexual offences and marital matters. But the secular justices of the peace were given statutory powers to deal with bastardy cases, especially those involving poor people who might be a burden on the poor rates. The London Bridewell, founded as a workhouse to cure idleness, in practice whipped and incarcerated large numbers of sexual offenders. At the end of the seventeenth century, when the coercive powers of the church courts were rapidly disappearing, voluntary Societies for Reformation of Manners, powered by strong religious sentiments, were founded in London and some other large towns to address what were perceived to be growing problems of prostitution and other forms of vice.[13]

The family household was thus the focus of ideas that gave it an importance far beyond the spheres of procreation, the upbringing of children, private conjugal relations, and domestic consumption that we associate it with today. As like as not it was also an important site of production, whether in manufacturing or in agriculture. It was the setting for much of the educational provision of the period (save for the more specialist kinds of book learning) and also important as the nursery of religious instruction. Developments associated with the Reformation and Counter-Reformation reinforced this role. In the sixteenth and seventeenth centuries, moreover, the role of the household as a political institution was re-emphasized. Jurists and moralists alike saw the family as the fundamental unit of civil society. Within it the husband was supposed to rule his wife, while husband and wife together exercised authority over children, servants and apprentices; the head of the household was hence answerable to higher authority for the conduct of those within his house. In the most developed versions of the political theory of the household, the 'government' of the householder over his wife, children and servants was seen as similar in nature to that of the prince over his subjects. Royal and patriarchal authority were mutually validating reflections of a divinely ordered hierarchy.[14]

What this meant for family relations in practice, and how far the tone and texture of family life changed over time, have been much debated. Historians have mostly abandoned the idea that relations between husbands and wives, parents and children were necessarily cold and authoritarian, even in the sixteenth and early seventeenth centuries when patriarchal theories were being most strongly promoted. The idea that there was a straightforward shift from patriarchal authoritarianism to companionate marriage by the early eighteenth century, as argued by Lawrence Stone, has likewise lost favour. Yet the notion that matrimonial relations were essentially unchanging in this period, as Alan Macfarlane has asserted in the case of England, is likewise unsatisfactory.[15] Ralph Houlbrooke has cautioned historians not to be misled by changes in the nature and abundance of source materials. Thus the shortage of personal letters between husbands and wives in the early part of the period, and the predominantly formal tone of such letters as do survive, should not necessarily be taken to show lack of sentiment in practice. As against this, it is now recognized that changes in the cultural milieu may themselves have had consequences in the emotional sphere. By the late seventeenth and eighteenth centuries, the freer expression of emotions in letters, diaries and the like, and the widespread availability of representations of emotions in drama, poetry and novels, helped to raise expectations and foster sentimental relationships.[16]

Apart from change over time, it is important to recognize that there was considerable variation from marriage to marriage, depending partly on the personal characteristics of particular husbands and wives – not to mention the diverse dynamics of relationships between children and their parents – but also on differences of occupational setting and social circumstance. If a wife was closely involved in her husband's business, whether this was farm production, textile manufacture, or buying and selling, the couple inevitably led their lives cheek by jowl. On the other hand, aristocratic husbands and wives might lead their lives largely in different spheres, as was to an extent true also when the husband pursued a professional career as a lawyer or physician. Such differences could not fail to affect relationships. Inevitably also there were mismatches between the pre-scriptions of moralists and jurists, the ideals that people actually aspired to, and everyday practice – invariably messier than how it was thought that things ought to be.

The basic legal framework affecting husband–wife relations was also more complex and more nuanced than is often realized. Very broadly, women surrendered property rights to their husbands on marriage. But they did not abrogate all claims and almost everywhere there existed a powerful notion of a communal fund administered for the benefit of both partners and their children. A marked feature of European (indeed Eurasian) society is the principle of dowry, whereby women had a claim on a share of the property of par-ents, characteristically bestowed at or before their marriage. In different parts of Europe, there developed a variety of means – some integral to systems of inheritance and family property law, others depending on individual initiative to create trusts or other special arrangements – whereby women's property rights within marriage were safeguarded.[17]

In many places, men had the legal right to coerce their wives physically, but this power was never untrammelled and was counterbalanced by a powerful ethos that not only con-demned cruelty but also fostered an expectation of good treatment. Over time these expectations were strengthened, not because of changes in basic ideas about the duties of husbands and wives, but as a result of the increasing diffusion of ideas that tended to soften social relations. Originating in higher or at least more educated social levels, the idea of 'civility', in particular, was so strong in fostering aspirations that its influence was rapidly diffused among people of middling social rank, certainly in towns and to an extent in the countryside as well. Changing theories about the physical constitution of women, promot-ing the idea that they were softer and more delicate, also had an impact. As a result, behaviour that in 1550 might have been regarded as harsh but acceptable – or even commendable if required to enforce patriarchal authority – was regarded two centuries later as cruel and unmanly. The simple reluctance of women to play their allotted role also played a part. Changing expectations are glimpsed in a Wiltshire case in 1690, when a woman contracting marriage 'made all the responses … very clear, without any scruple, until she came to the words "love, honour and obey", and then she boggled at the word "obey"'. But she carried on when she was assured that they were merely 'words of the [Book of] Common Prayer of course.'[18]

Yet at base the principle of female inferiority, and hence in the last resort the subjection of wives to the authority of their husbands, did remain extremely powerful. Thus women could by no means always count on good treatment; as ever, there were abused wives enough. On the other hand, the husband who lost control of his wife was everywhere despised. The cuckold whose wife had been unfaithful was the miserable object of derision; it was thought that fear of 'wearing the horns' could drive men mad. If a wife went as far as to beat her husband, the stock reaction in many areas was to stage a *charivari* or 'riding'.

This was a noisy, mocking demonstration, featuring a rider, often facing backwards, seated on a horse or ass, or astride a wooden pole. Sometimes the beaten husband himself was forced into this role; often a neighbour or an effigy was substituted; sometimes, yet again, both husband and wife were set 'bum to bum'. Some ridings were small in scale, but elaborate versions were truly spectacular events, enacted by hundreds of people and featuring the rough music of pots and pans, the raucous playing of musical instruments, parades of armed men, and even gunfire. The main participants, if they were not members of a youth group, as was sometimes the case in France, were usually people of lower social standing. But 'ridings' clearly made sense to all ranks of people, and they were often tolerated, if not actively encouraged, by the authorities. It is open to question whether these customs were a simple corrective, or whether they should rather be seen as a jocular reflection on the complexities of husband–wife relations, which rarely conformed exactly to prescription. Either way, the energy of *charivaris* testified to the power of the patriarchal ideal and the shocking spectacle of a termagant wife who turned the world upside down by transgressing so flagrantly the boundaries of permissible behaviour.[19]

Thus, from one angle, marriage was closely associated with dynasty, power, status, property and inheritance, and was thus highly desirable for all concerned. From another, the role of married householder might be seen as a burden or at least a challenge, carrying heavy social responsibilities and by no means easy to fulfil successfully. More basically, it was an intimate relationship that at best offered intense physical and emotional satisfactions but at worst was a hell on earth. This is why courtship was recognized to be so fraught with peril, quite apart from the practical difficulties of finding a suitable partner. It followed inevitably that courtship and marriage were shaped by a variety of expectations; were subject to many constraints, exercised not only by families but also by the wider community; and mediated through a complex of customs, practices and rituals. The task of deciphering these patterns is complicated by the nature and limitations of the available sources. Works of imaginative literature survive in abundance and have much to offer, but the interpretative problems they pose are formidable and they need to be used in tandem with real-life evidence. Legal records such as marriage contracts and wills have obvious utility, yet their formal nature limits the extent to which they can shed light on individual motives and emotions. Literature such as the German *Hausvaterbuch* and the household conduct books that had such a vogue in Elizabethan and early Stuart England are by their nature highly prescriptive, and cannot be taken as a safe guide either to the ideals that ordinary people subscribed to, or to life as it was led. Especially in the last respect, letters and diaries can offer richer pickings. But, as noted already, survivals are rare before the seventeenth century, if not later in some areas, and in any case tend to relate to the upper, or at least the better educated, ranks of society. The same is true of courtship narratives, which may be part and parcel of diaries, autobiographies or memoirs, or exist as independent items. The relatively rare survivals have the advantage of depicting events from the point of view of one or other of the two people involved in marriage negotiations; in particular, they not only shed light on matters such as the involvement of family and the intricacies of property negotiations, but may also illuminate the psychology – the hopes, fears and motives – of the participants.[20]

Sources bearing on the courtships of the peasantry and other lower social groups are inevitably in short supply. French historians writing in the 1960s and 1970s had recourse to the accounts of nineteenth- and early twentieth-century folklorists. The assumption was that the pace of change in peasant societies was so slow that these sources could, if handled cautiously, serve as windows on earlier periods. Nowadays such reasoning seems much less compelling, and it is moreover recognized that the prejudices – whether nostalgic, patronizing, or simply disparaging – of the educated, male, middle-class writers of such observations are a further barrier.[21] Contemporary church court records have proved a more valuable source, though they do have their pitfalls and limitations. In France, the bulk of survivals of *officialité* records – overall relatively restricted – are of most use for the study of courtship and marriage in the fifteenth and sixteenth centuries, though to an extent they have also been utilized for the late seventeenth. In some Protestant areas (late sixteenth- and early seventeenth-century Nîmes (Languedoc) is a prime example) the records of reformed discipline offer a rich source which is just beginning to be exploited fully.[22]

English historians have made extensive use of church court records for more or less the whole of the period. The materials include both disciplinary prosecutions – cases of bastardy, bridal pregnancy, and antenuptial fornication of all types shed much incidental light on courtship – and party-and-party suits over disputed marriage contracts or 'spousals'. They centred on a claim that a binding marriage contract in words of the present tense had been made between the parties, and the records of such cases, particularly the testimony of witnesses, commonly include not only an account of the words used in the contract ceremony, but also information – often extremely vivid – on prior meetings and negotiations, the exchange of gifts or 'tokens', and bargaining over money, land and goods. For the historian of the body, they also offer precious information on gestures: notably the clasping and unclasping of hands, repeated twice, that accompanied the words of contract; the 'loving kiss' that followed; and the mutual pledging in ale or wine that was a common embellishment.

Yet the apparent richness of these sources can easily mislead. As a matter of common form all marriage contract petitions set out a series of propositions that may be summarized as 'treaty and communication of marriage'; giving or exchange of gifts or 'tokens of marriage'; exchange of words of consent; acknowledgement of the contract by words and ritual actions in the presence of others; and the existence of a 'common fame' to this effect in the places where the couple were known. This gives the impression that courtship proceeded through a series of set stages and highlights the importance of gifts and tokens and of community recognition. Some historians, notably Diana O'Hara, have taken this impression at face value, but in reality practice was a great deal more fluid. By their very nature, moreover, spousals suits foreground the idea of a binding contract made in advance of the church wedding. Contemporaries recognized that by the late seventeenth century these were 'in great measure worn out of use'. But even for earlier periods there is great danger of exaggerating the significance of spousals – the folkloric nature of which appears to have a seductive fascination – and underestimating the social and legal importance of solemnization. Evidential problems of this sort help to explain why there are some sharp divergences of interpretation among historians of marriage contract litigation, though it is fair to say that regional differences, at present poorly understood, are an additional complication.[23]

What patterns emerge from the whole range of available sources? It is generally accepted that, merely in terms of family influence, people at the lowest social level had most freedom of choice. On the other hand, the least well-off were hampered by the strictures of poverty. It was not merely that lack of resources often forced people to delay the setting up of households, if it did not wholly prevent them. In many parts of Europe, the authorities actively sought to discourage poor people from getting married, especially in towns and cities. In Augsburg, for example, this policy was in action by the 1560s. In England, beginning in the late sixteenth century and increasingly in the seventeenth, even in rural parishes better-off people, represented by churchwardens and other office-holders, and sometimes aided and abetted by local clergy, deliberately stepped in to frustrate the marriages of the poor. This was the period when statutory poor relief funded by parish rates was becoming increasingly well established. The rate-payers were concerned that poor couples, if allowed to set up house together, would soon outrun their resources and burden the parish with a superfluity of poor children.[24]

Throughout Europe, at middling and upper social levels, the higher stakes in terms of status and property put a premium on the involvement of family and 'friends'. The extent of their power has been much debated. Some French historians, notably Jean-Louis Flandrin, have tended to assume that – in line with the letter of the law – family pressure was very strong, not only among the nobility but also among the better-off bourgeois and landed peasant society. Natalie Zemon Davis, while sympathetic to the idea that young people might have a degree of agency in the process, nonetheless suggested that obedience to parents was so strongly internalized that sons and daughters had little choice but to submit. On the other hand, even Flandrin admitted that over time there was an 'evolution towards the recognition of a right to inclination'; in other words, that parents had both a right and a duty to arrange marriages for their children, but not to insist on them if the latter expressed aversion. Already in 1978 René Pillorget was presenting a more nuanced picture, stressing how much it was in parents' interests to have a care for their children's happiness, and hence to give attention to their wishes; while more recent work, especially by historians concerned to demonstrate female agency, has mitigated the issue even further. In the case of England, a consensus rapidly emerged among historians reacting in the 1980s against the work of Lawrence Stone in the previous decade. It is now generally accepted that marriages that were wholly 'arranged' for dynastic or financial reasons were rare, except perhaps in the highest aristocratic circles. Across a very wide social spectrum, the ideal seems to have been the *multilateral* consent of all the interests involved. The early seventeenth-century moralist Matthew Griffith observed that 'on all parts there is commonly a willing consent and promise of marriage ... with consent of friends, and parties, some *Individuum Vagum*'s only excepted'.[25]

It is likewise recognized that powerful emotions, whether of love or aversion, could play an important part in matchmaking, and that personal attraction and sexual chemistry were crucial elements that parents ignored at their peril. To be sure, unbridled passion could be seen as a destructive force, indeed as a disease. This was especially so if it set children against their parents, or made individuals act in defiance of common sense; or if, in unrequited form, it corroded health and happiness; it was believed that, in extreme cases, people might die of love. On the other hand, the importance of love, or at least 'good liking', between the prospective bride and groom was seen as desirable. There was a rich vocabulary to describe the feelings of the heart and the behaviour to which they gave rise: 'love', 'fancy', 'fantasy', 'delight', 'dalliance', 'gestures of lovely liking'. By the later part of the period, if not at the beginning, notions of what we understand as romantic love were widely current and some parents were willing to accommodate them. The diary of Dudley Ryder, a law student in early eighteenth-century London, reveals him deeply besotted by a certain Sally Marshall. Though his father, a moderately prosperous draper in genteel circumstances, frankly expressed his grave doubts about her suitability, he also assured Dudley that if I was so deeply engaged in love as to interrupt me in my study or that I could not be easy without her, he could freely consent to my marrying of her, and would go himself to Mrs. Marshall and make up the match.[26]

Demographic and social realities also limited the power of parents. Given late ages at marriage and the prevalence of service and apprenticeship, many young people were not only physically at a distance from their families, but also hardly subject to their influence, by the time they came to contemplate marriage; indeed one or both parents might well be dead. Masters and mistresses sometimes acted *in loco parentis* in marriage matters, but their efforts, it would seem, were on the whole less effective than those of real parents. More generally, young people often enjoyed considerable freedom to meet and interact with their peers of the opposite sex. Some historians have been at pains to emphasize the contrary. Jean-Louis Flandrin, for example, stressed that formal distance governed relationships between young people in French peasant society. He was fain to admit that traditional patterns of sociability – pilgrimages, hiring and other fairs, *fêtes* and *veillées* (winter gatherings in barns to keep warm while spinning, telling stories and so on) – did offer many opportunities for contact, yet nonetheless insisted that the 'liberty of frequentation' was consistent with highly supervised gender relations and the parental control of marriage. More recent historians have been much more inclined to admit that many young people enjoyed a great deal of liberty. That this freedom could exist even in upper social levels is particularly evident in England, not least in royal court circles. Maids of honour and ladies in waiting may in theory have been closely chaperoned, but in practice they could easily evade these strictures.[27]

What, then, were the mechanisms for negotiating marriages and how were courtships conducted? Professional or amateur marriage brokers or go-betweens were often, but by no means invariably, employed. They were likely to be particularly useful in circumstances where there were ticklish issues of status and property at issue and, more basically, where information about suitable partners was not easy to come by; but there were also differences of regional and local custom. Also regionally diverse was the extent of community involvement. Famously in parts of France village youth groups staged *charivaris* when widows or widowers remarried – so reducing the pool of eligibles available to young people – or restricted the access of outsiders to local women. But in England such peasant customs were unknown.[28] The most fundamental rule of courtship practices was rooted in gender: normally the man, his family or their representatives made the first move. Beyond that, four basic models of courtship practice may be identified, albeit there were a number of hybrid forms and infinite variations in practice. In the first and most formal, that was most likely to occur in the wealthiest and most socially select circles, negotiations were undertaken by family representatives with their counterparts in the family of the prospective bride. In the most extreme cases, tantamount to arranged marriage, the young couple themselves had little if any individual choice and contact between them was restricted until agreement had been reached, or even until the actual wedding. In the second model, the man, usually with the consent and support of his own family, applied to the family of the woman on whom he had set his sights for permission to court her. This implied greater autonomy both on his part and, to an extent at least, on hers. Yet more freedom of choice was implicit in the third model, where a man made his addresses to a woman and, if these overtures were favourably received, one or both would seek the approval of their families. In these circumstances, property negotiations were likely to commence at a later stage of the proceedings, though they might then be very intense and, if agreement was not reached, the marriage might not go forward. The fourth model that was particularly prevalent among lower social groups, who could expect to inherit little or no property, but that was by no means wholly confined to them, involved little or no intervention by families. A man courted a woman and, if all went well, they agreed to marry. They might then seek the 'good will' of father, mother, or other family members, but in practice this was hardly more than a formality.

Cross-cutting the basic patterns of marriage formation were what Beatrice Gottlieb has splendidly characterized as 'cool' and 'warm' habits of courtship. Clearly, the more formal and distant the conduct of marriage negotiations, the more likely it was that amorous emotions, and their physical expression, would be kept in check; and this in turn depended on how high the stakes were, in terms of power, status and property. But the cool/warm spectrum also had personal and generational dimensions. It was perfectly possible for the young couple to develop warm inclinations, while their family negotiators did their best to restrain them and to keep a cool head themselves. In situations where there was little or no supervision of courtship, the couple might get very hot indeed. Gender politics also played a part. A hint, if not a promise, of marriage was a powerful ploy in seduction, while no doubt some women calculated that becoming pregnant was the best means they had of securing a partner.[29] If things went wrong the result could be an illegitimate birth with varying consequences: a source of scandal in high society; of hardship and shame for many women lower down the social scale; and a financial burden for the putative fathers, who in England, France and elsewhere were rigorously pursued to provide maintenance payments. Illegitimacy rates were nowhere very high but they did vary from region to region. They seem to have been higher in England than in France; and within England, births out of wedlock were more common in the north-west than elsewhere, at least until the seventeenth century.[30] Betrothal customs, it would seem, contributed to these contrasts: in Lancashire and Cheshire, spousals or 'handfasting' was commonly taken to license sexual relations in advance of the wedding in church, whereas elsewhere attitudes were more ambiguous, though everywhere in England the notion that a betrothed couple were 'man and wife before God' was commonly used as an excuse, if not a justification, for premarital sex. In France, the Counter-Reformation church viewed betrothal ceremonies or *fiançailles* with considerable suspicion, albeit with diverse outcomes in different parts of the kingdom. In the south the practice was anyway not strongly rooted in popular sentiment, so in many dioceses it proved possible to suppress it entirely. In northern France, on the other hand, the Church made *fiançailles* obligatory as a means of checking the validity of proposed unions, but insisted that the marriage ceremony should follow within a few days.[31]

In any event it is clear that the natural impulses of courting couples were a fact of life, but one that could to a large extent be accommodated within the normal processes of marriage formation. It is well established that in many parts of Europe, notably in England and to a lesser extent in France, a significant proportion of brides were pregnant at marriage; and, especially in lower social groups, this situation seems to have been viewed tolerantly or simply taken for granted. In some areas, such as Scandinavia, parts of Germany, and Piedmont (but not, it would seem, France and England) there were well-established 'bundling' customs, where courting couples were tacitly or openly allowed a great deal of physical intimacy – men visited women sleeping in haylofts in the summer, and couples were even allowed to lie together in one bed in the main house, perhaps with a bolster between them. These practices allowed intimacy to develop while safeguarding chastity; such was the theory, at least.[32]

The trials and tribulations of courtship having been surmounted, the actual wedding was an occasion for celebration. As the earlier parts of this discussion have indicated, the role of the Church in marriage celebrations varied in different parts of Europe and also changed over time. Inevitably, too, there were immense differences in the scale and scope of weddings. Partly this depended on the means of the couple and their families, but it was also a matter of how marriage fitted into wider patterns of kinship, patronage, and neighbourhood ties. A marriage could be (but was not necessarily) an occasion to demonstrate wealth, status and political clout. On the other hand, lavish weddings were, in theory at least, restricted by sumptuary laws in many parts of Europe. Fashion also played a part, to the extent that in some elevated social circles in the seventeenth century, there was a marked preference for the elegant simplicity of a quiet, secluded nuptial celebration. That said, a number of characteristic features of wedding celebrations may be identified. Strikingly they span the social scale. Indeed it is plain that some usages already had a talismanic significance; so customs that might at first sight seem coarse or plebeian were observed even by sophisticated members of the upper classes because they were the right thing to do – and it was perhaps unlucky to omit them. Usually the bride was led to the church, to the accompaniment of more or less raucous music, by relatives, friends and neighbours. The white bridal gown is a modern invention; but both bride and groom were dressed in their best, and if the woman lacked a suitable garment a kind neighbour might lend one. Ribbons and gloves were a common feature; sometimes the groom bestowed pairs of gloves on those who attended. The actual marriage ceremony was followed by a dinner, which might amount to a feast, where the woman 'sat like a bride'. Sometimes this was an act of lavish hospitality extended to the guests or even to all comers. But on occasion the guests contributed by paying for their own dinners, or the event was organized as a 'bride ale', designed to yield a profit for the benefit of the nuptial pair. Dinner was followed by dancing, sometimes including special measures traditionally regarded as meet for weddings. These morphed into pranks and horseplay, in which the bride's garters and stockings were likely to play a part. Finally the couple were assisted into bed, with any amount of decorous or indecorous ceremony. Thus their married life began.[33]

Notes

1 William Higford, *The Institution of a Gentleman*, London: A. W. for William Lee, 1660, p. 11.
2 For fuller treatment, see Michael Mitterauer and Reinhard Sieder, *The European Family: Patriarchy to Partnership from the Middle Ages to the Present*, trans. Karla Oosterveen and Manfred Hörzinger, Oxford: Basil Blackwell, 1982; Beatrice Gottlieb, *The Family in the Western World from the Black Death to the Industrial Age*, Oxford and New York: Oxford University Press, 1993; André Burguière, Christiane Klapisch-Zuber, Martine Segalen and Françoise Zonabend, *A History of the Family: Volume II. The Impact of Modernity*, trans. Sarah Hanbury Tenison, Cambridge, MA: Belknap Press, 1996, chs 1 and 2; Jack Goody, *The European Family: an Historico-Anthropological Essay*, Oxford: Blackwell, 2000; Katherine A. Lynch, *Individuals, Families, and Communities in Europe, 1200–1800: The Urban Foundations of Western Society*, Cambridge, Cambridge University Press, 2003. On France and England see François Lebrun, *La Vie conjugale sous l'Ancien Régime*, Paris: Armand Colin, 1975; Jean-Louis Flandrin, *Familles: parenté, maison, sexualité dans l'ancienne societe*, Paris: Hachette, 1976; Lawrence Stone, *The Family, Sex and Marriage in England, 1500–1800*, London: Weidenfeld & Nicolson, 1977; René Pillorget, *La Tige et le rameau. Familles*

anglaise et française XVIe–XVIIIe siècle, Paris: Calmann-Lévy, 1979; Ralph A. Houlbrooke, *The English Family, 1450–1700*, London and New York: Longman, 1984.

3   Steven Ozment, *When Fathers Ruled: Family Life in Renaissance Europe*, Cambridge, MA: Harvard University Press, 1983, pp. 80–89; Robert M. Kingdon, *Adultery and Divorce in Calvin's Geneva*, Cambridge, MA: Harvard University Press, 1995; Lawrence Stone, *Road to Divorce: England, 1530–1987*, Oxford: Clarendon Press, 1990.

4   R. B. Outhwaite, *Clandestine Marriage in England, 1500–1850*, London and Rio Grande: The Hambledon Press, 1995; Rebecca Probert, *Marriage Law and Practice in the Long Eighteenth Century*, Cambridge: Cambridge University Press, 2009.

5   Ozment, *When Fathers Ruled*, ch. 1; Trevor Dean and K. J. P. Lowe (eds), *Marriage in Italy, 1300–1650*, Cambridge: Cambridge University Press, 1998, pp. 2–7; Pillorget, *La Tige et le rameau*, ch. 1.

6   John Hajnal, 'European Marriage Patterns in Perspective' in D. V. Glass and D. E. C. Eversley (eds), *Population in History*, London: Edward Arnold, 1965, pp. 101–43; John Hajnal, 'Two Kinds of Preindustrial Household Formation System', *Population and Development Review* 8, 1982, pp. 449–94.

7   Tine De Moor and Jan Luiten van Zanden, 'Girl Power: The European Marriage Pattern and Labour Markets in the North Sea Region in the Late Medieval and Early Modern Period', *Economic History Review* 63, 2010, pp. 1–33.

8   Vivien Brodsky Elliott, 'Single Women in the London Marriage Market: Age, Status and Mobility, 1598–1619' in R. B. Outhwaite (ed.), *Marriage and Society: Studies in the Social History of Marriage*, London: Europa, 1981, pp. 81–100.

9   Marzio Barbagli, 'Three Household Formation Systems in Eighteenth- and Nineteenth-Century Italy' in David I. Kertzer and Richard Saller (eds), *The Family in Italy from Antiquity to the Present*, New Haven and London: Yale University Press, 1991, pp. 250–70.

10 Pillorget, *La Tige et le rameau*, pp. 171–83; Alain Collomp, 'Families: Habitations and Cohabitations' in Roger Chartier (ed.), *A History of Private Life III. Passions of the Renaissance*, trans. Arthur Goldhammer, Cambridge, MA, and London: Belknap Press, 1989, pp. 493–529; Lutz K. Berkner and John W. Shaffer, 'The Joint Family in the Nivernais', *Journal of Family History* 3, 1978, pp. 150–62.

11 Audiger [no forename], *La Maison reglée, et l'art de diriger la maison d'un grand seigneur*, 3rd edn, Amsterdam: Paul Marret, 1700 [1692], pp. 21–23, 99–100; Pillorget, *La Tige et le rameau*, pp. 86–87.

12 Pillorget, *La Tige et le rameau*, pp. 220–23; Eva Cantarella, 'Homicides of Honor: The Development of Italian Adultery Law over Two Millennia' in David I. Kertzer and Richard P. Saller (eds), *The Family in Italy from Antiquity to the Present*, New Haven and London: Yale University Press, 1991, pp. 229–44.

13 Martin Ingram, 'History of Sin or History of Crime? The Regulation of Personal Morality in England, 1450–1750' in Heinz Schilling with Lars Behrisch, *Institutionen, Instrumente und Akteure sozialer Kontrolle und Disziplinierung im frühneuzeitlichen Europa*, Frankfurt am Main: Vittorio Klostermann, 1999, pp. 87–103; Faramerz Dabhoiwala, *The Origins of Sex: A History of the First Sexual Revolution*, London: Allen Lane, 2012, prologue and ch. 1.

14 Susan Dwyer Amussen, *An Ordered Society: Gender and Class in Early Modern England*, Oxford: Basil Blackwell, 1988, ch. 2.

15 Goody, *European Family*, pp. 1–14; cf. Edward Shorter, *The Making of the Modern Family*, London: Collins, 1976; Stone, *Family, Sex and Marriage*; Alan Macfarlane, *Marriage and Love in England: Modes of Reproduction 1300–1840*, Oxford: Blackwell, 1986.

16 Houlbrooke, *English Family*, p. 4; Martin Ingram, 'Family and Household' in Arthur F. Kinney (ed.), *A Companion to Renaissance Drama*, Oxford, and Malden, MA: Blackwell, 2002, pp. 106–7.

17 Lynch, *Individuals, Families, and Communities*, p. 51; De Moor and Luiten van Zanden, 'Girl Power', pp. 7–11.

18 London Metropolitan Archives, DL/C/146, no. 28.

19 Daniel Fabre, 'Families: Privacy versus Custom' in Chartier (ed.), *A History of Private Life III*, pp. 531–69; Norbert Schindler, 'Guardians of Disorder: Rituals of Youthful Culture at the Dawn of the Modern Age' in Giovanni Levi and Jean-Claude Schmitt (eds), *A History of Young People in the West. Volume I: Ancient and Medieval Rites of Passage*, Cambridge, MA, and London: Belknap Press, 1997, pp. 240–82.

20 David Cressy, *Birth, Marriage and Death: Ritual, Religion, and the Life-Cycle in Tudor and Stuart England*, Oxford: Oxford University Press, 1997, chs 10–11.

21 Jean-Louis Flandrin, *Les Amours paysannes. Amour et sexualité dans les campagnes de l'ancienne France (XVIe–XIXe siècle)*, Paris: Gallimard, 1975, pp. 17–18ff.

22 Jean-Louis Flandrin, 'Les Créantailles troyennes (XVe–XVIIe siècle)' in Flandrin, *Le Sexe et l'occident. Évolution des attitudes et des comportements*, Paris: Seuil, 1981, pp. 61–82; Jacques Solé, *Être femme en 1500: la vie quotidienne dans le diocèse de Troyes*, Paris: Perrin, 2000; Suzannah Lipscomb, 'Crossing Boundaries: Women's Gossip, Insults and Violence in Sixteenth-Century France', *French History* 25, 2011, pp. 408–26.

23 Diana O'Hara, *Courtship and Constraint: Rethinking the Making of Marriage in Tudor England*, Manchester: Manchester University Press, 2000. Other studies, with varying emphases, include Ralph Houlbrooke, 'The Making of Marriage in Mid-Tudor England: Evidence from the Records of Matrimonial Contract Litigation', *Journal of Family History* 10, 1985, pp. 339–52; Peter Rushton, 'The Testament of Gifts: Marriage Tokens and Disputed Contracts in North-East England, 1560–1630', *Folk Life* 24, 1985–86, pp. 25–31; Peter Rushton, 'Property, Power and Family Networks: The Problem of Disputed Marriage in Early Modern England', *Journal of Family History* 11, 1986, pp. 205–19; Martin Ingram, *Church Courts, Sex and Marriage in England, 1570–1640*, Cambridge: Cambridge University Press, 1987, ch. 6; Laura Gowing, *Domestic Dangers: Women, Words and Sex in Early Modern London*, Oxford: Oxford University Press, 1996, ch. 5; Loreen L. Giese, *Courtships, Marriage Customs, and Shakespeare's Comedies*, Basingstoke: Palgrave Macmillan, 2006.

24 Lyndal Roper, *The Holy Household: Women and Morals in Reformation Augsburg*, Oxford: Clarendon Press, 1989, pp. 138–40; Steve Hindle, 'The Problem of Pauper Marriage in Seventeenth-Century England', *Transactions of the Royal Historical Society* 6th series, 8, 1998, pp. 71–89.

25 Flandrin, *Les Amours paysannes*, pp. 36–58, 87–88, 98–100; Natalie Zemon Davis, 'Ghosts, Kin and Progeny: Some Features of Family Life in Early Modern France', *Daedalus* 106:2, 1977, pp. 87–114 (108); Pillorget, *La Tige et le rameau*, pp. 49–63; Solé, *Être femme*, pp. 107–8, 111, 251–52; Ingram, *Church Courts, Sex and Marriage*, pp. 137–42.

26 Ingram, *Church Courts, Sex and Marriage*, p. 141; *The Diary of Dudley Ryder, 1715–1716*, ed. William Matthews, London: Methuen & Co., 1939, pp. 326–27.

27 Flandrin, *Les Amours paysannes*, pp. 110–21; Solé, *Être femme*, p. 111; Johanna Rickman, *Love, Lust and License in Early Modern England: Illicit Sex and the Nobility*, Aldershot: Ashgate, 2008.

28 Flandrin, *Les Amours paysannes*, pp. 108–10; Schindler, 'Guardians of Disorder', pp. 249–50.

29 Gottlieb, *Family*, pp. 62–64.

30 Lebrun, *La Vie conjugale*, pp. 96–103; Flandrin, *Les Amours paysannes*, pp. 207–30; Pillorget, *La Tige et le rameau*, ch. 6.

31 Richard Adair, *Courtship, Illegitimacy and Marriage in Early Modern England*, Manchester and New York: Manchester University Press, 1996; Burguière et al., *History of the Family. II*, p. 126.

32 Flandrin, *Les Amours paysannes*, pp. 122–27.

33 Gottlieb, *Family*, pp. 79–83; Cressy, *Birth, Marriage, and Death*, ch. 16.

18

MARRIAGE AND COMPANIONATE
IDEALS SINCE 1750

Kate Fisher

An apparent contradiction confronts the study of courtship and marriage in the nineteenth and twentieth centuries. At first sight, it would seem incontrovertible that the nineteenth and twentieth centuries have seen profound social, economic and cultural changes which have transformed European society and individuals' lives, choices, relationships and marriages. The context in which individuals choose to get married and what they expect or desire from the relationship has been fundamentally changed by, for example, the reorganization of communities following industrialization, the rise of city living, the demands of factory life, the changing religious landscape, the development of a yet-stronger middle class, the growth of a consumer culture within an increasingly advanced capitalist system, the emergence of feminism and changing ideas of gender roles within the family, the spread of birth control and contraception, and the invention of medicalized sexual identities.

Indeed much of the demographic evidence relating to the structure of marriage and courtship attests to such changes. Across northern western Europe (England, Scotland, northern France, the Netherlands, Germany and Austria) a unique and long-standing marriage regime dominated in which age at marriage was often comparatively high (25–26 for females and 27–28 for males) alongside a high proportion (10–20 per cent) of people never marrying. This regime is generally seen to divide Europe in half between east and west, though there was significant regional variation, and Mediterranean Europe in particular does not quite fit this picture.[1] Patterns changed during the twentieth century when, alongside the massive and sustained reduction in average family size, as a result of the widespread adoption of forms of birth control or family limitation (including abstinence, withdrawal and abortion alongside methods such as condoms, caps, the Pill and forms of sterilization/vasectomy), age at first marriage fell across northern and western Europe and the percentage of people marrying also rose – especially in Sweden, England and Norway, but also significantly in France, West Germany, Italy, Spain and Portugal (Ireland remained an exception). This increase in the popularity of marriage was accompanied in northern Europe by a massive rise in the levels of divorce (following legal changes), particularly after the 1960s (although the picture in southern and eastern Europe remained different with divorce remaining relatively rare until the 1970s and 1980s).[2] In the last decades of the twentieth century the structure of marriage has changed again across Europe: marriage rates have declined significantly and age at first marriage has also risen alongside the growth of various forms of cohabitation (as an alternative to marriage, as a form of 'trial' before marriage or as part of serial shorter-term relationships).[3] Yet, despite these transformations in the circumstances and social frameworks through which individual marriages and sexual relationships were lived, there is a strange continuity in historians' debates about marriage in very different centuries (eighteenth, nineteenth and twentieth).

The orthodox general interpretation of the twentieth century sees the period from 1900–1960 as encompassing the rise of the 'companionate marriage'. This is represented as a major transformation away from the previous patriarchal 'Victorian' marriage towards a 'new' form of romantic, intimate, loving and egalitarian partnership. This account is particularly dominant in the literature on Britain and north America, but European historians tell a similar story.[4] Yet, as shown in Martin Ingram's chapter, the general (albeit contested) consensus among historians of early modern courtship and marriage is that the 'companionate marriage' had been established as a dominant ideology much earlier, widely adopted at least by 1830, but well under way in the eighteenth century. As Sharon Marcus summarizes: 'Historians of kinship argue endlessly about exactly when it first became common to think of marriage as the union of soulmates ... [but] by the 1830s companionate marriage was the standard ... in all classes.'[5] So we are faced with a problem. If the companionate marriage had arrived in all classes across western Europe (and America) by at least 1830, how could it then emerge, develop and transform relationships in the twentieth century? How can the companionate marriage rise and rise and rise again? How can we make sense of this confusing literature?[6]

One route out would be to see the nineteenth century as a moment of backlash when the companionate ideal disappeared only to be resurrected at the start of the twentieth century.[7] However, and this is where the problem becomes yet more puzzling, historians of the nineteenth century, while much less concerned about the companionate marriage question, nonetheless frequently see companionate marriage as core to nineteenth-century western values too.[8] A. James Hammerton charts the rise of a 'companionate marriage' ideal in the mid-nineteenth century that was intimately linked to the separate spheres ideology.[9] Helena Michie characterizes the nineteenth century as a consolidation period when the 'new' companionate marriage ideal that stressed 'personal liking and sexual attraction' (which she prefers to call the 'conjugal marriage') continued to compete 'for cultural primacy with conceptions of marriage based on financial interest and familial ties ... gradually gaining ground and spreading across social classes'.[10] Jesse Battan presents twentieth-century companionate values as a development of nineteenth-century trends, arguing (with reference to America) that there was 'a profound shift in the emotional texture of married life in the nineteenth century' that marked 'an essential step in the emergence of the companionate model as the dominant ideal of marital behavior in the twentieth century'.[11] Thus, the picture remains puzzling with historians heralding the arrival of the companionate marriage again and again at various very different periods of history.

There are yet further grounds for concern. Although particularly dominant in historians' analyses of Britain and America, historians of Europe also chart changing marriage values in these terms, as do historians of non-European countries.[12] It seems extraordinary, given what we know about the diversity of European experiences, to see the 'companionate' marriage as having spread across Europe, America and the wider world. Indeed, scholarship has been increasingly critical of the various 'modernization' theories that once dominated world history and sensitive to the differences between European countries – and also between the 'West and the Rest' – alongside an increasing awareness of regional differences within nations: between rural/urban existence; between racially organized subcultures; among different religious groupings; between different social groups and classes. Although recent scholarship remains interested in transnational questions, it recognizes that ideas and debates, even as they appeared all over the globe, were always remade in particular local contexts.[13] As yet, however, the discussion of the companionate marriage has been relatively immune to such attacks, and it lingers on looking increasingly outdated.

This chapter seeks to make sense of the literature on companionate marriage, and highlights the limited usefulness of the 'companionate marriage' category for historians. It argues, first, that there is no discrete or concrete set of values, practices or beliefs associated with the companionate marriage. Rather it is a fluid concept with a wide range of permutations, whose important differences are elided and ignored when historians draw too loosely on the companionate marriage terminology. Second, the companionate marriage terminology is not merely loose but also itself tied up with the dynamics of nineteenth- and twentieth-century contestations about marriage. To use the term without sufficient care is to miss the complex politics at stake in its use. However, this is not to argue that the evidence drawn on by historians investigating the 'rise of companionate marriage' are not of historical significance. Between 1800 and 2000 there is a rich history of changing marital values, debates about the purpose and nature of marriage, and attempts to reform marriage, to be traced. In doing so, historians need to look behind the apparent similarities in the ways in which marriages are described and analyse the particular implications of such constructions in specific contexts. Historians need to avoid the unreflective adoption of overused and imprecise categories and concentrate instead on interrogating the politics of language within the sources to provide us with a much more nuanced picture of the contested ideals that underpinned marital relationships and a more sensitive mapping of historical change.

(Re)defining the companionate model

The first difficulty in adopting the conceptual framework of the 'companionate marriage' to analyse historical changes in marriage is that it is not entirely clear exactly what a companionate marriage is, and what it is not. Far from being a defined ideal, the concept itself embraces a number of possible meanings and has a varied (even conflicting) set of associations. This fuzziness is in part due to its multi-faceted history: the model has acquired ideologically diverse proponents in the course of its intellectual elaboration over several decades across a range of geographical locations. The term 'companionate marriage' first emerged in the twentieth century and has been at the heart of debates about marriage ever since. Yet during this period the companionate ideal has taken many forms. Initially, the 'companionate marriage' was used to refer to an open union, and the main thrust of the concept was that such unions could be freely entered into and left without the need for legal divorce (provided there were no children). This version of the 'companionate marriage' was popularized across America and Europe by American judge Ben Lindsey, in a series of radio addresses, magazine articles and lectures, and eventually an influential book in 1927.[14] This version of the companionate ideal became part of radical intellectual thinking on sexuality, free love, promiscuity and alternatives to state-formalized monogamy (although Ben Lindsey himself resisted such ideas). A central plank in Alexandra Kollontai's vision of a new morality rooted in women's economic independence and sexual autonomy, for example, was a similar version of the 'companionate marriage'.[15]

This was not the only version of the companionate marriage developed in the interwar period. Shortly after the use of the term 'companionate marriage' by Lindsey and Knight and its discussion in radical and reformist groups, it was used by American and British politicians and sociologists to champion a more traditional ideal of marital relations, rooted in a gendered division of marital roles. Linked specifically to a male breadwinner model of economic production, this version of the companionate ideal was focused less on the ideas of sexual freedom or female emancipation (though elements of these debates were present) and more on the nature of the interpersonal relationships between couples. Particularly influential in this discourse was Burgess and Locke's *The Family from Institution to Companionship*, which, although published in 1945, drew upon ideas that Burgess had been developing since the 1920s. It argued that 'patriarchal families' had been replaced by the 'companionate marriage', whose prominent factors were 'demonstration of affection; sharing of experiences; mutual confiding; sharing in the making of decisions; companionship'.[16] In France, sociologists such as Robert Boudet in 'La famille bourgeoise' or Pierre Drouin's article in *Le Monde*, 'Un nouveau type de couple' reveal the similar debates that occurred (slightly later) in post-war France,[17] while in Britain elements of Burgess' ideal are apparent in the models of marriage that underpinned the welfare reforms developed in the Beveridge report, that imagined a male breadwinner working in a team with his home-based wife.[18] This version of the companionate marriage was framed around the idea of the male breadwinner and the female 'homemaker'.[19]

Various elements of this version of the companionate ideal can be traced in a range of contemporary texts. Marriage manuals, such as Marie Stopes' *Married Love* and van de Velde's European best seller *Ideal Marriage*, can be read as guides to practising and achieving this type of companionate marriage.[20] Adrian Bingham has charted the various threads of the companionate ideal articulated through British newspapers. Jane Lewis has documented the relationship between an emerging Christian version of the companionate ideal and the development of the marriage guidance movement, and Stephen Brooke has charted the conflicting ways in which left-wing politics in Britain, particularly within the Labour Party, discussed a companionate ideology within a particular gender politics that emphasized the need to reform the working conditions of heroic male workers and improve the domestic conditions of mothers and children.[21] However, it would be a mistake to conclude that this vision was unified or discrete. This rendering of the companionate ideal had a variety of elements and emphases, articulated around fluid and ambiguous buzz terms such as sharing, mutuality, companionship, friendship, partnership, democracy, affection, love, sexual attraction, and joint decision making. Various different articulations of marital ideals around these companionate concepts took rather different forms.

By the 1960s and 1970s there was a further fragmentation in the ambiguous ideology of the companionate marriage ideal, with articulations of marriage models ever more focused on the issue of marital equality. Although the language of egalitarianism had been part of various understandings of the companionate ideal since the 1920s, increasingly those championing companionate models saw the equality of husbands and wives as the central plank of the concept.[22] At the same time, others attacked those who claimed to have witnessed the arrival of the companionate marriage by highlighting the ways in which such marriages remained unequal and structured by sexual subordination. Feminist sociologists in particular questioned the extent to which modern marriages were genuinely egalitarian or companionate, highlighting the imprecision in the concept of companionship and the hollowness of the egalitarianism it promised.[23] They pointed out the thin evidence support-ing the sociological surveys on the growth of companionship, the difficulties in determining what level of sharing of domestic activities or decision making distinguished a patriarchal from a companionate marriage, and the continuing tensions and conflicts within marriages about conjugal roles and gendered power relationships.[24] Ann Oakley, for example, con-cluded that 'only a minority of husbands give the kind of help that assertions of equality in modern marriage imply'.[25] This debate reconfigured the companionate marriage as one that required an equal relationship.

These shifts in the criteria used to determine what a companionate marriage looked like over the course of the twentieth century makes the attempt to explore the extent to which marriages in the twentieth century did, or did not, become more companionate exceed-ingly difficult, if not misguided. As Janet Finch and Penny Summerfield have pointed out, the 'comradely' marriage was used in the twentieth century to describe a wide range of domestic arrangements 'from the notion that there should be greater companionship between partners whose roles essentially were different, through the idea of marriage as "teamwork", to the concept of marriages based on "sharing" implying the breakdown of clearly demarcated roles'.[26] Similarly, Marcus Collins also notes that '"Modern Demo-cratic Marriage" went by many names – partnership marriage, symmetrical marriage, loose-knit, joint-conjugal marriage'. But few historians have dissected the different elements of the companionate marriage ideology or incorporated an understanding of the flexibility of the concept into their analysis. For Collins, all the different descriptions of marital ideologies 'meant one thing: companionship'.[27]

Yet more confusingly still (informed by twentieth-century configurations of the compa-nionate ideal) historians have, since the 1970s, asked whether marriages in earlier historical periods might also be investigated using the (ambiguous) framework of the companionate marriage. The understanding of the concept of companionate marriage employed by these historians is significantly different from that used by twentieth-century historians and sociologists, but equally ambiguous, fluid and intangible. Without any clear criteria for mapping or measuring marriages as companionate or not, historians nonetheless debate the extent to which marriages in earlier times involved affection or love between spouses, the centrality of sex to the relationship, and the degree to which couples shared interests or engaged in joint decision making. While all these elements in debates about the compa-nionate marriage in earlier times are related to the various twentieth-century marriage models, it is clear the companionate marriage in the eighteenth or nineteenth century looked very different to its twentieth-century counterparts. The dominance of the language of the companionate marriage in the historiography of the eighteenth and nineteenth centuries has endured, despite coming under sustained criticism since the early 1980s. For example, Wrightson and Houlbrooke both argued that there were no clearly defined dif-ferences between supposedly opposite marriage models: patriarchal and companionate. Linda Pollock presented the impossibility of categorizing marriages as companionate or patriarchal given the dynamic and changing nature of marital relations, and, more recently, Joanne Bailey has highlighted the failure of companionate marriage models to capture the complex of codes of masculinity and femininity or to help us understand the impact of structural, economic and cultural forces on the variety of marriage forms.[28]

Moreover, among historians of the eighteenth and nineteenth centuries the companionate marriage model acquired a particular focus, which was much less central to twentieth-century models. For these historians the companionate marriage is characterized by a courtship in which couples were free to choose a spouse on the grounds of love or affection without parental, kin or community interference. In this way the companionate marriage is presented as the antithesis of the arranged union (presumed to have dominated in earlier periods). This focus is also dominant in global cross-national studies, which differentiate western marriage from 'un-companionate' unions elsewhere in the world. Such literature champions a supposedly western focus on 'marriage for love' in opposition to other cultures where marriage is 'propagational', concerned with building family and community relationships through children.[29] Imperial historians also draw upon this construction: debates about marriage in imperial India, for example, such as colonial opposition to child betrothals, are often framed as a clash between a western 'companionate' model of marriage and indigenous practices.[30] However, this construction of the companionate marriage and the courtship practices associated with it is again ambiguous and difficult to map. Clearly differentiating between arranged and free unions has proved exceedingly difficult, as Martin Ingram's discussion of courtship and marriage before 1750 also shows, with structures of courtship involving a complex nexus of people (family, community and individual men and women) in the negotiation of emotional, economic, class and dynastic concerns in subtle and intricate ways. As F. M. L. Thompson notes, 'it is not at all clear that the romantic-liberal alternative model in which "pure" affection and attraction lead to love matches through random and unstructured contacts that somehow enable soulmates to get together, has any known historical place in any historical society.' Instead, marriage choices inevitably took place within 'powerful conventions and institutionalised rituals'.[31] Research into courtship in the twentieth century has revealed these subtle rituals, and individuals' narratives often downplayed the significance of passion or romance, highlighting rather the ways in which social convention, family pressure and pragmatism drew them into marriage.[32] Kertzer's research on Europe also collapses any easy distinction between companionate courtship and arranged marriages in outlining the structures which determined how and where young people met, and the ways in which these served to ensure that parental concerns regarding the choice of spouse by their children were subtly maintained and their children's behaviour policed.[33] Thus, the construction of the companionate marriage in opposition to arranged unions opposes criteria which are not readily distinguished, and historians should avoid pitting pragmatic choices in opposition to passionate ones and the individuals' desires against those of parents, family or community, in an attempt to categorize marriages according to ill-defined, unwieldy and imprecise companionate models.

These confusions are potentially resolved by acknowledging that there is no single model of companionate marriage, and that specific historical contexts determine the shape of debate about companionate ideals. Historians are, of course, aware that there are significant differences between the 'companionate' models of marriage circulating in the twentieth century and those that informed contested views of marriage in the nineteenth century, which were, in turn, distinct from the parameters framing companionate ideals in earlier centuries.[34] A close reading of the historiography on companionate models of marriage could produce subtle trajectories of the changing versions of these models. Each of the vague and fluid elements of the companionate ideals could be examined in this way. Taking, for example, the emotional bond between partners, it could be convincingly argued, using the early nineteenth century as a starting point, that a companionate marriage ideal that saw marriage as a relationship of affectionate friendship was increasingly dominant. Then, one might argue, this idea took on new threads, as it became cemented into Victorian society. In particular, it developed a new emphasis on the romantic element of the marital relationship, transforming the friendship model of the companionate marriage into one in which conceptions of love were central to the image of ideal relationships between men and women.[35] Subsequently, or so the argument would go, during the twentieth century, the companionate marriage ideal continued but was again reshaped to meet a newly sexualized world. At this point the sexual compatibility of partners became fundamental to companionate marriage models, alongside the romantic friendship that was also to underpin it. Thus, we might distinguish between Victorian companionate models in which sex was less central (where indeed the focus on romance was in tension with the passions of sex which were viewed as destabilizing and unpredictable), and twentieth-century models which viewed the romantic union between a married couple as requiring nourishment in the form of regular and mutually satisfying sexual encounters.[36] Similar accounts of the changes in models of companionate marriage could be produced for the other broad themes that underpin them: the patterns of courtship; the conceptions of power and authority; the framework of decision making; the negotiation of shared concerns, interests and activities; and so on. This would produce a dynamic history of companionate marriage which acknowledges the ways in which companionate marriage ideals shifted over time. However, we might argue that this would be an artificial and ultimately unhelpful attempt to cling on to the language of the companionate marriage. The continued use of this terminology to categorize marriage is detrimental in a variety of ways: it fails to focus on the significant differences between models of marriage, and it encourages historians to gloss over such distinctions, or to view them as subtle variations of each other. Moreover, such an approach ignores one of the most important aspects of the language of companionship – its rhetorical power – and a focus on the contestations over marriage is lost from the analysis. Not only was there no one companionate ideal, but various depictions of marriage, which drew upon a similar language, were directly opposed to each other.

The rhetorics of the companionate model

The continued and recurrent use of the terminology of the 'companionate marriage' to explore changing marital ideals or changing spousal relations during the nineteenth and twentieth centuries is more than just slippery linguistic imprecision. The companionate marriage is not simply a woolly set of interrelated ideas used rather too loosely by rather too many commentators, sociologists and historians. It is a set of ideas with changing but powerful political meanings and social significances. For those debating marriage during the twentieth century a companionate terminology became associated with progressive and positive ideals, and was widely adopted and appropriated by a range of different voices. During the twentieth century companionate language was used to support a range of different political standpoints with regard to marriage: as progressive and civilized, modern and anti-Victorian, radical and reformist, or conservative and traditional. A focus on the politics of such debates needs to be at the heart of historical analysis, as does an awareness that the different visions of the companionate marriage (outlined above) are indicative of these political tussles.[37]

It is equally important that historians recognize the ways in which much of the material available to twentieth-century historians to investigate the nature of individuals' experiences, such as social surveys, questionnaires, material from marriage guidance orga-nizations, the archives of social organizations, documents from welfare services, or responses to marital advice literature, is often inextricably linked to particular and specific socio-political perspectives on marriage. The politicized language of companionship is embedded in the documents historians rely upon and the history of marital relations cannot easily be separated from the complicated contemporary debates about the nature, history, problems and future of marriage – debates that were embroiled in social policy, class politics and social activism.

Most versions of a companionate ideal stressed the modernity of their model and used the term to denigrate other models of marriage as primitive, backward, old-fashioned or outdated. Burgess and Locke's version of the companionate marriage, articulated in *The Family from Institution to Companionship*, for example, presented the companionate marriage as the end point in the development of a civilized America which, following the rise in the status of women, the development of an industrial economy, secularization and urban life, had left primitive traditions of the past behind. Similarly, in 1931 Müller-Lyer distinguished the companionate marriage (which in this formulation was based on 'personal love') from less civilized forms of marriage in earlier times based on 'primitive love' or 'family love'.[38] To use the language of companionate models is to reinforce such politics of progress – politics which often reinforced class, regional and racial prejudices. Indeed, this association between the companionate marriage and progressive modernity has led some to detect an orientalist set of prejudices within the various articu-lations of the companionate marriage category in the twentieth century (particularly among sociologists and anthropologists).[39] The early twentieth-century language of companionship in marriage was part of the positioning by western Europe of itself as modern (urban, industrial, secular, individualistic) in direct and explicit contrast to pre-modern European societies on the one hand, and exotic, non-European ones on the other. The work of nineteenth-century anthropologists constructed a progressive and evo-lutionary narrative contrasting the civility of modern companionate models of marriage (this version tended to be patriarchal) as opposed to those found in primitive tribes or past societies; whereas during the twentieth century alternative viewpoints, such as those of Westermarck and Malinowski, highlighted the enduring appeal of companionate models of marriage (ones which emphasized the emotional bond between two individuals) across human history, which were deemed appropriate in savage and civilized societies alike.[40] Early twentieth-century politics of companionship were indebted to such anthropological material.[41] For example, Stephen Lassonde's work reveals the racial and imperial pre-judices that informed sociologists' investigations of courtship practices among Italian immigrant communities in America.[42] Such investigations drew on a language of back-wardness in criticizing the direct role played by immigrant parents in their children's courtships and of positive modernity in presenting American codes of dating as existing within a companionate framework, and as likely to create enduring partnerships of conjugal harmony.[43]

Similarly, the condemnation of forms of 'arranged marriage' in colonial contexts, such as India, also helped construct a western companionate model of marriage by choice and for love as superior and more civilized (a tendency which continues in modern discourses too).[44] There is thus a danger that historians, in continuing to debate whether or not, and when, the 'companionate marriage' took hold in western society, are unthinkingly reinfor-cing orientalist binaries and feeding a crude teleology which sees the 'companionate marriage' as a globally influential modern vision of marriage and changing marriage patterns across the world as examples of the spread of western values. To examine marriage patterns across the world and assess them on scales of 'companionateness' (given the fluid and imprecise nature of the category) as Hirsch and Wardlow point out, runs the risk of serving up 'reheated modernization theory in which inexorable social and economic changes produce progress – progress that can be measured by the degree to which the consumption styles, tastes and preferences of people around the world come to mimic those of western societies'.[45] The realities of differences between changing models of marriage across the globe are of course much more complex – but the rhetoric of companionship works to collapse such subtleties in the construction of a stark contrast between the modern and the primitive, between the West and the Rest.

Many versions of companionate models of marriage were part of a modernist project that articulated a progressive vision of a future world distinct from that of the recent past. The early twentieth-century politics of marriage reform were the politics of anti-Victorianism.[46] Our understanding of these companionate marriage models needs to focus on their role in the construction of an imagined Victorian past, and a modern anti-Victorian identity; they do not provide clear or straightforward evidence of the differences between models of marriage in these two centuries. During the early twentieth century a pervasive stereotype of Victorian marriage as a place of sexual repression and female oppression was developed, and the literature championing a new 'companionate' form of marriage, in a wide range of sources, draws heavily on this image. The invention of the emotionally distant and authoritarian 'Victorian' father, who in his working-class incarnation was in addition imagined as frequently both drunk and violent, gave rhetorical power to calls for marriage reform early in the century. This image has been thoroughly deconstructed by historians who have produced a far more subtle reading of Victorian family relationships. Work on family structures, models of masculinity and femininity, ideas about motherhood and fatherhood, and expressions of sexuality have significantly challenged the monolithic image of the Victorian father and re-evaluated the relationship between Victorian men and the home, their wives and their children.[47] Such literature reveals that there is no simple distinction between Victorian patriarchy and modern companionate models of marriage, and that in both centuries similar debates about the nature of domestic relations, the questions of conjugal power and authority, and the place of love, sex and affection in marriage were in constant flux, tension and negotiation. This literature has, however, had little impact on historians' discussion of companionate marriage models in the twentieth century, which often take the anti-Victorianism within the rhetoric of twentieth-century marriage reformers at face value. Marcus Collins, for example, recognizes that the 'Victorian family' was a stereotype that emerged early in the twentieth century as a 'portmanteau term' for all that was to be 'rejected' in the new century, yet concludes that the 'Victorians' reputation … was well earned'.[48] Jane Lewis, by contrast, highlights the underlying similarities in models of marriage across two centuries. Burgess and Locke's version of a companionate family – isolated from tradition or community control, where decisions were made by an affectionate and confiding couple, and in which a male breadwinner worked in partnership with a non-working wife – was not so distinct from Herbert Spencer's arch-Victorian family unit, articulated within a separate spheres framework that stressed the equality of spouses (whose biology equipped them to play different roles) and the importance of harmonious cooperation between men and women.[49] In this context, it is the politics of companionate marriage debates and the ways in which they relied upon a particular image of the past that requires further research.

An examination of the various voices championing different versions of marriage using the language associated with companionate models reveals the diversity of such views and the opposition between them. Far from being a related set of ideals around a companionate model which evolved over the course of the twentieth century, taking subtly different forms but united in a core set of values, companionate ideals are better viewed as a set of conflicting and contested ideas about the nature of marriage, and the form that any reform should take, that were in constant debate and dispute. The companionate language recurs in these very different views, as it constituted a set of desirable terms that were regularly appropriated by all sides. However, in framing the historical narrative as the 'rise of the companionate marriage', historians have elided such disputes and constructed a linear, evolutionary trajectory of change. Rather than seeing the twentieth century as a period when marriage was transformed along a new companionate model, historians need instead to focus on the interrelationship between the various contested models of marriage during this period, and the part played by the rhetoric of companionship in these debates. In particular, such histories need to draw out the opposition between different versions of the companionate marriage model. At one end we have 'conservative' versions of the companionate model, which, while adopting a language of anti-Victorianism, reformulated many of the themes that had been central to nineteenth-century understandings of companionate marriage, including the acceptance of a 'separate spheres' model of conjugal gender roles, based around a male breadwinner. At the other we have more radical attempts to overhaul marriage found in feminist, socialist and utopian visions of a changed future involving easier divorce or forms of free love alongside marriages of true equality between men and women.[50]

Important work in this area is already on-going. Some historians, for example, have recast our understanding of companionate marriage models espoused after World War I. Instead of framing these as in terms of a conservative backlash against the radical 'gender wars' of the first decades of the twentieth century, they argue we should see them as a sophisticated response to progressive critiques of marriage – a response which drew upon the positive language of companionship, where marriage was presented as a loving and egalitarian place and a natural home for the modern, enfranchised woman, while at the same time urging women to find fulfilment in the home as skilled mothers and domestic managers (supported and appreciated by their home-centred husbands).[51] A similar framework underpinned the debates about companionate marriage models after World War II. For Jane Lewis much of the literature on the companionate marriage in the post-war period should be viewed as part of a politicized project to 'modernize' the male breadwinner model of marriage to retain its appeal in the face of the social pressures that threatened to undermine it. It was an attempt to make the patriarchal values underlying the male breadwinner model appear more fulfilling to all parties and to incorporate the demands ushered in by women's changing legal and economic position. Patriarchal marriage could survive by refashioning itself as companionate and egalitarian.[52] In France too, post-war social scientists, journalists and policy makers heralded the arrival of a new modern French family whose egalitarian nature would provide personal fulfilment, intimacy and comfort.[53] It was equally focused on the 'Salaire Unique', that ensured a minimum income for a family with one (preferably male) earner.[54] These themes and tensions can be traced in a range of documents within which marriage was debated using the language of companionship: from government reports, sociological investigations, newsprint and women's magazines, to marriage guidance organizations and marriage manuals. These often drew upon some of the radical voices of sex reformers and feminists of the past 50 years. There was a heavy emphasis on an emotional intimacy between married couples, on the equality of the union, and on the centrality of mutual sexual pleasure – yet gender roles remained clearly delineated within a male breadwinner model.[55] Thus, the twentieth century – the period when the language of companionship first emerged – does not so much witness the growth of the companionate marriage, in any straightforward way, as reveal the political power of the rhetoric of companionship, mutuality and egalitarianism within marriage and its use by politicians, sociologists, the media, feminists, reform groups, and those providing marital advice, to describe a range of different visions of the ideal marriage.

The politics of debate about marriage also affects the nature of the sources available to historians to investigate individuals' experiences of marriage, what ideals and expectations informed men's and women's approaches to marriage, and how such ideals and experiences changed. Marital relationships became the focus of a number of sociological and anthropological studies in America and Europe (and elsewhere) throughout the twentieth century. Welfare organizations, social services and marriage guidance groups reported on the levels of companionship they witnessed, and news media reported on the state of the family across Europe. However, these surveys were themselves contributors to the contested debates about marriage during this period. In using such valuable evidence it is essential that historians recognize the place of such evidence in the politicized rhetoric of debate about marriage, and the ways in which their conclusions speak to the parameters of contestations around the nature of companionate models of marriage.

For example, changing attitudes towards the politics of class (and race) can be detected in much of the sociological survey material that explored the nature of marital relationships in communities across Europe and America. Throughout the first half of the twentieth century the study of marriage reflected a belief that middle-class marriages were ideal, and a desire to see the working classes emulate them. Such studies revealed a persistent anxiety that working-class communities remained trapped in an outdated 'Victorian' world of separate spheres and patriarchal authoritarianism.[56] In America, the influential study of life in 'Middle-town' concluded that this predominantly working-class community (in reality, Muncie, Indiana) had not yet adapted to modern values by adopting marriages of companionship. Evidence to the Family Welfare Association in the interwar period (analysed by Marcus Collins) supported a similar view that poor Londoners were living in uncompanionate unions where lower-class husbands and wives lived 'largely separate lives in households where spousal affection was secondary both to subsistence and the privileges exercised by men'.[57] By the 1950s, an optimistic mood and a belief in the possibility of reshaping class divisions, redistributing wealth and tackling social inequality, is reflected in sociological works which increasingly argued that companionate marriages were becoming common across all classes; an argument that was part of a general belief in the embourgeoisement of the working classes.[58] Young and Wilmott in 1957 claimed that in Bethnal Green in the East End of London, 'the old style of working-class family is fast disappearing … in place of the old comes a new kind of companionship between men and women which is one of the great transformations of our time'. A further study in 1973 confirmed these trends.[59] Geoffrey Gorer's *Exploring English Character* (1955) and his follow-up study *Sex and Marriage in England Today* (1971) argued that the traditional roles of husband

and wife had been replaced 'in favour of completely equal companionship, with all the emphasis on discussing things together and doing everything together, on being together all the time'.[60] Similar conclusions were drawn by sociologists across Europe and north America.[61]

Although the sources discussing marriage in early periods are not so embroiled in the politics of companionship that complicate the history of the twentieth century (as shown above), the politics of the twentieth-century debates about marriage have nevertheless had a direct effect on the writing of the history of earlier periods – writing which has itself further informed twentieth-century debate. The use of the language of companionship and egalitarianism among historians, which became prominent in the 1970s, to explore the emotional make-up of marriage in the early modern period, is reflected in the intellectual horizons of historians such as Lawrence Stone.[62] Indeed, the links are sometimes obvious: Peter Laslett was closely associated with Michael Young (co-author with Peter Willmott of *Family and Kinship in East London* and *The Symmetrical Family*).[63]

As a result, an ironic circularity faces us: the rhetoric and politics of marriage, equality and companionship, as debated in the twentieth century, created a linguistic framework subsequently used by historians to think about the sixteenth and seventeenth centuries (and earlier). In its turn this spawned a literature and debate which itself extended and refor-mulated later historians' and sociologists' understandings of the twentieth century. Anthony Fletcher, for example, clearly acknowledges the impact of Peter Laslett's *The World We Have Lost* on his categorization of modern companionate marriage: 'Marriage and the family have not declined in our time, but have become improved in most respects ... I do not know of any other period of British history in which the qualities and expectations of marriage and parenthood – in personal, social, or legal terms – were of as high a standard (and for the *whole* of the population) as they now are.'[64] This is not to criticize the dynamic interplay between historical writing and contemporary life; the flaws in the possibility of historians' methodological search for perfect objectivity have long been exposed, and, moreover, changing modern contemporary questions and issues drive historical inquiry in suggesting new areas and stimulating fresh questions and approaches. However, it does require close attention to the categories and concepts that we use and an awareness of their ever changing meanings.

Beyond the companionate marriage

We need to be much more cautious in our analysis of marriage, avoiding reliance on firm categories of marriage – e.g. as companionate or not; separate or not; patriarchal or not – but instead develop understandings of marriages fully attuned to precise ideological cate-gories and to the economic and social circumstances of precise historical moments and periods. Many historians are aware of the ways in which the established linguistic frame-works for understanding changes in marriage hinder, rather than help, the analysis. In a famous article, Amanda Vickery outlined the ways in which the problematic language of separate spheres impeded debate about women's roles in the nineteenth century.[65] Some historians considering the companionate marriage have come to similar conclusions: James Hammerton argues that 'to define patriarchal and companionate marriage as opposites is fundamentally misconceived'.[66] Each ideal embodied elements of the other; indeed they evolved, developed and changed in dynamic tandem. Similarly, Peter Stearns' subtle reading of the historical material on marriage and love, attachment, care, protection, provision, sex, desire, commitment, domesticity and gender roles, avoids making any crude differentiation between companionate and un-companionate in his characterization of changing models of marriage. He recognizes that emotional fulfilment was part of all marital ideals throughout the nineteenth and twentieth centuries, but argues that there were important shifts in the ways in which such emotional fulfilment was thought to be acquired.[67] Helena Michie also recognizes the problem. In the nineteenth century, she argues, the 'new' marital ideal should not be called 'companionate' since, although sharing was key to the ideal, it was unclear how much – or how little – of their lives and interests a couple would need to share in order to be companionate. Nor should it be called 'egalitarian' because *no* Victorian marriage ideal saw men and women as equals. Nor should it be called 'affective' marriage because, although the nineteenth-century ideal did emphasize the importance of love between husband and wife, such a categorization implies that previous marriage models did not also think love ought to be part of the equation between couples. As a result, she advocates labelling the increasingly popular nineteenth-century marriage model as 'conjugal' and understands this term as encapsulating Victorian ideas of togetherness and acceptance of the importance of sexual interest in marriage.[68]

What these subtle analyses of the terminology of marriage models indicate is the importance of paying close attention to the powerful rhetorics of marriage and of analysing the complicated contours of such debates.[69] Historians need to look behind apparent similarities in the ways in which marriages are modelled – as partnerships involving teamwork, sharing, companionship, mutuality, deference, and so on – and analyse the particular implications of such descriptions in specific contexts. Such an approach would be attuned to the intimate relationships between ideas about marriage (which often existed in tension and debate with each other) and the politics of such debates, in which key words might be appropriated by radically different voices to describe different conjugal models. Good examples of this approach can be found in the literature on marriage in colonial contexts, which focus on the uneasy translation of colonial values into imperial contexts and the ways in which such ideas were challenged or reshaped by indigenous practice. Rochanda Majundar explores the ideas about marriage developed by middle-class Bengalis in the late nineteenth and early twentieth centuries which drew in part upon western models, responding to western criticisms of child brides, adopting the language of romance and championing the idea that husbands and wives could be comrades. At the same time, the rhetoric of spouses as companions reinforced and reframed a continued expectation that marriage would be based on the concepts of self-sacrifice, conjugal duty and devotion, and organized hierarchically.[70] In her work on Egypt, Lila Abu-Lughod, in *Remaking Women: Feminism and Modernity in the Middle East*, goes beyond a simple understanding of the 'companionate' ideal as a fixed or unified set of values when exploring the ways in which such ideas were variously adapted and reshaped in a shifting Islamic context.[71]

Such an approach to the study of marriage also affects how historians approach the investigation of individual lives. Rather than asking whether or not, and to what extent, certain models of marriage affected individual choices, historians need to investigate the intricate ways in which individuals made sense of the varied, conflicting and changing debates about marriage that circulated around them. This analysis must be undertaken with care: individuals often draw on contemporary rhetoric, while reframing and interpreting values in new and distinct ways.[72] A range of recent treatments of the Victorian period have developed a subtle and careful analysis of Victorian models of marriage, masculinity and femininity, focusing on the tensions within circulating ideas and examining the complex ways in which individuals negotiated a path through such conflicting models of behaviour. In particular, work on masculinity has reframed understandings of men's approaches to marriage and the tensions between ideas about domestic manliness and marital authority and the different ways in which these were played out in different contexts.[73] In many instances it is clear that individuals held opposing values at the same time, and tried to steer a path that reconciled differing views and the varying expectations of the communities in which they lived. A good example is Stephen Lassonde's study into the ways young Italian immigrants in early twentieth-century America responded to changing marriage customs among young Anglo-American (middle-class, white) couples in New Haven who were attracted, on the one hand, by the rise of dating and the discourses of love, romance and sex within the context of emerging youth and consumer cultures and rising consumerism, but disconcerted, on the other, by the conflict between such practices and the expectations of their parents, or the customs of the Italian communities they inhabited. Similar conclusions are drawn by Elizabeth Alice Clement who charts the tensions between American 'companionate' courtship codes in which the couples were given considerable freedom to find a personally fulfilling love-match and Sicilian immigrant groups in New York who saw the maintenance of 'strictly supervised courtship', dowries and arranged matches as core to the preservation of Italian cultural purity in a foreign land.[74] In a British context, Claire Langhamer resists drawing on simplistic, vague companionate models in charting post-war British experiences of marriage. As a result, the tensions in individual experiences and relationships come to the fore heralding the emotional upheavals in social and cultural life in the decades that followed.[75]

Instead of charting the rise of the companionate marriage, the study of changing marital relationships should revolve around the analysis of debates about marital ideals; the investigation of the extent to which such messages were communicated to individuals, and in what terms; and the exploration of the ways in which individuals constructed their own relationships and negotiated their own forms of marriage in dialogue with contemporary marital ideals. Companionate marriage will remain a key concept for twentieth-century historians, but not one which they use to chart and describe the experiences of individuals. The companionate marriage is important for historians, but only insofar as it formed a conceptual framework used by historical actors to analyse their behaviour or justify their actions and beliefs.

Notes

1 John Hajnal, 'European Marriage Patterns in Perspective' in D. E. C. Eversley and D. V. Glass (eds), *Population in History: Essays in Historical Demography*, London: E. Arnold, 1965, pp. 101–43; John Hajnal, 'Two Kinds of Preindustrial Household Formation System', *Population and Development Review* 8:3, 1982, pp. 449–94; Mary S. Hartman, *The Household and the Making of History: A Subversive View of the Western Past*, Cambridge and New York: Cambridge University Press, 2004. On the regional complexities that are not captured by the east/west divide in the 'Western Marriage system' see David I. Kertzer and Marzio Barbagli, *The History of the European Family 2, Family Life in the Long Nineteenth Century, 1789–1913*, New Haven: Yale University Press, 2002, p. 308; Richard Wall, 'The Transformation of the European Family across the Centuries' in R. Wall, T. K. Hareven and J. Ehmer (eds), *Family History Revisited: Comparative Perspectives*, Newark: University of Delaware Press, 2001, pp. 217–41.

2 Tomas Sobotka and Laurent Toulemon, 'Overview Chapter 4: Changing Family and Partnership Behaviour: Common Trends and Persistent Diversity across Europe', *Demographic Research* 19:6, 2008, pp. 85–138.
3 Sobotka and Toulemon, 'Overview'.
4 See, for example, Ann Taylor Allen, *Women in Twentieth-Century Europe*, Basingstoke and New York: Palgrave Macmillan, 2008.
5 Sharon Marcus, *Between Women: Friendship, Desire, and Marriage in Victorian England*, Princeton: Princeton University Press, 2007, p. 6. Similarly, Helena Michie who concurs that 'sometime before the end of the eighteenth century English culture underwent a shift in regard to expectations about marriage, so that among the middle and upper classes ideals of marriage came to include and indeed to depend upon ideals of companionship and romantic love'. Helena Michie, *Victorian Honeymoons: Journeys to the Conjugal*, Cambridge and New York: Cambridge University Press, 2006, p. 19.
6 A further complication is that historians beyond Europe also chart the 'rise of the companionate marriage' in non-western cultures and in colonial contexts. Jennifer S. Hirsch and Holly Wardlow, *Modern Loves: The Anthropology of Romantic Courtship and Companionate Marriage*, Ann Arbor: University of Michigan Press, 2006.
7 This is the argument of Lawrence Stone who, in drawing upon the understanding that the twentieth century also saw the rise of the companionate marriage, claimed that the eigtheenth-century companionate marriage was destroyed by the nineteenth-century reassertion of patriarchy through marriages which championed separate spheres. Lawrence Stone, *The Family, Sex and Marriage in England, 1500–1800*, New York: Harper & Row, 1977, pp. 667–68.
8 Patricia Branca, *Women in Europe since 1750*; New York: St Martin's Press, 1978; Gisela Bock and Allison Brown, *Women in European History*, Malden, MA: Blackwell Publishers, 2001.
9 A. James Hammerton, *Cruelty and Companionship: Conflict in Nineteenth-Century Married Life*, London and New York: Routledge, 1992.
10 Michie, *Victorian Honeymoons*, p. 19.
11 J. F. Battan, 'The "Rights" of Husbands and the "Duties" of Wives: Power and Desire in the American Bedroom, 1850–1910', *Journal of Family History* 24:2, 1999, pp. 165–86 (178). Weiss argues that nineteenth-century companionate models of marriage were in opposition to patriarchal ones: Jessica Weiss, *To Have and to Hold: Marriage, the Baby Boom, and Social Change*, Chicago: University of Chicago Press, 2000.
12 Branca, *Women in Europe since 1750*; Bock and Brown, *Women in European History*.
13 On remediation, especially in local contexts, in relation to memory studies, see Astrid Erll and Ann Rigney, *Mediation, Remediation, and the Dynamics of Cultural Memory*, Berlin and New York: Walter de Gruyter, 2009. With regard to historiography, see Eckhardt Fuchs and Benedikt Stuchtey, *Across Cultural Borders: Historiography in Global Perspective*, Lanham, MD: Rowman & Littlefield, 2002. On local recontextualization, see Joan Wallach Scott, Cora Kaplan and Debra Keates (eds), *Transitions, Environments, Translations: Feminisms in International Politics*, New York: Routledge, 1997.
14 Melvin Knight, 'The Companionate Marriage and the Family', *Journal of Social Hygiene* 10:5, 1924, pp. 257–67; Ben B. Lindsey and Wainwright Evans, *Companionate Marriage*, New York: Boni & Liveright, 1927. On the articulation and reception of these ideas in America in the 1920s see Christina Simmons, *Making Marriage Modern: Women's Sexuality from the Progressive Era to World War II*, Oxford and New York: Oxford University Press, 2009; R. L. Davis, '"Not Marriage at All, but Simple Harlotry": The Companionate Marriage Controversy', *The Journal of American History* 94:4, 2008, pp. 1137–63. On the reception of Lindsey in Britain, see Jane Lewis, *The End of Marriage?: Individualism and Intimate Relations*, Cheltenham, UK, and Northampton, MA: Edward Elgar, 2001. These ideas spread to Europe too. See, for example, Lola Landaus, 'Kameradschaftsche', *Die Tat* 20:11, 1929, pp. 831–35. A translation into English can be found in A. Kaes, M. Jay and E. Dimendberg, *The Weimar Republic Sourcebook*, Berkeley: University of California Press, 1995, pp. 702–3.
15 Ingrid Sharp, 'Gender Relations in Weimar Berlin' in Christiane Schönfeld and Carmel Finnan (eds), *Practicing Modernity: Female Creativity in the Weimar Republic*, Würzburg: Königshausen & Neumann, 2006, pp. 1–13 (6–7). See also George Robb, 'Marriage and Reproduction' in Harry

Cocks and Matt Houlbrook (eds), *Palgrave Advances in the Modern History of Sexuality*, Basingstoke and New York: Palgrave Macmillan, 2006.

16 E. W. Burgess, 'The Romantic Impulse and Family Disorganization', *The Survey* 57, 1927, pp. 290–94; Ernest W. Burgess and Harvey J. Locke, *The Family: From Institution to Companionship*, New York: American Book Company, 1945. See also related texts such as: Robert O. Blood and Donald M. Wolfe, *Husbands and Wives: The Dynamics of Married Living*, New York: Free Press, 1960; Robert Staughton Lynd and Helen Merrell Lynd, *Middletown: a Study in Contemporary American Culture*, New York: Harcourt, Brace and Company, 1929. See also Lewis, *The End of Marriage*; Stephen Brooke, *Sexual Politics: Sexuality, Family Planning, and the British Left from the 1880s to the Present Day*, Oxford and New York: Oxford University Press, 2011.

17 Robert Boudet, 'La famille bourgeoise' in *Sociologie comparée de la famille contemporaine*, Paris: Centre national de la recherche scientifique, 1955, pp. 141–51; Pierre Drouin, 'Un nouveau type de couple', *Le Monde*, 4 April 1953. Boudet and Drouin cited in Rebecca Pulju, *Women and Mass Consumer Society in Postwar France*, Cambridge and New York: Cambridge University Press, 2011, pp. 108–9.

18 That this was a partnership of equals with separate roles and responsibilities was underpinned by Beveridge in the reasons given for women's receipt of benefits whether or not they worked and had their incomes taxed. They were entitled to social security benefits through their unpaid labour in the home which was of equal importance to society as their husbands' economic activity. See Ina Zweiniger-Bargielowska, *Women in Twentieth-Century Britain*, Harlow: Longman, 2001, pp. 327–28.

19 A. J. Cherlin, 'The Deinstitutionalization of American Marriage', *Journal of Marriage and Family* 66:4, 2004, pp. 848–61.

20 Ross McKibbin, introduction to a new edition of Marie Stopes' *Married Love*, reads the text as an ideological statement of the virtues of companionate marriage. Marie Carmichael Stopes and Ross McKibbin, *Married Love*, Oxford and New York: Oxford University Press, 2004.

21 Jane Lewis, David Clark and D. H. J. Morgan, *'Whom God Hath Joined Together': The Work of Marriage Guidance*, London and New York: Tavistock/Routledge, 1992; Brooke, *Sexual Politics*. See also Alana Harris, '"A Paradise on Earth, a Foretaste of Heaven": English Catholic Understandings of Domesticity and Marriage, 1945–65' in Lucy Delap, Ben Griffin and Abigail Wills (eds), *The Politics of Domestic Authority*, Basingstoke: Palgrave Macmillan, 2009, pp. 155–81.

22 See Ronald Fletcher, *The Family and Marriage in Britain: An Analysis and Moral Assessment*, Harmondsworth: Penguin, 1966; Michael Dunlop Young and Peter Willmott, *The Symmetrical Family: A Study of Work and Leisure in the London Region*, London: Routledge & Kegan Paul, 1973; Michael Dunlop Young and Peter Willmott, *Family and Kinship in East London*, London: Routledge & Kegan Paul, 1957.

23 Stephen Edgell, *Middle-Class Couples: A Study of Segregation, Domination, and Inequality in Marriage*, London and Boston: G. Allen & Unwin, 1980; Jennifer Platt, 'Some Problems in Measuring the Jointness of Conjugal Role-Relationships', *Sociology* 3:3, 1969, pp. 287–97; Diana Leonard, *Sex and Generation: A Study of Courtship and Weddings*, London and New York: Tavistock Publications, 1980; S. Edgell, 'Marriage and the Concept of Companionship', *The British Journal of Sociology* 23:4, 1972, pp. 452–61; Andrew Tolson, *The Limits of Masculinity*, London: Tavistock, 1977.

24 David Clark and J. D. Haldane, *Wedlocked?: Intervention and Research in Marriage*, Cambridge: Polity Press, 1990. See also, H. I. Hartmann, 'The Family as the Locus of Gender, Class, and Political Struggle: The Example of Housework', *Signs* 6:3, 1981, pp. 366–94; Colin Bell and Howard Newby, 'Husbands and Wives: The Deferential Dialectic' in Diana Leonard and Sheila Allen (eds), *Sexual Divisions Revisited*, London: Macmillan, 1991, pp. 25–44.

25 Ann Oakley, *The Sociology of Housework*, Bath: Martin Robertson, 1974, p. 138. On these debates in Britain see Marcus Collins, *Modern Love: An Intimate History of Men and Women in Twentieth Century Britain*, London: Atlantic, 2003, ch. 6. See also Lewis, *The End of Marriage?*

26 Janet Finch and Penny Summerfield, 'Social Reconstruction and the Emergence of Companionate Marriage, 1945–59' in Jacqueline L. Burgoyne and David Clark (eds), *Marriage, Domestic Life, and Social Change: Writings for Jacqueline Burgoyne, 1944–88*, London and New York: Routledge, 1991, pp. 7–32 (7).

27 Collins, *Modern Love*, p. 93.
28 Keith Wrightson, *English Society: 1580–1680*, London: Hutchinson, 1982, ch. 4; Ralph A. Houlbrooke, *The English Family, 1450–1700*, London and New York: Longman, 1984; Linda A. Pollock, 'Rethinking Patriarchy and the Family in Seventeenth-Century England', *Journal of Family History* 23:1, 1998, pp. 3–27, p. 20; Joanne Bailey, *Unquiet Lives: Marriage and Marriage Breakdown in England, 1660–1800*, Cambridge: Cambridge University Press, 2003.
29 Carol R. Ember and Melvin Ember, *Encyclopedia of Sex and Gender: Men and Women in the World's Cultures*, New York: Kluwer Academic/Plenum Publishers, 2003, p. 945.
30 Meena Khandelwal, 'Arranging Love: Interrogating the Vantage Point in Cross-Border Feminism', *Signs* 34:3, 2009, pp. 583–609; Jyoti Puri, *Woman, Body, Desire in Post-Colonial India: Narratives of Gender and Sexuality*, New York: Routledge, 1999; Jasodhara Bagchi, *Indian Women, Myth and Reality*, Hyderabad: Sangam Books, 1995; Asha Nadkarni, '"World-Menace": National Reproduction and Public Health in Katherine Mayo's Mother India', *American Quarterly* 60:3, 2008, pp. 805–27.
31 Francis M. L. Thompson, *The Rise of Respectable Society: A Social History of Victorian Britain, 1830–1900*, London: Fontana Press, 1989, p. 109.
32 Simon Szreter and Kate Fisher, *Sex before the Sexual Revolution: Intimate Life in England, 1918–1963*, Cambridge and New York: Cambridge University Press, 2010, ch. 4; Claire Langhamer, 'Love and Courtship in Mid-twentieth-century England', *The Historical Journal* 50:1, 2007, pp. 173–96; Judy Giles, '"You Meet 'Em and That's It": Working Class Women's Refusal of Romance between the Wars in Britain' in Lynne Pearce and Jackie Stacey (eds), *Romance Revisited*, London: Lawrence and Wishart, 1995, pp. 279–92.
33 David I. Kertzer and Marzio Barbagli, *Family Life in the Twentieth Century*, New Haven: Yale University Press, 2003, p. 320.
34 Hirsch and Wardlaw advocate this approach to western companionate models and stress the importance of examining 'local versions of companionate marriage': Hirsch and Wardlow, *Modern Loves*, p. 2. Cynthia Dunn points out the different expectations of companionate marriages in contemporary Japan and modern USA: Cynthia D. Dunn, 'Cultural Models and Metaphors for Marriage: An Analysis of Discourse at Japanese Wedding Receptions', *Ethos* 32:3, 2004, pp. 348–73 (365). Martin Richards and Jane Elliot reflect British sociological opinion in acknowledging that 'the notion of a companionate marriage is a complex one requiring careful analysis': Martin P. M. Richards and B. Jane Elliot, 'Sex and Marriage in the 1960s and 1970s' in Burgoyne and Clark, *Marriage, Domestic Life, and Social Change*, pp. 33–54.
35 Thompson, *The Rise of Respectable Society*, p. 111.
36 Stephanie Coontz, *Marriage, a History: From Obedience to Intimacy or How Love Conquered Marriage*, New York: Viking, 2005; P. N. Stearns and M. Knapp, 'Men and Romantic Love: Pinpointing a 20th-century Change', *Journal of Social History* 27, 1993, pp. 769–93.
37 David Morgan, 'Ideologies of Marriage and Family Life' in Burgoyne and Clark, *Marriage, Domestic Life, and Social Change*, pp. 114–38.
38 Franz Carl Müller-Lyer, *The Evolution of Modern Marriage: A Sociology of Sexual Relations*, London: G. Allen & Unwin, 1930.
39 Hirsch and Wardlow, *Modern Loves*.
40 Elizabeth Fee, 'The Sexual Politics of Victorian Social Anthropology', *Feminist Studies* 1:3/4, 1973, pp. 23–39; Rosemary Jann, 'Darwin and the Anthropologists: Sexual Selection and Its Discontents', *Victorian Studies* 37:2, 1994, pp. 287–306; Andrew P. Lyons and Harriet Lyons, *Irregular Connections: A History of Anthropology and Sexuality*, Lincoln: University of Nebraska Press, 2004. For one such debate, where the connection between anthropological material and contemporary concerns about marriage are made explicit see Robert Briffault, Bronislaw Malinowski and Ashley Montagu, *Marriage, Past and Present: A Debate between Robert Briffault and Bronislaw Malinowski*, Boston: P. Sargent, 1956.
41 Lyons and Lyons, *Irregular Connections*.
42 Researchers found among these Italian immigrants a view that romance was an unstable basis for marriage. However, this is not a view confined to 'old-fashioned', southern European models of marriage but was equally part of some progressive companionate voices in America in the 1920s. Stearns and Knapp, 'Men and Romantic Love'.

43 Lassonde does not challenge companionate categories however, and sees the conflict between American and immigrant communities as one of old-fashioned versus companionate values. He does, however, recognize that there is no clear distinction between these two communities, a blurring he explains as indicative of, on the one hand, the gradual and piecemeal transition from Victorian to companionate models in America, and, on the other, the eagerness of young Italian immigrants to adopt modern American values. I suggest that we should, instead, read such evidence as indicative of the futility of categorizing complex customs and relationships according to ill-defined marriage models. Stephen Lassonde, *Learning to Forget: Schooling and Family Life in New Haven's Working Class, 1870–1940*, New Haven: Yale University Press, 2005.

44 Dipesh Chakrabarty, 'The Difference-Deferral of (a) Colonial Modernity: Public Debates on Domesticity in British Bengal', *History Workshop Journal* 36:1, 1993, pp. 1–34; Dipesh Chakrabarty, 'Postcoloniality and the Artifice of History: Who Speaks for "Indian" Pasts?', *Representations* 37, 1992, pp. 1–26.

45 Hirsch and Wardlow, *Modern Loves*, p. 11.

46 Robb, 'Marriage and Reproduction'.

47 See, for example, John Tosh, *A Man's Place: Masculinity and the Middle-Class Home in Victorian England*, New Haven and London: Yale University Press, 1999; Martin Francis, 'The Domestication of the Male? Recent Research on Nineteenth- and Twentieth-century British Masculinity', *The Historical Journal* 45:3, 2002, pp. 637–52; Joanna Bourke, 'Sexual Violence, Marital Guidance, and Victorian Bodies: An Aesthesiology', *Victorian Studies* 50:3, 2008, pp. 419–36; Margaret Marsh, 'Suburban Men and Masculine Domesticity, 1870–1915', *American Quarterly* 40:2, 1988, pp. 165–86; Eleanor Gordon and Gwyneth Nair, 'Domestic Fathers and the Victorian Parental Role', *Women's History Review* 15:4, 2006, pp. 551–59.

48 Collins, *Modern Love*, pp. 5, 30.

49 Lewis, *The End of Marriage?*, pp. 45–46. Spencer's text took an evolutionary narrative in which marriage was seen as progressing from primitive polygamy and promiscuity to a civilized, harmonious, cooperative marriage of separate spheres. Spencer also argued that his model of marriage was one that particularly recognized women's superior status. For Spencer progressive marriage valued women by protecting them from the harsh demands of labour and isolating them from the evils of the market economy.

50 Brooke, *Sexual Politics*; Collins, *Modern Love*; Hammerton, *Cruelty and Companionship*; Carol Dyhouse, *Feminism and the Family in England, 1880–1939*, Oxford and New York: Basil Blackwell, 1989; Joanne Ellen Passet, *Sex Radicals and the Quest for Women's Equality*, Urbana: University of Illinois Press, 2003; Lynn Abrams, *The Making of Modern Woman: Europe 1789–1918*, Harlow: Longman, 2002; Christina Simmons, 'Women's Power in Sex Radical Challenges to Marriage in the Early-twentieth-century United States', *Feminist Studies* 29:1, 2003, pp. 169–98.

51 Adrian Bingham, *Gender, Modernity, and the Popular Press in Inter-war Britain*, Oxford and New York: Clarendon, 2004; Renate Bridenthal, 'Something Old, Something New: Women between the Two World Wars' in Renate Bridenthal and Claudia Koonz (eds), *Becoming Visible: Women in European History*, Boston: Houghton Mifflin, 1977, pp. 473–97; Susan Kingsley Kent, *Sex and Suffrage in Britain 1860–1914*, London: Routledge, 1990.

52 Lewis, *The End of Marriage?* On Europe see Chiara Saraceno, 'Social and Family Policy' in Kertzer and Barbagli, *Family Life in the Twentieth Century*, pp. 238–69 (255–65); Robb, 'Marriage and Reproduction'.

53 Pulju, *Women and Mass Consumer Society*, p. 96.

54 Pulju, *Women and Mass Consumer Society*, p. 98.

55 Claire Langhamer, 'Adultery in Post-war England', *History Workshop Journal* 62:1, 2006, pp. 86–115 (90).

56 On the middle-class prejudices informing investigations of working-class life see, for example, Peter Gurney, 'Intersex and Dirty Girls: Mass-observation and Working Class Sexuality in England in the 1930s', *Journal of the History of Sexuality* 8:2, 1997, pp. 256–90.

57 Collins, *Modern Love*.

58 Angela Davis, 'A Critical Perspective on British Social Surveys and Community Studies and Their Accounts of Married Life *c.* 1945–70', *Cultural and Social History* 6:1, 2009, pp. 47–64; Richards and Elliot, 'Social Reconstruction'.

59 Young and Willmott, *Family and Kinship*; Young and Willmott, *The Symmetrical Family*.

60 Geoffrey Gorer, *Exploring English Character, by Geoffrey Gorer*, London: Cresset Press, 1955; Geoffrey Gorer, *Sex and Marriage in England Today: A Study of the Views and Experience of the under-45s*, London: Nelson, 1971.

61 John Mogey, 'Sociology of Marriage and Family Behavior 1957–68', *Current Sociology* 17:1–3, 1969, pp. 5–51; J. H. Goldthorpe, D. Lockwood, F. Bechhofer and J. Platt, *The Affluent Worker*, Cambridge: Cambridge University Press, 1968; Richard B. Hoggart, *The Uses of Literacy: Aspects of Working-class Life*, London: Chatto & Windus, 1957, p. 319; Ferdynand Zweig, *The Worker in an Affluent Society: Family Life and Industry*, London: Heinemann, 1961; Agnes Pearl Jephcott, *Married Women Working*, London: Allen & Unwin, 1962. This literature saw the un-companionate marriage as limited to isolated communities, such as those inhabited by miners. Madeline Kerr, *The People of Ship Street*, London and New York: Routledge & Kegan Paul/Humanities Press, 1958; Norman Dennis, Fernando Henriques and Clifford Slaughter, *Coal Is Our Life. An Analysis of a Yorkshire Mining Community*, London: Tavistock, 1969.

62 Although Lawrence Stone, for example, was not directly involved in British or American sociological thinking, political activism or public policy making (he moved to the USA in 1963), he recognized that contemporary debates about marriage framed, constrained and inspired his work. He saw the present as establishing questions and frameworks for thinking about the past, and the past in turn as providing perspectives of relevance to modern existence. Lawrence Stone, 'Family Values in a Historical Perspective', *The Tanner Lectures on Human Values*, delivered at Harvard University, 16–17 November 1994.

63 Michael Young was himself a major player in the post-war politics of the family and Labour Party policy making; he was a key author of the Labour Party's 1945 manifesto which developed a whole range of welfare policies based on the notion of a 'companionate' family built around a male breadwinner. Laslett and Young worked together in in the early 1960s on the development of educational through television programming, which led in 1971 to the founding of the Open University.

64 Fletcher, *The Family and Marriage in Britain*, p. 12.

65 Amanda Vickery, 'Golden Age to Separate Spheres? A Review of the Categories and Chronology of English Women's History', *The Historical Journal* 36:2, 1993, pp. 383–414. Critics of Vickery see in her work a simplistic rejection of Leonore Davidoff and Catherine Hall's *Family Fortunes: Men and Women of the English Middle-Class 1780–1850*, London: Routledge, 1986, which charted the transformation of middle-class women's lives and their increasingly exclusion from work and politics, but Vickery's chief achievement is to insist that historians interrogate their analytical categories and remain sensitive to the precise, changing and contested meanings of social frameworks in the past. Anna Clark, 'Review of Amanda Vickery *The Gentleman's Daughter. Women's Lives in Georgian England*', *Reviews in History*, no. 57 [http:www.history.ac.uk/reviews/review/57]. See also Linda K. Kerber, 'Separate Spheres, Female Worlds, Woman's Place: The Rhetoric of Women's History', *The Journal of American History* 75:1, 1988, pp. 9–39.

66 Hammerton, *Cruelty and Companionship*, p. 169.

67 Stearns and Knapp, 'Men and Romantic Love'.

68 Michie, *Victorian Honeymoons*, p. 20.

69 See, for example, Alison Light's use of the idea of 'conservative modernity' in thinking about changes in marital ideals: Alison Light, *Forever England: Femininity, Literature and Conservatism between the Wars*, London: Routledge, 1991.

70 Rochona Majumdar, *Marriage and Modernity: Family Values in Colonial Bengal*, Durham, NC: Duke University Press, 2009. See also David Kopf, *The Brahmo Samaj and the Shaping of the Modern Indian Mind*, Princeton, NJ: Princeton University Press, 1979.

71 Lila Abu-Lughod, *Remaking Women: Feminism and Modernity in the Middle East*, Princeton, NJ: Princeton University Press, 1998.

72 Szreter and Fisher, *Sex before the Sexual Revolution*.

73 Hammerton, *Cruelty and Companionship*.

74 Lassonde, *Learning to Forget*; Elizabeth Alice Clement, *Love for Sale: Courting, Treating, and Prostitution in New York City, 1900–1945*, Chapel Hill: University of North Carolina Press, 2006. See also the historians who study marriage in twentieth-century Italy and the differences between various models of marriage in Italy, and the distinctiveness of rural Sicilians.

75 Claire Langhamer, 'Love, Selfhood and Authenticity in Post-war Britain', *Cultural and Social History* 9:2, 2012, pp. 277–97.

Part X

REPRODUCTION

19

REPRODUCTION, *C.*1500–1750

Lianne McTavish

In his matrimonial treatise of 1687, *Tableau de l'amour, consideré dans l'estat du mariage* [translated in 1703 as *The Mysteries of Conjugal Love Revealed*], French physician Nicolas Venette cautioned against certain sexual positions. According to him:

> The genital parts of men are not contrived to caress standing; our health receiving great inconveniences in a posture so opposed to generation. ... Nor is a sitting posture becoming an orderly love; it being difficult for the parts to join, and the seed to be received in order to form a child accomplished in all its parts. ... Instead of getting children, a woman is rendered barren by this posture; what perchance is the product of such caresses is either small or imperfect.[1]

Venette nevertheless recognized that having sex in the missionary position was not always possible; fat men or pregnant women might prefer to couple side by side, 'like foxes'. The 'back way' was also commendable, for it would encourage the seed to fall into its proper place inside the womb. By highlighting fertility, the physician from La Rochelle implied that sex was acceptable and healthy only when it was devoted to procreation. Yet his book was popular because it also contained references to bodily pleasures and such topics as deformed genitalia and simulated virginity. These elements help to explain why the *Tableau de l'amour* was augmented, re-edited and reprinted under various titles until the middle of the twentieth century, appearing in German, Dutch, Spanish, Italian, English, and Portuguese.[2]

Venette's engaging treatise addresses key issues covered in this chapter, including theories of conception, the formation of the embryo, qualities of the womb, and nature of pregnancy. His text reveals early modern understandings of the hierarchical relationship between men and women, efforts to overcome sterility, and fears about the production of so-called monsters, referred to above as the small or imperfect products resulting from unruly sex. At the same time, the *Tableau de l'amour* obliquely offers information about a range of potentially taboo topics, including contraception. Readers might have been intrigued by Venette's contention that sex in a seated position would impede fertility, and were perhaps encouraged to attempt it with precisely that goal in mind. There are, however, several topics that the physician overlooked, including the work of female midwives. Why does his description of pregnancy virtually ignore these women, when they remained the primary birth assistants throughout the early modern period?

351

The following analysis of reproductive beliefs and practices in western Europe between 1500 and 1750 proceeds in a more or less chronological fashion, moving from theories of conception to methods of contraception, the management of pregnancy, experience of childbirth, and construction of parenthood. During the early modern period, the life cycle did not always unfold so neatly, and this chapter also considers unwanted pregnancies, difficult labours, monstrous deliveries, high infant mortality rates, and the ways in which parents reacted to the death of a child. Even as the discussion below examines historical sources that indicate how early modern people both understood and responded to these events, it engages with contemporary debates about the past. Scholars offer diverse arguments about early modern problems that remain relevant today, including the effectiveness of various forms of birth control, the status of the female body, and the power invested in medical looking (as Michael Stolberg and Malcolm Nicolson have discussed earlier in this volume). A fundamental goal of this chapter is to shed light on these disagreements, drawing attention to the gaps in our comprehension of the early modern period, as well as to the sometimes limited source material on which current research is based.

Scholars are for the most part obliged to found their arguments on the surviving or accessible written sources, including medical texts, recipe books, or popular sex manuals like that of Venette. Demographic information, including statistics provided from baptismal records or death certificates, can also be useful sources of information, but such records are often scarce before the eighteenth century, when careful parish or state records were not kept in a modern, methodical fashion. In any case, the interpretation of these sources remains a contested issue, with modern scholars divided over how to collect and understand historical evidence. Many published medical treatises, for instance, tell us more about the opinions of individual early modern authors than the beliefs or practices of the time. This insistence on individuals is itself open to question, for authors often adhered to written conventions rather than striving for self-expression. At the same time, their texts were meant to promote their own reputations within the competitive medical marketplace of the early modern period, and were not simply, or even primarily, designed to convey knowledge.[3] Despite including what could be considered popular information, Venette, for example, was a privileged physician and his book dismissed female midwives while defending the dominance of men like him within the medical hierarchy, as indicated below. This chapter thus necessarily refers to a host of early modern medical and popular writings, as well as visual images, interpreting them both in terms of their generic conventions, and the broad historical and cultural context in which they were received.

Enhancing fertility

Venette's assertion that sex was primarily meant to produce children was commonplace. Most early modern people expected women to become pregnant within the first few years of marriage. A childless union would produce suspicions of sterility, impotence, or physical malformation, leading couples to seek advice from family members, local wise women, and perhaps even surgeons or physicians such as Venette. Various printed texts describe the fertility tests recommended by medical practitioners. In her obstetrical treatise, *The Midwives Book* of 1671, English midwife Jane Sharp echoed ancient and medieval sources by explaining how to determine which partner was more fruitful than the other by soaking barley in their urine.[4] The sample of the fertile person would sprout first, whereas a lack of growth would confirm sterility. If both pots of barley flowered, then fertility was considered possible with various treatments. Sharp concurred with dominant opinion by arguing that sterility usually stemmed from wombs that were too cold, humid, or otherwise inhospitable to seed. Conception – typically understood to result from the coagulation of male and female seed – would not occur in a womb that was tightly shut, or tilted to one side in a manner that permitted the seed to escape.

These conditions were mentioned in the Hippocratic corpus – some 50 to 70 texts written during the fourth and fifth centuries BC – which suggested the use of ointments, fumigations, and vaginal pessaries to soften and open the womb.[5] In the sixteenth century, the French physician Laurent Joubert noted that women wore Saint John's herbs about their loins to encourage conception, while administering herbal douches to warm up their wombs. According to him, such practices could backfire if used by lascivious women because their wombs were already too hot and simply roasted the seed.[6] This discussion was based on humoural theories that considered women to be naturally cold and moist, needing to be 'warmed up' in order to conceive or to achieve the orgasms necessary for conception to occur.[7] It also implied that both immoderate passion and moral impurity could cause sterility in women who became unnaturally hot, standard explanations for the supposed lack of fertility in prostitutes.

Although women and their defective wombs were often blamed as the cause of infertility, men could also be faulted for producing an inadequate supply of cold, thin seed. Productive sperm was ideally warm, viscuous, and white.[8] Male impotence could be treated by the ingestion of windy foods like peas and beans, or aphrodisiacs such as candied sea holly and oysters.[9] Venette mentioned some well-known remedies – eating egg yolks, cock testicles, and mild wine – but focused on exotic substances known to excite the 'secret parts', including ground crocodile skin and minerals such as borax.[10] Impotence and sterility caused by witchcraft required, however, a different approach. According to Angus McLaren, during the early modern period popular belief held that potions, charms, or a magical ligature knotted during a wedding ceremony could render couples infertile. A man could try urinating through his wife's wedding ring to break the spell.[11] If none of these methods improved a husband's performance, a wife might seek the dissolution of their marriage. Pierre Darmon has studied impotence trials held in France during the early modern period, noting that sometimes the accused man was made to prove his virility with his wife in a potentially humiliating sexual display before witnesses.[12]

The female body was, however, more regularly scrutinized than the male body for its reproductive capacities. Venette argued that only those capable of sexual activity leading to reproduction could marry, arguing that girls as young as 8 or 9 should be inspected by physicians, so that any impediments to future menstruation or sexual intercourse could be remedied at an early stage.[13] This reproductive surveillance of girls and young women was increasingly recommended by medical authorities during the seventeenth and eighteenth centuries. French writers such as Nicolas Puzos, Jean-Louis Baudelocque, and Antoine Petit provided detailed instructions about how to examine unmarried women, using visual and tactile methods to ensure that their pelvises would be able to support future pregnancies.[14] In 1694, the French surgeon Philippe Peu conveyed similar information in a more anecdotal form by describing his lucky escape from marriage to a religious woman whose father he admired. The surgeon avoided the union after realizing that the young woman's body was deformed by rickets. When she married another man, she quickly became pregnant but died before giving birth.[15] Peu portrayed the young woman as both undesirable and doomed because she could not become a mother.

Recent work by Sarah Toulalan affirms that fertility and sexual desire were conflated during the early modern period. Analysing seventeenth-century English pornography, she argues that sex was viewed as pleasurable only when conception could or actually did result.[16] Toulalan's research reveals a striking change of attitude from the early modern to the modern period because pornography now typically features sexual bodies severed from their reproductive capacities. In her study of English erotic culture during the eighteenth century, Karen Harvey highlights this difference, finding that early modern people could associate sexual desire with medical and scientific knowledge. She cites examples of young men using the engravings in obstetrical treatises, sometimes labelled images of the womb and surrounding organs, as bawdy forms of masturbatory entertainment.[17] In contrast, few readers would find titillating today's gynaecology textbooks, which represent the uterus in terms of mechanical function and purport to offer an objective kind of medical training or sexual education.

Undermining fertility

Despite the early modern celebration of conception, diminished fertility was of great interest to many people. Venette provided advice about how to avoid sexual excitement (steer clear of painted nude figures, erotic novels, and copulating animals) while hinting that certain sexual positions would inhibit the effective delivery of seed to the womb, as noted above.[18] Historians once assumed that early modern women had little or no control over their fertility, and were essentially victims of their biology.[19] According to E. P. Thompson, women were simply uninterested in limiting their pregnancies because of high infant mortality rates, which saw about one in four children die before the age of 10.[20] Demographic studies have since shown, however, that early modern families had on average only four to six children, born years apart from one another rather than at a constant rate. The number of births markedly declined once a woman reached her mid-thirties, suggesting the deliberate avoidance of pregnancy.[21] Scholars increasingly recognize that a range of contraceptive methods were used, such as abstinence, late marriage, *coitus interruptus*, and prolonged breast feeding, known to hinder fertility. Other techniques of birth control included wearing amulets, inserting vaginal pessaries of rue and ground lily root combined with castoreum or viscuous mixtures meant to plug the cervix, and administering douches designed to cool the womb, rendering it less hospitable to seed.[22] Records indicate that men wore condoms made of sheepskin and animal intestines by the seventeenth century, but primarily did so to protect themselves from disease rather than as a form of contraception.[23]

Scholars nevertheless disagree about the precise nature and effectiveness of the contraceptive methods used during the early modern period. John Riddle argues that a wide range of popular and medical recipes consistently recommended the same ingredients to avoid or end pregnancy, including pomegranate skin, rue, myrtle, myrrh, and pennyroyal. His conclusion that safe and effective methods of contraception were widely employed is based on modern laboratory experiments that reconstitute the historical recipes and test them on animals.[24] Patricia Crawford nevertheless doubts the efficacy of early methods of birth control, given the clearly high incidence of unwanted pregnancies outside of marriage, a point not addressed by Riddle.[25] Directly critical of Riddle, Helen King challenges both his methodology and conclusions. According to her, by relying on laboratory testing Riddle mistakenly assumes that chemistry is a universal language and that the herbs themselves have not varied over time.[26] A recent study by Joan Thirsk convincingly demonstrates that plants, including herbs and vegetables, have changed in appearance, odour, and taste since the early modern period.[27]

Historians similarly debate the incidence and effectiveness of early modern abortion techniques. Discussions typically take a long view, considering ancient and medieval as well as early modern source material. The Hippocratic corpus notes that abortion was something women were 'always doing'.[28] Written long after the death of the historical Hippocrates, the Hippocratic Oath appears to contradict this statement by forbidding doctors to administer abortive pessaries. Yet the Oath fails to mention other possible methods, suggesting that pessaries may have been considered particularly dangerous.[29] According to Ann Ellis Hanson, other texts in the Hippocratic corpus discuss abortion as if there were no prohibitions against it.[30] Several later publications consider abortion rather openly. The second-century Greek physician Soranus, for example, argued that abortion was medically indicated if a woman was too young to bear children or suffered from a physical impairment that made it difficult for her to carry a child to term.[31] Despite some contradictory evidence and an unfortunate lack of detailed information, it seems that abortions were not unusual during antiquity.

Along similar lines, there is evidence of both the use and prohibition of abortifacients during the Middle Ages and the early modern period. Male authors of medical and obstetrical treatises occasionally declared that women should not drink herbal concoctions in order to empty their wombs, implying that this activity was far from rare.[32] Selected medical men referred to herbs that would expel a dead foetus from the womb in coded terms, apparently worried that women and other readers would use their recipes to procure abortions. Though the surgeon Denis Fournier, for instance, wrote his *L'accoucheur méthodique* [The methodical man-midwife] in French, he used Latin to convey remedies designed to assist in removing a dead child or retained afterbirth, hoping that this learned language would prevent those without a university education from accessing particular kinds of knowledge.[33] Fournier may also have been worried, however, about potential negative responses to his publication from other medical men. In 1575, the physicians of the Faculté de Médecine in Paris attempted to impede the dissemination of a book written by barber-surgeon Ambroise Paré, arguing that it was, among many other things, immoral. Paré defended his discussion of the causes of miscarriage, claiming that he was urging caution in women, not assisting them in procuring abortions, as charged.[34] Though this case was primarily informed by the ongoing rivalries between physicians, surgeons, and barber-surgeons – the latter groups were not supposed to prescribe or publish information about internal remedies – it indicates that the spectre of abortion could be invoked in attempts to lower the status of a medical practitioner. All the same, most obstetrical treatises, including that of state physician of Worms and Frankfurt am Main, Eucharius Roesslin, in 1513, explained the causes of miscarriage, noting that excessive eating, bathing, and movement (especially jumping backwards while dancing lewdly) could dislodge a pregnancy.[35] In his treatise of 1668, the French surgeon man-midwife François Mauriceau insisted that pregnant women should avoid bumpy carriage rides, raising their arms over their heads, carrying heavy things, and extreme fits of anger. Regardless of what such authors intended, unhappily pregnant women may have attempted these activities in the hopes of provoking a miscarriage.[36]

These and other allusions to abortion make it difficult to determine the social status of pregnancy termination. The handful of female midwives who wrote treatises during the early modern period, for example, advised against providing abortives to clients. In volume one of her publication of 1609, the French royal midwife Louise Bourgeois described a case study in which a woman who was three-and-a-half months pregnant miscarried a tiny foetus with a visible head, spine, and partially formed limbs. Bourgeois disparaged those with little regard for this creature, arguing that it was wrong to prevent a child endowed with only a vegetative soul from receiving its sensitive and rational souls. She alluded to the tripartite theory of development, which held that a foetus was finally infused with a rational or immortal soul only after its parts were formed, at around six months' gestation.[37] Bourgeois' polemical tone suggests that it was customary to disregard unformed foetuses, and that she was challenging a majority view. There is more to the story, though, for with her apparent condemnation of abortion the royal midwife portrayed herself as someone consistently dedicated to preserving the contents of the womb. This representation countered the negative association of female midwives with danger and death increasingly produced by those male midwives striving to become more active within the lying-in chamber. Bourgeois staunchly declared that she was not responsible for the demise of that or any other foetus, shielding herself from general criticism and blame.[38]

In an open letter to her daughter published in 1617, Bourgeois advised the young midwifery apprentice against delivering women in her own home, noting that she had made that mistake early in her own career. In this case, the royal midwife disparaged the act of helping women to give birth secretly, in a location hidden from neighbours and family members.[39] Such clandestine births were frowned upon not only because they protected women from the social approbation attached to illicit sex and any resulting pregnancies, but also because the local authorities might become financially responsible for children abandoned or deposited at a foundling hospital; they furthermore assumed that secret births would encourage infanticide.[40] These fears encouraged both the legislative and literal surveillance of the bodies of unmarried women. Laura Gowing argues that when unwed women were suspected of being secretly pregnant in sixteenth- and seventeenth-century England, they were subjected to 'the investigating eyes and hands' of a group of matrons, older, married women with children, who would search the bodies of unmarried women for signs of pregnancy, squeezing their breasts to see if they produced milk.[41] In his broader study of medieval and early modern short fiction, Etienne van de Walle finds that frank discussions of birth control are relatively common in the literature, but that unwanted pregnancies are described in terms of clandestine birth rather than abortion. He argues that secret deliveries, child abandonment, and infanticide should be classified as important early modern forms of birth control.[42] His suggestion runs counter to modern understandings that associate birth control with the prevention of conception, not the disposal of newborns. It nevertheless provides a potentially startling reminder that early modern people often constructed such categories as fertility, sexual desire, contraception, abortion, and the unborn in a manner virtually unrecognizable to the modern reader.

Distinctions between contraception and abortion were more fluid during the early modern period than they are today. Intervention at an early stage of the pregnancy, before any kind of ensoulment (thought to occur at around 30 days for male and 45 days for female embryos) fell within the realm of contraception rather than abortion. Even the medieval Catholic Church distinguished between formed and unformed embryos and foetuses, though it consistently legislated against early abortions from the fourth century onward according to John T. Noonan.[43] It was, however, quite difficult to diagnose pregnancy during the early modern period. The cessation of menstruation or an increasingly expanding belly did not exclusively indicate conception, and may have pointed to other conditions. Throughout the early modern period, medical practitioners hesitated before declaring a woman pregnant. According to the French surgeon man-midwife Jacques Guillemeau in 1609, men would look ridiculous if the swollen wombs of their apparently pregnant clients produced menses, water, or wind instead of a child. He and other medical men considered the interior of the female body a dark and mysterious realm able to foster substances both natural and unnatural.[44] Barbara Duden argues that pregnancy was primarily confirmed by early modern women when they felt 'quickening' or movement inside their bodies, usually at around four months' gestation.[45] By interpreting their embodied experience, women were authorized to name and announce publicly their condition. Duden contrasts this historical form of female agency with the medical procedures that today have made pregnancy an objective condition confirmed by hormonal tests and ultrasound machines.[46]

Early modern medical practitioners and laypeople alike considered the womb to be crucial to women's overall health, providing far more than a location in which conception could occur. According to Cathy McClive, it was important for early modern women to maintain regular and abundant menstrual bleeding.[47] Medical writers argued that the uterus was in constant communication with the organs surrounding it, both collecting and expelling impurities from the entire body in the form of menstruation. Numerous early modern sources describe recipes for 'bringing on the menses' in order to restore this flow when it had become blocked by illness or stagnation. From a modern point of view, this is a coded way to describe an early abortion. Riddle assumes that early modern women were in fact procuring abortions whenever they sought to restore menstrual function. Yet King argues that Riddle does not fully appreciate early modern constructions of the female body, and that not every recipe designed to encourage menstruation was an abortifacient.[48] According to Carla Spivack, early modern people viewed as minimal and unworthy of discussion the distinction between encouraging menstrual bleeding and causing a miscarriage before any signs of quickening.[49] An early modern woman who had not menstruated for several months might fear the potentially harmful effects of retained menses, and legitimately procure treatments designed to cleanse her womb.

Like medical sources, legal discussions of abortion during the early modern period should be carefully interpreted, with sensitivity to the variability of historical categories and circumstances. In her discussion of abortion in England, Spivack notes that while in a small number of cases law seems to classify abortion as murder without reference to stages of foetal development, there are other cases and historical sources which appear to regard abortion as far from serious.[50] The situation is complicated because no singular or unified legal system existed in medieval and early modern England.[51] Examining particular cases brought to the feudal appeals system, Spivack contends that women sued for assaults causing the deaths of foetuses in their wombs as a form of harm to their interests and bodies, without recognizing the foetus as a person.[52] She highlights the ambivalent status of abortion in the legal records in early modern England, concluding that it is not possible to make absolutist statements on the subject.[53] Spivack's cautious approach to the history of abortion in early modern England can be extended to all of Europe. Although there are numerous representations of birth control and abortion in medical, popular, and legal texts, they do not gel into a generalized, authoritative picture. Nor is it clear what the 'average' early modern person thought about these subjects, for most historical sources stem from particular authors who produced texts within the bounds of literary and medical conventions. In the end, it seems that early modern people had regular recourse to birth control and abortion, but the efficacy and safety of their practices remain an open question.

Managing childbirth

Female midwives cared for pregnant women and assisted with their deliveries throughout the early modern period, though they were increasingly criticized by male medical practitioners as noted above. Venette disparaged French female midwives at various points in his treatise, insisting that they lacked the anatomical knowledge necessary to undertake their duties, which included examining rape victims, diagnosing pregnancy, and supporting labouring women.[54] Before the 1970s, scholars had accepted such denunciations at face value, arguing that when dangerously uninformed female midwives were replaced by men equipped with scientific training and the forceps, childbearing women were saved from death and destruction.[55] This heroic narrative is, however, no longer considered accurate by experts in the field. Medical historians and literary critics working primarily on early modern English, French, Dutch, and German sources have shown that after undergoing lengthy apprenticeships, many female midwives were not only well-educated, respected members of their communities, but were also able to manage various complications in childbirth.[56] Men were nevertheless involved in providing gynaecological and, to a certain degree, obstetrical care during the early modern period. Monica Green places the expansion of European gynaecology firmly within the sixteenth century.[57] Inside the birthing chamber, however, men were usually called to assist at deliveries only after days of unsuccessful labour, when the child was likely dead and the life of the mother in peril. Not welcomed with open arms, these men were initially associated with both sexual impropriety and death. Yet they slowly increased their reputations and abilities, managing to attend even the uncomplicated deliveries of wealthy, urban French and English women by the eighteenth century. The complex medical, social, and cultural factors that encouraged the increased participation of men in childbirth have long been of interest to scholars, producing a substantial historiography informed by continual debate and revision.

Barbara Ehrenreich and Deirdre English broke new ground by arguing that women were systematically driven out of medical practice by men, with female midwives persecuted as witches because of their intimate understanding of women's bodies.[58] Despite challenging the traditional narrative that featured men marching triumphantly into the lying-in chamber to save the lives of women and children, subsequent research by historians has disproved many of the arguments of Ehrenreich and English, particularly the idea that female midwives were identified as witches.[59] According to Adrian Wilson, pregnant women were not the unwilling victims of male medical ambition. In fact, the expansion of male midwifery in England was encouraged by those women striving to increase their social status. He argues that literate, wealthy English women sought to distinguish themselves from the lower orders during the eighteenth century by hiring more costly men-midwives to assist at their deliveries. Because the men were called earlier to intervene in difficult and even normal labours, they gained increasing opportunities to deliver live children, sometimes with the aid of forceps or other surgical instruments, ultimately improving their reputations and distancing them from an exclusive association with death.[60]

My own research suggests reasons why female midwives may have invited male medical practitioners into the birthing room, an act that did not necessarily undermine their own authority.[61] Early modern French obstetrical publications are replete with what I call 'blame narratives': stories in which both male and female midwives attempted to dissociate themselves from guilt when labouring women died or were seriously injured, often by proclaiming their innocence and directing blame at other practitioners. With reference to the competitive medical world of early modern France, I contend that female midwives, including Louise Bourgeois, could call for male assistance to diffuse their responsibility in dangerous labours, sometimes even shifting the blame onto men who were less vulnerable within the medical hierarchy. In 1671 Marguerite de La Marche, the head midwife at the Parisian hospital, the Hôtel-Dieu, advised female midwives to turn the child inside the womb to deliver it feet first (podalic version) only after protecting themselves from blame by requesting a physician's help and warning the suffering woman's relatives of the danger.[62] Such efforts to share or transfer responsibility could nevertheless backfire. Men's medical reputations would improve if they successfully delivered a labouring female client, revealing them as competent, life-saving practitioners worth hiring in the future.

This discussion of selected recent publications on early modern midwifery shows that they now focus on particular geographical regions and source materials, rather than generalizing about all of early modern Europe. Both childbirth practices and the participation of men in the birthing room varied according to the location and class status of clients. In England childbirth became part of medicine between 1720 and 1770, whereas in France male expansion occurred at a slower rate and was always relatively rare in rural and southern areas.[63] Eighteenth-century France even saw the revival of the female midwife, in the form of Madame du Coudray, hired by Kings Louis XV and Louis XVI to teach her methods throughout the country.[64] The situation in Italy was in striking contrast to the rest of Europe, for there men never dominated the practice of childbirth. Nadia Maria Filippini attributes this situation to the disapproval of both the Catholic Church and the general populace, yet notes that by the eighteenth century the public role of the female midwife had been reduced to attending normal births.[65] The material culture of childbirth in Italy was additionally unique for it included Tuscan *deschi da parto*, painted wooden trays as well as majolica dishes used to present food and drink to the newly delivered woman.[66] Italian childbirth has nevertheless received less scholarly attention than birth in other parts of Europe, likely because of the long-standing interest in the expansion of male midwifery.

The regulation of female midwives also varied according to region, but gradually began to increase towards the end of the fifteenth century. The earliest French statute, which appeared in 1560, dealt with the instruction, examination, licensing, and registration of midwives in addition to instituting a code of moral conduct.[67] The regulation of midwives occurred during the sixteenth and seventeenth centuries in England. There the moral character and religious affiliation of midwives continued to be of greater concern to the authorities than the women's medical competence. David Harley has shown that the training of midwives was a rather informal affair in northern England, with women applying for a midwifery licence only after they had been reported for practising without one.[68] Somewhat more formal licensing practices were present in what is now Germany and Poland. According to Lynne Tatlock, the German midwife Justine Siegemund wrote her 1690 treatise, *The Court Midwife*, in the form of a dialogue to recall the catechism used to license midwives.[69] In many northern cities, female midwives were asked rote questions about female anatomy, obstetrical techniques, and religious duties by city authorities who expected to be provided with the standard, memorized responses. Repetition was a common form of learning during the early modern period, but it was not the primary kind of knowledge appreciated by women themselves.

Though female midwives such as Louise Bourgeois and Jane Sharp insisted that a theoretical understanding of the female anatomy was requisite to the ideal female midwife, they continued to value the education provided by an intimate, physical experience of pregnancy and childbirth. In her obstetrical treatise, Bourgeois referred to her own multiple pregnancies, ridiculing those women who had given birth only once or twice and yet discussed the subject in the presence of older, wiser women.[70] Sharp claimed that it was the 'natural propriety of women to be much seeing into that Art [i.e., midwifery]' even as this natural form of knowing had to be augmented by a 'long and diligent practice, and be communicated to others of our own sex'.[71] Female midwives insisted that women were superior to male practitioners within the birthing room because of their firsthand experiences of menstruation, gynaecological conditions, or childbirth.[72] According to them, midwifery was a female practice buoyed by the information exchanged orally among women. Notions of a unified women's culture have nevertheless been challenged by such scholars as Adrian Wilson and Laura Gowing, who document divisions between early modern English women according to their social and marital status, as noted above.[73]

All the same, continuing beliefs in the authority of a fleshly knowledge of childbirth valorized maternity while potentially excluding men from the birthing room. Male surgeons and physicians wishing to expand their practices responded by arguing that childbirth was in fact a medical condition requiring expert intervention, especially in those difficult cases when an unborn child presented an arm or leg first, rather than its head. In early modern France, surgeon men-midwives portrayed female midwives as unskilled workers who simply assisted nature, but could do little if complications arose.[74] By emphasizing the dangers of childbirth, these men not only implied that female birthing assistants could not be trusted to provide adequate care, but left descriptions that have encouraged contemporary scholars to exaggerate the risks of early modern pregnancy. Despite some evidence that women indeed feared childbirth, deaths in the lying-in chamber were not commonplace during the early modern period. Such scholars as Alain Bideau, Roger Schofield, and Irvine Loudon have undertaken comparative studies of maternal mortality rates in early modern Europe, suggesting that they were much lower than the 8 to 15 per cent estimated by previous researchers. Their most thorough evidence, however, stems from the eighteenth and nineteenth centuries, rather than from the earlier periods.[75]

Even as early modern male medical practitioners produced a rather negative representation of maternity, they could not simply dismiss the bodily authority of women. Admitting that the female body was an important source of knowledge, the men insisted that their own physical and surgical experience of the womb, acquired through touch, gave them the hands-on knowledge valued by their female clients. Some men-midwives even discussed the pregnancies and labours experienced by their close female relatives, including wives and sisters, to bolster their claims to bodily authority. Many male authors of French obstetrical treatises referred to the physical labour they undertook while assisting at difficult births, describing themselves as becoming more exhausted than the newly delivered woman.[76] These discussions indicate that during the early modern period male midwives aspiring to improve their reputations and expand their practices had to please labouring women as well as their female relatives and friends.

Ambivalent wombs

This evidence of the continuing respect given to female experiences of pregnancy and birth in early modern Europe is at odds with long-standing arguments focused on the negative representation of maternity. Since the 1980s, feminists have argued that early modern authors regularly portrayed the female body as both unstable and in need of patriarchal control. Drawing primarily on medical texts, these scholars contend that although understandings of the female body changed during the early modern period, pregnancy was consistently considered a disease, menstruation was identified with pollution, and female sexuality was viewed as a social danger.[77] Gail Kern Paster, for example, discusses the overwhelming association of the womb with shame in obstetrical treatises published during the sixteenth and seventeenth centuries.[78] More recent feminist work strives, however, to present a more diverse picture of the early modern female body. As noted earlier, Cathy McClive examines an array of medical writings to demonstrate that menstruation was primarily considered a sign of women's health and well-being in early modern France.[79] Other academics claim that women's understandings of their bodies could vary significantly from accounts proffered by medical authorities. In her investigation of letters sent between 1559 and 1568 by Catherine de Médicis to her daughter at the Spanish Court, Susan Broomhall notes that the French Queen drew on her personal experiences of childbearing to dispense advice about menstrual cycles and fertility.[80] The female body, and the womb in particular, were in fact portrayed both in positive and negative terms throughout the early modern period.

Katharine Park argues that modernist accounts of the history of the body tend to underestimate 'the co-existence of dramatically different views of the body within a single culture – and often within a single individual'.[81] This diversity is nowhere more apparent than in early modern discussions of female physiology. In his account of the reproductive organs in 'De l'anatomie de tout le corps humain' of 1575, for example, the French barber-surgeon Ambroise Paré claimed that *l'amarry*, or the womb, was an organ exclusive to women, but also noted that women's organs were congruent with those of men, noting that that which the man had outside of his body, the woman had on the inside.[82] Like Paré, later authors of obstetrical treatises discussed the womb as a remarkable organ that was distinctive to women, without dismissing the Galenic theory of women's reproductive parts as inverted versions of the male organs. In his *Traité des hermaphrodits, parties génitales, accouchemens des femmes* of 1612, the French surgeon Jacques Duval did not only claim that women's genital parts were noble and perfect.[83] He continued that ancient writers such as Artistotle and Galen were absolutely right to point out the similitude between male and female reproductive members, but also insisted on the idiosyncratic nature of the womb, including its bottle-like shape.[84] The early modern womb was held to be both unique and comparable to other organs.

Adhering to disparate theories was not specific to the early modern period. Joan Cadden has shown that there was no single model of sexual distinction in later medieval Europe; instead, concepts stemming from a variety of sources were applied in different contexts.[85] Helen King returns to ancient texts to argue that this diversity of views about the female body was already present in the Hippocratic corpus, texts which informed Galen's ideas.[86] Such research, along with work by other scholars, provides a substantial challenge to Thomas Laqueur's claim that before the eighteenth century in Europe, the Galenic 'one-sex' model was dominant, depicting male and female bodies that varied in degree rather than substance.[87] Though his coherent narrative of change from a 'one-sex' to a 'two-sex' model is appealing, many historians continue to recognize the eclecticism of theories of sexual difference in the past as well as the present. This debate continues in large part because of the different sources used by various scholars. In her critique of Laqueur's 'one-sex' body thesis, King points out that he relies on English translations of Galen, without referring to the Greek texts that contain contradictory evidence.[88]

In keeping with these diverse views, women's bodies were associated both with positive and negative forms of productivity. On one hand, women were understood as actively involved in conception, pregnancy, and labour. Though a few early modern authors followed Aristotle by arguing that women contributed only matter to the embryo, in the form of menstrual blood, as indicated above the majority of them adhered to the Galenic two-seed theory, arguing that both men and women contributed semen, which mixed together and 'cooked' inside the womb to form the embryo. This idea continued long after 1650, when the English physician William Harvey had proclaimed that 'all animals are in some part produced out of an egg'.[89] The French surgeon and man-midwife Pierre Dionis, for instance, was reluctant to adopt Harvey's view, but by the late 1690s he finally agreed that conception occurred by means of the encounter between male sperm and female egg.[90] This more mechanical theory potentially diminished the status of the womb because it emphasized the vivifying power of male semen. Even when authors ascribed to the ovum theory, however, they continued to argue that women actively participated in the gestation of the embryo, influencing its growth through their nutrition, actions, and emotions. This important maternal role persisted throughout the pregnancy, extending to the birth itself. Many authors of early modern obstetrical treatises described how fully formed foetuses initiated labour, struggling to leave the womb once they became cramped by its restrictive size, or lacked an adequate food supply.[91] Yet medical writers also recognized that the delivery could not proceed without women's physical participation and labour pains. Thus even as understandings of conception began to shift, women were rarely described as mere containers for the foetus, or as purely passive during labour and delivery.

On the other hand, negative portrayals could become dominant, depending on regional and historical circumstances. In her study of popular beliefs in early modern England, Mary Fissell finds that during the seventeenth century positive descriptions of the vivifying powers of the womb were displaced by negative accounts of its potential to harbour disease and wickedness.[92] Fissell contends that as pregnancy gradually lost its connection with the miraculous – particularly in Protestant areas that downplayed the role of the Virgin Mary – the female body was linked with the monstrous and abnormal. Texts produced in such Catholic countries as France continued to portray the womb as an organ crucial to the creation of life, but similarly associated it with disease. In 1668, Mauriceau, for example, argued that the uterus was the source of most female illnesses even as it remained crucial to women's health because of its purgative function.[93] Furthermore, the womb was associated with the production of monsters throughout the early modern period. According to Marie-Hélène Huet, early modern medical writers and laypeople alike believed that a mother's thoughts could negatively affect her unborn child, especially during the early stages of pregnancy.[94] If a pregnant woman gazed at a devil-like figure in a painting, she might give birth to a hairy child, or even one with dark skin. If she longed for strawberries but could not fulfil her desire, the child might emerge from the womb with a red birthmark on its body, demonstrating the impact of maternal longing. Huet argues that such theories were related to contemporary anxieties about the force of paternity, suggesting that malformation resulted when women dominated the act of procreation. Women's ability to reshape the contents of their own wombs could nevertheless have highlighted the maternal role in gestation, potentially raising women's status. The emphasis on female agency was contrary to the long-standing idea that male seed was dominant in conception. For the most part, however, recognition of maternal intervention occurred when the birth went horribly awry, reinforcing paternal superiority as both natural and desirable.

Tales of monstrous birth were continually recounted in conversation and pamphlets from the Middle Ages through to the eighteenth century, and have been thoroughly analysed by Lorraine Daston and Katharine Park.[95] These authors contend that multiple explanations existed for cases of monstrous birth. The unusual or monstrous offspring could act as religious warnings or portents; they could be objects worthy of delight and appreciation; or they could be examined carefully in the quest to discover their natural causes. According to Daston and Park, the reaction which came to dominate was largely shaped by local political and economic circumstances. Reports of a winged hermaphrodite born in sixteenth-century Ravenna, for example, were linked with disaster because enemy forces were about to invade the city. Daston and Park argue that European elites came to reject this fascination with monstrous birth by the late seventeenth century, striving to create distinctions between 'high' and 'low' culture. Yet particular cases of abnormal or hybrid birth continued to arouse a broad public well into the eighteenth century. Most famously, an English maidservant claimed in 1726 to have given birth to rabbits.[96] She reported having longed for rabbits while pregnant and, despite suffering a miscarriage, having ultimately produced animal parts from her body. Given the continuing references to the power of the maternal imagination, Toft's story was not implausible, and she was examined by various court physicians, including Nathaniel St André, a surgeon and anatomist to King George I, who seemed to find her tale credible.[97] The London man-midwife Sir Richard Manningham eventually revealed Toft as a fraud, after a porter admitted to smuggling a rabbit into her bedchamber.[98] This incident inspired numerous scholarly and popular written descriptions, as well as vividly engraved images showing rabbits emerging from beneath Toft's skirt, which testify to the popular absorption with questions about the unruly female body, the relationship between humans and animals, and the gullibility of elite medical practitioners.

Vision and visuality

Monstrous births indicate the important status of vision, particularly when women gazed upon an image and it was conveyed to the impressionable matter in their womb. Looking at monsters once they were born was also of great interest to many early modern people, a point highlighted by Merry Wiesner-Hanks in her discussion of the Gonzales sisters, young women with long, fine hair covering most of their bodies.[99] When the learned Ulisse Aldrovandi encountered Antoinetta Gonzales in Bologna in 1594, he carefully described her face, which was hairy except for the areas around her nostrils and mouth, and the more bristly fur on her back. His report, along with woodcuts depicting the girl and her family, were later published in *Monstrorum historia*, a collection of human and animal abnormalities that circulated widely.[100] These and other images are now among the most important early modern sources related to the famously hairy Gonzales family, and Wiesner-Hanks analyses them carefully. Yet portraits of Antoinetta Gonzales tell us more about how she was displayed in court culture and figured as a spectacle for experts, aristocrats, and the broad audiences for the *Monstrorum historia*, than what she may actually have looked like.

Such early modern representations of monsters convey the historical practices of looking at beings considered abnormal or unnatural, contributing to scholarly considerations of visuality, in which vision is approached as an historical and cultural act, rather than a biological ability.[101] In the portrait of Antonietta Gonzales by Lavinia Fontana, made during the 1590s, for example, the girl's hairy face contrasts sharply with her fine clothing and the white ruff that encircles her neck. This deliberate comparison between the animalistic head and civilized body is highlighted again when Antonietta's slender fingers are shown holding a piece of paper on which her biography has been written. In this case, her cultivated hands and possible literacy appear to be at odds with her unkempt face. The portrait suggests that during the early modern period, people with unusual features were understood as hybrid characters that defied binary distinctions; they were openly looked upon as confusing and fascinating spectacles that were at once horrible and sympathetic.

Though representations of monstrous births were especially popular, images of conventional childbirth have also survived, providing information about the visual politics of the lying-in chamber. These sources have not been as thoroughly pursued by historians or literary critics with more training in textual analysis and careful archival research than visual methodologies. Many representations depict scenes of lying-in, in which the newly delivered woman reclines on a bed in the background, while nurses tend to the newborn in the foreground. Religious paintings of the births of Saint Anne, Saint John, and the Virgin, for example, draw on these conventions, alluding to contemporary birthing rituals.[102] Medical representations of pregnancy and birth feature anatomical portrayals of the female reproductive organs and diagrammatic renderings of the unborn child in the womb.[103] These visual documents make arguments, and do not simply reflect historical realities or reveal what early modern people thought about the parturient body.

An unusual early modern image of the lying-in chamber was added to the 1707 Dutch translation of the obstetrical treatise written by Louise Bourgeois, originally published in 1626 (see Figure 19.1). The designer and engraver are unknown, but the representation was not meant to transform Bourgeois' beliefs into a visual format. She had died in 1636, having no role in the continued reproduction of her treatise. The image itself does not correspond with any of the doctrines or case studies described in her book. It might have been added primarily to increase the aesthetic and monetary value of the translated treatise. Yet it communicates significant messages about the relationship between revelation and concealment, portraying a labouring woman assisted by a male midwife with a sheet tied around his neck. This sheet covers her lower body, making it impossible for him to see what his hands are doing. The female attendants gathered around the parturient woman are likewise unable to gaze at her body. Instead they look towards each other, while the birthing woman directs her eyes upward, as if appealing to the heavens for relief. None of the women looks directly at the seated male figure, who is almost entirely hidden from their view. The sheet falls across his shoulders and upper back in a manner echoing the bed draperies that frame the scene. These visual features highlight the themes of covering and uncovering in the image, while enhancing the theatricality of the event taking place.

The engraved birthing scene is idealized, and does not display what typically occurred when a man arrived to assist at a difficult labour. The draperies covering the labouring female body accord with the advice repeated in numerous obstetrical treatises, which noted

Figure 19.1 Woman in labour assisted by a man-midwife, from Louise Bourgeois' *Het begin en ingang van alle menschen in de wereld*, Dutch trans. *of Observations diverses sur la stérilité, perte de fruict, foecondité, accouchements et maladies des femmes et enfants nouveaux naiz*, Leyden, 1707. Courtesy of the National Library of Medicine, Bethesda, MD.

that women should be covered both for warmth and to shield them from shame.[104] The man-midwife is similarly protected from view, something unlikely to have happened. Only his back is offered to our prying eyes, and the women present in the birthing room discreetly look away from him. According to their own published accounts, male practitioners were regularly scrutinized within the birthing room. In order to gain the confidence of the labouring woman, as well as her friends and family members, male midwives strove to convey desirable physical qualities, such as cleanliness and proper attire, while disguising negative displays of fear or dangerous surgical instruments.[105] Female looking was potentially more significant than male looking within the early modern birthing room, something ignored in accounts that associate the increased practice of medical men with their application of a powerful medical gaze able to transform the female body into an object, medicalizing the experiences of both pregnancy and birth.[106]

Though admitted to the lying-in chamber in cases of emergency, men were usually excluded from the celebrations held after a successful labour, when women would gather around the bed of a newly delivered woman to eat, drink, and chat. This female event was regularly ridiculed in a literary genre called *les caquets de l'accouchée*, or the cackle of the confined woman, which portrayed the women as harridans discussing their extramarital sexual exploits. The narrator of the *caquets de l'accouchée* was often represented as a male visitor or member of the family, hidden behind a curtain to eavesdrop on the bawdy and intimate discussions of inebriated women.[107] In this case, the male interloper concealed himself behind drapery in order to have aural rather than visual access to the explicit kind of corporeal knowledge associated with women.

Historicizing parenthood

Images of monstrous births and descriptions of difficult labours may have created some anxiety about the act of procreation. Deaths in childbed were relatively low, especially in contrast to the high infant mortality rates; as many as one in four children died before reaching the age of 10.[108] Historians have long considered the specificity of parenting, trying to discover how early modern men and women felt about and interacted with their children. According to the early research of Philippe Ariès, there was really no such category as 'childhood' during the early modern period, when parents avoided forming emotional bonds with their offspring because of their limited chance for survival.[109] Ariès drew attention to a neglected area of study, but much subsequent historical work has disproven his theories, arguing that conceptions of childhood existed in the past, but varied according to time and place. In 1565 the physician Simon de Vallambert, for example, wrote the first work on pediatrics to appear in the French language, *Cinq Livres, de la manière de nourrir et gouverner les enfans dès leur naissance* [Five Books, on the manner of feeding and governing children from their birth], dividing childhood into distinct age classifications for the purpose of diagnosing disease: (1) from birth to 7 months; (2) from the first appearance of teeth to 2 years; (3) from 2 to 7 years; and (4) from 7 to 14 years.[110] Increasingly popular during the early modern period, similar parenting manuals offered advice about how to select a nurse for a newborn child, whether or not women should breastfeed their own children, how often to bathe a child, and how to recognize and treat various illnesses, in addition to the moral and religious education children should receive.[111] This and similar publications suggest that parents may have valued their children intensely during the early modern period, precisely because child loss through illness, disease, and accident was so commonplace.

Modern scholars have reconsidered the relationship between parents and their children, drawing on diaries, account books, and advice literature to argue that parents were indeed close to children, suffering devastating grief upon their early demise.[112] The nature of these relationships varied according to the economic status of particular individuals and families. In her study of the experiences of single mothers in seventeenth-century England, Laura Gowing concludes that parenthood was economically determined, with the affective ties between poor families and their children mediated through the authority of the parish, especially in such cities as London.[113] In his study of popular responses to stillbirth, Jacques Gélis argues that while early modern Europeans could resign themselves to the physical death of a child, they were tormented by thoughts of its spiritual death; an unbaptized child was forbidden burial in consecrated ground, and would remain forever in a state of limbo.[114] Hoping for a miracle, relatives might take the child to a *sanctuaire à répit* and lay its body before a sacred image of the Virgin while praying for its temporary resurrection and subsequent baptism. Gélis' study reveals that this practice was not uncommon in rural parts of north-eastern France, as well as in Belgium, Austria, and Switzerland from the sixteenth through the eighteenth centuries. Between 1569 and 1593 in Faverney in Haute-Saône there were, for example, 459 registered cases of children baptized after their brief return to life.[115] Drawing on accounts of miraculous resurrections recorded by the curés of various sanctuaries, Gélis provides a vivid picture of the ritual, finding that those caring for the child's body frequently travelled long distances on foot to a reputed sanctuary. His work contributes to an expanding literature that explores the ways in which parents could be devoted to their children, extending definitions of the early modern family.

Conclusions

Understandings of reproduction during the early modern period were diverse and often contradictory; they varied according to context, region, and the social status as well as education of particular people. While many ideas about the body were retained throughout the early modern period – a valorization of fertility, reliance on female midwives, fascination with monstrous birth – others changed over time. The Galenic two-seed theory of conception had a powerful hold in both popular and medical writings, for example, but it was gradually replaced by the ovum theory, which became dominant by the eighteenth century. At the same time, even as the female body remained a source of first-hand knowledge about maternity throughout the early modern period, men continued to expand their practices in the birthing room; yet men did not become the primary birthing assistants until the early twentieth century. Monstrous births, such as Mary Toft's production of rabbits, sustained the attention of medical practitioners and laypeople alike, during a time when monsters were increasingly explained in terms of such natural phenomena as maternal injury rather than the force of the maternal imagination. The Toft case provides a particularly striking instance of how older ideas could coexist in tension with newer ones, before being displaced by them.

The preservation of traditional ideas alongside more recent theories similarly occurs in current scholarship on the early modern period. Assertions of the overwhelmingly negative status of women's unruly bodies continue to be made, even as evidence of respect for the productivity of the maternal body is revealed. Narratives of the male takeover of the birthing room have not been entirely undermined by the numerous scholarly accounts that show the ongoing esteem for female midwives, women who were often quite well trained. And the influence of Ariès' arguments about the relative lack of parental devotion remains, despite the recent descriptions of a range of sources revealing the emotional bonds between early modern family members. In the end, ongoing uncertainly about early modern reproduction will ensure that debate and revision continue to be central to this active and exciting field of study.

Notes

1 Nicolas Venette, *Tableau de l'amour, consideré dans l'estat du mariage*, Amsterdam: J. and G. Jansson, 1687, p. 222. Translation is from Nicholas de Venette, *Conjugal Love Reveal'd*, London: T. Hinton, 1720, p. 127.

2 For the different editions and translations of Venette's treatise see Colette Piau-Gillot, 'Heurs et Malheurs du *Tableau de l'amour conjugal* de Nicolas Venette', *Dix-Huitième Siècle* 19, 1987, pp. 365–77 and Roy Porter, 'Spreading Carnal Knowledge or Selling Dirt Cheap? Nicolas Venette's "Tableau de l'amour conjugal" in Eighteenth-Century England', *Journal of European Studies* 14:4, 1984, pp. 233–55.

3 Lianne McTavish, *Childbirth and the Display of Authority in Early Modern France*, Aldershot: Ashgate, 2005.

4 Jane Sharp, *The midwives book, or the whole art of midwifry discovered*, London: Simon Miller, 1671, p. 164.

5 Sue Blundell, *Women in Ancient Greece*, Cambridge, MA: Harvard University Press, 1995, p. 105.

6 Laurent Joubert, *Popular Errors*, trans. Gregory David de Rocher, Tuscaloosa: University of Alabama Press, 1989, p. 122.

7 For straightforward accounts of humoural theory see Roy Porter, *Medicine: A History of Healing*, New York: Marlowe and Company, 1997, p. 20, and Audrey Eccles, *Obstetrics and Gynaecology in Tudor and Stuart England*, Kent, OH: Kent State University Press, 1982, p. 17.

8 Pierre Darmon, *Le mythe de la procréation à l'âge baroque*, Paris: J.-J. Pauvert, 1977, pp. 44–45.

9 Eccles, *Obstetrics and Gynaecology*, p. 36.

10 Venette, *Tableau de l'amour*, pp. 201–4.

11 Angus McLaren, *Reproductive Rituals: The Perception of Fertility in England from the Sixteenth to the Nineteenth Century*, New York: Methuen, 1984, p. 41.

12 Pierre Darmon, *Le Tribunal de l'impuissance: Virilité et défaillances conjugales dans l'ancienne France*, Paris: Seuil, 1979.

13 Venette, *Tableau de l'amour*, p. 69.

14 Nicolas Puzos, *Traité des accouchemens*, Paris: Desaint and Saillant, 1759; Jean-Louis Baudelocque, *Principes sur l'art des accouchemens*, Paris: Méquignon, 1787; Antoine Petit, *Traité des maladies des femmes enceintes*, Paris: Baudouin, 1799.

15 Philippe Peu, *La pratique des accouchemens*, Paris: Boudot, 1694, p. 107.

16 Sarah Toulalan, '"The Act of Copulation Being Ordain'd by Nature as the Ground of all Generation": Fertility and the Representation of Sexual Pleasure in Seventeenth-Century Pornography in England', *Women's History Review* 15:4, 2006, pp. 521–32.

17 Karen Harvey, *Reading Sex in the Eighteenth Century: Bodies and Gender in English Erotic Culture*, Cambridge: Cambridge University Press, 2004, p. 181.

18 Venette, *Tableau de l'amour*, p. 192.

19 Edward Shorter, *A History of Women's Bodies*, New York: Basic Books, 1982.

20 E. P. Thompson, 'Eighteenth-Century English Society: Class Struggle without Class?', *Social History* 3, 1978, pp. 133–65 (157–58); Jean-Louis Flandrin, *Families in Former Times: Kinship, Household and Sexuality*, trans. R. Southern, Cambridge: Cambridge University Press, 1979.

21 David Herlihy and Christiane Klapisch-Zuber, *Tuscans and their Families: A Study of the Florentine Catasto of 1427*, New Haven, CT: Yale University Press, 1985; Alfred Perrenoud, 'Espacement et arrêt dans le côntrole de naissances', *Annales de demographie historique*, 1988, 59–78; Peter Clark (ed.), *Small Towns in Early Modern Europe*, Cambridge: Cambridge University Press, 1995.

22 Jean Claude Bologne, *La naissance interdite*, Paris: Olivier Orban, 1988, pp. 138–64; McLaren, *Reproductive Rituals*, pp. 81–82; John T. Noonan, *Contraception: A History of its Treatment by the Catholic Theologians and Canonists*, Cambridge, MA: Harvard University Press, 1986, pp. 200–12.

23 Robert Jütte, *Contraception: A History*, trans. Vicky Russell, Cambridge: Polity Press, 2008, pp. 96–98; Bologne, *La naissance interdite*, pp. 154–55.

24 John M. Riddle, *Contraception and Abortion from the Ancient World to the Renaissance*, Cambridge, MA: Harvard University Press, 1992; John M. Riddle, *Eve's Herbs: A History of Contraception and Abortion in the West*, Cambridge, MA: Harvard University Press, 1997.

25 Patricia Crawford, 'Sexual Knowledge in England, 1500–1750' in Roy Porter and Mikuláš Teich (eds), *Sexual Knowledge, Sexual Science: The History of Attitudes to Sexuality*, Cambridge: Cambridge University Press, 1994, pp. 82–106 (99).

26 Helen King, *Hippocrates' Woman: Reading the Female Body in Ancient Greece*, London: Routledge, 1998, pp. 144–45.

27 Joan Thirsk, *Food in Early Modern England: Phases, Fads, Fashions 1500–1760*, London: Hambledon Continuum, 2006.

28 Nancy Demand, *Birth, Death, and Motherhood in Classical Greece*, Baltimore, MD: Johns Hopkins University Press, 1994, p. 22.

29 Thomas Rütten, 'Receptions of the Hippocratic Oath in the Renaissance', *Journal of the History of Medicine and Allied Sciences* 51:4, 1996, pp. 456–83 (466).

30 Ann Ellis Hanson, 'Hippocrates: Diseases of Women 1', *Signs* 1:2, 1975, pp. 567–84 (567).

31 Monica H. Green, 'Constantinus Africanus and the Conflict between Religion and Science' in G. R. Dunstan (ed.), *The Human Embryo: Aristotle and the Arabic and European Traditions*, Exeter: University of Exeter Press, 1990, pp. 47–69 (52).

32 Bologne, *La naissance interdite*, p. 166.

33 Denis Fournier, *L'accoucheur méthodique*, Paris: The Author, 1677, p. 213.

34 Ambroise Paré, *Responce de M. Ambroise Paré, premier chirurgien du Roy, aux calomnies d'aucuns médecins, et chirurgiens, touchant ses œuvres*, n.l.: n.p., n.d., pp. 8–9.

35 Wendy Arons, *Eucharius Rösslin: When Midwifery Became the Male Physician's Province. The Sixteenth Century Handbook 'The Rose Garden for Pregnant Women and Midwives'*, Jefferson, NC: McFarland and Company, 1994, pp. 83–84.

36 François Mauriceau, *Des maladies des femmes grosses et accouchées*, Paris: J. Hénault, 1668, p. 105.

37 McTavish, *Childbirth*, p. 203.

38 Lianne McTavish, 'Blame and Vindication in the Early Modern Birthing Room', *Medical History* 50:4, 2006, pp. 447–64.

39 Louise Bourgeois, *Observations diverses sur la stérilité, perte de fruict, foecondité, accouchements et maladies des femmes et enfants nouveaux naiz*, ed. Françoise Olive, Paris: Côte-Femmes, 1992 [1652], p. 177.

40 Joanne M. Ferraro, *Nefarious Crimes, Contested Justice: Illicit Sex and Infanticide in the Republic of Venice, 1557–1789*, Baltimore, MD: Johns Hopkins University Press, 2008; Susan C. Staub, *Nature's Cruel Stepdames: Murderous Women in the Street Literature of Seventeenth Century England*, Pittsburgh, PA: Duquesne University Press, 2005; Mark Jackson, *Infanticide: Historical Perspectives on Child Murder and Concealment, 1550–2000*, Aldershot: Ashgate, 2002.

41 Laura Gowing, *Common Bodies: Women, Touch, and Power in Seventeenth-Century England*, New Haven, CT: Yale University Press, 2003, p. 78.

42 Etienne van de Walle, '"Marvellous Secrets": Birth Control in European Short Fiction, 1150–1650', *Population Studies* 54, 2000, pp. 321–30.

43 Noonan, *Contraception*.

44 Jacques Duval, *Des Hermaphrodits, accouchemens des femmes et traitement qui est requis pour les relever en santé*, Rouen: P. Geuffroy, 1612, p. 111; Jacques Guillemeau, *De l'Heureux accouchement des femmes*, Paris: N. Buon, 1609, p. 2; G. Mauquest de La Motte, *Traité complet des accouchemens naturels, non naturels et contre nature*, Leiden: J. A. Langerak, 1729, p. 49. See also Cathy McClive, 'The Hidden Truths of the Belly: The Uncertainties of Pregnancy in Early Modern Europe', *Social History of Medicine* 15:2, 2002, pp. 209–27.

45 Barbara Duden, *The Woman Beneath the Skin: A Doctor's Patients in Eighteenth-Century Germany*, trans. Thomas Dunlap, Cambridge, MA: Harvard University Press, 1991 [1987].

46 Barbara Duden, *Disembodying Women: Perspectives on Pregnancy and the Unborn*, trans. Lee Hoinacki, Cambridge, MA: Harvard University Press, 1993; Lianne McTavish, 'The Cultural Production of Pregnancy: Bodies and Embodiment at a New Brunswick Abortion Clinic', *Topia: Canadian Journal of Cultural Studies* 20, 2008, pp. 23–42.

47 Cathy McClive, 'Bleeding Flowers and Waning Moons: A History of Menstruation in France, *c.* 1495–1761', Unpublished Doctoral Thesis, University of Warwick, 2000.

48 King, *Hippocrates' Woman*, pp. 144–45.

49 Carla Spivack, 'To "Bring Down the Flowers": The Cultural Context of Abortion Law in Early Modern England', *William and Mary Journal of Women and the Law* 14:1, 2007, pp. 107–51 (123).

50 Spivack 'To "Bring Down the Flowers"', p. 109.

51 Spivack 'To "Bring Down the Flowers"', p. 110.

52 Spivack 'To "Bring Down the Flowers"', pp. 139–40.

53 Spivack 'To "Bring Down the Flowers"', p. 110.

54 Venette, *Tableau de l'amour*, pp. 76, 87, 269.

55 Irving Samuel Cutter and Henry R. Viets, *A Short History of Midwifery*, Philadelphia, PA: Saunders, 1964; Thomas Rogers Forbes, *The Midwife and the Witch*, New Haven, CT: Yale University Press, 1966.

56 Hilary Marland (ed.), *The Art of Midwifery: Early Modern Midwives in Europe*, London: Routledge, 1993; Wendy Perkins, *Midwifery and Medicine in Early Modern France: Louise Bourgeois*, Exeter: University of Exeter Press, 1996; Nina Rattner Gelbart, *The King's Midwife: A History and Mystery of Madame du Coudray*, Berkeley, CA: University of California Press, 1998; Doreen Evenden, *The Midwives of Seventeenth-Century London*, Cambridge: Cambridge University Press, 2000; Lynne Tatlock, *The Court Midwife: Justine Siegemund*, Chicago, IL: Chicago University Press, 2005.

57 Monica H. Green, *Making Women's Medicine Masculine: The Rise of Male Authority in Pre-Modern Gynaecology*, Oxford: Oxford University Press, 2008.

58 Barbara Ehrenreich and Deidre English, *Witches, Midwives, and Nurses: A History of Women Healers*, New York: The Feminist Press, 1973.

59 David Harley, 'Historians as Demonologists: The Myth of the Midwife Witch', *Social History of Medicine* 3:1, 1990, pp. 1–26; Jane P. Davidson, 'The Myth of the Persecuted Female Healer', *Journal of the Rocky Mountain Medieval and Renaissance Association* 14, 1993, pp. 115–29.

60 Adrian Wilson, *The Making of Man-Midwifery: Childbirth in England 1660–1770*, London: UCL Press, 1995.

61 McTavish, 'Blame and Vindication'.

62 Marguerite de La Marche (du Tertre), *Instruction familière et utile aux sages-femmes pour bien pratiquer les accouchemens*, Paris: L. d'Houry, 1710, p. 7.

63 Lisa Forman Cody, *Birthing the Nation: Sex, Science, and the Conception of Eighteenth-Century Britons*, Oxford: Oxford University Press, 2005; Mireille Laget, *Naissances: L'accouchement avant l'âge de la clinique*, Paris: Seuil, 1982; Jacques Gélis, *La sage-femme ou le médecin: une nouvelle conception de la vie*, Paris: Fayard, 1988.

64 Gelbart, *The King's Midwife*.

65 Nadia Maria Filippini, 'The Church, the State and Childbirth: The Midwife in Italy during the Eighteenth Century' in Hilary Marland (ed.), *The Art of Midwifery*, pp. 152–75.

66 Jacqueline Marie Musacchio, *The Art and Ritual of Childbirth in Renaissance Italy*, New Haven, CT: Yale University Press, 1999.

67 Richard L. Petrelli, 'The Regulation of French Midwifery during the *Ancien Régime*', *Journal of the History of Medicine* 27, 1971, pp. 276–92; Gélis, *La sage-femme ou le médecin*, pp. 40–55.

68 David Harley, 'Provincial Midwives in England: Lancashire and Cheshire, 1660–1760' in Marland (ed.), *The Art of Midwifery*, pp. 27–48.

69 Tatlock, *The Court Midwife*, p. 4.

70 Bourgeois, *Observations diverses*, p. 143.

71 Sharp, *The Midwives Book*, p. 3.

72 McTavish, *Childbirth*, p. 87.

73 Wilson, *The Making of Man-Midwifery*; Gowing, *Common Bodies*.

74 McTavish, *Childbirth*, p. 42.

75 Alain Bideau, 'Accouchement "naturel" et accouchements à "haut risque"', *Annales de demographie historique*, 1981, pp. 4–66; Roger Schofield, 'Did the Mothers Really Die? Three Centuries of Maternal Mortality in "The World We Have Lost"' in Lloyd Bonfield *et al.* (eds), *The World We Have Gained*, Oxford: Blackwell, 1986, pp. 231–60; Irvine Loudon, *Death in Childbirth: An International Study of Maternal Care and Maternal Mortality 1800–1950*, Oxford: Clarendon, 1992.

76 McTavish, *Childbirth*, p. 159.

77 Yvonne Knibiehler and Catherine Fouquet, *La femme et les médecins: analyse historique*, Paris: Hachette, 1983; Evelyne Berriot-Salvadore, *Les femmes dans la société française de la Renaissance*, Geneva: Droz, 1990.

78 Gail Kern Paster, *The Body Embarrassed: Drama and the Disciplines of Shame in Early Modern England*, Ithaca, NY: Cornell University Press, 1993.

79 McClive, 'Bleeding Flowers and Waning Moons'.

80 Susan Broomhall, *Women's Medical Work in Early Modern France*, Manchester: Manchester University Press, 2004, pp. 214–31.

81 Katherine Park, 'Was There a Renaissance Body?' in Allen J. Grieco, Michael Rocke and Fiorella Gioffredi Superbi (eds), *The Italian Renaissance in the Twentieth Century*, Florence: Leo S. Olschki, 2002, pp. 21–35.

82 Ambroise Paré, *Deux livres de chirurgie, de la génération de l'homme*, Paris: A. Wechel, 1573, p. 85.

83 Duval, *Des Hermaphrodits*, p. 19.

84 Duval, *Des Hermaphrodits*, pp. 342–43.

85 Joan Cadden, *Meanings of Sex Difference in the Middle Ages: Medicine, Science, and Culture*, Cambridge: Cambridge University Press, 1993.

86 Helen King, 'The Mathematics of Sex: One to Two, or Two to One?', *Studies in Medieval and Renaissance History*, 3rd series, Vol. 2, New York: AMS Press, 2005, pp. 47–58.

87 Thomas Laqueur, *Making Sex: Body and Gender from the Greeks to Freud*, Cambridge, MA: Harvard University Press, 1990.

88   King, 'The Mathematics of Sex'.

89   William Harvey, *Exercitationes de generatione animalium*, London: Pulleyn, 1651.

90   Pierre Dionis, *Dissertation sur la génération de l'homme*, Paris: L'Houry, 1698.

91   Guillemeau, *De l'Heureux accouchement des femmes*, p. 168.

92   Mary Fissell, *Vernacular Bodies: The Politics of Reproduction in Early Modern England*, Oxford: Oxford University Press, 2004, pp. 52–73.

93   Mauriceau, *Des maladies des femmes grosses et accouchées*, p. 1; Pierre Dionis, *Traité general des accouchemens*, Paris: d'Houry, 1718, p. 68.

94   Marie-Hélène Huet, *Monstrous Imagination*, Cambridge, MA: Harvard University Press, 1993.

95   Lorraine Daston and Katharine Park, *Wonders and the Order of Nature, 1150–1750*, New York: Zone Books, 1998.

96   Dennis Todd, *Imagining Monsters: Miscreations of the Self in Eighteenth-Century England*, Chicago: University of Chicago Press, 1995.

97   Nathaniel St. André, *A Short Narrative of an Extraordinary Delivery of Rabbits, Perform'd by Mr. John Howard Surgeon at Guilford*, London: J. Clarke, 1727.

98   Richard Manningham, *An Exact Diary of What was Observ'd during a Close Attendance Upon Mary Toft, The Pretended Rabbet-Breeder of Godalming in Surrey*, London: J. Roberts, 1726.

99   Merry Wiesner-Hanks, *The Marvelous Hairy Girls: The Gonzales Sisters and Their Worlds*, New Haven, CT: Yale University Press, 2009.

100 Wiesner-Hanks, *The Marvelous Hairy Girls*, p. 3.

101 See, for example, Hal Foster (ed.), *Vision and Visuality*, Seattle: Bay, 1988.

102 Pierre Bertrand, 'Graver la naissance au XVIIe siècle', *Ethnologie française* 26:2, 1996, pp. 329–39.

103 McTavish, *Childbirth*, pp. 173–215.

104 Lianne McTavish, 'Concealing Spectacles: Childbirth and Visuality in Early Modern France' in Mark Cheetham, Elizabeth Legge and Catherine Soussloff (eds), *Editing (Out?) The Image*, Toronto: University of Toronto Press, 2008, pp. 95–114.

105 McTavish, *Childbirth*, pp. 57–79.

106 Lynne Tatlock, 'Speculum Feminarum: Gendered Perspectives on Obstetrics and Gynecology in Early Modern Germany', *Signs* 17:4, 1992, pp. 725–60; Roberta McGrath, *Seeing Her Sex: Medical Archives and the Female Body*, Manchester: Manchester University Press, 2002.

107 Domna C. Stanton, 'Recuperating Women and the Man behind the Screen' in James Grantham Turner (ed.), *Sexuality and Gender in Early Modern Europe: Institutions, Texts, Images*, Cambridge: Cambridge University Press, 1993, pp. 247–65.

108 Flandrin, *Families in Former Times*.

109 Philippe Ariès, *Centuries of Childhood: A Social History of Family Life*, trans. Robert Baldick, New York: Random, 1960.

110 Simon de Vallambert, *Cinq Livres, de la manière de nourrir et gouverner les enfans dès leur naissance*, ed. C. H. Winn, Geneva: Droz, 2005 [1565], p. 254.

111 Louis Haas, *The Renaissance Man and His Children: Childbirth and Early Childhood in Florence*, New York: St Martin's Press, 1998; Douglas A. Brooks (ed.), *Printing and Parenting in Early Modern England*, Ashgate: Aldershot, 2005.

112 Stephen E. Ozment, *Ancestors: The Loving Family in Old Europe*, Cambridge, MA: Harvard University Press, 2001. More recently see Hannah Newton, *The Sick Child in Early Modern England, 1580–1720*, Oxford: Oxford University Press, 2012.

113 Laura Gowing, 'Giving Birth at the Magistrate's Gate: Single Mothers in the Early Modern City' in Stephanie Tarbin and Susan Broomhall (eds), *Women, Identities and Communities in Early Modern Europe*, Aldershot: Ashgate, 2008, pp. 137–50.

114 Jacques Gélis, *Les enfants des limbes: Mort-nés et parents dans l'Europe chrétienne*, Paris: l'Audibert, 2006.

115 Gélis, *Les enfants des limbes*, p. 75.

20

REPRODUCTION SINCE 1750

Helen Blackman

During the 1890s, Everett Millais, son of the painter Sir John Everett Millais, spent some time trying to fertilize dogs without them copulating. He reported his results to the embryologist Walter Heape, who was undertaking similar experiments with artificial fertilization in other species. Heape in turn was working with Francis Galton, as they investigated ways in which to make human fertilization more efficient. More than a century later and the problems that they encountered in their experiments are all but overcome, though their motivation, the efficient breeding of the right type of human, occupies a more controversial place in history. Many of the motivations behind improving human reproductivity have a far from kindly motive – much of the concern in the early twentieth century came about because of a dearth of healthy soldiers. Successful reproduction was deemed of national importance in the context of military and imperial imperatives. The first section of this chapter examines the ways in which population became a resource to be encouraged and controlled. Men of science such as Heape were very aware of the wider concerns attached to their work. Heape was the first person to perform embryo transfer experiments successfully but he was not concerned with giving women more choice and certainly not with giving them more power. In fact he feared that women were trying to escape their reproductive destinies. Despite the presence of a number of married women with children in the suffrage movement, Heape saw voting women as likely to be un(re)productive 'waste products' of society:

> we are thus confronted with the probability, that extended power given to women will result in the waste products of our Female population gaining power to order the habits and regulate the work of those women who are of real value to us as a nation.[1]

In popular, medical and scientific discourse about reproduction women and women's roles were discussed far more often than were men and the roles they played. Throughout the period under discussion the male role in reproduction was rarely problematized. Thus women and the degree of control they have over their bodies is one of the key themes in this chapter. The state often played a part in trying to control reproduction: states have encouraged some sections of society to reproduce and at times forcibly prevented others from so doing. Women have been urged to stay at home. They have had to debate their right to access birth control and fight for the possibility of having an abortion. They have seen childbirth, previously a female domain, become dominated by often male obstetricians. Reproduction has been at once the most private and personal subject, and yet also the most public and political.

After examining the ways in which reproduction has been of interest to the state, in the second section I move on to discuss changes in biomedical knowledge about reproduction, in particular the female cycle. This leads naturally into a discussion of contraception, as women gained more control over their fertility and could make decisions about whether and when to conceive. In section four I then discuss genetics and embryology as it became possible for scientists to manipulate both fertilization and then the development of the embryo. Finally I turn to obstetrics, one of the key sites for women's struggles to gain control over reproduction.

Population and family structure

From the sixteenth to the nineteenth centuries, fertility rates remained relatively stable. From the mid-nineteenth century they dropped in both America and western Europe until by 1914 family size had halved. The age at which women first gave birth rose, and from 1870 to 1920 there was a dramatic drop in family size in Europe until families with only two children seemed relatively normal. Birth control was used to bring about this lowering of fertility rates, although why this is so is less than clear. Explanations include rising expectations, the protection of prosperity and the possibility that the working classes were copying their social superiors. This change in population growth, at a time when the population was regarded as a resource for promoting industry and empire, caused concern amongst politicians, medical men, and some vocal sections of the middle classes.[2]

During the eighteenth and nineteenth centuries, family structure underwent substantial change. As production moved out of the domestic sphere and into specifically commercial sites, women were less likely to act as business partners in a family concern. In the case of the middle classes, homes were relocated to the suburbs and domestic chores were done by servants. Thus the role of (middle-class) woman as mother was more and more emphasized. Working-class women also found themselves pushed more into the home, as legislation reduced their working hours. Children were not allowed to work at all and so they became potentially more a burden than a contributor to family income.[3] Generally, fertility rates were lower amongst the literate than amongst the illiterate from the same class. Aspirations changed as more information became available and large families were no longer the expected norm. As industrialization increased, so the population became a category for analysis and became something via which wealth could be generated. From the late seventeenth century, political and economic writers praised large populations as a resource that could bring military and industrial strength. It was in the state's interest to preserve and invest in the life of its population. Vital statistics could be used to count people and to work out the conditions which encouraged the most productive reproduction. The newly emergent medical profession could help to maintain optimum conditions. Increasingly, in an industrialized world, midwifery and the diseases of women and children became particularly important.[4]

From 1739 onwards the population in Britain began to fall. Then this reversed during the nineteenth century: at the 1801 census the population was 11 million, 100 years later it had risen to 37 million. However, from 1870 the birth rate began to fall.[5] Throughout most of the nineteenth century there had been around 34 births per 1,000 of the population but this dropped significantly. This fall in fertility occurred throughout Europe, although it was particularly marked in Britain. The decline in fertility was noted to have taken effect earliest among the middle classes, with sections of the poorest and less well-educated communities retaining high average numbers of children per family well into the twentieth century. Men of science and medical men often made comparisons between highly strung domestic animals and middle-class women who did not want to breed, in contrast to their less well-bred and more prolific sisters in the 'lower' classes.[6] By the early twentieth century, it was evident that fertility was declining amongst all women of marriageable age. Concerns about a drop in fertility and degeneration of breeding stock presented medical men and men of science with an opportunity. Investigating aspects of human reproduction was not highly valued in the scientific world, but if investigators could show that their studies could be useful in 'improving' human society, then they could raise the status of those studies.[7]

From the mid-nineteenth century, America and many European countries feared degeneration, which they were beginning to see as a natural corollary of progress. Just as man had become civilized, so he could revert to a savage state, and indeed civilization could contain the seeds of its own destruction for the pressures of modern life could lead to stress and eventually to disease. Men of science, writers, intellectuals and politicians worried that populations were degenerating. Evolution, they argued, by its very nature could be progressive or regressive: if you could evolve from a lower life form, you could also degenerate into that lower life form.[8] At the same time there were widespread fears amongst the middle classes that fertility rates were falling in the middle classes but increasing in the worst sections of the working classes, producing concern that the middle classes would be rapidly out-bred and that society would suffer as a consequence. From these fears came the science of eugenics.[9] Broadly speaking eugenics could be divided into positive eugenics (encouraging the 'right' people to breed) and negative eugenics (discouraging the 'wrong' people from breeding). Much of the impetus behind developing contraceptives, particularly from campaigners such as Marie Stopes, was eugenic in nature. To try to curb this problem of degeneration, eugenists sought to control who could breed. They lacked the knowledge to manipulate fundamental hereditary material, but they could attempt to decide who was allowed to reproduce.

In London during the 1880s and 1890s there were fears of a large underclass of unfit people. Rumours abounded that there were no third generation Londoners. Other fears emerged. Were the unfit being allowed to breed? By giving out help under the Poor Law, was a residuum being kept? And if the middle classes were limiting family size, were they interfering with a natural system? Large families were associated with prosperity and town stock had been replenished from the countryside. But were the British regressing and how could fertility be controlled – reduced in some quarters and encouraged in others – in order to bring about a better, fitter race? A plethora of national and local eugenic societies were founded, of which perhaps the best known was the Eugenics Education Society founded in 1907 to spread ideas about heredity and encourage eugenic marriages.

From the 1890s the so-called 'high-grade defective' became the focus of attention. They were described as being intelligent enough to function independently and so escape general notice, while actually being relatively unintelligent, producing children who might not be productive members of society. Concern increased until in 1903 a Committee on Physical Deterioration was founded. The following year a Royal Commission on the Care and Control of the Feeble Minded was also set up. When they reported in 1908 they identified a high-grade class who were particularly worrying because they were not covered by legislation and could function in society, but might produce 'low-grade deficients'.[10] The Commission estimated that there were more feeble-minded people than previously thought and that they were dangerous because they were unidentified. The higher grades had escaped detection and, they argued, their condition was inherited. Defectives were prolific and causing social problems. They made up the population of workhouses and prisons, were on relief or casually employed.[11] The women, the Commission argued, were often prostitutes and spread venereal diseases. In fact, there was no concrete evidence of this type of heredity in humans. As the biologist J. B. S. Haldane discussed in a 1955 lecture on eugenics, the knowledge of human heredity then current was not adequate to encourage positive eugenics and in his opinion, legislators were not capable of framing laws that would not be 'grossly unjust and inefficient'.[12]

Some countries, most notably various American states, and some Scandinavian countries, resorted to sterilization of the 'unfit'. In Britain there was no compulsory sterilization, although the Mental Deficiency Act of 1913 segregated the mentally deficient from the general population. The Brock Committee of 1932–34 investigated sterilization and there were hopes that this would lead to a Royal Commission and then to legislation. The Eugenics Society welcomed the report and argued that sterilization was politically feasible. Nonetheless, ministers worried about public opinion, rightly so, and sterilization never became law. In the eugenics movement, the state sought control over reproduction, trying to bring about 'improvement' on the population level. With little or no understanding of genetics, such control could not be forthcoming. However, as I discuss in the next section, throughout the period this chapter covers, medical and scientific knowledge of the reproductive body was rapidly improving.

The female cycle and changing views of the body

The way the human body in general and the female body in particular were understood changed markedly during the period under consideration. Basic anatomy became better understood, particularly as microscopy improved. Spermatozoa and then the mammalian egg were observed, then chromosomes (the string-like material within a cell's nucleus) were also seen. In the early twentieth century knowledge of genetics and the role of genes in heredity were developed, until in 1953 the structure of DNA was discovered. Alongside this better understanding of fertilization and heredity came a greater knowledge of what was going on within the body. The female cycle, initially believed to be triggered by the nervous system, came to be understood in terms of hormones. Along with this knowledge, various reproductive sciences arose, developed, and separated from one another. Until the twentieth century, the mechanism for inheritance, the transfer of material from one generation to another, was the source of much speculation. Darwin suggested pangenesis, in which gemmules in the blood carried information down to the next generation. This theory was tested by his cousin Francis Galton using blood transfusions and the results seemed negative.[13] French naturalist J. B. Lamarck argued that characteristics acquired during the lifetime of an individual could be inherited by the offspring of that individual, a theory first discredited and towards the end of the twentieth century found to have some limited truth.

While it was understood that men and women had to have sex to reproduce, exactly what happened after that was by and large unknown. Even the length of pregnancy was doubtful, with some women claiming that they must have been pregnant for 10 or 11 months (whether or not they were believed depended on the doctor's view of their reliability as a witness). The existence of spermatozoa was established by microscopist Antonie van Leeuwenhoek in 1677. The mammalian egg was first identified in 1827 by the embryologist Karl Ernst von Baer. However, it was some time before the nature of the interaction between egg and sperm was better understood. Following Aristotle's views on the functions of men and women in reproduction, some investigators posited that the sperm was equivalent to a plant seed whereas the egg acted like the soil. It was also thought that the sperm might give the egg a kind of lightning jolt and spur it into life.

We know now that the human female reproductive cycle lasts around 21 to 35 days. Doctors take the beginning of menstruation as the start date for the cycle, with menstruation lasting perhaps five days although there is much variation. Ovulation takes place roughly mid-cycle when there is a thick vascular lining to the womb. The egg dies fairly quickly, the lining sloughs off and begins to be shed. This cycle is now thought to be governed by hormones whereas until the early twentieth century it was thought to be governed neurologically. The exact purpose of menstruation remains unclear, although from at least the Middle Ages through to the present time there have been two essential theories – either it is a kind of mini-abortion or it has some kind of cleansing function.[14] Despite the paucity of knowledge about the human menstrual cycle, much influence was attributed to it. The sexologist Henry Havelock Ellis summed up many of the attitudes to women and the menstrual cycle in various of his works. Ellis published widely in the 1890s and well into the twentieth century, often summing up a wide range of literature, medical, anthropological, popular and wide ranging in time span. In *Man and Woman*, Ellis cited sources who held that 'women … only have intervals of health in the course of a continual disease' and who thought that 'woman is not only invalided but wounded'.[15] Although Ellis criticized these sources, he used similar language himself to describe menstruation, arguing that women always lived on the upward or downward slope of a curve. He illustrated this with a graph showing their variations in bodily functions over the course of a month – a graphic illustration of women's abnormality compared to men's.

In Ellis's eyes, and those of many of his contemporaries, menstruation was functionally abnormal, because it meant that a woman was not pregnant. Menstruation then became the 'abortion of a decidua'.[16] As Ellis placed an increasing emphasis on motherhood and continued to see menstruation as abortion, he was almost bound to describe its effects on women in negative terms. However, his negative thinking extended to all aspects of women's lives. He argued that 'a pregnant woman is at the climax of her most normal physiological life' yet went on to say that, 'owing to the tension thus involved she is specially liable to suffer from any slight shock or strain'.[17] That passage perhaps best sums up Ellis's attitude to women – they are at their healthiest when reproducing, yet that is also when they are at their most vulnerable. Ellis was medically trained, although practised little. His comments were fairly typical of the rather ambiguous attitudes that doctors had to menstruation and to the normality, or otherwise, of female physiology. As reproductive beings, women were often portrayed as primarily bodily, and also as lacking control of their bodies.

While the human female cycle was mysterious, almost anyone involved in animal husbandry knew that female mammals had a cycle which varied in length according to species. Animal breeders knew that animals such as horses, dogs and cows were only fertile when 'on heat' but beyond this practical knowledge, little was known about what occurred within the female body, although female animals were generally believed to be much more heavily influenced by their reproductive capacities than were their male counterparts. Then in 1844 the French zoologist Felix Archimedes Pouchet demonstrated that animals in heat were ovulating, thereby linking animal behaviour to a physiological change. He also argued that menstruation and heat were analogous and that by this reasoning, women ovulated during menstruation. This idea became widespread in western medicine, with doctors advising that a woman's most fertile time was while she was menstruating and pondering why sex during this time could seem so disgusting to both men and women. Doctors also wondered why it was that orthodox Jews managed to have children given religious strictures on sex during menstruation and for some days after. This was viewed as a puzzle, but not one that overturned the theory that ovulation occurred during menstruation, with some doctors hinting that perhaps Jews did not observe this regulation quite so strictly. Later, in the twentieth century, Jewish practices were used as evidence that ovulation was mid-cycle.

In the mid-1860s E. F. W. Pflüger argued that menstruation had a neurological cause. Pflüger thought that the enlarged Graafian follicle distended the ovary; this then sent nerve impulses to the spinal cord, causing pelvic engorgement and then, finally, menstruation, which released the engorgement.[18] Pflüger's was one of various theories that menstruation had a neurological causation: the controversial Birmingham gynaecologist Robert Lawson Tait argued that the tubal nerve caused menstruation and that removal of the Fallopian tubes brought about cessation of the menses. Clinical evidence was sometimes used to reinforce these theories, hence in 1879 obstetrician A. L. Galabin observed that menstruation often occurred after removal of both ovaries and so argued that 'the probable conclusion is that the immediate source of the menstrual nisus, and of its periodical recurrence, lies rather in the nervous centres than in the ovaries'.[19] However, alongside this theory ran the idea that perhaps menstruation had another cause. In 1849 Arnold Adolph Berthold, a German physiologist, removed the testes from a male bird and then regrafted them onto another part of the body. He found that doing so prevented the effects of castration. Experiments such as these were later widely repeated, demonstrating that whatever influence was at work, it did not come via the nerves for the grafting experiments severed any neurological connection. In 1855 the well-known French physiologist Claude Bernard suggested the idea of internal secretions. From here developed the idea of hormones, from a Greek word meaning to excite. Gradually physiologists realized that glands in the body excrete chemicals into the bloodstream which cause a number of effects on the body.

Investigations into menstruation were difficult. Doctors could feel uncomfortable talking to women about such a personal bodily function and some advised talking to husbands instead, arguing that men were more reliable witnesses anyway.[20] Interested gynaecologists collected anatomical specimens when they could but it was difficult to acquire the internal reproductive organs of normal healthy women. Organs taken from women dying in hospital of fever could be questioned if the evidence they presented seemed to disagree with accepted theories. Accidental deaths could produce good samples but suicides were disputed in case the suicide had been prompted by an imbalance in the reproductive system. Healthy women of reproductive age seldom die and leave their organs in a state suitable for investigation.[21] And if they did, they seldom left doctors a record of when they last menstruated. Physiologists, obstetricians and gynaecologists acquired what specimens they could in an effort to understand the relationship between ovulation and menstruation. They found examples in which ovulation could be seen at menstruation, before it, after it and in the middle of the cycle. Individual variation between women combined with a paucity of specimens meant that conclusions were difficult to draw.

Short of human material, investigators then turned to other animals, which in some ways was more confusing. Bats ovulate, have sex and then store the sperm for several months before becoming pregnant. Rabbits, an obvious choice as they are easy to keep and breed readily, only ovulate if they have sex. Larger animals such as cows seemed closer to humans in many ways, but required large amounts of space to keep and bred relatively infrequently. Choosing a suitable model for human menstruation proved difficult. The cycle needed to be similar if it could be compared, but how to know if it was similar or not? Cows have a 21-day cycle and looked like good models, but we now know that there are different reasons behind the bleeding in cows and in humans. Heape and other investigators chose primates since they were closest in evolutionary terms and there were similarities such as bleeding during their cycle. Heape was also convinced that female animals had a lot in common no matter what the species, whereas males and females of the same species had little in common. Heape was beset by difficulties: he became ill while collecting monkeys in India; he had to be careful where he collected them since they were commonest in areas where religion protected them; and he was unable to work in India so transported the monkeys back to England where the cold climate affected their menstrual cycle. Heape eventually published detailed descriptions of what happened to the primate uterus during menstruation, but he was unable to work out the connection between menstruation and ovulation.[22]

In the late 1880s, F. Lataste, working in France, correlated cytological changes in the vaginal epithelium with cyclic changes in the ovary.[23] However, the standard work referred to in most histories is that of Hitschmann and Adler and their 1908 paper on the histology of the menstrual cycle.[24] They showed that symptoms which had been classified as inflammatory disease were a normal part of the cycle. Further work by German investigators enabled clinical and laboratory workers to correlate changes in the uterus and vagina with changes in the corpus luteum (the yellow body that forms on the ovary after the release of an egg, now known to secrete hormones). The idea that the body might rely on chemical messages had ancient roots. Both the Greeks and the Romans thought that consuming testicles of some animals would give you certain powers. However, as ideas about internal secretions took hold in the late nineteenth century, they became tied up with quackery. In the late 1880s Charles Édouard Brown-Séquard, once a famous neurophysiologist, somewhat notoriously announced that he had rejuvenated himself by injecting extracts taken from dogs' testicles. He suggested that ovarian extract might do the same for women and reported on a Parisian midwife who had given herself ovarian extract made from pigs' ovaries, with similar benefits. Ovarian extracts are difficult to make and we now know that it depends on the point of the cycle at which the extract is taken. But early experimenters concluded that ovarian extracts produced minimal effects, a conclusion which chimed with the idea that ovaries were weaker than testes. Brown-Séquard became associated with quackery and extracts were sold under his name, without his knowledge. Many unscrupulous people were prepared to cash in on ideas about rejuvenation and the elixir of life, and to use the name of a famous scientist to do so. Brown-Séquard thought that the adrenals, thyroid, pancreas, liver, spleen and kidneys secreted substances into the bloodstream, and that these could be used in treatments. In 1893 he published a paper in the *British Medical Journal* on the therapeutic use of liquids extracted from glands and other organs.[25]

Despite the shaky start, gradually the idea of hormone extracts was taken more seriously, based on knowledge gained in both clinical and laboratory settings. Previously baffling diseases such as cretinism could be treated using hormone extracts and experiments, like Berthold's removal and re-grafting of glands in laboratory animals, helped provide an explanation for clinical observations. Between 1923 and 1932 oestrogen and progesterone were isolated and their effects on the female cycle became clearer. In 1927 Edgar Allen showed that menstrual bleeding follows within a few days of removal of the ovaries and that giving oestrogen for a few days after the operation fended off menstruation, leading researchers to believe that oestrogen secretion normally prevented menstruation. Gradually a map was built up showing when hormones needed to be given to bring about certain results. George Corner, working on monkeys, found that small injections of progesterone would delay menstruation for days or weeks.[26] As more became known about the effects of hormones, a hormonal contraceptive seemed increasingly likely. Although contraception could involve complex discussions between couples over what to use, the hormonal contraceptive pill gave women more control over their fertility than they had ever had before.

Contraception

Personal methods used to control fertility and conception are, by their nature, difficult for historians to investigate. Condoms of some form had been around for centuries, probably millennia. They were difficult to use, made of materials such as sheep gut with a ribbon to close off the end. Rubber condoms became available from the mid-nineteenth century, but they were expensive and associated with disease and prostitution. Women could use various barrier methods such as sponges soaked in vinegar, or caps; diaphragms were available from the mid-nineteenth century but had to be fitted by a doctor so were generally restricted to wealthier women. After sexual intercourse a woman might use a douche. None of the available methods were particularly reliable and women would often nurse for an extended period in the belief that lactation gave some protection against conception. Post conception, women were able to resort to abortion although it carried many health risks and its legal status was often complex. In Britain, for example, prior to 1803 abortion was legal before the foetus quickened, that is before the woman felt the foetus move and became aware that it was alive. However, the discovery of the mammalian ovum in 1827 changed ideas about when life began and, amongst medical professionals, what counted as abortion. For many women, however, they were not asking for an abortion, but were restoring their periods. Abortion became increasingly common during the nineteenth and twentieth centuries resulting in landmark cases. An Act of 1867 made pre-quickening abortion illegal and the 1929 Infant Preservation Act allowed abortion only to preserve the life of the mother.[27]

From the 1870s contraception was associated with the sins of modernity: materialism, socialism and feminism. Knowledge of contraceptives was passed from person to person but an 1857 British statute banned explicit advertising of contraception. Twenty years later Charles Bradlaugh and Annie Besant were prosecuted for republishing a birth control tract by Charles Knowlton. The Comstock Act passed in America in 1873 similarly made it illegal to distribute contraceptives or contraceptive advice through the mail. Thus contraceptive advice became both illegal and illicit.[28] There was an odd tension in the late nineteenth and early twentieth centuries between attempts by states to intervene in reproduction, and the need to keep issues of sex hidden away and personal. This was still the situation when research began into hormonal contraceptives. Knowledge of contraception was considered 'dirty' and scientific research into fertility and contraception was accorded a low status. The contraceptive pill has a complex history and historiography, as social issues intertwined with biochemical and biomedical research.[29] Development of the pill required a view of the body as hormonal, a knowledge of the role of hormones in the human female cycle, artificial production of those hormones in sufficient quantities, and the will and ability to carry out clinical trials.

The pill is one of the most widely consumed drugs in the world and has been seen as a cure for rising global population and the ills associated with it. But it is also a drug taken for extended periods of time by people who are well, raising safety concerns.[30] Yet despite controversies, women fought to be allowed to trial it, reasoning that whatever the risks from the pill, they were probably less than the risks from repeated pregnancies and frequent childbirth. The pill meant women gaining more control over their fertility, their bodies and their lives. In 1956, when the first large trial of the pill was carried out, women formed 32 per cent of the American workforce, and earned around a fifth of its total income; half a century later, the figures were 46 per cent and well over a third. Despite problems it is used by over 90 million women worldwide. The pill has had enormous social effects and in 1993 the *Economist* magazine ranked it one of the seven wonders of the modern world along with the microprocessor, the telephone, jumbo jets, offshore oil platforms, the hydrogen bomb and the Tranquillity base, the site of man's first landing on the moon. Though now used mainly by couples in stable relationships, it has been credited with bringing about a sexual revolution.

Doctors knew that progesterone would in theory prevent egg production. However, it was difficult to give women progesterone since natural progesterone is quickly broken down by the body, and large doses are needed to have any effect if it is taken by mouth. The alternative, daily injections, was simply impractical. Then, in the 1930s, Russell Marker of Pennsylvania State University found that, for hundreds of years, Mexican women had been eating wild yams of the Dioscorea genus for contraception, apparently successfully. Marker found that diosgenin, a chemical abundant in yams, has a structure that is similar to that of progesterone. He succeeded in producing progesterone from the diosgenin raw material in the early 1940s. Many chemists then tried to make a substance that would have the same effects as progesterone, but survive the human digestive system. In 1951 chemist Carl Djerassi succeeded in producing norethindrone in his lab in Mexico City, a steroid that would do just that. Earlier, in 1950, Gregory Goodwin Pincus, a biologist at the Worcester Foundation for Experimental Biology, in Massachusetts, was invited by the Planned Parenthood Federation of America to develop a contraceptive that would be reliable, simple and practical. During the 1950s, Pincus studied norethindrone, which had been sent to him by Djerassi. Pincus was helped and funded by Margaret Sanger and Katharine Dexter McCormick, who was one of the first women graduates of Massachusetts Institute of Technology and an heiress. McCormick also funded the first clinical trials, which were conducted by John Rock, a gynaecologist, with patients in his private practice. In 1956, *Science* announced the success of Rock's clinical trials, and Rock came to be regarded as a co-developer of the pill.

In the USA, on 9 May 1960, the Food and Drug Administration approved norethindrone, but it was not the first oral contraceptive to be marketed. G. D. Searle & Co. was the first on the market with Enovid. In 1960, Frank B. Colton, a research chemist at Searle, had developed Enovid, which contains mestranol and norethynodrel. But by 1964, norethindrone had become the most widely used active ingredient of the pill. For the first time, women had a reliable method of controlling their fertility themselves, meaning they could prevent unwanted pregnancies, and space out those pregnancies they did want. However, biomedical knowledge of reproduction was increasing apace throughout the twentieth century. Managing reproduction was no longer about stopping unwanted pregnancies: infertile couples could be helped to overcome their problems to produce much-wanted children. And further than this, the embryo itself could be manipulated.

Genetics and embryology

Even as humans were struggling to control the most basic aspects of reproduction, so they were also fantasizing about gaining control of its most complex aspects. In the early nineteenth century, Mary Shelley posited a world in which a man of science could infuse life into remains found in charnel houses to create a new human being. Over 100 years later, Aldous Huxley, grandson of the naturalist T. H. Huxley, envisaged a world in which reproduction was no longer natural and children were raised in hatcheries. Increasingly in the twentieth century these fantasies came to seem not too distant as our understanding of development and genetics increased apace.

Until the second half of the nineteenth century, inheritance was little understood and was not clearly separated from the development of an animal during its lifetime. Then, during the 1880s August Weismann began to argue that what affected the protoplasm of a cell could not affect its nucleus and that material contained in the nucleus was carried down from one generation to another. If material in the nucleus was not affected by external changes then any changes that occurred in an organism during its lifetime could not be carried down through the generations. Thus developmental changes were separated from heredity and gradually, scientific disciplines began to reflect this split. Geneticists came to study what was happening in the cell nucleus, while embryologists studied development, concentrating on what was happening outside of the nucleus.[31] Heape carried out embryo transfer experiments to see what effect the uterine environment had on embryos. He began his experiments in April 1890, helped by a Manchester surgeon. His experiments were carried out to investigate the effects a foster-mother would have on her offspring, and how foreign ova developing would affect other offspring. He transferred early embryos between different and quite distinct breeds of rabbit. Heape concluded that the womb had no effect on the appearance of the newly born rabbits, since the breeds remained distinct despite the transfers. The results of his experiment are now overshadowed by his ability to transfer embryos between wombs and then to see them carried to full term.[32]

Heape also experimented with artificial insemination in mammals, believing it would 'throw light on the physiological relations of coition and insemination, ovulation and fertilization, and on certain of the causes which induce sterility in mammals, which will be of great interest to physiologists and of great value to practical breeders'.[33] He worked with Galton, who was by then a prominent eugenist, in order to try to make the process of fertilization more efficient, by wasting fewer spermatozoa. The main problem he found was preserving the spermatozoa without killing them or having them succumb to bacterial infection.[34] By the 1930s artificial fertilization was reasonably common on farms and rapidly becoming commoner, partly for the economic reasons Heape had foretold and partly because it is much easier to use artificial fertilization than it is to deal with a stallion, bull, ram or boar. Gradually, scientists, clinicians and animal breeders were gaining the control they required, control over who or what became pregnant and when. But increasingly they were also to gain an even more controversial control over the development of the embryo itself.

In 1903, the biologist William Bateson, a sometime colleague of Heape's at Cambridge University, coined the term 'genetics'. Initially, Bateson saw the study of variation within species as key to answering questions about heredity and the development of species. In his search for work on variation Bateson became interested in the research of Gregor Mendel. Mendel published his work in the 1860s when it went largely unnoticed yet it later struck a chord with Bateson because it combined detailed mathematical work with careful observation. Mendel's ideas were rediscovered almost simultaneously around 1902 by Tschermak, Carl Correns and Hugo de Vries who all republished and promoted them. The 3:1 ratios of colour variation that Mendel found in the flowers of pea plants were one of the drivers behind the development of genetics. Over the course of the twentieth century, geneticists came to locate hereditary material in the chromosomes, strings of material found in the nuclei of cells. By the 1930s they had found that these chromosomes consisted of deoxyribonucleic acid (DNA) and then in 1953 the structure of DNA was discovered. By the 1990s, geneticists were able to clone higher mammals, that is, to create a genetically identical copy of an animal using its adult cells. Debate continues over the possibility of cloning human beings but, given that Dolly was the only survivor of 277 attempts to clone a sheep, ethical considerations make it a very distant dream.

More realistically, clinicians have acquired greater control over human reproduction in other ways. In 1978 the first 'test tube baby' was born; that is, a child born from an egg fertilized in vitro, outside of the human body and then implanted into a womb. There were fears that such children would develop differently from those fertilized in vivo, and indeed children born by IVF do show higher incidences of some diseases. Nonetheless, IVF has given many couples with fertility problems the chance to have children. However, IVF raised other issues. Several eggs are taken from a woman, fertilized and allowed to grow in vitro. Only some of these will be implanted but fertility specialists generally implant several in the hope that at least one will be carried to full term. This leaves the problem of what to do with any 'spare' fertilized eggs not implanted, and, occasionally, what to do if a woman ends up pregnant with a relatively high number of foetuses, endangering the survival chances of any of them. It also raised the spectre of selection. It is possible to genetically screen embryos not just for possible genetic diseases but for sex difference, as well as other traits. Thus couples could potentially choose which embryos to implant, based on certain selected characteristics. Many of these questions were explored by the Warnock Committee in the early 1980s, with an agreement reached that prior to 14 days it is admissible to conduct research on embryos, as they have no nervous system. At that stage the embryo was not, it was argued, a potential life but was a collection of cells.[35] However, in the United States such research remains more contentious. At this very early stage in development, an embryo consists of stem cells, that is, non-specialist cells that have the potential to develop into any cell in the human body. It is this potentiality that marks them out from adult cells, which are fixed in their form. Although it seems likely that research into stem cells may bring about cures for many diseases, debates over whether or not this is ethical are set to continue.

Just over a century ago, zoologist F. H. A. Marshall produced a textbook entitled *The Physiology of Reproduction*. He described most of the latest knowledge of animal reproduction in just one volume. Later editions ran to several volumes and now, no single textbook can cover the ground. Marshall had begun his career working with Scottish zoologist James Cossar Ewart. Ewart had speculated:

> Can science do anything to make the work of the breeder less uncertain and haphazard? Can it help in the production of new forms, and stereotype them when once realised, so that they may be reproduced, 'repeated' with as much certainty as statues are turned out of a mould? Science is incapable either of creating or, except to a limited extent, controlling life, but yet it may help the breeder to so influence the vital forces in operation that the desired goal is reached without unnecessary waste of time or energy.[36]

Ewart's dream became reality and the department he worked in at Edinburgh University became the Institute of Animal Genetics in 1919, the organization that eventually became the Roslin Institute where Dolly the sheep was cloned. Cloned animals may not become economically useful for some time yet, but our ability to control the fertility and reproduction of non-human animals has seen farming, and by extension human society, transformed. Our ability to control our own reproduction remains much more problematic and increasingly it is not lack of scientific or medical knowledge that holds us back, but a fear of just where that knowledge might lead us. In cloning, we take an adult cell and attempt to give it the properties of an omnipotent stem cell, a cell that has the potential to grow into every different type of cell of which a body consists. In doing so, we turn back not just individual development, but millions of years of evolutionary development to trick a specialized cell into once more becoming primitive. In so doing, we unleash an extraordinary amount of power.

Yet for all this increasing control over fertility, the complexity of the relationship between a developing embryo and its mother means that currently it seems highly unlikely that biomedicine will ever be able to replace the mother and the uterine environment that she provides. Science has provided control over when to become pregnant, it has helped the infertile to reproduce and it has enabled humans to manipulate the development of their offspring and those of other species. However, the act of giving birth itself is one of the most contested sites of control: in giving birth, women all but relinquish power over their bodies to the medical profession, but it was not always so.

Obstetrics

If eugenists were concerned with reproduction at the level of the state, obstetrics provided a means to control some aspects of reproduction on an individual level. Birth had traditionally been a female concern, but in western Europe and the US during the eighteenth and nineteenth centuries it increasingly came to be overseen by men. Obstetrics played a key role in the organization of medicine as a profession, particularly the organization of general practice, as gaining control over the lying-in chamber gave an entry to family practice. So who has control over the birth? Is the child delivered? Does it deliver itself? Does the woman deliver herself or does a doctor or midwife deliver her? As midwifery gave way to man-midwifery and then to obstetrics, birth increasingly came under the control of professional men.[37]

During the seventeenth century childbirth had been very much a female preserve, and a male practitioner, usually a surgeon, was called upon to assist only if the case proved difficult. The decision to call him was made by the midwife, patient and family. We do not fully know how skilled midwives might have been, although they were usually licensed to practise. They usually qualified by giving birth themselves and then attending other births in the company of an experienced midwife. At the beginning of the eighteenth century the birth process was still female dominated, but by the end of the century women of all classes might call in a man-midwife and all surgeon-apothecaries would also be man-midwives or accoucheurs. Along with these changes, the eighteenth century saw the growth of lying-in hospitals. The change was gradual. Initially the man-midwife was called in only in emergencies, then the man-midwife started to attend with the midwife, then he attended on his own.

There are two main theories as to how the man-midwife came to prominence. The increase in man-midwifery coincided with the introduction of forceps – instruments for removing the foetus. They had been developed by the Chamberlen family in the seventeenth century and their design kept secret until the 1730s. But the use of forceps alone seems an unlikely explanation. For one thing forceps were unpopular, for another midwives could use them. There are relatively few deliveries in which they would actually have been useful, or that would have resulted in a good outcome for mother and child. The other explanation historians put forward is that man-midwifery became fashionable for the upper classes and was then emulated by the middle and working classes. But this leaves open the question of why the upper classes opted for the man-midwife. It is more likely the increasing realization amongst medical men that much hinged on being present at the birth process. By being there they could come to treat mother and child and from there could treat the rest of the family. The rise in man-midwifery was as much as anything a political campaign on the part of medical practitioners.

During the nineteenth century obstetricians held an odd position. They were not obviously placed within the tripartite system of surgeon, apothecary or physician. The term 'man-midwife' was viewed by some as compromise. The term was accorded little respect, although arguably it made midwifery a part of medicine. In fact members of the Royal College of Surgeons and the Royal College of Physicians were banned from practising midwifery by 1800, leaving midwifery unregulated. But then at that stage all practice was unregulated. Rural practitioners claimed they had to act as surgeons, apothecaries and midwives, hence they became known as general practitioners. In 1826 a group of practitioners banded together to form the Obstetrical Society. They sought a recognized system of instruction, but their very existence marked them out as separate from other medicine rather than a part of it and they disbanded early on. Obstetrics was still not deemed to be a profession and was accorded a low status as a female concern. However, after the registration of births and deaths became compulsory in 1837, it became clear just how many women were dying in childbirth: 6 per 1,000 births (in modern developed countries the death rate is now counted per 100,000 births). Gradually the Colleges began to accept obstetrics as a real concern and in 1852 the surgeons repealed their clause against it and began to offer examinations in it.[38] Then shortly afterwards, in 1859, a group of practitioners including Tyler Smith and Robert Barnes formed the Obstetrical Society. In this second incarnation it was to be more successful. Both Barnes and Smith were in some ways radical, writing for Thomas Wakley and the *Lancet*. They aimed to reduce maternal mortality and to improve the political status of obstetrics. Although they had members from the provinces, they were a primarily London movement.[39]

The Society was formed in the aftermath of the 1858 Medical Education Act. The Act and the creation of the General Medical Council helped consolidate a very diverse profession, although it could not fully conceal the continuing rifts within medicine. Obstetrics was thus an ill-regarded part of an ill-regarded vocation. To improve their status, both medics in general and obstetricians in particular adopted, shaped and promoted a masculine, gentlemanly science. Science was seen as a way of uniting medicine and giving it status. An important part of that status was the exclusion of women. Science itself was still working to acquire professional status – if medicine and science were yoked together then they could enhance each other. With this in mind, some practitioners reduced obstetrics to basic mechanics. Essentially they were trying to extract the child out of a small space, a question they argued of basic mechanical forces, forces beyond female comprehension. As the French practitioner Velpeau expressed it:

> the science of obstetrics is one of the most important and positive branches of medicine ... Its most essential principles, being drawn from the laws of mechanics, or based upon the most exact anatomical facts, have far outstripped those speculative systems with which the healing art, properly so called, has often been the sad plaything, and gives to the resources it employs a degree of precision which causes it to approach in certainty the mathematical sciences.[40]

As a leading article in the *British Medical Journal* in 1856 made clear, for obstetrics to be scientific it had to exclude women, for 'we, in England, answer that exactly as the art has gradually ennobled itself to a science, so the mere midwife has given way to the obstetrician'.[41] Science, drawing on popular opinion, labelled woman as irrational and therefore incapable of scientific thought. To increase their status, medical men thus had to exclude women from their profession.

Women were often linked with beliefs such as homeopathy, which were perceived as irrational. In 1877 Robert Barnes, speaking at the annual meeting of the British Medical Association, against allowing women to take examinations in obstetrics, referred to 'the rashness of lawyers, ... of pedagogues and their fledgelings, of anti-vivisectionists, the advocates of the rights of women, of the opponents of the Contagious Diseases Acts, of homœopaths, mesmerists, *et hoc genus omne*' and called them all a 'restless band of crochet-mongers'.[42] His comments clearly illustrate the hierarchy adopted by protagonists for experiment and science. By linking all these groups together, Barnes, playing on a number of prejudices, labelled them all as inferior meddlers by association. But by moving into a traditionally female sphere, obstetricians faced a very real problem. Their character often came under attack. The author George Morant, in *Hints to Husbands* (1857), argued that women were 'invaded *by the presence, and violated by the actual contact* of the *man*-midwife'.[43] The midwife had opportunities which, according to some worried observers, would lead naturally into adultery. In addition to this fear, obstetricians were generally held in low esteem; the surgeon Anthony Carlisle argued in 1834 that 'it is an imposture to pretend that a medical man is required at a labour'.[44] This was not an uncommon attitude. In the 1870s, obstetricians at University College Hospital had to operate in separate premises in Gower Street, for they were not considered to be surgeons. In order to counteract these claims, obstetricians frequently argued that they acted in the name of a neutral, objective science which drew upon a gentlemanly code of honour.

Part of the problem was male involvement with the patient. The other issue was the extent to which men were taking away women's jobs. However, although women's education was beginning to be looked upon more favourably, their entry into the professions was still resisted. Thus Barnes argued:

> We repudiate utterly the proposition that there is one standard which it is necessary to attain to qualify for the treatment of the diseases of men; and another, a lower, standard to qualify for the treatment of the diseases of women. The new doctrine that there is a special, an inferior, kind of medical knowledge that is good enough to apply to the care of women is the most transcendent of all medical heresies, the most flagrant wrong, the grossest insult ever inflicted on woman. And all this under the plea of doing justice to woman! ... Have the mass of women no right? Is it not their dearest right to be protected by man? Even against their own sex?[45]

The fight to enhance the status of obstetrics continued into the second half of the nineteenth century. In 1884, by which time the Obstetrical Society had been seen to make little headway, the British Gynaecological Society was founded. In the UK, although the status of obstetrics improved, midwifery continued to coexist with it. However, in the light of maternal mortality statistics, and amongst fears of a degenerating population, there was substantial public and political pressure for some kind of regulation of midwifery. The 1890s saw the founding of two separate societies pushing for regulation. The main argument against it was that regulation might confer too much status on what some saw as just quackery.

In 1901 two cases gained much publicity. In one, in Kent, the husband and father offered three doctors half a guinea now and the other half later if they would attend his parturient wife, who had been attended by a midwife. They all refused, since they did not want to follow a midwife. The woman died. In another case in Stepney the husband called a doctor who refused to attend because he did not want to cover for an unqualified practitioner. The midwife concerned was then charged with manslaughter. The question arose, if you do not have a booked onset call, who is responsible for any deaths that occur?[46] Some doctors blamed any family who could not afford a doctor for want of thrift, even though the call-out fee could be as much as a week's wages for a respectable clerk or servant. The medical profession backed the doctors concerned in the Kent and Stepney cases, but this caused public feeling to turn against them. In 1902 another midwifery bill was introduced to Parliament, with medical men in the House both opposing and supporting it. Much of the debate focused on whether midwifery should be practised solely by those qualified. There were fears that allowing unlicensed practice would encourage abortions, but midwifery would then be in an unusual position, for, while medicine in the UK was regulated, unlicensed practitioners were not banned as such. A compromise was reached when it was agreed that unqualified practice would be outlawed from 1910, allowing time for the provision of qualified midwives to everyone.

This Act was unusual for it actually banned the practice of unqualified women, whereas the 1858 Medical Act had left it to the public to choose between qualified and unqualified practitioners. This meant that women could be prosecuted for practising midwifery without a licence, but men were free to practise, qualified or not. The Act imposed state registration upon midwives but placed them under local authority supervision by Medical

Officers of Health, giving them a lower status than doctors and ranking them with nurses. In addition, midwives did not regulate themselves; the majority of those on the Midwives Board were medically qualified men. Registration was much later than for other branches of medicine – partly because medical men were loath to allow through a bill which permitted women to practise medicine at all. Yet in contrast to the situation in America, midwifery persisted in the UK. Even at the end of the nineteenth century, over 90 per cent of deliveries were home deliveries by midwives and/or GPs.

The debate over whether or not birth is a natural process and the extent to which it might automatically need medical intervention is still very much alive. Historical and cross-cultural comparisons show that the answer is not clear-cut. There were thousands of maternal deaths in the western world during the period 1900–1940, deaths which were preventable using the standards of care available at the time. In Scandinavia the norm was home births overseen by a trained midwife and there maternal mortality was extremely low. In Britain births were attended by either midwives or GPs, usually in the mother's home. Emergency cases were then taken to hospital. Maternal mortality in Britain was mid-ranking in this period. In the US the midwife was written out of the picture, and maternal mortality was the highest in the western world.[47] Numerous national and regional studies have shown that the lowest maternal mortality occurred where trained midwifes attended home births, and where doctors did not interfere. Maternal mortality in Britain was higher in part because of forceps deliveries in which hygiene was not adhered to. In the US obstetric education was low and midwives were heavily criticized with little evidence. Better training helped the situation. In the mid-1930s the discovery of sulphonamide drugs produced dramatic results and, as a result of war, there was better access to blood transfusion. High maternal mortality rates dropped in the US and western Europe, though the debate over the naturalness or otherwise of the birth process continues.

In the mid-twentieth century home births were common but gradually birth came to be seen as a medical rather than a natural process and women were persuaded that the safest place to give birth was the hospital. In the twenty-first century, whether overseen by obstetricians or midwives, the vast majority of births in the western world take place in hospitals rather than at home. There are variations between countries, with home births prevalent in the Netherlands and all but unheard of in the US and the UK. However, there have been countermoves by various individuals and organizations, in particular Sheila Kitzinger in the UK and Citizens for Midwifery in the US. In the US, it is often midwives who lead these campaigns, despite their relative lack of status and resources in comparison with obstetricians within hospital settings.[48] Campaigners argue that in many cases home births are just as safe, if not safer, for both mother and child. They aim to provide women with information so that they can make an informed choice about how they give birth and to reclaim birth as a natural process that does not automatically require medical intervention. Essentially, they are trying to shift power over childbirth towards parents.

In 1750, around one in 30 women in the US died in childbirth.[49] Couples had little control over whether sex would result in pregnancy and as a result, it was not uncommon for women to become pregnant almost yearly. Just as individuals had little control, so doctors and men of science knew little of the process of fertilization or the changes embryos underwent. Any proposed mechanisms for heredity were speculative. The state lacked the ability or the knowledge to control reproduction, even as the population itself was increasingly reviewed as a resource. In the twenty-first century women in the west can be relatively confident in the safety of birth and increasingly are regaining control over where to give birth. Births can be spaced and infertile couples can at least take some action to counteract their infertility. Scientists understand fertilization, embryological growth and heredity to the extent that even higher mammals can be cloned. Our control over reproduction causes great concern, reflected in legislation that seeks to curb embryological research. Despite the many changes during this time period, some issues occur repeatedly. Reproduction is still seen as a largely female domain, whether or not they are in control of it. And throughout debates over the control and management of reproduction there is a tension between the public and the private and over who should have control of this most fundamental process.

Notes

1 Walter Heape, *Sex Antagonism*, London: Constable, 1913, p. 208.
2 Anna Davin, 'Imperialism and Motherhood', *History Workshop Journal* 5, 1978, pp. 9–65; Simon Szreter, *Fertility, Class and Gender in Britain, 1860–1940*, Cambridge: Cambridge University Press, 1996; Richard A. Soloway, *Demography and Degeneration: Eugenics and the Declining Birthrate in Twentieth-Century Britain*, London, and Durham, NC: University of North Carolina Press, 1995.
3 Leonore Davidoff and Catherine Hall, *Family Fortunes: Men and Women of the English Middle Class*, London: Routledge, 1986; Catherine Hall, *White, Male and Middle Class: Explorations in Feminism and History*, Oxford: Polity Press, 1992.
4 Davin, 'Imperialism and Motherhood'; Szreter, *Fertility, Class and Gender*.
5 Soloway, *Demography and Degeneration*.
6 See, for example, J. Matthews Duncan, *On Sterility in Woman: Being the Gulstonian Lectures Delivered in the Royal College of Physicians in February, 1883*, London: Churchill, 1884.
7 Adele E. Clarke, *Disciplining Reproduction: Modernity, American Life and the Problems of Sex*, London: University of California Press, 1998; Ornella Moscucci, 'Hermaphroditism and Sex Difference: The Construction of Gender in Victorian England' in Marina Benjamin (ed.), *Science and Sensibility: Gender and Scientific Enquiry, 1780–1945*, Oxford: Blackwell, 1991, pp. 174–99.
8 E. Ray Lankester, *Degeneration: A Chapter in Darwinism*, London: Macmillan, 1880; Daniel Pick, *Faces of Degeneration: A European Disorder, c. 1848–1918*, Cambridge: Cambridge University Press, 1989.
9 I will refer to eugenics as a science rather than as a pseudoscience for it was intended as a science. It was closely associated with reproductive physiology and to refer to it as a pseudoscience is to make an ahistorical judgement.
10 David Barker, 'The Biology of Stupidity: Genetics, Eugenics and Mental Deficiency in the Inter-War Years', *British Journal for the History of Science* 22, 1989, pp. 347–75.
11 A. M. Paterson, 'The Child as an Asset of the Empire', *Liverpool Medico-Chirurgical Journal* 31, 1911, pp. 235–53.
12 J. B. S. Haldane, 'The Prospects of Eugenics', *New Biology* 22, 1957, pp. 7–23 (22).
13 Rasmus G. Winther, 'Darwin on Variation and Heredity', *Journal of the History of Biology* 33, 2000, pp. 425–55.
14 George W. Corner, 'Our Knowledge of the Menstrual Cycle, 1910–50', *Lancet* 257, 1951, pp. 919–53; Patrick Geddes and J. Arthur Thomson, *The Evolution of Sex*, London: Walter Scott, 1889, p. 245.
15 Havelock Ellis, *Man and Woman*, London: Walter Scott, 1894, p. 247.
16 Ellis, *Man and Woman*, p. 111; Havelock Ellis, *Studies in the Psychology of Sex*, Vol. 1, New York: Random House, 1936, p. 95.
17 Ellis, *Studies in the Psychology of Sex*, Vol. 4, p. 9.
18 Hans H. Simmer, 'Pflüger's Nerve Reflex Theory of Menstruation: The Product of Analogy, Teleology and Neurophysiology', *Clio Medica* 12, 1977, pp. 57–90; John G. Gruhn and Ralph R. Kazer, *Hormonal Regulation of the Menstrual Cycle: The Evolution of Concepts*, London: Plenum Medical Book Company, 1989, pp. 31–32.

19 Alfred L. Galabin, *The Student's Guide to the Diseases of Women*, London: Churchill, 1879, p. 29.

20 On the unreliability of women as witnesses see Robert Lawson Tait, 'Note on the Influence of Removal of the Uterus and its Appendages on the Sexual Appetite', *British Gynaecological Journal* 4, 1888, pp. 310–91 (312).

21 For a debate over the suitability of evidence when investigating menstruation, see George J. Engelmann, 'The Mucous Membrane of the Uterus, with Especial Reference to the Development and Structure of the Decidua', *American Journal of Obstetrics* 8, 1875, pp. 30–87; John Williams, 'On the Structure of the Mucous Membrane of the Body of the Uterus and its Periodical Changes', *Obstetrical Journal* 2, 1875, pp. 681–96 and 753–67; John Williams, 'The Mucous Membrane of the Body of the Uterus', *Obstetrical Journal* 3, 1875–76, pp. 496–504.

22 Walter Heape, 'The Menstruation of Semnopithecus Entellus', *Philosophical Transactions* 185, 1894, pp. 11–467; Walter Heape, 'The Menstruation and Ovulation of Macacus Rhesus, with Observations on the Changes Undergone by the Discharged Follicle, Part II', *Philosophical Transactions* 188, 1897, pp. 135–65.

23 Michael J. O'Dowd and Elliot E. Philipp, *The History of Obstetrics and Gynaecology*, London: Parthenon Publishing Group, 1994, p. 257.

24 F. Hitschmann and L. Adler, 'The Structure of the Endometrium of Sexually Mature Women with Special Reference to Menstruation', *Mschr. Geburtsh. Gynaekol.* 27, 1908, pp. 1–82.

25 Chandak Sengoopta, 'Glandular Politics: Experimental Biology, Clinical Medicine, and Homosexual Emancipation in Fin-de-siècle Central Europe', *Isis* 89, 1998, pp. 445–73.

26 G. W. Corner, 'The Early History of Oestrogenic Hormones', *Journal of Endocrinology* 31, 1964–65, pp. iii–xvii.

27 On contraception in general see Angus McLaren, *Reproductive Rituals: The Perception of Fertility in England from the Sixteenth to the Nineteenth Century*, London: Methuen, 1984; on abortion see, for example, Barbara Brookes and Paul Roth, '*Rex vs. Bourne* and the Medicalisation of Abortion' in Michael Clark and Catherine Crawford (eds), *Legal Medicine in History*, Cambridge: Cambridge University Press, 1994, pp. 314–43.

28 On the low status of reproductive research see Clarke, *Disciplining Reproduction*.

29 See, for example, Lara Marks, *Sexual Chemistry: A History of the Contraceptive Pill*, London: Yale University Press, 2001; Nelly Oudshoorn, *Beyond the Natural Body: An Archaeology of Sex Hormones*, London: Routledge, 1994; Beth Bailey, 'Prescribing the Pill: Politics, Culture, and the Sexual Revolution in America's Heartland', *Journal of Social History* 30, 1997, pp. 827–56; Clarke, *Disciplining Reproduction*; Carl Djerassi, *This Man's Pill: Reflections on the 50th Birthday of the Pill*, Oxford: Oxford University Press, 2001; David Farber (ed.), *The Sixties: From Memory to History*, London; Chapel Hill: University of North Carolina Press, 1995.

30 Suzanne White Junod and Lara Marks, 'Women's Trials: The Approval of the First Oral Contraceptive Pill in the United States and Great Britain', *Journal of the History of Medicine* 57, 2002, pp. 117–60, (120).

31 August Weismann, *The Germ-Plasm: A Theory of Heredity*, trans. W. Newton Parker and Harriet Rönnfeldt, London: Walter Scott, 1893; on developments in genetics and embryology see Scott F. Gilbert, 'Cellular Politics: Ernest Everett Just, Richard B. Goldschmidt, and the Attempt to Reconcile Embryology and Genetics' in Keith R. Benson, Jane Maienschein and Ronald Rainger (eds), *The Expansion of American Biology*, London: Rutgers University Press, 1991, pp. 311–46.

32 Walter Heape, 'Preliminary Note on the Transplantation and Growth of Mammalian Ova within a Uterine Foster-mother', *Proceedings of the Royal Society* 48, 1890, pp. 457–58; J. D. Biggers, 'Walter Heape, FRS: A Pioneer in Reproductive Biology. Centenary of His Embryo Transfer Experiments', *Journal of Reproductive Fertility* 93, 1991, pp. 173–86.

33 Walter Heape, 'The Artificial Insemination of Mammals and Subsequent Possible Fertilisation or Impregnation of Their Ova', *Proceedings of the Royal Society* 61, 1897, pp. 52–63.

34 Helen Blackman, 'Embryological and Agricultural Constructions of the Menstrual Cycle' in Andrew Shail and Gillian Howie (eds), *Menstruation: A Cultural History*, Basingstoke: Palgrave, 2005, pp. 117–29.

35 Michael Mulkay, 'The Triumph of the Pre-Embryo: Interpretations of the Human Embryo in Parliamentary Debate over Embryo Research', *Social Studies of Science* 24, 1994, pp. 611–39.

36 J. C. Ewart, *The Penycuik Experiments*, London: Adam and Charles Black, 1899, p. xx.

37 Adrian Wilson, *The Making of Man-Midwifery: Childbirth in England, 1660–1770*, Cambridge, MA: Harvard University Press, 1995; William Ray Arney, *Power and the Profession of Obstetrics*, London: University of Chicago Press, 1985; Ornella Moscucci, *The Science of Woman: Gynaecology and Gender in England, 1800–1929*, Cambridge: Cambridge University Press, 1993.

38 Davin, 'Imperialism and Motherhood'; Moscucci, *The Science of Woman*; Soloway, *Demography and Degeneration*.

39 Moscucci, *The Science of Woman*, p. 66.

40 Alfred A. L. M. Velpeau, *A Complete Treatise on Midwifery*, trans. Charles D. Meigs, 4th edn, Philadelphia: Lindsay and Blakiston, 1852, p. 21.

41 'Shall we have Female Graduates in Medicine?', *Association Medical Journal* 4, 1856, pp. 653–55 (654).

42 Robert Barnes, 'The Scientific and Political Position of Obstetrics', *Obstetrical Journal* 5, 1877–78, pp. 457–73 (470).

43 George Morant, *Hints to Husbands: A Revelation of the Man-Midwife's Mysteries*, London: Simpkin, Marshall & Co., 1857, p. 24, cited in Moscucci, *The Science of Woman*, p. 118.

44 W. R. Merrington, *University College Hospital and its Medical School: A History*, London: Heinemann, 1976, p. 142.

45 Barnes, 'The Scientific and Political Position of Obstetrics', p. 471.

46 Irvine Loudon, 'The Making of Man-midwifery', *Bulletin of the History of Medicine* 70, 1996, pp. 507–15.

47 Arney, *Power and the Profession of Obstetrics*.

48 Katherine Beckett and Bruce Hoffman, 'Challenging Medicine: Law, Resistance, and the Cultural Politics of Childbirth', *Law & Society Review* 39, 2005, pp. 125–70 (126).

49 Charlotte G. Borst and Kathleen W. Jones, 'As Patients and Healers: The History of Women and Medicine', *OAH Magazine of History* 19, 2005, pp. 23–26 (23).

Part XI

PROSTITUTION

21

THE BODY OF THE PROSTITUTE

Medieval to modern

Kathryn Norberg

Perceptions of the body of the prostitute underwent important changes in the early modern period. The advent of syphilis, the Protestant and Catholic Reformations and especially the growth of the state transformed the prostitute from a member of society into an outright criminal. After hundreds of years of medieval toleration, prostitution became a criminal activity, prohibited and punished (albeit not very effectively) by the new state. Despite these sweeping changes, early modern prostitution is less well known and less studied than either medieval or nineteenth-century equivalents. Lack of documents is almost certainly the reason. Criminalization drove prostitution underground and forced prostitutes to hide their identities. Early modern cities may have teemed with whores, but we know neither their numbers nor their names because they easily evaded arrest. Courts were too few and police non-existent, so trials and arrest records – the foundations of the history of prostitution – are lacking. Historians have had to look elsewhere for sources and they have found them in the records of religious confraternities, convents, hospitals and workhouses where prostitutes were incarcerated so that they might be 'saved'. Religious institutions, whether Protestant or Catholic, played a leading role in the repression of prostitution so historians have been preoccupied with the attitudes and actions inspired by the great religious revival of the period. Scholars have also paid attention to a new kind of prostitute, the elite courtesan. In sixteenth- and seventeenth-century Rome and Venice, courtesans lived openly and led public lives. They were celebrated in paintings and poetry, images and texts which established models for the representation of prostition that survived well into the eighteenth century. Texts, whether literary, pornographic or medical, constitute the major source during much of the early modern period, and the contributions of literary scholars have been fundamental to the field. But in the eighteenth century, different kinds of souces, such as arrest records, trials and interrogations, became available as states managed to put significant numbers of policemen on the street. Women's lives became harder but the prostitute's misery was the historian's good fortune: after 1730, the nascent police forces of cities like London and Paris provide the sources of social history, and we can ascertain much more clearly the features of common prostitution.

This chapter adopts both literary and social historical approaches. But it emphasizes the emergence of the prostitute's body as a distinct, even alien form. In 1500, the prostitute had no clear outlines or particular characteristics. She was a woman, therefore lusty and weak like all her sisters. She was a sinner too vulnerable to the blandishments of the flesh, but so were all women or even men. Then rather late in the period around 1750, a new notion of the prostitute's body emerged which emphasized not the similarity between women and prostitutes, but the chasm that separated them. In the late eighteenth century, the prostitute became a diseased and freakish 'creature' more like an animal than a woman and subject to special police and administrative procedures. But before this great change could occur another had to precede it: the passage in the sixteenth century from medieval to early modern concepts of prostitution.

Medieval toleration

In late medieval Europe, prostitutes were neither criminalized nor marginalized.[1] Instead, they were tolerated and woven into the social fabric. The urban growth of the twelfth through the fifteenth centuries had created towns ruled by city fathers and populated by unmarried apprentices, journeymen and clerics. These single men posed a threat because without wives they lusted after the spouses and daughters of the ruling 'fathers'. Prostitution made cohabitation possible; it provided an outlet for the young men's sexual urges and medieval theology supplied a rationale. Saint Augustine himself had endorsed prostitution as a means of preserving the honour of virgins and wives by providing an alternative source of satisfaction to young, unmarried men.[2] Elites embraced the 'Augustinian justification' and established official, municipally sponsored brothels in the towns of southern France, and in Paris, Seville and London. As cities grew, so too, apparently, did tolerated prostitution: in Toulouse (1425), Frankfurt (1369), Munich (1433) and Strasbourg (1469) municipally owned brothels were in full operation by the late fifteenth century.[3] In commercial cities like Florence and Seville, brothels occupied a kind of red light district, a series of streets, enclosed by a wall in Seville, where prostitution was authorized and often policed by a special court or fiscal authority.[4] Life in the brothels was regulated by the city fathers or authorities. They determined who could go to the brothel (native bachelors), who could not (Jews, priests and married men) and when it was open (any time except Sundays and holy days). Prostitutes paid a special tax, as did pimps and brothel managers, known as brothel *padres*, *Frauenwirte* or abbesses, depending on the city. Business was good: in 1497 the Nuremberg *Frauenwirt* was one of the most highly taxed members of the community.

We have some information regarding the kind of women who ended up working in the *prostibulum*, or official brothels in the Rhone valley. Most were between 18 and 25 years of age and about a third came from outside the town. A substantial number had 'drifted' into prostitution after being the concubine or lover of a master artisan or priest. Many had been gang raped by the youth of the city who used rape as a means of 'punishing' women who engaged in illicit affairs.[5] Surprisingly, prostitutes were neither scorned nor stigmatized. In Germany, the official prostitutes were included among the town guilds and marched in civic processions. Authorized prostitutes attended mass and presented the city fathers with flowers on feast days and at municipal festivals. When an official prostitute retired, she was promised a place in the small but numerous asylums for repentant prostitutes established by pious Christians.[6]

The advent of criminalization

Then, between 1500 and 1550, toleration ended and a long era of criminalization began. First the brothels disappeared. In the 1530s in Germany and France, around 1550 in

Florence and as late as 1620 in Seville, authorized city brothels closed their doors. At the same time, edicts and laws criminalizing prostitution were promulgated. Spain's Philip IV prohibited brothels in his kingdom in 1623. In France, the great royal ordinance of 1560, the Edict of Blois, also banned prostitution. After 300 years, toleration and regulation ended and three centuries of prohibition and criminalization began. Why? The most obvious explanation is the appearance of syphilis. Before 1494, syphilis was unknown in Europe. However, it was widespread in the western hemisphere as conquistador and historian Bernardo dell Castillo (1492–1585) asserted in his writings. The old notion that syphilis came from the New World appears to be true. Spanish physician Rodrigo Ruiz Diaz de Isla (1462–1542) claims to have seen syphilis as early as 1493 among the crew men who accompanied Columbus. From its first appearance in Spain, syphilis then journeyed to Italy with the Spanish troops sent in 1495 to assist the King of Naples. On 5 July 1495 at the Battle of Fornovo French mercenaries fell down sick in the field. The new disease was baptized the French or the Neapolitan disease depending on one's perspective. Thereafter syphilis spread north reaching Scandinavia by 1497 and into Scotland.[7] From the outset physicians had no doubt that the disease was spread by sexual intercourse. 'Through sexual contact,' the Venetian physician Alexander Benedetto wrote, 'an ailment which is new or at least unknown to previous doctors, called the French sickness, has worked its way from the west to this spot (Italy) as I write.' The same physician also associated syphilis with prostitutes: the infected French troops, he observed, had wintered from January to May in Naples where they 'made merry', that is, consorted with whores.[8]

Superficially, venereal disease appears to explain the end of municipally regulated and tolerated prostitution, but a close look at the chronology of brothel closures suggests otherwise. The first wave of closings occurred almost 25 years after the appearance of syphilis, at a time when the disease had waned in intensity. The Augsburg brothel closed in 1523, the Basel brothel in 1534, Ulm in 1537 and Regensberg as late as 1553. In France, it was not until 1530 that the Montpellier *prostibulum* shut its doors. Moreover, some large commercial cities kept their official brothels and red light districts open. Seville and Florence had corralled prostitutes into particular streets where authorized (and unauthorized) brothels were located. In Seville, the area called the *Mancebia* consisted of several streets in the oldest part of the city which operated off and on, with greater or lesser restrictions until well into the seventeenth century.[9] In 1629, the Seville authorities did not close the official red light district but rather subjected it to closer regulation. In response to an outbreak of syphilis, a wall was built around the district to quarantine violence and restrict the movement of prostitutes. Venereal disease did not revolutionize prostitution; indeed its impact was surprisingly limited. There were two responses to venereal disease: prohibition or (as in the case of Seville) regulation. Both were deployed, but prohibition eventually won out thanks in large part to the religious revival of the sixteenth century, the Protestant and Catholic Reformations.[10]

The two reformations

From the start, Protestants condemned prostitution. Martin Luther (1483–1546) did so without equivocation. He referred to prostitutes as 'murderers or worse poisoners' and suggested that they be tortured and 'broken on the wheel'.[11] He regarded prostitutes as a threat to young men, a spur not a remedy for licentiousness, and the cause not the cure for adultery and fornication. Significantly, Luther rejected the Augustinian justification for prostitution: 'It is unchristian', Luther wrote, 'that public houses should be tolerated among Christians' all of whom, Luther observed, 'were baptized into chastity'. Marriage, Luther emphasized, was the only cure for lust, as Saint Paul himself had asserted. 'I certainly know,' Luther wrote, ' what some say about this … that it would be difficult to end it, that it is better to have such houses than to bring married women or maidens … to dishonor.' But marriage – the earlier the better – was, Luther argued, the only Christian cure for lust. As for prostitution, Luther advocated strict prohibition. He praised Fredrick the Elector who had banned camp followers from his armies and urged 'the temporal and Christian government' to do away with brothels and the prostitutes who filled them.[12]

Reformed communities in Germany and Switzerland did just that. While not unaware of the health risks posed by prostitutes, most city governments made it clear that religious and moral concerns were paramount, as happened in Augsburg. Contemporaries attributed the closing of the Augsburg municipal whorehouse in 1535 to the 'promptings of the Lutheran preachers'.[13] According to Lyndal Roper, an atmosphere of 'intense popular piety and high expectation' preceded the closing of the official brothel.[14] Preachers and city fathers exhorted prostitutes to repent and provided clothing so that the women might begin a new life suitably attired. Condemnation of the priests and monks who cavorted with prostitutes rang from the city's pulpits but was soon followed by criticism of prostitutes themselves. Both prostitutes and priests were ordered to leave the city in 1536. Gradually prostitutes were 'demonized', depicted as she-devils who corrupted men and, contrary to the Augustinian view, undermined the Christian community. In 1537, a comprehensive, disciplinary law was enacted which prescribed sentencing before a special court for prostitutes and those who consorted with them. At least 110 individuals were convicted and another 58 were closely questioned.[15] Sexual deviance, whether adultery, fornication or prostitution, was the target, and just about any woman was suspect. In Amsterdam, Calvinists seized control of the municipal government in 1578 and quickly rendered illegal almost all forms of sexuality outside marriage, including prostitution.[16] A series of repressive measures followed which culminated in the creation of the *Spinnhuis*, a former beggars' prison turned into a woman's workhouse, or prison. There, female criminals of all sorts, including prostitutes, were incarcerated and subjected to a regimen of discipline and work. Protestant elites throughout Europe established workhouses where female prisoners, including prostitutes, could be incarcerated and exposed to the healing power of work. In England, the Bridewell prison was opened in London in 1553.

Catholics took a somewhat different approach. Catholic theology emphasized contrition and conversion, mainly within the confines of a special convent devoted to such 'repentant' women. Such institutions had been constructed in the fourteenth century, but by 1500 most were in decline or had vanished altogether. In the late sixteenth and early seventeenth centuries, devout Catholic laywomen and reforming bishops created new institutions designed to support the contrition of the former prostitute and to rescue her from the clutches of sin if necessary. In France alone, two new religious orders, the sisters of the Refuge and the congregation of Notre Dame du Refuge, arose and gradually spread throughout France. Similar institutions appeared in Italy and Spain.[17] Despite the regimen of mass and Catholic devotion, these convents were little different from the *Spinnhuis* and Bridewell established by Dutch and English Protestants. Claims that the inmates were 'repentant' were unfounded. Few entered the Catholic 'asylums' of their own free will. Most were sent by secular courts which 'sentenced' women to the convents, often over the objections of the nuns in charge. Hard work, self-abnegation and strict obedience were required in the Catholic institutions just as they were in Protestant asylums. Confinement was the preferred remedy for prostitutes throughout Europe and discipline through work and prayer the cure prescribed by both confessions.

As these penal institutions show, Catholic and Protestant attitudes towards prostitution were surprisingly similar. Spanish theologians did argue, like their medieval forerunners, that prostitutes should be 'saved'. But they also called for the abolition of prostitution and the closing of authorized brothels. Both Catholics and Protestants rejected the Augustinian justification for venal sex. In his *Manuale di Confessori* (1578), priest Martin Navarro argued (like Luther) that men who went to brothels were made more intemperate, more likely to mistreat honest women and engage in fornication. Another theologian, Juan Mariana, condemned prostitution and regretted that Catholic tolerance of prostitutes made intolerant Protestants look more righteous.[18] In Italy, Charles Borromeo called prostitutes 'cankers' and condemned them for creating 'occasions to sin'.[19] Reformed Catholics were only slightly less zealous than their Protestant counterparts when it came to prohibiting prostitution. The case of Rome is instructive. In the summer of 1566, Pope Pius V initiated a campaign to clean up the holy city including (famously) painting fig leaves on nude images.[20] Prostitutes were included in the purification effort: Pius ordered prostitutes to leave the city and some complied, a few being robbed and killed for their goods on the highways.[21] Others' attempts at expulsion followed as a part of general campaigns to rid the holy city of the most visible forms of vice. In 1592, Pope Clement VIII issued yet another decree threatening the prostitutes with exile but only if they failed to move to a particular quarter.[22] The inhabitants objected so the prostitutes were relegated to the Campo Marzia, a newer neighbourhood further from the centre of the city. Thereafter the corralling of prostitutes into particular streets or quarters 'like Jews' became the preferred solution. Gradually, containment replaced prohibition.

Unable to eliminate prostitution, Catholic and Protestant authorities alike settled for quarantining it, that is, limiting the sex trade to special 'reserved' quarters. Even in Calvinist Amsterdam, the city fathers quietly abandoned prohibition in the course of the seventeenth century and settled by the early eighteenth century for limiting the city's brothels to certain streets.[23] In Catholic Seville, the authorities did the same. Considering the quiet but pervasive reassertion of tolerance in the early eighteenth century, recent historians have argued that we should not overestimate the commitment of early modern Europeans to the criminalization and condemnation of prostitution.[24] Protestant and Catholic moralists did continue to denounce prostitution, but the authorities of both confessions quietly adopted a more flexible stance. Even in the sixteenth and seventeenth centuries, prosecution of prostitutes was very selective, a fact exemplified by the appearance of a new kind of whore, the courtesan.

The rise of the courtesan

The high-priced, cultivated and exclusive prostitute was born in Rome where the expression 'courtesan' first surfaced at the papal court.[25] There clerics attached to the Holy See could not marry so they sought out venal women to accompany them on their social rounds. Being educated, these men preferred prostitutes who could carry on conversation and act appropriately. Because they frequented the papal court, these women became known as 'courtesans'. Hierarchical distinctions among prostitutes were new: the medieval *prostibulum* had provided only one class of service and all prostitutes were considered equal.

With the rise of new urban elites, a class of men (clerics and bureaucrats) emerged that did not want to share their women with rowdy soldiers. They wanted a whore who reflected their own status and personified their superiority over the common rabble. Just how many refined courtesans actually existed is hard to know. The term came to be used loosely and was applied to just about any venal woman.[26] Still, we know the names of a few women who were superior to common prostitutes in wealth and learning. Imperia, Tullia D'Aragona and Veronica Franco enjoyed genuine renown thanks to the praise lavished upon them by men of letters. Writers socialized with courtesans; Franco was herself a poet.[27] Artists too praised the courtesan and painted her portrait. Usually the courtesan was not named but presented as Flora or Bella or the Danae. Art historians long assumed that these portraits depicted prostitutes, but the identity of the beauties on these canvases is impossible to determine.[28] In any event, the images were astonishing in their beauty. Not a single pox mark or blemish appeared on these white complexions, testimony yet again to Europeans' ability to ignore venereal disease when it suited them.

The women portrayed by Italian artists were rich, wearing jewels, silks and garments embroidered with gold and silver. Courtesans were imagined to be wealthy and the notion was not without some foundation. Drawing on an array of documents including tax records, notarial documents and personal papers, Tessa Storey has found that about 40 per cent of the prostitutes in the Campo Marzia district of Rome were 'comfortable', while an additional 10 per cent owned property. Storey has also studied the courtesans' homes and jewelry and concludes that the Roman authorities had reason to issue in 1564 a sumptuary law, forbidding courtesans from wearing silks, gold and jewels: they did indeed possess such luxuries.[29] Not all courtesans were rich, but all 'honest' courtesans were free from criminal prosecution.[30] The Roman authorities called 'honest courtesans' those prostitutes who had registered with the Corte Savella and paid a tax. These women could live wherever they wished, own property and ply their trade without fear of interference or imprisonment.[31] 'Dishonest' prostitutes were women who hid their prostitution and sought to evade the authorities. The freedom enjoyed by 'honest' courtesans sometimes perturbed the authorities who tried to devise ways of controlling them. Between 1594 and 1606 a special police force known as the Birri was created to arrest women found in carriages, theatres and gardens, a clear attempt to monitor and control 'honest' courtesans.[32] The measure had little success, though, and courtesans continued to blur the boundaries between honest and dishonest women.

The prostitute's voice

During the Renaissance, courtesans challenged other boundaries by erupting into print. In 1536, Pietro Aretino (1492–1556) published the *Ragionamenti*, the first work of this period in which a prostitute speaks, and it set the tone for many prostitute texts to come, as Ian Moulton has discussed in chapter 11. Inspired by classical models, the *Ragionamenti* takes the form of a dialogue between Nana, a seasoned prostitute, and her inexperienced daughter, Pippa. Occasionally Pippa's godmother, the procuress Antonia, joins the conversation, which turns on the lubricity of women and the tricks of the courtesan's trade. Significantly, Nana aims to entertain with broad humour and farce. But Nana's babble is not pointless: she is a critical observer who exposes the lust of nuns and the hypocrisy of 'honest' wives. Part of her humour is satire aimed at social institutions and religious prejudices; but she is also a trickster, a clever, independent woman who deceives men and takes their money. The *Ragionamenti* had imitators in the sixteenth and seventeenth centuries. First came Lorenzo Veniero's *La puttana errante* (*The Wandering Whore*) in the 1530s and later Ferrante Pallavicino's *La retorica delle puttanne* (*The Rhetoric of Whores*) in 1642. Like the *Ragionamenti*, both texts were humorous, establishing the burlesque as the register in which whores spoke. Both texts were, like their model, also dialogues. Many more were to follow including two French classics: *L'Ecole des filles* (*The School of Venus*) and Nicolas Chorier's *Alyosiae* (*Dialogues of Luisa Sigea*).[33] These French texts like their Italian models featured sexually explicit conversations between an experienced wife/mother and her less knowledgeable girl/daughter. The French texts departed from the Italian model in that the women are ladies rather than prostitutes, but they are just as lusty as Nana and Pippa. Apparently, seventeenth-century readers found the notion of honest women talking about sex completely credible.[34] The old stereotype of women as sexually insatiable, whatever their status, still held. As Lotte C. van der Pol observes, in the seventeenth century 'the image of the whore was in fact an extension of the contemporary image of women in general'.[35] Every woman, van der Pol continues, 'was regarded as a whore at heart and therefore a potential prostitute', or possibly a raunchy conversationalist.

Mockery came naturally to the prostitute and many of the texts which incorporate her voice are satirical and political. In France, the uprising known as the Fronde produced a flood of pamphlets both pro- and anti-monarchy. Among these could be found pamphlets in which courtesans bemoaned the lack of business brought on by the civil war and even provided a satirical commentary on Mazarin and the royal forces.[36] In Restoration London, pamphlets signed by 'Companies of whores' and 'The Poor-Whores' pretended to be 'petitions' written by prostitutes and addressed to the authorities. These texts voiced both anti-Catholic and seemingly anti-monarchical sentiments.[37] The political viewpoint of these pseudo-prostitute tracts is not always easy to define, but its sources were Renaissance tracts like *The Wandering Whore* and the 'carnivalesque' traditions of male drinking and whoring.[38] In France, the 'cabaret poetry' of Théophile de Viau (1590–1626) and the other *Parnasse satirique* poets (so called because their verse was collected in the book of the same name) celebrated wine, women and an unfettered sexual life.[39] Unlike their English counterparts, the cabaret poets had no overtly political aims. Rather they used the figure of the prostitute, or more often the bawd, to mock the pastoral poetry of their day and to satirize its odes to an idealized female beauty.[40] The aged procuress with sagging breasts and wart-encrusted skin reminded the reader that all beauty was transitory and deceptive. Religion too was a sham. In this poetry, monks and priests patronize the procuress and she is only too happy to masquerade as the prude if it allows her to seduce girls more easily. The whore exists mainly to make visible the hypocrisy and duplicity of 'good' society. The Earl of Rochester (1647–80) employs the prostitute in his verse in a similar fashion. In the poem 'A Ramble in Saint James's Park' Rochester compares prostitutes and honest women and insinuates that there is little difference between the two.[41] In neither English nor French texts is the prostitute celebrated; rather she is mocked and used to debase those who associated with her.

Another kind of prostitute is depicted in *Die Ertzbetrügerin und Landstörtzerin Courasche* (*The Deceitful and Vagbond Courasche*, sometimes translated inaccurately as *The Life of Courage: The Notorious Thief, Whore and Vagabond*) written by Hans Jakob Christoffel von Grimmelshausen (1621–76) around 1670.[42] Courasche is crafty like the *picara* (vagabond) of the sixteenth-century Spanish novels. She is also voluble like Aretino's Nana, for she tells her own story, and she is old and diseased like the French bawds portrayed by the cabaret poets. She differs however from her predecessors in that the Thirty Years Wars and its horrors are the background to her story and her milieu is the army. Usually overlooked by historians, the camp follower may have been the most common form of prostitute in early modern Europe. She is certainly the most typical, for the great armies of the sixteenth and early seventeenth centuries brought her into being. Camp followers participated in the activity that sustained these huge, polyglot armies: plunder.[43] They also acted as sutlers, washerwomen and 'wives', providing food, clothing and, of course, sex. Whatever their numbers, the camp followers were certainly the most feared and reviled of prostitutes, for they frequented dangerous elements – soldiers and deserters – and travelled with a floating population of vagrants, beggars and thieves that terrified early modern Europeans.

The emergence of national armies in the seventeenth and eighteenth centuries did little to diminish the association between prostitutes, military men and criminality. As part of a general military reform, Louis XIV's ministers increased the powers of the local commandant empowering him to arrest prostitutes and remand them to the appropriate municipal authorities.[44] The military police swept through barracks and fortresses arresting prostitutes and handing them over to the municipal authorities for sentencing. Women captured by the military police regularly constituted a significant portion of the prostitutes sentenced in citadels like Metz, or cities like Paris. The tendency of soldiers to function as pimps and bullies did little to endear them to city dwellers, or to improve the army prostitute's reputation. As always, her companions were deserters, vagrants and thieves, a rootless and therefore dangerous population that bothered townsmen and police alike. The association of these itinerants with prostitutes was of long standing and it produced some of the earliest laws against prostitution.[45] One of the first French ordinances criminalizing prostitutes, promulgated by Louis IX in 1254, expelled vagrants and prostitutes from Paris as well as deserters, pickpockets and beggars. Prostitutes continued to be confused with other criminal elements: in 1777, the Parisian police chief still asked his policemen to monitor 'prostitutes and vagabonds' as well as unemployed domestics, deserters, artisans without masters and libertines, a sign of the city's greater complexity and urbanization. But still prostitutes were regarded as a threat to public security and a source of crime and disorder.

Policing prostitution

The maintenance of order by the burgeoning state was the primary motive (far outweighing religion or disease) for the criminalization of prostitution in early modern Europe.[46] If policies towards prostitution looked similar in different parts of Europe, it was because all areas of Europe experienced the extension of state power. The new states sought to secure public tranquillity (and quell popular complaint) by organizing armed bands of men, that is, police. In the sixteenth century, southern cities like Florence, Rome and Seville created special authorities to maintain order in their red light districts and siphon off some of the profits generated by the sex trade. The Roman *Birri* and the Florentine *Onesta* policed taverns, collected taxes and occasionally adjudicated disputes in the brothel quarters, but their duties were much more circumscribed than those of a modern police force. Only in 1667 would Louis XIV begin the process of building a true police force by creating the office of *surintendant de police* (police chief) in Paris. This officer answered directly to the king and presided over everything from printing to prostitution. All forms of 'disorder', whether theft, vagrancy, infractions of guild rules, filthy streets or dirty books, came under his purview.

It took almost a century for the Parisian police to become a large, significant force in the prosecution of prostitution. In 1750, there were 720 policemen who patrolled the city streets; in 1789 there were almost 1,500, or one policeman for every 193 inhabitants.[47] By 1720, these functionaries possessed the means to incarcerate prostitutes quickly and with little interference from the courts. Patrolmen and police inspectors apprehended women and brought them before a police commissioner who remanded them to the St Martin prison. There they waited until the second Friday of each month when the police chief judged hundreds of individuals, including a large number of women, for a variety of crimes including prostitution. The women were usually sentenced to the Salpetrière prison for periods of up to three years. The whole process, while perfectly legal, was arbitrary, autocratic and without hope of appeal. In London, a different system – but with many of the same effects – existed. For much of the 1700s, no law criminalized prostitution. To be sure, in 1650 the Puritan Parliament had passed an ordinance making all kinds of sexual behaviour outside marriage including fornication, adultery and sodomy punishable by whipping, exile and even death. But the law proved impossible to enforce and was generally ignored. Consequently, prostitutes who were bound over for trial – when they actually were detained – were indicted for disorderly behaviour or some other lesser charge. The lack of statutes specifically outlawing prostitution and the fragmentation of judicial authority made the policing of prostitution in London haphazard at best. In the early eighteenth century, a group of London moralists took matters into their own hands forming the Society for the Reformation of Manners. The members identified prostitutes through a network of spies and then had warrants signed by justices of the peace. Eventually the prostitute was served with a warrant and locked up in a bridewell. At its most active in 1722, the London Society had 7,451 prostitutes bound over for trial according to its own publications. But the Society's influence was relatively short-lived: by 1738, it could boast of only 545 prosecutions.[48]

With the Society gone, prosecution of prostitution fell to the parish watch or patrol. In 1735, a series of laws known as the Watch Acts sought to reform and make more efficient the night watch. Concern with public order rather than with vice prompted the issuing of these acts. Watchmen were enjoined to arrest 'all Nightwalkers, Malefactors, Rogues, Vagabonds and all disorderly persons whom they shall find disturbing the public peace'.[49] While the number of the men varied from parish to parish, most parishes had relatively large police forces. St James, Westminster, employed 65 watchmen, six beadles and two inspectors, the whole being augmented by eight sergeants and 32 additional watch in the months from October to March. Each watchman was assigned a fixed beat and was expected to apprehend and escort assorted miscreants, including night walkers or prostitutes, to the parish guard house. There, the drunks, thieves and prostitutes would wait to be bound over for trial in the morning. Only a fraction of those locked in the watch house ever made it to trial. Watchmen enjoyed considerable discretion and could release prisoners at will. Compromise and accommodation – not law – determined which prostitutes went to trial and which went free, and there is evidence that many female first offenders were warned and released.

How effective were these nascent police forces? Many, perhaps most, London watchmen simply turned a blind eye to the soliciting on their beat. Nor was enforcement consistent or regular. Prostitution was controlled primarily through occasional 'sweeps' or mass arrests. In December 1789, for example, a sweep of the Strand resulted in 50 arrests, more than occurred in Westminster during the whole year of 1785.[50] Parisian authorities too launched occasional sweeps against prostitutes. Police commissioners would carry out these sweeps in their assigned quarters and arrest dozens of prostitutes. Persecution intensified after 1760. According to a data sample constructed by Bénabou, 2,068 women in total were arrested in the years 1765, 1766 and 1770, or approximately 688 a year; this was at least six times the number arrested in the early seventeenth century.[51] It is impossible to know what percentage of the working prostitutes these figures represent, but it is clear that these bursts of persecution failed to eradicate prostitution (and probably did not intend to do so). Street-walkers disappeared from the streets temporarily, but soon returned or were replaced by others. Sweeps were not an effective means of eliminating prostitution; they only erased its most visible manifestation – street solicitation – temporarily. Nevertheless, the new police actions created difficulties and hardships for prostitutes. As the number of policemen increased, so too did the instances of bribery and extortion. In Amsterdam, several spectacular trials in the first half of the eighteenth century revealed that authorities regularly extorted money from client and prostitute alike.[52] In Paris, police corruption was so extensive that the royal government brought several police inspectors to trial between 1716 and 1720.[53] Testimony revealed that Parisians of all sorts were held for ransom, blackmailed, and terrorized by the police, but prostitutes were most likely to be victimized. The women had to pay policemen for 'protection' from arrest or, that failing, release from the Salpetrière prison. Bullies and *souteneurs* (pimps) probably multiplied because now more than ever before the prostitute needed someone to subdue angry clients and intimidate neighbours who might complain to the police. The police of early modern Europe were not entirely effective, but they certainly made the lives of prostitutes much harder. Whatever else they did, the new police forces created written records, specifically arrest records that allow us to put a face on the average prostitute. These documents are far from a perfect source. The arrest process itself was arbitrary: watchmen apprehended women who were drunk or out after curfew and processed them as if they were prostitutes. But it is all this growing documentation, the Paris police records, the London watch books and the Amsterdam Confessions, that allow us to create a profile of the early modern prostitute.

Youth was her most striking characteristic. Whether she was an inhabitant of Amsterdam, London or Paris, the prostitute was aged between 18 and 29 years (just like today's prostitutes); on average she was 25. Children did not tend to figure among the apprehended. The youngest prostitute questioned by John Fielding in 1758 was 16; none younger can be found in the Paris or Amsterdam data.[54] Nor was the average prostitute a country girl gone astray in the big city. Usually she was a migrant: 75 per cent of the Paris prostitutes arrested in Bénabou's sample were born outside Paris.[55] But she was not a peasant girl: migrants to both Paris and Amsterdam came from medium-sized towns where, most likely, they had already engaged in prostitution.[56] The early modern prostitute was also unmarried. Aged between 21 and 25, most prostitutes had *yet* to be married and hoped to find a spouse in the big city. What they found was economic hardship: no longer under parental authority, they had yet to establish a new family economy. These young women were therefore unusually vulnerable to economic crises and unemployment. Prostitution provided a solution at least for a while but eventually these same women probably married, for they disappear from the police records. Marriage brought some economic stability and no further need to sell sex.

The prostitutes worked in an array of trades either before or during their time as prostitutes. The Parisian women sent before the police chief claimed to have exercised over

200 professions from seamstresses to peddlers to simple day labourers. Surprisingly, the typical prostitute was *not* a domestic servant, for servants constituted less than 10 per cent of the Parisian prostitutes whose details were recorded.[57] In Amsterdam, the proportion was similar. Domestic servants, van der Pol reasons, received room and board which relieved them of the need to house and feed themselves. Unlike seamstresses and street vendors, domestic servants were not desperate to pay for food and shelter.[58] No particular occupation made women likely to take up prostitution; just about all the occupations exercised by women appear in the arrest lists. Other factors may have contributed to a woman's 'fall'. Thanks to a law which forced Amsterdam's brides to register their marriages, Lotte van der Pol is able to contrast the city's prostitutes with honest women of the same age. She found that the prostitutes were more likely than the brides to be migrants and much more likely to have been orphaned of one or both parents. The prostitutes were also mainly self-supporting, wage earners.[59] Clearly economic vulnerability caused by loss of family, low wages and temporary employment pushed women into prostitution.

Working conditions varied considerably in the world of venal sex. Some prostitutes worked 'outdoors'; that is, they solicited publicly on the street, from windows, and in public gardens and promenades. In London, Amsterdam and Paris, specific streets and public thoroughfares were haunted by prostitutes. These 'strolls' as they would be known coincided with major axes in the city where traffic was heavy, like the rues St Denis and St Martin in Paris, or along Piccadilly and the Strand in London. Prostitutes also clustered around places of amusement like Drury Lane or the Palais Royal. Operas and theatres attracted prostitutes who solicited clients right outside the house. In the course of the eighteenth century, the Paris opera burned down and was relocated several times; each time, the prostitutes followed. While street solicitation grew, brothels probably declined or changed in size and organization. Bars and taverns remained places of prostitution; most had rooms upstairs that could be used for the satisfaction of clients. The traditional, residential brothel was overshadowed by the multiplication of rooming houses which tolerated, and indeed benefited from prostitution. The rooming house provided shelter and some protection from the police in return for exceptionally high rent, sometimes charged by the day. In London, the parish authorities did nothing to prohibit the houses and there were complaints. In 1751, public outcry led to the Disorderly Houses Act which provided rewards to individuals who would denounce owners of bawdy houses and rooming houses where prostitutes clustered.[60] But the denunciations and fines levied on the owners had little effect. As soon as they were cited, brothel and rooming house owners would simply disappear so evading arrest. In Paris, too, rooming houses tended to multiply but more traditional brothels did not vanish. On the contrary, they operated with almost complete impunity because the police used madams and bawds as informers. Police chief Berryer de Ravenoville (1747–58) employed hundreds of spies and informers among whom were the most famous madams of the day. But 'tolerance' did not preclude bursts of persecution. The police descended in the middle of the night on brothels and arrested every prostitute in the house and packed them off to the St Martin jail. These measures (like the police sweeps of the streets) were designed not to eliminate prostitution but rather to quell public outcry and terrify prostitutes and madams into submission to the police.

One might ask if the general populace supported these punitive measures. Popular attitudes are hard to discern and are often contradictory. On the one hand, crowds did not defend prostitutes when the police arrested them, as crowds often did when it was a question of beggars. Neighbours' complaints usually occasioned police action against a brothel. Honest artisans and hard-working day labourers and their wives did not hesitate to complain about the drunken clients and noisy youth who insulted their wives and created mayhem in their apartment buildings. On the other hand, months, even years, often passed before the neighbours complained, indicating long periods of not just toleration but of peaceful cohabitation. Most Europeans were willing to coexist with the brothel upstairs provided no pimps or drunken clients harassed them or caused scandal in the house. Otherwise, they would overcome their fear of reprisals and report the whores. With the advent of the police, however, the power of the general populace to determine who should be punished and who tolerated greatly declined. Henceforth, the authorities, not the labouring poor, determined which women got arrested and which went free.

From criminalization to regulation

Elite attitudes towards prostitution did not change in the early eighteenth century. Bernard Mandeville's *Modest Defense of Public Stews* (1735) notwithstanding, early eighteenth-century English and French subjects tended to regard prostitution as harshly as their forerunners. Sophie Carter demonstrates that Hogarth's *A Harlot's Progress*, printed in 1732, portrays the prostitute in the traditional manner as duplicitous, dangerous and doomed.[61] The Abbé Prévost's *Manon Lescaut* published around 1730 also recapitulates familiar themes. Though technically innovative, the story of Manon and the Chevalier des Grieux is an old one: the tale of a promising young man laid low by a scheming and greedy whore. In both cases, the notion of the prostitute as predator still prevailed. But around 1750, this changed: the prostitute became a biological threat, and not just to a few clients but to society as a whole. The century's foremost venereologist, Jean Astruc (1684–1766), believed that while syphilis was less deadly than in the past, it was almost certainly more widespread.[62] According to one social commentator, France contained no less than 200,000 syphilitics.[63] Syphilis many believed was poisoning the artisan class and destroying the army. English physician William Buchan (1725–1805) observed that 'what was formerly called the gentleman's disease is now equally common among the lowest ranks of society'.[64] For these impoverished, the London Lock Hospital was founded in 1748 to provide treatment for venereal disease free of charge. The French worried that syphilis was undermining the French population because it killed babies and rendered adults infertile. The future of France, not just a rake's health, was now at risk.

Like venereal disease, prostitution was also increasing or so moralists proclaimed. Sebastien Mercier estimated the number of prostitutes in Paris at 30,000 while other authors spoke of 40,000, or even 50,000, out of a population of about 650,000.[65] In 1756, one observer went so far as to conclude that 100,000 Frenchwomen were 'more or less public and engaged in prostitution'.[66] In 1797, Patrick Colquhoun claimed that 50,000 women sold their bodies on the streets suggesting that 10 per cent of London's female population engaged in prostitution.[67] Such estimates were exaggerations reflecting an author's anxiety or personal agenda more than reality.[68] What prompted such extravagant estimates was probably the visibility of prostitution, manifested in the growth of street solicitation. Now stationed along boulevards, near theatres and popular amusements, in public parks and gardens, prostitutes appeared to be everywhere. For Mercier, street-walkers 'gathered in the busiest places where the neighbours and passers-by could witness their indecencies and hear their licentious talk'.[69] Along public streets, prostitutes 'hunted' and 'attacked' men. They were not women as in the past but rather *créatures* (creatures), *fauves* (wild beasts), *rapaces* (rapacious animals). Thus, gradually the notion that prostitutes were fundamentally different from other women grew. The belief promoted by eighteenth-century domesticity that women were inherently asexual made the old notion of the lusty woman unthinkable. In England, the contradiction between prostitute and feminine asexuality was resolved by making prostitutes victims. Bawds and libertines tricked women into prostitution and a life that was fundamentally alien to them. The Magdalene hospital, established in London in 1767, provided a remedy, a place where hapless prostitutes could be 'redeemed' and their modesty restored.[70] The effect of these changes was to separate prostitutes from ordinary women, indeed from the general population. Prostitutes now required their own police, special dispensaries and hospitals, as well as separate quarters and houses were they could be isolated and hidden from the healthy, upright population.

However, late eighteenth-century moralists never dreamed of eradicating prostitution. They might criticize the existing police force, arguing, as many did, that it failed to arrest prostitutes and allowed them to exist in return for bribes. In France, they decried the ineffectiveness of convents and hospitals and looked for new, non-religious solutions proposed by doctors, writers and policemen rather than theologians. But throughout Europe, reorganization not prohibition was the goal. In 1770, novelist Restif de la Bretonne suggested in his essay *Le Pornographe ou les idées d'un honnête homme sur un projet de règlement pour les prostituées* that the trade be tolerated and regulated so as to assure good hygiene, universal access and the continued increase of the population.[71] Less prescriptive but equally utopian was the period's most famous prostitution novel, John Cleland's *Memoirs of a Woman of Pleasure*, known today as *Fanny Hill*. Written in 1748, on the cusp of the changes in attitudes towards prostitution, *Fanny Hill* reveals both old notions about mercenary sex and new hopes for an orderly and healthy prostitution. The brothel of Mrs Brown is disorderly, vicious, and the bawd herself greedy and abusive. Her body, described at length by Cleland, is that of the Renaissance prostitute, lusty and insatiable, flabby and exhausted from repeated intercourse. Fanny flees to Mrs Cole's brothel where rationality prevails and ungovernable lust is banned. Mrs Cole, like her girls, is clean, neat and honest. Prostitution here is sanitized and controlled; it is in every aspect 'healthy'.[72] Cleland's vision of a 'healthy' prostitution is not without similarity to the regulatory projects adopted in Europe during the nineteenth century. By 1780, the prostitute's body had been defined as diseased and different from the 'normal' female body. Before, prostitutes were just women who had fallen prey to the universal call of the flesh. Prostitutes might be dangerous and crafty but they were not a species apart. Now prostitutes were freaks, utterly different from ordinary women (or men for that matter) and subject to a host of special regulations and police procedures. The early modern period prepared the way for the nineteenth-century notion of the prostitute that emphasized her body as a 'social evil', a biological threat to humankind.

Notes

1 On the measures and laws which protected prostitutes and included them in the city see Jacques Rossiaud, *Amours vénales la prostitution en Occident XIIe-XVIe siècle*, Paris: Flammarion, 2010, pp. 279–88.

2 James A. Brundage, *Law, Sex and Christian Society in Medieval Europe*, Chicago: University of Chicago Press, 1987, pp. 436–548.

3 Jacques Rossiaud, *Medieval Prostitution*, trans. Lydia Cochrane, Chicago: University of Chicago Press, 1988.

4 Francisco Vásquez Garcia and Andrés Moreno Mengibar, *Poder y prostitución en Sevilla*, Seville: Universidad de Sevilla, 1995, pp. 1–61; Richard Trexler, 'La prostitution florentine, au XVIème siècle', *Annales: Economies, Sociétés Civilisations* 36, 1981, pp. 983–1015.

5 Rossiaud, *Medieval Prostitution*, pp. 10–33.

6 The appearance of unofficial prostitutes, plying their trade outside the official brothel and in defiance of the authorities, indicated that official prostitution was in trouble. In many cities, the official brothel closed for lack of business; Rossiaud, *Medieval Prostitution*, pp. 65–70.

7 This discussion of syphilis is based upon Claude Quétel, *History of Syphilis*, Baltimore: Johns Hopkins University Press, 1990. See also chapter 25, this volume.

8 Alexander Benedetto cited in Quétel, *History of Syphilis*, p. 36.

9 See Vásquez Garcia and Moreno Mengibar, *Poder y prostitución*, pp. 1–61; Trexler, 'La prostitution florentine'.

10 Calls for stricter morality were heard before the two Reformations. In the Rhone valley and Burgundy, preachers in the 1490s harped upon society's corruption and condemned licentiousness, including prostitution. In Italy, Florentine friar Girolamo Savanarola (1452–98) condemned vice and railed against the frequenting of prostitutes; see Rossiaud, *Medieval Prostitution*, pp. 33–53.

11 Martin Luther, 'Table Talk' cited in Susan G. Karant-Nunn and Merry E Wiesner-Hanks (eds), *Luther on Women: A Sourcebook*, Cambridge: Cambridge University Press, 2003, p. 157.

12 Luther cited in Karant-Nunn and Weisner, *Luther on Women*, pp. 156–58.

13 Lyndal Roper, 'Discipline and Respectability: Prostitution in Reformation Augsburg', *History Workshop Journal* 19, 1985, pp. 3–28 (4).

14 Roper, 'Discipline and Respectability', p. 10.

15 Roper, 'Discipline and Respectability', p. 21.

16 Lotte C. van der Pol, 'The Whore, the Bawd and the Artist: The Reality and Imagery of Seventeenth-Century Dutch Prostitution', *Journal of Historians of Netherlandish Art* 2, 2010, pp. 1–12 (2).

17 On the new prostitutes' asylums in Italy see Sherrill Cohen, *The Evolution of Women's Asylums from 1500*, New York: Oxford University Press, 1992, which includes several chapters on Florence's Convertite and Malarmite convents. For Spanish examples, see Mary Elizabeth Perry, *Gender and Disorder in Early Modern Spain*, Princeton: Princeton University Press, 1990.

18 John Brackett, 'The Florentine Onesta and the Control of Prostitution, 1403–1680', *The Sixteenth Century Journal* 24, 1993, pp. 273–300.

19 Charles Borromeo cited in Tessa Storey, *Carnal Commerce in Counter-Reformation Rome*, Cambridge: Cambridge University Press, 2008, p. 4.

20 Storey, *Carnal Commerce*, p. 71.

21 Storey, *Carnal Commerce*, p. 76.

22 Storey, *Carnal Commerce*, pp. 7–8.

23 Lotte C. van der Pol, *The Burgher and the Whore: Prostitution in Early Modern Amsterdam*, trans. Liz Waters, Oxford: Oxford University Press, 2011, pp. 112–15.

24 Storey, *Carnal Commerce*, pp. 234–52.

25 See Paul Larivaille, *La vie quotidienne des courtisanes en Italie au temps de la Renaissance*, Paris: Hachette, 1975, pp. 28–30.

26 The label 'courtesan' also became degraded with time. In France, for example, 'courtesan' was used indiscriminately to refer to all women who sold sex. Even in Rome, the expression became 'devalued' after 1560 and was applied to all prostitutes of any standing or wealth; see Storey, *Carnal Commerce*, p. 122.

27 Margaret Rosenthal, *The Honest Courtesan: Veronica Franco, Citizen and Writer in Sixteenth-Century Venice*, Chicago: University of Chicago Press, 1992.

28 Carol M. Schuler, 'The Courtesan in Art: Historical Fact or Modern Fantasy?', *Women's Studies* 19, 1991, pp. 209–22.

29 Tessa Storey, 'Clothing Courtesans: Fabrics, Signals and Experiences' in Catherine Richardson (ed.), *Clothing Culture, 1350–1650*, London: Ashgate, 2004, pp. 95–108.

30 Elizabeth S. Cohen reminds us not to 'romanticize' the courtesan whose numbers were probably quite small; see Elizabeth S. Cohen, '"Courtesans" and "Whores": Words and Behavior in Roman Streets', *Women's Studies* 19, 1991, pp. 201–8.

31 Storey, *Carnal Commerce*, p. 116.
32 Storey, *Carnal Commerce*, pp. 97, 111.
33 On these classics of French pornography see Joan DeJean, *The Reinvention of Obscenity: Sex, Lies and Tabloids in Early Modern France*, Chicago: University of Chicago Press, 2002.
34 See Sarah Toulalan, *Imagining Sex: Pornography and Bodies in Seventeenth-Century England*, Oxford: Oxford University Press, 2007, p. 275.
35 van der Pol, *The Burgher and the Whore*, p. 76.
36 See, for example, Pierre Variquet, *La capture de deux courtisanes italiennes habillées en hommes, faite par le corps de garde de la porte Saint-Honoré, qui portaient des intelligences secrètes au cardinal Mazarin … avec la lettre d'un partisan*, Paris: P. Variquet, 1649.
37 See James Grantham Turner, *Libertines and Radicals in Early Modern London*, Cambridge: Cambridge University Press, 2002, pp. 181–96; Tim Harris, 'The Bawdy House Riots of 1668', *The Historical Journal* 29, 1986, pp. 537–56.
38 On the whore petitions, see Melissa M. Mowry, *The Bawdy Politic in Stuart England, 1660–1714*, Aldershot: Ashgate, 2004, pp. 105–27. This argument is made by Turner, *Libertines and Radicals*, pp. 197–252.
39 See Claire Guadiana, *The Cabaret Poetry of Théophile de Viau*, Tubingen: Nar, 1981.
40 Bawds also predominated in Spanish picaresque novels like Fernando de Rojas' *La Celestina: Tragicomedia de Calisto y Melibea*, Burgos: n.p., 1499.
41 John Wilmot, Earl of Rochester, 'A Ramble in Saint James's Park', Representative Poetry Online [http://rpo.library.utoronto.ca/poems/ramble-st-jamess-park] (accessed 25 April 2012).
42 Johann Grimmelshausen, *Die Ertzbetrügerin and Landstörtzerin Courasche*, roughly translated as *The Life of Courage: The Notorious Thief, Whore and Vagabond*, trans. Mike Mitchell, New York: Daedulus Books, 2001 [1669].
43 See John Lynn, *Women, Armies and Warfare in Early Modern Europe*, Cambridge: Cambridge University Press, 2008.
44 G. Bardin, *Dictionnaire de l'armée de terre*, Paris: Librairie militaire, 1865, p. 417. On Louis XIV's reform of the army see John Lynn, *Giant of the Grand Siècle: The French Army 1610–1715*, Cambridge: Cambridge University Press, 1998.
45 Rossiaud, *Amours vénales*, p. 294.
46 Vásquez Garcia and Moreno Mengibar, *Poder y prostitución en Sevilla*, p. 33.
47 Alan Williams, *The Police of Paris*, Durham, NC: University of North Carolina Press, 1980, p. 67.
48 Tony Henderson, *Disorderly Women in Eighteenth-Century London: Prostitution and Control in the Metropolis, 1730–1830*, London: Longman, 1999, p. 89.
49 'An Act for the Better Regulating the Nightly Watch … ' (1737) cited in Henderson, *Disorderly Women*, p. 90.
50 Henderson, *Disorderly Women*, p. 126.
51 Erica-Marie Bénabou, *La prostitution et la police des moeurs aux XVIIIe siècle*, Paris: Perrin, 1987, pp. 267–68.
52 van der Pol, *The Burgher and the Whore*, pp. 116–40.
53 Robert Cheype, *Recherches sur le procès des inspecteurs de police 1716–1720*, Paris: Presses Universitaires de France, 1975.
54 Henderson, *Disorderly Women*, p. 23; van der Pol, *The Burgher and the Whore*, p. 142; Bénabou, *La prostitution*, p. 268.
55 Bénabou, *La prostitution*, p. 268. London data comes from a later period, 1814–26, and concerns only Southwark. Native-born Londoners constituted the single largest group among the women detailed but overall 60 per cent of the detainees were migrants mainly from Ireland and the West Counties; see Henderson, *Disorderly Women*, p. 19.
56 van der Pol, *The Burgher and the Whore*, pp. 143–44. Data on the origins of London prostitutes comes from a much later period, approximately 1825. Consequently it has not been offered here as a comparison; see Henderson, *Disorderly Women*, pp. 18–22.
57 The figure was much higher (40 per cent in Montpellier) for prostitutes arrested in the French provinces; see Colin Jones, 'Prostitution and the ruling class in eighteenth-century Montpellier', *History Workshop Journal* 6, 1978, pp. 7–28. See also Geneviève Hébert, 'Les femmes de mauvaise vie dans la communauté (Montpellier, 1713–42)', *Histoire Sociale* 72, 2003, pp. 492–512.

58 van der Pol, *The Burgher and the Whore*, pp. 146–47.

59 van der Pol, *The Burgher and the Whore*, pp. 145–47.

60 Henderson, *Disorderly Women*, pp. 148–49.

61 Sophie Carter, *Purchasing Power: Representing Prostitution in Eighteenth-Century English Popular Print Culture*, Aldershot: Ashgate, 2004, pp. 7–50.

62 Astruc quoted in Randolph Trumbach, *Sex and the Gender Revolution*, Vol. 1, Chicago: University of Chicago Press, 1998, p. 197. See also part XIII on 'Sexual disease' in this volume.

63 Dr Jean Stanislas Mittié cited in Bénabou, *La prostitution*, p. 416.

64 William Buchan cited in Trumbach, *Sex and the Gender Revolution*, p. 198.

65 Sebastien Mercier cited in Bénabou, *La prostitution*, pp. 446–47.

66 Ange Goudemar cited in Bénabou, *La prostitution*, p. 447.

67 Patrick Colquoun cited in Trumbach, *Sex and the Gender Revolution*, p. 70.

68 Such exaggerated estimations of the number of prostitutes were an old phenomenon and one that has not entirely disappeared. See Elizabeth S. Cohen's remarks on estimating the number of prostitutes in Rome in '"Courtesans" and "Whores"', p. 202.

69 Mercier cited in Bénabou, *La prostitution*, p. 448.

70 On the Magdalene hospital and its literature see Donna T. Andrew, *Philanthropy and Police: London Charity in the Eighteenth Century*, Princeton: Princeton University Press, 1989; Sarah Lloyd, 'Pleasure's Golden Bait: Prostitution, Poverty and the Magdalene Hospital in Eighteenth-Century London', *History Workshop Journal* 41, 1996, pp. 48–70; Mary Peace, 'Asylum, Reformatory or Penitentiary? Secular Sentiments vs Proto-Evangelical Religion in *The Histories of Some of the Penitents in the Magdalen House* (1760)' in Ann Lewis and Markman Ellis (eds), *Prostitution and Eighteenth-Century Culture*, London: Pickering and Chatto, 2012, pp. 141–56; Jennie Batchelor, 'Mothers and Others: Sexuality and Maternity in Eighteenth-Century Prostitution Narratives' in Lewis and Ellis, *Prostitution and Eighteenth-Century Culture*, pp. 157–69.

71 On prostitution and depopulation see Bénabou, *La prostitution*, pp. 417–30.

72 Andrew Elfenbein, 'The Management of Desire in Memoirs of a Woman of Pleasure' in Patsy Fowler and Alan Jackson (eds), *Launching 'Fanny Hill': Essays on the Novel and its Influences*, New York: AMS Press, 2003, pp. 27–48, p. 28. This reading of Fanny Hill was suggested by Lena Olsson, 'Idealized and Realistic: Portrayals of Prostitution in John Cleland's *Memoirs of a Woman of Pleasure*' in Patsy S. Fowler and Alan Jackson (eds), *Launching 'Fanny Hill': Essays on the Novel and its Influences*, New York: AMS Press, 2003, pp. 81–101.

22

PROSTITUTION FROM 1800

Maria Luddy

'Before 1980, the prostitute was "pornographic"', states Timothy Gilfoyle in his review essay on the historiography of prostitution.[1] The subject has now become 'respectable'. Since the 1980s there have been numerous studies of prostitution and prostitutes reflecting the changing landscape of social and cultural history, and the development of women's and gender history. In the 1980s and 1990s much of the history of prostitution focused on the attempts made to control prostitution, regulate it, protect public morality, and secure social order. Sexuality, particularly as associated with prostitution, morality and health became subjects of political campaigning, by women and men, and helped shape the individual's relationship to the state. These earlier works, particularly that of Walkowitz, also show women who worked as prostitutes to be dynamic figures who exerted some agency in their own lives.[2] More recent studies of prostitution situate commercial sex within the contexts of social, political, religious, and economic developments. It is now recognized that sex, gender, class and race shape, and shaped, commercial sex. The practices of prostitution, its relationship to power and authority, the politics of sexuality, the diversity of the experience of prostitutes, the ways in which venereal diseases have shaped public health policy, the impact of international debates on issues such as 'trafficking' and the rights of women and children, together with the impact of regulation on the colonies suggest how these new histories of prostitution are reshaping our understanding of the impact of what is never simply an act of sexual commerce.[3]

Prostitutes had a very public presence in nineteenth- and twentieth-century European towns and cities. It was most often their visibility that caused anxiety, not only about the use of public space, but also the contamination of that space. Many of the discussions that developed around prostitution focused on the idea of contagion, either in the spread of disease or immorality; prostitution was itself believed to be contagious. Within the United Kingdom the prostitute could be described in a number of ways as a 'fallen woman', 'unfortunate', 'woman of bad character', 'woman of notorious character', 'nymph of the pave', among other names. It was clear to contemporaries what type of woman was being referred to. Prostitution, as a subject, was much discussed and written about in the nineteenth and twentieth centuries, as journalists, medical doctors, rescue workers, and policy makers described and tried to offer remedies to the 'problem' of prostitution. In this chapter I want to focus on the perception of prostitutes and prostitution, its extent, attempted regulation and control, and its association with disease. The definition of prostitution used in this chapter follows that of Outshoorn as 'the exchange of sex or sexual services for money or other material benefits', and commercial sex as 'men buying the sexual services of women, within a set of social relations implying unequal power relationships between the sexes'.[4] What will not be discussed here is the wider sex industry, or 'sex work' more generally, which includes lap dancing, phone sex or pornography. Utilizing the concept of Kelly *et al.*, prostitution here means 'face to face contact, in which some form of sexual/bodily contact takes place, most commonly penetrative sex'.[5]

The extent of prostitution

Prostitution was a 'hidden occupation', and only found its way into official statistics through police monitoring of arrests, or, in the later twentieth century, through focused research. Women drifted in and out of prostitution, therefore the numbers of women engaged in this occupation fluctuated according to general economic conditions and personal circumstances. Nineteenth-century contemporaries attempted to estimate the numbers of such women. William Logan, a missionary worker, claimed that in Leeds in 1840, which had a population of 160,000, 700 prostitutes earned an average of 30 shillings a week serving 14,000 men. Logan noted the fate that awaited a prostitute: 'Girls soon come down from the first-class houses to the second, then to the third, then down to the situation of a servant in one of their houses and finally, to the grave.'[6] He suggested some solutions for the problem of prostitution believing that the law should punish procuresses, brothels should be suppressed and the sale of alcohol should be restricted. He also advocated that prostitutes should not be allowed to parade in the streets.

In 1860 there were said to be 25,000 women working as prostitutes in the city of London; in 1900 the police estimated that 8,000 women worked as prostitutes; and just after World War II it was estimated that there were about 2,000 prostitutes operating in the city. In 2008 the United Kingdom Network of Sex Work Projects estimated that there were between 50,000 and 80,000 selling sex in the UK.[7] At the turn of the twentieth century it was believed that Germany contained between 100,000 and 200,000 prostitutes, with an estimated 40,000 prostitutes working in Berlin by 1909. During periods of war, such as World Wars I and II, prostitution around military camps and in port towns appears to have been particularly extensive. In Paris during World War I it was estimated that there were 5,000 licensed and over 70,000 unlicensed prostitutes working in the city.

Recent investigations of prostitution suggest that in 1993 an estimated 600 to 800 prostitutes worked within the city of Glasgow. There were few brothels in the city, but it was accepted that in the past the majority of women working as prostitutes were alcohol-dependent, and by the mid-1990s most were drug-dependent.[8] In 2000 there were estimated to be 25,000 women selling sex in the Netherlands, with about 150,000 in Germany. In the Netherlands, where prostitution is regulated, about one-third of towns have a visible sex industry, including 'window prostitution', and designated zoned street areas, and an estimated 1,270 licensed sex establishments.[9] However, a completely accurate figure for the numbers of women who work as prostitutes in any particular country cannot be given due to the amount of clandestine prostitution that exists.

Throughout the nineteenth century there was considerable discussion of prostitution, its causes and possible remedies. In 1843 the Reverend Ralph Wardlaw described prostitution as a 'sin' that, if not stopped, would cause the 'deterioration of national character, and to the consequent exposure of the nations among whom it abounds weakness, decline, and fall'.[10] Dr William Tait, a surgeon in the Edinburgh Lock hospital, published a book on prostitution in Edinburgh in 1840, based on the women he came into contact with in his medical practice. Tait wrote of all levels of prostitution, from the street-walker to the middle-class prostitute, and he recognized that poverty was its root cause, a finding which was unsurprising in a city where women were often unemployed or very poorly paid. The solutions he put forward to rid society of prostitutes were economically based. He suggested price fixing for various women's trades, such as needlework. Tait also considered that the law should be much stricter in areas such as procuring, street-walking and brothel-keeping.

Another contemporary writer, Dr Michael Ryan, in his book *Prostitution in London* published in 1839, suggested the following reasons as to why women became prostitutes:

> seduction; neglect of parents; idleness; the low price of needle and other female work; the employment of young men milliners and drapers in shops in place of women; the facilities of prostitution [i.e. the provision of brothels]; prevalence of intemperance; music and dancing in public houses, saloons and theatres; the impression that males are not are not equally culpable as females; female love of dress and of superior society; the seductive promises of men; the idea that prostitution is indispensable, poverty; want of education; ignorance; misery; innate licentiousness; improper prints, books and obscene weekly publications.[11]

Women, of course, became prostitutes for a wide variety of reasons. A Frenchwoman, Julie Daubie, wrote in 1866 that 'The inadequate pay of the urban working woman sometimes drives her ... to complete her budget by the sale of her body'.[12] Henry Mayhew, who investigated the lives of the poor in London in the 1840s, and whose findings appeared in the newspaper the *Morning Chronicle*, spoke to women who had taken up prostitution. One woman, who worked as a seamstress, told him, 'It was the little money I got by my labour that led me to go wrong. Could I have honestly earnt enough to have subsisted upon, to find me in proper food and clothing, such as is necessary, I should not have gone astray.'[13] Married women, along with single and widowed women, found their way into prostitution. One woman in Belfast noted she had been occasionally obliged to frequent a 'house of ill fame ... looking for my living'.[14] In Dublin in 1911, May Madden was in the courts for smashing the windows of Eliza Byrne, and was sentenced to nine months. She told the court that she had been in despair, 'that her husband had wanted her to support him by going on the streets'.[15]

Some contemporary commentators believed that the 'temptations' of city life, such as the music halls, the independence young women might have in moving from the country to the city where they would no longer be under the control of parents, and a love of finery led innocent young country women into prostitution. Not only was prostitution viewed as a source of physical disease but prostitutes were themselves regarded as sites of moral infection. A witness to a hospital commission noted that 'If we allowed these swell ladies from Mecklenburgh Street to flit about in pink wrappers and so on, it would be a distinct inducement to others less hardened to persevere in that life in the hope that probably they would arrive at similar distinction'.[16] Poverty was a major driving force in women entering prostitution. Women worked as waitresses or as unskilled labourers, or in domestic service, all unreliable and poorly paid occupations. In Berlin in 1873 evidence suggests that about 38 per cent of registered prostitutes had worked as domestic servants.[17] However, women also made active choices to enter prostitution because they believed it offered a viable means of earning a living. Nevertheless, the problems of poverty and addiction remained a constant for many of those women who worked the streets. In a 1997 newspaper article a 27-year-old Stoke on Trent woman, who worked the streets, commented:

> I sell my body every night to make a living. We all know each other on the street and help each other out, we'll pass a driver onto someone else if we've had quite a few that night and they haven't. I don't know how to stop. How else can I pay rent, buy food and cigarettes and pay for the heroin I sometimes need to top up my methadone prescription ... I don't think about the future, I can't. The only thing I want is to have my babies back but I can't do that yet ...[18]

Some current research suggests that it is primarily poverty, rather than drug abuse that brings women onto the street, and keeps them there.[19]

The 'Wrens of the Curragh'

It is difficult to hear the voices of women who worked as prostitutes. Such voices tend to be mediated through criminal reports, court records, or journalists. Their lives can be reconstructed to some extent from official records, but few have left accounts of their own.[20] However, there is one particular group of nineteenth-century women who worked as prostitutes, the 'Wrens of the Curragh', about whom we have some substantial information. These women worked as prostitutes in a military encampment, the Curragh army camp in County Kildare, Ireland, from the 1850s to the second decade of the twentieth century. While there was a tacit acceptance of prostitution in the vicinity of the camp, boundaries were created around these women to separate them from 'respectable' society. These boundaries were enforced by the police, the military authorities and the local civilian population. For some, the very presence of these women in the Curragh 'defiled' it,[21] and the women were often recorded as 'infesting' the camp with their presence.[22] These women were sexually immodest, often drunk and used foul language. While they were named as individuals when appearing before a magistrate, or in death, they were, to commentators and the general public, a collective mass of licentiousness. It is their collective existence that was the threat to 'respectable' society rather than their individual selves. The military authorities, the police and the local civilian population attempted, often without success, to limit the movements of these women and to confine them to particular geographical areas. However, while the authorities attempted to regulate the behaviour of these women it is clear that the 'wrens' often successfully resisted such regulation. These women provoked both fear and fascination.

The most extensive information on them comes from the journalist, James Greenwood, who visited the area in the 1860s and published a series of articles, between 15–19 October 1867, on the women in the *Pall Mall Gazette*. Greenwood was a journalist, writer and novelist, and a social explorer of Victorian society.[23] His work on the 'Wrens' was reprinted as a pamphlet and appeared in a collection of his writings.[24] Greenwood has little new to say on the causes of prostitution but his journalistic efforts in recording the life of the 'wrens' has preserved their story. Greenwood described the living conditions of these women:

> heaps of furze are built and furnished for human occupation; and here and there outside them were squatted groups of those who dwelt therein. ... Not one or two,

but several groups – half naked, flagrant – indicating a considerable colony ... Altogether there are ten bushes, with about sixty inhabitants. In them they sleep, cook, eat, drink, receive visits, and perform all the various offices of life. If they are sick, there they lie. Brothers, mothers and fathers go to see them there. There sometimes – such occurrences do happen – they lie in child-bed; and there sometimes they die.[25]

The number of women living as 'wrens' fluctuated between 60 and 100, depending on troop movements and the season of the year.[26] Like other women who worked as prostitutes, for some of the 'wrens' at least, prostitution was a seasonal occupation. Harvesters, for example, were known to join the band of women when they were not working, and the numbers of women at the Curragh declined during the winter when many of them returned to the city.[27] The ages of the women living at the Curragh varied, from young women under 20 to women in their fifties and sixties.[28] This age range is typical of that of women who worked as prostitutes in the nineteenth century.

Greenwood moves on to describe the women's living conditions:

the nests have an interior space of about nine feet long by seven feet broad; and the roof is not more than four and a half feet from the ground. You crouch into them, as beasts crouch into cover; and there is no standing upright until you crawl out again. They are rough, misshapen domes of furze ... the walls are some twenty inches thick ... There is no chimney – not even a hole in the roof, which generally slopes forward ... The door is a narrow opening nearly the height of the structure – a slit in it, kept open by two rude posts, which also serve to support the roof. To keep it down, and secure from the winds that drive over the Curragh so furiously, sods of earth are placed on top, here and there, with a piece of corrugated iron ... as an additional protection from the rain. Flooring there is none of any kind whatever, nor any attempt to make the den snugger by burrowing down into the bosom of the earth ... the nest is nothing but a furzy hole, such as, for comfort, any wild beast may match anywhere, leaving cleanliness out of the question.[29]

While these women lived under terrible conditions Greenwood noted a certain bond of solidarity amongst those who occupied the 'nests'. The women pooled their limited financial resources and collectively lived off any earnings they made. 'None of the women have any money of their own,' Greenwood noted, 'what each company get is thrown into a common purse, and the nest is provisioned out of it ... It is an understanding that they take it in turns to do the marketing, and to keep the house when the rest go wandering at night.'[30] The 'colony' was also 'open to any poor wretch who imagines that there she can find comfort'. With some degree of sentimentalization Greenwood wrote that the poor women who followed soldiers to the camp were 'made as welcome amongst the wrens as if they did not bring with them certain trouble and an inevitable increase to the common poverty'.[31]

The 'wrens' represented depravity to the local community and because of the very nature of their occupation they were often shunned by the local population, and, in many instances, treated quite badly. One individual, writing of the 1840s when he had served at the camp, stated that it was 'quite common for the priest, when he met one of them ["wrens"] to seize her and cut her hair off close'.[32] Not surprisingly the clergy had little time for these women. The same soldier recalled the priest coming into the barracks at Newbridge to request a fatigue party of soldiers, who, with the permission of their commanding officer and the priest at their head, 'went out and burned down the shelter these unfortunates ["wrens"] had built'.[33] At the Curragh many local shopkeepers would not serve the women in their shops. In the 1880s the parish priest of the district would not allow any of his parishioners to give shelter to the women.[34] The outcast status of women who worked as prostitutes, and their supposed lack of humanity is revealed in a comment noted by Greenwood. One 'gentleman', for example, remarked to him, with apparent amazement, that the women 'used cups and saucers just like ordinary people'.[35]

The double standard of sexual morality which operated in the nineteenth and twentieth centuries allowed men to often excuse bad behaviour towards women who worked as prostitutes. Although there is evidence of some camaraderie between prostitutes and their soldier customers, sexual commerce often degenerated into violence. Prostitutes were vulnerable to violence and sexual assault was a relatively common occurrence. Although we have no idea of the level of sexual assault on women generally in the nineteenth century it would seem likely that the 'reputation' of the woman involved would play a role in prosecuting the perpetrator. Loss of reputation, which women such as the 'wrens', or prostitutes more generally, suffered because of their occupation set the context for sexual violence. For many men, especially soldiers, sexual reputation was fluid and unlikely to be damaged by accusations of assaults on prostitutes. Prostitution was the most visible transgression of the sexual code, and prostitutes had lost their right to 'respectability' as a result of their occupation. In studies of the history of rape, as can be seen in the next chapter, it is clear that the 'character' and 'reputation' of the victim were important elements in securing convictions.[36] More recent studies of prostitution document the 'common, frequent and pervasive' violence experienced by women who sell sex.[37] Even where regulation is strong and prostitution is managed there is still a high level of physical and sexual abuse.[38]

Regulation

Controlling prostitution, and the diseases associated with it, were major concerns of governments in the nineteenth and twentieth centuries. The primary response of governments to the problems of prostitution was the segregation and punishment of prostitutes. Where male responsibility for sexual promiscuity and disease transmission was recognized, it was rarely punished. A system of regulation against prostitution operated in Berlin from 1792. The regulations ordered that no one could open a brothel without the permission of the police. Much of the regulation that had been introduced across Europe by the 1860s took its outline from the Napoleonic legislation introduced first in Paris in 1802, which provided facilities for prostitutes to be examined for venereal disease. The examination was then made mandatory, and the police began to register the women to ensure compliance with the medical inspections.[39] The classic French work on prostitution, *De La Prostitution dans la Ville de Paris*, was written by a medical doctor, A. J. B. Parent-Duchatelet, published in 1836, and was highly influential. He saw prostitutes as a part of society, and like 'drains and refuse dumps', they contributed 'to the maintenance of social order and harmony'.[40] Dr William Acton's work on prostitution was renowned in its day. He believed that prostitutes were the source of venereal disease and felt that the state should introduce a system of regulation, which would attempt to control the movement, and health, of women who worked as prostitutes. While calls for the regulation of prostitution were common, some individuals popularized the concept of prostitution as a necessary evil and argued that prostitution should be controlled rather than suppressed. The view that prostitution should be controlled gained popularity in the United Kingdom from the 1850s with many contemporaries seeing prostitution as a health issue. There was a growing belief, particularly amongst the medical profession, that prostitution should be regulated for medical rather than for moral reasons.

In the decades of the 1830s and 1840s there was considerable unease in Europe about sexual immorality, disease, the fear of social upheaval and the perceived dangers of the poorer classes to the stability of society.[41] Official concern with prostitution and its links with the spread of venereal diseases saw the introduction of a range of regularity measures that sought to control the body of the prostitute. Venereal diseases were considered morally and physically corrupting. They were infused with shame and were evidence of illicit sexual activity. They destroyed the health of men and women and of possible future generations. They signalled sexual impropriety and transgression. The idea of venereal diseases evoked images of decay, disgust, of madness and of death.[42] The prostitute was believed to be the major site of venereal infection, as is discussed by both Kevin Siena and Lesley Hall in Part XIII.

The anxiety amongst the Berlin authorities in the nineteenth century centred on the spread of venereal disease. If a prostitute transmitted a venereal disease to a client she was liable to three months' imprisonment and also had to pay for the client's medical treatment. The authorities also forced the client to pay for the medical treatment of the prostitute if it was proved he had passed a disease to her. More specific legislation to deal with prostitutes was introduced in Germany from 1871. Women who worked as prostitutes had to carry identity cards, thus a system of registration existed which marked out and stigmatized women who worked as prostitutes. As in other countries where prostitution was regulated, in Germany prostitutes were confined to particular districts of towns and cities. They were not, for example, supposed to be seen near railway stations, at dance halls or other places where the public gathered. Like their counterparts in Paris they were also liable to have enforced medical examinations. By 1850 in France there were two main features to regulation: controlling the movement of women and protecting public health.[43] Sweden established a regulatory system that understood women to be the sole source of venereal diseases. Various laws passed in the decades between the 1830s and 1870s saw prostitutes in Stockholm registering with the police and undergoing regular medical inspections. One historian has argued that these regulations were limiting the freedom of a group of women in Sweden at the same time that other women were gaining wider civil liberties in that country. Here, then, sexual regulation was helping to define women's citizenship.[44] The implementation of regulation was different in different countries but the common factor was the targeting of women who worked as prostitutes.

The Contagious Diseases Acts

In the nineteenth century the level of venereal diseases in the British armed forces became an issue of concern for the authorities. The Crimean war (1854–56) brought the level of ill health in the army to the nation's attention. The statistics of the Army Medical Department showed that the incidence of venereal disease was increasing. By 1864 venereal disease was responsible for one out of every three sick cases in the army. The logic for the military men was that paid sex had to be made safe for the soldier and sailor. The army authorities, along with many medical men, believed that it was prostitutes who spread venereal diseases. If they could be controlled and treated then it was less likely that soldiers and sailors would contract these diseases. Therefore to combat the spread of venereal disease the government introduced a series of acts, known as the Contagious Diseases Acts (CDA), which allowed for the enforced medical inspection of women who were believed to be prostitutes. The Acts, first introduced in 1864 and extended in 1866 and 1869, applied to a number of naval ports and garrison towns in England and Ireland. Some of the 'subjected districts', as they were called, were Portsmouth, Aldershot, Southport and Colchester in England. The Acts, however, applied only to women. Under the first Act of 1864 special plain-clothes police were organized under the direction of the War Office and Admiralty to enforce the bill. There was no legal definition of a 'prostitute' in the nineteenth century and all that was needed for a conviction was for a policeman to swear before a magistrate that he had seen the woman solicit a man. The magistrate then issued a summons for the woman to be medically examined at a certified hospital. If the woman refused then she could be imprisoned for two months. If a woman underwent the examination and was discovered to suffer from a venereal disease then she was detained in hospital for up to three months. In 1866 the detention period in hospital was extended to six months and then to nine months in 1869 when there were 18 subjected districts.

Women who were taken up under the Acts were registered as prostitutes, forced to undergo a medical examination, and, if diseased, confined to hospital until cured. Men who had venereal disease were not treated in confinement like the women. The authorities believed that men who contracted venereal diseases could look after themselves and find medical attention. They believed that women had to be confined to hospital if they were to be treated effectively. The military authorities certainly approved of the Acts and felt that they reduced the incidence of venereal disease and were thus beneficial to the soldiers. Many medical men also approved of the Acts, again believing that they offered protection to the women's clients, and they saw the Acts as an issue of public health control. There was little public reaction to the introduction of the Contagious Diseases Acts until the government attempted to extend the Acts to other garrison towns in 1869. It was from 1869 that sustained opposition to the Acts emerged.

The Contagious Diseases Acts were contentious and assumed cultural and political meanings never intended when they were introduced. They blurred the boundaries between the political and the sexual, they were seen to interfere in private life, and threatened the freedom of the working classes. They were gender and class specific and a substantial opposition developed towards them. In 1869 the National Association for the Repeal of the Contagious Diseases Acts was formed to prevent the extension of the Acts, but did not look for their abolition. There were no women present at this original meeting and as a result women formed their own society called the Ladies' National Association for the Repeal of the Contagious Diseases Acts (the LNA). Josephine Butler was a leading figure in the repeal movement and she organized and led the LNA. The objections raised about the Acts were based on a number of premises. Women objected on the grounds that the Acts applied only to them. Many campaigners believed that they sanctioned vice as the government, in treating women for venereal disease, was allowing prostitution to flourish rather than attempting to eradicate it. The Acts, it was believed, reinforced the double standard of sexual morality in operation and they were an abuse of civil rights since the

Acts did not define a prostitute, so any woman acting in a disreputable manner in public could be taken in by the police. It was also argued that repressive legislation could not stop the spread of disease, allowed too much state interference in private affairs, and gave the police too much power.

The methods used by the repeal campaigners involved organizing petitions, deputations, lobbying, meetings, and writing letters, pamphlets and books to rally support. Annual meetings which lasted a couple of days were organized to gain maximum publicity and support for the campaign. *The Shield* was a weekly newspaper published to support the repeal campaign. It took the government quite a while to acknowledge opposition to the Acts. Neither the Liberals nor the Conservatives initially supported repeal, making it difficult to have the issue raised in Parliament. The governments of the day were also more concerned about imperial affairs than this campaign. The government did, however, appoint a number of commissions to investigate the Acts. In 1871, for example, a Royal Commission was appointed but the LNA and other repeal groups refused to cooperate with it, distrusting the government's motives. The Commission favoured the continuance of the Acts. Throughout the 1870s repeal bills were introduced but received only minority support. By the mid-1870s, however, Liberal support for repeal was growing. In 1874 an influential Liberal MP, James Stansfield, spoke out against the Acts. This was an important turning point in the repeal campaign and the press began to take notice. He had both prestige and political experience and he was also an adviser to Josephine Butler. Eventually, because of the level of support for repeal, the Liberal administration of 1883 suspended the Acts and they were repealed in 1886.

Many prostitutes were able to escape legal restrictions, particularly if they managed to stay out of the way of the police. It seems that police forces throughout the United Kingdom often dealt leniently with prostitutes. Clampdowns on prostitution occurred most frequently when there was a public outcry against the presence of prostitutes on the streets, or if women who worked as prostitutes were thought to be disturbing the peace. The police often had an ambivalent attitude towards prostitution. Many members of the police force thought it futile to prosecute prostitutes. Harassment by police often forced the women to move to different areas of a town or city, but did little to stop them working as prostitutes. It was the street-walking prostitutes who attracted most attention from the police; those women who worked from brothels generally suffered less harassment. Some policemen appear to have had relationships with prostitutes and there was much room here for corruption. There were rumours that the police often demanded money from prostitutes, an accusation often made by rescue workers. However, while it is clear that some police officers had relationships with prostitutes, it is more difficult to prove that bribery or blackmail formed a large part of the relationship between police and prostitutes.

It is difficult to know if the Acts were effective in controlling venereal diseases. On the surface they seemed to work as the incidence of venereal disease appeared to decline. However, problems were raised by the diagnosis and treatment of venereal diseases in this period. There was no cure for venereal diseases until the introduction of salvarsan in 1909 and then the later use of antibiotics. Mercury was used in the treatment of syphilis and inflicted considerable damage on the patient. But women were adept at escaping the CDA's regulations. It appears likely that women, rather than be arrested, registered and confined to hospital, moved out of the subjected districts and worked elsewhere. For example, in Maidstone in Kent in 1866 there were 91 women registered as prostitutes. By 1871 there were only 45 left in the district. Many moved into the countryside, beyond the limits of the Acts, where they continued to work. The repeal of the CDA in 1886 did not mark the end of British regulationism. British administration of commercial sexuality spread throughout the colonies and regulationist regimes were still in place well into the twentieth century in various locations, including India and Hong Kong.[45]

The attempted regulation of prostitution is a feature of a number of European governments' policy and legislation in the twentieth century. Research has revealed that although the criminalization of prostitution in London increased during the early twentieth century it failed to confine or restrict prostitution to any single area of the city.[46] In Edinburgh, by contrast, police toleration of prostitution around Leith docks in the 1950s helped to restrict the location of prostitution in the city.[47] In Germany, it has been argued that there was an ambivalent approach to prostitution under the Nazi regime.[48] After World War II prostitution was formally prohibited in East Germany and a registrations system, similar to that which operated in the nineteenth century, was in place in West Germany. By the 1970s the growth of brothels was evident in many German cities, and towns operated a number of 'red light districts'. The *Prostitutuinsgesetz* (Prostitution Act) came into force in January 2001 which declared that neither selling nor buying sex were prohibited but were subject to zoning restrictions. Trafficking was criminalized in 2005.[49] In Spain brothels had been illegal from 1956 but many continued to operate from clubs. From 1963 the Spanish authorities attempted to suppress prostitution and judges had powers to incarcerate women in institutions or ban them from towns and cities. In 1995 all offences relating to the selling of sex were repealed and legal measures are now confined to 'addressing the exploitation of prostitution'.[50] It has been argued that the Spanish government has been one of the most proactive and progressive in Europe in dealing with violence against women.[51] Kelly *et al.*'s recent study of various prostitution regimes across Europe and in Australia and New Zealand concludes that 'far more prohibitions apply to selling sex than buying. ... The Swedish regime has an attractive symmetry and clarity with selling always decriminalized and buying always illegal.'[52] There is still confusion in many countries about how best to deal with the problems raised by prostitution and the sexual exploitation of women.

The issue of the trafficking of women, further discussed by Shani D'Cruze in chapter 24 on sexual violence, has become the aspect of prostitution that perhaps attracts most attention in contemporary society. This is not a new development however. After the abolition of the CDA in 1886 'purity campaigners' turned their attention to the 'white slave trade' which was understood as a vile trade that saw young, innocent women forced into prostitution. It was believed that no woman would willingly become a prostitute, and therefore those individuals, mostly men, othered as foreign or Jewish, who lured women into prostitution needed to be targeted. The idea of 'white slavery' gained notoriety throughout Europe and other parts of the world in the late nineteenth and early twentieth centuries. It linked race and sexual exploitation in powerful ways, the otherness of the foreign debasing and exploiting young, vulnerable white women for sexual pleasure and monetary gain. How prevalent it was, or even its actual existence have been questioned and the 'scare' had more to say about cultural and racial differences, and the fear of foreign men in particular, than about the nature of prostitution.[53]

However, the subject of women being trafficked into prostitution has become an issue of international concern in recent years. It is a controversial subject, much written about and its terms and meanings disputed. Jo Doezema argues that there is a 'global myth' of trafficking in women that takes many forms. She further argues that the 'notion of consent is central to a perspective on prostitution as a legitimate employment choice'.[54] It has been argued that the majority of 'trafficking victims' are aware that the jobs they will work in are in the sex industry; what is not clarified for them are the conditions under which they will work.[55] Ambivalence in dealing with prostitution and women who work as prostitutes appear to be the hallmarks of government policy and legislation in European countries generally. The issue of consent or prostitution as a choice is difficult because some states view supporting a drug habit by prostitution as an 'unfree' choice. It has been shown that trying to see prostitution as a form of employment similar to other forms of employment is problematic, as regulations fail to be properly enforced. The link between prostitution and criminality, and exploitation by pimps, does not seem to have been reduced by legislation. There is still a high level of violence associated with prostitution and legislation has had little impact in reducing it. As Kelly *et al.* suggest, 'to be effective prostitution regimes need to develop holistic responses that address women who sell, men who buy and those who profit simultaneously'.[56]

Evidence suggests that many women who were prostitutes had no interest in reforming. Betty Mackay, an 'emaciated, wasted-looking woman', was charged in 1862 in Belfast with having been drunk and disorderly. It was noted that 'the prisoner is a woman of ill fame [and] has been a habitual frequenter of the court during the last thirty-five years. In the course of her vicious career she has undergone many imprisonments and refused all attempts at rehabilitation.'[57] Though often considered 'vicious' the women who worked as prostitutes displayed their humanity in many ways. Elizabeth Finnegan, a 26-year-old single mother and prostitute from Clones, was convicted on 5 July 1883 at the County Monaghan Assizes for stealing £110. She was sentenced to five years' penal servitude at Mountjoy from where she corresponded regularly with the master of the Monaghan workhouse to ensure the care of her child while she served her sentence.[58]

The rescue of 'fallen women'

Another aspect of regulation, or attempted regulation, can be seen in efforts made to rescue 'fallen women'. Prostitutes were considered sinners and rescue workers attempted to persuade them to leave their occupation. Women philanthropists played a significant role in rescue work. Many established rescue homes, or Magdalen asylums, to provide shelter, accommodation and an opportunity for 'fallen women' to reform. These homes were named after the sinner Mary Magdalen, a follower of Jesus, who was perceived as the ideal sinner reformed. The first Magdalen asylum was established in London in 1758 and took in all women willing to reform. The only women denied access to this refuge were black women. A number of black women worked as domestic servants in London in this period, and black women who worked in brothels were considered 'exotic'. Many of the rescue homes were run by religious groups or organizations. Magdalen asylums have been little researched in most European countries, though they were a significant feature of rescue work particularly in France and Italy. Mahood's work on prostitution in nineteenth-century Scotland provides some insight into the operation of Magdalen asylums in that country.[59] Other than this there are, as far as I am aware, no published histories of Magdalen asylums in other European countries. There is however considerable information available on these institutions in Ireland.[60] In Ireland the major providers of rescue homes, or Magdalen asylums were congregations of female religious, particularly the Good Shepherd Sisters, a French congregation that also ran institutions in France, the Sisters of

Charity and the Sisters of Mercy.[61] By 1880 Magdalen asylums were a well-established feature of the Irish institutional landscape.

Penitents, as the women who entered these institutions were called, most often gained entry by making their own way to the refuge. It is clear that lay Magdalen philanthropists generally excluded the admission of hardened prostitutes. From the case histories provided in some of the annual reports, many of the women appear not to have been prostitutes at all, or at least their lives were constructed in a particular way to appeal to subscribers. Many were described as 'seduced' women who, on abandonment by their seducers and families, turned to the asylums for protection. It was also probably easier to reclaim young and 'seduced' women than hardened prostitutes. And the greater the success rate claimed by the asylums in the reform of penitents the more justification they had for their existence and the greater their claim on public support, on which the lay asylums depended, particularly in their earlier years. The reports of these asylums included case histories of young, vulnerable females in an attempt to engage public sympathy. These case histories humanized the women, made them 'worthy' of care and encouraged the public to subscribe to the refuges. The only requirement common to all these institutions in allowing entry was the expressed desire on the part of the penitent to reform.

Organization and funding

What was life like for the women who entered these institutions? Once within the walls of a refuge the penitents were generally issued with a uniform, one outfit for Sundays and another for everyday wear. In some institutions the women were separated into different classes. A strict regime was followed in the asylums which stripped the women of their former identity and moulded a new one for them. Penitents were forbidden to use their own names or to speak of their past. In religious-run asylums they were given the name of a saint. But even in rejecting their past the penitents were never allowed to forget that they had sinned. Their daily life was made up of prayer, labour, recreation and silence. This programme of reform and discipline made no allowance for maternal feeling. The children of penitents were not allowed into these asylums, and it is unclear what became of them. All contacts with their past life were broken. They could not write or receive letters without the matron first reading them. They were rarely allowed visitors and, if they were, they had to meet them with the matron present. The control these institutions attempted to exert over the women even extended to selecting topics of conversation among the inmates: 'all occasions which might give rise to improper mental associations are ... carefully guarded against ... all light and trifling conversation is strictly inhibited'.[62]

Within the asylums the inmates had to do a certain amount of work. A programme of religious instruction coupled with laundry work was normally followed. To effect reform and rehabilitation the homes inculcated a sense of guilt in the penitents and united this with lessons in sobriety and industry. The conversion of the inmates depended on them being constantly employed; an idle life was considered to be prejudicial to their good. The aim was not only to keep the inmates busy but also to train them for new occupations once they had left the asylum. All the asylums engaged in needle and laundry work. Although the main reason given was the desire to discipline the penitents and to give them a trade, such work was also a vital source of financial support for the institutions. These charities raised funds through annual charity sermons, subscriptions, donations and legacies. The institutions run by nuns are of especial interest in regard to the idealized picture of women common in the nineteenth century. In these refuges the 'purest' women looked after the most 'impure'. As in other charitable endeavours in which they became involved, female religious provided an extensive, organized network of refuges that operated throughout many parts of Europe. The regimes in these refuges were similar throughout Europe with Orders and Congregations of nuns following the same guidebooks.

From the evidence available from Ireland entering a refuge was, for the majority of women, a matter of choice. While it is true that many such women had only the work-house or the Magdalen asylum to turn to in times of utter distress, it would appear that the second was the favoured option of many. The length of stay in the asylums varied from one day for some women to an entire lifetime, of 30 or 40 years, for others. It was gen-erally women who entered in their teens or who were in their thirties or older, who remained in the homes. The decision to stay was made by the women themselves and, although the nuns certainly did not encourage women to leave, they had little choice in the matter if the woman was determined to go. It would seem, from the number of re-entries, that some women may have used the asylums as a temporary shelter and once they thought it possible to return to the outside world they did so. It is obvious also that the diet within the homes was of a higher standard than that to be obtained elsewhere, and this may have encouraged some women to stay. The stability of life within a refuge, and the order and discipline imposed, may have given a sense of security to others and made it an attractive option to remain.

Restrictions were placed on women's physical space within these institutions. There was, of course, no room for vanity and the most public aspect of vanity, the women's hair, was to be cut on entrance to the asylum. This, it was believed, was a means of ensuring that the women would stay in the asylum at least until their hair grew back. Cutting their hair was also a test for their motivation on entering as the nuns believed that some women entered for the purpose of procuring.[63] Surveillance was the main tool in maintaining discipline in the asylums. It is significant that the Good Shepherd nuns who worked directly with the women were called *surveillantes*.[64] The Good Shepherd Sisters were advised that,

> in the church, at their work, and especially during the recreation hours and in the dormitory, be watchful over our dear children ... a lamp should burn all night in their dormitory ... let your watchfulness extend itself to every one ... if you ... leave them to themselves you may be the cause of the loss of their souls.[65]

The Sisters were further warned that 'we should not, at recreation nor elsewhere, allow two children to be alone ... there should be no corners in which some could hide from the eyes of the Mistress. It is in such places that the demon lies in wait.'[66] The women within these asylums were watched 24 hours a day, but that did not prevent them from being disruptive. Insubordination, violence, madness, or a refusal to attend to religious duties or ceremonies, were the reasons usually given for dismissal. Women resisted the regimes in the asylums by escaping, refusing to take part in religious rituals, and refusing to work. One penitent in the Donnybrook asylum in Dublin was dismissed after 10 years in resi-dence. She was described as 'extremely slothful, irreligious and [having] a shocking tongue'.[67] Another woman in Limerick was expelled in 1891 after a month in the home. It was her sixth time in the refuge and the record of her dismissal states 'not to be admitted again ... a very bad spirit'.[68] Being disruptive was one way in which the penitents could express dissatisfaction with the institution; it was also a way for them to assert their individuality and personality. One woman in the Good Shepherd Asylum in Waterford was expelled in 1897 'for rebellion'. Another, in the same community, was expelled because of her 'troublesome disposition'. Yet another was sent away as she was 'very easily led into mischief'.[69] In the Good Shepherd Asylum in Belfast a number of women were expelled for 'striking', or refusing to work.[70] Those who were most disruptive were the ones excluded by the Sisters.

Many women were most active in their twenties and thirties and had given up prostitution by the time they reached 40.[71] Of the women who entered, and remained, in the refuges the majority had either entered very young, at 16, or were in their late thirties. It would seem that the latter group had given up their life on the streets and purposely entered the refuges with the intention of 'retiring'. Unless they had saved enough money to establish a business, or had married, there was very little choice for them other than the workhouse. Many of the women who entered and left the refuges on a regular basis were in their twenties and thirties and were obviously using the homes as a temporary refuge from their occupation. One other fact that emerges from the evidence of the registers is that the majority of women involved were without an immediate family. Most often both parents were dead, and in some few instances parents had emigrated without taking their children with them. The home was often disrupted by the death of one parent with the surviving parent remarrying, and in a number of cases it seems that the children of the first marriage were not welcome in the new home. The disruption of the family and migration to large centres of population would have removed the woman from the constraints of family life and expectations. The need to support herself, and perhaps the desire to be independent, may have made prostitution a viable option in a world where there was little else a woman could do to maintain an existence.[72]

All of the lay Magdalen asylums altered their function and purpose in the twentieth century. A number closed and those that continued in rescue work essentially became homes for unmarried mothers. Many of the lay Magdalen asylums adapted themselves to meet this newly recognized client or had closed due to an absence of clients. While lay-run asylums were changing their function by the early years of the twentieth century, convent-run asylums continued taking in a variety of girls and women as Magdalens. The perception of Magdalen asylums in twentieth-century Ireland is extremely negative. Undoubtedly, women were institutionalized and harshly treated in these institutions. While they might have been places of welfare in the nineteenth century, this may not be the case in the twentieth century. From some of the documentary evidence of government files, and the oral testimonies of women who were in these institutions, it appears that women were held against their will, they engaged in unpaid labour and lost whatever rights both the law and the constitution granted to them as Irish citizens. From the late nineteenth century it is evident that the asylums were beginning to be used by Catholic parents to hide the 'shame' visited on their families by wayward or pregnant daughters. It is also evident that some of the women being brought to these asylums were 'simple' and again were being hidden by their families. While the records of these institutions are closed to historians we can judge them only in the context of the oral histories that have been presented to us in television documentaries. For much of the twentieth century the concern of the church, the state and the general public with sexual immorality allowed these institutions to exist. The dominance of the Catholic Church in Irish society, and the network of welfare institutions that they ran, for which they were not generally publicly accountable, allowed a system to emerge where abuses were rife and where, until very recently, there was little public interest or government concern about the individuals maintained in these institutions.

Since 1991 Magdalen asylums have been written about in newspapers, women's magazines, plays have been produced, novels and a number of historical works have been published on these institutions. Peter Mullan's film, *The Magdalen Sisters*, released in Ireland in 2002, had the most lasting and powerful impact on the public's understanding of these institutions. The popularity of the film raises a number of interesting questions for the historian, not least how to provide a balanced history of a very difficult subject.

In contemporary society the representation of prostitution can be extreme. On one level it is 'glamorized', evident in such television series as *The Secret Diaries of a Call Girl*, starring Billie Piper, which aired between 2007 and 2011. Piper's character, university-educated Hannah, is a high-class escort. She has considerable control over her working life, and is wined and dined at fancy restaurants. Whether such programmes really influence how the public understand prostitution is a moot point. Clichés and stereotypes still abound, though some more sophisticated understanding of the lives of prostitutes was evident in the reporting of the five women murdered in Ipswich in December 2006. There was public outrage over TV and radio bulletins announcing that five 'prostitutes' had been murdered. Journalists agreed that in the early stages of reporting these crimes the language used about the women had been inappropriate, and public reaction to that coverage brought a greater journalistic depth to these women's stories. The *Guardian* newspaper in particular profiled the women as individuals whose life circumstances and choices were complex.[73]

Whatever historians have to note about prostitution, social scientists, feminists, health workers, policy makers and others also have provocative things to say about prostitution. There is little that is not debated, beginning with the words and phrases used to write and speak about prostitution. There is also little consensus among academics, policy makers and campaigners about how to tackle sex work.[74] Debates abound around the levels of intervention required, 'exit strategies' for those engaged in sex work, the needs of sex workers, how to tackle the clients of sex workers, what legal sanctions should be in place, how the economic configuration of society shapes sex work, and the commodification of women's bodies. Phoenix argues that while prostitutes and sex workers remain 'othered' they retain low status in society and the violence they experience is viewed in some parts of the media as 'deserved'. She also argues that while many women remain economically marginal they will engage in sex work to ensure a living.[75] Prostitution has always been a complex subject. There are no easy solutions to the exploitation that exists within this world and it is clear that the arguments and debates about sex work will continue for decades to come.

Notes

1 Timothy J. Gilfoyle, 'Prostitution in history: from parables of pornography to metaphors of modernity', *American Historical Review* 104:1, 1999, pp. 117–41 (117).
2 See, for example, Ida Blom, *Medicine, Morality and Political Culture: Legislation on Venereal Disease in Five Northern European Countries, c. 1870-c. 1995*, Lund, Sweden: Nordic Academic Press, 2012; Jill Harsin, *Policing Prostitution in Nineteenth-Century Paris*, Princeton, NJ: Princeton University Press, 1985; Mary Gibson, *Prostitution and the State in Italy, 1860–1915*, New Brunswick, NJ: Rutgers University Press, 1986; Judith R. Walkowitz,

Prostitution and Victorian Society: Women, Class and the State, Cambridge: Cambridge University Press, 1980.

3 For some of the more recent histories see the following: Elizabeth Clement, 'Prostitution' in H. G. Cocks and M. Houlbrook (eds), *The Modern History of Sexuality*, Basingstoke: Palgrave Macmillan, 2006, pp. 206–30; Victoria Harris, *Selling Sex in the Reich: Prostitutes in German Society, 1914–1945*, Oxford: Oxford University Press, 2010; Gail Hershatter, *Dangerous Pleasures: Prostitution and Modernity in Twentieth-Century Shanghai*, Berkeley: University of California Press, 1997; Philip Howell, *Geographies of Regulation: Policing Prostitution in Nineteenth-Century Britain and the Empire*, Cambridge: Cambridge University Press, 2009; Julia Laite, *Common Prostitutes and Ordinary Citizens: Commercial Sex in London, 1885–1960*, Basingstoke: Palgrave Macmillan, 2012; Philippa Levine, *Prostitution, Race and Politics: Policing Venereal Disease in the British Empire*, London: Routledge, 2003; Maria Luddy, *Prostitution and Irish Society, 1800–1940*, Cambridge: Cambridge University Press, 2007; Yvonne Svanström, *Policing Public Women: The Regulation of Prostitution in Stockholm, 1812–1820*, Stockholm: Atlas Akkademi, 2000; Luise White, *The Comforts of Home: Prostitution in Colonial Nairobi*, Chicago: Chicago University Press, 1990.

4 Joyce Outshoorn, 'Introduction: prostitution, women's movements and democratic politics' in Joyce Outshoorn (ed.), *The Politics of Prostitution: Women's Movements, Democratic States and the Globalisation of Sex Commerce*, Cambridge: Cambridge University Press, 2004, pp. 1–20 (4).

5 Liz Kelly, Maddy Coy and Rebecca Davenport, *Shifting Sands: A Comparison of Prostitution Regimes Across Nine Countries*, Child & Woman Abuse Studies Unit (CWASU), London Metropolitan University, 2009; http://www.turnofftheredlight.ie/wp-content/uploads/2011/02/Shifting_Sands_UK-HOMe-Office.pdf (accessed 7 January 2012).

6 William Logan, *An Exposure, from Personal Observations, of Female Prostitution in London, Leeds and Rochdale, and Especially in the City of Glasgow, with Remarks on the Cause, Extent, Results and Remedy of the Evil*, Glasgow: Gallie and Flecksfield, 1843.

7 Laite, *Common Prostitutes*, p. 29; Ruth Morgan Thomas, 'From "toleration" to zero tolerance: a view from the ground in Scotland' in Jo Phoenix (ed.), *Regulating Sex for Sale: Prostitution Policy Reform in the UK*, Bristol: Policy Press, 2009, pp. 137–58 (141).

8 *Report of the Working Party on Prostitution to the United Kingdom Programme Action Committee of Soroptimist International*, n.p., n.d., *c.* 2000, p. 4.

9 Kelly *et al.*, *Shifting Sands*.

10 Ralph Wardlaw, *Lectures on Magdalenism, Its Nature, Extent, Effects, Guilt, Causes and Remedy*, New York: Redfield, 1843.

11 Michael Ryan, *Prostitution in London, with a comparative view of that of Paris and New York, with an account of the nature and treatment of various diseases, caused by the abuses of the reproductive function*, London: H. Bailliere, 1839.

12 Harsin, *Policing Prostitution*, p. 210.

13 William Acton, *Prostitution Considered in its Moral, Social and Sanitary Aspects in London and other Large Cities and Garrison Towns*, London: J. Churchill, 1851, 2nd edn 1869. Henry Mayhew, *London Labour and the London Poor*, London: Charles Griffin and Company, 1861/2.

14 Deposition of Rose Ann Henry, Crown File at Belfast Assize Courts, Belf1/1/2/39, Public Record Office, Northern Ireland.

15 The sentence was not implemented and the recorder said he would see what could be done for the woman: *Irish Independent*, 11 October 1911.

16 Dublin Hospitals Commission, Report of the Committee of Inquiry, H.C. 1887, xxxv, [c.5042], p. 94.

17 Harris, *Selling Sex in the Reich*, p. 51.

18 *Staffordshire Evening Sentinel*, 10 March 1997.

19 Margaret Melrose, 'The government's new prostitution strategy: a cheap fix for drug-using sex workers', *Community Safety Journal* 6:1, 2007, pp. 18–26.

20 Victoria Harris reconstructs the life of one woman, Cornelie Baur, who worked as a prostitute in Germany from 1907 to the late 1930s. See Harris, *Selling Sex in the Reich*, pp 1–8.

21 Memorial to Colonel J. Colborne, Curragh Camp, 1 September 1859. OPW 486/59, OPW files, National Archives, Ireland.

22 Letter from Major Bellaris to Headquarters, Curragh, 12 September 1859. OPW 486/59, OPW files National Archives, Ireland.

23 Jeffrey Richards, 'Introduction' to James Greenwood, *The Seven Curses of London*, Oxford: Basil Black-well, 1981[1869], p. vi. For a fascinating insight into Greenwood's workhouse stay see Seth Koven, *Slumming: Sexual and Social Politics in Victorian London*, Princeton: Princeton University Press, 2004, ch. 2.

24 James Greenwood, *The Wrens of the Curragh*, London: Tinsley Bros., 1867; Greenwood, *The Seven Curses of London*.

25 Greenwood, *Wrens*, pp. 11, 17.

26 *Leinster Express*, 2 February 1865.

27 Kilmainham papers, Ms 1069, April 1878, p. 313, National Library of Ireland.

28 Evidence of Mr Curtis, Select Committee, 1882: Q. 11,277. Greenwood, *Wrens*, p. 25.

29 Greenwood, *Wrens*, pp. 14–15.

30 Greenwood, *Wrens*, p. 31.

31 Greenwood, *Wrens*, p. 27.

32 *All The Year Round*, 26 November 1864.

33 *All The Year Round*, 26 November 1864.

34 Kilmainham Papers, vol. 71, p. 105.

35 Kilmainham Papers, pp. 34–35.

36 See, for instance, Shani D'Cruze, *Crimes of Outrage: Sex, Violence and Victorian Working Women*, Dekalb, IL: Northern Illinois University Press, 1998; Shani D'Cruze (ed.), *Everyday Violence in Britain, 1850–1950*, London: Longman, 2000; Anna Clark, *Women's Silence, Men's Violence: Sexual Assault in England, 1770–1845*, London: Pandora, 1987.

37 C. Williamson and G. Folaron, 'Violence, risk and survival strategies of street prostitution', *Western Journal of Nursing Research* 23:5, 2001, pp. 463–75 (467).

38 Kelly *et al.*, *Shifting Sands*, p. 40.

39 Harsin, *Policing Prostitution*, p. xvi.

40 Alain Corbin, *Women for Hire: Prostitution and Sexuality in France after 1850*, Cambridge, MA: Harvard University Press, 1990, p. 4.

41 Judith R. Walkowitz, 'Dangerous sexualities' in Geneviève Fraisse and Michelle Perrot (eds), *A History of Women in the West, Volume IV: Emerging Feminism from Revolution to World War*, Harvard: Belknap Press, 1993, pp. 369–98 (376).

42 For the euphemisms and beliefs expressed about venereal diseases see, for example, *The Times*, 12 and 24 June 1875, 6 and 23 May 1878, 7 and 11 August 1882.

43 Harris, *Selling Sex in the Reich*, pp. 9–14: Harsin, *Policing Prostitution*, p. 54.

44 Svanström, *Policing Public Women*. See also Blom, *Medicine, Morality and Political Culture*.

45 See Howell, *Geographies of Regulation*, and Levine, *Prostitution, Race and Politics*.

46 Laite, *Common Prostitutes*.

47 Roger Davidson and Gayle Davis, '"A festering sore on the body of society": the Wolfenden Committee and female prostitution in mid-twentieth century Scotland', *Journal of Scottish Historical Studies* 24:1, 2005, pp. 80–98.

48 Harris, *Selling Sex*, pp. 183–85.

49 Kelly *et al.*, *Shifting Sands*, pp. 18–19.

50 Kelly *et al.*, *Shifting Sands*, p. 28.

51 Kelly *et al.*, *Shifting Sands*, p. 28.

52 Kelly *et al.*, *Shifting Sands*, p. 55.

53 Levine, *Prostitution, Race and Politics*, pp. 245–50. See the chapters by Jonathan Burton and Antoinette Burton in this volume for further discussion of this point.

54 Jo Doezema, *Sex Slaves and Discourse Masters: The Construction of Trafficking*, London: Zed Books, 2010, p. 170.

55 Marjan Wijers and Lin Lap-Chew, *Trafficking in Women, Forced Labour and Slavery-Like Practices in Marriage, Domestic Labour and Prostitution*, Utrecht and Bangkok: Foundation against Trafficking in Women/Global Alliance Against Trafficking in Women, 1997.

56 Kelly *et al.*, *Shifting Sands*, p. 62.

57 *Belfast Newsletter*, 27 November 1862.

58 Elizabeth Finnegan, GPB, PEN 1885/99, National Archives Ireland.

59 Linda Mahood, *The Magdalenes: Prostitution in the Nineteenth Century*, London: Routledge, 1990. See also Paula Bartley, *Prostitution: Prevention and Reform in England 1860–1914*, London: Routledge, 1999, which includes a discussion of rescue work.

60 There is an Irish government inquiry currently under way into the links between the govern-ment and convent-run Magdalen asylums in Ireland from 1922. The report is likely to be published in Spring 2013.

61 For a full list of Magdalen asylums in Ireland see Luddy, *Prostitution and Irish Society*, ch. 3.

62 *Annual Report, Asylum for Penitent Females*, Dublin: n.p., 1831, p. 11.

63 *Guide for the Religious Called Sisters of Mercy*, Dublin: n.p., 1831, p. 59.

64 See *Practical Rules for the Use of the Religious of the Good Shepherd for the Direction of the Classes*, Angers: n.p., 1898. The guidance in this book appears not to have changed over the nineteenth or even the twentieth century.

65 *Conferences and Instructions of the Venerable Mother Mary Euphrasia Pelletier*, London: n.p., 1907, pp. 372–78.

66 *Rules for the Direction of Classes*, p. 138.

67 Penitent 721, Ms Register of the Asylum, Religious Sisters of Charity Archive, Donnybrook, Dublin.

68 Ms Register of the Asylum, Good Shepherd Convent, Limerick.

69 Penitents 582, 601, 667, Ms Register Good Shepherd Convent, Waterford.

70 Ms Register, Good Shepherd Asylum, Belfast, pp. 56, 64.

71 Luddy, *Prostitution and Irish Society*, ch. 2.

72 For the origins of prostitutes in England see Walkowitz, *Prostitution and Victorian Society*, ch. 1.

73 *Guardian*, 14, 17, 18 December 2006, 22 February 2008.

74 Jo Phoenix, 'Frameworks of understanding' in Phoenix, *Regulating Sex for Sale*, pp. 1–28 (1–5).

75 Maggie O'Neill, 'Community safety, rights, redistribution and recognition: towards a coordinated prostitution strategy?' in Phoenix, *Regulating Sex for Sale*, pp. 47–66 (49–53).

Part XII

SEXUAL VIOLENCE AND RAPE

23

SEXUAL VIOLENCE AND
RAPE IN EUROPE, 1500–1750

Garthine Walker

Sexual violence and rape may seem transhistorical, for sexual acts we may categorize as coerced, violent and/or violatory appear to have been known in all historical periods. Yet we must not assume that rape and other forms of sexual aggression have no history. Nor should we suppose that the direction of historical change follows an obvious or inevitable pattern. The specific circumstances, general contexts, and collective and individual meanings attributed to sexual violence may change over time and are matters for historical investigation. This chapter begins by sketching out approaches to the history of sexual violence, paying particular attention to accounts of change during the early modern era. Sexual violence and rape in the period 1500–1750 is then discussed in four sections: the first establishes the legal frameworks within which sexual violence was situated; the second considers the practical difficulties inherent in accusing, prosecuting, convicting and punishing rape; the third clarifies the nature and significance of the early modern crime of abduction and other forms of sexual violence as 'property' crimes. Finally, we revisit the issue of change over time.

Writing the history of rape

Sexual violence became the subject of historical enquiry in the 1970s when feminists turned their attention to it. This early work assumed that the experience of both female victims and male perpetrators differed little over time and between cultures. From this perspective, articulated most forcefully in radical feminist accounts such as Susan Brownmiller's *Against Our Will: Men, Women and Rape* (1975), which attended to the issue of men's sexual violence from Ancient Babylonian society to 1970s America, sexual violence and rape were the *inevitable* consequences of men's nature, a primary means by which men as a group maintain political and social dominance over *all* women in patriarchal societies.[1] The maxim that all men are potential rapists was not restricted to feminist analyses. Edward Shorter, responding to Brownmiller in 1977, asserted that male libidinal drives appear to be historically constant even if rape itself was not. Early modern European society with its late age of marriage and proscription of pre- and extra-marital sexual activity contained 'a huge, restless mass of sexually frustrated men' for whom rape and sexual violence was a primary and inevitable release.[2] More recently, certain contributions from the perspective of evolutionary psychology naturalize male sexual violence in ways that appear to offer an explanation and, arguably, an *apologia* for this apparent constant of gender relations.[3] Although presumably not the authors' intention, this position may contribute to the notion that ultimately women are responsible for both avoiding and inviting rape. If sexually aggressive men merely act out 'natural' sexual impulses, the onus is on women not to conduct themselves in a manner that might encourage them. Such ideas about rape – 'rape myths' – are evident in many cultural media, from the popular press, cinema and television to surveys of popular opinion and verdicts in rape cases. However, even things that seem the same may be understood or experienced differently in particular times, places and contexts.

Much historical writing about sexual violence in fact tends to combine an essentialist acceptance that men have a natural propensity for sexual aggression with an account of change over time in which men gradually learn to control their drives and urges as they become more modern. Sexual violence effectively provides a gauge of how 'modern' any given society is and vice versa. The precise nature, chronology and meaning of changes identified vary. One study of the development of attitudes to sex and behaviour argued that countless pre-marital pregnancies in early modern Europe ensued from 'a chance meeting in an inappropriate location, at an age when [male] sexual urges became too demanding'. Many such encounters probably 'bordered on rape: stereotypes of the time, if not of nature, demanded it'.[4] Others have argued that although the process of civilization by which male violence became stigmatized and criminalized began in the pre-modern sixteenth century, only in the later eighteenth and nineteenth centuries were modern sensibilities sufficiently developed for rape to be viewed as 'a crime against a woman as a person rather than as the property of her husband or father'.[5] Another account identifies the same new attitude to rape as a form of interpersonal violence against women but locates it earlier, in the seventeenth century; here, the old view is one of rape as a sexual offence for which women were partly culpable. Either way, 'modern' society acknowledges women to be the victims of rape while 'pre-modern' society does not.

Not everyone views changes in attitudes to rape since 1500 as positive for women. In the tradition of socialist-feminist history, Anna Clark argued in 1983 that one of the (many) negative consequences for women of industrialization and the development of separate spheres ideology was that women came to be held *more* culpable for illicit sexual activity after 1750. In other words, as women were supposed to remain in the private domestic sphere, they had no business being out and about without male protection and putting themselves in situations where they were fair game for the men who raped them. The implication that women brought rape upon themselves made it harder for them to report it.[6] A related argument is found in histories of sexuality inspired by the work of Michel Foucault, which similarly eschew the notion that changing attitudes to and practices of sexual behaviours were necessarily positive for women. The 'first recognizably modern sexual identities' in the eighteenth century constructed women as the potential victims of dangerous male sexual urges, a discourse that was then used to maintain and strengthen a 'new and debilitating' model of passive, asexual femininity. This emphasis on women as weak and vulnerable victims was one way in which rape 'became a discursive mechanism through which female agency was limited'.[7]

Wherever we might stand on these issues of continuity and change, we might agree on an aspect of rape that is historically constant: a victim of rape does not consent to sex or only 'consents' to it under duress. Thus, accused men seek, in historically variable ways, to prove that victims consented of their free will; victims seek to disprove their own complicity and to prove the rapist used actual or threatened force. Arguments concerning if and when force (physical or otherwise) may legitimately be used against women may not be the same in all times and places. But if a woman is forced to have sex against her will, whether by physical force or not, from her perspective it is not legitimate.

Sexual coercion and law in Europe, 1500–1750

In all early modern jurisdictions, rape was rarely prosecuted and had a low conviction rate. Yet generalizing about sexual violence in early modern Europe is less straightforward than might at first appear. This is not due only to an absence of evidence about rape – although rape was without doubt vastly under-reported. Problems also arise from the disparity of evidence that *does* exist. Laws governing rape and sexual violence, and the procedures of the various tribunals in which cases were heard, varied widely both within and beyond state boundaries. Such variations could have a significant impact on how, when, against whom, by whom, and with what effect such acts were reported, prosecuted and punished. In early modern Europe, 'rape' denoted a range of incidents related to but not limited to those consonant with the type of coerced sex associated with rape today.

Nevertheless, as European legal systems and bodies of law shared roots in Roman, Germanic and Canon law, the legal foundations of rape were similar across the continent. Rape commonly required three criteria: sexual intercourse, defined as penile penetration of the vagina (sometimes stipulating ejaculation too); force (the degree and nature of which varied), and the (necessarily female) victim's non-consent. There were, however, a number of specific legal categories of rape depending on the status of the perpetrator and/or victim, the relationship between them, and the circumstances in which the act occurred. These differed from place to place, over time, and by tribunal. For example, in parts of Europe, the rape of a virgin (*defloratio, estupro, stupro forzoso*), an unmarried or widowed woman, a married woman (by a man other than her husband), a nun, a noblewoman (by a commoner), and an heiress, were each offences in their own right or subcategories to which particular rules applied. The rape of children was everywhere viewed as especially shocking. In some countries, sexual intercourse with female children under the age of consent (12 years) counted as rape even if the child had assented and no physical force was used. The dynamics of European colonial rule prompted further distinctions: an aggravated category of rape enacted by enslaved or black men on white women and a diminished one by white men on slave or indigenous women. Throughout Europe, rape was associated in legislation and language with abduction: the violent and forcible carrying away of women or minors with the intention to marry them to the abductor or someone else. Abduction and rape, abduction with the intention to forcibly marry (*rapt, raptus*), and abduction and clandestine marriage (elopement, *ravissment, raptus de seduction, estupro*) were all legal categories of offence. Precise definitions varied. In Spain, for instance, the term *estupro* technically meant both rape and seduction, but in practice the courts distinguished between *estupro* (seduction by promise of marriage) and *stupro forzoso* (rape), while rape was also known as *fuerza de mujer*. Certain acts of sexual coercion, even those involving high degrees of physical violence, did not legally constitute 'rape' at all, as may be seen in legislation concerning sexual intercourse as a consequence of 'persuasion' and 'seduction'. Moreover, marital rape was not legally recognized in early modern Europe (nor was it in France until 2006, in the UK, Eire, Germany, the Netherlands, Switzerland, and all US states until the 1990s, or Austria until 1989). Laws prohibiting prostitutes from bringing charges of rape were also widespread.

While not all of the activities mentioned above were designated offences everywhere over the entire period, their range and the spectrum of penalties they carried indicates the complexity of the topic of sexual violence in early modern Europe. Contemporaries did not view them all as equally heinous nor meriting similar punishment. The temporal and geographic incidences of court cases concerning sexual violence can also give a false impression of universality. For instance, in the early sixteenth century, the courts in Venice, Dijon and south-eastern England regularly heard cases of abduction of women of high social status and child rape, yet in Seville these offences were seldom prosecuted at all. Meanwhile, the *only* form of rape routinely sued in Rome's main criminal court was *defloratio* (the rape of virgins).[8] Practices and rituals of sexual violence also took particular forms in certain places. Gang rapes of prostitutes and other women allegedly of 'low morals' in the cities in southern Italy, France and Spain in the late fifteenth and sixteenth centuries appear to have been unfamiliar elsewhere. Similarly, sexual aggression towards young women during wedding celebrations formed a rite of violence only in some German communities.[9] When early modern historians discuss 'rape', then, we cannot take for granted that their sources refer to the same thing. In one study of sexual and domestic violence in seventeenth-century Holland, the author is unclear even about the status of rape and its prosecution in her own sources. We are told not only that no Dutch law against rape existed in the sixteenth and seventeenth centuries until 1656, when a marriage law that criminalized the 'seduction' of 'honourable' young girls included forcing or goading them to have sex in its remit, but also that previously only abduction and incest were covered by Dutch legislation (of 1540 and 1580, which presumably acknowledged the possibility of forced coition). Yet the author proceeds to discuss accusations, convictions and sentences for rape and attempted rape as early as 1618 and of married women.[10] Without a clearer statement of what the 'crime' of rape consisted of we do not know if we are comparing like with like.

Procedural and penal differences in the complex and overlapping jurisdictions of early modern Europe complicate an already complex picture. Between 1500 and 1750, few European 'countries' were unified states with centralized criminal justice systems. Most of the territory comprising what we now know as Germany, Switzerland, Italy, and much of central Europe was made up of independent or quasi-autonomous kingdoms, principalities, duchies, bishoprics and city-states, each with its own laws and legal institutions. Judicial practices were diverse even in the constituent parts of composite political units such as the Habsburg monarchy or the Holy Roman Empire. Thus, numerous German territories within the latter adopted aspects of the Empire's legal code of 1532, the *Constitutio Criminalis Carolina*, yet retained their existing legal institutions. Even the relatively centralized French state contained several provinces that possessed distinct legal traditions and privileges. The Parlement de Paris, in its role as the highest court of appeal, thus standardized sentences and punishments over only one half of the country. While England imposed its legal system upon Wales in 1536, Scotland retained its separate legal system in the Act of Union of 1707. In addition, rape was not solely a criminal matter. Like other sexual offences, rape came within the jurisdiction of the church courts or, in Reformation Germany, under the secular moral or 'marriage' courts. It also led to civil actions by which compensation was sought for the damage done to the victim. Penalties for rape varied accordingly.

Rape in the abstract was condemned as a most heinous offence. A Spanish almanac of 1619 was typical in proclaiming rape, like murder and tyranny, to be a 'great misery' portended by the comet of that year.[11] Most criminal law codes categorized rape with murder, sodomy, and other 'notorious offences' that merited capital punishment. Convicted rapists were, for instance, decapitated in areas adhering to the *Carolina*, decapitated or hanged in parts of the Dutch Republic, broken on the wheel or hanged in France, and hanged in England and Wales and in Ireland. The odiousness of rape was reflected in further penal conventions. In England and Ireland, rape was added (in 1576 and 1612 respectively) to the list of aggravated felonies for which the death penalty could not be commuted to branding. In several of England's colonies, rapists (particularly if they were slaves) were hanged in chains. In Venice, in 1513, an ordained priest who was convicted of robbing and raping 16 women was decapitated and quartered, his quarters displayed on the gibbet.[12]

Rape was not, however, an exclusively capital crime. Sentences for raping a minor in sixteenth-century Venice included the amputation of a hand and blinding; in Sardinian customary law rape incurred a fine, but if it had not been paid within 15 days the offender was to have a foot amputated.[13] The *Carolina* stipulated a penalty of 'body *or* life', leaving open the option of mutilation followed by banishment; in practice, convicted rapists were rarely executed. In the Dutch Republic, punishments for rape in Rotterdam were whipping, branding and banishment, not death, while in Amsterdam judges had the discretion to pass capital or corporal sentences.[14] Condemned rapists in French and Spanish courts in the sixteenth and early seventeenth centuries were among those reprieved and dispatched to a lifetime of servitude in the galleys. We ought not *automatically* to designate non-capital punishments as 'lenient'; certainly not all were intended to be so. Many men found the conditions of slavery in the galleys so insufferable that they deserted at the risk of being executed if caught. Banishment, too, was one of the most rigorous and severe punishments available. The Rotterdam man who, on a second conviction for rape, was sentenced to severe whipping, branding, 12 years' incarceration at hard labour, and thereafter life banishment from the city (thereby losing his family, home, occupation and community) is unlikely to have found his punishment modest.[15] In Russia, men were sentenced to pay hefty compensation to provide dowries for the young women they raped, as well as being sentenced to beatings and exile, while Byzantine secular law stipulated that the rapist give one-third of his property to the victim and have his nose cut off.[16] Ecclesiastical punishments for rape were also supposed to reflect the gravity of the offence. While these ranged from excommunication (social and spiritual death) and penance to imprisonment and money fines, canon law did not, in theory, regard rape lightly: it was classed as an *enormis delicta* along with assassination and treason, so much so that French canon lawyers opined in the sixteenth century that it was no sin for a woman to kill in self-defence a man who raped her. Indeed, in 1541, the (secular) Parlement de Paris pardoned Agnès Fauresse for doing just that.[17] Yet not all forms of sexual coercion, even those involving physical force, were treated as 'rape'. Distinctions between 'persuasion', 'seduction' and 'rape' were particularly muddy. The offence of 'persuading' a virgin or widow to have sexual intercourse in parts of Reformation Germany was punishable by one month's imprisonment.[18] In Catholic Europe, the highest penalties imposed on priests who raped women during confession (a sacrament, after all) were the same as those for seduction without force and even solicitation: they were prohibited from hearing confession, removed from their parishes, and sometimes sent to live in a monastery.[19] In Venice, the rape of a nun was not differentiated from entering convent grounds without official approval.[20] Sexual violence and rape in early modern Europe thus has more than one history, none of which can be other than sketched here. Let us turn nevertheless to an aspect of rape that was common enough everywhere.

Evidence, proofs and culpability

In early modern Europe, formal prosecutions for rape were few in absolute and relative terms. Between 1562 and 1695, tribunals in Frankfurt dealt with only two rape trials, while those in Geneva heard no more than two or three each decade. In seventeenth-century Delft and Rotterdam, a mere 14 men were prosecuted for rape or sexual assault, and only eight for rape in Amsterdam in the seventeenth and eighteenth centuries. In Ireland, about 12 rape cases were tried each year, grand juries having already thrown out over half of those initiated.[21] The Parlement de Paris, with jurisdiction as a court of appeal over one half of the land mass and population of France, heard fewer than three every ten years during the sixteenth and seventeenth centuries.[22] If formal charges of rape were few, convictions were fewer. Producing proof of the legal criteria for rape, penile-vaginal penetration, force (actual or threatened violence), and the victim's non-consent, was extremely difficult. Witness testimony was crucial in both inquisitorial legal systems based on Romano-canon law and in accusatorial systems such as English common law. Yet even eye-witnesses (uncommon in rape cases) or ear-witnesses (perhaps less so) to an alleged rape could seldom declare confidently whether these criteria were present. Describing rape necessarily involved a description of sex. This worked to the advantage of accused men, who were able to deflect an accusation of rape by asserting that they *had* enjoyed sexual intercourse but with the consent of the woman concerned. Consent was thus the central issue.

For early modern courts to accept that a woman had been raped, her non-consent had clearly to have been communicated to her assailant at the time and to others afterwards. During the assault she had to shout or scream and resist physically. If her cries brought no one to the scene she should alert others as soon as possible, thereby creating witnesses to her physical resistance – demonstrated by bruises, cuts, and lacerations in the genital area and elsewhere, torn or soiled clothing, dishevelled hair, and emotional distress. Proof of rape thus required female bodies to reveal truths about their experiences. Yet adult or post-pubescent women's bodies, or rather other people's readings of them, were apt to betray them (for child rape, see below). It simply was not the case that 'the display of a mutilated body trumps testimony every time'.[23] It depended on whose body, whose testimony. Even mutilated bodies had to be interpreted, and midwives and surgeons' expert opinions were valued over victims' first-hand accounts of what had happened. Moreover, an initially convincing tale might be negated in the later light of pregnancy, for conception was widely taken to signify consent. Women who reported a rape only after finding themselves pregnant were doubly damned, for the legal time limit within which rape could be disclosed had by then long passed. In the Duchy of Württemberg, for instance, this was a month; under English statute law, 40 days; in the Italian city-state of Ferrara, 15.[24] A woman's silence was interpreted as a form of collaboration with her assailant, suggesting her consent after the act if not before.

In practice, cases frequently boiled down to one person's word against another's. If a man denied that penetrative sex had occurred or claimed it was consensual, there was little a woman could do to persuade legal officials that it was he and not she who was lying.

Men's testimony was generally privileged over women's, adults' over children's, masters' over servants', those of higher over those of lower social status. This was particularly relevant in rape given that alleged victims were always female, and often maidservants or children, and defendants were adult males often in positions of authority over them. In late seventeenth- and early eighteenth-century Geneva, for example, nearly two-thirds of rape victims were domestic servants.[25] It is no coincidence that young, unmarried low-born women had the poorest chance of successfully prosecuting rape.

Moreover, secular and religious campaigns to control and punish moral offences laid the burden of responsibility for sexual misconduct on women. At best, this might mean that judges dismissed cases where they deemed victims had by 'word or deed' encouraged defendants.[26] At worst, victims of sexual violence were themselves punished. In Catholic Europe, many were sent to asylums to undergo a programme of moral reform.[27] In Württemberg after 1646, unmarried pregnant women who claimed they had been raped by soldiers were to be punished for fornication on the grounds that they were probably liars.[28] Dutch women and girls who had allegedly not cried out for help during an attack were punished for fornication or adultery alongside their assailants, while children molested or raped by male relatives over a period of time were treated as accessories to incest. Some children (boys as well as girls) convicted of incest were subject to corporal punishment and life banishment.[29] In these regions, penalties for fornication included various terms of imprisonment, forced labour, monetary fines, even banishment. Those who spoke out about rape could also find themselves prosecuted for slander and defamation by the men they accused.[30]

Confronted by this host of difficulties, it is hardly surprising that rape was seldom prosecuted. Many rapes were dealt with in other ways, as when a rapist was charged with simple assault, for example. In Venice such demotion of 'regular' rape cases involving adult women has been interpreted as evidence of Venetian government and society's contempt for women.[31] Yet dealing with rape by alternative means also suggests women's determination to bring rapists to account. English and Welsh women, for instance, prosecuted sexual assailants for simple assault in lower criminal courts where sentences were light but where a conviction was almost guaranteed; others complained to magistrates out of sessions to secure a peace bond that kept their aggressor away from them in future.[32] Meanwhile, successful civil actions against rapists resulted not only in financial compensation for victims but also a moral victory over an assailant whose reputation was by definition tarnished.[33] Both married and single women used these strategies.

Married women were generally better served by the legal process in cases of sexual violence (by men other than their husbands) than were unmarried women. This was not, as is commonly supposed, because early modern wives were viewed as their husbands' 'property', making husbands the legal and therefore more successful victims in such cases. Coverture in fact applied only in limited contexts. Wives, not their husbands, were the official victims in cases of violence and sexual violence. Rather, unless there was evidence to the contrary, a married woman's complaint of rape or sexual assault was not undermined by doubts about her chastity. Canon law jurists stated explicitly that a married woman who was raped was not guilty of adultery or other sin 'even if she voluntarily placed herself in the situation that led to the assault'. It was, tellingly, a married woman whom the Parlement de Paris pardoned in 1541 for inflicting a mortal wound on the man trying to rape her.[34] This was not, however, the experience of all married women. The Delft Assize court in 1658 sentenced Neeltje Cornelis to 40 years' imprisonment for adultery and incest after she had been raped several times by her brother; in 1670, another married woman whose husband was absent, was banished for 50 years after she became pregnant by a neighbour whom she said had raped her; for his part, he was banished for ten years, for adultery.[35]

One form of sexual violence, however, stands out from all others: the rape of girls under the age of consent (12). Child rape formed the largest category formally prosecuted, had the highest conviction rate, and resulted in the severest sentences. This may seem surprising given that the word of a child was not normally privileged over that of an adult – children's sworn testimony was usually inadmissible in court because they were considered incapable of understanding the nature and significance of an oath. How was it, then, that children's claims of rape were afforded greater credence than those of adult women or teenage girls? Above all else, the legal age of consent informed the ways in which courts dealt with child rape. Consent, as previously noted, was the key issue in rape cases of females of all ages. If a child had not attained the age at which the law recognized that she was capable of giving or withholding consent to sexual intercourse, the idea that she consented to sex with an adult was problematic. Some states formalized this in legislation: in England, it became statutory rape in 1576 even with the child's consent.[36] Early modern children under the age of consent were widely considered not to have attained what we might term 'the age of knowledge', of which their presumed ignorance of the implications of perjury was just one instance. This had especial import in sexual offences. Sexual intercourse involved 'carnal knowledge', but the notion that a child could 'know' an adult in this manner was dubious. Children were also believed to lack sufficient understanding of rape as a sexual act and the physical capacity to experience it as such. It was on a similar premise that boys under the age of 14 (the male age of consent) were presumed in law not to be able to carry out a rape. Thus, the responsibility and complicity widely attributed to women for sexual encounters did not apply in the same way to little girls. Indeed, Luther's interpretation of the rape of Dinah (Genesis 34) rested on this very point: as an 'infant' of no more than 11 or 12 years of age, Dinah's experience of sex constituted no sin on her part, nor was she responsible in any way for it, for 'at that age they do not even know they are alive or are girls'.[37] Although not everyone concurred with Luther's standpoint, sixteenth- and seventeenth-century court records suggest a consensus that sexual language was not so incriminating when uttered by children. Girls aged 11 or younger typically gave more graphic accounts of sex than teenage or adult women. Mary Golding, an English labourer's daughter aged 9, for instance, explained that her assailant had 'thrust a great thing into her privy parts and hurt her grievously and then felt something wet to come from him'.[38] In sixteenth-century Venice, cases of child rape or incest were the *only* ones that gave much detail of the sexual act.[39]

Child rape nonetheless had to be supported by evidence. Rapes and molestation of children were often discovered by a third party, usually the child's mother or other adult, not revealed by the child's spontaneous accusation. Questions were asked when children found it painful to sit down or walk, had bruised, swollen or torn genitals, or suffered vaginal bleeding or an unhealthy discharge. Immediately upon noticing her 7-year-old had a strange discharge, Caterina Brighenti took her to a midwife in Venice who confirmed that the discharge was a symptom of venereal disease; the little girl had been raped.[40] Such intervention of adults positioned children at one remove from their abusers, which perhaps contributed to children's stories of rape being more readily accepted by the courts than those told by post-pubescent girls and women.

Absent from this account of child rape is the rape of boys. Early modern rape legislation did not apply to male victims of any age: forced sexual intercourse of men and sexual intercourse with boys was legally constituted as sodomy. As such, it comes within the purview of other sections of this volume. We might nonetheless note briefly some differences between legal attitudes to rape and sodomy. Although early modern culture clearly recognized that it was possible for a man or boy to be forced to have sexual intercourse by another man, and despite acknowledgement of distinctions between 'active' and 'passive' participants in male-on-male sex, both parties in an act of sodomy were legally culpable. This is of a different order to the culpability ascribed to women for sexual encounters because, unlike heterosexual activity, same-sex sexual activity, as defined legislatively, transgressed scripturally defined boundaries in all circumstances. Men and boys who countered accusations of sodomy with claims that they had been sodomized against their will rarely found themselves exonerated. In Spain, inquisitors' definition of non-consent in sodomy cases was so narrow that there was scarcely any form of physical resistance strenuous enough to meet their criteria. Thus, an 18-year-old Valencian who accused a slave of attempting to sodomize him in 1581 was himself banished from the city for four years. Sodomizing little boys was clearly more shocking to early modern people, and was reflected in the punishments imposed: a 21-year-old shoemaker who 'raped' a young boy in Barcelona in 1575, for instance, was sentenced to an unknown number of lashes and to spend the rest of his life as a galley slave.[41] In sodomy trials in Frankfurt am Main, the allegations about which the Lutheran authorities were most concerned were those where the defendants had forced young boys to have sex with them.[42] In most parts of Europe, where sodomy was a capital crime, this meant, perhaps, that boys who had been raped were even less likely than girls or women to report the crime. The history of male rape is yet to be written.

Abduction, seduction and rape as property crimes

Histories of sexual violence often assert that before the 'modern' period, rape was a property crime, a form of theft, because women and children were effectively the property of men. The victim of rape was not the female who had been violated but rather her father or husband, the man to whom she 'belonged'; it was damage to his honour, not hers, that was of primary concern.[43] In fact, this was not so, even where rape was conceptualized as the theft of honour, and although a woman's honour was indeed central to that of her household and family. The *Carolina* of 1532, for example, expected women to be the complainants in rape cases precisely because the honour stolen was hers, not that of her male relatives. In Spain, and other parts of Europe, secular and ecclesiastical prosecutions that sued for coerced sex were frequently initiated by the women concerned, not by men on their behalves. Where the plaintiffs were husbands or married couples, the women were nonetheless perceived to be the wronged parties, and while adults, of course, had to prosecute cases where children had been violated, they did so not as victims of theft, but as parents or guardians of children in their care.[44]

The supposition that rape was a property crime is based partly upon the conflation of rape and abduction, a related – yet distinct – offence. The confusion is understandable: not only was the term for abduction *rapt*, but abduction was a criterion in late medieval canon law definitions of rape. Moreover, secular abduction laws did focus primarily on 'the protection of ... property and not the welfare of women'.[45] This, however, was not because women were constituted legally or socially as male property. The 'property' that the laws were designed to protect was not the body of the woman or child abducted but rather any inheritance, dowry or other financial settlement that could be claimed by the abductor or other person who married her. Heiresses and heirs were viewed as the transmitters *of* property stolen, yet medieval jurists nonetheless classed *rapt* not as a property crime, nor even a sexual offence, but a crime of violence against the person. While abduction laws were not identical throughout Europe, common categories existed: abduction and forced marriage; abduction and rape intended to result in the marriage of the abductee and rapist; clandestine marriage following the cynical seduction of the bride by the 'abductor', and elopement. Punishments ranged from execution, imprisonment and corporal punishment to fines, compensation and – to our eyes shockingly – marriage to the girl abducted, often taking account of the abductee's age and the degree of physical violence and deception used by the abductor.[46] Where abduction laws were concerned with property transmitted by marriage, it was prosecuted by the wealthy and in some jurisdictions pertained exclusively to the abduction and subsequent marriage of heiresses and sometimes also male heirs under the age of consent. It is certainly possible to argue that many elite women and children were treated as commodities in both the open marriage market and the illicit one in which abduction played a role.[47] However, this is not evidence that rape itself was a property crime, nor that women generally were, or were treated as if they were, men's property.

The subject position of abductees is potentially ambiguous. The offence of abduction entailed the carrying away of a woman or child against someone's will – always against that of her parent or guardian but, paradoxically, not necessarily against the will of the 'abductee'. In most jurisdictions, abduction was defined by its purpose: marriage without the consent of the latter's parents or guardian. Many women and girls were undoubtedly coerced into marrying, but not all. An abducted girl might be the victim of sexual violence before and/or after marriage, but equally she might give her full and free consent to such pre- or post-nuptial fornication and the incident still come within the remit of abduction. It is in this context, and not that of 'woman as property', that the notions both of consent *after the fact* of rape and of the marrying rapist are best understood.[48]

By 1500, the canon law option of marriage between rapist and victim (permissible only after the offender had undergone penance and with the full and free consent of the girl and her family) provided a loophole allowing young people to marry despite parental opposition. Abduction legislation developed to counter clandestine marriage, whether preceded by elopement, 'seduction', 'persuasion', or defloration, by removing the financial incentive: the bride's dowry or inheritance. The focus was therefore not sexual violence *per se* but rather the validity and potentially disastrous consequences of clandestine marriage.[49] For instance, despite ecclesiastical injunctions to the contrary, secular French legislation defined *all* unions that took place against parents' wishes as *rapt* even when they were consensual and involved no violence or other coercion. An edict of 1557 permitted parents to disinherit children who married covertly, and in 1579 marrying a minor of either sex without parental consent became potentially capital, although in practice pardons were routinely issued and, after the mid-seventeenth century, payment of damages was increasingly the sentence imposed.[50] Nor did abduction cases always involve heiresses to substantial fortunes (except where stipulated by law): in later eighteenth-century Ireland, for example, cases arose where non-elite parents had contested plans for marriages desired by their children.[51]

Similar concerns underlie some rape, seduction and defloration cases. In southern Europe, families of girls who had been raped took assailants to court in attempts to secure marriage between them, or at least to gain compensation to fund a generous dowry for a future marriage to someone else.[52] More startling from our perspective, perhaps, is the evidence of young women who, for the same ends of marriage or a dowry, themselves prosecuted men who had allegedly raped them or deceived them into sexual intercourse. Girls bringing suits to the Governor's Court in Rome for *stuprum* or defloration, including those in which rape was alleged, spoke from a range of subject positions, notwithstanding legal constraints on what could be said for a successful legal outcome: 'The girls spoke with differing language and with differing emphases ... not only dismay, fear, and anger, but also love and ambition, that is, personal feelings and intentions which fitted only in part with what their world would have had them say'.[53] Another study relates a case pursued there in 1570, in which the defendant, the complainant and her stepfather each modified their position until they reached a mutually agreeable outcome. The appositely named Innocentia prosecuted a young man called Vespasiano for *stuprum* as a means of securing marriage, claiming that he had courted, then raped and deflowered her, and afterwards promised marriage before changing his mind on discovering the paltry dowry her stepfather was prepared to provide. Vespasiano admitted to wooing her, three nights of consensual sex, and a betrothal, but insisted that he was not guilty of *stuprum* because Innocentia was no virgin. After the judge negotiated a better dowry with Innocentia's stepfather, Vespasiano publicly retracted his earlier claim and asserted that he had indeed deflowered his now-intended bride.[54]

The notion that young women or their families pressed for marriage only because non-virgins were too badly tainted to attract any other suitor is, therefore, misplaced. Nor was this known only in Italy.[55] In Basel, the Reformation ordinance of 1529 had mandated that men had to marry women whom they had 'deceived ... in a seductive manner' to have sex with them, albeit with the proviso that the women had not 'provoked' them in any way, and four years later was abolished by authorities that feared it encouraged rather than discouraged fornication. Nonetheless, at the end of the sixteenth century, Maria Verborgen and her father evoked this ordinance (as well the *Carolina* and Exodus 22:16) to compel the fellow who had raped her after inviting her to meet him in a secluded garden.[56] In the 1680s, a Muscovite nobleman was ordered to give 500 roubles to Mavrutka Ventysleeva for her dowry as well as being sentenced to a beating and exile to a monastery; in another case, the sum of one-third of the rapist's property was claimed.[57] As we saw above, women of the lower orders were in an extremely weak position when it came to avoiding or seeking justice for physical, emotional and sexual violence to which they were subjected. Yet despite this, some women successfully negotiated the law from a position of weakness. For lower-class girls especially, Elizabeth Cohen argues,

> [e]ven in the aftermath of experiences in which standard morality and parental expectations, on the one hand, and the persistent demands and even physical force of would-be lovers, on the other, left girls scant room for manoeuvre, some of them spoke to the judges not as passive victims but as participants in the making of their own fate.[58]

In early modern Europe, then, the 'property' that was lost and/or acquired in abduction, seduction and even rape and their prosecution was not simply or exclusively that of women's bodies, and the 'ownership' of such was not always someone other than the woman or girl herself.

Conclusion: sexual violence, rape and 'progress'

Many aspects of sexual violence and rape in early modern Europe outlined above may seem familiar. We could add to this endemic reports of rape by soldiers in wartime,[59] and the vulnerability of ethnic groups to sexual violence, such as that perpetrated by Inquisitors on Morisco women in sixteenth-century Spain.[60] Yet – as Jonathan Burton and Antoinette Burton discuss later in this volume – the early modern period, with European invasions and colonization of the New World, marked the beginning of generations of indigenous women being subjected to sexual violence on 'an unprecedented scale', with women and girls as young as 12 being raped, kept as concubines, or forced into prostitution by Europeans.[61] Such phenomena do not sit easily with teleological views of history as progress. Evidence of changes regarding sexual violence and rape in Europe itself also problematizes such a position. In eighteenth-century France, trials for child rape increased in absolute and relative terms, but in England prosecutions for rape (including child rape) decreased, while at the same time the acquittal rate increased. Yet historians have explained these as consequences of the *same* thing: the emergence of modern sensibilities. In England, this allegedly made it unthinkable for children to describe their own abuse in sexual language and so silenced children who had been abused, while in France, the same historical phenomena fostered a 'keener sensibility towards sexual violence' and 'a new sensibility to child rape' in particular, and so more child rapes were reported than ever before.[62]

Changes in punishments available for rape between the fifteenth and eighteenth centuries similarly demand that we scrutinize value judgements attached to a teleological view of the past. On the one hand, one might associate 'mild' corporal or monetary punishments for rape with the 'traditional' or 'backward' values of a society in which violence against women was not taken seriously. Rape was not a capital offence in all of England's North American colonies, for instance, in the seventeenth century: in Massachusetts and New York, adultery and incest were de-capitalized in the later seventeenth century, while rape *became* a hanging offence in the eighteenth.[63] The hardening of sentences for rape may be viewed as evidence of the development of modern sensibilities, an indication that violence against women was becoming less tolerated. Yet, from a related perspective, establishing the death penalty for rape could be seen as going *against* the trend of modernization. In sixteenth-century France, the rape of a prostitute was legally recognized, but in 1555 it was declared so insignificant a crime that it was no longer worthy of punishment – again, it is not entirely clear where this fits in a conventional account.[64] Change did not move in only one obvious or inevitable direction, nor did apparently unchanging phenomena always mean the same thing.

Notes

1   Susan Brownmiller, *Against Our Will: Men, Women, and Rape*, New York: Simon and Schuster, 1975. See also Kate Millett, *Sexual Politics*, New York: Doubleday, 1970; Susan Griffin, 'Rape: the all-American crime', *Ramparts* 10:3, 1971, pp. 26–35; Andrea Dworkin, *Woman Hating*, New York: E. P. Dutton, 1974.

2 Edward Shorter, 'On writing the history of rape', *Signs* 3, 1977, pp. 471–82 (474).

3 Randy Thornhill and Craig T. Palmer, *A Natural History of Rape: Biological Bases of Sexual Coercion*, Cambridge, MA: MIT Press, 2000.

4 Jean-Louis Flandrin, *Sex in the Western World: The Development of Attitudes and Behaviour*, trans. Sue Collins, London: Routledge, 1991, p. 262; first published in French in 1981.

5 Martin J. Wiener, 'The Victorian criminalization of men' in Pieter Spierenburg (ed.), *Men and Violence: Gender, Honor, and Rituals in Modern Europe and America*, Columbus, OH: Ohio State University Press, 1998, pp. 197–212 (199–200, 206).

6 Anna Clark, 'Rape or seduction? A controversy over sexual violence in the nineteenth century' in London Feminist History Group (ed.), *The Sexual Dynamics of History: Men's Power, Women's Resistance*, London: Pluto Press, 1983, pp. 13–27.

7 Tim Hitchcock, *English Sexualities, 1700–1800*, London and New York: Palgrave Macmillan, 1997, pp. 101, 108.

8 James A. Brundage, *Law, Sex and Christian Society in Medieval Europe*, Chicago: University of Chicago Press, 1990, p. 530; Elizabeth S. Cohen, 'No longer virgins: self-presentation by young women in late Renaissance Rome' in Marilyn Migiel and Juliana Schiesari (eds), *Refiguring Woman: Perspectives on Gender and the Italian Renaissance*, Ithaca: Cornell University Press, 1991, pp. 169–91.

9 Flandrin, *Sex in the Western World*, pp. 273–74; Edward Muir, *Ritual in Early Modern Europe*, 2nd edn, New York: Cambridge University Press, 2005, pp. 34–35; Susan C. Karant-Nunn, *The Reformation of Ritual: An Interpretation of Early Modern Germany*, London and New York: Routledge, 1997, p. 38.

10 Manon van der Heijden, 'Women as victims of sexual and domestic violence in seventeenth-century Holland: criminal cases of rape, incest, and maltreatment in Rotterdam and Delft', *Journal of Social History* 33:3, 2000, pp. 623–44 (624–25, 639 n. 22).

11 Geoffrey Parker, 'Crisis and catastrophe: the global crisis of the seventeenth century reconsidered', *American Historical Review* 113:4, 2008, pp. 1053–79 (1061–62).

12 Marino Sanudo, *Venice, Città Excelentissima: Selections from the Renaissance Diaries of Marin Sanudo*, ed. Patricia H. Labalme and Laura Sanguineti White, trans. Linda L. Carroll, Baltimore: Johns Hopkins University Press, 2008, pp. 130–31.

13 Ruggiero, *Boundaries of Eros*, p. 95; Brundage, *Law, Sex and Christian Society*, p. 531.

14 Heijden, 'Women as victims', p. 625; Pieter Spierenburg, *The Spectacle of Suffering: Executions and the Evolution of Repression from a Preindustrial Metropolis to the European Experience*, Cambridge: Cambridge University Press, 1984, p. 124.

15 Heijden, 'Women as victims', p. 625.

16 Nancy Shields Kollmann, *By Honor Bound: State and Society in Early Modern Russia*, Ithaca: Cornell University Press, 1999, pp. 43, 74–76.

17 James A. Brundage, 'Rape and seduction in the medieval canon law' in Vern L. Bullough and James A. Brundage (eds), *Sexual Practices and the Medieval Church*, Buffalo, NY: Prometheus Books, 1982, pp. 141–48 (143, 145–46); Natalie Zemon Davis, *Fiction in the Archives: Pardon Tales and their Tellers in Sixteenth-Century France*, Bloomington: Stanford University Press, 1990, pp. 81, 96–97.

18 Lyndal Roper, *Oedipus and the Devil: Witchcraft, Sexuality and Religion in Early Modern Europe*, London and New York: Routledge, 2003 [1994], p. 62.

19 Merry E. Wiesner-Hanks, *Christianity and Sexuality in the Early Modern World: Regulating Desire, Reforming Practice*, London and New York: Routledge, 2000, p. 119.

20 Mary Laven, 'Sex and celibacy in early modern Venice', *Historical Journal* 44:4, December 2001, pp. 865–88 (885).

21 Julius R. Ruff, *Violence in Early Modern Europe, 1500–1800*, Cambridge: Cambridge University Press, 2001, p. 141; Heijden, 'Women as victims', p. 625; Michael Durey, 'Abduction and rape in Ireland in the era of the 1798 Rebellion', *Eighteenth-Century Ireland/Iris an dá chultúr* 21, 2006, pp. 27–47 (34–35).

22 Georges Vigarello, *A History of Rape: Sexual Violence in France from the Sixteenth to the Twentieth Century*, trans. Jean Birrell, Oxford: Polity, 2001, p. 54.

23 Quoting Frances Ferguson, 'Rape and the rise of the novel', *Representations* 20:1, 1987, pp. 88–112 (90).

24 Ulinka Rublack, *The Crimes of Women in Early Modern Germany*, Oxford: Oxford University Press, 2001, pp. 184; 1275 Statute of Westminster; Brundage, *Law, Sex and Christian Society*, p. 484.

25 Ruff, *Violence in Early Modern Europe*, p. 142.

26 Joel Francis Harrington, *Reordering Marriage and Society in Reformation Germany*, Cambridge: Cambridge University Press, 1995, p. 256; Ulinka Rublack, 'State formation, gender and the experience of governance in early modern Württemberg' in Ulinka Rublack (ed.), *Gender in Early Modern German History*, Cambridge: Cambridge University Press, 2002, pp. 200–220 (205).

27 Wiesner-Hanks, *Christianity and Sexuality*, p. 125.

28 Rublack, *Crimes of Women*, pp. 239, 184.

29 Heijden, 'Women as victims', pp. 629–32.

30 Steve Hindle, 'The shaming of Margaret Knowsley: gossip, gender and the experience of authority in early modern England', *Continuity & Change* 9, 1994, pp. 391–419.

31 Ruggiero, *Boundaries of Eros*, pp. 95–96.

32 Garthine Walker, *Crime, Gender and Social Order in Early Modern England*, Cambridge: Cambridge University Press, 2003, pp. 49, 55–63; Garthine Walker, 'Re-reading rape and sexual violence in early modern England', *Gender & History* 10, 1998, pp. 1–25.

33 Brundage, 'Rape and seduction', p. 145.

34 Davis, *Fiction in the Archives*, pp. 189 n. 11, 96–97; Brundage, *Law, Sex and Christian Society*, pp. 396–97.

35 Heijden, 'Women as victims', pp. 630–31, 628.

36 The age set by this statute was 10 years, causing inconsistency in practice as the age of consent was 12 – as it was elsewhere in Europe.

37 Joy A. Schroeder, 'The rape of Dinah: Luther's interpretation of a biblical narrative', *Sixteenth Century Journal* 28, 1997, pp. 775–91.

38 Cited in Laura Gowing, 'Bodies and stories' in Margaret Mikesell and Adele Seeff (eds), *Culture and Change: Attending to Early Modern Women*, Cranbury, NJ, and London: Associated University Presses, 2003, pp. 317–32 (327–28).

39 Walker, 'Re-reading rape'; Ruggiero, *Boundaries of Eros*, p. 90.

40 Nadia Maria Filippini, 'The church, the state and childbirth: the midwife in Italy during the eighteenth century' in Hilary Marland (ed.), *The Art of Midwifery: Early Modern Midwives in Europe*, London and New York: Routledge, 1993, pp. 153–76 (153).

41 Cristian Berco, 'Producing patriarchy: male sodomy and gender in early modern Spain', *Journal of the History of Sexuality* 17, 2008, pp. 351–76 (361–63).

42 Maria R. Boes, 'On trial for sodomy in early modern Germany' in Tom Betteridge (ed.), *Sodomy in Early Modern Europe*, Manchester: Manchester University Press, 2002, pp. 27–46.

43 Julia Rudolph, 'Rape and resistance: women and consent in seventeenth-century English legal and political thought', *Journal of British Studies* 39:2, 2000, pp. 157–84; Marcia L. Welles, *Persephone's Girdle: Narratives of Rape in Seventeenth-Century Spanish Literature*, Nashville: Vanderbilt University Press, 2000; Gayle K. Brunelle, 'Review of Georges Vigarello, *A History of Rape: Sexual Violence in France from the 16th to the 20th Century*, trans. Jean Birrell, Cambridge: Polity Press, 2001', *The Historian* 65:3, 2003, pp. 773–74.

44 Isabel V. Hull, *Sexuality, State and Civil Society in Germany, 1700–1815*, Ithaca: Cornell University Press, 1997, p. 62; Abigail Dyer, 'Seduction by promise of marriage: law, sex, and culture in seventeenth-century Spain', *Sixteenth Century Journal* 34, 2003, pp. 439–55.

45 Quoting Nazife Bashar, 'Rape in England between 1550 and 1700' in London Feminist History Group (ed.), *The Sexual Dynamics of History: Men's Power, Women's Resistance*, London: Pluto Press, 1983, pp. 28–42 (30).

46 Garthine Walker, '"Strange kind of stealing": abduction in early modern Wales' in Michael Roberts and Simone Clarke (eds), *Women and Gender in Early Modern Wales*, Cardiff: University of Wales Press, 2000, pp. 55–62; James Richard Farr, *Authority and Sexuality in Early Modern Burgundy (1550–1730)*, Oxford and New York: Oxford University Press, 1995, p. 90; Brundage, 'Rape and seduction', pp. 141–42.

47 For abduction and marital strategies among the European elite, see Henk van Nierop, *The Nobility of Holland: From Knights to Regents, 1500–1650*, Cambridge: Cambridge University Press, 1993, pp. 82–92; Sanudo, *Venice, Città Excelentissima*, pp. 132–34; Walker, 'Strange kind of stealing'.

48 Brundage, 'Rape and seduction', pp. 141–43.
49 Daniela Lombardi, 'Intervention by church and state in marriage disputes in sixteenth- and seventeenth-century Florence' in Trevor Dean and K. J. P. Lowe (eds), *Crime, Society and the Law in Renaissance Italy*, Cambridge: Cambridge University Press, 1994, pp. 142–56; Harrington, *Reordering Marriage*.
50 Flandrin, *Sex in the Western World*, p. 65; Wiesner-Hanks, *Christianity and Sexuality*, p. 121; Stuart Carroll, *Blood and Violence in Early Modern France*, Oxford: Oxford University Press, 2006, p. 241; Farr, *Authority and Sexuality*, p. 108.
51 Durey, 'Abduction and rape in Ireland', p. 33.
52 Thomas Cohen, 'Bourdieu in bed: the seduction of Innocentia (Rome, 1570)', *Journal of Early Modern History* 7:1–2, 2003, pp. 55–85 (70).
53 Elizabeth S. Cohen, 'No longer virgins', p. 176.
54 Thomas Cohen, 'Seduction of Innocentia'.
55 Elizabeth S. Cohen, 'No longer virgins', p. 174.
56 Susanna Burghartz, 'Tales of seduction, tales of violence: argumentative strategies before the Basel Marriage Court', *German History* 17:1, 1999, pp. 41–56 (47–48).
57 Kollmann, *By Honor Bound*, pp. 73, 75–76.
58 Elizabeth S. Cohen, 'No longer virgins', pp. 177.
59 Brian Sandberg, '"Generous Amazons came to the breach": besieged women, agency and subjectivity during the French Wars of Religion', *Gender & History* 16:3, 2004, pp. 654–88 (662–65); Parker, 'Crisis and catastrophe', p. 1066; C. Arnold Snyder and Linda Agnès Huebert Hecht (eds), *Profiles of Anabaptist Women: Sixteenth-Century Reforming Pioneers*, Hecht Waterloo, Ontario: Wilfrid Laurier University Press, 1996, pp. 215–18.
60 Ronald E. Surtz, 'Morisco women, written texts, and the Valencia Inquisition', *Sixteenth Century Journal* 32:2, 2001, pp. 421–33 (429–32).
61 Karen Vieira Powers, *Women in the Crucible of Conquest: The Gendered Genesis of Spanish American Society, 1500–1600*, Albuquerque, NM: University of New Mexico Press, 2005, p. 95; John F. Chuchiak, 'The sins of the fathers: Franciscan friars, parish priests, and the sexual conquest of the Yucatec Maya, 1545–1808', *Ethnohistory* 54, 2007, pp. 69–127; Matthew Restall, *The Maya World: Yucatec Culture and Society, 1550–1850*, Stanford, CA: Stanford University Press, 1997.
62 Vigarello, *History of Rape*, pp. 78, 80–81; Bashar, 'Rape in England', p. 38; Elizabeth A. Foyster, *Marital Violence: An English Family History, 1660–1875*, Cambridge: Cambridge University Press, 2005, p. 148.
63 Stuart Banner, *The Death Penalty: An American History*, Cambridge, MA: Harvard University Press, 2003, pp. 6–10.
64 Sara F. Matthews Grieco, 'The body, appearance and sexuality' in Arlette Farge and Natalie Zemon Davis (eds), *A History of Women: Renaissance and Enlightenment Paradoxes*, Cambridge, MA: Belknap Press, 1993, pp. 46–84 (66).

24

SEXUAL VIOLENCE SINCE 1750

Shani D'Cruze

Writing the history of sexual violence

Interest in the history of sexual violence was once confined mostly to legal historians, particularly those who researched the medieval period and the intricacies of the laws on abduction (*raptus*) and rape.[1] Traditional legal history created a narrative of rational improvement in the law and in this view the modern age saw rape and sexual assault appropriately categorized within the criminal law on violence against the individual. Most other historians viewed sexual violence itself as an ahistorical phenomenon and outside their purview. In the post-war era social historians, often of the political left, became motivated to research the histories of societies as a whole, and of the poor as well as the rich, rather than the political and social elites who had hitherto taken more of the attention of academic historians.[2] This project opened up new questions and examined different sources and thus developed new methodologies. Sexual violence intersected with social histories of family and community relationships, including courtship, marriage and reproduction. Historians have outlined major shifts in sexual cultures which may have obscured and even have increased the violence in heterosexual practice by the nineteenth century. Furthermore, the developing field of the history of sexuality, directly or indirectly taking inspiration from Foucault, has historicized intimate and bodily matters earlier assumed to be physiological constants.[3] If sexuality has become more central in modern subjectivities, then arguably sexual violence has become more of an attack on personal identity.

The social history of crime aimed to explore criminality both for what it could reveal about class relations and as a means of researching the social lives of working people.[4] In the history of interpersonal violence in Europe a broad paradigm of the long-term decline of public violence into the modern age has come to be broadly accepted. This change was not least prompted by the stricter policing of violence, including sexual violence, by criminal justice systems since the early nineteenth century.[5] Nevertheless, much sexual violence continued to be ignored by criminal justice and it cannot automatically be assumed to mirror the general trend. Historians of crime were initially more interested in property crime and other kinds of violence, but more recently have addressed sexual violence either as an aspect of interpersonal violence or from a gender history perspective.[6]

The greater social liberalization of the 1960s–1980s which provided the social and cultural context for these academic developments also had political dimensions, not least in gender relations. Women's history was one of the direct academic outcomes. A key argument of New Wave Feminism was the recognition of sexuality and 'private' life as a site of gender subordination.[7] Women's historians applied a feminist politics to researching the history of work, family, reproduction and sexual violence.[8] Often the main concern was with male sexual violence against women and girls, and some work in this area tended to read modern feminist perceptions of sexual violence back into the past. Feminist academics have since refined and developed gender theory which, alongside the 'cultural turn' in social history more generally, has enabled the recognition both of how sexual violence changes its meaning in tandem with shifts in sexual culture and also of how sexual violence is written into the history of the modern state, through the law, the growth of professions (in particular medicine) and, indeed, in how European states and nations have been imagined.[9]

This chapter will explore the connections between these historiographical trends by discussing, first, the shift in sexual cultures between the eighteenth and nineteenth centuries, and second, by tracing the differing place of sexual violence in European criminal justice systems and hence in the history of state and nation. It will then examine the intersections between law, medicine and psychologically derived theories of sex in the twentieth century and how feminist interventions eventually disturbed this situation. Lastly, it will consider sexual violence in warfare. Most recently, systematic sexual violence was integral to the wars in Bosnia and Croatia in the 1990s even as other European states were expanding their definitions of criminal sexual violence.

Sexual cultures and sexual violence

The 1970s saw social-historical writing, outside that influenced by gender theory, which sought the origins of the modern nuclear family grounded in affectionate, intimate, heterosexual social relationships. For Edward Shorter, marital intimacy was achieved comparatively recently, through the more egalitarian sexual bargains possible between wage earners in industrializing society.[10] Shorter responded directly to Susan Brownmiller's (1975) radical feminist claim that 'From prehistoric times to the present ... rape has ... [been] ... a conscious process of intimidation in which all men keep all women in a state of fear'.[11]

Shorter argued that sexual violence was not an historical constant since the social conditions of sexuality had changed over time. He suggested that the rape of adult women actually declined by the late nineteenth century because of the greater opportunities for consensual sex in industrial society (including earlier marriage and contraception).[12] His argument is problematic, however, since he assumed that the twentieth-century model of male heterosexuality as an innate drive requiring libidinous release applied equally to the sixteenth and seventeenth centuries when (he argued) patterns of late marriage and strict social control made for male sexual frustration that found an outlet in rape.[13]

Lawrence Stone located the origins of the modern family in the eighteenth-century middle classes. This social group formed companionate, affective familial relations in contrast to both the emotionally distanced medieval extended family and the reserved, hierarchical nuclear families inspired by seventeenth-century 'puritan' religious culture.[14] By implication, therefore, sexual violence was deviant behaviour that happened elsewhere than in the modernizing, companionate family. This very mid-twentieth-century view of family, sex and marriage also accords with the view that sexual violence declined historically alongside other interpersonal violence. More recent work constructs rather different meta-narratives of change in sexual culture. These writers suggest that with the approach of modernity, sexuality became more central to identity, but that sexual violence became increasingly an aspect of masculine sexuality. In tandem with his argument about the eighteenth-century formation of homosexual identities, Randolph Trumbach finds that masculine heterosexuality that was exclusively focused on sex with females took priority over more heterogeneous sexual economies.[15] Heterosexual men wanted to demonstrate their difference from the 'sodomites' by penetrative sex with women and avoiding masturbation and same-sex practices. Amongst the middle and upper classes the cultures of sensibility and romance which Lawrence Stone describes gave a certain gloss to the brutish tendencies of heterosexual masculinities. Amongst working people, where increasing numbers of young women were domestic servants, subjected to intersecting grids of authority and highly vulnerable to sexual predation, sexual violence was just the nastier end of a continuum of courtship. Rape could lead to marriage. Trumbach's overall argument has been criticized.[16] However, his view of sexuality as a site of increasing gender subordination between heterosexual men and women by the nineteenth century finds echoes in the work of Tim Hitchcock who argues that Enlightenment cultures of 'sensibility' produced narratives of sexual seduction. Predatory masculine phallocentrism and penetrative intercourse matched to an increasingly subservient female response were prioritized; hence the increasing numbers of illegitimate births by the early 1800s.[17]

These models of changing (hetero)sexualities may indicate that heterosex acquired an increasing potential for male-on-female sexual violence as the modern era dawned, and indeed, as male-on-male public violence began to be restrained.[18] However, seventeenth-century rape narratives recount comparable sexual behaviour.[19] Possibly there was a shift in emphasis across more heterogeneous sexual cultures, rather than signalling entirely new behaviours. However, effective neutralizations of sexual violence were certainly becoming available, embedded in sexual cultures that thought about seduction and romance. Arguably, this cultural shift prefigured changes in European law and criminal justice that paid greater attention to both sexual and other interpersonal violence. Such changes did not necessarily help women and children complainants in court, but have been related to shifts in gender relations and the symbolic role of the (middle-class) family in European imaginaries of nation.

Sexual violence and nineteenth-century law

Across the nineteenth century more sexual violence came to court. The Old Bailey Sessions Papers for London show an average of only 29 defendants tried for rape per decade between the 1750s and 1810s, and of these only 4.5 on average were convicted. On the rural Norfolk Assize circuit there were a mere 15 convictions and 11 executions for rape between 1768 and 1818 and a further four convictions and three executions for buggery and sodomy.[20] Only seven Parisian women brought cases between 1760 and 1790. After 1850 cases were more numerous and conviction rates had improved. Seven defendants were convicted of rape at the Old Bailey in the 1820s, 85 in the 1840s and 196 in the 1880s. Around 50 per cent per decade of those prosecuted were convicted between the 1840s and 1900s compared to 17 or 18 per cent in the 1810s and 1820s. In France, the *Compte général de la justice criminelle* saw double the numbers of cases against adults, from 136 to 203, between 1830 and 1860, while those against children rose from 107 to 684.[21]

Following the 1789 French Revolution, the 1791 Legal Code stated simply that rape was punishable by six years in irons. By 1863 rape was established as a crime of violence against an individual victim of either sex. Other sexual violence was criminalized as indecent assault. The death penalty was replaced by forced labour in 1832.[22] By the 1880s in both Britain and France intercourse with a woman who had been deceived, drugged, or was asleep could be tried as rape.[23] French law remained substantially unchanged until the 1970s.

Russia codified its laws along more 'European' lines in the nineteenth century. However, the feudal nature of Russian rural society meant that Russian law remained a complex amalgam. Women, minors and peasants (who were unfree serfs until 1861) lacked full juridical status. The Criminal Code of 1845 positioned sexual crime other than rape as public disorder, not as personal injury. The punishment for rape differed according to social status and the relationship between victim and perpetrator. Although rape was a crime against 'female honour and chastity', that honour chiefly belonged to the patriarchal family and community.[24]

In late eighteenth-century English law, rape was a capital felony. By 1800 force, vaginal penetration and emission were all required. The common law offences of assault with intent to rape or ravish, or to attempt carnal knowledge attracted far lighter punishment. Sodomy was a capital felony for both parties even with consent. Evidence of penetration and ejaculation was necessary, confirmed by two witnesses. Unsurprisingly, few acts of sodomy came to court, especially where the sex was consensual. Most cases involving homosexual sex were tried as assault. The evidential requirements were less exacting and the penalties were usually imprisonment or the pillory.[25] The late eighteenth-century expansion of capital punishment was dismantled by the 1840s. There was also a progressive codification of the laws against violence and greater use of prison sentences. Martin Wiener interprets these developments as a 'civilizing offensive' which imposed new levels of discipline on many kinds of interpersonal violence.[26] Given class bias and because far more violent crime was (and is) committed by men than by women, these laws took greatest effect against working-class men. Capital punishment for rape and sodomy was discontinued in 1836.[27] Along with increases in the age of sexual consent and the creation of the offence of gross indecency between men in 1885,[28] these provisions shaped the English law on sexual violence until the late twentieth century. However, legal definitions were ambiguous. Indecent assault comprised 'what all right-minded men, men of sound and wholesome feelings would say was indecent'. 'Sodomy' came to describe a range of male–male sexual practices.[29] The Italian Criminal Code of 1889 categorized rape amongst crimes against the family and explicitly refused the protection of the law to women who had no family honour to defend, such as prostitutes.[30] It is a depressing historical constant that criminal convictions for sexual violence have generally been harder to obtain than for other crimes. The reasons for this are located in the prevailing complex of gender relations at any historical moment and how these intersected with the workings of criminal justice.

Sexual violence and gender relations in the nineteenth century

Over the nineteenth century rape shed its residual ambiguities as in some senses a crime against property and was written into statute law as a crime of violence.[31] Sexual violence articulated gender (and class) relations in changing ways; as Vigarello argues, French law took greater account of the moral violence done to victims' reputations and social standing.[32] Nevertheless, the idea of sexual 'fallenness' further emphasized women's responsibility to preserve their own chastity, now constituted as the more vulnerable to predatory male sexuality.

Anna Clark suggested a shift in England between 1770 and 1845 from an earlier 'libertine' cultural model where sexual violence was simply one of many kinds of violence to which the less powerful were vulnerable, to a 'chivalric' mode where women and girls were taught that to preserve their chastity they should rely on the protection of men (particularly husbands and fathers). At the same time, the rapist was constructed as monstrous and therefore distanced from respectable men. In both Britain and France he was sometimes an upper-class libertine – the Marquis de Sade being the quintessential French example – but was soon established as a marginal, working-class deviant.[33] His gender opposite was the prostitute, the symbolic embodiment of social marginality and dangerously excessive (irredeemably fallen) female sexuality. This doubled construction bolstered male authority in the home and made it harder for women to make full use of the criminal justice process. In mid-nineteenth-century France the criminal justice system policed sexuality more heavily, controlling pornography and prosecuting increased numbers of sexual offences. Prostitution was systematically controlled. This did not mean blanket sexual repression, but cultural renegotiations about the public manifestations of sexuality which took place partly in reaction to deep-rooted social change, population migration and urban growth. The family, on the model of middle-class, gendered domesticity, symbolized social order, even as it seemed challenged by an increase in adultery and a certain relaxation of sexual morality from the 1870s.[34]

Sexual violence and coercion in all-male locations (in the Navy or the universities) was hardly unknown.[35] However, for most of the nineteenth century homosexual sexual practices did not shape a man's or a boy's social value in the same way as loss of chastity did for women and girls. Women lacking a good character rarely obtained a verdict; they were already so thoroughly fallen that criminal justice systems could not imagine how rape or indecency harmed them. A woman or girl established her moral (and thus her social) value through her sexual chastity. The very experience of sexual violence damaged complainants' respectability and credibility as witnesses.[36] Nineteenth-century Ireland seems the exception that proved the rule. Conley has found a greater cultural acceptance of women's violence in dispute resolution or for retribution. In the few sexual violence cases conviction rates mirrored those for other violence. Irish courts convicted for rape regardless of the status and relationship of the victim and the accused.[37]

The issue of consent was at the heart of the law on rape. Consent was a matter of contract and an exercise of reason. However, nineteenth-century women and children were thought to need protection by the law (and by men in the family) because their capacities as reasoning individuals were limited and were, indeed, undermined by the very feminine sexuality which stimulated men's sexual attraction, potentially to the point of violence.[38] Judges were required to warn juries against convicting on uncorroborated victim testimony in British trials for sexual offences until 1994.[39] Imprecise definitions of sexual violence meant that judicial discretion remained extensive. There are instances of judges refusing to hear evidence against an apparently respectable defendant. Criminal justice systems became more complex and professionalized in the nineteenth century. Trials took longer and, especially in adversarial legal systems, complainants regularly faced prolonged and hostile cross-examination. Lower courts frequently tried rape as a lesser offence. However, this did provide limited justice when pursuing a case into the higher court would be expensive and with a good chance of an acquittal.[40]

Nevertheless, as Wiener argues, concerns to discipline male violence meant that courts could be sympathetic to victims of sexual assault who presented a narrative that accorded to dominant stereotypes.[41] The melodramatic seduction narrative became a common discursive terrain on which courts, the fast-growing nineteenth-century press and other print culture, as well as female and child witnesses could discuss sexual violence and the moral violence it entailed, though it required that they adopt appropriately vulnerable and sexually passive subject positions. These were 'crimes of outrage'. Testimony was masked by euphemism. Witnesses explained that 'he did what he should not do' or 'he effected his purpose'. If a nineteenth-century 'civilizing offensive' taught men restraint, it also taught women the demeanour of femininity and the need for 'protection'.[42] Punishing some men for serious sexual violence distanced hegemonic manly masculinities from 'real' rapists. By the 1900s, the identification of sexual violence with deviance and marginality became authorized by the emergent discourses of criminology, psychiatry and psychology. The moral violence of sexual assault was reinterpreted as victims' psychological trauma.

Sexual violence against minors

Much sexual violence that came to court involved minors. European legal codes established or raised specified ages below which minors were not expected to understand the nature of intercourse nor to resist physically. In Russia an age of consent for girls was set at 14 in the 1845 Criminal Code. Naples specified 12 in 1819. A French law of 1832 introduced an age of consent for boys and girls of 11, which was raised to 13 in 1863. English law was muddled and contradictory. In 1800, at its lowest estimate, the age of consent for girls was 10 and 14 for boys. The age for girls was raised progressively to 16 by 1885.[43] The cult of the innocent child intertwined with Victorian ideologies of the family. However, some children, particularly girls, were thought to display premature and precocious sexuality. In eighteenth-century France child victims of sexual abuse could themselves be prosecuted. In the 1880s there were scares over 'white slavery' and the trafficking of English teenagers to Belgian brothels which brought stories of virgin English children violated by foreigners into sharp public focus.[44] However, it was argued in the House of Lords that working-class girls might 'inveigle men to accompany them to houses of ill-fame', incite them into intercourse and subsequently blackmail them.[45]

Child abuse was identified with poor material environments, either the sexual dangers of the urban working-class neighbourhood or the uncivilized brutalities of the rural village.[46] Nineteenth-century medical knowledges claimed authority to interpret the bodily signs and symptoms of sexual abuse. However, into the twentieth century doctors very often preferred to explain injuries and infections through poor hygiene, bad parenting or masturbation. Incest was directly criminalized in Britain only in 1908. Sexually abused girls were often institutionalized.[47] A moralistic discourse accompanied scientific and therapeutic approaches to both offender and victim well into the twentieth century and is evident in popular perceptions of the paedophile into the twenty-first.[48]

Producing deviant sexual identities in the twentieth century

Joanna Bourke combines a feminist politics with a gender historian's attention to discourse and subjectivity and argues that rape discourses produce the subjects they claim to describe.[49] Historically shifting means have distanced sexual offenders from dominant models of sexual practice by creating deviant sexual identities: the rapist or the paedophile. If nineteenth-century sexual offenders were positioned as marginal and working class, twentieth-century discourses located sexual violence in specific, pathological (male) individuals. Offenders' bodies and minds were more carefully scrutinized. The Italian criminologist Lombroso worked to an evolutionary model which positioned sexual offenders as atavistic throwbacks. Krafft-Ebbing and other criminal psychiatrists elaborated taxonomies of sexual perversion. A recognition that sexual offenders could behave normally in other areas of life, combined with an increased cultural interest in sensual pleasure and its emotional power, implied that 'normal' sexual emotions might be dangerously close to perverted desire.[50]

These changing understandings of sexual violence went alongside new theories of sex. Sexology was an innovative secular, scientific explanation which acknowledged the importance of sexual pleasure for both women and men. Sexology privileged and naturalized a model of sexual practice based on sharp gender dichotomies, where masculinity was the active, aggressive principle. Psychologist Helene Deutsch argued that women desired and fantasized rape. Havelock Ellis argued in 1948, 'Rooted in the sexual instinct ... we find a delight in roughness, violence, pain and danger'. While many women found sexology liberating, it concealed much sexual violence as ordinary heterosexual practice.[51]

Sexual violence was distinguished from normal (hetero)sexuality by its pathological nature, where it focused on an inappropriate sexual choice, especially children, or where it involved extreme physical violence. By the 1970s theories of victim precipitation provided a psychological framework for victim blaming.[52] However, cure or control of offenders seemed a possibility and psychiatry and psychology became integrated into penal systems, until a renewed emphasis on punitiveness emerged in the 1990s. Psychiatric interventions produced the culturally potent but therapeutically ambiguous figure of the sexual psychopath. Intrinsically amoral and consequently incurable, this identification allowed compliant sex offenders to occupy legitimated if deviant subject positions.[53] Bourke traces how, from the early twentieth century there were attempts to treat sex offenders by sterilization or castration both surgical and chemical, lobotomy and leucotomy (destroying neural pathways in the brain through surgery), with ambiguous results.[54]

Psychological analysis was too protracted and expensive to be used on any scale, though from the 1920s in Britain behaviouralist techniques were used to reorient rapists' patterns of sexual arousal. Homosexuals were amongst those who received therapy for their sexual 'deviance'. Better educated offenders appeared more suited to softer 'talking cures'. More forceful interventions were applied to resistant prisoners. Punishment and control have been disproportionately directed towards men who were already disadvantaged, often by race or class. The British register of sexual offenders was created in 1997 and the range of actual or indeed predicted offenders and the information they are required to lodge with the police has since been extended. Such measures tend to identify already marginalized individuals, though some Swiss data suggests the social conventionality of middle-aged, professional men obsessed with accessing Internet child pornography.[55]

Feminism and the law

Nineteenth-century feminists identified sexuality as a site of women's oppression.[56] Between the wars, some feminists campaigned for birth control or to change the law to allow abortion,[57] but overall sexological models predominated and feminist attention to sexuality decreased until the 1970s when New Wave Feminism adopted fresh analyses of sexual violence as a matter of gender power. In France, feminist intervention had a direct effect on the law. The gang rape of two women who were camping in a secluded spot led to a public campaign in 1978, which, as Vigarello argues, put rape itself on trial and drew on a very different language about rape than the melodramatic allusive nineteenth-century discourse. As a result, the definition of rape in French law was significantly broadened.[58]

British statute law resisted reform, despite feminist activism. The 1975 judgment in DPP v Morgan found that a defendant was not guilty of rape if he believed the complainant had consented, however unreasonable his belief was.[59] Women complaining of sexual violence were still regularly disbelieved and treated harshly by police and criminal justice. The myths that it was impossible to rape a resisting woman, that women and girls lie about rape or that they say 'no' when they mean 'yes', were widely accepted. In 1982 in Britain a man was merely fined for raping a young woman hitchhiker. A judge commented that 'it is the height of imprudence for any girl to hitchhike at night. ... She is in the true sense asking for it.' There was public protest after a 1982 TV documentary on police work showed hostile treatment of a rape complainant by Thames Valley Police.[60] There was mounting public pressure for criminal justice systems to reform prejudicial attitudes and practices. The Italian Supreme Court decided in 1998 that since a young woman raped by her driving instructor had been wearing jeans, her consent could be assumed. The court held that her (tight) jeans could not have been removed without cooperation. The decision provoked a protest by women Members of Parliament – wearing jeans.[61]

From the 1980s several European states broadened the scope of their laws, included such offences as sexual harassment,[62] and rethought the definitions of rape and sexual assault. Despite criticism that it ignored the fact that rape was a predominantly masculine offence, gender neutrality was introduced in Sweden in 1984, in Austria and Belgium in 1989, in France in 1992 and later in Finland and Germany.[63] The exemption for rape in marriage was also progressively removed. In France, marital rape had become an offence in 1980, though case law remained ambiguous into the early 1990s. Austria, Ireland, Scotland and Spain all criminalized marital rape in the 1980s, and England and Wales, Germany, Macedonia, Finland and Hungary followed suit by the late 1990s. There were attempts to improve victims' experience of the criminal justice process (for example, better interviewing and medical services as well as rape shield laws to protect complainants' identities in court) and to make criminal investigations more efficient.[64]

The wilful transmission of HIV became identified as a form of assault.[65] In Britain the 2003 Sexual Offences Act included penetration of the mouth as well as the anus or vagina as rape and created an offence of sexual penetration by other objects. This Act also weighted the balance of proof towards the complainant and expanded the law on child sexual abuse. However, it has been questioned whether modern legislation is becoming so far shaped by one model of sexuality that it can act to criminalize other preferences. The 1990 'Spanner' trials of homosexual men found guilty of assault following consensual sado-masochistic sex was later taken to the European Court of Human Rights.[66]

Sexual violence in modern society

Feminists have unsurprisingly often addressed sexual violence as a women's issue. However, this made it difficult to address the sexual violence carried out by women and also obscured the problems faced by male victims. Understandably, the gay community were also reluctant to draw attention to sexual violence in homosexual relationships, though this accounted for comparatively few of the sexual assaults experienced by men.[67] The recognition of the psychological trauma of sexual violence was eventually extended to male victims. Rape of men was specifically criminalized in Britain (1994), Portugal (1998), Romania (1997) and Cyprus (2001). Modern criminologists argue that forced sex dominates and humiliates, not least in the context of masculine socialities predicated on aggressiveness, misogyny and homophobia. Male rape is generally an expression of heterosexuality rather than homosexuality and has little to do with eroticism. A 1990s study based on British police data indicated that male victims were no more likely to resist physically than female ones. In England and Wales 150 cases were tried in 1995 and 732 in 2001–2; by comparison, 9,734 rapes of women reported in 2001–2.[68]

Although involving a very small minority of offenders, the modern understanding of the varied and subtle violence possible in sexuality has recently brought a sometimes troubled recognition of women perpetrators, in part driven by an anti-feminist backlash. Bourke draws attention to Victorian working-class mothers who prostituted their daughters and domestic servants who abused the children in their care. Early twentieth-century psychiatric discourses framed such acts as 'nymphomania'. Some commentators claim that sexually violent women have acted at the behest of men. Recently, the sexual abuse of prisoners by female as well as male US soldiers during the Iraq war have demonstrated both the violent agency of these women and how they were adversely positioned within an aggressive and abusive military culture.[69] Sexual violence against men and women in prisons is deeply ingrained in inmate subcultures and reinforces the deep inequalities in prison societies. Until recently prison rape was regarded as an ineradicable effect of the depraved natures of criminals. In a 1990s French survey, 21 per cent of prisoners admitted to some level of involvement. The victims are the young, the weak, or those constituted punishable (from homosexuals to sex offenders) and the aggressors do not situate themselves as homosexual. In 1996 two prisoners prompted the first trial for prison rape that had been heard in a French assize court and the same year three warders were jailed for sexual abuse.[70]

After decades where the sexual abuse of children and teenagers had been subsumed within the partly disciplinary and partly welfarist measures addressed to 'problem families' and 'wayward girls' the issue re-emerged. In France rape of minors below 15 (including incest) rose from 100 cases in 1984 to 578 in 1993, and cases of sexual abuse recorded but not prosecuted reached 5,500 in 1995. The identification of numbers of children as sexually abused in Cleveland (UK) turned on medical diagnoses. Children were taken into care, some apparently mistakenly. Later moral panics about 'satanic' child abuse have proved more indicative of cultural anxiety than actual practices. By 2000 the psychopathic rapist-murderer of children was the quintessential monster. More than one investigation seemed to signal *fin de siècle* failures in criminal justice, community, family life and national culture. The Dutroux case in Belgium brought together 300,000 people to demonstrate against the inadequate investigation of this serial rapist-murderer, and the largest gathering in Belgium since World War II at the victims' funerals. Information technology and sexual tourism have added further dimensions to the shadowy threat of child abuse.[71]

Changes in European statute law and to an extent in criminal justice and policing practices seem to provide apparent grounds for optimism. However, this is undermined by the – albeit very incomplete – data on the incidence of sexual violence and the attrition between the growing numbers of complaints and the numbers of offenders found guilty and sentenced. In England and Wales there were 240 rape cases in 1947 compared to 6,281 in 1997. Of a 2002 nationally representative sample in Sweden, 34 per cent reported experiencing sexual violence since they were 15. Surveys in Finland (1997) and Lithuania (2001) show similar situations. A 1970s Scottish study found that a quarter of cases reported as rape or attempt to ravish were marked as 'no crime' by the police. The Scottish Procurator Fiscal decided not to initiate proceedings in 30 per cent of the cases referred to him (a much higher rate than for other crimes). The British conviction rate was 24 per cent in 1985; but by 1996 only 13 per cent of reported rapes ended in any kind of conviction, and only 6 per cent in a conviction for rape. More date and acquaintance rapes were being reported, for which conviction rates were lower. Black complainants were less likely to be taken seriously in the UK and elsewhere.[72] In Sweden in 2001 only 13 per cent of reported rapes were prosecuted and convictions obtained in only 7 per cent. Countries as different as Iceland, Slovenia, Poland and Portugal all have declining conviction rates. However, some countries, including Hungary, France, Germany and Latvia, had improved conviction rates.[73] Sentences of ten years and over were handed out in 13 per cent of French cases in 1978 and 35 per cent in 1992. Nevertheless, in 1990 40 per cent of the cases tried in French lower courts as indecent assaults or indecent behaviour were actually rapes.[74] Across Europe there has been a great variety in the levels of reporting, prosecution and conviction since the 1970s. The trends have not moved together and have not increased as far as might be expected given the higher visibility of sexual violence. If law codes and (sometimes) criminal justice practice have changed since the 1960s, sexual violence is still prevalent in modern Europe.

Sexual violence and warfare

War brings about the movement of people(s), disturbs the prevailing gender order and disrupts dominant social conventions. Although such conditions have provided opportunities for pleasurable and consensual sexual activity, they have also brought to our attention the near ubiquitous, but 'quite distinct historically and geographically specific ways' that sexual violence has figured in the spectrum of torture, killing and mutilation visited on defeated and often civilian populations.[75] Mixed-race children born out of wartime sexual relations, including violent ones, have been thought to compromise the national identity of the defeated.[76] Even though rape was a serious contravention of most modern western military codes, it has often been condoned by military authorities. Since until very recently combatant military forces have been composed almost entirely of men. The gender dimensions of wartime rape have been stark. Rape provided a key sexual component to military masculinities and emphasized the feminized vulnerabilities of the defeated. At some moments it was a deliberate technique of genocide and cultural annihilation. Practices such as gang rape acted as recreation and social bonding amongst combatants. Coerced sex was also part of a more general appropriation of female bodies which included forced prostitution and domestic labour.[77]

In World War II, sexual violence was committed by all combatant armies. Between 1942 and 1945 American GIs in Europe raped around 14,000 civilian women in England, France and Germany. At least 110,000 women were raped by 'liberating' Russian soldiers in and around Berlin in 1945. As well as Nazi supporters, the victims included Jewish women and forced labourers. French soldiers committed rape on a large scale in Southern Baden Wittenberg. Moroccan mercenaries fighting with the remnants of the Free French Army in Italy were explicitly given licence to rape and plunder. Very often the victims of sexual violence were then murdered, mutilated or tortured. Many women submitted to coerced sex or prostitution rather than face starvation or death. Nazi attempts at genocide included forced sterilizations (of both women and men), abortions and other medicalized violence in the concentration camps.[78]

The most recent large-scale example on European territory was the use of rape as a weapon of genocide by Serbian forces in Bosnia-Herzegovina in 1992–93. The infliction of pain, terror and humiliation on the immediate victims was only part of the purpose. Sexual violence was by no means confined to the Serbians in the complicated nexus of conflict between the states emerging from the former Yugoslavia. In the 1980s in the province of Kosovo, stories of rape encapsulated ethnic Serbian fears of the majority (Muslim) Kosovan Albanians, fears that were later realized in the Kosovan war of 1998–99.[79] In this region babies traditionally took the name and ethnic identity of their father. When conflict escalated in Bosnia-Herzegovina sexual violence became a key dimension of warfare.[80] The systematic sexual violence perpetrated by the army of the Republika Sprska was part of a strategy which, combined with massacre and deportation, aimed to annihilate Bosnian (Muslim) families, culture and claims to nationhood, not least by the demographic impact of the half-Serbian babies conceived through these rapes. As well as sexual violence embedded in everyday contexts of workplace, neighbourhood, or (parodied) domesticity, rape was also used in a targeted and highly organized way. Women were taken to dedicated camps where they were raped over a period of weeks or months until they conceived and were released only when their pregnancies were too far developed for abortion. Although the appropriation of female reproductive capacity through violence as a means of destroying an enemy were hardly original ideas, the historical, political and military context left the newly created Bosnian state particularly vulnerable.[81]

Despite the existence since the mid-nineteenth century of international legal conventions intended to protect civilian populations in warfare, most sexual violence remained unprosecuted.[82] Though the Americans did court martial numbers of soldiers for rape committed during World War II, the racial inequalities in military justice meant that black soldiers were not only more likely to be court martialled, but also more likely to be severely punished.[83] In 1945 tribunals at Nuremberg and Tokyo investigated major war crimes committed by the Axis Powers. Unlike in Tokyo, Nuremberg paid little attention to crimes of sexual violence (including forced sterilization and prostitution).[84] It was a further half century before the International Crime Tribunal for the former Yugoslavia argued for the explicit inclusion of wartime rape as a form of torture as well as a crime against humanity, and prosecuted rape in several trials.[85] The Statute of the International Criminal Court (1998, applied from 2002) has further extended the law in this area.[86] Nevertheless, the direct effect on the violences in war and conflict cannot be expected to be great. In fact, in the wars of the twenty-first century, if anything, the distinction between combatants and non-combatants seems to have collapsed ever further.

Conclusion

Much recent research on the history of sexual violence since 1750 has been either undertaken by feminists or prompted by responses to feminist polemics. Other strands in the historiography were prompted by social historians seeking to map the history of the modern family, historians of crime and violence and more recently by historians of sexuality. Researchers have come to appreciate that much of the earlier work was underpinned by present-minded constructions of sexuality and sexual violence, and that its historical meanings are more complex and harder to reach. Therefore, in the current state of knowledge, how should the modern history of sexual violence be understood? Over time, sexual violence has been differently conceptualized in the criminal law, depending on the kind of harm it was thought to do. At the beginning of the modern period it was a moral offence which tainted the victim as much as the offender. In the nineteenth century rape was positioned as a serious crime of violence, often liable to capital punishment, but for this reason charges of rape were difficult to prove. In the case of sodomy, where there was no issue of abduction, the transgression against moral and religious order was paramount. Therefore any elements of violence or coercion were less visible.

This trend followed alongside greater strictures against interpersonal violence in general, and a decrease in reported violent crime. Consequently, the law most readily recognized sexual violence where it was accompanied by physical violence, though greater account came to be taken of the moral violence that damaged a victim's social standing. Sexual violence against men by women was essentially invisible. By the mid-twentieth century 'psy' discourses had not only constructed different models of the perpetrators of sexual violence, they had also enabled the harm of sexual violence to be reinterpreted as psychological trauma. Over the first half of the century sexual violence was less of a public issue. The interlocking of penal and welfare measures focused on children and families masked both the power relations and the violence it entailed. At the same time the development of psychiatry and psychology opened up ways of treating as well as punishing sexual offenders.

By 2000 sexual violence, in law and in public perception, had become a far wider concept than it had been in 1750. From the 1970s feminists formulated analyses of sexual violence as the rough end of patriarchal power relations. Slowly, a wider range of sexual violence moved into visibility and eventually there were changes in laws and (unevenly) in criminal justice practice. However, none of this has reduced its prevalence. Women detained for terrorism in Spain report sexual violence alongside other maltreatment and torture. Adolescent and dating cultures have a good deal of intrinsic aggressiveness conducive to sexual violence. In a modern model of sexuality which emphasizes intimacy, rapists have mimicked dating.[87] Although international law on war rape is now better formulated, on a global scale sexual violence remains a common practice in warfare. The history of sexual violence is hardly an optimistic one.

Notes

1 Alan Harding, *The Law Courts of Medieval England*, London: George Allen & Unwin, 1973; J. B. Post, 'Ravishment of Women: The Statutes of Westminster' in J. H. Baker (ed.), *Legal Records and the Historian*, London: Royal Historical Society, 1978, pp. 150–64. For work on the medieval period which takes gender into account see citations in Garthine Walker, chapter 23, this volume.

2 For an overview, see Peter Burke, *New Perspectives on Historical Writing*, 2nd edn, Cambridge: Polity, 2001.

3 For a recent overview of work on the history of sexuality, see Anna Clark, *The History of Sexuality in Europe: A Sourcebook and Reader*, New York: Routledge, 2010. Areas of evolutionary psychology still argue the unchanging nature of male sexual violence, for a critique of which see Joanna

Bourke, 'Who is the "rapist"?: crimes of sexual violence and theories of evolution' in Efi Avdela, Shani D'Cruze and Judith Rowbotham (eds), *Problems of Crime and Violence in Europe, 1780–2000*, Lewiston, Queenston, Lampeter: Edwin Mellen Press, 2010, pp. 311–36.

4 For a brief overview, see Clive Emsley, 'Historical perspectives on crime' in Mike Maguire, Rod Morgan and Robert Reiner (eds), *The Oxford Handbook of Criminology*, 4th edn, Oxford: Oxford University Press, 2007, pp. 122–38.

5 The thesis of a long-term civilizing process was proposed by Norbert Elias. Norbert Elias, *The Civilizing Process, Vol 1, The History of Manners*, trans. Edmund Jephcott, 2 vols, Oxford: Blackwell, 1978, 1982. For a recent outline of the concept and the debate, Stuart Carroll, 'Introduction' in Stuart Carroll (ed.), *Cultures of Violence: Interpersonal Violence in Historical Perspective*, Basingstoke: Palgrave, 2007, pp. 1–46.

6 Martin J. Wiener, *Men of Blood: Violence, Manliness and Criminal Justice in Victorian England*, Cambridge: Cambridge University Press, 2004; Shani D'Cruze, *Crimes of Outrage: Sex, Violence and Victorian Working Women*, London: UCL Press, 1998; Louise A. Jackson, *Child Sexual Abuse in Victorian England*, London: UCL Press, 2000.

7 For an overview, Bonnie S. Anderson and Judith P. Zinsser, *A History of Their Own: Women in Europe from Prehistory to the Present*, 2nd edn, New York: Oxford University Press, 2000, vol. 2, p. ix.

8 A recent collection of key articles is Fiona Montgomery and Christine Collette (eds), *The European Women's History Reader*, London, New York: Routledge, 2001.

9 As an entry into these debates, Sue Morgan (ed.), *The Feminist History Reader*, London: Routledge, 2006.

10 Edward Shorter, *The Making of the Modern Family*, New York: Basic Books, 1975; Edward Shorter, *A History of Women's Bodies*, New York: Basic Books, 1982.

11 Susan Brownmiller, *Against our Will: Men, Women and Rape*, New York: Martin Secker and Warburg, 1975, pp. 14–15.

12 Edward Shorter, 'On writing the history of rape', *Signs* 3, 1977, pp. 471–82.

13 Roy Porter, 'Rape – Does it have a historical meaning?' in Sylvana Tomaselli and Roy Porter (eds), *Rape: An Historical and Cultural Enquiry*, Oxford: Blackwell, 1986, pp. 216–36 (231–32).

14 Lawrence Stone, *Family, Sex and Marriage in England, 1500–1800*, London: Weidenfeld and Nicolson, 1977.

15 Randolph Trumbach, *Sex and the Gender Revolution: Vol. 1, Heterosexuality and the Third Gender in Enlightenment London*, Chicago: University of Chicago Press, 1998.

16 See reviews by Thomas Laqueur, *American Historical Review* 106:4, 2001, pp. 1456–57; Robert Shoemaker, *Reviews in History* [http://www.history.ac.uk/reviews/review/78] (accessed 9 July 2010).

17 Tim Hitchcock, *English Sexualities, 1700–1800*, Basingstoke: Macmillan, 1997.

18 Robert Shoemaker, 'The decline of public insult in London 1660–1800', *Past & Present* 169, 2000, pp. 97–131; Robert Shoemaker, 'Male honour and the decline of public violence in eighteenth-century London', *Social History* 26, 2001, pp. 190–208.

19 Garthine Walker, 'Re-reading rape and sexual violence in Early Modern England', *Gender & History* 10:1, 1998, pp. 1–25, and chapter 23, this volume.

20 Antony E. Simpson, 'Masculinity and control: the prosecution of sex offenses in eighteenth-century London', Ph.D. thesis, New York University, 1984, pp. 811–13; Clive Emsley, *Crime and Society in England, 1750–1900*, 3rd edn, Harlow: Longman, 2005, p. 262.

21 *Old Bailey Sessions Papers* [www.oldbaileyonline.org]; Georges Vigarello, *A History of Rape: Sexual Violence in France from the Sixteenth to the Twentieth Century*, trans. Jean Birell, Cambridge: Polity, 2001, pp. 28, 78, 146.

22 Vigarello, *Rape*, pp. 50, 87, 133.

23 Vigarello, *Rape*, pp. 135–36; Joanna Bourke, *Rape: A History from 1860 to the Present*, London: Virago, 2007, pp. 58–61.

24 Laura Engelstein, 'Gender and the juridical subject: prostitution and rape in nineteenth-century Russian criminal codes', *Journal of Modern History* 60, 1988, pp. 458–95.

25 Hitchcock, *English Sexualities*, pp. 60–61.

26 V. A. C. Gatrell, *The Hanging Tree: Execution and the English People 1770–1868*, Oxford: Oxford University Press, 1994; Wiener, *Men of Blood*, pp. 86–87, 91; Caroll, 'Introduction'; Vigarello, *Rape*.

27 In England and Wales, capital punishment was actually repealed in 1841 for rape and in 1861 for sodomy.

28 Criminal Law Amendment Act, 1885.

29 Kim Stevenson, '"Ingenuities of the female mind": legal and public perceptions of sexual violence in Victorian England, 1850–90' in Shani D'Cruze (ed.), *Everyday Violence in Britain, 1850–1950: Gender and Class*, Harlow: Pearson, 2000, pp. 89–103, esp. p. 96; Jeffrey Weeks, *Coming Out: Homosexual Politics in Britain from the Nineteenth Century to the Present*, London: Quartet, 1977, p. 14.

30 Iştar Gözaydin, 'Adding injury to injury: the case of rape and prostitution in Turkey' in John T. Parry (ed.), *Evil, Law and the State: Perspectives on State Power and Violence*, Amsterdam: Rodopi, 2006, pp. 59–70 (59).

31 Nafize Bashar, 'Rape in England between 1550 and 1700' in London Feminist History Group (ed.), *The Sexual Dynamics of History*, London: Pluto, 1987, pp. 28–42 (34–35). For discussion and qualification see Garthine Walker, chapter 23, this volume.

32 I do not use the term *victims* to imply any sort of inadequate agency on the part of those who have experienced sexual violence, but to indicate that they have been victimized by the role of sexual violence in modern cultures.

33 Clark, *Women's Silence*; Vigarello, *Rape*, pp. 69–72; Bourke, *Rape*, p. 121.

34 Peter Gay, *The Bourgeoise Experience: Victoria to Freud, vol. 1, The Education of the Senses*, New York: Oxford University Press, 1984, pp. 359–60; Angus Mclaren, 'Some secular attitudes toward sexual behavior in France, 1760–1860', *French Historical Studies* 8, 1974, pp. 604–25 (606, 610); Anne-Marie Sohn, 'The Golden Age of Male Adultery: The Third Republic', *Journal of Social History* 28, 1995, pp. 469–91.

35 Hitchcock, *English Sexualities*, p. 64.

36 Clark, *Women's Silence*; Carolyn A. Conley, 'Rape and Justice in Victorian England', *Victorian Studies* 29, 1986, pp. 519–36; Carolyn A. Conley, *The Unwritten Law: Crime and Justice in Victorian Kent*, New York and Oxford: Oxford University Press, 1991.

37 Carolyn A. Conley, 'No Pedestals: Women and Violence in Late-Nineteenth-Century Ireland', *Journal of Social History* 28, 1995, pp. 801–18.

38 Conley, 'Rape', p. 5.

39 Kim Stevenson, 'Observations on the Law Relating to Sexual Offences: The Historic Scandal of Women's Silence', *Web Journal of Current Legal Issues* 4, 1999 [http://webjcli.ncl.ac.uk/1999/issue4/stevenson4.html].

40 Wiener, *Men of Blood*, p. 90; Conley, 'Rape'; Conley, *The Unwritten Law*; D'Cruze, *Crimes of Outrage*; Vigarello, *Rape*, p. 133.

41 Conley, 'Rape', p. 526.

42 Vigarello, *Rape*, p. 131; D'Cruze, *Crimes of Outrage*; Stevenson, 'Ingenuities'; Kim Stevenson, 'Crimes of Moral Outrage: Victorian Encryptions of Sexual Violence' in Judith Rowbotham and Kim Stevenson (eds), *Criminal Conversations: Victorian Crimes, Social Panic and Moral Outrage*, Champaign, IL: University of Illinois Press, 2003, pp. 232–46; Wiener, *Men of Blood*.

43 Englestein, 'Gender and the juridical subject'; Vigarello, *Rape*, pp. 54, 94–95, 132; Jackson, *Child Sexual Abuse*, p. 13; Antony E. Simpson, 'Vulnerability and the age of female consent: legal innovation and its effect on prosecutions for rape in eighteenth-century London' in G. S. Rousseau and Roy Porter (eds), *Sexual Underworlds of the Enlightenment*, Manchester: Manchester University Press, 1987, pp. 181–205 (182–85); Shani D'Cruze, 'Protection, harm and social evil: the age of consent, *c.* 1885–*c.* 1940' in Parry (ed.), *Evil, Law and the State*, pp. 31–46.

44 Frank Mort, *Dangerous Sexualities: Medico-Moral Politics in England since 1850*, 2nd edn, London: Routledge, 2000, pp. 102–6; Lucy Bland, *Banishing the Beast: English Feminism and Sexual Morality, 1885–1914*, London: Penguin, 1995, ch. 3; Deborah Gorham, '"The Maiden Tribute of Modern Babylon" Revisited', *Victorian Studies* 21, 1978, pp. 353–79; Judith Walkowitz, *City of Dreadful Delight: Narratives of Sexual Danger in Late-Victorian London*, London: Virago, 1992, ch. 3.

45 House of Lords, 1883 [280] 1390.

46 Jackson, *Child Sexual Abuse*, pp. 4, 72–75. Fabienne Giuliani, 'Monsters in the Village? Incest in nineteenth-century France', *Journal of Social History* 42, 2009, pp. 919–32 (929–32); Vigarello, *Rape*, pp. 121–23, 166–68.

47 Jackson, *Child Sexual Abuse*, pp. 71, 68; Pamela Cox, *Gender, Justice and Welfare: Bad Girls in Britain, 1900–1959*, Basingstoke: Palgrave Macmillan, 2003, ch. 6.

48 Roger Davidson, '"This pernicious delusion": law, medicine, and child sexual abuse in early-twentieth-century Scotland', *Journal of the History of Sexuality* 10, 2001, pp. 62–77.

49 Bourke, *Rape*, p. 398.

50 Vigarello, *Rape*, pp. 166, 180–85, Simon A. Cole, *Suspect Identities: A History of Fingerprinting and Criminal Identities*, Cambridge MA: Harvard University Press, 2002, ch. 2.

51 Nicola Garvey, *Just Sex? The Cultural Scaffolding of Rape*, London: Routledge, 2005, pp. 19–20, 22; Havelock Ellis, *On Life and Sex*, London: Heinemann, 1948, p. 95.

52 Menachem Amir, *Patterns in Forcible Rape*, Chicago: University of Chicago Press, 1971.

53 Amir, *Patterns*.

54 Bourke, *Rape*, pp. 147–57.

55 Bourke, *Rape*; Andreas Frei, Nuray Erenay, Volker Dittmann and Marc Graf, 'Paedophilia on the internet – a study of thirty three convicted offenders in the Canton of Lucerne', *Swiss Medical Weekly* 135, 2005, pp. 488–94.

56 Mort, *Dangerous Sexualities*, part 3.

57 Lesley A. Hall, *Sex, Gender and Social Change in Britain since 1880*, Basingstoke: Macmillan, 2000, chs 6 and 7; Lesley A. Hall (ed.), *Outspoken Women: An Anthology of Women's Writing on Sex, 1870–1969*, London: Routledge, 2005.

58 Vigarello, *Rape*, pp. 206–9, 211.

59 Jennifer Temkin, 'Women, Rape and Law Reform' in Tomaselli and Porter, *Rape*, pp. 16–40 (26, 36). For a detailed outline of British law at this period see Jennifer Temkin, *Rape and the Legal Process*, 2nd edn, Oxford: Oxford University Press, 2002, ch. 2.

60 Zsuzsanna Adler, *Rape on Trial*, London: Routledge, 1987, pp. 2, 3; Temkin, *Rape and the Legal Process*, p. 3.

61 Rachel A. Van Cleave, 'Sex, Lies and Honour in Italian Rape Law', *Suffolk University Law Review* 38, 2005, pp. 427–54 (esp. 447).

62 Jeanne Gregory and Sue Lees, *Policing Sexual Assault*, London: Routledge, 1999, ch. 2; Sharon Valente and Callie Wight, 'Military Sexual Trauma: Violence and Sexual Abuse', *Military Medicine* 172, 2007, pp. 259–65.

63 Vigarello, *Rape*, pp. 215–18; Linda Regan and Liz Kelly, *Rape: Still a Forgotten Issue*, Briefing Document, Rape Crisis Europe, 2003, p.16.

64 Vigarello, *Rape*, p. 221; Temkin, *Rape and the Legal Process*, pp. 83–84; Regan and Kelly, *Rape*, pp. 16–17.

65 Rosa Valls, Lidia Puigvert and Elena Duque, 'Gender Violence Among Teenagers: Socialisation and Prevention', *Violence Against Women* 14, 2008, pp. 759–85.

66 Kim Stevenson, Anne Davies and Michael Gunn, *Blackstone's Guide to the Sexual Offences Act 2003*, Oxford: Oxford University Press, 2003; Chris White, 'The Spanner Trials and the Changing Law on Sadomasochism in the UK', *Journal of Homosexuality* 50, 2006, pp. 167–87.

67 Bourke, *Rape*, pp. 246–47.

68 Philip Rumney and Martin Morgan-Taylor, 'Recognising the Male Victim: Gender Neutrality and the Law of Rape, Part Two', *Anglo-American Law Review* 26:3, 1997, pp. 330–56 (330, 337); Gregory and Lees, *Policing Sexual Assault*, pp. 115–16 [www.homeoffice.gov.uk, recorded-crime-1898-2002.xls].

69 Bourke, *Rape*, pp. 218–34.

70 Bourke, *Rape*, ch. 12; Vigarello, *Rape*, pp. 222–23.

71 Vigarello, *Rape*, pp. 226–30, 234–37; Catherine Itzin, *Home Truths About Child Abuse: A Reader*, London: CRC Press, 2000.

72 Temkin, 'Women, Rape and Law Reform', pp. 20–23; Philip N. S. Rumney, 'The Review of Sex Offences and Rape Law Reform: Another False Dawn?', *The Modern Law Review* 64:6, 2001, pp. 890–910 (892, n. 18); Regan and Kelly, *Rape*, p. 7; Bourke, *Rape*, p. 395

73 Regan and Kelly, *Rape*, pp. 8–13.

74 Vigarello, *Rape*, pp. 212–14.

75 Dagmar Herzog (ed.), *Brutality and Desire: War and Sexuality in Europe's Twentieth Century*, Basingstoke: Palgrave, 2009, p. 4.

76 Kjersti Ericsson and Eva Simonsen (eds), *Children of World War Two*, Oxford: Berg, 2005, pp. 252, 232–33.

77 For a sensitive discussion of these issues in World War I, see Ruth Harris, 'The "Child of a Barbarian": Rape, Race and Nationalism in France during the First World War', *Past and Present* 141, 1993, pp. 170–206.

78 J. Robert Lilly, *Taken by Force: Rape and American GIs during World War II*, Basingstoke: Palgrave, 2007; Ericsson and Simonsen, *Children*, p. 233; Ruth Seifert, 'The Second Front: the Logic of Sexual Violence in Wars', *Women's Studies International Forum* 19, 1996, pp. 35–43; Tommaso Baris, 'French Expeditionary Corps in Italy: Violence of the "Liberators" in the Summer of 1944', *Vingtième siècle-revue d'histoire* 93, 2007, pp. 47–61; Kelly Dawn Askin, *War Crimes Against Women: Prosecution in International War Crimes Tribunals*, The Hague: Martinus Nijhoff, 1997, pp. 59, 72 n. 238; Ruth Seifert, 'War and Rape: A Preliminary Analysis' in Alexandra Stiglmayer (ed.), *Mass Rape: The War against Women in Bosnia-Herzegovina*, Lincoln, NE: University of Nebraska Press, 1994, pp. 54–72 (64).

79 This conflict escalated into a full-blown war in 1998–99.

80 Bülent Diken and Carsten Bagge Lausten, 'Becoming Abject: Rape as a Weapon of War', *Body and Society* 11:1, 2005, pp. 111–28 (114–15).

81 Stiglmayer, *Mass Rape*; Vigarello, *Rape*, p. 223.

82 Anne-Marie de Brouwer, *Supra-national Criminal Prosecution of Sexual Violence: The ICC and the Practice of the ICTY and ICTR*, Antwerp: Intersentia, 2005, p. 5.

83 Lilly, *Taken by Force*.

84 Askin, *War Crimes*, pp. 73, 88; de Brouwer, *Supra-national*, pp. 6–7.

85 Lene Hansen, 'Gender, Nation, Rape: Bosnia and the Construction of Security', *International Feminist Journal of Politics* 3:1, 2001, pp. 55–75 (56); Statute of the International Tribunal, adopted 25 May 1993 as amended 13 May 1998; Blaskic IT-95-14; Furundzija IT-95-17/1; Celebici IT-96-21; all listed on [www.un.org/icty].

86 de Brouwer, *Supra-national*, p. 85.

87 Rosa Valls *et al.*, 'Gender Violence'; Bourke, *Rape*, p. 408.

Part XIII

SEXUAL DISEASE

25

'THE VENEREAL DISEASE', 1500–1800

Kevin Siena

Historians rely on periodization, the practice of defining certain eras as distinct from others. Like rivers that help form geographic boundaries, historians use great events to demarcate ages. The dawn of early modernity is marked by a litany of developments in the vicinity of 1500 said to terminate the middle ages: Gutenberg's press, Columbus' journey, Luther's shattering of Christian unity, Copernicus' transposition of earth and sun. After these events, we are told, the middle ages were no more. Although it is not invoked with the same gravity as these legends of textbooks, yet another event changed European life at the close of the fifteenth century: the 1494 emergence of a lethal disease that will eventually be called syphilis. For the history of sexuality it helps ring in a new age.

The disease spawned one of history's longest recorded debates, running into this its sixth century. Did it return with Columbus or was it a new strain of an existing disease? Nowadays syphilis' origin falls to paleopathologists studying pre- and post-Columbian bones on opposite sides of the Atlantic. But for all the power of techniques like carbon dating, the jury is still out.[1] The tide of opinion has long supported the view characterized by Alfred Crosby's phrase 'the Columbian Exchange', which sees Europeans and Americans trading smallpox for syphilis.[2] In these histories white sailors' bodies shuttle microbes across the ocean introducing them to ill-prepared populations with bad consequences for Europe and genocidal ones for America.[3] With recent awareness of environmentalism and globalization, meta-narratives on the global history of disease, in which the Columbian exchange plays a central role, have been powerful.[4] However, recent analysis of pre-Columbian English skeletons with possible signs of syphilitic damage ensures that the debate continues.[5]

For paleopathologists the history of syphilis hinges on the presence or absence of a bacterium, *Treponema pallidum*. However, other scholars resist reducing the disease to the pathogen. As it turns out, identifying past people's diseases is more complex than it first appears. First, bacteria mutate. Even if, as is almost certainly the case, some sixteenth-century people were infected with venereal syphilis caused by *Treponema pallidum*, it is difficult to know how closely sixteenth-century versions of the organism resemble samples from today. Descriptions of the initial outbreak suggest that it was highly lethal, weakening in later decades, although this is debated.[6] Its apparent early intensity has several possible explanations: a particularly virulent strain of the bacterium, its horrible initial effects on a population with little immunological protection, or the intense fear of sufferers describing a new scourge in particularly frightening ways.

Another difficulty in identifying the disease stems from the fact that contemporaries did not call it 'syphilis', a term from Giorolomo Fracastoro's epic poem, *Syphilis sive Morbus Gallicus* (1530) which did not come into general usage until the nineteenth century. Before then commentators used terms like 'the Great Pox', 'the venereal disease' or the 'French Disease' (in Latin *Lues Venerea* or *Morbus Gallicus*). Translating these terms as 'syphilis', as many have done and some continue to do, is a prime example of retrodiagnosis, applying modern disease categories to the past.[7] We must be cautious because even if some diagnosed with 'the Great Pox' harboured *Treponema pallidum* many others surely did not. For example, doctors conflated syphilis and gonorrhoea. 'The venereal disease' was at least two diseases, and it was likely many more. It is probable that patients with various reproductive, genito-urinary, and even dermatological conditions were also diagnosed with *Lues Venerea*. Finally, the sort of evidence required for a diagnosis today – a blood test, to take an obvious example – is hardly available. In its place we have mainly *textual* descriptions of symptoms, recorded in the vocabulary of a completely different medical world-view. Jon Arrizabalaga, John Henderson and Roger French made a convincing case that scholars should be cautious before proclaiming syphilitic those patients described with 'apostumes', 'buboes', or a 'running of the reins'.[8] Most historians have followed their lead limiting themselves to contemporary terms rather than the anachronistic 'syphilis'.[9] This approach has enormous up-sides, avoiding the pitfalls of retrodiagnosis and forcing scholars to think like their subjects. Since identifying precisely which modern disease struck someone in the sixteenth century may be well nigh impossible, socio-cultural historians tend to focus on how premodern people constructed their illnesses. A potential difficulty of this approach, as well as with lines of inquiry informed by discourse analysis that explore the disease as a text,[10] is that it becomes possible to think of diseases as merely cultural constructs, the product of men's minds rather than something ravaging their material bodies. Whatever it was, the pox was no figment of the imagination. People suffered and died, something that all approaches must allow ways to acknowledge.[11] Historian Laura McGough and epidemiologist Emily Erbelding are surely right to suggest that interdisciplinary cooperation offers the most promising way forward in a field that benefits from so many methodological approaches.[12]

That said, there can be no denying that culture informed all aspects of the disease. The shock to Europe's system that the new disease administered, for its newness, lethality and connection to sexuality, guaranteed a profound range of responses. Indeed, one early response stymies those too keen to pronounce a complete break with the middle ages. Sexually transmitted disease (STD) was not entirely new in the 1490s; medievalists have their own of sorts, leprosy.[13] Anna Foa and Sander Gilman each point to echoes of medieval leprosy in early presentations of the pox. Some doctors even argued that the pox was leprosy. Foa suggests that for many it was too frightening to accept inhabiting an unstable world where new diseases appeared from nowhere. Plague was terrible and struck unannounced. But Europeans had a history with it; they understood it as part of their world. A completely new disease, never before seen, was an altogether different kind of monster. Europeans reassured themselves by crafting the pox as an old disease for which they had ready discursive, visual and institutional tools.[14] It was no accident that England's first pox hospitals were refurbished lazarettos.[15] Visual artists similarly recycled medieval material, presenting the poxed in ways traditionally used to display lepers, especially as dejected and covered in spots.[16] Jonathan Gil Harris has shown how such blemishes were deployed not just in pictures but in written texts as well, marking the poxed as morally corrupt, as lepers had long been.[17] Medieval legacies lingered in the early modern world.

Most theorists rejected that the pox *was* leprosy. Yet many assumed that it was somehow related to leprosy. Initial discussions of the disease centred on the siege of Naples by the French armies of Charles VIII in 1494.[18] A likely version of the story is that Charles' troops took the city but were decimated by widespread infection that accompanied sex with diseased prostitutes. However, for some even sex with prostitutes seemed too mundane a cause for such a catastrophic turn of events. A monstrous disease demanded a monstrous origin. Fantasy, rumour and medical theory blended in elaborate ideas about its origin, many linked to leprosy. Several authorities asserted that the disease arose from sex between menstruating Neapolitan prostitutes and lepers.[19] Others reasoned that the soldiers had been poisoned. In tales similar to anxieties about plague-spreaders, wine casks or wells at Naples were poisoned with lepers' blood, shifting the act of pathogenesis from sex to a monstrous kind of cannibalism. Jews were the culprits in some versions, the relative coincidence of their expulsion from Spain (1492) and the rise of the epidemic offering circumstantial evidence for anti-Semitic connections between Jews and the disease.[20]

Blaming it on Jews was but one example of a common reaction to the pox: projection. Many names mimicked the French Disease, merely substituting other enemies: the Spanish Sickness, the Neapolitan Disease, the Disease of the Turk, and so on. By 1660 Thomas Pecke could ask in a pithy epigram: 'Born an Italian; bred in France; quoth Fame,/Which Country strives, to give the Pox a name?'[21] The trend reveals the power of the disease to smear, casting other nations and people as filthy, dangerous and depraved. It also demonstrates how strongly Europeans wished to free themselves by pinning blame for the disease on others.[22] Increasingly, indigenous Americans were cast in this villainous role in syphilis' historical morality play. Numerous stereotypes lent support to the American origin theory, none more important than exotic depictions of savage sexuality. Polygamy, for example, was held up by commentators like Amerigo Vespucci as exemplifying uncontrollable lust that must necessarily spin out of control: 'They have as many wives as they desire; they live in promiscuity without regard to blood relations; mothers lie with sons, brother with sisters; they satisfy their desires as they occur to their libidos as beasts do.'[23] Such tropes helped liken natives to animals and contributed to their dehumanization in much European rhetoric.[24] Moreover, Europeans readily believed that a deadly disease might arise from such wild practices. Jean de Léry's comments on a Frenchman in Brazil served warning about New World sexual culture.

> [He] wallowed in all sorts of bawdiness among the savage women and girls, and had reaped his earnings so well, that his body and his face were as covered and defigured by these *Pians* [i.e. sores] as if he had been a true leper.[25]

The epidemic provides important context for explorations of constructions of New World peoples. Indeed, reciprocal readings are useful. On the one hand, there is no question that the disease was a rhetorical tool; just as it was useful to castigate the French, it enabled Europeans of all stripes to demonize (and help justify dominating) indigenous peoples. However, the reverse has been considered less and may be just as useful. Contact occurred simultaneously with the sudden rise of a sexual epidemic assumed to come from America. Early texts about American peoples were thus written against a backdrop of Europe's scramble to make sense of the disease, which may help explain why the trope of the hypersexual native emerged so powerfully in the early sixteenth century. Notably, theories linking the disease to cannibalism perpetuated similar stereotypes.[26]

Cannibalism notwithstanding, theorists frequently assumed that a sexual disease must have a sexual origin; whether French soldiers with leprous prostitutes, lepers with menstruating prostitutes, or even men with animals,[27] the pox was sexual to its core, its very production stemming from impure sex. This assumption found its most influential expression in theories presenting promiscuous women's bodies as sites for disease-production. The core idea was that the 'seeds' of men and women could degrade into a deadly poison inside the womb. Jacques de Béthencourt may have first proposed the idea in 1527, speculating that the pox arose either from an unnatural mixture of men's and women's seed or else the mixture of the male seed and the menses.[28] Menstruation was considered excreta, rendering the vagina imagined as a site of filth frequently linked to illnesses.[29] Andrew Boorde's description of the vulva makes the point: 'there may brede many diseases as ulcers, skabbes, apostumes, fissures, fystles, festures, the Pockes and burnynge of an harlot'.[30] By 1596 Béthencourt's theory evolved when Italian physician Aurilius Minadoi presented the disease as arising not from a mixture of a man's seed and the menses, but from the mixture of different *men's* seed. The subtle change had major consequences, presenting female promiscuity as the cause of the disease.[31] Now the body of a woman with multiple sex partners became pathogenic. As the seventeenth century wore on doctors like Daniel Sennert in Germany and Nicholas de Blégny in France enhanced its credibility by casting it in the language of the early Scientific Revolution.[32] No longer were Jews, lepers or cannibals responsible. The danger was firmly located in women's bodies. In prior theories a single cataclysmic act spawned the pox, but now the disease could be born anew again and again, whenever women slept with multiple men. All women became potential threats. This development parallels Mary Fissell's view that women's bodies became increasingly dangerous as the period progressed. She explores a range of popular genres, describing the seventeenth century as a time when 'the womb goes bad', the female reproductive organs becoming subjects of intense anxiety.[33] Fissell does not consider the womb's power to generate the pox, but the heterogeneous seed theory exemplifies the cultural drift she detects. Its rise in the seventeenth century also corresponds with the shift to the two-sex model of anatomy, a feature of which is the absence of female seed in reproduction.[34] When both bodies shared the same organs men and women contributed seed equally. But in the new anatomy only men produced seed, rendering the female reproductive role passive incubation. Indeed, the shift from Béthencourt's early sixteenth-century version to Minadoi's and subsequent seventeenth- and eighteenth-century versions shows the same disappearance of the female seed and the same emphasis on the womb as incubator, in this case a monstrous incubation of filth rather than the sublime nurturing of new life.

In accord with cutting-edge medical theory and prevailing winds of gender, the theory was popular. However, it found challengers because it logically argued against the American origin of the disease: promiscuity is ancient, so too must be the pox. Opponents supported that its principles had merit – the womb was filthy and a mixture of different semen was dangerous – but they rejected it because they were convinced the pox was American.[35] Whores or Indians? Doctors took sides. The conflict was resolved by the leading eighteenth-century authority on the disease, French physician Jean Astruc, who transported the theory to America, blaming promiscuous women and natives simultaneously. White women's bodies were too cool for the process of 'putrefaction' by which seeds corrupted into pox. But women in hot climates generated disease readily. Describing Haiti, Astruc merged the stereotypes of the hypersexual native and the menstruating woman, confidently asserting:

The men, through the violence of their lust, lay like beasts with the first woman they meet with, and as the women through an excess of incontinence, promiscuously admitted all that offered. ... Nay whilst their menses were upon them they would impudently invite and press men to lie with them at that time, their lust breaking out of them as in brutes, through the heat of the womb with greater rage than at any time. No wonder then that the different acrid, and heterogeneous seed of several men blended together, amixed with a sharp and virulent menstrual blood and reposited in the over heated womb of very filthy women should by Time, Heterogeneity, and the Heat of its Receptacle soon corrupt, and constitute the first seeds of the Venereal Disease.

What was true of the Caribbean held true for all warm non-European climates, '[for] there must have been in them the like Heat of the Air as in Hispanola, a like Disposition to Impurity, and the same propensity to promiscuous copulation'.[36] The process of projection was completed, the New World origin secured, buttressed by powerful moralizing about female sexuality.

Such moralizing was hardly new. Indeed we must return to the beginning of the story to assess the pox's impact on European morality and the reciprocal influence of Europe's moral climate on the reception of the disease. Andrew Cunningham and Ole Peter Grell remind us that the pox entered a culture of 'apocalyptic expectations, eschatological speculations and millenarian dreams'.[37] Sixteenth-century mentalities were hardwired to interpret major phenomena like wars, famines and natural disasters as signs of divine wrath or diabolic intervention. Hence the advent of the pox was interpreted as a sign of divine displeasure. Indeed, at the base of all early origin theories was a basic premise that few disputed. God caused the disease. As early as 1495 Emperor Maximilian I declared that for their sins his subjects suffered earthquakes, famine and especially 'the evil pocks'.[38] It was to Maximilian that Joseph Grünpeck dedicated the most influential astrological interpretation of the pox, presenting an astral conjunction as the means by which God sent the disease.[39] Sixteenth-century Spanish physician Francisco Lopez de Villalobos spoke for many when he declared, 'surely it is sent by God as pain and penalty'.[40] Apocalyptic preacher Girolamo Savonarola interpreted both the Italian Wars and the resulting pox epidemic as clear signs of God's wrath and the need to purge sin.[41]

This millenarian trend intensified with the cultural revolution that was the Reformation. Once it became clear that the schism was not likely to be mended peacefully, Europe descended into the era of 'confessionalization', when the main religious camps propagated hot and cold styles of war to establish theirs as the sole religion.[42] The period witnessed increased surveillance, fiery proselytizing, and intense policing of popular culture, especially after 1550. Authorities initially sought to monitor belief. However, the need for moral purity to succeed in what was interpreted as a struggle between good and evil soon enlarged the scope of surveillance to include wider policing of behaviour, including drinking, swearing, gambling, Sabbath-breaking and especially sexuality.[43] This context enhanced the sense that the pox was a punishment, a clear sign of wickedness and an invitation for regulation. Lest there be any mistake, Luther and Calvin made their opinions clear. Luther called the pox 'one of the great signs of the day of Judgement'.[44] While Calvin, as usual, went even further, lamenting that sinners ignored this obvious sign:

I ask you, after fifty years is it not seen that God has raised up new illnesses against fornication? Whence came this pox, all these foulnesses which there is no need to list? Whence do all these things come, unless God has deployed vengeances that were unknown previously? The world was amazed, and for a time it is true that people were terrified; but even today they have not observed the hand of God. And today we are accustomed to know that the despisers of God, those who are dissolute in their lives, the fornicators, when they abandon themselves to every villainy, only thumb their noses. If God strikes them with some sort of leprosy, as this truly is, so that they are eaten by cancer or other foulness, they do not leave off following their course, and do nothing but jeer.[45]

Perhaps no one will ever dare attempt it, but there is ample material for a poxed history of the Reformation. The disease was an ever-present slur in propaganda like *The Whore of Babylon's Pockey Priest*, the English anti-popish pamphlet about an infected Catholic priest. His infection allowed Protestant Englishmen to expose the hypocrisy of the allegedly celibate priesthood and even demonize the Mass, suggesting that he infected parishioners when his tainted spittle corrupted the communion wafer.[46] By 1550 there was no denying the overwhelming sense that the pox was a divinely ordained tool sent to purify a world of sin, a mood captured in William Bulleyn's 1562 assurance of the disease's sacred mission: 'to strike, the filthy stinking corrupted bodies of His disobedient children, which have lived in most shameless lust and lechery, among painted stinkyng harlots for which offence they be smitten with the plague, called the French Pox'.[47]

Eamon has suggested that the Reformation-era interpretation of the pox as filth and punishment also helps explain why painful mercury purges remained its main treatment.[48] Just as zealots enacted violent rites of purification of the social body involving fire and water,[49] the corrupted physical body needed similar harsh cleansing. The pox had to be ejected from the body forcefully, much like the statues of saints, vernacular bibles or other pollutants. Patients' pain enduring what we would call mercury poisoning was viewed as a fitting part of their punishment.[50] However, we face a chicken-and-egg question about the relationship between the pox and puritanism. The sixteenth century's increased asceticism, more stringent attitudes towards morality and the policing of sexuality make it worth asking whether the pox played a causative role in these developments. Sociologist Stanislav Andreski believed that it did. For Andreski syphilis ushered in a period of anxiety and moralizing that produced both puritanism and even the witchcraze.[51] However, his thesis overreaches. The witchcraze, for example, was too complex a process, stretching over far too long a period (indeed, it was under way before the pox arrived) to be explained monocausally.[52] Moreover, a recent exploration of the pox in witch trials has suggested that the disease played little role.[53] Witchcraft was the work of the devil, and trials usually involved attempts to explain catastrophes that lacked natural explanations. The pox was too widespread and its transmission too commonly understood. When infection occurred there was no need to search for witches. God sent the pox, not the devil, and he sent it by way of well-known means. Still, Andreski offered a core insight that cannot be discounted, notwithstanding Claudia Stein's recent contention that the pox caused fewer cultural shockwaves than traditionally thought.[54] It may not have been a *deus ex machina*, but the presence of such a disfiguring and lethal sexually transmitted disease must have contributed in no small way to the changing moral climate – and certainly to the restrictive attitudes towards sexuality – that characterized the century and a half after 1500.

Prostitution, for example, became a target. Protestants and Catholics closed brothels in cities across Europe. Whereas medieval prostitutes had been seen to offer a kind of necessary service, providing an outlet for unmarried men, saving respectable wives and daughters from sexual predation, they were increasingly portrayed as a threat. It is difficult to know whether it was the Reformation's emphasis on moral purity or the fear of deadly disease driving this development. Luther himself invoked the pox when railing against whores, making it difficult to discern whether he feared the epidemic or merely seized an opportunity to deploy a powerful image.[55] Historians have certainly made the case that the pox inspired reform.[56] For example, Henry VIII's closure of the London 'stews' is often attributed to the epidemic.[57] The world was changing in other ways, however, and other scholars attribute the crackdown on prostitution to the effects of urban crowding. As populations rebounded from the Black Death cities saw large numbers of poor migrants moving in from the countryside. The policing of prostitutes, who were frequently impoverished migrants, was part of the wider drive to discipline a growing urban underclass. Early public health initiatives exemplify these efforts, and tellingly prostitutes were among those policed by early Italian health boards, notably during plague-outbreaks that *preceded* the advent of the pox.[58] That said, Guido Ruggiero sees little doubt that the presence of the disease intensified these efforts, enabling authorities to present prostitutes as themselves a form of pollution in the body politic to be purged.[59]

Above all other personages, the prostitute remained the figure most closely associated with sexual disease throughout its 500-year history in the West. While medical theories about mixing seed suggested any woman could generate the pox, in practice discussions usually centred on women who sold sex. The didactic power of such imagery is captured well in Figure 25.1, Giuseppe Maria Mitelli's 1692 *La Vita Infelice Della Meretrice Compartita Ne Dedeci Mesi Dell Anno Lunaro* (*The unhappy life of the prostitute divided according to the twelve months of the lunar year*).

A kind of moralizing calendar, it narrates a prostitute's demise from beautiful young girl to decimated corpse. In the spring and summer images she takes on different lovers, but as the story proceeds into autumn the dark denouement takes form. Imprisoned in September, she is attacked and mutilated in October. But it is in the November image (see Figure 25.2) that the pox takes over, driving home a series of powerful messages. Reduced from beauty and material comfort, she crumbles into poverty, begging in the streets. Decimated by illness, she is both disabled and disfigured, her collapsed nose a tell-tale sign of syphilitic infection.[60] A former client shares her fate, he, too, noseless and on crutches. Pointing to his baldness, another well-known symptom, he publicly insults her for infecting him. In ways typical of contemporary discussions Mitelli casts the male as the victim with the woman as the undoubted source of infection.[61] Perhaps the most telling figure, however, is the other man mocking her pathetic state. The impoverished and dying woman is simultaneously the subject of scorn and ridicule. She is to be laughed at because she deserves every bit of her misery – and hated because she has spread that misery throughout society. The pox was a common subject of satire throughout the seventeenth and eighteenth centuries, though this has been interpreted differently. While some assert that the pox's presence in humour indicates a light-hearted attitude towards the disease as it became normalized,[62] others suggest more convincingly that such depictions were usually quite biting.[63] The laughter in Mitelli's image is hardly humorous. Lest anyone miss the message, Mitelli's moral tale ends (see Figure 25.2) much like Hogarth's similar *Harlot's Progress* of the following century where the prostitute lies in a hospital dead of the pox.

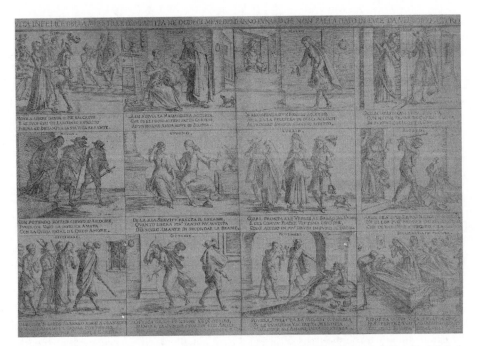

Figure 25.1 Giuseppe Maria Mitelli, *La Vita Infelice Della Meretrice Compartita Ne Dedeci Mesi Dell Anno Lunaro* (1692). Courtesy of the British Museum.

Figure 25.2 Giuseppe Maria Mitelli, *La Vita Infelice Della Meretrice Compartita Ne Dedeci Mesi Dell Anno Lunaro* (1692). Images for November and December. Courtesy of the British Museum.

This image of the hospital also raises the issue of institutional care, a vital subject in the history of this disease, one which demands another return to the Reformation. Some studies mistakenly argue that the poxed were barred from hospitals, deemed undeserving of charity until the Enlightenment when tolerant attitudes began to prevail.[64] However, once medical historians explored institutional records they found evidence of early hospital care for pox victims all over Europe.[65] English hospitals retooled former lazarettos in the early sixteenth century, and when estimates become possible we see care on a large scale. In some London hospitals over 20 per cent of patients entered the so-called 'foul wards'.[66] Elsewhere pox hospitals appeared even earlier, 1495 in Augsburg and 1499 in Genoa.[67] Why authorities provided hospital care remains a vital question. In England, I have argued that as much as the poxed were scorned, strong messages of Christian mercy and a powerful sense that the social dilemma was simply too big to ignore led city officials to deem them worthy of care.[68] In counter-Reformation Italy authorities also saw an opportunity. Here the importance of the Reformation must be considered. When Protestants dismantled Catholic institutions they transferred the Church's social welfare tasks to municipalities. But whereas Protestant Europe saw a dramatic change in the welfare landscape, Catholic cities witnessed continuity with hospitals remaining closely aligned with religious institutions. When the pox hit Italy religious orders and confraternities sprang to action building so-called *Incurabili* hospitals throughout the peninsula.[69] In the poxed, Catholic reformers saw an opportunity to save souls and purify Christendom. *Incurabili* hospitals thus performed a double role, mending people's bodies but also promoting their repentance.

This was especially true of female patients. It was out of these *Incurabili* hospitals that grew affiliated asylums for the saving of fallen women. Women treated in hospital were often transferred to these frequently cloistered asylums to undergo reclamation through chastity, work and moral re-education. These asylums literally institutionalized the double standard, demanding that men only need physical treatment, while women needed additional moral therapy. Populated by female 'penitents', these asylums are sometimes viewed as the first true 'penitentiaries', institutions that sought not just to segregate individuals from society but to transform them into new kinds of socially acceptable people, a project Foucault argues lies at the heart of modernity.[70] Historians debate these asylums. Laura McGough offers a critical reading of them, pointing out several key features. Noteworthy is the fact that some specifically targeted beautiful girls, who were seen as a greater threat in the spreading of disease, and that some asylums institutionalized girls before they had ever had sex, let alone caught the disease, making the quarantining of beauty a preventative health measure.[71] Sherrill Cohen recognizes their policing power over vulnerable women, but suggests that in some cases the asylums did help women forced to sell sex to survive.[72] There is little debate that the fallen women's asylums that grew out of pox hospitals demonstrate how sexual disease offered a powerful opportunity for authorities to target particular kinds of women for forms of policing that would continue into the twentieth century.

It took over 200 years for such asylums to appear in England, a curious and revealing phenomenon. Italian influence on English medicine was significant.[73] Yet the fallen woman's asylum as an arm of the pox hospital is absent until almost 1790. This disparity invites one to make the point that we are due for a synthesis that brings together what we have learned about the French Disease in various case studies. Such a synthesis will have to address patterns pointing to a possible confessional divide between Protestant and Catholic Europe. Reclamation of fallen women is in line with Catholic teachings emphasizing the redemptive power of 'good works'. Sin is everywhere, but salvation is possible through one's own sacred efforts. It was precisely this idea that Luther attacked, emphasizing salvation through faith alone. Sin for Protestants, especially Calvinists, was more permanent: acts of charity are fine, but they cannot alleviate sin, which is always on our heads and which only God can wash away after death.[74] Comparisons between Protestant and

Catholic hospitals have suggested that this theological cleavage resulted in an important distinction. Catholic institutions merged moral and material missions more closely than did Protestant ones which focused more exclusively on physical healing.[75] As late as 1747 officials at an English pox hospital still wiped their hands of the responsibility to save patients' souls: 'It is our part to relieve the distressed, theirs to amend their lives.'[76] Thus in the sixteenth century, fallen women's asylums made more sense in the Catholic context of sacramental redemption.[77] Moreover, they were frequently administered by nuns and some were established as convents, meaning that the possibility for this model in Protestant countries suffered a major setback with Protestant closure of convents – to say nothing of the loss of Mary Magdalen with the rest of the saints.

Attitudes towards the disease in Catholic Italy were harsh, as Mitelli's images clearly suggest, but redemption was possible. The presence of asylums to save prostitutes may thus indicate a slightly more forgiving culture. Four other contextual differences offer support to this view. First, keeping with hospitals, English evidence suggests that a strong stigma attended public admission of the disease, leading only the absolutely desperate to seek hospitalization because it demanded public disclosure of infection. Moreover, when they did have to enter hospitals patients frequently tried to access care under the guise of other ailments to avoid the designation 'foul'.[78] By contrast, Cristian Berco's research on Catholic Toledo suggests that even some respectable patients who could afford private care chose to utilize the public hospital.[79] Second, the demand for discreet care in England to avoid public acknowledgement of infection also impacted upon the medical marketplace. English empirics emphasized secrecy in advertisements and some offered female assistants to treat women discreetly.[80] David Gentilcore's study of similar practitioners in Italy finds no evidence of this same drive to keep the disease secret at all costs.[81] Third, a comparison of attitudes to prophylaxis finds a similar pattern of greater tolerance in Mediterranean Catholic contexts, and harsher moralizing in northern Protestant countries, where some doctors refused to discuss how to protect oneself from the disease for fear of helping people to sin without punishment.[82] Finally, perhaps the clearest evidence of a particularly strict climate in Protestant England is the practice of publicly whipping venereal patients when discharged from the hospital, something not yet discovered in Catholic hospitals.[83] It is too early to say definitively that religion is the key to all these differences, but it would make sense. In Catholic societies where redemption through practices like confession were part of daily life welcoming sinners back into the fold, it is possible that a slightly more forgiving culture may have existed in which the need to hide the disease was not quite as great, where safe sex was discussed more openly and where even diseased prostitutes might be forgiven, albeit within a very constrained institution. By contrast in Protestant societies, especially those influenced by Calvinism, more puritanical attitudes towards the disease may have prevailed, leading to a silencing on prophylaxis, a powerful drive to hide one's infection, no institutions geared towards redemption, and shaming spectacles of corporeal punishment to issue powerful public warnings literally on the backs of the diseased.

England eventually witnessed fallen women's asylums attached to venereal disease hospitals, but not until the late eighteenth century, when the London Lock Hospital established its Lock Asylum for the Reception of Penitent Female Patients (1788). The Lock Hospital resulted not from Reformation zeal but rather Enlightened philanthropy and the sheer need for hospital beds in a city growing by the thousands every year.[84] Rates of infection may have worsened in the eighteenth century, although the impossibility of identifying the pox perfectly means we will never know for sure. However, historians have suggested that sex itself was changing in the eighteenth century in ways that may have spread more disease. Tim Hitchcock and Randolph Trumbach argue that sex became defined more narrowly, centring more exclusively on heterosexual penetration, with practices like masturbation, oral or anal sex – especially between men – increasingly decried, policed and ultimately practised less. Sexuality became wed more fundamentally to identity, and the need to prove a new masculinity inspired increased sexual predation, use of prostitutes and greater rates of heterosexual intercourse, especially outside of marriage. Trumbach suggests this new sexual economy brought wider spread of disease.[85] While we lack concrete rates of infection, we do know that eighteenth-century hospitals were overwhelmed with patients who needed care, faced great competition to get beds, went on waiting lists and who often gave up and sought care in places like workhouses. Records of those institutions as well as McGough's analysis of Venetian death records also demonstrate that men and women suffered similar incidence of the pox.[86] These data overturn claims that the disease struck mainly men and just a small population of female prostitutes.[87] While there was a lively homosexual subculture that likely witnessed transmission between men, studies have found much silence on the issue in multiple contexts.[88]

The eventual arrival of fallen women's asylums in eighteenth-century London signals continuities and changes. Reformers hoping to control the disease still focused on women. Female sexuality remained the target of policing, and prostitutes remained central in plans to control the disease.[89] However, the mood of discussions changed. Increasingly late Enlightenment reformers presented prostitutes and fallen women in sentimental terms, frequently as victims of seduction in need of protection. Partially to elicit benefactions, governors of venereal disease hospitals and asylums crafted the image of their inmates sympathetically, emphasizing how women had been infected by rogues promising marriage or else forced into prostitution by poverty.[90] The Lock Asylum promised to transform prostitutes into the kinds of women who could, in theory, become the wives and mothers the nation needed. The shift in emphasis from the hypersexual prostitute spreading disease by preying on men to sympathetic portrayals of more passive victims of seduction exemplifies the eighteenth-century shift in gender ideals usually described in terms of 'separate spheres'.[91] Venereal disease was a compelling example of why the public sphere was dangerous for women, who were better off in the safe confines of the home, where the Lock Asylum promised to return them. Population concerns and the threat to national strength represented by widespread infection and the low birth rates and the sickly children that accompanied it made the gender politics of disease and hospitalization a national concern. Donna Andrew demonstrates how venereal disease hospitals were part of a larger pro-natalist thrust in eighteenth-century philanthropy which, in the name of a strong state, targeted objects of charity who would promote population, namely children, mothers and potential mothers (i.e. fallen women).[92] The Lock Asylum's mission to reclaim diseased women thus illustrates the intersection of the new domesticity with the emerging impulse to manage population – a drive Foucault terms biopower – forces that each intensified in the nineteenth century.[93]

Despite great promises, the asylums themselves had poor success rates. Women quite willing to accept the disciplinary regimes in the hospital frequently resisted subsequent attempts to save them in the asylum. In 1796, against 94 'success' stories of women returned to families or jobs, the Lock Asylum admitted that 112 women had run away.[94] Capturing the voices of such women is difficult, but their actions speak volumes. Much scholarship on premodern sexual disease necessarily focuses on images of the disease in contemporary rhetoric.[95] Indeed, the pox was ever-present in political criticism, standing as a blemish on the national character or pollutant of the body politic, especially the monarch's person.[96] Sufferers' lived experiences, however, are less easily accessed though they can be studied. Diarists wrote about infection, and historians willing to work through institutional records find many sources highlighting the survival strategies of people facing the unique challenges of being 'foul' in the age before antibiotics.[97] Patient-centred history is more difficult for the poor, women, or those like the poxed who actively tried to conceal their conditions.[98] But evidence survives to capture some sense of what it meant to suffer this disease in the premodern age. It is telling, for example, that so many suicides stemmed from despair directly traceable to the pain, disfigurement, disability, unemployment and stigma that attended the pox.[99] When treatment was both painful and ineffectual and the disease itself stigmatized, patients used every available resource in a struggle that a great many lost. Their stories have begun to be recovered, but there remains a great deal of work to do.

Notes

1 See O. Dutour, G. Pálfi, J. Berato and J. Brun (eds), *L'origine de la syphilis en Europe: Avant ou après 1493?*, Paris: Editions Errance, 1994.

2 Alfred W. Crosby, *The Columbian Exchange: Biological and Cultural Consequences of 1492*, Westport, CT: Greenwood, 1972.

3 Kenneth F. Kiple and Stephen V. Beck (eds), *Biological Consequences of the European Expansion, 1450–1800*, Aldershot: Ashgate, 1997; Noble David Cook, *Born to Die: Disease and New World Conquest, 1492–1650*, Cambridge: Cambridge University Press, 1998.

4 For example, Sheldon Watts, *Epidemics and History: Disease, Power and Imperialism*, New Haven: Yale University Press, 1999.

5 Tanya E. von Hunnius, Charlotte A. Roberts, Anthea Boylston and Shelley R. Saunders, 'Histological identification of syphilis in pre-Columbian England', *American Journal of Physical Anthropology* 129:4, 2006, pp. 559–66.

6 Laura J. McGough and Emily Erbelding, 'Historical Evidence of Syphilis and other Treponemes' in Justin D. Radolf and Sheila A. Lukehart (eds), *Pathogenic Treponema: Molecular and Cellular Biology*, Hethersett: Caister Academic Press, 2006, pp. 183–96 (189).

7 David Harley, 'Rhetoric and the Social Construction of Sickness and Healing', *Social History of Medicine* 12, 1999, pp. 407–35; Andrew Cunningham, 'Identifying Diseases in the Past: Cutting through the Gordian Knot', *Asclepio* 54, 2002, pp. 13–34.

8 Jon Arrizabalaga, John Henderson and Roger K. French. *The Great Pox: The French Disease in Renaissance Europe*, New Haven: Yale University Press, 1997, pp. 1–19.

9 Most recently see Claudia Stein, *Negotiating the French Pox in Early Modern Germany*, Burlington, VT: Ashgate, 2009, pp. 23–66.

10 A brilliant example is Jonathan Gil Harris, '(Po)X Marks the Spot: How to "Read" "Early Modern" "Syphilis" in *The Three Ladies of London*' in Kevin Siena (ed.), *Sins of the Flesh: Responding to Sexual Disease in Early Modern Europe*, Toronto: Center for Renaissance and Reformation Studies, 2005, pp. 109–32.

11 Rosenberg's idea that diseases are culturally 'framed' enables the practice of cultural history without negating biology. Charles E. Rosenberg, 'Framing Disease: Illness, Society, and History' in Charles E. Rosenberg and Janet Golden (eds), *Framing Disease: Studies in Cultural History*, New Brunswick: Rutgers University Press, 1992, pp. xiii–xxvi. However, conflicts between what might be termed cultural and social histories of medicine remain. Roger Cooter, 'Framing the end of social history of medicine' in Frank Huisman and John Harley Warner (eds), *Locating Medical History*, Baltimore: Johns Hopkins University Press, 2004, pp. 309–37.

12 McGough and Erbelding, 'Historical Evidence of Syphilis', p. 192.

13 Peter Lewis Allen, *The Wages of Sin: Sex and Disease, Past and Present*, Chicago: University of Chicago Press, 2000, pp. 33–35; Carole Rawcliffe, *Leprosy in Medieval England*, Woodbridge: Boydell, 2006, pp. 84–87.

14 Anna Foa, 'The New and the Old: The Spread of Syphilis (1494–1530)' in Guido Ruggiero and Edward Muir (eds), *Sex and Gender in Historical Perspective*, Baltimore: Johns Hopkins University Press, 1990, pp. 26–45.

15 Kevin Siena, 'The Clean and the Foul: Paupers and the Pox in London Hospitals, *c.*1550–*c.*1700' in Siena, *Sins of the Flesh*, pp. 264–66.

16 Sander Gilman, *Disease and Representation: Images of Illness from Madness to AIDS*, Ithaca: Cornell University Press, 1988, pp. 245–54.

17 Harris, '(Po)X Marks the Spot'.

18 Claude Quétel, *The History of Syphilis*, Baltimore: Johns Hopkins University Press, 1990, pp. 9–11.

19 Foa, 'The New and the Old', p. 39.

20 Foa, 'The New and the Old', pp. 35–40. On plague-spreaders see William G. Naphy, *Plagues Poisons and Potions: Plague-Spreading Conspiracies in the Western Alps, 1530–1640*, Manchester: Manchester University Press, 2002.

21 T. Pecke, *Parnassi puerperium*, London: James Cottrel, 1660, p. 23.

22 Dorothy Nelkin and Sander Gilman, 'Placing Blame for Devastating Disease', *Social Research* 55, 1988, pp. 361–78.

23 Cited in Foa, 'The New and the Old', pp. 31–32.

24 On imaginations about native sexuality see Peter Mason, *Deconstructing America: Representations of the Other*, London: Routledge, 1990, and Felicity Nussbaum, 'Polygamy, *Pamela* and the prerogative of Empire' in Ann Bermingham and John Brewer (eds), *The Consumption of Culture, 1600–1800: Image, Object, Text*, London: Routledge, 1995, pp. 217–36.

25 Cited in Guy Poirier, 'A Contagion at the Source of Discourse on Sexualities: Syphilis during the French Renaissance' in Claire L. Carlin (ed.), *Imagining Contagion in Early Modern Europe*, New York: Palgrave, 2005, p. 169.

26 William Eamon, 'Cannibalism and Contagion: Framing Syphilis in Counter-Reformation Italy', *Early Science and Medicine* 3, 1998, pp. 1–31.

27 Jean Astruc, *A Treatise of the Venereal Disease*, Vol. 1, London: W. Innys, 1754, p. 74.

28 Quétel, *History of Syphilis*, p. 53–54.

29 Ottavia Niccoli, '"Menstruum Quasi Monstruum": Monstrous Births and Menstrual Taboo in the Sixteenth Century' in Muir and Ruggiero (eds), *Sex and Gender*, pp. 1–25.

30 Andrew Boorde, *Brevyary of Helthe*, London: Wyllyam Myddelton, 1547, ch. 237.

31 Winfried Schleiner, 'Infection and Cure through Women: Renaissance Constructions of Women', *Journal of Medieval and Renaissance Studies* 24, 1994, pp. 499–517 (506); Kevin Siena, 'Pollution, Promiscuity, and the Pox: English Venereology and the Early Modern Discourse on Social and Sexual Danger', *Journal of the History of Sexuality* 8, 1998, pp. 553–74; Marie E. McAllister, 'Stories of the Origin of Syphilis in Eighteenth-Century England: Science, Myth, and Prejudice', *Eighteenth-Century Life* 24:1, 2000, pp. 33–40.

32 Daniel Sennert, *Two Treatises. The First of the Venereal Pocks*, London: Peter Cole, 1660, p. 15; Nicolas de Blegny, *New and Curious Observations Concerning the Art of Curing the Venereal Disease*, London: n.p., 1676, pp. 3–8.

33 Mary Fissell, *Vernacular Bodies: The Politics of Reproduction in Early Modern England*, Oxford: Oxford University Press, 2004 pp. 53–89.

34 Thomas Laqueur, *Making Sex: The Body and Gender from the Greeks to Freud*, Cambridge, MA: Harvard University Press, 1990.

35 Thomas Nedham, *A Treatise of a Consumption and the Venereal Disease*, London: n.p., 1700, pp. 9–13.

36 Astruc, *A Treatise of the Venereal Disease*, pp. 92–94.

37 Andrew Cunningham and Ole Peter Grell, *The Four Horsemen of the Apocalypse: Religion, War, Famine and Death in Reformation Europe*, Cambridge: Cambridge University Press, 2000, p. 1.

38 Cited in R. P. T. Davenport-Hines, *Sex, Death and Punishment: Attitudes to Sex and Sexuality in Britain since the Renaissance*, London: Fontana Press, 1990, pp. 26–27.

39 Darin Hayton, 'Joseph Grünpeck's Astrological Explanation of the French Disease' in Siena, *Sins of the Flesh*, pp. 81–106.

40 *The Medical Works of Francisco Lopez de Villalobos*, trans. George Gaskoin, London: Churchill and Sons, 1870, p. 106.

41 Arrizabalaga *et al.*, *The Great Pox*, pp. 38–55.

42 The classic model is Wolfgang Reinhard, 'Pressures Towards Confessionalization? Prolegomena to a Theory of the Confessional Age' in C. Scott Dixon (ed.), *The German Reformation*, Oxford: Blackwell, 1999, pp. 169–91.

43 On Reformation-era social and moral discipline see R. Po-Chia Hsia, *Social Discipline in the Reformation: Central Europe 1550–1750*, London: Routledge, 1989; Lyndal Roper, *The Holy Household: Women and Morals in Reformation Augsburg*, Oxford: Oxford University Press, 1991.

44 Cited in Mark W. Eberle, 'Lucas Cranach's Cupid as Honey Thief Paintings: Allegories of Syphilis?', *Comitatus* 10, 1979, pp. 21–30 (24).

45 Cited in Bernard Cottret, *Calvin: A Biography*, London: Continuum, 2003, p. 306.

46 Anon., *The Whore of Babylon's Pockey Priest*, London: Thomas Fox, 1679.

47 William Bulleyn, *Bulwarke of Defence*, London: J. Kyngston, 1562. fol. LX.

48 Eamon, 'Cannibalism and Contagion', pp. 19–20, 25–26.

49 Natalie Zemon Davis, *Society and Culture in Early Modern France*, Stanford: Stanford University Press, 1975, pp. 178–81.

50 Owsei Temkin, 'On the History of "Morality and Syphilis"' in Temkin, *The Double Face of Janus and Other Essays in the History of Medicine*, Baltimore: Johns Hopkins University Press, 1977, pp. 472–84.

51 Stanislav Andreski, *Syphilis, Puritanism, and Witch Hunts: Historical Explanations in the Light of Medicine and Psychoanalysis with a Forecast about AIDS*, New York: St Martin's Press, 1989.

52 For a multi-causal investigation see Brian Levack, *The Witch Hunt in Early Modern Europe*, New York: Longman, 2006.

53 Laura J. McGough, 'Demons, Nature, or God? Witchcraft Accusations and the French Disease in Early Modern Venice', *Bulletin of the History of Medicine* 80, 2006, pp. 219–46.

54 Claudia Stein, *Negotiating the French Pox in Early Modern Germany*, Farnham: Ashgate, 2009, pp. 9–11, 177.

55 *Luther: Letters of Spiritual Counsel*, trans. Theodore G. Tappert, Vancouver: Regent College Publishing, 2003, pp. 292–93.

56 Vern L. Bullough and Bonnie Bullough, *Women and Prostitution: A Social History*, Buffalo: Prometheus, 1987, pp. 139–56.

57 Johannes Fabricius, *Syphilis in Shakespeare's England*, London: Kingsley, 1994, p. 17.

58 Ann G. Carmichael, *Plague and the Poor in Renaissance Florence*, Cambridge: Cambridge University Press, 1986, pp. 123–25.

59 Guido Ruggiero, *Binding Passions: Tales of Magic, Marriage, and Power at the End of the Renaissance*, Oxford: Oxford University Press, 1993, p. 50; Michelle Laughran, 'The Body, Public Health, and Social Control in Sixteenth-Century Venice', Ph.D. diss., The University of Connecticut, 1998.

60 Sander Gilman, *Picturing Health and Illness: Images of Identity and Difference*, Baltimore: Johns Hopkins University Press, 1995, pp. 67–92.

61 Bruce Thomas Boehrer, 'Early Modern Syphilis', *Journal of the History of Sexuality* 1:2, 1990, pp. 197–214 (199).

62 Rose Zimbardo, 'Satiric Representation of Venereal Disease: The Restoration versus the Eighteenth-Century Model' in Linda E. Merians (ed.), *The Secret Malady: Venereal Disease in Eighteenth-Century Britain and France*, Lexington: University of Kentucky Press, 1996, pp. 183–94.

63 Raymond A. Anselment, *Realms of Apollo: Literature and Healing in Seventeenth-Century England*, Newark: University of Delaware Press, 1995, pp. 131–71.

64 Allen, *The Wages of Sin*, pp. 42–43, 57–58.

65 Arrizabalaga *et al.*, *The Great Pox;* Kevin Siena, *Venereal Disease, Hospitals and the Urban Poor: London's 'Foul Wards' 1600–1800*, Rochester: University of Rochester Press, 2004; Robert Jütte, 'Syphilis and Confinement: Hospitals in Early Modern Germany' in Norbert Finzsch and Robert Jütte (eds), *Institutions of Confinement: Hospitals, Asylums, and Prisons in Western Europe and North America, 1500–1950*, Cambridge: Cambridge University Press, 1996, pp. 97–116; Stein, *Negotiating the French Pox;* M. López Terrada, 'El tratamiento de la sífilis en un hospital renacentista: La sala del mal de siment del Hospital General de Valencia', *Asclepio* 41, 1989, pp. 19–50.

66 Siena, *Venereal Disease*, pp. 70–73, 110.
67 Stein, *Negotiating the French Pox*, p. 84; Arrizabalaga *et al.*, *The Great Pox*, p. 147.
68 Siena, 'Clean and the Foul', pp. 278–80.
69 Arrizabalaga *et al.*, *The Great Pox*, pp. 145–233.
70 Michel Foucault, *Discipline and Punish: The Birth of the Prison*, New York: Vintage, 1977. Analysing asylums for prostitutes Sherrill Cohen argues that Foucault's chronology needs to be pushed earlier, noting that women faced a 'panoptic regime' long before the nineteenth century. *The Evolution of Women's Asylums Since 1500*, Oxford: Oxford University Press, 1992, p. 6.
71 Laura J. McGough, 'Quarantining Beauty: The French Disease in Early Modern Venice' in Siena, *Sins of the Flesh*, pp. 211–37. For Laura J. McGough's fuller study see *Gender, Sexuality and Syphilis in Early Modern Venice: The Disease that Came to Stay*, Basingstoke: Palgrave Macmillan, 2011.
72 Sherrill Cohen, 'Asylums for Women in Counter-Reformation Italy' in Sherrin Marshall (ed.), *Women in Reformation and Counter-Reformation Europe: Public and Private Worlds*, Bloomington: Indiana University Press, 1989, pp. 166–88.
73 E. P. Chaney, '"Philanthropy in Italy": English observations on Italian hospitals, 1545–1789' in Thomas Riis (ed.), *Aspects of Poverty in Early Modern Europe*, Stuttgart: Klett-Cotta, 1981, pp. 183–217.
74 Euan Cameron, *The European Reformation*, Oxford: Oxford University Press, 1991, pp. 79–93, 111–35.
75 See the tandem collections Ole Peter Grell and Andrew Cunningham (eds), *Health Care and Poor Relief in Protestant Europe, 1500–1700*, London: Routledge, 1997, and Ole Peter Grell, Andrew Cunningham and Jon Arrizabalaga (eds), *Health Care and Poor Relief in Counter-Reformation Europe*, London: Routledge, 1999.
76 Cited in Siena, *Venereal Disease*, p. 196.
77 Cohen emphasizes the confessional divide on the spread of female asylums, *The Evolution of Women's Asylums*, pp. 127–30.
78 Cohen, *The Evolution of Women's Asylums*, pp. 79–81.
79 Cristian Berco, 'Textiles as Social Texts: Syphilis, Material Culture and Gender in Golden Age Spain', *Journal of Social History* 44:3, 2011, pp. 785–810. Thanks to Dr Berco for letting me read an advanced copy.
80 Kevin Siena, 'The "Foul" Disease and Privacy: The effects of venereal disease and patient demand on the medical marketplace in early modern London', *Bulletin of the History of Medicine* 75, 2001, pp. 199–224.
81 David Gentilcore, 'Charlatans, the Regulated Marketplace, and the Treatment of Venereal Disease in Italy' in Siena, *Sins of the Flesh*, pp. 57–80.
82 Winfried Schleiner, 'Moral Attitudes Towards Syphilis and its Prevention in the Renaissance', *Bulletin of the History of Medicine* 68, 1994, pp. 389–410.
83 Siena, 'Clean and the Foul', pp. 276–78.
84 See Linda E. Merians, 'The London Lock Hospital and the Lock Asylum for Women' in Merians, *The Secret Malady*, pp. 128–45, and Siena, *Venereal Disease*, pp. 181–250.
85 Tim Hitchcock, *English Sexualities 1700–1800*, London: Macmillan, 1997; Randolph Trumbach, *Sex and the Gender Revolution: Volume One: Heterosexuality and the Third Gender in Enlightenment London*, Chicago: University of Chicago Press, 1998, esp. pp. 196–275.
86 Siena, *Venereal Disease*, p. 225; McGough, 'Demons, Nature or God', p. 228.
87 Edward Shorter, *Women's Bodies: A Social History of Women's Encounters with Health, Ill-Health, and Medicine*, New Brunswick: Transactions Publications, 1991, pp. 263–67.
88 Cristian Berco, 'Syphilis and the Silencing of Sodomy in Juan Calvo's *Tratado del morbo gálico*' in K. Borris and G. Rousseau (eds), *The Sciences of Homosexuality in Early Modern Europe*, London: Routledge, 2007, pp. 92–114; Kevin Siena, 'The Strange Medical Silence on Same-sex Transmission of the Pox, *c.* 1660–*c.*1760' in Borris and Rousseau, *Sciences of Homosexuality*, pp. 115–34. See also Mary Hewlett, 'The French Connection: Syphilis and Sodomy in Late-Renaissance Lucca' in Siena, *Sins of the Flesh*, pp. 239–60.
89 See, for example, Bernard Mandeville, *A Modest Defence of Public Stews*, London: A. Moore, 1724, or Anon., *A Safe-Conduct through the Territories of the Republic of Venus. Containing, a practicable proposal for the prevention and final eradication of a certain disease*, London: n.p., 1794, esp. pp. 55–135.

90 Merians, *The Secret Malady*, p. 138.
91 For the standard model see Leonore Davidoff and Catherine Hall, *Family Fortunes: Men and Women of the English Middle Class, 1780–1850*, Chicago: University of Chicago Press, 1987.
92 Donna T. Andrew, *Philanthropy and Police: London Charity in the Eighteenth Century*, Princeton: Princeton University Press, 1989, pp. 98–134.
93 Michel Foucault, *The Birth of Biopolitics*: *Lectures at the Collège de France, 1978–79*, Basingstoke: Palgrave MacMillan, 2008.
94 Merians, *The Secret Malady*, p. 140.
95 Studies of literary deployments of pox imagery have been vital to understanding the formation of its associations with corruption, stigma and moral decay. Important examples include Fabricius, *Syphilis in Shakespeare's England*; Anselment, *Realms of Apollo*, pp. 131–71; Margaret Healy, *Fictions of Disease in Early Modern England*, Basingstoke: Palgrave, 2001, pp. 123–87; and the literary chapters in Siena, *Sins of the Flesh*, and Merians, *The Secret Malady*.
96 Ann A. Huse, 'Pox Britannica: The French Disease in the Age of Rochester' in Elizabeth Lane Furdell (ed.), *Textual Healing: Essays on Medieval and Early Modern Medicine*, Leiden: Brill, 2005, pp. 223–40; Lynn Hunt, *The Invention of Pornography: Obscenity and the Origins of Modernity, 1500–1800*, New York: Zone Books, 1993, p. 307.
97 See, for example, William Ober's investigation of James Boswell's many bouts with VD, *Boswell's Clap and Other Essays: Medical Analyses of Literary Men's Afflictions*, Carbondale: Southern Illinois University Press, 1979.
98 Roy Porter, 'The Patient's View: Doing Medical History from Below', *Theory and Society* 14, 1985, pp. 175–98.
99 Kevin Siena, 'Suicide as an Illness Strategy in the Long Eighteenth Century' in John Weaver and David Wright (eds), *Histories of Suicide: International Perspectives on Self-Destruction in the Modern World*, Toronto: University of Toronto Press, 2008, pp. 53–72 (63–65).

26

SEXUAL DISEASES SINCE 1750

Lesley A. Hall

A good deal has been written about sexually transmitted diseases (STDs) in modern Europe: however, although some areas and periods have received a good deal of attention, there are still significant lacunae in the story. The medical narrative of developing understandings of the venereal diseases and the development of effective means of treatment has tended to focus on the contributions of significant figures and possibly rather smoothes out a more complex picture of controversies and contested ideas. Attention has also been paid to governmental attempts to control the spread of these diseases through strategies of prevention, although how detailed and nuanced the historiography is of these varies greatly from area to area. There are many additional detailed specific studies that could shed light on understandings of and responses to these diseases in particular places and at particular times, while there is also a need for further syntheses based on comparative data and in particular looking at the international dimension. There have been discernible waves of rising and falling public concern over the diseases.[1] The historical narrative to date has tended to reflect this, since interest in these diseases generated public debate involving state officials, doctors, organized religion and various other interest groups, leaving a rich trail of documentary evidence. So far we know much less about what was going on between the obvious peaks in the narrative.

The state of knowledge

During the late eighteenth and the early part of the nineteenth century, confusion reigned over medical understandings of sexually transmitted diseases, although their mode of transmission had long been obvious. The most prevalent and recognized diseases in the European context were syphilis, gonorrhoea, and soft chancre (chancroid), but these were not always differentiated. The influential John Hunter, author of the *Treatise on the Venereal Disease* (1786), argued for a single 'venereal poison' though this was not universally accepted: Benjamin Bell, in his *Treatise on Gonorrhoea Virulenta and Lues Venerea* (1793), concluded that syphilis and gonorrhoea were quite distinct.[2]

The treatment of choice for syphilis was mercury, although medical opinions differed about the best means of administering this. It produced extremely unpleasant side effects but did ameliorate dermatological manifestations, while, as syphilis was a remitting disease, it could appear to have been eradicated when the second stage had run its course and the disease become quiescent. The often protracted period of apparent good health between the secondary stage and the very diverse array of conditions caused by tertiary syphilis meant that the latter were not necessarily attributed to the earlier infection, and in a significant minority of cases, these later complications did not develop. Gumma, deep lesions that eroded flesh and penetrated to the bone, particularly though not exclusively in the nasal area, had long been recognized as one long-term effect, as had the effects on bones. Although the Italian morbid anatomist Morgagni had identified lesions of the heart and arteries, the various manifestations in other internal organs were denied by Hunter and largely neglected by other authorities; they were easy to confuse with other diseases.[3] The congenital effects of syphilis were well known, although the exact mechanism by which the disease was transmitted was still a matter of conjecture, whether it was infection from the mother's primary chancre during passage through the birth canal, or infection while still in utero.[4]

Gonorrhoea was considered, if not an early symptom of syphilis, a less dangerous disease. It was believed to be generated by toxic substances formed in the genital tracts of promiscuous women, in particular prostitutes – its symptoms were often slight and invisible in infected women – and communicated to men, in whom the effects were much more obvious and observable in the form of discharge, inflammation and painful urination. Treatments were both local (urethral lavage, the passage of sounds into the urethra) and systemic, with the patient being bled and purged, or administered herbal remedies. Mercury was often given as a matter of course. Repeated infections in the male might lead to 'gleet', a persistent discharge, or stricture of the urethra, though in some cases this was the effect of vigorous local treatment with caustics and cauterization.[5] It could cause long-term systemic effects (endocarditis and rheumatic afflictions in the male, and in women it could cause sterility), but these connections would take many decades and the rise of bacteriology to reveal. Chancroid was sometimes viewed as a mild form of syphilis. It formed painful ulcers on the genitals and swollen lymph nodes in the groin. In conditions of poor hygiene it could develop into rapidly progressing sloughing necrotic ulceration of the genital area.[6] There were a number of other venereal diseases: some were not recognized as separate entities until diagnostic methods became more sophisticated; others were rare in Europe and largely confined to ports.

Because of the stigma of these diseases there was a particularly high level of quack activity offering treatment, and in particular these made a point of cure without mercury. There were some attempts at personal prophylaxis, for example, the use of animal skin condoms to prevent infection, but these devices were relatively expensive and hard to obtain except in large cities.[7] Certain specialist hospitals were founded for, or became dedicated to, the treatment of patients with venereal diseases. This was partly due to the reluctance of many other hospitals to admit these long-term stay troublesome patients, partly to acts of philanthropy, and partly to do with the desire of members of the medical profession to make a position for themselves in a competitive medical marketplace.[8] They also provided sites where doctors could experiment with various remedies on the incarcerated sufferers.

There are however numerous unexplored areas and unanswered questions within this story. Siena has vividly revealed how sufferers accessed treatment in London during the eighteenth century, but less is known about the situation elsewhere or in the later period before the early twentieth century and the introduction in many European countries of publicly funded clinics.

Prostitution had long been seen as playing a central role in circulating these diseases, with infection spreading like spokes from a wheel-hub.[9] It was argued that for the civilian population pursing illicit sex was a matter of private morality, and contracting a venereal disease was considered by many to be a just punishment for sin; but the pragmatics of maintaining military and naval forces in a condition of fighting fitness led military doctors to endeavour to control diseases that were extremely prevalent in the armed forces and which negatively affected efficiency. French army surgeons, according to Quétel, set up military hospitals to treat camp-followers, an initiative stymied by the resistance of the nuns in nursing orders.[10] Ballhatchet in his pioneering study *Race, Sex and Class under the Raj* revealed that inspection and surveillance of the prostitutes resorted to by troops in India long preceded the development of the Contagious Diseases Acts in the metropole.[11] The influence of Empire upon these developments has been further elaborated by Philippa Levine in *Prostitution, Race, and Politics: Policing Venereal Disease in the British Empire.*[12]

Priorities of national defence long continued to inflect policies to protect troops. During the twentieth century Catholic and pro-natalist states such as Spain and Italy issued to their military for defence against VD the prophylactic condoms whose contraceptive use they forbade. The concern for the health of the Army and Navy did not carry over into any equivalent concern for sailors in the mercantile marines, whose health was less critical to national defence. Hall's research indicates that shipowners for a long time resisted any obligation to treat these like other diseases, penalizing sufferers and discharging them if incapacitated.[13]

The regulatory model of control

While concern over venereal diseases among the civilian population was less acute, there were some endeavours, particularly with the rise of new concepts of public health and sanitation, to limit their spread. In the interests of public order and decency, most European countries were increasingly instituting forms of regulation to control the visible manifestations of the sex trade, and, it has been argued, medical inspection soon became incorporated into these systems although it was not the initial reason for them. The much-cited pioneer and exemplar in this was France.[14] Regulation was applied by local municipal authorities as part of administrative practices for local good order and public health, rather than as monolithic statutory legislation at the national level, or was even, as Baldwin has suggested, introduced as improvised policing practices.[15] Although licensing systems were developed to bring women prostituting themselves outside brothels into the system of inspection, this seldom gained effective cooperation, although more local studies may nuance this picture. There was general resistance to having contact with the policing system, or to being inscribed as prostitutes, since once 'on the register' it was very hard to get off and reintegrate into wider society. All countries with systems of regulation experienced a continuing problem of clandestine prostitution, along with police corruption, blackmail and bribery.

Strong claims were made for the hygienic benefit of regulation and enforcing regular medical inspection of prostitutes. Even some contemporary observers were sceptical, noting the cursory and careless nature of inspections as carried out by the designated police surgeons, a low-status post within the medical profession and held by doctors seldom particularly competent. Furthermore, the time allowed for individual inspections was extremely brief, and for most of the nineteenth century diagnosis was haphazard: it seems extremely probable that not only were many cases of infection missed, unless they were in the most active and obvious stage, but also that women with non-venereal genital ailments were diagnosed and incarcerated.[16]

Mooij acutely observes that systems of medical control and surveillance are dependent upon the collusion of the parties being controlled and their internalization of the medical discourses involved. For prostitutes and brothelkeepers, regulation had few perceived benefits. The examination was unpleasant, and diagnosis as infected meant that the woman was unable to work and might well be incarcerated for treatment until apparently recovered. There were therefore very strong incentives for the development of stratagems to disguise the symptoms of disease, as well as bribery of officials to issue the relevant certificate.[17] The preventive effect of inspections was severely limited by the fact that a woman certified clean could contract VD almost immediately afterwards and infect large numbers of customers before her next inspection. At best, the system might remove some women from circulation during the most infectious stages of syphilis or gonorrhoea. However, the way in which the examinations were conducted was also likely to have conveyed cross-infection through inadequate cleansing of instruments and surgeons' hands.

An apparently clearer understanding of venereology among the medical profession was brought about by the work of Philippe Ricord, an American-born French doctor, whose *Traité pratique des maladies vénériennes* (1838), brought a new if somewhat spurious clarity and confidence to the picture. By use of the speculum Ricord did greatly improve understanding of the manifestations of venereal diseases in women. He also clearly distinguished syphilis from gonorrhoea. He identified syphilis as a specifically human disease, mostly confined to the genitalia, which went through three stages, curable with mercury, and only contagious during the first stage, not during the secondary, a significant error he was eventually forced to retract. He also taught that the soft chancre of chancroid and the hard chancre of syphilis were both syphilitic. Taithe has suggested that the primacy obtained by Ricord in this field was multi-factorial, owing a fair amount to his ability to negotiate a complex medico-political landscape, and to his construction of syphilis within a 'morally neutral' medical paradigm in a regulationist nation; thus his characterization of the disease meshed effectively with wider social attitudes.[18]

A different, but less successful, approach was that of Joseph-Alexandre Auzias-Turenne, a much more marginal figure within the French medical establishment. He questioned the claim that syphilis was specific to humanity and obtained facilities to experiment on monkeys, though he failed to produce convincing results. He then turned to the possibility of inoculation on an analogy with smallpox, arguing that vaccinating would do away with the need for regular inspection, and that similar prophylaxis could be applied to other high-risk groups such as soldiers and sailors. He performed several 'syphilizations' upon himself and a small clinical sample. The clear-cut benefits of smallpox inoculation and vaccination were not perceptible in the case of syphilis, in spite of the misleading similarity of popular terminology as 'The Great Pox'. A series of commissions, led by Ricord, condemned his work. Nonetheless, the idea of syphilization was taken up in several other European countries, most notably by Professor Boeck in Norway, though it never became a dominant paradigm. Even so, the research undertaken from this angle had implications which undercut Ricord's benign model of a containable and curable disease.[19]

The whole area was less clear-cut than a simple dichotomy between these two approaches, simplifying a complex and contested picture, would suggest. There was little advance in treatment. Mercury remained the treatment of choice, although in rather less heroic measures, and precise methods of application were the subject of continuing debate. There was some interest in potassium iodide, which had superior efficacy in the amelioration of late gummata and bone disease. Alternative systems of medicine, such as homeopathy, claimed to provide a remedy. There were also attempts to prevent the disease from spreading by cauterizing or even excising the primary chancre: mutilating operations which did not, however, stop secondary symptoms developing.[20] Obtaining treatment was also not necessarily easy. Members of the more prosperous classes could usually obtain discreet treatment from a private physician, although such was the stigma that it was reported that even those who would normally consult elite practitioners resorted to quacks. For those dependent upon charity or social welfare provisions legitimate medical treatment was often hard to access. The case of Sweden was unusual even among the other Nordic countries: a compulsory state tax supported special isolation wards (the *kurhus*) throughout the country, and treatment, by private physicians acting as state employees within these institutions, was free for the poor. This was in a context of significant social controls, such as the obligation to report cases to the authorities, and compulsory incarceration.[21] Baldwin argues that this was due to perceptions of non-sexual transmission of syphilis, and Sweden being a predominantly rural society in which venereal diseases were widely prevalent outside the urban context which was such an influential element in moral panics in other parts of Europe.[22] Many general hospitals would not accept patients with VD as in-patients, and specialist hospitals were seldom sufficient to the need for their services. In some cases these were also strongly associated with prostitution.

Changing paradigms

Changes to the existing paradigm of sexually transmitted diseases, who was responsible for them, and means of control emerged, arguably, and rather counter-intuitively, from the British Isles, notorious for both prudery and a laissez-faire attitude towards prostitution. Britain had not had any form of regulation in place: prostitution was not illegal (though associated activities, such as annoyance through soliciting, were), and far from there being any kind of medical/moral divide in views on the subject, eminent medical men went publicly on record to define venereal diseases as God's punishment for sin and to argue that man and medical science should not tamper with them.[23] However, there was also a groundswell of medical and other opinion that was influenced by continental, especially French, policies, that saw these as something which could usefully be imported, against the background of rising sanitary concern in a period of rapid industrialization and urbanization.

As a result of the medical debacle of the Crimean War (1854–56), government investigations into the health of the Army and Navy revealed the extremely high level of venereal infection in the armed forces. Britain had a small professional Army and Navy (unlike those continental nations which required all males to undertake a compulsory period of military service) and a large and growing Empire, which had recently been shaken by the Indian Mutiny (1857–58). Questions of military fitness were therefore a matter of acute concern. A series of Contagious Diseases Acts were passed (1866, 1867, 1869) instituting medical surveillance of prostitutes in designated port and garrison towns. Women suspected of practising prostitution could be compulsorily examined and, if deemed to be infected, incarcerated in a Lock Hospital until considered to be cured. The responses to these Acts and the campaigns both for their extension beyond this narrow remit and for their repeal have been extensively documented and debated.[24] The Acts, unlike the complex and entangled local systems of regulation which existed over large parts of Continental Europe, were national and monolithic. They were visible in ways in which local administrative procedures conducted discreetly as business as usual were not. They aroused significant outcry from diverse and overlapping groups of the population, on several grounds: the violation of traditional British civil liberties; the affront to Christian morality involved in rendering vice safe; and also from an increasingly organized working class protesting the class bias of the Acts. They also became a cause for women campaigners already involved in the critique of existing male-dominated society and agitating for remedies.

These women, spearheaded by the charismatic Josephine Butler, raised a central and critical question: Was prostitution an unfortunate necessity determined by uncontrollable male sexual drives? This shifted the emphasis from the role of the prostitute to the role of the male in sustaining prostitution as an institution and disseminating venereal diseases.[25] The debate is sometimes framed as being about medicalization and a scientific approach versus moralism but the picture was far from clear-cut. Some doctors objected to inspection not only on the basis of its sanitary inefficacy but also on moral grounds, and were hostile to suggestions of prophylactic measures, while some individuals and organizations in the moralist camp nonetheless advocated a much tighter control over prostitutes while conceding their necessity.

Aided by the entry of women (in however limited numbers) into the medical profession, a discourse developed emphasizing the extent to which immoral men were the conduits for visiting venereal infection upon their innocent wives and children. Worboys has demonstrated how this discourse was not just buttressed by, but itself assisted in the paradigm shift in the understanding of gonorrhoea in the later decades of the nineteenth century. In 1876 Emil Noeggerath determined the major pathogenic role of gonorrhoea in pelvic inflammatory disease, causing general ill-health and, in some cases, sterility in women, and the existence of latent stages of infection. He also claimed that gonorrhoea was far more common than previously assumed with a large proportion of infected men infecting their wives in turn. Added to the discovery of the gonococcus responsible for gonorrhoea by Neisser in 1879, the resulting realization that much ill-health and infertility in 'respectable' women, with further repercussions on their offspring, was due to asymptomatic gonorrhoeal infection from their husbands brought about the reversal of the previous gendering of the disease, as something nasty given by bad women to men, to something given by immoral men to decent women, threatening their health, the well-being of their offspring, and endangering the reproductive health of the nation itself.[26] This feminist message was taken a stage further by the British suffragist doctor Louisa Martindale in her 1908 pamphlet *Under the Surface*, which placed the blame on the civil, economic and social disadvantages of women which deprived them of the power to challenge sexual exploitation. This standpoint was simplified by Christabel Pankhurst into the catchy slogan, 'Votes for Women and Chastity for Men', in *The Great Scourge*, 1913.

The relatively cheerful Ricordian view of syphilis as limited, briefly contagious and curable was also undergoing challenges. The extent and diversity of tertiary syphilis was becoming apparent to clinicians (as well as the degree to which assorted disabilities in children were due to congenital syphilis), although Gayle Davis' work on the understanding of General Paralysis of the Insane reveals how such new ideas about its aetiology were disseminated only very slowly and partially.[27] Doubt was thrown on the efficacy of mercury as curative rather than palliative. Increasing emphasis was laid on the need to delay marriage if the prospective groom was found to be infected, and the disastrous consequences of ignoring this. Doctors in all nations seem to have been inclined to conceal from wives, at least in the case of middle- and upper-class families, that the root of their persistent ill-health, and that of their offspring, was due to disease communicated by the husband through conjugal intercourse.[28] While, given the fallibility of the sources available, it is not possible to say that incidence of venereal diseases was actually increasing, it is certainly probable that better record-keeping was revealing their extent. Again, French venereologists took the lead in the medical discourse: Fournier presented a gloomy and somewhat nihilistic picture of the ravages of syphilis and the lack of obvious recourse for cure or care.

Various factors were entwined in this reconstruction of ideas around sexually transmitted diseases. There were changes in the organization of prostitution as more informal sexual marketplaces developed, and international traffic was facilitated by improved public transportation. Mooij has pointed out the relevance of changes in the balance of political power in many European nations, of a growing sense of mutual dependency within complex societies, of concern in all classes for respectability, and of new classes and interest groups being drawn into the political process.[29] All these and other factors intersected with wider *fin-de-siècle* anxieties, the rise of eugenics, and a general sense that, although many threats to public health had been greatly reduced by the successes of the sanitarian project, others still seemed impervious to remedy. Concerns over national fitness manifested and played out differently in different nations but sexually transmitted diseases usually figured.

The French remained largely wedded to regulation, even if 'neo-regulationist' legislation and administrative practices tidied up some of the worst abuses and shortcomings of the system. In other countries, more strongly influenced by the 'abolitionist' campaign originating in Britain and preached widely throughout Europe by Josephine Butler and her adherents, other solutions were sought. In the Netherlands, for example, free clinics for treatment were set up in 1903, intended to be destigmatizing by emphasizing the benefit to the innocently infected. A wider knowledge of the existence of the diseases and their effects was also deemed desirable, and there were moves to initiate this enlightenment among young people as a preventive measure. The desirability of premarital health examinations was suggested, as was the possibility of male sexual abstinence until marriage. Nonetheless, the persisting association of the diseases with immorality and stigma meant that constraints due to taboo persisted: private and state medical insurance schemes might specifically exclude sexually transmitted diseases from benefits, and hospitals might only admit the 'innocently' infected.[30] Works of literature and art drew implicitly or explicitly upon the theme of venereal diseases – Ibsen's play *Ghosts*, the New Woman novels of British writers of the 1890s, Brieux's play *Les Avariés (Damaged Goods)*, paintings by Munch – as both evils in themselves and metaphor for social and psychological ills. The increasing cultural pervasiveness of the motif of syphilis led to medical observations of a new psychosomatic disorder: syphilophobia, the fear of having contracted syphilis.

Venereology continued to be stigmatized as a medical speciality, in spite of the eminence of figures such as Fournier. Although potentially lucrative as private practice, it did not accrue less tangible social and professional capital, even though the quacks who preyed on the fears of the public about infection and the severity of orthodox treatment were strongly condemned. However, the subject was gaining ground: in spite of diverse national approaches embedded in specific histories and political and medical systems, sexually transmitted disease was recognized as a problem of transnational significance, with international medical conferences being held in 1899 and 1902.

New prospects, traditional responses, and new actors

Schaudinn and Hoffman finally identified the organism which causes syphilis in 1905. However, the development of the diagnostic Wasserman test in the following year depressingly revealed the prevalence of latent syphilis and the extent to which mercurial treatment might have alleviated symptoms, but failed to destroy the spirochaete. But in 1909 Paul Ehrlich and his assistant Japanese student Sahachiro Hata at the National Institute for Experimental Therapeutics in Frankfurt found that the 606th substance that they tested as a possible 'magic bullet' against the spirochaete was the one they were seeking; this was the arsenical preparation Salvarsan. Sent some for testing, the British venereologist L. W. Harrison observed that 'it stopped the clock' instead of merely slowing the spirochaete down.[31]

Putting it to practical use, however, was more complicated. There were issues of toxicity, and the side effects in some cases were lethal. The strength of dosage and how often it should be given had to be worked out. The compelling and optimistic 'bullet' metaphor concealed the fact that the drug had to be administered for a period of well over a year, by painful intramuscular injection, until the patient's Wasserman test passed as clear, and doctors required training. Above all, how were the infected and the cure to be brought together? In the Netherlands there was already, as previously mentioned, a network of public VD clinics, but comparable systems did not exist in all European countries. In the United Kingdom, this solution, unlikely to reignite the resistance generated by the Contagious Diseases Acts, gave impetus to demands for a Royal Commission to investigate venereal disease and its prevention, appointed in 1913, finally reporting in 1916.

While it is sometimes argued that it was World War I, and the associated issues of the proliferation of venereal diseases, which brought these into the realm of public debate, it is clear that the subject had become speakable well before the War. A case can be made that the overtness of the concerns over sexually transmitted disease in the wartime context was very largely due to the pre-existing climate of widespread discussion as to what should be done about the problem. Different nations pursued different strategies to counter this traditional concomitant of warfare, and, as Mark Harrison has documented, even one combatant nation might practise different policies in different contexts.[32] While some nations continued to rely on medically inspected regimental brothels, new approaches were also being promoted. It had already been noted that calomel (mercury) ointment could provide a reasonable degree of protection, and in some instances condoms were distributed, although in both cases effective use rather depended upon sobriety. Early treatment ablution stations for the disinfection of soldiers returning to quarters were also provided. In spite of these measures, rates of infection soared, even in non-combatant nations. However, the more effective diagnosis and treatment of syphilis among men in the armed forces may have had some impact on its significant decline between the wars.

What to do about venereal diseases became a problem for all nations, with different national solutions affected by particular local factors. Sweden, with its long tradition of state medical interventionism, passed its influential *Lex Veneris* in 1918. While examinations and treatment were free, those who were infected were obliged to submit to treatment, and physicians were required to report patients to the authorities. Marriage was forbidden to anyone who might transmit VD and it was a criminal offence to expose another person to the risk of infection.[33] In the UK, by contrast, the system was less coercive and more persuasive, with the establishment of a substantial network of government-funded free, confidential and voluntary clinics. The task of propaganda and public education, however, was outsourced to a voluntary organization, the National Council for Combatting Venereal Diseases, later renamed the British Social Hygiene Council.[34] In Weimar Germany, a network of Advice Centres, largely funded by social insurance, provided diagnosis and advice but treatment was by referral to local practitioners. The majority of patients attended under compulsion, but a large minority voluntarily. More stringent compulsion was initiated by the 1927 VD Act.[35] In Spain a network of dispensaries for treatment gradually developed in spite of financial difficulties, and in 1928 the Primo de Rivera Dictatorship Penal Code criminalized the transmission of VD. Regulation of prostitution was only abolished by the Republic in 1935.[36] Regulation similarly retained its place in Italy and indeed more rigorous measures were introduced under the Fascist government, although free special clinics were also established.[37] While free anti-venereal dispensaries for outpatient treatment were established in all French towns with populations over 10,000 between the wars, and there were also significant health education initiatives,[38] regulation remained one of the pillars of French preventive strategies.[39]

While it might appear that there was a distinction between nations which retained a focus on prostitution and regulation versus those which applied their policies to the whole population, eschewing categorizing into 'guilty' or 'innocent' and aiming at treating VD like any other disease, actual practice often differed and continued to weigh more heavily upon women engaging in 'illicit behaviour'.[40] Propaganda in Soviet Russia leaned heavily on the image of the prostitute as the conduit of infection, and contrasted the benefits of male scientific medicine to the evil done by female folk-healers.[41] There were new perceptions of the routes by which the diseases were transmitted, shifting from spokes radiating from a hub of infection to a chain along which it was passed. But the new player was defined as 'the girlfriend', the 'amateur', the young girl with unprecedented freedoms, a symbol of changing sexual and social mores, engaging in sexual activity either for fun or in exchange for presents rather than for basic economic survival.[42] Ironically, in some debates, she was contrasted with the professional prostitute, who, it was argued, 'knew how to take care of herself' and was wise in the ways of prophylaxis, thus shifting from being the cause of infection to a preventive strategy.[43] Anxieties about this figure tended to reflect concerns about social change rather than the actual statistics of disease transmission.

A number of improvements in treatment developed. Besides the continuing refining of treatment protocols using Salvarsan, Julius Wagner von Jauregg developed in 1917 a cure for hitherto intractable late neurosyphilis through giving the subjects malaria, the high fever from which destroyed the spirochaete.[44] In the mid-1930s the first antibiotic, sulphonamide, was found to be effective in curing gonorrhoea, abolishing the need for long-drawn-out painful and invasive treatments.[45] Wasserman testing of pregnant women (who might not even know they were infected) and treatment lowered the incidence of congenital syphilis. There were also developments, given the new model of a 'chain', of prevention through contact-tracing of individuals who were known to have had sexual relations with patients who had already presented at clinics, using the relatively new profession of trained social workers in collaboration with doctors and nurses.[46] Concomitantly, there was increasing concern over the defaulting patient who failed to continue treatment until cured and non-infectious. In some cases this was due to occupational reasons, for example, sailors of the mercantile marines were unable to make regular visits to the same clinic and often lacked access to doctors. This international problem was addressed by the Brussels agreement of 1924 which instituted treatment of sailors at port clinics without distinction of nationality and the provision of record cards to track the course of treatment.[47] There was also the rise of a distinction between the good citizen who took care of his health by using prophylaxis, seeking early treatment if infected, and continuing this until cure, and the irresponsible defaulter. Infection became not just a bodily or even moral ailment, but the signifier of more general social dysfunction.[48]

The incidence of sexually transmitted diseases generally fell in Europe throughout the interwar period, varying from country to country, with a slight rise in the early 1930s. With the increased concern over these diseases statistics were probably fuller and more accurate than they had ever been. Infections took a sharp turn upward with the outbreak of World War II, even in neutral nations. Scarce rubber supplies were directed into the manufacture of condoms. Measures to control the spread of infection were increased, including the resources of modern mass media and advertising methodology to alert the public to the risks and to the availability of treatment. A major advance in treatment came with the development by the Allies in 1942 of penicillin, which cured syphilis within weeks. However, limited supplies meant that venereal diseases came low on the priority list for this new miracle drug.[49]

Dying diseases and new ones to worry about

Concern around sexually transmitted diseases generally remained high in the years immediately following the War. In the Netherlands the late 1940s were comparable to the turn of the century in the level of public preoccupation.[50] Michaela Freund has described the high level of anxiety around VD and the consequent intensive policing of women in British-occupied post-war Hamburg involving collaboration between British and German authorities.[51] It is plausible that issues around invasion and occupation may well have influenced intensity of concern. In contrast, concern over VD almost dropped off the map in the UK: though 1946 was a peak year for numbers of infections, there was a rapid decline in resources available for public education, while little attention was paid to provisions made for these 'dying diseases' when setting up the National Health Service.[52]

This was a precursor to the more general lack of interest of the 1950s. The development of antibiotics inspired confidence that these age-old scourges would soon disappear. However, although antibiotics theoretically meant that specialist venereological skills were not so necessary, continuing stigma meant that VD clinics continued to be well patronized by the infected and the worried well. It also became apparent that several minor venereal afflictions had previously been occluded by, or identified as, the major diseases: trichomoniasis, non-gonococcal urethritis, chlamydia, bacterial diseases often asymptomatic or presenting vague, barely noticed, symptoms, and only becoming visible when treatment for gonorrhoea failed.[53] This calm began to be disturbed in the late 1950s and early 1960s, as slight rises in reported infections occurred in the context of the rise of a new and threatening social group, teenagers, and the arrival in several European nations of significant numbers of immigrants. Homosexuality was also becoming more visible. Panic proliferated about these groups, although, as Mooij points out, the bulk of infections were still to be found among native heterosexuals aged 20 to 30.[54]

While HIV/AIDS is the sexually transmitted disorder which has had the most dramatic impact and gained the most attention during recent decades, formerly minor and disregarded sexually transmitted ailments have also become of greater epidemiological significance during the second half of the twentieth century and the beginning of the twenty-first. Chlamydia was identified in the early years of the twentieth century, but considered of little interest: the extent of unsuspected infections was revealed in the antibiotic era when it failed to respond.[55]

It is now (in 2010) the most common sexually transmitted disease in the UK and a cause for considerable concern. It is largely asymptomatic but complications can lead to permanent infertility in women and increased likelihood of ectopic pregnancy. It is so prevalent among the under-25s that a free national screening programme is now in place.[56] Even before the first reports of AIDS, an incurable sexually transmitted viral condition was in the news. There had been accounts in medical literature of genital herpes since the early eighteenth century, but uncertainty reigned until the 1950s as to whether it was merely a non-venereal condition of the genitalia.[57] Around 1980 this previously rather obscure condition erupted into a full blaze of publicity and panic. While the traditional venereal diseases were by then perceived as curable (even though antibiotic resistant strains of gonorrhoea had emerged), and the various 'new' bacterial venereal diseases were also responsive to modern medicine, herpes was incurable, recurrent, and lacked effective treatment. Although the panic over what was believed to be increasing incidence was widespread in Europe, this was largely driven by concerns emanating from the USA. Mooij hypothesizes that anxieties over herpes were a way of dealing with disenchantment over the failed promises of 1960s sexual liberationism, by enabling a reframing of sexual discipline in the direction of greater caution without complete retreat into moral orthodoxy.[58] It may also be relevant that press attention to the subject occurred just about the time that acyclovir provided an effective treatment.

Genital warts (human papilloma virus) had been clinically reported for many centuries, but were often assumed to be the by-product of another venereal disease. The role of sexual transmission, and high degree of contagion, was not definitively established until the early 1950s. As with herpes, the condition is incurable and may recur. A major concern is the implication of certain strains in the development of cervical cancer. This has led to the development of a vaccine and advocacy of inoculating girls before they become sexually active, a proposal which has caused significant degrees of moral panic in certain groups. It has also raised questions about why the focus is so traditional, given that men, though less likely to be severely affected, are equally implicated in spreading the disease.[59] Hepatitis B was discovered to be sexually transmitted in the 1970s, with a particularly high incidence among homosexual men, although it is also prevalent in certain specific occupational groups. It is currently incurable and can develop serious complications, although a vaccine is available.[60]

None of these diseases had the dramatic impact of HIV/AIDS, which, like herpes, first made itself felt via reports from the USA. Part of the impact was doubtless due to its being an apparently entirely new disease, sexually transmitted, with highly visible symptomatology, and lethal, as well as, in the initial reports, manifesting primarily in homosexual men, a population which had become a great deal more visible while remaining the focus of suspicion and phobia. It arose at a time when the historic STDs were considered no longer a problem, indeed almost forgotten. Nonetheless, responses were strongly inflected by traditional motifs. As in earlier panics, there were fears that infection perceived to be generated in a stigmatized group might explode into the wider population. There has been a great deal of almost instant historiography of the rise of HIV/AIDS and policy responses as well as the social impact of the disease.

A significant activist role was taken by gay men in several countries, although this tended to occlude the presence of other less visible and articulate victim populations. There was a good deal of controversy within the gay community over appropriate measures of prevention and control. As with herpes, it provided a site for the sometimes heated articulation of concerns over the consequences of sexual liberation and sexual practices within the gay subculture.[61] Peter Baldwin argues for the influence of specific historical national and regional responses to STDs upon the evolution of HIV/AIDS policies. He compares the harsh interventionism of the Swedish sanitary state to the British liberal consensual voluntarist tradition of provision of treatment and public education; whereas the Germans (except in Bavaria, which pursued a particular draconian regime) became obliged to reconsider the persisting legacy of Nazi public health legislation in formulating their response.[62] Mooij, however, suggests that HIV/AIDS brought about (at least within the Netherlands) some significant ruptures with historical tradition. There arose a different mode of classification of those infected, one based on the mode of infection: through sexual activity, through non-sexual blood contact (including intravenous drug use), or by perinatal transmission. Furthermore, the risk of infection was related to specific acts not necessarily associated with one particular group, and the model for the transmission of infection became, rather than spokes radiating from the hub of a wheel, or a chain, a diffuse network.[63] With the rise of effective treatments (though not cure), the problem has shifted from one of an acute disease moving through rapid deterioration to death, to managing a chronic condition.[64]

The discourse of 'safe sex' which arose as a result of the HIV/AIDS epidemic, but generalizable across the range of sexually transmitted threats to health in twenty-first-century Europe, required explicit discussions of actual sexual praxis. This introduced an entirely new note: instead of 'bad sex' being illicit sex which might also result in disease, and 'good sex' being licit sex between married couples, 'good sex' is reframed as sexual activity between any partners which minimizes the danger of adverse consequences and maximizes pleasure. There are still issues: 'safe sex' in respect of one threat may still not avail against another (for example, condoms do not protect against HPV), there is no one simple solution, no 'magic bullet'. STDs remain a site not just about issues of public health and disease control but constantly invoking wider questions about society, responsibility, morality, gender, sexuality and citizenship.

Notes

1 Annet Mooij, *Out of Otherness: Characters and Narrators in the Dutch Venereal Disease Debates 1850–1990*, Amsterdam: Rodopi, 1998, pp. 12–16.
2 J. D. Oriel, *The Scars of Venus: A History of Venereology*, London: Springer-Verlag, 1994, pp. 27–35.
3 Oriel, *Scars of Venus*, pp. 45–46.
4 Oriel, *Scars of Venus*, p. 59;
5 Oriel, *Scars of Venus*, pp.115–24.
6 Oriel, *Scars of Venus*, p. 103.
7 Kevin Brown, *The Pox: The Life and Near Death of a Very Social Disease*, Stroud: Sutton Publishing, 2006, p. 51.
8 T. J. Wyke, 'The Manchester and Salford Lock Hospital', *Medical History* 19, 1975, pp. 73–86; David Innes Williams, *The London Lock: A Charitable Hospital for Venereal Disease 1746–1952*, London: Royal Society of Medicine Press, 1995; Kevin P. Siena, *Venereal Disease, Hospitals, and the Urban Poor: London's 'foul wards,' 1600–1800*, Rochester, NY: University of Rochester Press, 2004.

9 Mooij, *Out of Otherness*, p. 137.

10 Claude Quétel, *History of Syphilis*, London: Polity Press, 1990; first published as *Le Mal de Naples: Histoire de la Syphilis*, Paris: Editions Seghers, 1986, p. 102.

11 K. Ballhatchett, *Race, Sex, and Class under the Raj: Imperial Attitudes and Policies and their Critics, 1793–1905*, London: Weidenfield and Nicolson, 1980, ch. 1, 'Lock Hospitals and Lal Bazaars', pp. 10–39.

12 Philippa Levine, *Prostitution, Race, and Politics: Policing Venereal Disease in the British Empire*, London: Routledge, 2003.

13 Lesley A. Hall, 'What shall we do with the poxy sailor? Venereal diseases in the British mercantile marine, 1850–1950', *Journal for Maritime Research* 6:1, 2004, pp. 113–44.

14 Alain Corbin, *Women for Hire: Prostitution and Sexuality in France after 1850*, Cambridge, MA: Harvard University Press, 1990; first published as *Les filles de noce: Misère sexuelle et prostitution aux 19e et 20e siècles*, Paris: Aubier Montagne, 1978, pp. 9–16.

15 Peter Baldwin, *Contagion and the State in Europe, 1830–1930*, Cambridge: Cambridge University Press, 1999, pp. 364–65.

16 Baldwin, *Contagion and the State*, p. 374.

17 Mooij, *Out of Otherness*, pp. 35–37.

18 Oriel, *Scars of Venus*, pp. 35–40; Quétel, *History of Syphilis*, pp. 109–11; Bertrand Taithe, 'The Rise and Fall of European Syphilisation: The Debates on Human Experimentation and Vaccination of Syphilis, *c.* 1845–70' in Franz Eder, Lesley A. Hall and Gert Hekma (eds), *Sexual Cultures in Europe: Themes in Sexuality*, Manchester: Manchester University Press, 1999, pp. 34–57.

19 Taithe, 'The Rise and Fall of European Syphilisation'; Quétel, *History of Syphilis*, pp. 112–14.

20 Quétel, *History of Syphilis*, pp. 114–18; Oriel, *Scars of Venus*, pp. 86–89.

21 Anna Lundberg, '"Passing the Black Judgement": Swedish social policy on venereal disease in the early twentieth century' in Roger Davidson and Lesley A. Hall (eds), *Sex, Sin and Suffering: Venereal Disease and European Society since 1870*, London: Routledge, 2001, pp. 29–43.

22 Baldwin, *Contagion and the State*, pp. 408–9.

23 *Report of the Committee Appointed to Enquire into the Pathology and Treatment of Venereal Disease, with the View to Diminish its Injurious Effects on the Men of the Army and Navy* Cd. 4031, London: HMSO, 1868, Minutes of Evidence, Q. 3898.

24 D. Dunsford, 'Principle versus expediency: a rejoinder to F. B. Smith', *Social History of Medicine* 5, 1992, pp. 503–13; P. McHugh, *Prostitution and Victorian Social Reform*, London: Croom Helm, 1980; Levine, *Prostitution, Race, and Politics*; Frank Mort, *Dangerous Sexualities: Medico-moral Politics in Britain since 1830*, London: Routledge and Kegan Paul, 1987, pp. 174–76; F. B. Smith, 'The Contagious Diseases Acts reconsidered', '"Unprincipled expediency": a comment on Deborah Dunsford's paper', *Social History of Medicine* 3, 1990, pp. 197–215, *Social History of Medicine* 5, 1992, pp. 515–16; Judith R. Walkowitz, *Prostitution and Victorian Society: Women, Class and the State*, Cambridge: Cambridge University Press, 1980.

25 Mooij, *Out of Otherness*, pp. 53–54.

26 Oriel, *Scars of Venus*, pp. 125–34; Michael Worboys, 'Unsexing gonorrhoea: bacteriologists, gynaecologists, and suffragists in Britain, 1860–1920', *Social History of Medicine* 17, 2004, pp. 41–59.

27 Gayle Davis, *The Cruel Madness of Love: Sex, Syphilis and Psychiatry in Scotland, 1880–1930*, Amsterdam: Rodopi, 2008.

28 Petra de Vries, '"The Shadow of Contagion": gender, syphilis and the regulation of prostitution in the Netherlands, 1870–1914' in Davidson and Hall, *Sex, Sin and Suffering*, pp. 44–60.

29 Mooij, *Out of Otherness*, pp. 61–67.

30 Lutz Sauterteig, '"The Fatherland is in Danger, Save the Fatherland!": venereal disease, sexuality and gender in Imperial and Weimar Germany' in Davidson and Hall, *Sex, Sin and Suffering*, pp. 76–92; Lesley A. Hall, 'Venereal Diseases and Society in Britain, from the Contagious Diseases Acts to the National Health Service' in Davidson and Hall, *Sex, Sin and Suffering*, pp. 120–36.

31 L. W. Harrison, 'Ehrlich *versus* syphilis, as it appeared to L. W. Harrison', *British Journal of Venereal Diseases* 30, 1954, pp. 2–6.

32 Mark Harrison, 'The British Army and the problem of venereal disease in France and Egypt during the First World War', *Medical History* 34, 1995, pp. 133–58.

33 Lundberg, '"Passing the Black Judgement"'.
34 Hall, 'Venereal Diseases and Society in Britain'.
35 Sauterteig, '"The Fatherland is in Danger"'.
36 Ramón Castejón-Bolea, 'Doctors, Social Medicine and VD in Late-Nineteenth and Early Twentieth-Century Spain' in Davidson and Hall, *Sex, Sin and Suffering*, pp. 61–75.
37 Bruno Wanrooij, '"The Thorns of Love": sexuality, syphilis and social control in modern Italy' in Davidson and Hall, *Sex, Sin and Suffering*, pp. 137–59.
38 Quétel, *History of Syphilis*, pp. 176–92.
39 Quétel, *History of Syphilis*, pp. 241–47.
40 Lundberg, '"Passing the Black Judgement"'.
41 Frances Bernstein, 'Visions of Sexual Health and Illness in Revolutionary Russia' in Davidson and Hall, *Sex, Sin and Suffering*, pp. 93–119.
42 Mooij, *Out of Otherness*, pp. 124–43.
43 Lesley A. Hall, '"The Reserved Occupation"? Prostitution in the Second World War', *Women's History Magazine* 41, June 2002, pp. 4–9.
44 Oriel, *The Scars of Venus*, pp 95–96.
45 Oriel, *The Scars of Venus*, pp. 146–47.
46 Roger Davidson, '"Searching for Mary, Glasgow": contact tracing for sexually transmitted diseases in twentieth-century Scotland', *Social History of Medicine* 9:2, 1996, pp. 195–214; Mooij, *Out of Otherness*, 'Promiscuous Girls', pp. 124–78.
47 Hall, 'What shall we do with the poxy sailor?'
48 Lesley A. Hall, '"War Always Brings It On": War, STDs, the military, and the civilian population in Britain, 1850–1950' in Roger Cooter, Mark Harrison and Steve Sturdy (eds), *Medicine and Modern Warfare, Clio Medica* 55, Amsterdam: Rodopi, 2000, pp. 205–33; Mooij, *Out of Otherness*, pp.154–64.
49 D. J. Campbell, 'Venereal diseases in the armed forces overseas (2)', *British Journal of Venereal Diseases* 22, 1946, pp. 149–68; F. A. E. Crew (ed.), *History of the Second World War: United Kingdom Medical Series: The Army Medical Services: Administration II*, London: HMSO, 1955, p. 238.
50 Mooij, *Out of Otherness*, pp. 143–53.
51 Michaela Freund, 'Women, venereal disease and the control of female sexuality in post-war Hamburg' in Davidson and Hall, *Sex, Sin and Suffering*, pp. 205–19.
52 Hall, 'Venereal Diseases and Society in Britain'; Lesley A. Hall, 'Birds, bees and general embarrassment: sex education in Britain, from social purity to Section 28' in Richard Aldrich (ed.), *Public or Private Education?: Lessons from History*, London: Woburn Press, 2004, pp. 98–115; David Evans, 'Sexually transmitted disease policy in the English National Health Service, 1948–2000: continuity and social change' in Davidson and Hall, *Sex, Sin and Suffering*, pp. 237–52.
53 Mooij, *Out of Otherness*, pp. 188–89; Evans, 'Sexually transmitted disease policy'; Oriel, *Scars of Venus*, pp. 155–65.
54 Mooij, *Out of Otherness*, pp. 180–88; Evans, 'Sexually transmitted disease policy'; Roger Davidson, *Dangerous Liaisons: A Social History of Venereal Disease in Twentieth-Century Scotland*, Amsterdam: Rodopi, 2000, pp 237–58.
55 Oriel, *The Scars of Venus*, pp. 161–65.
56 http://www.netdoctor.co.uk/diseases/facts/chlamydia.htm (accessed November 2010).
57 Oriel, *The Scars of Venus*, pp. 149–55.
58 Mooij, *Out of Otherness*, pp. 198–208.
59 Margaret P. Battin, Leslie P. Francis, Jay A. Jacobson and Charles B. Smith, *The Patient as Victim and Vector*, Oxford: Oxford University Press, 2009, pp. 248–79.
60 Mooij, *Out of Otherness*, p. 189.
61 Peter Baldwin, *Disease and Democracy: The Industrialized World Faces AIDS*, Berkeley, CA: University of California Press, 2005, pp. 165–201.
62 Baldwin, *Disease and Democracy*, pp. 227–43.
63 Mooij, *Out of Otherness*, pp. 220–47.
64 Srdan Matic, Jeffrey V. Lazarus and Martin C. Donoghoe (eds), *HIV/AIDS in Europe: Moving from Death Sentence to Chronic Disease Management*, Copenhagen, Denmark: World Health Organization, 2006.

Part XIV

BODIES, SEX AND RACE

27

WESTERN ENCOUNTERS WITH SEX AND BODIES IN NON-EUROPEAN CULTURES, 1500–1750

Jonathan Burton

Michel Foucault's landmark *History of Sexuality* (1976) has little to say about sexual acts and identities outside of Europe. In confining his study to Europe, Foucault sought to avoid universalizing gestures that might apply European categories of analysis to all cultures or measure non-European processes and progress along a timeline derived from European experience. Yet desire and sexuality rarely defer to geospatial partitions, and the period across which Foucault imagines a transformation in European sexual discourse coincides with the era often described as the 'age of expansion', when colonialism, diplomacy, piracy, and trade brought Europeans into increasing contact with non-European texts, goods, people and information. This is not merely a temporal coincidence. Rather, as Mark Johnson argues, European sexual identities were 'created and sustained by contrasts drawn with the practices of "Others" imagined to fall outside the norm's cultural and geographical parameters'.[1]

This chapter elaborates on how European encounters with non-European peoples informed early modern conceptions of sexuality. In doing so, it demonstrates how early modern notions of sexual difference often served racial regimes, while race frequently marked the limits of sexuality. Though they are frequently narrated separately, the history of sexuality is as indissoluble from the history of race as histories of early modern Europe are undetachable from world history. Thus I will consider here some of the limits of Foucault's *History of Sexuality* before attempting to illustrate how early modern conceptions of race and sexuality explain and even prop up his account. To do so, I will concentrate primarily on the ways in which European perceptions and understandings of western sexual customs and bodies altered as a result of experiences and observations of the practices and mores in other places, as well as how varied and changing ideas about race structured and affected European attitudes towards, and beliefs about, bodies and sexuality. In turning to Europe's encounters with non-European peoples, we join in a scholarly movement precipitated by the rise of postcolonial studies and particularly Dipesh Chakrabarty's call, in *Provincializing Europe* (2000), for an unsettling of the predominant 'first Europe, then elsewhere' style of historicism.[2] Thus, as recent historians of sexuality abandon an area studies model committed to national borders and consider instead the global histories of sexuality, we begin to deterritorialize traditions of sexuality and ultimately decentre fixed notions of belonging and difference. Sexual cultures, we shall see, were never unique to particular geographies or cultures but instead were produced along criss-crossing pathways, and woven in and out of various spaces and times.

Foucault did not omit the non-European world entirely from his history. In fact, *The History of Sexuality* makes use of the contrasting mode described by Johnson, figuring the non-European world as 'Other' to Europe's emerging sexual order. Thus, in a crucial passage of Volume 1 describing the 'two great procedures for producing the truth of sex', Foucault differentiates the *scientia sexualis* that developed in Europe from an earlier *ars erotica* that he locates in China, Japan, ancient Rome, and 'the Arabo-Moslem societies'.[3] Where a 'will to knowledge regarding sex … characterizes the [*scientia sexualis* of the] modern Occident',[4] the *ars erotica* is distinguished by an understanding of sexuality as:

> drawn from pleasure itself, understood as a practice and accumulated as experience; pleasure is not considered in relation to an absolute law of the permitted and the forbidden, nor by reference to a criterion of utility, but first and foremost in relation to itself; it is experienced as pleasure, evaluated in terms of its intensity.[5]

The first thing to notice here is how, in separating pleasure from knowledge, and art from science, Foucault creates overlapping dichotomies between East and West, and the pre-modern and the modern. The division of experience (body) and science (mind) apportions sensation to the non-European world and judiciousness to Europe. While he later allows that pleasure migrated into analysis and the *ars erotica* never disappeared entirely in the West, his history otherwise draws clear lines demarcating 'our civilization' (i.e. the scientific modernity of Europe) both from its own past and from a non-European world that, by implication, remains fixed on pleasure and culturally belated.[6] As I will discuss in greater depth later in this chapter, the idea of non-European stagnation would also be crucial to the development and hardening of racial categories, which reciprocally drew on and brought into being sexual categories.

Because they both depend on implied timelines and notions of progress or stagnancy, histories of race and sexuality are not only bound together but also bound up with ideas about modernity. In Foucault's account of modernity, the emergence of sexual identities is crucial. *The History of Sexuality* famously emphasizes the conceptual break that occurs when, under the *scientia sexualis*, the modern category 'homosexual' is distinguished from the pre-modern 'sodomite'. Whereas the 'sodomite' was the perpetrator of 'forbidden acts', the category 'homosexual' could be applied to anyone inclined to the illicit, even if that inclination resulted in no action.[7] In other words, where sodomy comprised acts performed by an otherwise undifferentiated individual, homosexuality was a psychological state possessed by a distinct type of person. Of course, Foucault is not describing a change in people, only a change that occurs – purportedly in the West – in the way people are described and understood. The European break with the *ars erotica* is achieved, Foucault avers, when a culture of confession is inscribed in scientific discourses, codifying the demand to speak about sex and rendering sexuality broadly causal, interpretable, and subject to intervention. Foucault does not contemplate a structurally equivalent break with the past or the institutional classification of sexual identities outside of Europe, and in the absence of such a history the cultures of the *ars erotica* are rendered static and unchanging.

A number of commentators have questioned the hard lines of Foucault's division. One line of questioning follows from David Halperin's suggestion in a chapter entitled

'Forgetting Foucault' that 'we need to find ways of asking how different historical cultures fashioned different sorts of links between sexual acts, on the one hand, and sexual tastes, styles, dispositions, characters, gender presentations, and forms of subjectivity, on the other'.[8] While several important studies in an early wave of response to Foucault sought to push back the emergence of modern sexual identities to earlier moments in European history – distinguishing, for example, between acts of 'sodomy' and the identity, 'sodomite' in sixteenth-century Europe – these efforts most often concentrate on single European cultures and consequently redound to European exceptionalism and by implication render the non-European world ever more stagnant.[9] Even Halperin's own vision of 'different historical cultures' is largely confined to Europe as evinced by his commitment to the notion that distinctly modern sexual identities were produced with the development of western scientific discourses such as medicine, psychiatry and forensics.[10]

More recent explorations of early modern sexual cultures outside of Europe knock off balance the Foucauldian division of eastern/premodern/*ars erotica* and western/modern/ *scientia sexualis* by suggesting that an instrumental discourse of sexuality also developed in non-western cultures. In the classical Chinese texts of *ars erotica*, for example, Richard Shusterman locates a deep concern with health issues that 'clearly trump[s]' any attention to pleasure.[11] If the attention here to medical matters and sexual science does not take precisely the same form as western texts, a structural analogy is undeniable and refutes any sharp contrast of *ars erotica* and *scientia sexualis*. In addition, the concern with health in Chinese *ars erotica* helps to make visible how variations within the *ars erotica* can be as dramatic as any contrast drawn between the *ars erotica* and *scientia sexualis*. Similarly, the classical Indian *ars erotica* served a variety of functions by linking sustained sexual attraction in marriage to a general social stability maintained through domestic harmony. 'The expressed goal of even the *Kama Sutra* itself', Shusterman points out, 'is not merely the satisfaction of erotic or more broadly sensual desire. It is rather to deploy and educate one's desires in order to cultivate and refine the mastery of one's senses so that one can emerge a more complete and effective person'.[12] If, per Foucault, the *scientia sexualis* is a cultural discourse implicated in the 'games of power' played by competing discourses, then both the Chinese and Indian cases clearly challenge western exceptionalism as they use discursive tools to channel desire into cultural ideals such as family and heterosexual propriety.[13]

A second line of questioning concerns the Foucauldian dichotomy between acts and identities which, scholars point out, is difficult to sustain in light of performative notions of identity.[14] As Dina Al-Kassim observes, it makes little sense 'to suppose that economies of sodomy are free of identity or that they are not dominated by the specter of identity'.[15] Yet what is achieved through this false dichotomy is an overlapping partition of East and West that links the premodern to the eastern in opposition to and 'guarantee[ing] the [European] modernity of the modern'.[16] Al-Kassim's epilogue to the recent collection *Islamicate Sexualities* (2008) joins several earlier chapters in unsettling the East/West divide by showing that 'in the East the policing of the state's citizenry proceeded via the institution of heterosexual norms'.[17] In particular, Kathryn Babayan's chapter on female companionship in Safavi Iran demonstrates that concerns with the threats posed to heterosexual marriage by celibacy and boy gazing motivated a project of sexual regulation in sixteenth-century Safavi society.

The vexed question of acts and identities is more easily discerned when we consider an episode from Leo Africanus' 1526 *Geographical Historie of Africa*. After announcing that the people of Morocco are 'so notoriously addicted' to the 'horrible vice of sodomy' that 'they could scarce see any young stripling who escaped their lust', Africanus goes on to detail for his European readers the lifestyle of Fezzan innkeepers:

> The innkeepers of Fez ... go apparaled like women, and shave their beards, and are so delighted to imitate women, that they will not only counterfeit their speech, but will sometimes also sit down and spin. Each one of these hath his concubine, whom he accompanieth as if she were his own lawful wife; albeit the said concubines are not only ill-favoured in countenance, but notorious for their bad life and behavior ... . The innkeepers have a consul over them, and they pay tribute unto the governor of the city. And when the king hath occasion to send forth an army, then they, as being most meet for the purpose, are constrained largely to victual the camp ... . The very company of these innkeepers is so odious and detestable in the sight of all honest men, all learned men, and merchants, that they will in no wise vouchsafe to speak unto them. And they are firmly enjoined not to enter into the temple, the bourse, nor into any bath. Neither yet are they permitted to resort unto those inns which are next unto the great temple, and wherein merchants are usually entertained. All men in a manner are in utter detestation of these wretches, but because the king hath some use of them ... they are borne withal, whether the citizens will or no.[18]

I have quoted here from John Pory's 1600 English translation, but as Ian Smith points out, Pory's translation of his French source 'superimposes the rhetoric of the "heterosexual" couple', obscuring the fact that each innkeeper has a male concubine – *un concubin*, not *une concubine*.[19] In this, the French edition is faithful to Ramusio's first print edition of the *Geographical Historie* which uses the masculine term *concubino* (not the feminine *concubina*). Africanus' manuscript never uses the term 'concubine'; however, it explicitly describes the innkeepers taking another man as a husband (*tene uno homo al modo del Marito*).[20] For Guy Poirier, the innkeepers' cohabitation with male partners 'reveals the existence of a true homosexual subculture'.[21] Poirier's assertion is more convincing when we consider the response to the innkeepers' 'sodomitical' acts – their transvestism, shaving, and performance of women's work: not only are they shunned by many and forbidden from certain locations, they are also formally recognized by governing bodies that confer on them a categorical identity in placing them under the authority of a particular official and tax structure, and especially in enlisting their unique service in military operations. In other words, the line between acts and identities blurs when the innkeepers and their concubines are acknowledged as a distinct community and hence instrumentalized. For Foucault asserts that one of the distinguishing marks of the *scientia sexualis* is its use of sexuality as a 'dense transfer point for relations of power' including those between 'an administration and a population'.[22] Examples like this suggest that sexual identities were neither exclusive to the early modern West nor the product of a certain (i.e. western) 'modernity'. They reveal that divisions of the West and the Rest, as well as notions of modernity, often depend upon elision, mistranslation, or applications of culturally specific categories of analysis. Furthermore, certain examples raise the possibility that, rather than emerging in Europe and only later being exported to the rest of the world, European notions of sexual identity may have also formed through encounters with non-European cultures and then filtered back into the urban centres of Europe. Certainly William Biddulph acknowledged the possibility of European emulation when he complained in 1609 of the illicit acts of European Catholics in Turkey, 'these are the virtues which many Christians learn by sojourning long in heathen countries'.[23]

The case of the New World berdache goes a great way towards scuttling ideas of a European vanguard of sexual identities. 'Berdache' was a term used to describe Indian men across the Americas who dressed and behaved as if they were women. The precise sexual praxis of the berdaches remains subject to some debate; however, most European commentators surmised from their effeminacy that the berdaches were sexually passive sodomites. In the earliest European encounters with indigenous Americans, the berdaches were taken as representative of entire indigenous cultures. In most cases, this kind of stereotyping was used to justify military conquest or worse: when the Milanese Girolamo Benzoni documented his travels in the New World between 1541 and 1556, he cited Columbus' justification of the enslavement of native peoples where the second reason listed is that the Indians are 'pathics' (the passive partner in homosexual anal intercourse) who 'wear no beard'.[24] Earlier still, Hernán Cortés claimed in 1519 that the natives of Mexico 'all are sodomites and engage in this abominable sin'.[25] Yet stories about ubiquitous sodomy were swiftly challenged by accounts that recognized the berdaches as a distinct and distinctly recognized subculture. Just seven years after Cortés' letter, Fernandez de Oviedo described somewhat more precisely how:

> Indians who are lords and chieftains and who sin [against nature] keep young men [*tienen mozos*] publicly with them whom they consort in this infamous sin. And once they fall into this guilt [of sodomy], these passive *mozos* then put on skirts like women … , and the other things that women wear. And they do not bear arms, nor do they do anything that men do. Rather, they involve themselves in common household services, like sweeping and mopping and other customary tasks of women … . In the language of Cueva, these passives are called *camayoa*. So when among them one Indian wants to insult another or vituperatively to deride him as effeminate and mean, he is called *camayoa*.[26]

If, in Europe, public acknowledgement of sodomy was extremely rare outside of legal trials, the American berdache comprised a clearly defined minority in his culture. In other words, the berdache, or in Oviedo's case the *camayoa*, was a recognized identity, not a set of acts to which anyone might be inclined. For this reason, Rudi C. Bleys suggests that we need to take seriously the possibility that narratives of non-western sodomy 'facilitated the institution of a discourse about same sex-praxis' in European urban centres, where sexual subcultures were beginning to emerge.[27] In other words, the turn to a non-European archive of sexual histories unsettles the Foucauldian timeline and more generally the 'first Europe, then elsewhere' style of historicism.

We should not, however, draw from this example a linear relationship between sexual cultures observed outside of Europe and those emerging in Europe, with the latter simply following the former. Relationships between sexual cultures are double-jointed, with each utilizing, transforming or expanding the scope of the other. Moreover, as contact between different groups proliferated in new and unexpected ways, so too did unregulated sexuality across nations, peoples and groups, as well as unsanctioned forms of sexuality within groups. The frequency of conversion, or 'going native', and of cross-cultural desire makes it still more difficult to draw any simple lines between European and non-European sexualities. Moreover, there are important distinctions that can be made between European cultures, which frequently condemned one another for sexual excesses.[28] Yet, there are undeniably ways in which European perceptions of other cultures shaped European thought about bodies and sex. Most apparent across the landscape of early modern European writings is a pattern of external condemnation and internal disavowal, a 'readiness, even eagerness, to recognize homosexuality in an alien context ... in marked contrast to its reluctance to do so within'.[29] 'Aberrant' sexualities – intemperance, hermaphroditism, lesbianism, and 'sodomy' in its various forms - are attributed to people across the globe, and Europe is defined by contrast as the locus of temperance, heterosexuality, religiously sanctioned monogamy, and reproductive imperatives. Not only does this discourage the recognition and emergence of non-normative sexualities in the West, it also bolsters the idea of foreign cultures fixed on pleasure, and ripe for sexual exploration, idiosyncrasy and profligacy.

Imagining non-European sexualities as different also meant imagining non-European bodies as different. According to Thomas Laqueur, prior to the seventeenth century male and female bodies were not seen as distinct. Instead, they were 'arrayed according to their degree of metaphysical perfection, their vital heat, along an axis whose telos was male'.[30] Under this model there were frequent accounts of European men said to lactate and pictures of a boy Jesus with breasts. Girls were imagined to be able to turn into boys with the heat of exertion, and men who associated too much with women were said to be at risk of regressing into femininity. Yet over the course of the early modern period these stories were increasingly shifted to non-European subjects, operating as a matrix for European discernment of foreign bodies. Consequently, as European bodies were progressively seen as normative, non-European bodies were systematically imagined as intemperate and unstable. And as the one-sex model was shifted to the non-European world, a new model of biological divergence began to develop in the service of European patriarchy. That is, differential treatment of men and women might be justified on the basis of their divergent physiologies.

A number of scholars have recognized that histories of European bodies and sexuality will always be incomplete when they ignore the broader world in which Europeans travelled, settled, did business, and brokered alliances. In the same year that Bleys published his study of European ethnographic accounts of male-to-male sexual behaviour, Anne Laura Stoler made a related argument in *Race and the Education of Desire*, her rereading of Foucault's *History of Sexuality*. Stoler begins from two contentions, pushing both the temporal and geospatial boundaries of European sexual identity formation: first, she argues that 'Europe's eighteenth- and nineteenth-century discourses on sexuality ... cannot be charted in Europe alone' and must instead 'be traced along a more *circuitous imperial* route'; and second, 'imperial discourses on sexuality have not been restricted to bourgeois culture in the colonies alone', but significantly impacted metropolitan sexualities.[31] While acknowledging the legacy of pre-Enlightenment encounters, Bleys and Stoler both argue for eighteenth-century empire and travel as crucially formative for nineteenth-century identity formations, both at the core of empire and in the peripheries. Not only is the *scientia sexualis* seen to be 'embedded deeply in the intellectual innovations of the eighteenth century',[32] it is also fundamentally shaped 'in the production of historical Others, in the broader force field of empire where technologies of sex, self, and power were defined as European and Western as they were refracted and remade'.[33]

Stoler and Bleys each draw on the work of George Mosse, emphasizing the importance of notions of degeneracy for establishing bourgeois civility in eighteenth-century Europe.[34]

Yet the two part ways significantly in their differing considerations of the relationships between degeneracy, race and sexuality. For Bleys, eighteenth-century travel reports and ethnographies corroborated constructions of 'sodomite' identity, and ultimately propped up claims about the degeneracy of non-western peoples. Although degeneracy has been a critical trope in constructions of racial difference dating at least as far back as Jean Bodin's 1566 *Method for the Easy Comprehension of History*, Bleys restricts his use of the term to describe only the way in which European discourse located cultures along a single timeline of progress and civility so that sodomites and pederasts could be imagined as present only in the most 'culturally stagnant' societies.[35] Here we can see again how ideas about sexuality and modernity are bound together. Yet after noting the ways in which tropes of degeneracy could be shifted from one cultural site to another long before the Enlightenment, Bleys stops distinctly short of identifying race as a crucial component in European sexual identities:

> The generalizing constructions of an Oriental sexual morality, regardless of religious creed, social circumstance or cultural context, may lead us to believe that here were laid the germs of a racialist theory of human sexuality. Yet the Europeans' ever recurrent ascription of sodomy to almost all people of the New Worlds calls for skepticism towards such an interpretation of the evidence. How important was the weight of race identity, when sodomy was common currency among Muslims, Indian Americans, and Asians at once?[36]

Like many scholars of the history of race, Bleys is reluctant to recognize 'race' in the early modern world.[37] For her part, Stoler argues that racial classification may not have been scientifically 'legitimated' until the nineteenth century, but that a 'prior technology of sexuality' prepared the way for racisms.[38] Consequently, she urges us to see 'bourgeois sexuality and racialized sexuality not as distinct kinds … but as dependent constructs in a unified field'.[39]

Before pursuing the idea of race and sexuality as dependent constructs, it is first necessary to address Bleys' reluctance to use the term 'race' and Stoler's suggestion that, prior to the nineteenth century, 'race' lacked scientific legitimacy. Bleys and Stoler tend to follow the numerous theorists and historians of race who invoke premodern times only as a foil for later, more 'racialized' periods. This difference is also asserted by many early modernists, who argue that it is anachronistic to study race in the early modern period because then the term connoted family, class or lineage rather than the classifications of modern imperial times, and also because the defining features of later racial ideologies – the quasi-biological notion that physical traits denoted distinct types of human beings with distinct moral and social features – had not yet come into being. The particular reasons for Bleys' scepticism are never fully elaborated, though his implication that race might be disconnected from religious and cultural contexts betrays a common assumption about the relative forces of 'cultural' and 'scientific' forms of difference. The sense that 'scientific' have been somehow more pernicious than 'cultural' forms of difference also informs Stoler's notion of 'legitimated' racial classifications. Yet if earlier vocabularies of race seem less biological than post-Enlightenment ones, it is partly because a full-fledged discourse of biology or genetic transmission had not developed in the earlier period, and not because 'cultural difference' is a necessarily benign idea. Racial thought does not arise out of disciplines such as biology and anthropology, but rather in various disciplinary formations and ways of ordering knowledge, which are themselves shaped by the histories of cross-cultural encounters. Rather than imagining that nothing could legitimate racial classifications with the force of science, it makes more sense to consider what modes of discourse exercised analogous power in the early modern period.[40]

To question the bifurcation of 'culture' and 'science' is necessarily to emphasize the place of religion, gender, class and sexuality as central to the formation and workings of racial ideologies. This is not the place for a full-scale examination of the broad spectrum of discourses and practices of difference marshalled by early modern racial vocabularies.[41] However, the mingling of discourses that I am describing may be recognized in the ways that early modern concerns with interracial sexuality and mixed-race children drew together and mystified religious and somatic vocabularies, especially in circumstances with the potential for cultural mixture. If, in the late medieval and early modern periods, race and sexuality were not yet linked through common scientific terms or protocols, they were no less significantly bonded through religious discourse. Thus on the 1628 occasion of an English renegade's 'Return from Argier', Edward Kellet preached a sermon denouncing Jewish converts to Christianity as 'these Christian-Jews or Jewish Christians [who] would join Moses and Christ, forgetting the substance of the precepts given unto them. ... Thou shalt not let thy cattle gender with diverse kind, thou shalt not sow thy field with a mingled seed.'[42] Pronounced in a sermon most concerned with Christian conversions to Islam, Kellet's fear of a mingling of Jewish and Christian 'seed' anticipates later laws against inter-group sex by suggesting that the two were physically incompatible. Of course, learned writers including Jean Bodin and George Abbot had roundly dismissed the notion, introduced by Herodotus, that men of certain cultures produce 'seed', or semen, manifestly different from others. But Kellet's undeterred application of Leviticus 19 points not only towards the relative authority of scripture versus scientific empiricism, but also to the critical role played by religion in ushering in quasi-biological notions of difference, as well as the importance of sexuality in policing the borders of race.

In unseating western science from its position as the unique determinant of modern racial discourses, we also begin to expose the European bias in histories of sexuality that divide East from West. When histories of race exclude the sixteenth and seventeenth centuries from extended consideration and begin their analyses from the eighteenth century or later, they sustain the historical backdrop against which a division of eastern *ars erotica* from western *scientia sexualis* appears to make sense. That is, historical narratives in which pre-scientific technologies of classification are deemed less potent associate western science with modernity while corroborating the notion that there is a single modernity towards which all cultures progress at uneven rates. Ironically, this notion of modernity is not only culturally specific, it is built on the very ideas of progress and civility undergirding early modern racial discourses. This is not to say that racial discourses precede and determine sexual discourses. Rather, the European incarnation of the *scientia sexualis* develops in tandem and mutual service with a consolidation of European forms of racism. More specifically, the linking together of cultural stagnation and sexual degeneracy works symbiotically with contemporaneous modes of racial classification that themselves achieve 'legitimacy' by 'drawing on an earlier racial lexicon, on that of the struggle of the races', whereby races are located along a timeline of civility/normativity.[43] Put in simpler terms, if sexual 'degeneracy' was a marker of cultural stagnation, it could also be used to assert the 'backwardness' of a race of people. And in turn, that backwardness could reciprocally suggest the 'degeneracy' of a race.

Early modern constructions of difference often begin from or work to defend the idea of a single timeline along which cultures may progress or degenerate. Take, for example, the striking juxtaposition of images in Theodore de Bry's widely disseminated *A briefe and true report of the land of Virginia* (1590) of ancient Picts, their bodies dyed red with woad, with the painted bodies of Virginia natives. The comparison of Native Americans and ancient Britons validated colonization by suggesting that a more civilized (i.e. European) culture might help Native Americans move towards civility as they once had. William Strachey further justified European settlement in the New World by pointing out that Roman colonization endowed hitherto barbarous Britons with the 'powerful discourse of divine reason (which makes us only men, and distinguisheth us from beasts … .)'.[44] While Strachey's notion of progressive civility might suggest that the Native Americans could 'catch up' with European colonizers, this was rarely if ever acknowledged to happen. Thus while Michel de Montaigne's description of 'naked' Brazilians so 'near their original naturality … [t]he laws of nature do yet command them', might appear to praise untainted indigenous virtue, the same tropes were easily yoked to the language of degeneracy.[45] The Spanish theologian Francisco de Vitoria went so far as to suggest that an alleged inability to progress cast doubt on the very humanity of the Indians: 'It would seem that for these barbarians the same applies as to the feebleminded, for they cannot govern themselves better than simpleminded idiots. They are not even better than beasts and wild animals.'[46] Once the stagnation of a culture was established it was logical to cite the practices and mores of that place as expressions of degeneracy. From there could proceed a cycle of mutual recursion where sexual practices might attest to racial degeneracy, which in turn would verify sexual aberrance, which then further substantiated racial degeneracy, and so on. Thus, in 1599 George Abbot can turn swiftly from describing the peoples of the New World as 'simple' to charging them with a litany of sins including 'sodomie, incest, and all kind of adulterie'.[47] And John Bulwer's description of hermaphrodites in Florida and Virginia can, in turn, reinforce racial hierarchies in suggesting that when 'there is such corruption of life and manners, and so great lust … it is no wonder if men altogether degenerate into beasts'.[48]

The real potency of cultural ideas of difference (such as the notion of degeneracy) lies not only in their utility for enforcing domination, but also in their exceptional transferability. This was particularly important in the face of the powerful and sophisticated cultures of China, India, and the Ottoman Empire, where Europeans found themselves increasingly accused of backwardness and simplicity. Thus while Europeans connected simplicity to sexual aberrance in the New World, precisely the opposite could happen in Asia and the Near East where Europeans condemned urbane cultures as dissolute. For example, the same George Abbot who I just quoted on the simplicity of Native Americans acknowledges in the same text the Chinese assertion that 'all other nations do see but with one eye, but they themselves [the Chinese] have two'.[49] In 1616, Sir Thomas Roe recognized that the gifts he presented to the Mughal Emperor Jahangir were deemed cheap and so 'extremely despised … that they laugh at us for such as wee bring'.[50] By 1636 Henry Blount was ready to confess that 'the Turkes … are the only moderne people … [and] he who would behold these times in their greatest glory, could not finde a better scene then Turky'.[51] Yet in a number of texts like these, the very qualities that elevated Europeans over Native Americans might be cited in condemnation of non-European cultures. Thus, the English writer William Harrison willingly concedes that many non-European cultures 'in pregnancy of wit, nimbleness of limbs, and politic inventions … generally exceed us' but immediately counters, 'these gifts of theirs do often degenerate into mere subtlety, instability, unfaithfulness, and cruelty'.[52] Just as the degeneracy of Native Americans was confirmed with evidence of their perversions, it was lasciviousness, polygamy, and various forms of sodomy that most often marked eastern degeneracy. Thus we find a great proliferation of texts on the 'Old Worlds' of the East featuring sodomites, tribades (women who used their enlarged clitoris to pleasure other women), and especially harems complete with willing women, eunuchs, and lust-consumed potentates. The Scottish traveller William Lithgow is fairly representative of European observers when he describes the Turks as 'extremely inclined to all sorts of lascivious luxury, and generally addicted, besides all their sensual and incestuous lusts, unto sodomy, which they account as a dainty to digest all their other libidinous pleasures'.[53] Descriptions of dissolute Ottoman sultans offered particular hope for the decline of Europe's most proximate threat by suggesting the Empire might collapse from sexual corruption. Riches and power were imagined as transforming the militaristic Turkish prince into a feminized palace idler. Richard Knolles assured the readers of his monumental *The Generall Historie of the Turkes* (1603) by describing the soldiers in Constantinople, 'a city abounding with all manner of pleasure ... become much more effeminate and slothful' and 'their late voluptuous and effeminate emperours corrupted with the pleasures of Constantinople' and 'far degenerating from their warlike progenitors'.[54] In short, where simplicity was alleged to draw Native Americans to sexual degeneracy, it was instead the sophistication and power of eastern cultures that supposedly led them to degenerate.[55]

Virtually every early modern traveller to Africa, Asia and America, and every commentator on Jews and Muslims, as well as the Irish, has something to say about their sexual habits. Such observations are woven in a variety of increasingly racialized ways into the fabric of human difference. As European encounters with the non-European world widened, older tropes about particular places were reiterated and recirculated, to new and diverse effects. Thus Leo Africanus draws on Herodotus' suggestion that in Egypt effeminized men keep house and do 'women's work' such as spinning not only in his account of Egypt but also in his description, quoted above, of the innkeepers of Fez. The idea of men 'addicted' to sodomy appears in descriptions of Brazilians, Chinese, Moroccans, Persians, Turks and Pacific Islanders. Similarly, the shared terms and tropes describing feminized men around the world – such as the Egyptian, Jewish and Brazilian men that John Bulwer describes 'endowed with large breasts, swelling with milk, which are sufficient for the suckling and nursing up of infants' – attest to the ways in which aspects of difference were drawn from one location or people and conceptually assimilated to others in ways that conferred value or contempt, and in turn facilitated political practice.[56] The nearly ubiquitous idea of men variously feminized or 'addicted' to sodomy is matched by the notion of lustful non-European women – from the women of Fez and Turkey alleged to have sex with one another, to the Guinean, Jewish, and Native American said to desire white men. Alone, the idea of intemperate non-European women was used in policing the desires of European women, while paired with notions of feminized non-European men it could justify the heterosexual aggressions of European men in non-European settings.[57]

Lust and intemperance are also frequently attributed to African men, though sodomy is notably less prominent in European writings on Africa. This may have to do with the fact that, as Africans were enslaved in greater numbers, it was in the interest of Europeans to see them as a self-replenishing commodity. As Mary Floyd Wilson demonstrates, classical works depict Africans as no more wanton than northerners. Only with the growth of the

African slave trade were traits like hypersexuality *consistently* linked to black skin. Yet because this was in direct contradiction to the logic of classical humouralism, writers like Jean Bodin and Giovanni Botero took it upon themselves to reassign the meaning of humoural complexions.[58] At the same time, we find an increasing number of European texts, like Pieter de Marees' *A description and historicall declaration of the golden Kingdome of Guinea* (1604), attesting to African men's 'great privy members'.[59] Of course, reports of black men's oversized penises go back as far as the Greek historian Ctesias Indica's fifth-century BCE account of black, Indian pygmies. But the idea takes on new meaning in the context of slavery when John Bulwer observed that 'genital parts put a difference between nation and nation'.[60] Thus, in explaining the outsized penises of Mandingo men, Richard Jobson's *The Golden Trade* (1623) turns to the tale of Noah's curse: the Mandingo, he writes, are of 'the race of Canaan, the son of Ham' and are 'furnished with such members as are after a sort burdensome unto them' because Ham gazed upon his father's genitalia.[61] Whereas older versions of this story linked Ham's curse to both blackness and servitude, African slavery encouraged a connection of Noah's curse with African hypersexuality and fecundity.

Early modern writers drew on and adapted a number of ideas concerning sexuality that gained strength and authority with each new iteration. The early modern tendency to locate sodomy in cultural difference, for example, can be dated as far back as Herodotus' treatment of the Egyptians in his *History*. Yet stories such as those about Egyptian bestiality were also adapted and transformed with shifting racial discourses. Herodotus, writing at least two centuries before the circulation of the Old Testament, never uses the term 'sodomy'. Yet the adoption of this term gives a religious valence to medieval tales of human copulation with animals (and 'devils') in the non-Christian worlds of India and Africa. When *The Voyages de Jehan de Mandevelle Chevalier* (c. 1366) discusses hybrid unions in the East, the author draws on Christian discourse, suggesting that Ham's female progeny copulate with 'the fiends of hell' to produce 'many other diverse shape against kind'. Several centuries later, Jean Bodin drew instead on humoural discourse in attributing the 'promiscuous coition of men and animals' in Africa to the fact that southerners, as a result of their cool, dry complexions (dominated by black bile), 'are seized by frenzy more easily than northerners' and 'g[i]ve themselves over to horrible excesses'.[62] Bodin's contemporary, the Spanish physician Juan Huarte, anticipates later debates meant to determine whether whites and blacks were of the same species in citing instances of apes and other animals having sex with women to argue (reviving Herodotus) for the divergent strength of various species' 'seed'. We can see in this nonlinear sequence how, as a consequence of European encounters with non-European peoples, earlier theories about human 'seed' and tales of hybrid unions could ultimately become the basis of pseudo-scientific discourse about human types.

We need to be cautious not to mistake this as a clear and linear progression from cultural forms of difference into scientific racism. Throughout history, mechanisms for assigning different values to human beings arise and mutate, go dormant, resurface, relocate, and adapt anew. No single idea about race dominated early modern European thinking. Certainly identities were claimed, adjusted, disavowed, and imposed on the basis of skin colour, but early modern forms of racial difference also existed in relation to questions of religion, diet, nationality, lineage, human nature, the human body, and of course sexuality. Thus, just five years after Huarte's *The Examination of Men's Wits* was translated into English, George Abbot's *A briefe description of the whole worlde* (1599) returned to climatic theories of difference in speculating that Africa 'being very hot, and full of wildernesses, which have in them little water ... contrary kinds have conjunction the one with the other so that there ariseth a new kind of species'.[63] Likewise John Bulwer returns to religious discourse in 1650 in suggesting the Guinea drill baboon he witnessed near Charing Cross 'proceeded from the wicked copulation of man and beast, the devil cooperating'. It is crucial here to note that Bulwer is writing more than 40 years after the publication of Edward Topsell's *The History of Four-Footed Beasts and Snakes* (1607). Topsell too described apes 'so venerous that [they] will attempt to ravish women'.[64] Yet his earlier discussion actually anticipates nineteenth-century comparative anatomy and racial craniometry as he encourages the comparison of apes and black people in sexual terms by suggesting that 'men that have low and flat nostrils are libidinous as apes that attempt women'.[65] By 1634, this connection was made explicit by Thomas Herbert, who had no doubt that Africans 'have no better predecessors than monkeys'.[66] If, by the end of the century, Edward Tyson could identify the 'Orang-outan' as a creature between man and beast, reproducing illustrations from Topsell and underscoring the connections of early modern writings with a later, quasi-biological discourse about race, it was not because this was the only and inevitable discourse of racial difference. It was merely the one that seemed most credible and thus most forcefully addressed arguments for the abolition of slavery and increasing concerns with interracial sex.

Shifting theories of racial difference put pressure on ideas about interracial sex, and concerns with interracial sex in turn shaped theories of racial difference. As cross-cultural contact increased over the course of the early modern period, observers from Pietro Martire d'Anghiera to Thomas Browne remarked on the fact that men at the same latitude in South America and Africa had different skin colours and hair types, invalidating the climatic theory of difference that had been used to distinguish groups since Ptolemy's *Tetrabiblos*. At the same time, Hippocratic humoural theory, emphasizing the environmental determination of types, was revived by authors like Bodin, but it too became increasingly difficult to sustain as Europeans settled in non-European outposts and Africans and Native Americans were brought back to Europe without experiencing perceptible changes. The unsettling of these two theories of difference weakened more than discursive barriers. Early modern writers remarked increasingly on their rivals and peers entering into carnal relations with non-Europeans: Jean Bodin and Jan Huighen Van Linschoten each detail Portuguese relations with Indian women, while Pieter de Marees condemns Portuguese affairs with African women; William Biddulph and William Lithgow express disapproval of the liaisons between European men and Muslim women; George Best reports the marriage of an English woman to an 'an Ethiopian as black as a coal'; and numerous English and Spanish texts report on Spanish relations with Africans and Native Americans.[67] That these reports appear concurrently with the litany of accusations of non-European excess and sodomy suggests that Europeans turned to cultural forms of difference such as sexuality to restore the divisions once sustained by 'scientific' systems such as climatic theory and humouralism.[68]

Of course this is not the end of the story. The rise, or more accurately reanimation and reorientation, of scientific racism is one of the best-mined veins of cultural history. For the sake of this chapter, I have only had the space to point out that much of the 'science' behind eighteenth- and nineteenth-century racial discourse was rooted in earlier forms of cultural difference. In addition, 'scientific racism' shared with its predecessors an overpowering concern with and compulsion to address perceived sexual threats that could defile Europe's women or bring about the degeneracy of its men. Figuring non-European peoples as biologically distinct, or even subhuman, was simply the latest way of discouraging interracial sex; it was no less harmful or effective than it had been, in another context, to paint them as irreligious. Continually adjusting to cultural shifts, race is always an amalgam of unstable and evolving ideas. Thus we cannot trace a discrete line of development to which ideas of sexuality may have contributed or responded. Yet what this chapter should make clear is that the histories of race and sexuality cannot be told separately any more than the history of early modern Europe can be told apart from the history of the early modern world.

What this means for future scholarship on bodies, race, and sex is that restricting our gaze to Europe – as Foucault attempted to do – can provide no safeguard against universalizing histories, nor can it even supply a thorough vision of European sexualities. Disciplinary boundaries that have effectively partitioned European and non-European histories must be crossed, and scholars of English, French, Spanish or Italian cultures will need to turn to non-European archives or partner with colleagues in adjacent, non-European fields. The vanguard of identity studies lies in a sort of interdisciplinarity that, unfortunately, most academic institutions have not yet fostered. Thus, the challenge before us involves not only expanding our vision to include new places and sources, but also to turn our attention to the sites from which we survey the field, considering how our institutional settings encourage and sustain a kind of tunnel vision.

Notes

1 Mark Johnson, 'Sexuality' in David Atkinson, David Sibley, Peter Jackson and Neil Washbourne (eds), *Cultural Geography: a Critical Dictionary of Key Concepts*, New York: I. B. Tauris, 2005, p. 124.
2 Dipesh Chakrabarty, *Provincializing Europe: Postcolonial Thought and Historical Difference*, Princeton: Princeton University Press, 2000, p. 7.
3 Michel Foucault, *The History of Sexuality: An Introduction*, vol. 1, New York: Vintage Books, 1990 [1976], p. 57.
4 Foucault, *The History of Sexuality*, p. 65.
5 Foucault, *The History of Sexuality*, p. 57.
6 Foucault, *The History of Sexuality*, p. 58.
7 Foucault, *The History of Sexuality*, p. 43.
8 David M. Halperin, *How to do the History of Homosexuality*, Chicago: University of Chicago Press, 2004, pp. 43–44.
9 Halperin, *How to do the History*, pp. 30, 58. The literature on sexual identities in early modern Europe is too vast to sum up here. However, those interested in the question of acts and identities might begin with Kenneth Borris and George S. Rousseau (eds), *The Sciences of Homosexuality in Early Modern Europe*, New York: Routledge, 2007; Alan Bray, *Homosexuality in Renaissance England*, New York: Columbia University Press, 1995; Joseph Cady, '"Masculine love", Renaissance writing, and the "new invention" of homosexuality', *Journal of Homosexuality* 23, 1992, pp. 9–40; Martin Bauml Duberman, Martha Vicinus and George Chauncey Jr. (eds), *Hidden from History: Reclaiming the Gay and Lesbian Past*, New York: Meridian, 1989; Kent Gerard and Gert Hekma (eds), *The Pursuit of Sodomy: Male Homosexuality in Renaissance and Enlightenment Europe*, New York: Routledge, 1989; and Valerie Traub, *The Renaissance of Lesbianism in Early Modern England*, New York: Cambridge University Press, 2002. Amy Richlin argues for pushing the emergence of sexual identities as far back in European history as late imperial Rome in 'Not before Homosexuality: The Materiality of the *Cinaedus* and the Roman Law against Love between Men', *Journal of the History of Sexuality* 3:4, 1993, pp. 523–73.
10 For analogous arguments about the development of race, see note 35 below.
11 Richard Shusterman, 'Asian *Ars Erotica* and the Question of Sexual Aesthetics', *Journal of Aesthetics & Art Criticism* 65:1, January 2007, pp. 55–68 (60).
12 Shusterman, 'Asian *Ars Erotica*', p. 62.

13 Robert A. Nye, 'Sexuality' in Teresa A. Meade and Merry E. Wiesner-Hanks (eds), *A Companion to Gender History*, Malden, MA: Blackwell, 2004, p. 13.

14 Even if, as Halperin cautions, it has been misreading disciples of Foucault, rather than Foucault himself, who have converted the dichotomy of acts and identities from 'a heuristic analytical distinction into an ill-founded historical dogma' (p. 44), the distinction pervades histories of sexuality.

15 Dina Al-Kassim, 'Epilogue: Sexual Epistemologies, East in West' in Kathryn Babayan and Afsaneh Najmabadi (eds), *Islamicate Sexualities: Translations across Temporal Geographies of Desire*, Cambridge, MA: Harvard University Press, 2008, p. 309. Al-Kassim adds here that the migration of the pleasures of the *ars erotica* into the analysis of the *scientia sexualis* amounts to a 'haunting excess that escapes the control of erotic technique and state regulation [and thereby] complicates efforts to distinguish premodern from modern sexualities'.

16 Al-Kassim, 'Epilogue', p. 300.

17 Al-Kassim, 'Epilogue', p. 307.

18 J. L. Africanus, A *Geographical Historie of Africa*, London: Eliot's Court Press, 1600, Vol. III, p. 130.

19 Ian Smith, 'The Queer Moor: Bodies, Borders, and Barbary Inns' in Jyotsna Singh (ed.), *Companion to the Global Renaissance: English Literature and Culture in the Era of Expansion*, Malden, MA: Blackwell, 2009, p. 194.

20 Transcriptions and translations of Ramusio's edition and of Africanus' manuscript, held in the Vatican, appear in Natalie Davis, *Trickster Travels: A Sixteenth-Century Muslim Between Worlds*, New York: Hill and Wang, 2006, pp.118–19, 356 note 73.

21 Guy Poirier, 'Masculinities and Homosexualities in French Renaissance Accounts of Travel to the Middle East and North Africa' in Jacqueline Murray and Konrad Eisenbichler (eds), *Desire and Discipline: Sex and Sexuality in the Premodern West*, Toronto: University of Toronto Press, 1999, p. 162. While a counter-argument might be extrapolated from Richard Trexler's argument in *Sex and Conquest: Gendered Violence, Political Order and the European Conquest of the Americas*, Ithaca: Cornell University Press, 1999, that the indigenous berdaches of Spanish colonial South America developed only as 'signs of their masters' power and authority' (p. 129), this only proves the point that sexual identities were conferred and instrumentalized outside of Europe, and long before the period identified by Foucault.

22 Foucault, *The History of Sexuality*, p. 103.

23 Ania Loomba and Jonathan Burton (eds), *Race in Early Modern England: A Documentary Companion*, New York: Palgrave Macmillan, 2007, p. 172.

24 G. Benzoni, *History of the New World*, trans. W. H. Smyth, London: Hakluyt Society, 1857, p. 53.

25 Hernán Cortés, *Letters from Mexico*, ed. Anthony Pagden, New Haven: Yale University Press, 2001, p. 37.

26 Trexler, *Sex and Conquest*, p. 91.

27 Rudi C. Bleys, *The Geography of Perversion: Male-to-male Sexual Behaviour outside the West and the Ethnographic Imagination, 1750–1918*, New York: New York University Press, 1995, p. 44.

28 For the Italian-English interface, see Duncan Salkeld, 'Alien Desires: Travellers and Sexuality in Early Modern London' in Thomas Betteridge (ed.), *Borders and Travellers in Early Modern Europe*, Aldershot, Hampshire, and Burlington, VT: Ashgate, 2007.

29 Bray, *Homosexuality in Renaissance England*, p. 75.

30 Laqueur, *Making Sex*, p. 6.

31 Ann Laura Stoler, *Race and the Education of Desire: Foucault's History of Sexuality and the Colonial Order of Things*, Durham, NC: Duke University Press, 1995, p. 7.

32 Bleys, *The Geography of Perversion*, p. 2.

33 Stoler, *Race and the Education of Desire*, p. 195.

34 George Mosse, 'Nationalism and Sexuality in Nineteenth Century Europe', *Culture and Society* 20:5, 1983, pp. 75–84.

35 Bodin's contention that 'men as well as plants degenerate little by little when the soil has been changed' (quoted in Loomba and Burton, *Race in Early Modern England*, p. 94) combined with his linkage of temperance and climate clearly demonstrates the earlier relevance of Bleys' argument for the development of a European 'geography of perversion' emphasizing an alleged relationship between the environment and sexual activity.

36 Bleys, *The Geography of Perversion*, p. 31.
37 See, for example, K. A. Appiah, 'Race' in Frank Lentricchia and Thomas McLaughlin (eds), *Critical Terms for Literary Study*, Chicago: University of Chicago Press, 1990, pp. 274–87; Paul Gilroy, *Against Race: Imagining Political Culture Beyond the Colour Line*, Cambridge, MA: Harvard University Press, 2000, p. 31; Roberto Bernasconi and Tommy Lott, *The Idea of Race*, Indianapolis: Hackett Publishing Company, 2000; and Brian Niro, *Race*, New York: Palgrave, 2003. Ivan Hannaford's *Race, The History of an Idea in the West*, Baltimore: Johns Hopkins University Press, 1996, does consider the classical period but concludes that racism was the product of Enlightenment categories. Joyce Chaplin contends that racism was not engendered in English thought until the development of Atlantic slavery, in 'Race' in David Armitage and Michael J. Braddick (eds), *The British Atlantic World, 1500–1800*, New York: Palgrave, 2002, pp. 154–72.
38 Stoler, *Race and the Education of Desire*, pp. 68, 22.
39 Stoler, *Race and the Education of Desire*, p. 97. For Stoler, the interrelation of race, sex, and degeneracy is crucial to understanding how 'racism is inscribed in the mechanisms of the state via the emergence of biopower' (p. 84). Foucault defines 'biopower' in *The History of Sexuality* as 'an explosion of numerous and diverse techniques for achieving the subjugation of bodies and the control of populations' (p. 140). For our purposes, it is helpful to think of the *scientia sexualis* as one among those various techniques and institutions comprising biopower.
40 For a related argument regarding medieval forms of difference, see the introduction to Geraldine Heng, *Empire of Magic: Medieval Romance and the Politics of Cultural Fantasy*, New York: Columbia University Press, 2003.
41 See the introduction to Loomba and Burton, *Race in Early Modern England*, pp. 1–36.
42 Edward Kellet, *A returne from Argier. A sermon preached at … the re-admission of a relapsed Christian into our Church*, London: T. Harper, 1628, p. 19.
43 Stoler, *Race and the Education of Desire*, p. 68.
44 William Strachey, *The historie of travaile into Virginia Britannia*, ed. R. H. Major, London: Hakluyt Society, 1849, pp. 17–19.
45 Loomba and Burton, *Race in Early Modern England*, p. 161.
46 Cited in Tzvetan Todorov, *The Conquest of America: The Question of the Other*, trans. Richard Howard, New York: Harper & Row, 1984, p. 181.
47 George Abbot, *A briefe description of the whole worlde*, London: T. Judson, 1599, sigs. S2^r–S3^r.
48 Loomba and Burton, *Race in Early Modern England*, p. 244.
49 Loomba and Burton, *Race in Early Modern England*, p.146.
50 Sir Thomas Roe, 'To the East India Company' [24 November 1615] in William Foster (ed.), *The Embassy of Sir Thomas Roe to India*, London: Oxford University Press, 1926, pp. 76–77.
51 Henry Blount, *A Voyage into the Levant*, London: J[ohn] L[eggatt] for Andrew Crooke, 1636, p. 2.
52 Loomba and Burton, *Race in Early Modern England*, p.104.
53 Loomba and Burton, *Race in Early Modern England*, p. 219.
54 Richard Knolles, *The Generall Historie of the Turkes*, London: A. Islip, 1603, sigs. Ggggg1^v–2^r.
55 Just as recursiveness characterizes the relationship of racial and sexual discourses, so too do tropes of sexuality shuttle between cultures, adapting each time to their new or revisited settings, so that William Strachey's description of Chief Powhatan details the powerful Algonquin's 'sensual heathenism' and 'polygamy' with reference to 'the Turk' and his seraglio.
56 Loomba and Burton, *Race in Early Modern England*, p. 242.
57 See Mason, *Deconstructing America*, p. 110.
58 Mary Floyd-Wilson, *English Ethnicity and Race in Early Modern Drama*, New York: Cambridge University Press, 2003, p. 47.
59 Loomba and Burton, *Race in Early Modern England*, p. 211.
60 Loomba and Burton, *Race in Early Modern England*, p. 243.
61 Loomba and Burton, *Race in Early Modern England*, p. 205–6.
62 Loomba and Burton, *Race in Early Modern England*, p. 96.
63 Loomba and Burton, *Race in Early Modern England*, p. 148.
64 Loomba and Burton, *Race in Early Modern England*, p. 166.
65 Loomba and Burton, *Race in Early Modern England*, p. 166.
66 Sir Thomas Herbert, *A relation of some yeares travaile, begunne anno 1626*, London: William Stansby and Jacob Bloome, 1634, p. 17.

67 In Loomba and Burton, *Race in Early Modern England*.
68 Here I seek to complicate the teleology of Gary Taylor's assertion in *Buying Whiteness* that the Columbian discovery of the Americas initiated a search for an explanation to replace Ptolemy which would eventually yield the taxonomy of Linnaeus and scientific racism (p. 67). Scientific explanations would only become compelling again with the rise of disciplines such as biology and anthropology, which were themselves shaped in cultural conjunctures.

28

'THE ROOTS THAT CLUTCH'

Bodies, sex and race since 1750

Antoinette Burton

> What are the roots that clutch, what branches grow
> Out of this stony rubbish?
> T. S. Eliot, *The Waste Land* (1922)

Since the publication of volume 1 of Michel Foucault's *The History of Sexuality* in 1979, scholars have come to view the body as critical to all facets of the history of public and private life: to politics, consumption, discipline, punishment – indeed, to the very construction of the modern western self. What Foucault called biopower was foundational to the emergence of modern state bureaucracies; it was indispensable to the creation of 'rational' citizen/subjects as well. In modern European history, the body has undoubtedly had a distinctive career as a vector of labour and violence, reproduction and atrocity, alterity and civility. Yet, if bodies have served as lightning rods for politics of all kinds, the body has also been nothing more or less than the scandal of the state, in many senses of the term.[1] For the agencies of modern power have struggled with, and often failed in, the project of fixing bodies, striving to make them legible to dominant forms of power and stable as sites of profitability. Whether corralling labour for capital or ensuring the reproduction of norms of masculinity and femininity for social order, the modern state has relied on docile bodies for its own sustainability – determining to make them conform if they resisted incorporation into the body politic. In the process, state power has often violated, reshaped and otherwise deformed the body: most commonly in the name of progress and civilization and with a very specific iteration of a 'universal' white, male, heterosexual and middling class model always in view.

In this chapter I make two arguments about the body that grow out of a quarter of a century's scholarship in modern European history. First, I suggest that race and sex – as categories and as the basis for people's actual historical experiences – have been lived through the body and that the body is, therefore, one key way of thinking about them together. Although early work in feminist history emphasized the recovery of women's experience and gender as a discrete category of analysis, in fact most scholars have come to understand that sex and race are inseparable: that women and men live as embodied racial subjects and that gender is one modality of many in which race is lived.[2] Similarly, histories of race and class need to be understood as shaped by sexuality and gendered experience: whether we are speaking of white women's work or black men's politics, sex and race are entangled variables and must be examined as co-constitutive of how people lived and how power worked as well. As we shall see, tracking bodies helps illuminate in concrete ways how interrelated these forces were and how crucially concerns about managing them shaped both the imagination and the direction of modern European history.

Critical to this claim is my second argument: namely, that empire and colonialism have not operated only outside the boundaries of Europe, but have had a formative impact on the body politic of modern 'European' histories writ large.[3] Research undertaken in the wake of Edward Said's 1978 book *Orientalism*, which argued for the central role of imperial policies and power in the making of modern European culture, has shown how linked empires and their colonies were, not just symbolically but via the continual traffic of commodities, ideas and – of course – bodies between them.[4] These histories are what might be properly called 'postcolonial' because they were set in motion by the beginnings of mid-twentieth-century decolonization. As Frantz Fanon so famously remarked, 'Europe is literally the creation of the Third World'.[5] Just as the convergence of sex and race is most spectacularly visible through the history of the body, so too the making of modern European politics and society is arguably most powerfully legible via analyses of bodies in contact, in motion, in thrall to and elusive of colonial regimes of power.[6]

Arguments about the role of empire in the making of modern history have come to be fairly widely accepted in English, and to a lesser extent in French and German historiography. We should be careful to limit or at the very least to qualify their portability across all of 'Europe' – not least because of the variety of 'other' empires (Ottoman, Russian) that pressed against its frontiers and the dominance of its 'western' domains over its eastern, central and southeastern quarters. Nonetheless, what Foucault called biopower was always already imperial biopower, in large part because ambitious European men and women, whether agents of government or non-state actors, imagined lands beyond their various nation-states to be their god-given possessions and drafted the body – whether 'native' or 'metropolitan' – in the service of all manner of imperial projects. As the product of fitful and even capricious collisions between 'western' and 'non-western' subjects, the nations of the modern west were made by empire; and bodies were crucial to the forms that imperial modernity took.

As students of non-western empires have been quick to point out, the categories of imperial modernity and imperial biopower are hardly unique to European imperialism. Japan's rise to power in the twentieth century was built on the backs of all manner of colonial subjects, and its identity as a would-be global imperial power was bound up inextricably with its sense of demographic dominion, with all the raced, classed and sexualized systems and imaginaries that that entailed. The emergence of Japan on the world historical stage in the later nineteenth century throws the exceptionality of the European experience into question and raises doubts about the segregation of the western imperial body politic from Asian and Eurasian imperial histories.[7] These are subjects that limits of space, regrettably, prevent me from taking up in detail here. In any case, if we heed the work of postcolonial histories and take colonial modernity as our point of departure, Foucault's terms of embodiment are invariably colonial biopower, colonial governmentality, and colonial subjectivity. Our task is to understand the body and its geopolitical careers not simply as indices of a national story, but as part of the multi-faceted histories of empire as well.

A word of caution here. Sex, race and the body as I am using them are not intended to point to some kind of essential, self-evident identity. In keeping with feminist historiographical practice, I intend them as indicators of historical process, formation, consolidation and change rather than as timeless or given characteristics of either people or groups. Like colonial modernity itself, the body and its features are as much the effects of particular configurations of power as they are the properties of individuals or collectivities *per se*. Without putting too fine a point on it, histories of the post-1750 world that Europeans imagined and tried to shape are, inevitably, accounts of new forms of gender, sexuality, racial identity and embodiment produced in the crucible of imperial power, both 'at home' and in the empire itself. In some instances these new identities represented radical breaks with the recent or distant past; in others, they were differences of degree rather than of kind. In contrast to the regimes that sought to fix them as homogeneous and autonomous, the bodies that undergirded modern European histories were always in the process of becoming, and were, above all, contingent on the time and place in which they emerged. To acknowledge this is to concede that sex and race have no *a priori* histories, but are, as Joan Scott argued for gender, agents of historically specific, embodied forms of power.[8] As we shall see, we must admit to the body as more than incidental to the fate of polities, nations and empires.[9] In both the aggregate and the particular, bodies have consistently, and most often insistently, shaped the forms and meanings of the global imperial world in ways we have only begun to fully countenance. What follows is a thematic narrative of the post-1750 period that attempts to re-centre the body as both a sign of the imperial modern, and as one of its most powerfully raced and sexualized agents as well.

Working bodies: slavery and geopolitics, 1750–1900

To begin with slavery is to ground the history of modern European politics, economics and culture in the materiality of the unfree body and to posit the origins of western industrial power outside the metropole – to argue, in other words, that the 'miracle' of modern European progress (in all its supposed providentiality and inevitability) was contingent on the simultaneous embrace and disavowal of the work of enslaved bodies in the plantation complex and its cognate spaces. Although accounts of slavery as a system tend to emphasize the North Atlantic plantation complex, in fact it was the Portuguese who established the first plantations on the west coast of Africa, giving rise to a global exploitation system rooted in the subjugation of bodies to regimes of extraction and exportation that were linked in turn to global imperial power and ambition. At the same time, the significance of the transatlantic slave system for modern European imperial history commands our attention precisely because it embedded the raced, sexualized body at the heart of proto-industrial production and the liberal political imaginary in the west *tout court*. Across the Caribbean – that is to say, across English, French, Spanish and Dutch possessions in the seventeenth and eighteenth centuries – biopower was black and its sustainability into future generations was predicated on the reproductive capacity of the enslaved woman.[10] Her labour, be it as a field hand or as a vessel for the procreation of more field hands, helped to guarantee whatever profits there were from plantation holdings and thus shaped the political economies of London and Paris and the very lifeways of its inhabitants. Postcolonial theorist and Jamaica-born black Briton Stuart Hall's sardonic claim that 'I am the sugar at the bottom of the English cup of tea' captures perfectly the reciprocal dynamic that undergirded colonial modernity: the interdependence of core and periphery and the constitutive impact of imperial investments on the body politic at all levels 'at home'.[11] Events surrounding the French Revolution – specifically the role that uprisings in

St Domingue and Guadeloupe played in shaping new constitutional forms and the whole constellation of ideas and ideals around 'liberté, fraternité, egalité' – illustrate just how influential slave biopower could be on ostensibly 'national' events and their legacies, not least for producing race and blackness itself as markers of cultural difference with profound political consequences. As Laurent Dubois has so persuasively argued, the very notions of French republicanism and citizenship were borne out of these struggles over, through and by the bodies of slaves and ex-slaves.[12]

As significantly, new subjectivities were produced in and around this struggle, subjectivities that were deeply embodied even as they served to shore up abstractions (like that of the universal rights-bearing citizen) and civic ideals (like rational/economic man) that sought distance from corporality and its apparent irrational messiness. So, for example, images of enslaved men and women, archived in coins struck for the English abolitionist cause, circulated widely as emblems of both economic exploitation and the urgency of freedom in the early nineteenth century. As scholars of British anti-slavery movements have demonstrated, such images also enabled new forms of both whiteness and femininity. The spectre of the enslaved woman on bended knee drew middle-class British women into the cause, offering them the opportunity to see themselves as economic actors (with the power of the sugar boycott), political agents (with the power to impact petitions and ultimately effect abolitionist legislation), and maternal custodians (with the power to patronize black women, slave and free) as well.[13] These new, proto-feminist identities depended on the silence of the slave woman whose body was on the line, both literally and figuratively, in the abolitionist cause; this, despite the record of resistance we have among women of African descent, as individuals and as part of collective protest. For western missionaries of all national origins and denominational stripes, slavery remained the focal point of a reformist identity well into the nineteenth century as they tracked ongoing labour exploitation (like 'Chinese slavery' in South Africa) in campaigns that could bring them into heated conflict with colonial officialdom in situ.[14] Thanks to their work, it was not uncommon for ordinary, workaday inhabitants of the metropole to see evidence of reform projects – whether evangelical or lay – in the form of black and brown bodies, which turned up in all manner of exhibitions (as specimens) and drawing-rooms (as servants) in capital cities from London to Amsterdam and beyond.[15]

The exhibitionary complex that dominated cultural production across nineteenth-century Europe as well as the political economies that produced it rested on the abjection of racialized, sexualized bodies, often bringing state and non-state actors into spectacular, not to mention profitable, collaboration. Such spectacles might also give white workers 'at home', whose conditions Friedrich Engels was not above likening to slavery in the 1840s, a sense of investment in imperial projects that offered them affiliation with racial superiority – especially if they identified as Christians. Though they certainly pre-dated the high noon of European imperialism, these imperial identities were newly embodied in the gentleman explorer (David Livingstone) and even the gentleman reformer (E. D. Morel). They were also available to the western feminist (like Josephine Butler) willing to articulate a custodial relationship with her enslaved colonial 'sisters'.[16]

In the British empire, 'emancipation' occasioned the emergence of a whole new set of identities rooted in the labouring body of colour. Prime among these was the indentured labourer, or coolie, a term related to the Urdu word for slave that in the Caribbean meant someone of South Asian descent, but more broadly was applied to 'Asian' labourers who worked on plantations, railways and mines from Queensland to South Africa to Shanghai.

Coolie labour was at a premium after the abolition of the slave trade. Systems of recruitment and of work discipline were male-dominated, though the presence of women as wives, sexual partners and workers was consequential not just to the economies of post-abolition Britain but to its overall imperial stability as well. 'Coolie' was a term of description and of scorn. Perhaps most infamously, Mohandas Gandhi was known as the 'coolie lawyer', a phrase that conjures the power of the term to reduce recalcitrant subjects of colour – even Guildhall-trained barristers – to the racialized body. Elsewhere, as in the German colony of Tanzania, for example, slavery remained a reality, if an uneven one, well into the nineteenth century, with manumission policies (via the '*Freibriefe*' of the 1890s) allowing some men and women access to a variety of lived experiences and identities in the free market, including as landowners and entrepreneurs.[17] When abolition did occur, it was as much at the hands of Africans as it was by fiat on the part of the German colonial state. The Tanzanian case reminds us of the role that slaves played in shaping European political economies domestic and foreign up to the threshold of the twentieth century, as well as the malleability of regimes of colonial biopower that may appear totalizing. It also points to the limits of histories of slavery based exclusively on the transatlantic slavery model. Its Indian Ocean world counterpart, though eclipsed in western histories, was equivalent in scope and scale; though the hard and fast connections between race and slavery, between enslavement and bondage, and between colour and status that tended to characterize the New World system did not necessarily obtain.[18] In time, those differences impacted upon how competition for resources would shape intra-European rivalries and ultimately, the contours of the twentieth-century world, as German, French, Italian and British interests on the African continent took centre stage in the guise of 'the scramble for Africa'. This is at least in part because the legacy of slavery linked questions of biopolitical management to crises of geopolitical confidence between the French Revolution and World War I.

Body politics: suffrage and citizenship, 1850–1920

If the legacy of slavery is one material link between biopower and the history of European politics in the age of empire, the career of liberalism (with a small 'l') in the nineteenth century is another. For decades the history of liberalism – as a party project, as a civilizational ideal and as a presumptively modern western phenomenon – rested on a doubly durable foundation: the insularity of post-Enlightenment Europe from its racially 'inferior' empires and the segregation of the 'rational' public sphere from its preternaturally gendered other, the privacy of the home. Feminist scholarship has chipped away at the latter proposition, demonstrating how and why, like the domains nominated as 'masculine' or 'feminine', and the public and the private spheres were relational, overlapping and mutually constitutive.[19] Indeed, feminist histories have gone so far as to demonstrate that the so-called naturalness of this public/private divide is itself a consequence of mainly nineteenth-century discourses invested in aligning a new industrial order with a specific sexual order: wife at home (the angel of the house/child rearer) and husband in the world (the office clerk/business man/wage earner). That this distribution of bodies across such a wide swathe of space was a bourgeois ideal, linked with modes of capitalist production, is evident from its transnational circulation and its enshrinement at the centre of virtually every European socio-economic order by the end of the nineteenth century. The species of body management at its heart was viewed as the hallmark of 'polite and commercial peoples worldwide'.[20] In Foucauldian terms, its success was contingent on the internalization of specific, and highly gendered, dispositions of character and virtue – of middle-class manliness and gentility on the part of both sexes – and, it goes without saying, on the embrace of a normative system that recognized only two sexes, conjugally exclusive and racially endogamous.

What impact does the embeddedness of Europe's historical experience in imperial acquisition, expansion and maintenance have on our explanatory framework for this biopolitical project? If modern market-driven industrial capitalism was built on the backs of free slaves and indentured workers kept in train by a combination of colonial military force and less formal but nonetheless real commercial infrastructure – if capital was, effectively, imperial capital[21] – and if (as above) gender relations in the metropole were effectively produced out of new forms of market capitalism, then 'European' ideals and practices of domesticity were by extension deeply indebted to the impact of the empire writ large on 'the nation'. In this chain of logic, the heteronormative domestic scene was not merely incidentally or allusively imperial; nor was it a formulation originated 'at home' and transported wholesale to 'lesser breeds without the law' as the ultimate signifier of civilization. Domesticity – shorthand here for white bourgeois conjugality and all its cultural entailments – was consolidated either as a consequence of collisions with other, 'primitive' forms of hearth and home, or at the very least in dialectical relationship to them. In a reformulation of Said's argument in *Orientalism*, I suggest that the 'self' of European domesticity was contingent on, made through, necessitated by, its colonized 'other', variously represented by non-white female sexual availability, non-nuclear family forms, and ethnographic notions of 'primitive' accumulation. Or, to follow Cooper and Stoler, metropole and colony constantly 'played off' each other in ways that are particularly visible in bourgeois domestic forms.[22]

While European domesticity was consolidated by way of contrast with 'other' forms most intensively post-1750, we can also see traces of the process in earlier empires, specifically the Spanish in Mexico. Here, the collision of ecclesiastical imperialism with African practices of sexual intercourse and socio-sexual mixing helped consolidate an aggressive, evangelical program of household monogamy designed to guarantee white supremacy and Catholic hegemony.[23] The two (conjugality and whiteness) were as linked as they were fragile, thereby foretelling both the ferocious western European preoccupation with the conjugal couple and the precarious vulnerability of their domestic arrangements to challenges within and beyond the household that defined them. Here I follow Elizabeth Povinelli's lead by emphasizing that the racially pure/white, domesticated conjugal couple emerged and was established as the humanizing ground of all legitimate subjects in the context of modern liberal governance in the wake of the age of revolutions of the late eighteenth century. Contrary to conventional wisdom, and despite its sacralization,[24] it is not the security but the fragility of heterosexuality that has compelled the national/imperial state to be so invested in managing the domains of modern biopolitical power: marriage, divorce, reproduction, miscegenation, sexual orientation and family life.[25] Only when we recognize the colonial genealogies of, and the colonial pressures on, this investment can we fully appreciate how bound up the political career of liberalism in the west has been with the exigencies and insecurities of imperial power, embodied in that highly naturalized rights-bearing individual: the white, straight western Christian family man.

The history of democracy in Britain is a case in point. At virtually every legislative moment of constitutional change in the Victorian period – that is to say, at critical moments when the electorate was expanded to include greater numbers and new categories of voting people – imperial crises helped to produce an ostensibly more 'liberal' polity but one also re-dedicated to whiteness, maleness and middle-class status: dedicated, in short, to that family man. So, for example, both of the Great Reform Acts of 1832 and 1867, which created larger and more diverse electorates, occurred in the wake of major imperial upheavals in Jamaica – crises which engendered debates about the racial character of representative government and drew women and feminists (like John Stuart Mill) into transnational conversations about the sex, gender and colour of the British citizen/subject.[26] The question of embodiment was absolutely consequential here, as contests over the sexual and racial fitness of would-be citizens dominated public discourse in ways that shaped the legislative outcome and reconfirmed the white male character of Victorian politics expressly by closing out women and non-whites. The Third Reform Act (1884) is a possible exception to the imperial plotline of Victorian constitutionalism, though it was quickly followed by a crisis over Irish Home Rule and the explosion of Indian nationalism onto the domestic political scene – giving rise to controversies about who was fit not just to vote but to serve as a representative in the imperial Parliament as well. The routine exclusion of women voters and representatives combined with the election of an Indian man – Dadhabai Naoroji – to Westminster in 1892 demonstrates how discriminating liberal democracy was with respect to raced and sexed bodies in this period. Though Indian self-government was still just a distant point on the endlessly deferred horizon, metropolitan observers were growing into the conviction that the capacity of colonized subjects to manage themselves, their womenfolk and their own bodily habits was critical to evaluations of their fitness for participation in political life (eventually). Naoroji, for his part, had to distance himself from accusations that he was a 'black man' rather than a lighter skinned Parsee in order to win the election; in so doing, he both contributed to Victorians' sense of their own liberal inclusivity and ratified the racial distinctions between black and brown that grew directly out of British imperial hierarchies in India, Africa and the Indian Ocean world.[27]

The role that anxieties about national purity – itself a categorical standard bearer of concerns about sex and race – played in these contests over the direction of western geopolitics is something I will return to below. Suffice to say that the reproductive capacity of the middle-class English wife was considered essential to democratic virtue: arguments against women's suffrage were cast as a defence of white women's wombs against the corrupting influences of higher education, employment outside the home and activity anywhere near the vicinity of the hustings. Contemporary science was instrumental here, producing 'evidence' of the bodily degradation white women would suffer by such exposure; contemporary feminism, for its part, made the bodily suffering of Indian women at the hands of both Indian men and the colonial state the *sine qua non* of their own claims to inclusion in the body politic.[28] The centrality of sex, race and the body to the history of liberal political thinking and policy was not limited either to the question of women's suffrage or to women's bodies *per se*. As the work of Mrinalini Sinha has shown, colonized men were perforce failed men: in her example, 'effeminate Bengalis', whose bodily weakness and embrace of child marriage effectively placed them outside the pale of self-government.[29]

Though I have focused on the English case, there is every indication that the notion of bodily fitness (indeed, of bodily ideals of 'humanness' itself) shaped by imperial and/or racial anxieties left its mark on the fate of regimes across nineteenth-century Europe;

regimes which had, of course, variegated relations to liberalism and democracy. In France, for example, the overlap of labour questions connected to immigration on the one hand, and events in the colonial empire on the other, eventuated in heated public debates, and ultimately policy-making, designed explicitly to arrest *fin-de-siècle* population decline and degeneration, and so to reclaim 'French' citizenship and safeguard the racial destiny of the nation.[30] Meanwhile, images of racialized/sexualized bodies flooded the marketplace through commercial advertising and trademarking, delivering messages about how colonized Asian and African peoples could, and should, look and act to a wide spectrum of the early Third Republic. Africans as plantation workers remained a popular visual theme; in this sense the black body was fixed in time and place at a moment when colonial labourers were restive, and at times downright insubordinate, in response to the depredations of imperial capital.[31] Particularly telling is the role of white Frenchwomen in this context: as in Britain, despite the fact that their bodily capacity was also at stake, and of course because of it, they pathologized workers of colour even as they claimed that contact with French 'civilization' would uplift them and that French national interests would be served by their assimilation to the body politic. Crises of labour, the presence of mobile, racialized bodies and the limits that even liberal forms of governance placed on women's speech and action in public had similar echoes in the Netherlands and its colonies, where miscegenation was a major preoccupation of colonial law and metropolitan officialdom, and motherhood a site of anxiety and regulation.[32] In Amsterdam, too, the figure of the respectable Dutch working girl emerged as emblematic of Dutch industry and national pride in a global marketplace by the end of the nineteenth century. A co-production of national pride and imperial competition, of metropolitan needs and colonial realities, she was shadowed by the figure of the Javanese carpet weaver, her double and her other.[33] We need more work that historicizes how class identities and materialities were cross-hatched by colonialism, especially work that does not presume that the flow of such categories was from west to east. Like domesticity, class itself was rarely fully formed 'at home', borrowing instead from racial and gendered hierarchies for its social meaning and its political power.

Bodies for the nation: racial purity, imperial war and the international order, 1870–1940

To say that anxiety about the threats to racial supremacy in Europe – what we might call the imperilled project of white imperial biopower – shaped the fate of the first part of the twentieth century would be an understatement. This was in part because anti-colonial nationalists and nationalisms erupted across the landscapes of the later nineteenth century, demonstrating the limits of imperial politics and culture to metropolitan audiences very much aware of the fact of empire. But it was also because people of colour of all kinds made their way into metropolitan spaces, challenging the putative whiteness of the European heartland by competing with white labour and mixing with white men and women in new, and what were perceived as dangerous, forms of social/sexual intercourse. In many places, this migrancy was not seasonal or temporary but, for all kinds of global and local economic reasons, created more, and historically unprecedented, permanent settlements of people of colour in Europe's cities – as well as populations of mixed-race children who were seen as threats because they were representatives of 'sujétion and citoyenneté'.[34] It is frankly hard to overestimate the impact of the movement of people of

BODIES, SEX AND RACE SINCE 1750

colour in and out of the metropole and across the European political and cultural imagination on the world order from the 1880s onward. These moving subjects literally pressed themselves against extant 'legal and political justifications of immigration control' and thereby challenged the long-standing link between territorial sovereignty and the capacity of nations to fix bodies inside borders.[35] The very intensity of attempts to regulate national/imperial limits (through passports, pass laws, cartes d'identités, and other kinds of citizenship machinery) signalled the increasingly precarious nature of those borders, not to mention the permeability of the racially pure social/political Rousseauian contract. Indeed, the mobility of brown, black and yellow bodies was so unsettling to the dominant social order that white men produced elaborate mechanisms for keeping them in place, as is evident from the networks of intellectual and practical exchange through which regulatory policies were developed to shore up the 'global colour line'. One powerful example is the appropriation of the literacy test in the US south from British efforts to disenfranchise voters of colour in Natal – both instruments of colonial governmentality, albeit it in different settings and in response to historically particular forms of racialized political order.[36] Such transnational cross-fertilization was not limited to an Anglo-American brotherhood, and it could make for surprising collaborations, as in the case of the German businessmen who financed African-American experts from the Tuskegee Institute in Alabama in order to help their colonial operations to more efficiently extract raw materials from Togo into factories of mittel Europa – a tack soon imitated by other colonial powers.[37]

Such borrowings suggest that claims about the superiority of whiteness, particularly as the locus of technological genius or capitalist savvy, were under siege in the pre-war period. The apparent naturalness of white male supremacy as the basis for domination of the international order was undermined in even more melodramatic ways in the wake of the Boer War, which was a pyrrhic victory for the British, and the Russo-Japanese war, which propelled a non-western nation onto the world stage – a nation capable of felling a western foe and mobilizing huge and growing numbers of colonized peoples – as an apparent competitor in the global imperial arena. The interdependence of biopower, race and empire in the new century was palpably clear to contemporaries, who worried openly about 'yellow peril' (a phrase attributed to Kaiser Wilhelm II) and 'black scourge' and their impact on western civilization. Yet the linkages between bio-imperial anxiety and war on a global scale rarely feature in explanatory frameworks for the Great War, which even now is most often historicized through reference to the international treaty system and the balance of power, rather than via an analysis of the competition for resources, for the labour power of subject bodies, and for the racial stability and global dominance at stake therein. W. E. B. Dubois understood World War I as an imperial contest, writing eloquently about the African roots of war in 1915 in *The Atlantic Monthly*:

Consider a moment the desperate flames of war that have shot up in Africa in the last quarter of a century: France and England at Fashoda, Italy at Adua, Italy and Turkey in Tripoli, England and Portugal at Delagoa Bay, England, Germany, and the Dutch in South Africa, France and Spain in Morocco, Germany and France in Agadir, and the world at Algeciras. ... From Fashoda to Agadir, repeatedly the spark has been applied to the European magazine and a general conflagration narrowly averted. We speak of the Balkans as the storm-centre of Europe and the cause of war, but this is mere habit. The Balkans are convenient for occasions, but the ownership of materials and men in the darker world is the real prize that is setting the nations of Europe at each other's throats to-day.[38]

Unsurprisingly, perhaps, Dubois saw with particular vividness that dominion over black bodies and their labour capacity was one root cause of the war. Whether roots or tendrils, imperial projects like the German colonization of southwest Africa had a significant, if not necessarily a predictive, effect on the character of the German military in World War I and beyond. As Isabel Hull's research illuminates, German generals and even the common soldier were materially impacted by the extermination orders issued against the Herero in 1905–6; that campaign, with its shift from mere 'pursuit' of tribal resisters to orders for their 'annihilation', helped to shape an imperial identity for German military culture. Routines learned in the context of colonial warfare were later applied to the bodies of European enemy populations in ways that were to have world historical consequences well beyond the armistice of 1918.[39]

A number of factors made the immediate post-war period a dense moment for biopolitical crisis on a global scale. The influenza pandemic (the 'Spanish flu') swept the world from east to west, preying on populations already vulnerable from wartime displacement and malnutrition, and felling rich and poor alike.[40] The combination of the flu outbreak and the process of 'demobbing', or the demobilization of troops back into European countries looking for work in 1918–20, created conditions of instability rooted in demographic shifts and anxieties about the body that, in turn, impacted upon the post-war landscape in politically consequential ways. The year 1919 was a momentous, and arguably a globally revolutionary, year with unrest from Chicago to London to India and beyond – unrest that derived in part from economic contraction and job competition, in part from the political fallout in the wake of the 'peace' of Versailles. In Britain the violence of 1919 was highly racialized: black troops returning to metropolitan hospitals, employment lines and bread queues were set up by white soldiers and civilians; resentment of black Britons' sexual dalliances and relationships with white women were also an issue.[41] The post-war era inaugurated all kinds of proximities heretofore available, of course, but accelerated by interwar immigration, the rise of racialized commercial and residential zones, and the cultural intermixing at the heart of Europe it engendered.[42] That these intimate geographies made their way into the very centre of modernist life and thought cannot be gainsaid, as the preoccupations of that quintessential flaneur, Walter Benjamin, with the African quarters of Marseilles, and its prostitutes, aptly demonstrate.[43] That the intimate struggles in and over these spaces – which involved the regulation of prostitution and concerns, official and unofficial, about miscegenation and the survivability of the white race – were linked to larger questions of imperial crisis in pre-postcolonial South Asia, Africa, Indonesia there can also be little doubt. As Philippa Levine has shown, the regulation of prostitution was clearly 'a conscious instrument of imperial dominance' aimed at the protection of western troops from disease and the policing of the boundary between black and white, and, indeed, between white and anything that could sully it, including prostitutes who were Eurasian and Jewish.[44]

These were matters of heightened geopolitical significance in the wake of Versailles, which reshaped the international order into a new kind of imperial landscape, with American power ascendant.[45] As historians rethink the twentieth century they are coming to understand the impact of World War I in a variety of ways, and, in the process, the boundaries of Europe are proving as porous to US influence as to that of 'extra-territorial' imperial power – making the Tuskegee/Togo experiment cited above less anomalous than symptomatic of larger, if historiographically marginalized, geopolitical circuitries grounded in mobile, labouring, racialized bodies. In Victoria de Grazia's view, American capitalism was a kind of 'irresistible empire' in both material and symbolic terms, not least because of the rearrangement of middle- and aspirant middle-class desires around mass consumption, itself structured by the interwar years and all manner of racialized and appetitive fantasies with long imperial histories.[46] It thus makes little sense to cordon off American power from the story of European body politics: the US was increasingly influential in shaping the contours of Europe in many dimensions, and in ways that foretold much of the rest of the history of the twentieth century.

The political career of Gandhi, and of Indian nationalism more generally, is a case in point. Historians of both empire and India have tended to stage his nationalist politics as a core-periphery question, and it's easy enough to see how his much-discussed transformation from English-trained barrister to dhoti-wearing swadeshi advocate represents a body politics – his dhoti, his abstinence, his vegetarianism – whose terms of engagement were addressed directly to Britain, and London/Whitehall within it. Yet it is also true that Gandhi and as importantly, more radical sectors of the anti-imperial movement out of India, had audiences and active cells in the United States. The traffic in anti-colonial ideas moved in many directions and was carried by a variety of bodies as well. Mrinalini Sinha's work on the Mother India controversy of the late 1920s ratifies this interpretation even as it reveals how foundational the struggle over women's bodies – viewed in this case through the lens of child marriage and the Sarda Act of 1929 – was to interwar debates about colonial governmentality and biopower. Sinha's argument is that these debates circulated not just in Britain but transatlantically, reaching into and drawing upon Anglo-American narratives and histories of race, gender and body that resonated powerfully in the new imperial/international geopolitical order.[47] If the proliferation of 'Sambos' in Paris is anything to go by, even European regimes of race were figured at least in part through reference to American imagery, especially after the dust settled on Versailles – another example of the multi-axial work of colonial modernity and the co-production of new identities in its centripetal spaces.[48]

How women and children – the most obvious and available biopower of the post-war order – were to be managed was a matter of enormous concern in the interwar period. Such projects obviously had long histories: in Britain the rise of the welfare state grew directly out of the Boer War and the eugenic fears that followed, while in the 'Bohemian lands' of the multinational Hapsburg empire, German and Czech nationalists used the prospect of orphanages, camps and infant welfare clinics to win loyalties and bodies for their cause.[49] In post-war France, the debate over abortion and contraception and maternity raged, while in parts of the Middle East like Syria and Lebanon, the French civilizing mission morphed into something akin to 'paternal republicanism' in response to a catastrophic social crisis whose management was rooted in the stability and docility of the child-bearing body.[50] During this same period, European capitals served as the meeting and testing grounds for anti-colonial activities of all kinds: Paris for Leopold Senghor and Ho Chi Min, Berlin for Virendranath Chattopadhyaya and Brussels for the relatively short-lived League Against Imperialism.[51] On the face of it these men and the movements they sponsored may seem only remotely connected to the problem of sex, race and the body we have been tracking here. At the same time, their mere bodily presence in these aspirationally white spaces was disruptive of norms of territoriality and sovereignty predicated on hard and fast distinctions between legitimate European subjects and 'other' forms of embodiment, whether political or cultural. And despite the presence of women and feminists, both western and non-western, in numerous associational forums on the geopolitical stage across the world in the interwar period, even (and especially) anti-imperial nationalism remained a masculine affair.[52] It might even be considered a continuation, albeit in less stringent forms, of the kinds of collaborative patriarchies that undergirded early forms of legal, cultural and political power from earlier moments of colonial modernity.[53] Western feminists, for their part, struggled continuously with the challenges posed to them by the embodied presence of colonial women among them, women of colour seeking rights to recognition in a global order whose transnationalism they recognized as an avenue to power in a changing world sooner and with more savvy than their European 'sisters' did.[54]

Though the project of 'blurring the line' between nation and empire – or alternatively, of taking an outright global perspective – might have payoffs for colonizers and colonized alike, these were not mere abstract benefits.[55] Like the 'universals' by which European power was so enthralled during the period under consideration, the advantages sought and gained by both imperialists and anti-colonial nationalists redounded to real bodies whose flesh and bone not only matter in the history of colonial modernity and its governmentalities, but cannot be reduced simply to statistics or official policy – even in a new, more seamless narrative of an 'integrated' postcolonial history. The stories of these bodies and what was at stake for them in interwar colonial power struggles must be re-sutured to extant histories of class, ethnicity and even gender so that we can more fully appreciate whether, how, and to what degree the body, sex and race were critical referents for the European colonial modern up through to the end of World War II. How to thread the story of Nazi biopolitics through analyses of colonial governmentality remains a challenging question, historiographically and methodologically – especially since, in some respects, Germany's postcolonial history begins, as Pascal Grosse so insightfully observes, with World War I.[56] Some historians have stressed genealogical continuities, as between biological experiments on Africans and those in concentration camps; others have emphasized correspondences between projects or policies of racial reproduction. Still others have chosen a historically nuanced, ethnographically dense biographical approach as a way of tracking the simultaneity of pathologizing practices at the site of the colonized/Jewish body.[57] Clearly there is congruence between Germany's continental and overseas expansion ambitions; their complementarity is rooted, at the very least, in a 'shared ideological core of biologism'.[58] Perhaps most tellingly, this debate often founders on the shoals of German exceptionalism, a problem that plagues comparative work in European history, and would seem to be exacerbated by the spectre of a transnational and/or comparative European colonial history.

And yet the possibilities for juxtaposing, if not harmonizing, histories of colonialism ostensibly internal to Europe – examining, for example, the parameters of racial difference in 'colonial Poland', as Kristin Kopp does, or those of what Josef Borocz calls 'the never-colonial, yet always imperial, histories of various, clearly recognizable localities within Europe' – with histories of colonialism in extra-national spaces ought to be fruitful ones.[59] This is especially true when we understand bodies sexed and raced rather than borders *per se* as the 'roots that clutch' at the foundations of modern Europe. If the 'Final Solution' is modern Europe's paradigmatic event, its representative problem, it is also the culmination of its entanglements, bodily and otherwise, with colonialism and the exigencies of imperial biopolitics. As one destination for my narrative arc, it offers unfulfilled possibilities for a new beginning for histories of a fully embodied European colonial modern, if not for new models of co-production between nation and empire and, one suspects, in the spaces in between.

Notes

1 Here I draw on Rajeswari Sunder Rajan, *The Scandal of the State: Women, Law and Citizenship in Postcolonial India*, Durham, NC: Duke University Press, 2003.

2 Paul Gilroy, *The Black Atlantic: Modernity and Double Consciousness*, Cambridge, MA: Harvard University Press, 1993, p. 85.

3 As the work of Ann Stoler has demonstrated, this move requires a critique of Foucault, a recontextualization of his theoretical corpus so that it accounts for the work of imperialism in the making of the cavernous bureaucracies and interventionist capillaries of the modern state. See Ann Laura Stoler, *Race and the Education of Desire: Foucault's History of Sexuality and the Colonial Order of Things*, Durham, NC: Duke University Press, 1995.

4 Edward Said, *Orientalism*, London: Vintage, 1978.

5 Frantz Fanon, *The Wretched of the Earth*, New York: Grove Press, 1968, p. 102.

6 See Antoinette Burton (ed.), *After the Imperial Turn: Thinking With and Through the Nation*, Durham, NC: Duke University Press, 2003.

7 Sabine Fruhstuck, *Colonizing Sex: Sexology and Social Control in Modern Japan*, Berkeley, CA: University of California Press, 2003; Tani E. Barlow (ed.), *Formations of Colonial Modernity in East Asia*, Durham, NC: Duke University Press, 1997.

8 Joan Scott, *Gender and the Politics of History*, New York: Columbia University Press, 1988.

9 Though I begin at 1750 there are a number of possible chronologies for the onset of modernity and/or European hegemony. See Leila Abu-Lughod, *Before European Hegemony: The World System AD 1250–1350*, Oxford: Oxford University Press, 1991, and Andrew Gunder Frank, *Re-Orient: Global Economy in the Asian Age*, Berkeley, CA: University of California Press, 1998.

10 Jennifer Morgan, *Laboring Women: Reproduction and Gender in New World Slavery*, Philadelphia: University of Pennsylvania Press, 2004.

11 Stuart Hall, 'Old and New Identities, Old and New Ethnicities' in Anthony D. King (ed.), *Culture, Globalization and the World System*, Minneapolis: University of Minnesota Press, 1991, pp. 41–68 (48–49).

12 Laurent Dubois, *A Colony of Citizens: Revolution and Slave Emancipation in the French Caribbean, 1787–1804*, Chapel Hill: University of North Carolina Press, 2004.

13 Clare Midgley, *Women Against Slavery: The British Campaigns*, London and New York: Routledge, 1992.

14 Kevin Grant, *A Civilized Savagery: Britain and the New Slaveries in Africa, 1884–1926*, London and New York: Routledge, 2005.

15 Maria Grever and Berteke Waaldijk, *Transforming the Public Sphere: The Dutch National Exhibition of Women's Labor in 1898*, Durham, NC: Duke University Press, 2004; Saloni Mathur, *India by Design: Colonial History and Cultural Display*, Berkeley, CA: University of California Press, 2007.

16 Antoinette Burton, *Burdens of History: British Feminists, Indian Women and Imperial Culture, 1865–1915*, Chapel Hill, NC: University of North Carolina Press, 1994.

17 Jan-Georg Deutsch, 'The "Freeing" of Slaves in German East Africa: The Statistical Record, 1890–1914' in Suzanne Miers and Martin Klein (eds), *Slavery and Colonial Rule in Africa*, London and New York: Routledge, 1999, pp. 109–32 and *Emancipation without Abolition in German East Africa, c. 1884–1914*, Oxford: James Currey, 2006.

18 See Gwyn Campbell, 'Slave Trades and the Indian Ocean World' in John Hawley (ed.), *India in Africa, Africa in India: Indian Ocean Cosmopolitanisms*, Bloomington, IL: Indiana University Press, 2008, pp. 17–51.

19 For Britain see Catherine Hall, *White, Male and Middle Class: Explorations in Feminism and History*, London and New York: Routledge, 1992.

20 C. A. Bayly, *The Birth of the Modern World, 1780–1814*, Oxford: Blackwell, 2004, pp. 114–19.

21 Ellen Meskins Wood, *Empire of Capital*, Brooklyn, NY, and London: Verso, 2003.

22 Said, *Orientalism*; Frederick Cooper and Ann Stoler (eds), *Tensions of Empire: Colonial Cultures in a Bourgeois World*, Berkeley, CA: University of California Press, 1997, esp. pp. 4, 12, 22.

23 Herman Bennett, *Africans in Colonial Mexico: Absolutism, Christianity, and Afro-Creole Consciousness, 1570–1640*, Bloomington, IN: Indiana University Press, 2003.

24 Judith Surkis, *Sexing the Citizen: Morality and Masculinity in France, 1870–1920*, Ithaca, NY: Cornell University Press, 2006, ch. 6.

25 Elizabeth Povinelli, *The Empire of Love: Toward a Theory of Intimacy, Genealogy and Carnality*, Durham, NC: Duke University Press, 2006.

26 Catherine Hall, 'The Rule of Difference: Gender, Class and Empire in the Making of the 1832 Reform Act' in Catherine Hall, Ida Blom and Karen Hagemann (eds), *Gendered Nations: Nationalism and Gender Order in the Long Nineteenth Century*, Oxford: Berg, 2000, pp. 107–35; Catherine Hall, Keith McClelland and Jane Rendall, *Defining the Victorian Nation: Class, Race, Gender and the Reform Act of 1867*, Cambridge: Cambridge University Press, 2000.

27 Antoinette Burton, 'Tongues Untied: Lord Salisbury's "Black Man" and the Boundaries of Imperial Democracy', *Comparative Studies in Society and History* 43:2, 2000, pp. 632–59.

28 See Burton, *Burdens of History*.

29 Mrinalini Sinha, *Colonial Masculinity: The 'Manly' Englishman and the 'Effeminate' Bengali in the Late Nineteenth Century*, Manchester: Manchester University Press, 1995.

30 Elisa Camiscioli, *Reproducing the French Race: Immigration, Intimacy, and Embodiment in the Early Twentieth Century*, Durham, NC: Duke University Press, 2009.

31 Dana S. Hale, 'French Images of Race on Product Trademarks during the Third Republic' in Sue Peabody and Tyler Stovall (eds), *The Color of Liberty: Histories of Race in France*, Durham, NC: Duke University Press, 2004, pp. 131–46.

32 Elsbeth Locher-Scholten, *Women and the Colonial State Essays on Gender and Modernity in the Netherlands Indies 1900–1942*, Chicago: University of Chicago Press, 2000; Ann Laura Stoler, *Carnal Knowledge and Imperial Power: Race and the Intimate in Colonial Rule*, Berkeley and London: University of California Press, 2002.

33 Grever and Waaldijk, *Transforming the Public Sphere*.

34 Pascal Grosse, 'What does German Colonialism have to do with National Socialism? A Conceptual Framework' in Eric Ames, Marcia Klotz and Lora Wildenthal (eds), *Germany's Colonial Pasts*, Lincoln, NE: University of Nebraska Press, 2005, pp. 115–34 (127); Emmanuelle Saada, *Les Enfants de la Colonie: Les Métis de l'Empire Français Entre Sujétion et Citoyenneté*, Paris: Editions de la Découverte, 2007.

35 Adam McKeown, *Melancholy Order: Asian Migration and the Globalization of Borders*, New York: Columbia University Press, 2008, p. 9.

36 Marilyn Lake and Henry Reynolds, *Drawing the Global Colour Line: White Men's Countries and the International Challenge of Racial Equality*, Cambridge: Cambridge University Press, 2008.

37 Andrew Zimmerman, 'Booker T. Washington and the German Empire: Race and Cotton in the Black Atlantic', *Bulletin of the German Historical Institute* 43, Fall 2008, pp. 9–20.

38 W. E. B. Dubois, 'The African Roots of War', http://www.webdubois.org/dbAfricanRWar.html.

39 Isabel Hull, *Absolute Destruction: Military Culture and the Practices of War In Imperial Germany*, Ithaca, NY: Cornell University Press, 2004.

40 Outbreaks of disease occurred well before the official epidemic affected European troop strength throughout the war, leading some contemporary observers to question the viability of West Africans fighting for France for extended military service. See Michael A. Osborne, 'Constructions and Functions of Race in French Military Medicine' in Peabody and Stovall (eds), *The Color of Liberty*, pp. 206–36 (218–19).

41 Peter Fryer, *Staying Power: The History of Black People in Britain*, London: Pluto Press, 1984, pp. 298–316.

42 Yael Fletcher, 'Unsettling Settlers: Colonial Migrants and Racialized Sexuality Interwar Marseilles' in Antoinette Burton (ed.), *Gender, Sexuality and Colonial Modernities*, London and New York: Routledge, 1999, pp. 80–94.

43 Fletcher, 'Unsettling Settlers'.

44 Philippa Levine, *Prostitution, Race and Politics: Policing Venereal Disease in the British Empire*, London and New York: Routledge, 2003.

45 Erez Manela, *The Wilsonian Moment: Self-Determination and the International Origins of Anti-Colonial Nationalism*, Cambridge, MA: Harvard University Press, 2007.

46 Victoria de Grazia, *Irresistible Empire: America's Advance through Twentieth Century Europe*, Cambridge, MA: Harvard University Press, 2005.

47 Mrinalini Sinha, *Spectres of Mother India: The Global Restructuring of an Empire*, Durham, NC: Duke University Press, 2006.

48 Leora Auslander and Thomas Holt, 'Sambo in Paris: Race and Racism in the Iconography of the Everyday' in Peabody and Stovall, *The Color of Liberty*, pp. 147–85.

49 Anna Davin, 'Imperialism and Motherhood', *History Workshop Journal* 5:1, 1978, pp. 9–66; Tara Zahra, '"Each Nation Only Cares for its Own": Empire, Nation, and Child Welfare Activism in the Bohemian Lands, 1900–1900', *American Historical Review* 111:5, 2006, pp. 1378–1402.

50 Mary Louise Roberts, *Civilization Without Sexes: Reconstructing Gender in Postwar France, 1917–1927*, Chicago: Chicago University Press, 1994; Elizabeth Thompson, *Colonial Citizens: Republican Rights, Paternal Privilege, and Gender in French Syria and Lebanon*, New York: Columbia University Press, 2000.

51 Gary Wilder, *The French Imperial Nation-State: Negritude and Colonial Humanism between the Two World Wars*, Chicago: Chicago University Press, 2005; Brent Hayes Edwards, 'The Shadow of Shadows', *positions* 11:1, 2003, pp. 11–49; Nirode K. Barooah, *Chatto: The Life and Times of an Indian Anti-Imperialist in Europe*, Oxford: Oxford University Press, 2004.

52 Leila Rupp, *Worlds of Women: The Making of an International Women's Movement*, Princeton, NJ: Princeton University Press, 1997; Charlotte Weber, 'Between Nationalism and Feminism: The Eastern Women's Congresses of 1930 and 1932', *Journal of Middle East Women's Studies* 4:1, 2008, pp. 83–106.

53 See Lata Mani, *Contentious Traditions: The Debate on Sati in Colonial India*, Berkeley, CA: University of California Press, 1998.

54 See Fiona Paisley, '"Performing Interracial Harmony": Settler Colonialism at the 1934 Pan-Pacific Women's Conference in Hawai'i' in Tony Ballantyne and Antoinette Burton (eds), *Moving Subjects: Gender, Mobility and Intimacy in an Age of Global Empire*, Champaign, Il.: University of Illinois Press, 2008, pp. 127–47.

55 Frederick Cooper, 'Provincializing France' in Ann Laura Stoler, Carole McGranahan and Peter C. Perdue (eds), *Imperial Formations*, Santa Fe, NM: School for Advanced Research, 2007, pp. 341–78.

56 Grosse, 'What does', p. 131.

57 Tina Campt, *Other Germans: Black Germans and the Politics of Race, Gender and Memory*, Ann Arbor: University of Michigan Press, 2003.

58 Grosse, 'What does', p. 120.

59 Kristin Kopp, 'Constructing Racial Difference in Colonial Poland' in Eric Ames, Marcia Klotz and Lora Wildenthal (eds), *Germany's Colonial Pasts*, Lincoln, NE: University of Nebraska Press, 2005, pp. 76–96; Jozsef Borocz, 'Goodness is Elsewhere: The Rule of European Difference', *Comparative Studies in Society and History* 48:1, 2006, pp. 110–38 (134).

AFTERWORD

On 'compulsory sexuality', sexualization, and history

Lisa Downing

My aim in this short afterword is neither to summarize the chapters of this book and provide contextualization for them, as that was one of the tasks fulfilled by the editors' introduction, nor to provide a 'final word' to the collection by writing a conclusion. Rather, I intend to highlight some tensions, problems and areas deserving further scrutiny that my reading of this book suggested to me, and to underscore how the historical analyses carried out here resonate with contemporary cultural and intellectual debates about sex, gender and the body.

Michel Foucault famously wrote that he wished his life's work to be understood as a 'history of the present'.[1] Without apprehending the specificity of shifts in ways of thinking in the past, he suggests, we cannot understand the world in which we live today. This adage has been adopted especially by those who concern themselves with the history – and contemporaneity – of sexuality and the body. As witnessed throughout this book, although some authors take issue with the accuracy of certain of Foucault's broad historical claims, his insights regarding the techniques and technologies of knowledge by which persons came to be understood as 'types' of sexual subject, and sexuality to be constituted as the very secret at the heart of identity itself, have been indispensable for the epistemologies shaping critical humanities perspectives on sex and bodies in the present. Foucault's insights have had significant influence on the queer and deconstructive gender theory that have proliferated in the Anglo-American academy in the last three decades of the twentieth- and first two decades of the twenty-first centuries. While post-structuralist branches of theory are often accused of a woeful ahistoricism, queer theory in particular, with its rich indebtedness to a historian of systems of thought, can benefit from embracing more explicitly an engagement with historicity, as certain recent publications in the field have begun to do.[2] Collections such as the current one, issuing from a history of sexuality perspective, sit between the agendas of corrective historical scholarship and 'queer' political resistance, and are necessary reading for those scholars of sexuality whose principal remit is the present.

The application of historically focused work to contemporary debates can offer a valuable corrective to the inward-looking and present-centred nature of some current thinking on sexual cultures. The recent upsurge of speculation and worry about the 'sexualization' of culture – particularly the sexualization of children – in the Anglo-American world marks a specific articulation of anxiety about sex and its influences. This debate is carried out by a range of disparate interested commentators, including the religious right, keen to protect the 'moral virtue' of the young, the UK coalition government who pledged to investigate the alleged phenomenon in 2011, feminists of all stripes, and scholars from the fields of media and cultural studies. The divisiveness of the issue is particularly visible in the case of feminist debates. On the one hand, 'radical' feminists argue that the ready availability of pornography and sexualized images in the media both reflect and contribute to a misogynistic culture in which girls and women are objectified as the sex class.[3] Other, more 'liberal' or 'sex-positive' feminists argue that this is an over-simplification of the situation, and claim that radical feminism's affiliation to the monolithic position of class-based analysis refuses to pay attention to individual girls' and women's different experiences of facets of 'raunch' culture.[4] Both positions, however, risk ignoring that, as Lisa Z. Sigel points out in her chapter on modern pornography, analyses of the cultural meanings of the phenomena of explicit representation and media images of sex are routinely compromised by the search for universals in the meaning of the genre and the neglect of historical particularities. Likewise, it is crucial that an understanding of the discourses of contagion and corruption that have haunted debates about pornography and censorship, and that found a high point of expression in the nineteenth century with the now discredited theory of degeneration, is brought to bear on such contemporary problems. These historically located discourses continue to haunt – and to obfuscate – our thinking about issues of obscenity. Similarly, the presumed innocence of children – and the way in which we think about children as qualitatively different from the default subject, the adult – are products of a historically recent worldview, as explored in chapters by Julie-Marie Strange and Sarah Toulalan. If we are to separate knee-jerk conservative moral panics from nuanced analyses of the realities of lived, embodied, sexed and gendered experiences, existing in networks of unequally distributed social power relations, an eye to the past is critical.

If panics about 'sexualization' need to be nuanced and historically inflected, it is nevertheless the case that we are witness to an extraordinary and often gleeful proliferation of discourses and debates about sex in our present moment. This may remind us of Foucault's insights in the first volume of the *History of Sexuality* (1976) regarding the extent to which one characteristic of the modern period is that a specific sort of pleasure is found in *talking* about sex (to the detriment of *doing* sex), where such talk included the salacious, the analytic, the confessional and the pathologizing (what he terms 'a kind of generalised discursive erethism'[5]). In light of this trend, we may ask, with some justification, as historians of sexuality or contemporary sexuality studies scholars, *how* to study sexuality without simply contributing to this endless proliferation of discourse, this parade of truth claims about a ubiquitous and centred 'sexuality'. Although this is a genuine concern, it is doubtless the case that, if sex saturates the worldview of our contemporary moment, then simply refusing to talk about it does not constitute an appropriate or efficacious intervention (or lack thereof) either. In 1980, Adrienne Rich famously described heterosexuality's ubiquity, and consequent capacity to pass as natural, as 'compulsory heterosexuality'.[6] Heterosexuality could be described as 'compulsory' for Rich since one cannot, in our present moment, choose not to engage with this ideological norm. The most one can do is resist it – and thereby risk social sanctions and even violence. Careful historical scholarship of the kind undertaken in this volume by Randolph Trumbach, which shows just how recent a phenomenon 'heterosexuality' is in European culture, is useful in helping us to question the universality and prevalence of such compulsory systems – which questioning is evidently not intended to detract from the very real effects of heteronormativity in the present. Using Rich's terminology, we might analogously describe the sex logorrhoea and over-exposure of postmodernity, one local and situated articulation of which is 'sexualization of culture', as 'compulsory sexuality'. Within any compulsory system, the ethical and strategic imperative lies on the side of asking how one might engage with the system to which one is compulsorily subjected in order to show up the interests and iniquities within that system.

Speaking critically and with historical precision of the saturation of sex, normative and otherwise, is important because none of us, as social and embodied subjects, can 'refuse' to engage with it. We can resist dominant versions of sexual narratives and dogmatic discourses of correct bodily practices and presentations, but – as Foucault modelled in expounding his theory of power – we cannot *opt out* of the system in which they circulate. We are always already implicated in, and, I have suggested above, ethically obligated to respond to, the system of compulsory sexuality in which we find ourselves. The chapters in this book contribute to redressing persistent common misunderstandings of sex as natural and enduring across time and place. They also, however, inevitably find themselves engaging with – even if it is to reject – authority discourses about sex *and* the epistemological and logical means by which these discourses establish their truths.

One temptation faced by the historian/critical humanities scholar is that of transposing official, pathologizing knowledge with an alternative – and more egalitarian – discourse, that nevertheless can risk proposing a universalizing version of 'truth'. For example, in his excellent chapter, Ivan Crozier asserts that the truth of the 'perverted' subject's diversity of experience is not found in constraining psychiatric diagnostic criteria, 'official categories' being 'of little help in understanding these practices', but rather in a certain kind of location and experience. He writes: 'It is in the anonymous darkness of the club, with cries obscured by the pounding rhythms of other bodies in motion, that these pleasures and the people who enjoy them thrive.' This assumption – that resistance can best be found in subcultures and alternative communities that offer 'bodies and pleasures' outside of official discourse – is, of course, a recognizable post-Foucauldian gesture. Yet, Foucault and Crozier both risk setting up an alternative set of truth claims to the medical ones, claims that in themselves rest on stereotypes about certain kinds of subjects: all perverts enjoy loud music and communal nocturnal encounters; all gay men enjoy the anonymity of sex in bathhouses, etc. The latter set of claims, even when they issue from community contexts, are no more all-encompassingly 'true' than those claims about the pathological or fixated nature of perverted sexuality or the arrested development of homosexual psychology that issue from the psy sciences. Both assume there is a kind of person who is 'the homosexual' or 'the pervert'. And in both cases, a norm is still being established. In setting up the paradigm of 'the clubbing pervert', the 'antisocial', shy, or privacy-loving person with a non-normative sexuality is inevitably othered from the paradigm for proper perversion ('proper' according to those self-identifying perverts who share a taste for clubbing, as well as for their sexual practices). Thus, subcultures, communities, and left-wing academic writing may unwittingly police identities through discourse in ways that are not identical with, but are analogous to, official forms of knowledge, and that similarly produce a subject that is in keeping with their specific overriding ideologies (e.g. a pro-pleasure, sex-positive politics).

What many of the chapters highlight – whether explicitly, as their aim, or incidentally, as an effect of the very processes by which history is written – are the ways in which some forms of sexuality and some bodily practices have been excessively produced and policed, while others have been subject to considerably less discursive construction and scrutiny. Taking notice of which acts and bodily practices are most discussed in the book is worthwhile, since it is a barometer of both current academic tastes *and* of historical biases. On the one hand, those sexual identities, practices, etc. that have been the most frequently represented and discussed in 'official' authority discourses about sex (Crozier describes homosexuality as the 'the initial sexual "aberration" around which the field of sexology first emerged') will inevitably continue to be most widely treated, as they have the richest and most complex discursive histories – and they thereby reveal something about the concerns, obsessions and fears of those making 'official' history. Equally, however, continuing to pay attention to the most widely represented sexual and bodily phenomena risks contributing to the 'canonization' of certain forms of sexual identity, expression and practice – and of certain historical narratives – at the expense of others.

Bisexuality and asexuality are particularly significant modalities of identity that have arisen in counter- or reverse-discursive forms in recent years, as modes of resistance to dominant narratives of both sexual orientation organized on the principles of binary sexed and gendered attraction, and to compulsory sexuality.[7] Bisexuals are often ignored, thought 'not to exist', as per the familiar charge that 'a bisexual' is 'really' an insufficiently 'out' gay man, or a woman whose 'heteroflexibility' is designed to titillate men (accounting for some lesbians' suspicion of bisexual women and reluctance to date them[8]). Histories of sexuality have been rather silent on the subject of asexuality, understood in the current sense of an identity or 'orientation', rather than historically as a projection onto certain groups and classes of an 'innate nature' (such as women in the eighteenth century, following discourses of domesticity, as Kathryn Norberg shows). A genealogy of asexuality might show that its discursive predecessors are celibacy, a disciplinary practice of clerics, and the medicalized diagnoses of frigidity and impotence.[9] Such a genealogy would offer a unique insight into the ways in which identity formation can issue from silences, stigmas and stereotypes and would demonstrate an unusual temporal drag.[10] In parallel cases (e.g. homosexuality and fetish/BDSM), the historical gap between pathologization and the establishment of subcultures is much shorter, making asexuality a unique test case. It is not a reproach to the authors of the chapters contained in this book that they have less to say about such identity formations that have only recently concretized into subcultures and movements in the Internet age, and begun to attract sparse academic attention, but it will be important for future scholarship to incorporate these emergent voices, identities and practices into an account of the past and contemporary landscapes of sexuality. It is also instructive to note how those subjects embodying less discursively well-established identity positions can find themselves marginalized even within putatively non-normative spaces such as queer and feminist communities (as demonstrated by the example of biphobia within lesbian and gay contexts).

The editors of this book have insisted upon the importance of paying particular and explicit attention to the ways in which 'sexuality' has to be understood as an always already embodied set of experiences and as a history of the body, as well as the product of discursive activity. Foucault made it clear that the body and its experiences are the centre around which 'perpetual spirals of power and pleasure'[11] orbit in the modern period, yet Foucault himself is somewhat guilty of enacting, however unwittingly, a body/discourse split in his carving out of *scientia sexualis* as the dominant form of western sexuality, as distinct from the eastern *ars erotica*. In such a formulation, not only is the West split off from its 'other', as Jonathan Burton points out in his chapter, but also the body is 'othered', to the extent that it is orientalized, with respect to the 'rational' and 'scientific' West. Similarly, Foucault's claim that 'the rallying point for the counterattack against the deployment of sexuality ought not to be sex-desire, but bodies and pleasures', and his assertion that these would be new, previously unsung ways of experiencing the erotic, undermine his insistence elsewhere that the pleasure- and pain-experiencing body *is the very locus* where the disciplining of subjects occurs, the very target of disciplinary power.[12]

The recent broad turn to the body and to experience in many humanities and social sciences disciplines, including psychology's flirtation with phenomenology,[13] and queer theory's engagement with 'affect',[14] suggests a broader recognition of the tendency of much academic theory and practice to evacuate the bodily, the emotional, the tactile, the haptic – in short, those areas of experience traditionally associated with the irrational – from its remit. It also constitutes an attempt to remedy this de-corporealization of academia. What is particularly valuable about the current book's approach is that it sets up ways of thinking about the historicity and contemporaneity of the sexual subject that privilege neither abstract theory and dry discourse over engagement with the body, nor personal testimony and individual bodily experience over the broader analysis of class and consideration of historical power relations. Understanding that the body is at the epicentre of operations of social power as it functions around age, sex, gender, class, race and sexuality is central to the chapters in this book. As Antoinette Burton insists: 'we must admit to the body as *more than incidental* to the fate of polities, nations and empires' [my italics]. Paradigmatically, then, the authors seek to locate the body and its experiences in political, as well as historical and theoretical contexts and to remind us that if we ignore the presence and power of the material body, we engage with only half the story of the history of sexuality.

Notes

1 Michel Foucault, *Discipline and Punish* [1975], trans. Alan Sheridan, Harmondsworth: Penguin, 1991, p. 31.
2 See, for example, Elizabeth Freeman, *Time Binds: Queer Temporalities, Queer Histories*, Durham, NC: Duke University Press, 2011, and Heike Bauer and Matt Cook (eds), *Queer 50s: Rethinking Sexuality in the Postwar Years*, Basingstoke: Palgrave Macmillan, 2012.
3 See, for example, Susannah Paasonen, Kaarina Nikunen and Laura Saarenmaa (eds), *Pornification: Sex and Sexuality in Media Culture*, Oxford: Berg, 2007.
4 Feona Attwood is a proponent of the more nuanced, and also more individualistic, approach to the problem of sexualization of culture. See, for example, Attwood, 'Sexed Up: Theorizing the Sexualization of Culture', *Sexualities* 9:1, 2006, pp. 77–94, and Attwood (ed.), *Mainstreaming Sex: The Sexualization of Western Culture*, London and New York: I. B.Tauris, 2009. For more on the term 'raunch culture', see Ariel Levy, *Female Chauvinist Pigs: Women and the Rise of Raunch Culture*, New York: Free Press, 2005.
5 Michel Foucault, *The Will to Knowledge: The History of Sexuality, vol. 1*, trans. Robert Hurley, Harmondsworth: Penguin, 1990, p. 32.
6 Adrienne Rich, 'Compulsory Heterosexuality and Lesbian Existence' [1980] *Blood, Bread, and Poetry* [1986], New York: Norton, 1994.
7 An academic journal devoted to the study of bisexuality, *The Journal of Bisexuality*, published in the USA by the Taylor & Francis Group, was founded in 2000. Relatively little academic work in the critical humanities and social sciences exists on asexuality. In 2012, Anthony F. Bogaert published a book entitled *Understanding Asexuality* with Rowman and Littlefield.
8 *Diva* magazine, a British publication which defines its intended readership as 'lesbians and bi women', lately faced widespread criticism on the Internet for the alleged biphobia of one of its

articles about relationships between lesbians and bisexual women: http://www.divamag.co.uk/category/lifestyle/can-lesbians-and-bisexuals-find-love-together.aspx.

9 For an excellent recent history of frigidity, see Peter Cryle and Alison Moore, *Frigidity: An Intellectual History*, Basingstoke: Palgrave Macmillan, 2011.

10 'Temporal drag' is Elizabeth Freeman's term (see, for example, *Time Binds*). It punningly suggests both 'drag' in the sense of a gap in time and the performativity of sexed and gendered identities. Freeman advocates the necessity for sex- and gender-identity-based movements in the present to be aware of the historical contexts to which they owe their specificity.

11 Foucault, *The Will to Knowledge*, p. 45.

12 Foucault, *The Will to Knowledge*, p. 157.

13 See especially Darren Langdridge, *Phenomenological Psychology: Theory, Research and Method*, Harlow: Pearson Education, 2007.

14 See especially Sara Ahmed, *The Cultural Politics of Emotion*, London and New York: Routledge, 2004, and *Queer Phenomenology: Orientations, Objects, Others*, Durham, NC: Duke University Press, 2006.

SELECT BIBLIOGRAPHY

Abbott, Mary, *Life Cycles in England 1560–1720: Cradle to Grave*, London and New York: Routledge, 1996.

Abrams, Lynn, *The Making of Modern Woman: Europe 1789–1918*, Harlow: Longman, 2002.

Abu-Lughod, Lila, *Remaking Women: Feminism and Modernity in the Middle East*, Princeton, NJ: Princeton University Press, 1998.

——*Before European Hegemony: The World System AD 1250–1350*, Oxford: Oxford University Press, 1991.

Ackerknecht, Erwin H., *Medicine at the Paris hospital, 1794–1848*, Baltimore: Johns Hopkins Press, 1967.

Adair, Richard, *Courtship, Illegitimacy and Marriage in Early Modern England*, Manchester and New York: Manchester University Press, 1996.

Adler, Zsuzsanna, *Rape on Trial*, London: Routledge, 1987.

Aldrich, Robert, *Colonialism and Homosexuality*, London, New York: Routledge, 2003.

Allen, Ann Taylor, *Women in Twentieth-Century Europe*, Basingstoke and New York: Palgrave Macmillan, 2008.

Allen, Peter Lewis, *The Wages of Sin: Sex and Disease, Past and Present*, Chicago: University of Chicago Press, 2000.

Alloula, Malek, *The Colonial Harem*, Minneapolis: University of Minnesota Press, 1986.

Amir, Menachem, *Patterns in Forcible Rape*, Chicago: University of Chicago Press, 1971.

Amussen, Susan Dwyer, *An Ordered Society: Gender and Class in Early Modern England*, Oxford: Basil Blackwell, 1988.

Anderson, Bonnie S. and Judith P. Zinsser, *A History of Their Own: Women in Europe from Prehistory to the Present*, 2nd edn, New York: Oxford University Press, 2000.

Andreski, S., *Syphilis, Puritanism, and Witch Hunts: historical explanations in the light of medicine and psychoanalysis with a forecast about AIDS*, New York: St Martin's Press, 1989.

Andrew, Donna T., *Philanthropy and Police: London Charity in the Eighteenth Century*, Princeton: Princeton University Press, 1989.

Andrews, Walter G. and Mehmet Kalpakli, *The Age of Beloveds: Love and the Beloved in Early-Modern Ottoman and European Culture and Society*, Durham, NC: Duke University Press, 2005.

Anselment, Raymond A., *Realms of Apollo: Literature and Healing in Seventeenth-Century England*, Newark: University of Delaware Press, 1995.

Ariès, Philippe, *Centuries of Childhood: A Social History of Family Life*, trans. Robert Baldick, New York: Random, 1960.

Ariès, Philippe, Georges Duby *et al.* (eds), *A History of Private Life*, 5 vols, Cambridge, MA, and London: Belknap Press of Harvard University Press, 1987.

Arney, William Ray, *Power and the Profession of Obstetrics*, London: University of Chicago Press, 1985.

Arnold, Janet, *Queen Elizabeth's Wardrobe Unlock'd*, Leeds: Maney, 1988.

Arons, Wendy, *Eucharius Rösslin: When Midwifery Became the Male Physician's Province. The Sixteenth Century Handbook 'The Rose Garden for Pregnant Women and Midwives'*, Jefferson, NC: McFarland and Company, 1994.

Arrizabalaga, Jon, John Henderson and Roger K. French, *The Great Pox: The French Disease in Renaissance Europe*, New Haven: Yale University Press, 1997.

Ashelford, Jane, *The Art of Dress: Clothes and Society 1500–1914*, London: The National Trust, 1996.

——, *Dress in the Age of Elizabeth I*, London: Batsford, 1988.

Askin, Kelly Dawn, *War Crimes Against Women: Prosecution in International War Crimes Tribunals*, The Hague: Martinus Nijhoff, 1997.

Attwood, Feona (ed.), *Mainstreaming Sex: The Sexualization of Western Culture*, London and New York: I. B. Tauris, 2009.

Babayan, Kathryn and Afsaneh Najmabadi (eds), *Islamicate Sexualities: Translations across Temporal Geographies of Desire*, Cambridge, MA: Harvard University Press, 2008.

Bagchi, Jasodhara, *Indian Women, Myth and Reality*, Hyderabad: Sangam Books, 1995.

Bailey, Amanda, *Flaunting: Style and the Subversive Male Body in Renaissance England*, Toronto: University of Toronto Press, 2007.

Bailey, Joanne, *Unquiet Lives: Marriage and Marriage Breakdown in England, 1660–1800*, Cambridge: Cambridge University Press, 2003.

Baines, Barbara J., *Representing Rape in the English Early Modern Period*, Lewiston: Edwin Mellen Press, 2003.

Bakhtin, Mikhail, *Rabelais and His World*, trans. Hélène Iswolsky, Bloomington: Indiana University Press, 1984.

Baldwin, Frances Elizabeth, *Sumptuary Legislation and Personal Regulation in England*, Baltimore: Johns Hopkins University, 1926.

Baldwin, Peter, *Disease and Democracy: The Industrialized World Faces AIDS*, Berkeley, CA: University of California Press, 2005.

——, *Contagion and the State in Europe, 1830–1930*, Cambridge: Cambridge University Press, 1999.

Ballhatchett, K., *Race, Sex, and Class under the Raj: Imperial Attitudes and Policies and their Critics, 1793–1905*, London: Weidenfeld and Nicolson, 1980.

Banner, Stuart, *The Death Penalty: An American History*, Cambridge, MA: Harvard University Press, 2003.

Barlow, Tani E. (ed.), *Formations of Colonial Modernity in East Asia*, Durham, NC: Duke University Press, 1997.

Barooah, Nirode K., *Chatto: The Life and Times of an Indian Anti-Imperialist in Europe*, Oxford: Oxford University Press, 2004.

Barret-Ducrocq, Françoise, *Love in the Time of Victoria: Sexuality, Class and Gender in Nineteenth-Century London*, London: Verso, 1991.

Bartley, Paula, *Prostitution, Prevention and Reform in England, 1860–1914*, London: Routledge, 2000.

Battin, Margaret P., Leslie P. Francis, Jay A. Jacobson and Charles B. Smith, *The Patient as Victim and Vector*, Oxford: Oxford University Press, 2009.

Bauer, Heike and Matt Cook (eds), *Queer 50s: Rethinking Sexuality in the Postwar Years*, Basingstoke: Palgrave Macmillan, 2012.

Bayly, C. A., *The Birth of the Modern World, 1780–1814*, Oxford: Blackwell, 2004.

Beaujot, Ariel, *Victorian Fashion Accessories*, London: Berg, 2012.

Bell, Rudolph M., *How to Do It: Guides to Good Living for Renaissance Italians*, Chicago: Chicago University Press, 1999.

Bellini, Ligia, *A Coisa Obscura: mulher, sodomia e inquisição no Brasil colonial*, São Paulo: Brasilense, 1987.

Bénabou, Erica-Marie, *La prostitution et la police des moeurs aux XVIIIe siècle*, Paris: Perrin, 1987.

Benjamin, Jessica, *The Bonds of Love: Psychoanalysis, Feminism, and the Problem of Domination*, New York: Pantheon, 1988.

Bennett, Herman, *Africans in Colonial Mexico: Absolutism, Christianity, and Afro-Creole Consciousness, 1570–1640*, Bloomington: Indiana University Press, 2003.

Berco, Cristian, *Sexual Hierarchies, Public Status: Men, Sodomy and Society in Spain's Golden Age*, Toronto: University of Toronto Press, 2007.

Berger, John, Sven Blomberg, Chris Fox, Michael Dibb and Richard Hollis, *Ways of Seeing*, London: British Broadcasting Corporation and Penguin Books, 1972.

Berger, Stefan, *Writing the Nation: A Global Perspective*, Basingstoke: Palgrave, 2007.

Berman, Marshall, *All That Is Solid Melts Into Air: The Experience of Modernity*, London: Verso, 1983.

Bernard, G. W., *The King's Reformation: Henry VIII and the Remaking of the English Church*, New Haven: Yale, 2005.

Bernasconi, Roberto and Tommy Lott, *The Idea of Race*, Indianapolis: Hackett Publishing Company, 2000.

Berriot-Salvadore, Evelyne, *Les femmes dans la société française de la Renaissance*, Geneva: Droz, 1990.

Betteridge, Tom (ed.), *Sodomy in Early Modern Europe*, Manchester: Manchester University Press, 2002.

Bignamini, Ilaria and Martin Postle, *The Artist's Model: Its Role in British Art from Lely to Etty*, Nottingham: Nottingham University Art Gallery, 1991.

Bingham, Adrian, *Family Newspapers? Sex, Private Life, and the British Popular Press 1918–1978*, Oxford: Oxford University Press, 2009.

——, *Gender, Modernity, and the Popular Press in Inter-War Britain*, Oxford and New York: Clarendon, 2004.

Birke, Lynda, *Feminism and the Biological Body*, Edinburgh: Edinburgh University Press, 1999.

Blaikie, Andrew, *Illegitimacy, Sex and Society in North-East Scotland, 1750–1900*, Oxford: Oxford University Press, 1994.

Bland, Lucy, *Banishing the Beast, English Feminism and Sexual Morality, 1885–1914*, London: Penguin, 1995.

Blanshard, Alastair J. L., *Sex, Vice and Love from Antiquity to Modernity*, Chichester: Wiley-Blackwell, 2010.

Blench, J. W., *Preaching in England in the Late Fifteenth and Sixteenth Centuries*, Oxford: Basil Blackwell, 1964.

Bleys, Rudi C., *The Geography of Perversion: Male-to-male Sexual Behaviour outside the West and the Ethnographic Imagination, 1750–1918*, New York: New York University Press, 1995.

Bloch, Iwan, *Sexual Life in England*, London: Alfred Aldor, 1938.

——, *The Sexual Life of Our Time: In Its Relations To Modern Civilization*, London: Rebman, 1909; translated from the German *Das Sexualleben unserer Zeit in seinen Beziehungen zur modernen Kultur*, Berlin: Marcus Verlagsbuchhandlung, 1906.

Blom, Ida, *Medicine, Morality and Political Culture: Legislation on Venereal Disease in Five Northern European Countries, c. 1870-c. 1995*, Lund, Sweden: Nordic Academic Press, 2012.

Blood, Robert O. and Donald M. Wolfe, *Husbands and Wives: The Dynamics of Married Living*, New York: Free Press, 1960.

Blundell, Sue, *Women in Ancient Greece*, Cambridge, MA: Harvard University Press, 1995.

Bock, Gisela and Allison Brown, *Women in European History*, Malden, MA: Blackwell Publishers, 2001.

Bogaert, Anthony F., *Understanding Asexuality*, Lanham, MD: Rowman and Littlefield, 2012.

Bologne, Jean Claude, *La naissance interdite*, Paris: Olivier Orban, 1988.

Bongiorno, Frank, *The Sex Lives of Australians: A History*, Collingwood: Black Inc., 2012.

Borhan, Pierre and Gilles Mora, *Men for Men: Homoeroticism and Male Homosexuality in the History of Photography, 1840–2006*, London: Jonathan Cape, 2007.

Borris, Kenneth and George S. Rousseau (eds), *The Sciences of Homosexuality in Early Modern Europe*, New York: Routledge, 2007.

Boswell, John, *The Marriage of Likeness: Same-sex Unions in Pre-Modern Europe*, London: Harper Collins, 1995.

——, *Christianity, Social Tolerance and Homosexuality: Gay People in Europe From the Beginning of the Christian Era to the Fourteenth Century*, Chicago: University of Chicago Press, 1980.

Bottomley, Frank, *Attitudes to the Body in Western Christendom*, London: Lepus Books, 1979.

Bourke, Joanna, *Rape: A History from 1860 to the Present*, London: Virago, 2007.

Bowers, Toni, *The Politics of Motherhood: British Writing and Culture, 1680–1760*, Cambridge: Cambridge University Press, 1996.

Branca, Patricia, *Women in Europe since 1750*, New York: St Martin's Press, 1978.

SELECT BIBLIOGRAPHY

Braudel, Fernand, *Civilisation and Capitalism 15th–18th Century*, trans. Siân Reynolds, *Vol. 1 The Structures of Everyday Life: The Limits of the Possible*, London: Collins, 1981.

Bray, Alan, *The Friend*, Chicago: University of Chicago Press, 2003.

——, *Homosexuality in Renaissance England*, London: Gay Men's Press, 1982; New York: Columbia University Press, 1995.

Breward, Christopher, *The Hidden Consumer: Masculinities, Fashion and City Life 1860–1914*, Manchester: Manchester University Press, 1999.

——, *The Culture of Fashion: A New History of Fashionable Dress*, Manchester: Manchester University Press, 1995.

Briffault, Robert, Bronislaw Malinowski and Ashley Montagu, *Marriage, Past and Present: A Debate between Robert Briffault and Bronislaw Malinowski*, Boston: P. Sargent, 1956.

Brockliss, Laurence and Colin Jones, *The Medical World of Early Modern France*, Oxford: Oxford University Press, 1997.

Brook, Barbara, *Feminist Perspectives on the Body*, London and New York: Longman, 1999.

Brooke, Stephen, *Sexual Politics: Sexuality, Family Planning, and the British Left from the 1880s to the Present Day*, Oxford and New York: Oxford University Press, 2011.

Brooks, Douglas A. (ed.), *Printing and Parenting in Early Modern England*, Aldershot: Ashgate, 2005.

Broomhall, Susan, *Women's Medical Work in Early Modern France*, Manchester: Manchester University Press, 2004.

Brooten, Bernadette, *Love Between Women: Early Christian Responses to Female Homoeroticism*, Chicago: University of Chicago Press, 1996.

Brown, Kathleen, *Foul Bodies: Cleanliness in Early America*, New Haven: Yale University Press, 2009.

Brown, Kevin, *The Pox: The Life and Near Death of a Very Social Disease*, Stroud: Sutton Publishing, 2006.

Brownmiller, Susan, *Against Our Will: Men, Women, and Rape*, New York: Simon & Schuster, 1975.

Brundage, James A., *Law, Sex and Christian Society in Medieval Europe*, Chicago: University of Chicago Press, 1987.

Bullough, Vern L. and Bonnie Bullough, *Women and Prostitution: A social history*, Buffalo, NY: Prometheus, 1987.

Bullough, Vern L. and James A. Brundage (eds), *Sexual Practices and the Medieval Church*, Buffalo, NY: Prometheus Books, 1982.

Burgess, Ernest W. and Harvey J. Locke, *The Family: From Institution to Companionship*, New York: American Book Company, 1945.

Burgoyne, Jacqueline L. and David Clark (eds), *Marriage, Domestic Life, and Social Change: Writings for Jacqueline Burgoyne, 1944–88*, London and New York: Routledge, 1991.

Burguière, André, Christiane Klapisch-Zuber, Martine Segalen and Françoise Zonabend, *A History of the Family: Volume II. The Impact of Modernity*, trans. Sarah Hanbury Tenison, Cambridge, MA: Belknap Press, 1996.

Burke, Peter, *New Perspectives on Historical Writing*, 2nd edn, Cambridge: Polity Press, 2001.

Burton, Antoinette, *Burdens of History: British Feminists, Indian Women and Imperial Culture, 1865–1915*, Chapel Hill, NC: University of North Carolina Press, 1994.

—— (ed.), *After the Imperial Turn: Thinking With and Through the Nation*, Durham, NC: Duke University Press, 2003.

Burton, Antoinette and Tony Ballantyne (eds), *Bodies in Contact: Rethinking Colonial Encounters in World History*, Durham, NC: Duke University Press, 2005.

Butler, Judith, *Precarious Life*, London and New York: Verso, 2004.

——, *Bodies that Matter: On the Discursive Limits of 'Sex'*, New York; London: Routledge, 1993.

——, *Gender Trouble: Feminism and the Subversion of Identity*, New York: Routledge, 1990.

Bynum, William F. and Helen Bynum (eds), *Dictionary of Medical Biography*, Westport: Greenwood Press 2007.

Bynum, W. F. and Roy Porter (eds), *Medicine and the Five Senses*, Cambridge: Cambridge University Press, 1993.

——, *Companion Encyclopedia of the History of Medicine*, London and New York: Routledge, 1993.

Cadden, Joan, *Meanings of Sex Difference in the Middle Ages: Medicine, Science, and Culture*, Cambridge: Cambridge University Press, 1993.

Caferro, William, *Contesting the Renaissance*, Oxford: Blackwell Publishing, 2011.

Califia, Pat, *Public Sex: The Culture of Radical Sex*, San Francisco: Cleis Press, 1994.

Cameron, Euan, *The European Reformation*, Oxford: Oxford University Press, 1991.

Camiscioli, Elisa, *Reproducing the French Race: Immigration, Intimacy, and Embodiment in the Early Twentieth Century*, Durham, NC: Duke University Press, 2009.

Campt, Tina, *Other Germans: Black Germans and the Politics of Race, Gender and Memory*, Ann Arbor: University of Michigan Press, 2003.

Canguilhem, Georges, *The Normal and Pathological*, New York: Zone Books, 1989.

Carden-Coyne, Ana, *Reconstructing the Body: Classicism, Modernism, and the First World War*, Oxford: Oxford University Press, 2009.

Carmichael, Ann G., *Plague and the Poor in Renaissance Florence*, Cambridge: Cambridge University Press, 1986.

Carroll, Stuart (ed.), *Cultures of Violence: Interpersonal Violence in Historical Perspective*, Basingstoke: Palgrave, 2007.

——, *Blood and Violence in Early Modern France*, Oxford: Oxford University Press, 2006.

Carter, Sophie, *Purchasing Power: Representing Prostitution in Eighteenth-Century English Popular Print Culture*, Aldershot: Ashgate, 2004.

Cavallo, Sandra, *Artisans of the Body in Early Modern Italy: Identities, Families and Masculinities*, Manchester: Manchester University Press, 2007.

Chakrabarty, Dipesh, *Provincializing Europe: Postcolonial Thought and Historical Difference*, Princeton: Princeton University Press, 2000.

Chamberlain, Geoffrey, *From Witchcraft to Wisdom: A History of Obstetrics and Gynaecology*, London: RCOG Press, 2007.

Chase, Karen, *The Victorians and Old Age*, Oxford: Oxford University Press, 2009.

Chauncey, George, *Gay New York: Gender, Urban Culture and the Making of the Gay Male World, 1890–1940*, New York: Basic Books, 1995.

Cheype, Robert, *Recherches sur le procès des inspecteurs de police 1716–1720*, Paris: Presses Universitaires de France, 1975.

Chinn, Carl, *They Worked All Their Lives: Women of the Urban Poor in England, 1880–1939*, Manchester: Manchester University Press, 1988.

Clark, Anna, *The History of Sexuality in Europe: A Sourcebook and Reader*, New York: Routledge, 2010.

——, *Desire: A History of European Sexuality*, London: Routledge, 2008.

——, *The Struggle for the Breeches: Gender and the Making of the British Working Classes*, London: Routledge, 1995.

Clark, David and J. D. Haldane, *Wedlocked?: Intervention and Research in Marriage*, Cambridge: Polity Press, 1990.

Clark, Kenneth, *The Nude: A Study in Ideal Form*, New York: Pantheon Books, 1956.

Clark, Peter (ed.), *Small Towns in Early Modern Europe*, Cambridge: Cambridge University Press, 1995.

Clarke, Adele E., *Disciplining Reproduction: Modernity, American Life and the Problems of Sex*, London: University of California Press, 1998.

Clement, Elizabeth Alice, *Love for Sale: Courting, Treating, and Prostitution in New York City, 1900–1945*, Chapel Hill: University of North Carolina Press, 2006.

Cleminson, Richard and Francisco Vázquez García, *Hermaphroditism, Medical Science and Sexual Identity in Spain, 1850–1960*, Cardiff: University of Wales Press, 2009.

Cobb, Matthew, *The Egg and Sperm Race: The Seventeenth-Century Scientists Who Unravelled the Secrets of Sex, Life and Growth*, London: The Free Press, 2006.

Cocks, H. G., *Nameless Offences: Homosexual Desire in the Nineteenth Century*, London: I. B.Tauris, 2003.

Cody, Lisa Forman, *Birthing the Nation: Sex, Science, and the Conception of Eighteenth-Century Britons*, Oxford: Oxford University Press, 2005.

Coghlan, Timothy Augustine, *The Decline in the Birth-Rate of NSW and Other Phenomenon of Child-Birth: An Essay in Statistics*, Sydney: William Applegate, 1903.

Cohen, Elizabeth and Thomas Cohen, *Words and Deeds in Renaissance Rome: Trials before the Papal Magistrates*, Toronto: Toronto University Press, 1993.

Cohen, Sherrill, *The Evolution of Women's Asylums Since 1500*, Oxford: Oxford University Press, 1992.

Cole, Shaun, *'Don We Now Our Gay Apparel': Gay Men's Dress in the Twentieth Century*, Oxford: Berg, 2000.

Cole, Simon A., *Suspect Identities: A History of Fingerprinting and Criminal Identities*, Cambridge, MA: Harvard University Press, 2002.

Collins, Marcus, *Modern Love: An Intimate History of Men and Women in Twentieth Century Britain*, London: Atlantic, 2003.

Conley, Carolyn A., *The Unwritten Law: Crime and Justice in Victorian Kent*, New York and Oxford: Oxford University Press, 1991.

Conway, Jill Ker, *The Road From Coorain*, Port Melbourne: William Heinemann Australia, 1993 [1989].

Cook, Harold J., *Trials of an Ordinary Doctor: Joannes de Groenevelt in Seventeenth-Century London*, Baltimore and London: The Johns Hopkins University Press, 1994.

Cook, Hera, *The Long Sexual Revolution: English Women, Sex and Contraception, 1800–1975*, Oxford: Oxford University Press, 2004.

Cook, Matt, *London and the Culture of Homosexuality*, Cambridge: Cambridge University Press, 2003.

Cook, Noble David, *Born to Die: Disease and New World Conquest, 1492–1650*, Cambridge: Cambridge University Press, 1998.

Coontz, Stephanie, *Marriage, A History: How Love Conquered Marriage*, New York: Penguin, 2006.

Cooper, Emmanuel, *Fully Exposed: The Male Nude in Photography*, 2nd edn, London: Routledge, 1995.

Cooper, Frederick and Ann Stoler (eds), *Tensions of Empire: Colonial Cultures in a Bourgeois World*, Berkeley: University of California Press, 1997.

Corbin, Alain, *Women for Hire: Prostitution and Sexuality in France after 1850*, Cambridge, MA: Harvard University Press, 1990.

Cottret, Bernard, *Calvin: A Biography*, London: Continuum, 2003.

Cox, Pamela, *Gender, Justice and Welfare: Bad Girls in Britain, 1900–1959*, Basingstoke: Palgrave Macmillan, 2003.

Cox-Rearick, Janet, *The Drawings of Pontormo*, Cambridge, MA: Harvard University Press, 2 vols, 1964.

Crawford, Katherine, *The Sexual Culture of the French Renaissance*, Cambridge: Cambridge University Press, 2010.

——, *European Sexualities, 1400–1800*, Cambridge: Cambridge University Press, 2007.

Cressy, David, *Travesties and Transgressions in Tudor and Stuart England: Tales of Discord and Dissension*, Oxford: Oxford University Press, 2000.

——, *Birth, Marriage and Death: Ritual, Religion and the Life-Cycle in Tudor and Stuart England*, Oxford: Oxford University Press, 1997.

Crompton, Louis, *Homosexuality and Civilization*, Cambridge, MA: Harvard University Press, 2003.

Crosby, Alfred W., *The Columbian Exchange: Biological and Cultural Consequences of 1492*, Westport, CO: Greenwood, 1972.

Crowther, Kathleen M., *Adam and Eve in the Protestant Reformation*, Cambridge: Cambridge University Press, 2010.

Cryle, Peter and Alison Moore, *Frigidity: An Intellectual History*, Basingstoke: Palgrave Macmillan, 2011.

Cumming, Valerie, *Understanding Fashion History*, London: Batsford, 2004.

Cunningham, Andrew, *The Anatomical Renaissance: The Resurrection of the Anatomical Projects of the Ancients*, Aldershot: Scolar Press, 1997.

Cunningham, Andrew and Ole Peter Grell, *The Four Horsemen of the Apocalypse: Religion, War, Famine and Death in Reformation Europe*, Cambridge: Cambridge University Press, 2000.

Cunnington, Phillis and Anne Buck, *Children's Costume in England 1300–1900*, London: A & C Black, 1965.

Cusset, Catherine (ed.), *Libertinage and Modernity*, New Haven and London: Yale University Press, 1998.

Cutter, Irving Samuel and Henry R. Viets, *A Short History of Midwifery*, Philadelphia, PA: Saunders, 1964.

Dabhoiwala, Faramerz, *The Origins of Sex: A History of the First Sexual Revolution*, London: Allen Lane, 2012.

Darmon, Pierre, *Le Tribunal de l'impuissance: Virilité et défaillances conjugales dans l'ancienne France*, Paris: Seuil, 1979.

——, *Le mythe de la procréation á l'âge baroque*, Paris: J.-J. Pauvert, 1977.

Darnton, Robert, *The Forbidden Best-Sellers of Pre-Revolutionary France*, New York: W. W. Norton & Company, 1995.

——, *Édition et sédition: L'Univers de la littérature clandestine au XVIIIe siécle*, Paris: Gallimard, 1991.

——, *The Literary Underground of the Old Regime*, Cambridge, MA: Harvard University Press, 1982.

Daston, Lorraine and Katharine Park, *Wonders and the Order of Nature, 1150–1750*, New York: Zone Books, 1998.

Davenport-Hines, R. P. T., *Sex, Death and Punishment: Attitudes to sex and sexuality in Britain since the Renaissance*, London: Fontana Press, 1990.

Davidoff, Leonore and Catherine Hall, *Family Fortunes: Men and Women of the English Middle Class, 1780–1850*, Chicago: University of Chicago Press, 1987.

Davidson, Arnold, *The Emergence of Sexuality*, Cambridge, MA: Harvard University Press, 2002.

Davidson, Roger, *Dangerous Liaisons: A Social History of Venereal Disease in Twentieth-Century Scotland*, Amsterdam: Rodopi, 2000.

Davidson, Roger and Lesley A. Hall (eds), *Sex, Sin and Suffering: Venereal Disease and European Society since 1870*, London: Routledge, 2001.

Davis, Gayle, *The Cruel Madness of Love: Sex, Syphilis and Psychiatry in Scotland, 1880–1930*, Amsterdam: Rodopi, 2008.

Davis, Mark, *Sex, Technology and Public Health*, Basingstoke: Palgrave, 2009.

Davis, Natalie Zemon, *Trickster Travels: A Sixteenth-Century Muslim Between Worlds*, New York: Hill & Wang, 2006.

——, *Fiction in the Archives: Pardon Tales and their Tellers in Sixteenth-Century France*, Bloomington: Stanford University Press, 1990.

——, *Society and Culture in Early Modern France*, Stanford: Stanford University Press, 1975.

Davis, Whitney, *Queer Beauty: Sexuality and Aesthetics from Winckelmann to Freud and Beyond*, New York: Columbia University Press, 2010.

Dawkins, Heather, *The Nude in French Art and Culture, 1870–1910*, New York: Cambridge University Press, 2002.

Dawkins, Richard, *The Selfish Gene*, 30th anniversary edition, Oxford: Oxford University Press, 2006 [New York: OUP, 1976].

D'Cruze, Shani (ed.), *Everyday Violence in Britain, 1850–1950*, London: Longman, 2000.

——, *Crimes of Outrage: Sex, Violence and Victorian Working Women*, London: UCL Press, 1998.

Dean, Mitchell, *Governmentality: Power and Rule in Modern Society*, London: Sage, 1999.

Dean, Trevor and K. J. P. Lowe (eds), *Marriage in Italy, 1300–1650*, Cambridge: Cambridge University Press, 1998.

de Brouwer, Anne-Marie, *Supra-national Criminal Prosecution of Sexual Violence: The ICC and the Practice of the ICTY and ICTR*, Antwerp: Intersentia, 2005.

de Grazia, Victoria, *Irresistible Empire: America's Advance through Twentieth Century Europe*, Cambridge, MA: Harvard University Press, 2005.

——, *How Fascism Ruled Women: Italy, 1922–1945*, Berkeley: University of California Press, 1993.

DeJean, Joan, *The Reinvention of Obscenity: Sex, Lies and Tabloids in Early Modern France*, Chicago: University of Chicago Press, 2002.

Dekker, Rudolf and Lotte van der Pol, *The Tradition of Female Transvestism in Early Modern Europe*, Basingstoke and London: Macmillan, 1989.

Deleuze, Gilles, *Coldness and Cruelty*, New York: Zone Books, 1991.

Demand, Nancy, *Birth, Death, and Motherhood in Classical Greece*, Baltimore, MD: Johns Hopkins University Press, 1994.

D'Emilio, John, *Sexual Politics, Sexual Communities: The Making of a Homosexual Minority in the United States, 1940–1970*, Chicago: University of Chicago Press, 1983.

D'Emilio, John and Estelle B. Freedman, *Intimate Matters: A History of Sexuality in America*, New York: Harper & Row, 1988.

Deneffe, Victor, *Le speculum de la matrice à travers les âges*, Antwerp: Caals, 1902.

Dennis, Norman, Fernando Henriques and Clifford Slaughter, *Coal Is Our Life. An Analysis of a Yorkshire Mining Community*, London: Tavistock, 1969.

Deutsch, Jan-Georg, *Emancipation without Abolition in German East Africa, c. 1884–1914*, Oxford: James Currey, 2006.

Díez, Xavier, *Utopia sexual a la premsa anarquista de Catalunya: la revista 'Etica-Iniciales' (1927–1937)*, Lleida: Pagès Editors, 2001.

di Lauro, Al and Gerald Rabkin, *Dirty Movies: An Illustrated History of the Stag Film, 1915–1970*, New York: Chelsea House, 1976.

Djerassi, Carl, *This Man's Pill: Reflections on the 50th Birthday of the Pill*, Oxford: Oxford University Press, 2001.

Doezema, Jo, *Sex Slaves and Discourse Masters: The Construction of Trafficking*, London: Zed Books, 2010.

Domenech, Fernando Benito, *The Paintings of Ribalta 1565/1628*, New York: Spanish Institute, 1988.

Donoghue, Emma, *Passions between Women: British Lesbian Culture, 1668–1801*, London: Scarlet Press, 1993.

Döpp, Hans-Jürgen, *Paris Eros: The Imaginary Museum of Eroticism*, New York: Parkstone Press, 2004.

Douglas, Mary, *Purity and Danger: An analysis of concepts of pollution and taboo*, London: Routledge & Kegan Paul, 1978 [1966].

——, *Natural Symbols*, Harmondsworth: Pelican Books, 1973.

Downing, Lisa and Robert Gillett (eds), *Queer in Europe: Contemporary Case Studies*, Farnham: Ashgate, 2011.

Dreger, Alice D., *Hermaphrodites and the Medical Invention of Sex*, Cambridge, MA; London: Harvard University Press, 1988.

Duberman, Martin Bauml, Martha Vicinus and George Chauncey Jr. (eds), *Hidden from History: Reclaiming the Gay and Lesbian Past*, New York: Meridian, 1989.

Dubois, Laurent, *A Colony of Citizens: Revolution and Slave Emancipation in the French Caribbean, 1787–1804*, Chapel Hill: University of North Carolina Press, 2004.

Duden, Barbara, *Disembodying Women: Perspectives on Pregnancy and the Unborn*, trans. Lee Hoinacki, Cambridge, MA: Harvard University Press, 1993.

——, *The Woman Beneath the Skin: A Doctor's Patients in Eighteenth-Century Germany*, trans. Thomas Dunlap, Cambridge, MA: Harvard University Press, 1991 [1987].

——, *Geschichte unter der Haut. Ein Eisenacher Arzt und seine Patientinnen um 1730*, Stuttgart: Klett, 1987.

Duerr, Hans Peter, *Intimität: Der Mythos vom Zivilisationsprozeß*, Frankfurt: Suhrkamp, 1994.

Duffin, Jacalyn, *To See with A Better Eye: A life of R. T. H. Laennec*, Princeton: Princeton University Press, 1998.

Duggan, Lisa and Nan Hunter, *Sex Wars: Sexual Dissent and Political Culture*, London and New York: Routledge, 1995.

Dutour, Olivier, G. Pálfi, J. Berato and J. Brun (eds), *L'origine de la syphilis en Europe: Avant ou après 1493?*, Paris: Editions Errance, 1994.

Dworkin, Andrea, *Pornography: Men Possessing Women*, New York: Putnam, 1982.

——, *Woman Hating*, New York: E.P. Dutton, 1974.

Dyhouse, Carol, *Feminism and the Family in England, 1880–1939*, Oxford and New York: Basil Blackwell, 1989.

Eccles, Audrey, *Obstetrics and Gynaecology in Tudor and Stuart England*, Kent, OH: Kent State University Press; London: Croom Helm, 1982.

Eder, Franz X., Lesley Hall and Gert Hekma, *Sexual Cultures in Europe: Themes in Sexuality*, Manchester: Manchester University Press, 1999.

Edgell, Stephen, *Middle-Class Couples: A Study of Segregation, Domination, and Inequality in Marriage*, London and Boston: G. Allen & Unwin, 1980.

Ehrenreich, Barbara, *The Hearts of Men: American Dreams and the Flight From Commitment*, Garden City, NJ: Anchor Press/Doubleday, 1983.

Ehrenreich, Barbara and Deidre English, *For Her Own Good: 150 Years of the Experts' Advice to Women*, London: Pluto Press, 1979.

——, *Witches, Midwives, and Nurses: A History of Women Healers*, New York: The Feminist Press, 1973.

Ekserdjian, David, *Parmigianino*, New Haven: Yale, 2006.

Elias, Norbert, *The Civilizing Process, Vol. 1, The History of Manners*, trans. Edmund Jephcott, 2 vols, Oxford: Blackwell, 1978, 1982.

——, *Über den Prozess der Zivilization: soziogenetische und psychogenetische Untersuchungen*, Bern: Franke Verlag, 1969.

Ellenzweig, Allen, *The Homoerotic Photograph: Male Images from Durieu/Delacroix to Mapplethorpe*, New York: Columbia University Press, 1992.

Ellinghaus, Katherine, *Taking Assimilation to Heart: Marriages of White Women and Indigenous Men in Australia and the United States, 1887–1937*, Lincoln, NE: University of Nebraska Press, 2006.

El-Rouayheb, Khaled, *Before Homosexuality in the Arab-Islamic World, 1500–1800*, Chicago: University of Chicago Press, 2005.

Ember, Carol R. and Melvin Ember, *Encyclopedia of Sex and Gender: Men and Women in the World's Cultures*, New York: Kluwer Academic/Plenum Publishers, 2003.

Emiliani, Andrea, *Federico Barocci (Urbino 1535–1612)*, Ancona: Ars, 2008.

Emsley, Clive, *Crime and Society in England, 1750–1900*, 3rd edn, Harlow: Longman, 2005.

Entwistle, Joanne, *The Fashioned Body: Fashion, Dress and Modern Social Theory*, Cambridge: Polity Press, 2000.

Epprecht, Marc, *Hungochani: The History of Dissident Sexuality in Southern Africa*, Montreal: McGill-Queens University Press, 2004.

Epstein, Steven, *Impure Science*, Berkeley: California University Press, 1997.

Epstein, William H., *John Cleland: Images of a Life*, New York: Columbia University Press, 1974.

Ericsson, Kjersti and Eva Simonsen (eds), *Children of World War Two*, Oxford: Berg, 2005.

Erll, Astrid and Ann Rigney, *Mediation, Remediation, and the Dynamics of Cultural Memory*, Berlin and New York: Walter de Gruyter, 2009.

Esteban, Mari Luz, *Antropología del cuerpo. Género, itinerarios corporales, identidad y cambio*, Barcelona: Edicions Bellaterra, 2004.

Evans, Tanya, *Unfortunate Objects: Lone Mothers in Eighteenth-Century London*, Basingstoke: Palgrave, 2005.

Evans, Tanya and Pat Thane, *Sinners? Scroungers? Saints?: Unmarried Motherhood in Twentieth-Century England*, Oxford: Oxford University Press, 2012.

Evenden, Doreen, *The Midwives of Seventeenth-Century London*, Cambridge: Cambridge University Press, 2000.

Fabricius, Johannes, *Syphilis in Shakespeare's England*, London: Kingsley, 1994.

Fagan, Brian M., *The Little Ice Age: How Climate Made History 1300–1850*, New York: Basic Books, 2000.

Fanon, Frantz, *The Wretched of the Earth*, New York: Grove Press, 1968.

Farber, David (ed.), *The Sixties: From Memory to History*, London; Chapel Hill: University of North Carolina Press, 1995.

Farr, James Richard, *Authority and Sexuality in Early Modern Burgundy (1550–1730)*, Oxford and New York: Oxford University Press, 1995.

Faull, Katherine M. (ed.), *Masculinity, Senses, Spirit*, Lewisburg: Bucknell University Press, 2011.

Featherstone, Lisa, *Let's Talk About Sex: Histories of Sexuality in Australia, 1901–1961*, Newcastle: Cambridge Scholars Press, 2012.

Fenton, James, *School of Genius: A History of the Royal Academy of Arts*, London: Royal Academy of Arts, 2006.

Ferraro, Joanne M., *Nefarious Crimes, Contested Justice: Illicit Sex and Infanticide in the Republic of Venice, 1557–1789*, Baltimore, MD: Johns Hopkins University Press, 2008.

Fisher, Kate, *Birth Control, Sex and Marriage in Britain 1918–60*, Oxford: Oxford University Press, 2006.

Fisher, Will, *Materializing Gender in Early Modern English Literature and Culture*, Cambridge: Cambridge University Press, 2006.

Fissell, Mary E., *Vernacular Bodies: The Politics of Reproduction in Early Modern England*, Oxford: Oxford University Press, 2004.

Flandrin, Jean-Louis, *Sex in the Western World: The Development of Attitudes and Behaviour*, trans. Sue Collins, London: Routledge, 1991.

——, *Families in Former Times: Kinship, Household and Sexuality*, trans. R. Southern, Cambridge: Cambridge University Press, 1979.

——, *Familles: parenté, maison, sexualité dans l'ancienne société*, Paris: Hachette, 1976.

——, *Les Amours paysannes. Amour et sexualité dans les campagnes de l'ancienne France (XVIe–XIXe siècle)*, Paris: Gallimard, 1975.

Fletcher, Ronald, *The Family and Marriage in Britain: An Analysis and Moral Assessment*, Harmondsworth: Penguin, 1966.

Flouret, Jean, *Nicholas Venette, Médecin Rochelais, 1633–1698*, La Rochelle: Editions Rupella, 1992.

Floyd-Wilson, Mary, *English Ethnicity and Race in Early Modern Drama*, New York: Cambridge University Press, 2003.

Flügel, John Carl, *The Psychology of Clothes*, London: Hogarth Press, 1930.

Forbes, Thomas Rogers, *The Midwife and the Witch*, New Haven, CT: Yale University Press, 1966.

Foster, Hal (ed.), *Vision and Visuality*, Seattle: Bay, 1988.

Foster, Thomas A. (ed.), *Long Before Stonewall: Histories of Same-Sex Sexuality in Early America*, New York: New York University Press, 2007.

Foucault, Michel, *The Birth of Biopolitics: Lectures at the Collège de France, 1978–79*, Basingstoke: Palgrave Macmillan, 2008.

——, *Discipline and Punish* [1975], trans. Alan Sheridan, Harmondsworth: Penguin, 1991.

——, *The History of Sexuality, Vol. 1, An Introduction*, trans. Robert Hurley, New York: Vintage, 1980 [1976].

——, *Herculine Barbin, Being the Recently Discovered Memoirs of a Nineteenth-Century French Hermaphrodite*, trans. Richard McDougall, New York: Pantheon Books, 1980.

——, *Discipline and Punish: The Birth of the Prison*, New York: Vintage, 1977.

——, *La naissance de la clinique*, 7th edn, Paris: Quadrige, 2003 [1973].

——, *Archaeology of Knowledge*, trans. Alan Sheridan, New York: Pantheon Books, 1972.

Foxcroft, Louise, *Hot Flushes, Cold Science: The History of the Modern Menopause*, London: Granta, 2009.

Foxon, David, *Libertine Literature in England, 1660–1745*, Hyde Park, NY: University Books, 1965.

Foyster, Elizabeth A., *Marital Violence: An English Family History, 1660–1875*, Cambridge: Cambridge University Press, 2005.

——, *Manhood in Early Modern England, Honour, Sex and Marriage*, London and New York: Longman, 1999.

Frank, Andrew Gunder, *Re-Orient: Global Economy in the Asian Age*, Berkeley, CA: University of California Press, 1998.

Frantz, David O., *Festum Voluptatis: A Study of Renaissance Erotica*, Columbus: Ohio State University Press, 1989.

Fraterrigo, Elizabeth, *Playboy and the Making of the Good Life in Modern America*, Oxford: Oxford University Press, 2009.

Freeman, Elizabeth, *Time Binds: Queer Temporalities, Queer Histories*, Durham, NC: Duke University Press, 2011.

French, Roger, *Dissection and Vivisection in the European Renaissance*, Aldershot: Ashgate, 1999.

Fruhstuck, Sabine, *Colonizing Sex: Sexology and Social Control in Modern Japan*, Berkeley, CA: University of California Press, 2003.

Fryer, Peter, *Staying Power: The History of Black People in Britain*, London: Pluto Press, 1984.

Fuchs, Eckhardt and Benedikt Stuchtey, *Across Cultural Borders: Historiography in Global Perspective*, Lanham, MD: Rowman & Littlefield, 2002.

Fuchs, Rachel, *Poor and Pregnant in Nineteenth Century Paris*, Berkeley: New Brunswick, 1992.

Gaisser, Julia Haig, *Catullus and his Renaissance Readers*, Oxford: Clarendon Press, 1993.

Garton, Stephen, *Histories of Sexuality, Antiquity to Sexual Revolution*, London: Equinox, 2004.

Garvey, Nicola, *Just Sex? The Cultural Scaffolding of Rape*, London, Routledge, 2005.

Gatrell, V. A. C., *The Hanging Tree: Execution and the English People 1770–1868*, Oxford: Oxford University Press, 1994.

Gay, Peter, *The Bourgeoise Experience: Victoria to Freud, Vol. 1, The Education of the Senses*, New York: Oxford University Press, 1984.

Gelbart, Nina Rattner, *The King's Midwife: A History and Mystery of Madame du Coudray*, Berkeley, CA: University of California Press, 1998.

Gélis, Jacques, *Les enfants des limbes: Mort-nés et parents dans l'Europe chrétienne*, Paris: l'Audibert, 2006.

——, *La sage-femme ou le médecin: une nouvelle conception de la vie*, Paris: Fayard, 1988.

Gentilcore, David, *Healers and Healing in Early Modern Italy*, Manchester: Manchester University Press, 1998.

Gerard, Kent and Gert Hekma (eds), *The Pursuit of Sodomy: Male Homosexuality in Renaissance and Enlightenment Europe*, New York: Routledge, 1989.

Getsy, David J., *Body Doubles: Sculpture in Britain, 1877–1905*, New Haven, CT: Yale University Press, 2004.

Gibson, Mary, *Prostitution and the State in Italy, 1860–1915*, New Brunswick, NJ: Rutgers University Press, 1986.

Giese, Loreen L., *Courtships, Marriage Customs, and Shakespeare's Comedies*, Basingstoke: Palgrave Macmillan, 2006.

Gilbert, Ruth, *Early Modern Hermaphrodites*, Basingstoke: Palgrave, 2002.

Gilman, Sander, *Picturing Health and Illness: Images of Identity and Difference*, Baltimore: Johns Hopkins University Press, 1995.

——, *Disease and Representation: Images of Illness from Madness to AIDS*, Ithaca: Cornell University Press, 1988.

Gilroy, Paul, *Against Race: Imagining Political Culture Beyond the Colour Line*, Cambridge, MA: Harvard University Press, 2000.

——, *The Black Atlantic: Modernity and Double Consciousness*, Cambridge, MA: Harvard University Press, 1993.

Gittings, Claire, *Death, Burial and the Individual in Early Modern England*, London: Croom Helm, 1984.

Gittins, Diana, *Fair Sex, Family Size and Structure, 1900–1939*, London: Hutchinson, 1982.

Goldthorpe, J. H., D. Lockwood, F. Bechhofer and J. Platt, *The Affluent Worker*, Cambridge: Cambridge University Press, 1968.

Goody, Jack, *The European Family: An Historico-Anthropological Essay*, Oxford: Blackwell, 2000.

Gorer, Geoffrey, *Sex and Marriage in England Today: A Study of the Views and Experience of the Under-45s*, London: Nelson, 1971.

——, *Exploring English Character*, London: The Cresset Press, 1955.

Gottlieb, Beatrice, *The Family in the Western World from the Black Death to the Industrial Age*, Oxford and New York: Oxford University Press, 1993.

Goulemot, Jean Marie, *Forbidden Texts: Erotic Literature and its Readers in Eighteenth-Century France*, trans. James Simpson, Cambridge, UK: Polity Press, 1994.

Gowing, Laura, *Common Bodies: Women, Touch, and Power in Seventeenth-Century England*, New Haven, CT: Yale University Press, 2003.

——, *Domestic Dangers: Women, Words and Sex in Early Modern London*, Oxford: Oxford University Press, 1996.

Gowing, Laura, Michael Hunter and Miri Rubin (eds), *Love, Friendship and Faith in Europe, 1300–1800*, Basingstoke: Palgrave Macmillan, 2005.

Grafton, Anthony and Lisa Jardine, *From Humanism to Humanities: The Institutionalizing of the Liberal Arts in Fifteenth- and Sixteenth-Century Europe*, Cambridge, MA: Harvard University Press, 1986.

Grant, Kevin, *A Civilized Savagery: Britain and the New Slaveries in Africa, 1884–1926*, London and New York: Routledge, 2005.

Green, James N., *Beyond Carnival: Male Homosexuality in Twentieth-Century Brazil*, Chicago: University of Chicago Press, 1999.

Green, Monica H., *Making Women's Medicine Masculine: The Rise of Male Authority in Pre-Modern Gynaecology*, Oxford: Oxford University Press, 2008.

Greenfield, Susan C. and Carol Barash, *Inventing Maternity: Politics, Science and Literature, 1650–1865*, Lexington: University Press of Kentucky, 1999.

Greer, Germaine, *The Beautiful Boy*, New York: Rizzoli, 2003.

——, *The Female Eunuch*, London: Paladin, 1970.

Gregory, Jeanne and Sue Lees, *Policing Sexual Assault*, London: Routledge, 1999.

Grell, Ole Peter and Andrew Cunningham (eds), *Health Care and Poor Relief in Protestant Europe, 1500–1700*, London: Routledge, 1997.

Grell, Ole Peter Andrew Cunningham and Jon Arrizabalaga (eds), *Health Care and Poor Relief in Counter-Reformation Europe*, London: Routledge, 1999.

Grever, Maria and Berteke Waaldijk, *Transforming the Public Sphere: The Dutch National Exhibition of Women's Labor in 1898*, Durham, NC: Duke University Press, 2004.

Griffiths, Paul, *Youth and Authority: Formative Experiences in England 1560–1640*, Oxford: Clarendon Press, 1996.

Grosz, Elizabeth, *Volatile Bodies: Toward a Corporeal Feminism*, Bloomington, IN: Indiana University Press, 1994.

Gruhn, John G. and Ralph R. Kazer, *Hormonal Regulation of the Menstrual Cycle: The Evolution of Concepts*, London: Plenum Medical Book Company, 1989.

Guadiana, Claire, *The Cabaret Poetry of Théophile de Viau*, Tubingen: Nar, 1981.

Guber, Susan and Joan Hoff (eds), *For Adult Users Only*, Bloomington, IN: Indiana University Press, 1989.

Haas, Louis, *The Renaissance Man and His Children: Childbirth and Early Childhood in Florence*, New York: St Martin's Press, 1998.

Hacking, Ian, *The Social Construction of What?*, Cambridge: Cambridge University Press, 1999.

Hall, Catherine, *White, Male and Middle Class: Explorations in Feminism and History*, London and New York: Routledge, 1992.

Hall, Catherine, Keith McClelland and Jane Rendall, *Defining the Victorian Nation: Class, Race, Gender and the Reform Act of 1867*, Cambridge: Cambridge University Press, 2000.

Hall, Lesley A. (ed.), *Outspoken Women; An Anthology of Women's Writing on Sex, 1870–1969*, London: Routledge, 2005.

——, *Sex, Gender and Social Change in Britain since 1880*, Basingstoke: Macmillan, 2000.

Halperin, David M., *How to do the History of Homosexuality*, Chicago: University of Chicago Press, 2004.

Hamer, Dean and Paul Copeland, *The Science of Desire: The Search for the Gay Gene and the Biology of Behaviour*, New York: Simon & Schuster, 1994.

Hamling, Tara and Catherine Richardson (eds), *Everyday Objects: Medieval and Early Modern Material Culture and its Meaning*, Farnham: Ashgate, 2010.

Hammerton, A. James, *Cruelty and Companionship: Conflict in Nineteenth-Century Married Life*, London and New York: Routledge, 1992.

Hankins, James, *Plato in the Renaissance*, 2 vols, Leiden and New York: Brill, 1990.

Hannaford, Ivan, *Race, The History of an Idea in the West*, Baltimore: Johns Hopkins University Press, 1996.

Harding, Alan, *The Law Courts of Medieval England*, London: George Allen & Unwin, 1973.

Harper, Catherine, *Intersex*, Oxford; New York: Berg, 2007.

Harrington, Joel Francis, *Reordering Marriage and Society in Reformation Germany*, Cambridge: Cambridge University Press, 1995.

Harris, Victoria, *Selling Sex in the Reich: Prostitutes in German Society, 1914–1945*, Oxford: Oxford University Press, 2010.

Harsin, Jill, *Policing Prostitution in Nineteenth-Century Paris*, Princeton, NJ: Princeton University Press, 1985.

Hart, Avril and Susan North, *Historical Fashion in Detail: The 17th and 18th Centuries*, London: V&A Publications, 1998.

Hartman, Mary S., *The Household and the Making of History: A Subversive View of the Western Past*, Cambridge and New York: Cambridge University Press, 2004.

Harvey, Karen, *Reading Sex in the Eighteenth Century: Bodies and Gender in English Erotic Culture*, Cambridge: Cambridge University Press, 2004.

Haste, Cate, *Rules of Desire: Sex in Britain World War I to the Present*, London: Pimlico, 1994 [1992].

Hau, Michael, *The Cult of Health and Beauty in Germany: A Social History, 1890–1930*, Chicago: University of Chicago Press, 2003.

Hausman, Bernice, *Changing Sex: Transsexualism, Technology, and the Idea of Gender*, Durham, NC, and London: Duke University Press, 1995.

Hayward, Maria, *Rich Apparel: Clothing and the Law in Henry VIII's England*, Farnham: Ashgate, 2009.

———, *Dress at the Court of King Henry VIII*, Leeds: Maney, 2007.

Healey, Dan, *Homosexual Desire in Revolutionary Russia: The Regulation of Sexual and Gender Dissent*, Chicago: University of Chicago Press, 2001.

Healy, Margaret, *Fictions of Disease in Early Modern England*, Basingstoke: Palgrave, 2001.

Heath, Kay, *Ageing by the Book: The Emergence of Midlife in Victorian Britain*, Albany: State University of New York Press, 2009.

Henderson, Tony, *Disorderly Women in Eighteenth-Century London: Prostitution and Control in the Metropolis, 1730–1830*, London: Longman, 1999.

Heng, Geraldine, *Empire of Magic: Medieval Romance and the Politics of Cultural Fantasy*, New York: Columbia University Press, 2003.

Herdt, Gilbert (ed.), *Third Sex, Third Gender: Beyond Sexual Dimorphism in Culture and History*, New York: Zone Books, 1996.

Herlihy, David and Christiane Klapisch-Zuber, *Tuscans and their Families: A Study of the Florentine Catasto of 1427*, New Haven, CT: Yale University Press, 1985.

Herndl, Diane Price, *Invalid Women: Figuring Feminine Illness in American Fiction and Culture, 1840–1940*, Chapel Hill: University of North Carolina Press, 1993.

Hershatter, Gail, *Dangerous Pleasures: Prostitution and Modernity in Twentieth-Century Shanghai*, Berkeley: University of California Press, 1997.

Herzog, Dagmar, *Sexuality in Europe: A Twentieth Century History*, Cambridge: Cambridge University Press, 2011.

——— (ed.), *Brutality and Desire: War and Sexuality in Europe's Twentieth Century*, Basingstoke: Palgrave, 2009.

———, *Sex After Fascism: Memory and Morality in Twentieth Century Germany*, Princeton: Princeton University Press, 2005.

———(ed.), *Sexuality and German Fascism*, Oxford and New York: Berghahn, 2004.

Hillman, David and Carla Mazzio (eds), *The Body in Parts: Fantasies of Corporality in Early Modern Europe*, New York and London: Routledge, 1997.

Hines, Sally and Tam Sanger (eds), *Transgender Identities: Towards a Social Analysis of Gender Diversity*, London: Routledge, 2010.

Hird, Myra J., *Sex, Gender and Science*, Basingstoke: Palgrave, 2004.

Hirsch, Jennifer S. and Holly Wardlow, *Modern Loves: The Anthropology of Romantic Courtship and Companionate Marriage*, Ann Arbor: University of Michigan Press, 2006.

Hitchcock, Tim, *English Sexualities, 1700–1800*, New York and London: St Martin's Press, 1997.

Hoggart, Richard B., *The Uses of Literacy: Aspects of Working-Class Life*, London: Chatto & Windus, 1957.

Hollander, Anne, *Sex and Suits*, New York: Knopf, 1994.

Horn, David, *The Criminal Body: Lombroso And The Anatomy Of Deviance*, New York: Routledge, 2003.

——, *Social Bodies: Science, Reproduction, and Italian Modernity*, Princeton, NJ: Princeton University Press, 1994.

Horrocks, Roger, *Male Myths and Icons: Masculinity in Popular Culture*, New York: St Martin's Press, 1995.

Houck, Judith A., *Hot and Bothered: Women, Medicine and Menopause in Modern America*, Cambridge, MA: Harvard University Press, 2006.

Houlbrook, Matt, *Queer London: Perils and Pleasures in the Gay Metropolis, 1918–1957*, Chicago: University of Chicago Press, 2005.

Houlbrooke, Ralph, *Death, Religion, and the Family in England, 1480–1750*, Oxford: Clarendon Press, 1998.

——, *The English Family, 1450–1700*, London and New York: Longman, 1984.

Houppert, Karen, *The Curse: Confronting the Last Unmentionable Taboo*, London: Profile, 2000.

Howell, Philip, *Geographies of Regulation: Policing Prostitution in Nineteenth-Century Britain and the Empire*, Cambridge: Cambridge University Press, 2009.

Hsia, R. Po-Chia, *Social Discipline in the Reformation: Central Europe 1550–1750*, London: Routledge, 1989.

Huet, Marie-Hélène, *Monstrous Imagination*, Cambridge, MA: Harvard University Press, 1993.

Hull, Isabel, *Absolute Destruction Military Culture and the Practices of War In Imperial Germany*, Ithaca, NY: Cornell University Press, 2004.

——, *Sexuality, State and Civil Society in Germany, 1700–1815*, Ithaca, NY: Cornell University Press, 1997.

Humphries, Steve, *A Secret World of Sex: Forbidden Fruit: The British Experience 1900–1950*, London: Sidgwick and Jackson, 1988.

Hunt, Alan, *Governance of the Consuming Passions: A History of Sumptuary Law*, London: Macmillan, 1996.

Hunt, Lynn (ed.), *The Invention of Pornography: Obscenity and the Origins of Modernity, 1500–1800*, New York: Zone Books, 1993.

Hyam, Ronald, *Empire and Sexuality: The British Experience*, Manchester: Manchester University Press, 1990.

Ingram, Martin, *Church Courts, Sex and Marriage in England, 1570–1640*, Cambridge: Cambridge University Press, 1987.

Iñiguez, Diego Angulo, *Murillo*, 3 vols, Madrid: Espasa-Calpe, 1981.

Israel, Jonathan I., *Enlightenment Contested: Philosophy, Modernity, and the Emancipation of Man, 1670–1752*, New York: Oxford University Press, 2009.

Itzin, Catherine, *Home Truths About Child Abuse: A Reader*, London: CRC Press, 2000.

Jackson, Louise A., *Child Sexual Abuse in Victorian England*, London: UCL Press, 2000.

Jackson, Mark, *Infanticide: Historical Perspectives on Child Murder and Concealment, 1550–2000*, Aldershot: Ashgate, 2002.

Jacquart, Danielle and Claude Thomasset, *Sexuality and Medicine in the Middle Ages*, trans. Matthew Adamson, Cambridge: Polity Press, 1988 [1985].

Jardine, Lisa, *Still Harping on Daughters: Women and Drama in the Age of Shakespeare*, New York: Columbia University Press, 1989, 2nd edn.

Jelavich, Peter, *Berlin Cabaret*, Cambridge, MA: Harvard University Press, 1993.

Jenkins, David (ed.), *Cambridge History of Western Textiles*, 2 vols, Cambridge: Cambridge University Press, 2003.

Jennings, Rebecca, *Tomboys and Bachelor Girls: A Lesbian History of Post-war Britain 1945–71*, Manchester: Manchester University Press, 2007.

——, *A Lesbian History of Britain: Love and Sex between Women since 1500*, Oxford; Westport, CT: Greenwood World Publishing, 2007.

Jensen, Erik N., *Body by Weimar: Athletes, Gender, and German Modernity*, Oxford: Oxford University Press, 2010.

Jephcott, Agnes Pearl, *Married Women Working*, London: Allen & Unwin, 1962.

Johnson, Donald Clay and Helen Bradley Foster (eds), *Dress Sense: Emotional and Sensory Experiences of the Body and Clothes*, Oxford: Berg, 2007.

Johnson, Janet Elise and Jean C. Robinson, *Living Gender after Communism*, Bloomington, IN: Indiana University Press, 2007.

Jones, Ann Rosalind and Peter Stallybrass, *Renaissance Clothing and the Materials of Memory*, Cambridge: Cambridge University Press, 2000.

Jones, Colin and Roy Porter (eds), *Reassessing Foucault: Power, Medicine and the Body*, London and New York: Routledge, 1994.

Jordanova, Ludmilla, *Sexual Visions: Images of Gender in Science and Medicine between the Eighteenth and Twentieth Centuries*, New York and London: Harvester Wheatsheaf, 1989.

Jütte, Robert, *Contraception: A History*, trans. Vicky Russell, Cambridge: Polity Press, 2008.

Karant-Nunn, Susan C., *The Reformation of Ritual: An Interpretation of Early Modern Germany*, London and New York: Routledge, 1997.

Karkazis, Katrina, *Fixing Sex: Intersex, Medical Authority, and Lived Experience*, Durham, NC; London: Duke University Press, 2008.

Karras, Ruth Mazo, *Sexuality in Medieval Europe: Doing unto others*, London: Routledge, 2005.

Katz, Jonathan, *The Invention of Heterosexuality*, Chicago: University of Chicago Press, 2007.

Kearney, Patrick J., *A History of Erotic Literature*, Hong Kong: Dorset Press, 1993.

Keele, Kenneth D., *The Evolution of Clinical Methods in Medicine*, London: Pitman, 1963.

Keller, Eve, *Generating Bodies and Gendered Selves: The Rhetoric of Reproduction in Early Modern England*, Seattle: University of Washington Press, 2007.

Kendrick, Walter, *The Secret Museum: Pornography in Modern Culture*, New York: Viking, 1987.

Kent, Susan Kingsley, *Gender and Power in Britain, 1640–1990*, London: Routledge, 1999.

——, *Sex and Suffrage in Britain 1860–1914*, London: Routledge, 1987.

Kerr, Madeline, *The People of Ship Street*, London and New York: Routledge & Kegan Paul/Humanities Press, 1958.

Kertzer, David I. and Marzio Barbagli, *Family Life in the Twentieth Century*, New Haven: Yale University Press, 2003.

——, *The History of the European Family 2, Family Life in the Long Nineteenth Century, 1789–1913*, New Haven: Yale University Press, 2002.

Kincaid, James, *Child-Loving: The Erotic Child and Victorian Culture*, London: Routledge, 1992.

King, Helen, *Midwifery, Obstetrics and the Rise of Gynaecology: The Uses of a Sixteenth Century Compendium*, Aldershot: Ashgate, 2007.

——, *The Disease of Virgins: Green-Sickness, Chlorosis and the Problems of Puberty*, London: Routledge, 2003.

——, *Hippocrates' Woman: Reading the Female Body in Ancient Greece*, London: Routledge, 1998.

Kingdon, Robert M., *Adultery and Divorce in Calvin's Geneva*, Cambridge, MA: Harvard University Press, 1995.

Kiple, Kenneth F. and Stephen V. Beck (eds), *Biological Consequences of the European Expansion, 1450–1800*, Aldershot: Ashgate, 1997.

Kipnis, Laura, *Bound and Gagged: Pornography and the Politics of Fantasy in America*, New York: Grove Press, 1996.

Knibiehler, Yvonne and Catherine Fouquet, *La femme et les médecins: analyse historique*, Paris: Hachette, 1983.

Knowles, David and R. Neville Hadcock, *Medieval Religious Houses, England and Wales*, New York: St Martin's Press, 1971.

Kohler, Michael (ed.), *The Body Exposed: Views of the Body: 150 Years of the Nude in Photography*, trans. John S. Southard and Glen Burns, Zurich: Edition Stemmle, 1995.

Kollmann, Nancy Shields, *By Honor Bound: State and Society in Early Modern Russia*, Ithaca: Cornell University Press, 1999.

Kon, Igor S., *The Sexual Revolution in Russia: From the Age of the Czars to Today*, New York: The Free Press, 1995.

Koonz, Claudia, *Mothers in the Fatherland: Women, the Family and Nazi Politics*, New York: St Martin's Press, 1987.

Kopf, David, *The Brahmo Samaj and the Shaping of the Modern Indian Mind*, Princeton, NJ: Princeton University Press, 1979.

Koven, Seth, *Slumming: Sexual and Social Politics in Victorian London*, Princeton: Princeton University Press, 2004.

Kuchta, David, *The Three-Piece Suit and Modern Masculinity: England, 1550–1850*, Berkeley: University of California Press, 2002.

Kulpa, Robert and Joanna Mizielińska, *De-Centring Western Sexualities: Central and Eastern European Perspectives*, Farnham: Ashgate, 2011.

Kunzle, David, *Fashion and Fetishism: Corsets, Tight-Lacing, and Other Forms of Body-Sculpture*, new edn, Stroud, Gloucestershire: Sutton, 2004.

——, *Fashion and Fetishism: a Social History of the Corset, Tight-Lacing, and Other Forms of Body-Sculpture in the West*, Totowa, NJ: Rowman and Littlefield, 1982.

Kusch, Martin, *Psychological Knowledge*, London: Routledge, 1995.

Laget, Mireille, *Naissances: L'accouchement avant l'âge de la clinique*, Paris: Seuil, 1982.

Laite, Julia, *Common Prostitutes and Ordinary Citizens: Commercial Sex in London, 1885–1960*, Basingstoke: Palgrave, 2012.

Lake, Marilyn and Henry Reynolds, *Drawing the Global Colour Line: White Men's Countries and the International Challenge of Racial Equality*, Cambridge: Cambridge University Press, 2008.

Landesman, Elisabeth, *Dirt for Art's Sake: Books on Trial from Madame Bovary to Lolita*, Ithaca: Cornell University Press, 2007.

Lang, Sabine, *Men as Women, Women as Men: Changing Gender in Native American Cultures*, Austin: University of Texas Press, 1998.

Langdridge, Darren, *Phenomenological Psychology: Theory, Research and Method*, Harlow: Pearson Education, 2007.

Laqueur, Thomas, *Solitary Sex*, New York: Zone Books, 2004.

——, *Making Sex: Body and Gender from the Greeks to Freud*, Cambridge, MA, and London: Harvard University Press, 1990.

Larivaille, Paul, *La vie quotidienne des courtisanes en Italie au temps de la Renaissance*, Paris: Hachette 1975.

Laslett, Peter, *Family Life and Illicit Love in Earlier Generations*, Cambridge: Cambridge University Press, 1977.

——, *The World We Have Lost: English Life before the Industrial Age*, New York: Charles Scribner's Sons, 1965.

Lassonde, Stephen, *Learning to Forget: Schooling and Family Life in New Haven's Working Class, 1870–1940*, New Haven, CT: Yale University Press, 2005.

Latour, Bruno, *Reassembling the Social: An Introduction to Actor-Network Theory*, Oxford and New York: Oxford University Press, 2005.

——, *We Have Never Been Modern*, trans. Catherine Porter, Cambridge, MA: Harvard University Press, 1993.

Lawn, Brian, *The Salernitan Questions: An Introduction to the History of Medieval and Renaissance Problem Literature*, Oxford: Clarendon Press, 1963.

Lebrun, François, *La Vie conjugale sous l'Ancien Régime*, Paris: Armand Colin, 1975.

Lemire, Beverly, *Dress, Culture and Commerce: The English Clothing Trade before the Factory, 1660–1800*, Basingstoke: Macmillan, 1997.

——, *Fashion's Favourite: The Cotton Trade and the Consumer in Britain, 1660–1800*, Oxford: Pasold Research Fund and Oxford University Press, 1991.

Leonard, Diana, *Sex and Generation: A Study of Courtship and Weddings*, London and New York: Tavistock Publications, 1980.

Leppert, Richard D., *The Nude: The Cultural Rhetoric of the Body in the Art of Western Modernity*, Boulder, CO: Westview Press, 2007.

Leupp, Gary, *Male Colors: The Construction of Homosexuality in Tokugawa Japan*, Berkeley: University of California Press, 1995.

Levack, Brian, *The Witch Hunt in Early Modern Europe*, New York: Longman, 2006.

LeVay, Simon, *Gay, Straight, and the Reason Why*, Oxford: Oxford University Press, 2010.

Levine, Laura, *Men in Women's Clothing: Anti-Theatricality and Effeminization 1579–1642*, Cambridge: Cambridge University Press, 1994.

Levine, Philippa, *Prostitution, Race and Politics: Policing Venereal Disease in the British Empire*, London and New York: Routledge, 2003.

Levine-Clark, Marjorie, *Beyond the Reproductive Body: The Politics of Women's Health and Work in Early Victorian England*, Ohio: Ohio University Press, 2004.

Levy, Ariel, *Female Chauvinist Pigs: Women and the Rise of Raunch Culture*, New York: Free Press, 2005.

Lewinski, Jorge, *The Naked and the Nude: A History of the Nude in Photographs, 1839 to the Present*, New York: Harmony Books, 1987.

Lewis, Jane, *The End of Marriage? Individualism and Intimate Relations*, Cheltenham, UK, and Northampton, MA: Edward Elgar, 2001.

Lewis, Jane, David Clark and D. H. J. Morgan, *'Whom God Hath Joined Together': The Work of Marriage Guidance*, London and New York: Tavistock/Routledge, 1992.

Light, Alison, *Forever England: Femininity, Literature and Conservatism between the Wars*, London: Routledge, 1991.

Lilly, J. Robert, *Taken by Force: Rape and American GIs during World War II*, Basingstoke: Palgrave, 2007.

Lindemann, Mary, *Medicine and Society in Early Modern Europe*, Cambridge: Cambridge University Press, 1999.

Lindsey, Ben B. and Wainwright Evans, *Companionate Marriage*, New York: Boni & Liveright, 1927.

Litten, Julian, *The English Way of Death: The Common Funeral Since 1450*, London: Robert Hale, 1991.

Llewellyn, Nigel, *The Art of Death: Visual Culture in English Death Ritual c.1500–c.1800*, London: Reaktion, 1991.

Locher-Scholten, Elsbeth, *Women and the Colonial State Essays on Gender and Modernity in the Netherlands Indies 1900–1942*, Chicago: University of Chicago Press, 2000.

Long, Kathleen P., *Hermaphrodites in Renaissance Europe*, Aldershot: Ashgate, 2006.

Loomba, Ania and Jonathan Burton, *Race in Early Modern England: A Documentary Companion*, New York: Palgrave, 2007.

Loude, Michel, *Littérature érotique et libertine au xviie siècle*, Lyon: Aléas, 1994.

Loudon, Irvine, *Death in Childbirth: An International Study of Maternal Care and Maternal Mortality 1800–1950*, Oxford: Clarendon, 1992.

Lovenduski, Joni and Vicky Randall, *Contemporary Feminist Politics: Women and Power in Britain*, Oxford: Oxford University Press, 1993.

Lucie-Smith, Edward, *Adam: The Male Figure in Art*, New York: Rizzoli, 1998.

Luddy, Maria, *Prostitution and Irish Society, 1800–1940*, Cambridge: Cambridge University Press, 2007.

Lynch, Katherine A., *Individuals, Families, and Communities in Europe, 1200–1800: The Urban Foundations of Western Society*, Cambridge: Cambridge University Press, 2003.

Lynd, Robert Staughton and Helen Merrell Lynd, *Middletown, a Study in Contemporary American Culture*, New York: Harcourt, Brace and Company, 1929.

Lynn, John, *Women, Armies and Warfare in Early Modern Europe*, Cambridge: Cambridge University Press, 2008.

——, *Giant of the Grand Siècle: The French Army 1610–1715*, Cambridge: Cambridge University Press, 1998.

Lyons, Andrew P. and Harriet Lyons, *Irregular Connections: A History of Anthropology and Sexuality*, Lincoln, NE: University of Nebraska Press, 2004.

Macfarlane, Alan, *Marriage and Love in England: Modes of Reproduction 1300–1840*, Oxford: Blackwell, 1986.

Mackie, Erin Skye, *Market à La Mode: Fashion, Commodity, and Gender in The Tatler and The Spectator*, Baltimore, MD: Johns Hopkins University Press, 1997.

Maclean, Ian, *The Renaissance Notion of Woman: A Study in the Fortunes of Scholasticism and Medical Science in European Intellectual Life*, Cambridge: Cambridge University Press, 1980.

Magarey, Susan, *Passions of the First-Wave Feminists*, Sydney: UNSW Press, 2001.

Mahon, Alyce, *Surrealism and the Politics of Eros, 1938–1968*, New York: Thames and Hudson, 2005.

Mahood, Linda, *The Magdalenes: Prostitution in the Nineteenth Century*, London: Routledge, 1990.

Majumdar, Rochona, *Marriage and Modernity: Family Values in Colonial Bengal*, Durham, NC: Duke University Press, 2009.

Manela, Erez, *The Wilsonian Moment: Self-Determination and the International Origins of Anti-Colonial Nationalism*, Cambridge, MA: Harvard University Press, 2007.

Mani, Lata, *Contentious Traditions: The Debate on Sati in Colonial India*, Berkeley, CA: University of California Press, 1998.

Marcus, Sharon, *Between Women: Friendship, Desire, and Marriage in Victorian England*, Princeton: Princeton University Press, 2007.

Marcus, Stephen, *The Other Victorians: A Study of Sexuality and Pornography in Mid-Nineteenth Century England*, New York: Basic Books, 1964.

Marks, Lara, *Sexual Chemistry: A History of the Contraceptive Pill*, London: Yale University Press, 2001.

Marland, Hilary (ed.), *The Art of Midwifery: Early Modern Midwives in Europe*, London and New York: Routledge, 1993.

Mason, Michael, *The Making of Victorian Sexual Attitudes*, Oxford: Oxford University Press, 1994.

Mason, Peter, *Deconstructing America: Representations of the Other*, New York: Routledge, 1990.

Mathur, Saloni, *India by Design: Colonial History and Cultural Display*, Berkeley, CA: University of California Press, 2007.

Matic, Srdan, Jeffrey V. Lazarus and Martin C. Donoghoe (eds), *HIV/AIDS in Europe: Moving from Death Sentence to Chronic Disease Management*, Copenhagen, Denmark: World Health Organization, 2006.

Mavor, Carol, *Pleasures Taken: Performances of Sexuality and Loss in Victorian Photographs*, London: I. B. Tauris, 1996.

Maynard, John, *Victorian Discourses on Religion and Sexuality*, Cambridge: Cambridge University Press, 1995.

McCalman, Iain, *Radical Underworld: Prophets, Revolutionaries, and Pornographers, 1795–1840*, Oxford: Clarendon Press, 1993.

MacDonald, Michael, *Witchcraft and Hysteria in Elizabethan London: Edward Jorden and the Mary Glover Case*, London: Routledge, 1991.

McGough, Laura J., *Gender, Sexuality and Syphilis in Early Modern Venice: The Disease that Came to Stay*, Basingstoke: Palgrave Macmillan, 2011.

McGrath, Ann, *Born in the Cattle*, Sydney: Allen and Unwin, 1987.

McGrath, Roberta, *Seeing Her Sex: Medical Archives and the Female Body*, Manchester: Manchester University Press, 2002.

McHugh, Paul, *Prostitution and Victorian Social Reform*, London: Croom Helm, 1980.

McKee, Robert Irwin, Edward J. McCaughan and Michelle Rocio Nasser (eds), *The Famous 41: Sexuality and Social Control in Mexico, 1901*, London: Palgrave Macmillan, 2003.

McKeown, Adam, *Melancholy Order: Asian Migration and the Globalization of Borders*, New York: Columbia University Press, 2008.

McKinnon, Catherine, *Only Words*, Cambridge, MA: Harvard University Press, 1996.

McLaren, Angus, *A History of Contraception from Antiquity to the Present Day*, Oxford: Basil Blackwell, 1991.

——, *Reproductive Rituals: The Perception of Fertility in England from the Sixteenth to the Nineteenth Century*, New York: Methuen, 1984.

McTavish, Lianne, *Childbirth and the Display of Authority in Early Modern France*, Aldershot: Ashgate, 2005.

Merians, Linda E. (ed.), *The Secret Malady: Venereal Disease in Eighteenth-Century Britain and France*, Lexington, KY: University of Kentucky Press, 1996.

Merrick, Jeffrey and Bryant T. Ragan Jr., *Homosexuality in Early Modern France*, New York: Oxford, 2001.

Merrington, W. R., *University College Hospital and its Medical School: A History*, London: Heinemann, 1976.

Michie, Helena, *Victorian Honeymoons: Journeys to the Conjugal*, Cambridge and New York: Cambridge University Press, 2006.

Midgley, Clare, *Women Against Slavery: The British Campaigns*, London and New York: Routledge, 1992.

Miller, James, *The Passion of Michel Foucault*, New York: Basic Books, 1993.

Millett, Kate, *Sexual Politics*, New York: Doubleday, 1970.

Minton, H. L., *Departing From Deviance*, Chicago: Chicago University Press, 2001.

Mitchell, Timothy, *Rule of Experts: Egypt, Techno-Politics, Modernity*, Berkeley: University of California Press, 2002.

Mitterauer, Michael and Reinhard Sieder, *The European Family: Patriarchy to Partnership from the Middle Ages to the Present*, trans. Karla Oosterveen and Manfred Hörzinger, Oxford: Basil Blackwell, 1982.

Monter, William, *Frontiers of Heresy: The Spanish Inquisition from the Basque Lands to Sicily*, Cambridge: Cambridge University Press, 1990.

Montgomery, Fiona and Christine Collette (eds), *The European Women's History Reader*, London, New York: Routledge, 2001.

Mooij, Annet, *Out of Otherness: Characters and Narrators in the Dutch Venereal Disease Debates 1850–1990*, Amsterdam: Rodopi, 1998.

Morgan, Jennifer, *Laboring Women: Reproduction and Gender in New World Slavery*, Philadelphia: University of Pennsylvania Press, 2004.

Morgan, Sue (ed.), *The Feminist History Reader*, London: Routledge, 2006.

Mort, Frank, *Dangerous Sexualities: Medico-moral Politics in Britain since 1830*, London: Routledge and Kegan Paul, 1987.

Mortimer, Ian, *Berkshire Probate Accounts, 1583–1712*, Reading: Berkshire Record Society, 1999.

Moscucci, Ornella, *The Science of Woman: Gynaecology and Gender in England, 1800–1929*, Cambridge: Cambridge University Press, 1990.

Mosse, George, *Nationalism and Sexuality: Middle-Class Morality and Sexual Norms in Modern Europe*, Madison, WI, and London: University of Wisconsin Press, 1985.

Moulton, Ian Frederick, *Before Pornography: Erotic Writing in Early Modern England*, New York: Oxford, 2000.

Mowry, Melissa M., *The Bawdy Politic in Stuart England, 1660–1714*, Aldershot: Ashgate, 2004.

Mudge, Bradford K., *The Whore's Story: Women, Pornography, and the British Novel, 1684–1830*, Oxford and New York: Oxford University Press, 2000.

Muir, Edward, *Ritual in Early Modern Europe*, 2nd edn, New York: Cambridge University Press, 2005.

Müller, Anja (ed.), *Fashioning Childhood in the Eighteenth Century: Age and Identity*, Aldershot: Ashgate, 2006.

Müller-Lyer, Franz Carl, *The Evolution of Modern Marriage: A Sociology of Sexual Relations*, London: G. Allen & Unwin, 1930.

Murdoch, Lydia, *Imagined Orphans: Poor Families, Child Welfare, and Contested Citizenship in London*, London: Rutgers University Press, 2006.

Murphy, Timothy F., *Gay Science: The Ethics of Sexual Orientation Research*, New York: Columbia University Press, 1997.

Murray, Stephen O. and William Roscoe (eds), *Boy Wives and Female Husbands: Studies in African Homosexualities*, New York: St Martin's Press, 1998.

Musacchio, Jacqueline Marie, *The Art and Ritual of Childbirth in Renaissance Italy*, New Haven, CT: Yale University Press, 1999.

Naphy, William G., *Plagues Poisons and Potions: Plague-Spreading Conspiracies in the Western Alps, 1530–1640*, Manchester: Manchester University Press, 2002.

——, *Sex Crimes: From Renaissance to Enlightenment*, Stroud: Tempus, 2002.

Nead, Lynda, *Victorian Babylon: People, Streets, and Images in Nineteenth-Century London*, New Haven, CT: Yale University Press, 2000.

——, *The Female Nude: Art, Obscenity, and Sexuality*, London: Routledge, 1992.

Netherton, Robin and Gale R. Owen-Crocker (eds), *Medieval Clothing and Textiles*, Woodbridge: The Boydell Press, series 2005–12.

Newton, Hannah, *The Sick Child in Early Modern England, 1580–1720*, Oxford: Oxford University Press, 2012.

Nicolson, Malcolm and J. E. E. Fleming, *Imaging and Imagining the Fetus: The Development of Obstetric Ultrasound*, Baltimore: Johns Hopkins Press, forthcoming.

Nietzsche, Friedrich, *Will to Power*, New York: Vintage Books, 1968.

Niro, Brian, *Race*, New York: Palgrave, 2003.

Noonan, John T., *Contraception: A History of its Treatment by the Catholic Theologians and Canonists*, Cambridge, MA: Harvard University Press, 1986.

Norton, Rictor, *Mother Clap's Molly House: The Gay Subculture in England, 1700–1830*, London: Gay Men's Press, 1992.

Noyes, John K., *The Mastery of Submission*, Ithaca: Cornell University Press, 1997.

Nussbaum, Felicity, *Torrid Zones: Maternity, Sexuality, and Empire in Eighteenth-Century English Narratives*, Baltimore: Johns Hopkins University Press, 1995.

Nye, Robert (ed.), *Sexuality*, Oxford: Oxford University Press, 1999.

Oakley, Ann, *The Sociology of Housework*, Bath: Martin Robertson, 1974.

——, *Sex, Gender and Society*, London: Maurice Temple Smith, 1972.

Ober, William, *Boswell's Clap and Other Essays: Medical analyses of literary men's afflictions*, Carbondale: Southern Illinois University Press, 1979.

O'Donnell, Katherine and Michael O'Rourke (eds), *Love, Sex, Intimacy and Friendship Between Men, 1550–1800*, Basingstoke: Palgrave Macmillan, 2003.

O'Dowd, Michael J. and Elliot E. Philipp, *The History of Obstetrics and Gynaecology*, London: Parthenon Publishing Group, 1994.

O'Hara, Diana, *Courtship and Constraint: Rethinking the Making of Marriage in Tudor England*, Manchester: Manchester University Press, 2000.

Oosterhuis, Harry, *Stepchildren of Nature: Krafft-Ebing, Psychiatry, and the Making of Sexual Identity*, Chicago and London: University of Chicago Press, 2000.

Oram, Alison, *Her Husband was a Woman! Women's Gender Crossing in Modern British Popular Culture*, London: Routledge, 2007.

Orgel, Stephen, *Impersonations: The Performance of Gender in Shakespeare's England*, Cambridge: Cambridge University Press, 1996.

Oriel, J. D., *The Scars of Venus: A History of Venereology*, London: Springer-Verlag, 1994.

Orrells, Daniel, *Classical Culture and Modern Masculinity*, Oxford: Oxford University Press, 2011.

——, *Sex: Antiquity and Its Legacy*, Oxford: I. B. Tauris/Oxford University Press, 2010.

Ottoway, Susannah R., *The Decline of Life: Old Age in Eighteenth-Century England*, Cambridge: Cambridge University Press, 2004.

Oudshoorn, Nelly, *Beyond the Natural Body: An Archeology of Sex Hormones*, London: Routledge, 1994.

Outhwaite, R. B., *Clandestine Marriage in England, 1500–1850*, London and Rio Grande: The Hambledon Press, 1995.

Outram, Dorinda, *The Body in the French Enlightenment*, New Haven: Yale University Press, 1989.

Ozment, Stephen E., *Ancestors: The Loving Family in Old Europe*, Cambridge, MA: Harvard University Press, 2001.

——, *When Fathers Ruled: Family Life in Renaissance Europe*, Cambridge, MA: Harvard University Press, 1983.

Paasonen, Susannah, Kaarina Nikunen and Laura Saarenmaa (eds), *Pornification: Sex and Sexuality in Media Culture*, Oxford: Berg, 2007.

Park, Katharine, *Secrets of Women: Gender, Generation, and the Origins of Human Dissection*, New York: Zone Books, 2006.

Parker, Rozsika, *The Subversive Stitch: Embroidery and the Making of the Feminine*, rev. edn, London: The Woman's Press, 1996.

Parry, John T. (ed.), *Evil, Law and the State: Perspectives on State Power and Violence*, Amsterdam: Rodopi, 2006.

Passet, Joanne Ellen, *Sex Radicals and the Quest for Women's Equality*, Urbana: University of Illinois Press, 2003.

Paster, Gail Kern, *The Body Embarrassed: Drama and the Disciplines of Shame in Early Modern England*, Ithaca, NY: Cornell University Press, 1993.

Payne, Lynda, *With Words and Knives: Learning Medical Dispassion in Early Modern England*, Aldershot: Ashgate, 2007.

Peabody, Sue and Tyler Stovall (eds), *The Color of Liberty: Histories of Race in France*, Durham, NC: Duke University Press, 2004.

Peakman, Julie, *Mighty Lewd Books: The Development of Pornography in Eighteenth-Century England*, Basingstoke: Palgrave Macmillan, 2003.

Pearl, Sharrona, *About Faces: Physiognomy in Nineteenth-Century Britain*, Cambridge, MA: Harvard University Press, 2010.

Peignot, Etienne Gabriel, *Dictionnaire critique, littéraire et bibliographique des principaux livres condamnés au feu, supprimés ou censurés*, Paris: Renouard, 1806.

Pelling, Margaret, *Medical Conflicts in Early Modern London: Patronage, Physicians, and Irregular Practitioners 1550–1640*, Oxford: Oxford University Press, 2003.

Perkins, Wendy, *Midwifery and Medicine in Early Modern France: Louise Bourgeois*, Exeter: University of Exeter Press, 1996.

Perrot, Philippe, *Fashioning the Bourgeoisie: A History of Clothing in the Nineteenth Century*, trans. Richard Bienvenu, Princeton: Princeton University Press, 1994.

Perry, Mary Elizabeth, *Gender and Disorder in Early Modern Spain*, Princeton: Princeton University Press, 1990.

Pevsner, Nikolaus, *Academies of Art Past and Present*, New York: Da Capo, 1973.

Pflugfelder, Gregory M., *Cartographies of Desire: Male–Male Sexuality in Japanese Discourse*, Berkeley: University of California Press, 1999.

Phillips, David and Graham Willett (eds), *Australia's Homosexual Histories: Gay and Lesbian Perspectives V*, Melbourne: Australian Centre for Lesbian and Gay Research and the Australian Lesbian and Gay Archives, 2000.

Phillips, John, *Sade: The Libertine Novels*, London: Pluto Press, 2001.

——, *Forbidden Fictions, Pornography and Censorship in Twentieth Century French Literature*, London: Pluto Press, 1999.

Phillips, Kim M. and Barry Reay, *Sex Before Sexuality: A Premodern History*, Cambridge: Polity Press, 2011.

Pia, Pascal (ed.), *L'Ecole des filles ou la philosophie des dames*, Paris: L'Or du Temps, 1969.

Pick, Daniel, *Faces of Degeneration: A European Disorder, c. 1848–1918*, Cambridge: Cambridge University Press, 1989.

Pillorget, René, *La Tige et le rameau. Familles anglaise et française XVIe–XVIIIe siècle*, Paris: Calmann-Lévy, 1979.

Pinker, Stephen, *The Blank Slate: The Modern Denial of Human Nature*, London: Penguin, 2002.

Pintard, René, *Le Libertinage érudit dans la première moitié du XVIIe siècle*, Paris: Slatkine, 2000.

Pinto-Correia, Clara, *The Ovary of Eve: Egg and Sperm and Preformation*, Chicago: Chicago University Press, 1997.

Pointon, Marcia R., *Naked Authority: The Body in Western Painting, 1830–1908*, Cambridge: Cambridge University Press, 1990.

Porter, Dorothy and Roy Porter, *Patient's Progress: Doctors and Doctoring in Eighteenth-Century England*, Cambridge and Oxford: Polity Press, 1989.

Porter, Roy, *Disease, Medicine and Society in England, 1550–1860*, 2nd edn, Cambridge: Cambridge University Press, 1993.

——, *Enlightenment: Britain and the Creation of the Modern World*, London: Penguin, 2001.

——, *The Greatest Benefit to Mankind: A Medical History of Humanity from Antiquity to the Present*, London: HarperCollins, 1997.

——, *Medicine: A History of Healing*, New York: Marlowe and Company, 1997.

Porter, Roy and Lesley Hall, *The Facts of Life: The Creation of Sexual Knowledge in Britain, 1650–1950*, New Haven, CT: Yale University Press, 1995.

Postle, Martin (ed.), *Johan Zoffany RA, Society Observed*, New Haven: Yale University Press, 2011.

Postle, Martin and William Vaughan, *The Artist's Model from Etty to Spencer*, London: Merrell Holberton, 1999.

Povinelli, Elizabeth, *The Empire of Love: Toward a Theory of Intimacy, Genealogy and Carnality*, Durham, NC: Duke University Press, 2006.

Powers, Karen Vieira, *Women in the Crucible of Conquest: The Gendered Genesis of Spanish American Society, 1500–1600*, Albuquerque, NM: University of New Mexico Press, 2005.

Prettejohn, Elizabeth, *Beauty and Art 1750–2000*, Oxford: Oxford University Press, 2005.

Probert, Rebecca, *Marriage Law and Practice in the Long Eighteenth Century*, Cambridge: Cambridge University Press, 2009.

Prosser, Jay, *Second Skins: The Body Narratives of Transsexuality*, New York: Columbia University Press, 1998.

Puglisi, Catherine, *Caravaggio*, London: Phaidon, 1998.

Pulju, Rebecca, *Women and Mass Consumer Society in Postwar France*, Cambridge and New York: Cambridge University Press, 2011.

Puri, Jyoti, *Woman, Body, Desire in Post-Colonial India: Narratives of Gender and Sexuality*, New York: Routledge, 1999.

Quétel, Claude, *The History of Syphilis*, Baltimore: Johns Hopkins University Press, 1990.

Rajan, Rajeswari Sunder, *The Scandal of the State: Women, Law and Citizenship in Postcolonial India*, Durham, NC: Duke University Press, 2003.

Rappaport, Erika Diane, *Shopping for Pleasure: Women in the Making of London's West End*, Princeton, NJ: Princeton University Press, 2000.

Rawcliffe, Carole, *Leprosy in Medieval England*, Woodbridge: Boydell, 2006.

Raymond, Janice G., *The Transsexual Empire*, London: The Women's Press, 1980.

Reigger, Kerreen, *The Disenchantment of the Home: Modernizing the Australian Family 1880–1940*, Melbourne: Oxford University Press, 1985.

Reiser, Stanley Joel, *Medicine and the Reign of Technology*, Cambridge: Cambridge University Press, 1978.

Restall, Matthew, *The Maya World: Yucatec Culture and Society, 1550–1850*, Stanford, CA: Stanford University Press, 1997.

Reynolds, Robert, *From Camp to Queer*, Carlton: Melbourne University Press, 2002.

Ribeiro, Aileen, *Fashion and Fiction: Dress in Art and Literature in Stuart England*, New Haven and London: Yale University Press, 2005.

Rickman, Johanna, *Love, Lust and License in Early Modern England: Illicit Sex and the Nobility*, Aldershot: Ashgate, 2008.

Riddle, John M., *Contraception and Abortion from the Ancient World to the Renaissance*, Cambridge, MA: Harvard University Press, 1992.

——, *Eve's Herbs: A History of Contraception and Abortion in the West*, Cambridge, MA: Harvard University Press, 1997.

Ridley, Matt, *The Red Queen: Sex and the Evolution of Human Nature*, London: Viking, 1993; repr. London: Penguin, 1994.

Riello, Giorgio, *A Foot in the Past: Consumers, Producers and Footwear in the Long Eighteenth Century*, Oxford: Pasold Research Fund and Oxford University Press, 2006.

Riley, Denise, *Am I that Name? Feminism and the Category of Women in History*, Basingstoke: Macmillan, 1988.

Robb, Graham, *Strangers: Homosexual Love in the 19th Century*, London: Picador Press, 2003.

Robbins, Ruth (ed.), *Medical Advice for Women, 1830–1915*, London: Routledge, 2009.

Roberts, Elizabeth, *Women and Families*, Oxford: Blackwell, 1995.

——, *A Woman's Place, An Oral History of Working Class Women, 1890–1940*, Oxford: Basil Blackwell, 1984.

Roberts, Mary Louise, *Civilization Without Sexes: Reconstructing Gender in Postwar France, 1917–1927*, Chicago: Chicago University Press, 1994.

Roberts, Robert, *The Classic Slum: Salford Life in the First Quarter of the Century*, Manchester: Penguin, 1971.

Robertson, Stephen, *Crimes against Children: Sexual Violence and Legal Culture in New York City, 1880–1960*, Chapel Hill and London: University of North Carolina Press, 2005.

Roche, Daniel, *The Culture of Clothing: Dress and Fashion in the 'ancien régime'*, trans. Jean Birrell, Cambridge: Cambridge University Press, 1994.

Rocke, Michael, *Forbidden Friendships: Homosexuality and Male Culture in Renaissance Florence*, New York: Oxford University Press, 1996.

Rodin, Alvin E., *The Influence of Matthew Baillie's Morbid Anatomy: Biography, Evaluation and Reprint*, Springfield: Thomas, 1973.

Roger, Jacques, *The Life Sciences in Eighteenth Century French Thought*, trans. Keith R. Benson, Stanford: Stanford University Press, 1997.

Roper, Lyndal, *Oedipus and the Devil: Witchcraft, Sexuality and Religion in Early Modern Europe*, London and New York: Routledge, 1994.

——, *The Holy Household: Women and Morals in Reformation Augsburg*, Oxford: Oxford University Press, 1989.

Roscoe, Will, *The Zuni Man-Woman*, Albuquerque: University of New Mexico Press, 1991.

Rose, Nikolas, *The Politics of Life Itself: Biomedicine, Power and Subjectivity in the 21st Century*, Princeton: Princeton University Press, 2007.

——, *Lifelines: Biology beyond Determinism*, Oxford and New York: Oxford University Press, 1997; repr. as *Lifelines: Life beyond the Gene*, Oxford and New York: Oxford University Press, 2003.

——, *Powers of Freedom: Reframing Political Thought*, Cambridge: Cambridge University Press, 1999.

Rosenthal, Margaret, *The Honest Courtesan: Veronica Franco, Citizen and Writer in Sixteenth-Century Venice*, Chicago: University of Chicago Press, 1992.

Rosenthal, Margaret and Ann Rosalind Jones, *The Clothing of the Renaissance World: Europe, Asia, Africa, The Americas; Cesare Vecellio's Habiti Antichi et Moderni*, London: Thames and Hudson, 2008.

Ross, Chad, *Naked Germany: Health, Race and the Nation*, Oxford and New York: Berg, 2005.

Rossiaud, Jacques, *Amours vénale: la prostitution en Occident XIIe–XVIe siécle*, Paris: Flammarion, 2010.

——, *Medieval Prostitution*, trans. Lydia Cochrane, Chicago: University of Chicago Press, 1988.

Rowbotham, Sheila, *Edward Carpenter: A Life of Liberty and Love*, London: Verso, 2008.

——, *Promise of a Dream: Remembering the Sixties*, London: Allen Lane, 2000.

Rublack, Ulinka, *Dressing Up: Cultural Identity in Renaissance Europe*, Oxford: Oxford University Press, 2010.

——, *The Crimes of Women in Early Modern Germany* Oxford: Oxford University Press, 1999.

Ruff, Julius R., *Violence in Early Modern Europe, 1500–1800*, Cambridge: Cambridge University Press, 2001.

Ruggiero, Guido, *Binding Passions: Tales of Magic, Marriage, and Power at the end of the Renaissance*, Oxford: Oxford University Press, 1993.

——, *The Boundaries of Eros: Sex Crime and Sexuality in Renaissance Venice*, New York: Oxford University Press, 1985.

Ruggiero, Guido and Edward Muir (eds), *Sex and Gender in Historical Perspective*, Baltimore: Johns Hopkins University Press, 1990.

Rupp, Leila, *Worlds of Women: The Making of an International Women's Movement*, Princeton, NJ: Princeton University Press, 1997.

Rydström, Jens, *Sinners and Citizens: Bestiality and Homosexuality in Sweden, 1880–1950*, Chicago: Chicago University Press, 2003.

Saada, Emmanuelle, *Les Enfants de la Colonie: Les Métis de l'Empire Français Entre Sujétion et Citoyenneté*, Paris: Editions de la Découverte, 2007.

Said, Edward, *Orientalism*, London: Vintage, 1978.

Salmond, Anne, *Aphrodite's Island: The European Discovery of Tahiti*, Berkeley: University of California Press, 2010.

Sawday, Jonathan, *The Body Emblazoned: Dissection and the Human Body in Renaissance Culture*, London: Routledge, 1995.

Schäfer, Daniel, *Old Age and Disease in Early Modern Medicine*, trans. Patrick Baker, London: Pickering & Chatto, 2011.

Schama, Simon, *The Embarrassment of Riches: An Interpretation of Dutch Culture in the Golden Age*, New York: Random House, 1987.

Schiebinger, Londa, *Feminism and the Body*, Oxford: Oxford University Press, 2000.

——, *Nature's Body: Gender in the Making of Modern Science*, Brunswick, NJ: Rutger's University Press, 1993.

——, *The Mind Has No Sex? Women in the Origins of Modern Science*, Cambridge, MA: Harvard University Press, 1989.

Schleiner, Winfried, *Medical Ethics in the Renaissance*, Washington, DC: Georgetown University Press, 1995.

Schmitt, Arno and Jahoeda Sofer (eds), *Sexuality and Eroticism among Males in Moslem Societies*, New York: Harrington Park Press, 1992.

Scott, Joan, *Gender and the Politics of History*, New York: Columbia University Press, 1988.

Scott, Joan Wallach, Cora Kaplan and Debra Keates (eds), *Transitions, Environments, Translations: Feminisms in International Politics*, New York: Routledge, 1997.

Sengoopta, Chandak, *The Most Secret Quintessence of Life: Sex, Glands, and Hormones, 1850–1950*, Chicago: University of Chicago Press, 2006.

Shannon, Brent Alan, *The Cut of His Coat: Men, Dress, and Consumer Culture in Britain, 1860–1914*, Athens, OH: Ohio University Press, 2006.

Shapin, Steven, *A Social History of Truth: Civility and Science in Seventeenth-Century England*, Chicago: Chicago University Press, 1995.

Shapiro, Barbara J., *A Culture of Fact: England, 1550–1720*, Ithaca, NY: Cornell University Press, 2003.

Shapiro, Michael, *Gender Play on the Shakespearean Stage: Boy Heroines and Female Pages*, Ann Arbor: University of Michigan Press, 1994.

Shorter, Edward, *Women's Bodies: A Social History of Women's Encounters with Health, Ill-Health, and Medicine*, New Brunswick: Transactions Publications, 1991.

——, *Bedside Manners: The Troubled History of Doctors and Patients*, New York: Simon & Schuster, 1985.

——, *A History of Women's Bodies*, New York: Basic Books, 1982.

——, *The Making of the Modern Family*, New York: Basic Books, 1975.

Showalter, Elaine, *The Female Malady: Women, Madness and English Culture, 1830–1980*, London: Virago, 1987.

Siedlecky, Stefania and Diana Wyndham, *Populate and Perish: Australian Women's Fight for Birth Control*, Sydney: Allen & Unwin, 1990.

Siena, Kevin, *Venereal Disease, Hospitals and the Urban Poor: London's 'Foul Wards' 1600–1800*, Rochester: University of Rochester Press, 2004.

——(ed.), *Sins of the Flesh: Responding to Sexual Disease in Early Modern Europe*, Toronto: Center for Renaissance and Reformation Studies, 2005.

Sigel, Lisa Z., *Governing Pleasures: Pornography and Social Change in England, 1815–1914*, New Brunswick: Rutgers University Press, 2002.

——(ed.), *International Exposure: Perspectives on Modern European Pornography, 1800–2000*, New Brunswick: Rutgers University Press, 2005.

Simmons, Christina, *Making Marriage Modern: Women's Sexuality from the Progressive Era to World War II*, Oxford and New York: Oxford University Press, 2009.

Simpson, Myrtle, *Simpson, the Obstetrician: A Biography*, London: Gollancz, 1972.

Sinha, Mrinalini, *Spectres of Mother India: The Global Restructuring of an Empire*, Durham, NC: Duke University Press, 2006.

——, *Colonial Masculinity: The 'Manly' Englishman and the 'Effeminate' Bengali in the Late Nineteenth Century*, Manchester: Manchester University Press, 1995.

Slack, Paul, *The Impact of Plague in Tudor and Stuart England*, London: Routledge & Kegan Paul, 1985.

Smail, Daniel Lord, *On Deep History and the Brain*, Berkeley: University of California Press, 2007.

Smith, Alison, *The Victorian Nude: Sexuality, Morality, and Art*, Manchester: Manchester University Press, 1997.

Smith, Clarissa, *One for the Girls! The Pleasures and Practices of Reading Women's Porn*, Bristol: Intellect Books, 2007.

Smith, Justin E. H., *The Problem of Animal Generation in Early Modern Philosophy*, Cambridge: Cambridge University Press, 2006.

Smith, Vera Irwin, *The Story of Ovum and Sperm: And How They Grew into the Baby Kangaroo Stories of Birth and Sex for Children*, Sydney: Australasian League of Honour, 1920.

Snyder, C. Arnold and Linda Agnès Huebert Hecht (eds), *Profiles of Anabaptist Women: Sixteenth-Century Reforming Pioneers*, Hecht Waterloo, Ontario: Wilfrid Laurier University Press, 1996.

Solé, Jacques, *Être femme en 1500: la vie quotidienne dans le diocèse de Troyes*, Paris: Perrin, 2000.

Soloway, Richard A., *Demography and Degeneration: Eugenics and the Declining Birthrate in Twentieth-Century Britain*, London and Durham, NC: University of North Carolina Press, 1995.

Sommer, Matthew H., *Sex, Law and Society in Late Imperial China*, Stanford: Stanford University Press, 2000.

Spierenburg, Pieter, *The Spectacle of Suffering: Executions and the Evolution of Repression from a Preindustrial Metropolis to the European Experience*, Cambridge: Cambridge University Press, 1984.

Spufford, Margaret, *The Great Reclothing of Rural England: Petty Chapmen and their Wares in the Seventeenth Century*, London: Hambledon Press, 1984.

——, *Small Books and Pleasant Histories: Popular Fiction and its Readership in Seventeenth-Century England*, Athens, GA: The University of Georgia Press, 1981.

Stallybrass, Peter and Allon White, *The Politics and Poetics of Transgression*, Ithaca, NY: Cornell University Press, 1986.

Staub, Susan C., *Nature's Cruel Stepdames: Murderous Women in the Street Literature of Seventeenth Century England*, Pittsburgh, PA: Duquesne University Press, 2005.

Stearns, Peter, *Sexuality in World History*, New York and London: Routledge, 2009.

Steele, Valerie, *The Corset: A Cultural History*, New Haven, CT: Yale University Press, 2001.

——, *Paris Fashion: a Cultural History*, 2nd edn, Oxford: Berg, 1998.

——, *Fashion and Eroticism: The Ideals of Feminine Beauty from the Victorian Era to the Jazz Age*, New York: Oxford University Press, 1985.

Stein, Claudia, *Negotiating the French Pox in Early Modern Germany*, Burlington, VT: Ashgate, 2009.

Stevenson, David, *The Beggar's Benison: Sex Clubs of Enlightenment Scotland and Their Rituals*, East Lothian: Tuckwell Press, 2001.

Stevenson, Kim, Anne Davies and Michael Gunn, *Blackstone's Guide to the Sexual Offences Act 2003*, Oxford: Oxford University Press, 2003.

Stewart, Mary Lynn, *For Health and Beauty: Physical Culture for Frenchwomen, 1880s–1930s*, Baltimore, MD: Johns Hopkins University Press, 2001.

Stewart, Philip, *Engraven Desire: Eros, Image, and Text in the French Eighteenth Century*, Durham, NC: Duke University Press, 1992.

Stocking, George W., *Victorian Anthropology*, New York: Free Press, 1987.

Stolberg, Michael, *A Cultural History of Uroscopy, 1500–1800*, Farnham: Ashgate, 2012.

——, *Experiencing Illness and the Sick Body in Early Modern Europe*, Basingstoke: Palgrave, 2011.

Stoler, Ann Laura, *Carnal Knowledge and Imperial Power: Race and the Intimate in Colonial Rule*, Berkeley and London: University of California Press, 2002.

——, *Race and the Education of Desire: Foucault's History of Sexuality and the Colonial Order of Things*, Durham, NC: Duke University Press, 1995.

Stoller, Robert, *Perversion: The Erotic Form of Hatred*, New York: Pantheon, 1975.

Stone, David M., *Guercino*, Florence: Cantini, 1991.

Stone, Lawrence, *Road to Divorce: England, 1530–1987*, Oxford: Clarendon Press, 1990.

——, *The Family, Sex and Marriage in England, 1500–1800*, London: Weidenfeld & Nicolson, 1977.

Stopes, Marie Carmichael and Ross Mckibbin, *Married Love*, Oxford and New York: Oxford University Press, 2004.

Stora-Lamarre, Annie, *L'Enfer de la Troisième République: Censeurs et Pornographes, 1880–1914*, Paris: Imago, 1990.

Storey, Tessa, *Carnal Commerce in Counter-Reformation Rome*, Cambridge: Cambridge University Press, 2008.

Štulhofer, Aleksandar and Theo Sandfort (eds), *Sexuality and Gender in Postcommunist Eastern Europe and Russia*, New York: The Haworth Press, 2005.

Styles, John, *The Dress of the People: Everyday Fashion in Eighteenth-Century England*, New Haven and London: Yale University Press, 2007.

Sulloway, Frank, *Freud: Biologist of the Mind*, Cambridge, MA: Belknap Press, 1979.

Surkis, Judith, *Sexing the Citizen: Morality and Masculinity in France, 1870–1920*, Ithaca, NY: Cornell University Press, 2006.

Svanström, Yvonne, *Policing Public Women: The Regulation of Prostitution in Stockholm, 1812–1820*, Stockholm: Atlas Akkademi, 2000.

Szreter, Simon, *Fertility, Class and Gender in Britain 1860–1940*, Cambridge: Cambridge University Press, 1996.

Szreter, Simon and Kate Fisher, *Sex Before the Sexual Revolution: Intimate Life in England, 1918–1963*, Cambridge: Cambridge University Press, 2010.

Talvacchia, Bette, *Taking Positions: On the Erotic in Renaissance Culture*, Princeton: Princeton University Press, 1999.

Tarrant, Naomi, *The Development of Costume*, Edinburgh: National Museum of Scotland, 1994.

Tatar, Maria, *Lustmord: Sexual Murder in Weimar Germany*, Princeton: Princeton University Press, 1995.

Tatlock, Lynne, *The Court Midwife: Justine Siegemund*, Chicago: Chicago University Press, 2005.

Taylor, Gary, *Buying Whiteness: Race, Culture, and Identity from Columbus to Hip Hop*, New York: Palgrave, 2005.

Taylor, Gordon Rattray, *Sex in History*, London: Thames & Hudson, 1953.

Tebutt, Melanie, *Women's Talk? A Social History of Gossip in Working-Class Neighbourhoods, 1880–1960*, Aldershot: Scholar Press, 1995.

Temkin, Jennifer, *Rape and the Legal Process*, 2nd edn, Oxford: Oxford University Press, 2002.

Temkin, Owsei, *The Double Face of Janus and Other Essays in the History of Medicine*, Baltimore: Johns Hopkins University Press, 1977.

Terry, Jennifer, *An American Obsession*, Chicago: Chicago University Press, 2000.

Thane, Pat, *Old Age in English History: Past Experiences, Present Issues*, Oxford: Oxford University Press, 2000.

Thirsk, Joan, *Food in Early Modern England: Phases, Fads, Fashions 1500–1760*, London: Hambledon Continuum, 2006.

——, *Economic Policy and Projects: The Development of a Consumer Society in Early Modern England*, Oxford: Clarendon Press, 1978.

Thompson, Elizabeth, *Colonial Citizens: Republican Rights, Paternal Privilege, and Gender in French Syria and Lebanon*, New York: Columbia University Press, 2000.

Thompson, Francis M. L., *The Rise of Respectable Society: A Social History of Victorian Britain, 1830–1900*, London: Fontana Press, 1989.

Thompson, Roger, *Unfit for Modest Ears: A Study of Pornographic, Obscene and Bawdy Works Written and Published in England in the Second Half of the Seventeenth Century*, Totowa, NJ: Rowman and Littlefield, 1979.

Thornhill, Randy and Craig T. Palmer, *A Natural History of Rape: Biological Bases of Sexual Coercion*, Cambridge, MA: MIT Press, 2000.

Todd, Dennis, *Imagining Monsters: Miscreations of the Self in Eighteenth-Century England*, Chicago: University of Chicago Press, 1995.

Todorov, Tzvetan, *The Conquest of America: The Question of the Other*, trans. Richard Howard, New York: Harper & Row, 1984.

Toepfer, Karl, *Empire of Ecstasy: Nudity and Movement in German Body Culture*, London, and Berkeley, CA: University of California Press, 1997.

Tolson, Andrew, *The Limits of Masculinity*, London: Tavistock, 1977.

Tomaselli, Sylvana and Roy Porter (eds), *Rape: An Historical and Cultural Enquiry*, Oxford: Blackwell, 1986.

Tosh, John, *A Man's Place: Masculinity and the Middle-Class Home in Victorian England*, New Haven and London: Yale University Press, 1999.

Toulalan, Sarah, *Imagining Sex: Pornography and Bodies in Seventeenth Century England*, New York: Oxford University Press, 2007.

Traub, Valerie, *The Renaissance of Lesbianism in Early Modern England*, New York: Cambridge University Press, 2002.

Treadwell, Penelope, *Johan Zoffany: Artist and Adventurer*, London, Paul Halberton, 2009.

Trexler, Richard, *Sex and Conquest: Gendered Violence, Political Order and the European Conquest of the Americas*, Ithaca, NY: Cornell University Press, 1999.

Trumbach, Randolph, *Sex and the Gender Revolution. Volume One: Heterosexuality and the Third Gender in Enlightenment London*, Chicago: University of Chicago Press, 1998.

——, *The Rise of the Egalitarian Family: Aristocratic Kinship and Domestic Relations in Eighteenth Century England*, New York: Academic Press, 1978.

Turner, Bryan, *The Body and Society: Explorations in Social Theory*, Oxford: Blackwell, 1984.

Turner, David, *Fashioning Adultery: Gender, Sex and Civility in England, 1660–1740*, Cambridge: Cambridge University Press, 2002.

Turner, James Grantham, *Schooling Sex: Libertine Literature and Erotic Education in Italy, France, and England, 1534–1685*, New York: Oxford University Press, 2003.

——, *Libertines and Radicals in Early Modern London: Sexuality, Politics, and Literary Culture, 1630–1685*, New York: Cambridge University Press, 2002.

Usborne, Cornelie, *Cultures of Abortion in Weimar Germany*, Munich: Berghahn Books, 2007.

——, *The Politics of the Body in Weimar Germany: Women's Reproductive Rights and Duties*, Ann Arbor: University of Michigan Press, 1992.

Vance, Carole S. (ed.), *Pleasure and Danger: Exploring Female Sexuality*, Boston and London: Routledge & Kegan Paul, 1984.

van der Lugt, Maaike, *Le ver, le démon et la vierge: les théories médiévales de la génération extraordinaire: une étude sur les rapports entre théologie, philosophie naturelle et médecine*, Paris: Les Belles Lettres, 2004.

van der Pol, Lotte C., *The Burgher and the Whore: Prostitution in Early Modern Amsterdam*, trans. Liz Waters, Oxford: Oxford University Press, 2011.

van Nierop, Henk, *The Nobility of Holland: From Knights to Regents, 1500–1650*, Cambridge: Cambridge University Press, 1993.

Vásquez García, Francisco and Andrés Moreno Mengibar, *Poder y prostitución en Sevilla*, Seville: Universidad de Sevilla, 1995.

Vezzosi, Alessandro, *Leonardo e lo Sport*, Florence: Giunti, 2004.

Vicinus, Martha, *Intimate Friends: Women Who Loved Women, 1778–1928*, Chicago: University of Chicago Press, 2004.

Vieillard, Camille, *L'urologie et les médecins urologues dans la médecine ancienne*, Paris: Rudeval, 1903.

Vigarello, Georges, *A History of Rape: Sexual Violence in France from the Sixteenth to the Twentieth Century*, trans. Jean Birrell, Cambridge: Polity Press, 2001.

——, *Concepts of Cleanliness: Changing Attitudes in France since the Middle Ages*, trans. Jean Birrell, Cambridge: Cambridge University Press, 1988.

Vincent, David, *Literacy and Popular Culture: England 1750–1914*, Cambridge: Cambridge University Press, 1989.

Vincent, Susan J., *The Anatomy of Fashion: Dressing the Body from the Renaissance to Today*, Oxford: Berg, 2009.

——, *Dressing the Elite: Clothes in Early Modern England*, Oxford: Berg, 2003.

von Nettesheim, Agrippa, *Die Eitelkeit und Unsicherheit der Wissenschaft und die Verteidigungsschrift*, ed. Fritz Mauthner, 2 vols, Munich: Müller, 1913.

Wack, Mary Frances, *Lovesickness in the Middle Ages: The Viaticum and Its Commentaries*, Philadelphia: University of Pennsylvania Press, 1990.

Wagner, Peter, *Eros Revived: The Erotica of the Enlightenment in England and America*, London: Secker & Warburg, 1988.

Walker, Garthine, *Crime, Gender and Social Order in Early Modern England*, Cambridge: Cambridge University Press, 2003.

Walkowitz, Judith, *City of Dreadful Delight: Narratives of Sexual Danger in Late-Victorian London*, London: Virago, 1994.

——, *Prostitution and Victorian Society: Women, Class and the State*, Cambridge: Cambridge University Press, 1980.

Wallace, Catherine, *Catching the Light: The Art and Life of Henry Scott Tuke, 1858–1929*, Edinburgh: Atelier Books, 2008.

Watts, Sheldon, *Epidemics and History: Disease, Power and Imperialism*, New Haven: Yale University Press, 1999.

Waugh, Thomas, *Hard to Imagine*, New York: Columbia University Press, 1996.

Wear, Andrew, *Knowledge and Practice in English Medicine, 1550–1680*, Cambridge: Cambridge University Press, 2000.

Webster, Mary, *Johan Zoffany 1733–1810*, New Haven: Yale University Press, 2011.

Weeks, Jeffrey, *Sex, Politics and Society: The Regulation of Sexuality since 1800*, London and New York: Longman, 1989.

——, *Coming Out: Homosexual Politics in Britain from the Nineteenth Century to the Present*, London: Quartet, 1977.

Weiss, Jessica, *To Have and to Hold: Marriage, the Baby Boom, and Social Change*, Chicago: University of Chicago Press, 2000.

Welles, Marcia L., *Persephone's Girdle: Narratives of Rape in Seventeenth-Century Spanish Literature*, Nashville: Vanderbilt University Press, 2000.

White, Luise, *The Comforts of Home: Prostitution in Colonial Nairobi*, Chicago: Chicago University Press, 1990.

Wiener, Martin J., *Men of Blood: Violence, Manliness and Criminal Justice in Victorian England*, Cambridge: Cambridge University Press, 2004.

Wiesner-Hanks, Merry, *The Marvelous Hairy Girls: The Gonzales Sisters and Their Worlds*, New Haven, CT: Yale University Press, 2009.

——, *Christianity and Sexuality in the Early Modern World: Regulating Desire, Reforming Practice*, London and New York: Routledge, 2000.

Wijers, Marjan and Lin Lap-Chew, *Trafficking in Women, Forced Labour and Slavery-Like Practices in Marriage, Domestic Labour and Prostitution*, Utrecht and Bangkok: Foundation against Trafficking in Women/Global Alliance Against Trafficking in Women, 1997.

Wilder, Gary, *The French Imperial Nation-State: Negritude and Colonial Humanism between the Two World Wars*, Chicago: Chicago University Press, 2005.

Wilkin, Rebecca M., *Women, Imagination and the Search for Truth in Early Modern France*, Aldershot: Ashgate, 2008.

Willett, Graham, *Living Out Loud: A History Of Gay and Lesbian Activism in Australia*, St Leonards, NSW: Allen & Unwin, 2000.

Williams, Alan, *The Police of Paris*, Durham, NC: University of North Carolina Press, 1980.

Williams, Craig A., *Roman Homosexuality: Ideologies of Masculinity in Classical Antiquity*, New York: Oxford University Press, 1999.

Williams, David Innes, *The London Lock: A Charitable Hospital for Venereal Disease 1746–1952*, London: Royal Society of Medicine Press, 1995.

Williams, Gordon, *A Dictionary of Sexual Language and Imagery in Shakespearean and Stuart Literature*, 3 vols, London: Athlone Press, 1994.

Williams, John Alexander, *Turning to Nature in Germany: Hiking, Nudism, and Conservation, 1900–1940*, Stanford: Stanford University Press, 2007.

Williams, Linda (ed.), *Porn Studies*, Durham, NC: Duke University Press, 2004.

Williams, Walter L., *The Spirit and the Flesh: Sexual Diversity in American Indian Culture*, Boston: Beacon, 1986.

Wilson, Adrian, *The Making of Man-Midwifery: Childbirth in England 1660–1770*, London: UCL Press, 1995.

Wilson, Glen and Qazi Rahman, *Born Gay: The Psychobiology of Sex Orientation*, London: Peter Owen, 2005.

Wiltenburg, Joy, *Disorderly Women and Female Power in the Street Literature of Early Modern England and Germany*, Charlottesville: University of Virginia Press, 1992.

Wood, Ellen Meskins, *Empire of Capital*, Brooklyn, NY, and London: Verso, 2003.

Wrightson, Keith, *Earthly Necessities: Economic Lives in Early Modern Britain*, New Haven, CT: Yale University Press, 2000.

——, *English Society: 1580–1680*, London: Hutchinson, 1982.

Young, Antonia, *Women Who Become Men: Albanian Sworn Virgins*, New York: Berg, 2000.

Young, Iris Marion, *On Female Body Experience: 'Throwing Like a Girl' and Other Essays*, Oxford: Oxford University Press, 2005.

Young, Michael Dunlop and Peter Willmott, *The Symmetrical Family: A Study of Work and Leisure in the London Region*, London: Routledge & Kegan Paul, 1973.

——, *Family and Kinship in East London*, London: Routledge & Kegan Paul, 1957.

Youngs, Deborah, *The Life Cycle in Western Europe, c.1300–c.1500*, Manchester: Manchester University Press, 2006.

Zöllner, Frank, *Leonardo da Vinci 1452–1519*, London: Taschen, 2011.

Zweig, Ferdynand, *The Worker in an Affluent Society: Family Life and Industry*, London: Heinemann, 1961.

Zweiniger-Bargielowska, Ina, *Managing the Body: Beauty, Health, and Fitness in Britain, 1880–1939*, Oxford: Oxford University Press, 2010.

——, *Women in Twentieth-Century Britain*, Harlow: Longman, 2001.

INDEX

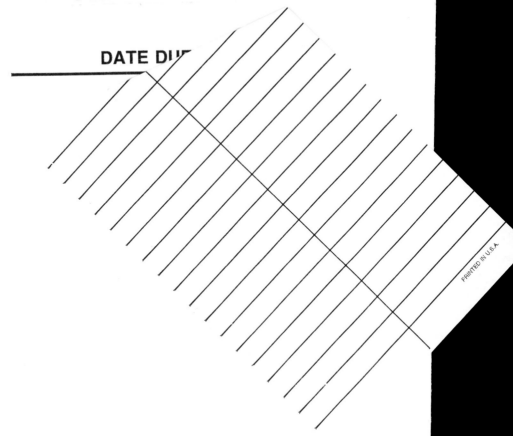

DATE DUE

PRINTED IN U.S.A.